DRAMA
PRINCIPLES & PLAYS

DRAMA
PRINCIPLES & PLAYS

Second Edition

Edited and with an Introduction by

Theodore W. Hatlen

University of California, Santa Barbara

PRENTICE-HALL, INC.

Englewood Cliffs, New Jersey

Library of Congress Cataloging in Publication Data

HATLEN, THEODORE W   comp.
   Drama.

   Bibliography: p.
   1. Drama—Collections.   2. Drama—History and
criticism.   I. Title.
PN6112.H35 1975   808.82   75-6826
ISBN 0-13-218982-8

Printed in the United States of America

10   9   8   7   6   5   4

Design and Picture Research by Anita Duncan

PRENTICE-HALL INTERNATIONAL, INC., *London*
PRENTICE-HALL OF AUSTRALIA, PTY. LTD., *Sydney*
PRENTICE-HALL OF CANADA, LTD., *Toronto*
PRENTICE-HALL OF INDIA PRIVATE LIMITED, *New Delhi*
PRENTICE-HALL OF JAPAN, INC., *Tokyo*

CONTENTS

Part Two   PLAYS

PREFACE

Reading a play well is often more difficult than seeing it well performed. In order to experience the full impact of a playwright's work, a reader must himself visualize and create all its dimensions. In a theatrical production the burden of interpretation is largely carried, with greater or lesser skill, by the director, actors and designers. Through speech, movement, gesture, rhythm, scenery, costume and lighting, the meaning and emotion of the play are communicated to the audience. The solitary reader misses the emotional contagion of a responsive audience, the atmosphere created by light, sound and speech, the cumulative effect of climactic action, and the personal qualities of the living actor. As an individual, you must exercise your imagination with cues from the printed page alone. To help you envision your own production, this anthology goes beyond the texts of the plays.

The opening section surveys the starting points and purposes of drama, its genres and techniques. This account may be read straight through, or piecemeal, and either before or after your own re-creation of a play.

Each play is accompanied by a series of production pictures which is intended to help you visualize the action of the play. To enhance your understanding and appreciation, study the illustrations carefully to see the relationship of performers and setting. Note carefully also the stage directions, and attempt to imagine the characters' movements and stage business. Reading some of the most arresting scenes aloud may help you to sense the emotional content of the play. As far as possible stage the play in your own mind. The plays are also accompanied by critical essays which were selected not only for their varied points of view but also as points of departure for student discussion and comment.

As a reader you have the opportunity for thoughtful analysis of the meaning, structure and symbolic aspects of the drama at your own pace. To appreciate a play fully is to realize that it is more than an evening's diversion in the theatre, more than so many words on a page; it is at once a personal statement of the dramatist and a clue to the culture that produced it. In addition to being significant landmarks of outstanding theatrical pieces, the plays were selected because of their universal and challenging themes—as contemporary as tomorrow's newspaper. The plays that follow are an invitation to a wide range of feeling and thought.

I am grateful to various persons and institutions for their assistance: to the many individuals and organizations who have allowed me to reproduce their illustrations, especially Dimitrios Harissiadis and Will Swalling; to my associates in the Department of Dramatic Art at the University of California, Santa Barbara; and to William Reardon, Colleen Ellis, Marty Swing, Patricia Peters, and Edna Hatlen.

THEODORE W. HATLEN

part one

PRINCIPLES

THEATER AND DRAMA
TRAGEDY
COMEDY

CHAPTER ONE

THEATER AND DRAMA

ORIGINS

Man has always sought ways to enlarge his world. He reinforces his own strength with a weapon—a stone, a club, a spear, a gun, a rocket, a bomb. He acts as far as he is able to insure good crops—he tills the land, plants the seed, irrigates the soil, and then, realizing that he is subject to forces beyond his control, invokes divine intervention to provide him with a good harvest. He links himself to the present with his mate and children and tribe. He projects himself beyond the grave with rites of passage which will insure him of an afterlife. These attempts of man to widen his experience and strengthen his power result from a complex cluster of motives—his needs to communicate, to survive, to understand, to secure recognition and status—which represent the basic longings to which he gives expression by means of his religious ceremonies.

It is in such rituals that we find the basic elements of drama—music, song, dance, costuming, impersonation, mimetic action and communal performance. Drama could not begin without the disciplined construction of an orderly sequence of words and actions representing a real or imaginary experience. But not all ritual becomes drama, because often the rites continue on as functional activities, never attaining the detachment necessary to transform them into works of art which can exist for their own sake. It was in ancient Greece that the remarkable transformation from ritual to drama took place.

It would be convenient if the steps in the origin and evolution of Greek drama were clearly marked and recorded, but unfortunately much of its background is obscure. However, certain inferences can be made from the evidence at hand.

Aristotle in his *Poetics*[1] informs us that "Tragedy...was first improvisation...originating with the leaders of the dithyramb. It advanced by slow degrees; each new element that showed itself was in turn developed." It seems clear from this statement that the rites were at first spontaneous expressions of the participants when they summoned the gods or rhapsodized on the coming of spring. The dithyramb seems to have been at first an improvised choral ode, a song of spring, which later became enriched as a part of a ceremonial rite in honor of the god Dionysus with the addition of dance and written verses by such poets as Pindar and Arion. Dionysus was the god of vegetation, wine and fertility—an appropriate divinity for representing man's oldest needs, food and family. Primitive societies invented rituals around seasonal celebrations in their efforts to induce fertility, good hunting and bountiful crops. In Greece, these objectives were centered in a single god whose relationship to fertility was not confined to vegetation, but included human fecundity as well, as is clearly evident from the

---

[1] All quotations from Aristotle are from S. H. Butcher, *Aristotle's Theory of Poetry and Fine Art* (London, Macmillan and Co., Ltd., 1907).

phallic rites associated with Dionysus. The legend of this god tells of his death and subsequent rebirth as a young man—a symbolic representation of the calendrical cycle of the death of the seed as it is buried in the ground in winter and its rebirth with the coming of spring. Some scholars, in tracing the origin of drama, emphasize the seasonal celebrations of seed and harvest. Others suggest that the roots of drama are to be found in the commemorative rites honoring dead heroes. In any case, the rituals from which drama emerged carried the emotional fervor of man's deepest urges and gave symbolic representation to his longest thoughts as he sought to orient himself to the universe.

In Aristotle's statement concerning the origin of Greek tragedy, he notes that "it advanced by slow degrees; each element that showed itself was in turn developed." We know that tragedy as a specific form was first mentioned in the seventh century B.C., that a century later its improvisatory nature gave way as tragedy became serious and more formalized, with poets writing verses in its form, and that by 534 B.C. it had developed sufficiently in form and substance so that Peisistratus inaugurated competition in tragedies as a part of the spring festivals in Athens.

The improvised dithyrambs probably were performed on threshing floors, just as today the Greeks make use of threshing floors as places for dancing. The altar of Dionysus was in the center and the dancers moved about it in a circular formation, setting the pattern for the orchestra circle of the later, fully developed theater architecture. At first the dithyrambs were a communal activity: everyone got into the act. When some of the worshippers broke away from the circle and became onlookers, it was possible to make the performance more specialized, with only the more proficient taking part and utilizing prepared verses and passages instead of the previous improvisations. As the spectators became more numerous, the locale of the celebration was moved to the base of an adjacent hillside so that the audience could more easily see the action. The separation of the participants from the viewers enhanced the possibility of developing an attitude of detachment in the audience, so that their enjoyment then included not only what was done, but also the *way* in which it was performed. As writers added their imaginative contributions, the original utilitarian basis for the ritual—the invocation of the supernatural to secure growth and fertility—lost some of its emphasis and the ceremony began to exist for its own sake, thus giving new freedom and sanction to the performers and poets.

An astonishing innovation then took place. Thespis appeared as the first actor. He broke away from the chorus and added the dramatic potential of impersonation. Instead of describing Dionysus, he became Dionysus, and in antiphonal response with the chorus and leaders he enlarged and enriched the ritual as a dramatic medium. When Aeschylus added the second actor another new thrust forward was given to drama, because the additional actor enabled the dramatist to *show in action* a dramatic conflict rather than merely talk about it. This primacy of action became a central tenet of Aristotelian criticism. The second actor enormously increased the potentialities of theatrical tension, which the playwrights were quick to exploit. Sophocles' addition of the third actor further enlarged the scope of the dramatist, providing him with the means of complicating his plot and devising more complex structural arrangements of his tragedies. As actors were added to the performance, the emphasis of the production shifted. While at first the chorus was the essential theatrical element, as the dramatic form evolved the playwright focused his attention on the speech and actions of individuals so that by the time Greek tragedy had reached its "golden age" the chorus had mere supporting role to the protagonists, in whom the dramatic conflict was now centered. In part this shift in emphasis was due to the change in dramatists' selection of materials; as they drew more and more heavily upon Greek myth and legend for their characters and situations, the individual roles became so powerful that they dominated the chorus.

The evolution of the physical theater was from the dancing circle, which all of the participants occupied, to three separate areas—the orchestra circle for the chorus, the huge theatron for the audience, which eventually became quite remote from the performers, and the *skene*, where the actors carried on the essential action of the play.

Play-giving, which was a religious obligation and celebration, centered in an annual spring festival called the City of Dionysia. On the opening day of the festival, which lasted for five or six days, a processional carried the image of Dionysus from his temple to the theater. The actual performances took place on the last three or four days, when each playwright presented three tragedies and a satyr-play. The productions were under state control and financed in part by wealthy patrons. The Athenian audience comprised practically the entire free population of the city, excepting the women. The people came early in morning and brought their day's food with them. As they watched the plays they knew that each was presented for one time only—a magnificent outpouring of talent and effort in honor of Dionysus.

Like tragedy, Greek comedy had its origin in rituals honoring Dionysus, but its development was separate. Playwrights and actors limited themselves to one type. Aristotle says that "comedy also sprang from improvisations, originating with the leaders of the phallic ceremonies which still survive in many of our cities." Old Comedy, which became

the important feature of the Lenaen festival, was officially recognized in 486 B.C. and reached its height of development in the comic genius of Aristophanes, as seen in such extant plays as *The Frogs*, *The Birds* and *Lysistrata*.

Just as Greek drama grew out of the rites performed in honor of Dionysus, so drama in the Middle Ages developed from the ritual performed in honor of the death and resurrection of Christ. Antiphonal singing was a part of the liturgy of the church as early as the fourth century, but genuine dialogue arose from the practice of inserting lines, known as tropes, into certain parts of the mass. An extant manuscript shows the introduction of a trope into the Easter service in the early part of the tenth century. From these tropes, which included mimetic action and the use of costumes and properties, serious plays developed through the addition of scenes, until long and complicated dramas were written and performed to dramatize the entire life of Christ.

As drama and its production became more complex it was moved out of the church and the various locales required in the expanding stories were represented by a series of "stations" or "mansions" placed in a churchyard or market place. Entire cycles of stories from the Bible and the lives of the saints placed so heavy a burden on the church for production that drama eventually passed into secular hands. In England, for example, the trade guilds, which often made use of "pageant wagons" to represent the various places for the action, took on the responsibility for producing plays. For a time drama existed precariously in the efforts of traveling companies of amateur players performing nondescript plays in improvised quarters. Ultimately the quality of drama improved markedly; the players, under noble patronage, became professionals working in the established theaters of Shakespeare's time.

THE CONVENTIONS OF THE THEATER

Drama, like all other forms of art, is conventionalized. That is to say, there are certain common agreements between spectator and theater-worker as to the manner of creation and production—certain ground rules that determine how the game is to be played. In painting, there is the convention that pigment is applied to a flat surface within a regular framework. Music is a conventionalized combination of sounds and rhythms that make almost no pretence of imitating nature. The spectator, as he enters the theater, becomes a partner to conventions in order that the drama can take place. He enters into the situation imaginatively by what Coleridge termed a "willing suspension of disbelief." In our contemporary theater, the spectator of a legitimate modern play often sees onstage characters and settings that resemble those of life: the speech suggests normal conversation and the characters' behavior follows familiar patterns. Actually, much of what the playgoer sees and hears is arbitrarily conventionalized even if the dramatist has written in a realistic style. Performer and audience tacitly agree that they will be separated from one another: usually the audience occupies the auditorium; the actor remains on stage. The separation of these two entities is facilitated by the darkened auditorium and the lighted stage, the architectural features of the elevated stage, a curtain that opens and closes, and the proscenium arch itself. There is also a psychological barrier at work, known as the "fourth wall," a contemporary convention that developed with realism in the late nineteenth century, in which the actors pretend that the audience does not exist and avoid direct communication across the footlights. Actually, the performer employs specific techniques to assure communication with everyone in the theater—by speaking louder and more clearly than in normal conversation, by turning his face at least partially toward the audience, by exaggerating his gestures and facial expressions. The drama itself is conventionalized. Its compressed structure, the arrangement into scenes or acts interrupted by intermissions and set changes, the climactic order of the action usually involving only a few characters—these are arbitrary practices of the playwright. Even the scenery that gives the illusion of actuality, with all the clutter and detail of real life, is patently artificial in the arrangement of exits and entrances, the grouping of furniture so that it "opens out" toward the audience, the arbitrary use of lighting, the enlarged scale of set pieces, the very use of scenic materials itself.

Conventions are not rigid, however. They change from time to time and even from one style of drama to another. In musical comedy, for example, everyone expects scenery that is frankly theatrical, performers who break into song and dance at the slightest provocation and to the accompaniment of a large orchestra, and a chorus of interlopers who hover in the immediate background ready to join instantly into the action of the production. In contemporary "arena," or center-staged productions, the audience is asked to accept such conventions as the absence of scenery, the intimacy of the surroundings, and the different kinds of movements and groupings which result from the playing area surrounded by spectators. As modern playwrights become

7

increasingly dissatisfied with realism, more and more attempts are made to free the theater from restricting conventions. For example, scenery is becoming frankly theatrical instead of representational. Now, for instance, a fragment of a wall may be picked out of the darkness by light to serve as a setting that a generation ago would have required a complete interior with three walls, a ceiling and practical doors. Dramatists are using freer forms for their plays. Dialogue may be poetic; asides, soliloquies and direct address may be reintroduced. Acting is oftentimes quite stylized, or the separation between spectator and performer deliberately broken down. The point is that theater conventions are subject to change as those who work in theater seek ways of expressing themselves more interestingly and completely, and as the established practices give way to new ones the spectator is obliged to make a corresponding adjustment.

Fashions in theatrical conventions have differed from time to time, and in order to understand the drama of any period it is essential to know the conventions underlying its productions. In the Greek theater, for example, performances were given outdoors and in the daytime as public ceremonies. Only three speaking characters appeared on stage at one time, and men played all of the female roles. Actors wore masks, special headpieces and footgear, and the plays dramatizing ancient legends and myths were written in verse. Greek dramas, presented usually in a single permanent setting with a simple story that occurred in a short space of time, also displayed little or no violence onstage. In the Elizabethan theater, like the Greek, all roles were played by male actors in an outdoor theater in the daytime with little or no use of illusionistic scenery. The plays, written in verse, were quite different from the Greek drama in form and content. The play usually was a complicated one involving several plot lines, comic matter was mixed with serious, high-born characters with low, and the playwright had openly ransacked history and literature for material that would tell an exciting story. Because plays were performed by professional actors in theaters whose dimensions and arrangement placed the actor in close proximity to the spectator, the subtleties of the language could be exploited. In addition, the convention of the large, unlocalized platform gave the dramatist a great deal of freedom in staging an animated and complicated narrative.

In each age, theater conventions have varied according to the influences of the playwrights, actors, audiences and physical theaters, and in turn, the conventions have affected all elements of the drama. In evaluating any drama, therefore, it is essential to recognize these conventions because of their influences in shaping the play and its production.

ELEMENTS OF DRAMA

In the previous sections we have suggested the appeals of drama and the variety of ways for studying its nature, among them analysis of dramatic structure. Let us examine the specific elements that constitute such a structure. In this discussion we will follow a pattern set down by Aristotle in his *Poetics*, perhaps the most significant and influential work on dramatic criticism ever written. Aristotle categorized drama into the following six elements, which are listed here in their order of importance as he viewed them:

Plot
Character
Thought
Diction
Music
Spectacle

We will not argue the relative importance of each of these items, but the student can use these six elements as a convenient frame of reference, not only in this chapter but in all considerations of dramatic literature. Hence, familiarity with Aristotle's dramatic categories and their component parts is necessary for subsequent discussions.

PLOT

Plot is, in Aristotle's words, "the life and soul of tragedy." As the formal aspect of a play, it is for the playwright what composition is for the painter and composer, namely, the arrangement of parts into a consistent and logical pattern. A play is not a series of separate events ordered chronologically like a timetable or the minutes of a meeting. Just as a motion picture editor arranges a meaningful sequence of film clips by relating each frame to every other, so, in a similar way, the playwright composes his events and builds the structure of his play. Dramatic structure is a concatenation, or linking of actions into an indivisible chain. Plots have varied from the tightly knit, simple structure of Greek tragedy to the loose episodes of medieval drama, bound together

by a theme, to the complicated action of the Elizabethans, who employed several sets of characters involved in a welter of overlapping situations, to the naturalists' attempt to avoid all semblance of structure in "slice-of-life" plays, and finally to contemporary experiments in expressionistic, "absurd" and "epic" drama that have little regard for disciplined construction. But despite differences in composition, the underlying pattern of Western drama reflects Aristotle's concept of organic unity—a series of actions that an audience can accept as "necessary and probable." Most of our plays involve human beings caught in decisive moments of struggle and conflict. Tension is increased as the drama moves toward a climax and an ultimate decision. In a Greek drama the central character finds himself in a situation that requires him to choose among courses of action and to endure the often dire consequences of his choice. Antigone must decide whether she will disrespect the funeral rites due her dead brother or bury him in defiance of the king's edict. Oedipus decides, whatever the cost, to rid his kingdom of the cause of the plague. Once the tragic hero makes a decision, pressure is brought to bear upon him, he refuses to be diverted from his course, and catastrophe ensues.

A play is composed of a series of units. Major divisions are the acts, which in turn may be divided into scenes, and these may be separated still further by a director into a series of "beats." "Scenes" in the French sense refer to any new grouping of characters. "Beats" are a director's device for separating small units of action for rehearsal purposes, such as Gloucester's attempt to jump off the cliff in *King Lear*, Jones's encounter with the crocodile in *The Emperor Jones*, and the killing of the canary in *Miss Julie*.

Greek tragedies have simple plots with a series of episodes involving two or three speaking characters, as for example in *Antigone*—Haimon and Creon, Antigone and Ismene, Antigone and Creon, Ismene and Antigone, and the guard and Creon. Between each of these episodes, which are of only a few minutes duration, the Chorus chants lyrical passages. In a compressed modern play such as *Miss Julie* the entire action is centered in three characters with only the interruption of the peasants' "ballet" to break the tension. These simple plots are in marked contrast to Shakespeare's structure of *King Lear*, in which more than a score of characters are directly involved in a variety of locales over a considerable span of time. But in each of these plays, the dramatist puts each scene or episode in its appropriate place in the sequence of action so that it is causally related to what happens before and after. It is this process of devising and arranging incidents that controls the progression of the action and which makes the art of playwriting a difficult one.

The plot is arranged to produce a cumulative effect by giving the play tension and emotional momentum. In addition, the plot provides explanation and meaning for the sum total of the parts. What incidents lead to Miss Julie's swift destruction? What events occur between the view of the swaggering Emperor Jones in the first scene and his destruction in the last one? What are the steps that mark the change in Major Barbara from a romantic to a realist? What events are necessary to reveal and undermine Möbius's real identity and purpose in *The Physicists?* The plot raises and answers these questions by providing the critical incidents that account for changes in the characters' fortunes.

In the nineteenth century the French critic Brunetière offered his celebrated "law of the drama," in which the basic tenet is that a play presents "the spectacle of the will striving toward a goal." While this concept is dif-

ficult to apply to all kinds of drama, there is a hard core of truth in it. Most plays do, in fact, deal with a group of characters striving toward goals—goals such as status, power, wealth, security, recognition, or affection. Usually the character is prevented from realizing his goal; obstacles are in his way and opposition often breaks into sharp and open conflict. Note the clashes in each episode of *Antigone*, beginning with the contention between the two sisters, then the clash of Creon and the guard, and finally of Creon and Antigone; the conflicts progressively build the emotional impact of the play as Sophocles dramatizes Antigone and the King, each striving toward a goal and running headlong into each other in the process. In *An Enemy of the People* the two Stockmann brothers run into sharp conflict with each other because of the differences in their goals. In comedy, the traditional plot is centered around a pair of lovers who are separated by social and economic barriers, parental disapproval, misunderstandings, a third person, or a cloud on his or her reputation. The pattern of action is concerned with eliminating such obstacles, as for example in *The Miser* where the lovers are initially thwarted by the greed of the father, Harpagon.

John Howard Lawson, in his *Theory and Technique of Playwriting*, advanced a theory of drama built on conflicts: "The essential nature of drama is a social conflict in which the conscious will is exerted . . ." Like Brunetière's theory, Lawson's contains much validity, although it seems inapplicable to works by Chekhov, Maeterlinck, and the current "absurdists," whose drama appears to be organized in a circular fashion rather than a linear one. Often these plays create a mood or show characters incapable of striving toward a goal, or who perhaps deny that a goal even exists. In Beckett's *Waiting for Godot*, the characters take no positive action. They do not know where they are headed. In Ionesco's *The Leader* the playwright dramatizes the act of waiting, but with the expectation that "the Leader" will come.

A common characteristic of all drama is the prevalence of *tension*. Without it, drama has little chance of holding attention. Usually, as Brunetière suggests, tension grows out of "striving toward a goal," and even in those plays of mood or those that lack striving, a sense of intensified feeling still arises from the expectancy of an arrival. In *The Leader*, the arrival does in fact take place, but the pattern is one of a joke—tension is aroused and given a sudden release in an unexpected direction. The same holds true of the plot of Beckett's *Act Without Words*. In Chekhov's plays, where most of the characters are frustrated and incapable of taking action, a sense of tension grows out of their dissatisfaction with their lives and conditions. They have memories and aspirations that are at odds with the hard facts of their present existence.

Generally speaking, each person will tend to form his own "theory" of plot, to derive his own emphases according to his separate analysis. For the purpose of such analysis plot may be said to consist of eleven basic aspects:

Exposition
Discovery and Reversal
Point of Attack
Foreshadowing
Complication
Climax
Crisis
Denouement
The Unities,
    of time
    of place
    of action

It is well to remember that although these aspects of plot may be separable in discussion, they may often coincide in any given play. The climax and crisis, for example, may occur at the same time, or exposition may be used for foreshadowing.

Exposition

When the curtain rises on a play, the dramatist faces the problem of capturing his audience's attention and providing necessary background so that it can understand subsequent action. He must show who the characters are, what their relationship is to one another, what motivates them, and usually some aspect of their environment. This is *exposition*. Notice in *The Miser* how quickly Molière sketches in the character relationships and the conflict. In *Miss Julie* Strindberg's first line is nearly a plot summary: "*Jean:* Miss Julie's mad again tonight: absolutely mad!" Likewise, Sophocles in the opening speeches of *Antigone* gives the audience important background information. The first scene of *King Lear* is an example of exposition, crammed full of antecedent information skillfully blended with dramatic action.

In most contemporary plays in which the dramatist is endeavoring to create the illusion of actuality, he ordinarily introduces his exposition into the play as an organic part of the action rather than as obvious information. Because exposition usually bulks rather large in the first act of a play, the writer must find ways to capture and hold the audience's interest while unobtrusively providing this necessary material. Many playwrights find it difficult to get their action underway, with the result that the opening scenes tend to drag. The television producer, conscious of this tendency in the opening moments of a play, often has resorted to the technique of beginning a production with an excerpt of violent action from the climax of the play in order to "hook" the spectator into the story.

Playwrights have used a variety of expository devices, such as "feather-duster scenes" of two minor characters bouncing information off one another toward the audience, or dumb-shows, confidants, narrators, choruses, asides, soliloquies, prologues, and all sorts of visual aids including slides, charts, maps, and motion pictures. The stage setting also serves as a means of providing background material for the audience. The modern dramatist takes considerable care to describe the locale of the play. Note, for example, Strindberg's explicit stage directions for the *Miss Julie* setting.

Discovery and Reversal

The playwright, in revealing his characters' motivations and objectives, their relationships, and their feelings, must possess the ability to invent and organize a series of interesting and compelling *discoveries* about his characters.

Exposition is a part of a general discovery process, but it deals primarily with antecedent or background material, whereas discovery per se includes events that may happen during the course of the action, as for example the death of Antigone, the acts of sadism by Goneril and Regan, and the discovery of the feigned illness of Grusha's husband in *The Caucasian Chalk Circle*.

Discovery scenes may be those of recognition such as in *The Miser*, Act V, Scene 5, when Anselm is reunited with his children, or when the true identity and purposes of the scientists is learned in *The Physicists. King Lear* is actually a long, torturous journey of discovery in which Lear finds compassion and love.

A *reversal* is a turning about, a sudden change in direction. Aristotle thought that discovery was most successful when it coincided with a reversal, as in *Oedipus the King* when Oedipus discovers the truth which brings on his catastrophe.

Point of Attack

Once the playwright provides sufficient background to hold the audience's attention, he starts a chain of events that constitute the main action of the play. The *point of attack* refers to that moment in the play when the precipitating force sets the mechanism into motion. The equilibrium that ordinarily exists at the rise of the first curtain is disturbed, turbulence results and a period of adjustment begins. King Lear mistakenly puts Cordelia to a foolish test; Creon forbids the burial of Polyneices; Miss Julie orders a servant to dance with her—these are characteristic points of attack, in which an inciting force triggers the course of action.

The location of the point of attack in the story is related directly to the physical theater and its conventions. The more flexible the stage, the freer the dramatic form and the greater the opportunity for an early attack and the presentation of a great deal of action. Medieval and Elizabethan playwrights, for example, exploited the freedom provided by their stages to tell complicated stories with many scenes and characters, while, in contrast, the Greek dramatists felt obliged to begin their stories as near as possible to the major crisis. In the most modern plays, because of the expense and limitations of staging a play, the tendency is to use a compact plot. As a consequence, the contemporary dramatist is likely to employ a relatively late point of attack.

Foreshadowing

In the exposition we have observed how the playwright must furnish the audience with background material. He also has the task of preparing the spectator for future developments. He does this by *foreshadowing*, that is, he makes the subsequent action credible by supplying carefully inserted clues in early parts of the play. Everyone is familiar with the techniques of foreshadowing, or "planting," employed by a mystery-story writer when he takes pains to drop hints—the butler is left-handed; the revolver is hidden in the desk drawer; the chauffeur has an assumed name. The dramatist is likewise obliged to prepare the audience for acceptance of the developments of the action.

Foreshadowing has several purposes: to make events appear believable, to build suspense, to create tension, to reveal character or aid in the development of climaxes, crises, and complications. It may also announce an entrance or establish atmosphere. Within the first few lines of Sophocles' play, Antigone makes the commitment that foreshadows her tragic end. Dürrenmatt sets a bizarre note when the opening curtain reveals a police investigation underway over the dead nurse in *The Physicists*. Strindberg skillfully prepares for Miss Julie's suicide by the slaughter of the bird and the presence of the razor. Warnings by Teiresias and the Chorus anticipate the catastrophes in *Antigone*. The absurdists, in order to make their point that much of modern life is meaningless, build up expectations through foreshadowing only to let them collapse into nothingness. But in general, the dramatist's use of foreshadowing indicates that he is aware of the need for an organic structure to his plot so that no turn of events will seem extraneous or incredible. The playwright values suspense more than surprise, and, while dramas may use the unexpected, good craftsmanship requires that the chain of events be foreshadowed.

Complication

A *complication* is any new force introduced into play which affects the direction of the course of action. Once the playwright has selected his characters, determined his theme, and planned the beginning and ending of his play, he constructs the plot through a series of complications. The point of attack, for example, is the first complication. Macgowan considers the complications so important that he says they are "the lifeblood of ninety-nine and ninety-nine hundredths percent of a play."

Let us consider for a moment the analogy of a three-stage rocket. Its destination is determined, its course charted and launching prepared. The mechanism is fired and the rocket is projected into space, but the initial impetus is insufficient to keep it moving; additional thrusts are needed from second- and third-stage firings to send the rocket soaring into its trajectory. In a similar way, the dramatist decides on his objective and sets his course of action. He precipitates the initial motion by means of a complication (the point of attack), but the plot, like the rocket, needs additional force to keep the mass moving forward and upward. Additional complications, like the rocket's secondary and tertiary firings, accelerate and increase the action until the play reaches its highest point. The thrust of a play follows a cumulative and climactic pattern from the introduction of the first complication to the major crisis, when the protagonist's fate is settled. Complications are utilized by the playwright in order to create a "straining forward of interest," to use George Pierce Baker's apt phrase. Their purpose is to intensify the emotions, arouse suspense, to illustrate and determine what happens to the characters—generally, to provide the building blocks of the play's plot structure.

Romeo falls in love with Juliet, but the situation is complicated by the enmity between the two families. This hostility is aggravated when Romeo slays Tybalt, causing a new complication, the banishment of Romeo. A further complication is raised when Juliet's father insists that she marry Paris immediately. In order to avoid this development, a plan is devised for Juliet to feign death through the use of a magic potion. But the letter disclosing the plan is not delivered to Romeo and the action is again further complicated. Romeo learns of Juliet's apparent death, goes to her and takes poison. Juliet awakens to find her lover dead—the final complication. She joins him in death, and this is the final action of the play. Shakespeare, like most playwrights, begins his play with a character trying to reach an objective, but complications intervene and require, as the play gathers momentum and intensity, a continuous readjustment of forces. This readjustment process is the heart of plot, and it is out of complications that the conflict of forces becomes apparent.

Climax

The *climax* is the culmination of a course of action, "the maximum disturbance of the equilibrium," "the moment of the most intense strain," "the crisis of maximum emotion and tension."

Actually, a play is a series of climaxes with moments of stability and adjustment in between. The action surges forward and upward, the tension mounting through minor climaxes, until the major climax is reached and the emotional impact of the play reaches its strongest point. The structure, in this respect, may resemble a boxing match between two opponents of similar strength and skill. In each round, there may be moments of climactic action with first one fighter gaining the advantage and then the other. In between the peaks of action are relatively quiet moments, rest periods between the rounds. In the frantic last round, the major climax is reached when one boxer succeeds in knocking out the other.

Notice the climactic pattern of action Strindberg employs in the seduction in *Miss Julie*. First we hear about her exploits with the servants at the dance; then she appears in person at the servants' quarters; she drinks beer (a servants' drink); she orders Jean to remove his livery and to sit with her; she removes something from his eye; she openly flirts with him and admires his French, his dancing, his physical strength. One by one, in scenes of gradual intensification, the barriers are removed between them. Similarly, her suicide is a carefully ordered structure of climactic action. This is basically the usual pattern of dramatic writing—an ordered sequence of mounting tension culminating in a major climax.

Crisis

Although the terms *crisis* and *climax* are sometimes used interchangeably because they may occur at the same time, we shall consider a crisis to mean a time of decision, a turning point, or a crossroads. After an accident, a patient hovers between life and death; he is at a moment of crisis and possibly of climax. A batter steps to the plate with the score tied and the bases loaded. The count reaches three balls and two strikes. The game is at a point of crisis and possibly at its climax too.

A crisis involves a clash of interests. The protagonist is faced with alternatives that will determine his fate. Grusha, about to flee from the revolt, discovers the abandoned child of the governor's wife and must decide whether or not to take the risk of rescuing him. Antigone must choose to bury her brother's body or obey the King. In *The Miser*, Harpagon and his son must decide which suitor is to win the girl. Sometimes a character makes his own decisions; sometimes they are thrust upon him. A crisis may lead to good fortune or to disaster depending upon the nature of the play and the author's intent.

A play, which is usually made up of a series of crises growing out of a series of complications, reaches its major crisis toward the play's end. Resolution of this crisis determines the ultimate outcome of the entire sequence of actions. A dramatist creates loaded situations which dramatize his characters caught in critical moments of their lives. For a time the outcome is in doubt; the protagonist teeters on the brink of success or failure. The hero's moment of suspension, before a decisive action occurs and settles his fate, is the final crisis.

Denouement

The *denouement* is the ending of the play, the final resolution. Julie takes her own life; Oedipus goes into exile; Romeo and Juliet are joined in death; the fate of the physicists falls into the hands of an insane female psychiatrist; the young couples are properly paired off and the miser, Harpagon, gets his comeuppance. It is the unravelling of the knot that the complications have formed, the committing of the protagonist to his ultimate fate. As a segment of the play, it occurs from the major crisis to the final curtain.

The denouement's function is to restore order, to unify and complete the course of action, and to provide an ending that seems necessary and probable as the result of the antecedent development. Indeed, the play's denouement is a fairly good index of the skill and integrity of the dramatist. The inept playwright may find his characters in an inextricable situation and resort to an implausible suicide, or to some other violent action, with the mistaken notion that these acts in themselves are "dramatic." In legitimate usage, violent action is the credible result of the characters themselves and their previous actions. Another kind of faulty ending occurs when the playwright uses an outside force to intervene and unsnarl the entanglements. The hero is incapable of working out his own salvation, so he must be rescued by the Cavalry, the Coast Guard, the Marines, the King or a miracle from on high. Still another weak denouement occurs when the playwright suddenly changes, for the sake of shock or surprise, to a direction which is contrary to his characters or violates the preceding action. As we have already suggested, however, the "absurdists" oftentimes deliberately twist the ending because the strange effect produced coincides with their view of life. Note, for example, the endings of *The Leader* and *Act Without Words*. Another questionable, though sometimes amusing denouement is the indeterminate ending in which the characters and the audience are left in doubt as to the outcome. Pirandello, in *Right You Are If You Think You Are*, makes an acceptable use of this device, but ordinarily the spectator likes to have the major questions answered before he goes home.

While the denouement of comedy usually shows the protagonist successful in overcoming obstacles to reach the land of his heart's desire, the denouement of tragedy often shows disaster. The denouements of both comedy and tragedy, however, frequently involve a complete reversal of the hero's status.

The Unities

Most dramatists have sought some means of creating *unity* in their plays—some way of providing a central focus. Aristotle suggested unity in an interlocking arrangement of the incidents with a "beginning, middle, and end." During the Renaissance, scholars insisted on imposing on the dramatist the alleged "classical" unities of time, place, and action. Actually, Aristotle mentions only time and action. He does not, as we have mentioned earlier, set down rules for dramatic composition; rather, his observations record the practices of the Greek playwrights of the preceding century. Aeschylus, Sophocles, and Euripides did not write according to law-like rules, but constructed their plays to meet the conventions of the theater and their own imaginations. They did not regard drama as a fixed and unchangeable form, but created their plays and methods of presentation to suit themselves. The notion that playwrights must observe rules or conform to the unities has had very little acceptance in the theater except in the neoclassic drama of France and England in the seventeenth century. In general, playwrights have written for popular approval rather than for academic acceptance.

UNITY OF TIME.   Aristotle wrote that "Tragedy endeavors, as far as possible to confine itself to a single revolution of the sun, or but slightly to exceed this limit." The Italian scholars of the Renaissance misapplied this *unity of time*, warping it to mean the portrayal of a maximum of twelve hours, and preferably of only the length of time which the play itself took. The Greek playwrights usually were close to Aristotle's observation, although there are several instances of plays requiring a longer span of time. Greek dramatists were not concerned with strict adherence to chronology. Their interest was centered on portrayal of characters and ideas rather than confining the action within a specific amount of elapsed time. Dramatists in other periods of theater history have felt free to use all of the time they needed. In practice, and as a natural concomitant of the compact nature of drama, the playwright has tended to restrict his action to a relatively short space of time. It will be noted that the majority of the plays in the text follow the unity of time.

UNITY OF PLACE.   Aristotle said nothing about *unity of place*, although it was customary for Greek tragic writers to use a single, or at the most two locales. Perhaps the continual presence of the chorus influenced this practice. Perhaps the fact of drama performed in a single locale set a precedent; or again, perhaps outdoor performances during daylight hours without the means of making rapid shifts of scenery conditioned playwriting. But more likely, a play which was centered on a few characters shown in the climactic and critical stages of their careers required no change of scenic background.

In medieval drama, the playwrights attempted to tell a complicated story and to put all of the action onstage. Shakespeare, and his fellow Elizabethans, followed this tradition. Furthermore, the architecture of the theater and the tastes of the audience encouraged the playwright to move about freely in time and space. Thus, *King Lear* has a variety of action in several locales over a considerable space of time. Similarly, Brecht in his "epic" drama *The Caucasian Chalk Circle* uses a wide latitude of time and place. While there are numerous plays that require freedom to move from place to place, the general tendency of the dramatist is to concentrate his action in order to keep his focus clear.

UNITY OF ACTION.   Aristotle said that the plot should be simple enough so that it might be held easily in the mind of the spectator. *Unity of action* means that the drama deals with a single course of events, involving little or no extraneous material, no mixture of comic and serious matter. The most important ingredient in the concept of unity is that all parts of the play be organically related. Again quoting from Aristotle: "The structural unity of the parts is such that, if any one of them is displaced or removed, the whole will be disjointed and disturbed. For a thing whose presence or absence makes no visible difference is not an organic part of the whole." It was, in fact, the practice of the Greek writers of tragedy to create simple, well-articulated plots. But the history of drama reveals that playwrights have often ignored the unity of action as Aristotle defined it, particularly in Elizabethan England where the physical theater, with its unlocalized platform, permitted the use of complicated stories and actions, and where the medieval tradition of mixing comedy with serious drama was an accepted practice. You will find examples in this text of complicated action in *King Lear* and *The Caucasian Chalk Circle* and simplicity of plot in *Miss Julie, Antigone, Look Back in Anger*, and *Ceremonies in Dark Old Men*.

In Elizabethan drama, playwrights often achieved a kind of unity of character by focusing the action on one dominant figure. Others have sought a unity of idea by selecting only those characters and incidents that were germane to the development and projection of their theme. Still others, ignoring structural unity, have achieved a unity of atmosphere. In any case, most dramatists have been cognizant of the need for finding some means to suggest a singleness of purpose or effect in

order to clarify and organize their creative efforts.

CHARACTER

In placing character as his second element, Aristotle started an endless argument. Many critics and playwrights insist that character is the most important element of drama. The controversy will undoubtedly continue, since there are valid arguments on both sides, but more importantly, the point needs to be made that plot and character are not mutually exclusive. Good drama requires both good plot and good characterization, for in the last analysis plot is character in action, and plot, in turn, is the result of what people are. The sequence of events is rooted in the characters' wills, desires, and objectives that are revealed in effective drama by skillful selection and organization.

The nature of the dramatic method and the conditions and conventions of the physical theater have exerted important influences on characterization. Unlike the novelist, who can demonstrate character by a wide range of incidents over a span of many years and under many conditions, who has, in addition, the opportunity to describe the character at length and to indicate the secret thoughts coursing through his head, the playwright must select a few key incidents that occur in a short space of time and in a few locales and must reveal character only by speech and behavior. The dramatist has no means of commenting directly on character. As a result, the characters in plays must be simplified, their qualities made clear in a few telling scenes. Because of the compression of the medium, characterization in drama often becomes one-dimensional, especially in farce and melodrama, and in the minor roles of most all plays.

As in all other aspects of drama, characterization has been exposed to a variety of fashions. In Greek, Elizabethan, and Japanese drama, the roles of women were played by men. Medieval drama often made use of allegorical figures representing single attributes of character, such as Wisdom, Greed, and Gluttony. Contemporary dramatists of realistic and naturalistic persuasion have endeavored to create the illusion of complicated character by piling up a wealth of physical details, by capitalizing on the significant trifle, and by searching for the psychological meaning beneath the act.

High tragedy deals primarily with "men as better than they are" but who, through some flaw of character, are led to great misfortune. Low comedy, on the other hand, deals with "men as worse than they are" but not with men who are altogether vicious or depraved. Medieval characters ranged from God to the Devil, from purest saint to most abject sinner. Some characters have been drawn on a heroic scale, masters of their fate, working out their destinies by dint of their own resources; other characters have been treated as hapless victims of an unfortunate heredity and environment, incapable of taking action, defeated, frustrated, and resigned. The expressionists have experimented with split personalities and characters effaced of all aspects of individuality, reducing them to X or Mr. Zero. During the last quarter of the nineteenth century, under the impact of the scientific method and the new developments in psychology, the playwright has generally become concerned with delineating characters with rich inner lives and complex motivations. Ibsen, Strindberg, and Chekhov were particularly successful in creating figures with the "stamp of life" upon them. Observe, for example, how complete a sense of character Strindberg creates with Julie and Jean in

a very short space of time. Dramatists in the twentieth century have continued to strive for the creation of solid characters whose motivations conform to the findings of contemporary psychology, with the result that many of our plays give the effect of case studies. Our modern writer is also interested in the interaction of characters, and his plays exploit the tensions and turbulence that result from the impact of one upon the other.

While he is restricted in scope, the playwright's very use of selection and heightening give clarity and directness to his figures. The fact that he is confined to a very few events places great weight upon them. The characters are brought into sharp focus because onstage all of their behavior is significant. The playwright cannot afford the diffuse haphazardness of real life or the leisurely indirectness of many novels.

Character may be delineated in four ways. First, by appearance, since the actor's physical qualities give an immediate stimulus to the audience. Many modern playwrights have a very specific image in mind and thus describe the character's appearance in considerable detail, as for example in the plays of Shaw.

Second, by speech, for the kind of language employed by the person, his manner of speaking, his voice quality, his inflection pattern, pitch, rate, and general vitality, all say something about him. The dramatist takes great care to write dialogue that makes an immediate impression about the characters. At the beginning of *Look Back in Anger*, Jimmy Porter's hostility toward his wife and his friend, and society in general, is vividly apparent from his scathing verbal attack on them. Although dialogue in most modern plays gives the impression of the give and take of normal conversation, some playwrights have found long speeches of reminiscence useful as a means both of conveying antecedent information and of revealing character to the listener. *Miss Julie* is an excellent example of this technique. Before the advent of realism in the nineteenth century, it was common practice for the playwright to use soliloquies and asides to let the audience know what the characters were thinking, as in Edmund's speech in *King Lear*, Act I, scene 2, and the monologues of Emperor Jones. Molière makes an amusing use of the aside in Act I, scenes 4 and 5, of *The Miser* when Harpagon, thinking himself alone, talks to the audience about his treasure, only to discover that there are other characters onstage who might have overheard him.

Third, through a character's external actions we have clues to his inner motivations. Sometimes the playwright may choose to create an initial impression that is misleading or ambiguous and then gradually reveal the truth as the play progresses. By the end of *Look Back in Anger* our original view of Jimmy Porter is markedly changed. Likewise, Dürrenmatt's major characters in *The Physicists* at the end of the play are not at all the characters they seem to be from their opening speeches. The more usual practice, however, is for the playwright to set the key to a character from the outset. Molière's Harpagon in his first appearance in Act I, scene 3, is shown as a testy skinflint, and the rest of the play goes on to detail action-by-action the completeness of his avarice. Miss Julie also indicates her character from her first entrance: she goes to the looking-glass, then strikes Jean in the face with her handkerchief, and a moment later plays the coquette by praising Jean's dancing.

Fourth, by what others say about a character and the way in which they react to him, we may begin to form an opinion before he even appears. We have already noted Jean's opening line about Miss Julie's madness;

the gossip that follows between the two servants provides a further damaging portrait of their mistress.

The sharpness of a character's image is in part dependent upon the structure of the drama. Plays written for a theater that permitted most of the essential action to appear onstage gave the playwright a greater opportunity to create a vivid and complex character than do those plays confined to a minimum of action. For example, one reason that King Lear is such a rich and interesting character is because we see him in combination with so many other characters and in such a variety of circumstances from a powerful king to a raving madman. When we contrast this variety of character exposure to that of Antigone, we realize how limited the Greeks were in delineating complex characterization. Some playwrights, notably Shakespeare, possessed the ability to sketch memorable characters in a very few lines, but most dramatists have felt the need of developing their roles at length in order to achieve personages that are convincing.

The credibility of a character is enhanced by the performance of the actor. The personal attributes of the performer add a dimension to the play which is difficult to describe and often impossible to predict in advance. In the hands of some actors villains have become heroic, heroines insipid, comic characters dull, and minor roles have run away with the play. It is a commonplace of the theater that flat, pedestrian material has, on occasion, been made by the actor to seem rich and captivating stuff, that talented performers have taken superficially contrived parts and infused them with the warmth and glow of scintillating life. In a sense, the playwright's conception of character is at the mercy of the actor. To the latter's credit, he very often extends and enlarges the original sketch into a fully rounded portrait.

THOUGHT

The third Aristotelian element, *thought*, refers to the reasoning aspect of drama. Thought is more than the intellectual content, since a character's reasons for his behavior are bound up with his emotions. Plays are not objective debates, mere presentations of factual data and logical arguments leading to a clear decision. Characters in drama make subjective decisions under pressure, while enmeshed in webs of conflicting emotional entanglements. In this respect, dramas are like the experiences of life with all of their complicating networks of feeling and meaning beyond the immediate moment.

In his opposition to Antigone, Creon presents arguments to support his edict. The episodes between him and Antigone, Haimon, the Chorus, and Teiresias nearly become organized debates. Ibsen's Dr. Stockmann attempts to present the scientific rationale back of his findings but the threat to the economic well-being of the community makes it impossible for others to accept his ideas. Möbius has laudatory reasons for his assumption of the role of an inmate in *The Physicists*, but his plans are undermined by the machinations of others. This rational background constitutes the thought element of individual characters.

In addition to the rationale of individual characters, thought also concerns a play's theme—a kind of "golden text" that summarizes the moral and indicates the symbolic meaning of the play as a whole, such as "love conquers all," "murder will out," or "niceness pays." Drama does not, however, always lend itself to such neat copybook maxims. A given play may convey a variety of interpretations to an audience. Many of the English public were profoundly shocked at Jimmy Porter's attack on contemporary life and institutions in *Look Back in Anger*, although many of the young so-called "angry" generation accepted him as their spokesman and champion. Some people regard Antigone as headstrong and foolish in openly defying Creon and thus deliberately choosing to die. The ideas of great dramas have, of course, been sources of endless critical contention. Is Shylock a comic or tragic figure? Is the tragedy of *Antigone* really that of Creon? Where varied interpretations of a play's meaning exist, the dramatist obviously did not openly make a statement of his theme. Unless a drama is freighted with an explicit message, it is open fairly to personal interpretations, and the individual reader and spectator is challenged to search his own mind in evaluating it.

On the other hand, the express purpose of some dramatists is to illustrate a theme. Medieval drama, for example, which was a sort of visual aid designed to frighten people into salvation, patently stated the point of the story. In the best known of all medieval plays, *The Moral of Everyman*, a Messenger prepares the audience to receive the moral in a prologue; at the end of the play a Doctor appears to reemphasize it in these words:

> This moral men may have in mind;
> Ye hearers, take it of worth, old and young,
> And forsake pride, for he deceiveth you in
>   the end.
> And remember Beauty, Five-Wits, Strength
>   and Discretion
> They all at the last do Everyman forsake,
> Save his Good-Deeds, there doth he take.
> But beware, and they be small
> Before God, he hath no help at all.

The outstanding German playwright Bertolt Brecht viewed the theater as a social force and thus deliberately avoided attempts to evoke emotional responses in order that his audience might be more aware of his political ideas. You will notice the interruption of continuity from time to time in *The Caucasian Chalk Circle.*

One of the most important contributions of Ibsen was his concern with dramatic themes that would provoke thought and discussion. His approach to the element of thought is clearly evident from the preliminary notes he made when in Rome while contemplating *A Doll's House.* In "Notes for a Modern Tragedy" he wrote:

There are two kinds of spiritual law, two kinds of conscience, one in man and another, altogether different, in woman. They do not understand each other; but in practical life the woman is judged by man's law, as though she were not a woman but a man.

The wife in the play ends by having no idea of what is right or wrong; natural feeling on the one hand and belief in authority on the other have bewildered her.

A woman cannot be herself in the society of the present day, which is an exclusively masculine society, with laws framed by men and with a judicial system that judges feminine conduct from a masculine point of view.

She has committed forgery, and she is proud of it; for she did it out of love for her husband, to save his life. But this husband with his commonplace principles of honor is on the side of the law and regards the question with masculine eyes.

Spiritual conflicts. Oppressed and bewildered by the belief in authority, she loses faith in her moral right and ability to bring up her children. Bitterness. A mother in modern society, like certain insects who go away and die when she has done her duty in the propagation of the race. Here and there a womanly shaking-off of her thoughts. Sudden return of anxiety and terror. She must bear it alone. The catastrophe approaches, inexorably, inevitably. Despair, conflict and destruction.

Although Ibsen, in describing his method of working on a play, acknowledges that he began with a clearly stated theme, he took considerable pains to present his thought by implication, indirection and innuendo rather than by direct statement. As a consequence, the spectator is not overly conscious of Ibsen's themes. Unlike the medieval writers, Ibsen did not point to a clear-cut solution to the problems he raised. His purpose was to provoke thought rather than to persuade the audience to adopt a specific plan of action. An interesting example of Ibsen's intention occurred in *An Enemy of the People.* In one scene in the original version, Dr. Stockmann alludes to biology to prove that there are certain individuals "bred" to superior comprehension of truths, and who, therefore, are natural leaders. This view has been taken by some to suggest that the playwright was a fascist. When Ibsen was attacked with this argument, he replied, "I do not mean the aristocracy of birth, or of the purse, or even the aristocracy of the intellect, I mean the aristocracy of character, of will, of mind—that alone can free us." Following Ibsen's example, many modern playwrights have found their source material in contemporary problems. The content of the plays of our day is often a direct reflection of contemporary thought as the playwright weighs values and motives by which men live, seek for individual fulfillment, or search for reality.

All playwrights, in representing men in action, dramatize their significant behavior and decisions, thus providing insight into the ways by which men live and move and have their being. In tragedy, the dramatist is concerned with the profoundest problems and the most elevated concepts of mankind, with the relation of his characters to their gods, the meaning of justice, the probing into good and evil. In comedy, the playwright may exploit the ridiculous aspects of human conduct. In some forms of drama, notably farce and melodrama, the dramatist may have little or no interest in the secondary meaning of the actions of his characters. The personages of his plays are concerned only with the actions themselves, not with the meaning of the actions. In creating this kind of drama the playwright has little reference to actuality except to require the external appearance of real life. He freely manipulates his characters according to the exigencies of his plot and excuses his essential dishonesty of thought and motivation on the grounds that he is concerned only with theatrical values.

Whatever the purpose of the playwright, the action of significant drama is as meaningful as an experience of life itself. The choices that the characters make, their behavior and motivation, and the sequence of the events of the play are all rewarding subjects for investigation. The playwright's attitude is inferable from his treatment of plot and character. He may be humane and sensible like Shakespeare and Molière; he may write with the scathing satire of Ben Jonson, the compassion of Chekhov and Hauptmann, the zeal of the early Odets, the incisive and perplexing probing of Pirandello, the bleak pessimism of Sartre and Beckett, or the comic audacity of Shaw. A play, then, is more than a passing diversion unrelated to life. It is, rather, a significant revelation of the human condition.

DICTION

Aristotle's fourth element is *diction*, by which is meant the language of the play, the words the actors speak. The function of diction is to provide a means for communicating the characters' thoughts, and ultimately to convey the playwright's total meaning to the audience. As John Howard Lawson says, "Speech puts the actual impact of events into words: it dramatizes forces which are not seen." In modern drama, the dramatist has a utilitarian basis for his dialogue. His lines must, as someone has suggested, "Advance the plot,

delineate character, or get a laugh." Good dialogue is a means to an end, not an end in itself, for the real merit of the drama does not reside so much in wording as in its solid structure, in the sequence of the plot, in the integrity and vividness of the characterization, and in the meaning of the action behind the facade of language.

Discourse in drama must be clear, because the language must be immediately apprehended by the listener; in the theater, one cannot turn back the page or pause to weigh and consider a line before hearing the next. The dialogue must be interesting despite the need for simplicity and economy. It should capture the spirit of life and character. As the Irish playwright, Synge, put it, "In a good play, every speech should be as fully flavored as a nut or an apple." Diction must be appropriate to the character and the situation, for lines do not exist in the theater as separate entities. They are always in context. They grow out of the emotionally charged incidents of the plot. The language of drama must be dynamic, its presentation a form of action. The dialogue thus shows the character's relationship to others, reflects the progression of the action, indicates what is happening inside the characters, reveals their suffering, growth or decline. It is a means of articulating the clash of wills and the conflicting motivations. It is also a means of establishing locale and character, as for example in the opening of *Ceremonies in Dark Old Men* and *The Emperor Jones*. In high comedy, agile dialogue, with characters shooting barbed verbal shafts at one another, may be a substitute for physical movement. The dramatist needs the poet's feeling for language—a rich imagination, a felicity for provocative imagery, an awareness of the weight, texture and arrangement of words. Dramatic dialogue is not contemplative or static; it is harnessed to action and change. Finally, good dialogue must be suited for oral expression. The lines must give the actor a basic pattern for performance. They must reveal fully the character's emotions and motivations as the actor interprets them before the audience.

Much of the serious drama preceding the nineteenth century was linked to poetry. The Greek and Elizabethan masters of drama were poets as well as playwrights. Their works, therefore, have an added literary and linguistic dimension, and their use of verse seems particularly appropriate to the elevated tragedies of high-born characters. In modern times, however, poetry gives way to prose when the naturalist and realist bring onstage contemporary, commonplace figures in the everyday pursuits of life. Many have lamented the absence of poetry in the contemporary theater; sporadic attempts have been made to recapture some of the enrichment of poetic speech, notably in the works of Maxwell Anderson, Christopher Fry, Bertolt Brecht, T. S. Eliot, and Federico Garcia Lorca. Although modern drama lacks elevated language, it is not true that all plays written in poetic form were successful. Indeed, the use of verse in the past was often puerile and ostentatious. Many poets had no sense of dramatic form or theatrical awareness. Oftentimes, their preoccupation with the language retarded the action, filled their plays with linguistic clutter, thus making the drama unstageworthy. The general use of prose in the contemporary theater has resulted in stage speech that tends to be flat and pedestrian, filled with the clichés of commonplace conversation. On the other hand, current emphasis on functional speech has produced texts of directness and clarity. In the hands of some modern playwrights, the dialogue is often vivid and evocative, as for example, in the plays of Tennessee Williams and Samuel Beckett. As Bernard Shaw points out, the modern drama has gained in what he calls the "discussion" element of drama. Shaw, of course, was especially fond of ventilating controversial issues, and his plays are full of shafts and barbs about all manner of problems, as is evident in *Major Barbara*.

Most modern playwrights tend to center their attention on dramatic experiences in which characters analyze and describe forces at work upon them. They do not simply pass through a series of adventures without cerebration. They talk over the issues and expose points of view, thus adding substance to contemporary dialogue. Consider, for example, the discussion elements that do so much to expose character in *Miss Julie*.

Over the years dramatists have utilized a variety of dialogue devices. One of the most interesting, devised by the Greeks, is *stichomythia*, that is, short lines of alternating dialogue. The Greek dramatist employed stichomythia as a method of building tension much as a motion picture editor uses rapid intercutting of film clips to increase intensity in exciting moments of a picture. Molière, in the seventeenth-century French theater, achieved comic stichomythia by breaking lines of dialogue into short bursts of speech by means of interruptions. You will find an example of this in *The Miser*, Act I, scene 3, and Act IV, scene 5.

Another linguistic device, one much favored by Shakespeare, is the soliloquy, a solo speech, generally an introspective analysis or a pondering of a future course of action. Playwrights, aware of rich psychological life beneath the surface, also used the convention of the soliloquy to reveal workings of the mind. The neoclassicists in France often replaced this device by the use of confidants for each of the leading characters, so that private thoughts, aimed at the ears of servants, friends, and duennas, reached the audience.

The use of extended narration for recounting offstage or antecedent action has been used from the Greeks to the present day. Effective examples are the messenger's description of the deaths of Antigone, Haimon, and Eurydice. Miss Julie's extended description of her family background is another case in point. In *The Caucasian Chalk Circle* you will note the use of a story-teller to bridge the action. An ingenious adaptation of the soliloquy is used by Beckett in *Krapp's Last Tape*, in which a single character contrasts his old age with his earlier life by listening to and commenting upon an old tape-recording of his voice.

A number of new playwrights have appeared recently who refuse to conform to established techniques and conventions of the theater. These so-called "absurdists" are of special interest in their rejection of dramatic structure and in their use of dialogue. Beckett, Ionesco, and Pinter, in particular, have written stage speech which, while intentionally pedestrian and hackneyed, is nevertheless remarkably evocative, as for example the dialogue in Ionesco's *The Leader*. Their use of clichés in short segments of sound, combined with frequent pauses, is strangely expressive in performance. At times this kind of dialogue has been used to satirize the vacuity of commonplace conversation. At other times the very flatness of the language has served as a kind of desperate cover to conceal the fear of silence.

Other dialogue devices have been used from time to time in the theater such as choral speeches, antiphonal passages between a leader and a group, staccato, telegraphic fragments of speech in expressionistic plays, extensive monologues, prologues and epilogues for exposition, foreshadowing or commenting on the action, bits of poetry, and involved conceits and epigrams. But the primary form of diction in most drama is compressed dialogue, which despite its conventions, gives to the listener the impression of natural speech.

MUSIC

Aristotle's fifth element is *music,* which refers to all of the auditory material of a play, including sound effects and the tonal patterns of the spoken words. Music encompasses all aspects of sound—pitch, rate, quality, duration, volume, and rhythm. We remember that Greek drama had its origin in choric dithyrambs, in which music, chanting, and dancing were integral parts of the performance. The speech of the Athenian playwrights was created in rich patterns of verse in which the sound, texture, and cadence of language were significant aspects. In the Oriental theater, music continues to play an essential part in the total effect. The language of the Elizabethans often was rich in lyricism that broke out into song. Melodrama was originally linked to music, and even though the spoken word came to dominate the genre, musical backgrounds were used to accompany exits and entrances of major characters and to reinforce the tensely emotional mood of the scenes.

In our contemporary drama, naturalism and realism have rejected music per se as an artificial intrusion, but even in realistic drama playwrights have occasionally made telling use of sound to enhance the mood of their plays. Chekhov, for example, was very conscious of the use of sounds in *Uncle Vanya.* In the final act of the play, a melancholy atmosphere is reinforced by the click of the counting beads, the scratch of the pen, the churring of a cricket, the tapping of the night watchman's cane, the soft strumming of a guitar, and the bells of the carriage as Dr. Astrov makes his departure. Strindberg too was aware of the evocative effect of music. In *Miss Julie* the dance and chorus music off-stage reinforce our awareness of the Midsummer Eve celebrations, and the sound of the bell heightens emotional feeling at the play's end. Other modern dramatists with a keen ear for the expressiveness of sound are Eugene O'Neill, Tennessee Williams, Maurice Maeterlinck, Federico Garcia Lorca, and Sean O'Casey. The nonrealistic playwrights, particularly the expressionists, have freely introduced music into their plays, as Brecht does in the songs in *The Caucasian Chalk Circle*.

The spoken word of all kinds of drama is allied to music in its appeal to the ear, and all successful playwrights have been mindful of the importance of rhythm and sound.

SPECTACLE

The sixth Aristotelian element of drama, *spectacle*, refers to all of the visual aspects of production—scenery, lighting, costume, makeup, and the business and movement of the actors. A glance at the descriptions of the stage settings and properties of the modern plays in this text will indicate how essential spectacle is for recent playwrights.

The kind and amount of spectacle have varied throughout theatrical history. In the Greek, Elizabethan, and Japanese Noh plays, virtually no representation of locale is required except that supplied by the architecture itself. Nonetheless, these plays are rich in spectacle, particularly in the use of striking costumes and in the action of the performers. The Greek chorus, the use of dance in Noh and Kabuki drama, and the vivid use of the entire ensemble in panoramic movement in Elizabethan plays, enhanced the visual appeal of the performances. With the development of the proscenium-arch theater during the Renaissance, a taste for pictorialism, for elaborate use of enormous and complicated settings, was cultivated because the arch provided a picture frame behind which changeable scenery could be devised. The realistic and naturalistic movements in the late nineteenth century gave spectacle a new importance in production because environment was widely accepted as a conditioning force in determining behavior. Hence spectacle came to assume an organic, psychological role in the theater, reinforcing the meaning of the play and serving as an expository device to relate character to its social milieu. This view of the function of spectacle is the current one, although there has been a tendency to temper the fashion for complete and factual representation of actuality by increasing simplicity and theatricalism, as for example in *The Caucasian Chalk Circle*.

While at times spectacle has dominated the stage, dwarfing or competing with the actor for the audience's attention, our present attitude is that visual aspects of theatrical production must provide appropriate psychological and physical environment for the drama, create atmosphere, and serve the actor's needs as he performs the play. Inasmuch as a play is intended to be acted, the display and the environment of that action contribute heavily to the impact of the play as theater.

CHAPTER TWO
TRAGEDY

Works of art are not subject to precise scientific classification because the artist, in this case the dramatist, works with a personal bent. He may also vary his style from time to time to suit a variety of purposes. We can, however, distinguish between drama that is serious (or at least makes a pretense of being serious) and drama that is intended to evoke laughter. Serious drama is usually termed tragedy and lighter drama comedy. In this chapter we will first discuss the nature of tragedy and then that of melodrama, and finally that species of play occupying a middle ground between tragedy and melodrama, which we will call *drame*.

Tragedy is a strange and mysterious country despite considerable efforts made to fix its boundaries and establish its configurations. Each adventurer must find his own way through an entangling jungle of conjecture and a luxuriant undergrowth of verbiage surrounding this territory. There is no short cut, no easy known way, because tragedy is a quality of experience each man must come to know for himself.

The first to chart his course and mark the way was Aristotle, who in his fourth-century B.C. work, the *Poetics*, sought to guide those who followed him. Although he found his original directions by the genius of dead-reckoning from relatively limited observation, we may still trace his progress with profit, so clearly did he designate his landmarks. As a consequence, we will continue to refer to him frequently, as we have in the preceding section. Aristotle's work is, however, open to varied interpretations and misinterpretations, partly because of his language, which is at points hastily constructed and even contradictory, and partly because of his examples, a number of which are from plays lost to us. Aristotelian doctrine, therefore, should be regarded as a lamp in the darkness, not the source of all light.

Aristotle places considerable emphasis on the structure of tragedy. Excellence of form in all kinds of art was a source of aesthetic pleasure to the Greeks. They saw things as parts of a whole. They delighted in the organization of a unified structure. Thus, while the *Poetics* is an analysis of tragedy, Aristotle's discussion frequently concerns all forms of dramatic writing and can serve as a commentary on play-making in general.

ARISTOTLE & TRAGEDY

Let us turn our attention to Aristotle's very significant definition of tragedy and then examine his terms.

Tragedy, then, is an imitation of an action that is serious, complete, and of a certain magnitude; in language embellished with each kind of artistic ornament, the several kinds being found in separate parts of the play; in the form of action, not of narrative; through pity and fear effecting the proper purgation of these emotions.

The origin of the word *tragedy* is a matter of conjecture. "Tragos" in Greek means goat;

"oide" means song. Tragedy was associated with goat-song or goat-singer in its early stages. The terms "tragic" and "tragedy" as we use them in everyday speech have little to do with "tragedy" as a form of drama. A person may speak of the "tragic" death of a small girl in an automobile accident. While tragedy usually involves catastrophe, it is not the calamity itself upon which attention is focused in drama. Death may even seem incidental, as in *Hamlet* when it occurs to such secondary characters as Polonius or Laertes. The validity of genuine tragedy is not concerned with the act of violence, but with what that act says about life—the struggle of the protagonist, the issues at stake, the effect of his suffering.

An *imitation* is not a mere copy, but is a created work of art fashioned by man. Its relation to reality is that the course of events of the drama are "necessary and probable."

An action refers to a sequence of incidents joined together into a unified whole. An action is the thing done.

Tragedy has been called the drama of *high seriousness*. It deals with the most profound and universal problems of man—his purpose and destiny, the nature of good and evil, a man's relationship to forces greater than himself, the consequences of individual responsibility. Tragedy is never frivolous, trivial, or mean. It goes far beyond diversion or amusement to investigate spiritual values and struggles.

Tragedy attains *magnitude* in the heroic stature of its characters, through the use of poetry, by the universality of its meaning and the loftiness of its ideas. Tragedies are elevated; they possess scale and scope far beyond the petty vicissitudes of daily existence. Magnitude of character is realized in tragedy through the use of high-born characters, persons of nobility and prominence who occupy "exposed positions;" people who, as Aristotle said, "are better than we are," such as Antigone, Creon, and King Lear.

A tragedy is *complete:* it has a beginning, a middle, and an end. Each of these parts is causally related, thus creating a unified effect and a plot that is a well-articulated structure having no extraneous material. The course of action is a "necessary and probable" linking of antecedents and consequents. Such unity and wholeness were fundamental to the Greek aesthetic view of life.

"By *language embellished with each kind of artistic ornament,*" Aristotle explains, "I mean that with rhythm and harmony or song superadded; and by the kinds separately, I mean that some portions are worked out with verse only, and others in turn with song."

The chief difference between the *dramatic* and *narrative form* is a result of the manner of presentation. A narrative may be written or told; drama must be presented with impersonation and action—it is "a thing done." The dramatic form puts the creative work of the playwright before an audience in the theater by means of the actor's performance. The arousal of *pity* and *fear* followed by the *proper purgation* (catharsis) of these emotions—these statements have intrigued and perplexed scholars and critics for generations. Although we will discuss these special effects of tragedy at length later, let us here state that *pity* goes beyond mere pathos to include the compassion that accompanies shared grief, and that *fear* transcends sheer fright to convey a sense of anxious concern and profound reverence. *Catharsis*, or *purgation*, suggests purification—a release of emotional tension that results in tranquillity.

With Aristotle's definition in mind, and acknowledging its shortcomings because of his limited basis for observation, let us consider some important principles that characterize tragedy.

PLOT

Aristotle lays great stress on plot—the "soul of tragedy." He discusses at length the essentials of dramatic structure, such as the necessity for a unified and complete sequence of interlocking action, the just proportions of the plot, and the proper use of such devices as reversal, discovery, and recognition. So broad is his consideration of plot that it may be applied to all forms of drama as well as specifically to tragedy.

What aspects of plot apply exclusively to tragedy? Certainly, Aristotle's concept of unity of action—a plot simple enough to be held easily in the mind of the spectator—does not apply to *King Lear* or to most Elizabethan drama. Shakespeare and his contemporaries disregarded unity, moreover, by blending comic and serious material, combining high- and low-born characters, mixing verse and prose, freely interweaving plots and sub-plots on the flexible Elizabethan stage. The general answer, then, is no, the structure of tragedy does not have its own special form. The plays of the Greeks, the Elizabethans, and the neo-classicists are too divergent in structure to fit a single pattern.

Certain generalizations, however, do apply to the treatment of dramatic materials. Tragedy usually deals with a positive and active protagonist caught in sharp conflict with opposing forces. In the ensuing struggle, he suffers greatly and moves from good fortune to misfortune, never in the opposite direction. Tragic conflicts are of a particular kind. The struggle does not involve such mundane considerations as economic or sociological problems. The struggle is ethical, spiritual. Often-times, the tragic hero is placed in a situation in which the courses of action open to him are at war with the moral order he has accepted. Tragic actions thus arise from inner conflicts that test the protagonist's integrity.

In the organization of the incidents, the playwright must solve the customary problems of plot construction; he must create climaxes, crises, reversals, discoveries and so forth, but always with a view toward what the events reveal about the hero. The interest is not only in the incidents themselves, but in what is going on inside, the effect on the protagonist's soul. When the dramatist adopts the opposite stance and makes the external action his primary concern, he writes melodrama. The writer of genuine tragedy constructs a plot that emphasizes "inwardness."

Because tragedy is relentlessly honest, the dramatist does not contrive to save the protagonist from catastrophe or spare him from suffering. Once Antigone has defied Creon's edict she is sent relentlessly to her doom. Shakespeare does not spare Lear from suffering. The playwright shows life as it is, not as one wishes it might be. Evil is shown along with the good. In the treatment of character, the protagonist is neither the white-washed, idealized hero of romanticism nor the black-hearted villain of melodrama. Man is shown as a mixture of clay and stardust. The tragic hero is usually an admirable character, but he possesses a flaw and his imperfection links him to us. In short, tragedy rests on a solid basis of integrity, making no concessions to desires for wish-fulfillment on the part of the audience.

TRAGIC CATHARSIS

The most significant element that distinguishes tragedy from other forms of drama is the tragic effect. Just what it is in tragedy that gives pleasure through pain is difficult to determine. Friedrich Schlegel felt that the tragic tone was one of "irrepressible melancholy," as the audience is consoled and elevated through witnessing human weakness exposed to the vagaries of fate and natural forces. Arthur Schopenhauer saw the meaning of tragedy as resignation and renunciation in the face of a miserable and desolate existence. On the other hand, H. A. Myers asserts that tragedy appeals to us because it satisfies our craving to discover, even in moments of utmost suffering and evil, patterns in life which are truly representative of life and therefore just. What constitutes the tragic effect in drama is thus capable of many interpretations.

Our individual sense of the tragic is complex and highly personalized; it is arrived at through our experience and awareness. In such plays as *Hamlet* and *Antigone,* as we seek to interpret the play with our experience and with our attitudes about life, we perceive values beyond what is explicit in the story and stage action. The play's events are raised to a universal level and move us, as Professor Alan Thompson says, ". . . to the impassioned contemplation of ultimates."

To understand the tragic effect, it is necessary to keep Aristotle's words "fear and pity" before us. What did he mean by them? Pity is not simply pathos, a soft sentiment of sorrow for one who is weak or unworthy. Pity is not contemptuous or patronizing. Implied in tragic pity is an equality, a sharing of grief. We enter into the experience of another through our sympathy and our fellow-feeling. We feel pity for the tragic hero as an act of compassion. Similarily, the meaning of the word fear must be extended beyond that of sheer fright or terror to include anxious concern, solicitude, awe, reverence, and apprehension. In tragedy, fear is not merely a hair-raising, spine-tingling reaction of the nervous system; it is an emotion that warms the heart and illuminates the mind. Fear carries a sense of wonder. The terms fear and pity, therefore, must be thought of in their most human and universal context, as involving a general concern for others rather than a private and personal identification with disaster.

Aristotle obviously intended that catharsis should be therapeutic. The tragic effect on the spectator is to purge away his fear and pity, to give him a sense of release and tranquillity. He is cleansed and exhilarated when he is liberated from his own emotional entanglements and disturbing passions. Fear gives way to certainty, even though that certainty is death. Pity goes beyond feeling and becomes understanding. The spectator leaves the theater "in calm of mind, all passion spent." The end result is, as Northrop Frye suggests, that the audience experiences a "kind of buoyancy." Or again, in Edith Hamilton's words, "the great soul in pain and death transforms and exalts pain and death." Myers universalizes the meaning more explicitly:

These are the main features of the tragic spirit. It lifts us above self-pity and reconciles us to suffering by showing that evil is a necessary part of the intelligible and just order of our experience. It lifts us above the divisive spirit of melodrama by showing that men are neither naturally good nor inherently evil. It saves us all from the pitfalls of utopianism and fatalism. It teaches moderation by showing that the way of the extremist is short, but at the same time it shows the man of principle that an uncompromising stand is not without its just compensations. And most important, it teaches us that all men are united in the kinship of a common fate, that all are destined to suffer and enjoy, each according to his capacity.

THE TRAGIC HERO

Another Aristotelian concept of fundamental importance to the understanding of tragedy is the nature of the tragic hero. The tragic hero is a good man, but not free from blemish—"an intermediate kind of personage" who, while not preeminently virtuous, is not depraved. His flaw is an error in judgement. This flaw, *hamartia,* has been the source of considerable controversy in that it appears to be neither uniformly applicable to all tragedies nor consistent with the variety of characters involved in catastrophes. How does one equate the suffering of Prometheus with that of Oedipus? Antigone with that of Medea? Hamlet with that of Macbeth? The degree of guilt seems to have little or nothing to do with justice. All tragic figures suffer greatly. Frequently, their fall seems to proceed not so much from crime and punishment as it does from cause and effect. They suffer because they occupy positions of responsibility. The tragic hero is a man of good intentions whose catastrophe may be the result of a flaw, not of guilt. He may fall because he errs as well as because he sins. He often elicits our pity because of his "undeserved misfortune." In this connection, we think of the protagonists who suffer beyond all desert—Julius Caesar, Antigone, Electra, Oedipus, Othello, and Lear. Tragedy does not exist to demonstrate justice. On the contrary, it may serve to remind us of the hard fact that much of life is filled with injustice. It is a mistake, therefore, to look to tragedy for a neat apportionment of reward and punishment. Some Greek tragedies deal with protagonists whose judgment is flawed by emotional pressure that causes them to lose their sense of balance and proportion. The Greek view of the good life was based on a sense of completeness and moderation in which the passions were controlled and tempered by reason. The tragic flaw is in the loss of the hero's sense of perspective. Caught in a web of circumstances, he becomes an extremist: he loses sight of the golden mean, fails to keep his balance on a high place, and at last slips to his downfall.

Aristotle's view of the tragic hero, and of his flaw, must not be regarded as an inflexible and all-inclusive definition. To make his concepts fit the few extant Greek tragedies, not to mention the plays of Shakespeare and his contemporaries, takes considerable stretching and straining. Aristotle is thus a frame of reference for discussing tragic heroes and their qualities rather than a rigid measure by which a play may or may not be justly labeled a tragedy.

The tragic hero is a man of significance, who in representing universal human qualities, represents us. He is an active agent rather than a passive, submissive victim of accident or fate. He struggles and suffers mightily, and in his travail affirms the greatness of the human spirit.

THE CREATION OF TRAGEDY

Tragedy, because of its defining characteristics, requires rather special circumstances for its creation. While numerous attempts have been made to write tragedy at many different times, playwrights in general have failed to ascend the heights because of deficiency of talent, shortness of vision, or prevailing circumstances that stunted their spiritual growth. Tragedy is thus *rare*.

What seem to be the social conditions

conducive to the writing of tragedy? Both the Golden Age of Greece and the England of Elizabeth I were periods and places of great intellectual stimulation. The human spirit was exalted, mankind ennobled. The world was no vale of shadows, but an exciting place full of enormous possibilities. Life was not bland or filled with despair. Man was dignified, hopeful, secure in his faith in the future and himself. He could extend himself in many directions. The spirit of such ages was congenial to tragedy because these cultures affirmed the worth and dignity of human life. The atmosphere of these times seems to conform to three basic assumptions that Oates and O'Neill give us as necessary for the creation of tragedy: "First, the dignity of man; second, the freedom of his will and his responsibility for the use which he makes of that will; and third, the existence in the universe of a super-human factor."[1] Such assumptions are positive expressions about life and its meaning. When the philosophical climate of an age rejects one or more of these points of view, tragedy of an elevated and affirmative nature is difficult to create.

Our modern temper with its doubts and skepticism about man and supernatural forces is considered by some to be inhospitable ground for the nurture of the tragic spirit. The political practice of raising the proletariat to a dominant position has changed our fashion in heroes from high-born and romantic characters to common, contemporary men. The materialism resulting from the Industrial Revolution has not only worked against individualism, but also has shifted our sense of values to a high regard for products and possessions. But most importantly, the impact of science has forced modern man to reorient his thinking, to question traditional Christian morality, to look with skepticism upon the dignity of man and see him rather as a part of the animal kingdom, "red in tooth and claw." The psychologist has caused us to look upon human behavior as a conditioned reflex. He studies the mechanism of conduct and explains man's choices and decisions on the basis of his emotions and drives.

The appropriate forms of expression which resulted from these changing attitudes were, as we shall see, realism and naturalism. The effect on drama was to drive out poetry, to emphasize the conditioning of behavior from a standpoint of heredity and environment, to depict contemporary characters involved in social problems in which interrelationships were extremely important, and to create a new significance for accurate representation of specific locale because of its influence on the action. It is obvious that these conditions were inhospitable to the creation of high tragedy. Among our contemporary playwrights, Arthur Miller has been most ambitious to recapture the tragic spirit especially as it relates to the common man. In such plays as *The Crucible* and *Death of a Salesman*, he shows that the ordinary man is quite capable of great suffering in the struggle to establish his personal dignity and to gain what Miller calls "his rightful position in society." While Miller's plays faithfully demonstrate his concern with the common man, the emphasis on environmental conditioning and the force of social pressures narrow the dramatist's vision so that his protagonists remain earthbound despite their travail. The existentialists have written seriously about the human conditions, but they have been restricted because their protagonists are cut off from

---

[1]Whitney J. Oates and Eugene O'Neill, Jr., eds., *The Complete Greek Drama* (New York, Random House, Inc., 1938), p. xxviii.

outside forces, even from their contem-poraries. The lack of faith and the restricted range of spiritual exploration negate the eleva-tion of tragedy. Now the "absurdists" have taken a yet more extreme position by denying even themselves and dramatizing life as being futile, meaningless, and grotesque.

John Mason Brown describes the dif-ficulties of writing modern tragedy, although he does see some hope:

A period of realism and an age of prose are not the only hindrances. The lost or dwindling religi-ous faith of many people; the encroachments of such a materialistic and earthboudn theology as Marxism; an increasing uncertainty as to accepted or acceptable standards; our living with the threat of mass annihilation; adjusting to the great changes in the stresses and basic concepts of our economic and social life; the emergence of the "little man" as the new hero for hero worship; the shrinkage of the individual's importance under the pressures of super-states or ever-growing bureaucracies; indeed, not only the notion but the realization that the century belongs to the common rather than the exceptional man—all these factors, widening or limiting, which have altered tragedy along with everything else. Because of them, one wonders if the tragic blueprint, cherished for so long as an

ideal, has not, at least in part, become a glorious anachronism.

Not that tragedy is dead or will ever die. Or that Man has lost his touch with the heroic. No one who has watched men, women, and children rise to the terrible trials of these past years can maintain that Man has become mean. The bigness of the so-called "little man" in the face of such trials and of daily living is one of the most hopeful facts of recent history. It is simply that the heroic has become different in scale and kind, and for this very reason tragedy needs to be rediscovered for our own times and in our own terms.[2]

Whether or not great tragedy can be writ-ten today is a matter of controversy. Cer-tainly, the temper of our times seems alien to the great traditions, although in the plays of Arthur Miller, Ugo Betti, and Paul Claudel we catch glimpses of an ancient grandeur, and in modern biography considerable evidence of man's spiritual capacity raises him again toward the tragic heights.

----

[2]John Mason Brown, "American Tragedy," *Satur-day Review*, August 6, 1949. Reprinted by permis-sion of the publishers.

SIGNIFICANCE OF CONTENT

Tragedy achieves significance because it is concerned with the deep and abiding ques-tions and problems that have perplexed man throughout the ages. As Nicoll says, tragedy puts us in ". . . contact with infinity. If we are religious, we shall say it is in contact with

the vast illimitable forces of the universe. Everywhere in tragedy there is this sense of being raised to loftier heights."[3] Tragedy is

----

[3]Allardyce Nicoll, *The Theory of Drama* (New York, Thomas Y. Crowell Co., 1931).

thus concerned with man's spiritual nature. It confronts suffering and evil with relentless honesty in such a way as to reveal both the weakness and nobility of man, his strength of will, and his capacity for suffering without breaking in the face of inevitable doom.

Although tragedy involves suffering, evil and death, it is a positive statement about life. As Nicoll says, "Death never really matters in a tragedy. . . . Tragedy assumes that death is inevitable and that its time of coming is of no importance compared with what a man does before his death."[4] Death may overtake the protagonist, but he is spiritually victorious. He is not an abject, craven victim of fate who goes cowering to his doom. The principles for which he lived and died survive his passing. The hero dies; heroism lives on. We admire the audacity of a man who, disregarding human frailty, reveals an astonishing capacity for suffering in matters of the spirit. His action, an affirmation of life, sustains our faith in mankind.

Professor H. A. Myers asserts that "tragedy best expresses its conceptions of the orderly and absolute nature of values;" and Professor Francis Fergusson observes that tragedy "celebrates the mystery of human nature and destiny with the health of the soul in view."

Tragedy is not the drama of small souls. It does not concentrate on man's physical environment or his welfare, nor with his getting and spending, his thing-collecting. On the contrary, tragedy lifts our vision beyond petty cares and mundane anxieties by forcing our attention to the great issues of life which bear a relationship to our spiritual welfare. Antigone is caught between her sacred obligation to the dead and obedience to the King. Entangled in a set of strong moral sensibilities, Hamlet bears the awful burden of avenging the death of his father. The conflicting characters in *Antigone* and *Hamlet* occupy places of great responsibility in contrast to the rather narrow lives of Jimmy and Alison Porter in *Look Back in Anger*, of the Parkers in *Ceremonies in Dark Old Men*, and of Jean and Miss Julie in *Miss Julie*. In contemporary serious drama the characters seem to be playing for small stakes and the effect of their suffering is personal rather than of great consequence.

The significant content of tragedy gives this form of drama a sense of universality. The effect of the play goes beyond the particular characters and the immediate circumstances to achieve an atmosphere of broad application. If even kings may suffer, how vulnerable are we? To the Greeks and Elizabethans the fate of the ruler was connected directly with that of his subjects. To witness genuine tragedy gives us not only a sense of elevation to our own separate lives, but also an acute awareness of our common frailty and humanity. The tragic hero's struggles and suffering thus ennoble and humble those who share the play.

In order to attain magnitude and elevation, however, let us remember that tragic events must be removed a step from our own lives. To perceive their great scope and grandeur, a certain amount of distance and perspective is required. High tragedy conveys a sense of aloofness and detachment, which in its most severe expression threatens to throw a chill of austerity over the drama and its characters. On the other hand, the problems dealt with by tragedy are so universal and the suffering of the protagonist so intense that we are drawn quite naturally into the action.

---

[4]*Ibid.*

MELODRAMA

The writer of melodrama is not interested in the literary aspects of drama; essentially he is an adept storyteller and craftsman with a shrewd sense of pace, rhythm, a feeling for climactic action, and an understanding of the audience for which he writes. Logic does not interest him so long as his script gives the impression of credibility. He achieves this credibility by involving his characters in exciting action and by creating the illusion of actuality through the use of realistic backgrounds, appropriate costuming, and dialogue that suggests the speech of everyday life.

Melodramatic plots rely on strong story lines because the writer knows that his audience is not primarily interested in probing character, listening to bright parlor talk, or considering perplexing social problems. His clientele wants to see familiar characters involved in stories told in scenes of clear and vigorous action. Hence, melodrama exaggerates climaxes and crises so that its structure becomes a series of peaks of action rather than a well-knit steady progression of logically related events. Characters are shown facing overwhelming odds—trapped, dangling, or marooned—holding out until help comes—the last bullet, the last drop of water, the last morsel of food, the last cent. Stock melodramatic situations include escapes, ambushes, shipwrecks, murders, duels, drownings, explosions, battles, rescues, fires, executions, rendezvous and all manner of natural phenomena—storms, avalanches, floods, eruptions: any situation in short, that places the characters in physical jeopardy.

Melodrama no longer occupies the central position that it did in the legitimate theater of the nineteenth century, but it continues today to have a very wide popular appeal in motion pictures and on television. Much of our current melodrama is much more sophisticated than that of a century ago. The visual aspects are far more credible, and the action may be psychological as well as physical. But the essentials of melodrama are almost always present in our "westerns," "whodunits," and our stories of war and adventure.

Professor H. A. Myers makes an interesting statement about character when he says, "In the black-and-white world of melodrama men are divided in two sharply opposed classes, represented by the unblemished hero and the unspeakable villain. . . . The first premise of melodrama is that there are two distinct kinds of men: The first premise of tragedy is that all men are essentially the same."[5] Nineteenth-century melodrama and our contemporary motion picture and television plays of action testify to the validity of Myers' observation. Characters are generally good or bad one-dimensional figures who pursue their objectives in a straight line, without thought, development, or psychological complexity. They do not think; they act. And as a result of their thoughtlessness, they become involved in all sorts of absurd entanglements, such as being caught on a train trestle at midnight without a lantern or match,

---

[5] Henry Alonzo Myers, *Tragedy: A View of Life* (Ithaca, Cornell University Press, 1956).

lost in the snow barefoot, or ensnared by the villain because they misjudged the character of their adversary. The writer of melodrama has little or no concern with delineating characters as substantial individuals who respond to the events in which they participate and who are conditioned by their environment and past experiences. Melodramatic characters are simple in heart and mind; they are objects of desire with whom the audience can readily identify itself. Hence, the heroes and heroines of melodrama are not the elevated figures of great tragedy; they are humble people drawn from everyday life. The villains, however, are often outsiders—foreigners, members of the upper crust, unscrupulous men of wealth.

The impact of melodrama relies heavily on music and spectacle. Melodrama, originally linked with music, has continued that association as a principal means of eliciting emotional response. In the nineteenth century, special theme music was used to announce entrances and exits of leading characters and to create the atmosphere for emotionally loaded scenes. With the coming of realism to the theater during the last quarter of the nineteenth century, music nearly disappeared. The makers of silent motion pictures soon learned to provide appropriate scores for piano or organ, and with the advent of sound films and television music has continued to be an important aspect of the production.

In the first half of the nineteenth century, theaters made use of two-dimensional stock pieces consisting of backdrops and wings, on which were painted a variety of backgrounds such as a kitchen, a palace, a prison, a grotto, a woodland glade. This system possessed two virtues—it was economic, and it made shifting rapid and easy. To change to a new setting, the backdrop was raised and the wings were slid back along their grooves to uncover the scenes directly behind them. Throughout the country theaters were equipped with stock sets, so that a touring company needed to bring only its special effects and costumes along. But as the taste for sensational novelties grew, productions became increasingly elaborate and expensive. Metropolitan stages became more complicated with bridges, traps, elevators, moving platforms, and various kinds of paraphernalia for producing fires, floods, explosions, and all manner of astounding displays. Two-dimensional scenery was replaced by built-up solid pieces, making the sets substantial and difficult to move. The producer David Belasco actually bought pieces of buildings and moved them intact onto the stage. Playwrights were obliged to create scenes calculated to exploit visual sensations. While sensational scenery called attention to itself, it was also used for more than pictorial representation. The setting was functional in that it served the actor's needs in particular scenes. A waterfall was not simply shown as an enlarged calendar picture for its visual appeal; it became a factor in the action when the hero struggled to save the heroine from plunging to her death. A railroad trestle was set on stage not merely for the novelty of showing a train, but also as a weapon of the villain who tied the heroine to the tracks while the approaching light and whistle of the train were seen and heard. The setting was an essential part of the action. Hence, a considerable amount of ingenuity was required by the stage mechanic to devise effects that were not only visually credible, but also utilitarian enough to be used in chases, fights, and escapes. The motion picture, the ideal medium for exploiting action, has shifted the elaboration of scenic requirements from stage to screen.

DRAME

Most serious modern playwrights have not aspired to scale the heights of tragedy, nor have they been content to confine themselves to sheer melodrama. They have tended to write middle-class plays for a middle-class audience, dealing with contemporary man in commonplace circumstances. This vast body of dramatic literature defies definition because of its great diversity, its technical experimentation and its mixture of several forms of writing at once. Some critics simply use the general term, drama, but we prefer, as a lesser evil, the French term *drame*, by which is meant a play of serious intent which deals for the most part with contemporary life. Just as realism has been the dominant mode of modern drama, likewise, the *drame* has been the preponderant form used by such writers as Henrik Ibsen, Anton Chekhov, Maxim Gorki, Sean O'Casey, Eugene O'Neill, Luigi Pirandello, Jean Anouilh, Clifford Odets, Arthur Miller, Tennessee Williams, John Osborne, and Friedrich Dürrenmatt.

Drame is allied to melodrama in that the playwright often attempts to involve the spectator in the action through identification with the characters and through suspense and tension. *Drame* differs from melodrama in that it may be interested in the realm of ideas—the issues at stake may be sociological and philosophical in implication, as in *An Enemy of the People, Look Back in Anger, Ceremonies in Dark Old Men*, and *The Physicists*. Characters may be involved in genuinely significant action. The effect of a *drame* may be to provoke thought and discussion after the curtain has gone down.

Drame is allied to tragedy in its seriousness of purpose, in its relentless honesty of treatment, in its concern with the meaning of human conduct. *Drame* differs from tragedy in its narrowness of vision, often with its emphasis on material, with temporary or local conditions that deny it universality, with its mechanistic or deterministic sense of values, and with its general lack of elevation. Frequently, the writer of *drames* is fascinated by the psychological complexities of character. His *dramatis personae* are not the stock characters of melodrama; they are individuals with subtle and complicated motivations. They are also not the tragic heroes of great stature who fall from high places, but are ordinary people painfully searching for meaning and security in a baffling world of shifting values.

Modern drama has been notable for its experimentation, but the bulk of serious theatrical fare falls in the general area of realism. It may be profitable to give some attention to this mode and departures from it.

Although playwrights throughout theater history have often intended to give their plots and characters the feeling of actuality, it was not until the nineteenth century that *realism* as a specific literary theory emerged. The intellectual revolution that was brought about by the advance of science and industrialism placed emphasis on the physical and material aspects of life and created the climate for realism. The works of Darwin, Freud, and Marx challenged the traditional views of man. He became an object of scientific study. His life and behavior were viewed as susceptible to explanation according to naturalistic laws and principles. Heredity and environment were conditioning factors behind his actions. The realist relied on meticulous observation, analysis, and recording of specific details. It was his mission to see, hear, and report everything.

This intellectual revolution had a profound effect on drama and the theater. The writer of popular nineteenth-century melodrama dramatized simple people in a complicated plot based on physical action. The realist reversed this method by showing complex characters in a simple plot involving psychological action. He caught the semblance of reality by making all aspects of his work seem logical and free from theatrical contrivances. The painted, two-dimensional stock sets gave way to the "box set," a setting of three continuous walls with practical doors and windows and the furniture properties of real life. Relying on observed facts of everyday existence, he brought the drama closer to actual experience. But the effect often achieved was to make the plot plausible at the expense of narrowing the scope of action and slowing down the pace. Critics of realism complain that in order to condense the action within a solid framework cluttered with detail, the realist sacrificed the free play of his imagination and trapped himself in the stuffy atmosphere of middle-class interiors.

The realist's interest in character caused him to probe into the complexities of motivation. He discarded the stock figures of the popular nineteenth-century theater because they did not jibe with his concept of behavior as rooted in the pressures of environment, the dynamics of childhood, and the interaction of biological drives and social inhibitions. A new gallery of characters, the ordinary and the downtrodden, took a central position on stage. They were shown at the critical moments of their lives, not necessarily those of violent physical action as in melodrama, but of the inner crises that penetrated the social façade and gave insight into their

desires, aspirations, and frustrations. The effect on playwriting was to deal with people of small stature, who were sometimes victims of circumstances, incapable of taking action against the forces that impinged on them. But the writers of realistic *drames* did contribute to the theater integrity of character and a concern with sound psychological motivation.

While realism has been the dominating mode of the contemporary theater, the *drame* has also moved in other directions. Two offshoots of realism were naturalism and expressionism.

The "naturalists" shared with the realists a similar background, but the former were much more emphatic in their mechanistic and deterministic view of life. Man is regarded as animalistic, a product of callous nature. The naturalist stresses the sordid and somber aspects of life; his characters are twisted rejects, the social outcast, the moral outlaw. The naturalist breaks sharply from the realist in his preoccupation with the ugly and squalid side of life. Émile Zola, the champion of naturalism, clamored for drama based on the scientific method, free from theatrical trickery. Attempts were made to write "slice-of-life plays," in which the usual dramatic structure was rejected in order to give the impression that what happened on stage was unorganized actuality.

In 1888 August Strindberg wrote *Miss Julie*, terming it "the Swedish drama's first naturalistic play." This *drame* is an excellent example of naturalism in its conflict of wills growing out of complicated motivations, the powerful use of biological drives, and the general atmosphere of amoral depravity. But technically the play does not follow strictly the tenets of naturalism. It is carefully structured toward a powerful climax, embodies careful foreshadowing and exposition and exhibits a clearcut beginning, middle, and end. In a very powerful way it displays nonetheless the naturalist's approach to character.

A second derivative of realism is expressionism, in which the dramatist argues that reality lies within. The observed facts of conventional behavior do not really show the vast jungle of primitive feelings and drives hidden beneath the surface. Hence, the expressionist strives to project the essential qualities of objects, experiences, and people from the inside out. The expressionist's method is to suppress the details of actuality and to experiment freely with ways of conveying his feelings, often in fantastic, distorted fragments. He flings open the windows of the mind and allows the spectator to look in upon the private, disordered, associative processes of his characters. In Rice's *The Adding Machine*, Mr. Zero's crime and punishment are shown; Kaiser's *From Morn to Midnight* tells the story of a bank clerk's theft, orgy of spending, and death; O'Neill's *Emperor Jones* is a kaleidoscopic depiction of the disintegration of a fugitive through fear. The events often are shown from the subjective and disoriented point of view of the protagonist caught in a nightmare world of grotesquerie. Expressionism never dominated the theater because of its lack of story appeal and its sometimes baffling use of symbols, but its bold theatricalism and effective use of light, form, and color make it a fascinating treatment of the *drame*.

Current playwrights seem to be increasingly impatient with the literal narrowness of realism and have struck off in many new directions, including the "absurdists," who are represented in this volume by Beckett and Ionesco. Another modern innovator writing in a serious vein was Brecht, who rejected the realistic mode to write "epic drama" —plays that are not concerned with the personal conflicts of an individual but with dynamics of social forces at work, as in *The Caucasian Chalk Circle*. Since Brecht was a man with a message, he utilized all the resources of the stage as visual support for his ideas.

CHAPTER THREE

COMEDY

Comedy wears many masks, appears in many guises, from the ill-fitting tattered rags of the drunken hobo to the elegant evening clothes of the most sophisticated aristocrat to the over-dressed finery of the fop. Comedy makes many appeals, from the belly-laugh to the well-concealed smile. Its armor includes such a variety of weapons as the rapier, the slap-stick, the barbed shaft, and the custard pie. It may invoke warm and sympathetic general laughter, or it may castigate a victim with a hard and ruthless derision. Comedy speaks many languages—epigrams, conceits, puns, obscenities, *bons mots*, double-meanings, and the gesture vocabulary of the silent mime. The field of comedy is broad enough to encompass many variations—the romantic comedy of Shakespeare, such as *As You Like It*, and his dark comedies like *A Winter's Tale;* the high comedy of Sheridan's *The School for Scandal;* a musical comedy such as *My Fair Lady;* a farce like Molière's *A Doctor in Spite of Himself* or his character comedy, *The Miser;* a Shavian satire, *Major Barbara;* an intimate revue, *Beyond the Fringe;* an Aristophanic thrust, *Lysistrata;* or a Jacques Tati pasqui-nade, *Mr. Hulot's Holiday.* And comedy includes the prefabricated television fare of Lucille Ball, Jack Benny, Flip Wilson, and situations built around the bewildering behavior of adolescents, the antics of their parents, and "fun in uniform."

THE NATURE OF COMEDY

To define comedy is first to acknowledge the difficulties and hazards of definition. What may make one person laugh may make another grieve. The lively oak of comedy cannot be crammed into a flower pot of simple definition when one considers all of its roots and branches, its variegated fruits and foliage. We usually label a play that ends happily as a comedy and one that ends unhappily as a tragedy. But even this broad generalization breaks down in some instances. Euripides chose to end *Alcestis* happily; Dante calls his great work, with its elevated theme and treat-ment, *The Divine Comedy.* While classicists and neoclassicists keep tragedy and comedy separate, many playwrights, notably the Eng-lish, blended comic and serious matter together, as in *Hamlet, Dr. Faustus,* and *Mac-beth.* Aristotle, in his *Poetics,* makes an impor-tant distinction in saying that in tragedy men are shown as "better than they are" and in comedy as "worse than they are." As Northrop Frye has pointed out, the qualifying words Aristotle uses for good and bad are *spoudaios* and *phaulos*, which have a figurative connotation of "weighty" and "light." Lightness of touch is certainly one of the hallmarks of comedy.

Perhaps it is sufficient to say that comedy has as its purpose to delight, entertain, or regale an audience through the presentation of characters, situations, and ideas in the spirit of fun. As tragedy achieves its catharsis through fear and pity, so comedy aims at its special catharsis through amusement and laughter that keep man close to sanity and balance, remind us of our human frailties and keep us humbly aware of what we are rather than what we might wish ourselves to be.

KINDS OF COMEDY

The problem of classification is also especially acute in comedy. Playwrights have a way of ignoring arbitrary pigeonholes and of mixing various kinds of comic matter to suit their dramatic purposes without regard to academic convenience. For example, Aristophanes frequently uses all manner of obscenities and physical humor characteristic of farce, but he blends this material with satirical thrusts at the ideas of his contemporaries, thus filling his comedies with political and philosophical ramifications. The perplexed scholar, in an attempt to catalogue this variety, has been forced to use the label of "Aristophanic" comedy. Shakespeare is similarly difficult to categorize because he writes in such a variety of ways—farcical, romantic, and "dark" comedies, sometimes mixing different styles in the same play.

The easiest generalization to make is that at the low end of the scale is the physical comedy of farce and at the other end the high comedy of manners or ideas. But the problem with the gradations in-between, as well as with the two extremes, is, as we have already

noted, that they are not mutually exclusive. Moreover, playwrights have compounded plays of all of the elements, blending them in various fashions so that they defy neat schematic compartmentalization. The juices of comedy have a way of bubbling over, penetrating all kinds of chinks and crannies. They are difficult to cork up in logic-tight containers. The safest conclusion seems to be that comedy ranges between high and low, between the physical and intellectual, and that it differs in kind from play to play according to the playwright's purposes. Perhaps the most essential ingredient for all kinds of comedy is the point of view we shall discuss subsequently as "the comic attitude."

PURPOSES OF COMEDY

Many thinkers consider comedy to have a useful and moral aim. Goldoni regarded comedy as a means to correct "faults and foibles"; Hazlitt, "to unmask ignorance and deceit"; Meredith, "to vindicate reason, common sense, rightness and justice, for no vain purpose ever"; Shaw, "for the correcting of pretentiousness, of inflation, of dullness." The French philosopher Henri Bergson, in his entertaining book *Laughter*, summarizes this function of comedy as the drama of criticism in these words: "Laughter is, above all, a corrective. Being intended to humiliate, it must make a painful impression on the person against whom it is directed. By laughter, society avenges itself for liberties taken with it."[1] When comedy serves such a purpose, the object of laughter is usually unsociable. This has little to do with morality, since we are inclined to laugh at a character's eccentricities

---

[1]Henri Bergson, *Laughter*, trans. by Cloudesley Brereton and Fred Rothwell (New York, The Macmillan Co., 1917).

rather than his vices or virtues, except insofar as they make him ludicrous. A comic character's deviation from the norm in speech, manners, or appearance causes us to laugh because we want to keep him in line. This corrective use of laughter is, of course, not confined to the theater inasmuch as the fear of ridicule is one of the primary forces in causing the members of society to conform. Hence, in comedy, the butt of the joke, by implication, suggests the sin of antisocial behavior.

But the purpose of comedy is not always critical. Laughter is shared in those situations when we laugh *with* a character rather than *at* him—a character who may be fully aware of his weakness, yet is appealing because we are reminded of our common human inconsistency. As instances of this kind of comic appeal, we think of characters caught in circumstances where they are embarrassed, fearful, and confused. Our laughter often becomes a bond of sympathy, not of ridicule. We do not isolate such characters from our approval; we share with them our universal experience as human beings. While some comedy is critical, it also exists on the level of sheer entertainment and delight and serves only secondarily as a means for releasing tensions and inhibitions, a purpose Freud saw, however, as the primary reason for the phenomenon of laughter.

THE COMIC ATTITUDE

Max Eastman has devoted considerable attention to analyzing the conditions essential for the "enjoyment of laughter" in his book by the same title.[2] He observes that humor depends upon the existence of a favorable circumstance, and concludes that "the condition in which joyful laughter most continually occurs is that of play." Laughter is not aroused by those situations where feelings are violent or deep. As a part of his evidence, Eastman cites the native response of a child who may welcome shock and disappointment as a pleasurable experience provided that an atmosphere of play has been established. If the child is teased, however, when he is tired or hungry, the fun is over; the atmosphere of play has been destroyed. Eastman's point of view is pertinent to our understanding of the comic attitude. How much emotional involvement should the audience be made to feel during a comedy? What is the basis for the comic attitude?

In Shakespeare's romantic comedies, the sentimental plays of Sheridan and Goldsmith in the eighteenth century, and in many of our contemporary works, the spectator is invited to enter into the emotions of the characters. We become concerned about the fortunes of the protagonist, and our sympathies and hostilities are aroused by the playwright's treatment of his characters; we take pleasure in seeing the hero achieve his objective, which is often accompanied by the jingle of money or wedding bells. The characters may be laughable, may at times appear foolish and weak, but the playwright does not criticize them. He treats them with tolerance and indulgence—the comic strip humor of "Peanuts." We laugh with the characters

[2]Max Eastman, *Enjoyment of Laughter* (New York, Simon & Shuster, Inc., 1942).

rather than at them, and our laughter is without malice.

On the other hand, Bergson argues that "laughter has no greater foe than emotion . . . Its appeal is to the intelligence, pure and simple." Myers supports Bergson in this view by saying, "without detachment, we cannot realize the effect of comedy, which transforms the frustrations of reason into laughter." This point of view is well taken, especially at the extremes of the comic scale—low comedy and high. In most farce, our enjoyment stems from the action itself, the momentary laugh, the sudden release. We recognize that farce is a form of play; we do not take its actions seriously. These are prefabricated characters racing through the convolutions of plot; they are not real people. No one experiences any genuine pain; the feelings do not penetrate the grease paint. Thus a detachment is achieved because we consciously watch the actions of an artificial world.

High comedy has a different basis for objectivity. Its appeal is intellectual. The reaction to it arises out of perception and insight rather than emotion. Sentiment is fatal to the aesthetic attitude required for intellectual wit and satire. Occasionally, the playwright lashes out too vigorously at his characters, stirring up an undertone of bitterness which destroys the comic effect. When Ben Jonson laid bare the human follies of avarice in *Volpone*, his unmerciful treatment of the brutal-

ity and viciousness of his characters threatened to dissipate the spirit of laughter. When Molière attacked greed in *The Miser*, he was careful to exaggerate the niggardliness of his protagonist so that little emotional attachment was possible. The character of Shylock in Shakespeare's *The Merchant of Venice* presents a perplexing challenge to the actor because of the wide range of emotions; he is at once an object of ridicule and at the same time a human being whose deep suffering intrudes upon the comic atmosphere.

The comic attitude requires a just sense of proportion so that the essential lightness of spirit is achieved, just as Eastman suggested in play with the child. The audience of comedy cannot be pushed too hard in any direction. Excessive sentimentality, bitterness, depravity, exaggeration—any conspicuous straining for effect, any flat dullness or heavy-footed plodding—upsets the niceness of balance which is so necessary to perform. In the words of Hegel:

Inseparable from the comic is an infinite geniality and confidence, capable of rising superior to its own contradiction, and experiencing therein no taint of bitterness nor sense of misfortune whatever. It is the happy frame of mind, a hale condition of the soul, which, fully aware of itself can suffer the dissolution of its aims.[3]

---

[3]G. W. F. Hegel, *The Philosophy of History*, trans. by J. Sisbree (New York, Colonial Press, 1899).

SOURCES OF LAUGHTER

The sources of comic effect have given scholar, critic, philosopher, and psychologist endless ground for speculation, and although

their efforts have resulted in no uncontroversial conclusions, we may find something of value in their ideas. Among the various comic theories, let us briefly examine the three which Allardyce Nicoll cites in his *The Theory of Drama* as the most prominent, and understand at the outset that a good deal of their validity depends upon personal interpretation and careful selection of examples. The three theories may be summarized as derision, incongruity, and automatism. You will recognize immediately the tendency of the theories to overlap because of the mercurial nature of comedy.

DERISION

Aristotle's observation that comedy deals with men as "worse than they are," implies a comic theory of derision or degradation. It is ordinarily used as a form of criticism to combat pretentiousness or ignorance. Its objective is to keep man balanced, humble, and human, the legitimate targets of derision are pomposity, hypocrisy, and sanctimoniousness. As in life, laughter is used to keep people in line, to insure conformity to a socially acceptable code of behavior. The satirist has always regarded comedy as a salutary scourge to castigate awkward behavior. Notice the use of comedy as criticism in the plays of Molière, Congreve, and Shaw in this text.

Greek comedy ridiculed physical deformities as well as those of conduct. Comic characters were intentionally distorted and misshapen in appearance through the use of masks, phallic symbols, and padded costumes. A man's attempts to rise above himself were often counteracted by the reminder of his biological needs. Aristophanes delighted in mocking men and gods by exhibiting them in all kinds of embarrassing physical situations. He was ruthless in aiming his shafts of wit at all levels of life. The pattern of derision, including all manner of physical humor,

coarse gags, barbed insults, and eccentric behavior, has continued throughout dramatic literature to the present time, especially in farce. The satirist exploits situations in which characters are debased and reduced to objects of scorn by such stock devices as physical beatings, bodily functions—situations in which man is caught off-balance, redhanded, under the bed, in the closet, in his underwear—in any of the circumstances of life in which he is exposed, his dignity punctured, his flaw revealed, reminding everyone of his kinship with the animal world. Even the most serious moments of life are not free from the threat of derision. For example, the sacred liturgy of the church was burlesqued by medieval performers in their *Feast of the Asses*. In a contemporary film, Jacques Tati in *Mr. Hulot's Holiday*, reduces the solemnity of a funeral to shambles when his leaking inner tube is mistaken for a wreath, hissing and writhing during the somber ceremony.

Degradation of character often involves a reversal of status. The deviant from normal social behavior wins the prize; the inflated person is brought down from his pedestal. Such common offenders against common sense and decent humanity as fools, fops, hypocrites, bumpkins, louts, misers, philanderers, braggarts, bores, and battle-axes are ridiculed into limbo because of their deformed behavior, their lack of wit or excess of ambition, greed, lust, or stupidity. And authority of any kind, when it becomes unbending and heavyhanded, is fair game for the barbs of satirists because the common man finds release and enjoyment in the discomfiture of those above him.

INCONGRUITY

Perhaps because it is the most elastic and extensive theory of comedy, the idea of incongruity has the widest application. Incongruity is the result of the tension of dissonance created by setting side by side two objects or people that are markedly or unexpectedly different, such as a large, fat woman matched with a small, skinny man, or a person out of place with his surroundings, say, someone wearing a bathing suit at the opera or formal clothes on the beach. The laugh-producing quality of the contrast usually depends on establishment of some kind of norm so that the degree of difference is emphasized. A distinct gap between the expected and the unexpected, between normal and abnormal, between intention and realization, results in comic discord and inconsistency.

Incongruity may take various forms—of situation, of character, or of dialogue. The comic situation, based on incongruity presents a contrast between the usual or accepted behavior and the unusual or unacceptable. A typical pattern is to place a character in unfamiliar surroundings that reveal his social incongruity, such as a country bumpkin in polite society, the socially elite in bucolic surroundings, an intellectual among barbarians, a clown or an inebriate in a dignified gathering, a sailor in a harem, a coed in a men's dormitory, a tramp in the mayor's bed. Some examples of incongruous comic situations are the father's failure to know his own children in *Major Barbara*, the extremely usurious demands made by Harpagon in loaning money in *The Miser* and Mr. Parker's interrupted lovemaking in *Ceremonies in Dark Old Men*.

Incongruity of character also involves a contrast between the ideal and the real, or between appearance and actuality: the miser's ridiculous attempts to serve as genial host while saving money on food and drink, or his ludicrous efforts to woo Marianna. An aspect of incongruity of character which also fits Bergson's automatism, described below,

is the inflexible character whose one-track mind separates him from the norm. An excellent illustration is again Harpagon and the miserliness which colors every facet of his life.

Incongruity of language occurs when the dialogue is in sharp contrast to the social context, such as the sudden interjection of vulgarity into a polite conversation, or when the language has the opposite effect to that intended by the speaker. Still another use of incongruous language is speech that is unexpected or inappropriate to the characters, such as refined epigrams spoken by rustics or wise sayings from the mouths of children.

Incongruity in its various forms suggests imbalance and disproportion; there is the implication of an upset equilibrium, "the disconnecting of one idea from another, or the jostling of one feeling against another."

AUTOMATISM

One of the most imaginative and provocative theories of comedy is that advanced by Bergson in his book, *Laughter*, in which he claims that the essence of the laughable is automatism—"something mechanical is encrusted on the living." Man becomes an object of laughter whenever he becomes rigid and machinelike, whenever he loses control of himself or breaks contact with humanity.

Automatism of character occurs when an individual loses his human flexibility and his behavior becomes mechanical in its repetition, or when a man becomes a puppet, no longer in control of his actions. The gist of Bergson's thinking is indicated by these representative statements about comedy and character:

We laugh every time a person gives the impression of being a thing.

Any individual is comic who automatically goes

his own way without troubling himself about getting in touch with the rest of his fellow beings. Rigidity, automatism, absentmindedness, and unsociability are all inextricably entwined, and all serve as ingredients to the making up of the comic in character.[4]

Bergson's point of view on one-sided characters is similar to that of Ben Jonson's comedy of "humours," in which he ridiculed those characters who were guilty of some imbalance, some excess.

> As when some one peculiar quality
> Doth so possess a man, that it doth draw
> All his effects, his spirits, and his powers
> In their confluctions, all to run one way
> This may be truly said to be a humour.

In such plays as *Epicene, Volpone,* and *The Alchemist,* Jonson makes comic figures of those who have lost control and succumbed to some individual trait of character that causes eccentric and antisocial behavior. Molière, in bringing low those guilty of excess, derided those who were too ambitious in *The Would-Be*

---

[4]Bergson, *Op. cit.*

Gentleman, those who were too clever in *The Affected Young Ladies,* too exacting in *Le Misanthrope,* too gullible in *Tartuffe,* and of course, too parsimonious in *The Miser.*

Bergson's theory is an interesting extension of the idea of incongruity, the jostling together of the human and the mechanical. By his ingenuity and persuasiveness, Bergson makes quite a plausible case for automatism, especially in regard to the comedies of Molière, but like other comic theories, automatism does not explain all of the sources of laughter, nor is it appropriate to all kinds of comic effect. Automatism must be recognized, nevertheless, as one of the explanations for the phenomenon of laughter, and we are indebted to Bergson for his stimulating analysis.

From the preceding discussion of representative theories of comedy, a case can be made for derision, incongruity, and automatism as significant factors in the comic effect. It is impossible, however, to fix comedy in a single rigid mold, even though recurrent patterns and mechanisms show through its diverse forms. The many faces of comedy will be increasingly evident as we consider its structure and content.

PLOT

Good comedy requires skillful plotting. A comedy is not simply a loosely knit accumulation of situations and gags. Laughs must be carefully timed and built, situations contrived and an appropriate atmosphere established. A comedy playscript is a score for playing, and, just as the composer must be fully cognizant of the possibilities of his music in the hands of musicians, the writer of comedy must, in a similar way, be fully aware of the techniques and resources of the actor which will animate his material. The comic writer is acutely concerned with man in his social environment. Basic patterns of comedy depict a character who deviates from the norm or who is out of place with his surroundings. The implicit contrasts and conflicts require adroit delineation of the social milieu in order to expose the laughable elements of conduct. Tragic writers may concentrate on heroic figures isolated from other characters and unaffected by their behavior, but comedy exploits the interaction of characters, the human scene, the group situation, the juxtaposition of characters. Comedy is more involved with the particular than with the universal. Its emphasis is on the here and now, not the long view. The playwright frequently develops timely allusions, local references, and contemporaneous characters. His material must have a sense of crispness and spontaneity. Comedy must not smell of the museum or the dead past. Hence, it is difficult for a comedy to survive its time and place of origin because many of its most telling targets are soon gone.

A typical Aristophanic plot shows how the leading character becomes inspired with a ridiculous idea that is vigorously opposed by others. The idea is tried out and the results are demonstrated. The play ends in revelry. In the subsequent development of comedy, the original pattern persists. A character strives for an objective but is thwarted because his goal is an impossible one, or because he misjudges his objectives and his opposition, or because he fights with the wrong weapons. His problem is solved when misunderstandings are cleared up and his true character emerges. The play ends happily, often with the lovers united in an embrace, a vestigial reminder of the orgiastic celebrations of Greek "old comedy." In any case, a comic plot usually involves an imbalance caused by the presence of some ridiculous element of error, ignorance, or ambition. The resultant conflicts and contrasts create comic tension that is released in laughter.

The plots of most comedies are made up of sharp complications that require careful craftsmanship in the use of exposition, climaxes, crises, discoveries, and the denouement. The tangled threads of action must be kept clear to the audience. This is tricky business in plays of rapid action, mixups, and misunderstandings. In previous centuries, the playwright's task was made much easier by the conventions of the aside and the soliloquy, which allowed the playwright to communicate directly with the audience in informing them of the schemes and tricks of the plot and of the disparity between truth and the pretense. The climaxes and crises of comedy demand technical mastery because the high points of the action often involve a social situation in which a number of people are caught in the same net, obliging the playwright to deal with very complex materials. Frequently, the emotional peaks are those of action and discovery, which require the playwright to have a strong sense of visual humor. Climaxes must be built and sustained without prolonging them beyond the limits of the material. The denouement must seem to be the logical result of the preceding action. The playwright's touch must be deft and sure to keep the pace rapid and to create the special climate of comedy which will insure laughter.

The materials from which comedies are made are venerable ones, as old as the theater itself. The sources of comic effect which the classic playwrights Aristophanes, Plautus, and Terence used to delight the audiences of Athens and Rome are still the stock in trade that you can see on your television or motion-picture screen tonight. Similarly, the devices of comedy which the playwright uses are well established. Let us consider three very common devices for evoking laughter, realizing that these are representative examples and by no means an exhaustive list.

COMIC DEVICES

One of the most reliable comic devices is that of teasing, or "gulling," which may take a variety of forms, such as the delay of news employed by Shakespeare when the nurse withholds Romeo's message from Juliet, or Molière's use of gulling in *The Miser* (Act V, scene 2) when Mr. James teases Harpagon with the slow revelation of truth about the loss of his casket. Another form of teasing occurs whenever characters are intentionally placed in embarrassing or awkward situations. A famous example is *The Taming of the Shrew*, at the point where Petruchio exposes Katharine to a series of teasings before "taming" her. After he has rudely taken her away following the wedding ceremony and has kept her from food and sleep, Petruchio tests Kate's subservience in this scene as he takes his starved, fatigued, and unkempt bride toward home:

PETRUCHIO: Come on, i' God's name; once more toward our father's.
Good Lord, how bright and goodly shines the moon!
KATHERINE: The moon! the sun: it is not moonlight now.
PETRUCHIO: I say it is the moon that shines so bright.
KATHERINE: I know it is the sun that shines so bright.
PETRUCHIO: Now, by my mother's son, and that's myself,
It shall be moon, or star, or what I list,
Or ere I journey to your father's house.
Go on, and fetch our horses back again.
Evermore cross'd and cross'd; nothing but cross'd!
HORTENSIO: Say as he says, or we shall never go.
KATHERINE: Forward, I pray since we have come so far,
And be it moon, or sun, or what you please;

And if you please to call it a rush-candle,
Henceforth, I vow it shall be so for me.
PETRUCHIO: I say it is the moon.
KATHERINE: I know it is the moon.
PETRUCHIO: Nay, then you lie: it is the blessed sun.
KATHERINE: Then, God be blessed, it is the blessed sun:
But sun it is not, when you say it is not;
And the moon changes even as your mind.
What you will have named, even that it is;
And so it shall be so for Katherine.

Another familiar plot mechanism of comedy is inversion. The entire play may be based on the turn-about of a downtrodden character who ultimately achieves status, as in such plays as *Born Yesterday* and *The Solid Gold Cadillac*. The young lovers overcome the blocking agents and are free to marry; the worm turns, the trickster gets caught in his own trap; the roles are reversed.

Another well-worn comic device is the use of the unfamiliar. A character or group of characters is placed in new surroundings or are engaged in unaccustomed activities. One form of this device is the process of teaching an inexperienced and oftentimes inexpert person; see, for example, the English lesson in Shakespeare's *Henry IV* and the dancing lesson in Molière's *Le Bourgeoise Gentilhomme*. The humor may be heightened by the additional twist of having the instructor as ignorant as his pupil. The awkward, embarrassed, or shy person making an adjustment to a new experience is used again and again for comic effect, such as that of the girls' first night in their basement apartment in *My Sister Eileen*, or Christopher Sly's adjustment to royal treatment in *The Taming of the Shrew*.

Perhaps these examples of comic devices

are sufficient to indicate some of the mechanisms of comedy. In the discussion of farce, additional comic patterns will be cited. The point is that the plots of comedy make use of fairly standardized devices that over the years have consistently produced laughter in the theater.

CHARACTER

Because comedy wears many guises its characters differ from each other considerably, not only in kind but also in treatment. A comic character may be the unconscious butt of ridicule, as is Harpagon in *The Miser* or Dogberry in *Much Ado About Nothing*. Sometimes, a character may be conscious of his plight and share his discomfiture with the audience, as does Falstaff in *Henry IV*. Again, a comic character may, through his wit and insight, direct the laughter toward an idea or situation, as does Undershaft at the "poor but honest" concept in *Major Barbara*. Sometimes a character may be comical because he inverts the norm as Judge Azdak does in *The Caucasian Chalk Circle* when he reverses the usual legal procedures and renders his verdicts according to his personal taste and feeling. A character may be comical because of his eccentric behavior, his lack of wit or judgment, his peculiar cast of mind, his delightful facility with language, his engaging animal spirits, his charming manner, or his buoyant attitude toward life. Character varies with the playwright's purpose.

Comic characters tend to be psychologically uncomplicated. The playwright is frequently more concerned about developing the intricacies of plot than he is about revealing depth of character. Hence he sketches his figures lightly or else resorts to easily recognizable types. The dramatist may deliberately create one-sided roles as a means of showing his characters' inhumanity in their fixations and inflexibility. Again, he may purposely keep his characters in the simple mold of stock figures in order to prevent excessive emotional attachment that might destroy the light atmosphere of comedy. As character becomes more genuine and complex, drama moves away from comedy.

The writer of comedy is closer to surface reality than the writer of tragedy. The comic dramatist is more concerned with the immediate, the temporal, the commonplace. Hence, despite the fact that characters in comedy may be types in that they are psychologically simple, they may give a superficial effect of actuality to an audience, especially when acted by consummate comedians whose personal attributes enlarge and deepen the original image of the playwright. Furthermore, the very nature of comic material is rooted in the kind of action that gives to the actor license and latitude to transform a spare outline into a full figure.

Bergson describes the comic character as one who is "generally comic in proportion to his ignorance of himself. The comic person is unconscious." Such character has a blind side that causes him to react in a ludicrous fashion. Harpagon, for example, is quite unaware that he is a comic figure. But, as we mentioned before, Bergson's point of view is too narrow for universal application. All comic characters are not unconscious or ignorant of their shortcomings. As we suggested earlier, laughter is shared with the character when we borrow some of his humiliation as the inept lover, the raw recruit, the bashful swain, or the shy maiden. Falstaff's follies infect us all. We do not laugh at him to punish him or to change him; we laugh because of the Falstaff in us. Laughter stems from sympathy as well as ridicule. Numerous comic characters, especially those from classic and neoclassic comedy, do fit neatly into Bergson's theory, but scores of comic roles, particularly in English and American plays, arouse our sympathy and affection only; a few of the examples are Rosalind in *As You Like It*, Viola in *Twelfth Night*, Billie in *Born Yesterday*, Marlow in *She Stoops to Conquer*, Professer Turner in *The Male Animal*, Charles Surface in *The School for Scandal*, and Tony in *They Knew What They Wanted*. The kind of response, whether critical or sympathetic, which a character elicits from an audience varies with the playwright's purpose.

THOUGHT

Most comedy does not bear a heavy burden of thought. The playwright is much more concerned with satisfying the needs of those spectators who come to the theater for diversion, who wish to avoid facing someone else's serious problems—spectators who, in short, have no immediate interest in receiving intellectual stimulation from the theater. They want to have a good time, to laugh and forget themselves. Because this attitude represents the dominating taste of those who come to see a comedy, the comic writer's efforts are concentrated on interesting the audience in a series of light-hearted actions and sympathetic characters whose involvements are not to be taken seriously. While laughter at such comedy may imply our acceptance of a code of behavior and a system of values, our attention is not centered on weighing the merits of conventional morality except insofar as it serves as a frame of reference for displaying the incongruous. In most comedy, the playwright is not questioning values; he is exposing ridiculous behavior. For his purposes, the comic action itself is more important than any deeper meaning the action may have.

A particular kind of comedy, however, reverses the point of view and makes of it a drama of criticism in which the appeal of the play is intellectual. This is known as high comedy. High comedy, social comedy, or the comedy of manners—each is a special form of drama with its own particular emphasis and techniques—are all the very antithesis of farce or low comedy in that they appeal to a limited, cultivated audience rather than a general, undiscriminating public, and in that they stress dialogue rather than action. High and low comedy do, however, possess one important similarity: both require an attitude of detachment, a freedom from emotional involvement.

High comedy is written for an audience that is urban and sophisticated and possesses a commonly accepted code of behavior, which is a matter of manners, not morals. Indeed, the Restoration audience was notorious for its immorality and licentiousness, and yet the period produced the most brilliant high comedy in English literature. It was the purpose of the high comedies of Congreve, Wycherley, and Vanbrugh to mock those who violated its manners. The objects of laughter were the gauche, the outsiders, the pretenders, whose absurd or awkward behavior caused them to lose their sense of balance. Ridicule was not a moral indictment but a reproof for antisocial conduct. In other periods of theater history, writers of high comedy have directed their criticism at more universal targets, like the foibles and follies of their age. Aristophanes scorned the militarists; Sheridan and Molière attacked hypocrisy and pretense; Shaw delighted in exposing the sham behind the sentimental and rigid precepts of Victorian behavior. High comedy is therefore a social weapon. Its implications extend beyond the immediate chuckle; its aim is to evoke thoughtful laughter. It is intended to have a residue of meaning. Writing in the *New York Times*, S. N. Behrman, a most successful American writer of high comedy sums up the playwright's point of view in this statement:

What makes the essence of high comedy is not the furniture of the room where the action takes place, but the articulateness of the characters, the plane on which they talk, the intellectual and moral climate in which they live . . . One of the endless sources of high comedy is seriousness of temperament and intensity of purpose in contrast with the triviality of the occasion.[5]

The techniques of high comedy rely heavily on language. Since it is addressed to an intellectual and cultivated audience, this kind of comedy employs bright repartee, conceits, epigrams, double-meanings, and all of the refinements and subtleties the writer can command. Note the scintillating repartee throughout *The Way of the World* and *Major Barbara*.

High comedy is an esoteric form of drama created for a particular kind of audience and demanding a special style of playing that is facile, suave, and artificial in keeping with the hothouse atmosphere of the play itself.

---

[5]S. N. Behrman, *New York Times*, O.12, 59, II, 7.

COMEDY IN PERFORMANCE

More than other forms of drama, comedy depends upon performance for its full effect. The timing of the actor, his ability to play a piece of business, to project a laugh line, to bring out the risible qualities of situation and character without destroying the light atmosphere—these are all needed for the complete realization of comedy.

To achieve its effect comedy employs a wide variety of language devices, from cleverly turned conceits and *bons mots* to crude puns, insults, vulgarisms, and deformed words. We have already observed some of its comic uses of diction in derision, automatism, and incongruity. Most successful comic writers have excellent ears for dialogue, and they take apparent delight in their verbal skill. Shakespeare as well as other Elizabethans was especially fond of exploiting language for comic effect. The rich texture of the rustics' speech in *A Midsummer Night's Dream*, the word-play of the doorkeeper in *Macbeth*, the banter of the grave diggers in *Hamlet* are all memorable in this aspect. Even in translation Molière's comic dialogue is notable for its tempo and cadence, and Shaw's repartee is incisive with its surprising twists and turns as he elaborates an idea. Congreve, an acknowledged master of bright conversation, gives thrust and parry to the dialogue throughout

The Way of the World, especially in the dialogue of Millamant and Mirabel.

The famous interrogation scene in Oscar Wilde's *The Importance of Being Earnest* depends for its full effectiveness on an actress who can convincingly reproduce Lady Bracknell's aristocratic speech as it modulates among tones of impersonal cross-examination, disapproval, dismay and utter disgust, as well as on an actor who can convey the mingled tones of eagerness, bewilderment and persistence on the part of the young suitor, Jack Worthing.

LADY BRACKNELL: . . . Are your parents living?

JACK: I have lost both my parents.

LADY BRACKNELL: Both? . . . That seems like carelessness. Who was your father? He was evidently a man of some wealth. Was he born in what the Radical papers call the purple of commerce, or did he rise from the ranks of the aristocracy?

JACK: I am afraid I really don't know. The fact is, Lady Bracknell, I said I had lost my parents. It would be nearer the truth to say that my parents seem to have lost me . . . I don't actually know who I am by birth. I was . . . well, I was found.

LADY BRACKNELL: Found!

JACK: The late Mr. Thomas Cardew, an old gentleman of a very charitable and kindly disposition, found me, and gave me the name of Worthing, because he happened to have a first-class ticket for Worthing in his pocket at the time. Worthing is a place in Sussex. It is a seaside resort.

LADY BRACKNELL: Where did the charitable gentleman who had a first-class ticket for this seaside resort find you?

JACK: (gravely) In a hand-bag.

LADY BRACKNELL: A hand-bag?

JACK: (very seriously) Yes, Lady Bracknell. I was in a hand-bag—a somewhat large, black leather hand-bag, with handles to it—an ordinary hand-bag in fact.

LADY BRACKNELL: In what locality did this Mr. James, or Thomas, Cardew come across this ordinary hand-bag?

JACK: In the cloak-room at Victoria Station. It was given to him in mistake for his own.

LADY BRACKNELL: The cloak-room at Victoria Station?

JACK: (*with deliberately oppressive honesty*) Yes. The Brighton line.

LADY BRACKNELL: The line is immaterial. (*moved to perorative sonorousness*) Mr. Worthing, I confess I feel somewhat bewildered by what you have just told me. To be born, or at any rate bred, in a hand-bag, whether it had handles or not, seems to me to display a contempt for the ordinary decencies of family life that remind one of the worst excesses of the French Revolution. And I presume you know what that unfortunate movement led to? As for the particular locality in which the handbag was found, a cloak-room at a railway station might serve to conceal a social indiscretion—has probably, indeed, been used for that purpose before now—but it could hardly be regarded as an assured basis for a recognized position in good society.

JACK: May I ask you then what you would advise me to do? I need hardly say I would do anything in the world to ensure Gwendolen's happiness.

LADY BRACKNELL: (*modulating into withering forthrightness*) I would strongly advise you, Mr. Worthing, to try and acquire some relations as soon as possible, and to make a definite effort to produce at any rate one parent, of either sex, before the season is quite over.

JACK: (*with a primitive unconcern for* LADY BRACKNELL'*s social demands*) Well, I don't see how I could possibly manage to do that. I can produce the hand-bag at any moment. It is in my dressing-room at home. I really think that should satisfy you, Lady Bracknell.

LADY BRACKNELL: (*as though contemplating an obscene horror*) Me, sir! What has it to do with me? You can hardly imagine that I and Lord Bracknell would dream of allowing our only daughter—a girl brought up with the utmost care—to marry into a cloak-room, and form an alliance with a parcel? Good morning, Mr. Worthing! (LADY BRACKNELL *sweeps out in majestic indignation.*)

One of the most puzzling aspects in the performance of comedy is the variety of response from audience to audience. A comic line or piece of business may arouse boisterous laughter at one performance and at the next be greeted by cold and stony silence. Friday and Saturday night audiences invariably out laugh a Monday or Tuesday night one. Young spectators are more demonstrative than older ones, and a scattered audience is less susceptible to laughter than a closely packed one. Within a given audience some individuals may often be convulsed with laughter while others remain aloof and unamused throughout the play.

In general, any easy social gathering helps create the climate for comedy. Laughter is a gesture that is social and contagious, but the audience must be in a light mood, easily susceptible to the courtship of comedy. Spectators must be wooed and won, not coerced. The comedian can lose the comic sympathy of his hearers by making them conscious of his efforts to be funny. Begin by saying to someone, "I'm going to tell you a very funny story," and you double your difficulty in getting a laugh because you have engaged the listener's critical faculties and he has focused on the means of your telling rather than the

end. Let one performer in a comedy strain for effect by being "consciously cute," and he is likely to alienate the audience for the production as a whole.

Comedy is a framework for action. The inanimate script is brought to life by the performer, but his skill is dependent upon the craftsmanship of the playwright. As the critic A. H. Thorndike says:

Comedy finds its purpose aided by skillful use of words as well as by gesture and mimicry. It avails itself of the arts of the theatre and of literature. It delights in song as well as dance, in epigram as well as grimace, in paradox as well as slap-jack, and it can stoop to punning as readily as to buffoonery. Whatever can be used in verse or fiction to amuse and delight can be employed in the drama with the additional advantage of impersonation. It combines the humor of words and voice, of the audible and visible. Its form and movement, construction and texture, person and speeches, are all dependent on literary art. Its greatest creative triumphs are won by the pen.[6]

---

[6] Ashley H. Thorndike, *English Comedy* (New York, The Macmillan Co., 1929).

FARCE

Just as the counterpart of tragedy is melodrama, the counterpart of high comedy is farce. As a form of drama, farce is very old, and as for its universal appeal, it has been and continues to be, along with melodrama, the most popular kind of entertainment presented in motion pictures and on television.

The purpose of farce is to entertain; the appropriate response to it is continuous and

unrestrained laughter. Farce has little intellectual content or symbolic significance, is not concerned with presenting a message, has slight residue of meaning, and makes no pretense of demanding serious consideration. In the journalistic fare of the theater, farce is the comic strip of the *Zam-Bang-Powie* school. Its appeal is simple, external and spontaneous.

Farce may involve a complete play such

as *The Comedy of Errors* and *Charley's Aunt*, or its techniques may be injected piecemeal into other forms of drama, as in *The Miser*. Critics may disparage farce as a degraded form of drama that "though it makes the unskillful laugh, cannot but make the judicious grieve." Farcical devices and characters have been employed, nevertheless, not only by dramatic hacks but also by some of the most preeminent playwrights, including Shakespeare, Molière, and Aristophanes.

The script of a farce must be regarded as a scenario for action. The distinctive essence of farce can be realized only in performance by accomplished comedians before a live audience. The gags, tricks, and devices that seem so absurd and flat in print may, in the hands of talented performers, move an audience to gales of laughter from which even the most sophisticated theatergoer cannot remain aloof, even though, on later reflection, he may wonder at his lack of judgment in responding to such stuff.

Because the enjoyment of laughter is one of man's favorite diversions, farce is the most popular of all forms of comedy. It demands no intellectual insight, no awareness of a social norm, no linguistic sensitivity in finding nuances of meaning—all of which are necessary for understanding other forms of comedy. The response to the farce is immediate and direct, offering no strain to the mind. Hence, this kind of laughing matter has a very wide appeal. The language barriers are slight because the performer in farce often expresses himself in the universal vocabulary of gesture and action. The enacted story is itself a kind of language which finds a ready audience.

PLOT

Farce is the comedy of situation. A good farcical plot is one that provides maximum opportunity for a series of complications, even though it has obviously been contrived and manipulated by the playwright. The structure of farce is a framework for vigorous, rapid, and exaggerated action in which the characters move rather than think and where getting a laugh justifies nearly any means. Once the engine is cranked up and set in motion, the speed is accelerated, and by unexpected blowouts, backfirings and explosions, the mechanism careens crazily through space, gathering momentum until it finally lurches to an awkward but happy ending in a cloud of steam with all of its parts still spinning; and while we have witnessed a whirlwind of activity, the machine has not really moved an inch in any direction.

The skill of plotting farce is determined by the dramatist's ingenuity in inventing a variety of entanglements to give the comedian a chance to play for laughs. The playwright usually exploits a basic situation that is highly improbable and atypical: a woodcutter reluctantly consents to become a court physician in order to cure the king's daughter of a feigned illness; two long-lost twin brothers, whose servants are another pair of twins, strive for reunion; two young Communists sharing a one-room apartment fall in love with each other's newly-wed wives; a shy writer of greeting-card verses becomes involved with a gang of race track touts because of his skill in predicting the winners; a young man wagers that he can tell the complete truth for twenty-four hours; a genial husband undertakes the precarious responsibility of simultaneously maintaining two separate wives and families, one each in Wilmington, Delaware, and Philadelphia, Pennsylvania. These are characteristic plot situations employed by writers of farce. Inventing a farcical plot requires ingenuity in manipulating situations, as well as a shrewd sense of the theater. The playwright must know precisely how, when and where to tickle the audience. A good example of a plot which illustrates the materials and organization that characterize this kind of comedy is the medieval farce, *Master Pierre Pathelin*.

An impoverished lawyer, Pierre Pathelin, assures his wife, Guillemette, that he has a plan for procuring some cloth. He visits the draper's shop, where he flatters the shopkeeper into giving him a piece of cloth. The draper is wary about parting with the cloth on credit, but Pathelin allays his fears by inviting him to visit his house, where the draper will get his money and share a roast goose dinner. The scene ends when Pathelin walks off with the cloth, leaving the draper to gloat over the price. Pathelin brings the cloth home to his delighted wife. When his dinner guest arrives, Pathelin climbs into bed, and his wife informs the hapless draper that her husband could not possibly have purchased any cloth—he has been seriously ill for some weeks. The draper goes away but returns immediately to find Pathelin feigning a ranting fit of madness. The draper becomes convinced that the devil has hoodwinked him. Another facet of the story then develops; the draper brings a shepherd into court, accused of having eaten several sheep belonging to the draper. The shepherd engages Pathelin to defend him, who feigning a toothache, masks his face until the draper makes his accusation. When Pathelin suddenly reveals his identity, the draper loses his wits and attacks the lawyer for stealing his cloth. The case becomes hopelessly lost in the confusing tangle of the two arguments. The bewildered judge tries to restore order by questioning the shepherd, who, following Pathelin's counsel, answers all questions by bleating like a sheep. The judge abandons the trial; Pathelin has succeeded. The distraught draper dashes off saying to Pathelin: "I am going to your house to see if you are here or there." When Pathelin demands his fee from his client, the shepherd's only reply is continued bleating. The trickster is himself victim of his own trick.

Earlier in the chapter, three representative theories of comedy were cited—derision, incongruity, and automatism—and three characteristic devices were discussed—teasing, inversion, and the unfamiliar. These theories and devices are also applicable to farce, although their use is generally on an elementary level. Low comedy exploits the physical aspects of man. His body, its desires and functions, are a primary source for comic material. Farcical situations usually depend upon visual humor—man is shown as the victim of his biological nature, not only sex but any drive, appetite or situation that makes him appear ridiculous, causes him to lose his balance, his control of himself or of his circumstances. Farcical characters move in an active physical world; they are out of place in the rarefied atmosphere of intellectual pursuits.

Familiar farcical devices are found in such standard patterns as mistaken identity, the funny costume, "caught in the act," or physical beatings or violence, but the action should not evoke genuine suffering in either the performer or the spectator. To elicit the audience's sympathy, or to give the effect of real pain, is to destroy the atmosphere for laughter. "A situation in which the actor really suffers," as W. H. Auden has pointed out, "can only be found comic by children, who see only the situation and are unaware of the suffering, as when a child laughs at a hunchback, or by human swine."[7] The comic possibilities of a situation are, moreover, enhanced when the recipient of the violence deserves chastisement for his antisocial behavior, such as Harpagon in *The Miser*. Farcical literature is filled with all kinds of fights, duels, beatings, spankings, combats, acci-

[7]W. H. Auden, "Notes on the Comic," in *The Dyer's Hand* (Random House, 1952), p. 371.

dents and tumbles. Standard gags are the "prat-fall," the black-eye, the sore foot, and the use of a cream pie.

CHARACTER

Farce usually deals with simple stock characters, often from ordinary walks of life. The romantic aspects of the story are frequently carried by pasteboard figures who have a talent for bumbling into awkward situations. The main burden of the comedy is in the hands of two kinds of characters—crafty manipulators, who keep the action going, and awkward, unlearned or unsuspecting characters, who are the targets of laughter. The manipulators are often tricky servants or parasites living by their wits; those preyed upon are rustics, foreigners, foolish old men, hypocrites and poseurs of all kinds. Low comedians may be a part of a farce, or they may be introduced into other kinds of plays, such as melodrama, for comic relief. In English comedy of the late eighteenth and early nineteenth centuries, low, farcical characters were injected into the plays in such roles as farmers, sailors, and Irishmen. Their ludicrous antics met with such popular favor that they frequently ran away with the show.

The speech and behavior of farcical characters is simplified as they race through the contrived mechanism of the plot. They do not think—they scheme, manipulate and act, often in devious ways, but always toward clearly defined objectives. Because farce involves so much acting based on situations, the actor is given exceptional opportunities to develop a full pattern of behavior. The playwright's original sketchy design may be filled out and enhanced by the lively performance and personality of an imaginative comedian so that, in the theater, the character becomes a memorable one.

THOUGHT

The writer of farce does not have a message. His aim is to divert the audience's attention by providing a pattern of comic behavior; his manipulation of character and situation aims only to serve his comic purpose. At the play's end, questions are answered, misunderstandings cleared up, the tangled threads of the story unravelled.

Because of its gay disrespect for conventional behavior, farce is sometimes criticized for its immorality; but actually farce is amoral, unconcerned with ethical implications, because the actions of its characters are removed from life and exist only in the theater through an unspoken agreement with the audience. Although farces may often include implicit criticisms of society and its mores, as for example attacks on pretentiousness and hypocrisy in works by Molière, Labiche, and Feydeau, they do not depend for their existence on such moralizing elements. They exist primarily as means of entertainment.

DICTION

Diction in farce is undistinguished by any literary pretensions. The linguistic devices of low comedy are puns, repetitions, "tag lines," wisecracks, insults, vulgarisms, and deformed language. Although the language of farce is non-literary, it requires a special talent. The dialogue of farce must sharply distinguish each character and accompany or thrust forward the action rather than impede it. Laugh lines demand a feeling for the flavor and cadence of language, for its angularities and crispness. The playwright must have an excellent sense of theater in order to pace his dialogue, build for laughs, make effective use of repetition, and realize the comic possibilities in arranging the incongruities of human speech. Writing effective farcical dialogue may seem an easy task to the reader but actually it is an exacting and rather rare skill.

SPECTACLE

Farce makes little demands of stage scenery except in occasional plays when the locale is an important aspect of the comic situation. In general, the main interest is in the actions of the character. The set designs should not hamper the actor but should give him ample space and opportunity for vigorous and rapid movement. The visual aspects of costume may be important in some instances and in nearly all cases the playing of farce will appeal to the eye in the use of pantomime and stage business. In farce, the fun is in the doing. Note the farcical comedy business called for by the stage directions of *The Miser*.

part two

PLAYS

ANTIGONE

KING LEAR

THE MISER

THE WAY OF THE WORLD

AN ENEMY OF THE PEOPLE

MISS JULIE

MAJOR BARBARA

THE EMPEROR JONES

THE CAUCASIAN CHALK CIRCLE

LOOK BACK IN ANGER

THE LEADER

ACT WITHOUT WORDS, I

THE PHYSICISTS

CEREMONIES IN DARK OLD MEN

ANTIGONE

Sophocles (c. 495-406 B.C.)

Translated and Edited by Peter D. Arnott

Sophocles was born at Colonus, near Athens. He stood high in the esteem of his contemporaries both as a playwright and as a man, being elected as one of the ten Athenian generals during the Samian War.

Sophocles followed the dramatic practices of Aeschylus and added the third actor. Although he wrote more than 120 plays, only seven are extant. In the yearly competition he won twenty-four victories and never finished lower than second. Sophocles is not regarded as being as original a thinker as Euripides or Aeschylus, but his mastery of dramatic techniques made him the greatest of the Greek playwrights.

Antigone (c. 441 B.C.) is the earliest of Sophocles' surviving plays. His masterpieces, *Oedipus the King* and *Oedipus at Colonus*, deal with Antigone's ill-fated father. Other surviving plays of Sophocles are *Electra*, *Philoctetes*, *The Trachnioe*, and *Ajax*.

Aristotle praised Sophocles as a dramatist who "saw life steadily and saw it whole." At the first dramatic festival following the death of Sophocles, the playwright Phrynichus paid this tribute: "Blessed is Sophocles, a happy and fortunate man who died after a long life; author of many beautiful tragedies, he came to a beautiful end and lived to see no evil day."

The Greek theater was made up of three main elements: the orchestra circle where the chorus danced and sang, the *skene* or stagehouse before which the actors usually performed, and the *theatron* occupied by the audience. It was a huge theater; the orchestra measuring 60 to 75 feet in diameter, and the 80 tiers of seats in the Theater of Dionysus on the Acropolis accommodated at least fifteen thousand spectators.

The dimensions of the theater compelled the actor to solve the problems of projection. His style of performance was necessarily enlarged by broad gesture, clear speech, and the use of masks, headdresses, and footgear to increase his size and expressiveness. Such exaggeration ruled out the illusion of realistic acting. This does not mean that the audience thought of the style as artificial; the actor's integrity and sense of conviction, and his ability to convey emotion and interpret the feeling and meaning of great poetry, gave his perfor-

mance validity despite the conventions of the theater.

All roles were played by male actors, and no more than three speaking characters appeared onstage at once. The performance of the chorus, retaining the circular movement of the original improvised dithyramb once performed on the threshing floor, was stylized in the use of dance and song. The length and positions of the entrances and exits and huge orchestra placed great emphasis on choric movement and affected its direction and quality, whereas the rhetorical nature of the drama, and the convention of not portraying violent action onstage, committed the actor to emphasize oral interpretation of the lines.

Opposite. A modern production of a Greek drama in the ancient theater at Epidaurus.

Left. A replica of a Greek tragic mask. Rome: Museo Nazionale.

Right. The ruins
of the Greek Theater
of Dionysus
in Athens today.

Left. Ismene pleads with Antigone
to obey the king's edict.
Photographs in this sequence
are of a modern production
staged at the Theater
of Epidaurus in Greece.

Below. The chorus of Theban elders
sing an ode in the middle
of the orchestra.

Left. Two strong wills in conflict as Antigone defies Creon's edict.

Right. Creon grieves over his dead son, Haemon.

CHARACTERS

ANTIGONE, *daughter of dead King Oedipus*
ISMENE, *her sister*
CHORUS *of Theban elders*
CREON, *uncle of* ANTIGONE *and* ISMENE, *King of Thebes*
GUARD
HAEMON, *son of* CREON, *betrothed to* ANTIGONE
TEIRESIAS, *a blind prophet*
FIRST MESSENGER
EURYDICE, *wife of* CREON
SECOND MESSENGER
GUARDS *and* ATTENDANTS

SCENE
Before the palace of CREON *in Thebes*

ANTIGONE

Enter ANTIGONE *and* ISMENE

ANTIGONE: Ismene, my dear, my mother's child, my sister,
What part of Oedipus' sad legacy
Has Zeus not laid in full on us who live?
There is nothing bitter, nothing of disaster,
No shame, no humiliation I have not seen
In the number of your sufferings and mine.
And now what is this order which they say
Our leader has announced throughout the city?
Do you know? Have you heard? Or do I have to tell you
10   That what has happened to our enemies
Is threatening to fall upon our friends?
ISMENE: I have heard no word of friends, Antigone,
To bring me comfort or to bring me pain
Since the time we two were robbed of our two brothers,
Dead in one day, and by each other's hand.
And now the Argive army overnight
Has disappeared, I am no nearer knowing
Whether my luck has changed for good or bad.
ANT: I know, too well. That is why I wanted to bring you
20   Outside the courtyard, to talk to you alone.
ISM: What is it? Trouble, you do not need to tell me.
ANT: What else, when Creon singles out one brother

10 *That what . . . friends?* the bodies of the warriors of Argos, who had aided Polyneices in his attempt on Thebes, had been left unburied; this punishment is now to be extended to Polyneices himself, although a Theban born

For a hero's grave, and lets the other rot?
They are saying he has laid Eteocles in the ground
With every rite and custom that is fitting
To give him honor with the dead below.
But Polyneices' body, that was killed
So pitifully, they say he has commanded
Should not be mourned or given burial
But lie unburied and unwept, a feast   30
For passing birds to gorge on at their pleasure.
And so, the rumor runs, has our good Creon
Decreed for you and me—for me, I say!
And is on his way here now, to spell it out
To those who have not heard. He does not take
This matter lightly. Anyone who disobeys
In any way will die by public stoning.
So there you have it. Now we shall soon find out
If you are a true-born daughter of your line,
Or if you will disgrace your noble blood!   40
ISM: But, my poor sister, if things are as you say,
What ways and means have I to set them straight?
ANT: Ask yourself, will you work with me, help me do it?
ISM: What adventure is this? What do you have in mind?
ANT: Will you help this hand of mine to lift the dead?
ISM: You mean to bury him? Against the law?
ANT: Bury my brother? Yes—and bury yours,
If you will not. No-one shall call me faithless.
ISM: You would not dare, when Creon has forbidden it!
ANT: He has no right to keep me from my own.   50
ISM: Oh sister, think of how our father died,

Hated, despised, and driven by the sins
He had himself laid bare, to turn his hand
Against himself, and strike out both his eyes.
And then his mother, wife—which shall I call her?
Knotted a noose, and took away her life.
Then the final blow, two brothers in one day,
Unhappy pair, each shedding kinsman's blood,
Lay hands on each other, and made one in death.
60   Now we two are alone. Think how much worse
Our deaths will be, if in despite of law
We brave the king's commandment and his
    power.
Let us not forget two things—that we were born
Women, and so not meant to fight with men:
And then, that we must do what our masters tell
    us—
Obey in this, and other things far worse.
I, then, will ask the kingdom of the dead
To pardon me; since I am no free agent,
I will yield to the powers that be. There is no sense
70   In meddling in things outside our sphere.
ANT: I shall not persuade you. You would not be
    welcome
To help me now, even if you wanted to.
Be what you want to be; but I intend
To bury him. It is a noble way to die.
I shall lie with him for love, as he loved me,
A criminal, but guiltless; for the dead
Have longer claims upon me than the living.
There is my lasting home. If you think fit
To dishonor the gods' commandments, then you
    may.
80   ISM: I mean them no dishonor; but when it means
Defying the state—I am not strong enough.
ANT: Let that be your excuse. Now I shall go
To heap the earth on my beloved brother.
ISM: Antigone, no! I am so afraid for you!
ANT: You need not fear for me. Look after your-
    self.
ISM: At least tell no-one what you mean to do.
    Keep it a secret, I shall do the same.
ANT: Oh no, denounce me! You will be in far
    worse trouble
For keeping silence, if you do not tell the world.
ISM: You have a hot heart where you should be
90   shivering.
ANT: I know I am giving pleasure where I should.
ISM: Yes, if you can. But you ask too much of
    yourself.

ANT: When I have no more strength, then I shall
    stop.
ISM: No point in starting, when the cause is hope-
    less.
ANT: Go on like this and you will make me hate
    you,
    And the dead will hate you too; you give him
    cause.
Leave me alone with my stupidity
To face this dread unknown; whatever it is,
Anything is better than to die a coward!
ISM: Then if your mind is made up, go. You are a
    fool,   100
And yet your own will love you for it.

Exit ANTIGONE; ISMENE *retires within the palace.*
Enter CHORUS *of Theban elders.*

CHORUS: Light of the morning sun, brightest that
    ever yet
Dawned upon the seven gates of Thebes;
Eye of the golden day, at last we see you
Rising over Dirke's streams,
Turning to rout the white-shielded warrior
That came from Argos in his array,
Winging his feet, and sending him flying home.
Polyneices' contentious quarrel
Was the cause of his coming here,   110
Winging over our country
Like an eagle clamoring,
Sheathed in snow-white feathers
With mail-clad men and waving plumes.
Over the housetops hovering, howling before
Our seven gates for blood to slake his spears;
But before he could suck his fill of Theban
Blood, before the Fire-god's flame
Leapt from the logs to embrace our ramparts,
He left, so loud the roaring of the war-cry   120
Behine him, as he fought the Theban dragon.
Zeus hates nothing more than a boastful tongue.
When he saw them coming, a mighty stream
Arrogant in their clanging gold
He brandished his thunderbolt and felled the
    man

105 *Dirke* river on the west of Thebes
125 *the man . . . ramparts* a famous incident in the Theban story. Capaneus, one of the seven heroes who
marched against the city, dared to defy Zeus and for his
presumption was struck down at the moment of his
triumph

Who had scaled our ramparts, and stood at his
    goal
With the cry of victory on his lips.
And over he tumbled, torch in hand,
He who a moment before
130   Had come at us like a man possessed,
Running berserk, with the hot breath of hatred.
Earth rang with his fall, and his threats went
    wide.
Then the God of War, our good yoke-fellow,
Lashed out, and assigned
To each of the rest their several deaths.
Seven captains stood before seven gates,
Matched against seven, and left their armor
In homage to Zeus, the arbiter of battles,
All but the ill-starred pair, who, born
140   Of one father and mother, leveled their spears
At each other; both won, and both fell dead.
But now the glorious name of Victory
Enters our chariot-proud
City, to laugh with us in our joy,
Let us put all memory of past war behind us
And visit the temples of the gods with song
And with nightlong dances; Bacchus, whose
    steps
Set the meadows dancing,
Come down to lead the procession!

Enter CREON

150   But here comes our country's ruler,
Creon, Menoeceus' son, our new lord
By the gods' new dispensations.
What counsel can he be pondering
To summon the elders by general decree
To meet in special conference together?
CREON: Gentlemen, the state has been in troubled
    waters,
But now the gods have set us back on course.
My summons came to you, of all the people,
To meet here privately, because I knew
160   Your constant reverence for Laius' throne,
And then, when Oedipus became our king,
After his death, I saw their children
Secure in your unswerving loyalty.
And now this double blow has taken both
His sons in one day, each struck down by the
    other.
Each with his brother's blood upon his hands,

The throne and all its powers come to me
As next of kin in order of succession.
But you can never know what a man is made of,
His character or powers of intellect,   170
Until you have seen him tried in rule and office.
A man who holds the reins of government
And does not follow the wisest policies
But lets something scare him from saying what
    he thinks,
I hold despicable, and always have done.
Nor have I time for anyone who puts
His popularity before his country.
As Zeus the omnipotent will be my witness,
If I saw our welfare threatened; if I saw
One danger-signal, I would speak my mind,   180
And never count an enemy of my country
To be a friend of mine. This I believe:
The state keeps us afloat. While she holds an even
    keel,
Then, and then only, can we make real friends.
By this creed I shall make Thebes prosperous;
And in accordance with it, I have published
My edict on the sons of Oedipus,
That Eteocles, who died a hero's death
While fighting to defend his fatherland
Should be entombed with every solemn rite   190
With which the glorious dead are sent to rest.
But his brother Polyneices, who returned
From exile, with intent to devastate
The country of his fathers, and to burn
The temples of his fathers' gods, to taste
His brother's blood, and make the rest his slaves,
Concerning him, it is proclaimed as follows:
That nobody shall mourn or bury him,
But let his body lie for dogs and birds
To make their meal, so men may look and
    shudder.   200
Such is my policy; foul play shall never
Triumph over honest merit, if I can help it,
But the man who loves his city shall receive
Honor from me, in his life and in his death.
CHORUS: Such is your pleasure, Creon, son of
    Menoeceus,
Concerning our city's friend and enemy,
And you have the power to order as you wish,
Not only the dead, but the living too.
CREON: Then see to it my orders are obeyed.
CHORUS: Lay this responsibility on someone
    younger!   210

CREON: No, not to guard the corpse; that has been
  seen to.
CHORUS: Then what else are you asking me to do?
CREON: Not to side with anyone who disobeys me.
CHORUS: No man is fool enough to ask for death.
CREON: That is what you would get. But hope of
  gain
  Has often led men on to their destruction.

Enter GUARD

GUARD: My lord, I won't say that I'm out of breath
  From hurrying, or that I've run here all the way,
  For several times my thoughts pulled me up short
220 And made me turn round to go back again.
  There was a voice inside me kept on saying
  "Why go, you fool? You're certain to be pun-
  ished."
  "Idiot, why hang about? If Creon hears
  The news from someone else, you'll smart for it."
  Arguing like this I went at snail's pace,
  And so a short road turned into a long one.
  But in the end, go forward won the day.
  There's nothing to say, but all the same I'll say it.
  I'm certain of one thing, at any rate,
230 That I can only get what's coming to me.
CREON: What is it that has put such fear in you?
GUARD: First let me say a word on my own
  account.
  I didn't do it, nor did I see who did,
  And it isn't right that I should take the blame for
  it.
CREON: A well-placed shot. You have covered
  yourself
  Well against attack. I see you mean to surprise
  me.
GUARD: A man thinks twice before he tells bad
  news.
CREON: Then tell me will you, and be on your
  way.
GUARD: Well, here it is: the corpse—someone has
  buried it.
240 The flesh, and did whatever else was fitting.
  And gone away; he sprinkled dry dust over
CREON: What are you saying? What man has dared
  to do this?
GUARD: I don't know. There was no mark of a
  pickaxe,
  No spade had been at work; the ground was hard,
  Dry and unbroken; we could find no tracks
  Of wheels; he left no trace, whoever did it.

And when the man who took the morning watch
Showed us, nobody knew what to make of it.
The corpse was out of sight—not in a tomb
But sprinkled with dust, as though someone had
  thrown it   250
To avoid bad luck. There was no sign of wild
  beasts
Or dogs around; the corpse was in one piece.
Then we all started cursing each other at once,
One sentry blaming the next; it would have come
To blows in the end, there was no-one there to
  stop us.
First one had done it, then the next man, then the
  next,
But we couldn't pin it down, all pleaded igno-
  rance.
We were ready to take red-hot irons in our hands,
To walk through fire, to swear an oath to heaven
That we were innocent, had no idea   260
Of who had planned it all, or done the work.
In the end, when there was no more point in
  searching,
One man said something which made every one
  of us
Shiver, and hang our heads; we didn't see
How we could argue with him, or if we listened
How we could save our necks. He said we
  couldn't
Keep the thing dark, but we must come and tell
  you.
So we did; and I was the unlucky one.
The lot picked me to receive the prize.
So here I am—about as pleased to be here   270
As I know you are to see me. Nobody
Has any love for the one who brings bad news.
CHORUS: My lord, since he began, I have been
  wondering
  Could this perhaps have been the work of heav-
  en?
CREON: Be quiet, before you make me lose my
  temper.
  Do you want to look like fools in your old age?
  What you suggest is intolerable,
  That the gods would give this corpse a second
  thought.
  Why should they try to hide his nakedness?
  In reward for services rendered? When he came   280
  To burn their marble halls and treasuries,
  To burn their land, make havoc of its laws?
  Or can you see the gods rewarding sinners?

Never. No, there were people in this town
Who took it hard from the first, and grumbled at
    me,
Furtively tossing their heads, not submitting
To the yoke as in duty bound, like contented
    men.
It was these people—of that I am convinced—
Who bribed the guards and urged them on to do
    it.
290 Of all the institutions of mankind
The greatest curse is money. It destroys
Our cities, it takes men away from home,
Corrupts men's honest minds, and teaches them
To enter on disreputable courses.
It shows them how to lead immoral lives
And flout the gods in everything they do.
But every one of the bribers will be caught
Sooner or later, they may be sure of that.
But by the reverence I owe to Zeus,
300 I tell you this upon my solemn oath,
That if you do not find the author of
This burial, and produce him before my eyes,
Death alone will be too good for you; you will be
Left hanging, till you tell about this outrage.
Then, when you next go stealing, you will know
What you may take, and learn for once and all
Not to love money without asking where
It comes from. You will find ill-gotten gains
Have ruined many more than they have saved.

GUARD: May I speak? Or shall I just turn round
310   and go?

CREON: Do you still need telling that your voice
    annoys me?

GUARD: Where does it hurt? In your ears or in your
    heart?

CREON: Is there any call for you to define my pain?

GUARD: The criminal troubles your mind, and I
    your ears.

CREON: Oh, you were born with a loose tongue, I
    can see.

GUARD: Maybe I was, but this I didn't do.

CREON: You did, and worse. You sold your life for
    money.

GUARD: How dreadful to judge by appearances,
    then be wrong.

CREON: Moralize as you please; but if you do not
    show me
    The men who did this thing, you will bear
320   witness
    That dishonest winnings bring you into trouble.

Exit CREON *to the palace*

GUARD: Well, I only hope he's caught; but
    whether he is
Or not—it's in the hands of fortune now—
You won't see me coming this way again.
I never thought I'd get away with this.
It's more than I hoped—the gods be praised for
    it.

Exit

CHORUS: The world is full of wonderful things
    But none more so than man,
    This prodigy who sails before the storm-winds,
    Cutting a path across the sea's gray face   330
    Beneath the towering menace of the waves.
    And Earth, the oldest, the primeval god,
    Immortal, inexhaustible Earth,
    She too has felt the weight of his hand
    As year after year the mules are harnessed
    And plows go back and forwards in the fields.
    Merry birds and forest beasts,
    Fish that swim in the deep waters,
    Are gathered into the woven nets
    Of man the crafty hunter.   340
    He conquers with his arts
    The beasts that roam in the wild hill-country;
    He tames the horses with their shaggy manes
    Throwing a harness around their necks,
    And the tireless mountain bull.
    Speech he has made his own, and thought
    That travels swift as the wind,
    And how to live in harmony with others
    In cities, and how to shelter himself
    From the piercing frost, cold rain, when the open 350
    Fields can offer but a poor night's lodging.
    He is ever-resourceful; nothing that comes
    Will find him unready, save Death alone.
    Then he will call for help and call in vain,
    Though often, where cure was despaired of, he
        has found one.
    The wit of man surpasses belief,
    It works for good and evil too;
    When he honors his country's laws, and the right
    He is pledged to uphold, then city
    Hold up your head; but the man   360
    Who yields to temptation and brings evil home
    Is a man without a city; he has
    No place in the circle of my hearth,
    Nor any part in my counsels.

Enter GUARD, *leading* ANTIGONE *prisoner*

But what is this? The gods alone know.
Is it Antigone? She and no other.
Oh unhappy daughter of
Your wretched father Oedipus,
What is it? Have they arrested you?
370   Have you broken the royal commandment?
Has your foolishness brought you to this?
GUARD: Here she is! This is the girl who did it!
We caught her burying him. But where is Creon?
CHORUS: Here, coming from the palace, just in
time.

Enter from the palace CREON *with* ATTENDANTS

CREON: Coming in time for what? What is it now?
GUARD: My lord, a man should never swear to
anything
Second thoughts belie the first. I could have
sworn
I wouldn't have come back here again in a hurry
After the tongue-lashing you gave me last time.
380   But there's no pleasure like the one that comes
As a surprise, the last thing you expected.
So here I am, breaking my solemn oath,
Bringing this girl, who was caught performing
The final rites. We didn't draw lots this time.
This piece of luck belongs to me, and no-one else.
So now, my lord, she's yours, for you to examine
And question as you wish. I've done my duty;
It's someone else's problem from now on.
CREON: This girl? Where did you take her?
What was she doing?
GUARD: Burying the man. That's all there is to
390   know.
CREON: Are you serious? Do you know what you
are saying?
GUARD: I saw her burying the corpse, the thing
You had forbidden. What could be clearer than
that?
CREON: You saw her? Captured her red-handed?
How?
GUARD: It happened this way. When we returned
to our posts
With your dreadful threats still ringing in our
ears
We swept off every bit of dust that covered
The corpse, and left the rotting carcass bare,
Then sat down on the brow of a hill to windward

Where the stench couldn't reach us. We kept our-
selves lively   400
By threatening each other with what would
happen
If anyone were careless in his duty.
And so time passed, until the sun's bright disk
Stood midway in the heavens, and the heat
Began to burn us. Suddenly a whirlwind
Raised a dust storm, a black blot on the sky,
Which filled the plain, played havoc with the
leaves
Of every tree in sight, and choked the air.
We shut our eyes and bore it; heaven sends
These things to try us. When it had gone at
last   410
There was the girl; she gave a shrill sharp cry
Like a bird in distress when it sees its bed
Stripped of its young ones and the nest deserted.
So she cried, when she saw the corpse left bare,
Raising her voice in grief, and calling down
Curses on the men who had done this thing.
Then at once she brought handfuls of dry dust,
Lifted a handsome vase, and poured from it
The three drink-offerings to crown the dead.
When we see it, out we run and close around her   420
In a moment. She was not at all put out.
We taxed her with what she had done, both then
And earlier; she admitted everything,
Which made me glad, but miserable too.
Nothing makes you happier than to get yourself
Out of trouble; but it's quite another thing
To get friends into it. But there's nothing
I wouldn't do, to keep myself from harm.
CREON: You there; yes, you, who dare not look me
in the face;
Do you admit this accusation or deny it?   430
ANT: Oh, I admit it. I make no denial.
CREON: (*to the* GUARD) Take yourself off, wherever
you want to go,
A free man. You are cleared of a serious charge.
(*to* ANTIGONE) Now tell me, you, and keep your
answers brief
Did you know there was an order forbidding
this?
ANT: Yes. How could I help it? Everybody knew.
CREON: And yet you dared to go against the law?
ANT: Why not? It was not Zeus who gave the
order.
And Justice living with the dead below

440 Has never given men a law like this
Nor did I think that your pronouncements were
So powerful that mere man could override
The unwritten and unfailing laws of heaven.
These live, not for today and yesterday
But for all time; they came, no man knows
   whence.
There is no man's resolve I fear enough
To answer to the gods for breaking these.
I knew that I must die—how could I help it?
Even without your edict; but if I die
450 Before my time is up, I count it gain.
For when a person lives as I do, in the midst
Of evils, what can death be but gain?
And so for me to happen on this fate
Is grief not worth a thought; but if I had left
My mother's son to lie a homeless corpse,
Then had I grieved. I do not grieve for this.
If what I do seems foolish in your sight
It may be that a fool condemns my folly.
CHORUS: This is her father's willful spirit in her,
460 Not knowing how to bend before the storm.
CREON: Come, you must learn that over-stubborn
   spirits
Are those most often humbled. Iron that has
Been hardened in the fire and cannot bend
You will find the first to snap and fly in pieces.
I have known high-mettled horses brought to
   order
By a touch on the bridle. Pride is not for those
Who live their lives at their neighbour's beck and
   call
This girl was already schooled in insolence
When she disobeyed the official proclamation.
470 And now she adds insult to injury
By boasting of it, glorying in her crime.
I swear, she is the man and I the woman
If she keeps her victory and goes unpunished.
No! Even though she be my sister's child,
If she were bound to me by ties more close
Than anyone who shares our household prayers
She and that sister of hers will not escape
The ultimate fate; for I accuse her too
Of equal guilt in plotting this burial.
480 So go and call her. I saw her indoors just now
Delirious, not knowing what she was saying.

Exeunt ATTENDANTS *to the palace*

A guilty mind betrays itself beforehand

When men go plotting mischiefs in the dark.
But no less do I hate the criminal
Who is caught, and tries to glorify his crime.
ANT: What more would you take from me than
   my life?
CREON: Not a thing. When I have that, I have all I
   want.
ANT: Then what are you waiting for? Your
   arguments
Fall on deaf ears; I pray they always will.
My loyalties are meaningless to you.   490
Yet, in the world's eyes, what could I have done
To earn me greater glory, than to give
My brother burial? Everybody here
Would cheer me, if they were not dumb with
   fear.
But royalty, among so many blessings,
Has power to say and do whatever it likes.
CREON: These Thebans take a different view from
   yours.
ANT: Not they. They only curb their tongues for
   your sake.
CREON: Then why be different? Are you not
   ashamed?
ANT: Ashamed? Of paying homage to a brother?   500
CREON: Was not the man he killed your brother
   too?
ANT: My brother, by one mother, by one father.
CREON: Then why pay honors hateful in his eyes?
ANT: The dead man will not say he finds them
   hateful.
CREON: When you honor him no higher than a
   traitor?
ANT: It was his brother died, and not his slave.
CREON: Destroying Thebes; while he died to pro-
   tect it.
ANT: It makes no difference. Death asks these
   rites.
CREON: But a hero asks more honor than a traitor.
ANT: Who knows? The dead may find no harm in
   this.   510
CREON: Even death cannot change hatred into
   love.
ANT: But I was born for love, and not for hate!
CREON: Then if you have to love, go down and love
   The dead; while I live, no woman shall rule me!

Enter ATTENDANTS *from the palace with* ISMENE)

CHORUS: Look, the gates open and Ismene comes

Weeping for love and sisterhood.
Her brows are clouded, shadowing
Her face flushed red, and teardrops
Fall on her lovely cheek.

520 CREON: And you, a viper lurking in my house,
Were sucking my life's blood, while I, unknow-
    ing.
Raised a twin scourge to drive me from my
    throne.
Come, answer me. Will you confess your share
In this burial, or deny all knowledge of it?

ISM: I did it—if my sister will allow me.
Half the blame is mine. I take it on myself.

ANT: No! Justice will not let you! You refused,
And I denied you any part in it.

ISM: But now you are in trouble. I am not
530 Ashamed to ride the storm out at your side.

ANT: Who did it, Hades and the dead can witness.
I love not those who only talk of love.

ISM: No, sister, do not reject me. Let
Me die with you and sanctify the dead.

ANT: You shall not share my death. You had no
    hand in this.
Do not say you had. My death will be enough.

ISM: What joy have I in life when you are gone?

ANT: Ask Creon. All your care has been for him.

ISM: Why do you want to hurt me? It does no
    good.

540 ANT: You are right. If I mock you it is for my pain.

ISM: Then tell me how I can help you, even now.

ANT: Save yourself. I do not grudge you your
    escape.

ISM: Then is poor Ismene not to share your fate?

ANT It was you who chose to live, and I to die.

ISM: At least I tried to move you from your choice.

ANT: One side approved your wisdom, the other
    mine.

ISM: And yet the offence is the same for both of us.

ANT: Be of good heart. You live; but I have been
Dead for a long time now, to serve the dead.

CREON: Here are two fools, one lately come to
550   folly,
The other since the day that she was born.

ISM: Indeed, my lord, such sense as nature gives
    us
Is not for ever. It goes in time of trouble.

CREON: Like yours, when you chose bad friends
    and evil ways.

ISM: How can I bear to live without my sister?

CREON: Sister? You have no sister. She is dead.

ISM: But will you kill your son's appointed bride?

CREON: I will. My son has other fields to plow.

ISM: He will never love another as he loved her.

CREON: No son of mine will wed an evil woman.   560

ISM: Haemon, my dearest! How your father
    wrongs you!

CREON: Let us have no further talk of marriages.

CHORUS: You will do it, then? You will rob your
    son of his bride?

CREON: Not I, but Death; yes, Death will break
    the match.

CHORUS: The decision stands, then, that the girl
    must die?

CREON: For you, and me. Let us have no more
    delay.
Servants, take them inside. From this time on
They must be women, not let out alone.
Even the boldest of us turns and runs
The moment he can see death closing in.   570

Exeunt ATTENDANTS *with* ANTIGONE *and* ISMENE

CHORUS: Blessed are those whose days have not
    tasted evil,
For once the gods have set a house tottering
The curse will never fade, but continues
From generation unto generation,
Like a storm rolling over the dark waters
Driven by the howling Thracian gales,
Stirring black mud from the bottom of the sea;
And the wind-torn headlands answer back
In a sullen roar, as the storm breaks over them.
I look on the house of Labdacus   580
And see how, from time immemorial,
The sorrows of the living have been heaped upon
The sorrows of those that died before them.
One generation does not set another
Free, but some god strikes them down
And they have no means of deliverance.
Over the last root of the house of Oedipus
Shone a ray of hope; but now this too has been
Laid low by a handful of bloody dust
Demanded by the gods of the underworld,   590
By unthinking words, and the heart's delirium.

561 *Haemon . . . wrongs you* it is uncertain whether this
line is spoken by Antigone or Ismene

Zeus, what man's transgression can restrain your
   power,
When neither Sleep, that encompasses all things,
Nor the months' unwearied and god-ordered
   march
Can arrest it? You do not grow old with the years
But rule in shining splendor as Olympus' king.
As it was in the past, this law will hold
Tomorrow and until the end of time:
600 That mortal life has a limited capacity.
When it aims too high, then the curse will fall.
For Hope, whose territory is unbounded,
Brings comfort to many, but to many others
Insane desires and false encouragement.
A man may go blindly on his way
Then walk into the fire and burn himself,
And so disillusion comes.
In his wisdom, someone coined the famous
   saying
That when a god leads a man's mind on
To destruction, sooner or later he comes
610 To believe that evil is good, good evil,
And then his days of happiness are numbered.

Enter HAEMON

But here is Haemon, your youngest son.
Does he come to grieve for the doom that has
   fallen
Upon Antigone, his promised bride,
To complain of the marriage that is taken from
   him?
CREON: We shall not need second sight to tell us
   that.
My son, have you heard that sentence has been
   passed
On your betrothed? Are you here to storm at me?
Or have I your good will, whatever I do?
HAEMON: Father, I am in your hands. You in your
   wisdom
620 Lay down for me the paths I am to follow.
There is no marriage in the world
That I would put before my good advisor.
CREON: Yes, keep this always in your heart, my
   son:
Accept your father's word as law in all things.
For that is why men pray to have
Dutiful children growing up at home,
To repay their father's enemies in kind

And honor those he loves no less than he does.
But a man is sowing troubles for himself
And enemies' delight—what else?—when he   630
Sires sons who bring no profit to their father.
So, my son, do not be led by passing fancy
To lose your head for a woman's sake. You know,
The warmth goes out of such embraces, when
An evil woman shares your home and bed.
False friends are deadlier than a festered wound.
So turn from her with loathing; let her find
A husband for herself among the dead.
For now that I have caught her, the only one
Of all the city to disobey me openly,   640
My people shall not see me break my word.
I shall kill her. Let her plead the sacred ties
Of kinship! If I bring up my own family
To flout me, there will be no holding others.
A man who sees his family obey him
Will have authority in public matters.
But if anyone offends, or violates the laws,
No word of praise shall he ever have from me.
Whoever the state appoints must be obeyed,
In little things or great things, right or wrong.   650
I should have confidence that such a man
Would be as good a ruler as a subject
And in a hail of spears would stand his ground
Where he was put, a comrade you could trust.
But disobedience is the worst of evils;
It is this that ruins cities, it is this
That makes homes desolate, turns brothers in
   arms
To headlong rout. But those who are preserved
Owe their lives, the greater part of them, to
   discipline.
And so we must stand up for law and order,   660
Not let ourselves be worsted by a woman.
If yield we must, then let us yield to a man.
Let no-one call us woman's underlings.
CHORUS: Unless the years have robbed me of my
   wits
You seem to have sound sense in what you say.
HAEMON: Father, the gods endow mankind with
   reason,
The highest quality that we possess.
It is not for me to criticize your words.
I could not do it, and would hate to try.
And yet, two heads are sometimes better than
   one;   670

At least, it is my place to watch, on your behalf,
All that men do and say and criticize.
Fear of your frown prevents the common man
From saying anything that would displease you,
But I can hear these murmurs in the dark,
The feeling in the city for this girl.
"No woman" they say "has ever deserved death
less,
Or died so shamefully in a noble cause.
When her brother fell in the slaughter, she would
not

680 Leave him unburied, to provide a meal
For carrion dogs or passing birds of prey.
Is she not, then, deserving golden honors?"
This is what men are whispering to each other.
Father, there is nothing dearer to my heart
Than your continuing prosperity.
What finer ornament could children have
Than a father's proud success—or he, than
theirs?
So wear an open mind; do not suppose
That you are right, and everyone else is wrong.

690 A man who thinks he has monopoly
Of wisdom, no rival in speech or intellect,
Will turn out hollow when you look inside him.
However wise he is, it is no disgrace
To learn, and give way gracefully.
You see how trees that bend to winter floods
Preserve themselves, save every twig unbroken,
But those that stand rigid perish root and branch,
And also how the man who keeps his sails
Stretched taut, and never slackens them, over-
turns

700 And finishes his voyage upside down.
Let your anger rest; allow us to persuade you.
If a young man may be permitted his opinion
I should say it would be best for everyone
To be born omniscient; but otherwise—
And things have a habit of falling out differ-
ently—
It is also good to learn from good advice.
CHORUS: My lord, if he speaks to the point you
ought to listen,
And Haemon, you to him. There is sense on both
sides.
CREON: And is a man of my age to be taught

710 What I should think by one so young as this?
HAEMON: Nothing that is not right; young though
I may be,

You should judge by my behavior, not my age.
CREON: What sort of behavior is it to honor rebels?
HAEMON: I would never suggest that the guilty
should be honored.
CREON: And is she not infected with this disease?
HAEMON: The people of Thebes unanimously deny
it.
CREON: Will the city tell me how I am to rule?
HAEMON: Listen to that! Who is being childish
now?
CREON: Is the state to listen to any voice but mine?
HAEMON: There is no state, when one man is its
master.   720
CREON: Is not the state supposed to be the ruler's?
HAEMON: You would do well as the monarch of a
desert.
CREON: It seems the woman has a champion here.
HAEMON: Then you are the woman! It is you I care
about!
CREON: Insolent cub! Will you argue with your
father?
HAEMON: I will, when I see you falling into error.
CREON: Am I wrong to respect my own preroga-
tives?
HAEMON: It is no respect, when you offend the
gods.
CREON: How contemptible, to give way to a
woman!
HAEMON: At least I do not give way to temptation.   730
CREON: But every word you say is a plea for her.
HAEMON: And for you, and for me, and for the
gods below.
CREON: You will never marry her this side of the
grave.
HAEMON: Then she will die—and take somebody
with her.
CREON: So! Do you dare to go so far? Are you
threatening me?
HAEMON: Is it threatening, to protest a wrong
decision?
CREON: You shall pay for this. A fine one to teach
wisdom!
HAEMON: If you were not my father, I should call
you a fool.
CREON: You woman's slave; do not try to wheedle
me!
HAEMON: Would you stop everyone from speaking
but yourself?   740
CREON: Indeed! I tell you, by the gods above us,

You shall pay for using such language to your father.

to the ATTENDANTS

Bring this abomination out, and let her die
Here, in his presence, at her bridegroom's side.
HAEMON: No, she will never perish at my side,
So do not think it. From this moment on
Your eyes will never see my face again.
So rave away, to those who have more patience!

Exit

CHORUS: My lord, he has gone away in angry haste.
Young tempers are fierce when anything pro-
750 vokes them.
CREON: Let him do or dream all men can do and more.
He shall never save those girls from punishment.
CHORUS: Do you mean to put the two of them to death?
CREON: You are right to ask. Not her whose hands are clean.
CHORUS: And how do you intend to kill the other?
CREON: I shall take her where nobody ever comes.
And shut her in a rocky vault alive,
With the minimum of food that is permitted
To stop pollution falling on the city.
760 There she may pray to Death, the only god
She worships, and perhaps he may forgive her.
If not, she will learn—but when it is too late—
That honoring the dead is wasted effort.

Exit

CHORUS: Love, whom we fight but never conquer,
Love, the ravager of proud possessions
Who keeps eternal vigilance
In the softness of a young girl's cheek,
You go wherever the wide seas go
And among the cottages of country-dwellers.
770 None of the immortal gods can escape you,
Nor man, whose life is as a single day,
And, to whoever takes you in, comes madness.
The minds of honest men you lead
Out of the paths of virtue to destruction.
Father is at odds with son
And it is you who set this quarrel in their hearts.
One glance from the eyes of a ready bride
Bright with desire, and a man is enslaved.

On the throne of the eternal laws
Love has a place, for there the goddess Aphrodite   780
Decides men's fates, and there is no withstanding her.

Enter ATTENDANTS *with* ANTIGONE *bound*

It is my turn now; at a sight like this
The voice of the laws cannot hold me back
Or stop the tears from pouring down my cheeks.
Here comes Antigone, on her way
To the bridal-chamber where all must go to rest.
ANT: See me, citizens of my fatherland, as I go out
On my last journey; as I look my last on the sun-
light,
Never to see it again; Death, who puts all to
sleep,
Takes me as I am,   790
With life still in me, to the shores of the midnight lake,
A bride with no choir to accompany her way,
With no serenade at the bedroom door;
I am to marry with the King of Darkness!
CHORUS: And so you go with honor and praise
Below to the caverns of the dead;
No sickness has wasted you away,
You do not pay the wages of the sword,
But will go to death a law unto yourself
As no human being has done before you.   800
ANT: I have heard of one, a stranger among us from Phrygia,
Tantalus' daughter, and her sad end on Mount Sipylus,
Growing slowly into stone as a tree is wrapped with ivy.
And the story goes
That her body pines in unceasing snow and rain
And tears from her streaming eyes pour upon her breast.
Her fate is mine; like her I go to rest.
CHORUS: But she was a goddess, born of gods,

780 *Aphrodite* goddess of love, or, more accurately, of sexual desire
792 *A bride . . . bedroom door* according to Greek custom bride and groom were accompanied home by singing friends, who also sang outside the wedding chamber in the evening
802 *Tantalus' daughter* Niobe, daughter of the King of Phrygia in Asia Minor, turned into stone as punishment for boasting herself superior to the gods

And we are mortals, mortal born.

810 When a woman has to die, it is
A great distinction, for her to share
The lot of those who are one removed from gods,
Both here, and in the manner of her death.

ANT: Oh, you make fun of me! Gods of my fathers!
Must you laugh in my face? Can you not wait till I am gone?
Oh, my city; Thebans, proud in your possessions;
Chariot-thundering plain, you at least will bear witness
How no friends mourn for my passing, by what laws
I go to my rock-barred prison, my novel tomb.

820 Luckless Antigone, an alien in both worlds,
Among the living and among the dead!

CHORUS: You have driven yourself to the furthest limit of daring
And run, my child, against the high throne
Where justice sits; and great has been your fall.
Perhaps you are paying the price of your father's sin.

ANT: You have touched the memory bitterest in my mind,
The dirge for my father that is never finished,
For the fate of us all, the famous house of Labdacus.
Oh, the curse born
In a mother's bed; doomed mother, sleeping with her son,

830 My father. Poor Antigone, what parents brought you
Into this world! Now I go to join them, accursed, unwed.
Oh, my brother, how ill-fated was your marriage.
Your dead hand has reached out to destroy the living.

CHORUS: Pious actions are a sort of piety.
But a man who has authority in his keeping
Can permit no offence against authority.
Your own willful temper has destroyed you.

ANT.: Friendless, unwept, without a wedding song,

They call for me, and I must tread my road.   840
Eye of heaven, light of the holy sun,
I may look on you no longer.
There is no friend to lament my fate,
No-one to shed a tear for me.

Enter CREON

CREON: Let me tell you, if songs and dirges before dying
Did any good, we should never hear the end of them.
Take her, and be quick about it. Lock her up
In her cavern tomb, as I have ordered you,
And leave her alone—to die, if she prefers,
Or live in her tomb, for that will be her home.   850
Whatever becomes of her our hands are clean.
But in this world she has a place no longer.

ANT: Tomb, bridal-chamber, my eternal home
Hewn from the rock, where I must go to meet
My own, those many who have died, and been
Made welcome by Persephone in the shadow-world.
I am the last, my death the worst of all
Before my allotted span of years has run.
But as I go I have this hope in heart,
That my coming may be welcome to my father,   860
My mother; welcome, dearest brother, to you.
For when you died, with my own hands I washed
And robed your bodies, and poured offerings
Over your graves. Now this is my reward,
Polyneices, for rendering such services to you.
Yet wisdom would approve my honoring you.
If I were a mother; if my husband's corpse
Were left to rot, I never should have dared
Defy the state to do what I have done.
What principle can justify such words?   870
Why, if my husband died I could take another;
Someone else could give me a child if I lost the first;
But Death has hidden my mother and father from me.
No brother can be born to me again.
Such was the principle by which I chose
To honor you; and for this Creon judges me guilty
Of outrage and transgression, brother mine!

---

833 *Oh, my brother* not Oedipus, but Polyneices, whose marriage with the daughter of the king of Argos had cemented the alliance against Thebes

856 *Persephone* queen of the dead
867 *If I were a mother . . . born to me again* this passage is possibly spurious, and omitted by some editors

And now he seizes me to lead me off,
880   Robbed of my bride-bed and my marriage song.
I shall never marry, never be a mother.
And so, in misery, without a friend,
I go still living to the pit of death.
Which of heaven's commandments have I
    broken?
Why should I look to the gods any longer
After this? To whom am I to turn for help
When doing right has branded me a sinner?
If the gods approve what is happening to me,
After the punishment I shall know my fault,
But if my judges are wrong, I wish them no
890   worse
Than what they have unjustly done to me.
CHORUS: Still the same tempestuous spirit carry-
    ing her along.
CREON: Then those who are charged with taking
    her
Shall have cause to repent their slowness.
ANT: Oh, that word has brought me
    Very near my death.
CREON: I can offer you no hope.
    Your punishment stands unchanged.
ANT: City of my father in the land of Thebes,
900   The time has come, they take me away.
Look, princes of Thebes; this is the last
Daughter of the house of your kings.
See what I suffer, and at whose hands,
For doing no less than heaven bids us do.

Exeunt ATTENDANTS, *leading off* ANTIGONE

CHORUS: So Danae in her beauty endured the
    change
From the bright sky to the brazen cell,
And there she was hidden, lost to the living
    world.
Yet she was of proud birth too, my daughter,

905 *Danae* the chorus adduce from mythology parallels to
Antigone's plight. Danae was imprisoned by her father in
a brazen tower to avert a prophecy that she would bear a
son who would grow up to kill him. But Zeus, king of the
gods, appeared to her in a shower of golden rain and
fathered her son Perseus, who grew up to fulfil the
prophecy. Lycurgus *son of Dryas* persecuted the worshippers of Dionysus, and as punishment for his insolence was
driven mad by the god and died. Cleopatra married
Phineus, King of Salmydessos in Thrace, and bore him
two sons. Phineus later imprisoned her and took a new
wife, who blinded the boys

And the seed of Zeus was trusted to her keeping
That fell in golden rain.   910
But the power of fate is terrible.
Wealth cannot keep you from its reach, nor war,
Nor city walls, nor the dark sea-beaten ships
And the king of the Edonians, the fiery-tempered
Son of Dryas, was held in bondage
For his savage taunts, at Dionysus' will,
Clapped in a rocky cell; and so the full
Flowering of his madness passed from him grad-
    ually
And he came to recognize
The god he had insulted in his frenzy.   920
He had sought to stop the women when the god
    was in them
And the Bacchic torches, and enraged the piping
    Muses.
And by the Dark Rocks at the meeting of two
    waters
Lie the shores of Bosporos and Thracian Salmy-
    dessos.
Here was a sight for the eyes
Of the city's neighbour, Ares—
The two sons of Phineus, blinded
By stepmother's fury, their sightless eyes
Appealing for vengeance, calling down a curse
On her bloody hands and the shuttle turned
    dagger.   930
Pining in grief they bewailed their cruel fate.
How sad their mother's marriage; but her line
Went back to the ancient family
Of Erechtheus—she was a child
Of the North Wind, nursed in distant caves,
Who played with her father's storms, a child of
    the gods
Running swift as a steed upon the high hills.
Yet on her too the gray Fates laid their hand, my
    daughter.

Enter TEIRESIAS, *led by a* BOY

TEIRESIAS: Princes of Thebes, we have come here
    side by side,

923 *Dark Rocks* at the entrance to what is now the Black Sea
924 *Bosporos* narrow strip of water separating Greece from
Asia Minor
926 *Ares* god of war, whose home was in the wild regions
of Thrace
934 *Erechtheus* legendary king of Athens

940   One pair of eyes for both of us. That is how
      Blind men must walk, supported by a guide.
CREON: What news have you for us, old Teiresias?
TEIR: I will tell you. Listen when the prophet
      speaks.
CREON: I have never yet disregarded your advice.
TEIR: And so have kept Thebes safely on her
      course.
CREON: I know my debt to you, and acknowledge
      it.
TEIR: Then listen. Once more you stand on the
      verge of doom.
CREON: What do you mean? I shudder at your
      words.
TEIR: You will know, when you hear the the warn-
      ings of my art.
950   As I took my place upon my ancient seat
      Of augury, where all the birds come flocking,
      I heard a noise I had never heard before,
      Their cries distorted in a scream of fury,
      And I knew that they were clawing, killing each
      other;
      The whirring of wings told a tale too clear.
      I was frightened, and went at once to light the
      altar
      And offer sacrifices; but from my offerings
      No flame sprang up. Fat melted on the thighs
      And oozed in slow drops down to quench the
      embers
960   And smoked and spluttered; and the gall was
      scattered
      Into the air. The streaming thighs were raw,
      Bare of the fat which once enfolded them.
      And so my rites had failed. I asked a sign
      And none was given, as I learnt from this boy
      here.
      He is my guide, as I am guide to others.
      Your counsels brought this sickness on our state.
      The altars of our city and our homes
      All are defiled by dogs and birds of prey
      Who feed on Oedipus' unhappy son.
970   And so the gods no longer accept our prayers,
      Our sacrifices, our burnt offerings.
      The birds no longer warn us with their cries;
      They have drunk the fat blood of a slaughtered
      man.
      Think on these things, my son. To err is human,
      But when we err, then happy is the man

      Who is not stubborn, and has sense enough
      To remedy the fault he has committed.
      Give the dead his due, and do not stab a man
      When he is down. What good to kill him twice?
      I have your interests at heart, and speak   980
      To help you. No advisor is more welcome
      Than when you profit from his good advice.
CREON: You circle me like archers, all of you,
      And I am made your target! Even the prophets
      Conspire against me. They have long been using
      me
      As merchandise, a thing to buy and sell!
      If profit is what you seek, go look abroad!
      There is silver in Sardis, gold in India.
      But you will not bury this man in his grave,
      No, not if the eagles of great Zeus himself   990
      Should lay his flesh before their master's throne.
      Not even that defilement frightens me
      Enough to bury him, for well I know
      No human being can defile the gods.
      The wisest of us, old Teiresias,
      Sink to the depths, when they hide their evil
      thoughts
      In fair-phrased speeches for the sake of money.
TEIR: If men only knew, would only realize—
CREON: Knew what? Another pronouncement!
      Let us hear!
TEIR: Good counsel is worth more than worldly
      riches.   1000
CREON: Just as stupidity is the greatest harm.
TEIR: Yet that is the sickness that has tainted you.
CREON: I do not want to call a prophet names.
TEIR: But you do, when you say my prophecies are
      false.
CREON: Men of your tribe were always money-
      seekers.
TEIR: And men of yours have always been
      dictators.
CREON: Have you forgotten you are speaking to
      your king?
TEIR: No. It was because of me that you saved
      Thebes.
CREON: You are a wise prophet but in love with
      evil.

988 *Sardis* city of Asia Minor containing the royal treasury

1010 TEIR: You will move me to tell the unutterable
secret.
CREON: Tell it—as long as there is no profit in it!
TEIR: I do not think so—as far as you are con-
cerned.
CREON: You will make no money out of my deci-
sion.
TEIR: Then listen well. Before the sun's swift
wheels
Have numbered many more days of your life,
You will surrender corpse for corpses, one
Begotten from the seed of your own loins,
Because you have sent this world to join the next
And cruelly lodged the living in the grave,
1020 But keep Death's property on earth, unburied,
Robbed of its honor, an unhallowed corpse.
This is not for you to say, nor for the gods
In heaven, but in doing this you wrong them.
And so the Avengers, Furies sent by Death
And by the gods, lie in waiting to destroy you
And snare you in the evils you have worked.
So watch, and you will see if I am bribed
To say these things. Before much time is out
The cries of men and womenfolk will fill your
house.
1030 And hatred rises against you in every city
Whose mangled sons were left for burial
To dogs, or beasts, or birds of prey, who bore
Their stinking breath to every soldier's home.
Archer you call me; then these are the arrows
I send into your heart, since you provoke me,
Sure arrows; you will not escape their sting.
Boy, take me to my home again, and leave him
To vent his fury on some younger man,
And learn to moderate his tongue, and bear
1040 A better spirit in his breast than now.

Exit

CHORUS: He has gone, my lord; his prophecies
were fearful.
As long as I remember, since my hair
Has turned from black to white, this man has
never
Made one false prophecy about our city.
CREON: I know it as well as you. My mind is
troubled.

1024 *Furies* supernatural pursuers of the wrongdoer

To yield is fatal; but to resist and bring
A curse on my proud spirit—that too is hard.
CHORUS: Son of Menoeceus, you must listen to
good advice.
CREON: What's to be done? Tell me and I will do it.
CHORUS: Go free the girl from her prison in the
rocks   1050
And give the corpse an honorable tomb.
CREON: Is this your advice? You think that I
should yield?
CHORUS: Yes, lord, as quickly as you can. The
gods
Move fast to cut short man's stupidity.
CREON: It is hard; but I resign my dear resolve.
We cannot fight against necessity.
CHORUS: Go do it now; do not leave it to another.
CREON: I will go as I am. Servants, be off with you,
Each and every one; take axes in your hands
And go to the hill you can see over there.   1060
Now that my judgment has been reversed
I shall be there to free her, as I imprisoned her.
Perhaps after all the gods' ways are the best
And we should keep them till our lives are done.

Exit

CHORUS: You who are known by many names,
Who blessed the union of Cadmus' daughter,
Begotten by Zeus the Thunderer, guarding
The land of Italy famed in story,
King of Eleusis, in the land-locked plain
Of Deo where the wanderer finds welcome,   1070
Bacchus whose home is Thebes, mother-city of
Bacchanals,
By Ismenus' tranquil waters where the fierce
dragon's teeth were sown.

1066 *Cadmus' daughter* Semele, mortal mother, by Zeus,
of Dionysus
1069 *Eleusis* home of the mystery-cult devoted to Demeter, goddess of the crops, and her daughter Persephone.
The worship of Dionysus had infiltrated into this rite
1070 *Deo* Demeter
1072 *By Ismenus'* . . . *were sown* Thebes was founded by
Cadmus, who killed a dragon guarding the site, near the
Ismenus River, and sowed the dragon's teeth in the
ground. From them sprang up armed men who fought
each other. All were killed but five, who became the
ancestors of the Thebans.

The fitful gleam of the torchlight finds you
Amid the smoke on the slopes of the forked
     mountains
Where tread your worshippers, the nymphs
Of Corycia, by Castalia's stream.
From Nysa's ivy-mantled slopes,
From the green shore carpeted with vines
You come, and they are no human lips that can
     cry
Your name, as you make your progress through
1080   the ways of Thebes.
For it is she you honor above all other cities,
And your mother too, who died by a bolt from
     heaven.
And now the whole city labors under
This grievous malady, come with healing feet
Down from the slopes of Parnassus or the sound-
     ing sea.
Conductor of the stars, whose breath is made of
     fire,
Lord of the voices that cry aloud in the night,
Son born of Zeus, appeared to us, oh lord,
With the Thyiads your servants who in nightly
     abandon
1090 Dance before you, Iacchus, the bringer of all
     blessings.

Enter MESSENGER

MESSENGER: You who live by Amphion's and
     Cadmus' walls,
No man's estate is ever so assured
That I would set it down as good or bad.
Fortune can raise us, fortune cast us down,
Depending on our luck, from day to day,
But for how long? No man can see the future.
For Creon was once blessed, as I count blessings;
He saved the land of Cadmus from its enemies,
Became its sole and undisputed king
1100 And ruled, proud father of a princely line.
Now everything is gone. A man who forfeits
All of life's pleasures I can count no longer
Among the living, but as dead in life.
So stack your house with treasures as you will
And live in royal pomp; when joy is absent

I would not give the shadow of a breath
For all the rest, compared with joy alone.
CHORUS: What is this new royal grief you come to
     tell us?
MESS: Death; and the living must answer to the
     dead.
CHORUS: Who killed? And who has been killed?
     Tell us.   1110
MESS: Haemon, and by a hand he knew too well.
CHORUS: By his father's hand? Or was it by his
     own?
MESS: His own, in anger for his father's murder.
CHORUS: Oh prophet, how much truth was in your
     words.
MESS: That is how things are. For the rest you
     must decide.

Enter EURYDICE

CHORUS: And here is Eurydice, the unhappy wife
     Of Creon; she is coming from the palace.
EURYDICE: People of Thebes, I heard what you
     were saying
As I was going from my house to offer
Devotions at the goddess Pallas' shrine.   1120
I stood there with my hand about to draw
The bolt, and my ears were greeted by this tale
Of family disaster. Terrified,
I fell back swooning in my servants' arms.
But tell again what you were telling then.
The first grief is over. I shall listen now.
MESS: Dear lady, I shall tell you what I saw
Omitting nothing, exactly as it happened.
Why should I give false comfort? You would
     soon
Know I was lying. Truth is always best.   1130
I attended on your husband to direct his way
Across the plain, where Polyneices' corpse,
Mangled by dogs, still lay unburied.
We prayed the goddess of the roads, and Pluto.
To have mercy on us and restrain their wrath,
Performed the ritual washing of the corpse,
Cut branches and cremated what was left of him
And raised a hillock of his native soil
Above him; then made for the cavern, where the
     girl
Waited for Death to share her rocky bed.   1140
Far off, one of us heard a piercing cry
Coming from that unholy bridal chamber

1076 *Corycia* cave on Mt. Parnassus *Castalia* fountain on
Mt. Parnassus sacred to the Muses
1077 *Nysa* legendary scene of the nursing of Dionysus
1091 *Amphion* legendary musician whose lyre-playing
charmed the stones to build a wall around Thebes

1134 *Pluto* god of the underworld

And came to report it to our master Creon.
As he approached, a cry of anguish came
To greet him, half-heard words; he groaned
aloud
And in his grief said "Creon, you are doomed;
Can my fear be true? Is the path I tread today
To be the bitterest path I ever trod?
The voice that greets me is my son's; men, run
ahead,
1150   Make for the tomb; there is an opening
Where someone has wrenched the stones away.
Squeeze inside
To the cell-mouth, see if it is Haemon's voice
I hear, or if the gods are mocking me."
And so, at our despairing master's bidding,
We made the search, and in the farthest corner
Of the tomb we saw her, hanged by the neck
In a noose of twisted linen, soft as silk,
While Haemon stood with his arms clasped
round her waist
Weeping for his bride now with the dead,
For his father's actions and his foredoomed
1160   marriage.
When he saw him his father gave a fearful cry
And went to him and called to him through his
tears
"Oh Haemon, what is this that you have done?
What has possessed you? Have you gone insane?
Come out, my son, I beg you, I implore you."
But the boy glared back at him wild-eyed,
Spat in his face, and without a word of answer
Drew his cross-hilted sword and thrust at him
But missed, as he jumped aside. Then in wild
remorse
1170   The poor wretch threw his weight upon the point
And drove it half into his side. As long as sense
Was left him, he clasped the girl in a limp em-
brace
And as his breath came hard, a jet of blood
Spurted from his lips, and ran down her pallid
cheek.
The bodies lie in each other arms. He has
Claimed his bride—in the next world, not in
this—
And he has given proof to all mankind
That of all human ills, bad counsel is the worst.

Exit EURYDICE *to the palace*

CHORUS: What would you make of this? Eurydice
1180   Has vanished without a word, good or bad.

MESS: It alarms me too. Yet I nourish the hope
That now she knows her loss she does not think
it proper
To mourn in public, but has gone inside
To set her maids to mourn for her bereavement.
She has learnt discretion and will not be foolish.
CHORUS: I am not so sure. To me this unnatural
silence
Is as ominous as the wildest excess of grief.
MESS: Well, I shall go in and see, in case
She is keeping some dark purpose hidden from us
In her grief-torn heart. You are right to be con-
cerned   1190
It is just as dangerous to be quiet.

Exit

CHORUS: But here is Creon coming himself
Bringing testimony all too plain,
The work of his and no other's madness,
If I may speak out, and his own wrongdoing.

Enter CREON *with* SERVANTS *bearing the body of*
HAEMON

CREON: Oh deadly end of stubborn sins
Born in the blindness of understanding!
See here, a son dead, a father who killed him.
Oh the fatal workings of my mind;
My son, to die so young,   1200
So soon to be taken from me
By my folly, not by yours.
CHORUS: Perhaps you see now too late what was
best.
CREON: Yes, I have learned my bitter lesson.
Some god must have chosen that moment
To crush me under his heavy hand
And hurl me into cruelty's ways,
Riding roughshod over all I held dear.
Oh, mankind, you were born to suffer!

Enter SECOND MESSENGER *from the palace*

MESSENGER: Master, you do not come empty-
handed; but there is   1210
More in store for you. You bear one load of grief
But soon you will see another, in your home.
CREON: My grief is here; is any worse to come?
MESS: Your wife is dead—true mother to her son
To the last, poor lady—by a wound still fresh.
CREON: Oh Death, ever-open door,
Do you have no mercy on me?
You who bring this tale of death and sorrow

What is this you are saying to me?
1220   What news is this, my boy?
My wife is dead? One more
To add to the pile of corpses?
MESS: See for yourself. It is no longer hidden.

The body of EURYDICE *is brought out*

CREON: Oh, here is another, a second blow.
What has fate in store for me after this?
I have but this moment lifted
My child in my arms, and again
I see a corpse brought out to greet me.
Oh wretched mother; oh my child.
MESS: There she lies at the altar, knife-point in her
1230   heart.
She mourned the noble fate of Megareus,
The first to die, then his; then closed her eyes
For ever, and with her dying breath called down
A curse on you for murdering her sons.
CREON: I am shaken with fear. Will nobody take
His two-edged sword and run me through?
For, oh, I am sick at heart.
Sorrow has made me his own.
MESS: Yes, she whose body you see lying here
1240   Laid the deaths of both sons at your door.
CREON: And what was the violent manner of her
leaving?
MESS: Her own hand drove the knife into her
heart
When she had heard them singing her son's
dirge.

1231 *Megareus* a minor incident in the siege of Thebes,
which Sophocles could expect his audience to know.
Megareus, son of Creon, sacrificed himself in an attempt
to appease the gods' wrath against the city.

CREON: Nobody else can bear the guilt,
No-one can take the blame from me.
I killed you, I, your unhappy father,
This is the truth.
Servants, take me away from this place.
Let me stay not a moment longer.
Creon has ceased to exist.   1250
CHORUS: Good advice, if there can be any good in
evil.
In present trouble the shortest way is best.
CREON: Let it come. What better fate could I ask
Than the fate which ushers in my life's last day?
Let it come, the best of all;
Let me never see tomorrow's dawn.
CHORUS: All in its proper time. We have things to
see
Here and now. The future is in other hands.
CREON: But everything I want was in that prayer.
CHORUS: Save your prayers. Whatever is going to
happen   1260
Is already fated. Nobody can change it.
CREON: Come, take this hot-headed fool away,
A fool who killed you, my son, in my blindness,
And you too, who are lying here; poor fool.
I do not know
Which way I am to take, where to lean;
My hands can do nothing right;
I am crushed beneath my fate.

Exit

CHORUS: To be happy it is first of all necessary
To be wise, and always remember   1270
To give the gods their due.
The measure of a proud man's boasting
Shall be the measure of his punishment
And teach him late in life
The nature of true wisdom.

THE *ANTIGONE*

by F. D. H. Kitto

The *Antigone* is accused, though more gently, of the same fault as the *Ajax*: the heroine drops out half-way through and leaves us to do our best with Creon, Haemon, and their fortunes.

We must recognize that if there is a fault it is a radical one, due to deliberate choice and not to oversight or to the inability of Sophocles to cope with a difficult situation. It is inevitable that so little should be said in the Exodus about her, that her lover's corpse but not hers is brought back, that Creon should at such length lament his own fate, least of all that Eurydice should be so unexpectedly introduced in order to kill herself immediately. Why Eurydice? Sophocles had no Elizabethan relish for corpses. She is relevant only to Creon. Clearly the close of the play is all Creon, deliberately so, for there is less of Antigone than might have been. Sophocles is not even making the best of a bad job.

The difficulty that we feel arises from our regarding Antigone as the chief character. If she is to this play what Oedipus and Electra are to theirs (and the *Antigone* is often criticized on this assumption), then the play is ill-balanced, but if the *Antigone* is more like the *Ajax* than the *Tyrannus*, the centre of gravity does not lie in one person, but between two. The *Ajax* is second-rate Sophocles until we feel the significance of Odysseus; the last part of the *Antigone* makes no sense until we realise that there is not one central character but two, and that of the two, the significant one to Sophocles was always Creon. It is simply a matter of looking at the dramatic facts. The older criticism (for of late things have taken a turn for the better) assumed that of course the play was about Antigone, and then set about explaining away the last scenes. The most satisfactory proof is performance. . . . But even without performance, we may note that Creon's part is half

---

From *Greek Tragedy* by F. D. H. Kitto, Methuen & Co., Ltd. Reprinted by permission.

as long again as Antigone's, a point which is less mechanical than it sounds, and that it is the more dynamic part. Hers is impressive and affecting enough, but his has the wider range and is the more elaborate. Her fate is decided in the first few verses and she can but go to meet it; most of the dramatic forces used in the play are deployed against Creon—the slight reserve with which the chorus receives his edict (211-14), the news that he has been defied, and that too by a woman, the opposition of Haemon, the disapproval of the city (691 ff.), the supernatural machinery of Teiresias, the desertion of the chorus (1098), the death of Haemon (foreshadowed), the death of Eurydice (unforeshadowed). Creon truly says

> Old sir, ye all like bowmen at a mark
> Let fly your shafts at me.

Antigone is indeed opposed, but not like this. Her tragedy is terrible, but it is foreseen and swift; Creon's grows before our eyes.

This must have been the balance that Sophocles designed; whether this reading saves the play from fault is not our business. Perhaps modern minds make more of Antigone than was intended (though as the argument of Sallustius explains why the play was called the *Antigone* we may perhaps infer that ancients felt the difficulty too), perhaps Antigone upset Sophocles's plans as Dido is held to have upset Vergil's; it is most likely that Sophocles did precisely what he set out to do, and that in this play, as in the *Ajax*, he built on a double foundation.

As to this double foundation, in the change from the bipartite structure of the *Ajax*, through the much less prominent double interest of the *Antigone*, to the splendid unity of the *Tyrannus* and the *Electra*, it is natural for us to see a technical development; but something much more important than technique is involved, and it is not in fact easy to picture a Sophocles learning the rudiments of his art at the age of forty-five. Between these two earlier plays and the next two there is a perceptible change of tragic emphasis. The *Ajax* and the *Antigone* are based on what we may call a purely ethical conception; this way of life is right and that one is wrong: "Not the thick-set and broad-shouldered prevail, but the wise, everywhere"; "To be stiffnecked is folly." Such a general idea naturally takes dramatic shape in an opposition between one who takes the wrong view and another who takes the right. In the second pair of plays the tragic idea is more philosophical, without of course ceasing to be ethical. One hero, more complex, more delicately poised, less catastrophic than either Ajax or Creon, fights not a moral law but his own nature. The moral and dramatic issue does not lie between him and another, but between the various facets of his own nature, assisted by the complexities of circumstance. Thus the one hero stands out more clearly from the other personages and a higher degree of unity follows. It is to some such fundamental change of outlook, not to the superficialities of dramatic technique, that we should turn if we wish to understand the development of Sophocles's form. Form, with him, is the same as thought; he did not need lessons from Aristotle.

The *Antigone* has been variously interpreted. The transcendental philosophers, who, from Plato onwards, have never been at their ease with the tragic poets, have done their worst with it, and have been discomfited. It has been a problem-play, the poet's condemnation of contemporary statecraft, his confession of a religious faith. What are the consequences of regarding it as primarily the tragedy of Creon?

First, I think we can afford to be reasonable about Antigone. Hegel had to assume that there was something seriously wrong with her; later critics, rejecting this preposterous view, were nevertheless careful to maintain (partly out of deference to Aristotle) that Antigone was not spotless. People are never spotless, especially heroes and heroines of tragedies. Antigone's hardness to Ismene therefore was exploited to the full—but this, surely, was no very striking blemish, hardly enough to spoil a perfect figure. We saw however in dealing with Pelasgus that the hamartia doctrine must either be interpreted reasonably or amended; Pelasgus had no fault in the *Supplices* not because he was a perfect man but because his character was irrelevant; equally we need not be assiduous in looking for saving faults in Antigone, because only part of her character comes into question here, the part which impels her to defy Creon; and where the blemish is there, only Hegel can tell us. The play is not a full-length portrait of Antigone, in which, let it be granted, perfection would be a little uninteresting. Her part is to suffer, and there is no dramatic canon which demands that victims should have faults: hardness and decisiveness were given her to explain her rebellion and her suicide. The chief *agent* is Creon; his is the character, his the faults and merits, which are immediately relevant to the play. If Sophocles is really inviting us to watch Creon, Antigone becomes much more natural, relieved of the burden of Aristotelianism, no longer the standard-bearer of the Unwritten Laws. On this, the last day of her life, she can be spared faults, as she can be spared heroics. Why indeed does she defy Creon? From a sense of religious duty? To Ismene, in the prologue, she mentions religious duty once—in an attempt to shame her sister. Her real thought comes out in phrases like

> He has no right to touch what is *mine*!—
> Yes, my brother and—though you deny it—yours.

She has a passionate feeling of what is due to her brother, to her race. Face to face with Creon's legality she indeed answers legally, and nobly, inspired to her highest eloquence, but essentially she is doing much more than championing one code against another; she is giving her whole being for her brother's honour. This leads to the genuineness of vv. 911-30. The confrontation with Creon over, we hear little more of her religious faith; she protests her innocence indeed, but the burden of her defence is again that her brother is hers to honour. Her tone is noticeably more personal. As the end draws near her defences fail one by one, until, in that marvellously moving and tragic speech which was not to the taste of those who saw in Antigone chiefly a martyr to the Higher Law, she abandons everything except the fact that she did it and had to do it. Facing death, deserted by the Chorus, she has no confidence even in the gods, and doubts her own impulse. For a husband, she says, No; for a son, No; but for a brother—

"Since my mother and my father have gone to the grave, there can be none henceforth that I can ever call my brother."

A frigid sophism borrowed from Herodotus? Yes, the finest borrowing in literature. This is the final tragedy of Antigone: *novissima hora est*—and she can cling to nothing but a frigid sophism.

If Antigone is more interesting than a mere antithesis to Creon, he is more than the stubborn fool who kills her. Sophocles was interested in his fate. He is, if not cruel, at least insensitive; like a tyrant, he is quick to suspect, and he does not know how to yield. But he has his own honesty, his own justification, and his own sense of responsibility. But what Creon is is not the whole of the story. We have this clear-cut moral issue between him and Antigone—itself a little too elementary to serve as the sole background for so subtle a thinker as Sophocles. We have too the clear-cut personal clash; it *is* noteworthy that from the beginning of her confrontation Antigone shows her contempt for this court. She wastes no time in trying to bridge what she knows to be an impassable gap. But behind all this there is the evolving tragedy of Creon. Creon may be what you like, but he is neither unintelligent nor irresponsible. He has his own field of action and his own principles; impulse, unwritten laws, are, he feels, not for him; he cannot move in this ampler region, and he sincerely feels he has no business to. In his own field he has thought things out and is confident of himself. We feel his confidence as soon as we hear his

> Citizens, for what concerns the State . . .

He has tradition and experience on his side, his maxims are sensible. True, a native stubbornness is given him, that he may defend his position to the dramatic end, but it is not from folly or willfulness that he originally takes up his position. But his confident judgement was wrong; his reason betrays him. It is true that but for his obstinacy he could have escaped with a lighter penalty, but the bitterness is that his judgement was wrong, and that Antigone's instinct was right; and in the end he has less to cling to than she. She goes "in the sure and certain hope that dear to thee will be my coming, Father"; he can say only

> Everything is turned to water in my hands.

"By far the biggest part of happiness," says the Chorus, "is Wisdom (*to phronein*)." And what is this? Not to behave impiously towards the gods is part of it. And what is this? Creon was honouring the gods after his fashion, Antigone after hers. How can you tell beforehand which is the right fashion? Alas! Piety is not an automatic thing; you may learn in time—*gera to phronein*. This is the tragedy of Creon.

KING LEAR

William Shakespeare (1564-1616)

Edited by R. C. Bald

Shakespeare's birthplace was Stratford-on-Avon, where he was given a grammar school education, shared his middle-class family's financial ups-and-downs, and married Ann Hathaway, who was eight years his senior. In the late 1580's Shakespeare went to London where he soon became connected with the theater, at first as an actor and then as a dramatist. The professional theaters were repertory companies consisting of small groups of men who were an acting and producing unit, and who usually had several playwrights creating new plays for them. Shakespeare was attached to the Lord Chamberlain's Company. He quickly won a reputation as a playwright and became a shareholder in the Globe Theater. His success in the theater made it possible for him to retire in 1611 to his native Stratford as a well-to-do gentleman.

Shakespeare's works are usually divided into four groups: (1) 1590-1594, a period of imitation and experimentation; (2) 1595-1600, tragedies and comedies; (3) 1601-1608, tragedies and satiric comedies; and (4) 1609-1611, dramatic romances. *King Lear* belongs to the third period, when Shakespeare was at the height of his powers. Other great works of this period were *Hamlet*, *Othello*, and *Macbeth*.

Shakespeare's theater was characterized by an open courtyard enclosed by roofed-over galleries three stories high. The main acting area was a large platform which projected into the center of the courtyard, placing the actor in intimate contact with his audience. There were seats in the galleries but the groundlings stood in the pit during the performance. Scenery was suggestive or absent altogether, and there was no drop curtain. In addition to the platform it is generally thought that two additional playing areas were available for the actor—a curtained area at stage level which could serve as an interior, and an elevated area at the second floor level. Physically, such a theater gave the playwright wonderful freedom and flexibility to move his characters around in time and space and to tell a complex and interesting story in which all of the essential action could be placed directly before the audience. All of the actors were males, the female roles being played by boys. Despite the paucity of scenery, the richness of costuming and the vigor of the action made the Elizabethan theater a spectacular one.

Ever since Aristotle, magnitude has been cited as one of the essential properties of tragedy, and it is perhaps because of this quality that *King Lear* is often regarded as the greatest Shakespearean tragedy. It is a play of such power and feeling that it nearly defies production. The spectator is almost inevitably caught up in the storm of passion that only through suffering and heartbreak ultimately gives way to compassion and understanding to reveal an enlarged vision of life.

Certainly it is a play to tax the resources of the theater and the actor to the utmost. In the past, producers have tried to adapt the play to the tastes of their audiences and the limitations of their stages and talent. In 1681 Nahum Tate tried to make *King Lear* more palatable by cutting the part of the Fool and rewriting the ending so that Cordelia survives to become the bride of Edgar. It wasn't until nearly a century and a half later that Charles Kean restored the full script only to stifle his productions with a superabundance of scenic display. Late in the nineteenth century, William Poel and the English Stage Society revived the Shakespearean architectural stage and recovered the play's original sweep and momentum.

Left.   An artist's schematic representation of the Shakespearian stage.

Left. The storm on the heath echoes Lear's own disordered nature.

Opposite. The broken-hearted Lear grieves over Cordelia's death.

Below. Edgar and the Fool try to soothe the mad Lear in the storm.

CHARACTERS

LEAR, *King of Britain*
KING OF FRANCE
DUKE OF BURGUNDY
DUKE OF CORNWALL
DUKE OF ALBANY
EARL OF KENT
EARL OF GLOUCESTER
EDGAR, *son to* GLOUCESTER
EDMUND, *bastard son to* GLOUCESTER
CURAN, *a courtier*
OLD MAN, *tenant to* GLOUCESTER
DOCTOR
LEAR'S FOOL
OSWALD, *Steward to* GONERIL
A CAPTAIN *under* EDMUND'S *command*
GENTLEMEN
A HERALD
SERVANTS *to* CORNWALL

GONERIL,
REGAN, } *daughters to* LEAR
CORDELIA,

KNIGHTS *attending on* LEAR, OFFICERS, MESSENGERS, SOLDIERS, ATTENDANTS

KING LEAR

ACT I

SCENE I

Enter KENT, GLOUCESTER, *and* EDMUND.

KENT: I thought the King had more affected the
Duke of Albany than Cornwall.

GLOU: It did always seem so to us; but now, in
the division of the kingdom, it appears not which
of the Dukes he values most, for equalities are
so weighed that curiosity in neither can make
choice of either's moiety.

KENT: Is not this your son, my lord?

GLOU: His breeding, sir, hath been at my charge.
I have so often blushed to acknowledge him that
now I am brazed to't.

KENT: I cannot conceive you.

GLOU: Sir, this young fellow's mother could;
whereupon she grew round-wombed, and had
indeed, sir, a son for her cradle ere she had a
husband for her bed. Do you smell a fault?

KENT: I cannot wish the fault undone, the issue
of it being so proper.

GLOU: But I have a son, sir, by order of law, some
year elder than this, who yet is no dearer in
my account. Though this knave came something
saucily into the world before he was sent for,
yet was his mother fair, there was good sport
at his making, and the whoreson must be acknowledged. Do you know this noble gentleman, Edmund?

EDM: No, my lord.

GLOU: My Lord of Kent. Remember him hereafter
as my honourable friend.

EDM: My services to your lordship.

KENT: I must love you, and sue to know you better.

EDM: Sir, I shall study deserving.

GLOU: He hath been out nine years, and away he
shall again.

(Sound a sennet.)

The King is coming.

Enter one bearing a coronet; then LEAR: *then the* DUKES
OF ALBANY *and* CORNWALL; *next,* GONERIL, REGAN,
CORDELIA, *with* FOLLOWERS.

LEAR: Attend the lords of France and Burgundy,
Gloucester.

GLOU: I shall, my lord.

(Exit.)

LEAR: Meantime we shall express our darker pur-
pose.
Give me the map there. Know that we have
divided
In three our kingdom; and 'tis our fast intent
To shake all cares and business from our age,
Conferring them on younger strengths while we
Unburthened crawl toward death. Our son of
Cornwall,

1 *more affected* preferred
6 *weighed* balanced *curiosity* careful investigation *make
choice of* distinguish between
7 *moiety* share
9 *breeding* begetting
11 *brazed* hardened
18 *proper* handsome
21 *account* estimation

97

And you, our no less loving son of Albany,
We have this hour a constant will to publish
Our daughters' several dowers, that future strife
May be prevented now. The princes, France and
  Burgundy,
Great rivals in our youngest daughter's love,
Long in our court have made their amorous
50 sojourn,
And here are to be answered. Tell me, my
  daughters
(Since now we will divest us both of rule,
Interest of territory, cares of state),
Which of you shall say doth love us most,
That we our largest bounty may extend
Where nature doth with merit challenge. Gon-
  eril,
Our eldest-born, speak first.
GON: Sir, I love you more than words can wield the
  matter;
Dearer than eyesight, space, and liberty;
60 Beyond what can be valued, rich or rare;
No less than life, with grace, health, beauty,
  honour;
As much as child e'er loved, or father found;
A love that makes breath poor, and speech
  unable.
Beyond all manner of so much I love you.
COR: (aside) What shall Cordelia speak? Love, and
  be silent.
LEAR: Of all these bounds, even from this line to
  this,
With shadowy forests and with champains
  riched,
With plenteous rivers and wide-skirted meads,
We make thee lady. To thine and Albany's
  issues
Be this perpetual. What says our second
70 daughter,
Our dearest Regan, wife of Cornwall?
REG: I am made of that self metal as my sister,
And prize me at her worth. In my true heart
I find she names my very deed of love,

Only she comes too short, that I profess
Myself an enemy to all other joys
Which the most precious square of sense
  possesses,
And find I am alone felicitate
In your dear Highness' love.
COR: (aside) Then poor Cordelia,   80
And yet not so, since I am sure my love's
More ponderous than my tongue.
LEAR: To thee and thine hereditary ever
Remain this ample third of our fair kingdom,
No less in space, validity, and pleasure
Than that conferred on Goneril. Now, our joy,
Although our last, and least, to whose young love
The vines of France and milk of Burgundy
Strive to be interessed, what can you say to draw
A third more opulent than your sisters? Speak.   90
COR: Nothing, my lord.
LEAR: Nothing?
COR: Nothing.
LEAR: Nothing will come of nothing; speak again.
COR: Unhappy that I am, I cannot heave
My heart into my mouth. I love your Majesty
According to my bond, no more nor less.
LEAR: How, how, Cordelia? Mend your speech a
  little,
Lest you may mar your fortunes.
COR: Good my lord,   100
You have begot me, bred me, loved me; I
Return those duties back as are right fit,
Obey you, love you, and most honour you.
Why have my sisters husbands, if they say
They love you all? Haply, when I shall wed,
That lord whose hand must take my plight shall
  carry
Half my love with him, half my care and duty.
Sure I shall never marry like my sisters,
To love my father all.
LEAR: But goes thy heart with this?   110
COR: Ay, good my lord.
LEAR: So young, and so untender?

46 *constant* determined
56 *nature* natural affection *with* along with *challenge* lay claim
58 *wield* express
67 *champains* fertile plains *riched* enriched
72 *self* very same
73 *prize . . . worth* bid you to value me as you value her
74 *my very deed of love* my love as I actually feel it

77 *most precious square of sense* most subtle sensibility
78 *felicitate* made happy
83 *hereditary* heirs
85 *validity* value
89 *be interessed* have a right to
97 *bond* tie of duty
106 *plight* pledge, troth
109 *all* exclusively

COR: So young, my lord, and true.
LEAR: Let it be so, thy truth then be thy dower;
  For by the sacred radiance of the sun,
  The mysteries of Hecate and the night,
  By all the operation of the orbs
  From whom we do exist and cease to be,
  Here I disclaim all my paternal care,
120 Propinquity and property of blood,
  And as a stranger to my heart and me
  Hold thee from this for ever. The barbarous
    Scythian,
  Or he that makes his generation messes
  To gorge his appetite, shall to my bosom
  Be as well neighboured, pitied, and relieved
  As thou my sometime daughter.
KENT: Good my liege—
LEAR: Peace, Kent,
  Come not between the dragon and his wrath.
130 I loved her most, and thought to set my rest
  On her kind nursery. Hence and avoid my sight!
  So be my grave my peace as here I give
  Her father's heart from her! Call France; who
    stirs?
  Call Burgundy! Cornwall and Albany,
  With my two daughters' dowers digest the third;
  Let pride, which she calls plainness, marry her.
  I do invest you jointly with my power,
  Preëminence, and all the large effects
  That troop with majesty. Ourself by monthly
    course
140 With reservation of an hundred knights,
  By you to be sustained, shall our abode
  Make with you by due turns, only we still retain
  The name, and all the addition to a king; the
    sway,
  Revenue, execution of the rest,

  Beloved sons, be yours, which to confirm
  This coronet part between you.
KENT: Royal Lear,
  Whom I have honoured as my king,
  Loved as my father, as my master followed,
  As my great patron thought on in my prayers— 150
LEAR: The bow is bent and drawn; make from the
    shaft.
KENT: Let it fall rather, though the fork invade
  The region of my heart! Be Kent unmannerly
  When Lear is mad. What wouldst thou do, old
    man?
  Think'st thou that duty shall have dread to speak
  When power to flattery bows? To plainness hon-
    our's bound
  When majesty falls to folly. Reserve thy state,
  And in thy best consideration check
  This hideous rashness. Answer my life my judg-
    ment,
  Thy youngest daughter does not love thee least, 160
  Nor are those empty-hearted whose low sounds
  Reverb no hollowness.
LEAR: Kent, on thy life no more.
KENT: My life I never held but as a pawn
  To wage against thine enemies, nor fear to lose it,
  Thy safety being the motive.
LEAR: Out of my sight!
KENT: See better, Lear, and let me still remain
  The true blank of thine eye.
LEAR: Now by Apollo— 170
KENT: Now by Apollo, King,
  Thou swearest thy gods in vain.
LEAR: O vassal! miscreant!
      (Lays his hand on his sword.)
ALB, CORN: Dear sir, forbear.
KENT: Kill thy physician, and the fee bestow
  Upon the foul disease. Revoke thy gift,
  Or, whilst I can vent clamour from my throat,
  I'll tell thee thou dost evil.
LEAR: Hear me, recreant,
  On thine allegiance, hear me! 180
  Since thou has sought to make us break our vow,

116 *mysteries* secret rites *Hecate* (goddess of the lower world)
117 *operation of the orbs* influence of the stars
120 *Propinquity and property of blood* close kinship and the rights pertaining to it
122 *Scythian* wild tribesman of inner Asia
123 *generation* offspring
131 *nursery* tender care *avoid* leave
132 *So be my grave* as I wish my grave may be *as* so
133 *from* away from *France* King of France
135 *digest* incorporate
138 *large effects* splendours
139 *course* regular order
143 *addition* title

156 *plainness* blunt speaking
157 *state* power
158 *best consideration* better judgment
162 *Reverb* reverberate, re-echo
164 *pawn* wager
165 *wage* stake
169 *blank* centre of target

Which we durst never yet, and with strained pride
To come betwixt our sentences and our power,
Which nor our nature nor our place can bear,
Our potency made good, take thy reward.
Five days we do allot thee for provision
To shield thee from disasters of the world,
And on the sixth to turn thy hated back
Upon our kingdom. If, on the tenth day follow-
ing,
190   Thy banished trunk be found in our dominions,
The moment is thy death. Away! By Jupiter,
This shall not be revoked.

KENT: Fare thee well, King; since thus thou wilt
appear,
Freedom lives hence, and banishment is here.
(*To* CORDELIA) The gods to their dear shelter take
thee, maid,
That justly think'st and hast most rightly said.
(*To* REGAN *and* GONERIL) And your large speeches
may your deeds approve,
That good effects may spring from words of love.
Thus Kent, O princes, bids you all adieu;
200   He'll shape his old course in a country new. *Exit.*

Flourish. Enter GLOUCESTER *with* FRANCE *and*
BURGUNDY; ATTENDANTS.

GLOU: Here's France and Burgundy, my noble
lord.

LEAR: My Lord of Burgundy,
We first address toward you, who with this king
Hath rivalled for our daughter. What in the least
Will you require in present dower with her,
Or cease your quest of love?

BUR: Most royal Majesty,
I crave no more than hath your Highness offered,
Nor will you tender less.

210 LEAR: Right noble Burgundy,
When she was dear to us, we did hold her so,
But now her price is fallen. Sir, there she stands.
If aught within that little seeming substance,
Or all of it, with our displeasure pieced,
And nothing more, may fitly like your Grace,
She's there, and she is yours.

BUR: I know no answer.

LEAR: Will you with those infirmities she owes,

Unfriended, new adopted to our hate,
Dowered with our curse, and strangered with   220
our oath,
Take her or leave her?

BUR: Pardon me, royal sir,
Election makes not up on such conditions.

LEAR: Then leave her, sir, for by the power that
made me
I tell you all her wealth. (*To* FRANCE) For you,
great king,
I would not from your love make such a stray
To match you where I hate; therefore beseech
you
To avert your liking a more worthier way
Than on a wretch whom nature is ashamed
Almost to acknowledge hers.   230

FRANCE: This is most strange,
That she that even but now was your best object,
The argument of your praise, balm of your age,
Most best, most dearest, should in this trice of
time
Commit a thing so monstrous to dismantle
So many folds of favour. Sure her offence
Must be of such unnatural degree
That monsters it, or your fore-vouched affection
Fallen into taint; which to believe of her
Must be a faith that reason without miracle   240
Should never plant in me.

COR: I yet beseech your Majesty,
If for I want that glib and oily art
To speak and purpose not, since what I well
intend,
I'll do't before I speak—that you make known
It is no vicious blot, murther, or foulness,
No unchaste action or dishonoured step,
That hath deprived me of your grace and
favour;
But even for want of that for which I am richer,
A still-soliciting eye, and such a tongue   250

182 *strained* excessive
185 *potency* power *made good* put into effect
214 *pieced* added
218 *infirmities* shortcomings *owes* possesses

220 *strangered* disowned
223 *Election* choice *makes not up* does not come to a decision
228 *avert* turn aside to
232 *best object* darling
233 *argument* subject
234 *trice* instant
238 *monsters it* turns it to a monster *fore-vouched* previously
declared
239 *taint* decay
250 *still-soliciting* always begging favours

As I am glad I have not, though not to have it
Hath lost me in your liking.
LEAR: Better thou
Hadst not been born than not to have pleased me
better.
FRANCE: Is it but this—a tardiness in nature
Which often leaves the history unspoke
That it intends to do? My Lord of Burgundy,
What say you to the lady? Love's not love
When it is mingled with regards that stands
260 Aloof from the entire point. Will you have her?
She is herself a dowry.
BUR: Royal King,
Give but that portion which yourself proposed,
And here I take Cordelia by the hand,
Duchess of Burgundy.
LEAR: Nothing. I have sworn, I am firm.
BUR: I am sorry then you have so lost a father
That you must lose a husband.
COR: Peace be with Burgundy!
270 Since that respects of fortune are his love,
I shall not be his wife.
FRANCE: Fairest Cordelia, that art most rich, being
poor,
Most choice, forsaken, and most loved, despised,
Thee and thy virtues here I seize upon,
Be it lawful I take up what's cast away.
Gods, gods! 'tis strange that from their coldest
neglect
My love should kindle to inflamed respect.
Thy dowerless daughter, King, thrown to my
chance,
Is queen of us, of ours, and our fair France.
280 Not all the dukes of waterish Burgundy
Can buy this unprized precious maid of me.
Bid them farewell, Cordelia, though unkind;
Thou losest here, a better where to find.
LEAR: Thou hast her, France; let her be thine; for
we
Have no such daughter, nor shall ever see
That face of hers again. Therefore be gone
Without our grace, our love, our benison.
Come, noble Burgundy.

Flourish. Exeunt LEAR, BURGUNDY, (CORNWALL,
ALBANY, GLOUCESTER, *and* ATTENDANTS).

255 *tardiness* reticence
259 *regards . . . point* irrelevant considerations
283 *where* place somewhere else
287 *grace* favour *benison* blessing

FRANCE: Bid farewell to your sisters.
COR: The jewels of our father, with washed eyes   290
Cordelia leaves you. I know you what you are,
And like a sister am most loath to call
Your faults as they are named. Use well our
father;
To your professéd bosoms I commit him;
But yet, alas, stood I within his grace
I would prefer him to a better place.
So farewell to you both.
GON: Prescribe not us our duty.
REG: Let your study
Be to content your lord, who hath received you   300
At fortune's alms. You have obedience scanted,
And well are worth the want that you have
wanted.
COR: Time shall unfold what plighted cunning
hides.
Who cover faults, at last shame them derides,
Well may you prosper!
FRANCE: Come, my fair Cordelia.
                        (*Exeunt* FRANCE *and* CORDELIA.)
GON: Sister, it is not little I have to say of what
most nearly appertains to us both. I think our
father will hence to-night.
REG: That's most certain, and with you; next   310
month with us.
GON: You see how full of changes his age is. The
observation we have made of it hath not been
little. He always loved our sister most, and with
what poor judgment he hath now cast her off
appears too grossly.
REG: 'Tis the infirmity of his age; yet he hath ever
but slenderly known himself.
GON: The best and soundest of his time hath
been but rash; then must we look from his age to   320
receive not alone the imperfections of long-ingraffed condition, but therewithal the unruly
waywardness that infirm and choleric years
bring with them.

290 *jewels* darlings *washed* tearful
294 *professe'd* filled with professions of devotion
296 *prefer* recommend
301 *At fortune's alms* out of mere charity *scanted* been lacking in
302 *the want . . . wanted* the same lack that you have shown
303 *plighted* folded
321 *long-ingraffed condition* long-established habits

REG: Such unconstant starts are we like to have
   from him as this of Kent's banishment.
GON: There is further compliment of leave-taking
   between France and him. Pray you let us hit
   together. If our father carry authority with such
330   dispositions as he bears, this last surrender of his
   will but offend us.
REG: We shall further think of it.
GON: We must do something, and i'th'heat.

(Exeunt.)

SCENE II

Enter (EDMUND *the*) *Bastard solus,* (*with a letter*).

EDM: Thou, Nature, art my goddess; to thy law
   My services are bound. Wherefore should I
   Stand in the plague of custom, and permit
   The curiosity of nations to deprive me,
   For that I am some twelve or fourteen moon-
      shines
   Lag of a brother? Why bastard? wherefore base?
   When my dimensions are as well compact,
   My mind as generous, and my shape as true,
   As honest madam's issue? Why brand they us
10   With base? with baseness? bastardy? base, base?
   Who, in the lusty stealth of nature, take
   More composition and fierce quality
   Than doth within a dull, stale, tired bed
   Go to the creating a whole tribe of fops
   Got 'tween asleep and wake? Well then,
   Legitimate Edgar, I must have your land.
   Our father's love is to the bastard Edmund
   As to the legitimate. Fine word 'legitimate'!

325 *inconstant starts* sudden wilfulness
329 *carry* exercise
330 *dispositions* irrational moods *bears* shows
331 *offend us* do us harm
333 *i'th'heat* at once
3 *Stand in the plague* submit to the afflictions of
4 *curiosity of* niceties accepted by
6 *Lag of* behind
7 *compact* shaped
8 *generous* gentlemanly
11 *lusty stealth of nature* surreptitious satisfaction of
natural desires
12 *composition* strength of constitution
15 *Got* begotten

Well, my legitimate, if this letter speed,
And my invention thrive, Edmund the base   20
Shall top the legitimate. I grow, I prosper:
Now, gods, stand up for bastards!

Enter GLOUCESTER.

GLOU: Kent banished thus? and France in choler
   parted?
   And the King gone to-night? prescribed his
   power?
   Confined to exhibition? All this done
   Upon the gad? Edmund, how now? What news?
EDM: So please your lordship, none.
GLOU: Why so earnestly seek you to put up that
   letter?
EDM: I know no news, my lord.
GLOU: What paper were you reading?   30
EDM: Nothing, my lord.
GLOU: No? What needed then that terrible dis-
   patch of it into your pocket? The quality of noth-
   ing hath not such need to hide itself. Let's see.
   Come, if it be nothing, I shall not need spectacles.
EDM: I beseech you, sir, pardon me. It is a letter
   from my brother that I have not all o'er-read; and
   for so much as I have perused, I find it not fit for
   your o'erlooking.
GLOU: Give me the letter, sir.   40
EDM: I shall offend either to detain or give it. The
   contents, as in part I understand them, are to
   blame.
GLOU: Let's see, let's see.
EDM: I hope, for my brother's justification, he
   wrote this but as an essay or taste of my virtue.
GLOU: (*reads*) This policy and reverence of age
   makes the world bitter to the best of our times,

19 *speed* succeed
20 *invention* plot
23 *choler* anger
24 *prescribed* limited
25 *exhibition* an allowance for his support
26 *Upon the gad* on the spur of the moment
32 *dispatch of it* hasty putting it out of sight
33 *The quality of nothing hath not such need* it is not the nature
of nothing to need
46 *essay or taste* trial or test
47 *policy and reverence of age* policy of reverence for age
48 *the best of our times* i.e., our youth

keeps our fortunes from us till our oldness cannot
50   relish them. I begin to find an idle and fond
bondage in the oppression of aged tyranny,
who sways, not as it hath power, but as it is
suffered. Come to me, that of this I may speak
more. If our father would sleep till I waked him,
you should enjoy half his revenue for ever, and
live the beloved of your brother

EDGAR.

Hum! Conspiracy? 'Sleep till I waked him, you
should enjoy half his revenue.' My son Edgar,
had he a hand to write this? a heart and brain
60   to breed it in? When came you to this? Who
brought it?

EDM: It was not brought me, my lord: there's the
cunning of it. I found it thrown in at the casement
of my closet.

GLOU: You know the character to be your brother's?

EDM: If the matter were good, my lord, I durst
swear it were his; but in respect of that, I would
fain think it were not.

70   GLOU: It is his.

EDM: It is his hand, my lord; but I hope his heart is
not in the contents.

GLOU: Has he never before sounded you in this
business?

EDM: Never, my lord. But I have heard him oft
maintain it to be fit that, sons at perfect age and
fathers declined, the father should be as ward to
the son, and the son manage his revenue.

GLOU: O villain, villain, his very opinion in the
80   letter! Abhorred villain, unnatural, detested,
brutish villain! worse than brutish! Go, sirrah,
seek him; I'll apprehend him. Abominable villain! Where is he?

EDM: I do not well know, my lord. If it shall please
you to suspend your indignation against my
brother till you can derive from him better testi-

mony of his intent, you should run a certain
course; where, if you violently proceed against
him, mistaking his purpose, it would make a
great gap in your own honour and shake in pieces   90
the heart of his obedience. I dare pawn down my
life for him that he hath writ this to feel my
affection to your honour, and to no other pretence of danger.

GLOU: Think you so?

EDM: If your honour judge it meet, I will place
you where you shall hear us confer of this and
by an auricular assurance have your satisfaction,
and that without any further delay than this very
evening.   100

GLOU: He cannot be such a monster.

EDM: Nor is not, sure.

GLOU: To his father, that so tenderly and entirely
loves him. Heaven and earth! Edmund, seek him
out; wind me into him, I pray you; frame the
business after your own wisdom. I would unstate
myself to be in a due resolution.

EDM: I will seek him, sir, presently; convey the
business as I shall find means, and acquaint
you withal.   110

GLOU: These late eclipses in the sun and moon portend no good to us. Though the wisdom of nature
can reason it thus and thus, yet nature finds
itself scourged by the sequent effects. Love cools,
friendship falls off, brothers divide. In cities,

87   *run a certain course* proceed without any danger of error
88   *where* whereas *violently proceed* act impetuously
90   *shake in pieces the heart* shatter the very centre
92   *feel* test
93   *pretence of danger* intention of doing harm
96   *meet* fitting
98   *auricular* aural
105   *wind me into him* for my sake win his confidence *frame the business* arrange the affair
106   *after your own wisdom* according to your own judg-
ment *unstate myself* surrender my rank and position
107   *to be in a due resolution* to be properly resolved (about the truth)
108   *presently* immediately *convey* manage
110   *withal* with it
112   *the wisdom of nature* scientific knowledge
114   *sequent* consequent

50   *idle* futile *fond* foolish
52   *who* which
53   *suffered* passively endured
63   *casement of my closet* window of my room
65   *character* handwriting
68   *in respect of that* i.e., on account of its subject matter *fain*
gladly
86   *derive* obtain

mutinies; in countries, discord; in palaces, treason; and the bond cracked 'twixt son and father. This villain of mine comes under the prediction, there's son against father; the King falls from bias of nature, there's father against child. We have seen the best of our time. Machinations, hollowness, treachery, and all ruinous disorders follow us disquietly to our graves. Find out this villain, Edmund; it shall lose thee nothing; do it carefully. And the noble and true-hearted Kent banished; his offence, honesty! 'Tis strange.

(Exit.)

EDM: This is the excellent foppery of the world that when we are sick in fortune, often the surfeit of our own behaviour, we make guilty of our disasters the sun, the moon, and the stars; as if we were villains on necessity, fools by heavenly compulsion, knaves, thieves, and treachers by spherical predominance, drunkards, lairs, and adulterers by an enforced obedience of planetary influence, and all that we are evil in by a divine thrusting on. An admirable evasion of whoremaster man, to lay his goatish disposition to the charge of a star! My father compounded with my mother under the Dragon's Tail, and my nativity was under Ursa Major, so that it follows that I am rough and lecherous. I should have been that I am, had the maidenliest star in the firmament twinkled on my bastardizing.

(Enter EDGAR.)

Pat! he comes, like the catastrophe of the old comedy. My cue is villanous melancholy, with a sigh like Tom o' Bedlam. O these eclipses do portend these divisions. Fa, sol, la, mi.

116 *mutinies* insurrections
120 *bias* natural course
124 *lose thee nothing* be to your advantage
127 *foppery* folly
128 *surfeit of* result of excesses in
132 *by spherical predominance* through the predominating influence of a certain planet
136 *thrusting on* urging
137 *goatish* lustful
139 *Dragon's Tail* a constellation *nativity* birth
140 *Ursa Major* the Great Bear, another constellation
146 *Tom o' Bedlam* a crazy beggar
147 *Fa . . . mi* (humming to himself)

EDG: How now, brother Edmund? What serious contemplation are you in?
EDM: I am thinking, brother, of a prediction I read this other day, what should follow these eclipses.
EDG: Do you busy yourself with that?
EDM: I promise you, the effects he writes of succeed unhappily, as of unnaturalness between the child and the parent, death, dearth, dissolutions of ancient amities, divisions in state, menaces and maledictions against king and nobles, needless diffidences, banishment of friends, dissipation of cohorts, nuptial breaches, and I know not what.
EDM: How long have you been a sectary astronomical?
EDM: Come, come, when saw you my father last?
EDG: The night gone by.
EDM: Spake you with him?
EDG: Ay, two hours together.
EDM: Parted you in good terms? Found you no displeasure in him by word or countenance?
EDG: None at all.
EDM: Bethink yourself wherein you may have offended him; and at my entreaty forbear his presence until some little time hath qualified the heat of his displeasure, which at this instant so rageth in him that with the mischief of your person it would scarcely allay.
EDG: Some villain hath done me wrong.
EDM: That's my fear. I pray you have a continent forebearance till the speed of his rage goes slower; and, as I say, retire with me to my lodging, from whence I will fitly bring you to hear my lord speak. Pray ye, go; there's my key. If you do stir abroad, go armed.
EDG: Armed, brother?
EDM: Brother, I advise you to the best: go armed.

153 *succeed* follow
156 *amities* friendships
158 *diffidences* causes of distrust *dissipation of cohorts* scattering of armed forces
161 *sectary astronomical* believer in astrology
171 *forbear* avoid
172 *qualified* moderated
174 *mischief* injury, harm *person* body
175 *allay* cool down
177 *have a continent forbearance* exercise self-control

I am no honest man if there be any good meaning toward you. I have told you what I have seen and heard, but faintly, nothing like the image and horror of it. Pray you, away!

EDG: Shall I hear from you anon?

190 EDM: I do serve you in this business.

(Exit EDGAR.)

A credulous father, and a brother noble,
Whose nature is so far from doing harms
That he suspects none, on whose foolish honesty
My practices ride easy; I see the business.
Let me, if not by birth, have lands by wit;
All with me's meet that I can fashion fit.

(Exit.)

SCENE III

Enter GONERIL and (her) Steward (OSWALD).

GON: Did my father strike my gentleman for chiding of his fool?

OSW: Ay, madam.

GON: By day and night he wrongs me. Every hour
He flashes into one gross crime or other
That sets us all at odds; I'll not endure it.
His knights grow riotous, and himself upbraids us
On every trifle. When he returns from hunting
I will not speak with him; say I am sick.
If you come slack of former services

10 You shall do well; the fault of it I'll answer.

OSW: He's coming, madam; I hear him.

GON: Put on what weary negligence you please,
You and your fellows; I'd have it come to question.
If he distaste it, let him to our sister,
Whose mind and mine I know in that are one,
Not to be overruled. Idle old man,
That still would manage those authorities
That he hath given away! Now, by my life,
Old fools are babes again, and must be used

With checks as flatteries, when they are seen .20 abused.
Remember what I have said.

OSW: Very well, madam.

GON: And let his knights have colder looks among you;
What grows of it, no matter. Advise your fellows so.
I would breed from hence occasions, and I shall,
That I may speak. I'll write straight to my sister
To hold my very course. Prepare for dinner.

(Exeunt.)

SCENE IV

Enter KENT (disguised).

KENT: If but as well I other accents borrow,
That can my speech defuse, my good intent
May carry through itself to that full issue
For which I razed my likeness. Now, banished Kent,
If thou canst serve where thou dost stand condemned,
So may it come, thy master, whom thou lovest,
Shall find thee full of labours.

Horns within. Enter LEAR, (KNIGHTS,) and
ATTENDANTS.

LEAR: Let me not stay a jot for dinner; go get it ready. *(Exit an ATTENDANT.)* How now? What art thou? 10

KENT: A man, sir.

LEAR: What dost thou profess? What wouldst thou with us?

KENT: I do profess to be no less than I seem, to serve him truly that will put me in trust, to love him that is honest, to converse with him that is wise and says little, to fear judgment, to fight when I cannot choose, and to eat no fish.

194 *practices* plots
196 *meet* profitable *fashion fit* manipulate aptly
4 *crime* offence
9 *come slack of former services* pay him less attention than previously
14 *distaste* dislike

20 *checks* rebukes *as* as much as *are seen abused* are clearly under a misapprehension
2 *defuse* disguise
4 *razed* completely altered *likeness* appearance
12 *What dost thou profess?* What is your occupation?
18 *eat no fish* i.e., am no papist

LEAR: What art thou?

20 KENT: A very honest-hearted fellow, and as poor as the King.

LEAR: If thou be'st as poor for a subject as he's for a king, thou art poor enough. What wouldst thou?

KENT: Service.

LEAR: Who wouldst thou serve?

KENT: You.

LEAR: Dost thou know me, fellow?

KENT: No, sir, but you have that in your counten-ance which I would fain call master.

30 LEAR: What's that?

KENT: Authority.

LEAR: What services canst thou do?

KENT: I can keep honest counsel, ride, run, mar a curious tale in telling it and deliver a plain message bluntly. That which ordinary men are fit for, I am qualified in, and the best of me is diligence.

LEAR: How old art thou?

KENT: Not so young, sir, to love a woman for sing-

40 ing, nor so old to dote on her for anything. I have years on my back forty-eight.

LEAR: Follow me; thou shalt serve me. If I like thee no worse after dinner, I will not part from thee yet. Dinner, ho, dinner! Where's my knave? my fool? Go you and call my fool hither.

(*Exit an* ATTENDANT.)

Enter (OSWALD *the*) *Steward.*

You, you, sirrah, where's my daughter?

OSW: So please you—   (*Exit.*)

LEAR: What says the fellow there? Call the clotpoll back. (*Exit a* KNIGHT.) Where's my fool, ho? I

50 think the world's asleep.

Enter KNIGHT.

How now? Where's that mongrel?

KNIGHT: He says, my lord, your daughter is not well.

LEAR: Why came not the slave back to me when I called him?

KNIGHT: Sir, he answered me in the roundest manner, he would not.

LEAR: He would not?

KNIGHT: My lord, I know not what the matter is, but to my judgment your Highness is not enter-   60 tained with that ceremonious affection as you were wont. There's a great abatement of kind-ness appears as well in the general dependants as in the Duke himself also and your daughter.

LEAR: Ha! say'st thou so?

KNIGHT: I beseech you pardon me, my lord, if I be mistaken, for my duty cannot be silent when I think your Highness wronged.

LEAR: Thou but rememberest me of mine own conception. I have perceived a most faint neglect   70 of late, which I have rather blamed as mine own jealous curiosity than as a very pretence and pur-pose of unkindness; I will look further into't. But where's my fool? I have not seen him this two days.

KNIGHT: Since my young lady's going into France, sir, the fool hath much pined away.

KNIGHT: No more of that; I have noted it well. Go you and tell my daughter I would speak with her. (*Exit* KNIGHT.) Go you, call hither my fool.   80

(*Exit an* ATTENDANT.)

Enter (OSWALD *the*) *Steward.*

O, you, sir, you, come you hither, sir. Who am I, sir?

OSW: My lady's father.

LEAR: 'My lady's father'? My lord's knave! You whoreson dog, you slave, you cur!

OSW: I am none of these, my lord; I beseech your pardon.

LEAR: Do you bandy looks with me, you rascal?

(*Strikes him.*)

OSW: I'll not be strucken, my lord.

KENT: Nor tripped neither, you base football play-   90 er.

(*Trips up his heels.*)

LEAR: I thank thee, fellow. Thou servest me, and I'll love thee.

34 *curious* complicated
48 *clotpoll* stupid fellow
56 *roundest* bluntest

60 *entertained* treated
63 *the general dependants* the servants in general
69 *rememberest* remindest
70 *conception* thought, impression *faint* unenthusiastic (*not* slight)
72 *curiosity* suspicion

KENT: Come, sir, arise, away; I'll teach you differences. Away, away! If you will measure your
lubber's length again, tarry; but away! Go to!
Have you wisdom? So.

(Pushes him out.)

LEAR: Now, my friendly knave, I thank thee.
There's earnest of thy service.

(Gives money.)

Enter FOOL.

100 FOOL: Let me hire him too. Here's my coxcomb.

(Offers KENT *his cap.)*

LEAR: How now, my pretty knave? How dost
thou?

FOOL: Sirrah, you were best take my coxcomb.

KENT: Why, fool?

FOOL: Why? For taking one's part that's out of
favour. Nay, an thou canst not smile as the wind
sits, thou'lt catch cold shortly. There, take my
coxcomb! Why, this fellow has banished two on's
110 daughters, and did the third a blessing against his
will. If thou follow him, thou must needs wear
my coxcomb.—How now, nuncle? Would I had
two coxcombs and two daughters!

LEAR: Why, my boy?

FOOL: If I gave them all my living, I'd keep my
coxcombs myself. There's mine! beg another of
thy daughters.

LEAR: Take heed, sirrah—the whip.

FOOL: Truth's a dog must to kennel; he must be
120 whipped out, when the Lady brach may stand by
th' fire and stink.

LEAR: A pestilent gall to me!

FOOL: Sirrah, I'll teach thee a speech.

LEAR: Do.

FOOL: Mark it, nuncle.

Have more than thou showest,
Speak less than thou knowest,

94 *differences* distinctions of rank
99 *earnest of* an advance for
100 *coxcomb* fool's cap
107 *smile as the wind sits* make yourself agreeable towards
those from whom favours come
120 *brach* bitch hound
122 *pestilent* plaguy *gall* source of irritation

Lend less than thou owest,
Ride more than thou goest,
Learn more than thou trowest,   130
Set less than thou throwest;
Leave thy drink and thy whore,
And keep in-a-door,
And thou shalt have more
Than two tens to a score.

KENT: This is nothing, fool.

FOOL: Then 'tis like the breath of an unfeed lawyer
—you gave me nothing for't. Can you make no
use of nothing, nuncle?

LEAR: Why, no, boy. Nothing can be made out of   140
nothing.

FOOL: *(to* KENT) Prithee tell him, so much of the rent
of his land comes to. He will not believe a fool.

LEAR: A bitter fool!

FOOL: Dost thou know the difference, my boy,
between a bitter fool and a sweet one?

LEAR: No, lad; teach me.

FOOL: That lord that counselled thee
To give away thy land,
Come place him here by me—   150
Do thou for him stand.
The sweet and bitter fool
Will presently appear;
The one in motley here,
The other found out there.

LEAR: Dost thou call me fool, boy?

FOOL: All thy other titles thou hast given away;
that thou wast born with.

KENT: This is not altogether fool, my lord.

FOOL: No, faith, lords and great men will not let   160
me. If I had a monopoly out, they would have
part on't. And ladies too, they will not let me
have all the fool to myself; they'll be snatching.
Give me an egg, nuncle, and I'll give thee two
crowns.

LEAR: What two crowns shall they be?

FOOL: Why, after I have cut the egg i' th' middle
and eat up the meat, the two crowns of the egg.

128 *owest* ownest
131 *set* stake *throwest* winnest
135 *score* twenty

When thou clovest thy crown i' th' middle and
gavest away both parts, thou borest thine ass on
thy back o'er the dirt. Thou hadst little wit in thy
bald crown when thou gavest thy golden one
away. If I speak like myself in this, let him be
whipped that first finds it so.

(*Sings*)   Fools had ne'er less grace in a year,
        For wise men are grown foppish,
        And know not how their wits to wear,
        Their manners are so apish.

LEAR: When were you wont to be so full of songs,
sirrah?
FOOL: I have used it, nuncle, ever since thou mad-
est thy daughters thy mother, for when thou gavest them the rod, and puttest down thine own
breeches,

(*Sings*)   Then they for sudden joy did weep,
        And I for sorrow sung,
        That such a king should play bo-peep
        And go the fools among.

Prithee, nuncle, keep a schoolmaster that can
teach thy fool to lie. I would fain learn to lie.
LEAR: An you lie, sirrah, we'll have you whipped.
FOOL: I marvel what kin thou and thy daughters
are. They'll have me whipped for speaking true;
thou'lt have me whipped for lying; and sometimes I am whipped for holding my peace. I had
rather be any kind o' thing than a fool, and yet I
would not be thee, nuncle. Thou hast pared thy
wit o' both sides and left nothing i' th' middle.
Here comes one o' the parings.

(*Enter* GONERIL.)

LEAR: How now, daughter? What makes that
frontlet on? Methinks you are too much o' late
i' th' frown.
FOOL: Thou wast a pretty fellow when thou hadst
no need to care for her frowning; now thou art an
O without a figure. I am better than thou art
now; I am a fool, thou art nothing. (*To* GONERIL)
Yes, forsooth, I will hold my tongue. So your
face bids me, though you say nothing. Mum,
mum!

200 *What makes that frontlet on?* Why do you wear that
frowning visage?

He that keeps nor crust nor crumb,   210
    Weary of all, shall want some.

(*Points at* LEAR) That's a shealed peascod.
GON: Not only, sir, this your all-licensed fool,
But other of your insolent retinue
Do hourly carp and quarrel, breaking forth
In rank and not-to-be-endured riots. Sir,
I had thought, by making this well known unto
    you,
To have found a safe redress, but now grow fear-
    ful,
By what yourself, too, late have spoke and done,
That you protect this course, and put it on   220
By your allowance; which if you should, the fault
Would not scape censure, nor the redresses sleep,
Which, in the tender of a wholesome weal,
Might in their working do you that offence
Which else were shame, that then necessity
Must call discreet proceeding.
FOOL: For you know, nuncle,

    The hedge-sparrow fed the cuckoo so long
    That it had it head bit off by it young.

So out went the candle, and we were left dark-   230
ling.
LEAR: Are you our daughter?
GON: I would you would make use of your good
    wisdom,
Whereof I know you are fraught, and put away
These dispositions which of late transport you
From what you rightly are.
FOOL: May not an ass know when the cart draws
    the horse?
    Whoop, Jug, I love thee!

212 *shealed peascod* shelled pea-pod
215 *carp* complain
216 *rank* unrestrained
218 *safe* sure
220 *put it on* encourage it
222 *redresses* remedies *sleep* be neglected
223 *tender* care *wholesome* healthy, well-ordered *weal* state,
commonwealth
224 *working* execution *offence* harm
225 *necessity* the circumstances of the case
226 *discreet* justifiable
229 *it* its
230 *darkling* in the dark
234 *fraught* supplied, stored

LEAR: Does any here know me? This is not Lear.
240　Does Lear walk thus? speak thus? Where are his
　　eyes?
　　Either his notion weakens, his discernings
　　Are lethargied. Ha, waking? 'Tis not so!
　　Who is it that can tell me who I am?

FOOL: Lear's shadow.

LEAR: I would learn that, for by the marks of sov-
　　ereignty,
　　Knowledge, and reason, I should be false per-
　　suaded
　　I had daughters.

FOOL: Which they will make an obedient father.

LEAR: Your name, fair gentlewoman?

250　GON: This admiration, sir, is much o' th' savour
　　Of other your new pranks. I do beseech you
　　To understand my purposes aright.
　　As you are old and reverend, you should be wise.
　　Here do you keep a hundred knights and squires,
　　Men so disordered, so deboshed, and bold
　　That this our court, infected with their manners,
　　Shows like a riotous inn. Epicurism and lust
　　Make it more like a tavern or a brothel
　　Than a graced palace. The shame itself doth
　　speak
260　For instant remedy. Be then desired
　　By her that else will take the thing she begs
　　A little to disquantity your train,
　　And the remainders that shall still depend
　　To be such men as may besort your age,
　　Which know themselves, and you.

LEAR: Darkness and devils!
　　Saddle my horses; call my train together!
　　Degenerate bastard, I'll not trouble thee;
　　Yet have I left a daughter.

270　GON: You strike my people, and your disordered
　　rabble
　　Make servants of their betters.

Enter ALBANY.

LEAR: Woe that too late repents! O, sir, are you
　　come?
　　Is it your will? Speak, sir! Prepare my horses.
　　Ingratitude, thou marble-hearted fiend,
　　More hideous when thou show'st thee in a child
　　Than the sea-monster!

ALB: Pray, sir, be patient.

LEAR: (*to* GONERIL) Detested kite, thou liest!
　　My train are men of choice and rarest parts,
　　That all particulars of duty know　　　　　　280
　　And in the most exact regard support
　　The worships of their name. O most small fault,
　　How ugly didst thou in Cordelia show,
　　Which, like an engine, wrenched my frame of
　　nature
　　From the fixed place, drew from my heart all love
　　And added to the gall. O Lear, Lear, Lear!
　　Beat at this gate that let thy folly in
　　　　　　　　　(*Strikes his head.*)
　　And thy dear judgment out! Go, go, my people.

ALB: My lord, I am guiltless, as I am ignorant
　　Of what hath moved you.　　　　　　　　290

LEAR: It may be so, my lord.
　　Hear, Nature, hear, dear goddess, hear!
　　Suspend thy purpose, if thou didst intend
　　To make this creature fruitful;
　　Into her womb convey sterility,
　　Dry up in her the organs of increase,
　　And from her derogate body never spring
　　A babe to honour her! If she must teem,
　　Create her child of spleen, that it may live
　　And be a thwart disnatured torment to her.　　300
　　Let it stamp wrinkles in her brow of youth,
　　With cadent tears fret channels in her cheeks,
　　Turn all her mother's pains and benefits
　　To laughter and contempt, that she may feel

241 *notion* understanding *discernings* perceptions
250 *admiration* astonishment *is much o'th' savour* has the
same flavour
255 *deboshed* debauched
257 *Epicurism* loose living
259 *graced* dignified
262 *disquantity* diminish
263 *depend* remain in service
264 *besort* suit

281 *regard* care, punctiliousness *support* uphold
282 *The worships of their name* their reputations
283 *show* appear
284 *engine* machine *frame of nature* whole natural structure
285 *the fixed place* its foundations
286 *gall* bitterness
288 *dear* precious
297 *derogate* debased
298 *teem* bear children
299 *spleen* malice
300 *thwart* perverse *disnatured* unnatural
302 *cadent* felling *fret* wear
303 *benefits* kindnesses

How sharper than a serpent's tooth it is
To have a thankless child! Away, away!

(Exit.)

ALB: Now, gods that we adore, whereof comes
this?

GON: Never afflict yourself to know more of it,
But let his disposition have that scope
310   That dotage gives it.

Enter LEAR.

LEAR: What, fifty of my followers at a clap?
Within a fortnight?

ALB: What's the matter, sir?

LEAR: I'll tell thee. (*To* GONERIL) Life and death! I
am ashamed
That thou hast power to shake my manhood thus,
That these hot tears, which break from me per-
force,
Should make thee worth them. Blasts and fogs
upon thee!
Th' untented woundings of a father's curse
Pierce every sense about thee! Old fond eyes,
320   Beweep this cause again, I'll pluck ye out,
And cast you, with the waters that you lose,
To temper clay. Yea, is it come to this?
Let it be so. I have another daughter,
Who I am sure is kind and comfortable.
When she shall hear this of thee, with her nails
She'll flay thy wolvish visage. Thou shalt find
That I'll resume the shape which thou dost think
I have cast off for ever.

(Exeunt LEAR, KENT, *and* ATTENDANTS.)

GON: Do you mark that, my lord?

330   ALB: I cannot be so partial, Goneril,
To the great love I bear you—

GON: Pray you, content. What, Oswald, ho!
(*To the* FOOL) You, sir, more knave than fool, after
your master!

FOOL: Nuncle Lear, nuncle Lear, tarry! Take the
fool with thee.

A fox, when one has caught her,
And such a daughter,
Should sure to the slaughter,
If my cap would buy a halter.
So the fool follows after.   *(Exit.)*

318 *untented* festering
319 *fond* foolish
322 *temper* soften
324 *comfortable* ready to give comfort

GON: This man hath had good counsel! A hundred   340
knights?
'Tis politic and safe to let him keep
At point a hundred knights; yes, that on every
dream,
Each buzz, each fancy, each complaint, dislike,
He may enguard his dotage with their powers
And hold our lives in mercy.—Oswald, I say!

ALB: Well, you may fear too far.

GON: Safer than trust too far.
Let me still take away the harms I fear,
Not fear still to be taken. I know his heart.
What he hath uttered I have writ my sister.   350
If she sustain him and his hundred knights,
When I have showed the unfitness—

Enter (OSWALD *the*) *Steward.*

How now, Oswald?
What, have you writ that letter to my sister?

OSW: Ay, madam.

GON: Take you some company, and away to horse,
Inform her full of my particular fear,
And thereto add such reasons of your own
As may compact it more. Get you gone,
And hasten your return. (*Exit* OSWALD.) No, no,   360
my lord,
This milky gentleness and course of yours,
Though I condemn it not, yet, under pardon,
You are much more at task for want of wisdom
Than praised for harmful mildness.

ALB: How far your eyes may pierce I cannot tell;
Striving to better, oft we mar what's well.

GON: Nay then—

ALB: Well, well, the event.

(Exeunt.)

SCENE V

Enter LEAR, KENT, GENTLEMAN, *and* FOOL.

LEAR: Go you before to Gloucester with these letters; acquaint my daughter no further with anything you know than comes from her demand out

342 *at point* fully armed
343 *buzz* rumour
349 *still* always
359 *compact* confirm
363 *at task* to blame

of the letter. If your diligence be not speedy, I shall be there afore you.

KENT: I will not sleep, my lord, till I have delivered your letter. *(Exit.)*

FOOL: If a man's brains were in's heels, were't not in danger of kibes?

10 LEAR: Ay, boy.

FOOL: Then I prithee be merry; thy wit shall ne'er go slipshod.

LEAR: Ha, ha, ha!

FOOL: Shalt see thy other daughter will use thee kindly, for though she's as like this as a crab's like an apple, yet I can tell what I can tell.

LEAR: What canst tell, boy?

FOOL: She'll taste as like this as a crab does to a crab. Thou canst tell why one's nose stands i' th'

20 middle on's face?

LEAR: No.

FOOL: Why, to keep one's eyes of either side's nose, that what a man cannot smell out, 'a may spy into.

LEAR: I did her wrong.

FOOL: Canst tell how an oyster makes his shell?

LEAR: No.

FOOL: Nor I neither; but I can tell why a snail has a house.

30 LEAR: Why?

FOOL: Why, to put's head in, not to give it away to

his daughters, and leave his horns without a case.

LEAR: I will forget my nature. So kind a father!— Be my horses ready?   *(Exit* GENTLEMAN.*)*

FOOL: Thy asses are gone about 'em. The reason why the seven stars are no more than seven is a pretty reason.

LEAR: Because they are not eight?

FOOL: Yes indeed. Thou wouldst make a good fool. 40

LEAR: To tak't again perforce! Monster ingratitude!

FOOL: If thou wert my fool, nuncle, I'ld have thee beaten for being old before thy time.

LEAR: How's that?

FOOL: Thou shouldst not have been old till thou hadst been wise.

LEAR: O, let me not be mad, not mad, sweet heaven!

Keep me in temper; I would not be mad!

Enter Gentleman.

How now? Are the horses ready?   50

GENT: Ready, my lord.

LEAR: Come, boy.

FOOL: She that's a maid now, and laughs at my departure,

Shall not be a maid long, unless things be cut shorter.

(Exeunt.)

9 *kibes* chilblains
12 *slipshod* in slippers (because of the chilblains)
18 *crab* crab apple

49 *in temper* normal, in control of myself

ACT II

SCENE I

*Enter (*EDMUND *the) Bastard and* CURAN, *meeting.*

EDM: Save thee, Curan.

CUR: And you, sir. I have been with your father and given him notice that the Duke of Cornwall and Regan his Duchess will be here with him this night.

EDM: How comes that?

CUR: Nay, I know not. You have heard of the news abroad—I mean the whispered ones, for they are yet but ear-kissing arguments?

EDM: Not I. Pray you, what are they? 10

6 *How comes that?* How does that happen?
9 *ear-kissing arguments* topics to be mentioned only with the mouth close to another's ear

CUR: Have you heard of no likely wars toward
   'twixt the two Dukes of Cornwall and Albany?
EDM: Not a word.
CUR: You may do, then, in time. Fare you well, sir.
                                (*Exit.*)
EDM: The Duke be here to-night? The better! best!
   This weaves itself perforce into my business.
   My father hath set guard to take my brother;
   And I have one thing, of a queasy question,
   Which I must act. Briefness and fortune, work!
20   Brother, a word! Descend! Brother, I say!

           Enter EDGAR.

   My father watches. O sir, fly this place;
   Intelligence is given where you are hid;
   You have now the good advantage of the night.
   Have you not spoken 'gainst the Duke of Corn-
     wall?
   He's coming hither, now i'th' night, i'th' haste,
   And Regan with him. Have you nothing said
   Upon his party 'gainst the Duke of Albany?
   Advise yourself.
EDG: I am sure on't, not a word.
30 EDM: I hear my father coming. Pardon me,
   In cunning I must draw my sword upon you;
   Draw, seem to defend yourself; now quit you
     well.—
   Yield! Come before my father. Light, ho, here!
   Fly, brother.—Torches, torches!—So farewell.
                     (*Exit* EDGAR.)
   Some blood drawn on me would beget opinion
   Of my more fierce endeavour. (*Stabs his arm.*) I
     have seen drunkards
   Do more than this in sport.—Father, father!—
   Stop, stop! No help?

   Enter GLOUCESTER, *and* SERVANTS *with torches.*

40 GLOU: Now, Edmund, where's the villain?
EDM: Here stood he in the dark, his sharp sword
     out,
   Mumbling of wicked charms, conjuring the
     moon

18 *of a queasy question* of a hazardous nature
19 *Briefness* speed
27 *Upon his party* in opposition to his faction
28 *Advise yourself* consider
32 *quit you well* fight vigorously

   To stand auspicious mistress.
GLOU: But where is he?
EDM: Look, sir, I bleed.
GLOU: Where is the villain, Edmund?
EDM: Fled this way, sir. When by no means he
   could—
GLOU: Pursue him, ho! Go after.
             (*Exeunt some* SERVANTS.)
   By no means what?
EDM: Persuade me to the murther of your lordship;   50
   But that I told him the revenging gods
   'Gainst parricides did all their thunders bend,
   Spoke with how manifold and strong a bond
   The child was bound to th' father—sir, in fine,
   Seeing how loathly opposite I stood
   To his unnatural purpose, in fell motion
   With his preparéd sword he charges home
   My unprovided body, latched mine arm;
   And when he saw my best alarumed spirits,
   Bold in the quarrel's right, roused to th' encoun-   60
     ter,
   Or whether gasted by the noise I made,
   Full suddenly he fled.
GLOU: Let him fly far.
   Not in this land shall he remain uncaught;
   And found—dispatch. The noble Duke my
     master,
   My worthy arch and patron, comes to-night.
   By his authority I will proclaim it,
   That he which finds him shall deserve our
     thanks,
   Bringing the murderous coward to the stake;
   He that conceals him, death.   70
EDM: When I dissuaded him from his intent
   And found him pight to do it, with curst speech
   I threatened to discover him. He replied,
   'Thou unpossessing bastard, dost thou think,
   If I would stand against thee, would the reposal

43 *stand auspicious mistress* incline her favours
51 *that* when
55 *loathly opposite* bitterly opposed
56 *fell* foul
58 *latched* caught
59 *alarumed* aroused
61 *gasted* scared
65 *dispatch* prompt execution
66 *arch* chief, lord
72 *pight* resolved *curst* angry
75 *reposal* placing

Of any trust, virtue, or worth in thee
Make thy words faithed? No. What I should
  deny
(As this I would, ay, though thou didst produce
My very character), I'ld turn it all
80 To thy suggestion, plot, and damnéd practice;
And thou must make a dullard of the world,
If they not thought the profits of my death
Were very pregnant and potential spurs
To make thee seek it.'
GLOU: O strange and fastenèd villain,
Would he deny his letter? I never got him.
                            (*Tucket within.*)
Hark, the Duke's trumpets! I know not why he
  comes.
All ports I'll bar; the villain shall not scape;
The Duke must grant me that. Besides, his
  picture
90 I will send far and near, that all the kingdom
May have due note of him, and of my land,
Loyal and natural boy, I'll work the means
To make thee capable.

Enter CORNWALL, REGAN, *and* ATTENDANTS.

CORN: How now, my noble friend? Since I came
  hither
(Which I can call but now) I have heard strange-
  ness.
REG: If it be true, all vengeance comes too short
Which can pursue the offender. How dost, my
  lord?
GLOU: O madam, my old heart is cracked, it's
  cracked!
REG: What, did my father's godson seek your life?
100 He whom my father named, your Edgar?
GLOU: O lady, lady, shame would have it hid!
REG: Was he not companion with the riotous
  knights
That tended upon my father?
GLOU: I know not, madam. 'Tis too bad, too bad!

EDM: Yes, madam, he was of that consort.
REG: No marvel then though he were ill affected.
'Tis they have put him on the old man's death,
To have the expense and waste of his revenues.
I have this present evening from my sister
Been well informed of them, and with such 110
  cautions
That, if they come to sojourn at my house,
I'll not be there.
CORN: Nor I, assure thee, Regan.
Edmund, I hear that you have shown your father
A childlike office.
EDM: It was my duty, sir.
GLOU: He did bewray his practice, and received
This hurt you see, striving to apprehend him.
CORN: Is he pursued?
GLOU: Ay, my good lord. 120
CORN: If he be taken, he shall never more
Be feared of doing harm. Make your own pur-
  pose,
How in my strength you please. For you,
  Edmund,
Whose virtue and obedience doth this instant
So much commend itself, you shall be ours,
Natures of such deep trust we shall much need;
You we first seize on.
EDM: I shall serve you, sir,
Truly, however else.
GLOU: For him I thank your Grace. 130
CORN: You know not why we came to visit you—
REG: Thus out of season, threading dark-eyed
  night.
Occasions, noble Gloucester, of some prize,
Wherein we must have use of your advice.
Our father he hath writ, so hath our sister,
Of differences, which I best thought it fit

77 *faithed* believed
79 *character* handwriting
80 *suggestion* instigation *practice* plotting
81 *make a dullard of the world* think the world full of fools
83 *pregnant and potential* obvious and powerful
85 *fastened* confirmed
86 *got* begot
93 *capable* able to inherit

105 *consort* company
106 *ill affected* disloyal
107 *put him on* incited him to attempt
108 *expense* spending
115 *childlike office* filial duty
117 *bewray* reveal *practice* plot
121-122 *he shall never more Be feared of doing harm* there will
be no fear of his ever doing any further harm
122 *purpose* plan
123 *How* howsoever *in my strength* within the scope of my
authority
133 *prize* importance

To answer from our home; the several messengers
From hence attend dispatch. Our good old
friend,
Lay comforts to your bosom, and bestow
140   Your needful counsel to our businesses,
Which craves the instant use.

GLOU: I serve you, madam.
Your Graces are right welcome.

(Exeunt. Flourish.)

SCENE II

Enter KENT *and (*OSWALD *the) Steward, severally.*

OSW: Good dawning to thee, friend; art of this
house?

KENT: Ay.

OSW: Where may we set our horses?

KENT: I'th' mire.

OSW: Prithee, if thou lov'st me, tell me.

KENT: I love thee not.

OSW: Why then, I care not for thee.

KENT: If I had thee in Lipsbury Pinfold, I would
10   make thee care for me.

OSW: Why dost thou use me thus? I know thee not.

KENT: Fellow, I know thee.

OSW: What dost thou know me for?

KENT: A knave, a rascal, an eater of broken meats;
a base, proud, shallow, beggarly, three-suited,
hundred-pound, filthy worsted-stocking knave;
a lily-livered, action-taking, whoreson, glass-
gazing, superservicable, finical rogue, one-
trunk-inheriting slave; one that wouldst be a
20   bawd in way of good service, and art nothing but
the composition of a knave, beggar, coward, pan-
der, and the son and heir of a mongrel bitch; one

137 *from* away from
138 *attend dispatch* are waiting to be sent off
141 *use* attention
4 *set* put
9 *in Lipsbury Pinfold* (equivalent to:) in my clutches
14 *broken meats* remains of the joint
15 *three-suited* (dependants received an allowance for three
suits a year)
17 *lily-livered* cowardly *action-taking* taking refuge in the
law *glass-gazing* looking at himself in the mirror
20 *in way of good service* to please those whom you serve

whom I will beat into clamorous whining, if thou
deny'st the least syllable of thy addition.

OSW: Why, what a monstrous fellow art thou, thus
to rail on one that's neither known of thee nor
knows thee!

KENT: What a brazen-faced varlet art thou, to deny
thou knowest me! Is it two days ago since I
tripped up thy heels and beat thee before the   30
King? *(Draws his sword.)* Draw, you rogue, for
though it be night yet the moon shines. I'll make
a sop o' th' moonshine of you. Draw, you whoreson cullionly barbermonger, draw!

OSW: Away! I have nothing to do with thee.

KENT: Draw, you rascal! You come with letters
against the King, and take Vanity the puppet's
part against the royalty of her father. Draw, you
rogue, or I'll so carbonado your shanks;
draw, you rascal! Come your ways!   40

OSW: Help, ho! murther! help!

KENT: Strike, you slave! Stand, rogue! Stand, you
neat slave! Strike!   *(Beats him.)*

OSW: Help, ho! murther! murther!

Enter EDMUND, *with his rapier drawn*, GLOUCESTER,
CORNWALL, REGAN, SERVANTS.

EDM: How now? What's the matter? Part.

KENT: With you, goodman boy, if you please!
Come, I'll flesh ye; come on, young master!

GLOU: Weapons? arms? What's the matter here?

CORN: Keep peace, upon your lives!
He dies that strikes again. What is the matter?   50

REG: The messengers from our sister and the King.

CORN: What is your difference? Speak.

OSW: I am scarce in breath, my lord.

KENT: No marvel, you have so bestirred your valour. You cowardly rascal, nature disclaims in
thee; a tailor made thee.

CORN: Thou art a strange fellow. A tailor make a
man?

KENT: A tailor, sir; a stonecutter or a painter could

24 *addition* description
33 *a sop o'th' moonshine* a corpse to soak up the moonbeams
34 *cullionly* base *barbermonger* fop
39 *carbonado* slash
46 *With you* I'll fight with you
47 *flesh* initiate
52 *difference* quarrel
54 *bestirred* agitated
55 *disclaims* renounces any share

60 not have made him so ill, though he had been but
two years o' the trade.

CORN: Speak yet, how grew your quarrel?

OSW: This ancient ruffian, sir, whose life I have
spared
At suit of his grey beard—

KENT: Thou whoreson zed, thou unnecessary letter! My lord, if you will give me leave, I will tread
this unbolted villain into mortar and daub the
walls of a jakes with him. 'Spare my grey beard,'
you wagtail?

70 CORN: Peace, sirrah;
You beastly knave, know you no reverence?

KENT: Yes, sir, but anger hath a privilege.

CORN: Why art thou angry?

KENT: That such a slave as this should wear a
sword,
Who wears no honesty. Such smiling rogues as
these,
Like rats, oft bite the holy cords atwain
Which are too intrinse to unloose; smooth every
passion
That in the natures of their lords rebel,
Bring oil to fire, snow to their colder moods;

80 Renege, affirm, and turn their halcyon beaks
With every gale and vary of their masters,
Knowing naught (like dogs) but following.
A plague upon your epileptic visage!
Smile you my speeches, as I were a fool?
Goose, an I had you upon Sarum Plain,
I'd drive ye cackling home to Camelot.

CORN: What, are thou mad, old fellow?

GLOU: How fell you out? Say that.

KENT: No contraries hold more antipathy

90 Than I and such a knave.

CORN: Why dost thou call him knave? What is his
fault?

KENT: His countenance likes me not.

CORN: No more perchance does mine, or his, or
hers.

KENT: Sir, 'tis my occupation to be plain;
I have seen better faces in my time
Than stands on any shoulder that I see
Before me at this instant.

CORN: This is some fellow
Who, having been praised for bluntness, doth
affect
A saucy roughness, and contrains the garb   100
Quite from his nature. He cannot flatter, he!
An honest mind and plain, he must speak truth!
An they will take it, so; if not, he's plain.
These kind of knaves I know which in this plain-
ness
Harbour more craft and more corrupter ends
Than twenty silly-ducking observants
That stretch their duties nicely.

KENT: Sir, in good faith, in sincere verity,
Under the allowance of your great aspect,
Whose influence, like the wreath of radiant fire   110
On flickering Phoebus' front—

CORN: What mean'st by this?

KENT: To go out of my dialect, which you discom-
mend so much. I know, sir, I am no flatterer. He
that beguiled you in a plain accent was a plain
knave, which for my part I will not be, though I
should win your displeasure to entreat me to't.

CORN: What was the offence you gave him?

OSW: I never gave him any.
It pleased the King his master very late   120
To strike at me upon his misconstruction,
When he, conjunct and flattering his displeasure,

65 *zed* (British name for the letter Z)
67 *unbolted* unsifted
68 *jakes* latrine
76 *atwain* apart
77 *intrinse* tangled *smooth* encourage
78 *rebel* rise up
80 *halcyon* fabled sea-bird which, if killed and hung up,
was supposed to act as a weathercock
81 *vary* variation
83 *epileptic* looking as if he were in a fit
84 *Smile you* do you smile at
85 *Sarum* Salisbury

92 *likes* pleases
94 *plain* plain-spoken
100 *constrains* forcibly assumes *garb* outward appearance
101 *from* contrary to
106 *silly-ducking* bowing ridiculously *observants*
obsequious attendants
107 *stretch* over-exert themselves in performing *nicely*
punctiliously
109 *aspect* regard
111 *Phoebus* the sun-god *front* forehead
115 *plain accent* downright speech
117 *win* overcome *to entreat* so that you would entreat
121 *misconstruction* misinterpretation (of what Oswald
had said)
122 *conjunct* taking sides with him

Tripped me behind; being down, insulted, railed
And put upon him such a deal of man
That worthied him, got praises of the King
For him attempting who was self-subdued,
And, in the fleshment of this dread exploit,
Drew on me here again.

KENT: None of these rogues and cowards

130   But Ajax is their fool.

CORN: Fetch forth the stocks!
You stubborn ancient knave, you reverent
    braggart,
We'll teach you—

KENT: Sir, I am too old to learn.
Call not your stocks for me; I serve the King,
On whose employment I was sent to you.
You shall do small respect, show too bold malice
Against the grace and person of my master,
Stocking his messenger.

140   CORN: Fetch forth the stocks! As I have life and
    honour,
There shall he sit till noon.

REG: Till noon? Till night, my lord, and all night
    too!

KENT: Why, madam, if I were your father's dog,
You should not use me so.

REG: Sir, being his knave, I will.

CORN: This is a fellow of the selfsame colour
Our sister speaks of. Come, bring away the
    stocks!

                    (Stocks brought out.)

GLOU: Let me beseech your Grace not to do so.
His fault is much, and the good King his master

150   Will check him for't. Your purposed low correc-
    tion
Is such as basest and contemnedest wretches
For pilferings and most common trespasses

Are punished with. The King must take it ill
That he, so slightly valued in his messenger,
Should have him thus restrained.

CORN: I'll answer that.

REG: My sister may receive it much more worse,
To have her gentleman abused, assaulted,
For following her affairs. Put in his legs.

                    (KENT is put in the stocks.)
Come, my good lord, away.   160

            (Exeunt all but GLOUCESTER and KENT.)

GLOU: I am sorry for thee, friend; 'tis the Duke's
    pleasure,
Whose disposition, all the world well knows,
Will not be rubbed nor stopped. I'll entreat for
    thee.

KENT: Pray do not, sir. I have watched and travel-
    led hard;
Some time I shall sleep out, the rest I'll whistle;
A good man's fortune may grow out at heels,
Give you good morrow!

GLOU: The Duke's to blame in this; 'twill be ill
    taken.

                    (Exit.)

KENT: Good King, that must approve the common
    saw,
Thou out of heaven's benediction comest   170
To the warm sun!
Approach, thou beacon to this under globe,
That by thy comfortable beams I may
Peruse this letter. Nothing almost sees miracles
But misery. I know 'tis from Cordelia,
Who hath most fortunately been informed
Of my obscured course: and (reads) 'shall find
    time
From this enormous state, seeking to give
Losses their remedies.' All weary and o'er-
    watched,
Take vantage, heavy eyes, not to behold   180

123 *behind* from behind *being down, insulted* when I was
down he insulted me
124 *such a deal of man* such appearance of manliness
125 *worthied* won him honour
126 *attempting* attacking *self-subdued* in full control of himself
127 *in the fleshment* encouraged by the success
129-130 *None . . . fool* There is not a rogue or coward
who does not behave as if Ajax (the Greek hero at Troy)
was a fool in comparison to him
138 *grace* honour
150 *check* reprove *low* implying disgrace
151 *contemnedest* most despised

155 *restrained* confined
156 *answer* accept responsibility for
163 *rubbed* hindered
164 *watched* been up late
166 *grow out at heels* wear out
169 *saw* saying
170 *heaven's benediction* i.e., the shade (on a very hot day)
172 *thou beacon* i.e., the sun
177 *obscured course* activities in disguise
178 *enormous* disordered
179 *o'erwatched* tired out

This shameful lodging.

Fortune, good night; smile once more, turn thy wheel.

(Sleeps.)

Enter EDGAR.

EDG: I heard myself proclaimed,
And by the happy hollow of a tree
Escaped the hunt. No port is free, no place
That guard and most unusual vigilance
Does not attend my taking. Whiles I may scape,
I will preserve myself; and am bethought
To take the basest and most poorest shape
190   That ever penury, in contempt of man,
Brought near to beast. My face I'll grime with filth,
Blanket my loins, elf all my hair in knots,
And with presented nakedness outface
The winds and persecutions of the sky.
The country gives me proof and precedent
Of Bedlam beggars, who, with roaring voices,
Strike in their numbed and mortified bare arms
Pins, wooden pricks, nails, sprigs of rosemary;
And with this horrible object, from low farms,
200   Poor pelting villages, sheepcotes, and mills,
Sometime with lunatic bans, sometime with prayers,
Enforce their charity. 'Poor Turlygod, poor Tom!'
That's something yet! Edgar I nothing am.

(Exit.)

Enter LEAR, FOOL, *and* GENTLEMAN.

LEAR: 'Tis strange that they should so depart from home,
And not send back my messenger.
GENT: As I learned,
The night before there was no purpose in them
Of this remove.

187 *attend my taking* wait to capture me
192 *elf* tangle
193 *outface* defy
195 *proof* example
196 *Bedlam* Bethlehem Hospital, the London hospital for the insane
197 *mortified* insensible
200 *pelting* petty
201 *bans* curses

KENT: Hail to thee, noble master!
LEAR: Ha!   210
Mak'st thou this shame thy pastime?
KENT: No, my lord.
FOOL: Ha, ha! he wears cruel garters.
Horses are tied by the head, dogs and bears by the neck, monkeys by the loins, and men by the legs. When a man's overlusty at legs, then he wears wooden nether-stocks.
LEAR: What's he that hath so much thy place mistook
To set thee here?
KENT: It is both he and she—   220
Your son and daughter.
LEAR: No
KENT: Yes.
LEAR: No, I say.
KENT: I say yea.
LEAR: No, no, they would not!
KENT: Yes, they have.
LEAR: By Jupiter, I swear no!
KENT: By Juno, I swear ay!
LEAR: They durst not do't;   230
The could not, would not do't. 'Tis worse than murther
To do upon respect such violent outrage.
Resolve me with all modest haste which way
Thou mightst deserve or they impose this usage,
Coming from us.
KENT: My lord, when at their home
I did commend your Highness' letters to them,
Ere I was risen from the place that showed
My duty kneeling, came there a reeking post,
Stewed in his haste, half breathless, panting   240
forth
From Goneril his mistress salutations;
Delivered letters, spite of intermission,
Which presently they read; on whose contents,
They summoned up their meiny, straight took horse,
Commanded me to follow and attend
The leisure of their answer, gave me cold looks,

217 *nether-stocks* stockings
232 *respect* duty owed (to Lear)
233 *Resolve* tell *modest* reasonable
239 *post* messenger
242 *intermission* interruption
243 *presently* immediately
244 *meiny* retinue

And meeting here the other messenger
Whose welcome I perceived had poisoned
   mine—
Being the very fellow which of late
250   Displayed so saucily against your Highness—
Having more man than wit about me, drew;
He raised the house with loud and coward cries.
Your son and daughter found this trespass worth
The shame which here it suffers.
FOOL: Winter's not gone yet if the wild geese fly
   that way.

   Fathers that wear rags
      Do make their children blind,
   But fathers that bear bags
260   Shall see their children kind.
   Fortune, that arrant whore,
   Ne'er turns the key to the poor.

But for all this, thou shalt have as many dolours
for they daughters as thou canst tell in a year.
LEAR: O, how this mother swells up toward my
   heart!
Hysterica passio! Down, thou climbing sorrow,
Thy element's below! Where is this daughter?
KENT: With the Earl, sir, here within.
REG: Follow me not;
270   Stay here.   (Exit.)
GENT: Made you no more offence but what you
   speak of?
KENT: None.
How chance the King comes with so small a
   number?
FOOL: An thou hadst been set i'th' stocks for that
question, thou'dst well deserved it.
KENT: Why, fool?
FOOL: We'll set thee to school to an ant, to teach
thee there's no labouring i'th' winter. All that fol-
low their noses are led by their eyes but blind
280   men, and there's not a nose among twenty but
can smell him that's stinking. Let go thy hold

when a great wheel runs down a hill, lest it break
thy neck with following it; but the great one that
goes upward, let him draw thee after. When a
wise man gives thee better counsel, give me mine
again. I would have none but knaves follow it,
since a fool gives it.

   That sir which serves and seeks for gain,
      And follows but for form,
   Will pack when it begins to rain   290
      And leave thee in the storm.
   But I will tarry, the fool will stay
      And let the wise man fly.
   The knave turns fool that runs away;
      The fool no knave, perdy.

KENT: Where learned you this, fool?
FOOL: Not i'th' stocks, fool.

   Enter LEAR *and* GLOUCESTER.

LEAR: Deny to speak with me? They are sick? they
   are weary?
They have travelled all the night? Mere fetches,
The images of revolt and flying off!   300
Fetch me a better answer.
GLOU: My dear lord,
You know the fiery quality of the Duke,
How unremovable and fixed he is
In his own course.
LEAR: Vengeance! death! confusion!
Fiery? What quality? Why, Gloucester, Glou-
   cester,
I'd speak with the Duke of Cornwall and his
   wife.
GLOU: Well, my good lord, I have informed them
   so.
LEAR: Informed them? Dost thou understand me,   310
   man?
GLOU: Ay, my good lord.
LEAR: The King would speak with Cornwall; the
   dear father
Would with his daughter speak, commands her
   service.
Are they informed of this? My breath and blood!
Fiery? the fiery Duke? Tell the hot Duke that—
No, but not yet, may be he is not well;

250 *Displayed* behaved
259 *bags* (of money)
262 *turns the key* (to open the door)
263 *dolours* (1) sorrows (2) dollars
264 *tell* count
265 *mother* choking passion
266 *Hysterica passio* hysteria

299 *fetches* excuses
300 *images* clear symptoms

Infirmity doth still neglect all office
Whereto our health is bound. We are not our-
selves
When nature, being oppressed, commands the
mind
320   To suffer with the body. I'll forbear,
And am fallen out with my more headier will,
To take the indisposed and sickly fit
For the sound man.—Death on my state! Where-
fore
Should he sit here? This act persuades me
That this remotion of the Duke and her
Is practice only. Give me my servant forth.
Go tell the Duke and's wife I'd speak with
them—
Now, presently. Bid them come forth and hear
me,
Or at their chamber door I'll beat the drum
330   Till it cry sleep to death.
GLOU: I would have all well betwixt you. *(Exit.)*
LEAR: O me, my heart, my rising heart! But down!
FOOL: Cry to it, nuncle, as the cockney did to the
eels when she put 'em i'th' paste alive. She
knapped 'em o'th' coxcombs with a stick and
cried 'Down, wantons, down!' 'Twas her brother
that, in pure kindness to his horse, buttered his
hay.

Enter CORNWALL, REGAN, GLOUCESTER, SERVANTS.

LEAR: Good morrow to you both.
340   CORN: Hail to your Grace!
                      (KENT here set at liberty.)
REG: I am glad to see your Highness.
LEAR: Regan, I think you are; I know what reason
I have to think so. If thou shouldst not be glad,
I would divorce me from thy mother's tomb,
Sepulchring an adultress. *(To KENT)* O, are you
free?
Some other time for that.—Beloved Regan,
Thy sister's naught. O Regan, she hath tied

Sharp-toothed unkindness, like a vulture, here! 350
            (Lays his hand on his heart.)
I can scarce speak to thee. Thou'lt not believe
With how depraved a quality—O Regan!
REG: I pray you, sir, take patience, I have hope
You less know how to value her desert
Than she to scant her duty.
LEAR: Say, how is that?
REG: I cannot think my sister in the least
Would fail her obligation. If, sir, perchance
She have restrained the riots of your followers, 360
'Tis on such ground, and to such wholesome end,
As clears her from all blame.
LEAR: My curses on her!
REG: O, sir, you are old;
Nature in you stands on the very verge
Of her confine. You should be ruled, and led
By some discretion that discerns your state
Better than you yourself. Therefore I pray you
That to our sister you do make return;
Say you have wronged her, sir. 370
LEAR: Ask her forgiveness?
Do you but mark how this becomes the house:
'Dear daughter, I confess that I am old;
               (Kneels.)
Age is unnecessary; on my knees I beg
That you'll vouchsafe me raiment, bed, and
food.'
REG: Good sir, no more; these are unsightly tricks.
Return you to my sister.
LEAR: *(rises)* Never, Regan!
She hath abated me of half my train,
Looked black upon me, struck me with her
tongue, 380
Most serpent-like, upon the very heart.
All the stored vengeances of heaven fall
On her ingrateful top; strike her young bones,
You taking airs, with lameness!
CORN: Fie, sir, fie!
LEAR: You nimble lightnings, dart your blinding
flames
Into her scornful eyes, infect her beauty,

317 *Infirmity* illness *office* duty
321 *fallen out* angry *more headier* too impetuous
325 *remotion* removal
326 *practice* plot, scheme
330 *cry sleep to death* shout at sleep so as to put an end to it
333 *cockney* squeamish woman
335 *knapped* rapped
347 *naught* wicked

353 *scant* come short of
362 *verge* edge
363 *confine* boundary
364 *state* state of mind
369 *the house* family relationships
371 *Age is unnecessary* old people are superfluous
376 *abated* curtailed

You fen-sucked fogs, drawn by the powerful
sun,
To fall and blast her pride!

REG: O the blest gods! so will you wish on me
When the rash mood is on.

LEAR: No, Regan, thou shalt never have my curse;
390   Thy tender-hefted nature shall not give
Thee o'er to harshness. Her eyes are fierce, but
thine
Do comfort, and not burn. 'Tis not in thee
To grudge my pleasures, to cut off my train,
To bandy hasty words, to scant my sizes,
And, in conclusion, to oppose the bolt
Against my coming in. Thou better know'st
The offices of nature, bond of childhood,
Effects of courtesy, dues of gratitude.
Thy half o' th' kingdom has thou not forgot,
400   Wherein I thee endowed.

REG: Good sir, to the purpose.

(*Tucket within.*)

LEAR: Who put my man i'th' stocks?

CORN: What trumpet's that?

REG: I know't—my sister's. This approves her letter,
That she would soon be here.

Enter (OSWALD *the*) *Steward.*

Is your lady come?

LEAR: This is a slave, whose easy-borrowed pride
Dwells in the fickle grace of her he follows.
Out, varlet, from my sight!

410   CORN: What means your Grace!

Enter GONERIL.

LEAR: Who stocked my servant? Regan, I have
good hope
Thou didst not know on't.—Who comes here? O
heavens!
If you do love old men, if your sweet sway
Allow obedience, if you yourselves are old,
Make it your cause! Send down, and take my
part!

(*To* GONERIL) Art not ashamed to look upon this
beard?—
O Regan, wilt thou take her by the hand?

GON: Why not by the hand, sir? How have I
offended?
All's not offence that indiscretion finds
And dotage terms so.   420

LEAR: O sides, you are too tough!
Will you yet hold? How came my man i'th'
stocks?

CORN: I set him there, sir; but his own disorders
Deserved much less advancement.

LEAR: You? Did you?

REG: I pray you, father, being weak, seem so.
If, till the expiration of your month,
You will return and sojourn with my sister,
Dismissing half your train, come then to me.
I am now from home, and out of that provision   430
Which shall be needful for your entertainment.

LEAR: Return to her, and fifty men dismissed?
No, rather I abjure all roofs, and choose
To wage against the enmity of the air,
To be a comrade with the wolf and owl—
Necessity's sharp pinch! Return with her?
Why, the hot-blooded France, that dowerless
took
Our youngest born, I could as well be brought
To knee his throne, and squire-like pension beg
To keep base life afoot. Return with her?   440
Persuade me rather to be slave and sumpter
To this detested groom.   (*Points at* OSWALD.)

GON: At your choice, sir.

LEAR: I prithee, daughter, do not make me mad.
I will not trouble thee, my child; farewell.
We'll no more meet, no more see one another.
But yet thou art my flesh, my blood, my
daughter,
Or rather a disease that's in my flesh,
Which I must needs call mine. Thou art a boil,
A plague sore, an embosséd carbuncle   450
In my corrupted blood. But I'll not chide thee;

390 *tender-hefted* gentle
394 *scant my sizes* reduce my allowances
395 *oppose the bolt* bolt the doors
397 *offices of nature* duties of daughter to father
398 *Effects* actions
404 *approves* confirms

423 *disorders* misbehaviour
424 *advancement* honorable treatment
431 *entertainment* maintenance
434 *wage* oppose myself
439 *knee* kneel before
441 *sumpter* pack-horse
450 *embossed* swelling *carbuncle* boil, wen

Let shame come when it will, I do not call it;
I do not bid the Thunder-bearer shoot
Nor tell tales of thee to high-judging Jove.
Mend when thou canst; be better at thy leisure;
I can be patient, I can stay with Regan,
I and my hundred knights.

REG: Not altogether so.
I looked not for you yet, nor am provided
460 For your fit welcome. Give ear, sir, to my sister,
For those that mingle reason with your passion
Must be content to think you old, and so—
But she knows what she does.

LEAR: Is this well spoken?

REG: I dare avouch it, sir. What, fifty followers?
Is it not well? What should you need of more?
Yea, or so many, sith that both charge and danger
Speak 'gainst so great a number? How in one
house
Should many people, under two commands,
470 Hold amity? 'Tis hard, almost impossible.

GON: Why might not you, my lord, receive attendance
From those that she calls servants, or from mine?

REG: Why not, my lord? If then they chanced to
slack ye,
We could control them. If you will come to me
(For now I spy a danger), I entreat you
To bring but five-and-twenty; to no more
Will I give place or notice.

LEAR: I gave you all—

REG: And in good time you gave it.

480 LEAR: Made you my guardians, my depositaries,
But kept a reservation to be followed
With such a number. What, must I come to you
With five-and-twenty? Regan, said you so?

REG: And speak't again, my lord. No more with
me.

LEAR: Those wicked creatures yet do look well-
favoured
When others are more wicked; not being the
worst

Stands in some rank of praise. (*To* GONERIL) I'll
go with thee.
Thy fifty yet doth double five-and-twenty,
And thou art twice her love.

GON: Hear me, my lord;   490
What need you five-and-twenty, ten, or five,
To follow in a house where twice so many
Have a command to tend you?

REG: What need one?

LEAR: O, reason not the need! Our basest beggars
Are in the poorest thing superfluous;
Allow not nature more than nature needs,
Man's life is cheap as beast's. Thou art a lady;
If only to go warm were gorgeous,
Why, nature needs not what thou gorgeous   500
wear'st,
Which scarcely keeps thee warm. But, for true
need—
You heavens, give me that patience, patience I
need!
You see me here, you gods, a poor old man,
As full of grief as age, wretched in both;
If it be you that stirs these daughters' hearts
Against their father, fool me not so much
To bear it tamely; touch me with noble anger,
And let not women's weapons, water drops,
Stain my man's cheeks! No, you unnatural hags!
I will have such revenges on you both   510
That all the world shall—I will do such things—
What they are yet, I know not, but they shall be
The terrors of the earth! You think I'll weep;
No, I'll not weep.
I have full cause of weeping, but this heart
                                        (*Storm and tempest.*)
Shall break into a hundred thousand flaws
Or ere I'll weep. O fool, I shall go mad!
                (*Exeunt* LEAR, GLOUCESTER, KENT, *and* FOOL.)

CORN: Let us withdraw; 'twill be a storm.

REG: This house is little; the old man and's people
Cannot be well bestowed.   520

453 *the Thunder-bearer* Jove
461 *mingle reason with* can bring common-sense to ap-
praise
467 *charge* expense
473 *slack* neglect
477 *notice* recognition
480 *depositaries* trustees
485 *well-favoured* handsome
496 *Are in the poorest thing superfluous* have some small
thing not absolutely necessary
498 *cheap* worthless, insignificant
499-500 *If . . . wear'st* If mere warm clothes were a sign
of luxury, then you could do without the luxury of your
clothes which, in actual fact, barely keep you warm
516 *flaws* fragments
517 *Or ere* before
520 *bestowed* lodged

GON: 'Tis his own blame hath put himself from rest
    And must needs taste his folly.
REF: For his particular, I'll receive him gladly
    But not one follower.
GON: So am I purposed.
    Where is Lord of Gloucester?
CORN: Followed the old man forth.

Enter GLOUCESTER.

    He is returned.
GLOU: The King is in high rage.
530 CORN: Whither is he going?
GLOU: He calls to horse, but will I know not
    whither.
CORN: 'Tis best to give him way; he leads himself.

523 *For his particular* as far as he is concerned
532 *give him way* let him go

GON: My lord, entreat him by no means to stay.
GLOU: Alack, the night comes on, and the bleak
    winds
    Do sorely ruffle. For many miles about
    There's scarce a bush.
REG: O, sir, to wilful men
    The injuries that they themselves procure
    Must be their schoolmasters. Shut up your doors.
    He is attended with a desperate train,   540
    And what they may incense him to, being apt
    To have his ear abused, wisdom bids fear.
CORN: Shut up your doors, my lord, 'tis a wild
    night.
    My Regan cousels well. Come out o'th' storm.
                                            (*Exeunt.*)

535 *ruffle* rage

ACT III

SCENE I

Storm still. Enter KENT *and a* GENTLEMAN
at several doors.

KENT: Who's there, besides foul weather?
GENT: One minded like the weather, most un-
    quietly.
KENT: I know you; where's the King?
GENT: Contending with the fretful elements,
    Bids the wind blow the earth into the sea,
    Or swell the curléd waters 'bove the main,
    That things might change or cease, tears his
    white hair,
    Which the impetuous blasts with eyeless rage
    Catch in their fury, and make nothing of,
10 Strives in his little world of man to outscorn
    The to-and-fro-conflicting wind and rain.
    This night, wherein the cub-drawn bear would
    couch,

6 *main* land
8 *eyeless* unseeing
9 *make nothing of* have no respect for
12 *cub-drawn* sucked dry by her cubs, hence ravenously
hungry *couch* lie hidden

    The lion and the belly-pinchéd wolf
    Keep their fur dry, unbonneted he runs,
    And bids what will take all.
KENT: But who is with him?
GENT: None but the fool, who labours to outjest
    His heart-struck injuries.
KENT: Sir, I do know you,
    And dare upon the warrant of my note   20
    Commend a dear thing to you. There is division
    (Although as yet the face of it is covered
    With mutual cunning) 'twixt Albany and Corn-
    wall,
    Who have (as who have not, that their great stars
    Throned and set high?) servants, who seem no
    less,
    Which are to France the spies and speculations
    Intelligent of our state. What hath been seen,
    Either in snuffs and packings of the Dukes,

20 *note* knowledge
21 *Commend* entrust *dear* important
24 *that* whom *great stars* high fortunes
26 *speculations* watchers
27 *Intelligent of* giving information of
28 *snuffs* causes of offence *packings* plots

Or the hard rein which both of them hath borne
30 Against the old kind King, or something deeper,
Whereof, perchance, these are but furnishings . .
But, true it is, from France there comes a power
Into this scattered kingdom, who already,
Wise in our negligence, have secret feet
In some of our best ports and are at point
To show their open banner. Now to you:
If on my credit you dare build so far
To make your speed to Dover, you shall find
Some that will thank you, making just report
Of how unnatural and bemadding sorrow
40 The King hath cause to plain.
I am a gentleman of blood and breeding,
And from some knowledge and assurance offer
This office to you.
GENT: I will talk further with you.
KENT: No, do not.
For confirmation that I am much more
Than my out-wall, open this purse and take
What it contains. If you shall see Cordelia
(As fear not but you shall), show her this ring,
50 And she will tell you who your fellow is
That yet you do not know. Fie on this storm!
I will go seek the King.
GENT: Give me your hand. Have you no more to
say?
KENT: Few words, but, to effect, more than all yet:
That, when we have found the King (in which
your pain
That way, I'll this) he that first lights on him
Holla the other.   (*Exeunt severally*.)

SCENE II

Storm still. Enter LEAR *and* FOOL.

LEAR: Blow, winds, and crack your cheeks! rage,
blow,
You cataracts and hurricanoes, spout
Till you have drenched our steeples, drowned
the cocks!

You sulphurous and thought-executing fires,
Vaunt-couriers of oak-cleaving thunderbolts,
Singe my white head! And thou, all-shaking
thunder,
Strike flat the thick rotundity o'th' world,
Crack Nature's moulds, all germains spill at
once,
That make ingrateful man!
FOOL: O nuncle, court holy water in a dry house is
better than this rain water out o' door. Good
nuncle, in, and ask they daughters' blessing!   10
Here's a night pities neither wise men nor fools.
LEAR: Rumble they bellyful! Spit, fire; spout, rain!
Not rain, wind, thunder, fire are my daughters;
I tax not you, you elements, with unkindness;
I never gave you kingdom, called you children;
You owe me no subscription. Then let fall
Your horrible pleasure. Here I stand your slave,
A poor, infirm, weak, and despised old man;
But yet I call you servile ministers,
That will with two pernicious daughters join   20
Your high-engendered battles 'gainst a head
So old and white as this. O, O, 'tis foul!
FOOL: He that has a house to put's head in has a
good headpiece.

The codpiece that will house
Before the head has any,
The head and he shall louse:
So beggars marry many.
The man that makes his toe
What he his heart should make   30
Shall of a corn cry woe,
And turn his sleep to wake.

31 *furnishings* pretexts
32 *power* army
33 *scattered* divided
40 *bemadding* maddening
41 *plain* complain
44 *office* duty
55 *to effect* in effect
56 *pain* effort
3 *cocks* weathercocks

4 *thought-executing* doing execution with the rapidity of
thought
5 *Vaunt-couriers* advance-couriers, harbingers
7 *rotundity* roundness
8 *germains* seeds
10 *court holy water* i.e., fulsome speeches
16 *tax* accuse
18 *subscription* submission
23 *high-engendered* engendered on high *battles* battalions
27-29 He who begets children before he has a house to
keep them in will become a lousy beggar
30 *beggars marry many* i.e., many beggars marry
31-34 The man who makes his toe and his heart change
places will get a corn on his heart and stay awake of
heartache

For there was never yet fair woman but she made
  mouths in a glass.

Enter KENT.

LEAR: No, I will be the pattern of all patience;
  I will say nothing.
KENT: Who's there?
40 FOOL: Marry, here's grace and a codpiece; that's a
  wise man and a fool.
KENT: Alas, sir, are you here? Things that love
  night
  Love not such nights as these. The wrathful skies
  Gallow the very wanders of the dark
  And make them keep their caves; since I was
  man,
  Such sheets of fire, such bursts of horrid thun-
  der,
  Such groans of roaring wind and rain, I never
  Remember to have heard; man's nature cannot
  carry
  The affliction nor the fear.
50 LEAR: Let the great gods,
  That keep this dreadful pudder o'er our heads,
  Find out their enemies now. Tremble, thou
  wretch,
  That has within thee undivulgéd crimes
  Unwhipped of justice. Hide thee, thou bloody
  hand,
  Thou perjured, and thou simular man of virtue
  That are incestuous; caitiff, in pieces shake
  That under covert and convenient seeming
  Hast practised on man's life. Close pent-up
  guilts,
  Rive your concealing continents, and cry
60 These dreadful summoners grace. I am a man
  More sinned against than sinning.
KENT: Alack, bareheaded?
  Gracious my lord, hard by here is a hovel;
  Some friendship will it lend you 'gainst the
  tempest;

35 *made mouths* practised smiling
40 *grace* a person of rank
44 *Gallow* terrify
48 *carry* bear up under
51 *pudder* hubbub
55 *simular* apparent
57 *covert* cover
58 *practised on* plotted against
59 *Rive* break open *continents* containers *cry grace* ask
mercy

Repose you there, while I to this hard house
(More harder than the stones whereof 'tis raised,
Which even but now, demanding after you,
Denied me to come in) return, and force
Their scanted courtesy.
LEAR: My wits begin to turn.   70
  Come on, my boy. How dost, my boy? Art cold?
  I am cold myself. Where is this straw, my fellow?
  The art of our necessities is strange,
  That can make vile things precious. Come, your
  hovel.
  Poor fool and knave, I have one part in my heart
  That's sorry yet for thee.
FOOL: (*sings*)

  He that has and a little tiny wit—
    With hey, ho, the wind and the rain—
  Must make content with his fortunes fit,   80
    For the rain it raineth every day.

LEAR: True, boy. Come bring us to this hovel.
                    (*Exeunt* LEAR *and* KENT.)
FOOL: This is a brave night to cool a courtesan. I'll
  speak a prophecy ere I go:

  When priests are more in word than matter;
  When brewers mar their malt with water;
  When nobles are their tailors' tutors,
  No heretics burned, but wenches' suitors;
  When every case in law is right,
  No squire in debt nor no poor knight;   90
  When slanders do not live in tongues,
  Nor cutpurses come not to throngs;
  When usurers tell their gold i'th' field,
  And bawds and whores do churches build:
  Then shall the realm of Albion
  Come to great confusión.
  Then come the time, who lives to see't,
  That going shall be used with feet.

This prophecy Merlin shall make, for I live before his time.   100
                    (*Exit.*)

67 *demanding after* asking for
69 *scanted* grudging
74 *vile* worthless
93 *tell* count
95 *Albion* England
99 *Merlin* the magician who aided King Arthur

SCENE III

Enter GLOUCESTER *and* EDMUND *with lights.*

GLOU: Alack, alack, Edmund, I like not this unnatural dealing. When I desired their leave that I
might pity him, they took from me the use of
mine own house, charged me on pain of perpetual displeasure neither to speak of him, entreat
for him, nor any way sustain him.

EDM: Most savage and unnatural!

GLOU: Go to; say you nothing. There is division
betwixt the Dukes, and a worse matter than that.
10 I have received a letter this night—'tis dangerous
to be spoken—I have locked the letter in my
closet. These injuries the King now bears will be
revenged home; there is part of a power already
footed; we must incline to the King. I will seek
him and privily relieve him. Go you and maintain talk with the Duke, that my charity be not of
him perceived; if he ask for me, I am ill and gone
to bed. If I die for't, as no less is threatened me,
the King my old master must be relieved. There
20 is strange things toward, Edmund; pray you be
careful.   (*Exit.*)

EDM: This courtesy, forbid thee, shall the Duke
Instantly know, and of that letter too.
This seems a fair deserving, and must draw me
That which my father loses—no less than all;
The younger rises when the old doth fall.
                                              (*Exit.*)

SCENE IV

Enter LEAR, KENT, *and* FOOL.

KENT: Here is the place, my lord; good my lord,
enter.
The tyranny of the open night's too rough
For nature to endure.   (*Storm still.*)

LEAR: Let me alone.

KENT: Good my lord, enter here.

LEAR: Wilt break my heart?

KENT: I had rather break mine own; good my lord,
enter.

13 *power* army
14 *footed* on the march *incline to* side with
20 *toward* in preparation
22 *forbid* forbidden
24 *deserving* action earning a reward

LEAR: Thou think'st 'tis much that this contentious
storm
Invades us to the skin; so 'tis to thee;
But where the greater malady is fixed,   10
The lesser is scarce felt. Thou'dst shun a bear,
But if thy flight lay toward the raging sea,
Thou'dst meet the bear i'th' mouth. When the
mind's free,
The body's delicate; the tempest in my mind
Doth from my senses take all feeling else
Save what beats there. Filial ingratitude!
Is it not as this mouth should tear this hand
For lifting food to't? But I will punish home!
No, I will weep no more. In such a night
To shut me out! Pour on; I will endure.   20
In such a night as this! O Regan, Goneril!
Your old kind father, whose frank heart gave all!
O, that way madness lies; let me shun that!
No more of that.

KENT: Good my lord, enter here.

LEAR: Prithee go in thyself, seek thine own ease;
This tempest will not give me leave to ponder
On things would hurt me more. But I'll go in.
(*To the* FOOL) In boy, go first.—You houseless
poverty—
Nay, get thee in; I'll pray, and then I'll sleep.   30
                                       (*Exit* FOOL.)
Poor naked wretches, wheresoe'er you are,
That bide the pelting of this pitiless storm,
How shall your houseless heads and unfed sides,
Your looped and windowed raggedness, defend
you
From seasons such as these? O, I have ta'en
Too little care of this! Take physic, pomp;
Expose thyself to feel what wretches feel,
That thou mayst shake the superflux to them
And show the heavens more just.

EDG: (*within*) Fathom and half, fathom and half!   40
Poor Tom!

Enter FOOL (*from the hovel*).

FOOL: Come not in here, nuncle, here's a spirit.
Help me, help me!

KENT: Give me thy hand. Who's there?

FOOL: A spirit, a spirit! He says his name's poor
Tom.

17 *as* as if
18 *home* to the utmost
34 *looped* full of loopholes
38 *superflux* superfluity

KENT: What art thou that dost grumble there i'th' straw? Come forth.

Enter EDGAR (*disguised as a madman*).

50 EDG: Away, the foul fiend follows me! Through the sharp hawthorn blows the cold wind. Humh! go to thy bed and warm thee.

LEAR: Didst thou give all to thy daughters, and art thou come to this?

EDG: Who gives anything to poor Tom, whom the foul fiend hath led through fire and through flame, through ford and whirlpool, o'er bog and quagmire; that hath laid knives under his pillow and halters in his pew, set ratsbane by his porridge, made him proud of heart, to ride on a bay 60 trotting horse over four-inched bridges, to course his own shadow for a traitor. Bless thy five wits, Tom's acold. O, do de, do de, do de; bless thee from whirlwinds, star-blasting, and taking! Do poor Tom some charity, whom the foul fiend vexes. There could I have him now—and there —and there again—and there!

(*Storm still*.)

LEAR: What, has his daughters brought him to this pass?
Couldst thou save nothing? Wouldst thou give 'em all?

FOOL: Nay, he reserved a blanket, else we had 70 been all shamed.

LEAR: Now all the plagues that in the pendulous air
Hang fated o'er men's faults light on thy daughters!

KENT: He hath no daughters, sir.

LEAR: Death, traitor! nothing could have subdued nature
To such a lowness but his unkind daughters.
Is it the fashion that discarded fathers
Should have thus little mercy on their flesh?
Judicious punishment, 'twas this flesh begot
Those pelican daughters.

EDG: Pillicock sat on Pillicock's Hill. 'Allow, 80 'allow, loo, loo.

FOOL: This cold night will turn us all to fools and madmen.

EDG: Take heed o'th' foul fiend; obey thy parents; keep thy word justly; swear not; commit not with man's sworn spouse; set not thy sweet heart on proud array. Tom's acold.

LEAR: What hast thou been?

EDG: A servingman, proud in heart and mind; that curled my hair, wore gloves in my cap, served the 90 lust of my mistress' heart and did the act of darkness with her; swore as many oaths as I spake words, and broke them in the sweet face of heaven; one that slept in the contriving of lust, and waked to do it. Wine loved I deeply, dice dearly, and in woman out-paramoured the Turk. False of heart, light of ear, bloody of hand, hog in sloth, fox in stealth, wolf in greediness, dog in madness, lion in prey! Let not the creaking of shoes nor the rustling of silks betray thy poor heart to 100 woman. Keep thy foot out of brothels, thy hand out of plackets, thy pen from lender's books, and defy the foul fiend. Still through the hawthorn blows the cold wind; says suum, mun, hey nonny. Dolphin my boy; boy, sessa! let him trot by. (*Storm still*.)

LEAR: Thou wert better in a grave than to answer with thy uncovered body this extremity of the skies. Is man no more than this? Consider him well. Thou owest the worm no silk, the beast no 110 hide, the sheep no wool, the cat no perfume. Ha, here's three on's are sophisticated! Thou art the thing itself; unaccommodated man is no more but such a poor, bare, forked animal as thou art. Off, off, you lendings! Come, unbutton here.

(*Tears at his clothes*.)

FOOL: Prithee, nuncle, be contented; 'tis a naughty night to swim in. Now a little fire in a wild field were like an old lecher's heart—a small spark, all the rest on's body cold. Look, here comes a walking fire. 120

60 *course* chase
63 *star-blasting* evil influence of planets *taking* infection
67 *pass* extremity
71 *pendulous* overhanging
74 *subdued* reduced
78 *Judicious* just
79 *pelican* (young pelicans were supposed to feed on the blood of their parents)

97 *light of ear* credulous of evil
102 *plackets* slits in the waists of petticoats
111 *cat* civet-cat
112 *sophisticated* (because they are clothed, in contrast to Edgar's nakedness)
113 *unaccomodated* unequipped

Enter GLOUCESTER *with a torch.*

EDG: This is the foul fiend Flibbertigibbet; he begins at curfew, and walks till the first cock. He gives the web and the pin, squirts the eye, and makes the harelip; mildews the white wheat, and hurts the poor creature of earth.

S'Withold footed thrice the 'old;
He met the nightmare, and her nine fold;
  Bid her alight
  And her troth plight,
130 And aroint thee, witch, aroint thee!

KENT: How fares your Grace?
LEAR: What's he?
KENT: Who's there? What is't you seek?
GLOU: What are you there? Your names?
EDG: Poor Tom, that eats the swimming frog, the toad, the todpole, the wall-newt and the water; that in the fury of his heart, when the foul fiend rages, eats cow-dung for sallets, swallows the old rat and the ditch-dog, drinks the green mantle of
140 the standing pool; who is whipped from tithing to tithing, and stock-punished and imprisoned; who hath had three suits to his back, six shirts to his body, horse to ride, and weapon to wear;

But mice and rats, and such small deer,
Have been Tom's food for seven long year.

Beware my follower; peace, Smulkin, peace, thou fiend!
GLOU: What, hath your Grace no better company?
EDG: The prince of darkness is a gentleman!
150 Modo he's called, and Mahu.
GLOU: Our flesh and blood, my lord, is grown so vile,
  That it doth hate what gets it.

123 *the web and the pin* cataract of the eye
126 *S'Withold* St. Withold *footed* crossed *'old* wold, upland plain
129 *her troth plight* pledge her word
130 *aroint* be gone
136 *todpole* tadpole *wall-newt* lizard *water* (newt)
138 *sallets* salads
139 *green mantle* scum
140 *tithing* district
145 *deer* animals
152 *gets* begets

EDG: Poor Tom's acold.
GLOU: Go in with me; my duty cannot suffer
  To obey in all your daughters' hard commands.
  Though their injunction be to bar my doors
  And let this tyrannous night take hold upon you.
  Yet have I ventured to come seek you out
  And bring you where both fire and food is ready.
LEAR: First let me talk with this philosopher; 160
  What is the cause of thunder?
KENT: Good my lord, take this offer; go into the house.
LEAR: I'll talk a word with this same learned Theban.
  What is your study?
EDG: How to prevent the fiend and to kill vermin.
LEAR: Let me ask you one word in private.
KENT: Importune him once more to go, my lord.
  His wits begin to unsettle.
GLOU: Canst thou blame him?

  (Storm still.)

  His daughters seek his death. Ah, that good 170
  Kent!
  He said it would be thus—poor banished man!
  Thou sayest the King grows mad: I'll tell thee, friend,
  I am almost mad myself. I had a son,
  Now outlawed from my blood; he sought my life
  But lately, very late. I loved him, friend,
  No father his son dearer; true to tell thee,
  The grief hath crazed my wits. What a night's this!
  I do beseech your Grace—
LEAR: O, cry you mercy, sir.
  Noble philosopher, your company. 180
EDG: Tom's acold.
GLOU: In, fellow, there, into th' hovel; keep thee warm.
LEAR: Come, let's in all.
KENT: This way, my lord.
LEAR: With him!
  I will keep still with my philosopher.
KENT: Good my lord, soothe him; let him take the fellow.
GLOU: Take him you on.
KENT: Sirrah, come on; go along with us.

164 *study* subject of special study
179 *cry you mercy* I beg your pardon
188 *Take him you on* take him ahead

190   LEAR: Come, good Athenian.

GLOU: No words, no words! hush.

EDG: Child Rowland to the dark tower came;
His word was still

Fie, foh, and fum!
I smell the blood of a British man.

(*Exeunt.*)

SCENE V

Enter CORNWALL *and* EDMUND.

CORN: I will have my revenge ere I depart his
house.

EDM: How, my lord, I may be censured, that
nature thus gives way to loyalty, something fears
me to think of.

CORN: I now perceive it was not altogether your
brother's evil disposition made him seek his
death, but a provoking merit, set awork by a re-
proveable badness in himself.

10   EDM: How malicious is my fortune that I must repent to be just! This is the letter he spoke of,
which approves him an intelligent party to the
advantages of France. O heavens! that this
treason were not—or not I the detector!

CORN: Go with me to the Duchess.

EDM: If the matter of this paper be certain, you
have mighty business in hand.

CORN: True or false, it hath made thee Earl of
Gloucester. Seek out where thy father is, that he
20   may be ready for our apprehension.

EDM: (*aside*) If I find him comforting the King, it
will stuff his suspicion more fully.—I will persevere in my course of loyalty, though the conflict
be sore between that and my blood.

CORN: I will lay trust upon thee, and thou shalt
find a dearer father in my love.

(*Exeunt.*)

192 *Child* candidate for knighthood
4 *something fears* somewhat concerns
7 *his* (Gloucester's)
8 *merit* desert (in Gloucester) *reprovable* blameworthy
12 *approves* proves *intelligent party* person giving information
20 *apprehension* arrest
24 *blood* kinship

SCENE VI

Enter KENT *and* GLOUCESTER.

GLOU: Here is better than the open air; take it
thankfully. I will piece out the comfort with what
addition I can; I will not be long from you.

(*Exit* GLOUCESTER.)

KENT: All the power of his wits have given way to
his impatience. The gods reward your kindness!

Enter LEAR, EDGAR, *and* FOOL.

EDG: Fraterretto calls me, and tells me Nero is an
angler in the lake of darkness. Pray, innocent,
and beware the foul fiend.

FOOL: Prithee, nuncle, tell me whether a madman
be a gentleman or a yeoman.   10

LEAR: A king, a king!

FOOL: No, he's a yeoman that has a gentleman to
his son, for he's a mad yeoman that sees his son a
gentleman before him.

LEAR: To have a thousand with red burning spits
Come hizzing in upon 'em—

EDG: The foul fiend bites my back.

FOOL: He's mad that trusts in the tameness of a
wolf, a horse's health, a boy's love, or a whore's
oath.   20

LEAR: It shall be done; I will arraign them straight.
(*To* EDGAR) Come sit thou here, most learned
justicer.
(*To the* FOOL) Thou, sapient sir, sit here. Now,
you she-foxes!

EDG: Look, where he stands and glares! Want'st
thou eyes at trial, madam?

Come o'er the bourn, Bessy, to me.

FOOL: Her boat hath a leak
And she must not speak
Why she dares not come over to thee.

EDG: The foul fiend haunts poor Tom in the voice   30
of a nightingale. Hopdance cries in Tom's belly

2 *piece out* add to
5 *impatience* inability to suffer further
7 *innocent* fool
16 *hizzing* hissing
21 *arraign* bring to trial *straight* at once
26 *bourn* brook

for two white herring. Croak not, black angel; I
have no food for thee.

KENT: How do you, sir? Stand you not so amazed.
Will you lie down and rest upon the cushions?

LEAR: I'll see their trial first; bring in their evidence.

(*To* EDGAR) Thou, robed man of justice, take thy
place.

(*To the* FOOL) And thou, his yokefellow of equity,
Bench by his side. (*To* KENT) You are o'th' commission,

40   Sit you too.

EDG: Let us deal justly.

     Sleepest or wakest thou, jolly shepherd?
       Thy sheep be in the corn;
     And for one blast of thy minikin mouth
       Thy sheep shall take no harm.

     Purr! the cat is gray.

LEAR: Arraign her first; 'tis Goneril. I here take my
oath before this honourable assembly, she kicked
the poor King her father.

50 FOOL: Come hither, mistress; is your name Goneril?

LEAR: She cannot deny it.

FOOL: Cry you mercy, I took you for a joint-stool.

LEAR: And here's another whose warped looks
proclaim
What store her heart is made on. Stop her there!
Arms, arms! sword! fire! Corruption in the
place!
False justicer, why has thou let her scape?

EDG: Bless thy five wits!

KENT: O pity, sir, where is the patience now
60   That you so oft have boasted to retain?

EDG: (*aside*) My tears begin to take his part so much
They mar my counterfeiting.

LEAR: The little dogs and all,
Tray, Blanch, and Sweetheart, see, they bark at
me.

EDG: Tom will throw his head at them. Avaunt,
you curs!

     Be thy mouth or black or white,
     Tooth that poisons if it bite;
     Mastiff, greyhound, mongrel grim,
     Hound or spaniel, brach or lym,   70
     Bobtail tyke or trundle-tail—
     Tom will make them weep and wail;
     For, with throwing thus my head,
     Dogs leap the hatch, and all are fled.

     Do, de, de, de. Sessa! Come, march to wakes and
fairs and market towns. Poor Tom, thy horn is
dry.

LEAR: Then let them anatomize Regan, see what
breeds about her heart. Is there any cause in
nature that makes these hard hearts? (*To* EDGAR)   80
You, sir, I entertain for one of my hundred; only
I do not like the fashion of your garments. You'll
say they are Persian; but let them be changed.

KENT: Now, good my lord, lie here and rest
awhile.

LEAR: Make no noise, make no noise; draw the curtains.
So, so, we'll go to supper i'th' morning.

FOOL: And I'll to bed at noon.

            Enter GLOUCESTER.

GLOU: Come hither, friend; where is the King my
master?

KENT: Here, sir, but trouble him not; his wits are   90
gone.

GLOU: Good friend, I prithee take him in thy arms;
I have o'erheard a plot of death upon him;
There is a litter ready; lay him in't
And drive toward Dover, friend, where thou
shalt meet
Both welcome and protection. Take up thy
master.
If thou shouldst dally half an hour, his life,
With thine, and all that offer to defend him,
Stand in assuréd loss. Take up, take up,

32 *white* fresh, unsmoked
39 *Bench* be seated *commission* group charged with the
execution of justice
44 *minikin* shrill
53 *Cry you mercy* I beg your pardon
54 *warped* distorted
55 *store* materials

70 *brach* bitch hound *lym* bloodhound
71 *tyke or trundle-tail* (common breeds of dogs)
78 *anatomize* dissect
79 *about* around
98 *Stand in assuréd loss* will certainly be lost

And follow me, that will to some provision
100   Give thee quick conduct.
KENT: Oppresséd nature sleeps;
    This rest might yet have balmed thy broken
        senses,
    Which, if convenience will not allow,
    Stand in hard cure. (*To the* FOOL) Come, help to
        bear thy master;
    Thou must not stay behind.
GLOU: Come, come, away!

    (*Exeunt all but* EDGAR.)
EDG: When we our betters see bearing our woes
    We scarcely think our miseries our foes.
    Who alone suffers suffers most i'th' mind,
110   Leaving free things and happy shows behind;
    But then the mind much sufferance doth o'erskip
    When grief hath mates, and bearing fellowship.
    How light and portable my pain seems now,
    When that which makes me bend makes the King
        bow.
    He childed as I fathered! Tom, away!
    Mark the high noises, and thyself bewray
    When false opinion, whose wrong thought de-
        files thee,
    In thy just proof repeals and reconciles thee.
    What will hap more to-night, safe scape the
        King!
120   Lurk, lurk.

    (*Exit*.)

SCENE VII

Enter CORNWALL, REGAN, GONERIL, (EDMUND
the) Bastard, *and* SERVANTS.

CORN: (*to* GONERIL) Post speedily to my lord your
    husband; show him this letter; the army of
    France is landed.—Seek out the traitor Glou-
    cester.

    (*Exeunt some of the* SERVANTS.)
REG: Hang him instantly.
GON: Pluck out his eyes.

CORN: Leave him to my displeasure. Edmund,
    keep you our sister company. The revenges we
    are bound to take upon your traitorous father are
    not fit for your beholding. Advise the Duke   10
    where you are going, to a more festinate prepara-
    tion; we are bound to the like. Our posts shall be
    swift and intelligent betwixt us. Farewell, dear
    sister; farewell, my Lord of Gloucester.

    Enter (OSWALD *the*) *Steward.*

    How now? Where's the King?
OSW: My Lord of Gloucester hath conveyed him
        hence.
    Some five or six and thirty of his knights,
    Hot questrists after him, met him at gate,
    Who, with some other of the lord's dependants,
    Are gone with him toward Dover, where they   20
        boast
    To have well-arméd friends.
CORN: Get horses for your mistress.
GON: Farewell, sweet lord, and sister.
CORN: Edmund, farewell.

    (*Exeunt* GONERIL, EDMUND, *and* OSWALD.)
    Go seek the traitor Gloucester,
    Pinion him like a thief, bring him before us.

    (*Exeunt other* SERVANTS.)
    Though well we may not pass upon his life
    Without the form of justice, yet our power
    Shall do a courtesy to our wrath, which men
    May blame, but not control.   30

    Enter GLOUCESTER, *brought in by two or three.*

    Who's there? the traitor?
REG: Ingrateful fox! 'tis he.
CORN: Bind fast his corky arms.
GLOU: What mean your Graces? Good my
        friends, consider
    You are my guests. Do me no foul play, friends.
CORN: Bind him, I say.

    (SERVANTS *bind him*.)
REG: Hard, hard. O filthy traitor!
GLOU: Unmerciful lady as you are, I'm none.

---

99 *provision* means of providing
100 *Give thee quick conduct* conduct you quickly
102 *balmed* healed
104 *Stand in hard cure* will be difficult to cure
111 *sufferance* suffering
112 *bearing* endurance
116 *high noises* discord among the great *bewray* reveal

11 *festinate* speedy
12 *bound* hastening *posts* messengers
13 *intelligent* communicative
18 *questrists* seekers
27 *pass upon* pass judgment upon
29 *do a courtesy to* put into effect
32 *corky* withered

CORN: To this chair bind him. Villain, thou shalt
find—

(REGAN *plucks his beard*.)

40 GLOU: By the kind gods, 'tis most ignobly done
To pluck me by the beard.

REG: So white, and such a traitor!

GLOU: Naughty lady,
These hairs which thou dost ravish from my chin
Will quicken, and accuse thee. I am your host.
With robber's hands my hospitable favours
You should not ruffle thus. What will you do?

CORN: Come, sir, what letters had you late from
France?

REG: Be simple-answered, for we know the truth.

50 CORN: And what confederacy have you with the
traitors
Late footed in the kingdom?

REG: To whose hands you have sent the lunatic
King:
Speak.

GLOU: I have a letter guessingly set down,
Which came from one that's of a neutral heart,
And not from one opposed.

CORN: Cunning.

REG: And false.

60 CORN: Where hast thou sent the King?

GLOU: To Dover.

REG: Wherefore to Dover? Wast thou not
charged at peril—

CORN: Wherefore to Dover? Let him first answer
that.

GLOU: I am tied to th' stake, and I must stand the
course.

REG: Wherefore to Dover, sir?

GLOU: Because I would not see thy cruel nails
Pluck out his poor old eyes; nor thy fierce sister
In his anointed flesh stick boarish fangs.
The sea, with such a storm as his bare head
70 In hell-black night endured, would have buoyed
up
And quenched the stellèd fires.

Yet, poor old heart, he holp the heavens to rain.
If wolves had at thy gate howled that stern time,
Thou shouldst have said, 'Good porter, turn the
key,
All cruels else subscribe.' But I shall see
The wingèd vengeance overtake such children.

CORN: See't shalt thou never. Fellows, hold the
chair.
Upon these eyes of thine I'll set my foot.

GLOU: He that will think to live till he be old,
Give me some help!—O cruel! O you gods!   80

REG: One side will mock another. Th' other too!

CORN: If you see vengeance—

I. SERV: Hold your hand, my lord!
I have served you ever since I was a child;
But better service have I never done you
Than now to bid you hold.

REG: How now, you dog?

I. SERV: If you did wear a beard upon your chin,
I'd shake it on this quarrel.

REG: What do you mean?   90

CORN: My villain!   (*Draw and fight*.)

I.SERV: Nay, then, come on, and take the chance
of anger.

REG: Give me thy sword. A peasant stand up thus?
(*She takes a sword and runs at him behind*.)

I. SERV: O, I am slain! My lord, you have one eye
left
To see some mischief on him. O!   (*He dies*.)

CORN: Lest it see more, prevent it. Out, vile jelly!
Where is thy lustre now?

GLOU: All dark and comfortless! Where's my son
Edmund?
Edmund, enkindle all the sparks of nature
To quit this horrid act.   100

REG: Out, treacherous villain!
Thou call'st on him that hates thee. It was he
That made the overture of thy treasons to us,
Who is too good to pity thee.

GLOU: O my follies! Then Edgar was abused.
Kind gods, forgive me that, and prosper him!

43 *Naughty* wicked
45 *quicken* come to life
47 *ruffle* violate
50 *confederacy* alliance
51 *footed* landed
64 *tied to th' stake* (like a bear at bear-baiting) *stand the course*
endure the onset (of the attacking dogs)
70 *buoyed* surged
71 *stellèd fires* stars

72 *holp* helped
74 *turn the key* open the door
75 *All cruels else subscribe* all other cruel creatures consent
to lay aside their cruelty
95 *some mischief on* some harm done on
99 *nature* filial duty
100 *quit* avenge
103 *made the overture of* revealed

REG: Go thrust him out at gates, and let him smell
His way to Dover.

(*Exit one with* GLOUCESTER.)

How is't, my lord? How look you?

110 CORN: I have received a hurt; follow me, lady.
Turn out that eyeless villain; throw this slave
Upon the dunghill. Regan, I bleed apace;
Untimely comes this hurt. Give me your arm.

(*Exit* CORNWALL, *led by* REGAN.)

2. SERV: I'll never care what wickedness I do,
If this man comes to good.

3. SERV: If she live long,

And in the end meet the old course of death,
Women will all turn monsters.

2. SERV: Let's follow the old Earl, and get the bedlam

To lead him where he would. His roguish madness

Allows itself to anything. 120

3. SERV: Go thou. I'll fetch some flax and whites of
eggs

To apply to his bleeding face. Now heaven help
him!

(*Exeunt*.)

117 *old* normal
124 *Allows* adapts

113 *Untimely* at an unfortunate time

ACT IV

SCENE I

Enter EDGAR.

EDG: Yet better thus, and known to be contemned,
Than still contemned and flattered. To be worst,
The lowest and most dejected thing of fortune,
Stands still in esperance, lives not in fear.
The lamentable change is from the best;
The worst returns to laughter. Welcome then,
Thou unsubstantial air that I embrace!
The wretch that thou hast blown unto the worst
Owes nothing to thy blasts.

Enter GLOUCESTER, *led by an* OLD MAN.

10 But who comes here?
My father, poorly led? World, world, O world!
But that thy strange mutations make us hate thee,
Life would not yield to age.

OLD MAN: O my good lord,
I have been your tenant, and your father's tenant,
These fourscore years.

1 *contemned* despised
3 *dejected* cast down
4 *still* always *esperance* hope
6 *laughter* mirth, happiness
13 *Life . . . age* i.e., men would not grow old and die

GLOU: Away, get theee away. Good friend, be
gone;
Thy comforts can do me no good at all;
Thee they may hurt.

OLD MAN: You cannot see your way. 20

GLOU: I have no way, and therefore want no
eyes;
I stumbled when I saw. Full oft 'tis seen
Our means secure us, and our mere defects
Prove our commodities. Oh dear son Edgar,
The food of thy abused father's wrath,
Might I but live to see thee in my touch,
I'd say I had eyes again.

OLD MAN: How now? Who's there?

EDG: (*aside*) O gods! Who is't can say 'I am at the
worst'?
I am worse than e'er I was. 30

OLD MAN: 'Tis poor mad Tom.

EDG: (*aside*) And worse I may be yet. The worst is
not
So long as we can say 'This is the worst.'

OLD MAN: Fellow, where goest?

GLOU: Is it a beggarman?

23 *secure* make careless *mere* absolute
24 *commodities* advantages
25 *food* object

OLD MAN: Madman and beggar too.

GLOU: He has some reason, else he could not beg.
   I'th' last night's storm I such a fellow saw,
   Which made me think a man a worm. My son
40   Came then into my mind, and yet my mind
   Was then scarce friends with him. I have heard
      more since.
   As flies to wanton boys are we to th' gods.
   They kill us for their sport.

EDG: (aside) How should this be?
   Bad is the trade that must play fool to sorrow,
   Angering itself and others.—Bless thee, master!

GLOU: Is that the naked fellow?

OLD MAN: Ay, my lord.

GLOU: Get thee away. If for my sake
50   Thou wilt o'ertake us hence a mile or twain
   I'th' way toward Dover, do it for ancient love,
   And bring some covering for this naked soul,
   Who I'll entreat to lead me.

OLD MAN: Alack, sir, he is mad!

GLOU: 'Tis the time's plague when madmen lead
      the blind.
   Do as I bid thee, or rather do thy pleasure.
   Above the rest, be gone.

OLD MAN: I'll bring him the best 'parel that I have,
   Come on't what will.   (Exit.)

60   GLOU: Sirrah naked fellow—

EDG: Poor Tom's acold. (Aside) I cannot daub it
   further.

GLOU: Come hither, fellow.

EDG: (aside) And yet I must.—Bless thy sweet eyes,
   they bleed.

GLOU: Know'st thou the way to Dover?

EDG: Both stile and gate, horseway and footpath.
   Poor Tom hath been scared out of his good wits.
   Bless thee, good man's son, from the foul fiend!
70   Five fiends have been in poor Tom at once: of
   lust, as Obidicut; Hobbididence, prince of
   dumbness; Mahu, of stealing; Modo, of murder;
   Flibbertigibbet, of mopping and mowing, who
   since possesses chambermaids and waiting wom-
   en. So, bless theee, master!

GLOU: Here, take this purse, thou whom the heavens' plagues
   Have humbled to all strokes; that I am wretched

Makes thee the happier. Heavens deal so still!
Let the superfluous and lust-dieted man,
That slaves your ordinance, that will not see   80
Because he does not feel, feel your power quick-
   ly;
So distribution should undo excess,
And each man have enough. Dost thou know
   Dover?

EDG: Ay, master.

GLOU: There is a cliff, whose high and bending
   head
   Looks fearfully in the confinéd deep.
   Bring me but to the very brim of it,
   And I'll repair the misery thou dost bear
   With something rich about me. From that place
   I shall no leading need.   90

EDG: Give me thy arm;
   Poor Tom shall lead thee.

               (Exeunt.)

SCENE II

Enter GONERIL *and* (EDMUND *the*) *Bastard.*

GON: Welcome, my lord. I marvel our mild husband
   Not met us on the way.

Enter (OSWALD *the*) *Steward.*

Now, where's your master?

OSW: Madam, within, but never man so changed.
   I told him of the army that was landed:
   He smiled at it. I told him you were coming;
   His answer was, 'The worse.' Of Gloucester's
      treachery
   And of the loyal service of his son
   When I informed him, then he called me sot
   And told me I had turned the wrong side out.   10
   What most he should dislike seems pleasant to
      him;
   What like, offsensive.

45 *play fool to* jest with
61 *daub it* dissemble
73 *mopping and mowing* grimacing and making faces
77 *strokes* (of misfortune)

79 *superfluous* having more than he needs
80 *slaves* makes subservient (*and hence* ignores)
82 *undo* do away with
86 *confinéd* shut in by land

GON: (*to* EDMUND) Then shall you go no further.
    It is the cowish terror of his spirit
    That dares not undertake; he'll not feel wrongs
    Which tie him to an answer. Our wishes on the
      way
    May prove effects. Back, Edmund, to my broth-
      er;
    Hasten his musters and conduct his powers.
    I must change names at home and give the distaff
20   Into my husband's hands. This trusty servant
    Shall pass between us; ere long you are like to
      hear
    (If you dare venture in your own behalf)
    A mistress's command. Wear this;
                         (*Gives a favour.*)
    spare speech;
    Decline your head. This kiss, if it durst speak,
    Would stretch thy spirits up into the air.
    Conceive, and fare thee well.
EDM: Yours in the ranks of death!   (*Exit.*)
GON: My most dear Gloucester!
    O, the difference of man and man!
30   To thee a woman's services are due;
    My fool usurps my body.
OSW: Madam, here comes my lord.   (*Exit.*)

             Enter ALBANY.

GON: I have been worth the whistle.
ALB: O Goneril,
    You are not worth the dust which the rude wind
    Blows in your face; I fear your disposition.
    That nature which contemns it origin
    Cannot be bordered certain in itself;
    She that herself will sliver and disbranch

    From her material sap, perforce must wither   40
    And come to deadly use.
GON: No more! The text is foolish.
ALB: Wisdom and goodness to the vile seem vile;
    Filths savour but themselves. What have you
      done?
    Tigers, not daughters, what have you performed?
    A father, and a gracious agéd man,
    Whose reverence even the head-lugged bear
      would lick,
    Most barbarous, most degenerate, have you
      madded.
    Could my good brother suffer you to do it?
    A man, a prince, by him so benefited!   50
    If that the heavens do not their visible spirits
    Send quickly down to tame these vile offences,
    It will come,
    Humanity must perforce prey on itself,
    Like monsters of the deep.
GON: Milk-livered man!
    That bearest a cheek for blows, a head for
      wrongs,
    Who has not in thy brows an eye discerning
    Thine honour from thy suffering; that not know-
      est
    Fools do those villains pity who are punished   60
    Ere they have done their mischief. Where's thy
      drum?
    France spreads his banners in our noiseless land,
    With pluméd helm thy state begins to threat,
    Whiles thou, a moral fool, sit'st still, and criest
    'Alack, why does he so?'
ALB: See thyself, devil!
    Proper deformity seems not in the fiend
    So horrid as in woman.
GON: O vain fool!

16 *tie him to an answer* demand retaliation from him
17 *prove effects* find fulfilment
18 *powers* forces
19 *distaff* staff used in spinning, and symbol of the woman's position in the home
21 *like* likely
23 *mistress's* lady-love's
26 *Conceive* understand
33 *I have been worth the whistle* i.e., you don't put yourself out much for me
37 *contemns* despises *it* its
38 *bordered certain in itself* contained within established limits
39 *sliver* sever
40 *material* forming part of its substance

41 *come to deadly use* turn to poison
42 *text* (of a sermon)
44 *savour* enjoy the taste of
47 *head-lugged* tugged along by the head
48 *madded* driven mad
52 *tame* check
53 *come* come to this, that
54 *Humanity* human kind
58 *discerning* capable of distinguishing
62 *France* the King of France *noiseless* unresisting
63 *threat* threaten
64 *moral* moralizing
67 *proper* appropriate

70 ALB: Thou changéd and self-covered thing, for shame
Bemonster not thy feature! Were't my fitness
To let these hands obey my blood,
They are apt enough to dislocate and tear
Thy flesh and bones. Howe'er thou art a fiend,
A woman's shape doth shield thee.
GON: Marry, your manhood mew!

Enter a GENTLEMAN.

ALB: What news?
GENT: O, my good lord, the Duke of Cornwall's dead,
Slain by his servant, going to put out
The other eye of Gloucester.
80 ALB: Gloucester's eyes?
GENT: A servant that he bred, thrilled with remorse,
Opposed against the act, bending his sword
To his great master, who thereat enraged,
Flew on him, and amongst them felled him dead;
But not without that harmful stroke which since
Hath plucked him after.
ALB: This shows you are above,
You justicers, that these our nether crimes
So speedily can venge! But O poor Gloucester!
90 Lost he his other eye?
GENT: Both, both, my lord.
This letter, madam, craves a speedy answer.
'Tis from your sister.
GON: *(aside)* One way I like this well;
But being widow, and my Gloucester with her,
May all the building in my fancy pluck
Upon my hateful life. Another way
The news is not so tart.—I'll read, and answer.
(Exit.)

70 *changed* i.e., into a fiend *self-covered* i.e., still the same in outward appearance
71 *bemonster* change into that of a monster *feature* appearance *my fitness* fitting for me
72 *blood* impulse
76 *Marry* tut *mew* restrain
81 *thrilled* pierced
82 *bending* turning
83 *To* towards
88 *justicers* judges *nether crimes* crimes down below
89 *venge* avenge
96 *building in fancy* structure built up in my imagination *pluck* pull down
97 *hateful* i.e., so that it will become hateful

ALB: Where was his son when they did take his eyes?
GENT: Come with my lady hither.
100 ALB: He is not here.
GENT: No, my good lord, I met him back again.
ALB: Knows he the wickedness?
GENT: Ay, my good lord; 'twas he informed against him,
And quit the house on purpose, that their punishment
Might have the freer course.
ALB: Gloucester, I live
To thank thee for the love thou showedst the King,
And to revenge thine eyes. Come hither, friend.
Tell me what more thou knowest.
(Exeunt.)

SCENE III

Enter KENT *and a* GENTLEMAN.

KENT: Why the King of France is so suddenly gone back—know you no reason?
GENT: Something he left imperfect in the state, which since his coming forth is thought of, which imports to the kingdom so much fear and danger that his personal return was most required and necessary.
KENT: Who hath he left behind him general?
GENT: The Marshall of France, Monsieur la Far.
10 KENT: Did your letters pierce the Queen to any demonstration of grief?
GENT: Ay, sir; she took them, read them in my presence,
And now and then an ample tear trilled down
Her delicate cheek. It seemed she was a queen
Over her passion, who, most rebel-like,
Sought to be king o'er her.
KENT: O, then it moved her?
GENT: Not to a rage; patience and sorrow strove
Who should express her goodliest. You have seen

102 *back* on the way back
11 *demonstration* display
13 *ample* overflowing *trilled* trickled
15 *passion* emotion
18 *rage* outburst
19 *express* reveal *goodliest* best, most beautifully

20 Sunshine and rain at once; her smiles and tears
Were like, a better way. Those happy smilets
That played on her ripe lip seemed not to know
What guests were in her eyes, which parted
thence
As pearls from diamonds dropped. In brief,
Sorrow would be a rarity most beloved,
If all could so become it.
KENT: Made she no verbal question?
GENT: Faith, once or twice she heaved the name of
father
Pantingly forth, as if it pressed her heart,
30 Cried 'Sisters, sisters! Shame of ladies! Sisters!
Kent! father! sisters! What, i'th' storm? i'th'
night?
Let pity not be believed!' There she shook
The holy water from her heavenly eyes,
And clamour moistened. Then away she started
To deal with grief alone.
KENT: It is the stars,
The stars above us, govern our conditions,
Else one self mate and mate could not beget
Such different issues. You spoke not with her
since?
40 GENT: No.
KENT: Was this before the King returned?
GENT: No, since.
KENT: Well, sir, the poor distresséd Lear's i'th'
town,
Who sometime, in his better tune, remembers
What we are come about, and by no means
Will yield to see his daughter.
GENT: Why, good sir?
KENT: A sovereign shame so elbows him; his own
unkindness,
That stripped her from his benediction, turned
her
50 To foreign casualties, gave her dear rights
To his dog-hearted daughters—these things
sting

His mind so venomously that burning shame
Detains him from Cordelia.
GENT: Alack, poor gentleman!
KENT: Of Albany's and Cornwall's powers you
heard not?
GENT: 'Tis so; they are afoot.
KENT: Well, sir, I'll bring you to our master Lear
And leave you to attend him. Some dear cause
Will in concealment wrap me up awhile.
When I am known aright, you shall not grieve   60
Lending me this acquaintance. I pray you go
Along with me.   (Exeunt.)

SCENE IV

Enter, with Drum and Colours, CORDELIA, DOCTOR,
and Soldiers.

COR: Alack, 'tis he! Why, he was met even now
As mad as the vexed sea, singing aloud,
Crowned with rank fumiter and furrow weeds,
With hardocks, hemlock, nettles, cuckoo flow-
ers,
Darnel, and all the idle weeds that grow
In our sustaining corn. A century send forth;
Search every acre in the high-grown field
And bring him to our eye. (*Exit an Officer*.) What
can man's wisdom
In the restoring his bereavéd sense?
He that helps him take all my outward worth.   10
DOCT: There is means, madam.
Our foster nurse of nature is repose,
The which he lacks. That to provoke in him
Are many simples operative, whose power
Will close the eye of anguish.
COR: All blest secrets,
All you unpublished virtues of the earth,
Spring with my tears; be aidant and remediate
In the good man's distress! Seek, seek for him!

21 *a better way* but after a better fashion
26 *become it* grace it, make it appear handsome
32 *believed* believed in
34 *clamour* her exclamations *moistened* turned into weeping
37 *conditions* characters
38 *one self mate and mate* the same two parents
44 *sometime* occasionally *better tune* moments of sanity
48 *sovereign* overruling *elbows* haunts
50 *casualties* risks

55 *powers* armies
58 *dear* important
61 *Lending* giving
3-4 *fumiter . . . hardocks . . .* cuckoo-flowers
5 *Darnel* varieties of weeds and wild flowers
6 *century* company, or troop, of soldiers
8 *can* can do
10 *worth* possessions
14 *simples* drugs
17 *virtues* efficacies

20   Lest his ungoverned rage dissolve the life
      That wants the means to lead it.

Enter MESSENGER.

MESS: News, madam.
      The British powers are marching hitherward.
COR: 'Tis known before. Our preparation stands
      In expectation of them. O dear father,
      It is thy business that I go about.
      Therefore great France
      My mourning and importuned tears hath pitied.
      No blown ambition doth our arms incite,
30   But love, dear love, and our aged father's right.
      Soon may I hear and see him!

(Exeunt.)

SCENE V

Enter REGAN *and* (OSWALD *the*) *Steward.*

REG: But are my brother's powers set forth?
OSW: Ay, madam.
REG: Himself in person there?
OSW: Madam, with much ado.
      Your sister is the better soldier.
REG: Lord Edmund spake not with your lord at
      home?
OSW: No, madam.
REG: What might import my sister's letter to him?
OSW: I know not, lady.
10   REG: Faith, he is posted hence on serious matter.
      It was great ignorance, Gloucester's eyes being
      out,
      To let him live; where he arrives he moves
      All hearts against us. Edmund, I think, is gone,
      In pity of his misery, to dispatch
      His nighted life; moreover, to descry
      The strength o'th' enemy.
OSW: I must needs after him, madam, with my let-
      ter.
REG: Our troops set forth to-morrow. Stay with
      us;

21 *means* i.e., reason
23 *powers* forces
29 *blown* swelling
4 *with much ado* with some difficulty
10 *is posted* has ridden hurriedly
11 *ignorance* miscalculation
15 *nighted* darkened (by blindness)

      The ways are dangerous.
OSW: I may not, madam.   20
      My lady charged my duty in this business.
REG: Why should she write to Edmund? Might not
      you
      Transport her purposes by word? Belike,
      Something—I know not what—I'll love thee
      much—
      Let me unseal the letter.
OSW: Madam, I had rather—
REG: I know your lady does not love her husband;
      I am sure of that; and at her late being here
      She gave the strange eliads and most speaking looks
      To noble Edmund. I know you are of her bosom.   30
OSW: I, madam?
REG: I speak in understanding. Y'are; I know't,
      Therefore I do advise you take this note.
      My lord is dead; Edmund and I have talked,
      And more convenient is he for my hand
      Than for your lady's. You may gather more.
      If you do find him, pray you give him this;
      And when your mistress hears thus much from
      you,
      I pray desire her call her wisdom to her.
      So fare you well.   40
      If you do chance to hear of that blind traitor,
      Preferment falls on him that cuts him off.
OSW: Would I could meet him, madam; I should
      show
      What party I do follow.
REG: Fare thee well.   *(Exeunt.)*

SCENE VI

Enter GLOUCESTER, *and* EDGAR (*like a Peasant*).

GLOU: When shall I come to the top of that same
      hill?

21 *charged* entrusted *in* with
23 *Transport* communicate *Belike* probably
29 *eliads* oglings
32 *speak in understanding* know what I am talking about
33 *take this note* take heed of this
35 *convenient* suitable
36 *gather* guess
39 *call her wisdom to her* come to her senses and behave
with discretion
42 *Preferment* promotion *cuts him off* ends his life
44 *What party I do follow* whose side I am on

EDG: You do climb up it now. Look how we la-
    bour.

GLOU: Methinks the ground is even.

EDG: Horrible steep.
    Hark, do you hear the sea?

GLOU: No, truly.

EDG: Why, then, your other senses grow imperfect
    By your eyes' anguish.

GLOU: So may it be indeed.
10 Methinks thy voice is altered, and thou speakest
    In better phrase and matter than thou didst.

EDG: Y'are much deceived. In nothing am I
    changed
    But in my garments.

GLOU: Methinks y'are better spoken.

EDG: Come on, sir, here's the place; stand still.
    How fearful
    And dizzy 'tis to cast one's eyes so low!
    The crows and choughs that wing the midway air
    Show scarce so gross as beetles. Halfway down
    Hangs one that gathers sampire—dreadful trade!
20 Methinks he seems no bigger than his head.
    The fishermen that walk upon the beach
    Appear like mice; and yond tall anchoring bark,
    Diminished to her cock; her cock, a buoy
    Almost too small for sight. The murmuring
    surge
    That on th'unnumbered idle pebble chafes
    Cannot be heard so high. I'll look no more,
    Lest my brain turn, and the deficient sight
    Topple down headlong.

GLOU: Set me where you stand.
30 EDG: Give me your hand. You are now within a
    foot
    Of th'extreme verge. For all beneath the moon
    Would I not leap upright.

GLOU: Let go my hand.
    Here, friend, 's another purse; in it a jewel
    Well worth a poor man's taking. Fairies and gods
    Prosper it with thee! Go thou further off;
    Bid me farewell, and let me hear thee going.

EDG: Now fare ye well, good sir.

GLOU: With all my heart.

EDG: (aside) Why I do trifle thus with his despair   40
    Is done to cure it.

GLOU: O you mighty gods!   (He kneels.)
    This world I do renounce, and, in your sights,
    Shake patiently my great affliction off.
    If I could bear it longer and not fall
    To quarrel with your great opposeless wills,
    My snuff and loathéd part of nature should
    Burn itself out. If Edgar live, O, bless him!
    Now, fellow, fare thee well.   (He falls.)

EDG: Gone, sir, farewell.—   50
    And yet I know not how conceit may rob
    The treasury of life when life itself
    Yields to the theft. Had he been where he
    thought,
    By this had thought been past.—Alive or dead?
    Ho you, sir! friend! Hear you, sir? Speak!—
    Thus might he pass indeed; yet he revives.
    What are you, sir?

GLOU: Away, and let me die.

EDG: Hadst thou been aught but gossamer, feath-
    ers, air,
    So many fathom down precipitating,   60
    Thou'dst shivered like an egg; but thou dost
    breathe,
    Hast heavy substance, bleed'st not, speak'st, art
    sound;
    Ten masts at each make not the altitude
    Which thou has perpendicularly fell;
    Thy life's a miracle. Speak yet again.

GLOU: But have I fallen, or no?

EDG: From the dread summit of this chalky bourn.
    Look up a-height; the shrill-gorged lark so far
    Cannot be seen or heard. Do but look up.

GLOU: Alack, I have no eyes.   70
    Is wretchedness deprived that benefit
    To end itself by death? 'Twas yet some comfort
    When misery could beguile the tyrant's rage
    And frustrate his proud will.

8 *anguish* pain
17 *choughs* jackdaws
19 *sampire* samphire, an aromatic plant that grows on the
face of cliffs
23 *cock* cockboat, dinghy
27 *the deficient sight, Topple* my sight, failing me (through
dizziness) cause me to topple
31 *verge* edge

46 *opposeless* irresistible
47 *snuff* burnt-out wick
51 *conceit* imagination
53 *Yields to the theft* is willing to be destroyed
54 *had thought been past* i.e., he would have been dead
63 *at each* one on top of the other
67 *bourn* brink
68 *a-height* on high *shrill-gorged* shrill throated
73 *beguile* elude

EDG: Give me your arm.
Up—so. How is't? Feel you your legs? You stand.

GLOU: Too well, too well.

EDG: This is above all strangeness.
Upon the crown o'th' cliff what thing was that
80 Which parted from you?

GLOU: A poor unfortunate beggar.

EDG: As I stood here below, methought his eyes
Were two full moons; he had a thousand noses,
Horns whelked and waved like the enridgéd sea;
It was some fiend. Therefore, thou happy father,
Think that the clearest gods, who make them honours
Of men's impossibilities, have preserved thee.

GLOU: I do remember now. Henceforth I'll bear
Affliction till it do cry out itself
90 'Enough, enough,' and die. That thing you speak of,
I took it for a man. Often 'twould say
'The fiend, the fiend'—he led me to that place.

EDG: Bear free and patient thoughts.

Enter LEAR, *mad*.

But who comes here?
The safer sense will ne'er accommodate
His master thus.

LEAR: No, they cannot touch me for coining;
I am the King himself.

EDG: O thou side-piercing sight!

100 LEAR: Nature's above art in that respect. There's
your press money. That fellow handles his bow
like a crow-keeper. Draw me a clothier's yard.
Look, look, a mouse! Peace, peace, this piece of
toasted cheese will do't. There's my gauntlet; I'll
prove it on a giant. Bring up the brown bills. O,
well flown, bird! i'th' clout, i'th' clout! Hewgh!
Give the word.

84 *whelked* curled, twisted
85 *father* old man
86 *who make them honours Of men's impossibilities* who win honour for themselves by deeds impossible to men
95 *safer sense* sound mind *accomodate* deck, clothe
96 *master* possessor
101 *press money* small sum paid in advance to recruits
102 *crow-keeper* boy to scare away crows
103 *clothier's yard* the standard length of an arrow
105 *on* against *bills* pikes
106 *i'th' clout* a bull's eye
107 *word* password

EDG: Sweet marjoram.

LEAR: Pass.

GLOU: I know that voice. 110

LEAR: Ha! Goneril with a white beard? They flattered me like a dog, and told me I had white hairs in my beard ere the black ones were there. To say 'ay' and 'no' to everything I said! 'Ay' and 'no' too was no good divinity. When the rain came to wet me once, and the wind to make me chatter, when the thunder would not peace at my bidding, there I found 'em, there I smelt 'em out. Go to, they are not men o' their words; they told me I was everything. 'Tis a lie—I am not ague-proof. 120

GLOU: The trick of that voice I do well remember.
Is't not the King?

LEAR: Ay, every inch a king!
When I do stare, see how the subject quakes.
I pardon that man's life. What was thy cause?
Adultery?
Thou shalt not die. Die for adultery? No.
The wren goes to't, and the small gilded fly
Does lecher in my sight.
Let copulation thrive; for Gloucester's bastard 130
son
Was kinder to his father than my daughters
Got 'tween the lawful sheets.
To't, luxury, pell-mell! for I lack soldiers.
Behold yond simpering dame,
Whose face between her forks presages snow,
That minces virtue, and does shake the head
To hear of pleasure's name.
The fitchew nor the soiléd horse goes to't
With a more riotous appetite.
Down from the waist they are Centaurs, 140
Though women all above.
But to the girdle do the gods inherit,
Beneath is all the fiend's.
There's hell, there's darkness, there is the sulphurous pit; burning, scalding, stench, consumption. Fie, fie, fie! pah, pah! Give me an ounce of civet, good apothecary, to sweeten my imagination. There's money for thee.

114 *'Ay' and 'no' too was no good divinity* i.e., flattery is false religion
134 *luxury* lust
135 *between . . . snow* suggests sexual frigidity
136 *minces* affects
138 *fitchew* polecat *soiléd* overfed on green grass
142 *But* only *inherit* enjoy possession
147 *civet* a perfume

GLOU: O, let me kiss that hand!

150   LEAR: Let me wipe it first; it smells of mortality.

GLOU: O ruined piece of nature, this great world
Shall so wear out to naught. Dost thou know me?

LEAR: I remember thine eyes well enough. Dost
thou squiny at me? No, do thy worst, blind
Cupid! I'll not love. Read thou this challenge;
mark but the penning of it.

GLOU: Were all the letters suns, I could not see.

EDG: (aside) I would not take this from report. It is,
And my heart breaks at it.

160   LEAR: Read.

GLOU: What, with the case of eyes?

LEAR: O, ho, are you there with me? No eyes in
your head, nor no money in your purse? Your
eyes are in a heavy case, your purse in a light. Yet
you see how this world goes.

GLOU: I see it feelingly.

LEAR: What, art mad? A man may see how this
world goes with no eyes. Look with thine ears.
See how yond justice rails upon yond simple
thief. Hark in thine ear; change places and,
handy-dandy, which is the justice, which is the

170   thief? Thou hast seen a farmer's dog bark at a
beggar?

GLOU: Ay, sir.

LEAR: And the creature run from the cur? There
thou mightst behold the great image of authority:
a dog's obeyed in office.

Thou rascal beadle, hold thy bloody hand!
Why dost thou lash that whore? Strip thine own
back.

180   Thou hotly lusts to use her in that kind
For which thou whip'st her. The usurer hangs
the cozener.
Through tattered clothes great vices do appear;
Robes and furred gowns hide all. Plate sins with
gold,
And the strong lance of justice hurtless breaks;
Arm it in rags, a pygmy's straw does pierce it.

None does offend, none—I say none! I'll able
'em.
Take that of me, my friend, who have the power
To seal th' accuser's lips. Get thee glass eyes
And, like a scurvy politician, seem
To see the things thou dost not. Now, now, now,   190
now!
Pull off my boots. Harder, harder! So.

EDG: O, matter and impertinency mixed,
Reason in madness!

LEAR: If thou wilt weep my fortunes, take my
eyes.
I know thee well enough; thy name is Gloucester.
Thou must be patient. We came crying hither;
Thou knowest, the first time that we smell the air
We wawl and cry. I will preach to thee. Mark.

GLOU: Alack, alack the day!

LEAR: When we are born, we cry that we are come   200
To this great stage of fools. This' a good block.
It were a delicate stratagem to shoe
A troop of horse with felt. I'll put't in proof,
And when I have stolen upon these sons-in-law,
Then kill, kill, kill, kill, kill, kill!

Enter a GENTLEMAN (with Attendants).

GENT: O, here he is! Lay hand upon him.—Sir,
Your most dear daughter—

LEAR: No rescue? What, a prisoner? I am even
The natural fool of fortune. Use me well;
You shall have ransom. Let me have a surgeon;   210
I am cut to th' brains.

GENT: You shall have anything.

LEAR: No seconds? All myself?
Why, this would make a man a man of salt,
To use his eyes for garden waterpots,
Ay, and laying autumn's dust.

GENT: Good sir—

LEAR: I will die bravely, like a smug bridegroom.
What!
I will be jovial. Come, come, I am a king;
My masters, know you that?   220

154 *squiny* squint
158 *take this from report* believe this on anyone's word
161 *case* sockets
164 *case* situation
166 *feelingly* (1) with my sense of touch (2) with intensity
171 *handy-dandy* which hand will you have? (in the child's
guessing game) i.e. take your pick
180 *kind* fashion
181 *cozener* sharper

192 *impertinency* irrelevance
198 *wawl* wail
201 *This' a good block* this is a hat in good style
202 *delicate* ingenious
209 *The natural fool of fortune* one born to be the sport of
fortune
213 *No seconds?* no one to help me?
215 *waterpots* watering cans
218 *smug* spruce

GENT: You are a royal one, and we obey you.

LEAR: Then there's life in't. Come, an you get it,
you shall get it by running. Sa, sa, sa, sa!

(*Exit running*.)

GENT: A sight most pitiful in the meanest wretch,
Past speaking of in a king! Thou hast a daughter
Who redeems nature from the general curse
Which twain have brought her to.

EDG: Hail, gentle sir.

GENT: Sir, speed you. What's your will?

230 EDG: Do you hear aught, sir, of a battle toward?

GENT: Most sure and vulgar. Every one hears that
Which can distinguish sound.

EDG: But, by your favour,
How near's the other army?

GENT: Near and on speedy foot; the main descry
Stands on the hourly thought.

EDG: I thank you, sir, That's all.

GENT: Though that the Queen on special cause is
here,
Her army is moved on.

240 EDG: I thank you, sir.

(*Exit* GENTLEMAN.)

GLOU: You ever-gentle gods, take my breath from
me;
Let not my worser spirit tempt me again
To die before you please!

EDG: Well pray you, father.

GLOU: Now, good sir, what are you?

EDG: A most poor man, made tame to fortune's
blows,
Who, by the art of known and feeling sorrows,
Am pregnant to good pity. Give me your hand;
I'll lead you to some biding.

250 GLOU: Hearty thanks.
The bounty and the benison of heaven
To boot, and boot!

Enter (OSWALD *the*) *Steward.*

OSW: A proclaimed prize; most happy!
That eyeless head of thine was first framed flesh
To raise my fortunes. Thou old unhappy traitor,
Briefly thyself remember; the sword is out
That must destroy thee.

GLOU: Now let thy friendly hand
Put strength enough to't.

(EDGAR *interposes*.)   260

OSW: Wherefore, bold peasant,
Darest thou support a published traitor? Hence,
Lest that the infection of his fortune take
Like hold on thee. Let go his arm.

EDG: Chill not let go, zir, without vurther 'cagion.

OSW: Let go, slave, or thou diest!

EDG: Good gentleman, go your gait, and let poor
voke pass. An chud ha' bin zwaggered out of my
life, 'twould not ha' bin zo long as 'tis by a vort-
night. Nay, come not near the old man. Keep   270
out, che vore ye, or Ise try whether your costard
or my ballow be the harder. Chill be plain with
you.

OSW: Out, dunghill!   (*They fight*.)

EDG: Chill pick your teeth, zir. Come no matter
vor your foins.

(OSWALD *falls*.)

OSW: Slave, thou has slain me. Villain, take my
purse.
If ever thou wilt thrive, bury my body,
And give the letters which thou findest about me
To Edmund Earl of Gloucester. Seek him out
Upon the British party. O, untimely death!
Death!   (*He dies*.)   280

EDG: I know thee well. A serviceable villain,
As duteous to the vices of thy mistress
As badness would desire.

GLOU: What, is he dead?

---

223 *Sa Sa* (a hunting cry)

229 *speed you* God prosper you

230 *toward* in preparation

231 *vulgar* of common knowledge

235 *on speedy foot* advancing rapidly *the main descry* sight of
the main body

236 *Stands on the hourly thought* is expected any hour

246 *made tame* accustomed

247 *art* experience *feeling* heartfelt

248 *pregnant to* productive of

249 *biding* refuge

252 *To boot, and boot* reward you again and again

253 *proclaimed* (because of the proclamation against
Gloucester)

256 *remember* prepare for heaven

261 *published* proclaimed

264 *Chill* I will *'cagion* occasion

266 *gait* way

267 *chud* I would

270 *vore* warn

271 *costard* head

272 *ballow* cudgel

275 *foins* thrusts

EDG: Sit you down, father; rest you.
  Let's see his pockets; these letters that he speaks of
  May be my friends. He's dead; I am only sorry
  He had no other deathsman. Let us see.
290 Leave, gentle wax; and, manners, blame us not.
  To know our enemies' minds, we'ld rip their hearts;
  Their papers, is more lawful.
                              (*Reads the letter*.)

Let our reciprocal vows be remembered. You
have many opportunities to cut him off. If your
will want not, time and place will be fruitfully
offered. There is nothing done, if he return the
conqueror. Then am I the prisoner, and his bed
my jail, from the loathed warmth whereof deliver
me, and supply the place for your labour.
300   Your (wife, so I would say) affectionate servant,

                              GONERIL.

  O indistinguished space of woman's will!
  A plot upon her virtuous husband's life,
  And the exchange my brother! Here in the sands
  Thee I'll rake up, the post unsanctified
  Of murtherous lechers; and in the mature time
  With this ungracious paper strike the sight
  Of the death-practised Duke. For him 'tis well
  That of thy death and business I can tell.
310 GLOU: The King is mad. How stiff is my vile sense,
  That I stand up, and have ingenious feeling
  Of my huge sorrows! Better I were distract.
  So should my thoughts be severed from my griefs,
  And woes by wrong imaginations lose
  The knowledge of themselves.
                              (*A drum afar off*.)
EDG: Give me your hand.
  Far off methinks I hear the beaten drum.
  Come, father, I'll bestow you with a friend.
                              (*Exeunt*.)

289 *deathsman* executioner
302 *indistinguished* limitless *will* lust
305 *rake up* bury hastily *post* messenger
308 *death-practised* whose death has been plotted
310 *stiff* strong
311 *ingenious feeling* feeling and apprehension
312 *distract* insane

SCENE VII

Enter CORDELIA, KENT, DOCTOR, *and* GENTLEMAN.

COR: O thou good Kent, how shall I live and work
  To match thy goodness? My life will be too short
  And every measure fail me.
KENT: To be acknowledged, madam, is o'erpaid.
  All my reports go with the modest truth;
  Nor more nor clipped, but so.
COR: Be better suited;
  These weeds are memories of those worser hours.
  I prithee put them off.
KENT: Pardon, dear madam,   10
  Yet to be known shortens my made intent.
  My boon I make it that you know me not
  Till time and I think meet.
COR: Then be't so, my good lord. (*To the* DOCTOR.)
  How does the King?
DOCT: Madam, sleeps still.
COR: O you kind gods,
  Cure this great breach in this abused nature!
  The untuned and jarring senses, O, wind up
  Of this child-changed father!
DOCT: So please your Majesty   20
  That we may wake the King? He hath slept long.
COR: Be governed by your knowledge, and proceed
  I'th' sway of your own will. Is he arrayed?

Enter LEAR *in a chair carried by Servants*.

GENT: Ay, madam. In the heaviness of sleep
  We put fresh garments on him.
DOCT: Be by, good madam, when we do awake him.
  I doubt not of his temperance.
COR: Very well.
                              (*Music*.)
DOCT: Please you draw near. Louder the music there!

5 *modest* moderate
6 *clipped* diminished
7 *suited* clothed
8 *weeds* garments
11 *made intent* intended plan
13 *meet* fitting
18 *wind up* (in order to tune again)
19 *child-changed* changed into a child again
27 *temperance* self-control

30 COR: O my dear father, restoration hang
         Thy medicine on my lips, and let this kiss
         Repair those violent harms that my two sisters
         Have in thy reverence made!
    KENT: Kind and dear princess!
    COR: Had you not been their father, these white
         flakes
         Had challenged pity of them. Was this a face
         To be opposed against the jarring winds,
         To stand against the deep dread-bolted thunder
         In the most terrible and nimble stroke
40   Of quick cross lightning? to watch—poor
         perdu!—
         With this thin helm? Mine enemy's dog,
         Though he had bit me, should have stood that
         night
         Against my fire; and was thou fain, poor father,
         To hovel thee with swine and rogues forlorn,
         In short and musty straw? Alack, alack!
         'Tis wonder that thy life and wits at once
         Had not concluded all.—He wakes. Speak to
         him.
    DOCT: Madam, do you; 'tis fittest.
    COR: How does my royal lord? How fares your
         Majesty?
50 LEAR: You do me wrong to take me out o'th' grave.
         Thou art a soul in bliss; but I am bound
         Upon a wheel of fire, that mine own tears
         Do scald like molten lead.
    COR: Sir, do you know me?
    LEAR: You are a spirit, I know. When did you die?
    COR: Still, still, far wide!
    DOCT: He's scarce awake. Let him alone awhile.
    LEAR: Where have I been? Where am I? Fair day-
         light?
         I am mightily abused. I should e'en die with pity,
60   To see another thus. I know not what to say;
         I will not swear these are my hands. Let's see,
         I feel this pin prick. Would I were assured
         Of my condition!
    COR: O, look upon me, sir,
         And hold your hand in benediction o'er me.
         No, sir, you must not kneel.

    LEAR: Pray, do not mock me.
         I am a very foolish fond old man,
         Fourscore and upward, not an hour more nor
         less;
         And, to deal plainly,   70
         I fear I am not in my perfect mind.
         Methinks I should know you, and know this
         man,
         Yet I am doubtful, for I am mainly ignorant
         What place this is, and all the skill I have
         Remembers not these garments; nor I know not
         Where I did lodge last night. Do not laugh at me;
         For (as I am a man) I think this lady
         To be my child Cordelia.
    COR: And so I am; I am!
    LEAR: Be your tears wet? Yes, faith. I pray weep   80
         not.
         If you have poison for me, I will drink it.
         I know you do not love me, for your sisters
         Have, as I do remember, done me wrong.
         You have some cause, they have not.
    COR: No cause, no cause.
    LEAR: Am I in France?
    KENT: In your own kingdom, sir.
    LEAR: Do not abuse me.
    DOCT: Be comforted, good madam. The great rage
         You see is killed in him; and yet it is danger   90
         To make him even o'er the time he has lost.
         Desire him to go in. Trouble him no more
         Till further settling.
    COR: Will't please your Highness walk?
    LEAR: You must bear with me.
         Pray you now, forget and forgive. I am old and
         foolish.
              (*Exeunt. Manent* KENT *and* GENTLEMAN.)
    GENT: Holds it true, sir, that the Duke of Cornwall
         was so slain?
    KENT: Most certain, sir.
    GENT: Who is conductor of his people?   100
    KENT: As 'tis said, the bastard son of Gloucester.
    GENT: They say Edgar, his banished son, is with
         the Earl of Kent in Germany.

31 *medicine* remedy
36 *challenged* compelled
40 *perdu* sentinel in an advance position
59 *abused* deceived
68 *fond* foolish

73 *mainly* greatly
88 *abuse* deceive
89 *rage* madness
91 *even o'er* catch up with
93 *Till further settling* till his mind becomes clearer
100 *conductor* leader

KENT: Report is changeable. 'Tis time to look about; the powers of the kingdom approach apace.

GENT: The arbitrement is like to be bloody.

104 *Report* rumour
105 *powers* armies
106 *apace* rapidly
107 *arbitrement* decision

Fare you well, sir.   (*Exit*.)

KENT: My point and period will be throughly wrought,
Or well or ill, as this day's battle's fought.   110
(*Exit*.)

109 *My point and period* the conclusion of my actions *throughly wrought* fully worked out
110 *Or . . . or* either . . . or

ACT V

SCENE I

Enter, with Drum and Colours; EDMUND, REGAN, GENTLEMAN, *and Soldiers.*

EDM: Know of the Duke if his last purpose hold,
Or whether since he is advised by aught
To change the course. He's full of alteration
And self-reproving. Bring his constant pleasure.
(*Exit an Officer*.)

REG: Our sister's man is certainly miscarried.

EDM: Tis to be doubted, madam.

REG: Now, sweet lord,
You know the goodness I intend upon you.
Tell me—but truly—but then speak the truth—
10   Do you not love my sister?

EDM: In honoured love.

REG: But have you never found my brother's way
To the forfended place?

EDM: That thought abuses you.

REG: I am doubtful that you have been conjunct
And bosomed with her, as far as we call hers.

EDM: No, by mine honour, madam.

REG: I never shall endure her. Dear my lord,
Be not familiar with her.

20   EDM: Fear me not.

2 *advised* influenced
3 *course* line of action agreed upon
4 *constant pleasure* fixed determination
5 *miscarried* come to harm
13 *forfended* forbidden
14 *That thought abuses you* if you think that, you are wrong
15 *doubtful* suspicious *conjunct* united
16 *as far as we call hers* in the fullest sense of the term

She and the Duke her husband!

Enter, with Drum and Colours, ALBANY, GONERIL, *Soldiers.*

GON: (*aside*) I had rather lose the battle than that sister
Should loosen him and me.

ALB: Our very loving sister, well bemet.
Sir, this I hear: the King is come to his daughter,
With others whom the rigour of our state
Forced to cry out. Where I could not be honest,
I never yet was valiant. For this business,
It touches us as France invades our land,
Not bolds the King, with others whom, I fear,   30
Most just and heavy causes make oppose.

EDM: Sir, you speak nobly.

REG: Why is this reasoned?

GON: Combine together 'gainst the enemy;
For these domestic and particular broils
Are not the question here.

ALB: Let's then determine
With th'ancient of war on our proceeding.

24 *bemet* met
26 *state* rule
27 *cry out* complain
29 *touches* concerns
30 *bolds* supports
31 *make* cause to
33 *Why is this reasoned?* why do you have to justify your actions?
35 *particular* personal *broils* quarrels
38 *ancient of war* experienced officers *proceeding* course of action

EDM: I shall attend you presently at your tent.

40 REG: Sister, you'll go with us?

GON: No.

REG: 'Tis most convenient. Pray you go with us.

GON: *(aside)* O, ho, I know the riddle.—I will go.

*Exeunt (EDMUND, REGAN, GONERIL and) both the
Armies. (As they are going out,) enter EDGAR
(disguised).*

EDG: If e'er your Grace had speech with man so
    poor,
  Hear me one word.

ALB: I'll overtake you.—Speak.

EDG: Before you fight the battle, ope this letter.
  If you have victory, let the trumpet sound
  For him that brought it. Wretched though I
    seem,

50 I can produce a champion that will prove
  What is avouchéd there. If you miscarry,
  Your business of the world hath so an end,
  And machination ceases. Fortune love you!

ALB: Stay till I have read the letter.

EDG: I was forbid it.
  When time shall serve, let but the herald cry,
  And I'll appear again.

ALB: Why, fare thee well. I will o'erlook thy paper.
                       (Exit EDGAR.)

Enter EDMUND.

EDM: The enemy's in view; draw up your powers.

60 Here is the guess of their true strength and forces
  By diligent discovery; but your haste
  Is now urged on you.

ALB: We will greet the time.   *(Exit.)*

EDM: To both these sisters have I sworn my
    love;
  Each jealous of the other, as the stung
  Are of the adder. Which of them shall I take?
  Both? one? or neither? Neither can be enjoyed,
  If both remain alive. To take the widow
  Exasperates, makes mad her sister Goneril,

70 And hardly shall I carry out my side

39 *presently* immediately
43 *riddle* hidden meaning
51 *avouchéd* alleged *miscarry* come to harm
53 *machination* plotting
59 *powers* forces
61 *discovery* investigation
63 *greet the time* act promptly
70 *side* plan, scheme

Her husband being alive. Now then, we'll use
His countenance for the battle, which being
  done,
Let her who would be rid of him devise
His speedy taking off. As for the mercy
Which he intends to Lear and to Cordelia—
The battle done, and they within our power,
Shall never see his pardon; for my state·
Stands on me to defend, not to debate. *(Exit.)*

SCENE II

*Alarum within. Enter, with Drum and Colours, the
Powers of France over the stage, CORDELIA with her
Father in her hand, and exeunt.*

Enter EDGAR and GLOUCESTER.

EDG: Here, father, take the shadow of this tree.
  For your good host; pray that the right may
    thrive.
  If ever I return to you again,
  I'll bring you comfort.

GLOU: Grace go with you, sir!
                       (Exit EDGAR.)

Alarum and retreat within. Enter EDGAR.

EDG: Away, old man; give me thy hand, away!
  King Lear hath lost, he and his daughter ta'en.
  Give me thy hand; come on!

GLOU: No further, sir. A man may rot even here.

EDG: What, in ill thoughts again? Men must en-   10
    dure
  Their going hence, even as their coming hither;
  Ripeness is all. Come on.

GLOU: And that's true too.   *(Exeunt.)*

SCENE III

*Enter, in conquest, with Drum and Colours, EDMUND:
LEAR and CORDELIA as prisoners; Soldiers, Captain.*

EDM: Some officers take them away. Good guard
  Until their greater pleasures first be known
  That are to censure them.

72 *countenance* authority, approval
78 *Stands on* compels *debate* argue (about rights and
wrongs)
sc. iii. 2 *greater pleasures* the determination of those of
higher rank
3 *censure* pass judgment on

COR: We are not the first
Who with best meaning have incurred the worst.
For thee, oppressèd king, I am cast down;
Myself could else outfrown false Fortune's
frown.
Shall we not see these daughters and these sis-
ters?

LEAR: No, no, no, no! Come, let's away to prison.
10   We two alone will sing like birds i'th' cage.
When thou dost ask me blessing, I'll kneel down
And ask of thee forgiveness. So we'll live,
And pray and sing, and tell old tales, and laugh
At gilded butterflies, and hear poor rogues
Talk of court news; and we'll talk with them
too—
Who loses and who wins; who's in, who's out—
And take upon's the mystery of things,
As if we were God's spies; and we'll wear out,
In a walled prison, packs and sects of great ones
20   That ebb and flow by the moon.

EDM: Take them away.

LEAR: Upon such sacrifices, my Cordelia,
The gods themselves throw incense. Have I
caught thee?
He that parts us shall bring a brand from heaven
And fire us hence like foxes. Wipe thine eyes.
The goodyears shall devour'em, flesh and fell,
Ere they shall make us weep! We'll see 'em
starved first.
Come.   (Exeunt LEAR and CORDELIA, guarded.)

EDM: Come hither, Captain; hark
30   Take thou this note (gives a paper). Go follow
them to prison.
One step I have advanced thee; if thou dost
As this instructs thee, thou dost make thy way
To noble fortunes. Know thou this, that men
Are as the time is; to be tender-minded
Does not become a sword. Thy great employ-
ment
Will not bear question. Either say thou'lt do't,

17 *take upon's* undertake to explain
18 *God's spies* i.e., angels sent down to report on human
affairs *wear out* outlast
23 *throw incense* i.e., sanctify
24 *brand* flaming torch
25 *like foxes* (as foxes were driven from their holes by fire
and smoke)
26 *goodyears* plagues *fell* hide, skin
35 *become a sword* befit a soldier
36 *bear question* admit discussion

Or thrive by other means.

CAPT: I'll do't, my lord.

EDM: About it! and write happy when thou hast
done.
Mark: I say instantly, and carry it so   40
As I have set it down.

CAPT: I cannot draw a cart, nor eat dried oats;
If it be man's work, I'll do't.   (Exit.)

Flourish. Enter ALBANY, GONERIL, REGAN, *Soldiers.*

ALB: Sir, you have showed to-day your valiant
strain,
And fortune led you well. You have the captives
Who were the opposites of this day's strife;
I do require them of you, so to use them
As we shall find their merits and our safety
May equally determine.

EDM: Sir, I thought it fit   50
To send the old and miserable King
To some retention and appointed guard;
Whose age has charms in it, whose title more,
To pluck the common bosom on his side
And turn our impressed lances in our eyes
Which do command them. With him I sent the
Queen,
My reason all the same; and they are ready
To-morrow, or at further space, to appear
Where you shall hold your session. At this time
We sweat and bleed, the friend hath lost his   60
friend,
And the best quarrels in the heat are cursed
By those that feel their sharpness.
The question of Cordelia and her father
Requires a fitter place.

ALB: Sir, by your patience,
I hold you but a subject of this war,
Not as a brother.

REG: That's as we list to grace him.

39 *write* consider yourself
40 *carry* execute
42 *cannot draw a cart nor eat dried oats* i.e., am not a horse
40 *strain* quality
46 *opposites of* opponents in
52 *retention* confinement
54 *pluck* win
55 *impressed lances* conscripted lancers *in our eyes* against us
61 *quarrels* causes *heat* heat of the moment
62 *feel their sharpness* have suffered for them
66 *subject of* subordinate in
67 *brother* equal
68 *list to grace* decide to honour

Methinks our pleasure might have been demanded

70 Ere you had spoke so far. He led our powers,
Bore the commission of my place and person,
The which immediacy may well stand up
And call itself your brother.

GON: Not so hot!
In his own grace he doth exalt himself
More than in your addition.

REG: In my rights
By me invested, he compeers the best.

GON: That were the most if he should husband
you.

80 REG: Jesters do oft prove prophets.

GON: Holla, holla!
That eye that told you so looked but asquint.

REG: Lady, I am not well, else I should answer
From a full-flowing stomach. General,
Take thou my soldiers, prisoners, patrimony;
Dispose of them, of me; the walls are thine.
Witness the world that I create thee here
My lord and master.

GON: Mean you to enjoy him?

90 ALB: The let-alone lies not in your good will.

EDM: Nor in thine, lord.

ALB: Half-blooded fellow, yes.

REG: (to EDMUND) Let the drum strike, and prove
my title thine.

ALB: Stay yet; hear reason. Edmund, I arrest thee
On capital treason; and, in thine attaint,
This gilded serpent (points to GONERIL). For
your claim, fair sister,
I bar it in the interest of my wife.
'Tis she is subcontracted to this lord,

And I, her husband, contradict your banes.
If you will marry, make your loves to me; 100
My lady is bespoke.

GON: An interlude!

ALB: Thou art armed, Gloucester. Let the trumpet
sound.
If none appear to prove upon thy person
Thy heinous, manifest, and many treasons,
There is my pledge (throws down a glove). I'll
prove it on thy heart,
Ere I taste bread, thou art in nothing less
Than I have here proclaimed thee.

REG: Sick, O, sick!

GON: (aside) If not, I'll ne'er trust medicine. 110

EDM: There's my exchange (throws down a glove).
What in the world he is
That names me traitor, villain-like he lies.
Call by thy trumpet. He that dares approach—
On him, on you, who not? I will maintain
My truth and honour firmly.

ALB: A herald, ho!

EDM: A herald, ho, a herald!

Enter a HERALD.

ALB: Trust to thy single virtue, for thy soldiers,
All levied in my name, have in my name
Took their discharge. 120

REG: My sickness grows upon me.

ALB: She is not well. Convey her to my tent.
(Exit REGAN, *led.)*
Come hither, herald. Let the trumpet sound,
And read out this.

CAPT: Sound, trumpet! *(A trumpet sounds.)*

HER: *(reads)* If any man of quality or degree within
the lists of the army will maintain upon Edmund,
supposed Earl of Gloucester, that he is a manifold traitor, let him appear by the third sound of
the trumpet. He is bold in his defence. 130

EDM: Sound! *(First trumpet.)*

HER: Again! *(Second trumpet.)*

HER: Again! *(Third trumpet.)*
(Trumpet answers within.)

---

71 *Bore the commission of my place and person* was my deputy
with full power to act
72 *The which immediacy* this direct relation to my authority
75 *grace* merit
76 *your addition* any rank you can confer
78 *compeers* equals
79 *That were the most if* he could rank so high only if
82 *looked but asquint* could not see straight
84 *a full-flowing stomach* overflowing anger
85 *patrimony* inheritance
86 *the walls are thine* you have overcome all my defences
90 *let-alone* power to hinder
92 *Half-blooded* base-born
95 *capital* punishable by death *in thine attaint* on the
same charge
98 *subcontracted* betrothed for a second time

99 *contradict* forbid *banes* banns
101 *bespoke* already promised
102 *An interlude* This is a farce
118 *single virtue* individual prowess
126 *quality or degree* rank or position
127 *lists* limits *upon* against

Enter EDGAR, *armed, a Trumpet before him.*

ALB: Ask him his purposes, why he appears
　　Upon this call o'th' trumpet.
HER: What are you?
　　Your name, your quality? and why you answer
　　This present summons?
EDG: Know my name is lost,
140　By treason's tooth bare-gnawn and canker-bit.
　　Yet am I noble as the adversary
　　I come to cope.
ALB: Which is that adversary?
EDG: What's he that speaks for Edmund Earl of
　　Gloucester?
EDM: Himself. What say'st thou to him?
EDG: Draw thy sword,
　　That, if my speech offend a noble heart,
　　Thy arm may do thee justice. Here is mine.
　　Behold, it is the privilege of mine honours,
150　My oath, and my profession. I protest,
　　Maugre thy strength, place, youth, and emi-
　　nence,
　　Despite thy victor sword and fire-new fortune,
　　Thy valour and thy heart, thou art a traitor,
　　False to thy gods, thy brother, and thy father,
　　Conspirant 'gainst this high illustrious prince,
　　And from th'extremest upward of thy head
　　To the descent and dust beneath thy foot,
　　A most toad-spotted traitor. Say thou no,
　　This sword, this arm, and my best spirits are
　　bent
160　To prove upon thy heart, whereto I speak,
　　Thou liest.
EDM: In wisdom I should ask thy name;
　　But since thy outside looks so fair and warlike,
　　And that thy tongue some say of breeding
　　breathes,
　　What safe and nicely I might well delay
　　By rule of knighthood, I disdain and spurn.
　　Back do I toss those treasons to thy head;
　　With the hell-hated lie o'erwhelm thy heart;

Which, for they yet glance by and scarcely
　　bruise,
This sword of mine shall give them instant way   170
Where they shall rest for ever. Trumpets, speak!
　　　　　　(*Alarums. Fight.* EDMUND *falls.*)
ALB: Save him, save him!
GON: This is mere practice, Gloucester.
　　By th'law of arms thou wast not bound to answer
　　An unknown opposite. Thou are not vanquish-
　　ed,
　　But cozened and beguiled.
ALB: Shut your mouth, dame,
　　Or with this paper shall I stop it. (*Shows her her let-
　　ter to* EDMUND.)—(*To* EDMUND). Hold, sir.
　　(*To* GONERIL) Thou worse than any name, read
　　thine own evil.
　　No tearing, lady! I perceive you know it.   180
GON: Say if I do—the laws are mine, not thine.
　　Who can arraign me for't?
ALB: Most monstrous!
　　Know'st thou this paper?
GON: Ask me not what I know.   (*Exit.*)
ALB: Go after he. She's desperate; govern her.
　　　　　　　　　　　　　(*Exit an Officer.*)
EDM: What you have charged me with, that have I
　　done,
　　And more, much more; the time will bring it out.
　　'Tis past, and so am I—But what are thou
　　That hast this fortune on me? If thou'rt noble,   190
　　I do forgive thee.
EDG: Let's exchange charity.
　　I am no less in blood than thou art, Edmund;
　　If more, the more th' hast wronged me.
　　My name is Edgar and thy father's son.
　　The gods are just, and of our pleasant vices
　　Make instruments to plague us.
　　The dark and vicious place where thee he got
　　Cost him his eyes.
EDM: Th' hast spoken right, 'tis true;   200
　　The wheel is come full circle, I am here.

137 *quality* rank
140 *canker-bit* eaten away
151 *Maugre* in spite of
152 *fire-new* newly forged
155 *Conspirant* conspiring
156 *extremest upward* very top
164 *say* trace　*breathes* expresses
165 *nicely* by a literal interpretation of the rules

169 *for* because
173 *mere practice* an outright plot against you
175 *opposite* opponent
176 *cozened* deceived
182 *arraign* indict
186 *govern* restrain
198 *got* begot
201 *wheel* (of Fortune)

ALB: Methought thy very gait did prophesy
A royal nobleness; I must embrace thee.
Let sorrow split my heart if ever I
Did hate thee, or thy father!

EDG: Worthy prince, I know't.

ALB: Where have you hid yourself?
How have you known the miseries of your
father?

EDG: By nursing them, my lord. List a brief tale,
210   And when 'tis told, O that my heart would burst!
The bloody proclamation to escape
That followed me so near (O, our lives' sweet-
ness!
That with the pain of death we would hourly die
Rather than die at once) taught me to shift
Into a madman's rags, t' assume a semblance
That very dogs disdained, and in this habit
Met I my father with his bleeding rings,
Their precious stones new lost; became his
guide,
Led him, begged for him, saved him from de-
spair;
220   Never (O fault!) revealed myself unto him
Until some half hour past, when I was armed,
Not sure, though hoping of this good success,
I asked his blessing, and from first to last
Told him my pilgrimage. But his flawed heart
(Alack, too weak the conflict to support)
'Twixt two extremes of passion, joy and grief,
Burst smilingly.

EDM: This speech of yours hath moved me,
And shall perchance do good; but speak you on;
230   You look as you had something more to say.

ALB: If there be more, more woful, hold it in;
For I am almost ready to dissolve,
Hearing of this.

EDG: This would have seemed a period
To such as love not sorrow; but another
To amplify too much, would make much more,
And top extremity.
Whilst I was big in clamour, came there a man,

Who, having seen me in my worst estate,
Shunned my abhorred society; but then, finding   240
Who 'twas that so endured, with his strong arms
He fastened on my neck, and bellowed out
As he'd burst heaven; threw him on my father;
Told the most piteous tale of Lear and him
That ever ear received; which in recounting
His grief grew puissant, and the strings of life
Began to crack. Twice then the trumpets sound-
ed,
And there I left him tranced.

ALB: But who was this?

EDG: Kent, sir, the banished Kent, who in disguise   250
Followed his enemy king and did him service
Improper for a slave.

Enter a GENTLEMAN *with a bloody knife.*

GENT: Help, help, O, help!

EDG: What kind of help?

ALB: Speak, man.

EDG: What means that bloody knife?

GENT: 'Tis hot, it smokes.
It came even from the heart of—O, she's dead!

ALB: Who dead? Speak, man.

GENT: Your lady, sir, your lady! and her sister   260
By her is poisoned; she confesses it.

EDM: I was contracted to them both. All three
Now marry in an instant.

Enter KENT.

EDG: Here comes Kent.

ALB: Produce their bodies, be they alive or dead.
(The bodies of GONERIL *and* REGAN *are brought in.)*
This judgment of the heavens, that makes us
tremble,
Touches us not with pity. Oh, is this he?
The time will not allow the compliment
That very manners urges.

KENT: I am come   270
To bid my king and master aye good night.
Is he not here?

239 *estate* condition
241 *endured* suffered
246 *grew puissant* overpowered him
248 *tranced* unconscious
252 *Improper for* too base even for
262 *contracted* engaged
263 *in an instant* at the same moment
268 *compliment* courtesy
269 *very manners* mere good manners

216 *habit* costume
217 *rings* sockets
224 *flawed* cracked
234 *period* point at which to conclude
236 *amplify too much* increase to excess
237 *top extremity* go beyond the highest possible point
238 *big in clamour* loud in lamentation

ALB: Great thing of us forgot!
Speak, Edmund, where's the King? and where's
Cordelia?
Seest thou this object, Kent?

KENT: Alack, why thus?

EDM: Yet Edmund was beloved.
The one the other poisoned for my sake,
And after slew herself.

280 ALB: Even so. Cover their faces.

EDM: I pant for life. Some good I mean to do,
Despite of mine own nature. Quickly send
(Be brief in it) to the castle, for my writ
Is on the life of Lear and on Cordelia.
Nay, send in time.

ALB: Run, run, O, run!

EDG: To who, my lord? Who has the office? Send
Thy token of reprieve.

EDM: Well thought on. Take my sword;

290 Give it to the Captain.

ALB: Haste thee for thy life.   (*Exit* EDGAR.)

EDM: He hath commission from thy wife and me
To hang Cordelia in the prison and
To lay the blame upon her own despair
That she fordid herself.

ALB: The gods defend her! Bear him hence a while.

(EDMUND *is borne off.*)

Enter LEAR, *with* CORDELIA (*dead*) *in his arms,*
(*EDGAR, CAPTAIN, and other following*).

LEAR: Howl, howl, howl, howl! O, you are men of
stones.
Had I your tongues and eyes, I'd use them so
That heaven's vault should crack. She's gone for
ever!

300 I know when one is dead, and when one lives;
She's dead as earth. Lend me a looking glass;
If that her breath will mist or stain the stone,
Why, then she lives.

KENT: Is this the promised end?

EDG: Or image of that horror?

ALB: Fall and cease!

LEAR: This feather stirs; she lives! If it be so,

It is a chance which does redeem all sorrows
That ever I have felt.

KENT: O my good master!   310

LEAR: Prithee away!

EDG: 'Tis noble Kent, your friend.

LEAR: A plague upon you, murderers, traitors all,
I might have saved her; now she's gone for ever.
Cordelia, Cordelia, stay a little. Ha!
What is't thou say'st? Her voice was ever soft,
Gentle, and low—an excellent thing in woman.
I killed the slave that was a-hanging thee.

CAPT: 'Tis true, my lords, he did.

LEAR: Did I not, fellow?   320
I have seen the day, with my good biting falchion
I would have made them skip. I am old now,
And these same crosses spoil me. Who are you?
Mine eyes are not o'th'best. I'll tell you straight.

KENT: If fortune brag of two she loved and hated,
One of them we behold.

LEAR: This is a dull sight. Are you not Kent?

KENT: The same—
Your servant Kent. Where is your servant Caius?

LEAR: He's a good fellow, I can tell you that.   330
He'll strike, and quickly too. He's dead and
rotten.

KENT: No, my good lord, I am the very man—

LEAR: I'll see that straight.

KENT: That from your first of difference and decay
Have followed your sad steps.

LEAR: You are welcome hither.

KENT: Nor no man else! All's cheerless, dark, and
deadly.
Your eldest daughters have fordone themselves,
And desperately are dead.

LEAR: Ay, so I think.   340

ALB: He knows not what he says, and vain is it
That we present us to him.

EDG: Very bootless.

Enter a CAPTAIN.

CAPT: Edmund is dead, my lord.

287 *office* duty
295 *fordid* put an end to
302 *stone* polished surface
304 *end* (of the world)
306 *Fall and cease!* let the heavens fall and all things come
to an end

321 *falchion* sword
323 *crosses* vexations
324 *straight* in a moment
333 *see* attend to
334 *your first of difference* the beginning of your decline
338 *fordone* done away with
339 *desperately* in despair
343 *bootless* useless

ALB: That's but a trifle here.
    You lords and noble friends, know our intent.
    What comfort to this great decay may come
    Shall be applied. For us, we will resign
    During the life of this old Majesty
350 To him our absolute power; *(to* EDGAR *and* KENT*)*
        you to your rights,
    With boot and such addition as your honours
    Have more than merited. All friends shall taste
    The wages of their virtue, and all foes
    The cup of their deservings.—O, see, see!
LEAR: And my poor fool is hanged! No, no, no life?
    Why should a dog, a horse, a rat, have life,
    And thou no breath at all? Thou'lt come no more,
    Never, never, never, never, never!
    Pray you undo this button. Thank you, sir.
360 Do you see this? Look on her! look, her lips!
    Look there, look there!   *(He dies.)*
EDG: He faints! My lord, my lord!

347 *this great decay* this great man in decay
351 *boot* increase *honours* honorable deeds

KENT: Break, heart, I prithee break.
EDG: Look up, my lord.
KENT: Vex not his ghost; O let him pass! He hates
        him
    That would upon the rack of this tough world
    Stretch him out longer.
EDG: He is gone indeed.
KENT: The wonder is, he hath endured so long.
    He but usurped his life.   370
ALB: Bear them from hence. Our present business
    Is general woe. *(To* KENT *and* EDGAR*)* Friends of
        my soul, you twain
    Rule in this realm, and the gored state sustain.
KENT: I have a journey, sir, shortly to go.
    My master calls me; I must not say no.
ALB: The weight of this sad time we must obey,
    Speak what we feel, not what we ought to say.
    The oldest hath borne most; we that are young
    Shall never see so much, nor live so long.
                        (Exeunt with a dead march.)

373 *gored* mauled, injured
376 *weight* sorrow *obey* submit to

ON *KING LEAR*

by Elder Olson

If the play is to be made tragic, what must the character of Lear be made to be? In the first place, if we are to feel any great pity for him, his misfortunes must be undeserved, which means that he must have elements of nobility in him. But he cannot be a perfect man; as Socrates remarks, the perfectly good man cannot be used as a tragic figure (an error that Addison made in his *Cato*, by the way); the perfect man cannot be humbled, he will not weep or lament, he is as safe as man can be, and even in his misfortunes we admire rather than pity him. Moreover, the act which Lear performs—that of deliberately banishing and disinheriting a loving daughter—is a peculiar one. If it is done deliberately and with full knowledge, it is a base and cold-hearted act. If it is done through sheer stupidity or whim or pettiness, it is regrettable, contemptible, perhaps ridiculous, but it is not tragic. To be made tragic, it must stem from compulsion or passion or incomplete knowledge; and though it is not a right action, it must *seem* right action—that is, it cannot be a piece of *knowing* injustice—to Lear at the time he commits it. Again, if it stems from some passion—anger, for instance—that anger will have to be of the right kind. No one is good or bad simply because he is angry; but different moral characters exhibit the same passion differently and under different circumstances: the petty man exhibits anger in a petty way and for causes which are important only to the petty, whereas the nobler man is indignant in a nobler way and for causes which are important only to the nobler. If Lear is to be angry, it must be with royal anger, such anger as befits a king, and for such cause as befits a king.

Let us examine the whole action. Critics have criticized everything about it; the irrational folly of dividing the kingdom, of demanding the profession of love, of disinheriting Cordelia; and it seems to me that not all of their objections are well taken. Why does Lear divide the kingdom? Because he is without male issue; consequently he has no real successor; consequently he wishes to avert war between the pretenders after his death by an equal division. Why does he abrogate authority? Because he is becoming too old to rule, and because he thinks that if the division is made in his lifetime and established as a going concern, there is less chance of war. And what is the point of his demanding the public profession of love? Well, in *part* it is this: if Lear is giving up his authority and still wants security and dignity, he can only trust to their *love*; and his insistence upon their public profession of it is an attempt to have it warranted and witnessed as a formal part of the compact of the delivery of property and power.

I say "in part" for there is more to it than that, but before I can explain I must digress a little. In Greek tragedy, while the tragic situation is usually brought about by the decrees of the Fates or by the intervention of gods in human affairs, as in the *Hippolytus*, or by a curse, as in the *Oresteia*, the tragic character *does* something that renders him especially liable and vulnerable to it. Roman tragedy, if Seneca is representative, is simply fatalistic; the characters are the passive instruments for the accomplishment of fate. But Shakespeare has worked out his own formula for the tragic *hamartia*, the tragic mistake; and so far as I know, it is one peculiar to him. A little review of some of the major tragic figures will make it clear. What is Hamlet? A philosopher and scholar by training and temperament, a speculative thinker who is not concerned with action. In what situation must he act? In a practical one, in which speculation is bound to be disastrous. What is Othello? A general, and a general must take the advice of his most trusted lieutenants. Othello is put in a situation in which it is disastrous to do so. Coriolanus is also a general; now, a general does not *solicit* support, he commands it; Coriolanus is put in a situation where he must solicit it. Macbeth is a soldier who has elevated himself by conspicuous courage; it is through taunting him about his courage that his wife at last drives him to murder Duncan. In brief, the thing is this: a character of conspicuous virtues and abilities, who has distinguished himself through them in one sphere, is thrown suddenly into a sphere of action in which to exercise them—and he *must* exercise them—is to invoke catastrophe. A far sadder notion than the Greek: we fall, not through our vices merely, but even through our virtues. The *hamartia*, the tragic error, is still there; but it has been transmuted into a mistake rendered inevitable by all that the character has been and has done. Disaster comes, not through the fates or the gods, but by human agency alone. In Lear's case, Lear is a feudal lord; he is thrown into a domestic sphere where the laws of feudality do not operate, for he is abrogating the authority on which feudality depends.

This strange act of his, then, *as Shakespeare constructs it*, is nothing other than that of a feudal lord demanding the profession of fealty from his vassals, as a condition of the conveyance of authority and property. He gives in this feudal way and he demands in this feudal way, for it is the only way he knows. He is still remaining king; he retains for himself "the name and all the additions to a king," not realizing that without army, kingdom, or authority, no king can be king. Look at these strangely formal speeches, with their legal phrasing, and everything becomes clear. After Goneril's answer, Lear responds:

> Of all these bounds, even from this line to this,
> With shadowy forests and with champains rich'd
> With plenteous rivers and wide-skirted meads,
> We make thee lady: to thine and Albany's issue
> Be this perpetual.

After Regan's answer, Lear says:

> To thee and thine hereditary ever
> Remain this ample third of our fair kingdom;
> No less in space, validity, and pleasure
> Than that conferred on Goneril.

These are the speeches of a feudal lord, to vassals who have professed fealty. Thus Shakespeare has solved one part of the problem; if now Lear is wrong, and of course he is, he at least is wrong on principle, and a kingly principle. Cordelia's famous obstinacy comes from her complete inability to understand the feudal character of Lear's action, as his own unfatherly response to her comes from the fact that here he is not acting as a father at all; he is acting in the role of lord to vassal. In his view it is particularly wounding that she, his favorite, should refuse to participate in what are to him necessary formalities, and her refusal casts doubt on her whole relation to him. How *can* she, in his view, be a loving daughter, when she refuses to take part in the only pact that hereafter can assure his continuing status as *king?* In *Julius Caesar*, Brutus comes to grief by imposing the ethical upon the political; Lear comes to grief by imposing the feudal upon the familial.

For the familial and the feudal do not mix. They are like countries with contrary laws, so that an act which is lawful in the one is criminal in the other. The one demands forms and contracts; the other depends wholly upon trust. A feudal lord may demand the exclusive loyalty of his vassal; a father can make no such demand upon his daughter's affection. The nature of love and affection is that they are inexhaustible, that consequently they cannot be limited to any one object. Hence any profession to that effect is by that very fact a *lie*. Cordelia knows this, and cannot make it. Lear does not; moreover, in demanding of love that it be secured to himself alone, he is committing an act, not of love, but of selfishness which is the contrary of love. Lear is ignorant of the nature of love; he must be taught it. He begins in selfishness, thinking of himself; let him end, himself forgotten, wholly absorbed in the beloved.

We have something of the character of Lear, now, for we know he must be the kind of man capable of an act such as I have described and for the reasons described; but he must also be capable of the tragic suffering and of what we may call, for the moment, the tragic resolution. I say "the" suffering and "the" resolution to imply both that these must be of a certain general kind and that these must be appropriate to *him* as a character. What shape must his sufferings take? He has sinned against love, demanded from it what it cannot give, what should not be demanded of it; his sufferings must be the atonement for this; he must discover the meaning of love through the privation of love. Without love and benevolence and the humane feelings, man becomes a beast, justice and law become empty forms, authority becomes mere force, and the world becomes the nightmare of cannibalistic nature where all prey on all. Lear has driven love away for the sake of empty forms; he must fall into that nightmare world and suffer in it. . . .

We must see Lear, then, in deteriorating fortunes; but his suffereings cannot come from these in themselves; they must come from a higher principle involved. Shall the daughters inflict bodily harm upon him? No; actual physical pain would indeed *detract* from his sufferings; they must be wholly mental even though they are experienced in circumstances of physical privation. Moreover, the harm or injury from the daughters must be kept as slight as possible; it must be the great principle involved which gives the offense its tragic magnitude. This alone must torment Lear; the point must even be emphasized that, whatever privation he may endure, he is insensible to it in comparison; it is no part of the real cause. Here we have, of course, the genesis of the storm scenes, and one of the themes of Lear's speeches during them.

Thus the main elements of the plot begin to take form: Lear must endure degradation from kingship, and to suffer from this *on principle*, i.e., as an affront to his *honor*, he must be proud; he must suffer ingratitude and betrayal, and to suffer from these *on principle* he must be just; he must suffer from the privation of affection, and to suffer from this as deeply as possible he must be the kind of man to whom affection is most necessary, and to whom affection may well outweigh all other things. Each of Shakespeare's great tragic heroes pays in his own personal coin, the kind that costs him most: the courageous Macbeth in moral terror, the intellectual Hamlet in doubt and confusion; and the proud, just, affectionate Lear must pay in the suffering of humiliation, injustice, and the privation of affection. What shall mark the extremity of his torment? Madness: he sees the world he has chosen and it maddens him. So Shakespeare's Lear is the only Lear to go mad, for he is the only Lear so fashioned that he is capable of the ultimate mental torment. To be profoundly shaken we must be profoundly made.

He is also the only Lear to come to an unhappy end; the Lears of the other versions have their kingdoms restored, and die of old age. Why must we have *this* ending? Is it made necessary or probable by the antecedent action? It is not. As a matter of fact the catastrophe *seldom* is in the great tragedies of Shakespeare. What in the plot necessitates that Emilia should come too late to save Desdemona? Hamlet's death-wound, poisoned though the sword is, is a mere possibility of combat. The defeat of Cordelia's forces is the mere fortune of war, and nothing prevents Edmund from speaking in time to save Cordelia. The catastrophe is no more probable than its contrary; and yet we must have the unhappy ending. Why? Because it is an *emotional* necessity.

But again we may ask: *why?* Because the bullfight is incomplete without death? Because tragedy, as some have thought, is basically ritualistic and hence sacrifice is demanded? Because, as Charles Lamb thought, our sympathies have otherwise been engaged in vain? None of these answers seem to me satisfactory. This is no point at which to embark on the poetics of tragedy; let me simply say that in every true tragedy the audience is compelled to transcend a *lower* set of moral values to a *higher;* it is compelled to fear and pity, for instance, only to acknowledge in the end that in a higher judgment there are worse evils than those it has been fearing and pitying; and by confronting great misery it has learned, momentarily at least, something of the great conditions upon which human happiness truly depends, and something of the high dignity of which man is capable. This, of course, is precisely the tragic *catharsis* of which Aristotle spoke. Frequently in tragedy—in *Lear*, for instance—the tragic hero himself experiences that transcendence of values, and his merest acknowledgment of that experience is in itself a human triumph. Lear must forget royal pride and the stings of ingratitude and all else, and realize the supreme value of love; he must put by his kingship and all the world, gladly, for the sake of his loved daughter; and then he must learn the value of love again as only loss can teach it; and so Cordelia must die. Her effort to save Lear, then, must be in vain; her death may follow naturally on her defeat; otherwise it will be difficult to bring about.

And so must Lear die. Ingratitude could only drive him to madness; love brings his death. . . .

We must note Shakespeare's very cunning strategy of representation in King Lear. Shakespeare is a great master of psychology; I don't mean this merely in its usual sense of his skillfully depicting his characters, but in the additional sense of his being very adroit in the manipulating of his audience. He knows that when people are extremely intent on something, a sudden interruption will be very startling; which is one reason why the knocking on the gate in Macbeth has such terrible force, for the audience is absorbed in the whispering murderers. He knows that a dreadful thing being done very quietly and slowly will seem all the more dreadful to an audience; which is one reason why Othello's coming to murder Desdemona is so powerful.

In King Lear he wants to arouse our sympathies with Lear to the utmost, and he knows that if we form an unfavorable opinion of someone who falls into misfortune we are far less sympathetic than if we had formed a favorable opinion of him. If, therefore, he can cause us first to look on Lear with some disfavor, and subsequently cause us to revise our opinions radically, he can work up our sympathetic emotions to an enormous pitch.

Look at what he allow us to see of Lear, step by step, and you will see how his strategy works. We *must not know too much about* Lear; we must see his faults first, then his virtues; and we must see his worse faults first, and then the lesser, and then the least; similarly, we must see his virtues in ascending order. Or rather I should say, what we *take* to be his faults; for many of his early actions as we get to know more of Lear are not what we took them for at all. To achieve this slow revelation Shakespeare uses the device of *ambiguous action*—that is, he invents actions for Lear, in the early part of the play, which on first sight look quite different from what they really are: his demand that his daughters profess their love publicly is, as I have interpreted it to you, the supreme example. His banishment of Cordelia is in any case a dreadful thing, but it is not a vicious moral action; it is a piece of folly, excusable in view of his character and his career. It looks like a cold-hearted action; it is nothing of the sort; the underlying cause is his deep affection for Cordelia; in his view she has publicly slighted him, and he feels the wound terribly because those we love have power to hurt us most. Critics, even eminent ones, have been somewhat insensitive on this point; they have taken Lear's early acts all at face value, and critized Shakespeare for making him arrogant or irascible or what-not. They have even criticized the play as beginning too abruptly, by contrast to the long introductory sequences in *Macbeth* or *Hamlet* or especially *Othello*, where the whole first act is nothing but introduction. But the reason for the difference is clear; in the other plays we must understand a great deal before the action begins, if the plot is to have its full effect; in *Lear*, on the other hand, if the plot is to have its full effect we must not know too much.

Shakespeare is not content simply to unfold gradually the character of Lear through his own actions; since so much of his behavior has to do with his interpretation of the characters of Goneril and Regan, they are gradually revealed to us as well. At first Lear seems to have but little ground for his resentment and anger, but as we know the sisters better we move into full accord with him. Why must Gloucester's eyes be put out on stage? It is a very horrible thing; but this is what Regan is capable of, and we must see it, not be told it, see with our own eyes exactly how it is done, to realize the full evil of her character. Why do she and her husband do it? Because Gloucester had a letter in his possession from Cordelia, whose forces had landed at Dover, and because Gloucester had helped the escape of Lear to Dover. If there was to be war the king had to be killed at once; Cornwall and Regan had already plotted his death; Gloucester had overheard and frustrated it. It would have been no easy death; we can gather that from her tearing out parts of Gloucester's beard, her fierce questioning of him, her insistence that his other eye be gouged out; indeed, before he loses his own eyes, Gloucester says "I would not see thy cruel nails/ Pluck out his poor old eyes," and he is referring to Lear.

The character of Albany has never been much discussed. Let me say one word about him. He has power to stop everything whenever he wishes; and we see him, in Act V, as the final agent of justice. Why does he not stop villainy and restore justice? Because, like the audience, he does not fully know; like the audience, he regards Lear somewhat unfavorably at first, and gradually learns the truth. In other words, he is part of Shakespeare's general strategy of representation; for the audience is moved also by the change in him.

FROM *THE EMPTY SPACE*

by Peter Brook

Both Shakespeare and Sartre would be fashioning plays according to their sense of truth: one author's inner material contains different intimations from the other's. The mistake would be to take events or episodes from a play and question them in the light of some third outside standard of plausibility—like 'reality' or 'truth'. The sort of play that Shakespeare offers us is never just a series of events: it is far easier to understand if we consider the plays as objects—as many faceted complexes of form and meaning in which the line of narrative is only one amongst many aspects—and cannot profitably be played or studied on its own.

Experimentally, we can approach Lear not as a linear narrative, but as a cluster of relationships. First, we try to rid ourselves of the notion that because the play is called *King Lear* it is primarily the story of one individual. So we pick an arbitrary point in the vast structure—the death of Cordelia, say, and now instead of looking towards the King we turn instead towards the man who is responsible for her death. We focus on this character, Edmund, and now we begin to pick our way to and fro across the play, sifting the evidence, trying to discover who this Edmund is. He is clearly a villain, whatever our standards, for in killing Cordelia he is responsible for the most gratuitous act of cruelty in the play—yet if we look at our first impression of him in the early scenes, we find he is by far the most attractive character we meet. In the opening scenes there is a denial of life in Lear's rusty ironclad power; Gloucester is tetchy, fussy and foolish, a man blind to everything except his inflated image of his own importance; and in dramatic contrast we see the relaxed freedom of his bastard son. Even if in theory we observe that the way he leads Gloucester by the nose is hardly moral, instinctively we cannot but side with his natural anarchy.

Not only do we sympathize with Goneril and Regan for falling in love with him, but we tend to side with them in finding Edmund so admirably wicked, because he affirms a life that the sclerosis of the older people seems to deny. Can we keep this same attitude of admiration towards Edmund when he has Cordelia killed? If not, why not? What has changed? Is it Edmund who has changed, through outside events? Or is it just the context that is different? Is a scale of value implied? What are Shakespeare's values? What is the value of a life? We flick through the play again and find an incident importantly situated, unrelated to the main plot, often quoted as an example of Shakespeare's slovenly construction. This is the fight between Edmund and Edgar. If we look closely, we are struck by one fact—it is not the powerful Edmund, but his younger brother who wins. In the first scenes of the play, Edmund had no trouble at all in outwitting Edgar—now five acts later in single combat it is Edgar who dominates. Accepting this as dramatic truth rather than romantic convention, we are forced to ask how it has come about. Can we explain it all quite simply in terms of moral growth—Edgar has grown up, Edmund has decayed—or is the whole question of Edgar's undoubted development from *naiveté* to understanding—and Edmund's visible change from freedom to entanglement—far more complex than a cut-and-dried question of the triumph of the good? Aren't we compelled in fact to relate this to all the evidence connected with the question of growth and decline, i.e. youth and age, i.e. strength and weakness? If for a moment we assume this point of view, then suddenly the whole play seems concerned with sclerosis opposing the flow of existence, of cataracts that dissolve, of rigid attitudes that yield, while at the same time obsessions form and positions harden. Of course the whole play is also about sight and blindness, what sight amounts to, what blindness means—how the two eyes of Lear ignore what the instinct of the Fool apprehends, how the two eyes of Gloucester miss what his blindness knows. But the object has many facets; many themes criss-cross its prismatic form. Let us stay with the strands of age and youth, and in pursuit of them move on to the very last lines of the play. When we read or hear them first our reaction is, "How obvious. What a trite end," for Edgar says:

> We that are young
> Shall never see so much, nor live so long.

The more we look at them the more troubling they become, because their apparent precision vanishes, making way for a strange ambiguity hidden in the naïve jangle. The last line is, at its face value, plain nonsense. Are we to understand that the young will never grow up, or are we to understand that the world will never again know old men? Both of these seems a pretty feeble winding up by Shakespeare of a consciously written masterpiece. However, if we look back through Edgar's own line of action, we see that although Edgar's experience in the storm parallels Lear's, it certainly has not wrought in him the intense inner change that has taken place in Lear. Yet Edgar acquired the strength for two killings—first Oswald, then his brother. What has this done to him—how deeply has he experienced this loss of innocence? Is he still wide-eyed? Is he saying in his closing words that youth and age are limited by their own definitions—that the only way to see as much as Lear is to go through Lear's mill, and then *ipso facto* one is young no longer. Lear lives longer than Gloucester—in time and in depth—and as a result he undoubtedly "sees" more than Gloucester before he dies. Does Edgar wish to say that it is experience of this order and intensity that really means "living long"? If so, the "being young" is a state with its own blindness—like that of the early Edgar, and its own freedom like that of the early Edmund. Age in turn has its blindness and decay. However, true sight comes from an acuteness of living that can transform the old. Indeed, it is clearly shown to us in the unfolding of the play that Lear suffers most and "gets farthest." Undoubtedly, his brief moment of captivity with Cordelia is as a moment of bliss, peace and reconciliation, and Christian commentators often write as though this were the end of the story—a clear tale of the ascent from the inferno through purgation to paradise. Unfortunately for this neat view the play continues, pitilessly, away from reconciliation.

> We that are young
> Shall never see so much, nor live so long.

The power of Edgar's disturbing statement—a statement that rings like a half-open question—is that it carries no moral overtones at all. He does not suggest for one moment that youth or age, seeing or not seeing, are in any way superior, inferior, more desirable or less desirable one than the other. In fact we are compelled to face a play which refuses all moralizing—a play which we begin to see not as a narrative any longer, but as a vast, complex, coherent poem designed to study the power and the emptiness of nothing—the positive and negative aspects latent in the zero. So what does Shakespeare mean? What is he trying to teach us? Does he mean that suffering has a necessary place in life and is worth cultivating for the knowledge and inner development it brings? Or does he mean us to understand that the age of titanic suffering is now over and our role is that of the eternally young? Wisely, Shakespeare refuses to answer. But he has given us his play, and its whole field of experience is both question and answer. In this light, the play is directly related to the most burning themes of our time, the old and the new in relation to our society, our arts, our notions of progress, our way of living our lives. If the actors are interested, this is what they will bring out. If we are interested, that is what we will find. Fancy dress, then, will be left far behind. The meaning will be for the moment of performance.

THE MISER

Molière (1622-1673)

Translated by Lloyd C. Parks

Jean Baptiste Poquelin, later Molière, one of the outstanding comic writers of the theater, was born in Paris, the son of an upholsterer who was in the service of the king. Molière was well educated but turned his back on a legal career to join a theatrical company, which suffered great economic hardships. For twelve years "The Theater Illustrious" toured the provinces playing under all kinds of conditions. During these years, Molière perfected his skill as an actor and began writing original plays for the company. When the troupe returned to Paris in 1658 and he was invited to play before the court, Molière won the favor of Louis XIV with one of his comedies, enabling the company to establish itself on a permanent basis in Paris.

Molière wrote some thirty plays, freely borrowing from Latin comedy and the devices and characters of the Italian improvised comedy. *The Miser*, for example, is an adaptation of Plautus's *The Pot of Gold*. He was especially successful with his satires of the foibles and follies of his contemporaries—avarice, hypocrisy, arrogance, sanctimoniousness and all manner of pretentiousness. His shafts of wit struck home so that he was constantly at odds with the church and the professions. Among the important plays of Molière are *Tartuffe, Don Juan, The Misanthrope, The Imaginary Invalid, The Would-Be-Gentleman* and *The School for Wives.*

In seventeenth-century France, plays were staged in a rectangular hall, partially as the result of following the shape of the Hotel de Bourgogne, the most prominent place for producing plays during the previous century, and partially because of the practice of converting roofed-over tennis courts into playhouses. The Palais Royal Theater, which Cardinal Richelieu built in 1637, was a rectangular hall that accommodated about 1500 people. Some spectators sat in seats on the ground floor level and others in the galleries along the sides of the hall placed at right angles to the stage. The acting area was behind the proscenium arch, the first such arch to appear in a French theater. Molière's troupe used the Palais Royal from 1660 to 1673. Although the theater was equipped with elaborate stage scenery for spectacular effects, Molière made little use of it in his comedies. *The Miser*, which was first produced in this theater in 1668, calls simply for a hall with a garden scene in the background.

Opposite. Harpagon, suspecting thievery, frisks his servant Flèche.

Below. The Harpagon family gathering. Photographs in this sequence are of the 1969 production at Lincoln Center in New York, with Robert Symonds as Harpagon, and Roger Robinson as Flèche.

PHOTOGRAPHS BY MARTHA SWOPE

Above. Harpagon is interested in a match—
"without a dowry."

Left. Harpagon is reunited
with his greatest love,
his moneybox.

Above. The set and the moral of the play.

Above. The Petit-Bourbon Theater, a room in the palace
of the Duke of Bourbon where Molière's company first performed.
The audience occupied the main floor and surrounding balconies
while the play took place within the frame of the proscenium arch,
seen here in the background. It was during this period
that the proscenium arch, with its closeable curtain
and changeable backdrop scenery, came into use.

CHARACTERS

HARPAGON, *father of* CLEANTH *and* ELISE, *and in love with* MARIANNE

CLEANTH, HARPAGON'S *son, and in love with* MARIANNE

ELISE, HARPAGON'S *daughter, and in love with* VALÈRE

VALÈRE, ANSELM'S *son, and in love with* ELISE

MARIANNE, ANSELM'S *daughter, and in love with* CLEANTH

ANSELM, *father of* VALÈRE *and* MARIANNE

FROSINE, *a woman of intrigue*

MASTER SIMON, *a broker*

MASTER JACQUES, HARPAGON'S *coachman and cook*

LA FLECHE, CLEANTH'S *valet*

DAME CLAUDE, HARPAGON'S *maid*

BRINDAVOINE, HARPAGON'S *lackey*

LA MERLUCHE, HARPAGON'S *lackey*

A COMMISSARY AND HIS CLERK

SCENE

Paris, HARPAGON'S *house*.

THE MISER

ACT ONE

Enter VALÈRE *and* ELISE.

VALÈRE: What is it, charming Elise? Are you melancholy? After all the obliging assurances you so kindly gave of faith in me? Alas! I see you sighing in the midst of my joy! Tell me, do you regret our engagement—to which my ardor has perhaps constrained you?

ELISE: No, Valère, I could not regret what I have done for you. I feel myself drawn by powers far too sweet, and I lack strength to wish that things were not as they are. But to tell the truth, I fear to think of the consequences. I am much afraid that I love you a little more than I ought.

VALÈRE: Ah! Elise, what can you have to fear from the kindness you have shown me?

ELISE: Alas! a hundred things: my father's wrath, reproaches from my family, the censure of the world—but most of all, Valère, a change in your heart and that criminal coldness with which those of your sex most often repay the over-ardent testimonies of innocent love.

VALÈRE: Oh! do not do me the wrong of judging me by others. Suspect me of anything, Elise, but not that I should fail in my duty to you. I love you too much for that, and I will love you as long as I live.

ELISE: Ah! that is the way you all talk. All men are alike in their speech; their actions alone reveal their differences.

VALÈRE: If our actions alone reveal what we are, then at least wait and judge my heart by mine; and do not invent crimes for me simply because unhappy apprehension has bred unjust fear. I beg you, do not kill me with mortal blows of outrageous suspicion. Give me time to convince you, by a thousand and one proofs, that my intentions are honorable.

ELISE: Alas! how easily we are persuaded by those we love! Yes, Valère, I think you have no room in your heart for deceit. I am convinced that you love me truly, and will always be faithful to me. I have no wish to doubt you; I am sad only because I fear I may be blamed by others.

VALÈRE: What is it that worries you?

ELISE: I would have nothing to fear if everyone saw you as I do. For in your very person I see enough to justify what I have done. My heart has all your merit for its defense, reinforced by that gratitude which Heaven has bade me owe you. Not an hour passes but I picture to myself the terrible catastrophe which brought us into one another's sight; your amazing generosity, which made you risk your life to preserve mine from the fury of the waves; the great pains you took, how tenderly you cared for me after lifting me from the water; and the assiduous homage of your ardent love, which neither time nor difficulty has discouraged; which causes you to neglect both family and fatherland; which detains

168

60 you in this place, and makes you hide your rank for my sake; and which has reduced you to wearing my father's livery. All of this has certainly made a wonderful impression on me, and in my eyes is justification enough for the engagement I have consented to. But perhaps that is not enough to justify it to the world, nor am I sure that every one feels as I do.

VALÈRE: For all that you have said, it is only
70 through my love that I pretend to merit your esteem, and as for your scruples, a father like yours is justification enough for anything you might do. His excessive avarice and the austere manner in which he lives with his children might well authorize far stranger things than this. Pardon me, charming Elise, for talking this way in front of you, but you know there is no good to be said on that score. But, if, as I hope, I can finally find my parents again, it will not be hard to win him over. I am waiting
80 impatiently for news of them, and I will go and inquire if it is much longer in coming.

ELISE: Oh! Valère, do not go away, I beg you. Think only of winning my father's confidence.

VALÈRE: You have seen how I go about it; you saw how artfully compliant I was obliged to be in order to introduce myself into his service—under what mask of sympathy and agreement I disguise my feelings to please him—what role I play to gain his affection. And I am making
90 admirable progress. I have discovered that, to win men over, there is no better way than to trick yourself out in their inclinations, fall in with their maxims, burn incense to their faults, and applaud everything they do. One need have no fear of overdoing complaisance. No matter how obviously you play on their feelings, the shrewdest men are always the greatest dupes when it comes to flattery. There is nothing so impertinent or so ridiculous that you can't
100 make them swallow it—if you season it well with praise. Sincerity, of course, suffers a little by this trade. But if you need certain men, you must adapt yourself to them. And, since there is no other way of winning them over, it is not the flatterers who are at fault, but those who wish to be flattered.

ELISE: Why don't you try to gain my brother's

support too—in the event my maid should decide to tell our secret?

VALÈRE: I cannot manage both of them at the same   110 time. The father's temperament and the son's are so opposed, it would be hard to accommodate the confidings of both at once. But you, for your part, could approach your brother, and avail yourself of his friendship to get him to act on our behalf. There he comes now. I'll withdraw. Use the occasion to sound him out, but don't disclose our affair unless you think the time is ripe.   *(Exit.)*

ELISE: I don't know if I will have the courage to   120 confide in him.

Enter CLEANTH.

CLEANTH: I am very happy to find you alone, Elise. I have been burning to unburden a secret to you.

ELISE: Here I am, ready to listen, Cleanth. What do you wish to tell me?

CLEANTH: A thousand things, Elise—all bound up in three words: I'm in love.

ELISE: You are in love?   130

CLEANTH: I am in love. But before I say more, I know I am dependent on my father; that the name of son subjects me to his wishes; that we should not commit ourselves without the consent of those who brought us into the world; that Heaven has made them the masters of our troth; that we are enjoined not to pledge it except by their direction; that having never been affected by foolish passions, they are in a condition to be deceived much less often than we are, and   140 can see more clearly what is best for us. I know that we ought to trust the light of their prudence rather than the blindness of our passion and that the extravagance of youth most often lures us toward the precipice of sorrow. I am telling all this to you, Elise, so that you won't take the trouble to tell it to *me*. For to tell the truth, my love will not listen. So, please do not make objections.

ELISE: Are you engaged, Cleanth, to her whom   150 you love?

CLEANTH: No, but I am resolved to be. And again I beg you not to offer any reasons to dissuade me.

ELISE: Am I such a stranger, Cleanth?

CLEANTH: No, Elise; but you are not in love. You do not know the violence that tender love does to our hearts. I mistrust your prudence.

ELISE: Alas! Cleanth, let us not talk of my prudence. There is no one who is not deficient in that at least once in a lifetime; and if I opened my heart to you, perhaps in your eyes I should seem far less prudent than you are.

CLEANTH: Ah! I wish to Heaven, that your heart, like mine . . .

ELISE: First of all, let us finish with your affair. Tell me, who is she. . . .

CLEANTH: A young lady who has lived but a short time in this neighborhood, and who seems to have been made to inspire love in all who see her. Nature never shaped anything more lovable. I felt transported the moment I saw her. Her name is Marianne and she lives under the protection of her mother—a good woman who is almost always ill, and whom her daughter holds in such loving regard, it is unbelievable. She waits on her, takes pity on her, and consoles her so tenderly that it touches your heart. She has the most charming way in the world of going about her business. A thousand graces shine through her every action. Such alluring sweetness, such engaging goodness, such adorable civility! such . . . Oh! Elise, if you could only see her!

ELISE: I see a great deal of her, Cleanth, through what you have told me. And to understand her, it is enough for me that you love her.

CLEANTH: I have discovered, in a roundabout way, that they are not very well provided for, and that even with frugal management, they can hardly stretch their income far enough to cover all their needs. Imagine, Elise, what a pleasure it would be to be able to raise the fortunes of the person one loves, adroitly to supply a little help for the modest needs of a virtuous family. And think how unpleasant it must be for me to be powerless to taste that pleasure because of my father's stinginess, to be powerless to surprise this beautiful girl with some proof of my love for her.

ELISE: Oh! Cleanth, I can easily conceive how exasperated you must feel.

CLEANTH: Ah! Elise, much more so than you can imagine. Really, have you ever seen anything more cruel than the rigorous economy he imposes on us, than this queer stinginess under which we languish? What good will wealth do us, if it comes only when we are past the age when we can most enjoy it, if even to maintain myself I am now obliged to go into debt on every side, and if I am reduced with you to seeking help from tradesmen to find the means to wear decent clothes? I really wanted to ask you to help me find out father's attitude toward my present feelings. If I find him contrary, I am resolved to go away, in the company of that wonderful creature, to enjoy whatever fortune Providence may offer us. I am having somebody look everywhere for money to borrow for this purpose; and, if your affairs are in the same state as mine, if father insists on opposing our desires, we will both leave him, and free ourselves of this tyranny, to which his insupportable avarice has so long subjected us.

ELISE: It is only too true that he gives us more reason every day to regret our mother's death, and that . . .

CLEANTH: I can hear his voice. Let us go somewhere else to conclude our confidences. Later we will join forces and assault his hard heart together.   *(Exeunt.)*

Enter HARPAGON *and* LA FLECHE.

HARPAGON: Get out of here at once, and don't answer back! Go on, leave my house! You mastermind of crime! You born gallows bait!

FLECHE: *(aside)* I have never seen anything so wicked as this cursèd old man, and I believe, begging your pardon, he has a devil in his flesh.

HARPAGON: Are you muttering between your teeth?

FLECHE: Why chase me out of the house?

HARPAGON: As though you didn't know why! Scoundrel! Go quickly before I beat you!

FLECHE: What have I done?

HARPAGON: You have done enough to make me want you to leave.

FLECHE: My master your son gave me orders to wait for him.

HARPAGON: Go and wait for him in the street, not

250 here in my house, standing there as stiff and straight as a post to watch what goes on and profit from everything. . . . I will not have someone continually spying on my business, a traitor whose cursèd eyes besiege all my actions, devour all I possess, and ferret about in every corner for something to steal.

FLÈCHE: How the deuce do you expect anyone to steal from you? Can you rob a man when he keeps everything under lock and key, and stands
260 guard day and night?

HARPAGON: I will lock up whatever I think should be locked up, and I will stand guard as I please. *(to audience)* There, isn't that the talk of a spy who watches everything you do? I tremble lest he suspect something about my money. *(to LA FLÈCHE)* Are you the kind of man who would go about spreading the story that I have money hidden away?

FLÈCHE: *Do* you have money hidden away?

270 HARPAGON: No, you rascal, I didn't say that. *(aside)* I'm losing my temper. *(to LA FLÈCHE)* I mean, would you go around spreading the story that I do have some—out of malice?

FLÈCHE: Hoho! what difference does it make to us, if you have or have not? Things are always the same for us anyway.

HARPAGON: Ha! you play the reasoner! I'll teach you how to reason with your ears. *(lifting his hand to give LA FLÈCHE a box on the ear)* One last
280 time—get out of here!

FLÈCHE: All right, I'm going.

HARPAGON: Wait. You're not taking anything of mine with you?

FLÈCHE: What could I take of yours?

HARPAGON: Come here, so I can see. Show me your hands.

FLÈCHE: There they are.

HARPAGON: *(sarcastically)* Your other hands.

FLÈCHE: My other hands?

290 HARPAGON: Yes.

FLÈCHE: *(good-humoredly)* There they are.

HARPAGON: *(pointing to LA FLÈCHE's breeches)* Have you put anything inside there?

FLÈCHE: See for yourself.

HARPAGON: *(feeling the knees of LA FLÈCHE's breeches)* These breeches are just right for hiding stolen goods, and I wish somebody had been hanged for it. . . .

FLÈCHE: Ah! how well a man like that deserves what he fears, and what pleasure it would give 300 me to steal from him.

HARPAGON: Eh?

FLÈCHE: What?

HARPAGON: What did you say about stealing?

FLÈCHE: I said that you are poking everywhere to see if I have stolen anything from you.

HARPAGON: That's what I intend to do.

FLÈCHE: *(aside)* A pox on avarice and the avaricious!

HARPAGON: How's that? What did you say? 310

FLÈCHE: What did I say?

HARPAGON: Yes. What did you say about avarice and the avaricious?

FLÈCHE: I said, a pox on avarice and the avaricious.

HARPAGON: Who are you talking about?

FLÈCHE: About avaricious men.

HARPAGON: And who are they, these avaricious men?

FLÈCHE: They are misers and villains. 320

HARPAGON: But who do you mean by that?

FLÈCHE: What are you so upset about?

HARPAGON: I am upset about what I ought to be upset about.

FLÈCHE: Do you think I mean you?

HARPAGON: I think what I think. But I want you to tell me who you were speaking to when you said that.

FLÈCHE: I . . . I was speaking to my beret.

HARPAGON: And I might well knock if off. 330

FLÈCHE: Would you stop me from cursing avaricious men?

HARPAGON: No, but I'll stop you from chattering and being insolent. Keep quiet.

FLÈCHE: I haven't named anybody.

HARPAGON: I'll thrash you if you talk.

FLÈCHE: If your nose feels snotty, blow it.

HARPAGON: Will you be quiet?

FLÈCHE: Yes, in spite of myself.

HARPAGON: Ah! ah! 340

FLÈCHE: *(showing him one of his waist-coat pockets)* Look, here's another pocket. Are you satisfied?

HARPAGON: Come now, give it back to me without any more searching.

FLÈCHE: What?

HARPAGON: What you took from me.

FLÈCHE: I took nothing from you.

HARPAGON: Are you sure?

FLÈCHE: Positive.

350 HARPAGON: Goodbye! Go to the devil!

FLÈCHE: Well, I must say, I have been very handsomely dismissed!

HARPAGON: At least I have laid something to your conscience.

(Exit LA FLÈCHE.*)*

That rascal of a valet makes me uneasy, and I don't care to see the limping cur around here. *(alone)* It's certainly no small worry having a large sum of money in this house, and it's a lucky

360 man who has his fortune well invested, and can carry what he needs for expenses on his own person. It's no little problem to find, in an entire house, a safe hiding place for it. Because, to my way of thinking, your strong-boxes are suspect; I'd never trust my money to one. In my opinion they are nothing but bait for thieves, they are what a thief always goes after first.

Enter CLEANTH *and* ELISE *unnoticed.*

Still, I don't know if it was wise to bury the ten

370 thousand écus I was paid yesterday in the garden. Ten thousand gold écus is a rather large sum to have about the house. *(noticing* CLEANTH *and* ELISE*)* Oh! Heavens! I must have given myself away! I must have been carried away by anxiety —and I think I spoke out loud while I was reasoning with myself all alone here. . . . What's the matter?

CLEANTH: Nothing, father.

HARPAGON: Have you been there very long?

380 ELISE: We have just come.

HARPAGON: You heard . . .

CLEANTH: What, father?

HARPAGON: There . . .

ELISE: What?

HARPAGON: What I just said.

CLEANTH: No.

HARPAGON: Yes, you did, you did.

370 *écus* The monetary units mentioned in the play had the following values: twelve *deniers*=one *sol;* twenty sols=one *franc;* three francs=one *écu;* ten francs=one *pistole;* twenty francs=one *gold louis*

ELISE: I beg your pardon, but we didn't.

HARPAGON: I can plainly see you heard something. I was talking to myself about how hard it 390 is to find money these days, and I said that anyone who happens to have ten thousand écus about the house is a very lucky man.

CLEANTH: We held back for fear of interrupting you.

HARPAGON: I am only too glad to let you know what I said. So you won't get it all wrong and think it is I who have the ten thousand écus.

CLEANTH: We don't concern ourselves with your affairs. 400

HARPAGON: Would to God I had that much money, ten thousand écus!

CLEANTH: I don't believe it.

HARPAGON: It would be a fine thing for me.

ELISE: These are matters . . .

HARPAGON: I could certainly use it.

CLEANTH: I think that . . .

HARPAGON: It would set me up very comfortably.

ELISE: You are . . .

HARPAGON: I wouldn't complain then, as I do 410 now, about how hard the times are!

CLEANTH: My God, father, you have no room to complain: everyone knows you are well-off.

HARPAGON: What! I am well-off? Those who say so are liars. Nothing could be more untrue. And those who go around spreading such a story are all villains.

ELISE: Don't be angry.

HARPAGON: It is very strange that my own children should betray me and become my enemies. 420

CLEANTH: Am I your enemy because I say you are well-off?

HARPAGON: Yes. That kind of talk and your extravagant spending will one day cause somebody to come here and to cut my throat, under the impression that my clothes are lined with money.

CLEANTH: What extravagant spending have I done?

HARPAGON: What? Is there anything more scandalous than the sumptuous clothes that you 430 parade all over the city? Yesterday I was criticizing your sister, but this is far worse. This cries out to Heaven for vengeance; and, taking you from head to foot, there is enough on you to buy a good piece of property. I have told you twenty times, son, that your ways displease me very much. You are breaking your neck to look like a marquis, and in order to go about dressed as you are, I am sure you must be stealing from me.

440 CLEANTH: Ha! how could I steal from you?

HARPAGON: How should I know? Then where do you get the means to keep up your fashionable appearance?

CLEANTH: I, father? Why, I gamble, and, since I am very lucky, I put all the money I win on my back.

HARPAGON: That is very ill-advised. If you are lucky at cards you ought to profit by it, and invest your money at an honest interest, so that one

450 day you will find it has . . . I should like very much to know, not to mention the rest, what good are all those ribbons you are garnished with from head to foot, as if half a dozen laces would not be enough to hold up your breeches? Is it really necessary to spend your money on wigs, when you can wear the hair that grows on your head, which doesn't cost a sou? I'll wager your wigs and ribbons alone are worth at least twenty pistoles. And twenty pistoles bring in eight

460 francs, six sols, and eight deniers a year, even at eight per cent interest.

CLEANTH: You are quite right.

HARPAGON: Enough of that; let us talk about something else. Eh? (aside, seeing CLEANTH and ELISE making signs to one another) I think they are signalling one another to pick my pockets. (to CLEANTH and ELISE) What do those signs mean?

ELISE: We were bargaining as to who should speak first, my brother or myself. Both of us have

470 something to tell you.

HARPAGON: And I, too, have something to tell both of you.

CLEANTH: It is about marriage, father, that we wish to speak with you.

HARPAGON: And it is marriage also that I want to discuss with you.

ELISE: Oh! father!

HARPAGON: Why "Oh! father!"? Is it the word, daughter, or the thing that frightens you?

480 CLEANTH: Marriage could be frightening in both respects, depending on how you mean it. And we are afraid that our inclinations might not agree with your choice.

453 *laces* ties lacing the breeches to the doublet. Men of fashion often ornamented their laces with ribbons

HARPAGON: Have a little patience. Don't get alarmed. I know what is best for you both, and neither one of you will have reason to complain of anything I intend to do. Now, to begin at the beginning, tell me, have you ever seen a girl named Marianne, who lives not far from here?

CLEANTH: Yes, father. 490

HARPAGON: (to ELISE) And you?

ELISE: I have heard of her.

HARPAGON: What do you think of this girl, Cleanth?

CLEANTH: An extremely charming person.

HARPAGON: Her physiognomy?

CLEANTH: Very honest and intelligent.

HARPAGON: Her air and manner?

CLEANTH: Exquisite, to be sure.

HARPAGON: Don't you think a girl like that is 500 worth some consideration?

CLEANTH: Yes, father.

HARPAGON: That she might be a very desirable match?

CLEANTH: Very desirable.

HARPAGON: That she looks very much as though she would make a good housewife?

CLEANTH: No doubt.

HARPAGON: And that a husband would be completely satisfied with her? 510

CLEANTH: Surely.

HARPAGON: There is one slight obstacle. I am afraid she may not have as much money as one might reasonably expect.

CLEANTH: Ah! father, money is no consideration when it is a question of marrying an honest woman.

HARPAGON: Pardon me if I disagree! But there is always this to be said: if a fortune does not measure up to one's expectations, one can always 520 try to make it up some other way.

CLEANTH: Of course.

HARPAGON: Well—I am happy to find that you agree with me, because her maidenly conduct and sweet disposition have won my heart and I am resolved to marry her. Provided she has some kind of property.

CLEANTH: Eh?

HARPAGON: What?

CLEANTH: You say you have resolved . . . 530

HARPAGON: To marry Marianne.

CLEANTH: Who? you, you?

HARPAGON: Yes. I, I, I! What do you mean by that?

CLEANTH: I feel dizzy all of a sudden. I think I'll go.

(Exit CLEANTH.*)*

HARPAGON: It will pass. Quick, go into the kitchen and drink a large glass of plain water. *(to* ELISE*)* There's one of your lily-livered dandies—no more constitution than a chicken! Well, daughter, that's what I have decided for myself. As for your brother, I have a certain widow in mind that someone spoke to me about this very morning. And as for you, I am going to give you to Signor Anselm.

ELISE: To Signor Anselm?

HARPAGON: Yes. A man who is mature, prudent and wise, who is not over fifty, and who is famous for his great wealth.

ELISE: I would rather not get married at all, father, if you please.

HARPAGON: And I, my little girl, my pet, would rather you did get married, if you please.

ELISE: I beg your pardon, father.

HARPAGON: I beg your pardon, daughter.

ELISE: I am Signor Anselm's most humble servant, but, with your permission, I will not marry him.

HARPAGON: I am your very humble valet, but with your permission, you shall marry him—this very evening.

ELISE: This very evening?

HARPAGON: This very evening.

ELISE: That shall never be, father.

HARPAGON: That shall be, daughter.

ELISE: No.

HARPAGON: Yes.

ELISE: I tell you, no.

HARPAGON: I tell you, yes.

ELISE: You shall never force me to do such a thing.

HARPAGON: I shall force you to do such a thing.

ELISE: I would kill myself sooner than marry such a husband.

HARPAGON: You will not kill yourself, and you shall marry him. Such audacity! Did you ever hear of a daughter talking to her father that way?

ELISE: Did you ever hear of a father marrying off his daughter that way?

HARPAGON: It is a match which will admit of no objection. And I will wager that everyone will approve my choice.

ELISE: And I will wager that no reasonable person could possibly approve it.

HARPAGON: Here is Valère. Would you be willing to let him be the judge of this matter for both of us?

ELISE: I'll consent to that.

HARPAGON: Will you abide by his decision?

ELISE: Yes. I will stand by whatever he says.

HARPAGON: It's settled then.

Enter VALÈRE.

Here, Valère. We have elected you to decide who is in the right, my daughter or myself.

VALÈRE: You, sir, there's no contradicting that.

HARPAGON: You know, of course, what we are talking about.

VALÈRE: No, but you couldn't be wrong; you are reason itself.

HARPAGON: Tonight I want to give her a husband who is as rich as he is wise, and the hussy tells me to my face she will have no part of him. What do you say to that?

VALÈRE: What do I say to that?

HARPAGON: Yes.

VALÈRE: Hoho!

HARPAGON: What?

VALÈRE: I say that fundamentally I am of your opinion; and that you couldn't possibly be wrong; but on the other hand, she is not absolutely in the wrong either, and . . .

HARPAGON: How so! Signor Anselm is a considerable match. He is a gentleman: noble, cultured, poised, intelligent and very rich; and he has no children left from his first marriage. Could she do better?

VALÈRE: True, but she might tell you that you are hurrying things somewhat, and that she ought to have a little time at least to find out whether she can adapt her temperament to . . .

HARPAGON: This is an opportunity that must be grasped by the forelock. This match offers me an advantage which I would find in no other. He has agreed to take her without a dowry and . . .

VALÈRE: Without a dowry?

HARPAGON: Yes.

VALÈRE: Ah! I have nothing more to say. You see, here is a reason that is entirely convincing; one can only defer to it. . . .

HARPAGON: To me it represents a considerable saving.

630 VALÈRE: Certainly. There's no denying it. It's true your daughter may suggest to you that marriage is a more important step than you are inclined to think; that it is a question of being happy or unhappy for the rest of one's life; and that a partnership which will last till death should never be entered on without great precaution.

HARPAGON: Without a dowry!

VALÈRE: You are right. That decides everything, naturally. Though there are those who might tell
640 you that in such matters you certainly ought to have some regard for your daughter's inclinations and that the great difference in age, in temperament, and in sensibility would render such a marriage liable to very unhappy accidents.

HARPAGON: Without a dowry!

VALÈRE: Oh! there's no gainsaying that, as everyone knows. Who the deuce would argue the point? Not that there aren't many fathers who are more interested in their daughters' happiness
650 than in the money they give with them; who would never sacrifice them to their own interest; and who seek, above all else, to insure that sweet conformity in marriage which is a continuous source of honor, tranquility and joy, and which . . .

HARPAGON: Without a dowry!

VALÈRE: Very true. That closes every mouth. Without a dowry? An irrefutable argument!

HARPAGON: Wait! I think I hear a dog barking.
660 (aside) Is someone trying to get at my money? (to VALÈRE) Don't move; I'll be back in a minute.

(Exit HARPAGON.)

ELISE: Are you joking, Valère, talking to him this way?

VALÈRE: I don't want to sour him. This way I cam better accomplish my own ends. Opposing his ideas to his face is a sure way to spoil everything. There are certain minds you have to take by the bias. Some temperaments are inimical to any
670 kind of resistance: they stiffen themselves against the truth, and always balk when they confront the straight road of reason. You can guide them where you want to take them only by leading them in a roundabout way. Pretend that you con-

sent to what he wants; you will be more certain to get your way in the end. . . .

ELISE: But this marriage, Valère?

VALÈRE: We'll break it on the bias.

ELISE: What can we contrive if it is to be concluded tonight? 680

VALÈRE: You must ask them to delay it. Feign a sickness.

ELISE: But they will discover the pretense—if they call in the doctor.

VALÈRE: Are you joking? Do doctors know anything about sickness? Come now, with doctors you can have any sickness you please, and they will find reasons for your having it, and tell you where it comes from.

690
Enter HARPAGON.

HARPAGON: (aside) It was nothing, thank God!

VALÈRE: As a last resort we could run away and leave all this behind. And if your love, Elise, is capable of firmness . . . (seeing HARPAGON) Yes, a daughter should obey her father. She should have no concern for what her husband is like; and, when such a powerful argument as *without a dowry* intervenes, she should be ready to accept whatever is given her.

HARPAGON: Good! That was well said, that! 700

VALÈRE: Sir, I beg pardon if I have been too forward, and for having made so bold as to talk to her this way.

HARPAGON: What do you mean? I am delighted. And I want to give you absolute power over her. (to ELISE) There's no good running away. (ELISE *moves to the end of the stage.*) I give him the same authority over you that God gave me, and I expect you to do everything he tells you.

VALÈRE: (to ELISE) After that how can you resist 710 my remonstrances! Sir, I will follow her and continue the lessons I have been giving her.

HARPAGON: Yes, you will oblige me. Truly . . .

VALÈRE: I think it is good to pull in the reins with her.

HARPAGON: That's right, you should. . . .

VALÈRE: Don't worry about a thing; I am sure I can manage this.

678 *by the bias* by indirection

HARPAGON: Do, do as you like. I am going to take a
little walk through the city. I'll be back shortly.

VALÈRE: Yes, money is the most precious thing
in the world, and you ought to thank God for
the honest father He has given you. He knows
what it takes to live. When someone offers to take
a girl without a dowry, she ought not to
look any further. Everything is included in
without a dowry; it takes the place of beauty,
youth, birth, honor, intelligence and
probity.

(*Exeunt* VALÈRE *and* ELISE)

HARPAGON: Ah! bravo, bravo! Spoken like an
oracle. Lucky the man with such a servant!

ACT TWO

CLEANTH *is on stage. Enter* LA FLÈCHE.

CLEANTH: Ah! you traitor! What new mischief
have you been getting into? Didn't I give you
orders? . . .

FLÈCHE: Yes sir! I came here with every intention
of waiting for you, but your father, the most
ungracious man in the world, chased me out of
the house, in spite of myself, and I came close to
getting a beating.

CLEANTH: How goes our business? Things are
more pressing than ever. Since I last saw you, I
have discovered that my own father is my rival.

FLÈCHE: Your father is in love?

CLEANTH: Yes; and I had all the trouble in the
world to keep him from seeing how much this
news distressed me.

FLÈCHE: Him, dabbling in love? What the devil
can he be thinking of? Does public opinion mean
nothing to him? Was love made for men built like
that?

CLEANTH: It must be for my sins that he has got
this idea into his head.

FLÈCHE: For what reason do you keep your love a
secret from him?

CLEANTH: So that he will be less suspicious. So
that he won't suspect my actions should it become necessary to try and prevent his marriage.
What answer did they give you?

FLÈCHE: By Heaven, sir, those that have to borrow are in a very bad way! A man has to put up
with strange things when he is reduced, as you
are, to putting himself into the hands of sharks.

CLEANTH: You couldn't get the money?

FLÈCHE: Not exactly. Our Master Simon, the
broker, who was recommended to us as an energetic, determined man, assures me he has left no
stone unturned to serve you—and that your face
alone has won his heart.

CLEANTH: Will I get the fifteen thousand francs I
asked for?

FLÈCHE: Yes, but there are some trifling conditions attached—which you must accept, if you
expect anything to be done.

CLEANTH: Did he let you speak to the man who is
supposed to lend the money?

FLÈCHE: Oh, really, it is not so simple as all that.
He took more pains to hide himself than you do
yourself; it is all much more mysterious than you
might think. They will by no means tell his
name and they are going to bring you together
today in a private house, so that he can learn from
your own lips who your family is and what
your expectations are. But I don't have the slightest doubt that your father's name alone will make
things easy for you.

CLEANTH: And especially the fact that our mother
is dead, whose property no one can take from me.

FLÈCHE: Here are a few articles which he himself
dictated to our go-between, to be shown to you
before any action will be taken.

"Supposing that the lender is satisfied with the
collateral offered, and that the borrower has
reached his majority and is from a family whose
estate is large, solid, assured and free from all
encumbrance, a valid and precise contract will be
drawn up in the presence of a notary, the most

honest man available, who, for that reason, must be chosen by the lender, to whom it is of the utmost importance that the contract be properly
70 drawn up."

CLEANTH: I have no objection to that.

FLÈCHE: "The lender, in order not to burden his conscience with any scruples, intends to charge no more than six percent interest."

CLEANTHE: Six per cent interest? By Jove, an nonest fellow indeed! There is no reason to complain about that.

FLÈCHE: Indeed not!

"But, since the said lender does not have the
80 sum required in his own house, and because, in order to oblige the borrower, he is forced to borrow himself at the rate of twenty per cent, it is only fair that the said, first borrower should pay this interest without prejudice to the other, considering that it is only to oblige him that the said lender will borrow the sum requested."

CLEANTH: What the devil! What Jew, what Arab am I dealing with? That's more than twenty-five per cent interest!

90 FLÈCHE: That's right. That's what I told him. You had better look into it yourself.

CLEANTH: What is there to look into? I need money. I will have to agree to anything.

FLÈCHE: That's what I told him.

CLEANTH: Is there something else?

FLÈCHE: Only a small item.

"Of the fifteen thousand francs that are requested, the lender can count on only twelve thousand francs in cash. As for the remaining
100 thousand écus, the borrower must take them in furniture, clothing, and jewelry, a list of which follows this note, and which the said lender has, in all good faith, priced as moderately as he possibly can."

CLEANTH: What does he mean by that?

FLÈCHE: Listen to the list.

"First: one four-poster bed, with Hungarian point lace handsomely sewn on olive-colored cloth, with six chairs, and a counterpane of the
110 same material; all in good condition and lined with changeable red and blue taffeta.

"In addition: one bedstead canopy of good, dry rose-colored serge, with silk fringes."

CLEANTH: What does he expect me to do with that?

FLÈCHE: Hold on.

"In addition: a set of tapestries; the subject of which is *The Amours of Gombaut and Macaea*.

"In addition: one large walnut table, with twelve columns, or turned pillars, pulling out at either end, and fitted with half-a-dozen joint
120 stools under it."

CLEANTH: My God! What good will that do me?

FLÈCHE: Be patient.

"In addition: three large muskets inlaid with mother-of-pearl, with three matching tripods.

"In addition: one brick furnace with two retorts and three recipients, very useful for anyone interested in distilling.

"In addition: a Bologna lute with all its strings, or a few lacking.
130
"In addition: a troll-madam table and a chess board, with a goose game restored from the Greeks; all very fine to pass away the time when one has nothing to do.

"In addition: a lizard skin, three feet long, and half-filled with straw—a very agreeable curiosity to hang from a bedroom ceiling.

"The total mentioned above, easily worth more than four thousand, five hundred francs, is reduced in price to one thousand écus by the
140 moderation of the lender."

CLEANTH: May the plague choke him and his moderation, the traitor! Cut-throat that he is! Have you ever heard of such usury? Can't he be satisfied with the furious interest he demands, without making me take all the junk he has heaped up, for three thousand francs? I won't get more than two hundred écus for the lot! And yet I must resign myself and consent to whatever he wants. He is in a position to make
150 me accept anything. The dog has me by the throat.

FLÈCHE: Sir, I see you taking the very same road, no offense intended, that Panurge followed to his ruin: taking money in advance, buying dear and selling cheap, and eating your wheat in the blade.

117 *The Amours . . . Macaea* a popular rustic romance of the time
131 *troll-madam* game played with ivory balls rolled into numbered holes or compartments
154 *Panurge* the improvident rascal in Rabelais' *Gargantua and Pantagruel*

CLEANTH: What would you have me do? You see what your men are reduced to be the cursèd avarice of their fathers! Is it any wonder, after this, that the sons should wish their fathers' death?

FLÈCHE: I must confess, the stinginess of yours would infuriate the calmest man in the world. I am not strongly inclined toward the gallows, thank God, and when I am with my colleagues, seeing them taking big chances for small gains, I always know when to pull my iron out of the fire, and when it is prudent to drop out of any adventure that smells ever so little of the gallows. But, to tell the truth, the way your father acts tempts me very much to steal from him. And I think, if I did rob him, I would be doing a good deed.

CLEANTH: Give me the note; I want to look it over again.

Enter MASTER SIMON *and* HARPAGON.

SIMON: Yes sir, he is a young man in need of money. The state of his affairs obliges him to find some, and he will agree to anything you prescribe.

HARPAGON: But are you convinced, Master Simon, that I will run no risk? Are you acquainted with the name, the fortune and the family of the party for whom you are speaking?

SIMON: No, I cannot give you any definite information about him; and it was only by chance that he was directed to me; but he himself will enlighten you about everything. And his man assures me that you will be satisfied when you meet him. All I can tell you is that his family is very rich, that his mother is already dead, and that he will guarantee, if you wish it, that his father will die before eight months are out.

HARPAGON: That is something, indeed. Charity, Master Simon, obliges us to make others happy when it is in our power to do so.

SIMON: To be sure.

FLÈCHE: (*low to* CLEANTH) What does this mean? Our Master Simon talking to your father!

CLEANTH: (*low to* LA FLÈCHE) Could they have told him who I am? or have you betrayed me?

SIMON: (*noticing* CLEANTH *and* LA FLÈCHE) Aha! you are in a hurry! Who told you this was the house?

(*to* HARPAGON) In any event, sir, it was not I who revealed your name and lodgings. But, in my opinion, no great harm has been done: they are discreet fellows, and now you can discuss your business together.

HARPAGON: What?

SIMON: This is the gentleman who wants to borrow the fifteen thousand francs, the one I was telling you about.

HARPAGON: What! you rascal! It is you who abandon yourself to such culpable extremities!

CLEANTH: What! father, it is you who carry on this shameful business!

(*Exit* MASTER SIMON *and* LA FLÈCHE.)

HARPAGON: It is you who want to ruin yourself by such deplorable borrowing!

CLEANTH: It is you who seek to enrich yourself by this criminal usury!

HARPAGON: Do you dare, after that, to show your face to me?

CLEANTH: Do your dare, after that, to show your face to the world?

HARPAGON: Tell me, aren't you ashamed to descend to such debauchery, to hurl yourself into horrible expenditure, and shamefully to squander the wealth that your ancestors have amassed for you by the sweat of their brows?

CLEANTH: How can you help but blush for disgracing your class this way with this trade you practise, sacrificing your honor and reputation to your insatiable desire to pile écu on écu and outdoing, in point of interest, the most infamous subtleties ever invented by the most notorious usurers?

HARPAGON: Get out of my sight, scoundrel, get out of my sight!

CLEANTH: Who is the greater criminal in your opinion: the man who buys money because he needs it, or the man who steals money but has no use for it?

HARPAGON: Leave the room I tell you, and stop chafing my ears.

(*Exit* CLEANTH.)

I am not a bit sorry that this has happened; it is a warning to me to watch everything he does more closely than ever.

Enter FROSINE.

FROSINE: Sir . . .

HARPAGON: Wait a moment. I'll be back to talk with you. *(aside)* It's about time I take a peek at my money.   *(Exit.)*

Enter LA FLECHE.

FLECHE: The whole thing is very amusing. He must surely have a large store of supplies somewhere in the house, because we couldn't find a thing that's listed on the inventory he gave us.

FROSINE: Ah! it's you, my poor La Flèche! To what do we owe this meeting?

FLECHE: Aha! it's you, Frosine! What are *you* doing here?

FROSINE: What I do everywhere else: play the go-between in negotiations, make myself useful to others, and profit as much as I possibly can by whatever slight talent I may have. You know that in this world one is obliged to live by one's wits. And for women like myself Heaven has provided no other source of income than intrigue and persistency.

FLECHE: Do you have some business with the master of the house?

FROSINE: Yes, I am transacting some small business for him— for which I hope to be compensated.

FLECHE: By him? Ah! in faith, you'll have to be pretty sharp to get anything out of *him*; I warn you, money costs very dearly in this house.

FROSINE: There are certain services that are wonderfully effective.

FLECHE: I am your humble servant. But you don't know Signor Harpagon, yet. Signor Harpagon is of all humans the least human, the hardest and tightest mortal of all mortals. No service can push his gratitude far enough to make him unclench his fists. Of praise, esteem, benevolent words and friendship as much as you like, but money?—nothing doing. There is nothing more dry and withered than his favors and caresses, and "give" is a word for which he has such an aversion that he never says "I give," but "I lend, you good-day."

FROSINE: Mercy me! I know the art of milking a man. I have the secret for bringing out his tenderness, for tickling his heart, for finding his soft spot.

FLECHE: Useless here! If money is involved, I defy you to touch the man in question. On that score he is a Turk; and his turkery is the despair of all who know him; you could be dying, and he wouldn't turn a hair. In a word, he loves money more than reputation, honor or virtue, and the sight of anyone who expects to be paid throws him into convulsions. It wounds him mortally. It pierces his heart. It tears out his entrails. And if . . . He's coming back; I must be going.   *(Exit.)*

Enter HARPAGON.

HARPAGON: *(aside)* All is as it should be. *(to* FROSINE*)* How now! What is it, Frosine?

FROSINE: Ah! Mercy me, how well you are looking! You are the very picture of health!

HARPAGON: Who? I?

FROSINE: Never have I seen your color so fresh and jovial.

HARPAGON: Really?

FROSINE: Never in your life were you as young as you are now; I see men of twenty-five who are older than you.

HARPAGON: Nevertheless, Frosine, I'm a good sixty years old.

FROSINE: Well, what is that, sixty years old? A worry indeed! It's the bloom of life, that is. And now you are entering on a man's prime season.

HARPAGON: That's true. However, twenty years less wouldn't do me any harm, as I see it.

FROSINE: Are you joking? You have no need of them. You bid fair to live to be a hundred.

HARPAGON: Do you think so?

FROSINE: Of course. You show every indication. Hold still a bit. Oh, there it is! There it is! Between your two eyes!—a sign of long life!

HARPAGON: Do you know something about these things?

FROSINE: Certainly. Show me your hand. Ah! Mercy me, what a life line!

HARPAGON: How's that?

FROSINE: Don't you see how far that line goes?

HARPAGON: Well, yes. What does it mean?

FROSINE: By my faith, I said a hundred years but you will pass the one hundred and twenty mark.

HARPAGON: Is it possible?

FROSINE: You deserve a beating. I tell you, you

will bury your children and your children's children.

HARPAGON: So much the better! How goes our little transaction?

350 FROSINE: Need you ask? Did anyone ever see me start anything I couldn't finish? I have an especially wonderful talent for marriages. There aren't two people in the world that I couldn't find a way to couple in no time at all. If I had the notion, I believe I could marry the Grand Turk to the Republic of Venice. But, to be sure, there wasn't any such great difficulty involved in this affair. Since I have business at their house, I have already discussed you at length with both 360 of them; and I told the mother what plans you had conceived for Marianne, on seeing her pass through the street and take the air at her window.

HARPAGON: She answered . . .

FROSINE: She received the proposition with joy! And when I informed her that you are very desirous her daughter should be present tonight at the signing of the marriage contract which is to take place here, she readily consented. And she has entrusted her daughter to me for the 370 evening.

HARPAGON: I am obliged, Frosine, to give a supper for Signor Anselm, and I would like her to attend this feast.

FROSINE: A good idea. After dinner, she is to pay your daughter a visit; from here she plans to go and see the fair; and afterwards she can come back for supper.

HARPAGON: Fine! They can go together in my carriage. Which I will lend them.

380 FROSINE: That will suit her perfectly.

HARPAGON: But, Frosine, have you talked to the mother about the money she can give her daughter? Did you tell her she ought to help a little, herself? That she should make some special effort? That she should bleed herself for an occasion like this? For, I tell you again, no one marries a girl unless she brings something in.

FROSINE: What! This is a girl who will bring you twelve thousand francs a year.

390 HARPAGON: Twelve thousand francs a year?

FROSINE: Yes. First of all: those who raised and

nurtured her were very sparing on food. She is a girl used to living on salad, milk, cheese, and apples, and consequently doesn't require a richly set table, or fancy jellies or barley syrup all the time, or all the other delicacies that most women must have. And this is no trifling matter. It will make a difference of at least three thousand francs a year. Besides, she feels that true elegance lies in simplicity, and she doesn't care for magni- 400 ficent clothes, or rich jewelry, or sumptuous furniture—things which young ladies are usually so passionately addicted to. And that little item is worth more than four thousand francs a year. What's more, she has a tremendous aversion to cards—a thing not common in women nowadays. I know of one in our neighborhood who, at thirties and forties, mind you, lost twenty thousand francs this year! But suppose we take only a quarter of that. Five thousand francs a 410 year for cards, and four thousand francs for clothes and jewelry, make nine thousand francs. And we will figure one thousand écus for food. Isn't that your twelve thousand francs a year—every sou of it?

HARPAGON: Yes, not bad: but this account has nothing real in it.

FROSINE: I beg your pardon. Is the great sobriety that she will bring to your marriage nothing real? Or her inheritance of a great love for simplicity 420 in dress? Or the acquisition of a great fund of hatred for cards?

HARPAGON: It is a mockery to try and make up a dowry out of the expenses that she won't put me to. I won't give a receipt for something I don't receive. I must be able to touch something.

FROSINE: Mercy me! you will touch enough. They spoke to me about a certain country where they have some property. You shall be the master of it. 430

HARPAGON: That remains to be seen. But Frosine, there is something else that bothers me. The girl is young, as you can see, and young people usually like only their own kind, and seek only their company. I am afraid that a man of my age might not be to her taste, and that this might cause some little disorder in my house, which would not suit me at all!

355 *Grand Turk* the Sultan. Turkey and Venice were conventional instances of irreconcilable hostility.

408 *thirties and forties* the card game *trent et quarante* or *rouge et noir*, distantly related to blackjack

FROSINE: Ah! how little you know her! This is
440   another thing about her that I was going to men-
           tion. She has a frightful aversion to all young
           men, and feels no love except for the old.

HARPAGON: Her?

FROSINE: Yes, her. I wish you could hear her on
           that subject. She can't so much as stand the sight
           of a young fellow; but she is in ecstasy, she
           tells me, when she can look at a handsome old
           man with a majestic beard. For her, the oldest
           are the most charming. And I warn you not
450   to go and make yourself look younger than you
           are. She likes a man to be sixty at the very least.
           It wasn't four months ago, that, all set to be
           married, she broke off the marriage on the spot
           because her lover let it be known he was only
           fifty-six years old—and didn't use spectacles to
           sign the contract.

HARPAGON: Just for that?

FROSINE: Yes. She says she simply couldn't be
           satisfied with a man of fifty-six, and above all,
460   she is for the nose that wears spectacles.

HARPAGON: Really, this is something altogether
           new!

FROSINE: It goes much deeper than most people
           know. Like most young girls she has a few paint-
           ings and a few prints in her room, but what
           do you think the subjects are? Adonises? Cephal-
           uses? Parises? or Apollos? No. They are hand-
           some portraits of Saturn, of King Priam, of old
           Nestor, and good father Anchises on his son's
470   shoulders!

HARPAGON: That is admirable! I should never have
           suspected it. And I am very happy to learn she
           has that kind of disposition. In fact, had *I* been
           a woman, I wouldn't have liked young men at
           all.

FROSINE: I can well believe you. What are they
           but fancy drugs? And to love them, ha! They
           are nothing but handsome idiots, goodlooking
           fops that make you envy their complexions. I'd
480   really like to know what there is to them!

HARPAGON: As for me, I can't understand it. I don't
           know why some women are so fond of them.

FROSINE: They must be stark mad. To find youth
           amiable! Is there any common sense in it? Are

466 *Adonises . . . Anchises* types of youthful beauty con-
trasted with types of elderly worth

they men, these young dandies? Can you become
attached to one of those animals?

HARPAGON: That's what I have always said—with
           their effeminate, milk-fed voices, and their three
           little wisps of beard turned up like cat's whiskers,
           with their mouse-colored wigs, and their sloppy   490
           breeches, and their puffed-out stomachs!

FROSINE: They are well-built, indeed, compared
           with a person like you (*to the audience*) There's
           a man for you! There is someone who is a
           pleasure to look at! This is how a man should
           be made and dressed to inspire love.

HARPAGON: You like the way I look?

FROSINE: I should say! You are ravishing, you
           ought to have your portrait painted. Turn round
           a bit, if you please. You couldn't be better. Let   500
           me see you walk. (*to the audience*) Here is a body
           that is trim, supple and tall as it ought to be.
           And not marked by any infirmity.

HARPAGON: None to speak of, thank God! (*coughs*)
           Except my catarrh that bothers me from time
           to time.

FROSINE: That is nothing. Your catarrh is not
           unbecoming to you. You cough gracefully.

HARPAGON: But tell me, hasn't Marianne seen me
           yet? Hasn't she noticed me at all, passing by   510
           her house?

FROSINE: No. But we have talked about you a great
           deal. I sketched a portrait of your person for
           her. And I did not fail to boast of your merits
           and the advantage it would be for her to have
           a husband like you.

HARPAGON: You have done well. And I thank you.

FROSINE: I would like, sir, to ask a small favor
           of you. I have a lawsuit that I am on the point
           of losing for want of a little money; and you   520
           could easily assure my winning this suit if you
           would show me some little kindness. (HARPAGON
           frowns.) Ah! how well you will please her! What
           a marvellous impression your old-fashioned ruff
           will make! But she will be especially charmed
           by your breeches, attached to your doublet with
           laces; they'll make her go wild over you. A laced-
           up lover will seem to her a wonderful treat.

HARPAGON: Really, it delights me to hear you say
           it.   530

FROSINE: To tell the truth, sir, this suit is of the
           utmost importance to me. I am ruined if I lose
           it, and the least bit of help would set everything

right for me. (HARPAGON *frowns.*) I wish you could have seen the rapture in her face when she heard me speak of you. Her eyes sparkled with joy as I recited your qualities. In short, I left her in a state of extreme impatience to see this marriage entirely concluded.

540 HARPAGON: You have given me great pleasure, Frosine. And I must confess, I am under all the obligation in the world to you.

FROSINE: I beg you, sir, to give me the slight help I need. It will put me on my feet again. And I will be eternally indebted to you.

HARPAGON: Goodbye! I must get my mail ready.

FROSINE: I assure you, sir, you couldn't relieve me in a greater need.

HARPAGON: I will leave orders, so my coach will 550 be ready to take you to the fair.

FROSINE: I would not importune you, were I not forced to do so—out of necessity.

HARPAGON: And I'll see to it that supper is ready early so that you won't get sick.

FROSINE: Do not refuse me this favor, I beg of you.

HARPAGON: I am going. There, someone is calling me. I'll see you by and by.

(*Exit* HARPAGON.)

FROSINE: May the fever rack you! Cur! Villain! 560 The devil take you! The miser was deaf to all my attacks. Nevertheless I must not drop his suit: for in any case, there is the other party. I am sure of a good reward from them!

ACT THREE

On stage; HARPAGON, CLEANTH, ELISE, VALÈRE, DAME CLAUDE, MASTER JACQUES, BRINDAVOINE *and* LA MERLUCHE.

HARPAGON: Here, all of you come here. I want to give you orders for this evening, and assign everyone a job. Step forward, Dame Claude. Let's begin with you. Good, I see you are already armed. I consign to you the task of cleaning up the house; but be especially careful not to

10 rub the furniture too hard, or you'll wear it out. Furthermore, I assign you to see to the bottles during supper. And if any of them are carried off, or if anything is broken, you will be responsible, and I'll deduct it from your wages.

JACQUES: (*aside*) A convenient punishment.

HARPAGON: (*to* DAME CLAUDE) Go. . . .

(*Exit* DAME CLAUDE.)

You, Brindavoine, and you, La Merluche, are appointed to rinse the glasses, and to serve the

20 wine—but only when someone is thirsty. And don't follow the example of those impudent lackies who go and *incite* people to drink and put the notion in their heads when they aren't even thinking about it. Wait until they have

asked you more than once, and remember always to bring a lot of water.

JACQUES: (*aside*) Yes, pure wine goes to the head.

MERLUCHE: Shall we take our canvas smocks off, sir?

HARPAGON: Yes, when you see the guests coming, 30 and be careful not to spoil your clothes.

BRINDAVOINE: You know very well, sir, that one side of my doublet is covered with a big spot of lamp-oil.

MERLUCHE: And I, sir, have a big hole in the back of my breeches, and I can be seen, begging your pardon . . .

HARPAGON: Peace! Keep that side discreetly turned toward the wall, and always show your front side to the world. And you, always hold your 40 hat like this (*holds his hat over his chest*) when you serve.

(*Exeunt* LA MERLUCHE *and* BRINDAVOINE.)

And as for you, my daughter, keep an eye open when they clear away the table, and see to it that nothing goes to waste. That's a proper job for a young girl. But meanwhile, prepare yourself to receive my fiancée, who is coming to pay

you a visit, and take you to the fair with her.
Did you hear what I said?

ELISE: Yes, father.

HARPAGON: And you, my son, the dandy whose latest escapade I was so good as to forgive, don't you go getting any ideas either and make sour faces at her.

CLEANTH: I father? Sour faces? And for what reason?

HARPAGON: By God, we know the drift of children whose fathers remarry, and how they feel toward what is called a stepmother. But, if you would like me to forget your last prank, I especially recommend that you treat this person to some of your most cheerful looks and give her the best reception you possibly can.

CLEANTH: To tell you the truth, father, I cannot promise you to be very glad she is to become my stepmother. I should be lying if I told you I would. But as for receiving her well and showing her a pleasant face, I promise to obey you punctually on that score.

HARPAGON: At least take care you do.

CLEANTH: You will see you will have no reason to complain.

HARPAGON: You will do wisely.

(*Exeunt* CLEANTH *and* ELISE.)

Valère, help me with this. Oh, there you are, Master Jacques! Come here. I have saved you for the last.

JACQUES: Is it to your coachman, sir, or is it to your cook you wish to speak? For I am one and the other.

HARPAGON: To the two of you.

JACQUES: But to which of us first?

HARPAGON: To the cook.

JACQUES: One moment then if you please. (*Takes off his coachman's coat and appears dressed as a cook.*)

HARPAGON: What the deuce kind of ceremony is this?

JACQUES: You have only to speak.

HARPAGON: I have committed myself, Master Jacques, to give a supper tonight.

JACQUES: (*aside*) This is miraculous!

HARPAGON: Tell me now, will you give us a fine feast?

JACQUES: Yes, if you will give me a good deal of money.

HARPAGON: What the devil! always money! It seems they have nothing else to say: money, money, money! That's the sword they keep by their bed, money!

VALÈRE: I have never heard a more impertinent answer. How miraculous it is to be able to set out a fine feast when you have a lot of money! It is the easiest thing in the world to do, and there is no man so poor in wit that he couldn't do as much. But it is a clever man who can talk about providing a fine feast for little money!

JACQUES: A fine feast for little money?

VALÈRE: Yes.

JACQUES: By my faith, Mr. Steward, you would oblige us if you would let us in on your secret—and if you will take my place as cook! You meddle so much in this house already, you might as well be the factotum.

HARPAGON: Be quiet. What will we need?

JACQUES: There is your steward who will provide a fine feast at small cost.

HARPAGON: Ha! I want you to answer me.

JACQUES: How many will you be at table?

HARPAGON: We will be eight or ten. When there is enough for eight, there is plenty for ten.

VALÈRE: Naturally.

JACQUES: Very well, we will need four kinds of soup and five other dishes. Soups, entrées . . .

HARPAGON: What the devil! That's enough to feed a whole city.

JACQUES: Roast . . .

HARPAGON: (*putting his hand over* MASTER JACQUES' *mouth*) Ah! traitor, you are eating up all my money!

JACQUES: Side dishes . . .

HARPAGON: (*putting his hand over* MASTER JACQUES' *mouth again*) More?

VALÈRE: Do you want to make everybody split open? Do you think our master invites people in order to *murder* them with food? Go and read the rules of health a while—and ask the doctors if there is anything more prejudicial to man than excessive eating.

HARPAGON: He is right.

VALÈRE: Learn, Master Jacques, you and the like of you, that a table overloaded with food is a cut-throat; that if you want to prove yourself a friend to those you invite, frugality should reign at the meals you serve; and that, according to

the saying of the ancients, we should eat to live,
and not live to eat.

HARPAGON: Oh! but that was well said! Come here,
I want to embrace you for that saying. It is the
150   most beautiful sentence I have ever heard in my
life. We should live to eat, and not eat to li . . .
No, that isn't it. How was it you said it?

VALÈRE: We should eat to live, and not live to eat.

HARPAGON: Yes, do you hear that? Who was the
great man who said it?

VALÈRE: At the moment I can't recall his name.

HARPAGON: Remember to write it down for me.
I want to have it carved in gold letters above
the mantelpiece in my dining room.

160   VALÈRE: I won't forget. And as for your supper,
you have only to leave it to me. I will order
things to be done as they should be.

HARPAGON: Take care of it then.

JACQUES: So much the better; it will mean less trouble for me.

HARPAGON: We should have those things that
people don't eat much of, that satisfy the
appetite quickly: a nice mutton stew, rather fat
with some kind of a meat-pie well garnished and
170   chestnuts to go with it. Yes, that! And let there
be a lot of it.

VALÈRE: Leave everything to me.

HARPAGON: Now, Master Jacques, my coach must
be cleaned up.

JACQUES: One moment. That was addressed to the
coachman. *(Exit, and reappears in his coachman's
coat.)* You said . . . ?

HARPAGON: That you should clean up my coach,
and have my horses ready to drive to the fair.

180   JACQUES: Your horses, sir? Faith, they are in no
condition to walk. I won't say they are down
on their litters. The poor beasts don't have any,
so I'd be speaking very improperly. But you
make them observe such strict fasts that they
are now no more than ideas or ghosts or appearances of horses.

HARPAGON: No wonder they are sick; they do
nothing.

JACQUES: And because they do nothing, sir, must
190   they eat nothing? It would be much better for
them, poor animals, to work a lot, and to eat
accordingly. It breaks my heart to see them so
weak, because, to tell the truth, I have so much
affection for my horses, that when I see them

suffer, it's just as though it were myself. Every
day I take food out of my own mouth to feed
them; it is a very hard nature, sir, that feels
no pity for the next one.

HARPAGON: It won't be much work for them to
go as far as the fair.   200

JACQUES: No, sir, I haven't the courage to drive
them, and it would lie on my conscience if I
hit them with the whip, in the condition they're
in. How do you expect them to pull a carriage?—they can't even pull themselves.

VALÈRE: Sir, I will ask our neighbor Picard if he
will be good enough to drive them. Besides, we
shall need him here to help prepare the supper.

JACQUES: Very well! I'd still rather they died under
someone else's hands and not mine.   210

VALÈRE: Master Jacques is intent on cavilling.

JACQUES: Mister Steward is intent on seeming
indispensable.

HARPAGON: Peace!

JACQUES: Sir, I can't stand flatterers, and I see what
he is doing. He continually restricts the bread,
the wine, the wood, the salt, and the candles
just to scratch your ear, to win your favor. It
makes me angry. And it grieves me to hear what
people say about you every day. Because I feel   220
a real affection for you, in spite of myself; and
after my horses, you are the person I like most.

HARPAGON: Could I learn from you, Master
Jacques, what people say about me?

JACQUES: Yes, sir, if I could be sure it wouldn't
make you angry.

HARPAGON: No, not in the least.

JACQUES: Pardon me, but I know very well you'd
fly into a rage.

HARPAGON: Not at all. On the contrary, it will   230
give me great pleasure to learn what is said about
me.

JACQUES: Sir, since it is your wish, I tell you
frankly: people everywhere are laughing at you.
They taunt us with a thousand jokes about you
on all sides and they are never so happy as when
tearing you to ribbons or making up countless
stories about your stinginess. One says that you
have special almanacs printed, in which you have
doubled the quarter-days and vigils, so you can   240
take advantage of the fasts you impose on your

240 *quarter-days . . . vigils* periods of fasting

household. Another says you always have a quarrel ready to pick with your valets when it is time for holiday gifts, or when they are leaving, so you'll have a reason for not giving them anything. This one tells the story that you once tried to bring your neighbor's cat to court for eating up the remainder of a leg of mutton. Somebody else says that you yourself were caught coming to steal your horses' oats, and that in the dark your coachman, the one before me, gave you I don't know how many blows with his stick, which you didn't care to say anything about. Shall I go on? We can't go anywhere without hearing people pull you apart. You are the talk of the town, the laughingstock of the world. and they never refer to you except by the name of miser, cut-throat, villain, or shark.

HARPAGON: You are a fool, a scoundrel, a rascal, an insolent knave!   *(Beats him.)*

JACQUES: There! Didn't I say it would be that way? You wouldn't believe me. I warned you that you would get angry if I told you the truth.

HARPAGON: Then learn how to talk.

                                                (Exit HARPAGON.*)*

VALÈRE: As far as I can see, Master Jacques, you are poorly paid for your frankness.

JACQUES: By God! Mister Upstart, playing the man of importance, it is none of your business. Save your laughs for your own beating when you get it, and don't come laughing at mine.

VALÈRE: Ah! good Master Jacques, please don't be angry.

JACQUES: *(aside)* He's backing down. I'll pretend to be tough, and if he is fool enough to be afraid of me, I'll give him a little thrashing. Did you know, Mister Comedian, that I myself never laugh?—and that if you get my temper up you are likely to be laughing out of the other side of your mouth?

VALÈRE: Gently now!

JACQUES: Why gently? What if I don't feel like being gentle?

VALÈRE: Please!

JACQUES: You are an impertinent fellow.

VALÈRE: Good Master Jacques!

JACQUES: There is no such person as good Master Jacques. If I get a stick, I'll beat the importance out of you.

VALÈRE: *(picking up the stick on the table)* What did you say? a stick?

JACQUES: Oh! I wasn't talking about that one.

VALÈRE: Did you know, Mister Fool, that I am man enough to thrash you?

JACQUES: I don't doubt it.

VALÈRE: That you are, by any standard, nothing but a miserable cook?

JACQUES: I know very well.

VALÈRE: And that you don't know me yet?

JACQUES: I beg your pardon.

VALÈRE: You'll beat me, you say?

JACQUES: I was joking.

VALÈRE: And your joking is not to my taste. This will teach you that you're a scurvy joker. *(Beats him.)*   *(Exit* VALÈRE.*)*

JACQUES: A pox on sincerity! It's a wretched practice. Here and now I renounce it, and I will never tell the truth again. As for my master, I'll let that go—he has some right to beat me. But, as for this steward, I'll take my revenge if I can.

Enter FROSINE *and* MARIANNE.

FROSINE: Do you know, Master Jacques, if your master is at home?

JACQUES: Yes, he certainly is. I know it all too well!

FROSINE: Tell him, pray, that we are here.

                                    (Exit MASTER JACQUES.*)*

MARIANNE: Ah! Frosine, I am in such a strange state! If I must tell what I feel: I am very much afraid of this interview.

FROSINE: But why? What is it that worries you?

MARIANNE: Alas! Need you ask? Can't you imagine the alarm of a person just about to see the rack she is to be tortured on?

FROSINE: I can plainly see that Harpagon is not the rack you would choose to embrace if you're thinking of an agreeable death. And I know by your expression that the dandy you were telling me about is somewhere in your thoughts.

MARIANNE: Yes, Frosine. That I do not wish to deny. The respectful visits he paid at our house have had, I must confess, some effect on my heart.

FROSINE: But have you learned *who* he is?

MARIANNE: No, I don't in the least know *who* he is, but I do know he is fashioned in a way that inspires love and that, if the choice were left

at my disposal, I would take him sooner than
340 any other, and that he contributes not a little
to make me find the husband you would give
me a horrible torment.

FROSINE: Mercy me! all those dandies are agreeable
enough, and they play their parts very well, but
most of them are poor as churchmice. You would
do much better to take an old husband who will
leave you a lot of money. I will admit that the
senses will not find full measure on the side
which I am speaking for, and there are some
350 slightly distasteful details to be endured with
such a husband—but it won't be for long. His
death, believe me, will soon put you in a position
to pick a more attractive one, who will make
up for everything.

MARIANNE: Bless me, Frosine, it seems a very
strange business when, to be happy, one must
hope or wait for the demise of someone. And
death does not always lend itself to the plans
we make.

360 FROSINE: Are you joking? You are marrying him
only on the understanding that he will soon leave
you a widow. That ought to be one of the articles
in the contract. It would be very impertinent
in him not to die before three months are out.

Enter HARPAGON.

Speak of the devil . . .

MARIANNE: Ah! Frosine, what a face!

HARPAGON: Do not be offended, my beauty, if I
come to you wearing spectacles. I know that
370 your charms are striking enough—are visible
enough by themselves—that there is no need
of glasses to perceive them. But after all, it is
through glasses we observe the stars, and I maintain and guarantee that you are a star. And what
a star! The most beautiful star in the realm of
stars. Frosine, she doesn't say a word, and she
doesn't show, so it seems to me, that she is at
all pleased to see me.

FROSINE: That is because she is still all surprise.
380 And then, the girls nowadays are always shy
about showing straightway what is in their
hearts.

Enter ELISE.

HARPAGON: You are right. (*to* MARIANNE) Here,

darling beauty, is my daughter, who has come
to greet you.

MARIANNE: I acquit myself, madam, much too tar-
dily of this visit.

ELISE: You have done that, madam, which I ought
to have done. It was my place to anticipate you.   390

HARPAGON: You see how tall she is; but weeds grow
fast.

MARIANNE: (*aside to* FROSINE) Oh, what an unpleasant man!

HARPAGON: What does the beauty say?

FROSINE: That she thinks you are wonderful.

HARPAGON: You do me too much honor, adorable
darling.

MARIANNE: (*aside to* FROSINE) Such an animal!

HARPAGON: I am obliged for your sentiments.   400

MARIANNE: (*aside to* FROSINE) I can't stand any more
of this.

Enter CLEANTH.

HARPASON: Here is my son, who also comes to
pay you his respects.

MARIANNE: (*aside to* FROSINE) Ah! Frosine, what
a coincidence! This is the very person I spoke
to you about.

FROSINE: The adventure is fantastic.

HARPAGON: I see you are astonished to find that   410
I have such big children; but I shall soon be
rid of them both.

CLEANTH: Madam, to tell the truth, this is an
encounter which I by no means expected; and
my father surprised me not a little when he told
me a while ago of his intentions.

MARIANNE: I can say the same for myself. This
is an unforeseen meeting, which has surprised
me as much as it has you. I too was not at all
prepared for such an encounter.   420

CLEANTH: It is true that my father, madam, could
not make a handsomer choice, and the honor
of seeing you is a real joy for me; but for all
that, I will not assure you that I rejoice over
the design you may have to become my stepmother. That compliment, I confess, is too much
for me; it is a title, if you please, that I do not
want for you. This speech may seem brutal in
the eyes of some, but I am sure you are a person
who will take it in the right sense. You can easily   430
imagine, madam, that this is a marriage which

is bound to be somewhat repugnant to me; for you know what kind of man I am and how much it clashes with my interests. In short, you will not be offended if I tell you, with my father's permission, that if things depended on me, these nuptials would never take place.

HARPAGON: Your compliment is very impertinent! What a nice confession to make to her!

440 MARIANNE: And I, in answer to you, have this to say: our feelings are quite mutual. If it is true that you would find it repugnant to have me for a stepmother, it would be no less so for me, I assure you, to have you for a stepson. Do not think, pray, that it is I who seek to be the source of your uneasiness. I should be very sorry to cause you any displeasure; and if I did not see myself forced to it by an absolute power, I give you my word, I would never consent to a mar-

450 riage that pains you.

HARPAGON: She is right. A stupid compliment like that deserves a stupid answer. I beg pardon, my beauty, for my son's impertinence. He is a young ass who doesn't yet know the weight of his own words.

MARIANNE: I assure that what he said has not offended me in the least. On the contrary, it has been a pleasure to hear him express his true sentiments. I like that kind of confession from

460 him. If he had spoken in any other way, I would have far less esteem for him.

HARPAGON: It is very kind of you to forgive his faults this way. Time will make him wiser, and you will see that he will have a change of heart.

CLEANTH: No, father, it is not capable of change; and I earnestly entreat madam to believe that.

HARPAGON: Just see how extravagant he is! He goes on more rashly than ever.

CLEANTH: Would you have me belie my heart?

470 HARPAGON: Again! Would you mind changing the subject?

CLEANTH: Very well, since you wish me to speak in a different manner . . . Permit me, madam, to put myself in my father's place, to confess that I have never seen anything in the world as lovely as you; that I can conceive nothing to equal the happiness of pleasing you; and that the title of your husband is a glory, a felicity, that I would prefer to the destiny of the greatest

prince on earth. Yes, madam, the happiness of 480 possessing you, is in my estimation, the fairest of all fortunes; it is the goal of my whole ambition. I would do anything to make such a conquest; and the most powerful obstacles . . .

HARPAGON: Moderation, son, if you please.

CLEANTH: This is a compliment I am paying the lady, for you.

HARPAGON: By God! I have a tongue to express myself, and I have no need of a proxy the likes of you. Here, bring chairs. 490

FROSINE: No, it will be better for us to go directly to the fair. Then we'll be back early and have the whole time afterward to talk with you.

HARPAGON: Then tell them to hitch up the horses to the carriage. I beg you to excuse me, my beauty, for not having thought to give you a little refreshment before you start out.

CLEANTH: I have provided for that, father. I had them bring a few plates of Chinese oranges, some lemons, and some preserves; which I sent for 500 in your name.

HARPAGON: (aside to VALÈRE) Valère!

VALÈRE: He's out of his head.

CLEANTH: Do you think, father, that it isn't enough? Madam will please have the kindness to excuse it.

MARIANNE: It was not at all necessary.

CLEANTH: Have you ever, madam, seen more fire in a diamond than in this one you see on my father's finger? (Takes ring off HARPAGON's finger.) 510

MARIANNE: It is true that it shines quite brightly.

CLEANTH: You must see it from close up. (Puts ring on MARIANNE's hand.)

MARIANNE: It is very handsome, I must say, and it sparkles a great deal. (Begins to take ring off her finger.)

CLEANTH: No, no, madam; it is on hands much too lovely. My father makes you a present of it.

HARPAGON: I? 520

CLEANTH: Isn't it true, father, that you want the lady to keep it for love of you?

HARPAGON: (aside to CLEANTH) What is this?

CLEANTH: Foolish question. He makes a sign to me that I should make you accept it.

MARIANNE: I don't at all want . . .

CLEANTH: Are you joking? He has no intention of taking it back.

HARPAGON: (*aside*) I'm losing my temper.

530   MARIANNE: It would be . . .

CLEANTH: No, I tell you, you will offend him.

MARIANNE: Please . . .

CLEANTH: Out of the question.

HARPAGON: (*aside*) A pox . . .

CLEANTH: Your refusal is making him angry.

HARPAGON: (*aside to* CLEANTH) Ah! you traitor!

CLEANTH: You see he's getting desperate.

HARPAGON: (*aside to* CLEANTH) You murderer, you!

CLEANTH: Father, its not my fault. I am doing
540   what I can to oblige her to keep it, but she is determined.

HARPAGON: (*aside to* CLEANTH) Scoundrel!

CLEANTH: You are the cause, madam, of my father's quarreling with me.

HARPAGON: (*aside to* CLEANTH) Knave!

CLEANTH: You will make him ill. Please, madam, do not resist any longer.

FROSINE: Mercy me! what a fuss! Keep the ring if the gentleman wants you to have it.

550   MARIANNE: So that you won't fly into a rage, I will keep it for the time being; and I will find another opportunity to return it.

Enter BRINDAVOINE.

BRINDAVOINE: Sir, there's a man here who wants to talk to you.

HARPAGON: Tell him I am busy, and to come back some other time.

BRINDAVOINE: He says he has money for you.

HARPAGON: (*to* MARIANNE) Please excuse me. I'll be back presently.   560

Enter LA MERLUCHE *running; collides with* HARPAGON *and knocks him down.*

MERLUCHE: Sir . . .

HARPAGON: Ah! I am dying!

CLEANTH: What is it, father, are you hurt?

HARPAGON: The traitor must surely have been paid by my debtors to make me break my neck.

VALÈRE: (*to* HARPAGON) There's no harm done.

MERLUCHE: I beg your pardon, sir, I thought I did right to come running.   570

HARPAGON: What are you here for, murderer?

MERLUCHE: To tell you that neither of your horses has any shoes.

HARPAGON: Take them to the blacksmith, right away.

CLEANTH: While waiting for the horses to be shod, father, I will do the honors of the house for you, and conduct madam into the garden, where I shall have the refreshments served.

Exeunt FROSINE, ELISE, MARIANNE *and* CLEANTH.   580

HARPAGON: Valère, keep an eye on all that; and take care, pray, to save me as much as you can, so that we can send it back to the dealer.

VALÈRE: Rest assured.   (*Exit* VALÈRE.)

HARPAGON: Oh, impertinent son! You are trying to ruin me!

ACT FOUR

Enter CLEANTH, MARIANNE, ELISE *and* FROSINE.

CLEANTH: Let us go in again; we shall be much better off in here. There is no longer anyone suspect around, and we can speak freely.

ELISE: Yes, madam, my brother has confided to me the love he bears you. I know what pain and frustration such obstacles can cause; and it is a most kindly sympathy, I assure you, that provokes my interest in your adventure.

MARIANNE: It is a sweet consolation to see a person   10
like you interested in oneself, and I implore you, madam, always to cherish your generous friendship for me—so capable of softening the cruel blows of misfortune.

FROSINE: By my faith, you are unlucky people, both of you, for not having told me about your affair before all this happened. I could, no doubt, have warded off these troubles. I wouldn't have brought matters to such a pass as this.

20 CLEANTH: What can you expect? It is my evil
destiny has willed it so. But, dear Marianne,
what have you resolved to do?

MARIANNE: Alas! am I in a position to resolve anything? Dependent as I am, can I do more than
hope?

CLEANTH: Is there nothing in your heart to encourage me but barren hope? No benevolent pity?
No helpful kindness? No lively affection at all?

MARIANNE: What can I tell you? Put yourself in
30 my place, and see what I can do. Advise me.
Order me. I put myself in your hands. And I
believe you are too reasonable to demand more
of me than is allowed by honor and decorum.

CLEANTH: Alas! to what am I reduced if you limit
me to the pallid sentiments that rigorous honor
and scrupulous decorum will allow?

MARIANNE: But what would you have me do? Even
though I could ignore many of the niceties which
our sex is obliged to observe, I have too much
40 consideration for my mother. She has reared me
with extreme tenderness. I could never resolve
to do anything that would cause her displeasure.
Go and speak to her. Do everything in your
power to win her over. You may do and say
whatever you please; I give you my permission.
And if it is only a question of declaring in your
favor, I readily consent to make a confession
to her of all that I feel for you.

CLEANTH: Frosine, my poor Frosine, would you
50 help us?

FROSINE: By my faith, is there any need to ask? I
will with all my heart. You know that by nature
I am human enough. Heaven didn't give me a
heart of bronze, and I am only too eager to do
little services for people when I see they love
one another sincerely and honorably. What can
we do about this?

CLEANTH: Think a little, I beg you.

MARIANNE: Show us a way.

60 ELISE: Invent something that will undo what you
have done.

FROSINE: That is rather difficult. (to MARIANNE) As
to your mother, she is not altogether unreasonable: perhaps you could win her over, and make
her decide to transfer the gift she intends for
the father to the son. (to CLEANTH) But the worst
part of this is that your father is—your father.

CLEANTH: That's understood.

FROSINE: I mean he will bear a grudge if she refuses

him openly, and he will be in no humor afterward   70
to give his consent to your marriage. It will be
necessary, to do it well, that the refusal come
from himself. We must try by some means to
make her distasteful to him.

CLEANTH: You are right.

FROSINE: Yes, I am right. I know it very well.
That is what has to be done. But the deuce of
it is to find a way. Wait; if we had a woman,
getting on in years, with my talent, and who
could act well enough to counterfeit a lady of   80
quality, with the help of a train made up in
a hurry and some bizarre name of marchioness
or viscountess, who we could pretend comes
from Brittany, I could be clever enough to convince him that she was a rich person who, besides
her houses, had a hundred thousand écus in solid
silver, that she was hopelessly in love with him,
and wanted to be his wife so badly that she
would sign over all her property to him in a marriage contract. I don't in the least doubt that   90
he would lend an ear to the proposition. For,
in short, although he loves you very much, he
loves money a little more. And, once blinded
by this illusion, once he has consented to what
concerns you most, it will matter little afterward
if he is undeceived when he looks more closely
into the estate of our marchioness.

CLEANTH: This is all very well thought out.

FROSINE: Leave it to me. I just thought of a friend
of mine who is the very woman we want.   100

CLEANTH: Rest assured, Frosine, of my gratitude
if you succeed in this. But dear Marianne, let
us begin by persuading your mother; there is
still much to be done to break off this marriage.
For your part, I beseech you, make every effort
you possibly can. Use all the power that her
love for you gives you over her. Unfold your
eloquent graces without reserve—those all-
powerful charms that Heaven has located in your
eyes and lips. And forget none, please, of those   110
tender expressions, or those soft entreaties, or
those touching caresses to which, I am persuaded, no one could refuse anything.

Enter HARPAGON.

MARIANNE: I will do all in my power, and I won't
forget a thing.

HARPAGON: (*aside*) Hey! what's this? My son
kisses the hand of his future stepmother; and

120 his future stepmother does not offer much resistance. Could there be more to this than meets the eye?

ELISE: Here is my father.

HARPAGON: The carriage is ready. You can leave when you please.

CLEANTH: Since you are not going, father, I will drive them myself.

HARPAGON: No, stay. They can go just as well by themselves. I need you here.

(Exeunt FROSINE, ELISE *and* MARIANNE.)

130 HARPAGON: Oh! by the way, apart from the question of her becoming your stepmother, what do you think of this person?

CLEANTH: What do I think of her?

HARPAGON: Yes—of her manner, her figure, her beauty, and her wit?

CLEANTH: So so.

HARPAGON: What do you mean?

CLEANTH: To tell you frankly, I did not find her what I thought her to be. She has the manner
140 of an out-and-out coquette, her figure is rather awkward, her beauty is mediocre, and she has a very common kind of wit. But don't think, father, that I am trying to set you against her. Because, stepmother for stepmother, I like this one as much as I would any other.

HARPAGON: Nevertheless you were telling her a while ago . . .

CLEANTH: I did say a few nice things to her in your name—but that was to please you.

150 HARPAGON: So then, you don't feel the slightest inclination for her?

CLEANTH: I? None at all.

HARPAGON: That's too bad, for it puts an end to an idea that came into my head. Seeing her here made me reflect on my age, and I thought to myself that people might find fault with me for marrying such a young girl. This consideration made me abandon my plans; but, since I have already asked her to marry and am bound by
160 my word, I would have given her to you—if you had not shown such an aversion.

CLEANTH: To me?

HARPAGON: To you.

CLEANTH: In marriage?

HARPAGON: In marriage.

CLEANTH: Listen. It is true she is not much to my taste. But to make you happy, father, I will resign myself to marrying her—since it is your wish.

HARPAGON: Mine? I am more reasonable than you
170 think. I would not force your inclination.

CLEANTH: Pardon me, I will do myself this violence out of love for you.

HARPAGON: No, no. A marriage can never be happy where there is no affection.

CLEANTH: Affection is something, father, that will come afterwards, perhaps. They say that love is often the fruit of marriage.

HARPAGON: No, the venture ought not to be risked on the man's side. There may be painful con-
180 sequences to which I would not care to expose myself. If you had felt some inclination for her earlier, I would have had you marry her in my place. But since that is not the case, I will carry out my first plan, and marry her myself.

CLEANTH: Very well, father, since this is the way things are, I am obliged to bare my heart to you: I must reveal our secret. The truth is that I have loved her since the first time I saw her out walking, that my intention up to a while
190 ago was to ask you if I could have her for my wife, and that nothing has held me back but your declaration of your own sentiments and fear of displeasing you.

HARPAGON: Have you visited her?

CLEANTH: Yes, father.

HARPAGON: Very often?

CLEANTH: Often enough—for the time I had.

HARPAGON: Were you well received?

CLEANTH: Very well. But they did not know who I was. That is why Marianne was so surprised
200 a while ago.

HARPAGON: Did you declare your passion to her, and your intention of marrying her?

CLEANTH: Certainly, and I have even broached the subject a little to her mother.

HARPAGON: Did she give your proposal a hearing?

CLEANTH: Yes, a very civil one.

HARPAGON: And does her daughter return your love appreciably?

CLEANTH: If appearances are to be trusted, I am
210 persuaded, father, that she feels some affection for me.

HARPAGON: I am happy to learn such a secret. It is exactly what I wanted to know. And now, son, do you know what you will have to do? You will have to think, if you please, about getting over your love, about giving up your pursuit of this person whom I intend for myself, and about marrying, in a short time, the woman I have chosen for you!

CLEANTH: So, father, you have tricked me! Very well! Since things have come to this pass, I declare to you that I will never cease loving Marianne, that I will go to any limit to dispute the conquest with you, and though you have the mother's consent on your side, I will perhaps find others who will fight for me.

HARPAGON: What? You scoundrel! You have the audacity to stalk my game?

CLEANTH: It is you who are stalking mine: I knew her first.

HARPAGON: Am I not your father? Don't you owe me your respect?

CLEANTH: These are not matters in which the children are obliged to defer to their fathers. Love knows no master.

HARPAGON: I'll teach you to know me—by the mastery of a good stick.

CLEANTH: All your threats will do no good.

HARPAGON: Will you renounce Marianne?

CLEANTH: On no account.

HARPAGON: Bring me a stick, quickly.

Enter MASTER JACQUES.

JACQUES: Now, now, now! gentlemen, what is this? What can you be thinking of?

CLEANTH: I laugh at it all.

JACQUES: Ah! gently, sir.

HARPAGON: To talk with such impudence!

JACQUES: Oh! sir, please.

CLEANTH: I won't yield an inch.

JACQUES: Eh, what? to your father?

HARPAGON: Leave him to me. (*Menaces CLEANTH with his stick.*)

JACQUES: Eh, what? to your son? Once more, leave off, for my sake.

HARPAGON: I want to make *you*, Master Jacques, judge of this affair—to prove I am right.

JACQUES: I am willing. (*to CLEANTH*) Go a little farther off.

HARPAGON: I am in love with a girl! I want to marry, and that scoundrel has the impudence to be in love with the same girl at the same time, and intends, despite my orders, to marry her.

JACQUES: Ah! he is in the wrong.

HARPAGON: Isn't it a shocking thing for a son to enter into competition with his father? Shouldn't he, out of repsect, refrain from meddling where my affections are involved?

JACQUES: You are right. Let me talk to him. Stay here.   (*Goes to CLEANTH.*)

CLEANTH: Yes, of course, since he has chosen you for judge, I'll not back out. It isn't important to me who it is, and I too am willing to refer myself to you, Master Jacques, in this matter of our difference.

JACQUES: You do me great honor.

CLEANTH: I am very much taken with a young lady who returns all my interest, and who has tenderly received the offer of my heart; and my father has taken it into his head to trouble our love by making her an offer of marriage.

JACQUES: He is in the wrong, surely.

CLEANTH: Isn't he ashamed, at his age, to dream of marrying? Is it becoming in him to be amorous? Wouldn't he do better to leave that business to young fellows?

JACQUES: You are right; he is making a fool of himself. Let me say a few words to him. (*Returns to HARPAGON.*) Well, your son is not so strange as you make him out to be; he has submitted to reason. He says he knows that he owes you respect, that he was carried away by the heat of the argument, and that he will not refuse to submit to anything that pleases you, provided you intend to treat him better than you have done, and that you give him someone in marriage with whom he will have reason to be satisfied.

HARPAGON: Ah, tell him, Master Jacques, that with this provision, he may expect anything he *wants* from me; and that, Marianne excepted, he is at liberty to choose any girl he pleases.

JACQUES: Leave it to me. (*to CLEANTH*) Well, your father is not as unreasonable as you make him out to be, and he admitted to me that it was only rage that roused his temper, that he is angry only about the way you conducted yourself, and that he will be very much disposed to grant all your wishes provided you will go about it gently,

310 and show him the deference, respect, and submission that a son owes his father.

CLEANTH: Ah! Master Jacques, you can assure him that if he grants me Marianne, he will see that I will always be the most submissive man in the world, and that I will never do anything except by his wish.

JACQUES: (*going to* HARPAGON) It's done. He consents to what you ask.

HARPAGON: It's the happiest conclusion in the
320 world.

JACQUES: (*going to* CLEANTH) It's all decided. He is satisfied with your promises.

CLEANTH: Heaven be praised!

JACQUES: (*in the middle of the stage*) Gentlemen, you have only to talk together. Here you are in agreement now, and you were about to fall out because of a misunderstanding!

CLEANTH: My poor Master Jacques, I will be obliged to you for life.

330 JACQUES: It was nothing, sir.

HARPAGON: You have made me happy, Master Jacques, and you deserve a reward. (MASTER JACQUES *puts out his hand.*) Go—I shall remember it, I assure you.

JACQUES: I kiss your hand.

(*Exit* MASTER JACQUES.)

CLEANTH: I beg your pardon, father, for showing my temper in that way.

HARPAGON: It was nothing.

340 CLEANTH: I assure you, it gives me all the concern in the world.

HARPAGON: As for myself, it gives me all the joy in the world to see you reasonable.

CLEANTH: How good of you to forget my fault so quickly!

HARPAGON: One easily forgets his child's faults when one sees him return to the path of duty.

CLEANTH: What! you harbor no resentment for all my extravagance?

350 HARPAGON: You oblige me not to by the submission and respect you show.

CLEANTH: And I, I promise you, father, will bear the memory of your kindness to the grave.

HARPAGON: And I, I promise you that there is nothing you shall not have from me.

CLEANTH: Ah! father, I have nothing more to ask: you gave me all when you gave me Marianne.

HARPAGON: What?

CLEANTH: I say, father, that you have made me too happy. You gave me all when you agreed 360 to give me Marianne.

HARPAGON: Who said anything about giving you Marianne?

CLEANTH: You, father.

HARPAGON: I?

CLEANTH: Certainly.

HARPAGON: What! You are the one who promised to renounce her.

CLEANTH: I renounce her?

HARPAGON: Yes.
370
CLEANTH: Not in the least.

HARPAGON: You haven't abandoned your pretensions to her?

CLEANTH: On the contrary, I am more determined than ever.

HARPAGON: What! you rascal, again?

CLEANTH: Nothing can change my mind.

HARPAGON: Let me at you, traitor!

CLEANTH: Do whatever you please.

HARPAGON: I forbid you ever to see me again. 380

CLEANTH: It's all the same to me.

HARPAGON: I abandon you.

CLEANTH: Abandon me.

HARPAGON: I disown you as my son.

CLEANTH: So be it.

HARPAGON: I disinherit you.

CLEANTH: Anything you like.

HARPAGON: And I give you my curse.

CLEANTH: I have no need of your gifts.

(*Exit* HARPAGON.) 390

Enter LA FLÈCHE.

FLECHE: Ah! sir! I have found you just in time! Follow me quickly.

CLEANTH: What's the matter?

FLECHE: Follow me, I tell you—our troubles are over.

CLEANTH: What?

FLECHE: (*shows him the chest*) Here's your way out.

CLEANTH: How?

FLECHE: Your father's treasure. I dug it up! 400

CLEANTH: Where was it?

FLECHE: You shall know everything. Run. I hear him screaming.

(*Exeunt* LA FLECHE *and* CLEANTH.)

Enter HARPAGON.

HARPAGON: Stop thief! Stop thief! Stop assassin! Stop murderer! Justice, Divine Justice! I am ruined! I've been murdered! He cut my throat, he stole my money! Who can it be? What's become of him? Where is he? Where is he hiding? What shall I do to find him? Where shall I run? Where shan't I run? Isn't that he there? Isn't this he here? Who's this? (*Sees his own shadow and grabs his own arm*.) Stop! Give me back my money, you rogue. . . . Ah! it is myself. My mind is unhinged, and I don't know where I am, who I am, or what I am doing. (*Falls to his knees*.) Alas! my poor money, my poor money, my dear friend, they have taken you from me. And since they carried you off, I've lost my support, my consolation, my joy. Everything is at an end for me; I have no more to do in this world! I cannot live without you! It's finished. I can no more. (*Lies down*.) I am dying. I am dead. I am buried! Isn't there anybody who would like to bring me back to life by returning my dear money or by telling me who took it? (*rising to his knees*) What did you say? It was nobody. (*Stands.*) Whoever did the job must have watched very closely for his chance; for he chose exactly the time when I was talking to my treacherous son. (*Takes his hat and cane.*) I'll go out. I'll go and demand justice. I'll order them to torture everyone in my house for a confession: the maids, the valets, my son, my daughter—and myself too! What a crowd of people! Everybody I cast my eyes on arouses my suspicion, and everything seems to be my thief. Eh! what are you talking about there? About the man that robbed me? Why are you making that noise up there? Is my thief there? (*Kneels and addresses the audience*.) Please, if anyone has any information about my thief, I beg you to tell me. Are you sure he isn't hidden there among you? They all look at me and laugh. (*Rises*.) You will probably see that they all had a part in this robbery. Here, quick, commissaries, archers, provosts, judges, tortures, scaffolds, and executioners! I want to have everybody hanged. And if I don't recover my money, I'll hang myself afterward!

ACT FIVE

On stage: HARPAGON, *the* COMMISSARY *and his clerk.*

COMMISSARY: Leave me alone. I know my business, thank God! I didn't start investigating robberies yesterday. I wish I had a sack of francs for every man I've sent to the gallows!

HARPAGON: All the magistrates are interested in taking this case in hand. What's more, if no one sees to it that I recover my money, I shall demand justice from Justice herself!

COMMISSARY: We must follow the prescribed procedure. How much was it you said was in this moneybox?

HARPAGON: Ten thousand écus, to the sou.

COMMISSARY: Ten thousand écus?

HARPAGON: Ten thousand écus.

COMMISSARY: It was a considerable theft.

HARPAGON: No penalty would be too great for the enormity of the crime. If it goes unpunished, nothing is too sacred to be safe.

COMMISSARY: In what coin was the sum?

HARPAGON: In good gold louis and solid pistoles.

COMMISSARY: Whom do you suspect of this theft?

HARPAGON: Everybody! I want you to arrest the whole city and the suburbs!

COMMISSARY: We mustn't frighten anyone, take my word for it. We must try and obtain some evidence quietly. Then afterward we can proceed more rigorously in recovering the deniers that were taken from you.

Enter MASTER JACQUES *from the kitchen.*

JACQUES: I'll be back in a little while. First I want you to cut his throat. Then I want you to singe his feet. Then I want you to put him in boiling water. Then I want you to hang him from the ceiling.

HARPAGON: Who? The man who robbed me?

JACQUES: I was talking about the suckling pig your steward just sent me. I want to dress him for you according to my fancy.

HARPAGON: That is not the question. You must talk to this gentleman about something else.

COMMISSARY: Don't be frightened. I am not a man who would cause you scandal. Everything will be done quietly.

JACQUES: Is the gentleman one of your supper guests?

COMMISSARY: Now, my dear friend, you must hide nothing from your master.

JACQUES: Faith, sir, I will show you all I know: I will treat you the best I possibly can.

HARPAGON: We aren't talking about that.

JACQUES: If I can't give you as fine a feast as I want to, it's the fault of a certain gentleman, a certain steward, who has clipped my wings with the scissors of his economy.

HARPAGON: Traitor! We are investigating something more important than supper. I want you to give me information about the money that was stolen from me.

JACQUES: Did someone steal your money?

HARPAGON: Yes, you rascal! And I'll have you hanged if you don't give it back.

COMMISSARY: For Heaven's sake, don't bully him! I can see by his face he's an honest man. Without making us send him to jail, he will tell you everything you want to know. Yes, my friend, if you tell us what you know, no harm will come to you. You will be rewarded by your master, as you deserve to be. Just this morning someone took his money. Is it possible you don't have some information about this matter?

JACQUES: (aside) Exactly what I need to get my revenge on our steward! Ever since he came into this house he has been the favorite—only *his* advice is listened to. Then, too, the beating he gave me sticks in my craw.

HARPAGON: What are you mumbling about?

COMMISSARY: Leave him alone. He is preparing to give you satisfaction. I told you he is an honest man.

JACQUES: Sir, since you want me to tell you something about this business, I think it was a certain gentleman, a certain steward, who did the job.

HARPAGON: Valère?

JACQUES: Yes.

HARPAGON: He? Who seemed to be so trustworthy?

JACQUES: Himself. I think he is the one who robbed you.

HARPAGON: On what grounds do you think so?

JACQUES: On what grounds?

HARPAGON: Yes.

JACQUES: I think so . . . on the grounds that . . . I think so.

COMMISSARY: But it is necessary that you tell us what proof you have.

HARPAGON: Did you see him sneaking around the place where I kept my money?

JACQUES: Yes, certainly. Where did you keep your money?

HARPAGON: In the garden.

JACQUES: Exactly. I saw him sneaking through the garden. What was this money in?

HARPAGON: A moneybox.

JACQUES: That's it. I saw him with a moneybox.

HARPAGON: This moneybox . . . What did it look like? I'll soon see if it was mine.

JACQUES: What did it look like?

HARPAGON: Yes.

JACQUES: It looked like . . . it looked like a moneybox.

COMMISSARY: Of course. But describe it a little, so we can see . . .

JACQUES: It was a large moneybox.

HARPAGON: The one that was stolen from me was small.

JACQUES: Oh, yes—it was small if you want to look at it that way. I call it large on account of what it contained.

COMMISSARY: What color was it?

JACQUES: What color?

COMMISSARY: Yes.

JACQUES: It was the color of . . . yes, the color of it was . . . Can't you help me out a bit?

HARPAGON: Eh!

JACQUES: Wasn't it red?

HARPAGON: No, gray.

JACQUES: Oh! yes, grayish-red. That's what I meant to say.

HARPAGON: There isn't the slightest doubt. That is definitely it. Write, sir, write down his testimony. Heavens! who's to be trusted nowadays? You can't put your faith in anything! After this, I fear I am a man who might rob himself.

JACQUES: Sir, he is coming back. At least don't go and tell him it was I who told you this.

Enter VALÈRE.

HARPAGON: Advance. Come. Confess the darkest deed, the most horrible atrocity ever committed.

140 VALÈRE: What do you mean, sir?

HARPAGON: What! traitor, you do not even blush for your crime?

VALÈRE: What crime can you be talking of?

HARPAGON: What crime am I talking of? Infamous! As though you didn't know what I mean! It is useless for you to try and cover up. The deed has been discovered. Someone has just told me all. Really! How could you abuse my kindness that way—insinuate yourself into my house to

150 betray me—to play a trick of that kind on me!

VALÈRE: Sir, since someone has told you all, I shall not try to find a way out. I deny nothing.

JACQUES: (*aside*) Hoho! Could I have guessed right without thinking?

VALÈRE: It was my intention to speak to you about it, and I wanted to wait for more favorable conditions to do so. But since things are the way they are, I beg you not to be angry. Be good enough to hear my reasons.

160 HARPAGON: And what wonderful reasons can you give me, infamous thief?

VALÈRE: Ah! sir, I have not deserved those names. It is true I am guilty of an offense against you. But, after all, my fault is pardonable.

HARPAGON: How, pardonable? A premeditated crime? An assassination of this sort?

VALÈRE: Please don't lose your temper. When you have heard me, you will see that the evil done is not so great as you make it out.

170 HARPAGON: The evil is not so great as I make it out! What? My blood! My entrails!—You scoundrel!

VALÈRE: Your blood, sir, has not fallen into evil hands. I belong to a class which is not beneath it, and there is nothing in all this for which I cannot make full reparation.

HARPAGON: That is my intention precisely—that you shall make full restitution of what you have ravished from me.

VALÈRE: Your honor, sir, shall be fully satisfied. 180

HARPAGON: It has nothing to do with honor. But, tell me, what ever possessed you to do it?

VALÈRE: Alas! You are asking me?

HARPAGON: Yes I really am.

VALÈRE: A god who is his own excuse for everything he does: Love.

HARPAGON: Love?

VALÈRE: Yes.

HARPAGON: A beautiful love, a beautiful love indeed! Love of my gold louis. 190

VALÈRE: No, sir, it was not in the least your wealth that tempted me. That wasn't what dazzled me. And I swear I will make no claims whatsoever on your property, provided you let me keep what I have.

HARPAGON: I will do no such thing, by God! See how insolent he is! He wants to keep the proceeds of his theft.

VALÈRE: Do you call it a theft?

HARPAGON: Do I call it a theft! A treasure like 200 that!

VALÈRE: A treasure indeed! The most precious you have, without a doubt! But your giving me such a treasure would be no real loss to you. I ask you on bended knee to give me this enchanting treasure. If you want to do right you will grant my request.

HARPAGON: I will do nothing of the kind. What is he saying?

VALÈRE: We have promised to be faithful to one 210 another. We have vowed never to separate.

HARPAGON: Your vow is admirable. Your promise is amusing.

VALÈRE: We are engaged to an eternal union.

HARPAGON: I shall forbid the banns, I assure you.

VALÈRE: Naught but death can part us.

HARPAGON: You are certainly bewitched by my money.

VALÈRE: I have told you, sir, it was not selfish interest that drove me to do what I have done. 220 My heart was not impelled by the motives you suspect. A nobler idea was my inspiration.

HARPAGON: You'll see: it is out of Christian charity he wants to keep my money! But I'll set all to rights. The law, you brazen scroundrel, will make me amends for everything!

VALÈRE: You may proceed as you like in the matter. I am ready to suffer any violence that will please

230 you. But at least believe, I beg, that if any harm is done, I am the only one to accuse. Your daughter is in no way to blame for any of this.

HARPAGON: Certainly I believe that. It would be very strange, indeed, if my daughter had a part in this crime. But I want to get my treasure back. I want you to confess where you have carried it off to!

VALÈRE: I? Your treasure has not been carried off at all, but is here—at home.

HARPAGON: (*aside*) Oh, my dear moneybox! (*to* 240 VALÈRE) My treasure has not left the house?

VALÈRE: No, sir.

HARPAGON: Well. Tell me now, haven't you even . . . tampered a bit?

VALÈRE: I, tamper? Ah! you do us both a great wrong. The love that consumes me is wholly pure and respectful.

HARPAGON: (*aside*) He's consumed with love for my moneybox?

VALÈRE: I would have died rather than reveal to 250 your treasure a single offensive thought. It would have been an insult to so much honor and virtue.

HARPAGON: (*aside*) My moneybox honorable and virtuous?

VALÈRE: I limited my desires to the pleasure of merely seeing. No criminal act has profaned the passion that is inspired by those lovely eyes.

HARPAGON: (*aside*) My moneybox's lovely eyes? He talks like a lover discussing his mistress.

VALÈRE: Dame Claude, sir, knows the truth of this 260 adventure. She can bear witness . . .

HARPAGON: What! my maid is an accomplice in this business?

VALÈRE: Yes, sir, she stood as a witness at our engagement. But it was not until she had learned how honorable were my intentions that she helped me to persuade your daughter to pledge her fidelity to me and accept my pledge in return.

HARPAGON: (*aside*) Ha! Is his fear of the law making his mind wander? (*to* VALÈRE) Why confuse us 270 by bringing my daughter into this?

VALÈRE: I tell you, sir, I had all the trouble in the world to persuade modesty to grant what love desired.

HARPAGON: Whose modesty?

VALÈRE: Your daughter's. And it wasn't until yesterday that she was able to make up her mind and sign a mutual promise of marriage with me.

HARPAGON: My daughter signed a promise of marriage with you?

VALÈRE: Just as I, on my part, signed one with 280 her.

HARPAGON: O Heavens! Another disgrace!

JACQUES: (*to the* COMMISSARY) Write, sir, write.

HARPAGON: Aggravation of misfortune! Excess of despair! Come, sir, do the duty of your office. Draw me up an indictment against him as a thief and an instigator.

VALÈRE: Those are names which do not belong to me. When it is known who I am . . .

Enter ELISE, MARIANNE *and* FROSINE.   290

HARPAGON: Ah! profligate daughter! Unworthy of a father like me! This is how you put into practice the lessons I gave you! You let yourself become infatuated with an infamous thief! You promise him your hand without my consent! But you will be undone, both of you. (*to Elise*) Four good, strong walls will answer for your conduct. (*to* VALÈRE) A good, tall gallows will give me satisfaction for your audacity.

VALÈRE: It is not your passion that will judge the   300 matter. I will at least be heard before I am condemned.

HARPAGON: I was mistaken to say the gallows. You will be broken alive on the wheel.

ELISE: Ah! father, be a little more human in your sentiments, I beseech you. Do not push things to the violent extreme of paternal power. Do not let yourself be carried away by the first impulse of passion. Give yourself time. Consider what you wish to do. Take pains. Look more   310 closely at the person who has roused your wrath. He is not what your eyes have judged him to be. You will find it far less strange that I should have given myself to him when you learn that, were it not for him, you would have lost me long ago, and forever. Yes, father, he is the man who saved me from the great peril, the peril you know I was so close to in the water—the man to whom you owe the life of the same daughter who . . .   320

HARPAGON: All that is nothing. It would have been better for me had he let you drown and not do what he has done.

ELISE: Father, out of paternal love for me . . .

HARPAGON: No, no! I won't hear another word.

The law must do its duty.

JACQUES: (*aside*) You'll pay for the beating you gave me.

FROSINE: (*aside*) This is a queer mix-up.

330   *Enter* ANSELM.

ANSELM: What is it, Signor Harpagon? I see you are very much disturbed.

HARPAGON: Ah! Signor Anselm, you now behold the most unfortunate of men. Here is I don't know how much trouble and disorder to complicate the contract you came to sign! My money has been attacked! My honor has been attacked! And there stands a traitor, a profligate who has violated all that is most sacred to man—who

340   has insinuated himself into my house under the name of servant in order to steal my money and seduce my daughter!

VALÈRE: Who cares about this money that you make so much noise about?

HARPAGON: Yes, they have made each other a promise of marriage. This outrage is your concern, Signor Anselm. You are the man who ought to take action against him. Have him prosecuted by the law! Revenge yourself for his insolence!

350   ANSELM: I have no intention of forcing myself on anybody or of making any claims to a heart that has already given itself to another. But of course I am ready to fight for your interests. As if the cause were my own.

HARPAGON: This gentleman here is an honest commissary, who assures me that he will neglect no part of his official duty. (*to the* COMMISSARY) Indict him, sir, in due form! And make everything sound very criminal!

360   VALÈRE: I don't see what sort of crime you can make out of my passion for your daughter or what punishment you think I can be condemned to for our engagement. When it is known who I am . . .

HARPAGON: I don't give a damn for all those tales. Nowadays the world is only too full of thieves of nobility, of impostors who take advantage of their insignificance and impudently bedeck themselves with the first illustrious name they

370   take a fancy to.

VALÈRE: I'll have you know I am too honest to adorn myself with aught that is not mine. All Naples can testify to my birth.

ANSELM: Careful. Watch what you say. You run a greater risk here than you think. You have before you a man to whom all Naples is known and who can easily see through a trumped-up story.

VALÈRE: I am a man with nothing to fear. If you   380
know Naples, you know who Don Thomas d'Alburcy was.

ANSELM: Of course I know who he was. Few people were better acquainted with him than I.

HARPAGON: I don't give a damn for Don Thomas or Don Smith.

ANSELM: Please, let him talk. We will see what he has to say about him.

VALÈRE: I have this to say: it was he who brought me into the world.

ANSELM: He?   390

VALÈRE: Yes.

ANSELM: Come now. You deceive yourself. Try some other story that might be more successful. Don't expect to save yourself by this imposture.

VALÈRE: Watch what you say. This is no imposture. I advance no claim that I cannot easily justify.

ANSELM: What! You dare to call yourself the son of Thomas d'Alburcy?

VALÈRE: I dare. And I am ready to defend that   400
truth against no matter whom.

ANSELM: Fantastic audacity! Learn to your confusion that it was sixteen years ago, at the very least, that the man you speak of perished at sea with his wife and children while trying to save their lives from the cruel persecutions that accompanied the disorder at Naples and which precipitated the exile of more than one noble family.

VALÈRE: Yes, but learn to your own confusion,   410
that his seven-year-old son, with a single servant, was saved from the shipwreck by a Spanish vessel—and that the son then saved now speaks to you. Learn that the captain of that vessel, touched by my misfortune, took a liking to me and brought me up as his own son—that arms have been my occupation since the time I was able to hold them—that I learned a short time ago that my father is not dead, as I had always thought—that while passing through this city   420
in search of him an adventure planned by Heaven gave me a glimpse of charming Elise—that the

sight of her made me a slave to her beauty—and that the violence of my love and her father's severity made me resolve to enter into his house and send another in search of my parents.

ANSELM: What proof do you have beyond your bare word that this is not a fable you have constructed on a foundation of truth?

430 VALÈRE: The Spanish captain, a ruby signet that belonged to my father, an agate bracelet that my mother placed upon my arm, and old Pedro, the servant who with me was saved from the shipwreck.

MARIANNE: Alas! I myself can answer for what you have said. You are not deceiving us. Your account has made clear to me that you are my brother!

VALÈRE: You, my sister?

440 MARIANNE: Yes. My heart was moved the moment you opened your mouth. Our mother, whom you will see again, has diverted me a thousand times with the misfortunes of our family. Heaven did not suffer us either to perish in that unhappy shipwreck—but our lives were saved only at the expense of our liberty. They were pirates who took us, my mother and me, off the wreckage of our vessel. After ten years of slavery, we regained our liberty through a happy accident, 450 and returned to Naples. There we found that all our property had been sold and were not able to uncover any news of my father. We sailed for Genoa, where my mother went to gather up the sad remains of our dissipated family fortune. From there, fleeing the barbarous injustice of her kinsmen, she came to these parts, where she has lived scarcely more than a languishing life.

ANSELM: O Heaven—such are the signs of Thy 460 power! How clearly Thou has shown us that Thou alone canst work miracles! Embrace me, children both! Mingle your joy with that of your father!

VALÈRE: You are our father?

MARIANNE: Is it for you my mother has shed so many tears?

ANSELM: Yes, my daughter, yes, my son, I am Don Thomas d'Alburcy, whom Heaven saved from the waves with all the money he had with 470 him—and who, believing for more than sixteen years you all were dead, was preparing, after long voyages, to seek the consolation of a new family through marriage with a good and gentle young lady. When I saw how much my life would be in danger should I return to Naples, I abandoned the idea forever. Having found a way to sell what I had there, I established my residence here. Under the name of Anselm I sought to leave behind the sorrows of the name which has caused me so many reverses. 480

HARPAGON: Is that your son?

ANSELM: Yes.

HARPAGON: I hold you responsible for the ten thousand écus he stole from me.

ANSELM: He? He stole from you?

HARPAGON: He himself.

VALÈRE: Who told you?

HARPAGON: Master Jacques.

VALÈRE: It is you that say so?

JACQUES: Look, I'm not saying a thing. 490

HARPAGON: Yes. This gentleman is the commissary who took down his testimony.

VALÈRE: Can you believe me capable of such a villainous deed?

HARPAGON: Capable or not capable, I want my money back.

Enter CLEANTH *and* LA FLÈCHE.

CLEANTH: Torment yourself no longer, father. Accuse no one. I have uncovered some information about your affair, and I have come to tell 500 you that, if you will resign yourself to letting me marry Marianne, your money will be returned to you.

HARPAGON: Where is it?

CLEANTH: Don't worry. It's in a place that I will answer for. Everything depends on me. It only remains for you to tell me your decision. You can choose whether to give me Marianne or lose your moneybox.

HARPAGON: Nothing has been removed from it? 510

CLEANTH: Nothing. Let us see if it is your intention to subscribe to this marriage and join your consent to that of her mother—who has given her the liberty to choose between us two.

MARIANNE: But you do not realize that his consent is not enough, or that Heaven, along with my brother, whom you now behold (*Points to* VALÈRE.) has restored my father to me. You must win me from *him.*

520 ANSELM: Heaven, my children, did not restore me to you in order that I should oppose your desires. Signor Harpagon, you very well know that the choice of a young lady falls to the son and not to the father. Come now, don't make people say what is too obvious to need expression. Give your consent to this double ceremony as I have.

HARPAGON: Before I can make up my mind, I must see my moneybox.

530 CLEANTH: You shall see it safe and sound.

HARPAGON: I have no money to give my children for their marriages.

ANSELM: Oh well, I have some for both of them. Don't let that bother you.

HARPAGON: You will commit yourself to stand the cost of both these marriages?

ANSELM: Yes, I will commit myself. Are you satisfied?

HARPAGON: Yes, provided that you have me a suit made for the wedding.

ANSELM: Agreed. Come let us indulge the happiness which this joyous day bestows upon us. 540

COMMISSARY: Hold, gentleman! Hold on, one moment, if you please! Who is going to pay for all the writing I've done?

HARPAGON: We have no need of your writing.

COMMISSARY: No? But I, on the other hand, can't pretend to have done it for nothing.

HARPAGON: (points to MASTER JACQUES) As payment I give you this man. Take him and hang him. 550

JACQUES: Alas! what is a man supposed to do? They beat me before for telling the truth. Now they want to hang me for lying.

ANSELM: Signor Harpagon, you ought to pardon him his trickery.

HARPAGON: You'll pay the commissary then.

ANSELM: So be it. Let us go at once and share our joy with your mother.

HARPAGON: And I, to see my dear, dear moneybox.

FROM *MOLIÈRE*

by Hallam Walker

Late in 1668, Molière returned to the stage of the Palais-Royal to put on *L'Avare* (*The Miser*) which had been planned for a year. This full-scale comedy in prose was not versified for good reason since it constituted a definite experiment in a new style, with a "low" technique of expression called upon to treat "high" subject. Borrowing the material of Plautus's *Aulularia* and other miser plays, he set about creating a sharp satire of some ugly human traits and still retained his usual framework of farce routines and values. The merging of psychological realism with what amounts to stylized form of prose farce makes of *L'Avare* one of Molière's carefully conceived innovations. The use of prose in *Don Juan*, it will be recalled, was called for by the haste of composition, but the writer must have been interested in seeing what could be achieved in this style.

The rather dark picture of corruption of the human spirit by gold may have disappointed a public eager for gay entertainment, and we must consider just why this play should be termed a comedy and not a moral drama. The problem is the same as the one which confronted us in studying *Tartuffe* and *Don Juan*, for thematically *L'Avare* repeats much found in the plays about the imposter and the seducer. Motives of sex and power come to the fore again, nor are we surprised to observe that Molière has got around to linking them to the theme of wealth and greed. The threat by the dangerous individual to the social order is contained, as usual, and there is a familiar contrived ending to settle matters. The play may thus be classed as one with great dramatic and moral potential which is kept from taking these directions by the author's vigorous use of heavy comic techniques. The apparent scheme of running through a series of variations on a theme will remind us of the nature of the work, so that the pernicious effects of gold upon human love do not

---

overwhelm us with a moral lesson but rather serve as one variation of theme, the nature of possession in love.

The setting selected for the play is important. In a bourgeois living room of the period (what has become the "Molière room" of French theater) the unities of place and action take on a natural realism which may delude us into seeing the entire comedy in such terms. . . . The appearance of "real life" is a pure theatrical trick, however, for the real world is jammed by the comedy into a distorted and zany mold by the rigorous adherence to conventional farce and commedia patterns. . . .

Neither as brilliant as *Tartuffe* nor as challenging as *Don Juan*, *L'Avare* still commands our interest as an experiment in theatrical techniques which rely upon and reaffirm farce while suggesting the range of moral import possible in such theater. It has been observed that ideas of "identity, coincidence, duality, exclusion, incompatibility, tenderness, generosity, and vanity" are thematic, nor is the critic wrong in perceiving these things, but the analysis of the play's structure as a forceful juxtaposition of opposites which are calculated to split the work apart at its ends seems overdrawn. Fracture is threatened throughout the play (the stock Molière routine which parodies serious drama), but the strength of the ending is such in his dramaturgy that it banishes the threat of a real split and imparts a sense of joyous physical assembling of all parties. Harpagon is not banished from the scene so that the others may resume a normal existence (Tartuffe's fate) but is very much present in the contrived denouement, and he has his share of happiness, warped as it is by his mania. The impression of traditional comic sense and significance is so great that we may go briefly through the play and see how its parts are organically structured to lead us to such an ending.

In *L'Avare* the title suggests a verb which serves to set forth the action: "to possess." From start to finish, the unifying idea is happy possession of the object desired, whether this is the loved person or the chest of money. Joy of lovers, parental love, and the avarice of the miser can be brought together in meaningful combination at the end, but the play may be termed successful only if the thematic relationships are clearly developed throughout. . . . Engagements in debt and in love may be means or impediments to happiness, so the characters all find themselves trying to get a clear way to touch the treasure desired. Motives of sex and avarice are mutually illuminating, and for them to be fulfilled certain obstacles must be surmounted. Bonds of obligation of various sorts are stressed heavily through the comedy, with claims of filial loyalty, financial debts, bonds of love, relationships between servant and master, and respect for human values posing problems for the characters. Elise and Cléanth must liberate themselves from a tyrannical parent to marry; Cléanth must also break free from the usurer; Valère and Marianne have to overcome social and financial barriers; and the servants must circumvent the restrictions of the miser to serve him properly. In all respects, the play and its parts emphasize "becoming free to possess one's desire."

The cases of all figures are clear-cut, with the exception of that of Harpagon himself, and in this character, Molière displays great skill in showing shifting planes of values and impressions of the world about him. When Harpagon wavers in treading the thin line between normal and abnormal desires, the playwright devises speeches and business to exploit the duality and yet show the unifying theme of effort to reach his true desire. Lack of accurate perception of his own nature leads him into the position of wanting a young bride while being unwilling to spend enough money to keep up a suitable home for her. His gentleman's household has been reduced to a "phantom" with a skeleton force of starving servants and horses. He does not know what he must free himself from, and because this basic action of cutting self free from things goes against the grain of the acquisitive miser, he is in a position of simultaneously grasping and deciding what to reject. The movement of the comedy is thus a function of his increasing clarity about what his true fetters are, that is, human concerns with paternal and sexual love, kindness, generosity, and respect for others. The comical hesitations and shifts which he goes through are the essential normal touch in the characterization which otherwise would verge upon the monstrous. W. G. Moore comments, "This man obsessed by money is shown in situations which do not stress, as they do not deny, his wickedness; they illumine the range and the limits of his obsession. His own energy (a significant point) drives him into situations in which he becomes a man like the rest of us."

Thus, we are reminded not to put too much stock in the moral implications of the case of the miser, thwarted or not. He is a moral caricature, a stage figure, and the denouement and the broad farce style of scenes like the dinner indicate that all is in the realm of stage magic. Is the ending an evasion of the harsh realities of avarice and selfishness? It seems not, just because of the deliberate use of comic *lazzi* which kill any pretense at serious dramatic effect and which create a topsy-turvy world. Molière's aim is to put into motion a rapid series of staged actions, the sum of which is indicative of the meaning of the play. The sheer movement about a theme such as we have elicited is meaningful in itself, and the means employed in this movement are arrangements of analogies, symmetries, and repetitions on the subject of possession of property and love.

At the start of the play, in characteristic manner, the notion of deception by words is established as a structural element, and the deception of Cléanth by his father, for example, is introduced naturally. Elise says: "All men are alike in their words, and it is only their actions which reveal them to be different" (I, 1). Then too, Molière will constantly show us Harpagon deceiving himself by his words, as he goes so far as to think that he "loves" Marianne in the conventional sense of the word. The repeated gag line in his mouth, "Without a dowry!" is a good sample of his substitution of cant for values. As the characters labor to see their ways clear to surmounting all the obstacles before them, they are hindered by the language in which the situations must be discussed. Polite verbal intercourse, for one thing, hardly illuminates truth, as the author stressed in *Le Misanthrope*, and Elise has trouble communicating sincerely with her Valère: "Do not assassinate me . . . ." pleads the lover, and his mistress is not sure whether this is verbal smokescreen or sincere anguish. It is hard enough to possess truth about oneself without having matters obscured by meaningless verbiage.

The next element for expression of themes is that of "mask" as it is referred to by Valère. He complains that he must act in disguise as the *maître d'hôtel* in order to be near Elise, and he regrets his compromise with sincerity. But all the characters will play a false role to deceive others at some time in the comedy, with evil or good intentions. Maître Jacques's comic quick changes of costume from chef to coachman underscore in visual fashion this concept. Sincerity is played off against falseness, however, as Elise and Cléanth declare their loves, and Harpagon is quite truthful with himself in his frenzy about guarding his gold. The general tone of falsehood and suspicion dominates the first act, and it culminates in a scene in which Valère finds himself obliged to praise the miser's scheme to marry Elise to Anselm, "without a dowry."

The rest of the play does not bring in new techniques or ideas so much as it sets up developments of the material at hand, for we see Harpagon being a secret usurer to his own son behind the mask of his agent and deliberately trapping Cléanth into admitting his love for Marianne. The playwright devises a series of variations on his theme and finally ties the whole business up in a neat comic package by the ending which has been described. Rather than creating an effect of disruption and breach at the end, Molière marries together the conflicting parts of his work, the ugliness of greed and the beauty of love, by presenting simultaneously a traditional comic ending and a caricature of the tragic ending, abnormal sterility and death of the soul. The young people embrace each other, while the miser treats his chest of gold like a virgin bride; "They did not take anything away from you?" (V, 6). The use of the unnatural love in comic form is the master stroke which creates the ultimate unity of *L'Avare* as a work of art. The contributing elements of dupery, masking, and deceptive words are all brought to mind at the end, after they have created obstacles now swept aside. Through the medium of the clown, Maître Jacques, Molière recalls to us his essential building materials in the comedy: "They give me blows for telling the truth, and they want to hang me for lying" (V, 6). Right up to the end, his is a burlesque mirror of the essential action, stumbling into the pitfalls now passed by everyone else, confusing matters, and failing to gain what he wants. The satire on desire and possession is complete.

One is finally led to the conclusion that the play is so satisfactory because of the poetic and theatrical fitness of all of its parts and their arrangement, that is, the inevitability and the wholeness of the work show the hand of the master maker of comedy.

THE WAY
OF THE WORLD

William Congreve (1670-1729)

Edited by Henry Ten Eyck Perry

William Congreve's *The Way of the World* is regarded as an outstanding example of the comedy of manners. His first venture as a playwright was an immediate success—*The Old Bachelor*, written when Congreve was just twenty-three years old. He wrote four other plays in the popular vein, most notably *Love For Love*, perhaps Congreve's funniest play that follows the classic pattern of outwitting the irascible father and the aging lover. Another popular success was *The Mourning Bride*, a pseudo-serious work of his whose appeal was closer to the softer emotions.

In *The Way of the World*, Congreve is said to have written more to suit his own tastes which, unfortunately, did not coincide with those of the audience. The play was not well received despite a sparkling performance by Mrs. Ann Bracegirdle, one of the foremost actresses of the time. After this play, Congreve abandoned his career as a playwright.

One always cites the sparkling dialogue of the characters, and their agility in playing their social games against an urbane background in which pretense and foppery are all too apparent. But Congreve has also created two genuine sophisticates who beneath the hard, polished surface reveal the redeeming qualities of genuine feeling and understanding.

When the theater was reopened in England during the Restoration period, its conventions, strongly influenced by the French stage, were a sharp break with the past. Instead of boys playing female roles, women appeared on stage. The Elizabethan architectural stage with its bare platform was replaced by a proscenium arch theater with a deep apron backed by changeable pictorial scenery.

Moreover, instead of the mixed audience of Shakespeare's theater, the new audience was a narrow segment mostly from the aristocracy whose manners and attitudes are reflected in *The Way of the World.*

Opposite. Four players in the game of intrigue in the 1954-1955 Proscenium Productions revival at the Cherry Lane Theater in New York.

Below. Mirabell and Fainall keep abreast of the talk of the town in the 1937 production at the Feagin School of Dramatic Art.

Above. Lady Wishfort plans her strategy
for receiving Sir Rowland in the 1952 Lyric Theatre production
in Hammersmith, England, with Dame Margaret Rutherford
as Lady Wishfort.

Opposite. Lady Wishfort and her friend Mistress Marwood
in the 1965 Minnesota Theatre Company production
at the Tyrone Guthrie Theatre in Minneapolis,
with Jessica Tandy as Lady Wishfort,
and Nancy Wickwire as Mistress Marwood.

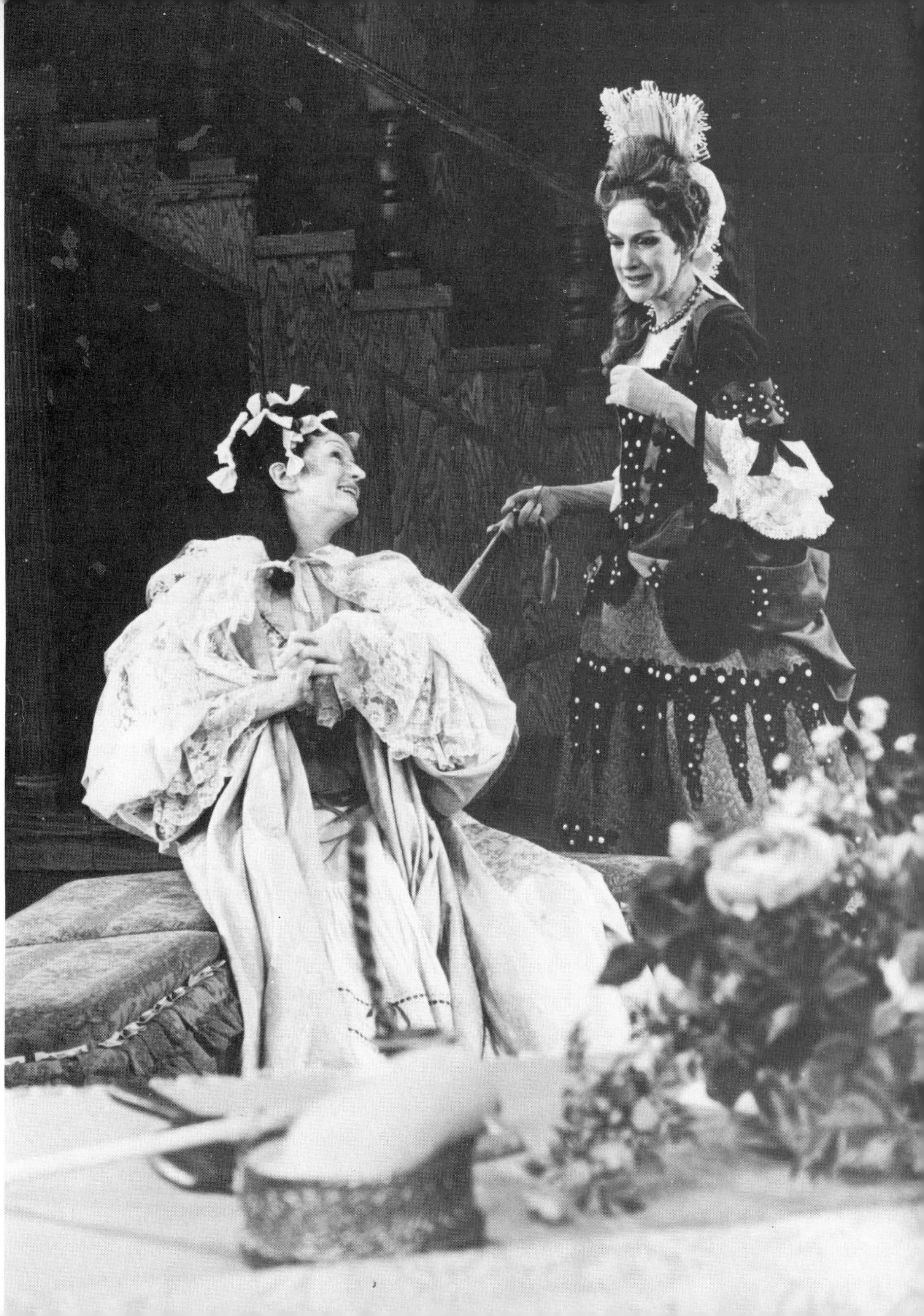

GUTHRIE THEATER COMPANY

Thomas Betterton,
director of the Lincoln's Inn Fields Theatre
and actor in many of the plays produced there.

PROLOGUE

SPOKEN BY MR. BETTERTON[1]

Of those few fools who with ill stars are curst,
Sure scribbling fools, called poets, fare the
    worst;
For they're a sort of fools which Fortune
    makes,
And after she has made 'em fools, forsakes.
With Nature's oafs[2] 'tis quite a different case,
For Fortune favours all her[3] idiot-race;
In her own nest the cuckoo-eggs[4] we find,
O'er which she broods to hatch the changeling-
    kind.
No portion for her own she has to spare,
So much she dotes on her adopted care.   10
    Poets are bubbles,[5] by the town drawn in,
Suffered at first some trifling stakes to win;
But what unequal hazards do they run!
Each time they write, they venture all they've
    won;
The squire that's buttered[6] still, is sure to be
    undone.
This author, heretofore, has found your fa-
    vour,
But pleads no merit from his past behaviour.

[1] *Mr. Betterton* Thomas Betterton played the part of
Fainall in *The Way of the World*.
[2] *oafs* children of elves; hence, deformed or stupid children
[3] *her* Nature's; in the next line "her own" refers to Fortune.
[4] *cuckoo-eggs* The cuckoo was well known for laying its
eggs in the nests of other birds for them to hatch.
[5] *bubbles* dupes
[6] *buttered* loaded with fulsome praise, flattered

To build on that might prove a vain presump-
    tion,
Should grants to poets made admit resump-
    tion;
And in Parnassus[7] he must lose his seat,   20
If it be found a forfeited estate.
But, if they're naught, ne'er spare him for his
    pains;
Damn him the more; have no commiseration
For dullness on mature deliberation.
He swears he'll not resent one hissed-off scene,
Nor, like those peevish wits, his play main-
    tain,
Who, to assert their sense, your taste arraign.[8]
Some plot we think he has, and some new
    thought;
Some humour too, no farce; but that's a fault.   30
Satire, he thinks, you ought not to expect;
For so reformed a town who dares correct?
To please, this time, has been his sole pre-
    tence;
He'll not instruct, lest it should give offence.
Should he by chance a knave or fool expose,
That hurts none here, sure here are none of
    those.
In short, our play shall (with your leave to
    show it)
Give you one instance of a passive poet,
Who to your judgments yields all resignation;
So save or damn, after your own discretion.   40

[7] *Parnassus* a mountain in Greece, sacred to Apollo and
the Muses
[8] *arraign* denounce

CHARACTERS

MEN

FAINALL, *in love with* MRS. MARWOOD.

MIRABELL, *in love with* MRS. MILLAMANT.

WITWOUD,
PETULANT,$\}$ *followers of* MRS. MILLAMANT.

SIR WILFULL WITWOUD, *half brother to* WITWOUD, *and nephew to* LADY WISHFORT.

WAITWELL, *servant to* MIRABELL.

WOMEN

LADY WISHFORT, *enemy to* MIRABELL, *for having falsely pretended love to her.*

MRS. MILLAMANT,[1] *a fine lady, niece to* LADY WISHFORT, *and loves* MIRABELL.

---

[1] *Mrs. Millamant* In Congreve's time the designation Mrs. was used for both married and unmarried women. The name Millamant suggests "mille amants," a thousand lovers.

MRS. MARWOOD, *friend*[2] *to* MR. FAINALL, *and likes* MIRABELL.

MRS. FAINALL, *daughter to* LADY WISHFORT, *and wife to* FAINALL, *formerly friend to* MIRABELL.

FOIBLE, *woman to* LADY WISHFORT.

MINCING, *woman to* MRS. MILLAMANT.

BETTY, *waiting-maid at a chocolate-house.*

PEG, *maid to* LADY WISHFORT.

Dancers, Footmen, and Attendants.

SCENE: *London*

The time equal to that of the presentation.

(Act I takes place in a chocolate-house; Act II in St. Jame's Park; Acts III, IV, and V in LADY WISHFORT's house.)

---

[2] *friend* a mild word for "mistress"

THE WAY OF THE WORLD

ACT I

A CHOCOLATE-HOUSE

MIRABELL *and* FAINALL, *rising from cards;* BETTY *waiting*

MIR: You are a fortunate man, Mr. Fainall.

FAIN: Have we done?

MIR: What you please. I'll play on to entertain you.

FAIN: No, I'll give you your revenge another time, when you are not so indifferent; you are thinking of something else now, and play too negligently. The coldness of a losing gamester lessens the pleasure of the winner. I'd no more play with a man that slighted his ill fortune than I'd make love to a woman who undervalued the loss of her reputation.

MIR: You have a taste extremely delicate and are for refining on your pleasures.

FAIN: Prithee, why so reserved? Something has put you out of humour.

MIR: Not at all. I happen to be grave to-day, and you are gay; that's all.

FAIN: Confess, Millamant and you quarrelled last night, after I left you; my fair cousin has some humours¹ that would tempt the patience of a Stoic.² What, some coxcomb came in, and was well received by her, while you were by.

MIR: Witwoud and Petulant, and what was worse, her aunt, your wife's mother, my evil genius;

or to sum up all in her own name, my old Lady Wishfort came in.

FAIN: Oh, there it is then! She has a lasting passion for you, and with reason. What, then my wife was there?

MIR: Yes, and Mrs. Marwood, and three or four more, whom I never saw before. Seeing me, they all put on their grave faces, whispered one another; then complained aloud of the vapours,³ and after fell into a profound silence.

FAIN: They had a mind to be rid of you.

MIR: For which reason I resolved not to stir. At last the good old lady broke through her painful taciturnity with an invective against long visits. I would not have understood her, but Millamant joining in the argument, I rose, and with a constrained smile, told her, I thought nothing was so easy as to know when a visit began to be troublesome. She reddened, and I withdrew, without expecting⁴ her reply.

FAIN: You were to blame to resent what she spoke only in compliance with her aunt.

MIR: She is more mistress of herself than to be under the necessity of such a resignation.

FAIN: What? though half her fortune depends upon her marrying with my lady's approbation?

MIR: I was then in such a humour that I should have been better pleased if she had been less discreet.

---

¹ *humours* states of mind, moods
² *Stoic* the school of Stoic philosophy taught that one should be indifferent to pleasure or pain.

³ *vapours* melancholy, the blues
⁴ *expecting* waiting for

213

FAIN: Now I remember, I wonder not they were weary of you. Last night was one of their cabal-nights;[5] they have 'em three times a week, and meet by turns at one another's apartments, where they come together like the coroner's inquest, to sit upon the murdered reputations of the week. You and I are excluded; and it was once proposed that all the male sex should be excepted.[6] But somebody moved that, to avoid scandal, there might be one man of the community; upon which motion Witwoud and Petulant[7] were enrolled members.

MIR: And who may have been the foundress of this sect? My Lady Wishfort, I warrant, who publishes her detestation of mankind, and full of the vigour of fifty-five, declares for a friend and ratafia;[8] and let posterity shift for itself, she'll breed no more.

FAIN: The discovery of your sham addresses to her, to conceal your love to her niece, has provoked this separation; had you dissembled better, things might have continued in the state of nature.

MIR: I did as much as man could, with any reasonable conscience; I proceeded to the very last act of flattery with her, and was guilty of a song in her commendation. Nay, I got a friend to put her into a lampoon,[9] and compliment her with the imputation of an affair with a young fellow, which I carried so far that I told her the malicious town took notice that she was grown fat of a sudden; and when she lay in a dropsy,[10] persuaded her she was reported to be in labour. The devil's in't, if an old woman is to be flattered further, unless a man should endeavour downright personally to debauch her; and that my virtue forbade me. But for the discovery of this amour I am indebted to your friend, or your wife's friend, Mrs. Marwood.

FAIN: What should provoke her to be your enemy, unless she has made you advances which you have slighted? Women do not easily forgive omissions of that nature.

MIR: She was always civil to me till of late. I confess I am not one of those coxcombs who are apt to interpret a woman's good manners to her prejudice,[11] and think that she who does not refuse 'em everything can refuse 'em nothing.

FAIN: You are a gallant man, Mirabell; and though you may have cruelty enough not to satisfy a lady's longing, you have too much generosity not to be tender of her honour. Yet you speak with an indifference which seems to be affected, and confesses you are conscious of a negligence.

MIR: You pursue the argument with a distrust that seems to be unaffected, and confesses you are conscious of a concern for which the lady is more indebted to you than is your wife.

FAIN: Fie, fie, friend! If you grow censorious, I must leave you. I'll look upon the gamesters in the next room.

MIR: Who are they?

FAIN: Petulant and Witwoud. (*To* BETTY) Bring me some chocolate.   (*Exit*)

MIR: Betty, what says your clock?

BET: Turned of the last canonical hour,[12] sir.

(*Exit*)

MIR: How pertinently the jade answers me! (*Looking on his watch*) Ha? almost one o'clock! O, y'are come!

Enter a SERVANT

Well, is the grand affair over? You have been something tedious.

SERV: Sir, there's such coupling at Pancras[13] that they stand behind one another, as 'twere in a country dance. Ours was the last couple to lead up,[14] and no hopes appearing of dispatch,[15] besides the parson growing hoarse, we were afraid his lungs would have failed before it came to our turn; so we drove round to Duke's Place,[16] and there they were riveted in a trice.

[5] *cabal-nights* evening parties of a small select society
[6] *excepted* left out
[7] *Witwoud and Petulant* Together they are equal to one man.
[8] *ratafia* a liqueur flavored with fruit kernels
[9] *lampoon* a personal satire in writing
[10] *dropsy* an abnormal accumulation of fluid in the body
[11] *prejudice* injury, disadvantage
[12] *canonical hour* in England, any of the hours from 8 A.M. to 3 P.M., before and after which a marriage cannot legally be performed in a parish church
[13] *Pancras* Pancras Church, where couples could marry without licenses
[14] *lead up* come up
[15] *dispatch* speed
[16] *Duke's Place* In Duke's Place was situated St. James's Church, where also marriages could be performed without licenses.

MIR: So, so, you are sure they are married.

SERV: Married and bedded, sir; I am witness.

MIR: Have you the certificate?

SERV: Here it is, sir.

MIR: Has the tailor brought Waitwell's clothes home, and the new liveries?

SERV: Yes, sir.

MIR: That's well. Do you go home again, d'ye hear, and adjourn the consummation till farther order; bid Waitwell shake his ears, and Dame Partlet[17] rustle up her feathers, and meet me at one o'clock by Rosamond's Pond,[18] that I may see her before she returns to her lady; and as you tender your ears, be secret.   (*Exit* SERVANT)

Re-enter FAINALL *and* BETTY

FAIN: Joy of your success, Mirabell; you look pleased.

MIR: Aye, I have been engaged in a matter of some sort of mirth, which is not yet ripe for discovery. I am glad this is not a cabal-night. I wonder, Fainall, that you who are married, and of consequence should be discreet, will suffer your wife to be of such a party.

FAIN: Faith, I am not jealous. Besides, most who are engaged are women and relations; and for the men, they are of a kind too contemptible to give scandal.

MIR: I am of another opinion. The greater the coxcomb, always the more the scandal; for a woman who is not a fool can have but one reason for associating with a man who is one.

FAIN: Are you jealous as often as you see Witwoud entertained by Millamant?

MIR: Of her understanding I am, if not of her person.

FAIN: You do her wrong; for, to give her her due, she has wit.

MIR: She has beauty enough to make any man think so, and complaisance[19] enough not to contradict him who shall tell her so.

FAIN: For a passionate lover, methinks you are a man somewhat too discerning in the failings of your mistress.

MIR: And for a discerning man, somewhat too passionate a lover; for I like her with all her faults, nay, like her for her faults. Her follies are so natural, or so artful, that they become her; and those affectations which in another woman would be odious, serve but to make her more agreeable. I'll tell thee, Fainall, she once used me with that insolence, that in revenge I took her to pieces, sifted[20] her, and separated her failings; I studied 'em, and got 'em by rote.[21] The catalogue was so large that I was not without hopes one day or other to hate her heartily; to which end I so used[22] myself to think of 'em that at length, contrary to my design and expectation, they gave me every hour less and less disturbance; till in a few days it became habitual to me to remember 'em without being displeased. They are now grown as familiar to me as my own frailties; and in all probability, in a little time longer I shall like 'em as well.

FAIN: Marry her, marry her! Be half as well acquainted with her charms as you are with her defects, and my life on't, you are your own man again.

MIR: Say you so?

FAIN: Aye, aye, I have experience; I have a wife, and so forth.

Enter a MESSENGER

MES: Is one Squire Witwoud here?

BET: Yes; what's your business?

MES: I have a letter for him, from his brother Sir Wilfull, which I am charged to deliver into his own hands.

BET: He's in the next room, friend; that way.
(*Exit* MESSENGER)

MIR: What, is the chief of that noble family in town, Sir Wilfull Witwoud?

FAIN: He is expected to-day. Do you know him?

MIR: I have seen him. He promises to be an extraordinary person; I think you have the honour to be related to him.

FAIN: Yes, he is half brother to this Witwoud by a former wife, who was sister to my Lady Wishfort, my wife's mother. If you marry Millamant, you must call cousins too.

MIR: I had rather be his relation than his acquaintance.

---

[17] *Dame Partlet* Pentelote, the hen; Foible is here so called.

[18] *Rosamond's Pond* a small pond in the southwest corner of St. James's Park

[19] *complaisance* civility

[20] *sifted* examined minutely

[21] *by rote* in a mechanical, routine order

[22] *used* accustomed

FAIN: He comes to town in order to equip himself for travel.

MIR: For travel! Why the man that I mean is above forty.

230 FAIN: No matter for that; 'tis for the honour of England that all Europe should know we have blockheads of all ages.

MIR: I wonder there is not an act of parliament to save the credit of the nation, and prohibit the exportation of fools.

FAIN: By no means; 'tis better as 'tis. 'Tis better to trade with a little loss than to be quite eaten up with being overstocked.

MIR: Pray, are the follies of this knight-errant[23] and 240 those of the squire his brother anything related?

FAIN: Not at all; Witwoud grows by the knight, like a medlar grafted on a crab.[24] One will melt in your mouth, and t'other set your teeth on edge; one is all pulp, and the other all core.

MIR: So one will be rotten before he be ripe, and the other will be rotten without ever being ripe at all.

FAIN: Sir Wilfull is an odd mixture of bashfulness and obstinacy. But when he's drunk, he's as lov-250 ing as the monster in *The Tempest*,[25] and much after the same manner. To give t'other[26] his due, he has something of good nature and does not always want wit.

MIR: Not always; but as often as his memory fails him, and his commonplace of comparisons.[27] He is a fool with a good memory and some few scraps of other folks' wit. He is one whose conversation can never be approved, yet it is now and then to be endured. He has indeed one good 260 quality, he is not exceptious;[28] for he so passionately affects the reputation of understanding raillery that he will construe an affront into a jest and call downright rudeness and ill language, satire and fire.

FAIN: If you have a mind to finish his picture, you have an opportunity to do it at full length. Behold the original!

Enter WITWOUD

WIT: Afford me your compassion, my dears! Pity me, Fainall! Mirabell, pity me! 270

MIR: I do from my soul.

FAIN: Why, what's the matter?

WIT: No letters for me, Betty?

BET: Did not a messenger bring you one but now, sir?

WIT: Aye, but no other?

BET: No, sir.

WIT: That's hard, that's very hard. A messenger, a mule, a beast of burden! He has brought me a letter from the fool my brother, as heavy as 280 a panegyric in a funeral sermon, or a copy of commendatory verses from one poet to another. And what's worse, 'tis as sure a forerunner of the author as an epistle dedicatory.

MIR: A fool, and your brother, Witwoud!

WIT: Aye, aye, my half brother. My half brother he is, no nearer upon honour.

MIR: Then 'tis possible he may be but half a fool.

WIT: Good, good, Mirabell, *le drôle!*[29] Good, good; hang him, don't let's talk of him. Fainall, how 290 does your lady? Gad, I say anything in the world to get this fellow out of my head. I beg pardon that I should ask a man of pleasure and the town a question at once so foreign and domestic.[30] But I talk like an old maid at a marriage, I don't know what I say; but she's the best woman in the world.[31]

FAIN: 'Tis well you don't know what you say, or else your commendation would go near to make me either vain or jealous. 300

WIT: No man in town lives well with a wife but Fainall. Your judgment, Mirabell?

MIR: You had better step and ask his wife, if you would be credibly informed.

WIT: Mirabell.

MIR: Aye.

---

[23] *knight-errant* wandering or traveling knight

[24] *a medlar grafted on a crab* A medlar resembles a crab apple; but the former is good to eat when it has begun to decay, the latter is always sour.

[25] *the monster in The Tempest* Caliban, or Sycorax, his sister, in the adaptation of Shakespeare's play by Dryden and Davenant produced in 1667

[26] *t'other* Witwoud

[27] *commonplace of comparisons* memorandum book for noting similarities

[28] *exceptious* apt to take exeptions, or to object

[29] *le drôle!* the facetious (fellow)!

[30] *foreign and domestic* foreign to one's interests and domestic in nature, with a reference to foreign and domestic public affairs

[31] *the best woman in the world* Witwoud refers to Mrs. Fainall.

WIT: My dear, I ask ten thousand pardons; gad, I have forgot what I was going to say to you!

MIR: I thank you heartily.

310 WIT: No, but prithee excuse me; my memory is such a memory.

MIR: Have a care of such apologies, Witwoud; for I never knew a fool but he affected to complain, either of the spleen[32] or his memory.

FAIN: What have you done with Petulant?

WIT: He's reckoning his money, my money it was. I have no luck to-day.

FAIN: You may allow him to win of you at play, for you are sure to be too hard for him at repartee;

320 since you monopolize the wit that is between you, the fortune must be his of course.

MIR: I don't find that Petulant confesses the superiority of wit to be your talent, Witwoud.

WIT: Come, come, you are malicious now, and would breed debates. Petulant's my friend, and a very honest fellow, and a very pretty fellow, and has a smattering—faith and troth, a pretty deal of an odd sort of a small wit; nay, I'll do him justice. I'm his friend, I won't wrong

330 him neither. And if he had any judgment in the world, he would not be altogether contemptible. Come, come, don't detract from the merits of my friend.

FAIN: You don't take your friend to be over-nicely bred?

WIT: No, no, hang him, the rogue has no manners at all, that I must own. No more breeding than a bum-baily,[33] that I grant you. 'Tis pity, faith; the fellow has fire and life.

340 MIR: What, courage?

WIT: Hum, faith I don't know as to that; I can't say as to that. Yes, faith, in a controversy he'll contradict anybody.

MIR: Though 'twere a man whom he feared, or a woman whom he loved.

WIT: Well, well, he does not always think before he speaks; we have all our failings. You're too hard upon him, you are, faith. Let me excuse him. I can defend most of his faults, except one or

350 two. One he has, that's the truth on't; if he were my brother, I could not acquit him. That indeed I could wish were otherwise.

32 *spleen* ill-humor coming from a diseased condition of the spleen

33 *bum-baily* a low order of bailiff, a lesser magistrate

MIR: Aye, marry, what's that, Witwoud?

WIT: Oh, pardon me! Expose the infirmities of my friend? No, my dear, excuse me there.

FAIN: What, I warrant he's unsincere, or 'tis some such trifle.

WIT: No, no, what if he be? 'Tis no matter for that; his wit will excuse that. A wit should no more be sincere than a woman constant; one 360 argues a decay of parts,[34] as t'other of beauty.

MIR: Maybe you think him too positive?[35]

WIT: No, no, his being positive is an incentive to argument, and keeps up conversation.

FAIN: Too illiterate?

WIT: That! that's his happiness; his want of learning gives him the more opportunities to show his natural parts.

MIR: He wants words?

WIT: Aye, but I like him for that now; for his want 370 of words gives me the pleasure very often to explain his meaning.

FAIN: He's impudent?

WIT: No, that's not it.

MIR: Vain?

WIT: No.

MIR: What! he speaks unseasonable truths sometimes, because he has not wit enough to invent an evasion?

WIT: Truths! ha! ha! ha! No, no; since you will 380 have it, I mean he never speaks truth at all, that's all. He will lie like a chambermaid, or a woman of quality's porter. Now that is a fault.

Enter a COACHMAN

COACH: Is Master Petulant here, mistress?

BET: Yes.

COACH: Three gentlewomen in a coach would speak with him.

FAIN: O brave Petulant! Three!

BET: I'll tell him. 390

COACH: You must bring two dishes of chocolate and a glass of cinnamon-water.[36]

(*Exeunt* BETTY *and* COACHMAN)

WIT: That should be too fasting strumpets, and a bawd troubled with wind.[37] Now you may know what the three are.

34 *parts* talent

35 *positive* dogmatic

36 *cinnamon-water* a mixture of sugar, spirits, powdered cinnamon, and hot water, used as a digestive cordial

37 *wind* air generated in the stomach or bowels

MIR: You are very free with your friend's acquaintance.

WIT: Aye, aye, friendship without freedom is as
400   dull as love without enjoyment, or wine without
toasting. But to tell you a secret, these are trulls[38]
whom he allows coach-hire, and something
more, by the week, to call on him once a day
at public places.

MIR: How!

WIT: You shall see he won't go to 'em, because
there's no more company here to take notice of
him. Why this is nothing to what he used to
do; before he found out this way, I have known
410   him call for himself.

FAIN: Call for himself? What dost thou mean?

WIT: Mean! Why he would slip you out of this
chocolate-house, just when you had been talking
to him; as soon as your back was turned, whip,
he was gone! Then trip to his lodging, clap on
a hood and scarf, and a mask, slap into a hackney-
coach, and drive hither to the door again in a
trice, where he would send in for himself; that
I mean, call for himself, wait for himself. Nay,
420   and what's more, not finding himself, sometimes
leave a letter for himself.

MIR: I confess this is something extraordinary. I
believe he waits for himself now, he is so long
a-coming. Oh! I ask his pardon.

Enter PETULANT *and* BETTY

BET: Sir, the coach stays.

PET: Well, well; I come. 'Sbud,[39] a man had as
good be a professed midwife as a professed
whoremaster, at this rate! To be knocked up
430   and raised at all hours, and in all places! Pox
on 'em, I won't come! d'ye hear, tell 'em I won't
come. Let 'em snivel and cry their hearts out.

FAIN: You are very cruel, Petulant.

PET: All's one, let it pass. I have a humour to be
cruel.

MIR: I hope they are not persons of condition[40]
that you use at this rate.

PET: Condition! Condition's a dried fig. If I am
not in humour! By this hand, if they were
440   your—a—a—your what-d'ye-call-'ems them-

selves, they must wait or rub off,[41] if I want
appetite.

MIR: What-d'ye-call-'ems! What are they, Witwoud?

WIT: Empresses, my dear; by your what-
d'ye-call-'ems he means sultana queens.

PET: Aye, Roxolanas.[42]

MIR: Cry you mercy!

FAIN: Witwoud says they are—

PET: What does he say th'are?   450

WIT: I? Fine ladies, I say.

PET: Pass on, Witwoud. Harkee,[43] by this light
his relations: two co-heiresses his cousins, and
an old aunt, who loves caterwauling better than
a conventicle.[44]

WIT: Ha! ha! ha! I had a mind to see how the
rogue would come off. Ha! ha! ha! Gad, I can't
be angry with him, if he had said they were my
mother and my sisters.

MIR: No!   460

WIT: No; the rogue's wit and readiness of invention
charm me. Dear Petulant!

BET: They are gone, sir, in great anger.

PET: Enough, let 'em trundle.[45] Anger helps complexion, saves paint.

FAIN: This continence is all dissembled; this is in
order to have something to brag of the next time
he makes court to Millamant, and swear he has
abandoned the whole sex for her sake.

MIR: Have you not left off your impudent preten-   470
sions there yet? I shall cut your throat some
time or other, Petulant, about that business.

PET: Aye, ay, let that pass. There are other throats
to be cut.

MIR: Meaning mine, sir?

PET: Not I. I mean nobody; I know nothing. But
there are uncles and nephews in the world, and
they may be rivals. What then? All's one for
that.

MIR: How! harkee Petulant, come hither. Explain,   480
or I shall call your interpreter.[46]

---

[38] *trulls* trollops, loose women

[39] *'Sbud* a corruption of "God's blood"

[40] *persons of condition* people of high social position

[41] *rub off* make off, clear out

[42] *Roxolanas* Roxolana is the Turkish Sultana in
Davenant's *The Siege of Rhodes*, first performed in
1656.

[43] *Harkee* corruption of "Hark ye"

[44] *conventicle* meetinghouse of a noncomformist sect

[45] *trundle* roll along

[46] *call your interpreter* summon someone or something (a
sword?) which will cause you to make an explanation

PET: Explain! I know nothing. Why, you have an uncle, have you not, lately come to town, and lodges by my Lady Wishfort's?

MIR: True.

PET: Why, that's enough. You and he are not friends; and if he should marry and have a child, you may be disinherited, ha?

MIR: Where hast thou stumbled upon all this truth?

490 PET: All's one for that; why, then say I know something.

MIR: Come, thou art an honest fellow, Petulant, and shalt make love to my mistress, thou sha't,[47] faith. What has thou heard of my uncle?

PET: I? Nothing I. If throats are to be cut, let swords clash! Snug's the word;[48] I shrug and am silent.

MIR: Oh, raillery, raillery! Come, I know thou art in the women's secrets. What, you're a cabalist; 500 I know you stayed at Millamant's last night, after I went. Was there any mention made of my uncle or me? Tell me. If thou hadst but good nature equal to thy wit, Petulant, Tony Witwoud, who is now thy competitor in fame, would show as dim by thee as a dead whiting's[49] eye by a pearl of orient; he would no more be seen by thee than Mercury is by the sun. Come, I'm sure thou wo't[50] tell me.

PET: If I do, will you grant me common sense then 510 for the future?

MIR: Faith, I'll do what I can for thee, and I'll pray that Heaven may grant it thee in the meantime.

PET: Well, harkee.

(MIRABELL *and* PETULANT *talk apart*)

FAIN: Petulant and you both will find Mirabell as warm a rival as a lover.

WIT: Pshaw! pshaw! That she laughs at Petulant is plain. And for my part, but that it is almost 520 a fashion to admire her, I should—Harkee, to tell you a secret, but let it go no further; between friends, I shall never break my heart for her.

FAIN: How!

WIT: She's handsome; but she's a sort of an uncertain woman.

FAIN: I thought you had died for her.

WIT: Umh—no—

FAIN: She has wit.

WIT: 'Tis what she will hardly allow anybody else. Now, demme,[51] I should hate that, if she were 530 as handsome as Cleopatra. Mirabell is not so sure of her as he thinks for.

FAIN: Why do you think so?

WIT: We stayed pretty late there last night, and heard something of an uncle to Mirabell, who is lately come to town, and is between him and the best part of his estate. Mirabell and he are at some distance, as my Lady Wishfort has been told; and you know she hates Mirabell worse than a Quaker hates a parrot, or than a fishmon- 540 ger hates a hard frost. Whether this uncle has seen Mrs. Millamant or not, I cannot say; but there were items of such a treaty being in embryo, and if it should come to life, poor Mirabell would be in some sort unfortunately fobbed,[52] i'faith.

FAIN: 'Tis impossible Millamant should hearken to it.

WIT: Faith, my dear, I can't tell; she's a woman, and a kind of a humourist.[53] 550

MIR: And this[54] is the sum of what you could collect last night?

PET: The quintessence. Maybe Witwoud knows more; he stayed longer. Besides, they never mind him; they say anything before him.

MIR: I thought you had been the greatest favourite.

PET: Aye, *tête à tête*, but not in public, because I make remarks.

MIR: You do?

PET: Aye, aye, pox, I'm malicious, man! Now he's 560 soft, you know; they are not in awe of him. The fellow's well-bred; he's what you call a whatd'ye-call-'em, a fine gentleman; but he's silly withal.

MIR: I thank you. I know as much as my curiosity requires. Fainall, are you for the Mall?[55]

FAIN: Aye, I'll take a turn before dinner.

WIT: Aye, we'll walk in the Park; the ladies talked of being there.

[47] *sha't* shalt
[48] *Snug's the word* The watchword is secrecy.
[49] *whiting's* a fish of the cod family
[50] *wo't* wilt
[51] *demme* damn me
[52] *fobbed* tricked
[53] *humourist* a person subject to humours or whims
[54] *And this* This speech resumes the private conversation between Mirabell and Petulant which has been going on during the dialogue of Fainall and Witwoud.
[55] *the Mall* a fashionable walk in St. James's Park

570 MIR: I thought you were obliged to watch for your brother Sir Wilfull's arrival.

WIT: No, no, he comes to his aunt's, my Lady Wishfort. Pox on him! I shall be troubled with him too; what shall I do with the fool?

PET: Beg him for his estate, that I may beg you afterwards; and so have but one trouble with you both.

WIT: O rare Petulant! Thou art as quick as fire in a frosty morning; thou shalt to the Mall with 580 us, and we'll be very severe.

PET: Enough, I'm in a humour to be severe.

MIR: Are you? Pray then walk by yourselves: let not us be accessory to your putting the ladies out of countenance with your senseless ribaldry, which you roar out aloud as often as they pass by you; and when you have made a handsome woman blush, then you think you have been severe.

PET: What, what? Then let 'em either show their innocence by not understanding what they 590 hear, or else show their discretion by not hearing what they would not be thought to understand.

MIR: But has not thou then sense enough to know that thou oughtest be most ashamed thyself, when thou hast put another out of countenance?

PET: Not I, by this hand! I always take blushing either for a sign of guilt or ill breeding.

MIR: I confess you ought to think so. You are in the right, that you may plead the error of your 600 judgment in defence of your practice.

Where modesty's ill manners, 'tis but fit
That impudence and malice pass for wit.

(*Exeunt*)

ACT II

ST. JAMES'S PARK

Enter MRS. FAINALL *and* MRS. MARWOOD

MRS. FAIN: Aye, aye, dear Marwood, if we will be happy, we must find the means in ourselves, and among ourselves. Men are ever in extremes, either doting or averse.[1] While they are lovers, if they have fire and sense, their jealousies are insupportable. And when they cease to love, (we ought to think at least) they loath; they look upon us with horror and distaste; they meet us 10 like the ghosts of what we were, and as from such, fly from us.

MRS. MAR: True, 'tis an unhappy circumstance of life that love should ever die before us; and that the man so often should outlive the lover. But say what you will, 'tis better to be left than never to have been loved. To pass our youth in dull indifference, to refuse the sweets of life because they once must leave us, is as preposterous as to wish to have been born old, because 20 we one day must be old. For my part, my youth may wear and waste, but it shall never rust in my possession.

MRS. FAIN: Then it seems you dissemble an aversion to mankind, only in compliance to my mother's humour?

MRS. MAR: Certainly. To be free,[2] I have no taste of those insipid dry discourses with which our sex of force must entertain themselves, apart from men. We may affect endearments to each other, profess eternal friendships, and seem to 30 dote like lovers; but 'tis not in our natures long to persevere. Love will resume his empire in our breasts; and every heart, or soon or late, receive and readmit him as its lawful tyrant.

MRS. FAIN: Bless me, how have I been deceived! Why you profess[3] a libertine!

[1] *averse* reluctant
[2] *free* frank
[3] *profess* proclaim yourself

MRS. MAR: You see my friendship by my freedom.[4] Come, be sincere, acknowledge that your sentiments agree with mine.

40 MRS. FAIN: Never!

MRS. MAR: You hate mankind?

MRS. FAIN: Heartily, inveterately.

MRS. MAR: Your husband?

MRS. FAIN: Most transcendently; aye, though I say it, meritoriously.

MRS. MAR: Give my your hand upon it.

MRS. FAIN: There.

MRS. MAR: I join with you; what I have said has been to try you.

50 MRS. FAIN: Is it possible? Dost thou hate those vipers, men?

MRS. MAR: I have done hating 'em, and am now come to despise 'em; the next thing I have to do, is eternally to forget 'em.

MRS. FAIN: There spoke the spirit of an Amazon, a Penthesilea![5]

MRS. MAR: And yet I am thinking sometimes to carry my aversion further.

MRS. FAIN: How?

60 MRS. MAR: Faith, by marrying; if I could but find one that loved me very well and would be throughly sensible of ill usage, I think I should do myself the violence of undergoing the ceremony.

MRS. FAIN: You would not make him a cuckold?[6]

MRS. MAR: No, but I'd make him believe I did, and that's as bad.

MRS. FAIN: Why had not you as good do it?

MRS. MAR: Oh, if he should ever discover it, he

70 would then know the worst, and be out of his pain; but I would have him ever to continue upon the rack of fear and jealousy.

MRS. FAIN: Ingenious mischief! Would thou wert married to Mirabell.

MRS. MAR: Would I were!

MRS. FAIN: You change colour.

MRS. MAR: Because I hate him.

MRS. FAIN: So do I; but I can hear him named. But what reason have you to hate him in par-

80 ticular?

MRS. MAR: I never loved him; he is, and always was, insufferably proud.

MRS. FAIN: By the reason you give for your aversion, one would think it dissembled; for you have laid a fault to his charge of which his enemies must acquit him.

MRS. MAR: Oh, then it seems you are one of his favourable enemies! Methinks you look a little pale, and now you flush again.

MRS. FAIN: Do I? I think I am a little sick o' the 90 sudden.

MRS. MAR: What ails you?

MRS. FAIN: My husband. Don't you see him? He turned short upon me unawares, and has almost overcome me.

Enter FAINALL *and* MIRABELL

MRS. MAR: Ha! ha! ha! He comes opportunely for you.

MRS. FAIN: For you, for he has brought Mirabell with him. 100

FAIN: My dear!

MRS. FAIN: My soul!

FAIN: You don't look well to-day, child.

MRS. FAIN: D'ye think so?

MIR: He is the only man that does, madam.

MRS. FAIN: The only man that would tell me so at least; and the only man from whom I could hear it without mortification.

FAIN: O my dear, I am satisfied of your tenderness; I know you cannot resent anything from me, 110 especially what is an effect of my concern.

MRS. FAIN: Mr. Mirabell, my mother interrupted you in a pleasant relation last night; I would fain hear it out.

MIR: The persons concerned in that affair have yet a tolerable reputation. I am afraid Mr. Fainall will be censorious.[7]

MRS. FAIN: He has a humour more prevailing than his curiosity and will willingly dispense with the hearing of one scandalous story, to avoid giving 120 an occasion to make another by being seen to walk with his wife. This way, Mr. Mirabell, and I dare promise you will oblige us both.

(*Exeunt* MRS. FAINALL *and* MIRABELL)

FAIN: Excellent creature! Well, sure if I should live to be rid of my wife, I should be a miserable man.

[4] *freedom* frankness

[5] *Penthesilea* Queen of the Amazons, a race or nation of female warriors

[6] *cuckold* a man whose wife is unfaithful to him

[7] *censorious* disapprovingly critical

MRS. MAR: Aye!

FAIN: For having only that one hope, the accomplishment of it, of consequence, must put an end to all my hopes; and what a wretch is he who must survive his hopes! Nothing remains when that day comes, but to sit down and weep like Alexander,[8] when he wanted other worlds to conquer.

MRS. MAR: Will you not follow 'em?

FAIN: Faith, I think not.

MRS. MAR: Pray let us; I have a reason.

FAIN: You are not jealous?

MRS. MAR: Of whom?

FAIN: Of Mirabell.

MRS. MAR: If I am, is it inconsistent with my love to you that I am tender of your honour?

FAIN: You would intimate, then, as if there were fellow-feeling between my wife and him.

MRS. MAR: I think she does not hate him to that degree she would be thought.

FAIN: But he, I fear, is too insensible.

MRS. MAR: It may be you are deceived.

FAIN: It may be so. I do now begin to apprehend it.

MRS. MAR: What?

FAIN: That I have been deceived, madam, and you are false.

MRS. MAR: That I am false! What mean you?

FAIN: To let you know I see through all your little arts. Come, you both [9] love him; and both have equally dissembled your aversions. Your mutual jealousies of one another have made you clash till you have both struck fire. I have seen the warm confession reddening on your cheeks and sparkling from your eyes.

MRS. MAR: You do me wrong.

FAIN: I do not. 'Twas for my ease to oversee[10] and wilfully neglect the gross advances made him by my wife; that by permitting her to be engaged, I might continue unsuspected in my pleasures, and take you oftener to my arms in full security. But could you think, because the nodding husband would not wake, that e'er the watchful lover slept?

MRS. MAR: And wherewithal can you reproach me?

FAIN: With infidelity, with loving another, with love of Mirabell.

[8] *Alexander* Alexander the Great, King of Macedon
[9] *both* both Mrs. Marwood and Mrs. Fainall
[10] *oversee* overlook

MRS. MAR: 'Tis false! I challenge you to show an instance that can confirm your groundless accusation. I hate him.

FAIN: And wherefore do you hate him? He is insensible, and your resentment follows his neglect. An instance? The injuries you have done him are a proof, your interposing in his love. What cause had you to make discoveries of his pretended passion? to undeceive the credulous aunt, and be the officious obstacle of his match with Millamant?

MRS. MAR: My obligations to my lady urged me; I had professed a friendship to her, and could not see her easy nature so abused by that dissembler.

FAIN: What, was it conscience then? Professed a friendship! Oh, the pious friendships of the female sex!

MRS. MAR: More tender, more sincere, and more enduring, than all the vain and empty vows of men, whether professing love to us, or mutual faith to one another.

FAIN: Ha! ha! ha! You are my wife's friend too.

MRS. MAR: Shame and ingratitude! Do you reproach me? You, you upbraid me? Have I been false to her, through strict fidelity to you, and sacrificed my friendship to keep my love inviolate? And have you the baseness to charge me with the guilt, unmindful of the merit? To you it should be meritorious, that I have been vicious; and do you reflect that guilt upon me, which should lie buried in your bosom?

FAIN: You misinterpret my reproof. I meant but to remind you of the slight account you once could make of strictest ties, when set in competition with your love to me.

MRS. MAR: 'Tis false; you urged it with deliberate malice! 'Twas spoke in scorn, and I never will forgive it.

FAIN: Your guilt, not your resentment, begets your rage. If yet you loved, you could forgive a jealousy; but you are stung to find you are discovered.

MRS. MAR: It shall be all discovered. You too shall be discovered; be sure you shall. I can but be exposed. If I do it myself, I shall prevent[11] your baseness.

FAIN: Why, what will you do?

[11] *prevent* anticipate

MRS. MAR: Disclose it to your wife; own what has passed between us.

FAIN: Frenzy!

MRS. MAR: By all my wrongs I'll do't! I'll publish to the world the injuries you have done me, both in my fame and fortune! With both I trusted you, you bankrupt in honour, as indigent[12] of wealth.

FAIN: Your fame I have preserved. Your fortune has been bestowed as the prodigality of your love would have it, in pleasures which we both have shared. Yet, had not you been false, I had ere this repaid it. 'Tis true, had you permitted Mirabell with Millamant to have stolen their marriage, my lady had been incensed beyond all means of reconcilement; Millamant had forfeited the moiety[13] of her fortune, which then would have descended to my wife. And wherefore did I marry, but to make lawful prize of a rich widow's wealth, and squander it on love and you?

MRS. MAR: Deceit and frivolous pretence!

FAIN: Death, am I not married? What's pretence? Am I not imprisoned, fettered? Have I not a wife? nay a wife that was a widow, a young widow, a handsome widow; and would be again a widow, but that I have a heart of proof,[14] and something of a constitution to bustle through the ways of wedlock and this world! Will you yet be reconciled to truth and me?

MRS. MAR: Impossible. Truth and you are inconsistent. I hate you, and shall for ever.

FAIN: For loving you?

MRS. MAR: I loathe the name of love after such usage; and next to the guilt with which you would asperse me, I scorn you most. Farewell!

FAIN: Nay, we must not part thus.

MRS. MAR: Let me go.[15]

FAIN: Come, I'm sorry.

MRS. MAR: I care not, let me go, break my hands, do! I'd leave 'em to get loose.

FAIN: I would not hurt your for the world. Have I no other hold to keep you here?

MRS. MAR: Well, I have deserved it all.

FAIN: You know I love you.

MRS. MAR: Poor dissembling! Oh, that—well, it is not yet—

FAIN: What? what is it not? what is it not yet? It is not yet too late—

MRS. MAR: No, it is not yet too late; I have that comfort.

FAIN: It is, to love another.

MRS. MAR: But not to loathe, detest, abhor mankind, myself, and the whole treacherous world.

FAIN: Nay, this is extravagance. Come, I ask your pardon. No tears. I was to blame; I could not love you and be easy in my doubts. Pray, forbear. I believe you. I'm convinced I've done you wrong; and any way, every way will make amends. I'll hate my wife yet more, damn her! I'll part with her, rob her of all she's worth, and we'll retire somewhere, anywhere to another world. I'll marry thee; be pacified. 'Sdeath,[16] they come; hide your face, your tears. You have a mask;[17] wear it a moment. This way, this way. Be persuaded.   (*Exeunt*)

Re-enter MIRABELL *and* MRS. FAINALL

MRS. FAIN: They are here yet.

MIR: They are turning into the other walk.

MRS. FAIN: While I only hated my husband, I could bear to see him; but since I have despised him, he's too offensive.

MIR: Oh, you should hate with prudence.

MRS. FAIN: Yes, for I have loved with indiscretion.

MIR: You should have just so much disgust for your husband as may be sufficient to make you relish your lover.

MRS. FAIN: You have been the cause that I have loved without bounds, and would you set limits to that aversion of which you have been the occasion? Why did you make me marry this man?

MIR: Why do we daily commit disagreeable and dangerous actions? To save that idol, reputation. If the familiarities of our loves had produced that consequence[18] of which you were apprehensive, where could you have fixed a father's name with credit, but on a husband? I knew Fainall to be a man lavish of his morals, an interested

---

[12] *indigent* destitute

[13] *moiety* half

[14] *proof* quality of having been proved or tried

[15] *Let me go.* Fainall has evidently seized Mrs. Marwood's hands.

[16] *S'death* i.e. God's death

[17] *mask* At this time masks were worn as substitutes for the modern veil; they were more reputable when used out-of-doors than at a play.

[18] *consequence* i.e. a child

and professing[19] friend, a false and a designing lover; yet one whose wit and outward fair behaviour have gained a reputation with the town enough to make that woman stand excused who has suffered herself to be won by his addresses. A better man ought not to have been sacrificed to the occasion; a worse had not answered to the purpose. When you are weary of him, you know your remedy.

320   MRS. FAIN: I ought to stand in some degree of credit with you, Mirabell.

MIR: In justice to you, I have made you privy to my whole design, and put it in your power to ruin or advance my fortune.

MRS. FAIN: Whom have you instructed to represent your pretended uncle?

MIR: Waitwell, my servant.

MRS. FAIN: He is an humble servant to Foible, my mother's woman, and may win her to your inter-

330   est.

MIR: Care is taken for that. She is won and worn by this time. They were married this morning.

MRS. FAIN: Who?

MIR: Waitwell and Foible. I would not tempt my servant to betray me by trusting him too far. If your mother, in hopes to ruin me, should consent to marry my pretended uncle, he might, like Mosca in *The Fox*[20] stand upon terms;[21] so I made him sure beforehand.

340   MRS. FAIN: So if my poor mother is caught in a contract, you will discover the imposture betimes, and release her by producing a certificate of her gallant's former marriage?

MIR: Yes, upon condition that she consent to my marriage with her niece, and surrender the moiety of her fortune in her possession.[22]

MRS. FAIN: She talked last night of endeavouring at a match between Millamant and your uncle.

MIR: That was by Foible's direction, and my

350   instruction, that she might seem to carry it[23] more privately.

MRS. FAIN: Well, I have an opinion of your success, for I believe my lady will do anything to get a husband; and when she has this, which you have provided for her, I suppose she will submit to anything to get rid of him.

MIR: Yes, I think the good lady would marry anything that resembled a man, though 'twere no more than what a butler could pinch out of a napkin.[24]   360

MRS. FAIN: Female frailty! We must all come to it, if we live to be old and feel the craving of a false appetite when the true is decayed.

MIR: An old woman's appetite is depraved like that of a girl. 'Tis the green sickness[25] of a second childhood; and, like the faint offer of a latter spring, serves but to usher in the fall, and withers in an affected bloom.

MRS. FAIN: Here's your mistress.

Enter MRS. MILLAMANT, WITWOUD, *and* MINCING   370

MIR: Here she comes, i'faith, full sail, with her fan spread and her streamers[26] out, and a shoal[27] of fools for tenders.[28] Ha, no, I cry her mercy!

MRS. FAIN: I see but one poor empty sculler,[29] and he tows her woman after him.

MIR: (*To* MRS. MILLAMANT) You seem to be unattended, madam. You used to have the *beau monde*[30] throng after you, and a flock of gay, fine perukes[31] hovering round you.

WIT: Like moths about a candle. I had like to have   380 lost my comparison for want of breath.

MRS. MIL: Oh, I have denied myself airs to-day. I have walked as fast through the crowd—

WIT: As a favourite just disgraced, and with as few followers.

MRS. MIL: Dear Mr. Witwoud, truce with your similitudes;[32] for I'm as sick of 'em—

---

[19] *interested and professing* self-interested and making only a pretense (of friendship)

[20] *The Fox* Ben Jonson's *Volpone: or The Fox* (1606)

[21] *stand upon terms* insist upon going through with the terms of a contract

[22] *her fortune in her possession* Mrs. Millamant's fortune in Lady Wishfort's possession

[23] *carry it* carry on the business (of marrying Mirabell's pretended uncle)

[24] *What a . . . napkin* referring to a butler's skill in pinching a napkin into a variety of fancy shapes

[25] *green sickness* an anemic disease of young women

[26] *streamers* flags that float in the wind; cf. Milton's description of Dalia, "Sails filled and streamers waving." *Samson Agonistes* 1. 718

[27] *shoal* school (as of fish), or throng

[28] *tenders* small vessels employed to attend other vessels

[29] *sculler* a boat rowed by one man with two sculls, or short oars; also, the man who uses the sculls.

[30] *beau monde* fashionable world

[31] *perukes* wigs

[32] *similitudes* similes, comparisons

WIT: As a physician of a good air. I cannot help it, madam, though 'tis against myself.

390 MRS. MIL: Yet, again! Mincing, stand between me and his wit.

WIT: Do, Mrs. Mincing, like a screen before a great fire. I confess I do blaze to-day; I am too bright.

MRS. FAIN: But, dear Millamant, why were you so long?

MRS. MIL: Long! Lord, have I not made violent haste? I have asked every living thing I met for you; I have inquired after you, as after a new fashion.

400 WIT: Madam, truce with your similitudes. No, you met her husband, and did not ask him for her.

MRS. MIL: By your leave, Witwoud, that were like inquiring after an old fashion, to ask a husband for his wife.

WIT: Hum, a hit! a hit! a palpable hit![33] I confess it.

MRS. FAIN: You were dressed before I came abroad.

MRS. MIL: Aye, that's true. Oh, but then I had—Mincing, what had I? Why was I so long?

410 MIN: O mem,[34] your laship[35] stayed to peruse a pecket[36] of letters.

MRS. MIL: Oh, aye, letters; I had letters. I am persecuted with letters. I hate letters. Nobody knows how to write letters, and yet one has 'em, one does not know why. They serve one to pin up one's hair.

WIT: Is that the way? Pray, madam, do you pin up your hair with all your letters? I find I must keep copies.

420 MRS. MIL: Only with those in verse, Mr. Witwoud. I never pin up my hair with prose. I fancy one's hair would not curl if it were pinned up with prose. I think I tried once, Mincing.

MIN: O mem, I shall never forget it.

MRS. MIL: Aye, poor Mincing tiffed[37] and tiffed all the morning.

MIN: Till I had the cremp[38] in my fingers, I'll vow, mem. And all to no purpose. But when your ladyship pins it up with poetry, it sits so pleasant the next day as anything. and is so pure and so crips.[39] 430

WIT: Indeed, so crips?

MIN: You're such a critic, Mr. Witwoud.

MRS. MIL: Mirabell, did you take exceptions last night? Oh, aye, and went away. Now I think on't, I'm angry. No, now I think on't, I'm pleased; for I believe I gave you some pain.

MIR: Does that please you?

MRS. MIL: Infinitely; I love to give pain.

MIR: You would affect a cruelty which is not in 440 your nature; your true vanity is in the power of pleasing.

MRS. MIL: Oh, I ask you pardon for that. One's cruelty is one's power; and when one parts with one's cruelty, one parts with one's power; and when one has parted with that, I fancy one's old and ugly.

MIR: Aye, aye, suffer your cruelty to ruin the object of your power, to destroy your lover, and then how vain, how lost a thing you'll be! Nay, 450 'tis true: you are no longer handsome when you've lost your lover; your beauty dies upon the instant. For beauty is the lover's gift; 'tis he bestows your charms, your glass is all a cheat. The ugly and the old, whom the looking-glass mortifies, yet after commendation[40] can be flattered by it, and discover beauties in it; for that reflects our praises, rather than your face.

MRS. MIL: Oh, the vanity of these men! Fainall, d'ye hear him? If they did not commend us, 460 we were not handsome! Now you must know they could not commend one, if one was not handsome. Beauty the lover's gift! Lord, what is a lover, that it can give? Why, one makes lovers as fast as one pleases, and they live as long as one pleases, and they die as soon as one pleases; and then, if one pleases, one makes more.

WIT: Very pretty. Why, you make no more of making of lovers, madam, than of making so many card-matches.[41] 470

MRS. MIL: One no more owes one's beauty to a lover than one's wit to an echo. They can but

---

[33] *a palpable hit* cf. Osric in *Hamlet*, V, ii, 1. 292

[34] *mem* contraction for "madam"

[35] *laship* i.e. ladyship

[36] *pecket* packet, or package

[37] *tiffed* dressed the hair

[38] *cremp* cramp

[39] *crips* a variation of "crisp" found in some provincial dialects

[40] *after commendation* after they have been commended, or praised

[41] *card-matches* pieces of cardboard dipped in melted sulphur and used as matches

reflect what we look and say; vain empty things if we are silent or unseen, and want a being.

MIR: Yet to those two vain empty things you owe two the greatest[42] pleasures of your life.

MRS. MIL: How so?

MIR: To your lover you owe the pleasure of hearing yourselves praised; and to an echo the pleasure of hearing yourselves talk.

WIT: But I know a lady that loves talking so incessantly, she won't give an echo fair play; she has that everlasting rotation of tongue, that an echo must wait till she dies, before it can catch her last words.

MRS. MIL: Oh, fiction! Fainall, let us leave these men.

MIR: Draw off Witwoud.

(*Aside to* MRS. FAINALL)

MRS. FAIN: Immediately. I have a word or two for Mr. Witwoud.

(*Exeunt* WITWOUD *and* MRS. FAINALL)

MIR: I would beg a little private audience too. You had the tyranny to deny me last night, though you knew I came to impart a secret to you that concerned my love.

MRS. MIL: You saw I was engaged

MIR: Unkind! You had the leisure to entertain a herd of fools; things who visit you from their excessive idleness, bestowing on your easiness that time which is the incumbrance of their lives. How can you find delight in such society? It is impossible they should admire you; they are not capable. Or if they were, it should be to you as a mortification, for sure to please a fool is some degree of folly.

MRS. MIL: I please myself. Besides, sometimes to converse with fools is for my health.

MIR: Your health! Is there a worse disease than the conversation of fools?

MRS. MIL: Yes, the vapours; fools are physic[43] for it, next to assafoetida.[44]

MIR: You are not in a course of fools?[45]

MRS. MIL: Mirabell, if you persist in this offensive freedom, you'll displease me. I think I must resolve, after all, not to have you; we shan't agree.

MIR: Not in our physic, it may be.

MRS. MIL: And yet our distemper,[46] in all likelihood, will be the same; for we shall be sick of one another. I shan't endure to be reprimanded nor instructed; 'tis so dull to act always by advice, and so tedious to be told of one's faults—I can't bear it. Well, I won't have you, Mirabell. I'm resolved—I think—you may go. Ha! ha! ha! What would you give that you could help loving me?

MIR: I would give something that you did not know I could not help it.

MRS. MIL: Come, don't look grave then. Well, what do you say to me?

MIR: I say that a man may as soon make a friend by his wit, or a fortune by his honesty, as win a woman with plain-dealing[47] and sincerity.

MRS. MIL: Sententious Mirabell! Prithee, don't look with that violent and inflexible wise face, like Solomon at the dividing of the child[48] in an old tapestry hanging.

MIR: You are merry, madam, but I would persuade you for one moment to be serious.

MRS. MIL: What, with that face? No, if you keep your countenance, 'tis impossible I should hold mine. Well, after all, there is something very moving in a love-sick face. Ha! ha! ha! Well, I won't laugh; don't be peevish. Heigho! now I'll be melancholy, as melancholy as a watchlight.[49] Well, Mirabell, if ever you will win me, woo me now. Nay, if you are so tedious, fare you well; I see they are walking away.

MIR: Can you not find in the variety of your disposition one moment—

MRS. MIL: To hear you tell me that Foible's married, and your plot like to speed? No.

MIR: But how came you to know it?

MRS. MIL: Without the help of the devil, you can't imagine; unless she should tell me herself. Which of the two it may have been, I will leave you to consider; and when you have done thinking of that, think of me.

(*Exeunt* MRS. MILLAMANT *with* MINCING)

MIR: I have something more—Gone! Think of you? To think of a whirlwind, though 'twere in a

---

[42] *two the greatest* two of the greatest
[43] *physic* medicine
[44] *assafoetida* an ill-smelling gum resin, used as a medicine to prevent or alleviate spasms
[45] *in a course of fools* taking a cure to get rid of fools

[46] *distemper* disease
[47] *plain-dealing* honest, outspoken expression of opinion
[48] *Solomon . . . child* cf. I Kings, III, 16-28
[49] *watch-light* a slow burning candle for night watches

whirlwind, were a case of more steady contemplation; a very tranquility of mind and mansion. A fellow that lives in a windmill has not a more whimsical dwelling than the heart of a man that is lodged in a woman. There is no point of the compass to which they[50] cannot turn, and by which they are not turned; and by one as well as another, for motion, not method, is their occupation. To know this, and yet continue to be in love, is to be made wise from the dictates of reason, and yet persevere to play the fool by the force of instinct. Oh, here come my pair of turtles![51] What, billing so sweetly? Is not Valentine's Day over with you yet?

Enter WAITWELL *and* FOIBLE

Sirrah, Waitwell, why sure you think you were married for your own recreation, and not for my conveniency.[52]

WAIT: Your pardon, sir. With submission, we have indeed been solacing[53] in lawful delights; but still with an eye to business, sir. I have instructed her as well as I could. If she can take your directions as readily as my instructions, sir, your affairs are in a prosperous way.

MIR: Give you joy, Mrs. Foible.

FOIB: O las,[54] sir, I'm so ashamed! I'm afraid my lady has been in a thousand inquietudes for me. But I protest, sir, I made as much haste as I could.

WAIT: That she did indeed, sir. It was my fault that she did not make more.

MIR: That I believe.

FOIB: But I told my lady as you instructed me, sir, that I had a prospect of seeing Sir Rowland, your uncle; and that I would put her ladyship's picture in my pocket to show him, which I'll be sure to say has made him so enamoured of her beauty, that he burns with impatience to lie at her ladyship's feet and worship the original.

MIR: Excellent Foible! Matrimony has made you eloquent in love.

WAIT: I think she has profited, sir. I think so.

FOIB: You have seen Madam Millamant, sir?

MIR: Yes.

FOIB: I told her, sir, because I did not know that you might find an opportunity; she had so much company last night.

MIR: Your diligence will merit more. In the meantime—   (*Gives money*)

FOIB: O dear sir, your humble servant!

WAIT: Spouse.[55]

MIR: Stand off, sir, not a penny! Go on and prosper, Foible; the lease shall be made good and the farm stocked,[56] if we succeed.

FOIB: I don't question your generosity, sir; and you need not doubt of success. If you have no more commands, sir, I'll be gone; I'm sure my lady is at her toilet and can't dress till I come. Oh, dear, I'm sure that (*looking out*) was Mrs. Marwood that went by in a mask; if she has seen me with you, I'm sure she'll tell my lady. I'll make haste home and prevent her. Your servant, sir. B'w'y,[57] Waitwell.   (*Exit*)

WAIT: Sir Rowland, if you please. The jade's so pert upon her preferment[58] she forgets herself.

MIR: Come, sir, will you endeavour to forget yourself, and transform into Sir Rowland?

WAIT: Why, sir, it will impossible I should remember myself. Married, knighted, and attended[59] all in one day! 'Tis enough to make any man forget himself. The difficulty will be how to recover my acquaintance and familiarity with my former self, and fall from my transformation to a reformation into Waitwell. Nay, I shan't be quite the same Waitwell neither; for, now I remember me, I'm married and can't be my own man again.

Aye, there's my grief; that's the sad change of life,
To lose my title, and yet keep my wife.

(*Exeunt*)

---

[50] *they* women
[51] *turtles* turtledoves
[52] *conveniency* convenience
[53] *solacing* taking comfort, or pleasure
[54] *O las* Alas

[55] *Spouse* Waitwell evidently tries to take from Foible the money which Mirabell has just given to her.
[56] *the lease . . . stocked* i.e. I shall be as good as my promise and do even more than that for you.
[57] *B'w'y* contraction for "God be with you," as is "Goodby"
[58] *so . . . preferment* so bold because of her advancement (to the state of a married woman)
[59] *attended* expected, waited for (with a pun upon "waited on")

ACT III

A ROOM IN LADY WISHFORT'S HOUSE

LADY WISHFORT *at her toilet*, PEG *waiting*

LADY WISH: Merciful! no news of Foible yet?

PEG: No, Madam.

LADY WISH: I have no more patience. If I have not fretted myself till I am pale again, there's no veracity in me! Fetch me the red; the red, do you hear, sweetheart? An arrant ash-colour, as I'm a person![1] Look you how this wench stirs! Why dost thou not fetch me a little red? Didst thou not hear me, mopus?[2]

PEG: The red ratafia does your ladyship mean, or the cherry-brandy?

LADY WISH: Ratafia, fool! No, fool! Not the ratafia, fool. Grant me patience! I mean the Spanish paper,[3] idiot; complexion, darling. Paint, paint, paint; dost thou understand that, changeling,[4] dangling thy hands like bobbins[5] before thee? Why dost thou not stir, puppet? thou wooden thing upon wires!

PEG: Lord, madam, your ladyship is so impatient! I cannot come at the paint, madam; Mrs. Foible has locked it up and carried the key with her.

LADY WISH: A pox take you both! Fetch me the cherry-brandy then. (*Exit* PEG) I'm as pale and as faint, I look like Mrs. Qualmsick, the curate's wife, that's always breeding. Wench, come, come, wench, what art thou doing? sipping? tasting? Save thee, dost thou not know the bottle?

Re-enter PEG *with a bottle and china cup*

PEG: Madam, I was looking for a cup.

---

[1] *a person* a person of distinction; "as I'm a person" is a favorite expression of Lady Wishfort's
[2] *mopus* mope, a dull, spiritless person
[3] *Spanish paper* a kind of cosmetic
[4] *changeling* a child secretly exchanged for another more desirable one in infancy; hence a simpleton or idiot
[5] *bobbins* pins or cylinders stuck in a pillow to form a design in making lace

LADY WISH: A cup, save thee! and what a cup hast thou brought! Dost thou take me for a fairy, to drink out of an acorn? Why didst thou not bring thy thimble? Hast thou ne'er a brass thimble clinking in thy pocket with a bit of nutmeg? I warrant thee. Come, fill, fill! So; again. (*One knocks*) See who that is. Set down the bottle first. Here, here, under the table. What, wouldst thou go with the bottle in thy hand, like a tapster? As I'm a person, this wench has lived in an inn upon the road, before she came to me, like Maritornes the Asturian[6] in *Don Quixote!* No Foible yet?

PEG: No, madam; Mrs. Marwood.

LADY WISH: Oh, Marwood; let her come in. Come in, good Marwood.

Enter MRS. MARWOOD

MRS. MAR: I'm surprised to find your ladyship in dishabillé[7] at this time of day.

LADY WISH: Foible's a lost thing; has been abroad since morning, and never heard of since.

MRS. MAR: I saw her but now, as I came masked through the park, in conference with Mirabell.

LADY WISH: With Mirabell! You call my blood into my face with mentioning that traitor. She durst not have the confidence! I sent her to negotiate an affair in which, if I'm detected,[8] I'm undone. If that wheedling villain has wrought upon Foible to detect me, I'm ruined. O my dear friend, I'm a wretch of wretches if I'm detected.

MRS. MAR: O madam, you cannot suspect Mrs. Foible's integrity.

LADY WISH: Oh, he carries poison in his tongue that would corrupt integrity itself! If she has given him an opportunity, she has as good as put her integrity into his hands. Ah, dear Marwood, what's integrity to an opportunity? Hark!

---

[6] *Maritornes the Asturian* in Cervantes' *Don Quixote,* Part I, Book III, Chapter ii
[7] *dishabillé* informal clothes
[8] *detected* exposed

228

I hear her! Go, you thing, and send her in. (*Exit* PEG) Dear friend, retire into my closet,[9] that I may examine her with more freedom. You'll pardon me, dear friend; I can make bold with you. There are books over the chimney. Quarles and Prynne,[10] and the *Short View of the Stage*,[11] with Bunyan's works,[12] to entertain you.

(*Exit* MRS. MARWOOD)

Enter FOIBLE

O Foible, where hast thou been? What hast thou been doing?

FOIB: Madam, I have seen the party.

LADY WISH: But what hast thou done?

FOIB: Nay, 'tis your ladyship has done, and are to do; I have only promised. But a man so enamoured, so transported! Well, here it is,[13] all that is left; all that is not kissed away. Well, if worshipping of pictures[14] be a sin, poor Sir Rowland, I say.

LADY WISH: The miniature has been counted like. But hast thou not betrayed me, Foible? Hast thou not detected me to that faithless Mirabell? What hadst thou to do with him in the Park? Answer me, has he got nothing out of thee?

FOIB: (*Aside*) So the devil has been beforehand with me. What shall I say? (*Aloud*) Alas, madam, could I help it, if I met that confident thing? Was I in fault? If you had heard how he used me, and all upon your ladyship's account, I'm sure you would not suspect my fidelity. Nay, if that had been the worst, I could have borne; but he had a fling at your ladyship too. And then

I could not hold; but i'faith I gave him his own.

LADY WISH: Me? what did the filthy fellow say?

FOIB: O madam! 'tis a shame to say what he said, with his taunts and his fleers, tossing up his nose. "Humh!" says he. "What, you are a hatching some plot," says he. "You are so early abroad, or catering," says he. "Ferreting for some disbanded[15] officer, I warrant. Half-pay is but thin subsistence," says he. "Well, what pension does your lady propose? Let me see," says he. "What, she must come down pretty deep now, she's superannuated," says he, "and—"

LADY WISH: Ods[16] my life, I'll have him, I'll have him murdered! I'll have him poisoned! Where does he eat? I'll marry a drawer[17] to have him poisoned in his wine! I'll send for Robin from Locket's[18] immediately.

FOIB: Poison him? Poisoning's too good for him. Starve him, madam, starve him; marry Sir Rowland, and get him disinherited. Oh, you would bless yourself to hear what he said!

LADY WISH: A villain! "superannuated!"

FOIB: "Humh," says he. "I hear you are laying designs against me too," says he, "and Mrs. Millamant is to marry my uncle" (he does not suspect a word of your ladyship); "but," says he, "I'll fit you for that." "I warrant you," says he. "I'll hamper you for that," says he. "You and your old frippery[19] too," says he. "I'll handle you—"

LADY WISH: Audacious villain! "handle" me; would he durst! "Frippery! old frippery!" Was there ever such a foul-mouthed fellow? I'll be married to-morrow; I'll be contracted to-night.

FOIB: The sooner the better, madam.

LADY WISH: Will Sir Rowland be here, sayest thou? When, Foible?

FOIB: Incontinently,[20] madam. No new sheriff's wife expects the return of her husband after knighthood with that impatience in which Sir Rowland burns for the dear hour of kissing your ladyship's hands after dinner.

LADY WISH: "Frippery! superannuated! frippery!" I'll frippery the villain; I'll reduce him to frippery

[9] *closet* a small room for privacy

[10] *Quarles and Prynne* Francis Quarles, a religious poet, author of *Emblems, Divine and Moral* (1635), and William Prynne, author of *Histrio-Mastix: The Player's Scourge* (1633), a Puritan attack upon the stage

[11] *the Short View of the Stage* Jeremy Collier's *A Short View of the Immorality and Profaneness of the English Stage* (1698), which had specifically attacked, among other plays, the earlier comedies of Congreve

[12] *Bunyan's works* In 1692 there had appeared in print one volume of "The Works of that Eminent Servant of Christ, Mr. John Bunyan."

[13] *here it is* the picture of Lady Wishfort which Foible has supposedly shown to "Sir Rowland"

[14] *worshipping of pictures* the worship of religious pictures in Roman Catholic churches

[15] *disbanded* discharged

[16] *Ods* a contraction of "God's"

[17] *drawer* a drawer of liquor, a waiter

[18] *Locket's* a fashionable tavern at Charing Cross

[19] *frippery* castoff clothes

[20] *Incontinently* immediately

and rags! A tatterdemalion![21] I hope to see him hung with tatters, like a Long-Lane penthouse[22] or a gibbet thief. A slander-mouthed railer! I warrant the spend-thrift prodigal's in debt as much as the million lottery,[23] or the whole court upon a birthday.[24] I'll spoil his credit with his tailor. Yes, he shall have my niece with her fortune, he shall!

FOIB: He! I hope to see him lodge in Ludgate[25] first, and angle into Blackfriars for brass farthings with an old mitten.

LADY WISH: Aye, dear Foible; thank thee for that, dear Foible. He has put me out of all patience. I shall never recompose my features to receive Sir Rowland with any economy[26] of face. This wretch has fretted me that I am absolutely decayed. Look, Foible.

FOIB: Your ladyship has frowned a little too rashly, indeed, madam. There are some cracks discernible in the white varnish.

LADY WISH: Let me see the glass. "Cracks," sayest thou? Why I am arrantly fleaed;[27] I look like an old peeled wall. Thou must repair me, Foible, before Sir Rowland comes, or I shall never keep up to[28] my picture.

FOIB: I warrant you, madam, a little art once made your picture like you; and now a little of the same art must make you like your picture. Your picture must sit for you, madam.

LADY WISH: But art thou sure Sir Rowland will not fail to come? Or will 'a not fail when he does come? Will he be importunate, Foible, and push? For if he should not be importunate, I shall never break decorums. I shall die with confusion, if I am forced to advance. Oh no, I can never advance! I shall swoon if he should expect advances. No, I hope Sir Rowland is better bred

than to put a lady to the necessity of breaking her forms. I won't be too coy neither. I won't give him despair; but a little disdain is not amiss, a little scorn is alluring.

FOIB: A little scorn becomes your ladyship.

LADY WISH: Yes, but tenderness becomes me best, a sort of dyingness. You see that picture has a sort of a—ha, Foible? a swimmingness in the eyes. Yes, I'll look so. My neice affects it; but she wants features. Is Sir Rowland handsome? Let my toilet be removed. I'll dress above. I'll receive Sir Rowland here. Is he handsome? Don't answer me. I won't know; I'll be surprised, I'll be taken by surprise.

FOIB: By storm, madam. Sir Rowland's a brisk man.

LADY WISH: Is he! Oh, then he'll importune, if he's a brisk man. I shall save decorums if Sir Rowland importunes. I have a mortal terror at the apprehension of offending against decorums. Nothing but importunity can surmount decorums. Oh, I'm glad he's a brisk man. Let my things be removed, good Foible. (*Exit*)

Enter MRS. FAINALL

MRS. FAIN: O Foible, I have been in a fright, lest I should come too late! That devil Marwood saw you in the Park with Mirabell, and I'm afraid will discover it to my lady.

FOIB: Discover what, madam?

MRS. FAIN: Nay, nay, put not on that strange face. I am privy to the whole design, and know that Waitwell, to whom thou wert this morning married, is to personate[29] Mirabell's uncle, and as such, winning my lady, to involve her in those difficulties from which Mirabell only must release her, by his making his conditions to have my cousin and her fortune left to her own disposal.

FOIB: O dear madam, I beg your pardon. It was not my confidence in your ladyship that was deficient; but I thought the former good correspondence between your ladyship and Mr. Mirabell might have hindered his communicating this secret.

MRS. FAIN: Dear Foible, forget that.[30]

[21] *A tatterdemalion* a ragged fellow
[22] *Long-Lane penthouse* a shed attached to a wall or building in Long Lane, noted for the sale of old clothes
[23] *the million lottery* a government scheme to raise a million pounds by the sale of lottery tickets
[24] *a birthday* the birthday of a member of the royal family
[25] *Ludgate* Prison in Blackfriars was used chiefly for debtors; a man at a grated window there solicited money for the prisoners from passers-by in the street.
[26] *economy* orderly arrangement
[27] *fleaed* flayed
[28] *keep up to* look as well as
[29] *personate* impersonate
[30] *forget that* Mrs. Fainall seems to give Foible money at this point.

FOIB: O dear madam, Mr. Mirabell is such a sweet, winning gentleman, but your ladyship is the pattern of generosity. Sweet lady, to be so good! Mr. Mirabell cannot choose but be grateful. I find your ladyship has his heart still. Now, madam, I can safely tell your ladyship our success. Mrs. Marwood had told my lady; but I warrant I managed myself. I turned it all for the better. I told my lady that Mr. Mirabell railed at her. I laid horrid things to his charge, I'll vow; and my lady is so incensed that she'll be contracted to Sir Rowland to-night, she says. I warrant I worked her up, that he may have her for asking for, as they say of a Welsh maidenhead.

MRS. FAIN: O rare Foible!

FOIB: I beg your ladyship to acquaint Mr. Mirabell of his success. I would be seen as little as possible to speak to him; besides, I believe Madam Marwood watches me. She has a month's mind;[31] but I know Mr. Mirabell can't abide her. (*Calls*) John! Remove my lady's toilet. Madam, your servant. My lady is so impatient, I fear she'll come for me if I stay.

MRS. FAIN: I'll go with you up the back stairs, lest I should meet her.   (*Exeunt*)

Re-enter MRS. MARWOOD *alone*

MRS. MAR: Indeed, Mrs. Engine,[32] is it thus with you? Are you become a go-between of this importance? Yes, I shall watch you. Why this wench is the *passe-partout*,[33] a very master-key to everybody's strong-box. My friend Fainall[34] have you carried it so swimmingly? I thought there was something in it; but it seems it's over with you. Your loathing is not from a want of appetite then, but from a surfeit. Else you could never be so cool to fall from a principal to be an assistant; to procure for him! "A pattern of generosity," that I confess. Well, Mr. Fainall, you have met with your match. O man, man! woman, woman! the devil's an ass; if I were

a painter, I would draw him like an idiot, a driveller with a bib and bells. Man should have his head and horns,[35] and woman the rest of him. Poor simple fiend! "Madam Marwood has a month's mind, but he can't abide her." 'Twere better for him you had not been his confessor in that affair, without[36] you could have kept his counsel closer. I shall not prove another pattern of generosity and stalk[37] for him, till he takes his stand to aim at a fortune. He has not obliged me to that with those excesses of himself; and now I'll have none of him. Here comes the good lady, panting ripe; with a heart full of hope, and a head full of care, like any chemist upon the day of projection.[38]

Re-enter LADY WISHFORT

LADY WISH: O dear Marwood, what shall I say for this rude forgetfulness? But my dear friend is all goodness.

MRS. MAR: No apologies, dear madam. I have been very well entertained.

LADY WISH: As I'm a person, I am in a very chaos to think I should so forget myself; but I have such an olio[39] of affairs, really I know not what to do. (*Calls*) Foible! I expect my nephew, Sir Wilfull, every moment too. (*Calls*) Why, Foible! He means to travel for improvement.

MRS. MAR: Methinks Sir Wilfull should rather think of marrying than travelling at his years. I hear he is turned of forty.

LADY WISH: Oh, he's in less danger of being spoiled by his travels. I am against my nephew's marrying too young. It will be time enough when he comes back and has acquired discretion to choose for himself.

MRS. MAR: Methinks Mrs. Millamant and he would make a very fit match. He may travel afterwards. 'Tis a thing very usual with young gentlemen.

---

[31] *a month's mind* a strong inclination (for Mirabell)

[32] *Mrs. Engine* i.e. the agent or tool, Foible, whose conversation with Mrs. Fainall has been overheard by Mrs. Marwood

[33] *passe-partout* that by which one can pass everywhere

[34] *My friend Fainall* Mrs. Fainall, whom Mrs. Marwood is reproaching for aiding Mirabell in his designs

[35] *horns* referring to the horns which were supposed to sprout on the head of a deceived husband, or cuckold

[36] *without* unless

[37] *stalk* walk behind something for the purpose of approaching game, here the fortune which Mirabell is going to take his position to aim at

[38] *projection* the last process of alchemy, in which base metal is transformed into gold or silver by an infusion of the "philosophers' stone"

[39] *olio* a miscellaneous collection

LADY WISH: I promise you I have thought on't; and since 'tis your judgment, I'll think on't again. I assure you I will; I value your judgment extremely. On my word, I'll propose it.

Re-enter FOIBLE

310   Come, come, Foible, I had forgot my nephew will be here before dinner. I must make haste.

FOIB: Mr. Witwoud and Mr. Petulant are come to dine with your ladyship.

LADY WISH: Oh, dear, I can't appear till I'm dressed. Dear Marwood, shall I be free with you again, and beg you to entertain 'em? I'll make all imaginable haste. Dear friend, excuse me.   (*Exeunt* LADY WISHFORT *and* FOIBLE)

Enter MRS. MILLAMANT *and* MINCING

320   MRS. MIL: Sure never anything was so unbred as that odious man! Marwood, your servant.

MRS. MAR: You have a colour; what's the matter?

MRS. MIL: That horrid fellow, Petulant, has provoked me into a flame. I have broke my fan. Mincing, lend me yours; is not all the powder out of my hair?

MRS. MAR: No. What has he done?

MRS. MIL: Nay, he has done nothing; he has only talked. Nay, he has said nothing neither; but

330   he has contradicted everything that has been said. For my part, I thought Witwoud and he would have quarrelled.

MIN: I vow, mem, I thought once they would have fit.[40]

MRS. MIL: Well, 'tis a lamentable thing, I swear, that one has not the liberty of choosing one's acquaintance as one does one's clothes.

MRS. MAR: If we had that liberty, we should be as weary of one set of acquaintance, though never

340   so good, as we are of one suit, though never so fine. A fool and a doily stuff[41] would now and then find days of grace, and be worn for variety.

MRS. MIL: I could consent to wear 'em, if they would wear alike; but fools never wear out, they are such *drap-de-Berry*[42] things! without one could give 'em to one's chambermaid after a day or two.

MRS. MAR: 'Twere better so indeed. Or what think you of the playhouse? A fine, gay glossy fool   350 should be given there, like a new masking habit, after the masquerade is over, and we have done with the disguise. For a fool's visit is always a disguise and never admitted by a woman of wit, but to blind[43] her affair with a lover of sense. If you would but appear barefaced now, and own Mirabell, you might as easily put off Petulant and Witwoud as your hood and scarf. And indeed 'tis time, for the town has found it; the secret is grown too big for the pretence.   360 'Tis like Mrs. Primly's great belly; she may lace it down before, but it burnishes[44] on her hips. Indeed, Millamant, you can no more conceal it than my Lady Strammel can her face, that goodly face, which, in defiance of her Rhenish-wine tea,[45] will not be comprehended[46] in a mask.

MRS. MIL: I'll take my death, Marwood, you are more censorious than a decayed beauty, or a discarded toast.[47] Mincing, tell the men they   370 may come up. My aunt is not dressing here; their folly is less provoking than your malice. (*Exit* MINCING) "The town has found it!" What has it found? That Mirabell loves me is no more a secret than it is a secret that you discovered it to my aunt, or than the reason why you discovered it is a secret.

MRS. MAR: You are nettled.[48]

MRS. MIL: You're mistaken. Ridiculous!

MRS. MAR: Indeed, my dear, you'll tear another   380 fan, if you don't mitigate those violent airs.

MRS. MIL: O silly! ha! ha! ha! I could laugh immoderately. Poor Mirabell! His constancy to me has quite destroyed his complaisance for all the world beside. I swear, I never enjoyed it him to be so coy. If I had the vanity to think he would obey me, I would command him to show more gallantry. 'Tis hardly well-bred to be so particular[49] on one hand, and so insensible on the other. But I despair to prevail, and so   390 let him follow his own way, ha! ha! ha! Pardon

---

[40] *fit* fought
[41] *doily stuff* a kind of woolen stuff
[42] *drap-de-Berry* woolen cloth from the province of Berry in France

[43] *blind* conceal
[44] *burnishes* shines forth
[45] *her Rhenish-wine tea* strong wine instead of tea
[46] *comprehended* enclosed
[47] *discarded toast* a person whose health used to be drunk
[48] *nettled* irritated
[49] *particular* specific in his attentions (to Mrs. Millamant)

me, dear creature, I must laugh, ha! ha! ha!
though I grant you 'tis a little barbarous, ha!
ha! ha!

MRS. MAR: What pity 'tis, so much fine raillery,
and delivered with so significant gesture, should
be so unhappily directed to miscarry!

MRS. MIL: Ha? Dear creature, I ask your pardon.
I swear I did not mind[50] you.

400 MRS. MAR: Mr. Mirabell and you both may think
it a thing impossible, when I shall tell him by
telling you—

MRS. MIL: Oh, dear, what? For it is the same thing
if I hear it, ha! ha! ha!

MRS. MAR: That I detest him, hate him, madam.

MRS. MIL: O madam, why so do I. And yet the
creature loves me, ha! ha! ha! How can one forbear laughing to think of it! I am a sibyl[51] if
I am not amazed to think what he can see in
410 me. I'll take my death, I think you are handsomer
and, within a year or two as young; if you could
but stay for me, I should overtake you, but that
cannot be. Well, that thought makes me
melancholy. Now, I'll be sad.

MRS. MAR: Your merry note may be changed sooner
than you think.

MRS. MIL: D'ye say so? Then I'm resolved I'll have
a song to keep up my spirits.

Re-enter MINCING

420 MIN: The gentlemen stay but to comb,[52] madam,
and will wait on you.

MRS. MIL: Desire Mrs.—, that is in the next room,
to sing the song I would have learned yesterday.
You shall hear it, madam, not that there's any
great matter in it, but 'tis agreeable to my
humour.

SONG

Set by MR. JOHN ECCLES *and sung by* MRS. HODGSON

I

Love's but the frailty of the mind,
    When 'tis not with ambition joined;
430 A sickly flame, which, if not fed, expires,
    And feeding, wastes in self-consuming fires.

II

'Tis not to wound a wanton boy
    Or amorous youth, that gives the joy;

⁵⁰ *mind* pay attention to
⁵¹ *sibyl* prophetess
⁵² *comb* i.e. their wigs

But 'tis the glory to have pierced a swain
For whom inferior beauties sighed in vain.

III

Then I alone the conquest prize,
    When I insult a rival's eyes;
If there's delight in love, 'tis when I see
That heart, which others bleed for, bleed
    for me.   440

Enter PETULANT *and* WITWOUD

MRS. MIL: Is your animosity composed, gentlemen?

WIT: Raillery, raillery, madam; we have no animosity. We hit off a little wit now and then, but
no animosity. The falling-out of wits is like the
falling-out of lovers; we agree in the main, like
treble and bass. Ha, Petulant?

PET: Aye, in the main, but when I have a humour
to contradict.

WIT: Aye, when he has a humour to contradict,   450
then I contradict too. What, I know my cue.
Then we contradict one another like two bat-
tledores; for condractions beget one another like
Jews.

PET: If he says black's black, if I have a humour
to say 'tis blue, let that pass; all's one for that.
I have a humour to prove it, it must be granted.

WIT: Not positively must, but it may, it may.

PET: Yes, it positively must, upon proof positive.

WIT: Aye, upon proof positive it must; but upon   460
proof presumptive it only may. That's a logical
distinction now, madam.

MRS. MAR: I perceive your debates are of importance and very learnedly handled.

PET: Importance is one thing, and learning's
another; but a debate's a debate, that I assert.

WIT: Petulant's an enemy to learning; he relies
altogether on his parts.

PET: No, I'm no enemy to learning; it hurts not
me.   470

MRS. MAR: That's a sign indeed it's no enemy to
you.

PET: No, no, it's no enemy to anybody but them
that have it.

MRS. MIL: Well, an illiterate man's my aversion;
I wonder at the impudence of any illiterate man
to offer to make love.

WIT: That I confess I wonder at too.

MRS. MIL: Ah! to marry an ignorant that can hardly
read or write!   480

PET: Why should a man be any further from being

234   CONGREVE

married, though he can't read, than he is from being hanged? The ordinary's[53] paid for setting the psalm, and the parish-priest for reading the ceremony. And for the rest which is to follow in both cases, a man may do it without book; so all's one for that.

MRS. MIL: D'ye hear the creature? Lord, here's company; I'll be gone.

490   (*Exeunt* MRS. MILLIMANT *and* MINCING)

Enter SIR WILFULL WITWOUD *in a country riding habit and a* SERVANT *to* LADY WISHFORT

WIT: In the name of Bartlemew and his fair,[54] what have we here?

MRS. MAR: 'Tis your brother, I fancy. Don't you know him?

WIT: Not I. Yes, I think it is he. I've almost forgot him; I have not seen him since the Revolution.[55]

SERV: (*To* SIR WILFULL) Sir, my lady's dressing.
500   Here's company; if you please to walk in, in the meantime.

SIR WIL: Dressing! What, it's but morning here, I warrant, with you in London; we should count it towards afternoon in our parts, down in Shropshire. Why then, belike, my aunt han't[56] dined yet, ha, friend?

SERV: Your aunt, sir?

SIR WIL: My aunt, sir! Yes, my aunt, sir and your lady, sir; your lady is my aunt, sir. Why, what,
510   dost thou not know me, friend? Why then send somebody hither that does. How long has thou lived with thy lady, fellow, ha?

SERV: A week, sir; longer than anybody in the house, except my lady's woman.

SIR WIL: Why then, belike thou dost not know thy lady, if thou seest her, ha, friend?

SERV: Why truly, sir, I cannot safely swear to her face in a morning, before she is dressed. 'Tis like I may give a shrewd guess at her by this
520   time.

SIR WIL: Well, prithee try what thou canst do; if thou canst not guess, inquire her out, dost hear,

[53] *ordinary's* clergyman appointed to prepare criminals for the death penalty.
[54] *Bartlemew and his fair* Bartholomew Fair, a fair held annually in West Smithfield on St. Bartholomew's Day, August 24
[55] *the Revolution* the Bloodless, or Glorious, Revolution of 1688
[56] *han't* hasn't

fellow? And tell her, her nephew, Sir Wilfull Witwoud, is in the house.

SERV: I shall, sir.

SIR WIL: Hold ye, hear me, friend; a word with you in your ear. Prithee who are these gallants?

SERV: Really, sir, I can't tell; here come so many here, 'tis hard to know 'em all.   (*Exit*)

SIR WIL: Oons,[57] this fellow knows less than a starl-   530 ing,[58] I don't think 'a knows his own name.

MRS. MAR: Mr. Witwoud, your brother is not behind-hand in forgetfulness; I fancy he has forgot you too.

WIT: I hope so. The devil take him that remembers first, I say.

SIR WIL: Save you, gentlemen and lady!

MRS. MAR: For shame, Mr. Witwoud; why don't you speak to him? And you, sir.

WIT: Petulant, speak.   540

PET: And you, sir.

SIR WIL: No offence, I hope. (*Salutes* MRS. MARWOOD)

MRS. MAR: No sure, sir.

WIT: This is a vile dog; I see that already. No offence! Ha! ha! ha! to him; to him, Petulant, smoke[59] him.

PET: It seems as if you had come a journey, sir; hem, hem.   (*Surveying him round*)

SIR WIL: Very likely, sir, that it may seem so.   550

PET: No offence, I hope, sir.

WIT: Smoke the boots, the boots; Petulant, the boots, ha! ha! ha!

SIR WIL: May be not, sir; thereafter[60] as 'tis meant, sir.

PET: Sir, I presume upon the information of your boots.

SIR WIL: Why, 'tis like you may, sir. If you are not satisfied with the information of my boots, sir, if you will step to the stable, you may inquire   560 further of my horse, sir.

PET: Your horse, sir! Your horse is an ass, sir!

SIR WIL: Do you speak by way of offence, sir?

MRS. MAR: The gentleman's merry, that's all sir. (*Aside*) 'Slife,[61] we shall have a quarrel betwixt a horse and an ass, before they find one another

[57] *Oons* a corruption of "God's wounds" like "Zounds"
[59] *a starling* supposed to be a particularly stupid bird.
[59] *smoke* make fun, or game, of
[60] *thereafter* according
[61] *'Slife* i.e. God's life

out. *(Aloud)* You must not take anything amiss from your friends, sir. You are among your friends here, though it may be you don't know it. If I am not mistaken, you are Sir Wilfull Witwoud.

SIR WIL: Right, lady; I am Sir Wilfull Witwoud, so I write myself; no offence to anybody, I hope; and nephew to the Lady Wishfort on this mansion.

MRS. MAR: Don't you know this gentleman, sir?

SIR WIL: Hum! What, sure 'tis not—yea by'r Lady, but 'tis. 'Sheart,[62] I know not whether 'tis or no. Yea, but 'tis, by the Wrekin.[63] Brother Anthony! What Tony, i'faith! What, dost thou not know me? By'r Lady, nor I thee, thou art so becravated and so beperiwigged. 'Sheart, why dost not speak? Art thou o'erjoyed?

WIT: Odso, brother, is it you? Your servant, brother.

SIR WIL: Your servant! Why, yours, sir. Your servant again, 'sheart, and your friend and servant to that, and a—*(puff)* and a flapdragon[64] for your service, sir! and a hare's foot, and a hare's scut[65] for your service, sir, an you be so cold and so courtly!

WIT: No offence, I hope, brother.

SIR WIL: 'Sheart, sir, but there is, and much offence! A pox, is this your Inns o' Court[66] breeding, not to know your friends and your relations, your elders and your betters?

WIT: Why, brother Wilfull of Salop,[67] you may be as short as a Shrewsbury cake, if you please. But I tell you 'tis not modish to know relations in town. You think you're in the country, where great lubblerly[68] brothers slabber[69] and kiss one another when they meet, like a call of serjeants[70] 'Tis not the fashion here; 'tis not indeed, dear brother.

SIR WIL: The fashion's a fool; and you're a fop, dear brother. 'Sheart, I've suspected this. By'r Lady, I conjectured you were a fop, since you began to change the style of your letters, and write in a scrap of paper, gilt round the edges, no broader than a *subpoena.*[71] I might expect this when you left off, "Honoured brother," and "hoping you are in good health," and so forth, to begin with a "Rat me,[72] knight, I'm so sick of a last night's debauch," ods heart, and then tell a familiar tale of a cock and a bull,[73] and a whore and a bottle, and so conclude. You could write news before you were out of your time, when you lived with honest Pumple[74] Nose, the attorney of Furnival's Inn;[75] you could entreat to be remembered then to your friends round the Wrekin. We could have gazettes,[76] then, and *Dawks's Letter,*[77] and the *Weekly Bill,*[78] till of late days.

PET: 'Slife, Witwoud, were you ever an attorney's clerk? of the family of the Furnivals? Ha! ha! ha!

WIT: Aye, aye, but that was but for a while, not long, not long. Pshaw! I was not in my own power then; an orphan, and this fellow was my guardian. Aye, aye, I was glad to consent to that man to come to London. He had the disposal of me then. If I had not agreed to that, I might have been bound prentice[79] to a felt-maker in Shrewsbury; this fellow would have bound me to a maker of felts.

SIR WIL: 'Sheart, and better than to be bound to a maker of fops, where, I suppose, you have served your time; and now you may set up for yourself.

[62] *'Sheart* i.e. God's heart, a favorite oath of Sir Wilfull's
[63] *the Wrekin* a hill in Shropshire
[64] *flapdragon* a raisin snatched from burning brandy and eaten
[65] *scut* short erect tail
[66] *Inns o' Court* the four societies of students and practitioners of the law in England
[67] *Salop* Shropshire, the capital of which is Shrewsbury
[68] *lubberly* clumsy
[69] *slabber* slobber
[70] *a call of serjeants* sergeants-of-law when called, or admitted to the status of barristers
[71] *subpoena* a writ commanding attendance at a court of law
[72] *Rat me* a form of cursing, short for "May God rot me," as is "Drat"
[73] *a familiar tale of a cock and a bull* a well-known cock-and-bull story, an extravagant tale
[74] *Pumple* i.e. Pimple
[75] *Furnival's Inn* one of the subordinate inns of court attached to Lincoln's Inn
[76] *gazettes* news-sheets
[77] *Dawks's Letter* a news-letter printed from type in imitation of handwriting
[78] *the Weekly Bill* the official publication of the deaths occurring in and around London
[79] *bound prentice* bound as an apprentice

MRS. MAR: You intend to travel, sir, as I'm informed.

SIR WIL: Belike I may, madam, I may chance to sail upon the salt seas, if my mind hold.

PET: And the wind serve.

SIR WIL: Serve or not serve, I shan't ask licence of you, sir; nor the weathercock your companion. I direct my discourse to the lady, sir. 'Tis like my aunt may have told you, madam. Yes, I
650 have settled my concerns,[80] I may say now, and am minded to see foreign parts. If an how that the peace[81] holds, whereby, that is, taxes abate.

MRS. MAR: I thought you had designed for France at all adventures.[82]

SIR WIL: I can't tell that; 'tis like I may, and 'tis like I may not. I am somewhat dainty in making a resolution, because when I make it, I keep it. I don't stand shill I, shall I,[83] then; if I say't, I'll do't. But I have thoughts to tarry a small
660 matter in town, to learn somewhat of your lingo[84] first, before I cross the seas. I'd gladly have a spice of your French, as they say, whereby to hold discourse in foreign countries.

MRS. MAR: Here's an academy in town for that use.

SIR WIL: There is? 'Tis like there may.

MRS. MAR: No doubt you will return very much improved.

WIT: Yes, refined, like a Dutch skipper from a whale-fishing.

670 *Re-enter* LADY WISHFORT *with* FAINALL

LADY WISH: Nephew, you are welcome.

SIR WIL: Aunt, your servant.

FAIN: Sir Wilfull, your most faithful servant.

SIR WIL: Cousin Fainall, give me your hand.

LADY WISH: Cousin Witwoud, your servant; Mr. Petulant, your servant. Nephew, you are welcome again. Will you drink anything after your journey, nephew, before you eat? Dinner's almost ready.

680 SIR WIL: I'm very well, I thank you, aunt; however, I thank you for your courteous offer. 'Sheart I was afraid you would have been in the fashion too, and have remembered to have forgot your relations. Here's your cousin Tony; belike I mayn't call him brother for fear of offence.

LADY WISH: O, he's a rallier,[85] nephew. My cousin's a wit; and your great wits always rally their best friends to choose.[86] When you have been abroad, nephew, you'll understand raillery better. (FAINALL *and* MRS. MARWOOD *talk apart*) 690

SIR WIL: Why then let him hold his tongue in the meantime, and rail when that day comes.

Re-enter MINCING

MIN: Mem, I come to acquaint your laship that dinner is impatient.

SIR WIL: Impatient? Why then belike it won't stay till I pull off my boots. Sweetheart, can you help me to a pair of slippers? My man's with his horses, I warrant.

LADY WISH: Fie, fie, nephew, you would not pull 700 of your boots here. Go down into the hall; dinner shall stay for you. My nephew's a little unbred; you'll pardon him, madam. Gentlemen, will you walk? Marwood?

MRS. MAR: I'll follow you madam, before Sir Wilfull is ready.

(*Exeunt all but* MRS. MARWOOD *and* FAINALL)

FAIN: Why then, Foible's a bawd, an errant,[87] rank, match-making bawd. And I, it seems, am a husband, a rank husband; and my wife a very 710 errant, rank wife, all in *the way of the world*. 'Sdeath, to be a cuckold by anticipation, a cuckold in embryo! Sure I was born with budding antlers, like a young satyr, or a citizen's child.[88] 'Sdeath! to be out-witted, to be out-jilted, out-matrimonied! If I had kept my speed like a stag, 'twere somewhat; but to crawl after, with my horns, like a snail, and be outstripped by my wife, 'tis scurvy wedlock.

MRS. MAR: Then shake it off. You have often 720 wished for an opportunity to part; and now you have it. But first prevent their plot; the half of Millamant's fortune is too considerable to be parted with, to a foe, to Mirabell.

---

[80] *concerns* business affairs

[81] *the peace* the Peace of Ryswick (1697), broken in 1701, the year after *The Way of the World* was first acted

[82] *at all adventures* at all costs

[83] *Shill I, shall I* cf. shilly-shally

[84] *lingo* language, here the French language

[85] *rallier* one who indulges in raillery, or jocose ridicule

[86] *to choose* by choice

[87] *errant* arrant

[88] *a citizen's child* the "citizens" of the business part of London were supposed to be frequently cuckolded by the fine gentlemen of the town

FAIN: Damn him! that had been mine, had you not made that fond[89] discovery. That had been forfeited, had they been married. My wife had added lustre to my horns by that increase of fortune; I could have worn' em tipped with gold, though my forehead had been furnished like a deputy-lieutenant's hall.

MRS. MAR: They may prove a cap of maintenance[90] to you still, if you can away with[91] your wife. And she's no worse than when you had her. I dare swear she had given up her game before she was married.

FAIN: Hum! that may be. She might throw up her cards; but I'll be hanged if she did not put Pam[92] in her pocket.

MRS. MAR: You married her to keep you; and if you can contrive to have her keep you better than you expected, why should you not keep her longer than you intended?

FAIN: The means, the means.

MRS. MAR: Discover to my lady your wife's conduct; threaten to part with her. My lady loves her, and will come to any composition[93] to save her reputation. Take the opportunity of breaking it, just upon the discovery of this imposture. My lady will be enraged beyond bounds, and sacrifice niece and fortune and all, at that conjuncture. And let me alone to keep her warm; if she should flag in her part, I will not fail to prompt her.

FAIN: Faith, this has an appearance.[94]

MRS. MAR: I'm sorry I hinted to my lady to endeavour a match between Millamant and Sir Wilfull; that may be an obstacle.

FAIN: Oh, for that matter leave me to manage him; I'll disable him for that. He will drink like a Dane;[95] after dinner, I'll set his hand in.

MRS. MAR: Well, how do you stand affected towards your lady?

FAIN: Why, faith, I'm thinking of it. Let me see. I am married already, so that's over. My wife has played the jade with me; well, that's over too. I never loved her, or if I had, why that would have been over too by this time. Jealous of her I cannot be, for I am certain;[96] so there's an end of jealousy. Weary of her I am, and shall be. No, there's no end of that; no, no, that were too much to hope. Thus far concerning my repose; now for my reputation. As to my own, I married not for it, so that's out of the question. And as to my part in my wife's, why she had parted with hers before; so bringing none to me, she can take none from me. 'Tis against all rule of play that I should lose to one who has not wherewithal to stake.

MRS. MAR: Besides, you forget, marriage is honourable.

FAIN: Hum! Faith, and that's well thought on. Marriage is honourable, as you say; and if so, wherefore should cuckoldom be a discredit, being derived from so honourable a root?

MRS. MAR: Nay, I know not; if the root be honourable, why not the branches?[97]

FAIN: So, so; why this point's clear. Well, how do we proceed?

MRS. MAR: I will contrive a letter which shall be delivered to my lady at the time when that rascal who is to act Sir Rowland is with her. It shall come as from an unknown hand, for the less I appear to know of the truth, the better I can play the incendiary. Besides, I would not have Foible provoked if I could help it, because you know she knows some passages. Nay, I expect all will come out; but let the mine be sprung first, and then I care not if I'm discovered.

FAIN: If the worst comes to the worst, I'll turn my wife to grass.[98] I have already a deed of settlement of the best part of her estate, which

---

[89] *fond* foolish

[90] *a cap of maintenance* a term in heraldry for a kind of cap, with two points like horns behind, borne in the arms of certain families; here, the cap is to be used for financial maintenance, or support.

[91] *away with* endure

[92] *Pam* the knave of clubs, the highest card in the game of loo. Fainall means that he does not believe, as Mrs. Marwood has just suggested, that his wife completely severed her relations with Mirabell at the time of her marriage.

[93] *composition* agreement

[94] *an appearance* a probability, or likelihood (of succeeding)

[95] *drink like a Dane* The Danes were notorious for overdrinking. Cf. *Hamlet* I, iv, ll. 17-22

[96] *certain* Jealousy is essentially a suspicion of rivalry, not a certainty of it.

[97] *the branches* i.e. of the cuckold's horns

[98] *turn my wife to grass* turn her out, as a beast to pasture

I wheedled out of her; and that you shall par-take[99] at least.

MRS. MAR: I hope you are convinced that I hate Mirabell now; you'll be no more jealous.

FAIN: Jealous! No, by this kiss. Let husbands be jealous; but let the lover still believe. Or if he doubt, let it be only to endear his pleasure, and prepare the joy that follows, when he proves his mistress true. But let husbands' doubts convert to endless jealousy; or if they have belief, let it corrupt to superstition and blind credulity. I am single, and will herd no more with 'em. True, I wear the badge, but I'll disown the order. And since I take my leave of 'em, I care not if I leave 'em a common motto to their common crest.

All husbands must or[100] pain or shame endure;
The wise too jealous are, fools too secure.

(Exeunt)

[99] partake share

[100] or either

ACT IV

SCENE CONTINUES

Enter LADY WISHFORT *and* FOIBLE

LADY WISH: Is Sir Rowland coming, sayest thou, Foible? and are things in order?

FOIB: Yes, madam, I have put wax-lights in the sconces, and placed the footmen in a row in the hall, in their best liveries, with the coachmen and postillion to fill up the equipage.

LADY WISH: Have you pulvilled[1] the coachmen and postillion, that they may not stink of the stable when Sir Rowland comes by?

FOIB: Yes, madam.

LADY WISH: And are the dancers and the music ready, that he may be entertained in all points with correspondence to his passion?

FOIB: All is ready, madam.

LADY WISH: And—well, and how do I look, Foible?

FOIB: Most killing well, madam.

LADY WISH: Well, and how shall I receive him? In what figure shall I give his heart the first impression? There is a great deal in the first impression. Shall I sit? No, I won't sit, I'll walk; aye, I'll walk from the door upon his entrance; and then turn full upon him. No, that will be too sudden. I'll lie, aye, I'll lie down. I'll receive him in my little dressing room; there's a couch. Yes, yes I'll give the first impression on a couch. I won't lie neither, but loll and lean upon one elbow; with one foot a little dangling off, jogging in a thoughtful way. Yes, and then as as soon as he appears, start, aye, start and be surprised, and rise to meet him in a pretty disorder. Yes, oh, nothing is more alluring than a levee[2] from a couch, in some confusion; it shows the foot to advantage, and furnishes with blushes and recomposing airs beyond comparison. Hark! there's a coach.

FOIB: 'Tis he, madam.

LADY WISH: Oh, dear, has my nephew made his addresses to Millamant? I ordered him.

FOIB: Sir Wilfull is set in to drinking, madam, in the parlour.

LADY WISH: Ods my life, I'll send him to her. Call her down, Foible; bring her hither. I'll send him as I go. When they are together, then come to me, Foible, that I may not be too long alone with Sir Rowland.   (Exit)

Enter MRS. MILLAMANT *and* MRS. FAINALL

FOIB: Madam, I stayed here, to tell your ladyship that Mr. Mirabell has waited this half hour for an opportunity to talk with you, though my lady's orders were to leave you and Sir Wilfull together. Shall I tell Mr. Mirabell that you are at leisure?

[1] pulvilled sprinkled with a sweet-scented powder

[2] levee the act of rising

MRS. MIL: No, what would the dear man have? I am thoughtful, and would amuse myself; bid him come another time.

"There never yet was woman made,[3]
Nor shall, but to be cursed."

(Repeating and walking about)

60   That's hard!

MRS. FAIN: You are very fond of Sir John Suckling today, Millamant, and the poets.

MRS. MIL: He? Aye, and filthy verses; so I am.

FOIB: Sir Wilfull is coming, madam. Shall I send Mr. Mirabell away?

MRS. MIL: Aye, if you please, Foible, send him away, or send him hither; just as you will, dear Foible. I think I'll see him; shall I? Aye, let the wretch come.   *(Exit FOIBLE)*

70   "Thyrsis, a youth of the inspired train."[4]

(Repeating)

Dear Fainall, entertain Sir Wilfull. Thou has philosophy to undergo[5] a fool; thou art married and hast patience. I would confer with my own thoughts.

MRS. FAIN: I am obliged to you, that you would make me your proxy in this affair; but I have business of my own.

Enter SIR WILFULL

80   O Sir Wilfull, you are come at the critical instant. There's your mistress up to the ears in love and contemplation; pursue your point, now or never.

SIR WIL: Yes; my aunt will have it so. I would gladly have been encouraged with a bottle or two, because I'm somewhat wary at first, before I am acquainted. *(This while MILLAMANT walks about repeating to herself)* But I hope, after a time, I shall break my mind; that is, upon further acquaintance. So for the present, cousin, I'll take my leave. If so be you'll be so kind to make   90   my excuse, I'll return to my company.

MRS. FAIN: Oh, fie, Sir Wilfull! What, you must not be daunted.

SIR WIL: Daunted! No, that's not it. It is not so much for that; for if so be that I set on't, I'll do't. But only for the present; 'tis sufficient till further acquaintance, that's all. Your servant.

MRS. FAIN: Nay, I'll swear you shall never lose so favourable an opportunity, if I can help it. I'll leave you together and lock the door.   100

(Exit)

SIR WIL: Nay, nay, cousin. I have forgot my gloves. What d'ye do? 'Sheart, 'a[6] has locked the door indeed, I think. Nay, Cousin Fainall, open the door! Pshaw, what a vixen trick is this? Nay, now 'a has seen me too. Cousin, I made bold to pass through as it were. I think this door's enchanted!

MRS. MIL: *(Repeating)*

"I prithee spare me, gentle boy,[7]
Press me no more for that slight toy—"   110

SIR WIL: Anan?[8] Cousin, your servant.

MRS. MIL: *(Repeating)*

"That foolish trifle of a heart—"

Sir Wilfull!

SIR WIL: Yes. Your servant. No offence, I hope, cousin.

MRS. MIL: *(Repeating)*

"I swear it will not do its part,
Though thou dost thine, employ'st thy power
and art."   120

Natural, easy Suckling!

SIR WIL: Anan? Suckling? No such suckling neither

---

[3] *There never yet was woman made* a quotation from a lyric poem by Sir John Suckling (1609-1642), which begins with these lines

[4] *Thyrsis, a youth of the inspired train* a quotation from *The Story of Phoebus and Daphne, Applied*, a poem by Edmund Waller (1606-1687), which begins as follows:

Thyrsis, a youth of the inspired train,
Fair Sacharissa loved, but loved in vain.
Like Phoebus sung the no less amorous boy;
Like Daphne she, as lovely, and as coy!

[5] *undergo* endure

[6] *'a* for "she" (more usually for "he")

[7] *I prithee spare me, gentle boy* A "Song" by Suckling begins with these lines, followed by those that Millamant quotes in her next two speeches.

[8] *Anan?* an expression equivalent to "What did you say?"

cousin, nor stripling; I thank Heaven, I'm no minor.

MRS. MIL: Ah, rustic! ruder than Gothic![9]

SIR WIL: Well, well, I shall understand your lingo one of these days, cousin; in the meanwhile I must answer in plain English.

MRS. MIL: Have you any business with me, Sir Wilfull?

SIR WIL: Not at present, cousin. Yes, I made bold to see, to come and know if that how you were disposed to fetch a walk this evening; if so be that I might not be troublesome, I would have fought[10] a walk with you.

MRS. MIL: A walk! What then?

SIR WIL: Nay, nothing. Only for the walk's sake, that's all.

MRS. MIL: I nauseate walking; 'tis a country diversion. I loathe the country and everything that relates to it.

SIR WIL: Indeed! hah! Look ye, look ye, you do? Nay, 'tis like you may. Here are choice of pastimes here in town, as plays and the like; that must be confessed indeed.

MRS. MIL: Ah, *l'étourdi!*[11] I hate the town too.

SIR WIL: Dear heart, that's much. Hah! that you should hate 'em both! Hah! 'tis like you may; there are some can't relish the town, and others can't away with the country. 'Tis like you may be one of those, cousin.

MRS. MIL: Ha! ha! ha! Yes, 'tis like I may. You have nothing further to say to me?

SIR WIL: Not at present, cousin. 'Tis like when I have an opportunity to be more private, I may break my mind in some measure. I conjecture you partly guess—however, that's as time shall try; but spare to speak and spare to speed,[12] as they say.

MRS. MIL: If it is of no great importance, Sir Wilfull, you will oblige me to leave me; I have just now a little business—

SIR WIL: Enough, enough, cousin, yes, yes, all a case,[13] when you're disposed, when you're disposed. Now's as well as another time; and another time as well as now. All's one for that. Yes, yes, if your concerns call you, there's no haste; it will keep cold, as they say. Cousin, your servant. I think this door's locked.

MRS. MIL: You may go this way, sir.

SIR WIL: Your servant; then with your leave I'll return to my company.

MRS. MIL: Aye, aye; ha! ha! ha!

"Like Phoebus sung the no less amorous boy."

Enter MIRABELL

MIR: "Like Daphne she, as lovely and as coy."

Do you lock yourself up from me, to make my search more curious?[14] Or is this pretty artifice contrived, to signify that here the chase must end and my pursuit be crowned, for you can fly no further?

MRS. MIL: Vanity! No. I'll fly and be followed to the last moment. Though I am upon the very verge of matrimony, I expect you should solicit me as much as if I were wavering at the grate of a monastery, with one foot over the threshold. I'll be solicited to the very last, nay and afterwards.

MIR: What, after the last?

MRS. MIL: Oh, I should think I was poor and had nothing to bestow, if I were reduced to an inglorious ease and freed from the agreeable fatigues of solicitation.

MIR: But do not you know that when favours are conferred upon instant[15] and tedious solicitation, that they diminish in their value, and that both the giver loses the grace, and the receiver lessens his pleasure?

MRS. MIL: It may be in things of common application; but never sure in love. Oh, I hate a lover that can dare to think he draws a moment's air independent on the bounty of his mistress. There is not so impudent a thing in nature as the saucy look of an assured man, confident of success. The pedantic arrogance of a very husband has not so pragmatical[16] an air. Ah! I'll never marry, unless I am first made sure of my will and pleasure.

---

[9] *Gothic* Goths, a barbarous Teutonic tribe.

[10] *fought* a provincial form of "fetched"

[11] *Ah l'étourdi!* Oh, the stupid (fellow)!

[12] *spare to speak and spare to speed* a proverb meaning "If you don't talk, you won't succeed"

[13] *all a case* all the same

[14] *curious* painstaking, difficult

[15] *instant* pressing, urgent

[16] *pragmatical* matter-of-fact, businesslike

MIR: Would you have 'em both before marriage? Or will you be contented with the first now, and stay for the other till after grace?

MRS. MIL: Ah! don't be impertinent.[17] My dear liberty, shall I leave thee? My faithful solitude, my darling contemplation, must I bid you then adieu? Ay-h adieu, my morning thoughts, agreeable wakings, indolent slumbers, all ye *douceurs*,[18] ye *sommeils du matin*,[19] I can't do't, 'tis more than impossible. Postively, Mirabell, I'll lie abed in a morning as long as I please.

MIR: Then I'll get up in a morning as early as I please.

MRS. MIL: Ah! idle creature, get up when you will. And d'ye hear, I won't be called names after I'm married; positively I won't be called names.

MIR: Names!

MRS. MIL: Aye, as wife, spouse, my dear, joy, jewel, love, sweetheart, and the rest of that nauseous cant, in which men and their wives are so fulsomely familiar; I shall never bear that. Good Mirabell, don't let us be familiar or fond, nor kiss before folks, like my Lady Fadler[20] and Sir Francis; nor go to Hyde Park together the first Sunday in a new chariot, to provoke eyes and whispers, and then never be seen there together again, as if we were proud of one another the first week, and ashamed of one another ever after. Let us never visit together, nor go to a play together. But let us be very strange and well-bred; let us be as strange as if we had been married a great while, and as well-bred as if we were not married at all.

MIR: Have you any more conditions to offer? Hitherto your demands are pretty reasonable.

MRS. MIL: Trifles! As liberty to pay and receive visits to and from whom I please; to write and receive letters, without interrogatories[21] or wry faces on your part; to wear what I please, and choose conversation with regard only to my own taste; to have no obligation upon me to converse with wits that I don't like, because they are your acquaintance, or to be intimate with fools, because they may be your relations. Come to dinner when I please; dine in my dressing-room when I'm out of humour, without giving a reason. To have my closet inviolate; to be sole empress of my tea-table, which you must never presume to approach without first asking leave. And lastly, wherever I am, you shall always knock at the door before you come in. These articles subscribed, if I continue to endure you a little longer, I may by degrees dwindle into a wife.

MIR: Your bill of fare is something advanced in this latter account. Well, have I liberty to offer conditions, that when you are dwindled into a wife, I may not be beyond measure enlarged into a husband?

MRS. MIL: You have free leave. Propose your utmost; speak and spare not.

MIR: I thank you. *Imprimis*[22] then, I covenant[23] that your acquaintance be general; that you admit no sworn confidante, or intimate of your own sex; no she friend to screen her affairs under your countenance, and tempt you to make trial of a mutual secrecy. No decoy-duck to wheedle you[24] a fop, scrambling[25] to the play in a mask; then bring you home in a pretended fright, when you think you shall be found out, and rail at me for missing the play, and disappointing the frolic which you had to pick me up and prove my constancy.

MRS. MIL: Detestable *imprimis*! I go to the play in a mask!

MIR: *Item*, I article that you continue to like your own face, as long as I shall; and while it passes current with me, that you endeavour not to new-coin it. To which end, together with all vizards for the day, I prohibit all masks for the night, made of oiled-skins and I know not what: hog's bones, hare's gall, pig-water,[26] and the marrow of a roasted cat. In short, I forbid all commerce with the gentlewoman in What-d'ye-call-it Court. *Item*, I shut my doors against all bawds with baskets, and pennyworths of muslin, china,

[17] *impertinent* not restrained within the bounds of propriety
[18] *douceurs* sweetnesses, pleasures
[19] *sommeils du matin* morning sleeps
[20] *Lady Fadler* To faddle is to fondle, or fuss. cf. fiddle-faddle
[21] *interrogatories* questionings
[22] *Imprimis* in the first place
[23] *covenant* make as the condition of a formal agreement
[24] *wheedle you* obtain for you by cajolery
[25] *scrambling* struggling unceremoniously
[26] *pig-water* The urine of pigs was used as an ingredient in cosmetics
[27] *atlases* atlas was a rich kind of satin made in the Orient.

"Prithee fill me the glass,
Till it laugh in my face,
With ale that is potent and mellow;
He that whines for a lass
Is an ignorant ass,
For a bumper[47] has not its fellow."

460

But if you would have me marry my cousin, say the word, and I'll do't. Wilfull will do't; that's the word. Wilfull will do't; that's my crest. My motto I have forgot.

LADY WISH: My nephew's a little overtaken,[48] cousin, but 'tis with drinking your health. O' my word you are obliged to him.

SIR WIL: *In vino veritas*,[49] aunt. If I drunk your health to-day, cousin, I am a borachio. But if you have a mind to be married, say the word, and send for the piper; Wilfull will do't. If not, dust it away, and let's have t'other round. Tony! Ods-heart, where's Tony? Tony's an honest fellow; but he spits after a bumper, and that's a fault.   (*Sings*)

470

"We'll drink, and we'll never ha' done, boys,
Put the glass then around with the sun, boys;
Let Apollo's example invite us;
For he's drunk every night,
And that makes him so bright,
That he's able next morning to light us."

480

The sun's a good pimple,[50] an honest soaker; he has a cellar at your Antipodes.[51] If I travel, aunt, I touch at your Antipodes; your Antipodes are a good, rascally sort of topsy-turvy fellows. If I had a bumper, I'd stand upon my head and drink a health to 'em. A match or no match, cousin with the hard name? Aunt, Wilfull will do't. If she has her maidenhead, let her look to't; if she has not, let her keep her own counsel in the meantime, and cry out at the nine months' end.[52]

490

MRS. MIL: Your pardon, madam, I can stay no longer. Sir Wilfull grows very powerful. Egh! how

he smells! I shall be overcome, if I stay. Come, cousin.

(*Exeunt* MRS. MILLAMANT *and* MRS. FAINALL)

LADY WISH: Smells! he would poison a tallow-chandler[53] and his family! Beastly creature, I know not what to do with him! Travel, quotha! aye, travel, travel, get thee gone, get thee but far enough, to the Saracens, or the Tartars, or the Turks, for thou art not fit to live in a Christian commonwealth, thou beastly pagan!

500

SIR WIL: Turks, no; no Turks, aunt: your Turks are infidels, and believe not in the grape. Your Mahometan, your Mussulman, is a dry stinkard.[54] No offence, aunt. My map says that your Turk is not so honest a man as your Christian. I cannot find by the map that your mufti[55] is orthodox; whereby it is a plain case that orthodox is a hard word, aunt, and (*hiccup*) Greek for claret.

510

(*Sings*)

"To drink is a Christian diversion,
Unknown to the Turk or the Persian:
Let Mahometan fools
Live by heathenish rules,
And be damned over tea-cups and coffee!
But let British lads sing,
Crown a health to the king,
And a fig for your sultan and sophy!"[56]

520

Ah, Tony!

Enter FOIBLE, *and whispers* LADY WISHFORT

LADY WISH: (*Aside to* FOIBLE) Sir Rowland impatient? Good lack! what shall I do with this beastly tumbril?[57] (*Aloud*) Go lie down and sleep, you sot! or, as I'm a person, I'll have you bastinadoed[58] with broomsticks. Call up the wenches with broomsticks.   (*Exit* FOIBLE)

530

SIR WIL: Ahey! Wenches, where are the wenches?

LADY WISH: Dear Cousin Witwoud, get him away, and you will bind me to you inviolably. I have an affair of moment that invades me with some precipitation. You will oblige me to all futurity.

[47] *bumper* a cap or glass filled to the brim
[48] *overtaken* overcome, intoxicated
[49] *In vino veritas* "(there is) truth in wine," a proverbial expression
[50] *a good pimple* a boon companion
[51] *Antipodes* the parts of the globe diametrically opposite where we are; also, the people who live there
[52] *the nine months' end* when a child will be born

[53] *tallow-chandler* a maker or seller of tallow candles
[54] *a dry stinkard* a stinking, paltry fellow who does not drink; referring to the Mahometan prohibition of wine and spirituous liquors
[55] *mufti* official expounder of Moslem law
[56] *sophy* a former title of the kings of Persia
[57] *tumbril* a farmer's cart
[58] *bastinadoed* beaten on the soles of the feet, as in an Oriental form of punishment

WIT: Come, knight. Pox on him, I don't know what to say to him. Will you go to a cock-match?

SIR WIL: With a wench, Tony? Is she a shake-bag,[59] Sirrah? Let me bite your cheek[60] for that.

540 WIT: Horrible! he has a breath like a bag-pipe! Aye, aye, come, will you march, my Salopian?[61]

SIR WIL: Lead on, little Tony; I'll follow thee, my Anthony, my Tantony.[62] Sirrah, thou shalt be my Tantony, and I'll be thy pig.

"And a fig for your sultan and sophy."

(*Exit singing with* WITWOUD)

LADY WISH: This will never do. It will never make a match; at least before he has been abroad.

550 *Enter* WAITWELL, *disguised as* SIR ROWLAND

Dear Sir Rowland, I am confounded with confusion at the retrospection of my own rudeness! I have more pardons to ask than the Pope distributes in the Year of Jubilee.[63] But I hope, where there is likely to be so near an alliance, we may unbend the severity of decorum and dispense with a little ceremony.

WAIT: My impatience, madam, is the effect of my transport; and till I have the possession of your adorable person, I am tantalized on the rack,

560 and do but hang, madam, on the tenter[64] of expectation.

LADY WISH: You have excess of gallantry, Sir Rowland, and press things to a conclusion with a most prevailing vehemence. But a day or two for decency of marriage—

WAIT: For decency of funeral, madam! The delay will break my heart; or, if that should fail, I shall be poisoned. My nephew will get an inkling of my designs, and poison me; and I would will-

570 ingly starve him before I die; I would gladly go out of the world with that satisfaction. That would be some comfort to me, if I could but

live so long as to be revenged on that unnatural viper.

LADY WISH: Is he so unnatural, say you? Truly I would contribute much both to the saving of your life, and the accomplishment of your revenge. Not that I respect myself, though he has been a perfidious wretch to me.

WAIT: Perfidious to you?   580

LADY WISH: O Sir Rowland, the hours that he has died away at my feet, the tears that he has shed, the oaths that he has sworn, the palpitations that he has felt, the trances and the tremblings, the ardours and the ecstacies, the kneelings and the risings, the heart-heavings and the handgripings, the pangs and the pathetic regards of his protesting eyes! Oh, no memory can register!

WAIT: What, my rival! Is the rebel my rival? 'A dies.   590

LADY WISH: No, don't kill him at once, Sir Rowland; starve him gradually, inch by inch.

WAIT: I'll do't. In three weeks he shall be barefoot; in a month out at knees with begging and alms. He shall starve upward and upward, till he has nothing living but his head, and then go out in a stink like a candle's end upon a save-all.[65]

LADY WISH: Well, Sir Rowland, you have the way. You are no novice in the labyrinth of love; you have the clue. But as I am a person, Sir Rowland,   600 you must not attribute my yielding to any sinister appetite, or indigestion of widowhood; nor impute my complacency to any lethargy of continence. I hope you do not think me prone to any iteration[66] of nuptials.

WAIT: Far be it from me—

LADY WISH: If you do, I protest I must recede, or think that I have made a prostitution of decorums; but in the vehemence of compassion, and to save the life of a person of so much impor-   610 tance—

WAIT: I esteem it so.

LADY WISH: Or else you wrong my condescension.

WAIT: I do not, I do not!

LADY WISH: Indeed you do.

WAIT: I do not, fair shrine of virtue!

LADY WISH: If you think the least scruple of carnality[67] was an ingredient—

---

[59] *a shake-bag* a gamecock of the largest size, i.e. a good subject for sport

[60] *bite your cheek* give you a violent kiss, as a sign of affection

[61] *Salopian* an inhabitant of Shropshire

[62] *Tantony* A corruption of "Saint Anthony" Saint Anthony was often represented as being attended by a pig.

[63] *the Year of Jubilee* the year in which the Pope proclaims remission of the entire temporal punishment that is ordinarily imposed for sin

[64] *tenter* a frame for stretching cloth; also, a tenter hook

[65] *save-all* a device in a candlestick to hold the ends of candles, so that they may be burned

[66] *iteration* repetition

[67] *carnality* sensuality

WAIT: Dear madam, no. You are all camphire[68] and frankincense, all chastity and odour.

LADY WISH: Or that—

Re-enter FOIBLE

FOIB: Madam, the dancers are ready; and there's one with a letter, who must deliver it into your own hands.

LADY WISH: Sir Rowland, will you give me leave? Think favourably, judge candidly, and conclude you have found a person who would suffer racks in honour's cause, dear Sir Rowland, and will wait on you incessantly.[69]   (*Exit*)

WAIT: Fie, fie! What a slavery have I undergone! Spouse, hast thou any cordial? I want spirits.

FOIB: What a washy[70] rogue art thou, to pant thus for a quarter of an hour's lying and swearing to a fine lady!

WAIT: Oh, she is the antidote to desire! Spouse, thou wilt fare the worse for't. I shall have no appetite to "iteration of nuptials" this eight-and-forty hours. By this hand I'd rather be a chair-man[71] in the dog-days[72] than act Sir Rowland till this time to-morrow!

Re-enter LADY WISHFORT, *with a letter*

LADY WISH: Call in the dancers. Sir Rowland, we'll sit, if you please, and see the entertainment. (*Dance*) Now, with your permission, Sir Rowland, I will peruse my letter. I would open it in your presence, because I would not make you uneasy. If it should make you uneasy, I would burn it. Speak, if it does. But you may see by the superscription it is like a woman's hand.

FOIB: (*Aside to* WAITWELL) By Heaven! Mrs. Marwood's; I know it. My heart aches. Get it from her.

WAIT: A woman's hand? No, madam, that's no woman's hand; I see that already. That's somebody whose throat must be cut.

LADY WISH: Nay, Sir Rowland, since you give me a proof of your passion by your jealousy, I promise you I'll make you a return, by a frank communication. You shall see it; we'll open it together. Look you here. (*Reads*) "Madam, though unknown to you." Look you there; 'tis from nobody that I know. "I have that honour for your character, that I think myself obliged to let you know you are abused. He who pretends to be Sir Rowland is a cheat and a rascal." Oh, heavens! what's this?

FOIB: (*Aside*) Unfortunate! all's ruined!

WAIT: How, how, let me see, let me see! (*reading*) "A rascal, and disguised and suborned[73] for that imposture." O villainy! O villainy! "by the contrivance of—"

LADY WISH: I shall faint, I shall die, I shall die, oh!

FOIB: (*Aside to* WAITWELL) Say 'tis your nephew's hand. Quickly, his plot, swear, swear it!

WAIT: Here's a villain! Madam, don't you perceive it? don't you see it?

LADY WISH: Too well, too well! I have seen too much.

WAIT: I told you at first I knew the hand. A woman's hand? The rascal writes a sort of a large hand, your Roman hand.[74] I saw there was a throat to be cut presently. If he were my son, as he is my nephew, I'd pistol him!

FOIB: Oh, treachery! But are you sure, Sir Rowland, it is his writing?

WAIT: Sure? Am I here? Do I live? Do I love this pearl of India? I have twenty letters in my pocket from him in the same character.[75]

LADY WISH: How!

FOIB: Oh, what luck it is, Sir Rowland, that you were present at this juncture! This was the business that brought Mr. Mirabell disguised to Madam Millamant this afternoon. I thought something was contriving, when he stole by me and would have hid his face.

LADY WISH: How, how! I heard the villain was in the house indeed; and now I remember, my niece went away abruptly, when Sir Wilfull was to have made his addresses.

[68] *camphire* camphor, supposed to lessen sexual desire
[69] *incessantly* instantly, immediately
[70] *washy* watery, weak
[71] *chair-man* a man whose business it is to carry people in a sedan chair
[72] *the dog-days* a period of from four to six weeks between early July and early September; the sultry, close part of the summer

[73] *suborned* persuaded by bribery to commit a foul deed
[74] *Roman hand* round and bold handwriting
[75] *character* handwriting

FOIB: Then, then, madam, Mr. Mirabell waited for her in her chamber, but I would not tell your ladyship to discompose[76] you when you were to receive Sir Rowland.

WAIT: Enough, his date is short.

FOIB: No, good Sir Rowland, don't incur the law.

WAIT: Law? I care not for law. I can but die, and 'tis in a good cause. My lady shall be satisfied of my truth and innocence, though it cost me my life.

710

LADY WISH: No, dear Sir Rowland, don't fight; if you should be killed, I must never show my face, or hanged. Oh, consider my reputation, Sir Rowland! No, you shan't fight. I'll go in and examine my niece; I'll make her confess. I conjure you, Sir Rowland, by all your love, not to fight.

WAIT: I am charmed, madam; I obey. But some proof you must let me give you; I'll go for a black box, which contains the writings of my whole estate, and deliver that into your hands.

720

LADY WISH: Aye, dear Sir Rowland, that will be some comfort; bring the black box.

WAIT: And may I presume to bring a contract to be signed this night? May I hope so far?

LADY WISH: Bring what you will; but come alive, pray come alive. Oh, this is a happy discovery!

WAIT: Dead or alive I'll come, and married we will be in spite of treachery; aye, and get an heir that shall defeat the last remaining glimpse of hope in my abandoned nephew. Come, my buxom widow.

730

Ere long you shall substantial proof receive,
That I'm an arrant[77] knight—

FOIB: (*Aside*) Or arrant[78] knave.   (*Exeunt*)

[76] *discompose* agitate, upset

[77] *arrant* errant, wandering
[78] *arrant* pre-eminently bad

ACT V

SCENE CONTINUES

Enter LADY WISHFORT *and* FOIBLE

LADY WISH: Out of my house, out of my house, thou viper! thou serpent, that I have fostered! thou bosom traitress, that I raised from nothing! Begone! begone! begone! go! go! That I took from washing of old gauze and weaving of dead hair, with a bleak blue nose, over a chafing-dish of starved embers, and dining behind a travers rag,[1] in a shop no bigger than a birdcage! Go, go! starve again, do, do!

10

FOIB: Dear madam, I'll beg pardon on my knees.

LADY WISH: Away! out! out! Go set up for yourself again! Do, drive a trade, do, with your three-pennyworth of small ware flaunting upon a packthread,[2] under a brandy-seller's bulk,[3] or against a dead wall by a ballad-monger! Go, hang out an old frisoneer-gorget,[4] with a yard of yellow colberteen[5] again. Do; an old gnawed mask, two rows of pins, and a child's fiddle; a glass necklace with the beads broken, and a quilted nightcap with one ear. Go, go, drive a trade! These were your commodities, you treacherous trull! this was the merchandise you dealt in, when I took you into my house, placed you next myself, and made you governante[6] of my whole family! You have forgot this, have you, now you have feathered your nest?

20

FOIB: No, no, dear madam. Do but hear me; have but a moment's patience. I'll confess all. Mr. Mirabell seduced me; I am not the first that he

30

[1] *travers rag* a rag used as a traverse or screen
[2] *packthread* strong thread or small twine
[3] *bulk* projecting part of a building used for a booth in which business is conducted; cf. bulk-head
[4] *frisoneer-gorget* a kind of covering for the neck and breast made of rough Frisian cloth
[5] *colberteen* a kind of French lace, the making of which was encouraged by Colbert, a minister of Louis XIV. It was not highly esteemed in the England of Congreve's day.
[6] *governante* housekeeper

has wheedled with his dissembling tongue. Your ladyship's own wisdom has been deluded by him; then how should I, a poor ignorant, defend myself? O madam, if you knew but what he promised me, and how he assured me your ladyship should come to no damage! Or else the wealth of the Indies should not have bribed me to conspire against so good, so sweet, so kind a lady as you have been to me.

40   LADY WISH: "No damage?" What, to betray me, to marry me to a cast-servingman?[7] to make me a receptacle, a hospital for a decayed pimp? "No damage?" O thou frontless[8] impudence, more than a big-bellied actress!

FOIB: Pray do but hear me, madam; he could not marry your ladyship, madam. No indeed; his marriage was to have been void in law, for he was married to me first, to secure your ladyship. He could not have bedded your ladyship; for

50   if he had consummated with your ladyship, he must have run the risk of the law[9] and been put upon his clergy.[10] Yes indeed; I inquired of the law in that case before I would meddle or make.[11]

LADY WISH: What, then I have been your property, have I? I have been convenient to you, it seems! While you were catering for Mirabell, I have been broker[12] for you? What, have you made a passive bawd of me? This exceeds all precedent;

60   I am brought to fine uses, to become a botcher[13] of second-hand marriages between Abigails and Andrews![14] I'll couple you! Yes, I'll baste you together, you and your Philander![15] I'll Duke's-

---

[7] a cast-servingman a discharged servant
[8] frontless shameless
[9] run the risk of the law i.e. for bigamy
[10] been put upon his clergy claimed the benefit of clergy, originally an exemption of clergymen from trial by a secular court, a privilege later extended to all clerici, or clerks, i.e. those who could read
[11] meddle or make intrude into another's private concerns. "Meddle and make" was a colloquial phrase.
[12] broker a marriage broker
[13] botcher mender or patcher
[14] Abigails and Andrews waiting-maids and menservants, from characters in Beaumont and Fletcher's The Scornful Lady and The Elder Brother respectively
[15] Philander lover, from a character in Beaumont and Fletcher's The Laws of Candy. Beaumont and Fletcher seem to have been favorite authors of Lady Wishfort's.

Place you, as I'm a person! Your turtle is in custody already; you shall coo in the same cage, if there be a constable or warrant in the parish.

(Exit)

FOIB: Oh, that ever I was born! Oh, that I was ever married! A bride! aye, I shall be a Bridewell-bride.[16] Oh!   70

Enter MRS. FAINALL

MRS. FAIN: Poor Foible, what's the matter?

FOIB: O madam, my lady's gone for a constable. I shall be had to a justice, and put to Bridewell to beat hemp. Poor Waitwell's gone to prison already.

MRS. FAIN: Have a good heart, Foible; Mirabell's gone to give security[17] for him. This is all Marwood's and my husband's doing.

FOIB: Yes, yes, I know it, madam; she was in my   80 lady's closet, and overheard all that you said to me before dinner. She sent the letter to my lady; and that missing effect, Mr. Fainall laid this plot to arrest Waitwell, when he pretended to go for the papers; and in the meantime Mrs. Marwood declared all to my lady.

MRS. FAIN: Was there no mention made of me in the letter? My mother does not suspect my being in the confederacy? I fancy Marwood has not told her, though she has told my husband.   90

FOIB: Yes, madam; but my lady did not see that part. We stifled the letter before she read so far. Has that mischievous devil told Mr. Fainall of your ladyship then?

MRS. FAIN: Aye, all's out, my affair with Mirabell, everything discovered. This is the last day of our living together; that's my comfort.

FOIB: Indeed, madam, and so 'tis a comfort if you knew all. He has been even with your ladyship;[18] which I could have told you long enough since,   100 but I love to keep peace and quietness by my good will. I had rather bring friends together than set 'em at distance. But Mrs. Marwood and

---

[16] a Bridewell-bride a bride in Bridewell Prison, a house of correction, where disreputable women were often punished by being made to beat hemp
[17] security bail
[18] He has been even with your ladyship Fainall has got even with his wife for her past affair with Mirabell by his own present affair with Mrs. Marwood.

he are nearer related than ever their parents thought for.

MRS. FAIN: Sayest thou so, Foible? Canst thou prove this?

FOIB: I can take my oath on it, madam; so can Mrs. Mincing. We have had many a fair word from Madam Marwood, to conceal something that passed in our chamber one evening when you were at Hyde Park and we were thought to have gone a-walking; but we went up unawares, though we were sworn to secrecy too. Madam Marwood took a book and swore upon it, but it was a book of verses and poems. So as long is it was not a Bible oath, we may break it with a safe conscience.

MRS. FAIN: This discovery is the most opportune thing I could wish. Now, Mincing?

Enter MINCING

MIN: My lady[19] would speak with Mrs. Foible, mem. Mr. Mirabell is with her; he has set your spouse at liberty, Mrs. Foible, and would have you hide yourself in my lady's closet till my old lady's anger is abated. Oh, my old lady is in a perilous passion at something Mr. Fainall has said; he swears, and my old lady cries. There's a fearful hurricane, I vow. He says, mem, how that he'll have my lady's fortune made over to him, or he'll be divorced.

MRS. FAIN: Does your lady or Mirabell know that?

MIN: Yes, mem; they have sent me to see if Sir Wilfull be sober and to bring him to them. My lady is resolved to have him, I think, rather than lose such a vast sum as six thousand pound. Oh, come, Mrs. Foible, I hear my old lady.

MRS. FAIN: Foible, you must tell Mincing that she must prepare to vouch[20] when I call her.

FOIB: Yes, yes, madam.

MIN: O yes, mem, I'll vouch anything for your ladyship's service, be what it will.

(*Exeunt* MINCING *and* FOIBLE)

Re-enter LADY WISHFORT, *with* MRS. MARWOOD

LADY WISH: O my dear friend, how can I enumerate the benefits that I have received from your good-ness? To you I owe the timely discovery of the false vows of Mirabell; to you I owe the detection of the impostor Sir Rowland. And now you are become an intercessor with my son-in-law, to save the honour of my house, and compound for the frailities of my daughter. Well, friend, you are enough to reconcile me to the bad world, or else I would retire to deserts and solitudes, and feed harmless sheep by groves and purling[21] streams. Dear Marwood, let us leave the world and retire by ourselves and be shepherdesses.

MRS. MAR: Let us first dispatch the affair at hand, madam. We shall have leisure to think of retirement afterwards. Here is one who is concerned in the treaty.

LADY WISH: O daughter, daughter, is it possible thou shouldst be my child, bone of my bone, and flesh of my flesh, and, as I may say, another me, and yet transgress the most minute particle of severe virtue? Is it possible you should lean aside to iniquity, who have been cast in the direct mould of virtue? I have not only been a mould but a pattern for you, and a model for you, after you were brought into the world.

MRS. FAIN: I don't understand your ladyship.

LADY WISH: Not understand? Why, have you not been naught?[22] have you not been sophisticated?[23] Not understand? Here I am ruined to compound[24] for your caprices and your cuck-oldoms. I must pawn my plate and my jewels, and ruin my niece, and all little enough.

MRS. FAIN: I am wronged and abused, and so are you. 'Tis a false accusation, as false as hell, as false as your friend there, aye, or your friend's friend, my false husband.

MRS. MAR: My friend, Mrs. Fainall? Your husband my friend? What do you mean?

MRS. FAIN: I know what I mean, madam, and so do you; and so shall the world at a time convenient.

MRS. MAR: I am sorry to see you so passionate, madam. More temper[25] would look more like innocence. But I have done. I am sorry my zeal

---

[19] *My lady* i.e. Mrs. Millamant. Mincing is Millamant's maid.

[20] *vouch* give evidence

[21] *purling* murmuring

[22] *naught* naughty, wicked

[23] *sophisticated* deprived of original innocence

[24] *compound* make composition, a payment to prevent prosecution for an offense

[25] *temper* temperateness

190 to serve your ladyship and family should admit of misconstruction, or make me liable to affronts. You will pardon me, madam, if I meddle no more with an affair in which I am not personally concerned.

LADY WISH: O dear friend, I am so ashamed that you should meet with such returns! (*To* MRS. FAINALL) You ought to ask pardon on your knees, ungrateful creature; she deserves more from you than all your life can accomplish. (*To* MRS. 200 MARWOOD) Oh, don't leave me destitute in this perplexity! No, stick to me, my good genius.

MRS. FAIN: I tell you, madam, you're abused. Stick to you? Aye, like a leech, to suck your best blood; she'll drop off when she's full. Madam, you shan't pawn a bodkin,[26] nor part with a brass counter,[27] in composition for me. I defy 'em all. Let 'em prove their aspersions; I know my own innocence, and dare stand trial. (*Exit*)

LADY WISH: Why, if she should be innocent, if she 210 should be wronged after all, ha? I don't know what to think; and, I promise you, her education has been unexceptionable.[28] I may say it; for I chiefly made it my own care to initiate her very infancy in the rudiments of virtue, and to impress upon her tender years a young odium[29] and aversion to the very sight of men. Aye, friend, she would ha' shrieked if she had but seen a man, till she was in her teens. As I'm a person 'tis true. She was never suffered to 220 play with a male child, though but in coats; nay, her very babies[30] were of the feminine gender. Oh, she never looked a man in the face but her own father, or the chaplain, and him we made a shift[31] to put upon her for a woman, by the help of his long garments and his sleek face, till she was going in her fifteen.[32]

MRS. MAR: 'Twas much she should be deceived so long.

LADY WISH: I warrant you, or she would never have borne to have been catechized by him; and have 230 heard his long lectures against singing and dancing, and such debaucheries, and going to filthy plays, and profane music-meetings, where the lewd trebles squeak nothing but bawdy, and the basses roar blasphemy. Oh, she would have swooned at the sight or name of an obscene play-book! And can I think, after all this, that my daughter can be naught? What, a whore? and thought it excommunication to set her foot within the door of a playhouse! O my dear friend, 240 I can't believe it, no, no! As she says, let him prove it, let him prove it.

MRS. MAR: Prove it, madam? What, and have your name prostituted in a public court? yours and your daughter's reputation worried at the bar by a pack of bawling lawyers? To be ushered in with an *O yes*[32] of scandal, and have your case opened by an old fumbling lecher in a quoif[34] like a man-midwife; to bring your daughter's infamy to light; to be a theme for legal punsters 250 and quibblers by the statute, and become a jest against a rule of court, where there is no precedent for a jest in any record, not even in Dooms-day Book;[35] to discompose the gravity of the bench, and provoke naughty interrogatories in more naughty law Latin, while the good judge, tickled with the proceeding, simpers under a grey beard, and fidges[36] off and on his cushion as if he had swallowed cantharides,[37] or sat upon cow-itch![38] 260

LADY WISH: Oh, 'tis very hard!

MRS. MAR: And then to have my young revellers of the Temple[39] take notes, like prentices at a

---

[33] *O yes* Oyez, "Hear ye," a cry used by court-criers to secure silence before making a proclamation

[34] *quoif* coif, a white cap formerly worn by English lawyers

[35] *Doomsday Book* the record of a great survey of the lands of England made in 1085-86, by order of William the Conqueror

[36] *fidges* fidgets

[37] *cantharides* a preparation of dried beetles used for medicinal purposes

[38] *cow-itch* cowhage, a tropical vine having pods covered with barbed hairs which cause violent itching

[39] *the Temple* The Inner and Middle Temple were two of the four Inns of Court.

---

[26] *a bodkin* a large-eyed blunt needle, or a kind of pin used by women to fasten their hair

[27] *a brass counter* a coin of base metal used as a token of payment

[28] *unexceptionable* beyond reproach

[29] *odium* hatred

[30] *babies* dolls

[31] *made a shift* used a trick

[32] *going in her fifteen* going into her fifteenth year

conventicle;[40] and after, talk it all over again in commons,[41] or before drawers in an eating-house.

LADY WISH: Worse and worse!

MRS. MAR: Nay, this is nothing; if it would end here, 'twere well. But it must, after this, be con-
270 signed by the shorthand writers to the public press; and from thence be transferred to the hands, nay into the throats and lungs of hawkers,[42] with voices more licentious than the loud flounder-man's,[43] or the woman that cries grey peas. And this you must hear till you are stunned; nay, you must hear nothing else for some days.

LADY WISH: Oh, 'tis insupportable! No, no, dear friend; make it up, make it up; aye, aye, I'll compound. I'll give up all, myself and my all,
280 my niece and her all, anything, everything for composition.

MRS. MAR: Nay, madam, I advise nothing; I only lay before you, as a friend, the inconveniences which perhaps you have overseen. Here comes Mr. Fainall; if he will be satisfied to huddle up all in silence, I shall be glad. You must think I would rather congratulate than condole with you.

Enter FAINALL

290 LADY WISH: Aye, aye, I do not doubt it, dear Marwood; no, no, I do not doubt it.

FAIN: Well, madam, I have suffered myself to be overcome by the importunity of this lady your friend, and am content you shall enjoy your own proper estate during life, on condition you oblige yourself never to marry, under such penalty as I think convenient.

LADY WISH: Never to marry?

FAIN: No more Sir Rowlands; the next imposture
300 may not be so timely detected.

MRS. MAR: That condition, I dare answer, my lady will consent to, without difficulty; she has already but too much experienced the perfidiousness of men. Besides, madam, when we retire to our pastoral solitude, we shall bid adieu to all other thoughts.

LADY WISH: Aye, that's true; but in case of necessity, as of health, or some such emergency——

FAIN: Oh, if you are prescribed marriage, you shall be considered; I will only reserve to myself the power to choose for you. If your physic be wholesome, it matters not who is your apothecary. 310 Next, my wife shall settle on me the remainder of her fortune, not made over already; and for her maintenance depend entirely on my discretion.

LADY WISH: This is most inhumanly savage, exceeding the barbarity of a Muscovite[44] husband.

FAIN: I learned from his Czarish majesty's retine,[45] in a winter evening's conference over brandy and pepper, amongst other secrets of matrimony and policy, as they are at present 320 practised in the northern hemisphere. But this must be agreed unto, and that positively. Lastly, I will be endowed, in right of my wife, with that six thousand pound, which is the moiety of Mrs. Millamant's fortune in your possession; and which she has forfeited (as will appear by the last will and testament of your deceased husband, Sir Jonathan Wishfort) by her disobedience in contracting herself against your consent or knowledge, and by refusing the offered match 330 with Sir Wilfull Witwoud, which you, like a careful aunt, had provided for her.

LADY WISH: My nephew was *non compos*,[46] and could not make his addresses.

FAIN: I come to make demands. I'll hear no objections.

LADY WISH: You will grant me time to consider?

FAIN: Yes, while the instrument[47] is drawing, to which you must set your hand till more sufficient deeds can be perfected; which I will take care 340

---

[40] *take notes, like prentices at a coventicle* indentured apprentices were supposed to take notes on the sermon in a meetinghouse for the use of their employers
[41] *commons* the dining hall of a collegiate institution
[42] *hawkers* peddlers
[43] *the loud flounder-man's* There was a well-known crier of flounders in the streets of London whose voice was loud and unrestrained.

[44] *Muscovite* Russian
[45] *his Czarish majesty's retinue* Peter the Great had visited England early in 1698.
[46] *non compos* not in his right senses
[47] *instrument* legal document

shall be done with all possible speed. In the meanwhile I will go for the said instrument, and till my return you may balance this matter in your own discretion.   (*Exit*)

LADY WISH: This insolence is beyond all precedent, all parallel; must I be subject to this merciless villain?

MRS. MAR: 'Tis severe indeed, madam, that you should smart for your daughter's wantonness.

350 LADY WISH: 'Twas against my consent that she married this barbarian, but she would have him, though her year[48] was not out. Ah! her first husband, my son Languish, would not have carried it thus.[49] Well, that was my choice, this is hers; she is matched now with a witness.[50] I shall be mad! Dear friend, is there no comfort for me? must I live to be confiscated[51] at this rebel-rate? Here come two more of my Egyptian plagues[53] too.

360 *Enter* MRS. MILLAMANT *and* SIR WILFULL WITWOUD

SIR WIL: Aunt, your servant.

LADY WISH: Out, caterpillar, call not me aunt! I know thee not!

SIR WIL: I confess I have been a little in disguise,[54] as they say. 'Sheart! and I'm sorry for't. What would you have? I hope I committed no offence, aunt, and if I did, I am willing to make satisfaction; and what can a man say fairer? If I have broke anything, I'll pay for't, and it cost a pound.

370 And so let that content for what's past, and make no more words. For what's to come, to pleasure you I'm willing to marry my cousin. So pray let's all be friends; she and I are agreed upon the matter before a witness.

LADY WISH: How's this dear niece? Have I any comfort? Can this be true?

MRS. MIL: I am content to be a sacrifice to your repose, madam; and to convince you that I had no hand in the plot, as you were misinformed,

380 I have laid my commands on Mirabell to come

---

in person, and be a witness that I give my hand to this flower of knighthood; and for the contract that passed between Mirabell and me, I have obliged him to make a resignation of it in your ladyship's presence. He is without, and waits your leave for admittance.

LADY WISH: Well, I'll swear I am something revived at this testimony of your obedience; but I cannot admit that traitor. I fear I cannot fortify myself to support his appearance. He is as terrible to 390 me as a Gorgon;[55] if I see him, I fear I shall turn to stone, petrify incessantly.

MRS. MIL: If you disoblige him, he may resent your refusal, and insist upon the contract still. Then 'tis the last time he will be offensive to you.

LADY WISH: Are you sure it will be the last time? If I were sure of that! Shall I never see him again?

MRS. MIL: Sir Wilfull, you and he are to travel together, are you not?   400

SIR WIL: 'Sheart, the gentleman's a civil gentleman, aunt; let him come in. Why, we are sworn brothers and fellow-travellers. We are to be Pylades and Orestes,[56] he and I. He is to be my interpreter in foreign parts. He has been overseas once already; and with *proviso* that I marry my cousin, will cross 'em once again, only to bear me company. 'Sheart, I'll call him in. An I set on't once,[57] he shall come in; and see who'll hinder him.   (*Exit*) 410

MRS. MAR: This is precious fooling, if it would pass; but I'll know the bottom of it.

LADY WISH: O dear Marwood, you are not going?

MRS. MAR: No far, madam; I'll return immediately.
                                        (*Exit*)

Re-enter SIR WILFULL *with* MIRABELL

SIR WIL: Look up, man, I'll stand by you; 'sbud an she do frown, she can't kill you; besides, harkee, she dare not frown desperately, because her face is none of her own. 'Sheart, an she should, her 420 forehead would wrinkle like the coat of a cream-cheese; but mum for that, fellow-traveller.

---

48 *her year* of formal mourning
49 *carried it thus* acted like this
50 *with a witness* effectually, with great force
51 *be confiscated* have one's property seized
52 *at this rebel-rate* in this rebellious, high-handed manner
53 *two more of my Egyptian plagues* a reference to the ten plagues of Egypt cf. *Exodus* VII-XII
54 *in disguise* not my natural self, intoxicated

55 *Gorgon* one of the three snaky-haired sisters whose hideous appearance turned the beholder to stone
56 *Pylades and Orestes* Pylades was the faithful friend of Orestes, son of Agamemnon and Clytemnestra
57 *An I set on't once* if I once set my heart on it

MIR: If a deep sense of the many injuries I have offered to so good a lady, with a sincere remorse and a hearty contrition, can but obtain the least glance of compassion, I am too happy. Ah, madam, there was a time! But let it be forgotten. I confess I have deservedly forfeited the high place I once held, of sighing at your feet. Nay, kill me not, by turning from me in disdain. I come not to plead for favour; nay, not for pardon. I am a suppliant only for your pity. I am going where I never shall behold you more.

SIR WIL: How, fellow-traveller! You shall go by yourself then.

MIR: Let me be pitied first, and afterwards forgotten. I ask no more.

SIR WIL: By'r lady, a very reasonable request, and will cost you nothing, aunt. Come, come, forgive and forget, aunt; why you must, an you are a Christian.

MIR: Consider, madam, in reality you could not receive much prejudice; it was an innocent device, though I confess it had a face of guiltiness. It was at most an artifice which love contrived, and errors which love produces have ever been accounted venial. At least think it is punishment enough that I have lost what in my heart I hold most dear, that to your cruel indignation I have offered up this beauty, and with her my peace and quiet; nay, all my hopes of future comfort.

SIR WIL: An he does not move me, would I may never be o' the quorum![58] An it were not as good a deed as to drink, to give her to him again, I would never take shipping! Aunt, if you don't forgive quickly, I shall melt, I can tell you that. My contract went no farther than a little mouth-glue, and that's hardly dry; one doleful sigh more from my fellow-traveller, and 'tis dissolved.

LADY WISH: Well, nephew, upon your account—ah, he has a false insinuating tongue! Well, sir, I will stifle my just resentment at my nephew's request. I will endeavour what I can to forget, but on *proviso* that you resign the contract with my niece immediately.

MIR: It is in writing, and with papers of concern; but I have sent my servant for it, and will deliver it to you with all acknowledgments for your transcendent goodness.

[58] *the quorum* the justices of the peace collectively

LADY WISH: (*Aside*) Oh, he has witchcraft in his eyes and tongue! When I did not see him, I could have bribed a villain to his assassination; but his appearance rakes the embers which have so long lain smothered in my breast.

Re-enter FAINALL *and* MRS. MARWOOD

FAIN: Your date of deliberation, madam, is expired. Here is the instrument; are you prepared to sign?

LADY WISH: If I were prepared, I am not empowered. My niece exerts a lawful claim, having matched herself by my direction to Sir Wilfull.

FAIN: That sham is too gross to pass on me, though 'tis imposed on you, madam.

MRS. MIL: Sir, I have given my consent.

MIR: And, sir, I have resigned my pretensions.

SIR WIL: And, sir, I assert my right; and will maintain it in defiance of you, sir, and of your instrument. 'Sheart, an you talk of an instrument, sir, I have an old fox[59] by my thigh shall hack your instrument of ram vellum[60] to shreds, sir! It shall not be sufficient for a *mittimus*[61] or a tailor's measure.[62] Therefore withdraw your instrument, sir, or, by'r lady, I shall draw mine.

LADY WISH: Hold, nephew, hold!

MRS. MIL: Good Sir Wilfull, respite[63] your valour.

FAIN: Indeed? Are you provided of your guard, with your single beef-eater[64] there? But I'm prepared for you, and insist upon my first proposal. You shall submit your own estate to my management and absolutely make over my wife's to my sole use, as pursuant to the purport and tenor of this other covenant. (*To* MRS. MILLAMANT) I suppose, madam, your consent is not requisite in this case; nor, Mr. Mirabell, your resignation; nor, Sir Wilfull, your right. You may draw your fox if you please, sir, and make a Bear-Garden[65] flourish somewhere else; for here it will not avail.

[59] *fox* a kind of sword
[60] *ram vellum* parchment prepared from sheepskin
[61] *a mittimus* a warrant of commitment to prison
[62] *a tailor's measure* parchment used by tailors in taking measurements
[63] *respite* delay
[64] *beef-eater* a yeoman of the royal guard
[65] *Bear-Garden* place for baiting bears; a scene of rowdiness

This, my Lady Wishfort, must be subscribed,
510   or your darling daughter's turned adrift, like a
leaky hulk, to sink or swim, as she and the current
of this lewd town can agree.

LADY WISH: Is there no means, no remedy to stop
my ruin? Ungrateful wretch! dost thou not owe
thy being, thy subsistence, to my daughter's fortune?

FAIN: I'll answer you when I have the rest of it
in my possession.

MIR: (*To* LADY WISHFORT) But that you would not
520   accept of a remedy from my hands—I own I
have not deserved you should owe any obligation
to me; or else perhaps I could advise—

LADY WISH: Oh, what? what? to save me and my
child from ruin, from want, I'll forgive all that's
past; nay, I'll consent to anything to come, to
be delivered from this tyranny.

MIR: Aye, madam, but that is too late; my reward
is intercepted. You have disposed of her who
only could have made me a compensation for
530   all my services. But be it as it may, I am resolved
I'll serve you; you shall not be wronged in this
savage manner.

LADY WISH: How! Dear Mr. Mirabell, can you be
so generous at last? But it is not possible. Harkee,
I'll break my nephew's match; you shall have
my niece yet, and all her fortune, if you can
but save me from this imminent danger.

MIR: Will you? I take you at your word. I ask
no more. I must have leave for two criminals
540   to appear.

LADY WISH: Aye, aye; anybody, anybody!

MIR: Foible is one, and a penitent.

Re-enter MRS. FAINALL, FOIBLE, *and* MINCING

MRS. MAR: O my shame! (MIRABELL *and* LADY
WISHFORT *go to* MRS. FAINALL *and* FOIBLE) These
corrupt things are brought and brought hither to
expose me.   (*To* FAINALL)

FAIN: If it must all come out, why let 'em know
it; 'tis but *the way of the world*. That shall not
550   urge me to relinquish or abate one tittle[66] of
my terms; no, I will insist the more.

FOIB: Yes indeed, madam; I'll take my Bible-oath
of it.

MIN: And so will I, mem.

LADY WISH: O Marwood. Marwood, art thou false?
my friend deceive me? Hast though been a
wicked accomplice with that profligate man?

MRS. MAR: Have you so much ingratitude and
injustice, to give credit against your friend to
the aspersions of two such mercenary trulls?   560

MIN: "Mercenary," mem? I scorn your words. 'Tis
true we found you and Mr. Fainall in the blue
garret; by the same token, you swore us to
secrecy upon Messalina's poems.[67]
"Mercenary?" No, if we would have been mercenary, we should have held our tongues; you
would have bribed us sufficiently.

FAIN: Go, you are an insignificant thing! Well,
what are you the better for this? Is this Mr.
Mirabell's expedient? I'll be put off no longer.   570
You thing, that was a wife, shall smart for this!
I will not leave thee wherewithal to hide thy
shame; your body shall be naked as your reputation.

MRS. FAIN: I despise you, and defy your malice!
You have aspersed me wrongfully. I have proved
your falsehood. Go you and your treacherous—I
will not name it, but starve together, perish!

FAIN: Not while you are worth a groat,[68] indeed,
my dear. Madam, I'll be fooled no longer.   580

LADY WISH: Ah, Mr. Mirabell, this is small comfort, the detection of this affair.

MIR: Oh, in good time. Your leave for the other
offender and penitent to appear, madam.

Enter WAITWELL, *with a box of writings*

LADY WISH: O Sir Rowland! Well, rascal?

WAIT: What your ladyship pleases. I have brought
the black box at last, madam.

MIR: Give it me. Madam, you remember your
promise.   590

LADY WISH: Aye, dear sir.

MIR: Where are the gentlemen?

WAIT: At hand, sir, rubbing their eyes; just risen
from sleep.

FAIN: 'Sdeath, what's this to me? I'll not wait your
private concerns.

Enter PETULANT *and* WITWOUD

[66] *tittle* a very small part

[67] *Messalina's poems* Messalina was the dissolute wife of the
Roman emperor, Claudius. "Messalina's" is probably an
error of Mincing's for "miscellaneous."

[68] *groat* an old English coin worth fourpence

PET: How now? What's the matter? Whose hand's out?[69]

WIT: Heyday! what, are you all got together, like players at the end of the last act?

MIR: You may remember, gentlemen, I once requested your hands as witnesses to a certain parchment.

WIT: Aye, I do; my hand I remember. Petulant set his mark.

MIR: You wrong him, his name is fairly written as shall appear. You do not remember, gentlemen, anything of what that parchment contained? (*Undoing the box*)

WIT: No.

PET: Not I. I writ. I read nothing.

MIR: Very well; now you shall know. Madam, your promise.

LADY WISH: Aye, aye, sir, upon my honour.

MIR: Mr. Fainall, it is now time that you should know that your lady, while she was at her own disposal, and before you had by your insinuations wheedled her out of a pretended settlement of the greatest part of her fortune—

FAIN: Sir! pretended!

MIR: Yes, sir. I say that this lady, while a widow, having it seems received some cautions respecting your inconstancy and tyranny of temper, which from her own partial opinion and fondness of you she could never have suspected—she did, I say, by the wholesome advice of friends and of sages learned in the laws of this land, deliver this same as her act and deed to me in trust, and to the uses within mentioned. You may read if you please (*holding out the parchment*), though perhaps what is inscribed on the back may serve your occasions.

FAIN: Very likely, sir. What's here? Damnation! (*reads*) "A deed of conveyance of the whole estate real of Arabella Languish, widow, in trust to Edward Mirabell." Confusion!

MIR: Even so, sir; 'tis the *way of the world*, sir, of the widows of the world. I suppose this deed may bear an elder[70] date than what you have obtained from your lady?

FAIN: Perfidious fiend! then thus I'll be revenged. (*Offers to run at* MRS. FAINALL)

SIR WIL: Hold, sir! Now you may make your Bear-Garden flourish somewhere else, sir.

FAIN: Mirabell, you shall hear of this, sir; be sure you shall. Let me pass, oaf! (*Exit*)

MRS. FAIN: Madam, you seem to stifle your resentment: you had better give it vent.

MRS. MAR: Yes, it shall have vent, and to your confusion; or I'll perish in the attempt. (*Exit*)

LADY WISH: O daughter, daughter, 'tis plain thou hast inherited thy mother's prudence.

MRS. FAIN: Thank Mr. Mirabell, a cautious friend, to whose advice all is owing.

LADY WISH: Well, Mr. Mirabell, you have kept your promise, and I must perform mine. First, I pardon, for your sake, Sir Rowland there, and Foible. The next thing is to break the matter to my nephew, and how to do that—

MIR: For that, madam, give yourself no trouble; let me have your consent. Sir Wilfull is my friend; he has had compassion upon lovers, and generously engaged a volunteer[71] in this action, for our service, and now designs to prosecute his travels.

SIR WIL: 'Sheart, aunt, I have no mind to marry. My cousin's a fine lady, and the gentleman loves her, and she loves him, and they deserve one another; my resolution is to see foreign parts. I have set on't, and when I'm set on't, I must do't. And if these two gentlemen would travel too, I think they may be spared.

PET: For my part, I say little; I think things are best off or on.[72]

WIT: I gad,[73] I understand nothing of the matter; I'm in a maze yet, like a dog in a dancing-school.

LADY WISH: Well, sir, take her, and with her all the joy I can give you.

MRS. MIL: Why does not the man take me? Would you have me give myself to you over again?

MIR: Aye, and over and over again; (*Kisses her hand*) for I would have you as often as possibly I can. Well, Heaven grant I love you not too well; that's all my fear.

SIR WIL: 'Sheart, you'll have time enough to toy[74] after you're married; or if you will toy now,

---

[69] *Whose hand's out?* Who is making trouble?

[70] *elder* earlier

[71] *engaged a volunteer* volunteered to take part

[72] *off or on* either way

[73] *I gad* Egad, i.e. by God

[74] *toy* play

let us have a dance in the meantime, that we who are not lovers may have some other employment besides looking on.

690   MIR: With all my heart, dear Sir Wilfull. What shall we do for music?

FOIB: Oh, sir, some that were provided for Sir Rowland's entertainment are yet within call.

(A dance)

LADY WISH: As I am a person, I can hold out no longer. I have wasted my spirits so to-day already that I am ready to sink under the fatigue; and I cannot but have some fears upon me yet that my son[75] Fainall will pursue some desperate
700   course.

MIR: Madam, disquiet not yourself on that account; to my knowledge his circumstances are such, he must of force[76] comply.[77] For my part, I will contribute all that in me lies to a reunion; in the meantime, madam, (To MRS. FAINALL) let me before these witnesses restore to you this deed of trust; it may be a means, well-managed, to make you live easily together.

From hence let those be warned, who mean to wed,   710
Lest mutual falsehood stain the bridal bed;
For each deceiver to his cost may find,
That marriage-frauds too oft are paid in kind.

(Exeunt omnes)

[75] my son i.e. my son-in-law

[76] of force necessarily
[77] comply acquiesce

EPILOGUE

SPOKEN BY MRS. BRACEGIRDLE[1]

After our Epilogue this crowd dismisses,
I'm thinking how this play'll be pulled to pieces.
But pray consider, ere you doom its fall,
How hard a thing 'twould be to please you all.
There are some critics so with spleen diseased,
They scarcely come inclining to be pleased;
And sure he must have more than mortal skill,
Who pleases any one against his will.
Then, all bad poets we are sure are foes,
10   And how their number's swelled, the town well knows;
In shoals I've marked 'em judging in the pit;
Though they're on no pretence for judgment fit,
But that they have been damned for want of wit.
Since when, they, by their own offences taught,
Set up for spies on plays, and finding fault.
Others there are whose malice we'd prevent;
Such who watch plays with scurrilous intent

To mark out who by characters are meant.
And though no perfect likeness they can trace,
Yet each pretends to know the copied face.   20
These with false glosses[2] feed their own ill nature,[3]
And turn to libel what was meant a satire.
May such malicious fops this fortune find,
To think themselves alone the fools designed;
If any are so arrogantly vain,
To think they singly[4] can support a scene,
And furnish fool enough[5] to entertain.
For well the learned and the judicious know
That satire scorns to stoop so meanly low
As any one abstracted[6] fop to show.   30
For, as when painters form a matchless face,
They from each fair one catch some different grace;
And shining features in one portrait blend,
To which no single beauty must pretend;
So poets oft do in one piece expose
Whole belles assemblées[7] of coquettes and beaux.

[1] Mrs. Bracegirdle Mrs. Anne Bracegirdle, one of the loves of Congreve's life, played the part of Mrs. Millamant in The Way of the World.

[2] glosses notes of explanation
[3] nature pronounced "nater" to rhyme with satire, "sater"
[4] singly alone
[5] furnish fool enough furnish enough of a fool
[6] abstracted separated from others
[7] belles assemblées fashionable gatherings

FROM *UNDERSTANDING DRAMA*

by *Cleanth Brooks & Robert B. Heilman*

CONGREVE'S ATTITUDE TOWARD HIS CHARACTERS

When we come to the important problem of Congreve's comment upon experience, we must first judge his attitudes toward his characters—a task complicated by the fact that these attitudes are far from meeting conventional expectations. In this matter such a seasoned critic as W. M. Thackeray has failed by misreading Congreve as a cynic, that is, one who believes the worst of human beings. It is ironic that such a charge should result from Congreve's method, which compliments the reader by assuming that the reader can distinguish good and bad even when the distinction is not made obvious.

Congreve, for instance, does not divide his characters into heroes and villains. He does not underline the goodness of his more admirable characters. He does not burn with righteous indignation when he presents such bad characters as Mrs. Marwood and Fainall; instead, he treats them with detachment by giving due play to their motives, their insight into others, their quickness, etc. He does not utterly deride the boobies such as the fops and Sir Wilfull; he allows them a measure of wit and acuteness. He does not present Mirabell as a flawless hero; instead he shows Mirabell very emphatically in "the way of the world" in his not only having had an affair with Millamant's cousin but also having married her off to the unpalatable Fainall as a cover-up; Congreve neither conceals these facts nor attempts to present

From *Understanding Drama: Twelve Plays* by Cleanth Brooks and Robert B. Heilman. Copyright 1945, 1948 by Holt, Rinehart and Winston, Inc.

Mirabell, in his new love for Millamant, as a changed or "converted" man. Finally, Congreve does not make Millamant into an obviously "sweet" or lovely heroine; she knows her way about in the world; she enjoys coquetry and the exercise of power; to grasp her essential charm we must see more than the glittering surface of her manner.

This is characterization at an adult level, and a naive reader may think that it makes sense only if we regard the author as a sardonic observer of an insoluble human muddle. Such a reader will think that Congreve ought to have had the characters whom he regards favorably reject the artificial life of society and embrace a more direct, spontaneous way of life—especially in the matter of love. The only character, however, who rejects society is Sir Wilfull; but, though we are meant to sympathize to some extent with Sir Willfull's shrewdness and honesty, it is clear that his gaucheries are still meant to be comic. That is, he is also measured by the author's criterion; though he aids the lovers, he does not himself provide a criterion for their conduct.

Society has its shortcomings, then, and the country also has its shortcomings. But this fact does not mean that Congreve believes that nowhere are values to be found. The fact that we reject some things which the characters do, while at the same time we accept other things, shows that a system of values is operating in the play. Our critical problem is to define them—not altogether an easy task since, though they do not coincide with, they do not wholly differ from, the standards of conduct upon which fashionable society in the play preens itself. Yet we should not make the mistake of thinking that Congreve approvingly presents a picture of a cynically heartless society. Nor, on the other hand, does he give us, with the ease of the sentimentalist, conventional reassurances about "natural" and spontaneous love, the victory of good over evil, and the triumph of "pure love." In fact, the elimination of all traces of sentimentality is one of the striking achievements of the play.

CONGREVE'S SYSTEM OF VALUES

What, then, are Congreve's values? *The Way of the World*, we may say, represents *values as achieved by discipline*. Discipline means control, order, the rejection of extremes. What we should go on to observe, then, is how, through the action of the play, Congreve does reject extremes.

Manners Versus Emotions. We are not asked to choose between raw, uninhibited but sincere emotion on the one hand, and artificial, insincere manners on the other. Such a dilemma is oversimple and therefore false. But many of the characters are caught in this dilemma: Sir Wilful is impaled on the former horn, Witwoud and Petulant on the latter. Sir Wilfull can say, "*The Fashion's* a fool . . ."; Witwoud can say (of Millamant), "And for my part, but that it is almost a *fashion* to admire her, I should—hark'ee— to tell you a secret, . . .—I shall never break my heart for her."

At one extreme, the matter-of-fact Sir Wilfull rejects romantic love, the niceties of courtship, gracefully extravagant compliments; when Millamant shows indifference to him, he dismisses the matter with: "When you're disposed, when you're disposed.

Now's as well as another time . . ." At the other extreme, the fops are lovers' conventions as ends in themselves, for nicety, delicacy of taste, and wit. But their emphasis lies on the mastery of the mechanism rather than on anything to be achieved by the mechanism. For them, therefore, the poetry of courtship is really as meaningless as it is for Sir Wilfull.

Congreve presents a nice irony here: opposite extremes tend to coalesce. When drunk, Petulant and Sir Wilfull take precisely the same line. Petulant, drunk, can say to Millamant: "If you are not handsome, what then, if I have a humor to prove it? If I shall have my reward, say so; if not, fight for your face the next time yourself. . . . I'll go to bed to my maid." When his chivalrous manners are peeled off—and they are worn by him merely as a modish garment—he is exactly like Sir Wilful, who scorns manners and cries out, at the mention of wenches, "Ahey! wenches; where are the wenches?"

Mirabell and Millamant. The problem of extremes also engages the hero and heroine, though for them discipline means not only the rejection of unsuitable extremes but also the reconciliation of objectives that, in the society in which they live are usually found in opposition. Millamant, for instance, would like to marry Mirabell and save her fortune too (maybe she *would* sacrifice it; since this is comedy, she is not really tested). But much more important—the play really hinges on this issue—is that Millamant wants to save, not only her lover and fortune, but romantic love and marriage too; to have marriage, but also a certain tone and dignity that, like romantic love—as she sees—do not always go with marriage.* The marriage is too often one of convenience, of money or social position; the poetry of love is dropped after courtship or hardened into a meaningless conventional form for appearance's sake. The problem of Mirabell and Millamant is to define and create a situation to discover a discipline, whereby love and dignity and marriage may be combined.

Congreve highlights this problem in two places. When Lady Wishfort, disillusioned, takes refuge in the mawkish poetry of "I would retire to deserts and solitudes, and feed harmless sheep by groves and purling streams. Dear Marwood, let us leave the world, and retire by ourselves and be shepherdesses" she shows what is *not* the way out—escape, an undisciplined jumping from one extreme to another. On the other hand, the famous bargaining scene in Act IV shows Mirabell and Millamant dealing directly with their problem—seeking the terms, the discipline, by which they may realize their complex objective. The serious implications are all there, though the tone is that finest comedy—one of urbane and witty gaiety. Sentimentalists may miss the feeling, the moralists may miss the seriousness (just as neither may know how to deal with Falstaff and Hal); Congreve's achievement is, like that of his characters, the avoidance of both lushness and solemnity.

---

*The phrase "romantic love" perhaps needs further definition, for the word "romantic" has been used in so many meanings and the whole phrase has become so vulgarized in recent years that its use here may be misleading. Yet we need a term which will not only assert the retention of a certain personal dignity in the relationship—as opposed to "love" that is selfishly possessive —but also one which will denote the retention of a certain spontaneity and charm as opposed to a matter-of-fact, sober-sides domestic partnership.

CONGREVE'S VARIATIONS ON THE THEME OF LOVE

Why is the bargaining scene so successful? For one thing, because the various stipulations and demands, though made in a manner that may suggest selfishness or indulgence of whim, actually embody sound critiques of conventional matrimony, of its trivialities and hypocrises. Taken alone, this critique itself might make Mirabell and Millamant look vain, condescending, and persnickety; but it is largely justified by the rest of the play. In fact, the relationship of Mirabell and Millamant is to be seen in the context of all the relationships of the play, from which it receives considerable qualification.

The theme is love, of which Congreve has presented an amazing number of variations—not for variety's sake, but as the background which defines the central problem of the play. The Fainalls, for instance, had married without love at all—he for money, she to cover up an amour. Lady Wishfort, whose chief concern is sex, is offered pretended passion by Waitwell, a parody of romantic courtship. Fainall and Marwood carry on an illicit relationship, marred by his distrust and her halfheartedness. Marwood's passion for Mirabell offers another variation, unrequited love, though the "love" is largely a medley of desire, pride, pique, and the wish to make Fainall jealous. Here we have a sharp contrast between her and Mrs. Fainall, who with equanimity sees her former lover laying suit to another woman. The desire for the contrast may have influenced Congreve here, since he leaves us somewhat uncertain about Mrs. Fainall's character; perhaps we are to assume that the earlier affair has burned itself out into a kind of general amiability, but the evidence does not clarify the matter finally. Then there are the bachelors—Sir Wilfull, Petulant, and Witwoud—to whom love is either a fashion or a convenience, and the servants, Waitwell and Foible, whose marriage, like that of the Fainalls, is one of convenience—in this case, their betters' convenience. Yet there is a variation here, for the pair seem to be in love: Foible sounds sincere enough when, upon her husband's being arrested, she wails about becoming "a Bridewell bride."

Ironically enough, they are the only happy couple in the play. It is perhaps significant that they are outside the world of fashion and its temptations. They can see it in perspective, and Congreve definitely presents them as seeing the other characters as they are. Ironically, they are not at the mercy of the conventions because they are *beneath* the conventions. Mirabell and Millamant must recognize the conventions, within which they aim for the same working relationship. Waitwell and Foible, by showing the possibility of domestic harmony, offer a kind of dramatic intimation of what Mirabell and Millamant may achieve.

The Way of the World represents, then, almost a symphonic pattern in which the theme of love receives a variety of treatments, ranging from the somber—the

Fainall-Marwood affair is bitter, perhaps, as Bonamy Dobrée has suggested, even verging on the tragic—to the burlesque, which we see in Waitwell's pretended assault on Lady Wishfort. Somewhere between those extremes Mirabell and Millamant must plot their course—facing the opposition not merely of the Marwoods who would "mar" their affair and of the Fainalls scheming to get their money, but, more importantly, of a society which, because of its own addiction to extremes (of conventionality, sentimentality, pretence, etc.), must naturally be opposed to their search for balance and discipline. But this latter struggle becomes also a struggle with themselves: have they the inner stamina to adhere to standards of their own? If not, Millamant will "dwindle into a wife" and Mirabell be "enlarged into a husband"—two phrases, by the way, which beautifully epitomize the stereotyped marital relationship in which the essential dignity of the individual is lost. The loss of that dignity is what Congreve shows in the others: Fainall is "enlarged," Mrs. Fainall is "dwindled," Marwood can talk independently to Fainall because she is not tied to him, Lady Wishfort is only too eager to dwindle.

Thus the way of the world gives meaning to the bargaining scene, in which the participants struggle with the world and with themselves. Millamant imposes conditions, but she is equally willing to have Mirabell impose conditions: "Speak and spare not," she says. Some of her chief injunctions regard their joint conduct rather than her own prerogatives. And if each one does speak at times for himself, how else could Congreve convey the terms of a self-imposed discipline. For each one to outline in detail his *own* schedule of good behavior would be very close to sentimentality. But the play does not become soft and effusive. Congreve always keeps the tone firm; the wit in the bargaining scene is conspicuous.

CONGREVE'S USE OF IRONY

Very important in Congreve's management of the bargaining scene—as well as in the whole treatment of the love-affair—is the irony. On one plane it is the irony of lovers doing the opposite of what is expected of them, namely, haggling over rights and privileges and working out itemized contracts. On another plane, there is the ironic contrast between the unimportance of many (not all) of the minutiae discussed and the real importance of the deep implications. If the details are trivial, the realism of the lovers is not trivial; and there is a real wistfulness—intensified by and yet, at the same time, protected from sentimentality by, the humor—in Millamant's exclamation, "Let us be as strange as if we had been married a great while, and as well-bred as if we were not married at all."

Thus Congreve has Mirabell and Millamant approach all issues through teasing and banter. They are aware of each other's faults, as they well may be, for they are also aware of their own. The amusing little scene in Act I in which Mirabell says, "I like her with all her faults—nay, like her for her faults," is significant. Mirabell is laughing at his mistress and also being ironic about his infatuation for her. Note the climax, in which he says of her frailties, "They are now grown as familiar to me as my own frailties, and in all probability in a little time longer I shall like 'em as well." To like her faults risks the sentimental, but the risk is completely countered by the playful, and yet shrewdly realistic, statement of his devotion to his own faults. His love is real, but he remains ironically perceptive.

There should be no doubt of the underlying genuineness of feeling: for one thing, no one but a lover (or an outright enemy) would take so much trouble to tease and joke about someone else. But the feeling may be missed by someone who takes the speeches only at their surface meaning, or someone who demands a direct avowal of feeling and has not the sophistication to grasp the fact that emotion may be presented indirectly.

Congreve makes matters sure, however, when he has Millamant say outright, "Well, if Mirabell should not make a good husband, I am a lost thing, for I find I love him violently"; she makes her confession, true, but even that she balances with a realistic view of future possibilities. Congreve demands more of us in Mirabell's comparable line at the close of the play, "Well, Heaven grant I love you not too well; that's all my fear." Reflection is needed to show us that the ironic playfulness would be possible only to one completely sure of his own feelings.

AN ENEMY
OF THE PEOPLE

Henrik Ibsen (1828-1906)

Adapted By Arthur Miller

The father of modern drama, Ibsen, was born in Skien, Norway. He felt the frustrations and restraints of the provincial life that he later was to protest against so vigorously in his plays. He struggled for recognition as a romantic poet and dramatist but attracted little attention. In 1851 he became associated with the national theater at Bergen as a playwright and director. Twelve years later he left Norway to live in Germany and Italy, where for more than a quarter of a century he continued to write plays.

His realistic period began with *Pillars of Society* in 1877, followed by *A Doll's House* and *Ghosts*. The public indignation aroused by his forthright treatment of social problems led him to write a scathing indictment of society in *An Enemy of the People*. Other notable plays of Ibsen are *Peer Gynt*, *The Master Builder*, *Rosmersholm*, *The Wild Duck* and *Hedda Gabler*.

ARTHUR MILLER (b. 1915)

Born a New Yorker, Miller attended the University of Michigan, where his aptitude for playwriting was so marked that he won three cash awards. After graduation he worked in the Federal Theater before becoming a script writer for the Columbia Broadcasting Company. His first professional production on Broadway was *The Man Who Had All the Luck*, in 1944, which did little to bring him recognition. Three years later, however, *All My Sons* won the Drama Critics Circle Award. His most successful play, *The Death of A Salesman*, appeared in 1949 to establish him as one of the foremost of contemporary playwrights. Other notable Miller plays are *The Crucible*, *A View from the Bridge*, and *After the Fall*.

Miller was attracted to Ibsen's *An Enemy of the People* because of its frontal attack on the hypocrisy of vested interests. In preparing his version of the play, he set out to transform the original dialogue into contemporary English while retaining the central theme. Miller's statement of his objective indicates his point of view:

Throughout the play I tried to peel away the trappings of the moment, its relatively accidental details which ring the dull green tones of Victorianism, and to show that beneath there still lives the terrible wrath of Henrik Ibsen, who could make a play as men make watches, precisely, intelligently, and telling not merely the minute and the hour but the age.

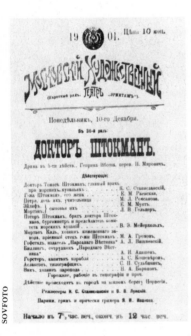

SOVFOTO

Above. The program
from a 1901 production
of "Dr. Shtokman"
at the Moscow Art Theatre.

Right. A Soviet sculpture
of "Dr. Shtokman,"
by S. N. Sudbinin.

SOVFOTO

Dr. Stockmann is eager
to publish the results of his findings
about the polluted springs.
Photographs in this sequence
are of the 1971 production
at Lincoln Center in New York,
with Stephen Elliott
as Dr. Stockmann,
and Barbara Casson
as Catherine Stockmann.

Opposite top. Catherine is concerned about the future of the family if Dr. Stockmann alienates the community.

Opposite bottom. Dr. Stockmann is branded by the mob as the "enemy of the people."

Below. Dr. Stockmann and his brother, the mayor, clash over the damaging report of pollution.

Dr. Stockmann and his family decide to stay
and fight for the truth.

CHARACTERS

MORTEN KIIL, *Mrs. Stockmann's father*

BILLING, *a junior newspaper editor*

MRS. STOCKMANN, *wife of* DR. STOCKMANN

PETER STOCKMANN, DR. STOCKMANN'S *brother, the Mayor*

HOVSTAD, *Editor of the People's Daily Messenger*

DR. STOCKMANN, *medical officer of the Baths*

MORTEN
EJLIF } *sons of* DR. *and* MRS. STOCKMANN

CAPTAIN HORSTER, *a ship's captain*

PETRA, *daughter of* DR. *and* MRS. STOCKMANN, *a teacher*

ASLAKSEN, *a publisher*

THE DRUNK

TOWNSPEOPLE

The action takes place in a Norwegian town.

AN ENEMY OF THE PEOPLE

ACT ONE

SCENE ONE

It is evening. DR. STOCKMANN's *living-room is simply but cheerfully furnished. A doorway* U. R. *leads into the entrance hall, which extends from the front door to the dining-room. Only a small part of the hallway is seen* U. R., *but there is a passageway extending back-stage from the front door to the dining-room. This dining-room will be described below. The point is that the passage-way is practical for actors, but unseen by the audience. There is a doorway or archway* U. L. *which leads into the dining-room. Just inside this doorway we see the* R. *end of a dining-room table. There is one dining-room chair downstage, one at* R. *of the table and two just above. A short distance up-stage of the end of the table that is visible to the audience is a sideboard or table with one chair on each side of it. The* R. *end of the dining-room table, the one visible to the audience, stands about halfway between* R. *and* L. *side of the sideboard or table. Down* L., *about two-thirds of the way to the curtain-line, is another door which leads into* STOCKMANN's *study and other rooms of the house.* U. L., *fitting into the corner of the room, is a tiled stove. Somewhat below this and to* R., *is a sofa with a table behind it.* D. L. *below door is an armchair, and near it another small chair. In* R. *foreground, somewhat to* R. *of* C., *are two chairs, a small table between them, on which stand a lamp and a bowl of apples. A bay window is in* R. *wall about halfway down-stage, and immediately below this is a bench or window seat.*

As the curtain rises KIIL *is busily eating in the dining room.* BILLING *is watching him.* KIIL *quickly rises and goes around* BILLING *to his coat and hat which are lying on upstage end of sofa.*

BILLING: (*Following him.*). You sure eat fast, Mr. Kiil!

KIIL: Eating don't get you anywhere, boy. (BILLING *helps him with his coat.*) Tell my daughter I went home.

BILLING: All right. (*He returns to dining-room and begins to eat.* KIIL *crosses to* D. R. *of* R. C. *table, sees apple, stops, takes it, bites it, likes it, takes another, which he puts into his pocket. Starts toward door* U. R. *but circles back to table and takes a third apple, which he puts into his pocket. He notices tobacco humidor on table, looks slyly up at dining-room, comes* D. *to* L. *of table and covertly fills his coat pocket with tobacco. As he sets the humidor down,* CATHERINE *enters* D. L. KIIL *starts off* U. R. CATHERINE *starts to put on apron.*)

CATHERINE: (*Crosses* D. C.). Father! You're not going, are you?

KIIL: Got all kinds of business to tend to.

CATHERINE: Oh, you're only going to sit alone in your room and you know it! Stay—Mr. Billing's here, and Mr. Hovstad's coming; it'll be interesting for you.

KIIL: No, I got all kinds of business. Only reason I come over was the butcher told me you bought roast beef today. And it was very tasty, dear.

CATHERINE: Why don't you wait for Tom? He only went for a little walk.

KIIL: (*Points to tobacco can on table.*). You suppose he'd mind if I filled my pipe?

CATHERINE: Oh, help yourself! (*He does so.*) And why don't you take some apples? (*Offering him bowl of apples.*) You should always have some fruit in your room, go ahead.

KIIL: No, no, wouldn't think of it.

40 CATHERINE: Why don't you move in with us, Father? I often wonder if you're eating.

KIIL: I'm eating. Well . . . (*Doorbell rings* U. R.) See you soon, Catherine.

CATHERINE: (*Crosses* U. C. *to door* U. R.) That must be Hovstad.

(KIIL *steps* R. *and lights his pipe.*)

PETER: (*Entering hall.*) . Good evening, Catherine. How are you tonight? (*Sees* KIIL.) Mr. Kiil!

KIIL: Your Honor! (*Takes big bite out of apple and goes out* U. R.)

50 CATHERINE: You mustn't mind him, Peter. He's getting terribly old. Wouldn't you like some supper?

PETER STOCKMANN (*Sees* BILLING *who has stepped into dining-room archway and given a suggestion of a salute.*). No . . . no, thanks.

CATHERINE: (*Nervously, quietly.*). He just sort of dropped by, Peter.

PETER: (CATHERINE *has taken his coat and hangs it up in* U. R. *hall.*). That's all right. I can't take

60 hot food in the evening, anyway. I stick to my tea and toast. Much healthier and more economical.

CATHERINE: (*Smiling.*). You sound as though Tom and I threw money out the window.

PETER: (*Crossing* D. C., *looks* U. *and then to* D. L. *door.*). Not you, Catherine. He wouldn't be home, would he?

CATHERINE: (*Following him.*). He went for a little walk with the boys.

70 PETER: You don't think that's dangerous—right after dinner? (*Loud knocking on door.* CATHERINE *crosses* U. R. *to door.*) *That* sounds like my brother. (PETER *crosses* R. C.)

CATHERINE: Tom? He hasn't knocked on the door for ten years. (HOVSTAD *enters* U. R., *coat and hat in hand.*) Mr. Hovstad! Come in, please.

HOVSTAD: (*Handing her hat and coat, then crossing* D.

R. *to* R. *of* PETER. CATHERINE *hangs up clothes in hallway* U. R.). Sorry I'm late. I was held up at the printing shop. (*A little surprised.*) Good 80 evening, Your honor. (CATHERINE *crosses* U. *around* R. *table to* L. *of* PETER.)

PETER: (*Sitting in* R. C. *chair.*). Hovstad. On business, no doubt.

HOVSTAD: Partly. It's about an article for the paper . . .

PETER: Ha! I didn't doubt it. I understand my brother has become a very prolific contributor to—what do you call it—(*Sarcastically.*) *The People's Daily Liberator?* 90

HOVSTAD: (*Holding his ground. Crosses* PETER.). *The People's Daily Messenger*, sir? (*Turning to* PETER.) The Doctor sometimes honors the *Messenger* when he wants to uncover the real truth of some subject.

PETER: The truth. Oh, yes, I see . . .

CATHERINE: (*Nervously crossing* D. *to* HOVSTAD.). Would you like to . . . (*Points to dining-room.*)

HOVSTAD: No, thanks.

PETER: I don't want you to think I blame the Doctor 100 for using your columns. After all, every performer goes for the audience that applauds him most. It's really not your paper I have anything against, Mr. Hovstad. (CATHERINE *busies herself with little housework things on sofa table, crossing from* D. *end of sofa to* U. *end.*)

HOVSTAD: I really didn't think so, Your Honor.

PETER: As a matter of fact, I happen to admire the spirit of tolerance in our town—it's magnificent. Just don't forget that we have it because we all 110 believe in the same thing; it brings us together.

HOVSTAD: Kirsten Springs, you mean?

PETER: The Springs, Mr. Hovstad, our wonderful new Springs. They've changed the soul of this town. Mark my words, Kirsten Springs are going to put us on the map, and there's no question about it.

CATHERINE: (*Moving* U. C. *of sofa table.*). That's what Tom says, too.

PETER: Everything is shooting ahead; real estate 120 going up, money changing hands every hour, business humming . . .

HOVSTAD: And no more unemployment.

PETER: Right. Give us a really good summer and sick people will be coming here in carloads, the

Springs will turn into a regular fad, a new Carlsbad. And for once, the well-to-do people won't be the only ones paying taxes in this town.

HOVSTAD: I hear reservations are really starting to come in?

PETER: Coming in every day. Looks very promising, very promising.

HOVSTAD: That's fine. (*To* CATHERINE.) Then the Doctor's article will come in handy.

PETER: He's written something again?

HOVSTAD: No, it's a piece he wrote during the winter recommending the water. But at the time, I let the article lie . . .

PETER: Why, some hitch in it?

HOVSTAD: Oh, no, I just thought it would have a bigger effect in the spring, when people start planning for the summer.

PETER: That's smart, Mr. Hovstad, very smart.

CATHERINE: (*Crossing* D. *to* L. *of* HOVSTAD.). Tom is always so full of ideas about the Springs; every day he . . .

PETER: Well, he ought to be, he gets his salary from the Springs, my dear.

HOVSTAD: Oh, I think it's more than that, don't you? Doctor Stockmann *created* Kirsten Springs.

PETER: (*Looking at* HOVSTAD.). You don't say! I've been hearing that lately, but I think I had a certain modest part . . .

CATHERINE: Oh, Tom always says . . .

HOVSTAD: I only meant the original idea was . . .

PETER: (*Rises, crosses* D. L.). My good brother is never at a loss for ideas. All sorts of ideas. But when it comes to putting them into action you need another kind of man, and I did think that at least people in this house would . . .

CATHERINE: But, Peter, dear . . . we didn't mean to . . . (*To* HOVSTAD, *helping him off stage toward dining-room a little.*) Go get yourself a bite, Mr. Hovstad, my husband will be here any minute.

HOVSTAD: (*Overlapping a little.*). Thank you, maybe just a little something . . . (*Enters dining-room through* U. L. *doorway, sits in* D. *chair.*)

PETER: (*Lowering his voice.*). Isn't it remarkable . . . Why is it that people without background can never learn tact?

CATHERINE: Why upset yourself, Peter? Can't you and Thomas share the honor, like good brothers?

PETER: The trouble is that certain men are never satisfied to share, Catherine.

CATHERINE: Nonsense. You've always gotten along beautifully with Tom . . . (DOCTOR THOMAS STOCKMANN, MORTEN, EJLIF *and* CAPTAIN HORSTER *are heard approaching.* CATHERINE *crosses up to hall* U. R.) That must be him now. (STOCKMANN, HORSTER *and the boys,* EJLIF *and* MORTEN, *enter* U. R. *joking and laughing, about racing each other home.*)

STOCKMANN: (*Taking off coat, revealing smoking-jacket underneath.*). Hey, Catherine! Here's another guest for you! Here's a hanger for your coat, Captain. (*During following,* CATHERINE *is trying to tell* STOCKMANN *about* PETER.)

HORSTER: I don't need . . .

STOCKMANN: Oh, that's right, you don't wear overcoats! (*Claps* MORTEN *on the behind.* MORTEN *spars a moment.*) Go on in, boys. You kids must be hungry all over again. (*Boys exit* U. R. *and appear in dining-room.*) Come here, Captain Horster, I want you to get a look at this roast. (HORSTER *crosses* L. *to dining-room, sits in* U. *chair.*)

CATHERINE: Tom, dear . . . (*Motions toward* PETER.)

STOCKMANN: (*Turns, sees* PETER.) Oh, Peter . . . (*Crosses above* R. *chairs to* PETER C., *holding out his hand.*) Say, now, this is really nice. (CATHERINE *crosses* D. R. *in front of table.*)

PETER: I'll have to go in a minute.

STOCKMANN: (*Crossing* R. *to* CATHERINE.) Oh, nonsense, not with the toddy on the table. You haven't forgotten the toddy, have you, Catherine? (*Kisses* CATHERINE.)

CATHERINE: (*Crossing* U. *dining-room.*). Of course not, I've got the water boiling. (*Goes into dining-room, closes portieres.*)

PETER: Toddy, too?!

STOCKMANN: (*Crosses to* PETER, *takes his arm, seats him in* R. C. *chair.*). Sure, just sit down and make yourself at home.

PETER: (*Resisting a little, but sitting.*). No thanks, I don't go in for drinking parties.

STOCKMANN: (*At* L. *of* PETER.). But this is no party.

PETER: What else do you call it? (*Looks toward dining-room.*) It's extraordinary how you people can consume all this food and live.

STOCKMANN: Why? What's finer than to watch young people eat! (*Nudging* PETER.) Peter, those are the fellows who are going to stir up the whole future.

PETER: Is that so?! What's there to stir up?

STOCKMANN: Don't worry, they'll let us know when the times comes. Old idiots like you and me, we'll be left behind like . . .

PETER: I've never been called *that* before.

STOCKMANN: (*Fixing book in bookcase.*). Oh, Peter, don't jump on me every minute, will you? You know your trouble, Peter—your impressions are blunted. You ought to sit up there in that crooked corner of the North for five years like I did and then come back here. It's like watching the first seven days of Creation.

PETER: Here?!

STOCKMANN: Things to work and fight for, Peter! Without that, you're dead. (*Calling.*) Catherine, are you sure the mailman came today?

CATHERINE: (*From dining-room.*). There wasn't any mail today.

STOCKMANN: (*Crossing to L. of PETER.*). And another thing, Peter, a good income; *that's* something you learn to value after you've lived on a starvation diet.

PETER: When did you starve?

STOCKMANN: Damned near! It was pretty tough going a lot of the time up there. And now, to be able to live like a prince—tonight, for instance, we had roast beef for dinner and by God, there was enough left for supper, too! (*Takes PETER's arm, tries to push him to dining-room.*) Please have a piece—come here.

PETER: (*At C.*) Oh, no, no—please, certainly not.

STOCKMANN: At least, let me show it to you! Come in here, we even have a table-cloth.

PETER: I saw it.

STOCKMANN: (*Offering fruit to PETER.*) Live to the hilt! That's my motto. Anyway, Catherine says I'm earning almost as much as we spend.

PETER: (*Declining fruit.*). Well, you're improving.

STOCKMANN: (*Crossing PETER U. to dining-room.*). Why can't I give myself the pleasure of having young interesting people around me? You'll see—when Hovstad comes in, we'll talk and . . .

PETER: (*Sitting in R. C. chair.*). Oh, yes, Hovstad. That reminds me—he told me he was going to print one of your articles.

STOCKMANN: One of my articles?

PETER: Yes, about the Springs—an article you wrote during the winter.

STOCKMANN: (*Checking his appointment book in front of sofa.*) Oh, that one—in the first place, I don't want that one printed right now.

PETER: No? It sounded to me as though it would be very timely.

STOCKMANN: Under normal conditions maybe so.

PETER: Well, what's abnormal about the conditions now?

STOCKMANN: (*In front of sofa, turns.*). I can't say that for the moment, Peter—at least not tonight. There could be a great deal abnormal about conditions—then again, there could be nothing at all.

PETER: Well, you've managed to sound mysterious. Is there anything wrong? Something you are keeping from me? Because I wish once in a while you'd remind yourself that I am chairman of the board for the Springs, as well as Mayor.

STOCKMANN: And I'd like you to remember that, Peter. (*Crosses D. behind sofa.*) Look, let's not get into each other's hair.

PETER: For God's sake, no—I don't make a habit of getting into people's *hair*. But I'd like to underline that everything concerning Kirsten Springs must be treated in a businesslike manner, through the proper channels and dealt with by the legally constituted authorities. I can't allow anything done behind my back in a roundabout way.

STOCKMANN: (*Crossing back to PETER with bowl of nuts, offering him some.*). When did I ever go behind your back, Peter?

PETER: (*Declining nuts, but STOCKMANN takes some.*). You have an ingrained tendency to go *your own way*, Thomas, and that simply can't go on in a well-organized society. The individual really must subordinate himself to the overall—or more accurately (*Indicating self.*) to the authorities who are in charge of the general welfare.

STOCKMANN: (*Crossing back behind sofa.*). Well, that's probably so, (*Cracks nut.*) but how the hell does that concern me, Peter?

PETER: (*Rises, crosses U. a step.*). My dear Thomas, this is exactly what you will never learn—but you had better watch out because some day you might pay dearly for it. (*Crosses U. R. to coat in hall U. R.*) Now I've said it—good-bye.

STOCKMANN: Are you out of your mind? (*Follows PETER U. R. C. behind table, carrying bowl.*) You're absolutely on the wrong track.

PETER: I am usually not—anyway, may I be excused? (*Nods into dining-room.*) Good-bye, Catherine. Good evening, gentlemen. (*He leaves* U. R. *The men mumble farewells.*)

CATHERINE: (*Entering from dining-room.*). He left?

STOCKMANN: (*Surprised at* PETER'S *behavior. Above* R. *chair.*). Yes, he did, and thoroughly burned up.

CATHERINE: (*At* U. C.). What'd you do to him now?

330 STOCKMANN: What does he want from me? He can't expect me to give him an accounting of every move I make—every thought I think, until I'm ready to do it.

CATHERINE: Why? What should you give him an accounting of?

STOCKMANN: Just leave that to me, Catherine. (*Crosses to bay window* R., *looking out, setting bowl on window seat.*) It is peculiar that the mailman didn't come today. (CATHERINE *goes to dining-*
340 *room. Men enter downstage from dining-room, opening portieres:* HORSTER L. *of* HOVSTAD; HOVSTAD *crosses* D. *to* L. *of* R. C. *chair;* BILLING *in front of* D. *end of sofa;* EJLIF *and* MORTEN R. *of* L. *chair.*)

BILLING: (*Stretching out his arms.*). After a meal like that, by God, I feel like a new man. This house is so . . .

HOVSTAD: (*Cutting him off.*). The Mayor certainly wasn't in a glowing mood tonight.

STOCKMANN: It's his stomach—he has a lousy
350 digestion.

HOVSTAD: (*Indicating* BILLING *and self.*). I think two editors from the *People's Daily Messenger* didn't help, either.

STOCKMANN: No, it's just that Peter is a lonely man —poor fellow, all he knows is official business and duties and then all that damn weak tea that he pours into himself. Catherine, may we have the toddy?

CATHERINE: (*From dining-room.*). I'm just getting it.

360 STOCKMANN: (*Takes* HORSTER *to sofa, crossing* HOVSTAD *and* BILLING.). Sit down here on the couch with me, Captain Horster—a rare guest like you—sit here. Sit down, friends. (HORSTER *sits on* D. *end of sofa.*)

HORSTER: This used to be such an ugly house; suddenly it's beautiful!

BILLING: (*To* HORSTER, *intimately, indicating* STOCKMANN.). Great man. (STOCKMANN, *embarrassed, turns to see to whom* BILLING *refers, sits;*

BILLING *crosses* U. *around to* R. *chair, sits. The men* 370 *rise as* CATHERINE *brings in from dining-rrom tray with pot, glasses, three bottles and sets it on table behind sofa, then crosses and sits in* L. *chair.*)

CATHERINE: (*Entering.*). Here you are. Help yourselves.

STOCKMANN: (*Fixing toddy.*). We sure will. (EJLIF *is tucking in* MORTEN'S *sweater.*) And the cigars, Ejlif—you know where the box is—and, Morten, get my pipe. (MORTEN *and* EJLIF *exit* L. *and* EJLIF *just overhears* STOCKMANN'S *suspicions about cigars.*) 380 I have a sneaking suspicion that Ejlif is snitching a cigar now and then, but I don't pay any attention. (MORTEN *re-enters* L. *and stands on* STOCKMANN'S R. *with his pipe.*) Catherine, you know where I put it? Oh, he's got it. Good boys! (EJLIF *re-enters* L. *with cigars, offers them to* HORSTER, HOVSTAD *and* BILLING *then sits* U. *of* MORTEN *on window seat* R. *eating nuts from bowl.* STOCKMANN *gives toddy to* HOVSTAD, BILLING *and* HORSTER *then returns to* U. *of sofa.*) Help yourselves, fellows. 390 I'll stick to the pipe—this one's gone through plenty of blizzards with me up in the north. (*Sits* U. *end of sofa.*) Skol! (BILLING *and* HOVSTAD *clink glasses,* HORSTER *and* STOCKMANN *clink glasses. All drink.* STOCKMANN *looks around.*) Home! (*All look at* STOCKMANN.) What an invention, heh!

CATHERINE: (*After a moment.*). Are you sailing soon, Captain Horster?

HORSTER: I expect to be ready next week.

CATHERINE: And then to America, Captain? 400

HORSTER: Yes, that's the plan.

BILLING: Oh, then you won't be home for the new election?

HORSTER: Is there going to be another election?

BILLING: Don't you know? (STOCKMANN *lights pipe.*)

HORSTER: No, I don't get mixed up in those things.

BILLING: But you are interested in public affairs, aren't you?

HORSTER: Frankly, I don't understand a thing about it. 410

CATHERINE: (*Sympathetically.*). Neither do I, Captain; maybe that's why I'm always to glad to see you.

BILLING: Just the same, you ought to vote, Captain.

HORSTER: Even if I don't understand anything about it?

BILLING: Understand? What do you mean by that? Society, Captain, is like a ship—every man should do something to help navigate the ship.

420 HORSTER: That may be all right on shore, but on board a ship it doesn't work out so well. (PETRA, *carrying hat and coat with textbooks and notepads under her arm, enters from hall* U. R.)

PETRA: Good evening. (*Men rise*, PETRA *removes her coat and hat and places books on hall chair* U. R. *There are mutual greetings.*)

STOCKMANN: (*Warmly.*). Good evening, Petra.

PETRA: (*Crosses* C. *to* STOCKMANN, *throwing kiss to* CATHERINE, *which she throws back.*) And here you

430 are lying around like lizards while I'm out slaving.

STOCKMANN: (*Embracing* PETRA *at* C.). Well, you come and be a lizard, too. (*To company.*) I look at her and I say to myself—how did I do it!

BILLING: (*Close to* HOVSTAD.). Great young woman. (*Crosses to* PETRA.) Shall I mix a toddy for you?

PETRA: Thank you, I had better do it myself—you always mix it too strong. Oh, Father, I forgot—I have a letter for you. (*Goes to hall* U. R. *brings*

440 *down book with letter in it.*)

STOCKMANN: (*Crosses after her. Alerted, sets drink on table, returns to* C.). Who's it from?

PETRA: (*Takes letter, backs* D. R. *then* C., STOCKMANN *follows her.*). I met the mailman on the way to school this morning and he gave me your mail, too, and I just didn't have time to run back.

STOCKMANN: And you don't give it to me until now!

450 PETRA: I really didn't have time to run back, Father.

CATHERINE: (*Standing.*). If she didn't have time . . .

STOCKMANN: Let's see it—come on, child . . . (*Slaps* PETRA's *fanny, takes letter, looks at envelope, recognizes it, crosses* D. R. C.) Yes, indeed.

CATHERINE: Is that the one you've been waiting for?

STOCKMANN: (*Crossing* L. *to study.*). I'll be right back. There wouldn't be a light on in my room, would

460 there? (CATHERINE *takes his glasses out of his pocket as he goes out.*)

CATHERINE: The lamp is on the desk burning away. (*Turns* C.)

STOCKMANN: (*Re-entering* L.). Please excuse me for a moment. (CATHERINE *puts his glasses in his hand as he goes back out* L. *Closes door.* CATHERINE *turns.*).

PETRA: What's that, Mother? (PETRA *crosses slowly to table, fixes drink.*)

CATHERINE: I don't know. The last couple of days he has been asking again and again about the mailman. 470

BILLING: Probably an out-of-town patient of his. (CATHERINE *sits.*)

PETRA: Poor Father, he's got much too much to do. (*She mixes her drink, comes around sofa.*) This ought to taste good.

HOVSTAD: (*Crossing to* PETRA.). By the way, what happened to that English novel you were to translate for us? 480

PETRA: I started to, but I got so busy . . .

HOVSTAD: Oh, have you been teaching evening school again?

PETRA: Two hours a night.

BILLING: Plus the high school every day?

PETRA: Yes, five hours, and every night a pile of lessons to correct . . .

CATHERINE: She never stops going.

HOVSTAD: Maybe that's why I always think of you 490 as kind of breathless, and . . . well, breathless.

PETRA: I love it. I get so wonderfully tired. (PETRA *sits.*)

BILLING: (*To* HORSTER.). She looks tired. (BILLING *crosses* R. *to* R. *chair, all sit.*)

MORTEN: (*Crossing to in front of* BILLING.). You must be a wicked woman, Petra. (BILLING *beckons* MORTEN, *who approaches;* EJLIF *follows with nut bowl.*)

PETRA: (*Laughing.*). Wicked?

MORTEN: You work so much. My teacher says that work is a punishment for our sins. 500

EJLIF: And you believe that?

CATHERINE: Ejlif! Of course he believes his teacher.

BILLING: (*Smiling.*). Don't stop him . . .

HOVSTAD: Don't you like to work, Morten?

MORTEN: Work? No.

HOVSTAD: Then what will you ever amount to in this world?

MORTEN: Me? I'm going to be a Viking.

EJLIF: You can't! You'd have to be a heathen!

MORTEN: So I'll be a heathen. 510

CATHERINE: (*Rising, crossing* R.; *men rise.*).   I think it's getting late, boys . . .

BILLING: I agree with you, Morten; I think . . .

CATHERINE: (*Interrupting* BILLING.). You certainly don't, Mr. Billing.

BILLING: Yes, by God, I do. I'm a real heathen and proud of it. (*Lifts* MORTEN. CATHERINE *tries to stop this violent exercise.*) You'll see, pretty soon we are all going to be heathens.

520 MORTEN: And then we can do anything we want——

BILLING: *Right!* You see, Morten . . .

CATHERINE: (*Interrupting.*). Don't you have any homework for tomorrow, boys? Better go in and do it.

EJLIF: Oh, can't we stay in here awhile?

CATHERINE: (*Takes bowl.*). No, neither of you—now run along.

EJLIF: Good night.

530 MORTEN: Good night. But I don't have any homework . . . (*Boys exit into hall* U. R. HOVSTAD *edges over to* PETRA. CATHERINE *picks up nut bowl, sets it on* R. *table.*)

HOVSTAD: You don't really think it hurts them to listen to such talk, do you? (*Enter* STOCKMANN L.)

CATHERINE: I don't know, but I don't like it. (*As* STOCKMANN *breaks for door* L.) Tom!

STOCKMANN: (*Crossing* C., *open letter in his hand.*) Boys, there is going to be news in this town!

540 BILLING: News?

CATHERINE: (*Crossing to* STOCKMANN *at* C.). What kind of news?   (*Together.*)

STOCKMANN: Hunh? — A terrific discovery, Catherine.

HOVSTAD: Really?

CATHERINE: That you made?   (*Together.*)

STOCKMANN: (*At* C. *of table.*). That I made. (*Walks back and forth.*) Now let the baboons running this town call me a lunatic! Now they'd better

550 watch out. Oh, how the mighty have fallen! (U. *above* R. *table.*)

PETRA: What is it, Father?

STOCKMANN: Oh, if Peter were only here! Now you'll see how human beings can walk around and make judgments like blind rats.

HOVSTAD: What in the world's happened, Doctor?

STOCKMANN: (*Above table.*). It is the general opinion, isn't it, that our town is a sound and healthy spot?

560 HOVSTAD: Of course.

CATHERINE: What happened?

STOCKMANN: Even a rather unusually healthy spot——Oh, God . . . (*Throws his arms up, holding glasses in* L. *hand,* CATHERINE *takes glasses from*

him, puts them in his pocket.) a place that can be recommended, not only to all people but sick people.

CATHERINE: But, Tom, what are you——?

STOCKMANN: And we certainly have recommended it. I myself have written and written about it, in the *People's Messenger*, pamphlets . . .   570

HOVSTAD: Yes, yes, but, Doctor, what are you trying to say?

STOCKMANN: The miraculous Springs that cost such a fortune to build. The whole Health Institute is a pest hole.

PETRA: Father! The Springs?

CATHERINE: Our Springs?   (*Together.*)

BILLING: That's unbelievable!

STOCKMANN: (*Crossing* R. *to* D. R., *then* L. *to* HORSTER.). You know the filth up in Windmill   580 Valley—that stuff that has such a stinking smell? It comes down from the tannery up there and the same damn poisonous mess comes right out into (*To* HORSTER.) the blessed, miraculous water we're supposed to *cure* people with!

HORSTER: You mean actually where our beaches are?

STOCKMANN: (*At* D. L.). Exactly.

HOVSTAD: How are you so sure about this, Doctor?   590

STOCKMANN: (*Crossing* C. *to* R. *of* HOVSTAD.). I had a suspicion about it a long time ago—last year there were too many sick cases among the visitors; typhoid and gastric disturbances.

CATHERINE: That *did* happen. (*To* BILLING.) I remember Mrs. Svensen's niece . . .

STOCKMANN: (*Crossing to* CATHERINE.). Yes, dear. At the time we thought that the visitors brought the bug, but later this winter I got a new idea and I started investigating the water.   600

CATHERINE: So that's what you've been working on!

STOCKMANN: I sent samples of the water to the University for an exact chemical analysis.

HOVSTAD: And that's what you have received?

STOCKMANN: (*Showing letter.*). This is it. It proves the existence of infectious organic matter in the water. (*A little pause.* HOVSTAD *is looking at* BILLING.)

CATHERINE: Well, thank God you discovered it in   610 time.

STOCKMANN: I think we can say that, Catherine.

CATHERINE: Isn't it wonderful!

HOVSTAD. And what do you intend to do now, Doctor?

STOCKMANN: Put the thing right, of course.

HOVSTAD: Do you think that can be done?

STOCKMANN: If not, the whole Institute is useless—but there's nothing to worry about—I am quite clear on what has to be done.

CATHERINE: But, Tom, why'd you keep it so secret?

STOCKMANN: What'd you want me to do?—go out and shoot my mouth off before I really knew? No, thanks, I'm not that crazy. (*He walks around, rubbing his hands.*) You don't realize what this means, Catherine—(*Crosses to* BILLING.) the whole water system has got to be changed.

CATHERINE: The *whole* water system? (*Fades to* L. *above sofa table.*)

STOCKMANN: The whole water system. The intake is too low, it's got to be raised to a much higher spot. The whole construction's got to be ripped out!

PETRA: Well, Dad, at least you can prove they should have listened to you!

STOCKMANN: Ha, she remembers!

CATHERINE: That's right, you did warn them . . .

STOCKMANN: Of course I warned them! When they started the damned thing I told them not to build it down there. But who am I, a mere scientist to tell politicians where to build a health institute! Well, now they're going to get it both barrels!

BILLING: This is tremendous . . . (*To* HORSTER.) He's a great man!

STOCKMANN: (*Turns.*). It's bigger than tremendous. Wait'll they see this. (*Crosses to* PETRA.) Petra, my report is on my desk . . .(PETRA *sets glass down, runs out* L.) And envelopes, Catherine! (CATHERINE *goes into dining-room;* PETRA *returns with report, gives it to* STOCKMANN.) Gentlemen, this final proof from the University and my report . . . (*Flicks pages.*) five solid, explosive pages . . .

CATHERINE: (*Returns, hands him envelopes.*). Is that big enough?

STOCKMANN: Fine. Right to the Board of Directors! (*Hands report, letter to* CATHERINE.) Will you give this to the maid . . . what's her name again?

CATHERINE: Randine, dear, Randine . . .

STOCKMANN: Tell our darling Randine to wipe her nose and run over to the Mayor right now.

(CATHERINE *stands looking at him as though she'd had a little pain.*) What's the matter, dear?

CATHERINE: I don't know . . .

PETRA: What's Uncle Peter going to say to this?

CATHERINE: That's what I'm wondering.

STOCKMANN: What can he say! He ought to be damn glad that such an important fact is brought out before we start an epidemic. Hurry, dear! (CATHERINE *goes into dining-room.*)

HOVSTAD: (*Crossing* R. *from behind sofa between* STOCKMANN *and* PETRA.) I would like to put a brief item about this discovery in the *Messenger*.

STOCKMANN: Yes, now I'd really be grateful for it.

HOVSTAD: Because the public ought to know soon.

STOCKMANN: Right away.

BILLING: By God, you'll be the leading man in this town, Doctor.

STOCKMANN: (*Crossing* BILLING *to* D. R.). Oh, there was nothing to it. Every detective gets a lucky break once in his life. But just the same, I . . .

BILLING: Hovstad, don't you think the town ought to pay Dr. Stockmann some tribute?

STOCKMANN: Oh, no, no . . .

HOVSTAD: Let's all put in a word for . . .

BILLING: (*Crossing* D. R. PETRA *takes drink from sofa table.*). I'll talk to Aslaksen about it. (CATHERINE *enters, crosses* C. HOVSTAD *picks up drink from* R. *table.*)

STOCKMANN: (*Crossing* C.). No, no, fellows, no fooling around. I won't put up with any commotion. Even if the Board of Directors want to give me an increase, I won't take it . . . (*To* CATHERINE.) I just won't take it, Catherine.

CATHERINE: That's right, Tom.

PETRA: (*Lifting glass.*). Skol, Father!

ALL: Skol, Doctor. (*They drink.*)

HORSTER: Doctor, I hope this will bring you great honor and pleasure.

STOCKMANN: Thanks, friends, thanks. There's one blessing above all others: to have earned the respect of one's neighbor is . . . is . . . Catherine, I'm going to dance! (*He grabs* CATHERINE, *starts singing and whirls her around. On second phrase,* PETRA *joins the circle. Boys enter* L., *go* R. *and stand on window seat.* HORSTER, HOVSTAD *and* BILLING *join the dancing circle. All are singing.*)

CATHERINE: (*Seeing boys, screams.*). Children! (*Boys run out* L.)

FAST CURTAIN

SCENE TWO

SCENE: *The same. The following morning.*

CATHERINE: (*Entering from dining-room with sealed letter, crosses above sofa to* D. L. *door.*). Are you there, Tom?

STOCKMANN: (*Off* L.). I just got in. (*Entering* D. L.; *his coat is buttoned wrong. Closes door.*) What's up?

CATHERINE: (*Giving him letter.*). From Peter. It just came.

STOCKMANN: (*Taking letter.*). Peter! Oh, let's see. (*Opens envelope, reads letter, crosses* C., *holding up letter to catch* R. *sunlight.*) "I am returning herewith the report you submitted . . . "

CATHERINE: (*Following him.*). Well, what does he say? Don't stand there!

STOCKMANN: (*Putting letter in his pocket.*). He just says he'll come around this afternoon.

CATHERINE: (*Buttoning his coat correctly.*). Oh. Well, maybe you ought to try to remember to be home then.

STOCKMANN: Oh, I sure will. I'm through with my morning visits, anyway.

CATHERINE: I'm dying to see how he's going to take it.

STOCKMANN: Why, is there any doubt? He'll probably make it look like he made the discovery, not me.

CATHERINE: But aren't you a little bit afraid of that?

STOCKMANN: Oh, underneath he'll be happy, Catherine. (*Kisses her. One arm is around her.*) It's just that Peter is so damn afraid that somebody else is going to do something good for this town.

CATHERINE: I wish you'd go out of your way and share the honors with him. Couldn't we say that he put you on the right track or something? (KIIL *enters hallway* U. R.)

STOCKMANN: (*Embracing* CATHERINE.). Oh, I don't mind—as long as it makes everybody happy.

KIIL: (*Pokes head into room from hall* U. R., *chuckling.*). Is it really true? (*Crosses* D. R. C.)

CATHERINE: (*Crosses* U. *of* R. C. *table.*). Father! Come on in.

STOCKMANN: (*A step to* KIIL.). Well, good morning!

KIIL: It better be true, or I'm going.

STOCKMANN: What had better be true?

KIIL: (*Crossing to* D. *of* R. *table.*). This crazy story about the water system. Is it true?

CATHERINE: Of course it's true.

STOCKMANN: How did you find out about it?

KIIL: Petra came flying by on her way to school this morning.

STOCKMANN: Oh, she did?

KIIL: Yes. I thought she was trying to make a fool out of me . . .

CATHERINE: Now, Father, why would she do that?

KIIL: Nothing pleases young people more than to make fools out of old people. But this is true, eh?

STOCKMANN: Of course it's true——(*Seating* KIIL *in* R.C. *chair.* CATHERINE *is above* R. *table.*) Sit down here. It's pretty lucky for the town, eh?

KIIL: (*Fighting his laughter.*). Lucky for the town?!

STOCKMANN: I mean that I made the discovery before it was too late.

KIIL: Tom, I never thought you had the imagination to pull your own brother's leg like this.

STOCKMANN: Pull his leg?

CATHERINE: But, Father, he's not . . .

KIIL: How does it go now? Let me get it straight. There's some kind of . . . like cockroaches in the waterpipes . . . ?

STOCKMANN: (*Laughing.*). No, not cockroaches . . .

KIIL: Well, some kind of little animals . . .

CATHERINE: Bacteria, Father . . .

KIIL: Ah, but a whole mess of them, eh?

STOCKMANN: Oh, there'd be millions and millions.

KIIL: And nobody can see them but you, is that it?

STOCKMANN: Yes, that's . . . well, of course, anybody with a micro . . . (*Breaks off.*) What are you laughing at?

CATHERINE: (*Smiling at* KIIL.). You don't understand, Father, nobody can actually see bacteria, but that doesn't mean they're not there . . .

KIIL: (*Chuckling.*). Good girl, you stick with him. By God, this is the best thing I ever heard in my life!

STOCKMANN: (*Smiling.*). What do you mean?

KIIL: But tell me, you think you are going to get your brother to actually believe this?

STOCKMANN: Well, we'll see soon enough!

KIIL: You really think he's that crazy?

STOCKMANN: I hope the whole town will be that "crazy," Morten.

KIIL: Ya, they probaby are, and it'll serve them right, too—they think they're so much smarter than us old-timers. Your good brother ordered them to bounce me out of the council, so they chased me out like a dog. (*Rising.*) Make jackasses out of all of them, Stockmann.

100   STOCKMANN: (*Interrupting.*). Yes, but Morten . . .

KIIL: Long-eared, short-tailed jackasses . . . Stockmann, if you can make the Mayor and his elegant friends grab at this bait, I will give a couple hundred crowns to charity, and right now, right on the spot.

STOCKMANN: (*Interrupting,* KIIL *crosses* L. C.). Well, that would be very kind of you, but I'm . . .

KIIL: I haven't got much to play around with, but if you can pull the rug out from under him with

110   this cockroach business, I'll give at least fifty crowns to charity. (HOVSTAD *enters the hall* U. R.) Maybe this'll teach them to put some brains back in City Hall!

HOVSTAD: (*Crossing* D. R.) Good morning! Oh, pardon me——

STOCKMANN: Come on in.

KIIL: (*Crossing to below table.*). Oh, this one is in on it, too?

HOVSTAD: What's that, sir?

120   STOCKMANN: Of course, he's in on it.

KIIL: Couldn't I have guessed that—and it's going to be in the papers, I suppose. You're sure tying down the corners, aren't you? Well, lay it on thick. I've got to go.

STOCKMANN: Oh, no, stay a while, let me explain it to you!

KIIL: (*Crossing* STOCKMANN *to* L. *of* HOVSTAD.) Oh, I get it, don't worry! Only you can see them, heh? That's the best idea I've ever heard in my

130   life. (*He goes out* U. R. CATHERINE *then goes off* R. *through dining-room, appears in hall* U. R. *closing portieres tightly.*)

CATHERINE: (*Laughing.*). But, Father, you don't understand about bacteria . . .

STOCKMANN: (*Laughing.*). The old badger doesn't believe a word of it.

HOVSTAD: What does he think you're doing?

STOCKMANN: Making an idiot out of my brother, imagine that?

140   HOVSTAD: (*Crossing* STOCKMANN *to* C.). You got a few minutes?

STOCKMANN: Sure, as long as you like.

HOVSTAD: Have you heard from the Mayor?

STOCKMANN: Only that he's coming over later.

HOVSTAD: I've been thinking about this since last

night . . . (*Crosses to* STOCKMANN.)

STOCKMANN: Don't say?

HOVSTAD: For you as a medical man, a scientist, this is a really rare opportunity. But I've been wondering if you realize that it ties in with a 150 lot of other things.

STOCKMANN: How do you mean? Sit down—— (*They sit,* STOCKMANN *in* R. *chair,* HOVSTAD *in* R. C. *chair.*) What are you driving at?

HOVSTAD: You said last night that the water comes from impurities in the ground——

STOCKMANN: It comes from the poisonous dump in Windmill Valley.

HOVSTAD: Doctor, I think it comes from an entirely different dump—the same dump that is poison- 160 ing and polluting our whole social life in this town.

STOCKMANN: For God's sake, Hovstad, what are you babbling about?

HOVSTAD: Everything that matters in this town has fallen into the hands of a few bureaucrats.

STOCKMANN: Well, they're not all bureaucrats——

HOVSTAD: They're all rich—all with old reputable names and they've got everything in the palm of their hands. 170

STOCKMANN: Yes, but they happen to have ability and knowledge.

HOVSTAD: Did they show ability and knowledge when they built the water system where they did?

STOCKMANN: No, of course not, but that happened to be a blunder and we'll clear it up now.

HOVSTAD: You really imagine it's going to be as easy as all that?

STOCKMANN: Easy or not easy, it's got to be done. 180

HOVSTAD: Doctor, I've made up my mind to give this whole scandal very special treatment.

STOCKMANN: Now wait—you can't call it a scandal yet.

HOVSTAD: Doctor, when I took over the *People's Messenger,* I swore I'd blow that smug cabal of old, stubborn, self-satisfied fogies to bits. This is the story that can do it.

STOCKMANN: But I still think we owe them a deep debt of gratitude for building the Springs. 190

HOVSTAD: The Mayor being your brother, I wouldn't ordinarily want to touch it, but I know you'd never let that kind of thing obstruct the truth.

STOCKMANN: Of course not, but . . .

HOVSTAD: I want you to understand me. I don't have to tell you I come from a simple family. I know in my bones what the underdog needs —he's got to have a say in the government of society—that's what brings out ability, intelligence, and self-respect in people.

STOCKMANN: I understand that, but . . .

HOVSTAD: I think a newspaper man who turns down any chance to give the underdog a lift is taking on a responsibility that I don't want. (*Rises, paces* C. *and back to table.*) I know perfectly well that in fancy circles they call it agitation, and they can call it anything they like if it makes them happy—but I have my own conscience!

STOCKMANN: (*Interrupting.*) I agree with you, Hovstad . . . (ASLAKSEN *knocks, then enters* U. R.) but this is just the water supply and . . . (STOCKMANN *rises, crosses* R. *and* U.) Damn it, come in.

ASLAKSEN: (*Entering from* U. R.). I beg your pardon, Doctor, if I intrude . . . (STOCKMANN *takes him by* R. *arm and brings him* D. C.)

HOVSTAD: (*Crossing* D. R.) Are you looking for me, Aslaksen?

ASLAKSEN: No, I didn't know you were here. I want to see the Doctor.

STOCKMANN: What can I do for you?

ASLAKSEN: Is it true, Doctor, what I hear from Mr. Billing that you intend to campaign for a better water system?

STOCKMANN: (*Offers chair.*). Yes, for the Institute—but it's not a campaign.

ASLAKSEN: I just wanted to call and tell you that we are behind you one hundred percent.

HOVSTAD: (*To* STOCKMANN.). There, you see . . .

STOCKMANN: Mr. Aslaksen, I thank you with all my heart, but, you see . . .

ASLAKSEN: We can be important, Doctor. When the little businessman wants to push something through, he turns out to be the majority, you know, and it's always good to have the majority on your side.

STOCKMANN: That's certainly true, but I don't understand what this is all about. It seems to me it's a simple, straightforward business. The water . . .

ASLAKSEN: Of course, we intend to behave with moderation, Doctor. I always try to be a moderate and careful man.

STOCKMANN: You are known for that, Mr. Aslaksen, but . . .

ASLAKSEN: Kirsten Springs are becoming a gold mine for this town. Especially for the little businessmen, and that's why, in my capacity as Chairman of the Property Owners' Association . . .

STOCKMANN: Yes . . .

ASLAKSEN: And furthermore, as a representative of the Temperance Society—you probably know, Doctor, that I am active for prohibition.

STOCKMANN: So I've heard.

ASLAKSEN: As a result, I come into contact with all kinds of people, and since I'm known to be a law-abiding and solid citizen, I have a certain influence in this town—(*Advancing a little to* HOVSTAD.) you might even call it a little power.

STOCKMANN: I know that very well, Mr. Aslaksen.

ASLAKSEN: That's why you can see that it would be practically nothing for me to arrange a demonstration.

STOCKMANN: Demonstration? What are you going to demonstrate about?

ASLAKSEN: The citizens of the town complimenting you for bringing this important matter to everybody's attention. Obviously it would have to be done with the utmost moderation so as not to hurt the authorities . . .

HOVSTAD: This could knock the big-bellies right into the garbage can!

ASLAKSEN: (*Crossing to* HOVSTAD.). No indiscretion or extreme aggressiveness toward the authorities, Mr. Hovstad! (HOVSTAD *crosses to window seat* R., *sits, takes notes.*) I don't want any wild-eyed radicalism on this thing. (ASLAKSEN *to* STOCKMANN.) I've had enough of that in my time, and no good ever comes of it, but for a good solid citizen to express his calm, frank and free opinion is something nobody can deny.

STOCKMANN: (*Shaking his hand.*). My dear Aslaksen, I can't tell you how it heartens me to hear this kind of support. I'm happy—I really am—I'm happy. Listen! Wouldn't you like a glass of sherry?

ASLAKSEN: I am a member of the Temperance Society, I——

STOCKMANN: Well, how about a glass of beer?

ASLAKSEN: I don't think I can go quite that far, Doctor. Well, good day, and I want you to remember that the little man is behind you like a wall. You have the solid majority on your side, because when the little man takes over . . .

STOCKMANN: *(Takes his arm, crosses* ASLAKSEN *in front and starts out* U. R.*)*. Thanks for that, Mr. Aslaksen—and good day.

ASLAKSEN: Are you going to the printing shop, Mr. Hovstad?

HOVSTAD: I just have a thing or two to attend to here.

ASLAKSEN: Very well. *(He leaves* U. R.; STOCKMANN *follows him into hall, then returns* D. R.*)*

HOVSTAD: *(Rising, puts notes in pocket, crosses* C.*)*. Well, what do you say to a little hypodermic for these fence-sitting deadheads? Everybody's afraid—afraid—they know perfectly well what's right, but they're afraid.

STOCKMANN: Why? I think that Aslaksen is a very sincere man.

HOVSTAD: Isn't it time we pumped some guts into these well-intentioned men of good-will? Under all their liberal talk, they still idolize authority and that's got to be rooted out of this town. This blunder of the water system has to be made clear to every voter. Let me print your report.

STOCKMANN: *(Turning away a little.)*. Not until I talk to my brother.

HOVSTAD: I'll write an editorial in the meantime, and if the Mayor won't go along with us——

STOCKMANN: I don't see how you can imagine such a thing!

HOVSTAD: Believe me, Doctor, it's entirely possible . . .

STOCKMANN: Listen. I promise you: he will go along and then you can print my report, every word of it.

HOVSTAD: On your word of honor?

STOCKMANN: *(Giving him manuscript.)*. Here it is, take it. It can't do any harm for you to read it. Return it to me later.

HOVSTAD: *(Takes manuscript, puts it in his pocket, starts out* U. R.*)*. Good day, Doctor.

STOCKMANN: Good day. You will see it's going to be easier than you think.

HOVSTAD: *(Stops.)*. I hope so, Doctor, sincerely. Let me know as soon as you hear from His Honor. *(Goes out* U. R.*)*

STOCKMANN: *(Crosses and looks in dining-room.)*. Catherine! Oh, you're home already, Petra.

PETRA: *(Entering dining-room from* L. *with glass of milk.)*. I just got back from school. *(Comes into room, kisses* STOCKMANN, *crosses to stove to warm back.* CATHERINE *enters from dining-room.)*

CATHERINE: Hasn't he been here yet?

STOCKMANN: Peter? No, but I just had a long chat with Hovstad. *(Leading* CATHERINE D. C.*)* He's really fascinated with my discovery and, you know, it has more implications than I thought at first. Do you know what I have backing me up?

CATHERINE: What, in heaven's name, have you got backing you up?

STOCKMANN: The solid majority.

CATHERINE: Is that good? *(PETRA crosses D., sits on D. arm of sofa.)*

STOCKMANN: Good? It's wonderful. You can't imagine the feeling, Catherine, to know that your own town feels like a brother to you. I haven't felt so at home in this town since I was a boy. *(Doorbell.)*

CATHERINE: That's the front door. *(She crosses* U. *around table to hall* U. R.; *lets* PETER *in.)*

STOCKMANN: Oh, it's Peter, then. Come in. *(PETER enters from hall* U. R. PETRA *rises.)*

PETER: *(Crossing D. R.)*. Good morning!

CATHERINE: Good morning.

STOCKMANN: It's nice to see you, Peter.

CATHERINE: How are you today?

PETER: Well, so-so . . . *(CATHERINE crosses* U. *to* R. *of* PETRA; PETER *to* STOCKMANN.*)* I received your thesis about the condition of the Springs yesterday. *(Crosses* L., *puts hat on* R. C. *table, crosses* C., *turns to face* STOCKMANN.*)*

STOCKMANN: I got your note. Did you read it?

PETER: I read it.

STOCKMANN: Well, what do you have to say? *(PETER clears his throat, glances aside.)*

CATHERINE: Come on, Petra. *(She and* PETRA *exit* L., *closing door.)*

PETER: *(After a moment.)*. Thomas, was it really necessary to go into this investigation behind my back?

STOCKMANN: Yes, until I was convinced myself, there was no point in . . .

PETER: And now you are convinced?

STOCKMANN: Well, certainly—aren't you, too, Peter? *(Pause.)* The University chemists corroborated . . .

PETER: You intend to present this document to the Board of Directors, officially, as the Medical Officer of the Springs?

STOCKMANN: Of course, something's got to be done, and quick.

PETER: You always use such strong expressions, Thomas. (*Sits* C. *of sofa*.) Among other things, in your report, you say that we *guarantee* our guests and visitors a permanent case of poisoning.

STOCKMANN: Yes, but, Peter, how can you describe it any other way? Imagine! Poisoned internally and externally!

PETER: So you merrily conclude that we must build a waste disposal plant—and reconstruct a brand new water system from the bottom up?

STOCKMANN: (*Taking* R. C. *chair, moves it* C. *as though to sit*.). Well, do you know some other way out? I don't.

PETER: I took a little walk over to the City Engineer this morning and in the course of conversation I sort of jokingly mentioned these changes—as something we might consider for the future, you know.

STOCKMANN: The future won't be soon enough, Peter.

PETER: The Engineer kind of smiled at my extravagance and gave me a few facts. I don't suppose you've taken the trouble to consider what your proposed changes would cost?

STOCKMANN: No, I never thought of that...

PETER: Naturally. Your little project would come to at least three hundred thousand crowns.

STOCKMANN: (*Sitting*.). That expensive?

PETER: Oh, don't look so upset—it's only money. The worst thing is that it would take some two years.

STOCKMANN: Two years?

PETER: At the least, and what do you propose we do about the Springs in the meantime—shut them up, no doubt! Because we'd have to, you know. As soon as the rumor gets around that the water is dangerous, we won't have a visitor left. And that's the picture, Thomas—you have it in your power to literally ruin your own town.

STOCKMANN: (*Rises*.). Now look, Peter! I don't want to ruin anything.

PETER: Thomas, your report has not convinced me that the conditions are as dangerous as you try to make them.

STOCKMANN: Now, listen, they are even worse than the report makes them out to be. Remember, summer is coming, and the warm weather.

PETER: *I* think you're exaggerating. A capable physician ought to know what precautions to take.

STOCKMANN: And then what?

PETER: The existing water supplies for the Springs are a fact, Thomas, and they've got to be treated as a fact. If you are reasonable and act with discretion, the Directors of the Institute will be inclined to take under consideration any means to reasonably and without financial sacrifices make possible improvements.

STOCKMANN: Dear God, do you think for one minute that I would ever agree to such trickery?

PETER: Trickery?

STOCKMANN: Yes, a trick, a fraud, a lie, a treachery—a downright crime against the public and against the whole community.

PETER: I said before that I'm not convinced that there is any actual danger.

STOCKMANN: Oh, you aren't? Anything else is impossible! My report is an absolute fact. (*Turns, violently replaces chair, steps* D.) The only trouble is that you and your administration were the ones who insisted that the water supply be built where it is, and now you're afraid to admit the blunder you committed. Damn it! Don't you think I can see through it all?

PETER: (*Rises, crosses* D. C.). All right, let's suppose that is true. Maybe I do care a little about my reputation. I still say I do it for the good of the town; without moral authority there can be no government. *And that is why, Thomas, it is my duty to prevent your report from reaching the Board*. Some time later I will bring up the matter for discussion. In the meantime, not a single word is to reach the public.

STOCKMANN: Oh, my dear Peter, do you imagine you can prevent that!

PETER: It will be prevented.

STOCKMANN: It can't be. There are too many people who already know about it.

PETER: Who? (*Angered*.) It can't possibly be those people from the *Daily Messenger* who...

STOCKMANN: Exactly. The liberal, free and independent press will stand up and do its duty!

PETER: You are an unbelievably irresponsible man, Thomas. Can't you imagine what consequences that is going to have for you?

STOCKMANN: For me?

PETER: Yes, for you and your family.

STOCKMANN: (*Turning away*.). What the hell are you saying now?

PETER: I believe I have the right to think of myself as a helpful brother, Thomas.

STOCKMANN: You have been and I thank you deeply for it.

PETER: Don't mention it. I often couldn't help myself. I had hoped that by improving your finances I would be able to keep you from running *completely* hog-wild.

STOCKMANN: You mean it was only for your own sake?

PETER: Partly yes. What do you imagine people think of an official whose closest relatives get themselves into trouble time and time again?

STOCKMANN: And that's what I've done?

PETER: You do it without knowing it—you're like a man with an automatic brain—as soon as an idea breaks into your head, no matter how idiotic it may be—you get up like a sleep-walker and start writing a pamphlet.

STOCKMANN: (*Steps to* PETER.). Peter, don't you think it's a citizen's duty to share a new idea with the public?

PETER: (*Crossing* D. L. C.). The public doesn't need new ideas—the public is much better off with old ideas.

STOCKMANN: You're not even embarrassed to say that?

PETER: (*Crossing to* STOCKMANN.). Now look, I am going to lay this out once and for all. You're always barking about authority. If a man gives you an order, he's persecuting you. Nothing is important enough to respect, once you decide to revolt against your superiors. All right, then, I give up. I'm not going to try to change you any more. I told you the stakes you are playing for here, and now I'm going to give you an order and I warn you, you'd better obey it if you value your career.

STOCKMANN: What kind of an order?

PETER: You are going to deny these rumors officially.

STOCKMANN: How?

PETER: You simply say that you went into the examination of the water more thoroughly and you find that you overestimated the danger.

STOCKMANN: I see!

PETER: And that you have complete confidence that whatever improvements are needed, the management will certainly take care of them.

STOCKMANN: My convictions come from the conditions of the water. My convictions will change when the water changes, and for no other reason.

PETER: What are you talking about convictions? You're an official, you keep your convictions to yourself!

STOCKMANN: To myself?!

PETER: As an official, I said. God knows as a private person that is something else, but as a subordinate employee of the Institute, you have no right to express any convictions or personal opinions about anything connected with policy!

STOCKMANN: Now you listen to me! I am a doctor and a scientist!!

PETER: What's this got to do with science?

STOCKMANN: And I have the right to express my opinion on anything in the world!

PETER: Not about the Institute—that I forbid.

STOCKMANN: You forbid!

PETER: I forbid you as your superior, and when I give orders you obey.

STOCKMANN: (*Turning away from* PETER.). Peter, if you weren't my brother . . .

PETRA: (*Throws* L. *door open, flies in,* CATHERINE *tries to restrain her,* PETRA *crosses to* L. *of* PETER.). Father! You aren't going to stand for this!

CATHERINE: (*Following* PETRA.). Petra, Petra . . .

PETER: What have you two been doing, eavesdropping?

CATHERINE: You were talking so loud we couldn't help . . .

PETRA: (*Interrupting*.). Yes, I was eavesdropping.

PETER: (*Crossing below* STOCKMANN *to his* R.). That makes me very happy.

STOCKMANN: (*Moving* L.). You said something to me about forbidding——

PETER: You forced me to.

STOCKMANN: So, you want me to spit in my own

face officially, is that it?

PETER: Why must you always be so colorful?

STOCKMANN: And if I don't obey?

PETER: Then we will publish our own statement, to calm the public.

STOCKMANN: Good enough! And I will write against you. I will stick to what I said, and I will prove that I am right and that you are wrong, and what will you do then?

PETER: Then I simply won't be able to prevent your dismissal.

STOCKMANN: (*Steps back.*). What! ⎫
PETRA: (*Steps to* C.). Father! ⎬ (*Together.*).
                                    ⎭

PETER: Dismissed from the Institute is what I said. If you want to make war on Kirsten Springs, you have no right to be on the Board of Directors.

STOCKMANN: You'd dare to do that?

PETER: Oh, no, you're the daring man.

PETRA: (*Crossing below* STOCKMANN, *who crosses* D. C., *head in hands.*). Uncle, this is a rotten way to treat a man like Father.

CATHERINE: (*Crossing below* STOCKMANN, *to* PETRA.). Will you be quiet, Petra.

PETER: So young and you've got opinions already—but that's natural. (*To* CATHERINE.) Catherine, dear, you're probably the only sane person in this house. Knock some sense into his head, will you? Make him realize what he's driving his whole family into.

STOCKMANN: (*Crossing below to* PETER, *puts family behind him.*). My family concerns nobody but myself.

PETER: His family and his own town!

STOCKMANN: I'm going to show you who loves his town. The people are going to get the full stink of this corruption, Peter, and then we will see who loves his town.

PETER: You love your town when you blindly, spitefully, stubbornly go ahead trying to cut off our most important industry?

STOCKMANN: That source is poisoned, man. We are getting fat by peddling filth and corruption to innocent people!

PETER: I think this has gone beyond opinions and convictions, Thomas. A man who can throw that kind of insinuation around is nothing but a traitor to society!

STOCKMANN: (*Striving to control self.*). How dare you to . . .?

CATHERINE: (*Running in front of* STOCKMANN; PETRA *pulls* STOCKMANN *back.*). Tom!

PETRA: (*Grabbing* STOCKMANN'S *arm.*). Be careful, Father!

PETER: (*Taking hat, starting out* U. R., *with dignity.*). I won't expose myself to violence. You have been warned. Consider what you owe yourself and your family. Good day! (*He exits* U. R., *leaving front door open.*

STOCKMANN: (*Pacing* D. R., *then back to* D. L.). He's insulted! *He's* insulted!

CATHERINE: (*Crossing* U. C., D. R., *then* L.). It's shameful, Thomas.

PETRA: (*Crossing* U. L. C., *to stove, then* R. *to look after* PETER, *back to* C. *at* R. *of* CATHERINE.). Oh, I would love to give him a piece of my mind.

STOCKMANN: (*Still pacing.*). It was my own fault—I should have shown my teeth right from the beginning. He called me a traitor to society. Me! Damn it all, that is not going to stick.

CATHERINE: Please, think; he's got all the power on his side.

STOCKMANN: Yes, but I have the truth on mine.

CATHERINE: Without power, what good is the truth? (*All turn and look at her.*)

STOCKMANN: (*Crosses to* CATHERINE.). That's ridiculous, Catherine. I have the liberal press with me and the majority, the solid majority. If that isn't power, what is?

CATHERINE: But for Heaven's sake, Tom, you aren't going to . . .?

STOCKMANN: What am I not going to do——?

CATHERINE: You aren't going to fight it out in public with your brother!

STOCKMANN: What the hell else do you want me to do?

CATHERINE: But it won't do you any earthly good—if they won't do it, they won't. All you'll get out of it is a notice that you're fired.

STOCKMANN: I am going to do my duty, Catherine. Me, the man he calls a traitor to society!

CATHERINE: And how about your duty to your family—the people you're supposed to provide for?

PETRA: Don't always think of us first, Mother.

CATHERINE: You can talk—if worst comes to worst, you can manage for yourself, but what about the boys, Tom, and you and me?

STOCKMANN: What about you? You want me to

be the miserable animal who'd crawl up the boots of that damn gang? Will you be happy if I can't face *myself* the rest of my life?

CATHERINE: Tom, Tom, there's so much injustice in the world—you've simply got to learn to live with it. If you go on this way, God help us, we'll have no money again. Is it so long since the North that you have forgotten what it was to live like we lived? (MORTEN *and* EJLIF *enter hall* U. R. *with school-books.* CATHERINE *sees them.*) Haven't we had enough of that for one lifetime? What will happen to them? We've got nothing if you are fired . . . ! (*The boys have entered heartily; they cross* D. R., *then to* R. *of family.*)

STOCKMANN: (*After seeing boys enter.*). Stop it! (*To boys, who are frightened by this scene.*) Well, boys, did you learn anything in school today?

MORTEN : We learned what an insect is . . .

STOCKMANN: You don't say!

MORTEN : (*To* STOCKMANN.). What happened here? (*Crosses to* L. *of* STOCKMANN; *to* CATHERINE.) Why is everybody . . .?

STOCKMANN: (*Calming boys.*). Nothing, nothing! You know what I'm going to do, boys? From now on, I'm going to *teach you what a man is!* (CATHERINE *cries.*)

MEDIUM FAST CURTAIN

ACT TWO

SCENE ONE

The Editorial Office of "The People's Daily Messenger." The front door of the office is D. R. U. R. *is* BILLING'S *desk and chair. A wastebasket is downstage of desk. A large table, covered with newspapers, measures, etc. is* C. *with two chairs,* U. *and* R. *A door leading to printing shop is* U.L. D.L. *is a door to a small room. The room is dingy and cheerless, the furniture shabby, the chairs dirty.*

BILLING *is sitting at his desk* U. R., *reading* STOCKMANN'S *manuscript. After a moment,* HOVSTAD *enters* U. L., *carrying a ruler.* BILLING *looks up.*

BILLING: Doctor not come yet?

HOVSTAD: (*Crossing to* BILLING, *looks over his shoulder.*). No, not yet. You finish it. (BILLING *holds up a hand to signal "just a moment." He reads on. After a moment he closes manuscript with a bang, glances up at* HOVSTAD *with some trepidation, then looks off.* HOVSTAD, *looking at* BILLING, *walks a few steps to* C. D. *table, sets ruler down, puts on coat.*) Well? What do you think of it?

BILLING: (*As though with some hesitation.*). It's devastating. The Doctor is a brilliant man. I swear I myself never really understood how incompetent those fat fellows are, on top. (*Holding manuscript, rises, waves it a little.*) I hear the rumble of revolution in this.

HOVSTAD: (*Glances at* U. L. *door, takes* BILLING D. R. C.). Sssh! Aslaksen's inside.

BILLING: Aslaksen's a coward. With all that moderation talk, all he's saying is he's yellow. You're going to print this, aren't you?

HOVSTAD: Sure, I'm just waiting for the Doctor to give the word. And if his brother hasn't given in, we put it on the press anyway.

BILLING: Yes, but if the Mayor is against this it's going to get pretty rough. You know that, don't you?

HOVSTAD: Just let him try to block that reconstruction—the little businessmen and the whole town'll be screaming for his head. Aslaksen'll see to that.

BILLING: (*Holding up manuscript.*). But the stockholders'll have to lay out a fortune of money if this goes through.

HOVSTAD: My boy, I think it's going to bust them! And when the Springs go busted, the people are finally going to understand the level of genius

40   that's been running this town. Those five sheets of paper are going to put in a liberal administration once and for all.

BILLING: It's a revolution. You know that? (*With hope and fear.*) I mean it, we're on the edge of a real revolution! (STOCKMANN *enters* D. R., *takes manuscript from* BILLING, *holds it out to* HOVSTAD, *but doesn't give it to him.*)

STOCKMANN: Put it on the press!

BILLING: (*Over* STOCKMAN'S *lines, crossing* U. L., *call-*
50   *ing into shop*.). Mr. Aslaksen! The Doctor's here! (*Crosses* D. *to* L. C.)

HOVSTAD: Wonderful! What'd the Mayor say?

STOCKMANN: The Mayor has declared war, so war is what it's going to be. (*Crosses back in front of* HOVSTAD.) And this is only the beginning! You know what he tried to do? . . . He actually tried to blackmail me! He's got the nerve to tell me that I'm not allowed to speak my mind without his permission. Imagine the shameless
60   effrontery!

HOVSTAD: He actually said it right out?

STOCKMANN: Right to my face! The trouble with me was I kept giving them credit for being our kind of people, but they're *dictators!* (ASLAKSEN *enters* U. L., *crosses* U. *to* R. *of* STOCKMANN.) They're people who'll try to hold power even if they have to poison the town to do it!

ASLAKSEN: Now take it easy, Doctor, you . . . mustn't always be throwing accusations. I'm
70   with you, you understand, but—moderation.

STOCKMANN: (*Cutting him off*.). What'd you think of the article, Hovstad?

HOVSTAD: It's a masterpiece. In one blow you've managed to prove beyond any doubt what kind of men are running us.

ASLAKSEN: May we print it now, then?

STOCKMANN: I should say *so!*

HOVSTAD: (*Reaching for manuscript*.). We'll have it ready for tomorrow's paper.

80   STOCKMANN: And, listen, Mr. Aslaksen, do me a favor, will you? You run a fine paper, but supervise the printing personally, heh? I'd hate to see the weather report stuck into the middle of my article.

ASLAKSEN: (*Laughs*.). Don't worry, there won't be a mistake this time!

STOCKMANN: Make it perfect, heh? Like you were printing money. You can't imagine how I'm

dying to see it in print. After all the lies in the papers, the half lies, the quarter lies—to finally   90
see the absolute, unvarnished truth about something important . . . ! And this is only the beginning. We'll go on to other subjects, and blow up every lie we live by! What do you say, Aslaksen?

ASLAKSEN: (*Nods in agreement, but.*). Just remember . . .

BILLING and HOVSTAD: (*Together with* ASLAKSEN.). "Moderation!" (BILLING *and* HOVSTAD *are greatly amused.*)   100

ASLAKSEN: (*To* BILLING *and* HOVSTAD.). I don't see what's so funny about that!

BILLING: (*Crossing above table to* STOCKMANN, *enthralled.* HOVSTAD *gives* L.). Doctor Stockmann . . . I feel as though I were standing in some historic painting. Goddammit, this is a historic day! Some day this scene'll be in a museum. Entitled, "The Day the Truth Was Born." (*All are embarrassed by this.* ASLAKSEN *and* HOVSTAD *look away.*)   110

STOCKMANN: (*Suddenly*.). Oh! I've got a patient half-bandaged down the road. (*Crosses to door* D. R., *returns and exclaims* "Oh," *gives* BILLING *manuscript.* BILLING *follows, takes manuscript from* STOCKMANN, *who exits* D. R.)

HOVSTAD: (*Moving to* ASLAKSEN.). I hope you realize how useful he could be to us.

ASLAKSEN: (*Crossing* HOVSTAD *to* D. L. C.). I don't like that business about "this is only the beginning." Let him stick to the Springs.   120

BILLING: (*Crossing* HOVSTAD *to* ASLAKSEN. HOVSTAD *takes manuscript from* BILLING, *studies it.*) What makes you so scared all the time?

ASLAKSEN: I have to live here. It'd be different if he were attacking the national Government or something, but if he thinks I'm going to start going after the whole town administration . . .

BILLING: What's the difference, bad is bad!

ASLAKSEN: Yes, but there is a difference. You attack the national Government, what's going   130
to happen? Nothing. They go right on. But a town administration—they're liable to be overthrown or something! I represent the small property owners in this town . . .

BILLING: Ha! It's always the same. Give a man a little property and the truth can go to hell!

ASLAKSEN: Mr. Billing, I'm older than you are; I've

seen fire-eaters before. (*Points to* BILLING's *desk*.)
You know who used to work at your desk before
140 you? Councilman Stensford—*Councilman!*

BILLING: Just because I work at a renegade's desk,
does that mean . . . ?

ASLAKSEN: You're a politician; a politician never
knows where he's going to end up. And, besides,
you applied for a job as secretary to the Magistrate, didn't you?

HOVSTAD: Billing!

BILLING: (*To* HOVSTAD.). Well, why not? If I get
it I'll have a chance to put across some good
150 things——(*Turns back to* ASLAKSEN.) I could put
plenty of big boys on the spot with a job like
that!

ASLAKSEN: All right, I'm just saying . . . People
change. Just remember, when you call me a coward—I may not have made the hot speeches,
but I never went back on my beliefs, either.
Unlike some of the big radicals around here,
I didn't change. Of course, I *am* a little more
moderate . . .

160 HOVSTAD: Oh, God!

ASLAKSEN: (*Glaring at* HOVSTAD.). I don't see what's
so funny about that! (*He goes out* D. L.)

BILLING: (*After watching him off*.). If we could get
rid of him, we . . .

HOVSTAD: Take it easy, he pays the printing bill,
he's not that bad. (*Crosses to* BILLING, *with manuscript*.) I'll get the printer on this . . . (*Starts out
to* U. L. *door*.)

BILLING: Say, Hovstad, how about asking Stock-
170 mann to back us? Then we could really put out
a paper!

HOVSTAD: What would he do for money?

BILLING: His father-in-law.

HOVSTAD: Kiil? Since when has he got money?

BILLING: I think he's loaded with it.

HOVSTAD: No! Really, as long as I've known him,
he's worn the same overcoat, the same suit . . .

BILLING: Yeah, and the same ring on his right hand.
You ever get a look at that boulder? (*Points to
180 his finger*.)

HOVSTAD: No, I never . . .

BILLING: All year he wears the diamond inside. But
on New Year's Eve, he turns it around. Figure it
out, when a man has no visible means of support,
what's he living on?—Money, right? Now, my
idea is . . . (PETRA *enters* D. R., *carrying a book*.)

PETRA: Hello.

HOVSTAD: (*Stepping down a little*.). Well, fancy seeing you here! Sit down, what . . . ?   190

PETRA: (*Tossing book on* BILLING's *desk with a certain peeve*.). I want to ask you something.

BILLING: (*Crossing* U. *to desk*.). What's that?

PETRA: That English novel you wanted translated.

HOVSTAD: Aren't you going to do it?

PETRA: (*Crossing to* HOVSTAD *at* C.). I don't get this.

HOVSTAD: You don't get what?

PETRA: This book is absolutely against everything
you people believe.   200

HOVSTAD: Oh, it isn't that bad . . . (*Looks at* BILLING;
neither has read it.)

PETRA: But, Mr. Hovstad, it says if you're good
there's a super-natural force that'll fix it so you
end up happy. And if you're bad, you'll be
punished. Since when does the world work that
way?

HOVSTAD: Yeah, but, Petra, this is a newspaper;
people like to read that kind of thing. They buy
the paper for that and then we slip in our political   210
stuff. A newspaper can't buck the public . . .

PETRA: You don't say! (*She starts to go out* D. R.
HOVSTAD *hurries to her, grabs her arm at door, holds
her*.)

HOVSTAD: Now, wait a minute. I don't want you
to go feeling that way. (*Holds out manuscript to
BILLING*.) Here, take this to the printer, will you?

BILLING: (*Taking it*.). Sure. (*He exits* U. L.)

HOVSTAD: (*Leading her back to* C.). I just want you
to understand something: I never even read that   220
book. It was Billing's idea.

PETRA: I thought he was a radical.

HOVSTAD: He is. But he's also a . . .

PETRA: A newspaper man.

HOVSTAD: Well, that, too. But I was going to say
that Billing is trying to get the job as secretary
to the Magistrate.

PETRA: What?

HOVSTAD: People are people, Miss Stockmann.

PETRA: But, the Magistrate! He's been fighting   230
everything progressive in this town for thirty
years.

HOVSTAD: Let's not argue about it, I just didn't
want you to go out of here with a wrong idea
of me. I guess you know that I . . . happen to
admire women like you. I've never had a chance
to tell you, but I . . . well, I want you to know

288 IBSEN

it. Do you mind? (*He smiles.*)

240 PETRA: No, I don't mind, but reading that book upset me. I really don't understand . . . Will you tell me why you're supporting my father?

HOVSTAD: What's the mystery? It's a matter of principle.

PETRA: But a paper that'll print a book like that has no principle.

HOVSTAD: Why do you jump to such extremes! You're just like . . .

PETRA: Like what?

HOVSTAD: I simply meant that . . .

250 PETRA: Like my father, you meant. You really have no use for him, do you?

HOVSTAD: (*Chiding a little, takes her arms, guides her back.*). Now wait a minute!

PETRA: What's behind this? Are you just trying to hold my hand or something?

HOVSTAD: I happen to agree with your father, and that's why I'm printing his stuff! Nothing would please me more than to hold your hand, Miss Stockmann, but I assure you this . . .

260 PETRA: You're trying to put something over, I think. Why are you in this?

HOVSTAD: Who are you accusing? Billing gave you that book, not me!

PETRA: But you don't mind printing it, do you? What're you trying to do with my father?—you have no principles, what are you up to here?! (ASLAKSEN, *manuscript in his hand, hurriedly enters from* D. L. *door, looking off. He closes door.*)

ASLAKSEN: My God! Hovstad! (*Sees* PETRA, *stops.*

270 PETRA, *frightened, jumps to* R. *of* HOVSTAD.) Miss Stockmann!

PETRA: I don't think I've been so frightened in my life. (*She goes out* D. R. HOVSTAD *starts after her.*)

HOVSTAD: (*Following her.*). Please, you mustn't think I . . .

ASLAKSEN: (*As* HOVSTAD *starts to move, following and stopping him.*). Where are you going? The Mayor's out there.

HOVSTAD: The Mayor!

280 ASLAKSEN: He wants to speak to you. He came in the back door. He doesn't want to be seen.

HOVSTAD: (*Crossing to* D. L. *door.*). What does he want?

ASLAKSEN: I'll watch for anyone coming in here.

HOVSTAD: (*Opening* D. L. *door.*). Come in, Your Honor!

PETER: (*Entering* D. L. *and looking the place over.*).

Thank you. (*He crosses* HOVSTAD. HOVSTAD *carefully closes* D. L. *door.*) It's clean! I always imagined this place would look dirty. But it's clean. (*Sets hat on* BILLING's *desk.*) Very nice, Mr. Aslaksen.

290

ASLAKSEN: Not at all, Your Honor. I mean to say I always . . .

HOVSTAD: (*Crossing to* L. *of table.*). What can I do for you, Your Honor? (*Offers him* U. L. *chair, but* PETER *is sitting in* L. C. *chair.*) Sit down?

PETER: I had a very annoying thing happen today, Mr. Hovstad.

HOVSTAD: That so?

300

PETER: It seems my brother has written some sort of . . . memorandum. About the Springs.

HOVSTAD: You don't say! (ASLAKSEN *starts to fade to* U. L. *door.*)

PETER: (*Looking at* HOVSTAD *now.*). Ah . . . he mentioned it . . . to you?

HOVSTAD: Ah . . . yes. I think he said something about it.

PETER: (*Points to manuscript, stopping* ASLAKSEN *at* U. L. *door.*) That's it, isn't it?

310

ASLAKSEN: This? (*Crosses to* R. *of* PETER.) I don't know, I haven't had a chance to look at it, the printer just handed it to me . . .

HOVSTAD: (*Crossing* U. *a little, speaking behind* PETER.). Isn't that the thing the printer wanted the spelling checked?

ASLAKSEN: That's it, it's only a question of spelling. I'll be right back . . .

PETER: I'm very good at spelling. (*Holds out his hand.*) Maybe I can help you?

320

HOVSTAD: No, Your Honor, there's some Latin in it . . . you wouldn't know Latin, would you?

PETER: Oh, yes. I used to help my brother with his Latin all the time. Let me have it. (ASLAKSEN *gives him manuscript.* PETER *looks at title on first page, then glances up at* HOVSTAD, *who avoids his eyes.*) You're going to print this?

HOVSTAD: I can't very well refuse a signed article. A signed article is the author's responsibility.

PETER: (*Holding up manuscript.*). Mr. Aslaksen, you're going to allow this?

330

ASLAKSEN: I'm the publisher, not the editor, Your Honor. My policy is, freedom for the editor.

PETER: You have a point; I can see that.

ASLAKSEN: (*Reaching for manuscript.*). So if you don't mind . . .

PETER: Not at all. (*But he holds on to manuscript.*)

This reconstruction of the Springs...

ASLAKSEN: I realize, Your Honor, it does mean
340   tremendous sacrifices for the stockholders...

PETER: Don't upset yourself. The first thing a
Mayor learns is that the less wealthy can always
be prevailed upon to demand a spirit of sacrifice
for the public good.

ASLAKSEN: I'm glad you see that.

PETER: Oh, yes. Especially when it's the wealthy
who are going to do the sacrificing. What you
don't seem to understand, Mr. Aslaksen, is that
so long as I am Mayor, any changes in those
350   baths are going to be paid for by a municipal
loan.

ASLAKSEN: A municipal . . . You mean you're
going to tax the people for this?

PETER: Exactly.

HOVSTAD: But the Springs are a private corporation...

PETER: (*Sets cane on table.*). The corporation built
Kirsten Springs out of its own money. If the
people want them changed, the people naturally
360   must pay the bill. The corporation is in no position to put out any more money. It simply can't
do it.

ASLAKSEN: That's impossible. People will never
stand for another tax. (*To* PETER.) Is this a fact,
or your opinion?

PETER: It happens to be a fact. Plus another fact
—you'll forgive me for talking about facts in
a newspaper office—but don't forget that the
Springs will take two years to make over. Two
370   years without income for your small businessmen, Mr. Aslaksen, and a heavy new tax,
besides. And all because . . . (*Throttling manuscript in his hand.*) because of this dream, this
hallucination that we live in a pest-hole...

HOVSTAD: That's based on science...

PETER: (*Throwing manuscript on table.*). This is based
on vindictiveness, on his hatred of authority,
and nothing else. (*Pounds fist on manuscript.*) This
is the mad dream of a man who is trying to
380   blow up our way of life! It has nothing to do
with reform or science or anything else but pure
and simple destruction! And I intend to see to
it that the people understand it exactly so!

ASLAKSEN: (*Hit by this.*). My God! Maybe...
(*Crosses* PETER *to* R. *of* HOVSTAD, *takes* HOVSTAD
D. L.) You sure you want to support this thing,
Hovstad?

HOVSTAD: (*Nervously.*). Frankly, I'd never thought
of it in quite that way. I mean... (*Crosses above*
ASLAKSEN; *to* PETER.) When you think of it
390   psychologically it's completely possible, of
course, that the man is simply out to... I don't
know what to say, Your Honor. I'd hate to hurt
the town in any way... I never imagined we'd
have to have a new tax.

PETER: You should have imagined it, because
you're going to have to advocate it. Unless, of
course, liberal and radical newspaper readers
enjoy high taxes... (*Takes own manuscript out of
inside coat pocket.*) You'd know that better than
400   I, of course. I happen to have here a brief story
of the actual facts. It proves that with a little
care, nobody need be harmed at all by the water.
Of course, in time we'd have to make a few
minor structural changes, and we'd pay for
those.

HOVSTAD: May I see that?

PETER: I want you to *study* it, Mr. Hovstad, and
see if you don't agree that... (BILLING *hurries
in quickly from* U. L., *closing door, comes* D. *around*
410   *back of table.*)

BILLING: Are you expecting the Doctor?

PETER: (*Alarmed, rising quickly, replacing manuscript
in pocket.*). He's here?

BILLING: (*Motioning to street at* R.). He's just crossing
the street. (ASLAKSEN *crosses quickly to* D. R. *door.*)

PETER: I'd rather not run into him here. How can
I...?

BILLING: (*Taking* PETER *to* D. L. *door.*). Right
420   this way, sir. Hurry up . . .

ASLAKSEN: (*At* R. *door, peeking.*). Hurry up!

PETER: (*Going out* D. L. *door with* BILLING.). Get
him out of here right away!

HOVSTAD: (*Covering* STOCKMANN's *manuscript with
papers on table, sitting in* D. C. *chair.*). Do something, do something! (ASLAKSEN *rushes to* BILLING's
*desk, turns chair up, sits and becomes very, very busy,
seating himself to cover hat.*)

STOCKMANN: (*Entering* D. R. *and crossing* C.). Any
430   proofs yet? (*Looks at* HOVSTAD, *then at* ASLAKSEN.)
I guess not, heh?

ASLAKSEN: (*Without turning.*). No, you can't expect
them for some time.

STOCKMANN: You mind if I wait?

HOVSTAD: (*Trying to smile.*). No sense in that, Doctor; it'll be quite a while yet.

STOCKMANN: (*Laughing, places his hand on* HOVSTAD's

back.). Bear with me, Hovstad, I just can't wait to see it in print.

440 HOVSTAD: We're pretty busy, Doctor, so . . .

STOCKMANN: (*Starting for* D. R. *door*.). Don't let me hold you up. That's the way to be, busy, busy. We'll make this town shine like a jewel! (*Exits* D. R. *After a moment he returns*.) Just one thing, I . . .

HOVSTAD: Couldn't we talk some other time? We're very . . .

STOCKMANN: Two words. Just walking down the street now, I looked at the people, in the stores,
450 driving the wagons, and suddenly I was . . . well, touched, you know? By their innocence, I mean. What I'm driving at is when this exposé breaks, they're liable to start making a saint out of me or something, and I . . . (*Moves to* ASLAKSEN.) Aslaksen, I want you to promise me that you're not going to try to get up any dinner for me, or . . .

ASLAKSEN: (*Rising*.). Doctor, there's no use concealing . . .

460 STOCKMANN: I knew it! Now look, I will simply not attend a dinner in my honor.

HOVSTAD: (*Rising*.). Doctor, I think it's time we . . . (CATHERINE *enters* D. R. *and crosses to* STOCKMANN.)

CATHERINE: I thought so! Thomas, I want you home. Now come. I want you to talk to Petra. (*She returns to* D. R. *door*.)

STOCKMANN: What happened? What are you doing here?

470 HOVSTAD: Something wrong, Mrs. Stockmann?

CATHERINE: (*Crossing to* HOVSTAD.). Doctor Stockmann is the father of three children, Mr. Hovstad!

STOCKMANN: Now look, dear, everybody knows that, what's the . . .

CATHERINE: (*Restraining an outburst at* STOCKMANN.). Nobody would believe it from the way you're dragging us into this disaster!

HOVSTAD: Oh, now, Mrs. Stockmann . . .

480 STOCKMANN: What disaster?

CATHERINE: (*To* HOVSTAD.). He treats you like a son and you want to make a fool of him.

HOVSTAD: (*Gives way*, CATHERINE *follows*.). *I'm* not making a . . .

STOCKMANN: Catherine, how can you accuse . . .

CATHERINE: (*To* HOVSTAD, *backs him to below table*.). He'll lose his job at the Springs, do you realize that? You print the article and they'll grind him up like a piece of flesh!

STOCKMANN: (*Putting hat on table*.). Catherine, 490 you're embarrassing me! I beg your pardon, gentlemen . . .

CATHERINE: Mr. Hovstad, what are you up to?

STOCKMANN: I won't have you jumping at Hovstad, Catherine!

CATHERINE: (*To* STOCKMANN.). I want you home! This man is not your friend!

STOCKMANN: He is my friend—any man who shares my risk is my friend! You simply don't understand that as soon as this breaks, everybody 500 in this town is going to come out in the streets . . . (*Picks up cane from table*.) and drive that gang of . . . (*He notices cane, recognizes it, looks at* HOVSTAD, *then* ASLAKSEN.) What's this? (*No reply. He looks from* ASLAKSEN *to desk, sees hat and picks it up on cane, comes* D. *As he goes to desk*, ASLAKSEN *crosses to* D. *of table*, CATHERINE *goes around* L. *and* U. *of table*.) What the hell is he doing here?

ASLAKSEN: All right, Doctor, now let's be calm and . . . 510

STOCKMANN (*Crossing* D. L., ASLAKSEN *and* HOVSTAD *give up*, CATHERINE *backs to* D. R. *end of table, looking at door*.). Where is he? What'd he do, talk you out of it? Hovstad! (*No reply*.) He won't get away with it; where'd you hide him? (*Opens door* D. L.)

ASLAKSEN: Be careful, Doctor! (PETER *enters* D. L. *and crosses* D. R. C. BILLING *enters* D. L. *and stands* D. L., *closes door*. PETER *is trying to hide his embarrassment*.)

STOCKMANN (*Crossing to* PETER *at* R. C.). Well, Peter! 520 Poisoning the water wasn't enough, you're working on the press now, eh?

PETER: My hat, please. And my stick. (STOCKMANN *puts on* PETER'S *hat*.) Now what's *this* nonsense? Take that off, that's official insignia!

STOCKMANN: I just wanted you to realize, Peter . . . (*Takes off hat*.) that anyone may wear this hat in a democracy, and . . . (*Handing him hat*.) that a free citizen is not afraid to touch it. And as for the baton of command, Your Honor, it can 530 pass from hand to hand. So don't gloat yet. (*Hands stick to* PETER.) The people haven't spoken. (*Turning to* HOVSTAD *and* ASLAKSEN.) And I have the people because I have the truth, my friends.

ASLAKSEN: (*Moving down*.). Doctor, we're not scientists; we can't judge whether your article is really true.

STOCKMANN: Then print it under my name; let *me* defend it!

540 HOVSTAD: (*Moving down.*). I'm not printing it. I'm not going to sacrifice this newspaper. When the whole story gets out the public is not going to stand for any changes in the Springs.

ASLAKSEN: His Honor just told us, Doctor. You see, there will have to be a new tax...

STOCKMANN: Ahhh! Yes. I see! That's why you're not scientists suddenly and can't decide if I'm telling the truth. Well, so.

HOVSTAD: Don't take that attitude. The point is...

550 STOCKMANN: (*Crossing to* ASLAKSEN; CATHERINE *gives* R.). The point, the point, oh, the point is going to fly through this town like an arrow, and I'm going to fire it! Will you print this article as a pamphlet? I'll pay for it.

ASLAKSEN: I'm not going to ruin this paper or this town. Doctor, for the sake of your family...

CATHERINE: (*Picking up hat from table, moving* D. *to* L. *of* STOCKMANN.). You can leave his family out of this, Mr. Aslaksen. God help me, I think 560 you people are horrible!

STOCKMANN: My article, if you don't mind!

ASLAKSEN: (*Giving it to him.*). Doctor, you won't get it printed in this town.

PETER: Can't you forget it? (*Indicating* HOVSTAD *and* ASLAKSEN.) Can't you see now that everybody...?

STOCKMANN: Your Honor, I can't forget it, and you will never forget it as long as you live. I'm going to call a mass meeting and I...

570 PETER: And who is going to rent you a hall?

STOCKMANN: Then I will take a drum and go from—(*Crosses to* PETER.) street to street proclaiming that the springs are befouled and poison is rotting the body politic!

PETER: And I believe you really are that mad!

STOCKMANN: (*Waving manuscript in his hand.*). Mad? Oh, my brother, you haven't even heard me raise my voice yet. Catherine? (*He holds out his* L. *arm, she takes it. They cross* PETER *and go stiffly* 580 *out* D. R. PETER *shakes his head regretfully, reaches into pocket, takes out his own manuscript, looks at* ASLAKSEN, *who crosses and takes it.* ASLAKSEN *quickly looks at* HOVSTAD, *who crosses and takes it.* HOVSTAD *looks at* BILLING, *who crosses and takes it, gestures a salute and exits* U. L. PETER *acknowledges* BILLING'S *salute as*)

FAST CURTAIN

SCENE TWO

A room in CAPTAIN HORSTER'S *house. The room is bare, as though unused for a long time. There is a platform* R. *of* C. *with a chair and a small table on it.* R. *of platform are two small chairs.* D. L. *is a highbacked chair. Two windows with shutters are in back wall. A shelf is between them. There is a doorway* D. R. *and an archway in* L. *wall, which leads to a doorway.*

At rise, the stage is empty. CAPTAIN HORSTER *enters from* R., *carrying a pitcher of water on a tray with two glasses. As he is putting these on the table,* BILLING *enters* L.

BILLING: Captain Horster?

HORSTER: (*Tidying up platform table; doesn't see* BILLING.). Oh, come in. I don't have enough chairs for a lot of people, so I decided not to have chairs at all.

10 BILLING: My name is Billing. Don't you remember, at the Doctor's house?

HORSTER: (*A little coldly.*). Oh yes, sure—I've been so busy I didn't recognize you. (*Crosses* BILLING *to* U. L. C. *window, looks out.*) Why don't those people come inside?

BILLING: I don't know. I guess they're waiting for the Mayor or somebody important so they can be sure it's respectable in here. I wanted to ask you a question before it begins, Captain. (HORSTER *crosses to* BILLING.) Why are you lending 20 your house for this? I never heard of you connected with anything political.

HORSTER: I'll answer that. I travel most of the year... Did you ever travel?

BILLING: Not abroad, no.

HORSTER: Well, I've been in a lot of places where people aren't allowed to say unpopular things. Did you know that?

BILLING: Sure, I've read about it.

HORSTER: (*Simply.*). Well, I don't like it. (*Starts to* 30 *go out* D. R.)

BILLING: (*Dutifully writes down "doesn't like it."*). One more question. (HORSTER *stops.*) What's your opinion about the Doctor's proposition to rebuild the Springs?

HORSTER: (*After a moment.*). Don't understand a thing about it. (HORSTER *sees some people in room* U.L., *through door.*) Come in. Come in. (NANSEN, HENRIK *and* EDVARD *enter* L. *and cross* U.C. BILLING *crosses* D. L.) I don't have enough chairs, so you'll 40 just have to stand. (HORSTER *goes out* D. R.)

HENRIK: (*As soon as* HORSTER *is off.*). Try the horn.

EDVARD: No, let him start to talk first.

NANSEN: (*Taking out horn.*). Wait'll they hear this! I could blow your moustache off with this! (HORSTER *has re-entered* R., *carrying two more glasses. Stops on seeing horn.*)

HORSTER: (*Setting things on table.*). I don't want any rough-house, you hear me? (CATHERINE *and* PETRA *enter* L.) Come in. I've got chairs just for you. (*As the women move to* HORSTER *at* C. PETRA *crosses* U. *of* CATHERINE *and reaches* HORSTER *first.*)

CATHERINE: (*Nervously.*). There's quite a crowd on the sidewalk. Why don't they come in?

HORSTER: I suppose they're waiting for the Mayor.

PETRA: Are all those people on his side?

HORSTER: Who knows? People are bashful . . . (BILLING *crosses to ladies at* C.) and it's so unusual to come to a meeting like this, I suppose they . . .

BILLING: (*Taking off hat.*). Good evening, ladies. (CATHERINE *and* PETRA *don't look at him.*) I don't blame you for not speaking. I just wanted to say I don't think this is going to be a place for ladies tonight.

CATHERINE: I don't remember asking your advice, Mr. Billing.

BILLING: I'm not as bad as you think, Mrs. Stockmann.

CATHERINE: Then why did you print the Mayor's statement and not a word about my husband's report? Nobody's had a chance to find out what he really stands for. Why, everybody on the street is against him already!

BILLING: If we printed his report it only would have hurt your husband.

CATHERINE: Mr. Billing, I've never said this to anyone in my life, but I think you're a liar. (*Suddenly* NANSEN, *who is directly behind* CATHERINE, *lets out a blast on his horn. The women jump.* HORSTER *moves the women* D. L. C., *then goes* U. *to the three men who have moved* U. L. C.)

HORSTER: You do that once more and I'll throw you out of here! (PETER *enters* L., *briskly and crosses to women. Behind him are* HEDVIG, GEORG, *and* GUNNAR, *who cross* D. R. *in front of chair.* BILLING *crosses to the men.*)

PETER: (*Nodding.*). Catherine? Petra? (HORSTER *crosses* D. *to* R. *of* PETER. GUNNAR *tries to get* EDVARD'S *attention.*)

PETRA: Good evening.

PETER: Why so coldly? He wanted a meeting and he's got it. (*To* HORSTER.) Isn't he here? (*A* DRUNK *crosses to* U. L. *group.* HEDVIG *and* GUNNAR *watch him.*)

HORSTER: The Doctor is going around town to be sure that there's a good attendance. (*He crosses* U. C. *and watches* DRUNK.)

PETER: Fair enough. By the way, Petra, did you paint that poster—the one somebody stuck on the town hall?

PETRA: If you can call it a painting, yes.

PETER: You know I could arrest you, it's against the law to deface the Town Hall.

PETRA: (*Holding out hands for handcuffs.*). Well, here I am.

CATHERINE: If you arrest her, Peter, I'll never speak to you!

PETER: (*Crossing* D. L., *laughing.*). Catherine, you have no sense of humor! (*He sees* HEDVIG, GUNNAR *and* GEORG *in front of his chair. They dart* U. *and he sits.* DRUNK, *egged on by the* U. L. *group, crosses* D. *to* HORSTER.)

DRUNK: Say, friend, who's runnin'! Who's the candidate?!

HORSTER: You're drunk, Mister. Now get out of here.

DRUNK: There's no law says a man who's drunk can't vote!

HORSTER: (*Crossing* DRUNK *in front of him, pushes* DRUNK *to* L. *door as crowd laughs.*). Get out of here, get out . . .

DRUNK: I wanna vote! I got a right to vote!

(ASLAKSEN *has entered* L. *and* HORSTER *pushes* DRUNK *into him.* ASLAKSEN *recoils upstage;* HORSTER *pushes* DRUNK *out door* L.)

ALAKSEN: (*Hurriedly and covertly crossing* D. *to* PETER.). Your Honor, (*Indicates* L. *door.*) he's . . .

STOCKMANN: (*Offstage.*). Right this way, gentlemen! (HOVSTAD *enters* L., *looks around, sees* PETER, *comes* D. *to* L. *of* ASLAKSEN.) In you go, come on, fellows . . . (PAUL *and* KNUT *enter* L., *followed by* STOCKMANN. *Then* TORA, PETER *and* FINN *enter* L. GUNNAR *crosses to* R. *of* HEDVIG *and* HANS, *who are in front of platform.*) Sorry, no chairs, gentlemen, but we couldn't get a hall, y'know, so just relax, it won't take long. (STOCKMANN *crosses* C., *sees* PETER.) Glad you're here, Peter!

PETER: Wouldn't miss it for the world.

STOCKMANN: (*Crossing to* CATHERINE *and* PETRA, *tak-*

140 *ing off hat and coat, giving them to* PETRA*.).* How do you feel, Catherine?

CATHERINE: Just promise me, don't lose your temper . . . (STOCKMANN *helps them to chairs.* CATHERINE *sits in* R. *chair,* PETRA *in* R. *chair. While* HORSTER *is looking* R. DRUNK *enters* L. *and crosses* D. R. C.*)*

DRUNK: Look, if you ain't votin', what the hell's going on here!

HORSTER: *(Starting after him.).* Did I tell you to
150 get out of here?

DRUNK: *(Imperiously.).* Don't push.

PETER: *(Rising.).* I order you to get out of here and stay out!

DRUNK: *(Imperiously.).* I don't like the tone of your voice! And if you don't watch your step I'm gonna tell the *Mayor* right now and he'll throw yiz all in the jug! *(Crowd is laughing,* DRUNK *turns to them.)* What're you, revolution here?! *(Amidst loud laughter,* DRUNK *turns and walks out* L.,
160 *immensely pleased with himself.)*

STOCKMANN: *(Mounting platform, quieting crowd.).* All right, gentlemen, we might as well begin. Quiet down, please. *(Crowd moves in* L. STOCKMANN *looks at* CATHERINE, *then at crowd.)* The issue is very simple . . .

ASLAKSEN: We haven't elected a chairman, Doctor.

STOCKMANN: I'm sorry, Mr. Aslaksen, this isn't a meeting; I advertised a lecture and I . . .

HENRIK: *(Raising hand.).* I came to a meeting, Doc-
170 tor, there's got to be some kind of control here.

STOCKMANN: What do you mean, control . . . what is there to control?

HEDVIG: Sure, let him speak, this is no meeting!

EDVARD: *(Stepping to* PETER*.).* Your Honor, why don't you take charge of this . . . ?

STOCKMANN: Just a minute now . . .

EDVARD: *(Crossing* L. *to in front of* HEDVIG*.).* Somebody responsible has got to take charge . . . *(To* HEDVIG*.)* There's a big difference of opinion here . . . *(Returning* L. *of* GUNNAR*.)*
180 STOCKMANN: What makes you so sure? You don't even know yet what I'm going to say.

NANSEN: I've got a pretty good idea what you're going to say and I don't like it! If a man doesn't like it here let him go where it suits him better, we don't want any trouble-makers here! *(A low grunt of assent from crowd.* STOCKMANN *looks at them.)*

STOCKMANN: Now look, friend, you don't know anything about me . . .
190 NANSEN: We know plenty about you, Stockmann.

STOCKMANN: From what, from the newspapers? How do you know I don't like this town? *(Holds up notes.)* I'm here to save the life of this town.

PETER: *(Rising quickly.).* Now just a minute, Doctor. *(Crowd quickly becomes silent from* L. *to* R.*)* I think the democratic thing to do is to elect a chairman.

EDVARD: *(Quickly raising his hand.).* I nominate the Mayor!
200 NANSEN: *(Quickly raising his hand.).* Second the Mayor!

PETER: No, no, no. That wouldn't be fair. We want a neutral person. I suggest Mr. Aslaksen who has always . . .

HEDVIG: I came to a lecture, I didn't . . .

NANSEN: *(To* HEDVIG*.).* What're you afraid of a fair fight? *(To* PETER*.)* Second Mr. Aslaksen! *(Crowd assents: "Very good choice," etc.)*

STOCKMANN: All right, if that's your pleasure. I
210 just want to remind you that the reason I arranged for this lecture was that I have a very important message for you people and . . . *(ASLAKSEN crosses* D. C.; STOCKMANN *gets off platform.)* I couldn't get it into the press and nobody would rent me a hall. *(To* PETER*.)* I just hope I'll be given time to speak here. *(To* ASLAKSEN*.)* Mr. Aslaksen? *(The crowd applauds* ASLAKSEN, *who mounts platform.* STOCKMANN *crosses to between* PETRA *and* CATHERINE. KNUT *crosses to* R. *of plat-*
220 *form.* NANSEN *crosses and talks to* BILLING. HOVSTAD *crosses* R. *and talks to* PETER. FINN *crosses* D. *to* L. *of* EDVARD. KIIL *enters* L. *and stands just* R. *of* GABRIEL.*)*

ASLAKSEN: I have just one word before we start. Whatever is said tonight, please remember, the highest civic virtue is moderation. *(He can't help turning to* STOCKMANN, *then looks over to* PETER.*)* Now if anybody wants to speak . . . *(DRUNK enters* L. *suddenly and crosses* C.*)*
230 DRUNK: I heard that! Since when you allowed to electioneer at the polls? *(Crowd pushes him back to door* L. *amid laughter.)* I'm gonna report this to the Mayor, goddammit! *(STOCKMANN crosses* D. L., *looks after* DRUNK.*)*

ASLAKSEN: Quiet, please, quiet. *(Complete quiet.)* Does anybody want the floor? *(STOCKMANN raises his hand but* PETER *also raises his, almost imperceptibly.)*

240   PETER: Mr. Chairman.

ASLAKSEN: *(Quickly.).* His Honor the Mayor will address the meeting. *(Great applause,* STOCKMANN *returns to his position* L. *of* PETRA. PETER *rises and crosses to platform, which he mounts.* EDVARD *pulls* GUNNAR *to get better view of* PETER. BILLING *crosses to* D. C. *edge of platform as* HENRIK *goes* U. L. C. *to talk to* NANSEN. KIIL *sits in the Mayor's chair,* D. R. HOVSTAD *crosses to behind* BILLING.*)*

250   PETER: Gentlemen, there's no reason to take very long to settle this tonight and return to our ordinary calm and peaceful life. Here's the issue: Doctor Stockmann, my brother—and believe me, it's not easy to say this—has decided to destroy Kirsten Springs, our Health Institute. . . .

Crowd is dead quiet.

STOCKMANN: Peter!

ASLAKSEN: Let the Mayor continue, please. There

260   mustn't be any interruptions.

PETER: He has a long and very involved way of going about it, but that's the brunt of it, believe me.

NANSEN: *(Rather quietly.).* Then what're we wasting time for? Run him out of town! *(*HENRIK *"plots" with* NANSEN. *Others agree;* HEDVIG *disagrees.)*

PETER: Now wait a minute. I want no violence here. I want you to understand his motives. He is a man, always has been, who is never happy

270   unless he is badgering authority, ridiculing authority, destroying authority. He wants to attack the Springs so he can prove that the Administration blundered in the construction.

STOCKMANN: *(To* ASLAKSEN*.).* May I speak, I . . .?

ASLAKSEN: The Mayor's not finished. *(*STOCKMANN *turns and steps* D. *distractedly.)*

PETER: Thank you. Now there are a number of people here who seem to feel that the Doctor has a right to say anything he pleases. After

280   all, we are a democratic country. Now God knows, in ordinary times, I'd agree a hundred percent with anybody's right to say anything. But these are not ordinary times. Nations have crises and so do towns. There are ruins of nations and there are ruins of towns all over the world,

and they were wrecked by people who in the guise of reform and pleading for justice and so on, broke down all authority and left only revolution and chaos.

STOCKMANN: *(Crossing* D. L. *of platform.).* What the   290
hell are you talking about!

ASLAKSEN: *(As crowd begins to murmur.).* I'll have to insist, Doctor . . .

STOCKMANN: I called a lecture, I didn't invite him to attack me. *(Crosses to crowd.)* He's got the press and every hall in town to attack me and I've got nothing but this room tonight. *(Crowd snarls and advances on* STOCKMANN.*)*

ASLAKSEN: I don't think you're making a very good impression, Doctor. *(Assenting laughter and catcalls.*   300
DRUNK *whistles loudly from arch* L. HORSTER *quiets him.* HOVSTAD *crosses* D. *then* U. *to* BILLING. GUNNAR *and* EDVARD *cross to* GABRIEL *to deplore situation.* STOCKMANN *backs away from crowd, dismayed, goes up to confer with family.* ASLAKSEN *rings and calls for quiet, finally gets it.)* Please continue, Your Honor.

PETER: Now this is our crisis. We know what this town was without our Institute. We could barely afford to keep the streets in condition; it was   310
a dead, third-rate hamlet. Today we're just on the verge of becoming internationally known as a resort. I predict that within five years the income of every man in this room will be immensely greater. *(*HENRIK *chuckles at this prospect.)* I predict that our schools will be bigger and better; and in time this town will be crowded with fine carriages; *(*GABRIEL *beams at* KIIL, *who glowers back.)* great homes will be built here, first-class stores will open all along Main Street.   320
(Crowd murmurs in appreciation.) I predict that if we were not defamed and maliciously attacked we will some day be one of the richest and most beautiful resort towns in the world.*(General applause.)* There are your choices. Now all you've got to do is ask yourselves a simple question—has any one of us the right, the "democratic" right as they like to call it, to pick at minor flaws in the Springs, to exaggerate the most picayune faults . . . *(Cries of "No, no!")* and to attempt to   330
publish these defamations for the whole world to see? We live or die on what the outside world thinks of us! I believe there is a line that must be drawn, and if a man decides to cross that

line, we the people must finally take him by the collar and declare, "You cannot say that." (*An uproar of assent.* HENRIK *and* NANSEN *cross* D. *after* STOCKMANN. BILLING *and* HOVSTAD *forcibly stop them and they return* U. R. C. EDVARD *reaches and pulls* GUNNAR *back* L. *out of danger.* GABRIEL *crosses to* FINN, *takes him* U. L. C. HORSTER *crosses* D. L.) All right, then. I think we all understand each other. Mr. Aslaksen, I move that Doctor Stockmann be prohibited from reading his report at this meeting. (*Ovation.* PETER *returns to his chair* D. R., *accepting the handshakes and plaudits of crowd. He finds* KIIL *sitting in his chair;* KIIL *disgustedly rises and scornfully gives* PETER *his place.* STOCKMANN *is behind his family at* L., *talking to them.* ASLAKSEN *is ringing bell and finally quiets the enthusiasm.*)

ASLAKSEN: Quiet, please! Please, now! I think we can proceed to the vote. (PETRA *claps* STOCKMANN *on the back.*)

STOCKMANN: Well, aren't you going to let me speak at all?

ASLAKSEN: Doctor, we are just about to vote on that question.

STOCKMANN: But damn it, man, I've got a right to . . .

PETRA: (*Moving behind* STOCKMANN.). Point of order, Father!

STOCKMANN: (*Remembering.*). Yes, point of order!

ASLAKSEN: Yes, Doctor? (STOCKMANN, *at a loss, turns to* PETRA *for further instruction.*)

PETRA: You want to discuss the motion.

STOCKMANN: That's right, damn it. I want to discuss the motion!

ASLAKSEN: Ah . . . (*Glances at* PETER, *who nods.*) All right, go ahead. (PETRA *sits.*)

STOCKMANN: (*Moving to* D. *of platform.*). Now listen. (*Pointing to* PETER.) He talks and he talks and he talks, but not a word about the facts. (*Holding up papers.*)

HENRIK: (*Snarling.*). We don't want to hear any more about the water!

NANSEN: You're just trying to blow up everything!

STOCKMANN: Well, judge for yourselves. Let me read . . . (*Crowd calls,* "No, no, no." *This rapidly builds into the biggest, noisiest reaction: shouting, horns blowing, bell ringing. Crutches and canes are waved in the air.* PETRA *and* CATHERINE *rise.*)

ASLAKSEN: (*Ringing for quiet.*). Please, please now, quiet. We can't have this uproar! (*Quiet finally comes.*) I think, Doctor, that the majority wants to take the vote before you start to speak. If they so will, you can speak, otherwise . . . majority rules, you won't deny that.

STOCKMANN: (*Turns and tosses notes to* PETRA.). Don't bother voting. I understand everything now. Can I have a few minutes?

PETER: (*Rising.*). Mr. Chairman . . .

STOCKMANN: (*Crossing* D. C.; *to* PETER.). I won't mention the Institute. (*Crowd recoils before him.*) I have a new discovery that's a thousand times more important than all the institutes in the world. (*To* ASLAKSEN.) May I have the platform?

ASLAKSEN: (*Looking over crowd to* PETER.). I don't see how we can deny him that as long as he confines himself to . . . (*Crowd discusses* ASLAKSEN's *decision.* HOVSTAD *fades* D. R. C.)

STOCKMANN: The Springs are not the subject. (*He mounts platform.* ASLAKSEN, CATHERINE, *and* PETRA *sit.* TORA *crosses to* U. *of* PETER; FINN *crosses* U. R.; BILLING *and* HOVSTAD *are* D. R. C.; HORSTER *crosses* L. C.; GABRIEL *crosses to in front of* PETER; EDVARD *and* GUNNAR *cross* U. R. C.; PAUL *crosses* D. C.; GEORG *puts bag of raisins in pocket.*) Before I go into my subject, I want to congratulate the "liberals" and "radicals" among us—like Mr. Hovstad . . . (BILLING *takes notes during* STOCKMANN's *speech.*)

HOVSTAD: What do you mean, radical! Where's your evidence to call me a radical! (DRUNK *enters* L. *and leans against the arch.*)

STOCKMANN: You got me there. There isn't any evidence. I guess there never really was. I just wanted to congratulate you on your self-control tonight—you who have fought in every parlor for the principle of free speech these many years.

HOVSTAD: I believe in democracy. When my readers are overwhelmingly against something, I'm not going to impose my will on the majority.

STOCKMANN: You have begun my remarks, Mr. Hovstad. (*Turns to crowd.*) Gentlemen, Mrs. Stockmann, Miss Stockmann, tonight I was struck by a sudden flash of light, a discovery second to none. But before I tell it to you, a little story. (*Slight improvisation of exasperation.*) I put in a good many years in the North of our country. Up there the rulers of the world are the great seal and the gigantic squadrons of duck. Man lives on ice, huddled together in a little pile of stone. His whole life consists of grubbing for food. Nothing more. He can barely speak his own language. And it came to me one day that it was romantic and sentimental for a man of my education to be tending these people. They had not yet reached the stage where they needed a doctor. If the truth were to be told, a veterinary would be more in order.

440 (*A murmur of displeasure works through crowd.*)

BILLING: Is that the way you refer to decent, hardworking people!

STOCKMANN: I expected that, my friend, but don't think you can fog up my brain with that magic word, the People! Not any more! Just because there is a mass of organisms with the human shape... (*Crowd reacts to this insult.*) they do not automatically become a People. That *honor* has to be *earned!* Nor does one automatically become

450 "A Man" by having human shape, and living in a house, and feeding one's face—and agreeing with one's neighbors. (*Slight reaction to this insult.*) That name *also* has to be earned. (*Crowd becomes quiet by the force of his words.*) Now, when I came to my conclusions about the Springs...

PETER: (*Rising.*) You have no right to...

STOCKMANN: That's a picayune thing to catch me on a word, Peter, I'm not going into the Springs. (*To crowd.*) When I became convinced of my

460 theory about the water, the authorities moved in at once, and I said to myself, I will fight them to the death because...

NANSEN: (*Quietly.*). What're you trying to make, a revolution here? (*To* GUNNAR.) He's a revolutionist!

STOCKMANN: (*Almost pleading to* NANSEN.) Let me finish! (*To crowd.*) I thought to myself—the majority, I have the majority! And let me tell you, friends, it was a grand feeling. Because

470 the reason I came back to this place of my birth was that I wanted to give my education to this town, I loved it, so I spent months without pay or encouragement and dreamed up the whole project of the Springs. And why? Not as my brother says, so that fine carriages could crowd our streets, but so that we might cure the sick, so that we might meet people from all over the world and learn from them, and become broader and more civilized—in other words, more like

480 Men, more like A People.

EDVARD: You don't like anything about this town, do you?

STOCKMANN: I don't admit it! I proclaim it now! I am in revolt against the age-old lie that the majority is *always* right! (*Crowd's reaction is astonished, stunned.*)

HOVSTAD: He's an aristocrat all of a sudden!

STOCKMANN: And more! I tell you now, that the majority is always wrong, and in this way!

PETER: Have you lost your mind! Stop talking   490 before...

STOCKMANN: Was the majority right when they stood by while Jesus was crucified? (*Silence.*) Was the majority right when they refused to believe that the earth moved round the sun, and let Galileo be driven to his knees like a dog? It takes fifty years for the majority to be right. The majority is never right until it *does* right.

HOVSTAD: I want to state right now, that although I've been this man's friend and I've eaten at his   500 table many times, I now cut myself off from him absolutely. (*Starts to leave* U. R.; GABRIEL, BILLING *and* FINN *restrain him.* EDVARD *and* GUNNAR *start off;* STOCKMANN'S *pleas bring them back.*)

STOCKMANN: Answer me this! Please, one more moment! A platoon of soldiers is walking down a road toward the enemy. Every one of them is convinced he is on the right road, the safe road. But two miles ahead stands one lonely man, the outpost. He sees that this road is dangerous,   510 that his comrades are walking into a trap. He runs back, he finds the platoon. Isn't it clear that this man must have the right to warn the majority, to argue with the majority, to fight with the majority if he believes he has the truth? Before many can know something, *one* must know it! (*His passion has made a silence.*) It's always the same. Rights are sacred until it hurts for somebody to use them. I beg you now—I realize the cost is great, the inconvenience is great, the   520 risk is great that other towns will get the jump on us while we're rebuilding...

PETER: Aslaksen, he's not allowed to...

STOCKMANN: Let me prove it to you! The water is poisoned!

NANSEN: (*Crosses to below platform, waving fist in air;* PETRA *rises and crosses to give* STOCKMANN *his report, but bumps into* NANSEN.). One more word about poison and I'm gonna take you outside! (*Crowd* *surges forward.* CATHERINE *pulls* PETRA *back* D. L. *Bell is ringing; crowd is roaring. Canes and crutches are waved in the air. Even the* DRUNK, *who has dozed off while leaning in archway* L., *starts to fight an imaginary opponent. All are violent "for the good of the town."* KIIL *takes this all in, then darts away off* L. HENRIK *has crossed, and is arguing with the women.* HEDVIG *screams when crowd moves forward, then runs* R. C. *with* HANS; GUNNAR *crosses to her.* HORSTER, *who has been pulling men out of the crowd, sees* HENRIK *with the two women and crosses to get him away, then stays* D. L. *to protect the women.* PETER *is standing* R. C., *watching all this.*)

PETER: That's enough! Now stop it! Quiet! There is not going to be any violence here!! (*People in the crowd look at* PETER *and become quiet. After a moment.*) Doctor, come down and give Mr. Aslaksen the platform.

STOCKMANN: I'm not through yet.

PETER: Come down or I will not be responsible for what happens.

CATHERINE: I'd like to go home; come on, Tom.

PETER: I move the Chairman order the speaker to leave the platform.

EDVARD: Sit down!

NANSEN: Get off that platform!   (*Together.*)
(*Others join in.*)

STOCKMANN: All right. Then I'll take this to out-of-town newspapers until the whole country is warned...

PETER: You wouldn't dare!

HOVSTAD: (*Breaking away* R. C.). You're trying to ruin this town, that's all, trying to ruin it.

STOCKMANN: You are trying to build a town on a morality so rotten that it will infect the country and the world! If the only way you can prosper is this murder of freedom and truth, then I say with all my heart—let it be destroyed, let the people perish! (*He jumps down from rear of platform and crosses to his family* D. R. HORSTER *helps him with his hat and coat. Crowd turns to* PETER *for action.*)

NANSEN: Arrest him!

HENRIK *and* FINN: He's a traitor! Traitor!

GABRIEL: Revolution!

ASLAKSEN: (*Ringing for quiet.*). I would like to sub-mit the following resolution: The people assem-bled here tonight, decent and patriotic citizens, in defense of their town and their country, declare, that Doctor Stockmann, Medical Officer of the Springs, is an enemy of the people and of this community.

CATHERINE: That's not true! He loves this town!

STOCKMANN: You damned fools, you fools! (*Crowd advances on* STOCKMANN.)

ASLAKSEN: (*Shouting over the din.*). Is there anyone against this motion? Anyone against? (*Crowd becomes quiet. After a moment.*)

HORSTER: (*Raises hand.*). I am. (*Crowd backs away.*)

ASLAKSEN: One?

DRUNK: (*Raises his hand, sleepily.*). Me, too! You can't do without a Doctor... (*Everyone looks back at* ASLAKSEN.) Anybody'll tell you...

ASLAKSEN: Anyone else? With all votes against two, this assembly formally declares Doctor Thomas Stockmann to be the people's enemy. In the future, all dealings with him by decent, patriotic citizens will be on that basis. The meet-ing is adjourned. (*Applause.* ASLAKSEN *and* BILLING *and* HOVSTAD *cross* D. R. *to* PETER; HOVSTAD *helps him on with coat.* HEDVIG *and* GEORG *cross* C.)

STOCKMANN: (*Stepping to* HORSTER.). Captain, do you have room for us on your ship to America?

HORSTER: Any time you say, Doctor. (NANSEN *steps* D., *looks at* HORSTER, *then crosses* R. R.)

STOCKMANN: Catherine! (*She takes his* R. *arm.*) Petra? (*She takes his* L. *arm. They start for door* U. L. *Crowd falls silent; a gauntlet is formed.* HEDVIG *looks at the three, then hides her boy's head, ashamed, and turns away herself. As the three start to move:*)

NANSEN: Doctor! (*Slight pause.*) You'd better get on that ship soon.

CATHERINE: (*Quickly.*). Let's go out the back door...

HORSTER: Right this way...

STOCKMANN: No, no! No back doors! (*To crowd.*) I don't want to mislead anybody—the enemy of the people is not finished in this town—not quite yet! And if anybody thinks...

HENRIK: (*Suddenly.*). Traitor! (*Quickly the noise builds.*)

EDVARD: Enemy! Enemy!

NANSEN: Throw him in the   (*Together.*)
    river! Come on, throw him in
    the river!

(Out of the noise, a chant emerges; soon the whole crowd is calling, "Enemy! Enemy!" stamping their feet on last syllable. Through the two lines the STOCKMANNS, *erect, move. Crowd is snapping at them like animals.*

STOCKMANN, PETER, BILLING, ASLAKSEN *and* HOVSTAD *are seen watching* D. L. *The whole stage throbs with the chant, "Enemy, enemy, enemy.")*   630
CURTAIN

ACT THREE

SCENE: *Same as* ACT I, SCENE I.

The following morning. Windows at R. *are broken. Disorder. There are small rocks around the room:* D. C., *under* C. *chair, under the* R. C. *chair, and in front of bay window.*

STOCKMANN *enters* D. L. *with robe over shirt and trousers; closes door. It's cold in the house. He picks up a stone from* D. C., *sets it on table where there is a little pile of rocks.*

STOCKMANN: Catherine! Tell what's-her-name there's still some rocks to pick up in here!

CATHERINE: (*Off* U. L.). She's not finished sweeping up the glass! (STOCKMANN *bends down to get another*
10   *stone under a chair when a rock is thrown through one of the last remaining panes. He whirls around and rushes to* U. *of window, looks out.* CATHERINE *runs in from dining-room door and crosses to* STOCKMANN. *They put their arms round each other.*) You all right?!

STOCKMANN: (*Looking out window.*). A little boy. Look at him run. (*Picking up stone in front of window.*) How fast the poison spreads—even to the children. (*Crosses and sets rock on* R. C. *table.*)

20   CATHERINE: (*Looking out window, has chill.*). It's hard to believe this is the same town . . .

STOCKMANN: I'm going to keep these like sacred relics. I'll put them in my will. I want the boys to have these in their homes to look at every day. (*Shudders.*) Cold in here. Why hasn't what's-her-name got the glazier here?

CATHERINE: (*Turns to him, steps* D.). She's getting him . . .

STOCKMANN: She's been getting him for two hours.
30   We'll freeze to death in here. (*Pulls muffler around neck.*)

CATHERINE: (*Unwillingly.*). He won't come here, Tom.

STOCKMANN: No! The glazier's afraid to fix my windows?

CATHERINE: You don't realize . . . people don't like to be pointed out. He's got neighbors, I suppose, and . . . (*A knock on* U. R. *door.*) Is that someone at the door? (*She goes to* U. R. *door.* STOCKMANN *picks up stone under* R. *chair.* CATHERINE *returns.*)   40
Letter for you.

STOCKMANN: (*Taking and opening it.*) What's this now?

CATHERINE: (*Picking up stone under* C. *chair.*). I don't know how we're going to do any shopping with everybody ready to bite my head off . . .

STOCKMANN: Well, what do you know! We're evicted!

CATHERINE: Oh, no!

STOCKMANN: He hates to do it, but with public   50
opinion what it is . . .

CATHERINE: (*Frightened, crosses* U. C.). Maybe we shouldn't have let the boys go to school today?

STOCKMANN: (*Crosses* U. R. *around table to* U. C.). Now don't get all frazzled again . . .

CATHERINE: But the landlord is such a nice man. If he's got to throw us out the town must be ready to murder us!

STOCKMANN: Just calm down, will you? (*Leads her to* C. *chair, sits, pulls her down on his* L. *knee.*) We'll   60
go to America and the whole thing'll be like a dream . . .

CATHERINE: But I don't want to go to America . . .
(*Noticing his pants.*) When did this get torn?

STOCKMANN: Must've been last night . . .

CATHERINE: Your best pants!

STOCKMANN: Well, it shows you, that's all. Man

goes out to fight for the truth should never wear his best pants. (*She half-laughs*.) Stop worrying, will you? You'll sew them up and in no time at all we'll be three thousand miles away . . .

CATHERINE: But how do you know it'll be any different there?

STOCKMANN: I don't know, it just seems to me in a big country like that, the spirit must be bigger. Still, I suppose they must have the solid majority there, too? I don't know, at least there must be more room to hide there.

CATHERINE: Think about it more, will you? I'd hate to go half around the world and find out we're in the same place.

STOCKMANN: You know, Catherine, I don't think I'm ever going to forget the face of that crowd last night.

CATHERINE: (*Puts shawl around him*.). Don't think about it . . .

STOCKMANN: Some of them had their teeth bared, like animals in a pack. And who leads them? Men who call themselves liberals! Radicals! (*She looks around at furniture, figuring*.) The crowd lets out one roar and where are they—my liberal friends! I bet if I walked down the street now not one of them would admit he ever met me! It's hard to believe, it's . . . Are you listening to me?

CATHERINE: I was just wondering what we'll ever do with this furniture if we go to America?

STOCKMANN: Don't you ever listen when I talk, dear?

CATHERINE: Why must I listen? *I* know you're right. (PETRA *enters* U. R. CATHERINE *sees her, rises*.) Petra! Why aren't you in school?

STOCKMANN: (*Rises, as* PETRA *crosses, steps back a little*.). What's the matter? (PETRA *crosses* D., *then* L. *to* STOCKMANN *at* C.; CATHERINE *comes* D. *a step and watches*. PETRA *kisses* STOCKMANN.)

PETRA: I'm fired.

CATHERINE: They wouldn't!

PETRA: As of two weeks from now. But I couldn't bear to stay there.

STOCKMANN: (*Shocked*.). Mrs. Busk fired you?

CATHERINE: Who'd ever imagine she could do such a thing?

PETRA: It hurt her. I could see it, because we've always agreed so about things. But she didn't dare do anything else . . .

STOCKMANN: The glazier doesn't dare fix the windows, the landlord doesn't dare let us stay on . . .

PETRA: The landlord!

STOCKMANN: Evicted, darling! Oh, God, on the wreckage of all the civilizations in the world there ought to be a big sign—"They Didn't Dare!"

PETRA: I really can't blame her, Father, she showed me three letters she got this morning . . .

STOCKMANN: From whom?

PETRA: They weren't signed . . .

STOCKMANN: Oh, naturally. The big patriots with their anonymous indignation, scrawling out the darkness of their minds onto dirty little slips of paper—that's morality, and *I'm* the traitor! What'd the letters say?

PETRA: Well, one of them was from somebody who said that he'd heard at the club that somebody who visits this house said I had radical opinions about certain things.

STOCKMANN: Oh, wonderful! Somebody heard that somebody heard that *she* heard that *he* heard!—Catherine, pack as soon as you can. I feel as though vermin were crawling all over me. (*He starts to door* D. L. HORSTER *enters* U. R. *immediately and crosses* D. R.)

HORSTER: Good morning!

STOCKMANN: (*Crossing to* HORSTER D. R. C.). Captain! You're just the man I want to see.

HORSTER: I thought I'd see how you all were . . .

CATHERINE: That's awfully nice of you, Captain . . . (*Stepping down and crossing to* L. *of* STOCKMANN.) and I want to thank you for seeing us through the crowd last night.

PETRA: Did you get home all right? We hated to leave you alone with that mob.

HORSTER: Oh, nothing to it. In a storm, there's just one thing to remember—it will pass.

STOCKMANN: Unless it kills you.

HORSTER: (*After a moment*.). You mustn't let yourself get too bitter.

STOCKMANN: I'm trying, I'm trying. But I don't guarantee how I'll feel when I try to walk down the street with "Traitor" branded on my forehead.

CATHERINE: Don't think about it. ⎫

HORSTER: Ah, what's a word? ⎭   (*Together*)

STOCKMANN: A word can be like a needle sticking in your heart, Captain. It can dig and corrode like an acid, until you become what they want you to be—really an enemy of the people.

HORSTER: You mustn't ever let that happen, Doctor.

170 STOCKMANN: Frankly, I don't give a damn any more. Let summer come, let an epidemic break out, then they'll know who they drove into exile. When are you sailing?

PETRA: (*Stepping* D. C.). You really decided to go, Father?

STOCKMANN: Absolutely. When do you sail, Captain?

HORSTER: (*Crossing* D. L. C. *to* L. *of* PETRA.) That's really what I came to talk to you about.

180 STOCKMANN: Why, something happen to the ship?

CATHERINE: (*Happily to* STOCKMANN.). You see! We can't go!

HORSTER: No, the ship will sail. But I won't be aboard.

STOCKMANN: No!

PETRA: You fired, too? 'Cause I was this morning!

CATHERINE: Oh, Captain, you shouldn't have given us your house...

HORSTER: Oh, I'll get another ship. It's just that

190 the owner, Mr. Vik, happens to belong to the same party as the Mayor, and I suppose when you belong to a party and the party takes a certain position... Because Mr. Vik himself is a very decent man...

STOCKMANN: Oh, they're all decent men!

HORSTER: No, really, he's not like the others...

STOCKMANN: He doesn't have to be. A party is like a sausage grinder—it mashes up clear heads, longheads, fatheads, blockheads, and what

200 comes out?—meatheads! (*Bell at* U. R. *door.* PETRA *goes to answer it.*)

CATHERINE: (*Crossing to* U. *of* R. C. *table.*). Maybe that's the glazier...

STOCKMANN: (Stepping to HORSTER.). Imagine, Captain... (*Pointing to door.*) He refused to come all morning. (PETER *enters* U. R. *and stands just below arch.* PETRA *stays in hall.*)

PETER: If you're busy...

STOCKMANN: (*Crossing to* D. *of* R. C. *table.* HORSTER

210 *crosses* D. L. C.). Just picking up rocks and broken glass. Come in, Peter. What can I do for you this fine, brisk morning? (*He demonstratively pulls his robe tighter around his throat.*)

CATHERINE: (*Indicating dining-room.*). Come inside, won't you, Captain?

HORSTER: (*Crossing* U.). Yes. I'd like to finish our talk, Doctor.

STOCKMANN: (*Stepping* L. *a little.*). Be with you in a minute, Captain. (HORSTER *exits into dining-room, preceded by* CATHERINE *and* PETRA. PETER 220 *says nothing, looking at the damage; he is standing* D. R.) Keep your hat on if you like, it's a little draughty in here today.

PETER: Thanks, I believe I will. (*Puts his hat on.*) I think I caught cold last night—that house was freezing.

STOCKMANN: I thought it was kind of warm—suffocating, as a matter of fact. What do you want?

PETER: May I sit down? (*Starts to sit in* R. C. *chair.*)

STOCKMANN: Not there, a piece of the solid 230 majority... (*Refers to window.*) is liable to open your skull! There. (*Indicates* D. L. *chair, sits, while taking a large envelope out of his breast pocket.*) Now don't tell me!

PETER: Yes. (*Hands him envelope.*)

STOCKMANN: (*Gets it and sets it on table, returns, sits on* R. C. *chair.*). I'm fired.

PETER: The Board met this morning. There was nothing else to do, considering the state of public opinion. (*Pause.*) 240

STOCKMANN: You look scared, Peter.

PETER: I... haven't completely forgotten that you're still my brother.

STOCKMANN: I doubt that.

PETER: You have no practice left in this town, Thomas.

STOCKMANN: People always need a doctor.

PETER: A petition is going from house to house. Everybody is signing it. A pledge not to call you any more. I don't think a single family will 250 dare refuse to sign it.

STOCKMANN: You started that, didn't you?

PETER: No. As a matter of fact, I think it's all gone a little too far. I never wanted to see you ruined, Thomas. This will ruin you.

STOCKMANN: No, it won't...

PETER: For once in your life, will you act like a responsible man?

STOCKMANN: Why don't you say it, Peter? You're afraid I'm going out of town to start publishing 260 things about the Springs, aren't you?

PETER: I don't deny that. (*Takes off hat.*) Thomas, if you really have the good of the town at heart you can accomplish everything without damaging anybody, including yourself. (*Pause.*)

STOCKMANN: What's this now?

PETER: Let me have a signed statement saying that in your zeal to help the town, you went overboard and exaggerated—put it any way you like, just so you calm anybody who might feel nervous about the water. If you'll give me that, you've got your job, and I give you my word you can gradually make all the improvements you feel are necessary. Now that gives you what you want...

STOCKMANN: You're nervous, Peter.

PETER: (*He is; steps back to sofa.*) I am not nervous!

STOCKMANN: (*Rises, stands* U. C. *of* PETER.). You expect me to remain in charge while people are being poisoned?

PETER: In time you can make your changes...

STOCKMANN: When—five years, ten years? You know your trouble, Peter? You just don't grasp, even now, that there are certain men you can't buy.

PETER: I'm quite capable of understanding that; but you don't happen to be one of those men. (*Slight pause.*)

STOCKMANN: What do you mean by that now?

PETER: You know damned well what I mean by that. Morten Kiil is what I mean by that.

STOCKMANN: Morten Kiil?

PETER: (*Rising.*). Your father-in-law, Morten Kiil.

STOCKMANN: I swear, Peter, one of us is out of his mind; what are you talking about?

PETER: Now don't try to charm me with that professional innocence...

STOCKMANN: What are you talking about?

PETER: You don't know that your father-in-law has been running around all morning buying up stock in Kirsten Springs?

STOCKMANN: (*Perplexed.*). Buying up stock?

PETER: Buying up stock, every share he can lay his hands on!

STOCKMANN: Well, I don't understand, Peter, what's that got to do with...?

PETER: (*Crossing* STOCKMANN *to* D. *of* R. C. *chair in agitation; takes off hat.*). Oh, come now, come now, come now...

STOCKMANN: (*Crossing to* D. *of sofa.*). I hate you when you do that! Don't just walk around gabbling "Come now, come now"—what the hell are you talking about?

PETER: Very well, if you insist on being dense. A man wages a relentless campaign to destroy confidence in a corporation. He even goes so far as to call a mass meeting against it. The very next morning, when people are still in a state of shock about it all, his father-in-law runs all over town picking up shares at half their value.

STOCKMANN: (*After a pause.*). My God!

PETER: And you have the nerve to speak to me about principles?

STOCKMANN: You mean you actually believe that I...

PETER: I'm not interested in psychology! I believe what I see! And what I see is nothing but a man doing a dirty, filthy job for Morten Kiil, and let me tell you, by tonight every man in this town'll see the same thing!

STOCKMANN: Peter, you, you...!

PETER: (*Pointing to study door* L.). Now go to your desk and write me a statement denying everything you've been saying or...

STOCKMANN: Peter, you're a low creature!

PETER: All right, then, you'd better get this one straight, Thomas. If you're figuring on opening another attack from out of town, keep this in mind: the morning it's published I will send out a subpoena for you and begin a prosecution for conspiracy. I've been trying to make you respectable all my life; now if you want to make the big jump there'll be nobody there to hold you back. Now do we understand each other?

STOCKMANN: Oh, we do, Peter! (KIIL *enters hall* U. R. PETER *starts for door and almost bumps into him.* STOCKMANN *crosses* U. *to* R. *of dining-room arch.*) Get the girl—what the hell is her name?—scrub the floors, wash down the walls, a pestilence has been here!

PETER: (*Turning to* STOCKMANN, *pointing to* KIIL.). Hah! (*He exits* U. R. KIIL *crosses* D. *to* R. *table; sits in* R. *chair.*)

STOCKMANN: (*Crossing* D. *to* L. *of* KIIL.). Morten, now what have you done? What's the matter with you? Do you realize what this makes me look like?! (KIIL *simply sits there, grinning up at him;*

takes some stock shares out of his inside coat pocket and sets them on table. STOCKMANN *breaks off on seeing them.*) Is that . . . them?

KIIL: That's them, yes. Kirsten Springs shares. And very easy to get this morning.

STOCKMANN: Morten, don't play with me, what's this all about?

KIIL: What are you so nervous about? Can't a man buy some stock without . . . ?

STOCKMANN: (*Moves to* KIIL.). I want an explanation, Morten.

KIIL: Thomas, they hated you last night.

STOCKMANN: You don't have to tell me that.

KIIL: But they also believed you. They'd love to murder you, but they believe you. (*Slight pause.*) The way they say it, the pollution is coming down the river from Windmill Valley.

STOCKMANN: That's exactly where it's coming from.

KIIL: Yes. And that's exactly where my tannery is.

STOCKMANN: (*Sitting, slowly.*). Well, Morten, I never made a secret to you that the pollution was tannery waste.

KIIL: I'm not blaming you. It's my fault. I didn't take you seriously. But it's very serious now. Thomas, I got that tannery from my father, he got it from his father; and his father got it from my great-grandfather. I do not intend to allow my family's name to stand for the three generations of murdering angels who poisoned this town.

STOCKMANN: I've waited a long time for this talk, Morten. I don't think you can stop that from happening.

KIIL: No, but you can.

STOCKMANN: I?

KIIL: (*Nudging the shares.*). I've bought these shares because . . .

STOCKMANN: Morten, you've thrown your money away: the Springs are doomed.

KIIL: I never throw my money away, Thomas. These were bought with your money.

STOCKMANN: My money? What . . . ?

KIIL: You've probably suspected that I might leave a little something for Catherine and the boys?

STOCKMANN: Well, naturally, I'd hoped you'd . . .

KIIL: (*Touches shares.*). I decided this morning to invest that money in some stock, Thomas.

STOCKMANN: (*Slowly getting up. Slight indication of* CATHERINE *off* L.). You bought that junk with Catherine's money . . . !

KIIL: People call me badger, and that's an animal that roots out things, but it's also some kind of a pig, I understand. I've lived a clean man and I'm going to die clean. You're going to clean my name for me.

STOCKMANN: Morten . . .

KIIL: Now I want to see if you really belong in a strait-jacket.

STOCKMANN: How could you dare do such a thing? What's the matter with you?

KIIL: Now don't get excited, it's very simple. If you should make another investigation of the water . . .

STOCKMANN: I don't *need* another investigation, I . . .

KIIL: If you think it over and decide that you ought to change your opinion about the water . . .

STOCKMANN: But the water is poisoned, it's poisoned!

KIIL: If you simply go on insisting the water is poisoned, (*Holds up shares.*) with these in your house, then there's only one explanation for you—you are absolutely crazy!

STOCKMANN: You're right! I'm mad! I'm insane!

KIIL: (*Rising.*). You must be! You're stripping the skin off your family's back—only a madman would do a thing like that!

STOCKMANN: Morten, Morten, I'm a penniless man, why didn't you tell me before you bought this junk?

KIIL: (*Crossing to* STOCKMANN.). Because you would understand it better if I told you after. (*Holds him by lapels with terrific force.* STOCKMANN *turns his face away.*) And Goddammit, I think you do understand it now! Don't you! Millions of tons of water come down that river. How do you know the day you made your tests there wasn't something unusual about the water?

STOCKMANN: (*Breaking* D. L. C.). No, I took too many samples.

KIIL: How do you know? (*Following him.*) Why couldn't those little animals have clotted up only in the patch of water you souped out of the river? How do you know the rest of it wasn't pure?

STOCKMANN: (*Crossing* KIIL *to* C. KIIL *follows.*). It's

not probable... people were getting sick last summer...

KIIL: They were sick when they came here, or they wouldn't have come!

460 STOCKMANN: Not intestinal diseases, skin diseases...

KIIL: The only place anybody gets a bellyache is here?! There are no carbuncles in Norway? Maybe the food was bad! Did you even think of the food?

STOCKMANN: (*With desire to agree with him*.). No... I didn't look into the food...

KIIL: Then what the hell makes you so sure it's the water?

470 STOCKMANN: Because I tested the water and...

KIIL: (*Turning to* STOCKMANN.). Admit it. We're all alone here... you have some doubt...

STOCKMANN: (*Crossing,* U. *around table, then* L. C.). Well, nothing is a hundred percent on this earth, but...

KIIL: Then you have a perfect right to doubt the other way! You have a scientific right! And did you ever think of some disinfectant? I bet you never even thought of that!

480 STOCKMANN: Not for a mass of water like that, you can't...

KIIL: Everything can be killed. That's science! (*Crosses to* STOCKMANN, *turning him around*.) Thomas, I never liked your brother, you have a perfect right to hate him...

STOCKMANN: I didn't do it because I hate my brother!

KIIL: (*During this speech,* STOCKMANN *slowly turns to face* KIIL.). Part of it, part of it, don't deny it!

490 You admit there's some doubt in your mind about the water, you admit there may be ways to disinfect it, and yet you went after your brother as though the only way to cure the thing was to blow up the whole Institute! There's hatred in that, boy, don't forget it. (*Crosses to* R. *table, picks up shares in* R. *hand, stands in front of* C. *chair*.) These can belong to you now, so be sure, be sure; tear the hatred out of your heart, stand naked in front of yourself—*are you*

500 *sure?*

STOCKMANN: What right have you to gamble my family's future on the strength of my convictions?

KIIL: Ah ha! Then the convictions are not really that strong!

STOCKMANN: I am ready to hang for my convictions! (*Crosses* R. *to* KIIL.) But no man has a right to make martyrs of others; my family is innocent. Sell back those shares, give her what belongs to her, I'm a penniless man!

510

KIIL: Nobody is going to say Morten Kiil wrecked this town. (*Crosses* R. *of* R. *chair, turns.*) You retract your "convictions," or these go to charity.

STOCKMANN: Everything?

KIIL: There'll be a little something for Catherine, but not much. I want my good name. It's exceedingly important to me.

STOCKMANN: (*Bitterly.*). And charity...

KIIL: Charity will do it, or you will do it. It's a serious thing to destroy a town.

520

STOCKMANN: Morten, when I look at you I swear to God I see the devil! (HOVSTAD *and* ASLAKSEN *enter* U. R.) You... (KIIL *almost bumps into* ASLAKSEN. STOCKMANN, U. R. C., *crosses* D. *below table, then* C.)

ASLAKSEN: (*Holds up hand defensively.*). Now don't get excited, please! (HOVSTAD *and* ASLAKSEN *smile a little at* KIIL.)

KIIL: Too many intellectuals here! (*He is standing below archway* U. R.)

530

ASLAKSEN: (*Apologetically.*). Doctor, can we have five minutes of...?

STOCKMANN: I've got nothing to say to you...

KIIL: I want an answer right away. You hear? I'm waiting. (*Exits* U. R.)

STOCKMANN: All right, say it quick. What do you want?

HOVSTAD: (*Crossing* D. *to* L. *of* R. C. *table,* ASLAKSEN *crossing* D. *to* R. *of* R. C. *table.*). We don't expect you to forgive our attitude at the meeting, but...

540

STOCKMANN: (*Grasping for the word.*). Your attitude was prone... prostrated... prostituted!

HOVSTAD: All right, call it whatever you want...

STOCKMANN: I've got a lot on my mind, so get to the point. What do you want?

ASLAKSEN: (*Crossing to* D. *of* R. C. *table.*). Doctor, you should have told us what was in back of it all. You could have had the *Messenger* behind you all the way.

HOVSTAD: You'd have had public opinion with you now. Why didn't you tell us?

550

STOCKMANN: Look, I'm very tired. Let's not beat around the bush . . .

HOVSTAD: (*Gestures toward door where* KIIL *went out*.). He's been all over town buying up stock in the Springs. It's no secret any more.

STOCKMANN: (*Slight pause*.). Well, what about it?

HOVSTAD: (*In a friendly way*.). You don't want me to spell it out, do you?

560   STOCKMANN: I certainly wish you would, I . . .

HOVSTAD: All right, let's lay it on the table. Aslaksen, you want to . . . ?

ASLAKSEN: No—no, go ahead.

HOVSTAD: Doctor, in the beginning we supported you. (*Slowly, to drive it into his head*.) We couldn't go on supporting you because, in simple language, we didn't have the money to withstand the loss in circulation. You're boycotted now? Well, the paper would have been boycotted, too,

570   if we'd stuck with you.

ASLAKSEN: You can see that, Doctor . . .

STOCKMANN: Oh, yes, but what do you want?

HOVSTAD: *The People's Messenger* can put on such a campaign that in two months you'll be hailed a hero in this town.

ASLAKSEN: (*Crossing to* R. *of* HOVSTAD.). We're ready to go.

HOVSTAD: We will prove to the public that you had to buy up the stock because the management

580   would not make the changes required for the public health. In other words, you did it for absolutely scientific, public-spirited reasons. (*Steps to* STOCKMANN.) Now, what do you say, Doctor?

STOCKMANN: You want money from me, is that it?

ASLAKSEN: Well, now, Doctor . . .

HOVSTAD: (*To* ASLAKSEN.). No, don't walk around it. (*To* STOCKMANN.) If we started to support you

590   again, Doctor, we'd lose circulation for a while. We'd like you—or Mr. Kiil, rather—to make up the deficit. (*Quickly, stepping to* STOCKMANN.) Now that's open and above-board and I don't see anything wrong with it. Do you? (*Pause.* STOCKMANN *looks at him, then crosses him and* ASLAKSEN *to window* R. *in thought*.)

ASLAKSEN: Remember, Doctor, you need the paper, you need it desperately.

STOCKMANN: (*Returns to* D. R. *of* R. *chair*.). No, there's

600   nothing wrong with it at all. I . . . I'm not at

all averse to cleaning up my name, although for myself it never was dirty. I don't *enjoy* being hated, if you know what I mean.

ASLAKSEN: Exactly.

HOVSTAD: Aslaksen, will you show him the budget? (ASLAKSEN *reaches into his pocket*.)

STOCKMANN: Just a minute. There is one point. I hate to keep repeating the same thing, but the water is poisoned.

HOVSTAD: (*Crossing* ASLAKSEN.). Now, Doctor . . .   610

STOCKMANN: Just a minute. The Mayor says that he will levy a tax on everybody to pay for the reconstruction. I assume you are ready to support that tax at the same time you're supporting me?

ASLAKSEN: That tax would be extremely unpopular.

HOVSTAD: Doctor, with you back in charge of the baths as Medical Officer, I have absolutely no fear that anything can go wrong . . .   620

STOCKMANN: In other words, you will clean up my name so that I can be in charge of the Corruption.

HOVSTAD: But we can't tackle everything at once. A new tax, there'd be an uproar!

ASLAKSEN: It would ruin the paper!

STOCKMANN: Then you don't intend to do anything about the water?

HOVSTAD: We have faith you won't let anyone get sick!

STOCKMANN: In other words, gentlemen, you are   630 looking for someone to blackmail into paying your printing bill.

HOVSTAD: (*Indignantly*.). We are trying to clear your name, Doctor Stockmann! And if you refuse to cooperate, if that's going to be your attitude . . .

STOCKMANN: Yes? Go on. What will you do?

HOVSTAD: (*Taking* ASLAKSEN'S R. *arm, starts to cross* STOCKMANN.). I think we'd better go.

STOCKMANN: (*Steps* D. *into their way*.). What will   640 you do? I would like you to tell me! Me, the man two minutes ago you were going to make into a hero—what will you do now that I won't pay you!

ASLAKSEN: Doctor, the public is almost hysterical!

STOCKMANN: To my face, tell me what you are going to do!

HOVSTAD: The Mayor will prosecute you for conspiracy to destroy a corporation, and without

650 a paper behind you, you will end up in prison!

STOCKMANN: And you'll support him, won't you? I want it from your mouth, Hovstad! This little victory you will not deny me. (HOVSTAD *crosses* STOCKMANN, *starts for* U. R. *door.* STOCKMANN *takes his* R. *arm, stops him.*) Tell the hero, Hovstad; you're going to go on crucifying the hero, are you not? Say it to me... you will not leave here until I get this from your mouth!

HOVSTAD: (*Stepping back, looking directly at him.*).
660 You are a madman. You are insane with egotism, and don't excuse it with humanitarian slogans, because a man who'll drag his family through a lifetime of disgrace is a demon in his heart! (*Advances on* STOCKMANN.) You hear me? A demon who cares more for the purity of a public bath than the lives of his wife and children. Doctor Stockmann, you deserve everything you're going to get! (HOVSTAD *starts to go* U. R. STOCKMANN *is struck by his ferocious conviction.*
670 ASLAKSEN *comes toward him, taking budget out of his pocket.*)

EJLIF: (*Off* R.). Mother!

ASLAKSEN: (*Nervously.*). Doctor, please, consider it; it won't take much money and in two months' time I promise you your whole life will change and...

EJLIF: (*Entering hall* U. R.). Mother! Mother!

CATHERINE: (*Without shawl, running to front door* U. R. *from dining-room behind bookcase.*). What hap-
680 pened? My God, what's the matter? (STOCKMANN, *alarmed, crosses* U. *as* CATHERINE *brings* MORTEN *down, followed by* EJLIF. PETRA *and* HORSTER *enter* U. R.; *she crosses* D. C.; *he crosses* D. L. C.; HOVSTAD *with* ASLAKSEN *on his* R. *give to* L. C.) Something happened! Look at him!

MORTEN: I'm all right. It's nothin'.

STOCKMANN: (*Very much the doctor.*). What happened here?

MORTEN: Nothin', Papa, I swear...

690 STOCKMANN: (*To* EJLIF.). What happened? Why aren't you in school?

EJLIF: The teacher said we better stay home the rest of the week.

STOCKMANN: The boys hit him?

EJLIF: They started calling you names so he got sore and began to fight with one kid and all of a sudden the whole bunch of them jumped on him.

CATHERINE: (*To* MORTEN.). Why did you answer?

MORTEN: (*Indignantly, to* STOCKMANN.). They 700
called him a traitor! (*To* EJLIF.). My father is no traitor!

EJLIF: But you didn't have to answer!

CATHERINE: (*Pushing* EJLIF *away a little.*). You should've known they'd all jump on you! They could have killed you!

MORTEN: I don't care!

STOCKMANN: (*To quiet him—and his own heart.*). Morten...

MORTEN: (*Pulls away from* STOCKMANN.). I'll kill 710
them! I'll take a rock and the next time I see one of them I'll kill him! (STOCKMANN *reaches for* MORTEN *who, thinking he will be chastised, starts to pull away.* STOCKMANN *catches him and starts gripping him against his chest.*) Let me go! Let me...

STOCKMANN: Morten... Morten... (MORTEN *cries in his arms.*)

MORTEN: They called you a traitor, an enemy...
(*He sobs.*) 720

STOCKMANN: Sssh. That's all. Wash your face. (*Turns to* ASLAKSEN *and* HOVSTAD.) Good day, gentlemen.

HOVSTAD: Let us know what you decide, and we'll...

STOCKMANN: I've decided. I am an enemy of the people...

CATHERINE: Tom, what are you saying?

STOCKMANN: To such people who teach their own children to think with their fists—to them I'm an enemy! And my boy... my boys... my 730
family... I think you can count us all enemies!

ASLAKSEN: Doctor, you could have everything you want...

STOCKMANN: Except the truth. I could have everything but that. The water is poisoned.

HOVSTAD: But you'll be in charge...

STOCKMANN: But the children are poisoned, the people are poisoned! If the only way I can be a friend of the people is to take charge of that corruption, then I am an enemy! The water is 740
poisoned, poisoned, poisoned, that's the beginning of it and that's the end of it! Now get out of here!

HOVSTAD: You know where you're going to end?

STOCKMANN: (*Taking umbrella from* ASLAKSEN.). I said get out of here! (HOVSTAD *and* ASLAKSEN *cross* STOCKMANN *and the boys.* CATHERINE *and the boys cross* U. C. *around* R. *table.* PETRA *crosses* R. *to* STOCKMANN. HOVSTAD *crosses* D. L. C.)

750 CATHERINE: What are you doing?

ASLAKSEN: You're a fanatic! You're out of your mind!

CATHERINE: What are you doing?

STOCKMANN: They want me to buy the paper, the public, the pollution of the Springs, buy the whole pollution of this town. They'll make a hero out of me for that! *(Furiously to* ASLAKSEN *and* HOVSTAD.) But I am not a hero, I am the enemy and now you're first going to find out

760 what kind of enemy I am! I will sharpen my pen like a dagger—you, all you "friends" of the people are going to bleed before I'm done! Go, tell them to sign the petitions, warn them not to call me when they're sick; beat up my children; and never let her... *(Points to* PETRA.) in the school again or she'll destroy the immaculate purity of the vacuum there! See to the barricades, the truth is coming, ring the bells, sound the alarm! The truth, the truth is out, and soon

770 it will be prowling like a lion in the streets!

HOVSTAD: Doctor, you're out of your mind. *(He and* ASLAKSEN *turn* U. R. *to go quickly.* STOCKMANN *runs after them.)*

STOCKMANN: Out of here, out of here!

EJLIF: *(Rushing at them.).* Don't you say that to him!

STOCKMANN: *(At ball.).* Out of here! *(He throws umbrella after them, slams the door* U. R. *behind them, crosses* C. *with* EJLIF *on his* R. *After a moment:)* I've had all the ambassadors of hell today, but

780 there'll be no more. Now, now listen, Catherine. Children, listen. We are besieged. They'll call for blood now, they'll whip the people like oxen... *(A rock comes through remaining pane of* R. *window.* MORTEN *starts for window.* STOCKMANN *stops him.* HORSTER *turns to face* STOCKMANN.) Stay away from there!

CATHERINE: The Captain knows where we can get a ship...

STOCKMANN: No ships!

PETRA: We're staying?   790

CATHERINE: But they can't go back to school, I won't let them out of the house!

STOCKMANN: We're staying.

PETRA: Good!

STOCKMANN: We must be careful now. We must live through this. Boys, no more school. I'm going to teach you. And Petra will. Do you know any kids, street louts, hookey-players... ?

EJLIF: Oh, sure!

STOCKMANN: We'll want about twelve of them to   800 start. But I want them good and ignorant, absolutely uncivilized. Can we use your house, Captain!

HORSTER: Sure, I'm never there.

STOCKMANN: Fine! We'll begin, Petra, and we'll turn out not taxpayers and newspaper subscribers, but free and independent people, hungry for the truth. Oh, I forgot! Petra, run to Grandpa and tell him... tell him... as follows... NO!   810

CATHERINE: *(Puzzled.).* What do you mean?

STOCKMANN: It means, my dear, that we are all alone. And there'll be a long night before it's day... *(A rock smashes through another window.* PETRA *starts for window;* STOCKMANN *holds her back.* HORSTER *crosses to* D. *of window, crouches low and looks out.)*

HORSTER: Half the town is out. *(*STOCKMANN *pulls family down low. All are crouching a little.)*

CATHERINE: What's going to happen? Tom! What's   820 going to happen? *(*HORSTER *crosses* D. R. C., *looks* U. *at family.)*

STOCKMANN: I don't know. But remember now, everybody. You are fighting for the truth, and that's why you're alone. And that makes you strong—we're the strongest people in the world ... *(Crowd noises build.)* And the strong must learn to be lonely.

CURTAIN

FROM "FOREWORD"

by Rolf Fjelde

... The gist of Ibsen's realistic style could be termed the method of reductive analysis. The playwright creates a setting which is partially localized ("a coastal town in southern Norway") and, in most cases, seemingly constrictive; and then, within this area of controlled inquiry, he sets in motion minutely individualized characters in a limited action that by no stretch of Brechtian imagination could be considered epic. The sense of larger dimensions that all great drama must evoke is achieved, nevertheless, through the fact that setting, character, and action are shaped to correspond at significant points with the deepest tendencies and conflicts of the age, against a background of the entire history of Western civilization. In *Enemy*, this pattern of equivalents receives a glancing reference in Act I, when Dr. Stockmann parallels the ferment of activity in the provincial seaport setting with a bustling metropolis in the great world, adding, as if to stress the analogy: "Oh, I'm well aware this is small scale compared with a lot of other places." Thus the mayor's assertion, moments later, that the individual must learn to subordinate himself to the whole, and the doctor's response throughout the play, countering that thesis to the utmost, together mirror a conflict polarizing that century of ascendant nationalism, one which culminates in the totalitarian coercions of the present age. (Brian Johnston has noted several respects in which Stockmann resembles a diminished contemporary version of Socrates, the unwelcome gadfly of his community. One might additionally observe that Ibsen's means of examining the failure of human possibility, his method of reductive analysis, is appropriately the reverse of the one identified with Socrates in *The Republic*: instead of discovering the fundamental moral traits of the individual writ large in the idea state, Ibsen discovers the fundamental moral deficiencies of his civilization writ small in the unidealized individuals of his symptomatic community.)

The second, weightier ingredient, one of substance more than style, comes in focus with the recognition that *An Enemy of the People* conducts an inquiry, through Ibsen's reductive method, into the merging conflict between two kinds of revolution—what might be called the traditional or conventional conception, and the new or modern conception. Traditional revolution has been the prevailing form on countless occasions throughout the past, from the insurrections of 1848 back to earliest classic antiquity. The scenario for this conception pits a champion of the oppressed masses, or a party of the people, against the repressive force of irrational authority vested in an individual tyrant or a small, self-perpetuating power elite. The traditional conception, holding the deprived majority to be right and the ruling minority to be wrong, adopts for its remedy the drastic expedient whereby Fortune's wheel, given a half turn, paradoxically yields a full revolution: the outs are swept in, the ups are brought down—but beyond a redistribution of material goods, nothing further is won. The new establishment, in fact, immediately generates a new underground, plotting *its* program for the next half turn of the wheel. Insecure in this knowledge, and aware of the self-interest behind his own rhetoric, the traditional revolutionist may betray a secret fear and guilt, which must be stifled under ever more vehement assertions of preemptive right, in terms of the rationalizations of his idealogy. Conventional revolution, the outgrowth of an autocratic system, is at one with a world-view that conceives history as repetitive or cyclical, a concept typical of classic antiquity, the Middle Ages, and the Renaissance.... Now, after more than three decades of reconsidering the nature of revolt in the perspectives of realism, Ibsen, in returning to the theme, assigned the traditional revolutionary role to the two journalists of the play, Hovstad and Billing.

The first impressions they give in Act I are deceiving, since they come filtered through the warm conviviality that radiates from the doctor's personality to dominate the scene. Only later, in Act III, is it revealed that they share the doctor's table, not for his company, but for Petra's, and less for her sake than for the sizable inheritance they calculate will be settle on her by Morten Kiil. Thus when Hovstad presents Stockmann with his plans to overthrow the incompetent leadership of the town, we still (Act II) have no grounds for dobuting his utter sincerity. The clique of the rich and established who have built the prosperity of the community have done so, he states, at the cost of one disastrous and inexusable mistake, the pollution which the doctor has discovered; they must accordingly be stripped of their power, not only for reason of that blunder, but also to demonstrate an ideological point that will advance the liberation of the oppressed masses, namely, by demolishing the myth of the infallibility of the ruling class. Yet, even as Stockmann is nodding in agreement, unexpectedly the guilt hidden in the traditional revolutionist breaks through the vehemence of Hovstad's argument. "You mustn't think badly of me," he abruptly interjects. "I'm no more self-seeking or power-hungry than most people." "But—whoever said you were?" replies the bewildered doctor. In this momentary disclosure, the end is foreshadowed: Hovstad's program for liberation will fail, not because he lacks a cause and an issue (the generation of 1848 had both), but because his commitment is compromised from the start, and, moreover, because, as Ibsen will shortly suggest, the conventional conception of revolution is no longer adequate to the changing reality of the times. By Act IV Hovstad has conformed his possibilities to his situation sufficiently to become the willing apologist of his publisher, Aslaksen, who in turn is the chosen spokesman for that well-greased axle of the wheels that run the town, Mayor Peter Stockmann. Thus, by several telescoped stages, Hovstad traverses a summation of what Ibsen must have witnessed of the radical's progress as a journey of accommodation, one terminated already by Billing, who cynically bids for a job on the municipal payroll of the government he proposes to overthrow. As the two factions of the majority learn their common interests and solidify in the turbulent public meeting, the process of reductive analysis reveals its larger conclusion: the traditional revolutionist proves indistinguishable from the established order he ostensibly attacks—if he fails, he joins it; if he succeeds, he supplants it and, after some ideological redecoration of the premises, finds himself in time practicing the same uses and abuses of power he had once protested.

Both the leaders of the community and its conventional rebels are self-proclaimed friends of the people; the bearer of the new conception of revolution is, of course, the man they jointly brand as an enemy of the people, Dr. Stockmann. If one asks what the difference is, at the core, between the old and new conceptions, the answer given by the play and supported elsewhere in Ibsen's writings would be, succinctly, if not simply: ideas. The traditional ins and outs, molding their lives to the expediencies of power, are essentially identical in character, whereas Stockmann is an outsider of another kind altogether, being obstinately committed to a new, unpopular truth that the majority will have to learn to live with.

TRAGEDY AND THE COMMON MAN

by *Arthur Miller*

In this age few tragedies are written. It has often been held that the lack is due to a paucity of heroes among us, or else that modern man has had the blood drawn out of his organs of belief by the skepticism of science, and the heroic attack on life cannot feed on an attitude of reserve and circumspection. For one reason or another, we are often held to be below tragedy—or tragedy above us. The inevitable conclusion is, of course, that the tragic mode is archaic, fit only for the very highly placed, the kings or the kingly, and where this admission is not made in so many words it is most often implied.

I believe that the common man is as apt a subject for tragedy in its highest sense as kings were. On the face of it this ought to be obvious in the light of modern psychiatry, which bases its analysis upon classic formulations, such as the Oedipus and Orestes complexes, for instances, which were enacted by royal beings, but which apply to everyone in similar emotional situations.

More simply, when the question of tragedy in art is not at issue, we never hesitate to attribute to the well-placed and the exalted the very same mental processes as the lowly. And finally, if the exaltation of tragic action were truly a property of the high-bred character alone, it is inconceivable that the mass of mankind should cherish tragedy above all other forms, let alone be capable of understanding it.

As a general rule, to which there may be exceptions unknown to me, I think the tragic feeling is evoked in us when we are in the presence of a character who is ready to lay down his life, if need be, to secure one thing—his sense of personal dignity. From Orestes to Hamlet, Medea to Macbeth, the underlying struggle is that of the individual attempting to gain his "rightful" position in his society.

Sometimes he is one who has been displaced from it, sometimes one who seeks to

---

attain it for the first time, but the fateful wound from which the inevitable events spiral is the wound of indignity, and its dominant force is indignation. Tragedy, then, is the consequence of a man's total compulsion to evaluate himself justly.

In the sense of having been initiated by the hero himself, the tale always reveals what has been called his "tragic flaw," a failing that is not peculiar to grand or elevated characters. Nor is it necessarily a weakness. The flaw, or crack in the character, is really nothing—and need be nothing, but his inherent unwillingness to remain passive in the face of what he conceives to be a challenge to his dignity, his image of his rightful status. Only the passive, only those who accept their lot without active retaliation, are "flawless." Most of us are in that category.

But there are among us today, as there always have been, those who act against the scheme of things that degrades them, and in the process of action everything we have accepted out of fear or insensitivity or ignorance is shaken before us and examined, and from this total onslaught by an individual against the seemingly stable cosmos surrounding us—from this total examination of the "unchangeable" environment —comes the terror and the fear that is classically associated with tragedy.

More important, from this total questioning of what has previously been unquestioned, we learn. And such a process is not beyond the common man. In revolutions around the world, these past thirty years, he has demonstrated again and again this inner dynamic of all tragedy.

Insistence of the rank of the tragic hero, or the so-called nobility of his character, is really but a clinging to the outward forms of tragedy. If rank or nobility of character was indispensable, then it would follow that the problems of those with rank were the particular problems of tragedy. But surely the right of one monarch to capture the domain from another no longer raises our passions, nor are our concepts of justice what they were to the mind of an Elizabethan king.

The quality in such plays that does shake us, however, derives from the underlying fear of being displaced, the disaster inherent in being torn away from our chosen image of what and who we are in this world. Among us today this fear is as strong, and perhaps stronger, than it ever was. In fact, it is the common man who knows this fear best.

Now, if it is true that tragedy is the consequence of a man's total compulsion to evaluate himself justly, his destruction in the attempt posits a wrong or an evil in his environment. And this is precisely the morality of tragedy and its lesson. The discovery of the moral law, which is what the enlightenment of tragedy consists of, is not the discovery of some abstract or metaphysical quantity.

The tragic right is a condition of life, a condition in which the human personality is able to flower and realize itself. The wrong is the condition which suppresses man, perverts the flowing out of his love and creative instinct. Tragedy enlightens —and it must, in that it points the heroic finger at the enemy of man's freedom. The thrust for freedom is the quality in tragedy which exalts. The revolutionary questioning of the stable environment is what terrifies. In no way is the common man debarred from such thoughts or such actions.

Seen in this light, our lack of tragedy may be partially accounted for by the turn which modern literature has taken toward the purely psychiatric view of life, or the purely sociological. If all our miseries, our indignities, are born and bred within our minds, then all action, let alone the heroic action, is obviously impossible.

And if society alone is responsible for the cramping of our lives, then the protagonist must needs be so pure and faultless as to force us to deny his validity as a character. From neither of these views can tragedy derive, simply because neither represents a balanced concept of life. Above all else, tragedy requires the finest appreciation by the writer of cause and effect.

No tragedy can therefore come about when its author fears to question absolutely everything, when he regards any institution, habit or custom as being either everlasting, immutable or inevitable. In the tragic view the need of man to wholly realize himself is the only fixed star, and whatever it is that hedges his nature and lowers it is ripe for attack and examination. Which is not to say that tragedy must preach revolution.

The Greeks could probe the very heavenly origin of their ways and return to confirm the rightness of laws. And Job could face God in anger, demanding his right and end in submission. But for a moment everything is in suspension, nothing is accepted, and in this stretching and tearing apart of the cosmos, in the very action of so doing, the character gains "size," the tragic stature which is spuriously attached to the royal or the high born in our minds. The commonest of men may take on that stature to the extent of his willingness to throw all he has into the contest, the battle to secure his rightful place in the world.

There is a misconception of tragedy with which I have been struck in review after review, and in many conversations with writers and readers alike. It is the idea that tragedy is of necessity allied to pessimism. Even the dictionary says nothing more about the word than that it means a story with a sad or unhappy ending. This impression is so firmly fixed that I almost hesitate to claim that in truth tragedy implies more optimism in its author than does comedy, and that its final result ought to be the reinforcement of the onlooker's brightest opinions of the human animal.

For, if it is true to say that in essence the tragic hero is intent upon claiming his whole due as a personality, and if this struggle must be total and without reservation, then it automatically demonstrates the indestructible will of man to achieve his humanity.

This possibility of victory must be there in tragedy. Where pathos rules, where pathos is finally derived, a character has fought a battle he could not possibly have won. The pathetic is achieved when the protagonist is, by virtue of his willingness, his insensitivity, or the very air he gives off, incapable of grappling with a much superior force.

Pathos truly is the mode for the pessimist. But tragedy requires a nicer balance between what is possible and what is impossible. And it is curious, although edifying, that the plays we revere, century after century, are the tragedies. In them, and in them alone, lies the belief—optimistic, if you will, in the perfectability of man.

It is time, I think, that we who are without kings, took up the bright thread of our history and followed it to the only place it can possibly lead in our time—the heart and spirit of the average man.

MISS JULIE

August Strindberg (1849-1912)

Translated by E. M. Sprinchorn

Sweden's outstanding playwright was born in Stockholm. He had a difficult and traumatic childhood and his adult years were filled with domestic torment and agonizing self-doubt. The experiences of his personal life are sharply revealed in many of his plays. He was a man of great imagination both in his plays and in his innovations in theatrical production.

Strindberg's plays fall into three periods. He first wrote romantic, historical plays before turning to realistic character studies in the late 1880s, such as *The Father* and *Miss Julie*. His final plays were experiments in expressionism, in which he probed into psychotic behavior in dream-like sequences, as in *The Spook Sonata* and *The Dream Play*.

Among the theatrical innovations suggested by Strindberg were an intimate theater, the abolition of footlights, and less makeup for the actors. "To make a real room of the stage, with the fourth wall missing, and a part of the furniture placed towards the audience, would probably produce a disturbing effect at present." The real wall of the set for *Miss Julie* was slanted diagonally across the stage to give it a more natural effect. "Having only a single setting, one may demand to have it real," Strindberg said. He objected to painted properties on the wall, and to the act divisions and intermissions in a play because they disrupted continuity. He filled in the pauses of the action by dance, pantomime and monologue. All of these indications suggest that Strindberg wished to stage his plays such as *Miss Julie* and *The Father* in an untheatrical fashion in order to give the impression of authenticity to match that of the characters in his plays.

Above. The flirtation begins.

Opposite top. Jean and Christine discuss Miss Julie's "wild" behavior.
Photographs in this sequence are of the 1966 production
at the McCarter Theatre at Princeton University.

Opposite bottom. Miss Julie comes to see Jean in the servants' quarters.

ALL PHOTOGRAPHS IN THIS SECTION BY
ALLISON DELARUE, PHOTOGRAPHER/
PRINCETON UNIVERSITY LIBRARY THEATRE COLLECTION

The "ballet" of the country people celebrating Midsummer Eve.

The tension grows between Jean and Julie.

CHARACTERS

MISS JULIE, *twenty-five years old*
JEAN, *valet, thirty years old*
CHRISTINE, *the cook, thirty-five years old*

The action of the play takes place in the kitchen of the Count's manor house on Midsummer Eve in Sweden in the 1880s.

MISS JULIE

The scene is a large kitchen. The walls and ceiling are covered with draperies and hangings. The rear wall runs obliquely upstage from the left. On this wall to the left are two shelves with pots and pans of copper, iron, and pewter. The shelves are decorated with goffered paper. A little to the right can be seen three-fourths of a deep arched doorway with two glass doors, and through them can be seen a fountain with a statue of Cupid, lilac bushes in bloom, and the tops of some Lombardy poplars. From the left of the stage the corner of a large, Dutch-tile kitchen stove protrudes with part of the hood showing. Projecting from the right side of the stage is one end of the servants' dining table of white pine, with a few chairs around it. The stove is decorated with branches of birch leaves; the floor is strewn with juniper twigs. On the end of the table is a large Japanese spice jar filled with lilacs. An icebox, a sink, a wash basin. Over the door a big, old-fashioned bell; and to the left of the door the gaping mouth of a speaking tube.

CHRISTINE is standing at the stove, frying something. She is wearing a light-colored cotton dress and an apron. JEAN enters, dressed in livery and carrying a pair of high-top boots with spurs. He sets them where they are clearly visible.

JEAN: Tonight she's wild again. Miss Julie's absolutely wild!

CHRISTINE: You took your time getting back!

JEAN: I took the Count down to the station, and on my way back as I passed the barn I went in for a dance. And there was Miss Julie leading the dance with the game warden. But then she noticed me. And she came right up and chose me for the ladies' waltz. And she's been dancing ever since like—like I don't know what. She's absolutely wild!

CHRISTINE: That's nothing new. But she's been worse than ever during the last two weeks, ever since her engagement was broken off.

JEAN: Yes, I never did hear all there was to that. He was a good man, too, even if he wasn't rich. Well, that's a woman for you.

He sits down at the end of the table

But, tell me, isn't it strange that a young girl like her—all right, young woman—prefers to stay home here with the servants rather than go with her father to visit her relatives?

CHRISTINE: I suppose she's ashamed to face them after that fiasco with her young man.

JEAN: No doubt. He wouldn't take any nonsense from her. Do you know what happened, Christine? I do. I saw the whole thing, even though I didn't let on.

CHRISTINE: Don't tell me you were there?

JEAN: Well, I was. They were in the barnyard one evening—and she was training him, as she called it. Do you know what she was doing? She was making him jump over her riding whip—training him like a dog. He jumped over twice, and she whipped him both times. But the third time, he grabbed the whip from her, broke it in a thousand pieces—and walked off.

CHRISTINE: So that's what happened. Well, what do you know.

JEAN: Yes, that put an end to that affair.—Now have you got something good for me, Christine?

CHRISTINE: *(Serving him from the frying pan).* Just a little bit of kidney. I cut it especially for you.

JEAN: *(Smelling it).* Wonderful! My special *délice.*

50 *(Feeling the plate)* Hey, you didn't warm the plate!

CHRISTINE: You're more fussy than the Count himself when you set your mind to it. *(She rumples his hair gently)*

JEAN: *(Irritated).* Cut it out! Don't muss up my hair. You know I don't like that!

CHRISTINE: Oh, now don't get mad. Can I help it if I like you?

JEAN *eats.* CHRISTINE *gets out a bottle of beer*

JEAN: Beer on Midsummer Eve! No thank you!
60   I've got something much better than that. *(He opens a drawer in the table and takes out a bottle of red wine with a gold seal)* Do you see that? Gold Seal. Now give me a glass—No, a wine glass of course. I'm drinking it straight.

CHRISTINE: *(Goes back to the stove and puts on a small saucepan).* Lord help the woman who gets you for a husband. You're an old fussbudget!

JEAN: Talk, talk! You'd consider yourself lucky if you got yourself a man as good as me. It hasn't
70   done you any harm to have people think I'm your fiancé. *(He tastes the wine)* Very good. Excellent. But warmed just a little too little. *(Warming the glass in his hands)* We bought this in Dijon. Four francs a liter, unbottled—and the tax on top of that.... What on earth are you cooking? It smells awful!

CHRISTINE: Some damn mess that Miss Julie wants for her dog.

JEAN: You should watch your language, Chris-
80   tine.... Why do you have to stand in front of the stove on a holiday, cooking for that mutt? Is it sick?

CHRISTINE: Oh, she's sick, all right! She sneaked out to the gatekeeper's mongrel and—got herself in a fix. And Miss Julie, you know, can't stand anything like that.

JEAN: She's too stuck-up in some ways and not proud enough in others. Just like her mother. The Countess felt right at home in the kitchen
90   or down in the barn with the cows but when she went driving, *one* horse wasn't enough for her; she had to have a pair. Her sleeves were always dirty, but her buttons had the royal crown on them. As for Miss Julie, she doesn't seem to care how she looks and acts. I mean, she's not really refined. Just now, down at the barn, she grabbed the game warden away from Anna and asked him to dance. You wouldn't see anybody in our class doing a thing like that. But that's what happens when the gentry try
100 to act like the common people—they become common!... But she *is* beautiful! Magnificent! Ah! those shoulders—those——and so forth, and so forth!

CHRISTINE: Oh, don't exaggerate. Clara tells me all about her, and Clara dresses her.

JEAN: Clara, pooh! You women are always jealous of each other. *I've* been out riding with her.... And how she can dance!

CHRISTINE: Listen, Jean, you *are* going to dance
110 with me, aren't you, when I am finished here?

JEAN: Certainly! Of course I am.

CHRISTINE: Promise?

JEAN: Promise! Listen if I say I'm going to do a thing, I do it.... Christine, I thank you for a delicious meal. *(He shoves the cork back into the bottle)*

MISS JULIE *appears in the doorway, talking to someone outside*

MISS JULIE: I'll be right back. Don't wait for me.
120
JEAN *slips the bottle into the table drawer quickly and rises respectfully.* MISS JULIE *comes in and crosses over to* CHRISTINE, *who is at the mirror*

MISS JULIE: Did you get it ready?

CHRISTINE *signals that* JEAN *is present*

JEAN: *(Polite and charming).* Are you ladies sharing secrets?

MISS JULIE: *Flipping her handkerchief in his face).* Don't be nosey!

JEAN: Oh, that smells good! Violets.
130
MISS JULIE: *(Flirting with him).* Don't be impudent! And don't tell me you're an expert on perfumes, too. I know you're an expert dancer.—No, don't look! Go away!

JEAN: *(Inquisitive, but deferential).* What are you cooking? A witch's brew for Midsummer Eve? Something that reveals what the stars have in store for you, so you can see the face of your future husband?

MISS JULIE: *(Curtly).* You'd have to have good eyes
140 to see that. *(To* CHRISTINE*)* Pour it into a small

bottle, and seal it tight. . . . Jean, come and dance a schottische with me.

JEAN: *(Hesitating).* I hope you don't think I'm being rude, but I've already promised this dance to Christine.

MISS JULIE: She can always find someone else. Isn't that so, Christine? You don't mind if I borrow Jean for a minute, do you?

CHRISTINE: It isn't up to me. If Miss Julie is gracious enought to invite you, it isn't right for you to say no, Jean. You go on, and thank her for the honor.

JEAN: Frankly, Miss Julie, I don't want to hurt your feelings, but I wonder if it is wise—I mean for you to dance twice in a row with the same partner. Especially since the people around here are so quick to spread gossip.

MISS JULIE: *(Bridling).* What do you mean? What kind of gossip? What are you trying to say?

JEAN: *(Retreating).* If you insist on misunderstanding me, I'll have to speak more plainly. It just doesn't look right for you to prefer one of your servants to the others who are hoping for the same unusual honor.

MISS JULIE: Prefer! What an idea! I'm really surprised. I, the mistress of the house, am good enough to come to their dance, and when I feel like dancing, I want to dance with someone who knows how to lead. After all I don't want to look ridiculous.

JEAN: As you wish. I am at your orders.

MISS JULIE: *(Gently).* Don't take it as an order. Tonight we're all just happy people at a party. There's no question of rank. Now give me your arm.—Don't worry, Christine. I won't run off with your boy friend.

JEAN gives her his arm and leads her out

PANTOMIME SCENE: *This should be played as if the actress were actually alone. She turns her back on the audience when she feels like it; she does not look out into the auditorium; she does not hurry as if she were afraid the audience would grow impatient.*

CHRISTINE *alone. In the distance the sound of the violins playing the schottische.* CHRISTINE, *humming in time with the music, cleans up after* JEAN, *washes the dishes, dries them, and puts them away in a cupboard. Then*

she takes off her apron, takes a little mirror from one of the table drawers, and leans it against the jar of lilacs on the table. She lights a tallow candle, heats a curling iron, and curls the bangs on her forehead. Then she goes to the doorway and stands listening to the music. She comes back to the table and finds the handkerchief that MISS JULIE *left behind. She smells it, spreads it out, and then, as if lost in thought, stretches it, smooths it out, folds it in four, and so on.*

JEAN enters alone

JEAN: I told you she was wild! You should have seen the way she was dancing. They were peeking at her from behind the doors and laughing at her. Can you figure her out, Christine?

CHRISTINE: You might know it's her monthlies, Jean. She always acts peculiar then. . . . Well, are you going to dance with me?

JEAN: You're not mad at me because I broke my promise?

CHRISTINE: Of course not. Not for a little thing like that, you know that. And I know my place.

JEAN: *(Grabs her around the waist).* You're a sensible girl, Christine. You're going to make somebody a good wife——

MISS JULIE, *coming in, sees them together. She is unpleasantly surprised*

MISS JULIE: *(With forced gaiety).* Well, aren't you the gallant beau—running away from your partner!

JEAN: On the contrary, Miss Julie. As you can see, I've hurried back to the partner I deserted.

MISS JULIE: *(Changing tack).* You know, you're the best dancer I've met—But why are you wearing livery on a holiday. Take it off at once.

JEAN: I'd have to ask you to leave for a minute. My black coat is hanging right here—*He moves to the right and points)*

MISS JULIE: You're not embarrassed because I'm here, are you? Just to change your coat? Go in your room and come right back again. Or else you can stay here and I'll turn my back.

JEAN: If you'll excuse me, Miss Julie. *(He goes off to the right. His arm can be seen as he changes his coat)*

MISS JULIE: *(To* CHRISTINE). Tell me something,

Christine. Is Jean your fiancé? He seems so intimate with you.

CHRISTINE: Fiancé? I suppose so. At least that's what we say.

MISS JULIE: What do you mean?

CHRISTINE: Well, Miss Julie, you have had fiancés yourself, and you know—

240 MISS JULIE: But we were properly engaged—!

CHRISTINE: I know, but did anything come of it?

JEAN comes back, wearing a cutaway coat and derby

MISS JULIE: *Très gentil, monsieur Jean! Très gentil!*

JEAN: *Vous voulez plaisanter, madame.*

MISS JULIE: *Et vous voulez parler francais!* Where did you learn to speak French?

JEAN: In Switzerland. I was *sommelier* in one of the biggest hotels in Lucerne.

MISS JULIE: But you look quite the gentleman in
250 that coat! *Charmant! (She sits down at the table)*

JEAN: Flatterer!

MISS JULIE: *(Stiffening).* Who said I was flattering you?

JEAN: My natural modesty would not allow me to presume that you were paying sincere compliments to someone like me, and therefore I assumed that you were exaggerating, or, in other words, flattering me.

MISS JULIE: Where on earth did you learn to talk
260 like that? Do you go to the theater often?

JEAN: And other places. I get around.

MISS JULIE: But weren't you born in this district?

JEAN: My father worked as a farm hand on the county attorney's estate, next door to yours. I used to see you when you were little. But of course you didn't notice me.

MISS JULIE: Did you really?

JEAN: Yes. I remember one time in particular—. But I can't tell you about that!

270 MISS JULIE: Of course you can. Oh, come on, tell me. Just this once—for me.

JEAN: No. No, I really couldn't. Not now. Some other time maybe.

243 *Très gentil* . . .
   . . . *parler française!*
      MISS JULIE. Very elegant, Mr. Jean! Very elegant.
      JEAN. You wish to joke, my lady.
      MISS JULIE. And you wish to speak French!

MISS JULIE: Some other time? That means never. What's the harm in telling me now?

JEAN: There's no harm. I just don't feel like it.—Look at her. *(He nods at* CHRISTINE, *who has fallen asleep in a chair by the stove)*

MISS JULIE: Won't she make somebody a pretty 280 wife! I'll bet she snores, too.

JEAN: No she doesn't. But she talks in her sleep.

MISS JULIE: *(Cynically).* Now how would you know she talks in her sleep?

JEAN: *(Coolly).* I've heard her . . . .

Pause. They look at each other

MISS JULIE: Why don't you sit down?

JEAN: I wouldn't take the liberty in your presence.

MISS JULIE: But if I were to order you—?

JEAN: I'd obey. 290

MISS JULIE: Well then, sit down.—Wait a minute. Could you get me something to drink first?

JEAN: I don't know what there is in the icebox. Only beer, I suppose.

MISS JULIE: *Only* beer! I have simple tastes. I prefer beer to wine.

JEAN takes a bottle of beer from the icebox and opens it. He looks in the cupboard for a glass and a saucer, and serves her

JEAN: At your service. 300

MISS JULIE: Thank you. Don't you want to drink, too?

JEAN: I'm not much of a beer-drinker, but if it's your wish—

MISS JULIE: My wish! I should think a gentleman would want to keep his lady company.

JEAN: That's a point well taken! *(He opens another bottle and takes a glass)*

MISS JULIE: Now drink a toast to me! *(*JEAN *hesitates)* You're not shy, are you? A big, strong man like 310 you? *(Playfully,* JEAN *kneels and raises his glass in mock gallantry)*

JEAN: To my lady's health!

MISS JULIE: Bravo! Now if you would kiss my shoe, you will have hit it off perfectly. *(*JEAN *hesitates, then boldly grasps her foot and touches it lightly with his lips)* Superb! You should have been an actor.

JEAN: *(Rising).* This has got to stop, Miss Julie! Someone might come and see us.

MISS JULIE: What difference would that make? 320

JEAN: People would talk, that's what! If you knew how their tongues were wagging out there just a few minutes ago, you wouldn't—

MISS JULIE: What sort of things did they say? Tell me. Sit down and tell me.

JEAN: *(Sitting down)*. I don't want to hurt your feelings, but they used expressions that—hinted at certain—you know what I mean. After all, you're not a child. And when they see a woman drinking, alone with a man—and a servant at that—in the middle of the night—well . . .

MISS JULIE: Well what?! Besides, we're not alone. Christine is here.

JEAN: Yes, asleep!

MISS JULIE: I'll wake her up then. *(She goes over to* CHRISTINE*)* Christine! Are you asleep? *(*CHRISTINE *babbles in her sleep)* Christine!—How sound she sleeps!

CHRISTINE: *(Talking in her sleep)*. Count's boots are brushed . . . put on the coffee . . . right away, right away, right . . . mm—mm . . . poofff . . . *(*MISS JULIE *grabs* CHRISTINE'S *nose)*

MISS JULIE: Wake up, will you!

JEAN: *(Sternly)*. Let her alone!

MISS JULIE: *(Sharply)*. What!

JEAN: She's been standing over the stove all day. She's worn out when evening comes. Anyone asleep is entitled to some respect.

MISS JULIE: *(Changing tack)*. That's a very kind thought. It does you credit. Thank you. *(She offers* JEAN *her hand)* Now come on out and pick some lilacs for me.

During the following, CHRISTINE *wakes up and, drunk with sleep, shuffles off to the right to go to bed*

JEAN: With you, Miss Julie?

MISS JULIE: Yes, with me.

JEAN: That's no good. Absolutely not.

MISS JULIE: I don't know what you're thinking. Maybe you're letting your imagination run away with you.

JEAN: I'm not. The other people are.

MISS JULIE: In what way? Imagining that I'm—*verliebt* in a servant?

JEAN: I'm not conceited, but it's been known to happen. And to these people nothing's sacred.

363 *verliebt in a servant?* in love with a servant?

MISS JULIE: Why, I believe you're an aristocrat!

JEAN: Yes, I am.

MISS JULIE: I'm climbing down—

JEAN: Don't climb down, Miss Julie! Take my advice. No one will ever believe that you climbed down deliberately. They'll say that you fell.

MISS JULIE: I think more highly of these people than you do. Let's see who's right! Come on! *(She looks him over, challenging him)*

JEAN: You know, you're very strange.

MISS JULIE: Perhaps. But then so are you. . . . Besides, everything is strange. Life, people, everything. It's all scum, drifting and drifting on the water until it sinks—sinks. There's a dream I have every now and then. It's coming back to me now. I'm sitting on top of a pillar that I've climbed up somehow and I don't know how to get back down. When I look down I get dizzy. I have to get down but I don't have the courage to jump. I can't hold on much longer and I want to fall; but I don't fall. I know I won't have any peace until I get down; no rest until I get down, down on the ground. And if I ever got down on the ground, I'd want to go farther down, right down into the earth. . . . Have you ever felt anything like that?

JEAN: Never! I used to dream that I'm lying under a tall tree in a dark woods. I want to get up, up to the very top, to look out over the bright landscape with the sun shining on it, to rob the bird's nest up there with the golden eggs in it. I climb and I climb, but the trunk is so thick, and so smooth, and it's such a long way to that first branch. But I know that if I could just reach that first branch, I'd go right to the top as if on a ladder. I've never reached it yet, but some day I will—even if only in my dreams.

MISS JULIE: Here I am talking about dreams with you. Come out with me. Only into the park a way. *(She offers him her arm, and they start to go)*

JEAN: Let's sleep on nine midsummer flowers, Miss Julie, and then our dreams will come true!

MISS JULIE *and* JEAN *suddenly turn around in the doorway.* JEAN *is holding his hand over one eye*

MISS JULIE: You've caught something in your eye. Let me see.

JEAN: It's nothing. Just a bit of dust. It'll go away.

MISS JULIE: The sleeve of my dress must have grazed your eye. Sit down and I'll help you. (*She takes him by the arm and sits him down. She takes his head and leans it back. With the corner of her handkerchief she tries to get out the bit of dust*) Now sit still, absolutely still. (*She slaps his hand*)

420 Do as you're told. Why, I believe you're trembling—a big, strong man like you. (*She feels his biceps*) With such big arms!

JEAN: (*Warmingly*). Miss Julie!

MISS JULIE: Yes, *monsieur Jean?*

JEAN: *Attention! Je ne suis qu'un homme!*

MISS JULIE: Sit still, I tell you!... There now! It's out. Kiss my hand and thank me!

JEAN: (*Rising to his feet*). Listen to me, Miss Julie—Christine has gone to bed!—Listen to me,

430 I tell you!

MISS JULIE: Kiss my hand first!

JEAN: Listen to me!

MISS JULIE: Kiss my hand first!

JEAN: All right. But you'll have no one to blame but yourself.

MISS JULIE: For what?

JEAN: For what? Are you twenty-five years old and still a child? Don't you know it's dangerous to play with fire?

440 MISS JULIE: Not for me. I'm insured!

JEAN: (*Boldly*). Oh, no you're not! And even if you are, there's inflammable stuff next door.

MISS JULIE: Meaning you?

JEAN: Yes. Not just because it's me, but because I'm a young man—

MISS JULIE: And irresistibly handsome? What incredible conceit! A Don Juan, maybe! Or a Joseph! Yes, bless my soul, that's it: you're a Joseph!

450 JEAN: You think so?!

MISS JULIE: I'm almost afraid so! (*JEAN boldly steps up to her, grabs her around the waist, kisses her. She slaps his face*) None of that!

JEAN: Are you still playing games or are you serious?

MISS JULIE: I'm serious.

JEAN: Then you must have been serious just a moment ago, too! You take your games too seriously and that's dangerous. Well, I'm tired of

460 your games, and if you'll excuse me, I'll return

425 *Attention!... homme!* Be careful! I'm only a man!

to my work. The Count will be wanting his boots on time, and it's long past midnight.

MISS JULIE: Put those boots down.

JEAN: No! This is my job. It's what I'm here for. But I never undertook to be a playmate for you. That's something I could never be. I consider myself too good for that.

MISS JULIE: You are proud.

JEAN: In some ways. Not in others.

MISS JULIE: Have you ever been in love? 470

JEAN: We don't use that word around here. But I've been interested in a lot of girls, if that's what you mean.... I even got sick once because I couldn't have the one I wanted—really sick, like the princes in the *Arabian Nights*—who couldn't eat or drink for love.

MISS JULIE: Who was the girl? (*JEAN does not reply*) Who was she?

JEAN: You can't make me tell you that.

MISS JULIE: Even if I ask you as an equal—ask 480 you—as a friend?... Who was she?

JEAN: You.

MISS JULIE: (*Sitting down*). How—amusing....

JEAN: Yes, maybe so. Ridiculous.... That's why I didn't want to tell you about it before. But now I'll tell you the whole story.... Have you any idea what the world looks like from below? Of course you haven't. No more than a hawk or eagle has. You hardly ever see their backs because they're always soaring above us. I lived 490 with seven brothers and sisters—and a pig—out on the waste land where there wasn't even a tree growing. But from my window I could see the wall of the Count's garden with the apple trees sticking up over it. That was the Garden of Eden for me, and there were many angry angels with flaming swords standing guard over it. But in spite of them, I and the other boys found a way to the Tree of Life.... I'll bet you despise me.

MISS JULIE: All boys steal apples. 500

JEAN: That's what you say now. But you still despise me. Never mind. One day I went with my mother into this paradise to weed the onion beds. Next to the vegetable garden stood a Turkish pavilion, shaded by jasmine and hung all over with honeysuckle. I couldn't imagine what it was used for. I only knew I had never seen such a beautiful building. People went in, and

505 *pavilion* a privy

came out again. And one day the door was left open. I sneaked in. The walls were covered with portraits of kings and emperors, and the windows had red curtains with tassels on them.—You do know what kind of place I'm talking about, don't you?... I—(*He breaks off a lilac and holds it under* MISS JULIE's *nose*) I had never been inside a castle, never seen anything besides the church. But this was more beautiful. And no matter what I tried to think about, my thoughts always came back—to that little pavilion. And little by little there arose in me a desire to experience just for once the whole pleasure of...*Enfin*, I sneaked in, looked about, and marveled. Then I heard someone coming! There was only one way out—for the upper-class people. But for me there was one more—a lower one. And I had no other choice but to take it. (MISS JULIE, *who has taken the lilac from* JEAN, *lets it fall to the table*) Then I began to run like mad, plunging through the raspberry bushes, ploughing through the strawberry patches, and came up on the rose terrace. And there I caught sight of a pink dress and a pair of white stockings. That was you. I crawled under a pile of weeds, under—well, you can imagine what it was like—under thistles that pricked me and wet dirt that stank to high heaven. And all the while I could see you walking among the roses. I said to myself, "If it's true that a thief can enter heaven and be with the angels, isn't it strange that a poor man's child here on God's green earth can't enter the Count's park and play with the Count's daughter."

MISS JULIE: (*Sentimentally*). Do you think all poor children have felt that way?

JEAN: (*Hesitatingly at first, then with mounting conviction*). If all poor ch—? Yes—yes, naturally. Of course!

MISS JULIE: It must be terrible to be poor.

JEAN: (*With exaggerated pain and poignancy*). Oh, Miss Julie! You don't know! A dog can lie on the sofa with its mistress; a horse can have its nose stroked by the hand of a countess; but a servant—! (*Changing his tone*) Of course, now and then you meet somebody with guts enough to work his way up in the world, but how often?—Anyway, you know what I did afterwards? I threw myself into the millstream with all my clothes on. Got fished out and spanked. But the following Sunday, when Pa and everybody else in the house went to visit Grandma, I arranged things so I'd be left behind. Then I washed myself all over with soap and warm water, put on my best clothes, and went off to church—just to see you there once more. I saw you, and then I went home determined to die. But I wanted to die beautifully and comfortably, without pain. I remembered that it was fatal to sleep under an alder bush. And we had a big one that had just blossomed out. I stripped it of every leaf and blossom it had and made a bed of them in a bin of oats. Have you ever noticed how smooth oats are? As smooth to the touch as human skin.... So I pulled the lid of the bin shut and closed my eyes—fell asleep. And when they woke me I was really very sick. But I didn't die, as you can see.——What was I trying to prove? I don't know. There was no hope of winning you. But you were a symbol of the absolute hopelessness of my ever getting out of the circle I was born in.

MISS JULIE: You know, you have a real gift for telling stories. Did you go to school?

JEAN: A little. But I've read a lot of novels and gone to the theater. And I've also listened to educated people talk. That's how I've learned the most.

MISS JULIE: You mean to tell me you stand around listening to what we're saying!

JEAN: Certainly! And I've heard an awful lot, I can tell you—sitting on the coachman's seat or rowing the boat. One time I heard you and a girl friend talking——

MISS JULIE: Really?... And just what did you hear?

JEAN: Well, now, I don't know if I could repeat it. I can tell you I was a little amazed. I couldn't imagine where you had learned such words. Maybe at bottom there isn't such a big difference as you might think, between people and people.

MISS JULIE: How vulgar! At least people in my class don't behave like you when we're engaged.

JEAN: (*Looking her in the eye*). Are you sure?—Come on now, it's no use playing the innocent with me.

MISS JULIE: He was a beast. The man I offered my love was a beast.

522 *Enfin* finally

JEAN: That's what you all say—afterwards.

MISS JULIE: All?

JEAN: I'd say so, since I've heard the same expression used several times before in similar circumstances.

MISS JULIE: What kind of circumstances?

JEAN: The kind we're talking about. I remember the last time I—

MISS JULIE: *(Rising).* That's enough! I don't want to hear any more.

JEAN: How strange! Neither did she! . . . Well, now if you'll excuse me, I'll go to bed.

MISS JULIE: *(Softly).* Go to bed on Midsummer Eve?

JEAN: That's right. Dancing with that crowd up there really doesn't amuse me.

MISS JULIE: Jean, get the key to the boathouse and row me out on the lake. I want to see the sun come up.

JEAN: Do you think that's wise?

MISS JULIE: You sound as if you were worried about your reputation.

JEAN: Why not? I don't particularly care to be made ridiculous, or to be kicked out without a recommendation just when I'm trying to establish myself. Besides, I have a certain obligation to Christine.

MISS JULIE: Oh, I see. It's Christine now.

JEAN: Yes, but I'm thinking of you, too. Take my advice, Miss Julie, and go up to your room.

MISS JULIE: When did you start giving me orders?

JEAN: Just this once. For your own sake! Please! It's very late. You're so tired, you're drunk. You don't know what you're doing. Go to bed, Miss Julie.——Besides, if my ears aren't deceiving me, they're coming this way, looking for me. If they find us here together, you're done for!

THE CHORUS *is heard coming nearer, singing*

Two ladies came from out the clover,
Tri-di-ri-di-ralla, tri-di-ri-di-ra.
And one of them was green all over,
Tri-di-ri-di-ralla-la.
They told us they had gold aplenty,
Tri-di-ri-di-ralla, tri-di-ri-di-ra.
But neither of them owned a penny.
Tri-di-ri-di-ralla-la.

619 *Midsummer Eve* A festive occasion, especially in northern lands, It is a festival ultimately of pagan origin which still retains some of its original license.

This wreath for you I may be plaiting,
Tri-di-ri-di-ralla, tri-di-ri-di-ra.
But it's for another I am waiting,
Tri-di-ri-ralla-la!

MISS JULIE: I know these people. I love them just as they love me. Let them come. You'll find out.

JEAN: No, Miss Julie, they don't love you! They take the food you give them, but they spit on it as soon as your back is turned. Believe me! Just listen to them. Listen to what they're singing——No, you'd better not listen.

MISS JULIE: *(Listening).* What are they singing?

JEAN: A dirty song— about you and me!

MISS JULIE: How disgusting! Oh, what cowardly, sneaking—

JEAN: That's what the mob always is—cowards! You can't fight them; you can only run away.

MISS JULIE: Run away? Where? There's no way out of here. And we can't go in to Christine.

JEAN: What about my room? What do you say? The rules don't count in a situation like this. You can trust me. I'm your friend, remember? Your true, devoted, and respectful friend.

MISS JULIE: But suppose—suppose they looked for you there?

JEAN: I'll bolt the door. If they try to break it down, I'll shoot. Come, Miss Julie! *(On his knees)* Please, Miss Julie!

MISS JULIE: *(Meaningfully).* You promise me that you—?

JEAN: I swear to you!

MISS JULIE *goes out quickly to the right.* JEAN *follows her impetuously*

THE BALLET. *The country people enter in festive costumes, with flowers in their hats. The fiddler is in the lead. A keg of small beer and a little keg of liquor, decorated with greenery, are set up on the table. Glasses are brought out. They all drink, after which they form a circle and sing and dance the round dance, "Two ladies came from out the clover." At the end of the dance they all leave singing.*

MISS JULIE *comes in alone; looks at the devasted kitchen; clasps her hands together; then takes out a powder puff and powders her face.* JEAN *enters. He is in high spirits*

JEAN: You see! You heard them, didn't you? You've got to admit it's impossible to stay here.

MISS JULIE: No, I don't. But even if I did, what
700   could we do?

JEAN: Go away, travel, get away from here!

MISS JULIE: Travel? Yes—but where?

JEAN: Switzerland, the Italian lakes. You've never
been there?

MISS JULIE: No. Is it beautiful?

JEAN: External summer, oranges, laurel trees,
ah . . . !

MISS JULIE: But what are we going to do there?

JEAN: I'll set up a hotel—a first-class hotel with
a first-class clientele.

710   MISS JULIE: Hotel?

JEAN: I tell you that's the life! Always new faces,
new languages. Not a minute to think about
yourself or worry about your nerves. No looking
for something to do. The work keeps you busy.
Day and night the bells ring, the trains whistle,
the busses come and go. And all the while the
money comes rolling in. I tell you it's the life!

MISS JULIE: Yes, that's the life. But what about
me?

720   JEAN: The mistress of the whole place, the star
of the establishment! With your looks—and your
personality—it can't fail. It's perfect! You'll sit
in the office like a queen, setting your slaves
in motion by pressing an electric button. The
guests will file before your throne and timidly
lay their treasures on your table. You can't
imagine how people tremble when you shove
a bill in their face! I'll salt the bills and you'll
sugar them with your prettiest smile. Come on,
730   let's get away from here—(He takes a timetable
from his pocket)—right away—the next train!
We'll be in Malmo at 6:30; Hamburg 8:40 in
the morning; Frankfurt to Basle in one day; and
to Como by way of the Gotthard tunnel in—let
me see—three days! Three days!

MISS JULIE: You make it sound so wonderful. But,
Jean, you have to give me strength. Tell me
you love me. Come and put your arms around
me.

740   JEAN: (Hesitates). I want to . . . but I don't dare.
Not any more, not in this house. I do love
you—without a shadow of a doubt. How can
you doubt that, Miss Julie?

MISS JULIE: (Shyly, very becomingly). You don't have

734 Como in northern Italy

to be formal with me, Jean. You can call me
Julie. There aren't any barriers between us now.
Call me Julie.

JEAN: (Agonized). I can't! There are still barriers
between us, Miss Julie, as long as we stay in
this house! There's the past, there's the Count.   750
I've never met anyone I feel so much respect
for. I've only got to see his gloves lying on a
table and I shrivel up. I only have to hear that
bell ring and I shy like a frightened horse. I
only have to look at his boots standing there
so still and proud and I feel my spine bending.
(He kicks the boots) Superstitions, prejudices that
they've drilled into us since we were children!
But they can be forgotten just as easily! Just
we get to another country where they have a   760
republic! They'll crawl on their hands and knees
when they see my uniform. On their hands and
knees, I tell you! But not me! Oh, no. I'm not
made for crawling. I've got guts, backbone. And
once I grab that first branch, you just watch
me climb. I may be a valet now, but next year
I'll be owning property; in ten years, I'll be living
off my investments. Then I'll go to Rumania,
get myself some decorations, and maybe—notice
I only say maybe—end up as a count!   770

MISS JULIE: How wonderful, wonderful.

JEAN: Listen, in Rumania you can buy titles. You'll
be a countess after all. My countess.

MISS JULIE: But I'm not interested in that. I'm leaving all that behind. Tell me you love me, Jean,
or else—or else what difference does it make
what I am?

JEAN: I'll tell you a thousand times—but later! Not
now. And not here. Above all, let's keep our
feelings out of this or we'll make a mess of every-   780
thing. We have to look at this thing calmly and
coolly, like sensible people. (He takes out a cigar,
clips the end, and lights it) Now you sit there and
I'll sit here, and we'll talk as if nothing had happened.

MISS JULIE: (In anguish). My God, what are you?
Don't you have any feelings?

JEAN: Feelings? Nobody's got more feelings than
I have. But I've learned how to control them.

MISS JULIE: A few minutes ago you were kissing   790
my shoe—and now—!

JEAN: (Harshly). That was a few minutes ago.
We've got other things to think about now!

MISS JULIE: Don't speak to me like that, Jean!

JEAN: I'm just trying to be sensible. We've been stupid once; let's not be stupid again. Your father might be back at any moment, and we've got to decide our future before then.—Now what do you think about my plans? Do you approve or don't you?

MISS JULIE: I don't see anything wrong with them. Except one thing. For a big undertaking like that, you'd need a lot of capital. Have you got it?

JEAN: (Chewing on his cigar). Have I got it? Of course I have. I've got my knowledge of the business, my vast experience, my familiarity with languages. That's capital that counts for something, let me tell you.

MISS JULIE: You can't even buy the railway tickets with it.

JEAN: That's true. That's why I need a backer —someone to put up the money.

MISS JULIE: Where can you find him on a moment's notice?

JEAN: You'll find him—if you want to be my partner.

MISS JULIE: I can't. And I don't have a penny to my name.

Pause

JEAN: Then you can forget the whole thing.

MISS JULIE: Forget—?

JEAN: And things will stay just the way they are.

MISS JULIE: Do you think I'm going to live under the same roof with you, as your mistress? Do you think I'm going to have people sneering at me behind my back? How do you think I'll ever be able to look my father in the face after this? No, no! Take me away from here, Jean—the shame, the humiliation.... What have I done? Oh, my God, my God! What have I done? (She bursts into tears)

JEAN: Now don't start singing that tune. It won't work. What have you done that's so awful? You're not the first.

MISS JULIE: (Crying hysterically). Now you despise me!—I'm falling, I'm falling!

JEAN: Fall down to me, and I'll lift you up again!

MISS JULIE: What awful hold did you have over me? What drove me to you? The weak to the strong? The falling to the rising! Or maybe it was love? Love? This? You don't know what love is!

JEAN: Want to bet? Did you think I was a virgin?

MISS JULIE: You're vulgar! The things you say, the things you think!

JEAN: That's the way I was brought up and that's the way I am! Now don't get hysterical and don't play the fine lady with me. We're eating off the same platter now.... That's better. Come over here and be a good girl and I'll treat you to something special. (He opens the table drawer and takes out the wine bottle. He pours the wine into two used glasses)

MISS JULIE: Where did you get that wine?

JEAN: From the wine cellar.

MISS JULIE: My father's burgundy!

JEAN: Should be good enough for his son-in-law.

MISS JULIE: I was drinking beer and you—!

JEAN: That shows that I have better taste than you.

MISS JULIE: Thief!

JEAN: You going to squeal on me?

MISS JULIE: Oh, God! Partner in crime with a petty house thief! I must have been drunk; I must have been walking in my sleep. Midsummer Night! Night of innocent games—

JEAN: Yes, very innocent!

MISS JULIE: (Pacing up and down). Is there anyone here on earth as miserable as I am?

JEAN: Why be miserable? After such a conquest! Think of poor Christine in there. Don't you think she's got any feelings?

MISS JULIE: I thought so a while ago, but I don't now. A servant's a servant—

JEAN: And a whore's a whore!

MISS JULIE: (Falls to her knees and clasps her hands together). Oh, God in heaven, put an end to my worthless life! Lift me out of this awful filth I'm sinking in! Save me! Save me!

JEAN: I feel sorry for you, I have to admit it. When I was lying in the onion beds, looking up at you on the rose terrace, I—I'm telling you the truth now—I had the same dirty thoughts that all boys have.

MISS JULIE: And you said you wanted to die for me!

JEAN: In the oat bin? That was only a story.

MISS JULIE: A lie, you mean.

JEAN: (Beginning to get sleepy). Practically. I think

890 I read it in a paper about a chimney sweep who curled up in a wood-bin with some lilacs because they were going to arrest him for nonsupport of his child.

MISS JULIE: Now I see you for what you are.

JEAN: What did you expect me to do? It's always the fancy talk that gets the women.

MISS JULIE: You dog!

JEAN: You bitch!

900 MISS JULIE: Well, now you've seen the eagle's back—

JEAN: Wasn't exactly its back—!

MISS JULIE: I was going to be your first branch—!

JEAN: A rotten branch—

MISS JULIE: I was going to be the window dressing for your hotel—!

JEAN: And I the hotel—!

MISS JULIE: Sitting at the desk, attracting your customers, padding your bills—!

JEAN: I could manage that myself—!

910 MISS JULIE: How can a human soul be so dirty and filthy?

JEAN: Then why don't you clean it up?

MISS JULIE: You lackey! You shoeshine boy! Stand up when I talk to you!

JEAN: You lackey lover! You bootblack's tramp! Shut your mouth and get out of here! Who do you think you are telling me I'm coarse? I've never seen anybody in my class behave as crudely as you did tonight. Have you ever seen

920 any of the girls around here grab at a man like you did? Do you think any of the girls of my class would throw themselves at a man like that? I've never seen the like of it except in animals and prostitutes!

MISS JULIE: (Crushed). That's right! Hit me! Walk all over me! It's all I deserve. I'm rotten. But help me! Help me to get out of this—if there is any way out for me!

JEAN: (Less harsh). I'd be doing myself an injustice

930 if I didn't admit that part of the credit for this seduction belongs to me. But do you think a person in my position would have dared to look twice at you if you hadn't asked for it? I'm still amazed—

MISS JULIE: And still proud.

JEAN: Why not? But I've got to confess the victory was a little too easy to give me any real thrill.

MISS JULIE: Go on, hit me more!

JEAN: (Standing up). No.... I'm sorry for what I said. I never hit a person who's down, especially 940 a woman. I can't deny that, in one way, it was good to find out that what I saw glittering up above was only fool's gold, to have seen that the eagle's back was as gray as its belly, that the smooth cheek was just powder, and that there could be dirt under the manicured nails, that the handkerchief was soiled even though it smelled of perfume. But, in another way, it hurt me to find that everything I was striving for wasn't very high above me after all, wasn't even 950 real. It hurts me to see you sink far lower than your own cook. Hurts, like seeing the last flowers cut to pieces by the autumn rains and turned to muck.

MISS JULIE: You talk as if you already stood high above me.

JEAN: Well, don't I? Don't forget I could make you a countess but you can never make me a count.

MISS JULIE: But I have a father for a count. You 960 can never have that!

JEAN: True. But I might father my own counts —that is, if—

MISS JULIE: You're a thief! I'm not!

JEAN: There are worse things than being a thief. A lot worse. And besides, when I take a position in a house, I consider myself a member of the family—in a way, like a child in the house. It's no crime for a child to steal a few ripe cherries when they're falling off the trees, is it? (He begins 970 to feel passionate again) Miss Julie, you're a beautiful woman, much too good for the likes of me. You got carried away by your emotions and now you want to cover up your mistake by telling yourself that you love me. You don't love me. You might possibly have been attracted by my looks—in which case your kind of love is no better than mine. But I could never be satisfied to be just an animal for you, and I could never make you love me. 980

MISS JULIE: Are you so sure of that?

JEAN: You mean there's a chance? I could love you, there's no doubt about that. You're beautiful, you're refined—(He goes up to her and takes her hand)—educated, lovable when you want to be, and once you set a man's heart on fire, I'll bet it burns forever. *(He puts his arm around her waist)* You're like hot wine with strong spices. One of your kisses is enough to—*(He attempts to lead her out, but she rather reluctantly breaks away from him)*

MISS JULIE: Let me go. You don't get me that way.

JEAN: Then how? Not by petting you and not with pretty words, not by planning for the future, not by saving you from humiliation! Then how, tell me how?

MISS JULIE: How? How? I don't know how! I don't know at all—I hate you like I hate rats, but I can't get away from you.

JEAN: Then come away *with* me.

MISS JULIE: *(Pulling herself together).* Away? Yes, we'll go away!——But I'm so tired. Pour me a glass of wine, will you? *(JEAN pours the wine.* MISS JULIE *looks at her watch)* Let's talk first. We still have a little time. *(She empties the glass of wine and holds it out for more)*

JEAN: Don't overdo it. You'll get drunk.

MISS JULIE: What difference does it make?

JEAN: What difference? It looks cheap.——What did you want to say to me?

MISS JULIE: We're going to run away together, right? But we'll talk first—that is, I'll talk. So far you've done all the talking. You've told me your life, now I'll tell you mine. That way we'll know each other through and through before we become traveling companions.

JEAN: Wait a minute. Excuse me, but are you sure you won't regret this afterwards, when you've surrendered your secrets?

MISS JULIE: I thought you were my friend.

JEAN: I am—sometimes. But don't count on me.

MISS JULIE: You don't mean that. Anyway, everybody knows my secrets.—My mother's parents were very ordinary people, just commoners. She was brought up, according to the theories of her time, to believe in equality, the independence of women, and all that. And she had a strong aversion to marriage. When my father proposed to her, she swore she would never become his wife.... But she did anyway. I was born —against my mother's wishes, as far as I can make out. My mother decided to bring me up as a nature child. And on top of that I had to learn everything a boy learns, so I could be living proof that women were just as good as men. I had to wear boy's clothes, learn to handle horses—but not to milk the cows. I was made to groom the horses and handle them, and go out hunting—and even had to try and learn farming! And on the estate all the men were set to doing the work of women, and the women to doing men's work—with the result that the whole place threatened to fall to pieces, and we became the local laughing-stock. Finally my father must have come out of his trance. He rebelled, and everything was changed according to his wishes. Then my mother got sick. I don't know what kind of sickness it was, but she often had convulsions, and she would hide herself in the attic or in the garden, and sometimes she would stay out all night. Then there occurred that big fire you've heard about. The house, the stables, the cowsheds, all burned down—and under very peculiar circumstances that led one to suspect arson. You see, the accident occurred the day after the insurance expired, and the premiums on the new policy, which my father had sent in, were delayed through the messenger's carelessness, and didn't arrive on time. *(She refills her glass and drinks)*

JEAN: You've had enough.

MISS JULIE: Who cares!——We were left without a penny to our name. We had to sleep in the carriages. My father didn't know where to turn for money to rebuild the house. Then Mother suggested to him that he might try to borrow money from an old friend of hers, who owned a brick factory, not far from here. Father takes out a loan, but there's no interest charged, which surprises him. So the place was rebuilt. *(She drinks some more)* Do you know who set fire to the place?

JEAN: Your honorable mother!

MISS JULIE: Do you know who the brick manufacturer was?

JEAN: Your mother's lover?

MISS JULIE: Do you know whose money it was?

JEAN: Let me think a minute.... No, I give up.

MISS JULIE: It was my mother's!

JEAN: The Count's, you mean. Or was there a marriage settlement?

MISS JULIE: There wasn't a settlement. My mother had a little money of her own which she didn't want under my father's control, so she invested it with her—friend.

JEAN: Who grabbed it!

MISS JULIE: Precisely. He appropriated it. Well, my father finds out what happened. But he can't go to court, can't pay his wife's lover, can't prove that it's his wife's money. That was how my mother got her revenge because he had taken control of the house. He was on the verge of shooting himself. There was even a rumor that he tried and failed. But he took a new lease on life and he forced my mother to pay for her mistakes. Can you imagine what those five years were like for me? I felt sorry for my father, but I took my mother's side because I didn't know the whole story. She had taught me to distrust and hate all men—you've heard how she hated men—and I swore to her that I'd never be slave to any man.

JEAN: But you got engaged to the attorney.

MISS JULIE: Only to make him slave to me.

JEAN: But he didn't want any of that?

MISS JULIE: Oh, he wanted to well enough, but I didn't give him the chance. I got bored with him.

JEAN: Yes, so I noticed—in the barnyard.

MISS JULIE: What did you notice?

JEAN: I saw what I saw. *He* broke off the engagement.

MISS JULIE: That's a lie! It was I who broke it off. Did he tell you that? He's beneath contempt!

JEAN: Come on now, he isn't as bad as that. So you hate men, Miss Julie?

MISS JULIE: Yes, I do.... Most of the time. But sometimes, when I can't help myself—oh.... *(She shudders in disgust)*

JEAN: Then you hate me, too?

MISS JULIE: You have no idea how much! I'd like to see you killed like an animal—

JEAN: Like a mad dog, without a moment's hesitation, right?

MISS JULIE: Right!

JEAN: But we don't have anything to shoot him with—and no dog! What are we going to do?

MISS JULIE: Go away from here.

JEAN: To torture ourselves to death?

MISS JULIE: No. To enjoy ourselves for a day or two, or a week, for as long as we can—and then—to die—

JEAN: Die? How stupid! I've got a better idea: start a hotel!

MISS JULIE: *(Continuing without hearing JEAN).* —on the shores of Lake Como, where the sun is always shining, where the laurels bloom at Christmas, and the golden oranges glow on the trees.

JEAN: Lake Como is a stinking hole, and the only oranges I saw there were on the fruit stands. But it's a good tourist spot with a lot of villas and cottages that are rented out to lovers. Now there's a profitable business. You know why? They rent the villa for the whole season, but they leave after three weeks.

MISS JULIE: *(Innocently).* Why after only three weeks?

JEAN: Because they can't stand each other any longer. Why else? But they still have to pay the rent. Then you rent it out again to another couple, and so on. There's no shortage of love —even if it doesn't last very long.

MISS JULIE: Then you don't want to die with me?

JEAN: I don't want to die at all! I enjoy life too much. And moreover, I consider taking your own life as a sin against the Providence that gave us life.

MISS JULIE: You believe in God? You?

JEAN: Yes, certainly I do! I go to church every other Sunday.—Honestly, I've had enough of this talk. I'm going to bed.

MISS JULIE: Really? You think you're going to get off that easy? Don't you know that a man owes something to the woman he's dishonored?

JEAN: *(Takes out his purse and throws a silver coin on the table).* There you are. I don't want to owe anybody anything.

MISS JULIE: *(Ignoring the insult).* Do you know what the law says—?

JEAN: Aren't you lucky the law says nothing about the women who seduce men!

MISS JULIE: What else can we do but go away from here, get married, and get divorced?

JEAN: Suppose I refuse to enter into this *mésalliance*?

MISS JULIE: *Mésalliance?*

JEAN: For me! I've got better ancestors than you. I don't have any female arsonist in my family.

MISS JULIE: How can you know?

1175 *mésalliance* misalliance

1180 JEAN: You can't prove the opposite because we don't have any family records—except in the police courts. But I've read the whole history of your family in that book on the drawing-room table. Do you know who the founder of your family line was? A miller—who let his wife sleep with the king one night during the Danish war. I don't have any ancestors like that. I don't have any ancestors at all! But I can become an ancestor myself.

1190 MISS JULIE: This is what I get for baring my heart and soul to someone too low to understand, for sacrificing the honor of my family—

JEAN: Dishonor!—I warned you, remember? Drinking makes one talk, and talking's bad.

MISS JULIE: Oh how sorry I am!... If only it had never happened!... If only you at least loved me!

JEAN: For the last time—What do you expect of me? Do you want me to cry? Jump over your 1200 whip? Kiss you? Do you want me to lure you to Lake Como for three weeks and then—? What am I supposed to do? What do you want? I've had more than I can take. This is what I get for involving myself with women.... Miss Julie, I can see that you're unhappy; I know that you're suffering; but I simply cannot understand you. My people don't behave like this. We don't hate each other. We make love for the fun of it, when we can get any time off from our work. But 1210 we don't have time for it all day and all night like you do. If you ask me, you're sick, Miss Julie. I'm sure that's it, Miss Julie.

MISS JULIE: You can be understanding, Jean. You're talking to me like a human being now.

JEAN: Well, be human yourself. You spit on me but you don't let me wipe it off—on you!

MISS JULIE: Help me, Jean. Help me. Tell me what I should do, that's all—which way to go.

JEAN: For Christ's sake, if only I knew myself!

1220 MISS JULIE: I've been crazy—I've been out of my mind—but does that mean there's no way out for me?

JEAN: Stay here as if nothing had happened. Nobody knows anything.

MISS JULIE: Impossible! Everybody who works here knows. Christine knows.

JEAN: They don't know a thing. And anyhow they'd never believe it.

MISS JULIE: (Slowly, significantly). But... it might happen again. 1230

JEAN: That's true!

MISS JULIE: And there might be consequences.

JEAN: (Stunned). Consequences! What on earth have I been thinking of! You're right! There's only one thing to do: get away from here! Immediately! I can't go with you—that would give the whole game away. You'll have to go by yourself. Somewhere—I don't care where!

MISS JULIE: By myself? Where?—Oh, no, Jean, I can't. I can't! 1240

JEAN: You've got to! Before the Count comes back. You know as well as I do what will happen if you stay here. After one mistake, you figure you might as well go on, since the damage is already done. Then you get more and more careless until—finally you're exposed. I tell you, you've got to get out of the country. Afterwards you can write to the Count and tell him everything—leaving me out, of course. He'd never be able to guess it was me. Anyway, I don't think 1250 he'd exactly like to find that out.

MISS JULIE: I'll go—if you'll come with me!

JEAN: Lady, are you out of your mind!? "Miss Julie elopes with her footman." The day after tomorrow it would be in all the papers. The Count would never live it down.

MISS JULIE: I can't go away. I can't stay. Help me. I'm so tired, so awfully tired.... Tell me what to do. Order me. Start me going. I can't think any more, can't move any more.... 1260

JEAN: Now do you realize how weak you all are? What gives you the right to go strutting around with your noses in the air as if you owned the world? All right, I'll give you your orders. Go up and get dressed. Get some traveling money. And come back down here.

MISS JULIE: (Almost in a whisper). Come up with me!

JEAN: To your room?... You're going crazy again! (He hesitates a moment) No! No! Go! Right now! (He takes her hand and leads her 1270 out)

MISS JULIE: (As she is leaving). Don't be so harsh, Jean.

JEAN: Orders always sound harsh. You've never had to take them.

JEAN, *left alone, heaves a sigh of relief and sits down at the table. He takes out a notebook and a pencil and begins to calculate, counting aloud now and then. The pantomime continues until* CHRISTINE *enters, dressed for church, and carrying* JEAN's *white tie and shirt front in her hand*

1280

CHRISTINE: Lord in Heaven, what a mess! What on earth have you been doing?

JEAN: It was Miss Julie. She dragged the whole crowd in here. You must have been sleeping awfully sound if you didn't hear anything.

CHRISTINE: I slept like a log.

JEAN: You already dressed for church?

1290

CHRISTINE: Yes, indeed. Don't you remember you promised to go to Communion with me today?

JEAN: Oh, yes, of course. I remember. I see you've brought my things. All right. Come on, put it on me. (*He sits down, and* CHRISTINE *starts to put the white tie and shirt front on him. Pause*)

JEAN: (*Yawning*). What's the lesson for today?

CHRISTINE: The beheading of John the Baptist, I suppose.

JEAN: My God, that will go on forever.—Hey, you're choking me!... Oh, I'm so sleepy, so

1300

sleepy.

CHRISTINE: What were you doing up all night? You look green in the face.

JEAN: I've been sitting here talking with Miss Julie.

CHRISTINE: That girl! She doesn't know how to behave herself!

Pause

JEAN: Tell me something, Christine....

CHRISTINE: Well, what?

JEAN: Isn't it strange when you think about it?

1310

Her, I mean.

CHRISTINE: What's so strange?

JEAN: Everything!

Pause. CHRISTINE *looks at the half-empty glasses on the table*

CHRISTINE: Have you been drinking with her?

JEAN: Yes!

CHRISTINE: Shame on you!—Look me in the eyes! You haven't...?

JEAN: Yes!

1320

CHRISTINE: Is it possible? Is it really possible?

JEAN: (*After a moment's consideration*). Yes. It is.

CHRISTINE: Oh, how disgusting! I could never have believed anything like this would happen! No. No. This is too much!

JEAN: Don't tell me you're jealous of her?

CHRISTINE: No, not of her. If it had been Clara—or Sophie—I would have scratched your eyes out! But her—? That's different. I don't know why.... But it's still disgusting!

JEAN: Then you're mad at her?

1330

CHRISTINE: No. Mad at you. You were mean and cruel to do a thing like that, very mean. The poor girl!... But let me tell you, I'm not going to stay in this house a moment longer, not when I can't have any respect for my employers.

JEAN: Why do you want to respect them?

CHRISTINE: Don't try to be smart. You don't want to work for people who behave immorally, do you? Well, do you? If you ask me, you'd be lowering yourself by doing that.

1340

JEAN: Oh, I don't know. I think it's rather comforting to find out that they're not one bit better than we are.

CHRISTINE: Well, I don't. If they're not any better, there's no point in us trying to be like them.—And think of the Count. Think of all the sorrows he's been through in his time. No, sir, I won't stay in this house any longer.... Imagine! You, of all people! If it had been the attorney fellow; if it had been somebody respectable—

1350

JEAN: Now just a minute—!

CHRISTINE: Oh, you're all right in your own way. But there's a big difference between one class and another. You can't deny that.——No, this is something I can never get over. She was so proud, and so sarcastic about men, you'd never believe she'd go and throw herself at one. And at someone like you! And *she* was going to have Diana shot, because the poor thing ran after the

1360

gatekeeper's mongrel!—Well, I tell you, I've had enough! I'm not going to stay here any longer. On the twenty-fourth of October, I'm leaving.

JEAN: Then what'll you do?

CHRISTINE: Well, since you brought it up, it's about time you got yourself a decent place, if we're going to get married.

JEAN: Why should I go looking for another place? I could never get a place like this if I'm married.

CHRISTINE: Well, of course not! But you could get

1370

a job as a doorkeeper, or maybe try to get a government job as a caretaker somewhere. The government don't pay much, but they pay regular. And there's a pension for the wife and children.

JEAN: (Wryly). Fine, fine! But I'm not the kind of fellow who thinks about dying for his wife and children this early in the game. I hate to say it, but I've got slightly bigger plans than that.

1380

CHRISTINE: Plans! Hah! What about your obligations? You'd better start giving them a little thought!

JEAN: Don't start nagging me about obligations! I know what I have to do without you telling me. (He hears a sound upstairs) Anyhow, we'll have plenty of chance to talk about this later. You just go and get yourself ready, and we'll be off to church.

1390

CHRISTINE: Who is that walking around up there?

JEAN: I don't know. Clara, I suppose. Who else?

CHRISTINE: (Starting to leave). It can't be the Count, can it? Could he have come back without anybody hearing him?

JEAN: (Frightened). The Count? No, it can't be. He would have rung.

CHRISTINE: (Leaving). God help us! I've never heard of the like of this.

1400

The sun has now risen and strikes the tops of the trees in the park. The light shifts gradually until it is shining very obliquely through the windows. JEAN *goes to the door and signals.* MISS JULIE *enters, dressed for travel, and carrying a small bird cage, covered with a towel. She sets the cage down on a chair*

MISS JULIE: I'm ready now.

JEAN: Shh! Christine's awake.

MISS JULIE: (She is extremely tense and nervous during the following). Did she suspect anything?

JEAN: She doesn't know a thing.——My God,

1410

what happened to you?

MISS JULIE: What do you mean? Do I look so strange?

JEAN: You're white as a ghost, and you've—excuse me—but you've got dirt on your face.

MISS JULIE: Let me wash it off. (She goes over to the wash basin and washes her face and hands) There! Do you have a towel? . . . Oh, look the sun's coming up!

JEAN: That breaks the magic spell!

MISS JULIE: Yes, we were spellbound last night, weren't we? Midsummer madness . . . Jean, listen to me! Come with me. I've got the money!

1420

JEAN: (Suspiciously). Enough?

MISS JULIE: Enough for a start. Come with me, Jean. I can't travel alone today. Midsummer Day on a stifling hot train, packed in with crowds of people, all staring at me—stopping at every station when I want to be flying. I can't, Jean, I can't! . . . And everything will remind me of the past. Midsummer Day when I was a child and the church was decorated with leaves—birch leaves and lilacs . . . the table spread for dinner with friends and relatives . . . and after dinner, dancing in the park, with flowers and games. Oh, no matter how far you travel, the memories tag right along in the baggage car . . . and the regrets and the remorse.

1430

JEAN: All right, I'll go with you! But it's got to be now—before it's too late! This very instant!

MISS JULIE: Hurry and get dressed! (She picks up the bird cage)

1440

JEAN: But no baggage! It would give us away.

MISS JULIE: Nothing. Only what we can take to our seats.

JEAN: (As he gets his hat). What in the devil have you got there? What is that?

MISS JULIE: It's only my canary. I can't leave it behind.

JEAN: A canary! My God, do you expect us to carry a bird cage around with us? You're crazy. Put that cage down!

1450

MISS JULIE: It's the only thing I'm taking with me from my home—the only living thing who loves me since Diana was unfaithful to me! Don't be cruel, Jean. Let me take it with me.

JEAN: I told you to put that cage down!——And don't talk so loud. Christine can hear us.

MISS JULIE: No, I won't leave it with a stranger. I won't. I'd rather have you kill it.

JEAN: Let me have the little pest, and I'll wring its neck.

1460

MISS JULIE: Yes, but don't hurt it. Don't—. No, I can't do it!

JEAN: Don't worry, I can. Give it here.

MISS JULIE *takes the bird out of the cage and kisses it*

MISS JULIE: Oh, my little Serena, must you die and leave your mistress?

JEAN: You don't have to make a scene of it. It's a question of your whole life and future. You're wasting time! *(JEAN grabs the canary from her, carries it to the chopping block, and picks up a meat cleaver. MISS JULIE turns away)* You should have learned how to kill chickens instead of shooting revolvers—*(He brings the cleaver down)*—then a drop of blood wouldn't make you faint.

MISS JULIE: *(Screaming)*. Kill me too! Kill me! You can kill an innocent creature without turning a hair—then kill me. Oh, how I hate you! I loathe you! There's blood between us. I curse the moment I first laid eyes on you! I curse the moment I was conceived in my mother's womb.

JEAN: What good does your cursing do? Let's get out of here!

MISS JULIE: *(Approaches the chopping block as if drawn to it against her will)*. No, I don't want to go yet. I can't.—I have to see.—Shh! I hear a carriage coming! *(She listens but keeps her eyes fastened on the chopping block and cleaver)* You don't think I can stand the sight of blood, do you? You think I'm so weak! Oh, I'd love to see your blood and your brains on that chopping block. I'd love to see the whole of your sex swimming in a sea of blood just like that. I think I could drink out of your skull. I'd like to bathe my feet in your ribs! I could eat your heart roasted whole!—You think I'm weak! You think I loved you because my womb hungered for your seed. You think I want to carry your brood under my heart and nourish it with my blood! Bear your child and take your name!—Come to think of it, what is your name anyway? I've never heard your last name. You probably don't even have one. I'd be Mrs. Doorkeeper or Madame Floorsweeper. You dog with my name on your collar—you lackey with my initials on your buttons! Do you think I'm going to share you with my cook and fight over you with my maid?! Ohhh!—You think I'm a coward who wants to run away. No, I'm going to stay. Come hell or high water, I don't care! My father comes home—finds his bureau broken into—his money gone. Then he rings—on that bell—two rings for the valet. And then he sends for the sheriff —and I tell him everything. Everything! Oh, it'll be wonderful to have it all over . . . If only it will be over. . . . He'll have a stroke and die.

Then there'll be an end to all of us. There'll be peace . . . and quiet . . . forever. . . . His coat of arms will be broken on the coffin; the Count's line dies out. But the valet's line will continue in an orphanage, win triumphs in the gutter, and end in jail!*

CHRISTINE *enters, dressed for church and with a hymn-book in her hand. MISS JULIE rushes over to her and throws herself into her arms as if seeking protection*

MISS JULIE: Help me, Christine! Help me against this man!

CHRISTINE: *(Cold and unmoved)*. This is a fine way to behave on a holy day! *(She sees the chopping block)* Just look at the mess you've made there! How do you explain that? And what's all this shouting and screaming about?

MISS JULIE: Christine, you're a woman, you're my friend! I warn you, watch out for this—this monster!

JEAN: *(Ill at ease and a little embarrassed)*. If you ladies are going to talk, I think I'll go and shave. *(He slips out to the right)*

MISS JULIE: You've got to understand, Christine! You've got to listen to me!

CHRISTINE: No, I don't. I don't understand this kind of shenanigans at all. Where do you think you're going dressed like that? And Jean with his hat on?—Well?—Well?

MISS JULIE: Listen to me, Christine! If you'll just listen to me, I'll tell you everything.

CHRISTINE: I don't want to know anything.

MISS JULIE: You've got to listen to me—!

CHRISTINE: What about? About your stupid behavior with Jean? I tell you that doesn't bother me at all, because it's none of my business. But if you have any silly idea about talking him into skipping out with you, I'll soon put a stop to that.

MISS JULIE: *(Extremely tense)* Christine, please don't get upset. Listen to me. I can't stay here, and Jean can't stay here. So you see, we have to go away.

*Most editions of *Miss Julie* have a speech by Jean at this point: "Now there speaks the royal blood! Brava, Miss Julie. Only you mustn't let the cat out of the bag about the miller and his wife." Strindberg wanted this speech expunged as not in keeping with Jean's character [Professor Sprinchorn's note].

CHRISTINE: Hm, hm, hm.

MISS JULIE: *(Suddenly brightening up).* Wait! I've got an idea! Why couldn't all three of us go away together?—out of the country—to Switzerland—and start a hotel. I've got the money, you see. Jean and I would be responsible for the whole affair—and Christine, you could run the kitchen, I thought. Doesn't that sound wonderful! Say yes! Say you'll come, Christine, then everything will be settled. Say you will! Please! *(She throws her arms around* CHRISTINE *and pats her)*

CHRISTINE: *(Remaining aloof and unmoved).* Hm. Hm.

MISS JULIE: *(Presto tempo).* You've never been traveling, Christine. You have to go out and see the world. You can't imagine how wonderful it is to travel by train—constantly new faces—new countries. We'll go to Hamburg, and stop over to look at the zoo—you'll love that. And we'll go to the theater and the opera. And then when we get to Munich, we'll go to the museums, Christine. They have Rubenses and Raphaels there—those great painters, you know. Of course you've heard about Munich where King Ludwig lived—you know, the king who went mad. And then we can go and see his castles—they're built just like the ones you read about in fairy tales. And from there it's just a short trip to Switzerland—with the Alps. Think of the Alps, Christine, covered with snow in the middle of summer. And oranges grow there, and laurel trees that are green the whole year round—*(JEAN can be seen in the wings at right, sharpening his straight razor on a strap held between his teeth and his left hand. He listens to* MISS JULIE *with a satisfied expression on his face, now and then nodding approvingly.* MISS JULIE *continues tempo prestissimo)*—And that's where we'll get a hotel. I'll sit at the desk while Jean stands at the door and receives the guests, goes out shopping, writes the letters. What a life that will be! The train whistle blowing, then the bus arriving, then a bell ringing upstairs, then the bell in the restaurant rings—and I'll be making out the bills—and I know just how much to salt them—you can't imagine how timid tourists are when you shove a bill in their face!—And you, Christine, you'll run the whole kitchen—there'll be no standing at the stove for you—of course not.

If you're going to talk to the people, you'll have to dress neatly and elegantly. And with your looks—I'm not trying to flatter you, Christine—you'll run off with some man one fine day—a rich Englishman, that's who it'll be, they're so easy to—*(slowing down)*—to catch—Then we'll all be rich—We'll build a villa on Lake Como.—Maybe it does rain there sometimes, but—*(more and more lifelessly)*—the sun has to shine sometimes, too—even if it looks cloudy.—And—then... Or else we can always travel some more—and come back... *(pause)*—here... or somewhere else....

CHRISTINE: Do you really believe a word of that yourself, Miss Julie?

MISS JULIE: *(Completely beaten).* Do I believe a word of it myself?

CHRISTINE: Do you?

MISS JULIE: *(Exhausted).* I don't know. I don't believe anything any more. *(She sinks down on the bench and lays her head between her arms on the table)* Nothing. Nothing at all.

CHRISTINE: *(Turns to the right and faces* JEAN*).* So! You were planning to run away, were you?

JEAN: *(Nonplused, lays his razor down on the table).* We weren't exactly going to run away! Don't exaggerate. You heard Miss Julie's plans. Even if she's tired now after being up all night, her plans are perfectly practical.

CHRISTINE: Well, just listen to you! Did you really think you could get me to cook for that little—

JEAN: *(Sharply).* You keep a respectful tongue in your mouth when you talk to your mistress! Understand?

CHRISTINE: Mistress!

JEAN: Yes, mistress!

CHRISTINE: Well of all the—! I don't have to listen—

JEAN: Yes, you do! You need to listen more and talk less. Miss Julie is your mistress. Don't forget that! And if you're going to despise her for what she did, you ought to despise yourself for the same reason.

CHRISTINE: I've always held myself high enough to—

JEAN: High enough to make you look down on others!

CHRISTINE: —enough to keep from lowering myself beneath my position. No one can say that the

Count's cook has ever had anything to do with
the stable groom or the swineherd. No one can
say that!

JEAN: Yes, aren't you lucky you got involved with
a decent man!

CHRISTINE: What kind of a decent man is it who
sells the oats from the Count's stables?

JEAN: Listen to who's talking! You get a commission on the groceries and take bribes from the
butcher!

CHRISTINE: How can you say a thing like that!

JEAN: And you tell me you can't respect your
employers any more! You! You!

CHRISTINE: Are you going to church or aren't you?
I should think you'd need a good sermon after
your exploits.

JEAN: No, I'm not going to church! You can go
alone and confess your own sins.

CHRISTINE: Yes, I'll do just that. And I'll come
back with enough forgiveness to cover yours,
too. Our Redeemer suffered and died on the
cross for all our sins, and if we come to Him
in faith and with a penitent heart, He will take
all our sins upon Himself.

JEAN: Grocery sins included?

MISS JULIE: Do you really believe that, Christine?

CHRISTINE: With all my heart, as sure as I'm standing here. It was the faith I was born into, and
I've held on to it since I was a little girl, Miss
Julie. Where sin aboundeth, there grace aboundeth also.

MISS JULIE: If I had your faith, Christine, if only—

CHRISTINE: But you see, that's something you can't
have without God's special grace. And it is not
granted to everyone to receive it.

MISS JULIE: Then who receives it?

CHRISTINE: That's the secret of the workings of
grace, Miss Julie, and God is no respecter of
persons. With him the last shall be the first——

MISS JULIE: In that case, he does have respect for
the last, doesn't he?

CHRISTINE: *(Continuing)*. —and it is easier for a
camel to go through the eye of a needle than
for a rich man to enter the kingdom of God.
That's how things are, Miss Julie. I'm going to
leave now—alone. And on my way out I'm going
to tell the stable boy not to let any horses out,
in case anyone has any ideas about leaving before
the Count comes home. Goodbye. *(She leaves)*

JEAN: She's a devil in skirts!—And all because of
a canary!

MISS JULIE: *(Listlessly)*. Never mind the canary....
Do you see any way out of this, any end to
it?

JEAN: *(After thinking for a moment)*. No.

MISS JULIE: What would you do if you were in
my place?

JEAN: In your place? Let me think.... An aristocrat, a woman, and—fallen.... I don't
know.——Or maybe I do.

MISS JULIE: *(Picks up the razor and makes a gesture
with it)*. Like this?

JEAN: Yes. But *I* wouldn't do it, you understand!
That's the difference between us.

MISS JULIE: Because you're a man and I'm a
woman? What difference does that make?

JEAN: Just the difference that there is—between
a man and a woman.

MISS JULIE: *(Holding the razor in her hand)*. I want
to! But I can't do it. My father couldn't do it
either, that time he should have done it.

JEAN: No, he was right not to do it. He had to
get his revenge first.

MISS JULIE: And now my mother is getting her
revenge again through me.

JEAN: Haven't you ever loved your father, Miss
Julie?

MISS JULIE: Yes, enormously. But I must have
hated him too. I must have hated him without
knowing it. It was he who brought me up to
despise my own sex, to be half woman and half
man. Who's to blame for what has happened?
My father, my mother, myself? Myself? I don't
have a self that's my own. I don't have a single
thought I didn't get from my father, not an emotion I didn't get from my mother. And that last
idea—about all people being equal—I got that
from him, my betrothed. That's why I say he's
beneath contempt. How can it be my own fault?
Put the blame on Jesus, like Christine does? I'm
too proud to do that—and too intelligent, thanks
to what my father taught me.... A rich man
can't get into heaven? That's a lie. But at least
Christine, who's got money in the savings bank,
won't get in.... Who's to blame? What difference does it make who's to blame? I'm still the
one who has to bear the guilt, suffer the consequences—

JEAN: Yes, but—

The bell rings sharply twice, MISS JULIE *jumps up.* JEAN *changes his coat*

1760   JEAN: The Count's back! What if Christine—? *(He goes to the speaking tube, taps on it, and listens)*
MISS JULIE: Has he looked in his bureau yet?
JEAN: This is Jean, sir! *(Listen. The audience cannot hear what the* COUNT *says)* Yes, sir! *(Listens)* Yes, sir! Yes, as soon as I can. *(Listens)* Yes, at once, sir! *(Listens)* Very good, sir! In half an hour.
MISS JULIE: *(Trembling with anxiety)*. What did he say? For God's sake, what did he say?
JEAN: He ordered his boots and his coffee in half
1770   an hour.
MISS JULIE: Half an hour then!... Oh, I'm so tired. I can't bring myself to do anything. Can't repent, can't run away, can't stay, can't live... can't die. Help me, Jean. Command me, and I'll obey like a dog. Do me this last favor. Save my honor, save his name. You know what I ought to do but can't force myself to do. Let me use your will power. You command me and I'll obey.
JEAN: I don't know—I can't either, not now. I don't
1780   know why. It's as if this coat made me—. I can't give you orders in this. And now, after the Count has spoken to me, I—I can't really explain it—but—I've got the backbone of a damned lackey! If the Count came down here now and ordered me to cut my throat, I'd do it on the spot.
MISS JULIE: Pretend that you're him, and that I'm you. You were such a good actor just a while ago, when you were kneeling before me. You
1790   were the aristocrat then. Or else—have you ever been to the theater and seen a hypnotist? *(JEAN nods)* He says to his subject, "Take this broom!" and he takes it. He says, "Now sweep!" and he sweeps.
JEAN: But the person has to be asleep!
MISS JULIE: *(Ecstatic)*. I'm already asleep. The

whole room has turned to smoke. You seem like an iron stove, a stove that looks like a man in black with a high hat. Your eyes are glowing like coals when the fire dies out. Your face is a white smudge, like ashes. *(The sun is now shining in on the floor and falls on* JEAN*)* It's so good and warm—*(She rubs her hands together as if warming them at a fire)*—and so bright—and so peaceful.   1800
JEAN: *(Takes the razor and puts it in her hand)* There's the broom. Go now, when the sun is up—out into the barn—and—*(He whispers in her ear)*
MISS JULIE: *(Waking up)*. Thanks! I'm going to get my rest. But tell me one thing. Tell me that the first can also receive the gift of grace. Tell me that, even if you don't believe it.   1810
JEAN: The first? I can't tell you that.——But wait a moment, Miss Julie. I know what I can tell you. You're no longer among the first. You're among—the last.
MISS JULIE: That's true! I'm among the very last. I am the last!—Oh! Now I can't go! Tell me just once more, tell me to go!
JEAN: Now I can't either. I can't!
MISS JULIE: And the first shall be the last....   1820
JEAN: Don't think—don't think! You're taking all my strength away. You're making me a coward. ... What! I thought I saw the bell move. No.... Let me stuff some paper in it.— Afraid of a bell! But it isn't just a bell. There's somebody behind it. A hand that makes it move. And there's something that makes the hand move——Stop your ears, that's it, stop your ears! But it only rings louder. Rings louder and louder until you answer it. And then it's too   1830
late. Then the sheriff comes—and then—*(There are two sharp rings on the bell.* JEAN *gives a start, then straightens himself up)* It's horrible! But there's no other way for it to end.—Go! *(*MISS JULIE *walks resolutely out through the door)*

The end

FROM "PREFACE" TO
MISS JULIE

by August Strindberg

Theatre has long seemed to me—in common with much other art—a *Biblia Pauperum*, a Bible in pictures for those who cannot read what is written or printed; and I see the playwright as a lay preacher peddling the ideas of his time in popular form, popular enough for the middle-classes, mainstay of theatre audiences, to grasp the gist of the matter without troubling their brains too much. For this reason theatre has always been an elementary school for the young, the semi-educated and for women who still have a primitive capacity for deceiving themselves and letting themselves be deceived—who, that is to say, are susceptible to illusion and to suggestion from the author. I have therefore thought it not unlikely that in these days, when that rudimentary and immature thought-process operating through fantasy appears to be developing into reflection, research and analysis, that theatre, like religion, might be discarded as an outworn form for whose appreciation we lack the necessary conditions. This opinion is confirmed by the major crisis still prevailing in the theatres of Europe, and still more by the fact that in those countries of culture, producing the greatest thinkers of the age, namely England and Germany, drama—like other fine arts—is dead.

Some countries, it is true, have attempted to create a new drama by using the old forms with up-to-date contents, but not only has there been insufficient time for these new ideas to be popularized, so that the audience can grasp them, but also people have been so wrought up by the taking of sides that pure, disinterested appreciation has become impossible. One's deepest impressions are upset when an applauding or a hissing majority dominates as forcefully and openly as it can in the theatre. Moreover, as no new form has been devised for these new contents, the new wine has burst the old bottles.

In this play I have not tried to do anything new, for this cannot be done, but only to modernize the form to meet the demands which may, I think, be made on this art today. To this end I chose—or surrendered myself to—a theme which claims to be outside the controversial issues of today, since questions of social climbing or falling, of higher or lower, better or worse, of man and woman, are, have been and will be of lasting interest. When I took this theme from a true story told me some years ago, which made a deep impression, I saw it as a subject for tragedy, for as yet it is tragic to see one favoured by fortune go under, and still more to see a family heritage die out, although a time may come when we have grown so developed and enlightened that we shall view with indifference life's spectacle, now seeming so brutal, cynical and heartless. Then we shall have dispensed with those inferior, unreliable instruments of thought called feelings, which become harmful and superfluous as reasoning develops.

The fact that my heroine rouses pity is solely due to weakness; we cannot resist fear of the same fate overtaking us. The hyper-sensitive spectator may, it is true, go beyond this kind of pity, while the man with belief in the future may actually demand some suggestion for remedying the evil—in other words some kind of policy. But to begin with, there is no such thing as absolute evil; the downfall of one family is the good fortune of another, which thereby gets a chance to rise, and, fortune being only comparative, the alternation of rising and falling is one of life's principal charms. Also, to the man of policy, who wants to remedy the painful fact that the bird of prey devours the dove, and lice the bird of prey, I should like to put the question: why should it be remedied? Life is not so mathematically idiotic as only to permit the big to eat the small; it happens just as often that the bee kills the lion or at least drives it mad.

That my tragedy depresses many people is their own fault. When we have grown strong as the pioneers of the French revolution, we shall be happy and relieved to see the national parks cleared of ancient rotting trees which have stood too long in the way of others equally entitled to a period of growth—as relieved as we are when an incurable invalid dies.

My tragedy "The Father" was recently criticised for being too sad—as if one wants cheerful tragedies! Everybody is clamouring for this supposed "joy of life," and theatre managers demand farces, as if the joy of life consisted in being ridiculous and portraying all human beings as suffering from St. Vitus's dance or total idiocy. I myself find the joy of life in its strong and cruel struggles, and my pleasure in learning, in adding to my knowledge. For this reason I have chosen for this play an unusual situation, but an instructive one—an exception, that is to say, but a great exception, one proving the rule, which will no doubt annoy all lovers of the commonplace. What will offend simple minds is that my plot is not simple, nor its point of view single. In real life an action—this, by the way, is a somewhat new discovery—is generally caused by a whole series of motives, more or less fundamental, but as a rule the spectator chooses just one of these—the one which his mind can most easily grasp or that does most credit to his intelligence. A suicide is committed. Business troubles, says the man of affairs. Unrequited love, say the women. Sickness, says the invalid. Despair, says the down-and-out. But it is possible that the motive lay in all or none of these directions, or that the dead man concealed his actual motive by revealing quite another, likely to reflect more to his glory.

I see Miss Julie's tragic fate to be the result of many circumstances: the mother's character, the father's mistaken upbringing of the girl, her own nature, and the influence of her fiancé on a weak, degenerate mind. Also, more directly, the festive mood of Midsummer Eve, her father's absence, her monthly indisposition, her pre-occupation with animals, the excitement of dancing, the magic of dusk, the strongly aphrodisiac influence of flowers, and finally the chance that drives the couple into a room alone—to which must be added the urgency of the excited man.

My treatment of the theme, moreover, is neither exclusively physiological nor psychological. I have not put the blame wholly on the inheritance from her mother, nor on her physical condition at the time, nor on immorality. I have not even preached a moral sermon; in the absence of a priest I leave this to the cook.

I congratulate myself on this multiplicity of motives as being up-to-date, and if others have done the same thing before me, then I congratulate myself on not being alone in my "paradoxes," as all innovations are called.

In regard to the drawing of the characters, I have made my people somewhat "characterless" for the following reasons. In the course of time the word character has assumed manifold meanings. It must have originally signified the dominating trait of the soul-complex, and this was confused with temperament. Later it became the middle-class term for the automaton, one whose nature had become fixed or who had adapted himself to a particular role in life. In fact a person who had ceased to grow was called a character, while one continuing to develop—the skilful navigator of life's river, sailing not with sheets set fast, but veering before the wind to luff again—was called characterless, in a derogatory sense, of course, because he was so hard to catch, classify and keep track of. This middle-class conception of the immobility of the soul was transferred to the stage where the middle-class has always ruled. A character came to signify a man fixed and finished: one who invariably appeared either drunk or jocular or melancholy, and characterization required nothing more than a physical defect such as a club-foot, a wooden leg, a red nose; or the fellow might be made to repeat some such phrase as: "That's capital" or: "Barkis is willin'!" This simple way of regarding human beings still survives in the great Molière. Harpagon is nothing but a miser, although Harpagon might have been not only a miser, but also a first-rate financier, an excellent father and a good citizen. Worse still, his "failing" is a dintinct advantage to his son-in-law and his daughter, who are his heirs, and who therefore cannot criticise him, even if they have to wait a while to get to bed. I do not believe, therefore, in simple stage characters; and the summary judgments of authors—this man is stupid, that one brutal, this jealous, that stingy, and so forth—should be challenged by the Naturalists who know the richness of the soul-complex and realise that vice has a reverse side very much like virtue.

Because they are modern characters, living in a period of transition more feverishly hysterical than its predecessor at least, I have drawn my figures vacillating, disinte-grated, a blend of old and new. Nor does it seem to me unlikely that, through newspapers and conversations, modern ideas may have filtered down to the level of the domestic servant.

My souls (characters) are conglomerations of past and present stages of civilization, bits from books and newspapers, scraps of humanity, rags and tatters of fine clothing, patched together as is the human soul. And I have added a little evolutionary history by making the weaker steal and repeat the words of the stronger, and by making the characters borrow ideas or "suggestions" from one another.

Miss Julie is a modern character, not that the half-woman, the man-hater, has not existed always, but because now that she has been discovered she has stepped to the front and begun to make a noise. The half-woman is a type who thrusts herself forward, selling herself nowadays for power, decorations, distinctions, diplomas, as formerly for money. The type implies degeneration; it is not a good type and it does not endure; but it can unfortunately transmit its misery, and degenerate men seem instinctively to choose their mates from among such women, and so they breed, producing offspring of indeterminate sex to whom life is torture. But fortunately they perish, either because they cannot come to terms with reality, or because their repressed instincts break out uncontrollably, or again because their hopes of catching up with men are shattered. The type is tragic, revealing a desperate fight against nature, tragic too in its Romantic inheritance now dissipated by Naturalism, which wants nothing but happiness—and for happiness strong and sound species are required.

But Miss Julie is also a relic of the old warrior nobility now giving way to the new nobility of nerve and brain. She is a victim of the discord which a mother's "crime" has produced in a family, a victim too of the day's complaisance, of circumstances, of her own defective constitution, all of which are equivalent to the Fate or Universal Law of former days. The Naturalist has abolished guilt with God, but the consequences of the action—punishment, imprisonment or the fear of it—he cannot abolish, for the simple reason that they remain whether he is acquitted or not. An injured fellow-being is not so complacent as outsiders, who have not been injured, can afford to be. Even if the father had felt impelled to take no vengeance, the daughter would have taken vengeance on herself, as she does here, from that innate or acquired sense of honour which the upper-classes inherit—whether from Barbarism or Aryan forebears, or from the chivalry of the Middle Ages, who knows? It is a very beautiful thing, but it has become a danger nowadays to the preservation of the race. It is the nobleman's *hara-kiri*, the Japanese law of inner conscience which compels him to cut his own stomach open at the insult of another, and which survives in modified form in the duel, a privilege of the nobility. And so the valet Jean lives on, but Miss Julie cannot live without honour. This is the thrall's advantage over the nobleman, that he lacks this fatal preoccupation with honour. And in all of us Aryans there is something of the nobleman, or the Don Quixote, which makes us sympathize with the man who commits suicide because he has done something ignoble and lost his honour. And we are noblemen enough to suffer at the sight of fallen greatness littering the earth like a corpse—yes, even if the fallen rise again and make restitution by honourable deeds. Jean, the valet, is a race-builder, a man of marked characteristics. He was a labourer's son who has educated himself towards becoming a gentleman. He has learnt easily, through his well-developed senses (smell, taste, vision)—and he also has a sense of beauty. He has already bettered himself, and is thick-skinned enough to have no scruples about using other people's services. He is already foreign to his associates, despising them as part of the life he has turned his back on, yet also fearing and fleeing from them because they know his secrets, pry into his plans, watch his rise with envy, and look forward with pleasure to his fall. Hence his dual, indeterminate character, vacillating between love of the heights and hatred of those who have already achieved them. He is, he says himself, an aristocrat; he has learned the secrets of good society. He is polished, but vulgar within; he already wears his tails with taste, but there is no guarantee of his personal cleanliness.

He has some respect for his young lady, but he is frightened of Kristin, who knows his dangerous secrets, and he is sufficiently callous not to allow the night's events to wreck his plans for the future. Having both the slave's brutality and the master's lack of squeamishness, he can see blood without fainting and take disaster by the horns. Consequently he emerges from the battle unscathed, and probably ends his days as a hotel-keeper. And even if *he* does not become a Roumanian Count, his son will doubtless go to the university and perhaps become a county attorney.

The light which Jean sheds on a lower-class conception of life, life seen from below, is on the whole illuminating—when he speaks the truth, which is not often, for he says what is favourable to himself rather than what is true. When Miss Julie suggests that the lower-classes must be oppressed by the attitude of their superiors, Jean naturally agrees, as his object is to gain her sympathy; but when he perceives the advantage of separating himself from the common herd, he at once takes back his words.

It is not because Jean is now rising that he has the upper hand of Miss Julie, but because he is a man. Sexually he is the aristocrat because of his virility, his keener senses and his capacity for taking the initiative. His inferiority is mainly due to the social environment in which he lives, and he can probably shed it with his valet's livery.

The slave mentality expresses itself in his worship of the Count (the boots), and his religious superstition; but he worships the Count chiefly because he holds that higher position for which Jean himself is striving. And this worship remains even when he has won the daughter of the house and seen how empty is that lovely shell.

I do not believe that a love relationship in the "higher" sense could exist between two individuals of such different quality, but I have made Miss Julie imagine that she is in love, so as to lessen her sense of guilt, and I let Jean suppose that if his social position were altered he would truly love her. I think love is like the hyacinth which has to strike roots in darkness *before* it can produce a vigorous flower. In this case it shoots up quickly, blossoms and goes to seed all at the same time, which is why the plant dies so soon.

As for Kristin, she is a female slave, full of servility and sluggishness acquired in front of the kitchen fire, and stuffed full of morality and religion, which are her cloak and scape-goat. She goes to church as a quick and easy way of unloading her household thefts on to Jesus and taking on a fresh cargo of guiltlessness. For the rest she is a minor character, and I have therefore sketched her in the same manner as the Pastor and the Doctor in "The Father," where I wanted ordinary human beings, as are most country pastors and provincial doctors. If these minor characters seem abstract to some people this is due to the fact that ordinary people are to a certain extent abstract in pursuit of their work; that is to say, they are without individuality, showing, while working, only one side of themselves. And as long as the spectator does not feel a need to see them from other sides, there is nothing wrong with my abstract presentation.

In regard to the dialogue, I have departed somewhat from tradition by not making my characters catechists who ask stupid questions in order to elicit a smart reply. I have avoided the symmetrical, mathematical construction of French dialogue, and let people's minds work irregularly, as they do in real life where, during a conversation, no topic is drained to the dregs, and one mind finds in another a chance cog to engage in. So too the dialogue wanders, gathering in the opening scenes material which is later picked up, worked over, repeated, expounded and developed like the theme in a musical composition.

The plot speaks for itself, and as it really only concerns two people, I have concentrated on these, introducing only one minor character, the cook, and keeping the unhappy spirit of the father above and behind the action. I have done this because it seems to me that the psychological process is what interests people most today. Our inquisitive souls are no longer satisfied with seeing a thing happen; we must also know how it happens. We want to see the wires themselves, to watch the machinery, to examine the box with the false bottom, to take hold of the magic ring in order to find the join, and look at the cards to see how they are marked.

MAJOR BARBARA

Bernard Shaw (1856-1950)

Shaw, like so many other English dramatists, was born in Dublin. He began his writing career as a novelist, but soon found himself a journalist-critic of music, painting, and literature. He became one of the leaders of the Fabian Society and was an outspoken champion of Socialism. Responding to his admiration for Ibsen and the need for striking new plays for the Independent Theater, Shaw turned his attention in 1892 to the theater, where he found a congenial outlet for his theatrical flair and dramatic talent.

His first two plays were forthright attacks on contemporary social problems—slum landlordism in *Widowers' Houses* and prostitution and sweatshop labor in *Mrs. Warren's Profes-*sion. His *Major Barbara* (1905) was another indictment of social ills.

Although Shaw departed from realistic problem plays, he continued to deal in his uncompromising fashion with the pervasive issues of modern society. While critical evaluation at first suggested that he was merely a clever showman, the impact of his work ultimately was acknowledged, until he was recognized as the creator of the most significant collection of dramatic literature in the twentieth century. Among the other notable plays of Shaw are *Heartbreak House, Man and Superman, Candida, Pygmalion, Caesar and Cleopatra, Arms and the Man,* and *Saint Joan.*

Opposite page. Barbara attempts to soften the young, tough Bill Walker.

Below. Undershaft makes a rare visit to his family.
Photographs in this sequence
are of the 1956 Broadway production,
with Charles Laughton as Undershaft, Glynis Johns as Barbara,
Eli Wallach as Bill Walker, and Burgess Meredith as Cusins.

FRIEDMAN-AB

Above. Undershaft comes to see
the Salvation Army in action.

Opposite top. Barbara and her fiancé, Cusins,
find a bright moment in their work with the Salvation Army.

Opposite bottom. Undershaft finds a warm welcome
for his tainted money, much to Barbara's dismay.

CHARACTERS

STEPHEN UNDERSHAFT, *son of* ANDREW UNDERSHAFT *and* LADY BRITOMART

LADY BRITOMART, *daughter of the* EARL OF STEVENAGE *and wife of* ANDREW
UNDERSHAFT

BARBARA UNDERSHAFT, *daughter of* ANDREW UNDERSHAFT *and* LADY BRITOMART;
a Major in the Salvation Army

SARAH UNDERSHAFT, *daughter of* ANDREW UNDERSHAFT *and* LADY BRITOMART

ADOLPHUS CUSINS, *fiancé of* BARBARA UNDERSHAFT

CHARLES LOMAX, *fiancé of* SARAH UNDERSHAFT

MORRISON, LADY BRITOMART's *butler*

ANDREW UNDERSHAFT, *husband of* LADY BRITOMART; *head of Undershaft and
Lazarus, munitions makers*

RUMMY (ROMOLA) MITCHENS, } *Regulars at the West Ham*
SNOBBY (BRONTERRE O'BRIEN) PRICE, } *Salvation Army shelter*

PETER SHIRLEY, *a discharged workman, poor but honest*

JENNY HILL, *a Salvation Army lass*

BILL WALKER, *a young tough*

MRS. BAINES, *a Salvation Army Commissioner*

BILTON, *a foreman in Undershaft and Lazarus*

MAJOR BARBARA

ACT ONE

It is after dinner in January 1906, in the library in Lady Britomart Undershaft's house in Wilton Crescent. A large and comfortable settee is in the middle of the room, upholstered in dark leather. A person sitting on it (it is vacant at present) would have, on his right, Lady Britomart's writing table, with the lady herself busy at it; a smaller writing table behind him on his left; the door behind on Lady Britomart's side; and a window with a window seat directly on his left. Near the window is an armchair.

Lady Britomart is a woman of fifty or thereabouts, well dressed and yet careless of her dress, well bred and quite reckless of her breeding, well mannered and yet appallingly outspoken and indifferent to the opinion of her interlocutors, amiable and yet peremptory, arbitrary, and high-tempered to the last bearable degree, and withal a very typical managing matron of the upper class, treated as a naughty child until she grew into a scolding mother, and finally settling down with plenty of practical ability and worldly experience, limited in the oddest way with domestic and class limitations, conceiving the universe exactly as if it were a large house in Wilton Crescent, though handling her corner of it very effectively on that assumption, and being quite enlightened and liberal as to the books in the library, the pictures on the walls, the music in the portfolios, and the articles in the papers.

Her son, Stephen, comes in. He is a gravely correct young man under 25, taking himself very seriously, but still in some awe of his mother, from childish habit and bachelor shyness rather than from any weakness of character.

STEPHEN: Whats the matter?

LADY BRITOMART: Presently, Stephen.

Stephen submissively walks to the settee and sits down. He takes up a Liberal weekly called The Speaker.

LADY BRITOMART: Dont begin to read, Stephen. I shall require all your attention.

STEPHEN: It was only while I was waiting—

LADY BRITOMART: Dont make excuses, Stephen. *(He puts down The Speaker).* Now! *(She finishes her writing; rises; and comes to the settee).* I have not kept you waiting very long, I think.

STEPHEN: Not at all, mother.

LADY BRITOMART: Bring me my cushion. *(He takes the cushion from the chair at the desk and arranges it for her as she sits down on the settee).* Sit down. *(He sits down and fingers his tie nervously).* Dont fiddle with your tie, Stephen: there is nothing the matter with it.

STEPHEN: I beg your pardon. *(He fiddles with his watch chain instead).*

LADY BRITOMART: Now are you attending to me, Stephen?

STEPHEN: Of course, mother.

LADY BRITOMART: No: it's not of course. I want something much more than your everyday matter-of-course attention. I am going to speak to you very seriously, Stephen. I wish you would let that chain alone.

STEPHEN: (*hastily relinquishing the chain*). Have I done anything to annoy you, mother? If so, it was quite unintentional.

LADY BRITOMART: (*astonished*). Nonsense! (*With some remorse*) My poor boy, did you think I was angry with you?

40 STEPHEN: What is it, then, mother? You are making me very uneasy.

LADY BRITOMART: (*squaring herself at him rather aggressively*). Stephen: may I ask how soon you intend to realize that you are a grown-up man, and that I am only a woman?

STEPHEN: (*amazed*). Only a—

LADY BRITOMART: Dont repeat my words, please: it is a most aggravating habit. You must learn to face life seriously, Stephen. I really cannot 50 bear the whole burden of our family affairs any longer. You must advise me: you must assume the responsibility.

STEPHEN: I!

LADY BRITOMART: Yes, you, of course. You were 24 last June. Youve been at Harrow and Cambridge. Youve been to India and Japan. You must know a lot of things, now; unless you have wasted your time most scandalously. Well, advise me.

60 STEPHEN: (*much perplexed*). You know I have never interfered in the household—

LADY BRITOMART: No: I should think not. I dont want you to order the dinner.

STEPHEN: I mean in our family affairs.

LADY BRITOMART: Well, you must interfere now; for they are getting quite beyond me.

STEPHEN: (*troubled*). I have thought sometimes that perhaps I ought; but really, mother, I know so little about them; and what I do know is so pain-70 ful! it is so impossible to mention some things to you—(*he stops, ashamed*).

LADY BRITOMART: I suppose you mean your father.

STEPHEN: (*almost inaudibly*). Yes.

LADY BRITOMART: My dear: we cant go on all our lives not mentioning him. Of course you were quite right not to open the subject until I asked you to; but you are old enough now to be taken into my confidence, and to help me to deal with 80 him about the girls.

STEPHEN: But the girls are all right. They are engaged.

LADY BRITOMART: (*complacently*). Yes: I have made a very good match for Sarah. Charles Lomax will be a millionaire at 35. But that is ten years ahead; and in the meantime his trustees cannot under the terms of his father's will allow him more than £800 a year.

STEPHEN: But the will says also that if he increases his income by his own exertions, they may dou-90 ble the increase.

LADY BRITOMART: Charles Lomax's exertions are much more likely to decrease his income than to increase it. Sarah will have to find at least another £800 a year for the next ten years; and even then they will be as poor as church mice. And what about Barbara? I thought Barbara was going to make the most brilliant career of all of you. And what does she do? Joins the Salva-100 tion Army; discharges her maid; lives on a pound a week; and walks in one evening with a professor of Greek whom she has picked up in the street, and who pretends to be a Salvationist, and actually plays the big drum for her in public because he has fallen head over ears in love with her.

STEPHEN: I was certainly rather taken aback when I heard they were engaged. Cusins is a very nice fellow, certainly: nobody would ever guess that he was born in Australia; but—

LADY BRITOMART: Oh, Adolphus Cusins will make 110 a very good husband. After all, nobody can say a word against Greek: it stamps a man at once as an educated gentleman. And my family, thank Heaven, is not a pig-headed Tory one. We are Whigs, and believe in liberty. Let snobbish people say what they please: Barbara shall marry, not the man they like, but the man *I* like.

STEPHEN: Of course I was thinking only of his income. However, he is not likely to be extrava-120 gant.

LADY BRITOMART: Dont be too sure of that, Stephen. I know your quiet, simple, refined, poetic people like Adolphus: quite content with the best of everything! They cost more than your extravagant people, who are always as mean as they are second rate. No: Barbara will need at least £2000 a year. You see it means two additional households. Besides, my dear, you must marry soon. I dont approve of the present fashion 130 of philandering bachelors and late marriages; and I am trying to arrange something for you.

STEPHEN: It's very good of you, mother; but perhaps I had better arrange that for myself.

LADY BRITOMART: Nonsense! you are much too young to begin matchmaking: you would be taken in by some pretty little nobody. Of course I dont mean that you are not to be consulted: you know that as well as I do. (STEPHEN *closes his lips and is silent*). Now dont sulk, Stephen.

STEPHEN: I am not sulking, mother. What has all this got to do with—with—with my father?

LADY BRITOMART: My dear Stephen: where is the money to come from? It is easy enough for you and the other children to live on my income as long as we are in the same house; but I cant keep four families in four separate houses. You know how poor my father is: he has barely seven thousand a year now; and really, if he were not the Earl of Stevenage, he would have to give up society. He can do nothing for us. He says, naturally enough, that it is absurd that he should be asked to provide for the children of a man who is rolling in money. You see, Stephen, your father must be fabulously wealthy, because there is always a war going on somewhere.

STEPHEN: You need not remind me of that, mother. I have hardly ever opened a newspaper in my life without seeing our name in it. The Undershaft torpedo! The Undershaft quick firers! The Undershaft ten inch! the Undershaft disappearing rampart gun! the Undershaft submarine! and now the Undershaft aerial battleship! At Harrow they called me the Woolwich Infant. At Cambridge it was the same. A little brute at King's who was always trying to get up revivals, spoilt my Bible—your first birthday present to me—by writing under my name, 'Son and heir to Undershaft and Lazarus, Death and Destruction Dealers: address Christendom and Judea.' But that was not so bad as the way I was kowtowed to everywhere because my father was making millions by selling cannons.

LADY BRITOMART: It is not only the cannons, but the war loans that Lazarus arranges under cover of giving credit for the cannons. You know, Stephen, it's perfectly scandalous. Those two men, Andrew Undershaft and Lazarus, positively have Europe under their thumbs. That is why your father is able to behave as he does.

He is above the law. Do you think Bismarck or Gladstone or Disraeli could have openly defied every social and moral obligation all their lives as your father has? They simply wouldnt have dared. I asked Gladstone to take it up. I asked the Times to take it up. I asked the Lord Chamberlain to take it up. But it was just like asking them to declare war on the Sultan. They wouldnt. They said they couldnt touch him. I believe they were afraid.

STEPHEN: What could they do? He does not actually break the law.

LADY BRITOMART: Not break the law! He is always breaking the law. He broke the law when he was born: his parents were not married.

STEPHEN: Mother! Is that true?

LADY BRITOMART: Of course it's true: that was why we separated.

STEPHEN: He married without letting you know this!

LADY BRITOMART: (*rather taken aback by this inference*). Oh no. To do Andrew justice, that was not the sort of thing he did. Besides, you know the Undershaft motto: Unashamed. Everybody knew.

STEPHEN: But you said that was why you separated.

LADY BRITOMART: Yes, because he was not content with being a foundling himself: he wanted to disinherit you for another foundling. That was what I couldnt stand.

STEPHEN (*ashamed*). Do you mean for—for—for—

LADY BRITOMART: Dont stammer, Stephen. Speak distinctly.

STEPHEN: But this is so frightful to me, mother. To have to speak to you about such things!

LADY BRITOMART: It's not pleasant for me, either, especially if you are still so childish that you must make it worse by a display of embarrassment. It is only in the middle classes, Stephen, that people get into a state of dumb helpless horror when they find that there are wicked people in the world. In our class, we have to decide what is to be done with wicked people; and nothing should disturb our self-possession. Now ask your question properly.

STEPHEN: Mother: have you no consideration for me? For Heaven's sake either treat me as a child, as you always do, and tell me nothing at all; or tell me everything and let me take it as best I can.

LADY BRITOMART: Treat you as a child! What do you mean? It is most unkind and ungrateful of you to say such a thing. You know I have never treated any of you as children. I have always made you my companions and friends, and allowed you perfect freedom to do and say whatever you liked, so long as you liked what I could approve of.

STEPHEN: (desperately). I daresay we have been the 240 very imperfect children of a very perfect mother; but I do beg you to let me alone for once, and tell me about this horrible business of my father wanting to set me aside for another son.

LADY BRITOMART: (amazed). Another son! I never said anything of the kind. I never dreamt of such a thing. This is what comes of interrupting me.

STEPHEN: But you said—

LADY BRITOMART: (cutting him short). Now be a good 250 boy, Stephen, and listen to me patiently. The Undershafts are descended from a foundling in the parish of St. Andrew Undershaft in the city. That was long ago, in the reign of James the First. Well, this foundling was adopted by an armorer and gun-maker. In the course of time the foundling succeeded to the business; and from some notion of gratitude, or some vow or something, he adopted another foundling, and left the business to him. And that foundling did 260 the same. Ever since that, the cannon business has always been left to an adopted foundling named Andrew Undershaft.

STEPHEN: But did they never marry? Were there no legitimate sons?

LADY BRITOMART: Oh yes: they married just as your father did; and they were rich enough to buy land for their own children and leave them well provided for. But they always adopted and trained some foundling to succeed them in the 270 business; and of course they always quarrelled with their wives furiously over it. Your father was adopted in that way; and he pretends to consider himself bound to keep up the tradition and adopt somebody to leave the business to. Of course I was not going to stand that. There may have been some reason for it when the Undershafts could only marry women in their own class, whose sons were not fit to govern great estates. But there could be no excuse for 280 passing over my son.

STEPHEN: (dubiously). I am afraid I should make a poor hand of managing a cannon foundry.

LADY BRITOMART: Nonsense! you could easily get a manager and pay him a salary.

STEPHEN: My father evidently had no great opinion of my capacity.

LADY BRITOMART: Stuff, child! you were only a baby: it had nothing to do with your capacity. Andrew did it on principle, just as he did every perverse and wicked thing on principle. When 290 my father remonstrated, Andrew actually told him to his face that history tells us of only two successful institutions: one the Undershaft firm, and the other the Roman Empire under the Antonines. That was because the Antonine emperors all adopted their successors. Such rubbish! The Stevenages are as good as the Antonines, I hope; and you are a Stevenage. But that was Andrew all over. There you have the man! Always clever and unanswerable when 300 he was defending nonsense and wickedness: always awkward and sullen when he had to behave sensibly and decently!

STEPHEN: Then it was on my account that your home life was broken up, mother. I am sorry.

LADY BRITOMART: Well, dear, there were other differences. I really cannot bear an immoral man. I am not a Pharisee, I hope; and I should not have minded his merely doing wrong things: we are none of us perfect. But your father didnt 310 exactly do wrong things: he said them and thought them: that was what was so dreadful. He really had a sort of religion of wrongness. Just as one doesnt mind men practising immorality so long as they own that they are in the wrong by preaching morality; so I couldnt forgive Andrew for preaching immorality while he practised morality. You would all have grown up without principles, without any knowledge of right and wrong, if he had been in the house. You 320 know, my dear, your father was a very attractive man in some ways. Children did not dislike him; and he took advantage of it to put the wickedest ideas into their heads, and make them quite unmanageable. I did not dislike him myself: very far from it; but nothing can bridge over moral disagreement.

STEPHEN: All this simply bewilders me, mother. People may differ about matters of opinion, or even about religion; but how can they differ 330 about right and wrong? Right is right; and wrong is wrong; and if a man cannot distinguish them properly, he is either a fool or a rascal: thats all.

LADY BRITOMART: *(touched).* Thats my own boy *(she pats his cheek)*! Your father never could answer that: he used to laugh and get out of it under cover of some affectionate nonsense. And now that you understand the situation, what do you
340   advise me to do?

STEPHEN: Well, what can you do?

LADY BRITOMART: I must get the money somehow.

STEPHEN: We cannot take money from him. I had rather go and live in some cheap place like Bedford Square or even Hampstead than take a farthing of his money.

LADY BRITOMART: But after all, Stephen, our present income comes from Andrew.

STEPHEN: *(shocked).* I never knew that.

350   LADY BRITOMART: Well, you surely didnt suppose your grandfather had anything to give me. The Stevenages could not do everything for you. We gave you social position. Andrew had to contribute something. He had a very good bargain, I think.

STEPHEN: *(bitterly).* We are utterly dependent on him and his cannons, then?

LADY BRITOMART: Certainly not: the money is settled. But he provided it. So you see it is not
360   a question of taking money from him or not: it is simply a question of how much. I dont want any more for myself.

STEPHEN: Nor do I.

LADY BRITOMART: But Sarah does; and Barbara does. That is, Charles Lomax and Adolphus Cusins will cost them more. So I must put my pride in my pocket and ask for it, I suppose. That is your advice, Stephen, is it not?

STEPHEN: No.

370   LADY BRITOMART: *(sharply).* Stephen!

STEPHEN: Of course if you are determined—

LADY BRITOMART: I am not determined: I ask your advice; and I am waiting for it. I will not have all the responsibility thrown on my shoulders.

STEPHEN: *(obstinately).* I would die sooner than ask him for another penny.

LADY BRITOMART: *(resignedly).* You mean that *I* must ask him. Very well, Stephen: it shall be as you wish. You will be glad to know that your grand-
380   father concurs. But he thinks I ought to ask

Andrew to come here and see the girls. After all, he must have some natural affection for them.

STEPHEN: Ask him here!!!

LADY BRITOMART: Do not repeat my words, Stephen. Where else can I ask him?

STEPHEN: I never expected you to ask him at all.

LADY BRITOMART: Now dont tease, Stephen. Come! you see that it is necessary that he should pay us a visit, dont you?

STEPHEN: *(reluctantly).* I suppose so, if the girls can-   390
not do without his money.

LADY BRITOMART: Thank you, Stephen: I knew you would give me the right advice when it was properly explained to you. I have asked your father to come this evening. (STEPHEN *bounds from his seat*). Dont jump, Stephen: it fidgets me.

STEPHEN: *(in utter consternation).* Do you mean to say that my father is coming here tonight—that he may be here at any moment?

LADY BRITOMART: *(looking at her watch).* I said nine.   400
(He gasps. She rises). Ring the bell, please. (STEPHEN *goes to the smaller writing table; presses a button on it; and sits at it with his elbows on the table and his head in his hands, outwitted and overwhelmed).* It is ten minutes to nine yet; and I have to prepare the girls. I asked Charles Lomax and Adolphus to dinner on purpose that they might be here. Andrew had better see them in case he should cherish any delusions as to their being capable of supporting their wives. *(The butler*   410
enters: LADY BRITOMART *goes behind the settee to speak to him).* Morrison: go up to the drawing room and tell everybody to come down here at once. (MORRISON *withdraws.* LADY BRITOMART *turns to* STEPHEN). Now remember, Stephen: I shall need all your countenance and authority. *(He rises and tries to recover some vestige of these attributes).* Give me a chair, dear. *(He pushes a chair forward from the wall to where she stands, near the smaller writing table. She sits down; and he goes to the armchair,*   420
into which he throws himself). I dont know how Barbara will take it. Ever since they made her a major in the Salvation Army she has developed a propensity to have her own way and order people about which quite cows me sometimes. It's not ladylike: I'm sure I dont know where she picked it up. Anyhow, Barbara shant bully me; but still it's just as well that your father should be here before she has time to refuse to meet him or make a fuss. Dont look nervous,   430

Stephen: it will only encourage Barbara to make difficulties. *I* am nervous enough, goodness knows; but I dont shew it.

SARAH *and* BARBARA *come in with their respective young men, Charles Lomax and Adolphus Cusins. Sara is slender, bored, and mundane. Barbara is robuster, jollier, much more energetic. Sarah is fashionably dressed: Barbara is in Salvation Army uniform. Lomax, a young man about town, is like many other young men about town. He is afflicted with a frivolous sense of humor which plunges him at the most inopportune moments into paroxysms of imperfectly suppressed laughter. Cusins is a spectacled student, slight, thin haired, and sweet voiced, with a more complex form of Lomax's complaint. His sense of humor is intellectual and subtle, and is complicated by an appalling temper. The lifelong struggle of a benevolent temperament and a high conscience against impulses of inhuman ridicule and fierce impatience has set up a chronic strain which has visibly wrecked his constitution. He is a most implacable, determined, tenacious, intolerant person who by mere force of character presents himself as–and indeed actually is–considerate, gentle, explanatory, even mild and apologetic, capable possibly of murder, but not of cruelty or coarseness. By the operation of some instinct which is not merciful enough to blind him with the illusions of love, he is obstinately bent on marrying Barbara. Lomax likes Sarah and thinks it will be rather a lark to marry her. Consequently he has not attempted to resist Lady Britomart's arrangements to that end.*

All four look as if they had been having a good deal of fun in the drawing room. The girls enter first, leaving the swains outside. Sarah comes to the settee. Barbara comes in after her and stops at the door.

BARBARA: Are Cholly and Dolly to come in?

LADY BRITOMART: (*forcibly*). Barbara: I will not have Charles called Cholly: the vulgarity of it positively makes me ill.

BARBARA: It's all right, mother: Cholly is quite correct nowadays. Are they to come in?

LADY BRITOMART: Yes, if they will behave themselves.

BARBARA: (*through the door*). Come in, Dolly; and behave yourself.

BARBARA *comes to her mother's writing table.* CUSINS *enters smiling, and wanders towards* LADY BRITOMART.

SARAH: (*calling*). Come in, Cholly. (LOMAX *enters, controlling his features very imperfectly, and places himself vaguely between* SARAH *and* BARBARA).

LADY BRITOMART: (*peremptorily*). Sit down, all of you. (*They sit.* CUSINS *crosses to the window and seats himself there.* LOMAX *takes a chair.* BARBARA *sits at the writing table and* SARAH *on the settee*). I dont in the least know what you are laughing at, Adolphus. I am surprised at you, though I expected nothing better from Charles Lomax.

CUSINS: (*in a remarkably gentle voice*). Barbara has been trying to teach me the West Ham Salvation March.

LADY BRITOMART: I see nothing to laugh at in that; nor should you if you are really converted.

CUSINS: (*sweetly*). You were not present. It was really funny, I believe.

LOMAX: Ripping.

LADY BRITOMART: Be quiet, Charles. Now listen to me, children. Your father is coming here this evening.

General stupefaction. LOMAX, SARAH, *and* BARBARA *rise:* SARAH *scared, and* BARBARA *amused and expectant.*

LOMAX: (*remonstrating*). Oh I say!

LADY BRITOMART: You are not called on to say anything, Charles.

SARAH: Are you serious, mother?

LADY BRITOMART: Of course I am serious. It is on your account, Sarah, and also on Charles's. (*Silence.* SARAH *sits, with a shrug.* CHARLES *looks painfully unworthy*). I hope you are not going to object, Barbara.

BARBARA: I! why should I? My father has a soul to be saved like anybody else. He's quite welcome as far as I am concerned. (*She sits on the table, and softly whistles 'Onward Christian Soldiers'*).

LOMAX: (*Still remonstrant*). But really, dont you know! Oh I say!

LADY BRITOMART: (*frigidly*). What do you wish to convey, Charles?

LOMAX: Well, you must admit that this is a bit thick.

LADY BRITOMART: (*turning with ominous suavity to* CUSINS). Adolphus: you are a professor of Greek. Can you translate Charles Lomax's remarks into reputable English for us?

CUSINS: (*cautiously*). If I may say so, Lady Brit, I think Charles has rather happily expressed what we all feel. Homer, speaking of Autolycus, uses the same phrase. πυκινὸν δόμον ἐλθεῖν means a bit thick.

LOMAX: (handsomely). Not that I mind, you know, if Sarah dont. (He sits)

LADY BRITOMART: (crushingly). Thank you. Have I your permission, Adolphus, to invite my own husband to my own house?

CUSINS: (gallantly). You have my unhesitating support in everything you do.

LADY BRITOMART: Tush! Sarah: have you nothing to say?

SARAH: Do you mean that he is coming regularly to live here?

LADY BRITOMART: Certainly not. The spare room is ready for him if he likes to stay for a day or two and see a little more of you; but there are limits.

SARAH: Well, he cant eat us, I suppose. I dont mind.

LOMAX: (chuckling). I wonder how the old man will take it.

LADY BRITOMART: Much as the old woman will, no doubt, Charles.

LOMAX: (abashed). I didn't mean—at least—

LADY BRITOMART: You didnt think, Charles. You never do; and the result is, you never mean anything. And now please attend to me, children. Your father will be quite a stranger to us.

LOMAX: I suppose he hasnt seen Sarah since she was a little kid.

LADY BRITOMART: Not since she was a little kid, Charles, as you express it with that elegance of diction and refinement of thought that seem never to desert you. Accordingly—er—(impatiently) Now I have forgotten what I was going to say. That comes of your provoking me to be sarcastic, Charles. Adolphus: will you kindly tell me where I was.

CUSINS: (sweetly). You were saying that as Mr. Undershaft has not seen his children since they were babies, he will form his opinion of the way you have brought them up from their behavior tonight, and that therefore you wish us all to be particularly careful to conduct ourselves well, especially Charles.

LADY BRITOMART: (with emphatic approval). Precisely.

LOMAX: Look here, Dolly: Lady Brit didnt say that.

LADY BRITOMART: (vehemently). I did, Charles. Adolphus's recollection is perfectly correct. It is most important that you should be good; and I do beg you for once not to pair off into opposite corners and giggle and whisper while I am speaking to your father.

BARBARA: All right, mother. We'll do you credit. (She comes off the table, and sits in her chair with ladylike elegance).

LADY BRITOMART: Remember, Charles, that Sarah will want to feel proud of you instead of ashamed of you.

LOMAX: Oh I say! theres nothing to be exactly proud of, dont you know.

LADY BRITOMART: Well, try and look as if there was.

MORRISON, pale and dismayed, breaks into the room in unconcealed disorder.

MORRISON: Might I speak a word to you, my lady?

LADY BRITOMART: Nonsense! Shew him up.

MORRISON: Yes, my lady. (He goes).

LOMAX: Does Morrison know who it is?

LADY BRITOMART: Of course. Morrison has always been with us.

LOMAX: It must be a regular corker for him, dont you know.

LADY BRITOMART: Is this a moment to get on my nerves, Charles, with your outrageous expressions?

LOMAX: But this is something out of the ordinary, really—

MORRISON: (at the door). The—er—Mr. Undershaft. (He retreats in confusion).

ANDREW UNDERSHAFT comes in. All rise. LADY BRITOMART meets him in the middle of the room behind the settee.

ANDREW is, on the surface, a stoutish, easygoing elderly man, with kindly patient manners, and an engaging simplicity of character. But he has a watchful, deliberate, waiting, listening face, and formidable reserves of power, both bodily and mental, in his capacious chest and long head. His gentleness is partly that of a strong man who has learnt by experience that his natural grip hurts ordinary people unless he handles them very carefully, and partly the mellowness of age and success. He is also a littly shy in his present very delicate situation.

LADY BRITOMART: Good evening, Andrew.

UNDERSHAFT: How d'ye do, my dear.

LADY BRITOMART: You look a good deal older.

UNDERSHAFT: (apologetically). I am somewhat older. (Taking her hand with a touch of courtship) Time has stood still with you.

LADY BRITOMART: *(throwing away his hand)*. Rubbish! This is your family.

UNDERSHAFT: *(surprised)*. Is it so large? I am sorry to say my memory is failing very badly in some things. *(He offers his hand with paternal kindness to* LOMAX*)*.

LOMAX: *(jerkily shaking his hand)*. Ahdedoo.

UNDERSHAFT: I can see you are my eldest. I am very glad to meet you again, my boy.

LOMAX: *(remonstrating)*. No, but look here dont you know—*(Overcome)* Oh I say!

LADY BRITOMART: *(recovering from momentary speechlessness)*. Andrew: do you mean to say that you dont remember how many children you have?

UNDERSHAFT: Well, I am afraid I—. They have grown so much—er. Am I making any ridiculous mistake? I may as well confess: I recollect only one son. But so many things have happened since, of course—er—

LADY BRITOMART: *(decisively)*. Andrew: you are talking nonsense. Of course you have only one son.

UNDERSHAFT: Perhaps you will be good enough to introduce me, my dear.

LADY BRITOMART: That is Charles Lomax, who is engaged to Sarah.

UNDERSHAFT: My dear sir, I beg your pardon.

LOMAX: Notatall. Delighted, I assure you.

LADY BRITOMART: This is Stephen.

UNDERSHAFT: *(bowing)*. Happy to make your acquaintance, Mr. Stephen. Then *(going to* CUSINS*)* you must be my son. *(Taking* CUSINS' *hands in his)* How are you, my young friend? *(To* LADY BRITOMART*)* He is very like you, my love.

CUSINS: You flatter me, Mr. Undershaft. My name is Cusins: engaged to Barbara. *(Very explicitly)* That is Major Barbara Undershaft, of the Salvation Army. That is Sarah, your second daughter. This is Stephen Undershaft, your son.

UNDERSHAFT: My dear Stephen, I beg your pardon.

STEPHEN: Not at all.

UNDERSHAFT: Mr. Cusins: I am much indebted to you for explaining so precisely. *(Turning to* SARAH*)* Barbara, my dear—

SARAH: *(prompting him)*. Sarah.

UNDERSHAFT: Sarah, of course. *(They shake hands. He goes over to* BARBARA*)* Barbara—I am right this time, I hope?

BARBARA: Quite right. *(They shake hands)*.

LADY BRITOMART: *(resuming command)*. Sit down, all of you. Sit down, Andrew. *(She comes forward and sits on the settee.* CUSINS *also brings his chair forward on her left.* BARBARA *and* STEPHEN *resume their seats.* LOMAX *gives his chair to* SARAH *and goes for another)*.

UNDERSHAFT: Thank you, my love.

LOMAX: *(conversationally, as he brings a chair forward between the writing table and the settee, and offers it to* UNDERSHAFT*)*. Takes you some time to find out exactly where you are, dont it?

UNDERSHAFT: *(Accepting the chair, but remaining standing)*. That is not what embarrasses me, Mr Lomax. My difficulty is that if I play the part of a father, I shall produce the effect of an intrusive stranger; and if I play the part of a discreet stranger, I may appear a callous father.

LADY BRITOMART: There is no need for you to play any part at all, Andrew. You had much better be sincere and natural.

UNDERSHAFT: *(submissively)*. Yes, my dear: I daresay that will be best. *(He sits down comfortably)*. Well, here I am. Now what can I do for you all?

LADY BRITOMART: You need not do anything, Andrew. You are one of the family. You can sit with us and enjoy yourself.

A painfully conscious pause. BARBARA *makes a face at* LOMAX, *whose too long suppressed mirth immediately explodes in agonized neighings.*

LADY BRITOMART: *(outraged)*. Charles Lomax: if you can behave yourself, behave yourself. If not, leave the room.

LOMAX: I'm awfully sorry, Lady Brit; but really you know, upon my soul! *(He sits on the settee between* LADY BRITOMART *and* UNDERSHAFT, *quite overcome)*.

BARBARA: Why dont you laugh if you want to, Cholly? It's good for your inside.

LADY BRITOMART: Barbara: you have had the education of a lady. Please let your father see that; and dont talk like a street girl.

UNDERSHAFT: Never mind me, my dear. As you know, I am not a gentleman; and I was never educated.

LOMAX: *(encouragingly)*. Nobody'd know it, I assure you. You look all right, you know.

CUSINS: Let me advise you to study Greek, Mr

Undershaft. Greek scholars are privileged men. Few of them know Greek; and none of them know anything else; but their position is unchallengeable. Other languages are the qualifications of waiters and commercial travellers: Greek is to a man of position what the hallmark is to silver.

BARBARA: Dolly: dont be insincere. Cholly: fetch your concertina and play something for us.

LOMAX: (jumps up eagerly, but checks himself to remark doubtfully to UNDERSHAFT). Perhaps that sort of thing isnt in your line, eh?

UNDERSHAFT: I am particularly fond of music.

LOMAX: (delighted). Are you? Then I'll get it. (He goes upstairs for the instrument).

UNDERSHAFT: Do you play, Barbara?

BARBARA: Only the tambourine. But Cholly's teaching me the concertina.

UNDERSHAFT: Is Cholly also a member of the Salvation Army?

BARBARA: No: he says it's bad form to be a dissenter. But I dont despair of Cholly. I made him come yesterday to a meeting at the dock gates, and take the collection in his hat.

UNDERSHAFT: (looks whimsically at his wife)!!

LADY BRITOMART: It is not my doing, Andrew. Barbara is old enough to take her own way. She has no father to advise her.

BARBARA: Oh yes she has. There are no orphans in the Salvation Army.

UNDERSHAFT: Your father there has a great many children and plenty of experience, eh?

BARBARA: (looking at him with quick interest and nodding). Just so. How did you come to understand that? (LOMAX is heard at the door trying the concertina).

LADY BRITOMART: Come in, Charles. Play us something at once.

LOMAX: Righto! (He sits down in his former place, and preludes).

UNDERSHAFT: One moment, Mr. Lomax. I am rather interested in the Salvation Army. Its motto might be my own: Blood and Fire.

LOMAX: (shocked). But not your sort of blood and fire, you know.

UNDERSHAFT: My sort of blood cleanses: my sort of fire purifies.

BARBARA: So do ours. Come down tomorrow to my shelter—the West Ham shelter—and see what we're doing. We're going to march to a great meeting in the Assembly Hall at Mile End. Come and see the shelter and then march with us: it will do you a lot of good. Can you play anything?

UNDERSHAFT: In my youth I earned pennies, and even shillings occasionally, in the streets and in public house parlors by my natural talent for stepdancing. Later on, I became a member of the Undershaft orchestral society, and performed passably on the tenor trombone.

LOMAX: (scandalized—putting down the concertina). Oh I say!

BARBARA: Many a sinner has played himself into heaven on the trombone, thanks to the Army.

LOMAX: (to BARBARA, still rather shocked). Yes; but what about the cannon business, dont you know? (To UNDERSHAFT) Getting into heaven is not exactly in your line, is it?

LADY BRITOMART: Charles!!!

LOMAX: Well; but it stands to reason, dont it? The cannon business may be necessary and all that: we cant get on without cannons; but it isnt right, you know. On the other hand, there may be a certain amount of tosh about the Salvation Army—I belong to the Established Church myself—but still you cant deny that it's religion; and you cant go against religion, can you? At least unless youre downright immoral, dont you know.

UNDERSHAFT: You hardly appreciate my position, Mr. Lomax—

LOMAX: (hastily). I'm not saying anything against you personally—

UNDERSHAFT: Quite so, quite so. But consider for a moment. Here I am, a profiteer in mutilation and murder. I find myself in a specially amiable humor just now because, this morning, down at the foundry, we blew twenty-seven dummy soldiers into fragments with a gun which formerly destroyed only thirteen.

LOMAX: (leniently). Well, the more destructive war becomes, the sooner it will be abolished, eh?

UNDERSHAFT: Not at all. The more destructive war becomes the more fascinating we find it. No, Mr. Lomax: I am obliged to you for making the usual excuse for my trade; but I am not ashamed of it. I am not one of those men who keep their morals and their business in watertight compartments. All the spare money my trade rivals spend on hospitals, cathedrals, and other receptacles for conscience money, I devote to experiments and researches in improved methods of destroying life and property. I have always done so; and I always shall. Therefore your Christmas card moralities of peace on earth and goodwill among men are of no use to me.

830   Your Christianity, which enjoins you to resist not evil, and to turn the other cheek, would make me a bankrupt. My morality—my religion—must have a place for cannons and torpedoes in it.

STEPHEN: (coldly–almost sullenly). You speak as if there were half a dozen moralities and religions to choose from, instead of one true morality and one true religion.

UNDERSHAFT: For me there is only one true
840   morality; but it might not fit you, as you do not manufacture aerial battleships. There is only one true morality for every man; but every man has not the same true morality.

LOMAX: (overtaxed). Would you mind saying that again? I didnt quite follow it.

CUSINS: It's quite simple. As Euripides says, one man's meat is another man's poison morally as well as physically.

UNDERSHAFT: Precisely.

850   LOMAX: Oh, that! Yes, yes, yes. True, True.

STEPHEN: In other words, some men are honest and some are scoundrels.

BARBARA: Bosh! There are no scoundrels.

UNDERSHAFT: Indeed? Are there any good men?

BARBARA: No. Not one. There are neither good men nor scoundrels: there are just children of one Father; and the sooner they stop calling one another names the better. You neednt talk to me: I know them. Ive had scores of them through
860   my hands: scoundrels, criminals, infidels, philanthropists, missionaries, county councillors, all sorts. Theyre all just the same sort of sinner; and theres the same salvation ready for them all.

UNDERSHAFT: May I ask have you ever saved a maker of cannons?

BARBARA: No. Will you let me try?

UNDERSHAFT: Well, I will make a bargain with you. If I go to see you tomorrow in your Salvation
870   Shelter, will you come the day after to see me in my cannon works?

BARBARA: Take care. It may end in your giving up the cannons for the sake of the Salvation Army.

UNDERSHAFT: Are you sure it will not end in your giving up the Salvation Army for the sake of the cannons?

BARBARA: I will take my chance of that.

UNDERSHAFT: And I will take my chance of the other. (They shake hands on it). Where is your   880
shelter?

BARBARA: In West Ham. At the sign of the cross. Ask anybody in Canning Town. Where are your works?

UNDERSHAFT: In Perivale St Andrews. At the sign of the sword. Ask anybody in Europe.

LOMAX: Hadnt I better play something?

BARBARA: Yes. Give us Onward, Christian Soldiers.

LOMAX: Well, thats rather a strong order to begin   890
with, dont you know. Suppose I sing Thourt passing hence, my brother. It's much the same tune.

BARBARA: It's too melancholy. You get saved, Cholly; and youll pass hence, my brother, without making such a fuss about it.

LADY BRITOMART: Really, Barbara, you go on as if religion were a pleasant subject. Do have some sense of propriety.

UNDERSHAFT: I do not find it an unpleasant subject,   900
my dear. It is the only one that capable people really care for.

LADY BRITOMART: (looking at her watch). Well, if you are determined to have it, I insist on having it in a proper and respectable way. Charles: ring for prayers.

General amazement. Stephen rises in dismay.

LOMAX: (rising). Oh I say!

UNDERSHAFT: (rising). I am afraid I must be going.

LADY BRITOMART: You cannot go now, Andrew: 910
it would be most improper. Sit down. What will the servants think?

UNDERSHAFT: My dear: I have conscientious scruples. May I suggest a compromise? If Barbara will conduct a little service in the drawing room, with Mr. Lomax as organist, I will attend it willingly. I will even take part, if a trombone can be procured.

LADY BRITOMART: Dont mock, Andrew.

UNDERSHAFT: (shocked—to BARBARA). You dont   920

think I am mocking, my love, I hope.

BARBARA: No, of course not; and it wouldnt matter if you were: half the Army came to their first meeting for a lark. *(Rising)* Come along. *(She throws her arm round her father and sweeps him out, calling to the others from the threshold)* Come, Dolly. Come, Cholly.

Cusins rises.

930 LADY BRITOMART: I will not be disobeyed by everybody. Adolphus: sit down. *(He does not).* Charles: you may go. You are not fit for prayers: you cannot keep your countenance.

LOMAX: Oh I say! *(He goes out).*

LADY BRITOMART: *(Continuing).* But you, Adolphus, can behave yourself if you choose to. I insist on your staying.

CUSINS: My dear Lady Brit: there are things in the family prayer book that I couldnt bear to hear you say.

940 LADY BRITOMART: What things, pray?

CUSINS: Well, you would have to say before all the servants that we have done things we ought not to have done, and left undone things we ought to have done, and that there is no health in us. I cannot bear to hear you doing yourself such an injustice, and Barbara such an injustice. As for myself, I flatly deny it: I have done my best. I shouldnt dare to marry Barbara—I couldnt look you in the face—if it were true. 950 So I must go to the drawing room.

LADY BRITOMART: *(Offended).* Well, go. *(He starts for the door).* And remember this, Adolphus *(he turns to listen)*: I have a very strong suspicion that you went to the Salvation Army to worship Barbara and nothing else. And I quite appreciate the very clever way in which you systematically humbug me. I have found you out. Take care Barbara doesnt. Thats all.

CUSINS: *(With unruffled sweetness).* Dont tell on me. *(He steals out).* 960

LADY BRITOMART: Sarah: if you want to go, go. Anything's better than to sit there as if you wished you were a thousand miles away.

SARAH: *(languidly).* Very well, mamma. *(She goes).*

LADY BRITOMART, *with a sudden flounce, gives way to a little gust of tears.*

STEPHEN: *(going to her).* Mother: whats the matter?

LADY BRITOMART: *(swishing away her tears with her handkerchief).* Nothing. Foolishness. You can go with him, too, if you like, and leave me with 970 the servants.

STEPHEN: Oh, you mustnt think that, mother. I—I dont like him.

LADY BRITOMART: The others do. That is the injustice of a woman's lot. A woman has to bring up her children; and that means to restrain them, to deny them things they want, to set them tasks, to punish them when they do wrong, to do all the unpleasant things. And then the father, who has nothing to do but pet them and spoil them, 980 comes in when all her work is done and steals their affection from her.

STEPHEN: He has not stolen our affection from you. It is only curiosity.

LADY BRITOMART: *(violently).* I wont be consoled, Stephen. There is nothing the matter with me. *(She rises and goes towards the door).*

STEPHEN: Where are you going, mother?

LADY BRITOMART: To the drawing room, of course. *(She goes out. Onward, Christian Soldiers, on the* 990 *concertina, with tambourine accompaniment, is heard when the door opens).* Are you coming, Stephen?

STEPHEN: No. Certainly not. *(She goes. He sits down on the settee, with compressed lips and an expression of strong dislike).*

ACT TWO

The yard of the West Ham shelter of the Salvation Army is a cold place on a January morning. The building itself, an old warehouse, is newly whitewashed. Its gabled

end projects into the yard in the middle, with a door on the ground floor, and another in the loft above it without any balcony or ladder, but with a pulley rigged over it for hoisting sacks. Those who come from this central gable end into the yard have the gateway leading to the street on their left, with a stone horsetrough just beyond it, and, on the right, a penthouse shielding a table from the weather. There are forms at the table; and on them are seated a man and a woman, both much down on their luck, finishing a meal of bread (one thick slice each, with margarine and golden syrup) and diluted milk.

The man, a workman out of employment, is young, agile, a talker, a poser, sharp enough to be capable of anything in reason except honesty or altruistic considerations of any kind. The woman is a commonplace old bundle of poverty and hard-worn humanity. She looks sixty and probably is forty-five. If they were rich people, gloved and muffed and well wrapped up in furs and overcoats, they would be numbed and miserable; for it is a grindingly cold raw January day; and a glance at the background of grimy warehouses and leaden sky visible over the whitewashed walls of the yard would drive any idle rich person straight to the Mediterranean. But these two, being no more troubled with visions of the Mediterranean than of the moon, and being compelled to keep more of their clothes in the pawnshop, and less on their persons, in winter than in summer, are not depressed by the cold: rather are they stung into vivacity, to which their meal has just now given an almost jolly turn. The man takes a pull at his mug, and then gets up and moves about the yard with his hands deep in his pockets, occasionally breaking into a stepdance.

THE WOMAN: Feel better arter your meal, sir?

THE MAN: No. Call that a meal! Good enough for you, praps; but wot is it to me, an intelligent workin man.

THE WOMAN: Workin man! Wot are you?

THE MAN: Painter.

THE WOMAN: *(sceptically).* Yus, I dessay.

THE MAN: Yus, you dessay! I know. Every loafer than cant do nothink calls isself a painter. Well, I'm a real painter: grainer, finisher, thirty-eight bob a week when I can get it.

THE WOMAN: Then why dont you go and get it?

THE MAN: I'll tell you why. Fust: I'm intelligent—ffff! it's rotten cold here *(he dances a step or two)*—yes: intelligent beyond the station o life into which it has pleased the capitalists to call me; and they dont like a man that sees through

em. Second, an intelligent bein needs a doo share of appiness; so I drink somethink cruel when I get the chawnce. Third, I stand by my class and do as little as I can so's to leave arf the job for me fellow workers. Fourth, I'm fly enough to know wots inside the law and wots outside it; and inside it I do as the capitalists do: pinch wot I can lay me ands on. In a proper state of society I am sober, industrious and honest: in Rome, so to speak, I do as the Romans do. Wots the consequence? When trade is bad—and its rotten bad just now—and the employers az to sack arf their men, they generally start on me.

THE WOMAN: Whats your name?

THE MAN: Price. Bronterre O'Brien Price. Usually called Snobby Price, for short.

THE WOMAN: Snobby's a carpenter, aint it? You said you was a painter.

PRICE: Not that kind of snob, but the genteel sort. I'm too uppish, owing to my intelligence, and my father being a Chartist and a reading, thinking man: a stationer, too. I'm none of your common hewers of wood and drawers of water; and dont you forget it. *(He returns to his seat at the table, and takes up his mug).* Wots your name?

THE WOMAN: Rummy Mitchens, sir.

PRICE: *(quaffing the remains of his milk to her.)* Your elth, Miss Mitchens.

RUMMY: *(correcting him).* Missis Mitchens.

PRICE: Wot! Oh Rummy, Rummy! Respectable married woman, Rummy, gittin rescued by the Salvation Army by pretendin to be a bad un. Same old game!

RUMMY: What am I to do? I cant starve. Them Salvation lasses is dear good girls; but the better you are, the worse they likes to think you were before they rescued you. Why shouldnt they av a bit o credit, poor loves? theyre worn to rags by their work. And where would they get the money to rescue us if we was to let on we're no worse than other people? You know what ladies and gentlemen are.

PRICE: Thievin swine! Wish I ad their job, Rummy, all the same. Wot does Rummy stand for? Pet name praps?

RUMMY: Short for Romola.

PRICE: For wot!?

RUMMY: Romola. It was out of a new book. Somebody me mother wanted me to grow up like.

PRICE: We're companions in misfortune, Rummy. Both on us got names that nobody cawnt pronounce. Consequently I'm Snobby and youre Rummy because Bill and Sally wasnt good enough for our parents. Such is life!

RUMMY: Who saved you, Mr. Price? Was it Major Barbara?

PRICE: No: I come here on my own. I'm going to be Bronterre O'Brien Price, the converted painter. I know wot they like. I'll tell em how I blasphemed and gambled and wopped my poor old mother—

RUMMY: (shocked). Used you to beat your mother?

PRICE: Not likely. She used to beat me. No matter: you come and listen to the converted painter, and youll hear how she was a pious woman that taught me prayers at er knee, an how I used to come home drunk and drag her out o bed be er snow white airs, an lam into er with the poker.

RUMMY: Thats whats so unfair to us women. Your confessions is just as big lies as ours: you dont tell what you really done no more than us; but you men can tell your lies right out at the meetins and be made much of for it; while the sort o confessions we az to make az to be wispered to one lady at a time. It aint right, spite of all their piety.

PRICE: Right! Do you spose the Army'd be allowed if it went and did right? Not much. It combs our air and makes us good little blokes to be robbed and put upon. But I'll play the game as good as any of em. I'll see somebody struck by lightnin, or hear a voice sayin 'Snobby Price: where will you spend eternity?' I'll av a time of it, I tell you.

RUMMY: You wont be let drink, though.

PRICE: I'll take it out in gorspellin, then. I dont want to drink if I can get fun enough any other way.

Jenny Hill, a pale, overwrought, pretty Salvation lass of 18, comes in through the yard gate, leading Peter Shirley, a half hardened, half worn-out elderly man, weak with hunger.

JENNY: (supporting him). Come! pluck up. I'll get you something to eat. Youll be all right then.

PRICE: (rising and hurrying officiously to take the old man off JENNY's hands). Poor old man! Cheer up,

brother: youll find rest and peace and happiness ere. Hurry up with the food, miss: e's fair done. (JENNY hurries into the shelter). Ere, buck up, daddy! she's fetchin y'a thick slice o breadn treacle, an a mug o skyblue. (He seats him at the corner of the table).

RUMMY: (gaily). Keep up your old art! Never say die!

SHIRLEY: I'm not an old man. I'm only 46. I'm as good as ever I was. The grey patch come in my hair before I was thirty. All it wants is three pennorth o hair dye: am I to be turned on the streets to starve for it? Holy God! Ive worked ten to twelve hours a day since I was thirteen, and paid my way all through; and now am I to be thrown into the gutter and my job given to a young man that can do it no better than me because Ive black hair that goes white at the first change?

PRICE: (cheerfully). No good jawrin about it. Your ony a jumped-up, jerked-off, orspittle-turned-out incurable of an ole workin man: who cares about you? Eh? Make the thievin swine give you a meal: theyve stole many a one from you. Get a bit o your own back. (JENNY returns with the usual meal). There you are, brother. Awsk a blessin an tuck that into you.

SHIRLEY: (looking at it ravenously but not touching it, and crying like a child). I never took anything before.

JENNY: (petting him). Come, come! the Lord sends it to you: he wasnt above taking bread from his friends; and why should you be? Besides, when we find you a job you can pay us for it if you like.

SHIRLEY: (eagerly). Yes, yes: thats true. I can pay you back: it's only a loan. (Shivering) Oh Lord! oh Lord! (He turns to the table and attacks the meal ravenously).

JENNY: Well, Rummy, are you more comfortable now?

RUMMY: God bless you, lovey! youve fed my body and saved my soul, havnt you? (JENNY, touched, kisses her). Sit down and rest a bit: you must be ready to drop.

JENNY: I've been going hard since morning. But theres more work than we can do. I mustnt stop.

RUMMY: Try a prayer for just two minutes. Youll work all the better after.

JENNY: *(Her eyes lighting up)*. Oh isnt it wonderful how a few minutes prayer revives you! I was quite lightheaded at twelve o'clock, I was so tired; but Major Barbara just sent me to pray for five minutes; and I was able to go on as if I had only just begun. *(To* PRICE*)* Did you have a piece of bread?

170

PRICE: *(with unction)*. Yes, miss; but Ive got the piece that I value more; and thats the peace that passeth hall hannerstennin.

RUMMY: *(fervently)*. Glory Hallelujah!

BILL WALKER, *a rough customer of about 25, appears at the yard gate and looks malevolently at* JENNY.

JENNY: That makes me so happy. When you say that, I feel wicked for loitering here. I must get to work again.

180   *She is hurrying to the shelter, when the newcomer moves quickly up to the door and intercepts her. His manner is so threatening that she retreats as he comes at her truculently, driving her down the yard.*

BILL: Aw knaow. Youre the one that took awy maw girl. Youre the one that set er agen me. Well, I'm gowin to ev er aht. Not that Aw care a carse for er or you: see? Bat Aw'll let er knaow; and Aw'll let you knaow. Aw'm gowing to give her a doin thatll teach er to cat awy from me.

190   Nah in wiv you and tell er to cam aht afore Aw cam in and kick er aht. Tell er Bill Walker wants er. She'll knaow wot thet means; and if she keeps me witin itll be worse. You stop to jawr beck at me; and Aw'll stawt on you: d'ye eah? Theres your wy. In you gow. *(He takes her by the arm and slings her towards the door of the shelter. She falls on her hand and knee.* RUMMY *helps her up again)*.

PRICE: *(rising, and venturing irresolutely towards* 200   BILL*)*. Easy there, mate. She aint doin you no arm.

BILL: Oo are you callin mite? *(Standing over him threateningly)* Youre gowin to stend ap for er, aw yer? Put ap your ends.

RUMMY: *(running indignantly to him to scold him)*. Oh you great brute— *(He instantly swings his left hand back against her face. She screams and reels back to the trough, where she sits down, covering her bruised face with her hands and rocking herself and moaning*
210   *with pain)*.

JENNY: *(going to her)*. Oh, God forgive you! How could you strike an old woman like that?

BILL: *(seizing her by the hair so violently that she also screams, and tearing her away from the old woman)*. You Gawd forgimme again and Aw'll Gawk forgive you one on the jawr thetll stop you pryin for a week. *(Holding her and turning fiercely on* PRICE*)* Ev you ennything to sy agen it?

PRICE: *(intimidated)*. No matey: she aint anything to do with me.   220

BILL: Good job for you! Aw'd pat two meals into you and fawt you with one finger arter, you stawved cur. *(To* JENNY*)* Nah are you gowin to fetch aht Mog Ebbijem; or em Aw to knock your fice off you and fetch her meself?

JENNY: *(writhing in his grasp)*. Oh please someone go in and tell Major Barbara— *(she screams again as he wrenches her head down; and* PRICE *and* RUMMY *flee into the shelter)*.

BILL: You want to gow in and tell your Mijor of   230   me, do you?

JENNY: O please dont drag my hair. Let me go.

BILL: Do you or downt you? *(She stifles a scream)*. Yus or nao?

JENNY: God give me strength—

BILL: *(striking her with his fist in the face)*. Gow an shaow her thet, and tell her if she wants one lawk it to cam and interfere with me. *(Jenny, crying with pain, goes into the shed. He goes to the form and addresses the old man)*. Eah: finish your   240   mess; and git aht o maw wy.

SHIRLEY: *(springing up and facing him fiercely, with the mug in his hand)*. You take a liberty with me, and I'll smash you over the face with the mug and cut your eye out. Aint you satisfied—young whelps like you—with takin the bread out o the mouths of your elders that have brought you up and slaved for you, but you must come shovin and cheekin and bullyin in here, where the bread o charity is sickenin in our stummicks?   250

BILL: *(contemptuously, but backing a little)*. Wot good are you, you aold palsy mag? Wot good are you?

SHIRLEY: As good as you and better. I'll do a day's work agen you or any fat young soaker of your age. Go and take my job at Horrockses, where I worked for ten year. They want young men there: they cant afford to keep men over forty-five. Theyre very sorry—give you a character and happy to help you to get anything suited to your years—sure a steady man wont be long out of a job. Well, let em try you. Theyll find the differ. What do you know? Not as much as how to beeyave yourself—laying your dirty fist across the mouth of a respectable woman!

BILL: Downt provowk me to ly it acrost yours: d'ye eah?

SHIRLEY: (*with blighting contempt*). Yes: you like an old man to hit, dont you, when youve finished with the women. I aint seen you hit a young one yet.

BILL: (*stung*). You loy, you aold soupkitchener, you. There was a yang menn eah. Did Aw offer to itt him or did Aw not?

SHIRLEY: Was he starvin or was he not? Was he a man or only a crosseyed thief and a loafer? Would you hit my son-in-law's brother?

BILL: Oo's ee?

SHIRLEY: Todger Fairmile o Balls Pond. Him that won £20 off the Japanese wrastler at the music hall by standin out 17 minutes 4 seconds agen him.

BILL: (*sullenly*). Aw'm nao music awl wrastler. Ken he box?

SHIRLEY: Yes: an you cant.

BILL: Wot! Aw cawnt, cawnt Aw? Wots thet you sy (*threatening him*)?

SHIRLEY: (*not budging an inch*). Will you box Todger Fairmile if I put him on to you? Say the word.

BILL: (*subsiding with a slouch*). Aw'll stend ap to enny menn alawv, if he was ten Todger Fairmawls. But Aw dont set ap to be a perfeshnal.

SHIRLEY: (*looking down on him with unfathomable disdain*). You box! Slap an old woman with the back o your hand! You hadnt even the sense to hit her where a magistrate couldnt see the mark of it, you silly young lump of conceit and ignorance. Hit a girl in the jaw and ony make her cry! If Todger Fairmile'd done it, she wouldnt a got up inside o ten minutes, no more than you would if he got on to you. Yah! I'd set about you myself if I had a week's feedin in me instead o two months' starvation. (*He turns his back on him and sits down moodily at the table*).

BILL: (*following him and stooping over him to drive the taunt in*). You loy! youve the bread and treacle in you that you cam eah to beg.

SHIRLEY: (*bursting into tears*). Oh God! it's true: I'm only an old pauper on the scrap heap. (*Furiously*) But youll come to it yourself; and then youll know. Youll come to it sooner than a teetotaller like me, fillin yourself with gin at this hour o the mornin!

BILL: Aw'm nao gin drinker, you oald lawr; bat wen Aw want to give my girl a bloomin good awdin Aw lawk to ev a bit o devil in me: see? An eah emm, talkin to a rotten aold blawter like you sted o givin her wot for. (*Working himself into a rage*) Aw'm gowin in there to fetch her aht. (*He makes vengefully for the shelter door*).

SHIRLEY: Youre going to the station on a stretcher, more likely; and theyll take the gin and the devil out of you there when they get you inside. You mind what youre about: the major here is the Earl o Stevenage's granddaughter.

BILL: (*checked*). Garn!

SHIRLEY: Youll see.

BILL: (*his resolution oozing*). Well, Aw aint dan nathin to er.

SHIRLEY: Spose she said you did! who'd believe you?

BILL: (*very uneasy, skulking back to the corner of the penthouse*). Gawd! theres no jastice in this cantry. To think wot them people can do! Aw'm as good as er.

SHIRLEY: Tell her so. It's just what a fool like you would do.

Barbara, brisk and businesslike, comes from the shelter with a note book, and addresses herself to SHIRLEY. BILL, *cowed, sits down in the corner on a form, and turns his back on them.*

BARBARA: Good morning.

SHIRLEY: (*standing up and taking off his hat*). Good morning, miss.

BARBARA: Sit down: make yourself at home. (*He hesitates; but she puts a friendly hand on his shoulder and makes him obey*). Now then! since youve made friends with us, we want to know all about you. Names and addresses and trades.

SHIRLEY: Peter Shirley. Fitter. Chucked out two months ago because I was too old.

BARBARA: (*not at all surprised*). Youd pass still. Why didnt you dye your hair?

SHIRLEY: I did. Me age come out at a coroner's inquest on me daughter.

BARBARA: Steady?

SHIRLEY: Teetotaller. Never out of a job before. Good worker. And sent to the knackers like an old horse!

BARBARA: No matter: if you did your part God will do his.

SHIRLEY: (suddenly stubborn). My religion's no concern of anybody but myself.

BARBARA: (guessing). I know. Secularist?

SHIRLEY: (hotly). Did I offer to deny it?

BARBARA: Why should you? My own father's a Secularist, I think. Our Father—yours and mine—fulfils himself in many ways; and I daresay he knew what he was about when he made a Secularist of you. So buck up, Peter! we can always find a job for a steady man like you. (SHIRLEY, disarmed and a little bewildered, touches his hat. She turns from him to BILL). Whats your name?

BILL: (insolently). Wots thet to you?

BARBARA: (calmly making a note). Afraid to give his name. Any trade?

BILL: Oos' afride to give is nime? (Doggedly, with a sense of heroically defying the House of Lords in the person of Lord Stevenage) If you want to bring a chawge agen me, bring it. (She waits, unruffled). Moy nime's Bill Walker.

BARBARA: (as if the name were familiar: trying to remember how). Bill Walker? (Recollecting) Oh, I know: youre the man that Jenny Hill was praying for inside just now. (She enters his name in her note book).

BILL: Oo's Jenny Ill? And wot call as she to pry for me?

BARBARA: I dont know. Perhaps it was you that cut her lip.

BILL: (defiantly). Yus, it was me that cat her lip. Aw aint afride o you.

BARBARA: How could you be, since youre not afraid of God? Youre a brave man, Mr. Walker. It takes some pluck to do our work here; but none of us dare lift our hand against a girl like that, for fear of her father in heaven.

BILL: (sullenly). I want nan o your kentin jawr. I spowse you think Aw cam eah to beg from you, like this demmiged lot eah. Not me. Aw downt want your bread and scripe and ketlep. Aw dont blieve in your Gawd, no more than you do yourself.

BARBARA: (sunnily apologetic and ladylike, as on a new footing with him). Oh, I beg your pardon for putting your name down, Mr. Walker. I didnt understand. I'll strike it out.

BILL: (taking this as a slight, and deeply wounded by it). Eah! you let maw nime alown. Aint it good enaff to be in your book?

BARBARA: (considering). Well, you see, theres no use putting down your name unless I can do something for you, is there? Whats your trade?

BILL: (still smarting). Thets nao concern o yours.

BARBARA: Just so. (Very businesslike) I'll put you down as (writing) the man who—struck—poor little Jenny Hill—in the mouth.

BILL: (rising threateningly). See eah. Awve ed enaff o this.

BARBARA: (quite sunny and fearless). What did you come to us for?

BILL: Aw cam for maw gel, see? Aw cam to tike her aht o this and to brike er jawr for er.

BARBARA: (complacently). You see I was right about your trade. (BILL, on the point of retorting furiously, finds himself, to his great shame and terror, in danger of crying instead. He sits down again suddenly). Whats her name?

BILL: (dogged). Er nime's Mog Ebbijem: thets wot her nime is.

BARBARA: Mog Habbijam! Oh, she's gone to Canning Town, to our barracks there.

BILL: (fortified by his resentment of Mog's perfidy). Is she? (Vindictively) Then Aw'm gowin to Kennintahn arter her. (He crosses to the gate; hesitates; finally comes back at BARBARA). Are you loyin to me to git shat o me?

BARBARA: I dont want to get shut of you. I want to keep you here and save your soul. Youd better stay: youre going to have a bad time today, Bill.

BILL: Oo's gowin to give it to me? You, preps?

BARBARA: Someone you dont believe in. But youll be glad afterwards.

BILL: (slinking off). Aw'll gow to Kenningtahn to be aht o reach o your tangue. (Suddenly turning on her with intense malice) And if Aw downt fawnd Mog there, Aw'll cam beck and do two years for you, selp me Gawd if Aw downt!

BARBARA: (a shade kindlier, if possible). It's no use, Bill. She's got another bloke.

BILL: Wot!

BARBARA: One of her own converts. He fell in love

with her when he saw her with her soul saved, and her face clean, and her hair washed.

BILL: (surprised). Wottud she wash it for, the carroty slat? It's red.

BARBARA: It's quite lovely now, because she wears a new look in her eyes with it. It's a pity youre too late. The new bloke has put your nose out of joint, Bill.

BILL: Aw'll put his nowse aht o joint for him. Not that Aw care a carse for er, mawnd thet. But Aw'll teach her to drop me as if Aw was dirt. And Aw'll teach him to meddle with maw judy. Wots iz bleedin nime?

BARBARA: Sergeant Todger Fairmile.

SHIRLEY: (rising with grim joy). I'll go with him, miss. I want to see them two meet. I'll take him to the infirmary when it's over.

BILL: (to SHIRLEY, with undissembled misgiving). Is thet im you was speakin on?

SHIRLEY: Thats him.

BILL: Im that wrastled in the music awl?

SHIRLEY: The competitions at the National Sportin Club was worth nigh a hundred a year to him. He's gev em up now for religion; so he's a bit fresh for want of the exercise he was accustomed to. He'll be glad to see you. Come along.

BILL: Wots is wight?

SHIRLEY: Thirteen four. (BILL's last hope expires).

BARBARA: Go and talk to him, Bill. He'll convert you.

SHIRLEY: He'll convert your head into a mashed potato.

BILL: (sullenly). Aw aint afride of im. Aw aint afride of ennybody. Bat e can lick me. She's dan me. (He sits down moodily on the edge of the horse trough).

SHIRLEY: You aint going. I thought not. (He resumes his seat).

BARBARA: (calling). Jenny!

JENNY: (appearing at the shelter door with a plaster on the corner of her mouth). Yes, Major.

BARBARA: Send Rummy Mitchens out to clear away here.

JENNY: I think she's afraid.

BARBARA: (her resemblance to her mother flashing out for a moment). Nonsense! she must do as she's told.

JENNY: (calling into the shelter). Rummy: the Major says you must come.

JENNY comes to BARBARA, purposely keeping on the side next to BILL, lest he should suppose that she shrank from him or bore malice.

BARBARA: Poor little Jenny! Are you tired? (Looking at the wounded cheek) Does it hurt?

JENNY: No: it's all right now. It was nothing.

BARBARA: (critically). It was as hard as he could hit, I expect. Poor Bill! You dont feel angry with him, do you?

JENNY: Oh no, no, no: indeed I dont, Major, bless his poor heart! (BARBARA kisses her; and she runs away merrily into the shelter. BILL writhes with an agonizing return of his new and alarming symptoms, but says nothing. RUMMY MITCHENS comes from the shelter).

BARBARA: (going to meet RUMMY). Now Rummy, bustle. Take in those mugs and plates to be washed; and throw the crumbs about for the birds.

RUMMY takes the three plates and mugs; but SHIRLEY takes back his mug from her, as there is still some milk left in it.

RUMMY: There aint any crumbs. This aint a time to waste good bread on birds.

PRICE: (appearing at the shelter door). Gentleman come to see the shelter, Major. Says he's your father.

BARBARA: All right. Coming. (SNOBBY goes back into the shelter, followed by BARBARA).

RUMMY: (stealing across to BILL and addressing him in a subdued voice, but with intense conviction). I'd av the lor of you, you flat eared pignosed potwalloper, if she'd let me. Youre no gentleman, to hit a lady in the face. (BILL, with greater things moving in him, takes no notice).

SHIRLEY: (following her). Here! in with you and dont get yourself into more trouble by talking.

RUMMY: (with hauteur). I aint ad the pleasure o being hintroduced to you, as I can remember. (She goes into the shelter with the plates).

SHIRLEY: Thats the—

BILL: (savagely). Downt you talk to me, d'ye eah? You lea me alown, or Aw'll do you a mischief. Aw'm not dirt under your feet, ennywy.

SHIRLEY: (calmly). Dont you be afeerd. You aint such prime company that you need expect to be sought after. (He is about to go into the shelter when BARBARA comes out, with UNDERSHAFT on her right).

550 BARBARA: Oh, there you are, Mr. Shirley! (*Between them*) This is my father: I told you he was a Secularist, didnt I? Perhaps youll be able to comfort one another.

UNDERSHAFT: (*startled*). A Secularist! Not the least in the world: on the contrary, a confirmed mystic.

BARBARA: Sorry, I'm sure. By the way, papa, what is your religion? in case I have to introduce you again.

560 UNDERSHAFT: My religion? Well, my dear, I am a Millionaire. That is my religion.

BARBARA: Then I'm afraid you and Mr. Shirley wont be able to comfort one another after all. Youre not a Millionaire, are you, Peter?

SHIRLEY: No; and proud of it.

UNDERSHAFT: (*gravely*). Poverty, my friend, is not a thing to be proud of.

SHIRLEY: (*angrily*). Who made your millions for you? Me and my like. Whats kep us poor? Keepin

570 you rich. I wouldnt have your conscience, not for all your income.

UNDERSHAFT: I wouldnt have your income, not for all your conscience, Mr. Shirley. (*He goes to the penthouse and sits down on a form*).

BARBARA: (*stopping* SHIRLEY *adroitly as he is about to retort*). You wouldnt think he was my father, would you, Peter? Will you go into the shelter and lend the lasses a hand for a while: we're worked off our feet.

580 SHIRLEY: (*bitterly*). Yes: I'm in their debt for a meal, aint I?

BARBARA: Oh, not because youre in their debt, but for love of them, Peter, for love of them. (*He cannot understand, and is rather scandalized*) There! dont stare at me. In with you; and give that conscience of yours a holiday (*bustling him into the shelter*).

SHIRLEY: (*as he goes in*). Ah! it's a pity you never was trained to use your reason, miss. Youd have

590 been a very taking lecturer on Secularism.

BARBARA *turns to her father.*

UNDERSHAFT: Never mind me, my dear. Go about your work; and let me watch it for a while.

BARBARA: All right.

UNDERSHAFT: For instance, whats the matter with that outpatient over there?

BARBARA: (*looking at* BILL, *whose attitude has never changed, and whose expression of brooding wrath has deepened*). Oh, we shall cure him in no time. Just 600 watch. (*She goes over to* BILL *and waits. He glances up at her and casts his eyes down again, uneasy, but grimmer than ever*). It would be nice to just stamp on Mog Habbijam's face, wouldnt it, Bill?

BILL: (*starting up from the trough in consternation*). It's a loy: Aw never said so. (*she shakes her head*). Oo taold you wot was in moy mawnd?

BARBARA: Only your new friend.

BILL: Wot new friend?

BARBARA: The devil, Bill. When he gets round people they get miserable, just like you. 610

BILL: (*with a heartbreaking attempt at devil-may-care cheerfulness*). Aw aint miserable. (*He sits down again, and stretches his legs in an attempt to seem indifferent*).

BARBARA: Well, if youre happy, why dont you look happy, as we do?

BILL: (*his legs curling back in spite of him*). Aw'm eppy enaff, Aw tell you. Woy cawnt you lea me alown? Wot ev I dan to you? Aw aint smashed your fice, ev Aw? 620

BARBARA: (*softly: wooing his soul*). It's not me thats getting at you, Bill.

BILL: Oo else is it?

BARBARA: Somebody that doesnt intend you to smash women's faces, I suppose. Somebody or something that wants to make a man of you.

BILL: (*blustering*). Mike a menn o me! Aint Aw a menn? eh? Oo sez Aw'm not a menn?

BARBARA: Theres a man in you somewhere, I suppose. But why did he let you hit poor little Jenny 630 Hill? That wasnt very manly of him, was it?

BILL: (*tormented*). Ev dan wiv it, Aw tell you. Chack it. Aw'm sick o your Jenny Ill and er silly little fice.

BARBARA: Then why do you keep thinking about it? Why does it keep coming up against you in your mind? Youre not getting converted, are you?

BILL: (*with conviction*). Not Me. Not lawkly.

BARBARA: Thats right, Bill. Hold out against it. 640 Put out your strength. Dont lets get you cheap. Todger Fairmile said he wrestled for three nights against his salvation harder than he ever wrestled with the Jap at the music hall. He gave in to the Jap when his arm was going to break. But he didnt give in to his salvation until his heart

CUSINS: It is a fair translation. The word means Loveliness.

UNDERSHAFT: May I ask—as Barbara's father—how much a year she is to be loved for ever on?

CUSINS: As for Barbara's father, that is more your affair than mine. I can feed her by teaching Greek: that is about all.

UNDERSHAFT: Do you consider it a good match for her?

CUSINS: (with polite obstinacy). Mr. Undershaft: I am in many ways a weak, timid, ineffectual person; and my health is far from satisfactory. But whenever I feel that I must have anything, I get it, sooner or later. I feel that way about Barbara. I dont like marriage: I feel intensely afraid of it; and I dont know what I shall do with Barbara or what she will do with me. But I feel that I and nobody else must marry her. Please regard that as settled.—Not that I wish to be arbitrary; but why should I waste your time in discussing what is inevitable?

UNDERSHAFT: You mean that you will stick at nothing: not even the conversion of the Salvation Army to the worship of Dionysos.

CUSINS: The business of the Salvation Army is to save, not to wrangle about the name of the pathfinder. Dionysos or another: what does it matter?

UNDERSHAFT: (rising and approaching him). Professor Cusins: you are a young man after my own heart.

CUSINS: Mr Undershaft: you are, as far as I am able to gather, a most infernal old rascal; but you appeal very strongly to my sense of ironic humor.

UNDERSHAFT mutely offers his hand. They shake.

UNDERSHAFT: (suddenly concentrating himself). And now to business.

CUSINS: Pardon me. We are discussing religion. Why go back to such an uninteresting and unimportant subject as business?

UNDERSHAFT: Religion is our business at present, because it is through religion alone that we can win Barbara.

CUSINS: Have you, too, fallen in love with Barbara?

UNDERSHAFT: Yes, with a father's love.

CUSINS: A father's love for a grown-up daughter is the most dangerous of all infatuations. I

apologize for mentioning my o
trustful fancy in the same bre

UNDERSHAFT: Keep to the point
her; and we are neither of us

CUSINS: That doesnt matter. T
wields here—the power that v
self—is not Calvinism, not Pr
Methodism—

UNDERSHAFT: Not Greek Pagan

CUSINS: I admit that. Barbara i
her religion.

UNDERSHAFT: (triumphantly)
Undershaft would be. Her
from within herself.

CUSINS: How do you suppose i

UNDERSHAFT: (in towering exc
Undershaft inheritance. I shal
to my daughter. She shall
and preach my gospel—

CUSINS: What! Money and gun

UNDERSHAFT: Yes, money and
dom and power. Command o
of death.

CUSINS: (urbanely: trying to bring
This is extremely interesting
Of course you know that yo

UNDERSHAFT: (with redoubled fo

CUSINS: Oh, mad as a hatter.
to my secret since I have dis
I am astonished. Can a madi

UNDERSHAFT: Would anyone
make them? And now (with
tion for question. Can a
Euripides?

CUSINS: No.

UNDERSHAFT: (seizing him by the
woman make a man of a
of a worm?

CUSINS: (reeling before the sto
sus—Mammoth Millionaire

UNDERSHAFT: (pressing him).
people or three in this Salv

CUSINS: You mean Barbara is

UNDERSHAFT: (pushing him lig
his equanimity suddenly and
Professor! let us call thin
names. I am a millionaire; y
is a savior of souls. What
with the common mob of

was going to break. Perhaps you'll escape that. You havnt any heart, have you?

BILL: Wot d'ye mean? Woy aint Aw got a awt the sime as ennybody else?

BARBARA: A man with a heart wouldnt have bashed poor little Jenny's face, would he?

BILL: (almost crying). Ow, will you lea me alown? Ev Aw ever offered to meddle with you, that you cam neggin and provowkin me lawk this? (He writhes convulsively from his eyes to his toes).

BARBARA: (with a steady soothing hand on his arm and a gentle voice that never lets him go). It's your soul thats hurting you, Bill, and not me. Weve been through it all ourselves. Come with us, Bill. (He looks wildly round). To brave manhood on earth and eternal glory in heaven. (He is on the point of breaking down). Come. (A drum is heard in the shelter; and BILL, with a gasp, escapes from the spell as BARBARA turns quickly. ADOLPHUS enters from the shelter with a big drum). Oh! there you are, Dolly. Let me introduce a new friend of mine, Mr. Bill Walker. This is my bloke, Bill: Mr. Cusins. (CUSINS salutes with his drumstick).

BILL: Gowin to merry im?

BARBARA: Yes.

BILL: (fervently). Gawd elp im! Gaw-aw-aw-awd elp im!

BARBARA: Why? Do you think he wont be happy with me?

BILL: Awve aony ed to stend it for a mawnin: e'll ev to stend it for a lawftawm.

CUSINS: That is a frightful reflection, Mr. Walker. But I cant tear myself away from her.

BILL: Well, Aw ken. (To BARBARA) Eah! do you knaow where Aw'm gowin to, and wot Aw'm gowin to do?

BARBARA: Yes: youre going to heaven; and youre coming back here before the week's out to tell me so.

BILL: You loy. Aw'm gowin to Kennintahn, to spit in Todger Fairmawl's eye. Aw beshed Jenny Ill's fice; and nar Aw'll git me aown fice beshed and cam beck and shaow it to er. Ee'll itt me ardern Aw itt her. Thatll mike us square. (To ADOLPHUS) Is thet fair or is it not? Youre a genlmn: you oughter knaow.

BARBARA: Two black eyes wont make one white one, Bill.

BILL: Aw didnt awst you. Cawnt you never keep

your mahth shat? Oy awst the genlmn.

CUSINS: (reflectively). Yes: I think youre right, Mr. Walker. Yes: I should do it. It's curious: it's exactly what an ancient Greek would have done.

BARBARA: But what good will it do?

CUSINS: Well, it will give Mr Fairmile some exercise; and it will satisfy Mr Walker's soul.

BILL: Rot! there aint nao sach a thing as a saoul. Ah kin you tell wevver Awve a saoul or not? You never seen it.

BARBARA: Ive seen it hurting you when you went against it.

BILL: (with compressed aggravation). If you was maw gel and took the word aht o me mahth lawk thet, Aw'd give you sathink youd feel urtin, Aw would. (To ADOLPHUS) You tike maw tip, mite. Stop er jawr; or youll doy afoah your tawm (With intense expression) Wore aht: thets wot youll be: wore aht. (He goes away through the gate).

CUSINS: (looking after him). I wonder!

BARBARA: Dolly! (indignant, in her mother's manner).

CUSINS: Yes, my dear, it's very wearing to be in love with you. If it lasts, I quite think I shall die young.

BARBARA: Should you mind?

CUSINS: Not at all. (He is suddenly softened, and kisses her over the drum, evidently not for the first time, as people cannot kiss over a big drum without practice. UNDERSHAFT coughs).

BARBARA: It's all right, papa, weve not forgotten you. Dolly: explain the place to papa: I havnt time. (She goes busily into the shelter).

UNDERSHAFT and ADOLPHUS now have the yard to themselves. UNDERSHAFT, seated on a form, and still keenly attentive, looks hard at ADOLPHUS. ADOLPHUS looks hard at him.

UNDERSHAFT: I fancy you guess something of what is in my mind, Mr Cusins. (CUSINS flourishes his drumsticks as if in the act of beating a lively rataplan, but makes no sound). Exactly so. But suppose Barbara finds you out.

CUSINS: You know, I do not admit that I am imposing on Barbara. I am quite genuinely interested in the views of the Salvation Army. The fact is, I am a sort of collector of religions; and the curious thing is that I find I can believe them all. By the way, have you any religion?

UNDERSHAFT: Yes.

CUSINS: Anything out of the common?

UNDERSHAFT: Only that there are two things necessary to Salvation.

CUSINS: (disappointed, but polite). Ah, the Church Catechism. Charles Lomax also belongs to the Established Church.

750 UNDERSHAFT: The two things are—

CUSINS: Baptism and—

UNDERSHAFT: No. Money and gunpowder.

CUSINS: (surprised, but interested). That is the general opinion of our governing classes. The novelty is in hearing any man confess it.

UNDERSHAFT: Just so.

CUSINS: Excuse me: is there any place in your religion for honor, justice, truth, love, mercy and so forth?

760 UNDERSHAFT: Yes: they are the graces and luxuries of a rich, strong, and safe life.

CUSINS: Suppose one is forced to choose between them and money or gunpowder?

UNDERSHAFT: Choose money and gunpowder; for without enough of both you cannot afford the others.

CUSINS: That is your religion?

UNDERSHAFT: Yes.

The cadence of this reply makes a full close in the conversation,
770 CUSINS *twists his face dubiously and contemplates* UNDERSHAFT. UNDERSHAFT *contemplates him.*

CUSINS: Barbara wont stand that. You will have to choose between your religion and Barbara.

UNDERSHAFT: So will you, my friend. She will find out that that drum of yours is hollow.

CUSINS: Father Undershaft: you are mistaken: I am a sincere Salvationist. You do not understand the Salvation Army. It is the army of joy, of love, of courage: it has banished the fear and
780 remorse and despair of the old hell-ridden evangelical sects: it marches to fight the devil with trumpet and drum, with music and dancing, with banner and palm, as becomes a sally from heaven by its happy garrison. It picks the waster out of the public house and makes a man of him: it finds a worm wriggling in a back kitchen, and lo! a woman! Men and women of rank too, sons and daughters of the Highest. It takes the poor professor of Greek, the most artificial and
790 self-suppressed of human creatures, from his meal of roots, and lets loose the rhapsodist in

him; reveals the true ...
him; sends him down th...
dithyrambs *(he plays a...
drum).*

UNDERSHAFT: You will a...

CUSINS: Oh, they are acc... ecstasies. However, if t... *pockets the drumsticks; u... it on the ground opposite*

UNDERSHAFT: Thank you...

CUSINS: You remember ... your money and gunp...

UNDERSHAFT: No.

CUSINS: *(declaiming).*

One ...
In money and guns...
And men in their ...
And seethe with a...
And they win thei... will;
And their hopes a... still;
But who'er can kn...
As the long days g...
That to live is happy...

My translation: what...

UNDERSHAFT: I think, ... to know, as the long... happy, you must fir... for a decent life, and... own master.

CUSINS: You are dam... *resumes his declamation*...

It is so hard a thi...
That the spirit of ...
The law that abides ...
The Eternal and Na... strong?
What else is Wisdom...
Or God's high grac...
To stand from fear s...
To hold a hand upli...
And shall not Barba...

UNDERSHAFT: Euripid...
he?

(He sits down again with a shrug of contempt for the mob).

CUSINS: Take care! Barbara is in love with the common people. So am I. Have you never felt the romance of that love?

UNDERSHAFT: *(cold and sardonic).* Have you ever
940 been in love with Poverty, like St Francis? Have you ever been in love with Dirt, like St Simeon! Have you ever been in love with disease and suffering, like our nurses and philanthropists? Such passions are not virtues, but the most unnatural of all the vices. This love of the common people may please an earl's grand-daughter and a university professor; but I have been a common man and a poor man; and it has no romance for me. Leave it to the poor to pretend
950 that poverty is a blessing: leave it to the coward to make a religion of his cowardice by preaching humility: we know better than that. We three must stand together above the common people: how else can we help their children to climb up beside us? Barbara must belong to us, not to the Salvation Army.

CUSINS: Well, I can only say that if you think you will get her away from the Salvation Army by talking to her as you have been talking to me,
960 you dont know Barbara.

UNDERSHAFT: My friend: I never ask for what I can buy.

CUSINS: *(in a white fury).* Do I understand you to imply that you can buy Barbara?

UNDERSHAFT: No; but I can buy the Salvation Army.

CUSINS: Quite impossible.

UNDERSHAFT: You shall see. All religious organizations exist by selling themselves to the rich.

970 CUSINS: Not the Army. That is the Church of the poor.

UNDERSHAFT: All the more reason for buying it.

CUSINS: I dont think you quite know what the Army does for the poor.

UNDERSHAFT: Oh yes I do. It draws their teeth: that is enough for me as a man of business.

CUSINS: Nonsense! It makes them sober—

UNDERSHAFT: I prefer sober workmen. The profits are larger.

980 CUSINS: —honest—

UNDERSHAFT: Honest workmen are the most economical.

CUSINS: —attached to their homes—

UNDERSHAFT: So much the better: they will put up with anything sooner than change their shop.

CUSINS: —happy—

UNDERSHAFT: An invaluable safeguard against revolution.

CUSINS: —unselfish—

UNDERSHAFT: Indifferent to their own interests, 990 which suits me exactly.

CUSINS: —with their thoughts on heavenly things—

UNDERSHAFT: *(rising).* And not on Trade Unionism nor Socialism. Excellent.

CUSINS: *(revolted).* You really are an infernal old rascal.

UNDERSHAFT: *(indicating* PETER SHIRLEY, *who has just come from the shelter and strolled dejectedly down the yard between them).* And this is an honest man! 1000

SHIRLEY: Yes; and what av I got by it? *(he passes on bitterly and sits on the form, in the corner of the penthouse).*

SNOBBY PRICE, *beaming sanctimoniously, and* JENNY HILL, *with a tambourine full of coppers, come from the shelter and go to the drum, on which* JENNY *begins to count the money.*

UNDERSHAFT: *(replying to* SHIRLEY*).* Oh, your employers must have got a good deal by it from first to last. *(He sits on the table, with one foot* 1010 *on the side form,* CUSINS, *overwhelmed, sits down on the same form nearer the shelter.* BARBARA *comes from the shelter to the middle of the yard. She is excited and a little overwrought).*

BARBARA: Weve just had a splendid experience meeting at the other gate in Cripps's lane. Ive hardly ever seen them so much moved as they were by your confession, Mr Price.

PRICE: I could almost be glad of my past wickedness if I could believe that it would elp to keep hathers 1020 stright.

BARBARA: So it will, Snobby. How much, Jenny?

JENNY: Four and tenpence, Major.

BARBARA: Oh Snobby, if you had given your poor mother just one more kick, we should have got the whole five shillings!

PRICE: If she heard you say that, miss, she'd be sorry I didnt. But I'm glad. Oh what a joy it will be to her when she hears I'm saved!

UNDERSHAFT: Shall I contribute the odd two- 1030 pence, Barbara? The millionaire's mite, eh? *(He takes a couple of pennies from his pocket).*

BARBARA: How did you make that twopence?

UNDERSHAFT: As usual. By selling cannons, torpedoes, submarines, and my new patent Grand Duke hand grenade.

BARBARA: Put it back in your pocket. You cant buy your salvation here for twopence: you must work it out.

UNDERSHAFT: Is twopence not enough? I can afford a little more, if you press me.

BARBARA: Two million millions would not be enough. There is bad blood on your hands; and nothing but good blood can cleanse them. Money is no use. Take it away. *(She turns to* CUSINS*).* Dolly: you must write another letter for me to the papers. *(He makes a wry face).* Yes: I know you dont like it; but it must be done. The starvation this winter is beating us: everybody is unemployed. The General says we must close this shelter if we cant get more money. I force the collections at the meetings until I am ashamed: dont I, Snobby?

PRICE: It's a fair treat to see you work it, miss. The way you got them up from three-and-six to four-and-ten with that hymn, penny by penny and verse by verse, was a caution. Not a Cheap Jack on Mile End Waste could touch you at it.

BARBARA: Yes; but I wish we could do without it. I am getting at last to think more of the collection than of the people's souls. And what are those hatfuls of pence and halfpence? We want thousands! tens of thousands! hundreds of thousands! I want to convert people, not to be always begging for the Army in a way I'd die sooner than beg for myself.

UNDERSHAFT: *(in profound irony).* Genuine unselfishness is capable of anything, my dear.

BARBARA: *(unsuspectingly, as she turns away to take the money from the drum and put it in a cash bag she carries).* Yes, isnt it? (UNDERSHAFT *looks sardonically at* CUSINS*).*

CUSINS: *(aside to* UNDERSHAFT*).* Mephistopheles! Machiavelli!

BARBARA: *(tears coming into her eyes as she ties the bag and pockets it).* How are we to feed them? I cant talk religion to a man with bodily hunger in his eyes. *(Almost breaking down)* It's frightful.

JENNY: *(running to her).* Major, dear—

BARBARA: *(rebounding).* No: dont comfort me. It will be all right. We shall get the money.

UNDERSHAFT: How?

JENNY: By praying for it, of course. Mrs Baines says she prayed for it last night; and she has never prayed for it in vain: never once. *(She goes to the gate and looks out into the street).*

BARBARA: *(who has dried her eyes and regained her composure).* By the way, dad, Mrs Baines has come to march with us to our big meeting this afternoon; and she is very anxious to meet you, for some reason or other. Perhaps she'll convert you.

UNDERSHAFT: I shall be delighted, my dear.

JENNY: *(at the gate: excitedly).* Major! Major! heres that man back again.

BARBARA: What man?

JENNY: The man that hit me. Oh, I hope he's coming back to join us.

BILL WALKER, *with frost on his jacket, comes through the gate, his hands deep in his pockets and his chin sunk between his shoulders, like a cleaned-out gambler. He halts between* BARBARA *and the drum.*

BARBARA: Hullo, Bill! Back already!

BILL: *(nagging at her).* Bin talkin ever sence, ev you?

BARBARA: Pretty nearly. Well, has Todger paid you out for poor Jenny's jaw?

BILL: Nao e aint.

BARBARA: I thought your jacket looked a bit snowy.

BILL: Sao it is snaowy. You want to knaow where the snaow cam from, downt you?

BARBARA: Yes.

BILL: Well, it cam from orf the grahnd in Pawkinses Corner in Kennintahn. It got rabbed orf be maw shaoulders: see?

BARBARA: Pity you didnt rub some off with your knees, Bill! That would have done you a lot of good.

BILL: *(with sour mirthless humor).* Aw was siving anather menn's knees at the tawn. E was kneelin on moy ed, e was.

JENNY: Who was kneeling on your head?

BILL: Todger was. E was pryin for me: pryin comfortable wiv me as a cawpet. Sow was Mog. Sao was the aol bloomin meetin. Mog she sez 'Ow Lawd brike is stabborn sperrit; bat downt urt is dear art.' Thet was wot she said. 'Downt urt is dear art'! An er blowk—thirteen stun four!—kneelin wiv all is wight on me. Fanny, aint it?

JENNY: Oh no. We're so sorry, Mr Walker.

BARBARA: *(enjoying it frankly).* Nonsense! of course

it's funny. Served you right, Bill! You must have done something to him first.

BILL: *(doggedly).* Aw did wot Aw said Aw'd do. Aw spit in is eye. E looks ap at the skoy and sez, 'Ow that Aw should be fahnd worthy to be spit upon for the gospel's sike!' e sez; an Mog sez 'Glaory Alleloolier!'; and then e called me Braddher, and dahned me as if Aw was a kid and e was me mather worshin me a Setterda nawt. Aw ednt jast nao shaow wiv im at all. Arf the street pryed; an the tather arf larfed fit to split theirselves. *(To* BARBARA*)* There! are you settisfawd nah?

BARBARA: *(her eyes dancing).* Wish I'd been there, Bill.

BILL: Yus: youd a got in a hextra bit o talk on me, wouldnt you?

JENNY: I'm sorry, Mr Walker.

BILL: *(fiercely).* Downt you gow being sorry for me: youve no call. Listen eah. Aw browk your jawr.

JENNY: No, it didnt hurt me: indeed it didnt, except for a moment. It was only that I was frightened.

BILL: Aw downt want to be forgive be you, or be ennybody. Wot Aw did Aw'll py for. Aw trawd to gat me aown jawr browk to settisfaw you—

JENNY: *(distressed).* Oh no—

BILL: *(impatiently).* Tell y' Aw did: cawnt you listen to wots bein taold you? All Aw got be it was bein mide a sawt of in the pablic street for me pines. Well, if Aw cawnt settisfaw you one wy, Aw ken anather. Listen eah! Aw ed two quid sived agen the frost; and Awve a pahnd of it left. A mite o mawn last week ed words with the judy e's gowing to merry. E give er wot-for; an e's bin fawnd fifteen bob. E ed a rawt to itt er cause they was gowin to be married; but Aw ednt nao rawt to itt you; sao put another fawv bob on an call it a pahnd's worth. *(He produces a sovereign).* Eahs the manney. Tike it; and lets ev no more o your forgivin an pryin and your Mijor jawrin me. Let wot Aw dan be dan an pide for; and let there be a end of it.

JENNY: Oh, I couldnt take it, Mr Walker. But if you would give a shilling or two to poor Rummy Mitchens! you really did hurt her; and she's old.

BILL: *(contemptuously).* Not lawkly. Aw'd give her anather as soon as look at er. Let her ev the lawr

o me as she threatened! She aint forgiven me: not mach. Wot Aw dan to er is not on me mawnd—wot she *(indicating* BARBARA*)* mawt call on me conscience—no more than stickin a pig. It's this Christian gime o yours that Aw wownt ev plyed agen me: this bloomin forgivin an neggin an jawrin that mikes a menn thet sore that iz lawf's a burdn to im. Aw wownt ev it, Aw tell you; sao tike your manney and stop thraowin your silly beshed fice hap agen me.

JENNY: Major: may I take a little of it for the Army?

BARBARA: No: the Army is not to be bought. We want your soul, Bill; and we'll take nothing less.

BILL: *(bitterly).* Aw knaow. Me an maw few shillins is not good enaff for you. Youre a earl's grendorter, you are. Nathink less than a andered pahnd for you.

UNDERSHAFT: Come, Barbara! you could do a great deal of good with a hundred pounds. If you will set this gentleman's mind at ease by taking his pound, I will give the other ninety-nine.

Bill, dazed by such opulence, instinctively touches his cap.

BARBARA: Oh, youre too extravagant, papa. Bill offers twenty pieces of silver. All you need offer is the other ten. That will make the standard price to buy anybody who's for sale. I'm not; and the Army's not. *(To* BILL*)* Youll never have another quiet moment, Bill, until you come round to us. You cant stand out against your salvation.

BILL: *(sullenly).* Aw cawnt stend aht agen music awl wrastlers and awtful tangued women. Awve offered to py. Aw can do no more. Tike it or leave it. There it is. *(He throws the sovereign on the drum, and sits down on the horse-trough. The coin fascinates* SNOBBY PRICE, *who takes an early opportunity of dropping his cap on it).*

Mrs Baines comes from the shelter. She is dressed as a Salvation Army Commissioner. She is an earnest looking woman of about 40, with a carressing, urgent voice, and an appealing manner.

BARBARA: This is my father, Mrs. Baines. *(*UNDERSHAFT *comes from the table, taking his hat off with marked civility).* Try what you can do with him. He wont listen to me, because he remembers what a fool I was when I was a baby. *(She leaves them together and chats with* JENNY*).*

MRS BAINES: Have you been shewn over the shelter, Mr Undershaft? You know the work we're doing, of course.

UNDERSHAFT: *(very civilly)*. The whole nation knows it, Mrs Baines.

MRS BAINES: No, sir: the whole nation does not know it, or we should not be crippled as we are for want of money to carry our work through the length and breadth of the land. Let me tell you that there would have been rioting this winter in London but for us.

UNDERSHAFT: You really think so?

MRS BAINES: I know it. I remember 1886, when you rich gentlemen hardened your hearts against the cry of the poor. They broke the windows of your clubs in Pall Mall.

UNDERSHAFT: *(gleaming with approval of their method)*. And the Mansion House Fund went up next day from thirty thousand pounds to seventy-nine thousand! I remember quite well.

MRS BAINES: Well, wont you help me to get at the people? They wont break windows then. Come here, Price. Let me shew you to this gentleman (PRICE *comes to be inspected*). Do you remember the window breaking?

PRICE: My ole father thought it was the revolution, maam.

MRS BAINES: Would you break windows now?

PRICE: Oh no, maam. The windows of eaven ave bin opened to me. I know now that the rich man is a sinner like myself.

RUMMY: *(appearing above at the loft door)*. Snobby Price!

SNOBBY: Wot is it?

RUMMY: Your mother's askin for you at the other gate in Cripps's Lane. She's heard about your confession (PRICE *turns pale)*.

MRS BAINES: Go, Mr Price; and pray with her.

JENNY: You can go through the shelter, Snobby.

PRICE: *(to MRS BAINES)*. I couldnt face her now, maam, with all the weight of my sins fresh on me. Tell her she'll find her son at ome, waitin for her in prayer. *(He skulks off through the gate, incidentally stealing the sovereign on his way out by picking up his cap from the drum)*.

MRS BAINES: *(with swimming eyes)*. You see how we take the anger and the bitterness against you out of their hearts, Mr Undershaft.

UNDERSHAFT: It is certainly most convenient and gratifying to all large employers of labor, Mrs Baines.

MRS BAINES: Barbara: Jenny: I have good news: most wonderful news. (JENNY *runs to her)*. My prayers have been answered. I told you they would, Jenny, didnt I?

JENNY: Yes, yes.

BARBARA: *(moving nearer to the drum)*. Have we got money enough to keep the shelter open?

MRS BAINES: I hope we shall have enough to keep all the shelters open. Lord Saxmundham has promised us five thousand pounds—

BARBARA: Hooray!

JENNY: Glory!

MRS BAINES: —if—

BARBARA: 'If!' If what?

MRS BAINES: —if five other gentlemen will give a thousand each to make it up to ten thousand.

BARBARA: Who is Lord Saxmundham? I never heard of him.

UNDERSHAFT: *(who has pricked up his ears at the peer's name, and is now watching BARBARA curiously)*. A new creation, my dear. You have heard of Sir Horace Bodger?

BARBARA: Bodger! Do you mean the distiller? Bodger's whisky!

UNDERSHAFT: That is the man. He is one of the greatest of our public benefactors. He restored the cathedral at Hakington. They made him a baronet for that. He gave half a million to the funds of his party: they made him a baron for that.

SHIRLEY: What will they give him for the five thousand?

UNDERSHAFT: There is nothing left to give him. So the five thousand, I should think, is to save his soul.

MRS BAINES: Heaven grant it may! Oh Mr. Undershaft, you have some very rich friends. Cant you help us towards the other five thousand? We are going to hold a great meeting this afternoon at the Assembly Hall in the Mile End Road. If I could only announce that one gentleman had come forward to support Lord Saxmundham, others would follow. Dont you know somebody? couldnt you? wouldnt you? *(her eyes fill with tears)* oh, think of those poor people, Mr. Undershaft: think of how much it

means to them, and how little to a great man
like you.

UNDERSHAFT: *(sardonically gallant)*. Mrs Baines: you
are irrestible. I cant disappoint you; and I cant
deny myself the satisfaction of making Bodger
1330   pay up. You shall have your five thousand
pounds.

MRS BAINES: Thank God!

UNDERSHAFT: You dont thank me?

MRS BAINES: Oh sir, dont try to be cynical: dont
be ashamed of being a good man. The Lord
will bless you abundantly; and our prayers will
be like a strong fortification round you all the
days of your life. *(With a touch of caution)* You
will let me have the cheque to shew at the meet-
1340   ing, wont you? Jenny: go in and fetch a pen and
ink. (JENNY *runs to the shelter door*).

UNDERSHAFT: Do not disturb Miss Hill: I have a
fountain pen (JENNY *halts. He sits at the table,
writes the cheque.* CUSINS *rises to make room for him.
They all watch him silently*).

BILL: *(cynically, aside to* BARBARA, *his voice and accent
horribly debased)*. Wot prawce selvytion nah?

BARBARA: Stop. (UNDERSHAFT *stops writing: they all
turn to her in surprise*). Mrs Baines: are you really
1350   going to take this money?

MRS BAINES: *(astonished)*. Why not, dear?

BARBARA: Why not! Do you know what my father
is? Have you forgotten that Lord Saxmundham
is Bodger the whisky man? Do you remember
how we implored the County Council to stop
him from writing Bodger's Whisky in letters of
fire against the sky; so that the poor drink-ruined
creatures on the Embankment could not wake
up from their snatches of sleep without being
1360   reminded of their deadly thirst by that wicked
sky sign? Do you know that the worst thing
I have had to fight here is not the devil, but
Bodger, Bodger, Bodger, with his whisky, his
distilleries, and his tied houses? Are you going
to make our shelter another tied house for him,
and ask me to keep it?

BILL: Rotten dranken whisky it is too.

MRS BAINES: Dear Barbara: Lord Saxmundham has
a soul to be saved like any of us. If heaven has
1370   found the way to make a good use of his money,
are we to set ourselves up against the answer
to our prayers?

BARBARA: I know he has a soul to be saved. Let

him come down here; and I'll do my best to
help him to his salvation. But he wants to send
his cheque down to buy us, and go on being
as wicked as ever.

UNDERSHAFT: *(with a reasonableness which* CUSINS
alone perceives to be ironical). My dear Barbara:
alcohol is a very necessary article. It heals the   1380
sick—

BARBARA: It does nothing of the sort.

UNDERSHAFT: Well, it assists the doctor: that is
perhaps a less questionable way of putting it.
It makes life bearable to millions of people who
could not endure their existence if they were
quite sober. It enables Parliament to do things
at eleven at night that no sane person would
do at eleven in the morning. Is it Bodger's fault
that this inestimable gift is deplorably abused   1390
by less than one per cent of the poor? *(He turns
again to the table; signs the cheque; and crosses it)*.

MRS BAINES: Barbara: will there be less drinking or
more if all those poor souls we are saving come
tomorrow and find the doors of our shelters shut
in their faces? Lord Saxmundham gives us the
money to stop drinking—to take his own business from him.

CUSINS: *(impishly)*. Pure self-sacrifice on Bodger's
part, clearly! Bless dear Bodger! (BARBARA *almost*   1400
breaks down as ADOLPHUS, *too, fails her*).

UNDERSHAFT: *(tearing out the cheque and pocketing the
book as he rises and goes past* CUSINS *to* MRS BAINES*)*.
I also, Mrs Baines, may claim a little disinteres-
tedness. Think of my business! think of the
widows and orphans! the men and lads torn to
pieces with shrapnel and poisoned with lyddite!
(MRS BAINES *shrinks; but he goes on remorselessly*)
the oceans of blood, not one drop of which is
shed in a really just cause! the ravaged crops!   1410
the peaceful peasants forced, women and men,
to till their fields under the fire of opposing
armies on pain of starvation! the bad blood of
the fierce little cowards at home who egg on
others to fight for the gratification of their
national vanity! All this makes money for me:
I am never richer, never busier than when the
papers are full of it. Well, it is your work to
preach peace on earth and good will to men.
(MRS BAINES's *face lights up again)*. Every convert   1420
you make is a vote against war. *(Her lips move
in prayer)*. Yet I give you this money to help

you to hasten my own commercial ruin. *(He gives her the cheque).*

CUSINS: *(mounting the form in an ecstasy of mischief).* The millennium will be inaugurated by the unselfishness of Undershaft and Bodger. Oh be joyful! *(He takes the drum-sticks from his pocket and flourishes them).*

430 MRS BAINES: *(taking the cheque).* The longer I live the more proof I see that there is an Infinite Goodness that turns everything to the work of salvation sooner or later. Who would have thought that any good could have come out of war and drink? And yet their profits are brought today to the feet of salvation to do its blessed work. *(She is affected to tears).*

JENNY: *(running to* MRS BAINES *and throwing her arms round her).* Oh dear! how blessed, how glorious

440 it all is!

CUSINS: *(in a convulsion of irony).* Let us seize this unspeakable moment. Let us march to the great meeting at once. Excuse me just an instant. *(He rushes into the shelter.* JENNY *takes her tambourine from the drum head).*

MRS BAINES: Mr. Undershaft: have you ever seen a thousand people fall on their knees with one impulse and pray? Come with us to the meeting. Barbara shall tell them that the Army is saved,

450 and saved through you.

CUSINS: *(returning impetuously from the shelter with a flag and a trombone, and coming between* MRS BAINES *and* UNDERSHAFT*).* You shall carry the flag down the first street. Mrs Baines *(he gives her the flag).* Mr. Undershaft is a gifted trombonist: he shall intone an Olympian diapason to the West Ham Salvation March. *(Aside to* UNDERSHAFT, *as he forces the trombone on him)* Blow, Machiavelli, blow.

460 UNDERSHAFT: *(aside to him, as he takes the trombone).* The trumpet in Zion! *(CUSINS rushes to the drum, which he takes up and puts on.* UNDERSHAFT *continues, aloud)* I will do my best. I could vamp a bass if I knew the tune.

CUSINS: It is a wedding chorus from one of Donizetti's operas; but we have converted it. We convert everything to good here, including Bodger. You remember the chorus. 'For thee immense rejoicing—immenso giubilo—immenso

470 giubilo.' *(With drum obbligato)* Rum tum ti tum tum, tum tum ti ta—

BARBARA: Dolly: you are breaking my heart.

CUSINS: What is a broken heart more or less here? Dionysos Undershaft has descended. I am possessed.

MRS BAINES: Come, Barbara: I must have my dear Major to carry the flag with me.

JENNY: Yes, yes, Major darling.

CUSINS: *(snatches the tambourine out of* JENNY's *hand and mutely offers it to* BARBARA*).* 1480

BARBARA: *(coming forward a little as she puts the offer behind her with a shudder, whilst* CUSINS *recklessly tosses the tambourine back to* JENNY *and goes to the gate).* I cant come.

JENNY: Not come!

MRS BAINES: *(with tears in her eyes).* Barbara: do you think I am wrong to take the money?

BARBARA: *(impulsively going to her and kissing her).* No, no: God help you, dear, you must: you are saving the Army. Go; and may you have a 1490 great meeting!

JENNY: But arnt you coming?

BARBARA: No. *(She begins taking off the silver S brooch from her collar).*

MRS BAINES: Barbara: what are you doing?

JENNY: Why are you taking your badge off? You cant be going to leave us, Major.

BARBARA: *(quietly).* Father: come here.

UNDERHSAFT: *(coming to her).* My dear! *(Seeing that she is going to pin the badge on his collar, he retreats* 1500 *to the penthouse in some alarm).*

BARBARA: *(quietly).* Father: come here.

BARBARA: *(following him).* Dont be frightened. *(She pins the badge on and steps back towards the table, shewing him to the others)* There! It's not much for £5000, is it?

MRS BAINES: Barbara: if you wont come and pray with us, promise me you will pray for us.

BARBARA: I cant pray now. Perhaps I shall never pray again. 1510

MRS BAINES: Barbara!

JENNY: Major!

BARBARA: *(almost delirious).* I cant bear any more. Quick march!

CUSINS: *(calling to the procession in the street outside).* Off we go. Play up, there! Immenso giubilo. *(He gives the time with his drum; and the band strikes up the march, which rapidly becomes more distant as the procession moves briskly away).*

MRS BAINES: I must go, dear. Youre overworked: 1520

you will be all right tomorrow. We'll never lose you. Now Jenny: step out with the old flag. Blood and Fire! (*She marches out through the gate with her flag*).

JENNY: Glory Hallelujah! (*flourishing her tambourine and marching*).

UNDERSHAFT: (*to* CUSINS, *as he marches out past him easing the slide of his trombone*). 'My ducats and my daughter'!

1530 CUSINS: (*following him out*). Money and gunpowder!

BARBARA: Drunkenness and Murder! My God: why hast thou forsaken me?

She sinks on the form with her face buried in her hands. The march passes away into silence. BILL WALKER *steals across to her.*

BILL: (*taunting*). Wot prawce selvytion nah?

SHIRLEY: Dont you hit her when she's down.

BILL: She itt me wen aw wiz dahn. Waw shouldnt Aw git a bit o me aown beck?

1540 BARBARA: (*raising her head*). I didnt take your money, Bill. (*She crosses the yard to the gate and turns her back on the two men to hide her face from them*).

BILL: (*sneering after her*). Naow, it warnt enaff for you. (*Turning to the drum, he misses the money*) Ellow! If you aint took it sammun else ez. Weres it gorn? Bly me if Jenny Ill didnt tike it arter all!

RUMMY: (*screaming at him from the loft*). You lie, you

1550 dirty blackguard! Snobby Price pinched it off the drum when he took up his cap. I was up here all the time an see im do it.

BILL: Wot! Stowl maw manney! Waw didnt you call thief on him, you silly aold macker you?

RUMMY: To serve you aht for ittin me acrost the fice. It's cost y'pahnd, that az. (*Raising a paean of squalid triumph*) I done you. I'm even with you. Uve ad it aht o y—(BILL *snatches up* SHIRLEY'S *mug and hurls it at her. She slams the loft door and*

1560 *vanishes. The mug smashes against the door and falls in fragments*).

BILL: (*beginning to chuckle*). Tell us, aol menn, wot o'clock this mawnin was it wen im as they call Snobby Prawce was sived?

BARBARA: (*turning to him more composedly, and with unspoiled sweetness*). About half past twelve, Bill. And he pinched your pound at a quarter to two. *I* know. Well, you cant afford to lose it. I'll send it to you.

BILL: (*his voice and accent suddenly improving*). Not if 1570 Aw wiz to stawve for it. Aw aint to be bought.

SHIRLEY: Aint you? Youd sell yourself to the devil for a pint o beer; only there aint no devil to make the offer.

BILL: (*unashamed*). Sao Aw would, mite, and often ev, cheerful. But she cawnt baw me. (*Approaching* BARBARA) You wanted maw saoul, did you? Well you ant got it.

BARBARA: I nearly got it, Bill. But weve sold it back to you for ten thousand pounds. 1580

SHIRLEY: And dear at the money!

BARBARA: No, Peter: it was worth more than money.

BILL: (*salvationproof*). It's nao good: you cawnt get rahnd me nah. Aw downt blieve in it; and Awve seen tody that Aw was rawt. (*Goint*) Sao long, aol soupkitchener! Ta, ta, Mijor Earl's Grendorter! (*Turning at the gate*) Wot prawce selvytion nah? Snobby Prawce! Ha! ha!

BARBARA: (*offering her hand*). Goodbye, Bill. 1590

BILL: (*taken aback, half plucks his cap off; then shoves it on again defiantly*). Git aht. (BARBARA *drops her hand, discouraged. He has a twinge of remorse*). But thets aw rawt, you knaow. Nathink pasnl. Naow mellice. Sao long, Judy. (*He goes*).

BARBARA: No malice. So long, Bill.

SHIRLEY: (*shaking his head*). You make too much of him, miss, in your innocence.

BARBARA: (*going to him*). Peter: I'm like you now. Cleaned out, and lost my job. 1600

SHIRLEY: Youve youth an hope. Thats two better than me.

BARBARA: I'll get you a job, Peter. Thats hope for you: the youth will have to be enough for me. (*She counts her money*). I have just enough left for two teas at Lockharts, a Rowton doss for you, and my tram and bus home. (*He frowns and rises with offended pride. She takes his arm*). Dont be proud, Peter: it's sharing between friends. And promise me youll talk to me and not let 1610 me cry. (*She draws him towards the gate*).

SHIRLEY: Well, I'm not accustomed to talk to the like of you—

BARBARA: (*urgently*). Yes, yes: you must talk to me. Tell me about Tom Paine's books and Brad-laugh's lectures. Come along.

SHIRLEY: Ah, if you would only read Tom Paine in the proper spirit, miss! (*They go out through the gate together*).

ACT THREE

Next day after lunch Lady Britomart is writing in the library in Wilton Crescent. Sarah is reading in the armchair near the window. Barbara, in ordinary fashionable dress, pale and brooding, is on the settee. Charles Lomax enters. He starts on seeing Barbara fashionably attired and in low spirits.

LOMAX: Youve left off your uniform!

Barbara says nothing; but an expression of pain passes over her face.

LADY BRITOMART: *(warning him in low tones to be careful)*. Charles!

LOMAX: *(much concerned, coming behind the settee and bending sympathetically over* BARBARA*)*. I'm awfully sorry, Barbara. You know I helped you all I could with the concertina and so forth. *(Momentously)* Still, I have never shut my eyes to the fact that there is a certain amount of tosh about the Salvation Army. Now the claims of the Church of England—

LADY BRITOMART: That's enough, Charles. Speak of something suited to your mental capacity.

LOMAX: But surely the Church of England is suited to all our capacities.

BARBARA: *(pressing his hand)*. Thank you for your sympathy, Cholly. Now go and spoon with Sarah.

LOMAX: *(dragging a chair from the writing table and seating himself affectionately by* SARAH*'s side)*. How is my ownest today?

SARAH: I wish you wouldn't tell Cholly to do things, Barbara. He always comes straight and does them. Cholly: we're going to the works this afternoon.

LOMAX: What works?

SARAH: The cannon works.

LOMAX: What? your governor's shop!

SARAH: Yes.

LOMAX: Oh I say!

CUSINS *enters in poor condition. He also starts visibly when he sees* BARBARA *without her uniform.*

BARBARA: I expected you this morning, Dolly. Didn't you guess that?

CUSINS: *(sitting down beside her)*. I'm sorry. I have only just breakfasted.

SARAH: But we've just finished lunch.

BARBARA: Have you had one of your bad nights?

CUSINS: No: I had rather a good night: in fact, one of the most remarkable nights I have ever passed.

BARBARA: The meeting?

CUSINS: No: after the meeting.

LADY BRITOMART: You should have gone to bed after the meeting. What were you doing?

CUSINS: Drinking.

LADY BRITOMART: ⎫ Adolphus!
SARAH: ⎪ Dolly!
BARBARA: ⎬ Dolly!
LOMAX: ⎭ Oh I say!

LADY BRITOMART: What were you drinking, may I ask?

CUSINS: A most devilish kind of Spanish burgundy, warranted free from added alcohol: a Temperance burgundy in fact. Its richness in natural alcohol made any addition superfluous.

BARBARA: Are you joking, Dolly?

CUSINS: *(patiently)*. No. I have been making a night of it with the nominal head of this household: that is all.

LADY BRITOMART: Andrew made you drunk!

CUSINS: No: he only provided the wine. I think it was Dionysos who made me drunk. *(To* BARBARA*)* I told you I was possessed.

LADY BRITOMART: You're not sober yet. Go home to bed at once.

CUSINS: I have never before ventured to reproach you, Lady Brit; but how could you marry the Prince of Darkness?

LADY BRITOMART: It was much more excusable to marry him than to get drunk with him. That is a new accomplishment of Andrew's, by the way. He usent to drink.

CUSINS: He doesnt now. He only sat there and completed the wreck of my moral basis, the rout

of my convictions, the purchase of my soul. He cares for you, Barbara. That is what makes him
80   so dangerous to me.

BARBARA: That has nothing to do with it, Dolly. There are larger loves and diviner dreams than the fireside onces. You know that, dont you?

CUSINS: Yes: that is our understanding. I know it. I hold to it. Unless he can win me on that holier ground he may amuse me for a while; but he can get no deeper hold, strong as he is.

BARBARA: Keep to that; and the end will be right. Now tell me what happened at the meeting?

90   CUSINS: It was an amazing meeting. Mrs Baines almost died of emotion. Jenny Hill simply gibbered with hysteria. The Prince of Darkness played his trombone like a madman: its brazen roarings were like the laughter of the damned. 117 conversions took place then and there. They prayed with the most touching sincerity and gratitude for Bodger, and for the anonymous donor of the £5000. Your father would not let his name be given.

100   LOMAX: That was rather fine of the old man, you know. Most chaps would have wanted the advertisement.

CUSINS: He said all the charitable institutions would be down on him like kites on a battlefield if he gave his name.

LADY BRITOMART: Thats Andrew all over. He never does a proper thing without giving an improper reason for it.

CUSINS: He convinced me that I have all my life
110   been doing improper things for proper reasons.

LADY BRITOMART: Adolphus: now that Barbara has left the Salvation Army, you had better leave it too. I will not have you playing that drum in the streets.

CUSINS: Your orders are already obeyed, Lady Brit.

BARBARA: Dolly: were you ever really in earnest about it? Would you have joined if you had never seen me?

120   CUSINS: (disingenuously). Well—er—well, possibly, as a collector of religions—

LOMAX: (cunningly). Not as a drummer, though, you know. You are a very clearheaded brainy chap, Dolly; and it must have been apparent to you that there is a certain amount of tosh about—

LADY BRITOMART: Charles: if you must drivel, drivel like a grown-up man and not like a schoolboy.

LOMAX: (out of countenance). Well, drivel is drivel,   130
dont you know, whatever a man's age.

LADY BRITOMART: In good society in England, Charles, men drivel at all ages by repeating silly formulas with an air of wisdom. Schoolboys make their own formulas out of slang, like you. When they reach your age, and get political private secretaryships and things of that sort, they drop slang and get their formulas out of the Spectator or The Times. You had better confine yourself to The Times. You will find   140
that there is a certain amount of tosh about The Times; but at least its language is reputable.

LOMAX: (overwhelmed). You are so awfully strong-minded, Lady Brit—

LADY BRITOMART: Rubbish! (MORRISON comes in). What is it?

MORRISON: If you please, my lady, Mr Undershaft has just drove up to the door.

LADY BRITOMART: Well, let him in. (MORRISON hesitates). Whats the matter with you?   150

MORRISON: Shall I announce him, my lady; or is he at home here, so to speak, my lady?

LADY BRITOMART: Announce him.

MORRISON: Thank you, my lady. You wont mind my asking, I hope. The occasion is in a manner of speaking new to me.

LADY BRITOMART: Quite right. Go and let him in.

MORRISON: Thank you, my lady. (He withdraws).

LADY BRITOMART: Children: go and get ready. (SARAH and BARBARA go upstairs for their out-of-door   160
wraps). Charles: go and tell Stephen to come down here in five minutes: you will find him in the drawing room. (CHARLES goes). Adolphus: tell them to send round the carriage in about fifteen minutes. (ADOLPHUS goes).

MORRISON: (at the door). Mr Undershaft.

UNDERSHAFT comes in. MORRISON goes out.

UNDERSHAFT: Alone! How fortunate!

LADY BRITOMART: (rising). Don't be sentimental, Andrew. Sit down. (She sits on the settee: he sits   170
beside her, on her left. She comes to the point before he has time to breathe). Sarah must have £800 a year until Charles Lomax comes into his property. Barbara will need more, and need it perma-

nently, because Adolphus hasnt any property.

UNDERSHAFT: *(resignedly)*. Yes, my dear: I will see to it. Anything else? for yourself, for instance?

LADY BRITOMART: I want to talk to you about Stephen.

UNDERSHAFT: *(rather wearily)*. Dont, my dear. Stephen doesnt interest me.

LADY BRITOMART: He does interest me. He is our son.

UNDERSHAFT: Do you really think so? He has induced us to bring him into the world; but he chose his parents very incongruously, I think. I see nothing of myself in him, and less of you.

LADY BRITOMART: Andrew: Stephen is an excellent son, and a most steady, capable, highminded young man. You are simply trying to find an excuse for disinheriting him.

UNDERSHAFT: My dear Biddy: the Undershaft tradition disinherits him. It would be dishonest of me to leave the cannon foundry to my son.

LADY BRITOMART: It would be most unnatural and improper of you to leave it to anyone else, Andrew. Do you suppose this wicked and immoral tradition can be kept up for ever? Do you pretend that Stephen could not carry on the foundry just as well as all the other sons of the big business houses?

UNDERSHAFT: Yes: he could learn the office routine without understanding the business, like all the other sons; and the firm would go on by its own momentum until the real Undershaft— probably an Italian or a German—would invent a new method and cut him out.

LADY BRITOMART: There is nothing that any Italian or German could do that Stephen could not do. And Stephen at least has breeding.

UNDERSHAFT: The son of a foundling! Nonsense!

LADY BRITOMART: My son, Andrew! And even you may have good blood in your veins for all you know.

UNDERSHAFT: True. Probably I have. That is another argument in favour of a foundling.

LADY BRITOMART: Andrew: dont be aggravating. And dont be wicked. At present you are both.

UNDERSHAFT: This conversation is part of the Undershaft tradition, Biddy. Every Undershaft's wife has treated him to it ever since the house was founded. It is mere waste of breath. If the tradition be ever broken it will be for an abler man than Stephen.

LADY BRITOMART: *(pouting)*. Then go away.

UNDERSHAFT: *(deprecatory)*. Go away!

LADY BRITOMART: Yes: go away. If you will do nothing for Stephen, you are not wanted here. Go to your foundling, whoever he is; and look after him.

UNDERSHAFT: The fact is, Biddy—

LADY BRITOMART: Dont call me Biddy. I dont call you Andy.

UNDERSHAFT: I will not call my wife Britomart: it is not good sense. Seriously, my love, the Undershaft tradition has landed me in a difficulty. I am getting on in years; and my partner Lazarus has at last made a stand and insisted that the succession must be settled one way or the other; and of course he is quite right. You see, I havent found a fit successor yet.

LADY BRITOMART: *(obstinately)*. There is Stephen.

UNDERSHAFT: Thats just it: all the foundlings I can find are exactly like Stephen.

LADY BRITOMART: Andrew!!

UNDERSHAFT: I want a man with no relations and no schooling: that is, a man who would be out of the running altogether if he were not a strong man. And I cant find him. Every blessed found-ling nowadays is snapped up in his infancy by Barnardo homes, or School Board officers, or Boards of Guardians; and if he shews the least ability he is fastened on by schoolmasters; trained to win scholarships like a racehorse; crammed with secondhand ideas; drilled and dis-ciplined in docility and what they call good taste; and lamed for life so that he is fit for nothing but teaching. If you want to keep the foundry in the family, you had better find an eligible foundling and marry him to Barbara.

LADY BRITOMART: Ah! Barbara! Your pet! You would sacrifice Stephen to Barbara.

UNDERSHAFT: Cheerfully. And you, my dear, would boil Barbara to make soup for Stephen.

LADY BRITOMART: Andrew: this is not a question of our likings and dislikings: it is a question of duty. It is your duty to make Stephen your suc-cessor.

UNDERSHAFT: Just as much as it is your duty to submit to your husband. Come, Biddy! these tricks of the governing class are of no use with me. I am one of the governing class myself; and it is waste of time giving tracts to a missionary. I have the power in this matter; and I am not to be humbugged into using it for your purposes.

LADY BRITOMART: Andrew: you can talk my head off; but you cant change wrong into right. And your tie is all on one side. Put it straight.

UNDERSHAFT: (disconcerted). It wont stay unless it's pinned (he fumbles at it with childish grimaces)–

STEPHEN comes in.

STEPHEN: (at the door). I beg your pardon (about to retire).

LADY BRITOMART: No: come in, Stephen. (STEPHEN comes forward to his mother's writing table).

UNDERSHAFT: (not very cordially). Good afternoon.

STEPHEN: (coldly). Good afternoon.

UNDERSHAFT: (to LADY BRITOMART). He knows all about the tradition, I suppose?

LADY BRITOMART: Yes. (To STEPHEN) It is what I told you last night, Stephen.

UNDERSHAFT: (sulkily). I understand you want to come into the cannon business.

STEPHEN: I go into trade! Certainly not.

UNDERSHAFT: (opening his eyes, greatly eased in mind and manner). Oh! in that case—

LADY BRITOMART: Cannons are not trade, Stephen. They are enterprise.

STEPHEN: I have no intention of becoming a man of business in any sense. I have no capacity for business and no taste for it. I intend to devote myself to politics.

UNDERSHAFT: (rising). My dear boy: this is an immense relief to me. And I trust it may prove an equally good thing for the country. I was afraid you would consider yourself disparaged and slighted. (He moves towards STEPHEN as if to shake hands with him).

LADY BRITOMART: (rising and interposing). Stephen: I cannot allow you to throw away an enormous property like this.

STEPHEN: (stiffly). Mother: there must be an end of treating me as a child, if you please. (LADY BRITOMART recoils, deeply wounded by his tone). Until last night I did not take your attitude seriously, because I did not think you meant it seriously. But I find now that you left me in the dark as to matters which you should have explained to me years ago. I am extremely hurt and

offended. Any further discussion of my intentions had better take place with my father, as between one man and another.

LADY BRITOMART: Stephen! (She sits down again, her eyes filling with tears).

UNDERSHAFT: (with grave compassion). You see, my dear, it is only the big men who can be treated as children.

STEPHEN: I am sorry, mother, that you have forced me—

UNDERSHAFT: (stopping him). Yes, yes, yes, yes: thats all right, Stephen. She wont interfere with you any more: your independence is achieved: you have won your latchkey. Dont rub it in; and above all, dont apologize. (He resumes his seat). Now what about your future, as between one man and another—I beg your pardon, Biddy: as between two men and a woman.

LADY BRITOMART: (who has pulled herself together strongly). I quite understand, Stephen. By all means go your own way if you feel strong enough. (STEPHEN sits down magisterially in the chair at the writing table with an air of affirming his majority).

UNDERSHAFT: It is settled that you do not ask for the succession to the cannon business.

STEPHEN: I hope it is settled that I repudiate the cannon business.

UNDERSHAFT: Come, come! dont be so devilishly sulky: it's boyish. Freedom should be generous. Besides, I owe you a fair start in life in exchange for disinheriting you. You cant become prime minister all at once. Havnt you a turn for something? What about literature, art, and so forth?

STEPHEN: I have nothing of the artist about me, either in faculty or character, thank Heaven!

UNDERSHAFT: A philosopher, perhaps? Eh?

STEPHEN: I make no such ridiculous pretension.

UNDERSHAFT: Just so. Well, there is the army, the navy, the Church, the Bar. The Bar requires some ability. What about the Bar?

STEPHEN: I have not studied law. And I am afraid I have not the necessary push—I believe that is the name barristers give to their vulgarity—for success in pleading.

UNDERSHAFT: Rather a difficult case, Stephen. Hardly anything left but the stage, is there? (STEPHEN makes an impatient movement). Well, come! is there anything you know or care for?

STEPHEN: *(rising and looking at him steadily)*. I know the difference between right and wrong.

UNDERSHAFT: *(hugely tickled)*. You dont say so! What! no capacity for business, no knowledge of law, no sympathy with art, no pretension to philosophy; only a simple knowledge of the secret that has puzzled all the philosophers, baffled all the lawyers, muddled all the men of business, and ruined most of the artists: the secret of right and wrong. Why, man, youre a genius, a master of masters, a god! At twenty-four, too!

STEPHEN: *(keeping his temper with difficulty)*. You are pleased to be facetious. I pretend to be nothing more than any honorable English gentleman claims as his birthright *(he sits down angrily)*.

UNDERSHAFT: Oh, thats everybody's birthright. Look at poor little Jenny Hill, the Salvation lassie! she would think you were laughing at her if you asked her to stand in the street and teach grammar or geography or mathematics or even drawing room dancing; but it never occurs to her to doubt that she can teach morals and religion. You are all alike, you respectable people. You cant tell me the bursting strain of a ten-inch gun, which is a very simple matter; but you all think you can tell me the bursting strain of a man under temptation. You darent handle high explosives; but youre all ready to handle honesty and truth and justice and the whole duty of man, and kill one another at that game. What a country! What a world!

LADY BRITOMART: *(uneasily)*. What do you think he had better do, Andrew?

UNDERSHAFT: Oh, just what he wants to do. He knows nothing and he thinks he knows everything. That points clearly to a political career. Get him a private secretaryship to someone who can get him an Under Secretaryship; and then leave him alone. He will find his natural and proper place in the end on the Treasury Bench.

STEPHEN: *(springing up again)*. I am sorry, sir, that you force me to forget the respect due to you as my father. I am an Englishman and I will not hear the Government of my country insulted. *(He thrusts his hands in his pockets, and walks angrily across to the window)*.

UNDERSHAFT: *(with a touch of brutality)*. The government of your country! *I* am the government of your country: I, and Lazarus. Do you suppose that you and half a dozen amateurs like you, sitting in a row in that foolish gabble shop, can govern Undershaft and Lazarus? No, my friend: you will do what pays us. You will make war when it suits us, and keep peace when it doesnt. You will find out that trade requires certain measures when we have decided on those measures. When I want anything to keep my dividends up, you will discover that my want is a national need. When other people want something to keep my dividends down, you will call out the police and military. And in return you shall have the support and applause of my newspapers, and the delight of imagining that you are a great statesman. Government of your country! Be off with you, my boy, and play with your caucuses and leading articles and historic parties and great leaders and burning questions and the rest of your toys. *I* am going back to my counting-house to pay the piper and call the tune.

STEPHEN: *(actually smiling, and putting his hand on his father's shoulder with indulgent patronage)*. Really, my dear father, it is impossible to be angry with you. You dont know how absurd all this sounds to me. You are very properly proud of having been industrious enough to make money; and it is greatly to your credit that you have made so much of it. But it has kept you in circles where you are valued for your money and deferred to for it, instead of in the doubtless very old-fashioned and behind-the-times public school and university where I formed my habits of mind. It is natural for you to think that money governs England; but you must allow me to think I know better.

UNDERSHAFT: And what does govern England, pray?

STEPHEN: Character, father, character.

UNDERSHAFT: Whose character? Yours or mine?

STEPHEN: Neither yours nor mine, father, but the best elements in the English national character.

UNDERSHAFT: Stephen: Ive found your profession for you. Youre a born journalist. I'll start you with a high-toned weekly review. There!

Before STEPHEN *can reply* SARAH, BARBARA, LOMAX, *and* CUSINS *come in ready for walking.* BARBARA *crosses the room to the window and looks out.* CUSINS *drifts amiably to the armchair.* LOMAX *remains near the door, whilst* SARAH *comes to her mother.*

470 STEPHEN *goes to the smaller writing table and busies himself with his letters.*

SARAH: Go and get ready, mamma: the carriage is waiting. (LADY BRITOMART *leaves the room*).

UNDERSHAFT: *(to* SARAH*).* Good day, my dear. Good afternoon, Mr. Lomax.

LOMAX: *(vaguely).* Ahdedoo.

UNDERSHAFT: *(to* CUSINS*).* Quite well after last night, Euripides, eh?

CUSINS: As well as can be expected.

UNDERSHAFT: Thats right *(To* BARBARA*)* So you are coming to see my death and devastation factory, Barbara?

480

BARBARA: *(at the window).* You came yesterday to see my salvation factory. I promised you a return visit.

LOMAX: *(coming forward between* SARAH *and* UNDERSHAFT*).* Youll find it awfully interesting. Ive been through the Woolwich Arsenal; and it gives you a ripping feeling of security, you know, to think of the lot of beggars we could kill if it came to fighting. *To* UNDERSHAFT *with sudden solemnity)* Still, it must be rather an awful reflection for you, from the religious point of view as it were. Youre getting on, you know, and all that.

490

SARAH: You dont mind Cholly's imbecility, papa, do you?

LOMAX: *(much taken aback).* Oh I say!

UNDERSHAFT: Mr. Lomax looks at the matter in a very proper spirit, my dear.

LOMAX: Just so. Thats all I meant, I assure you.

500

SARAH: Are you coming, Stephen?

STEPHEN: Well, I am rather busy—er—*(Magnanimously)* Oh well, yes: I'll come. That is, if there is room for me.

UNDERSHAFT: I can take two with me in a little motor I am experimenting with for field use. You wont mind its being rather unfashionable. It's not painted yet; but it's bullet proof.

LOMAX: *(appalled at the prospect of confronting Wilton Crescent in an unpainted motor).* Oh I say!

510

SARAH: The carriage for me, thank you. Barbara doesnt mind what she's seen in.

LOMAX: I say, Dolly, old chap: do you really mind the car being a guy? Because of course if you do I'll go in it. Still—

CUSINS: I prefer it.

LOMAX: Thanks awfully, old man. Come, my ownest. *(He hurries out to secure his seat in the carriage.* SARAH *follows him).*

CUSINS: *(moodily walking across to* LADY BRITOMART'S *writing table).* Why are we two coming to this Works Department of Hell? that is what I ask myself.

520

BARBARA: I have always thought of it as a sort of pit where lost creatures with blackened faces stirred up smoky fires and were driven and tormented by my father. Is it like that, dad?

UNDERSHAFT: *(scandalized).* My dear! It is a spotlessly clean and beautiful hillside town.

CUSINS: With a Methodist chapel? Oh do say theres a Methodist chapel.

530

UNDERSHAFT: There are two: a Primitive one and a sophisticated one. There is even an Ethical Society; but it is not much patronized, as my men are all strongly religious. In the High Explosives Sheds they object to the presence of Agnostics as unsafe.

CUSINS: And yet they dont object to you!

BARBARA: Do they obey all your orders?

UNDERSHAFT: I never give them any orders. When I speak to one of them it is 'Well, Jones, is the baby doing well? and has Mrs Jones made a good recovery?' 'Nicely, thank you, sir.' And thats all.

540

CUSINS: But Jones has to be kept in order. How do you maintain discipline among your men?

UNDERSHAFT: I dont. They do. You see, the one thing Jones wont stand is any rebellion from the man under him, or any assertion of social equality between the wife of the man with 4 shillings a week less than himself, and Mrs Jones! Of course they all rebel against me, theoretically. Practically, every man of them keeps the man just below him in his place. I never meddle with them. I never bully them. I dont even bully Lazarus. I say that certain things are to be done; but I dont order anybody to do them. I dont say, mind you, that there is no ordering about and snubbing and even bullying. The men snub the boys and order them about; the carmen snub the sweepers; the artisans snub the unskilled

550

560

laborers; the foremen drive and bully both the laborers and artisans; the assistant engineers find fault with the foremen; the chief engineers drop on the assistants; the departmental managers worry the chiefs; and the clerks have tall hats and hymnbooks and keep up the social tone by refusing to associate on equal terms with anybody. The result is a colossal profit, which comes to me.

CUSINS: (*revolted*). You really are a—well, what I was saying yesterday.

BARBARA: What was he saying yesterday?

UNDERSHAFT: Never mind, my dear. He thinks I have made you unhappy. Have I?

BARBARA: Do you think I can be happy in this vulgar silly dress? I! who have worn the uniform. Do you understand what you have done to me? Yesterday I had a man's soul in my hand. I set him in the way of life with his face to salvation. But when we took your money he turned back to drunkenness and derision. (*With intense conviction*) I will never forgive you that. If I had a child, and you destroyed its body with your explosives—if you murdered Dolly with your horrible guns—I could forgive you if my forgiveness would open the gates of heaven to you. But to take a human soul from me, and turn it into the soul of a wolf! that is worse than any murder.

UNDERSHAFT: Does my daughter despair so easily? Can you strike a man to the heart and leave no mark on him?

BARBARA: (*her face lighting up*). Oh, you are right: he can never be lost now: where was my faith?

CUSINS: Oh, clever clever devil!

BARBARA: You may be a devil; but God speaks through you sometimes. (*She takes her father's hands and kisses them*). You have given me back my happiness: I feel it deep down now, though my spirit is troubled.

UNDERSHAFT: You have learnt something. That always feels at first as if you had lost something.

BARBARA: Well, take me to the factory of death; and let me learn something more. There must be some truth or other behind all this frightful irony. Come, Dolly. (*She goes out*).

CUSINS: My guardian angel! (*To* UNDERSHAFT) Avaunt! (*He follows* BARBARA).

STEPHEN: (*quietly, at the writing table*). You must not mind Cusins, father. He is a very amiable good fellow; but he is a Greek scholar and naturally a little eccentric.

UNDERSHAFT: Ah, quite so, Thank you, Stephen. Thank you. (*He goes out*).

STEPHEN *smiles patronizingly; buttons his coat responsibly; and crosses the room to the door.* LADY BRITOMART, *dressed for out-of-doors, opens it before he reaches it. She looks round for others; looks at* STEPHEN; *and turns to go without a word.*

STEPHEN: (*embarrassed*). Mother—

LADY BRITOMART: Dont be apologetic, Stephen. And dont forget that you have outgrown your mother. (*She goes out*).

Perivale St. Andrews lies between two Middlesex hills, half climbing the northern one. It is an almost smokeless town of white walls, roofs of narrow green slates or red tiles, tall trees, domes, campaniles, and slender chimney shafts, beautifully situated and beautiful in itself. The best view of it is obtained from the crest of a slope about half a mile to the east, where the high explosives are dealt with. The foundry lies hidden in the depths between, the tops of its chimneys sprouting like huge skittles into the middle distance. Across the crest runs an emplacement of concrete, with a firestep, and a parapet which suggests a fortification, because there is a huge cannon of the obsolete Woolwich Infant pattern peering across it at the town. The cannon is mounted on an experimental gun carriage: possibly the original model of the Undershaft disappearing rampart gun alluded to by Stephen. The firestep being a convenient place to sit, is furnished here and there with straw disc cushions; and at one place there is the additional luxury of a fur rug.

Barbara is standing on the firestep, looking over the parapet towards the town. On her right is the cannon; on her left the end of a shed raised on piles, with a ladder of three or four steps up to the door, which opens outwards and has a little wooden landing at the threshold, with a fire bucket in the corner of the landing. Several dummy soldiers more or less mutilated, with straw protruding from their gashes, have been shoved out of the way under the landing. A few others are nearly upright against the shed; and one has fallen forward and lies, like a grotesque corpse, on the emplacement. The parapet stops short of the shed, leaving a gap which is the beginning of the path down the hill through the foundry to the town. The rug is on the firestep near this gap. Down on the emplacement behind the cannon is a trolley carrying a huge conical bombshell with a red band painted on it. Further to the right is the door of an office, which, like the sheds, is of the lightest possible construction.

———————

CUSINS *arrives by the path from the town.*

BARBARA: Well?

CUSINS: Not a ray of hope. Everything perfect! wonderful! real! It only needs a cathedral to be a heavenly city instead of a hellish one.

630 BARBARA: Have you found out whether they have done anything for old Peter Shirley?

CUSINS: They have found him a job as gatekeeper and timekeeper. He's frightfully miserable. He calls the time-keeping brainwork, and says he isnt used to it; and his gate lodge is so splendid that he's ashamed to use the rooms, and skulks in the scullery.

BARBARA: Poor Peter!

STEPHEN *arrives from town. He carries a fieldglass.*

640 STEPHEN: *(enthusiastically).* Have you two seen the place? Why did you leave us?

CUSINS: I wanted to see everything I was not intended to see; and Barbara wanted to make the men talk.

STEPHEN: Have you found anything discreditable?

CUSINS: No. They call him Dandy Andy and are proud of his being a cunning old rascal; but it's all horribly, frightfully, immorally, unanswerably perfect.

650 SARAH *arrives.*

SARAH: Heavens! what a place! *(She crosses to the trolley).* Did you see the nursing home!? *(She sits down on the shell).*

STEPHEN: Did you see the libraries and schools!?

SARAH: Did you see the ball room and the banqueting chamber in the Town Hall!?

STEPHEN: Have you gone into the insurance fund, the pension fund, the building society, the various applications of cooperation!?

660 UNDERSHAFT *comes from the office, with a sheaf of telegrams in his hand.*

UNDERSHAFT: Well, have you seen everything? I'm sorry I was called away. *(Indicating the telegrams)* Good news from Manchuria.

STEPHEN: Another Japanese victory?

UNDERSHAFT: Oh, I dont know. Which side wins does not concern us here. No: the good news is that the aerial battleship is a tremendous success. At the first trial it has wiped out a fort with three hundred soldiers in it.   670

CUSINS: *(from the platform).* Dummy soldiers?

UNDERSHAFT: *(striding across to* STEPHEN *and kicking the prostrate dummy brutally out of his way).* No: the real thing.

CUSINS *and* BARBARA *exchange glances. Then* CUSINS *sits on the step and buries his face in his hands.* BARBARA *gravely lays her hand on his shoulder. He looks up at her in whimsical desperation.*

UNDERSHAFT: Well, Stephen, what do you think of the place?   680

STEPHEN: Oh, magnificent. A perfect triumph of modern industry. Frankly, my dear father, I have been a fool: I had no idea of what it all meant: of the wonderful forethought, the power of organization, the administrative capacity, the financial genius, the colossal capital it represents. I have been repeating to myself as I came through your streets 'Peace hath her victories no less renowned than War.' I have only one misgiving about it all.   690

UNDERSHAFT: Out with it.

STEPHEN: Well, I cannot help thinking that all this provision for every want of your workmen may sap their independence and weaken their sense of responsibility. And greatly as we enjoyed our tea at that splendid restaurant—how they gave us all that luxury and cake and jam and cream for threepence I really cannot imagine!—still you must remember that restaurants break up home life. Look at the continent, for instance! Are   700 you sure so much pampering is really good for the men's characters?

UNDERSHAFT: Well you see, my dear boy, when you are organizing civilization you have to make up your mind whether trouble and anxiety are good things or not. If you decide that they are, then, I take it, you simply dont organize civilization; and there you are, with trouble and

710 anxiety enough to make us all angels! But if you decide the other way, you may as well go through with it. However, Stephen, our characters are safe here. A sufficient dose of anxiety is always provided by the fact that we may be blown to smithereens at any moment.

SARAH: By the way, papa, where do you make the explosives?

UNDERSHAFT: In separate little sheds, like that one. When one of them blows up, it costs very little; and only the people quite close to it are killed.

720 STEPHEN, *who is quite close to it, looks at it rather scaredly, and moves away quickly to the cannon. At the same moment the door of the shed is thrown abruptly open; and a foreman in overalls and list slippers comes out on the little landing and holds the door for* LOMAX, *who appears in the doorway.*

LOMAX: *(with studied coolness).* My good fellow: you neednt get into a state of nerves. Nothing's going to happen to you; and I suppose it wouldnt be the end of the world if anything did. A little 730 bit of British pluck is what you want, old chap. *(He descends and strolls across to* SARAH*).*

UNDERSHAFT: *(to the foreman).* Anything wrong, Bilton?

BILTON: *(with ironic calm).* Gentleman walked into the high explosives shed and lit a cigaret, sir: thats all.

UNDERSHAFT: Ah, quite so. *(Going over to* LOMAX*)* Do you happen to remember what you did with the match?

740 LOMAX: Oh come! I'm not a fool. I took jolly good care to blow it out before I chucked it away.

BILTON: The top of it was red hot inside, sir.

LOMAX: Well, suppose it was! I didn't chuck it into any of your messes.

UNDERSHAFT: Think no more of it, Mr. Lomax. By the way, would you mind lending me your matches.

LOMAX: *(offering his box).* Certainly

UNDERSHAFT: Thanks. *(He pockets the matches).*

750 LOMAX: *(lecturing to the company generally).* You know, these high explosives dont go off like gunpowder, except when theyre in a gun. When theyre spread loose, you can put a match to them without the least risk: they just burn quietly like a bit of paper. *(Warming to the scientific interest of the subject)* Did you know that, Undershaft? Have you ever tried?

UNDERSHAFT: Not on a large scale, Mr Lomax. Bilton will give you a sample of gun cotton when you are leaving if you ask him. You can experi- 760 ment with it at home. *(BILTON looks puzzled).*

SARAH: Bilton will do nothing of the sort, papa. I suppose it's your business to blow up the Russians and Japs; but you might really stop short of blowing up poor Cholly. *(BILTON gives it up and retires into the shed).*

LOMAX: My ownest, there is no danger. *(He sits beside her on the shell).*

LADY BRITOMART *arrives from the town with a bouquet.* 770

LADY BRITOMART: *(impetuously).* Andrew: you shouldnt have let me see this place.

UNDERSHAFT: Why, my dear?

LADY BRITOMART: Never mind why: you shouldn't have: thats all. To think of all that *(indicating the town)* being yours! and that you have kept it to yourself all these years!

UNDERSHAFT: It does not belong to me. I belong to it. It is the Undershaft inheritance.

LADY BRITOMART: It is not. Your ridiculous cannons 780 and that noisy banging foundry may be the Undershaft inheritance; but all that plate and linen, all that furniture and those houses and orchards and gardens belong to us. They belong to me: they are not a man's business. I wont give them up. You must be out of your senses to throw them all away; and if you persist in such folly, I will call in a doctor.

UNDERSHAFT: *(stooping to smell the bouquet).* Where did you get the flowers, my dear? 790

LADY BRITOMART: Your men presented them to me in your William Morris Labor Church.

CUSINS: Oh! It needed only that. A Labor Church! *(he mounts the firestep distractedly, and leans with his elbows on the parapet, turning his back to them).*

LADY BRITOMART: Yes, with Morris's words in mosaic letters ten feet high round the dome. NO MAN IS GOOD ENOUGH TO BE ANOTHER MAN'S MASTER. The cynicism of it!

UNDERSHAFT: It shocked the men at first, I am 800 afraid. But now they take no more notice of it than of the ten commandments in church.

LADY BRITOMART: Andrew: you are trying to put me off the subject of the inheritance by profane jokes. Well, you shant. I dont ask it any longer for Stephen: he has inherited far too much of your perversity to be fit for it. But Barbara has rights as well as Stephen. Why should not Adolphus succeed to the inheritance? I could manage the town for him; and he can look after the cannons, if thy are really necessary.

UNDERSHAFT: I should ask nothing better if Aldolphus were a foundling. He is exactly the sort of new blood that is wanted in English business. But he's not a foundling; and theres an end of it. (*He makes for the office door*).

CUSINS: (*turning to them*). Not quite. (*They all turn and stare at him*). I think—Mind! I am not committing myself in any way as to my future course —but I think the foundling difficulty can be got over. (*He jumps down to the emplacement*).

UNDERSHAFT: (*coming back to him*). What do you mean?

SARAH:
LADY BRITOMART: } Confession!
BARBARA:
STEPHEN:
LOMAX: Oh I say!

CUSINS: Yes, a confession. Listen, all. Until I met Barbara I thought myself in the main an honorable, truthful man, because I wanted the approval of my conscience more than I wanted anything else. But the moment I saw Barbara, I wanted her far more than the approval of my conscience.

LADY BRITOMART: Adolphus!

CUSINS: It is true. You accused me yourself, Lady Brit, of joining the Army to worship Barbara; and so I did. She bought my soul like a flower at a street corner; but she bought it for herself.

UNDERSHAFT: What! Not for Dionysos or another?

CUSINS: Dionysos and all the others are in herself. I adored what was divine in her, and was therefore a true worshipper. But I was romantic about her too. I thought she was a woman of the people, and that a marriage with a professor of Greek would be far beyond the wildest social ambitions of her rank.

LADY BRITOMART: Adolphus!!

LOMAX: Oh I say!!!

CUSINS: When I learnt the horrible truth—

LADY BRITOMART: What do you mean by the horrible truth, pray?

CUSINS: That she was enormously rich; that her grandfather was an earl; that her father was the Prince of Darkness—

UNDERSHAFT: Chut!

CUSINS: —and that I was only an adventurer trying to catch a rich wife, then I stooped to deceive her about my birth.

BARBARA: (*rising*). Dolly!

LADY BRITOMART: Your birth! Now Adolphus, dont dare to make up a wicked story for the sake of these wretched cannons. Remember: I have seen photographs of your parents; and the Agent General for South Western Australia knows them personally and has assured me that they are most respectable married people.

CUSINS: So they are in Australia; but here they are outcasts. Their marriage is legal in Australia, but not in England. My mother is my father's deceased wife's sister; and in this island I am consequently a foundling. (*Sensation*).

BARBARA: Silly! (*She climbs to the cannon, and leans, listening, in the angle it makes with the parapet*).

CUSINS: Is the subterfuge good enough, Machiavelli?

UNDERSHAFT: (*thoughtfully*). Biddy: this may be a way out of the difficulty.

LADY BRITOMART: Stuff! A man cant make cannons any better for being his own cousin instead of his proper self (*she sits down on the rug with a bounce that expresses her downright contempt for their casuistry*).

UNDERSHAFT: (*to* CUSINS). You are an educated man. That is against the tradition.

CUSINS: Once in ten thousand times it happens that the schoolboy is a born master of what they try to teach him. Greek has not destroyed my mind: it has nourished it. Besides, I did not learn it at an English public school.

UNDERSHAFT: Hm! Well, I cannot afford to be too particular: you have cornered the foundling market. Let it pass. You are eligible, Euripides: you are eligible.

BARBARA: Dolly: yesterday morning, when Stephen told us all about the tradition, you became very silent: and you have been strange and excited ever since. Were you thinking of your birth then?

900 CUSINS: When the finger of Destiny suddenly points at a man in the middle of his breakfast, it makes him thoughtful.

UNDERSHAFT: Aha! You have had your eye on the business, my young friend, have you?

CUSINS: Take care! There is an abyss of moral horror between me and your accursed aerial battleships.

UNDERSHAFT: Never mind the abyss for the present. Let us settle the practical details and leave your

910 final decision open. You know that you will have to change your name. Do you object to that?

CUSINS: Would any man named Adolphus—any man called Dolly!—object to be called something else?

UNDERSHAFT: Good. Now, as to money! I propose to treat you handsomely from the beginning. You shall start at a thousand a year.

CUSINS: *(with sudden heat, his spectacles twinkling with mischief)*. A thousand! You dare offer a miserable

920 thousand to the son-in-law of a millionaire! No, by Heavens, Machiavelli! you shall not cheat me. You cannot do without me; and I can do without you. I must have two thousand five hundred a year for two years. At the end of that time, if I am a failure, I go. But if I am a success, and stay on, you must give me the other five thousand.

UNDERSHAFT: What other five thousand?

CUSINS: To make the two years up to five thousand

930 a year. The two thousand five hundred is only half pay in case I should turn out a failure. The third year I must have ten per cent on the profits.

UNDERSHAFT: *(taken aback)*. Ten per cent! Why, man, do you know what my profits are?

CUSINS: Enormous, I hope: otherwise I shall require twenty-five per cent.

UNDERSHAFT: But Mr. Cusins, this is a serious matter of business. You are not bringing any capital into the concern.

940 CUSINS: What! no capital! Is my mastery of Greek no capital? Is my access to the subtlest thought, the loftiest poetry yet attained by humanity, no capital? My character! my intellect! my life! my career! what Barbara calls my soul! are these

no capital? Say another word; and I double my salary.

UNDERSHAFT: Be reasonable—

CUSINS: *(peremptorily)*. Mr. Undershaft: you have my terms. Take them or leave them.

UNDERSHAFT: *(recovering himself)*. Very well. I note 950 your terms; and I offer you half.

CUSINS: *(disgusted)*. Half!

UNDERSHAFT: *(firmly)*. Half.

CUSINS: You call yourself a gentleman; and you offer me half!!

UNDERSHAFT: I do not call myself a gentleman; but I offer you half.

CUSINS: This to your future partner! your successor! your son-in-law!

BARBARA: You are selling your own soul, Dolly, 960 not mine. Leave me out of the bargain, please.

UNDERSHAFT: Come! I will go a step further for Barbara's sake. I will give you three fifths; but that is my last word.

CUSINS: Done!

LOMAX: Done in the eye! Why, *I* get only eight hundred, you know.

CUSINS: By the way, Mac, I am a classical scholar, not an arithmetical one. Is three fifths more than half or less? 970

UNDERSHAFT: More, of course.

CUSINS: I would have taken two hundred and fifty. How you can succeed in business when you are willing to pay all that money to a University don who is obviously not worth a junior clerk's wages!—well! What will Lazarus say?

UNDERSHAFT: Lazarus is a gentle romantic Jew who cares for nothing but string quartets and stalls at fashionable theatres. He will be blamed for your rapacity in money matters, poor fellow! 980 as he has hitherto been blamed for mine. You are a shark of the first order, Euripides. So much the better for the firm!

BARBARA: Is the bargain closed, Dolly? Does your soul belong to him now?

CUSINS: No: the price is settled: that is all. The real tug of war is still to come. What about the moral question?

LADY BRITOMART: There is no moral question in the matter at all, Adolphus. You must simply 990 sell cannons and weapons to people whose cause is right and just, and refuse them to foreigners and criminals.

UNDERSHAFT: (*determinedly*). No: none of that. You must keep the true faith of an Armorer, or you dont come in here.

CUSINS: What on earth is the true faith of an Armorer?

UNDERSHAFT: To give arms to all men who offer
1000   an honest price for them, without respect of persons or principles: to aristocrat and republican, to Nihilist and Tsar, to Capitalist and Socialist, to Protestant and Catholic, to burglar and policeman, to black man, white man and yellow man, to all sorts and conditions, all nationalities, all faiths, all follies, all causes and all crimes. The first Undershaft wrote up in his shop IF GOD GAVE THE HAND, LET NOT MAN WITHHOLD THE SWORD. The second wrote up ALL HAVE THE
1010   RIGHT TO FIGHT: NONE HAVE THE RIGHT TO JUDGE. The third wrote up to Man THE WEAPON: TO HEAVEN THE VICTORY. The fourth had no literary turn; so he did not write up anything; but he sold cannons to Napoleon under the nose of George the Third. The fifth wrote up PEACE SHALL NOT PREVAIL SAVE WITH A SWORD IN HER HAND. The sixth, my master, was the best of all. He wrote up NOTHING IS EVER DONE IN THIS WORLD UNTIL MEN ARE PREPARED TO KILL
1020   ONE ANOTHER IF IT IS NOT DONE. After that, there was nothing left for the seventh to say. So he wrote up, simply, UNASHAMED.

CUSINS: My good Machiavelli, I shall certainly write something up on the wall; only, as I shall write it in Greek, you wont be able to read it. But as to your Armorer's faith, if I take my neck out of the noose of my own morality I am not going to put it into the noose of yours. I shall sell cannons to whom I please and refuse them
1030   to whom I please. So there!

UNDERSHAFT: From the moment when you become Andrew Undershaft, you will never do as you please again. Dont come here lusting for power, young man.

CUSINS: If power were my aim I should not come here for it. You have no power.

UNDERSHAFT: None of my own, certainly.

CUSINS: I have more power than you, more will. You do not drive this place: it drives you. And
1040   what drives the place?

UNDERSHAFT: (*enigmatically*). A will of which I am a part.

BARBARA: (*startled*). Father! Do you know what you are saying; or are you laying a snare for my soul?

CUSINS: Dont listen to his metaphysics, Barbara. The place is driven by the most rascally part of society, the money hunters, the pleasure hunters, the military promotion hunters; and he is their slave.   1050

UNDERSHAFT: Not necessarily. Remember the Armorer's Faith. I will take an order from a good man as cheerfully as from a bad one. If you good people prefer preaching and shirking to buying my weapons and fighting the rascals, dont blame me. I can make cannons: I cannot make courage and conviction. Bah! you tire me, Euripides, with your morality mongering. Ask Barbara: she understands. (*He suddenly reaches up and takes* BARBARA's *hands, looking powerfully into*   1060 *her eyes*) Tell him, my love, what power really means.

BARBARA: (*hypnotized*). Before I joined the Salvation Army, I was in my own power; and the consequence was that I never knew what to do with myself. When I joined it, I had not time enough for all the things I had to do.

UNDERSHAFT: (*approvingly*). Just so. And why was that, do you suppose?

BARBARA: Yesterday I should have said, because   1070 I was in the power of God. (*She resumes her self-possession, withdrawing her hands from his with a power equal to his own*). But you came and shewed me that I was in the power of Bodger and Undershaft. Today I feel—oh! how can I put it into words? Sarah: do you remember the earthquake at Cannes, when we were little children?—how little the surprise of the first shock mattered compared to the dread and horror of waiting for the second? That is how I feel in   1080 this place today. I stood on the rock I thought eternal; and without a word of warning it reeled and crumbled under me. I was safe with an infinite wisdom watching me, an army marching to Salvation with me; and in a moment, at a stroke of your pen in a cheque book, I stood alone; and the heavens were empty. That was the first shock of the earthquake: I am waiting for the second.

UNDERSHAFT: Come, come, my daughter! dont make too much of your little tinpot tragedy. What do we do here when we spend years of work and thought and thousands of pounds of solid cash on a new gun or an aerial battleship that turns out just a hairsbreadth wrong after all? Scrap it. Scrap it without wasting another hour or another pound on it. Well, you have made for yourself something that you call a morality or a religion or what not. It doesnt fit the facts. Well, scrap it. Scrap it and get one that does fit. That is what is wrong with the world at present. It scraps its obsolete steam engines and dynamos; but it wont scrap its old prejudices and its old moralities and its old religions and its old political constitutions. Whats the result? In machinery it does very well; but in morals and religion and politics it is working at a loss that brings it nearer bankruptcy every year. Dont persist in that folly. If your old religion broke down yesterday, get a newer and a better one for tomorrow.

BARBARA: Oh how gladly I would take a better one to my soul! But you offer me a worse one. *(Turning on him with sudden vehemence)*. Justify yourself: shew me some light through the darkness of this dreadful place, with its beautifully clean workshops, and respectable workmen, and model homes.

UNDERSHAFT: Cleanliness and respectability do not need justification, Barbara: they justify themselves. I see no darkness here, no dreadfulness. In your Salvation shelter I saw poverty, misery, cold and hunger. You gave them bread and treacle and dreams of heaven. I give from thirty shillings a week to twelve thousand a year. They find their own dreams; but I look after the drainage.

BARBARA: And their souls?

UNDERSHAFT: I save their souls just as I saved yours.

BARBARA: *(revolted)*. You saved my soul! What do you mean?

UNDERSHAFT: I fed you and clothed you and housed you. I took care that you should have money enough to live handsomely—more than enough; so that you could be wasteful, careless, generous. That saved your soul from the seven deadly sins!

BARBARA: *(bewildered)*. The seven deadly sins!

UNDERSHAFT: Yes, the deadly seven. *(Counting on his fingers)* Food, clothing, firing, rent, taxes, respectability and children. Nothing can lift those seven millstones from Man's neck but money; and the spirit cannot soar until the mill stones are lifted. I lifted them from your spirit. I enabled Barbara to become Major Barbara; and I saved her from the crime of poverty.

CUSINS: Do you call poverty a crime?

UNDERSHAFT: The worst of crimes. All the other crimes are virtues beside it: all the other dishonors are chivalry itself by comparison. Poverty blights whole cities; spreads horrible pestilences; strikes dead the very souls of all who come within sight, sound, or smell of it. What you call crime is nothing: a murder here and a theft there, a blow now and a curse then: what do they matter? they are only the accidents and illnesses of life: there are not fifty genuine professional criminals in London. But there are millions of poor people, abject people, dirty people, ill fed, ill clothed people. They poison us morally and physically: they kill the happiness of society: they force us to do away with our own liberties and to organize unnatural cruelties for fear they should rise against us and drag us down into their abyss. Only fools fear crime: we all fear poverty. Pah! *(turning on BARBARA)* you talk of your half-saved ruffian in West Ham: you accuse me of dragging his soul back to perdition. Well, bring him to me here; and I will drag his soul back again to salvation for you. Not by words and dreams; but by thirtyeight shillings a week, a sound house in a handsome street, and a permanent job. In three weeks he will have a fancy waistcoat; in three months a tall hat and a chapel sitting; before the end of the year he will shake hands with a duchess at a Primrose League meeting, and join the Conservative Party.

BARBARA: And will he be the better for that?

UNDERSHAFT: You know he will. Dont be a hypocrite, Barbara. He will be better fed, better housed, better clothed, better behaved; and his children will be pounds heavier and bigger. That will be better than an American cloth mattress in a shelter, chopping firewood, eating bread and treacle, and being forced to kneel down from time to time to thank heaven for it: knee drill, I think you call it. It is cheap work converting starving men with a Bible in one hand and a slice of bread in the other. I will undertake to convert West Ham to Mahometanism on the same terms. Try your hand on my men: their souls are hungry because their bodies are full.

BARBARA: And leave the east end to starve?

UNDERSHAFT: (*his energetic tone dropping into one of bitter and brooding remembrance*). I was an east ender. I moralized and starved until one day I swore that I would be a full-fed free man at all costs; that nothing should stop me except a bullet, neither reason nor morals nor the lives of other men. I said 'Thou shalt starve ere I starve'; and with that word I became free and great. I was a dangerous man until I had my will: now I am a useful, beneficent, kindly person. That is the history of most self-made millionaires, I fancy. When it is the history of every Englishman we shall have an England worth living in.

LADY BRITOMART: Stop making speeches, Andrew. This is not the place for them.

UNDERSHAFT: (*punctured*). My dear: I have no other means of conveying my ideas.

LADY BRITOMART: Your ideas are nonsense. You got on because you were selfish and unscrupulous.

UNDERSHAFT: Not at all. I had the strongest scruples about poverty and starvation. Your moralists are quite unscrupulous about both: they make virtues of them. I had rather be a thief than a pauper. I had rather be a murderer than a slave. I dont want to be either; but if you force the alternative on me, then, by Heaven, I'll chose the braver and more moral one. I hate poverty and slavery worse than any other crimes whatsoever. And let me tell you this. Poverty and slavery have stood up for centuries to your sermons and leading articles: they will not stand up to my machine guns. Dont preach at them: dont reason with them. Kill them.

BARBARA: Killing. Is that your remedy for everything?

UNDERSHAFT: It is the final test of conviction, the only lever strong enough to overturn a social system, the only way of saying Must. Let six hundred and seventy fools loose in the streets; and three policemen can scatter them. But huddle them together in a certain house in Westminster; and let them go through certain ceremonies and call themselves certain names until at last they get the courage to kill; and your six hundred and seventy fools become a government. Your pious mob fills up ballot papers and imagines it is governing its masters; but the ballot paper that really governs is the paper that has a bullet wrapped up in it.

CUSINS: That is perhaps why, like most intelligent people, I never vote.

UNDERSHAFT: Vote! Bah! When you vote, you only change the names of the cabinet. When you shoot, you pull down governments, inaugurate new epochs, abolish old orders and set up new. Is that historically true, Mr. Learned Man, or is it not?

CUSINS: It is historically true. I loathe having to admit it. I repudiate your sentiments. I abhor your nature. I defy you in every possible way. Still, it is true. But it ought not to be true.

UNDERSHAFT: Ought! ought! ought! ought! ought! Are you going to spend your life saying ought, like the rest of our moralists? Turn your oughts into shalls, man. Come and make explosives with me. Whatever can blow men up can blow society up. The history of the world is the history of those who had courage enough to embrace this truth. Have you the courage to embrace it, Barbara?

LADY BRITOMART: Barbara: I positively forbid you to listen to your father's abominable wickedness. And you, Adolphus, ought to know better than to go about saying that wrong things are true. What does it matter whether they are true if they are wrong?

UNDERSHAFT: What does it matter whether they are wrong if they are true?

LADY BRITOMART: (*rising*). Children: come home instantly. Andrew: I am exceedingly sorry I allowed you to call on us. You are wickeder than ever. Come at once.

BARBARA: (*shaking her head*). It's no use running away from wicked people, mamma.

LADY BRITOMART: It is every use. It shews your disapprobation of them.

BARBARA: It does not save them.

LADY BRITOMART: I can see that you are going to disobey me. Sarah: are you coming home or are you not?

SARAH: I daresay it's very wicked of papa to make

cannons; but I dont think I shall cut him on that account.

LOMAX: (*pouring oil on the troubled waters*). The fact is, you know, there is a certain amount of tosh about this notion of wickedness. It doesnt work. You must look at facts. Not that I would say a word in favor of anything wrong; but then, you see, all sorts of chaps are always doing all sorts of thing; and we have to fit them in somehow, dont you know. What I mean is that you cant go cutting everybody; and thats about what it comes to. (*Their rapt attention to his eloquence makes him nervous*). Perhaps I dont make myself clear.

LADY BRITOMART: You are lucidity itself, Charles. Because Andrew is successful and has plenty of money to give to Sarah, you will flatter him and encourage him in his wickedness.

LOMAX: (*unruffled*). Well, where the carcase is, there will the eagles be gathered, dont you know. (*To* UNDERSHAFT) Eh? What?

UNDERSHAFT: Precisely. By the way, may I call you Charles?

LOMAX: Delighted. Cholly is the usual ticket.

UNDERSHAFT: (*to* LADY BRITOMART). Biddy—

LADY BRITOMART: (*violently*). Dont dare call me Biddy. Charles Lomax: you are a fool. Adolphus Cusins: you are a Jesuit. Stephen: you are a prig. Barbara: you are a lunatic. Andrew: you are a vulgar tradesman. Now you all know my opinion; and my conscience is clear, at all events (*she sits down with a vehemence that the rug fortunately softens*).

UNDERSHAFT: My dear: you are the incarnation of morality. (*She snorts*). Your conscience is clear and your duty done when you have called everybody names. Come, Euripides! it is getting late; and we all want to go home. Make up your mind.

CUSINS: Understand this, you old demon—

LADY BRITOMART: Adolphus!

UNDERSHAFT: Let him alone, Biddy. Proceed, Euripides.

CUSINS: You have me in a horrible dilemma. I want Barbara.

UNDERSHAFT: Like all young men, you greatly exaggerate the difference between one young woman and another.

BARBARA: Quite true, Dolly.

CUSINS: I also want to avoid being a rascal.

UNDERSHAFT: (*with biting contempt*). You lust for personal righteousness, for self-approval, for what you call a good conscience, for what Barbara calls salvation, for what I call patronizing people who are not so lucky as yourself.

CUSINS: I do not: all the poet in me recoils from being a good man. But there are things in me that I must reckon with. Pity—

UNDERSHAFT: Pity! The scavenger of misery.

CUSINS: Well, love.

UNDERSHAFT: I know. You love the needy and the outcast: you love the oppressed races, the negro, the Indian ryot, the underdog everywhere. Do you love the Japanese? Do you love the French? Do you love the English?

CUSINS: No. Every true Englishman detests the English. We are the wickedest nation on earth; and our success is a moral horror.

UNDERSHAFT: That is what comes of your gospel of love, is it?

CUSINS: May I not love even my father-in-law?

UNDERSHAFT: Who wants your love, man? By what right do you take the liberty of offering it to me? I will have your due heed and respect, or I will kill you. But your love! Damn your impertinence!

CUSINS: (*grinning*). I may not be able to control my affections, Mac.

UNDERSHAFT: You are fencing, Euripides. You are weakening: your grip is slipping. Come! Try your last weapon. Pity and love have broken in your hand: forgiveness is still left.

CUSINS: No: forgiveness is a beggar's refuge. I am with you there: we must pay our debts.

UNDERSHAFT: Well said. Come! you will suit me. Remember the words of Plato.

CUSINS: (*starting*). Plato! You dare quote Plato to me!

UNDERSHAFT: Plato says, my friend, that society cannot be saved until either the Professors of Greek take to making gunpowder, or else the makers of gunpowder become Professors of Greek.

CUSINS: Oh, tempter, cunning tempter!

UNDERSHAFT: Come! choose, man, choose.

CUSINS: But perhaps Barbara will not marry me if I make the wrong choice.

BARBARA: Perhaps not.

CUSINS: (*desperately perplexed*). You hear!

BARBARA: Father: do you love nobody?

UNDERSHAFT: I love my best friend.

LADY BRITOMART: And who is that, pray?

UNDERSHAFT: My bravest enemy. That is the man who keeps me up to the mark.

1380 CUSINS: You know, the creature is really a sort of poet in his way. Suppose he is a great man, after all!

UNDERSHAFT: Suppose you stop talking and make up your mind, my young friend.

CUSINS: But you are driving me against my nature. I hate war.

UNDERSHAFT: Hatred is the coward's revenge for being intimidated. Dare you make war on war? Here are the means: my friend Mr. Lomax is sitting on them.

1390 LOMAX: (springing up). Oh I say! You dont mean that this thing is loaded, do you? My ownest: come off it.

SARAH: (sitting placidly on the shell). If I am to be blown up, the more thoroughly it is done the better. Dont fuss, Cholly.

LOMAX: (to UNDERSHAFT strongly remonstrant). Your own daughter, you know!

UNDERSHAFT: So I see. (To CUSINS). Well, my friend, may we expect you here at six tomorrow morning?

1400 CUSINS: (firmly). Not on any account. I will see the whole establishment blown up with its own dynamite before I will get up at five. My hours are healthy, rational hours: eleven to five.

UNDERSHAFT: Come when you please: before a week you will come at six and stay until I turn you out for the sake of your health. (Calling) Bilton! (He turns to LADY BRITOMART, who rises).
1410 My dear: let us leave these two young people to themselves for a moment. (BILTON comes from the shed). I am going to take you through the gun cotton shed.

BILTON: (baring the way). You cant take anything explosive in here, sir.

LADY BRITOMART: What do you mean? Are you alluding to me?

BILTON: (unmoved). No, maam. Mr. Undershaft has the other gentleman's matches in his pocket.

LADY BRITOMART: (abruptly). Oh! I beg your pardon. (She goes into the shed).

1420 UNDERSHAFT: Quite right, Bilton, quite right: here you are. (He gives BILTON the box of matches). Come,

Stephen. Come, Charles. Bring Sarah. (He passes into the shed).

BILTON opens the box and deliberately drops the matches into the fire-bucket.

LOMAX: Oh! I say (BILTON stolidly hands him the empty box). Infernal nonsense! Pure scientific ignorance! (He goes in).

SARAH: Am I all right, Bilton?

BILTON: You'll have to put on list slippers, 1430 miss: that's all. Weve got em inside. (She goes in).

STEPHEN: (very seriously to CUSINS). Dolly, old fellow, think. Think before you decide. Do you feel that you are a sufficiently practical man? It is a huge undertaking, an enormous responsibility. All this mass of business will be Greek to you.

CUSINS: Oh, I think it will be much less difficult than Greek.

STEPHEN: Well, I just want to say this before I 1440 leave you to yourselves. Dont let anything I have said about right and wrong prejudice you against this great chance in life. I have satisfied myself that the business is one of the highest character and a credit to our country. (Emotionally) I am very proud of my father. I—(Unable to proceed, he presses CUSINS' hand and goes hastily into the shed, followed by BILTON). BARBARA and CUSINS, left alone together, look at one another silently.

CUSINS: Barbara: I am going to accept this offer. 1450

BARBARA: I thought you would.

CUSINS: You understand, dont you, that I had to decide without consulting you. If I had thrown the burden of the choice on you, you would sooner or later have despised me for it.

BARBARA: Yes: I did not want you to sell your soul for me any more than for this inheritance.

CUSINS: It is not the sale of my soul that troubles me: I have sold it too often to care about that. I have sold it for a professorship. I have sold 1460 it for an income. I have sold it to pay taxes for hangmen's ropes and unjust wars and things that I abhor. What is all human conduct but the daily and hourly sale of our souls for trifles? What I am now selling it for is neither money nor position nor comfort, but for reality and for power.

BARBARA: You know that you will have no power, and that he has none.

1470 CUSINS: I know. It is not for myself alone. I want to make power for the world.

BARBARA: I want to make power for the world too; but it must be spiritual power.

CUSINS: I think all power is spiritual: these cannons will not go off by themselves. I have tried to make spiritual power by teaching Greek. But the world can never be really touched by a dead language and a dead civilization. The people must have power; and the people cannot have

1480 Greek. Now the power that is made here can be wielded by all men.

BARBARA: Power to burn women's houses down and kill their sons and tear their husbands to pieces.

CUSINS: You cannot have power for good without having power for evil too. Even mother's milk nourishes murderers as well as heroes. This power which only tears men's bodies to pieces has never been so horribly abused as the intellect-

1490 ual power, the imaginative power, the poetic, re-ligious power that can enslave men's souls. As a teacher of Greek I gave the intellectual man weapons against the common man. I now want to arm them against the lawyers, the doctors, the priests, the literary men, the professors, the artists, and the politicians, who, once in author-ity, are more disastrous and tyrannical than all the fools, rascals, and impostors. I want a power simple enough for common men to use, yet

1500 strong enough to force the intellectual oligarchy to use its genius for the general good.

BARBARA: Is there no higher power than that (pointing to the shell)?

CUSINS: Yes; but that power can destroy the higher powers just as a tiger can destroy a man: therefore Man must master that power first. I admitted this when the Turks and Greeks were last at war. My best pupil went out to fight for Hellas. My parting gift to him was not a copy of Plato's

1510 Republic, but a revolver and a hundred Undershaft cartridges. The blood of every Turk he shot—if he shot any—is on my head as well as on Undershaft's. That act committed me to this place for ever. Your father's challenge has beaten me. Dare I make war on war? I must. I will. And now, is it all over between us?

BARBARA: (touched by his evident dread of her answer). Silly baby Dolly! How could it be!

CUSINS: (overjoyed). Then you—you—you— Oh for my drum! (He flourishes imaginary drumsticks). 1520

BARBARA: (angered by his levity). Take care, Dolly, take care. Oh, if only I could get away from you and from father and from it all! if I could have the wings of a dove and fly away to heaven!

CUSINS: And leave me!

BARBARA: Yes, you, and all the other naughty mis-chievous children of men. But I cant. I was happy in the Salvation Army for a moment. I escaped from the world into a paradise of enthusiasm and prayer and soul saving; but the moment our 1530 money ran short, it all came back to Bodger: it was he who saved our people: he and the Prince of Darkness, my papa. Undershaft and Bodger: their hands stretch everywhere: when we feed a starving fellow creature, it is with their bread, because there is no other bread; when we tend the sick, it is in the hospitals they endow; if we turn from the churches they build, we must kneel on the stones of the streets they pave. As long as that lasts, there is no getting away from 1540 them. Turning our backs on Bodger and Undershaft is turning our backs on life.

CUSINS: I thought you were determined to turn your back on the wicked side of life.

BARBARA: There is no wicked side: life is all one. And I never wanted to shirk my share in what-ever evil must be endured, whether it be sin or suffering. I wish I could cure you of middle-class ideas, Dolly.

CUSINS: (gasping). Middle cl—! A snub! A social 1550 snub to me! from the daughter of a foundling!

BARBARA: That is why I have no class, Dolly: I come straight out of the heart of the whole people. If I were middle-class I should turn my back on my father's business; and we should both live in an artistic drawing room, with you reading the reviews in one corner, and I in the other at the piano, playing Schumann: both very superior persons, and neither of us a bit of use. Sooner than that, I would sweep out the guncot- 1560 ton shed, or be one of Bodger's barmaids. Do you know what would have happened if you had refused papa's offer?

CUSINS: I wonder!

BARBARA: I should have given you up and married the man who accepted it. After all, my dear old mother has more sense than any of you.

I felt like her when I saw this place—felt that I must have it—that never, never, never could
1570   I let it go; only she thought it was the houses and the kitchen ranges and the linen and china, when it was really all the human souls to be saved: not weak souls in starved bodies, sobbing with gratitude for a scrap of bread and treacle, but fullfed, quarrelsome, snobbish, uppish creatures, all standing on their little rights and dignities, and thinking that my father ought to be greatly obliged to them for making so much money for him—and so he ought. That is where
1580   salvation is really wanted. My father shall never throw it in my teeth again that my converts were bribed with bread. *(She is transfigured)*. I have got rid of the bribe of bread. I have got rid of the bribe of heaven. Let God's work be done for its own sake: the work he had to create us to do because it cannot be done except by living men and women. When I die, let him be in my debt, not I in his; and let me forgive him as becomes a woman of my rank.

1590 CUSINS: Then the way of life lies through the factory of death?

BARBARA: Yes, through the raising of hell to heaven and of man to God, through the unveiling of an eternal light in the Valley of The Shadow. *(Seizing him with both hands)* Oh, did you think my courage would never come back? did you believe that I was a deserter? that I, who have stood in the streets, and taken my people to my heart, and talked of the holiest and greatest things
1600   with them, could ever turn back and chatter foolishly to fashionable people about nothing in a drawing room? Never, never, never, never:

Major Barbara will die with the colors. Oh! and I have my dear little Dolly boy still; and he has found me my place and my work. Glory Hallelujah! *(She kisses him)*.

CUSINS: My dearest: consider my delicate health. I cannot stand as much happiness as you can.

BARBARA: Yes: it is not easy work being in love with me, is it? But its good for you. *(She runs to the* 1610 *shed, and calls, childlike)* Mamma! Mamma! (BILTON *comes out of the shed, followed by* UNDERSHAFT). I want Mamma.

UNDERSHAFT: She is taking off her list slippers, dear. *(He passes on to* CUSINS). Well? What does she say?

CUSINS: She has gone right up into the skies.

LADY BRITOMART: *(coming from the shed and stopping on the steps, obstructing* SARAH, *who follows with* LOMAX. BARBARA *clutches like a baby at her mother's* 1620 *skirt)*. Barbara: when will you learn to be independent and to act and think for yourself? I know as well as possible what that cry of 'Mamma, Mamma,' means. Always running to me!

SARAH: *(touching* LADY BRITOMART'S *ribs with her finger tips and imitating a bicycle born)*. Pip! pip!

LADY BRITOMART: *(highly indignant)*. How dare you say Pip! pip! to me, Sarah? You are both very naughty children. What do you want, Barbara? 1630

BARBARA: I want a house in the village to live in with Dolly. *(Dragging at the skirt)* Come and tell me which one to take.

UNDERSHAFT: *(to* CUSINS). Six o'clock tomorrow morning, Euripides.

THE END

LETTERS TO LOUIS CALVERT ON PLAYING UNDERSHAFT

by Bernard Shaw

Shaw was not content to write his plays and let it go at that. He was forever writing prefaces, comments, and advice such as the following letters and prefatory note.

From Derry Roscarberry, Ireland, July 23, 1905[1]

Dear Calvert—

Can you play the trombone? If not, I beg you to acquire a smattering of the art during your holidays. I am getting on with the new play scrap by scrap; and the part of the millionaire cannon founder is becoming more and more formidable. Broadbent and Keegan rolled into one, with Mephistopheles thrown in; that is what it is like. Business is Business will be cheap melodrama in comparison, Irving and Tree will fade into third class when Calvert takes the stage as Andrew Undershaft. It will be TREMENDOUS, simply. But there is a great scene at the end of the second act where he buys up the Salvation Army, and has to take part in a march to a big meeting. Barker will play the drum. You will have a trombone—or a bass-horn if you prefer that instrument—and it would add greatly to the effect if you could play it prettily. Besides if you took to music you could give up those confounded cigars and save your voice and your memory (both wrecks, like Mario's,[2] from thirty-seven cigars a day) for this immense part. It is very long, speeches longer than

From E. J. West, ed., *Shaw on Theatre*. Reprinted by permission of the Society of Authors, on behalf of the Bernard Shaw Estate.
[1] Shaw created the role of Andrew Undershaft expressly for Calvert, who had played Broadbent in 1904.
[2] Giovanni Mario (1810–1883) was a great but erratic mid-century tenor frequently referred to in Shaw's music criticism.

Keegan's and dozens of them, and infinite nuances of execution. Undershaft is diabolically subtle, gentle, self-possessed, powerful, stupendous, as well as amusing and interesting. There are the makings of ten Hamlets and six Othellos in his mere leavings. Learning it will half kill you; but you can retire the next day as pre-eminent and unapproachable. That penny-plain and twopence-colored pirate Brassbound will be beneath your notice then. I have put him off for another year, as I cannot get the right Lady Cicely. ———, unluckily, has read my plays at Margate and is now full of the most insane proposals—wants Brassbound instantly. With you and Kate Rorke for one thing. But the trombone is the urgent matter of the moment.

By the way, trombone players never get cholera nor consumption—never die, in fact, until extreme old age makes them incapable of working the slide.

G. Bernard Shaw.

Letter concerning a rehearsal, November 18.

My Dear Calvert—

I hope I did not worry you too much today at rehearsal. The fact is you are ruining the end of the second act by your enormous, desolating, oblivious-to-everybody absentmindedness. The reason I put on an understudy for Barbara was that you had driven Miss Russell almost out of her senses by letting the scene drop when she was doing her hardest to get hold of it. She did not complain; but I saw what was happening and acted on my own initiative. You see, it is all very well for you; you know that you can wake up at the last moment and do the trick; but that will not help out the unhappy victims who have to rehearse with you. And you forget your own weight. The moment you let the play go, it drops. You sit there, greatly interested (except when you are asleep) by the way to manage the play and the mistakes that all the rest are making, and trying to make out what is wrong with the whole scene. Of course, what is wrong is you. There is that frightful speech where Undershaft deliberately gives a horrible account of his business, sticking detail after detail of the horrors of war into poor bleeding Barbara to show her what Mrs. Baines will stand for £ 5000. Cusins, who sees it all, is driven into an ecstasy of irony by it; it is sort of a fantasia played on the nerves of both him and Barbara by Machiavelli-Mephistopheles. All that is needed to produce the effect is steady concentration, magnetic intensity. Irving, who could not do lots of things that you can do, could have done this superbly. But, you are evidently thinking of Lord knows what—the returns of your Sweet Nell Companies, or how Barker always drops his voice when he ought to raise it and emphasizes the wrong word, or what a monstrous thing it is that an idiot of an author should produce a play when he doesn't know the first rudiments of his business or—then you suddenly realize that the stage has been waiting for you ten minutes. There are moments when if we were not in a conspiracy to spoil you, we should rend you to pieces and wallow in your blood. Miss Russell has been working at the thing with the greatest enthusiasm, and when she tries to get into the rush of it, and is slacked down every time by your colossal indifference, she almost gives up in despair. If you were an insignificant actor it would not matter; they could run away from you; but they are not strong enough for this; the piece takes its time and intensity from you in spite of all they can do.

Mind, I quite appreciate your heroic study of the lines; and I don't complain of anything except the end of the second act; but for that I have no words strong enough to describe your atrocity; you will scream through endless centuries in hell for it, and implore me in vain to send you ices from heaven to cool your burning tongue. We have only one week more; and I have set my heart on your making a big success in the part. And you are taking it as easy as if Undershaft were -an old uncle in a farce. Spend tomorrow in prayer. My wife was horrified at my blanched hair and lined face when I returned from rehearsal today. And I have a blinding headache and can no more.

Your unfortunate,
G.B.S.

From Adelphi Terrace, November 29, day after opening

My Dear Calvert—

I see with disgust that the papers all say that your Undershaft was a magnificent piece of acting and *Major Barbara* a rottenly undramatic play, instead of pointing out that *Major B* is a masterpiece and that you are the most infamous amateur that ever disgraced the boards.

Do let me put ———into it. A man who could let the seven deadly sins go for nothing could sit on a hat without making an audience laugh. I have taken a box for Friday and had a hundredweight of cabbages, dead cats, eggs, and gingerbeer bottles stacked in it. Every word you fluff, every speech you unact, I will shy something at you. Before you go on the stage I will insult you until your temper gets the better of your liver. You are an impostor, a sluggard, a blockhead, a shirk, a malingerer, and the worst actor that ever lived or that ever will live. I will apologize to the public for engaging you. I will tell your mother of you.[3] Barbara played you off the stage; Cremlin dwarfed you; Bill annihilated you; Clare Greet took all eyes from you. If you are too lazy to study the lines I'll coach you in them. That last act MUST be saved or I'll withdraw the play and cut you off without a shilling.

Yours,
G.B.S.

[3]Calvert's parents, Mr. and Mrs. Charles Calvert, were the proprietors and leading actors of the Queen's Theatre, Manchester, one of the finest stock theatres in late nineteenth-century England. Shaw had long admired them; he had persuaded Mrs. Calvert after her retirement to return to the stage to play Catherine Petkoff in *Arms and the Man* in 1894.

TO AUDIENCES AT
MAJOR BARBARA

by Bernard Shaw

(Prefatory note circulated to the press when Grace George produced the play in America, 1915 and 1916; the note was purportedly written by "a playwright whose work is well known in this country, in England, and in Germany. He prefers to keep his identity a secret, but it may be said without betrayal of confidence that he knows intimately and admires greatly Bernard Shaw.")

Major Barbara is the third of a group of three plays of exceptional weight and magnitude on which the reputation of the author as a serious dramatist was first established, and still mainly rests. The first of the three, completed in 1903, the author's forty-seventh year, was *Man and Superman*, which has never been performed in its prodigious entirety in America, nor in England until the present year. The second, *John Bull's Other Island*, followed in 1904, and was an immediate success. The third of the series was *Major Barbara*, which arrived in 1905. It made demands on the audience but the demands were conceded. The audience left the theatre exhausted, but felt the better for it and came again. The second act, the Salvation Army act, was a play in itself. Regarded in that way, it may be said to be the most successful of all the author's plays.

The possibility of using the wooing of a man's soul for his salvation as a substitute for the hackneyed wooing of a handsome young gentleman for the sake of marrying him had occurred to Bernard Shaw many years before, when, in the course of his campaigns for socialism, he had often found himself on Sunday mornings address-

---

From E. J. West, ed., *Shaw on Theatre*. Reprinted by permission of the Society of Authors, on behalf of the Bernard Shaw Estate.

ing a Socialist meeting .in the open air in London or in the provinces while the Salvation Army was at work on the same ground. He had frequently, at the conclusion of his own meeting, joined the crowd round the Salvation lasses and watched their work and studied their methods sympathetically. Many of them sang, with great effect, songs in which the drama of salvation was presented in the form of a series of scenes between a brutal and drunken husband and a saved wife, with a thrilling happy ending in which the audience, having been persuaded by the unconscious art of the singer to expect with horror a murderous attack on the woman as her husband's steps were heard on the stairs, were relieved and delighted to hear that when the villain entered the room and all seemed lost, his face was lighted with the light of Heaven; for he too had been saved. Bernard Shaw was not at that time a playwright; but such scenes were not lost on him; the future dramatist was collecting his material everywhere.

Many years afterwards when he had acquired a considerable reputation as a critic of music, Bernard Shaw saw in a daily paper a silly remark describing some horrible noise as being almost as bad as a Salvation Army band. He immediately wrote to the paper pointing out that the Salvation Army bands were mostly good, and that some of them were of very conspicuous excellence. This compliment from an unexpected quarter made quite a commotion at the Army's headquarters in London. The general quoted it again and again in public, and the author was invited to attend one of the musical festivals of the Army. He did so and wrote an elaborate critical report on the bands, besides declaring that the performance of the "Dead March" from Handel's *Saul* at the great meeting at the Albert Hall in commemoration of Mrs. Booth by the combined bands of the Army, headed by the International Staff Band, was incomparably the finest he had ever heard, and the only one which showed any understanding of the magnificent triumphal character of the closing section.

Shaw took advantage of the relations thus established to ask the Army staff why they did not develop the dramatic side of their ritual by performing plays. He even offered to write a short play as a model of what might be done. The leaders of the Army, though interested and not themselves hostile to the proposal, could not venture to offend the deep prejudices against the theatre that still form part of English evangelism. They could only say rather doubtfully that if the author of a play could guarantee that everything in it had actually happened, that "it was all true," it might be possible to reconcile the stricter Salvationists to it. Shaw put forward the old defence made by Bunyan that parables were allowable; but he was met with the assurance that the Salvationists believed the parables to be records of facts as well as vehicles of instruction.

Finally, Mrs. Bramwell Booth told the author frankly that a subscription would be more useful to the social work of the Army than a model play; and so the matter dropped. But it bore fruit in *Major Barbara*; and during its run the spectacle was seen for the first time of a box filled with Salvation Army officials in uniform, sitting in a theatre and witnessing a play. Their testimony was useful. Some of the critics, in an inept attempt to be piously shocked, tried to present the play as a gibe at the Army, on the ground that the Salvationists were represented as being full of fun, and that they took money from the distiller. The Army received this with the scorn it deserved, declaring that Barbara's fun was perfectly correct and characteristic, and that the only incident that seemed incredible to them was her refusal to accept the money. Any good Salvationist, they said, would, like the commissioner in the play, take money from the devil himself, and make so good use of it that he would perhaps be converted, as there is hope for everybody.

The play, however, raises larger issues than those of popular Salvationism. Undershaft, with his terrible trade—so grimly flourishing just now—and his doctrine that money comes first, and that poverty is the worst of crimes and the only unbearable crime, strikes the deepest note in the play as Barbara sounds the highest. It was the allusions to Nietzsche which he provoked that elicited from the author the well-known preface in which he protested against the habit of the English critics of referring every trace of intellect in the English drama to Norwegian and German writers when all the doctrines which so surprised them were to be found in the literature of the English language. His reference to Samuel Butler as the greatest English exponent of Undershaft's doctrine of the importance of money was the beginning of the vogue of that remarkable writer which has persisted and spread ever since.

It is an open secret that the part of Adolphus Cusins, the very unusual *jeune premier* of the play, owes its originality to the fact that Mr. Gilbert Murray, the Regius professor of Greek at Oxford University, served the author as a very interesting model. He quotes his own famous translations of Euripides. Undershaft is perhaps the most exacting part that has fallen to the lot of an actor since Shakespeare's big parts; it belongs thoroughly to the new drama in which a tragedy and comedy and even broad fun, are so intimately bound up that it needs the greatest versatility and flexibility on the part of the actor, and the most alert vigilance on the part of the audience, to avoid confusing them.

It is curious that ten years should have elapsed between the production of *Major Barbara* in London and its first appearance on the American stage. It has been the subject of many proposals, but until today the artistic conditions have never seemed to the author favorable enough to warrant him in venturing on an authorization. Miss Grace George's appearance in London has doubtless had its weight in his decision. But Shaw has always said that for plays of this class, the great question is whether the audience will be a failure or a success.

THE EMPEROR JONES

Eugene O'Neill (1888-1953)

Eugene O'Neill was born in New York, the son of a famous melodramatic actor, James O'Neill. Eugene's early years were painful ones, as is evident in his autobiographical play, *Long Day's Journey Into Night*. His first one-act plays, based on his experiences as a seaman and prospector, were produced by the Provincetown Players in Massachusetts and later in New York. Critical recognition came to him in 1920 with the openings of both *The Emperor Jones* and *Beyond the Horizon*.

O'Neill rejected the traditional romantic drama and experimented with new forms and theatrical techniques. Among these experiments was his use of expressionism. The expressionistic playwright departs from the conventional carefully ordered structure of action to present a series of symbolic images, often distorted ones in seemingly irrational shapes and arrangements. In this play, O'Neill places his protagonist in a sequence of fragmentary scenes which dramatize the process of regression in Brutus Jones from a self-assured "Emperor" to an abject savage destroyed by his fears. In the chase that forms the central action of the play, the protagonist is pursued not only by his former subjects, but also by the dark forces in his own mind —the "nameless fears" that are a part of his collective unconscious. Because the expressionist conceives of his plays in theatrical terms making full use of imaginative production, scene designers have been especially attracted to such works as *The Emperor Jones*.

This is an important play in our theater for it brought to the attention of the public the first American playwright of international stature and provided an extraordinary example of imaginative theater.

O'Neill was awarded the Nobel prize for literature in 1936 and on three occasions won the Pulitzer Prize for drama. Outstanding plays of his are *The Hairy Ape, The Great God Brown, Desire Under the Elms, Mourning Becomes Electra, Strange Interlude, Anna Christie, The Iceman Cometh*, and *Long Day's Journey Into Night*.

Emperor Jones is seated in his throne talking to Smithers.
Sketches in this sequence are of the 1933 operatic version of *The Emperor Jones*,
staged by the Metropolitan Opera Company in New York,
with settings designed by Jo Mielziner.

"Jungle Terror"—Jones pursued by the Little Formless Fears.

"Snake Eyes"—Jones sees the ghost of Jeff,
a man he murdered in a gambling quarrel.

"Voodoo Dance"—the spirit of terror pursues Jones.

Left. At the beginning of the play,
Emperor Jones is confident
of his ability to make good his escape.
Photographs in this sequence are
of the 1925 British production,
with Paul Robeson as Emperor Jones.

Below. Jones retrogresses to his chain-gang days.

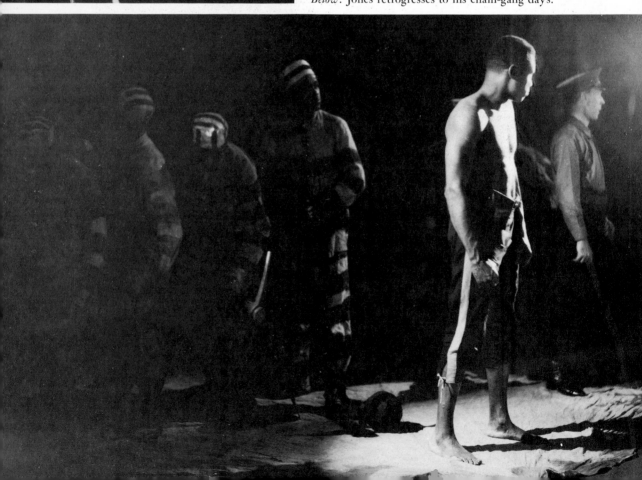

Jones as a slave on the auction block.

Jones is haunted by the memory of the witch doctor.

Jones is brought down by his fears—
and his own silver bullet.

CHARACTERS

BRUTUS JONES *Emperor*

HENRY SMITHERS, *a Cockney trader*

AN OLD NATIVE WOMAN

LEM, *A Native Chief*

SOLDIERS, ADHERENTS OF SUN

THE LITTLE FORMLESS FEARS

JEFF

THE NEGRO CONVICTS

THE PRISON GUARD

THE PLANTERS

THE AUCTIONEER

THE SLAVES

THE CONGO WITCH DOCTOR

THE CROCODILE GOD

The action of the play takes place on an island in the West Indies, as yet un-self-determined by white marines. The form of native government is, for the time being, an Empire.

THE EMPEROR JONES

SCENE ONE

The audience chamber in the palace of the Emperor–a spacious, high-ceilinged room with bare, white-washed walls. The floor is of white tiles. In the rear, to the left of center, a wide archway giving out on a portico with white pillars. The palace is evidently situated on high ground, for beyond the portico nothing can be seen but a vista of distant hills, their summits crowned with thick groves of palm trees. In the right wall, center, a smaller arched doorway leading to the living quarters of the palace. The room is bare of furniture with the exception of one huge chair, made of uncut wood, which stands at center, its back to rear. This is very apparently the Emperor's throne. It is painted a dazzling, eye-smiting scarlet. There is a brilliant orange cushion on the seat and another smaller one is placed on the floor to serve as a footstool. Strips of matting, dyed scarlet, lead from the foot of the throne to the two entrances.

It is late afternoon, but the sunlight still blazes yellowly beyond the portico, and there is an oppressive burden of exhausting heat in the air. As the curtain rises a native negro woman sneaks in cautiously from the entrance on the right. She is very old, dressed in cheap calico, barefooted, a red bandana handkerchief covering all but a few stray wisps of white hair. A bundle bound in colored cloth is carried over her shoulder on the end of a stick. She hesitates beside the doorway, peering back as if in extreme dread of being discovered. Then she begins to glide noiselessly, a step at a time, toward the doorway in the rear. At this moment Smithers appears beneath the portico.

Smithers is a tall, stoop-shouldered man about forty. His bald head, perched on a long neck with an enormous Adam's apple, looks like an egg. The tropics have tanned his naturally pasty face with its small, sharp features to a sickly yellow, and native rum has painted his pointed nose to a startling red. His little washy-blue eyes are red-rimmed, and dart about like a ferret's. His expression is one of unscrupulous meanness, cowardly and dangerous. His attitude toward Jones is that of one who will give vent to a nourished grudge against all superiority–as far as he dares. He is dressed in a worn riding suit of dirty white drill, puttees, spurs, and wears a white cork helmet. A cartridge belt with an automatic revolver is around his waist. He carries a riding whip in his hand. He sees the woman and stops to watch her suspiciously. Then, making up his mind, he steps quickly on tiptoe into the room. The woman, looking back over her shoulder continually, does not see him until it is too late. When she does, Smithers springs forward and grabs her firmly by the shoulder. She struggles to get away, fiercely but silently.

SMITHERS: (*tightening his grasp–roughly*) Easy! None o' that, me birdie. You can't wriggle out now. I got me 'ooks on yer.

WOMAN: (*seeing the uselessness of struggling, gives away to frantic terror and sinks to the ground, embracing his knees supplicatingly*). No tell him! No tell him, Mister!

SMITHERS: (*with great curiosity*) Tell 'im (*Then scornfully*) Oh, you mean 'is bloomin' Majesty. What's the gaime, any 'ow? What are you sneakin' away for? Been stealin' a bit, I s'pose. (*He taps her bundle with his riding whip significantly.*)

WOMAN: (*shaking her head vehemently*) No, me no steal.

SMITHERS: Bloody liar! But tell me what's up.

There's somethin' funny goin' on. I smelled it in the air first thing I got up this mornin'. You blacks are up to some devilment. This palace of 'is is like a bleedin' tomb. Where's all the 'ands? (*The woman keeps sullenly silent.* SMITHERS *raises his whip threateningly.*) Ow, yer won't, won't yer? I'll show yer what's what.

WOMAN: (*coweringly*) I tell, Mister. You no hit. They go—all go. (*She makes a sweeping gesture toward the hills in the distance.*)

SMITHERS: Run away—to the 'ills?

WOMAN: Yes, Mister. Him Emperor—Great Father—(*She touches her forehead to the floor with a quick, mechanical jerk.*) Him sleep after eat. Then they go—all go. Me old woman. Me left only. Now me go, too.

SMITHERS: (*his astonishment giving way to an immense mean satisfaction*) Ow! So that's the ticket! Well, I know bloody well wot's in the air—when they runs orf to the 'ills. The tom-tom 'll be thumping out there bloomin' soon. (*With extreme vindictiveness*) And I'm bloody glad of it, for one! Serve 'im right! Puttin' on airs, the stinkin' nigger! 'Is Majesty! Gawd blimey! I only 'opes I'm there when they takes 'im out to shoot 'im. (*Suddenly*) 'E's still 'ere all right, ain't 'e?

WOMAN: Yes. Him sleep.

SMITHERS: 'E's bound to find out soon as 'e wakes up. 'E's cunnin' enough to know when 'is time's come. (*He goes to the doorway on right and whistles shrilly with his fingers in his mouth. The old woman springs to her feet and runs out of the doorway, rear.* SMITHERS *goes after her, reaching for his revolver.*) Stop or I'll shoot! (*Then stopping indifferently.*) Pop orf, then, if yer like, yer black cow! (*He stands in the doorway, looking after her.*)

Jones enters from the right. He is a tall, powerfully-built, full-blooded negro of middle age. His features are typically negroid, yet there is something decidedly distinctive about his face—an underlying strength of will, a hardy, self-reliant confidence in himself that inspires respect. His eyes are alive with a keen, cunning intelligence. In manner he is shrewd, suspicious, evasive. He wears a light-blue uniform coat, sprayed with brass buttons, heavy gold chevrons on his shoulders, gold braid on the collar, cuffs, etc. His pants are bright red, with a light-blue stripe down the side. Patent leather laced boots with brass spurs, and a belt with a long-barreled, pearl-handled

revolver in a holster, complete his make-up. Yet there is something not altogether ridiculous about his grandeur. He has a way of carrying it off.

JONES: (*not seeing anyone—greatly irritated and blinking sleepily—shouts*) Who dare whistle dat way in my palace? Who dare wake up de Emperor? I'll git de hide frayled off some o' you niggers sho'!

SMITHERS: (*showing himself—in a manner half-afraid and half-defiant*) It was me whistled to yer. (*As* JONES *frowns angrily.*) I got news for yer.

JONES: (*putting on his suavest manner, which fails to cover up his contempt for the white man*) Oh, it's you, Mister Smithers. (*He sits down on his throne with easy dignity.*) What news you got to tell me?

SMITHERS: (*coming close to enjoy his discomfiture*) Don't you notice nothin' funny to-day?

JONES: (*coldly*) Funny? No, I ain't perceived nothin' of de kind!

SMITHERS: Then you ain't so foxy as I thought you was. Where's all your court? (*Sarcastically*) the Generals and the Cabinet Ministers and all?

JONES: (*imperturbably*) Where dey mostly runs to minute I closes my eyes—drinkin' rum and talkin' big down in de town. (*Sarcastically*) How come you don't know dat? Ain't you sousin' with 'em most every day?

SMITHERS: (*stung, but pretending indifference—with a wink*) That's part of the day's work. I got ter—ain't I—in my business?

JONES: (*contemptuously*) Yo' business!

SMITHERS: (*imprudently enraged*) Gawd blimey, you was glad enough for me ter take you in on it when you landed here first. You didn' 'ave no 'igh and mighty airs in them days!

JONES: (*his hand going to his revolver like a flash—menacingly*) Talk polite, white man! Talk polite, you heah me! I'm boss heah now, is you forgettin'? (*The Cockney seems about to challenge this last statement with the facts, but something in the other's eyes holds and cows him.*)

SMITHERS: (*in a cowardly whine*) No 'arm meant, old top.

JONES: (*condescendingly*) I accepts yo' apology. (*Lets his hand fall from his revolver.*) No use'n you rakin' up ole times. What I was den is one thing. What I is now's another. You didn't let me in on yo' crooked work out o' no kind feelin' dat time. I done de dirty work fo' you—and most o' de

brain work, too, fo' dat matter—and I was wu'th
money to you, dat's de reason.

SMITHERS: Well, blimey, I give yer a start, didn't
I—when no one else would. I wasn't afraid to
hire yer like the rest was—'count of the story
about your breakin' jail back in the States.

JONES: No, you didn't have no s'cuse to look down
on me fo' dat. You been in jail yo'self more'n
120 once.

SMITHERS: (furiously) It's a lie! (Then trying to pass
it off by an attempt at scorn) Garn! Who told yer
that fairy tale?

JONES: Dey's some things I ain't got to be tole.
I kin see 'em in folks eyes. (Then after a
pause—meditatively) Yes, you sho' give me a start.
And it didn't take long from dat time to git dese
fool woods' niggers right where I wanted dem.
(With pride) From stowaway to Emperor in two
130 years! Dat's goin' some!

SMITHERS: (with curiosity) And I bet you got er pile
o' money 'id safe someplace.

JONES: (with satisfaction) I sho' has! And it's in a
foreign bank where no pusson don't ever get
it out but me, no matter what come. You don't
s'pose I was holdin' down dis Emperor job for
de glory in it, did you? Sho'! De fuss and glory
part of it, dat's only to turn de heads o' de low-
flung bush niggers dat's here. Dey wants de big
140 circus show for deir money. I gives it to 'em
an' I gits de money. (With a grin.) De long green,
dat's me every time! (Then rebukingly) But you
ain't got no kick agin me, Smithers. I'se paid
you back all you done for me many times. Ain't
I pertected you and winked at all de crooked
tradin' you been doin' right out in de broad day?
Sho' I has—and me makin' laws to stop it at
de same time! (He chuckles.)

SMITHERS: (grinning) But, meanin' no 'arm, you
150 been grabbin' right and left yourself, ain't you?
Look at the taxes you've put on 'em! Blimey!
You've squeezed 'em dry.

JONES: (chuckling) No dey ain't all dry yet. I'se still
heah, ain't I?

SMITHERS: (smiling at his secret thought) They're dry
right now, you'll find out. (Changing the subject
abruptly) And as for me breaking laws, you've
broke 'em all yerself just as fast as yer made
'em.

160 JONES: Ain't I de Emperor? De laws don't go for

him. (Judiciously) You heah what I tells you,
Smithers. Dere's little stealin' like you does, and
dere's big stealin' like I does. For de little stealin'
dey gits you in jail soon or late. For de big stealin'
dey makes you Emperor and puts you in de
Hall o' Fame when you croaks. (Reminiscently)
If dey's one thing I learns in ten years on de
Pullman ca's listenin' to de white quality talk,
it's dat same fact. And when I gits a chance
to use it I winds up Emperor in two years.   170

SMITHERS: (unable to repress the genuine admiration
of the small fry for the large) Yes, you turned the
bleedin' trick, all right. Blimey, I never seen
a bloke 'as 'ad the bloomin' luck you 'as.

JONES: (severely) Luck? What you mean—luck?

SMITHERS: I suppose you'll say as that swank about
the silver bullet ain't luck—and that was what
first got the fool blacks on yer side the time
of the revolution, wasn't it?

JONES: (with a laugh) Oh, dat silver bullet! Sho'   180
was luck! But I makes dat luck, you heah? I
loads de dice! Yessuh! When dat murderin' nigger ole Lem hired to kill me takes aim ten feet
away and his gun misses fire and I shoots him
dead, what you heah me say?

SMITHERS: You said yer'd got a charm so's no lead
bullet 'd kill yer. You was so strong only a silver
bullet could kill yer, you told 'em. Blimey,
wasn't that swank for yer—and plain, fat-'eaded
luck?   190

JONES: (proudly) I got brains and I uses 'em quick.
Dat ain't luck.

SMITHERS: Yer knew they wasn't 'ardly liable to
get no silver bullets. And it was luck 'e didn't
'it you that time.

JONES: (laughing) And dere all dem fool bush niggers was kneelin' down and bumpin' deir heads
on de ground like I was a miracle out o' de Bible.
Oh, Lawd, from dat time on I has dem all eatin'
out of my hand. I cracks de whip and dey jumps   200
through.

SMITHERS: (with a sniff) Yankee bluff done it.

JONES: Ain't a man's talkin' big what makes him
big—as long as he makes folks believe it. Sho'
I talks large when I ain't got nothin' to back
it up, but I ain't talkin' wild just de same. I
knows I kin fool 'em—I knows it—and dat's back-
in' enough fo' my game. And ain't I got to learn
deir lingo and teach some of dem English befo'

210   I kin talk to 'em? Ain't dat wuk? You ain't never
learned ary word er it, Smithers, in de ten years
you been heah, dough yo' knows it's money in
yo' pocket tradin' wid 'em if you does. But you'
too shiftless to take de trouble.

SMITHERS: (*flushing*) Never mind about me. What's
this I've 'eard about yer really 'avin' a silver bullet
moulded for yourself?

JONES: It's playin' out my bluff. I has de silver
bullet moulded and I tells 'em when de time comes
220   I kills myself wid it. I tells 'em dat's 'cause I'm
de only man in de world big enuff to git me.
No use'n deir tryin'. And dey falls down and
bumps deir heads. (*He laughs.*) I does dat so's I
kin take a walk in peace widout no jealous nigger
gunnin' at me from behind de trees.

SMITHERS: (*astonished*) Then you 'ad it made—'onest?

JONES: Sho' did. Heah she be. (*He takes out his
revolver, breaks it, and takes the silver bullet out
of one chamber.*) Five lead an' dis silver baby at
230   de last. Don't she shine pretty? (*He holds it
in his hand, looking at it admiringly, as if strangely fascinated.*)

SMITHERS: Let me see. (*Reaches out his hand for it.*)

JONES: (*harshly*) Keep yo' hands whar dey b'long,
white man. (*He replaces it in the chamber and puts
the revolver back on his hip.*)

SMITHERS: (*snarling*) Gawd blimey! Think I'm a
bleedin' thief, you would.

JONES: No. 'Tain't dat. I knows you'se scared to
240   steal from me. On'y I ain't 'lowin' nary body
to touch dis baby. She's my rabbit's foot.

SMITHERS: (*sneering*) A bloomin' charm, wot?
(*Venomously*) Well, you'll need all the bloody
charms you 'as before long, s' 'elp me!

JONES: (*judicially*) Oh, I'se good for six months yit
'fore dey gits sick o' my game. Den, when I
sees trouble comin', I makes my get-a-way.

SMITHERS: Ho! You got it all planned, ain't yer?

JONES: I ain't no fool. I knows dis Emperor's time
250   is sho't. Dat why I make hay when de sun shine.
Was you thinkin' I'se aimin' to hold down dis
job for life? No, suh! What good is gittin' my
if you stays back in dis raggedy country? I wants
action when I spends. And when I sees dese
niggers gittin' up deir nerve to tu'n me out, and
I'se got all de money in sight, I resigns on de
spot and beats it quick.

SMITHERS: Where to?

JONES: None o' yo' business.

SMITHERS: Not back to the bloody States, I'll lay   260
my oath.

JONES: (*suspiciously*) Why don't I? (*Then with an easy
laugh*) You mean 'count of dat story 'bout me
breakin' from jail back there? Dat's all talk.

SMITHERS: (*skeptically*) Ho, yes!

JONES: (*sharply*) You ain't 'sinuatin' I'se a liar, is
you?

SMITHERS: (*hastily*) No, Gawd strike me! I was only
thinkin' o' the bloody lies you told the blacks
'ere about killin' white men in the States.   270

JONES: (*angered*) How come dey're lies?

SMITHERS: You'd 'ave been in jail if you 'ad, would-
n't yer then? (*With venom*) And from what I've
'eard, it ain't 'ealthy for a black to kill a white
man in the States. They burn 'em in oil, don't
they?

JONES: (*with cool deadliness*) You mean lynchin' 'd
scare me? Well, I tells you, Smithers, maybe
I does kill one white man back dere. Maybe
I does. And maybe I kills another right heah   280
'fore long if he don't look out.

SMITHERS: (*trying to force a laugh*) I was on'y spoofin'
yer. Can't yer take a joke? And you was just
sayin' you'd never been in jail.

JONES: (*in the same tone–slightly boastful*) Maybe I
goes to jail dere for gettin' in an argument wid
razors ovah a crap game. Maybe I gits twenty
years when dat colored man die. Maybe I gits
in 'nother argument wid de prison guard who
was overseer ovah us when we're walkin' de   290
roads. Maybe he hits me wid a whip an' I splits
his head wid a shovel an' runs away an' files
de chain off my leg an' gits away safe. Maybe
I does all dat an' maybe I don't. It's a story
I tells you so's you knows I'se de kind of man
dat if you evah repeats one word of it, I ends
yo' stealin' on dis yearth mighty damn quick!

SMITHERS: (*terrified*) Think I'd peach on yer? Not
me! Ain't I always been yer friend?

JONES: (*suddenly relaxing*) Sho' you has—and you   300
better be.

SMITHERS: (*recovering his composure–and with it his
malice*) And just to show yer I'm yer friend, I'll
tell yer that bit o' news I was goin' to.

JONES: Go ahead! Shoot de piece. Must be bad
news from de happy way you look.

SMITHERS: (*warningly*) Maybe it's gettin' time for you to resign—with that bloomin' silver bullet, wot? (*He finishes with a mocking grin.*)

310 JONES: (*puzzled*) What's dat you say? Talk plain.

SMITHERS: Ain't noticed any of the guards or servants about the place to-day, I 'aven't.

JONES: (*carelessly*) Dey're all out in de garden sleepin' under de trees. When I sleeps, dey sneaks a sleep, too, and I pretends I never suspicions it. All I got to do is to ring de bell an' dey come flyin', makin' a bluff dey was wukin' all de time.

SMITHERS: (*in the same mocking tone*) Ring the bell
320 now an' you'll bloody well see what I means.

JONES: (*startled to alertness, but preserving the same careless tone*) Sho' I rings. (*He reaches below the throne and pulls out a big common dinner bell which is painted the same vivid scarlet as the throne. He rings this vigorously–then stops to listen. Then he goes to both doors, rings again, and looks out.*)

SMITHERS: (*watching him with malicious satisfaction–after a pause–mockingly*) The bloody ship is sinkin' an' the bleedin' rats 'as slung their 'ooks.

330 JONES: (*in a sudden fit of anger flings the bell clatteringly into a corner*) Low-flung, woods niggers! (*Then catching* SMITHERS' *eye on him, he controls himself and suddenly bursts into a low, chuckling laugh.*) Reckon I overplays my hand dis once! A man can't take de pot on a bob-tailed flush all de time. Was I sayin' I'd sit in six months mo'? Well, I'se changed my mind, den. I cashes in and resigns de job of Emperor right dis minute.

SMITHERS: (*with real admiration*) Blimey, but you're
340 a cool bird, and no mistake.

JONES: No use'n fussin'. When I knows de game's up I kisses it good-bye widout no long waits. Dey've all run off to de hills, ain't dey?

SMITHERS: Yes—every bleedin' manjack of 'em.

JONES: Den de revolution is at de post. And de Emperor better git his feet smokin' up de trail. (*He starts for the door in rear.*)

SMITHERS: Goin' out to look for your 'orse? Yer won't find any. They steals the 'orses first thing.
350 Mine was gone when I went for 'im this mornin'. That's wot first give me a suspicion of wot was up.

JONES: (*alarmed for a second, scratches his head, then philosophically*) Well, den I hoofs it. Feet, do yo' duty! (*He pulls out a gold watch and looks at it.*)

Three-thuty. Sundown's at six-thuty or dereabouts. (*Puts his watch back–with cool confidence.*) I got plenty o' time to make it easy.

SMITHERS: Don't be so bloomin' sure of it. They'll be after you 'ot and 'eavy. Ole Lem is at the 360 bottom o' this business an' 'e 'ates you like 'ell. 'E'd rather do for you than eat 'is dinner, 'e would!

JONES: (*scornfully*) Dat fool no-count nigger! Does you think I'se scared o' him? I stands him on his thick head more'n once befo' dis, and I does it again if he come in my way—(*fiercely*). And dis time I leave him a dead nigger fo' sho'!

SMITHERS: You'll 'ave to cut through the big forest—an' these blacks 'ere can sniff and follow 370 a trail in the dark like 'ounds. You'd 'ave to 'ustle to get through that forest in twelve hours even if you knew all the bloomin' trails like a native.

JONES: (*with indignant scorn*) Look-a-heah, white man! Does you think I'm a natural bo'n fool? Give me credit fo' havin' some sense, fo' Lawd's sake! Don't you s'pose I'se looked ahead and made sho' of all de chances? I'se gone out in dat big forest, pretendin' to hunt so many times dat I knows it high an' low like a book. I could 380 go through on dem trails wid my eyes shut. (*With great contempt*) Think dese ig'nerent bush niggers dat ain't got brains enuff to know deir own names even can catch Brutus Jones? Huh! I s'pects not! Not on yo' life! Why, man, de white men went after me wid bloodhounds where I come from an' I jes' laughs at 'em. It's a shame to fool dese black trash around heah, dey're so easy. You watch me, man. I'll make dem look sick, I will. I'll be 'cross de plain to 390 de edge of de forest by time dark comes. Once in de woods in de night, dey got a swell chance o' findin' dis baby! Dawn tomorrow I'll be out at de oder side and on de coast whar dat French gunboat is stayin'. She picks me up, take me to the Martinique when she go dar, and dere I is safe wid a mighty big bankroll in my jeans. It's easy as rollin' off a log.

SMITHERS: (*maliciously*) But s'posin' somethin' 'appens wrong an' they do nab yer? 400

JONES: (*decisively*) Dey don't. Dat's de answer.

SMITHERS: But just for argyment's sake—what'd you do?

JONES: (*frowning*) I'se got five lead bullets in dis

gun good enuff fo' common bush niggers—an' after dat I got de silver bullet left to cheat 'em out o' gittin' me.

SMITHERS: (*jeeringly*) Ho, I was fergettin' that silver bullet. You'll bump yourself orf in style, won't yer? Blimey!

410

JONES: (*gloomily*) Yo' kin bet yo' whole roll on one thing, white man. Dis baby plays out his string to de end and when he quits, he quits wid a bang de way he ought. Silver bullet ain't none too good for him when he go, dat's a fac'! (*Then shaking off his nervousness—with a confident laugh*) Sho'! What is I talkin' about? Ain't come to dat yet an' I never will—not wid trash niggers like dese yere. (*Boastfully*) Silver bullet bring me luck,

420

anyway. I kin outguess, outrun, outfight, an' outplay de whole lot o' dem all ovah de board any time o' de day er night! Yo' watch me!

From the distant hills comes the faint, steady thump of a tom-tom, low and vibrating. It starts at a rate exactly corresponding to normal pulsebeat—72 to the minute—and continues at a gradually accelerating rate from this point uninterruptedly to the very end of the play.

Jones starts at the sound; a strange look of apprehension

430

creeps into his face for a moment as he listens. Then he asks, with an attempt to regain his most casual manner:

What's dat drum beatin' fo'?

SMITHERS: (*with a mean grin*) For you. That means the bleedin' ceremony 'as started. I've 'eard it before and I knows.

JONES: Cer'mony? What cer'mony?

SMITHERS: The blacks is 'oldin' a bloody meetin', 'avin' a war dance, gettin' their courage worked up b'fore they starts after you.

440

JONES: Let dem! Dey'll sho' need it!

SMITHERS: And they're there 'oldin' their 'eathen religious service—makin' no end of devil spells and charms to 'elp 'em against your silver bullet. (*He guffaws loudly.*) Blimey, but they're balmy as 'ell.

JONES: (*a tiny bit awed and shaken in spite of himself*) Huh! Takes more'n dat to scare dis chicken!

SMITHERS: (*scenting the other's feeling—maliciously*) Ternight when it's pitch black in the forest,

450

they'll 'ave their pet devils and ghosts 'oundin'

after you. You'll find yer bloody 'air 'll be standin' on end before to-morrow mornin'. (*Seriously*) It's a bleedin' queer place, that stinkin' forest, even in daylight. Yer don't know what might 'appen in there, it's that rotten still. Always sends the cold shivers down my back minute I gets in it.

JONES: (*with a contemptuous sniff*) I ain't no chicken-liver like you is. Trees an' me, we's friends, an' dar's a full moon comin' bring me light. And   460 let dem po' niggers make all de fool spells dey'se a min' to. Does yo' s'pect I'se silly enuff to b'lieve in ghosts an' ha'nts an' all dat ole woman's talk? G'long, white man! You ain't talkin' to me. (*With a chuckle*) Doesn't you knows dey's got to do wid a man who was member in good standin' o' de Baptist Church. Sho' I was dat when I was porter on de Pullman, an' befo' I gits into my little trouble. Let dem try deir heathen tricks. De Baptist Church done pertect me an' land dem   470 all in hell. (*Then with more confident satisfaction*) An' I'se got little silver bullet o' my own, don't forgit.

SMITHERS: Ho! You 'aven't give much 'eed to your Baptist Church since you been down 'ere. I've 'eard myself and 'ad turned yer coat an' was takin' up with their blarsted witch-doctors, or whatever the 'ell yer calls the swine.

JONES: (*vehemently*) I pretends to! Sho' I pretends! Dat's part o' my game from de fust. If I finds   480 out dem niggers believes dat black is white, den I yells it out louder 'n deir loudest. It don't git me nothin' to do missionary work for de Baptist Church. I'se after de coin, an' I lays my Jesus on de shelf for de time bein'. (*Stops abruptly to look at his watch—alertly.*) But I ain't got de time to waste no mo'e fool talk wid you. I'se gwine away from heah dis secon'. (*He reaches in under the throne and pulls out an expensive Panama hat with a bright multi-colored band and sets it jauntily   490 on his head.*) So long, white man! (*With a grin*) See you 'n jail some time, maybe!

SMITHERS: Not me, you won't. Well, I wouldn't be in yer bloody boots for no bloomin' money, but 'ere's wishin' yer luck just the same.

JONES: (*contemptuously*) You're de frightenedest man evah I see! I tells you I'se safe 's'f I was in New York City. It take dem niggers from now to dark to git up de nerve to start somethin'. By dat time I'se got a head start dey never kotch up wid.

SMITHERS: (*maliciously*) Give my regards to any ghosts yer meets up with.

JONES: (*grinning*) If dat ghost got money, I'll tell him never ha'nt you less'n he wants to lose it.

SMITHERS: (*flattered*) Garn! (*Then curiously*) Ain't yer takin' no luggage with yer?

JONES: I travels light when I wants to move fast. And I got tinned grub buried on de edge o' de forest. (*Boastfully*) Now say dat I don't look ahead an' use my brains! (*With a wide, liberal gesture*) I will all dat's left in de palace to you an' you better grab all you kin sneak away wid befo' dey gits here.

SMITHERS: (*gratefully*) Righto—and thanks ter yer. (*As* JONES *walks toward the door in rear–cautioningly*) Say! Look 'ere, you ain't goin out that way, are yer?

JONES: Does you think I'd slink out de back door like a common nigger? I'se Emperor yit, ain't I? And de Emperor Jones leaves de way he comes, and dat black trash don't dare stop him—not yit, leastways. (*He stops for a moment in the doorway, listening to the far-off but insistent beat of the tom-tom.*) Listen to dat roll-call, will yo'? Must be mighty big drum carry dat far. (*Then with a laugh*) Well, if dey ain't no whole brass band to see me off, I sho' got de drum part of it. So long, white man. (*He puts his hands in his pockets and with studied carelessness, whistling a tune, he saunters out of the doorway and off to the left.*)

SMITHERS: (*looks after him with a puzzled admiration*) 'E's got 'is bloomin' nerve with 'im, s'elp me! (*Then angrily*) Ho—the bleedin' nigger—puttin' on 'is bloody airs! I 'opes they nabs 'im an' gives 'im what's what! (*Then putting business before the pleasure of his thought, looking around him with cupidity.*) A bloke ought to find a 'ole lot in this palace that 'd go for a bit of cash. Let's take a look, 'Arry, me lad. (*He starts for the doorway on right as*)

The Curtain Falls

SCENE TWO: NIGHTFALL

The end of the plain where the Great Forest begins. The foreground is sandy, level ground, dotted by a few stones and clumps of stunted bushes cowering close against the earth to escape the buffeting of the trade wind. In the rear the forest is a wall of darkness dividing the world. Only when the eye becomes accustomed to the gloom can the outlines of separate trunks of the nearest trees be made out, enormous pillars of deeper blackness. A somber monotone of wind lost in the leaves moans in the air. Yet this sound serves but to intensify the impresison of the forest's relentless immobility, to form a background throwing into relief its brooding, implacable silence.

———————

JONES *enters from the left, walking rapidly. He stops as he nears the edge of the forest, looks around him quickly, peering into the dark as if searching for some familiar landmark. Then, apparently satisfied that he is where he ought to be, he throws himself on the ground, dog-tired.*

Well, heah I is. In de nick o' time, too! Little mo' an' it'd be blacker'n de ace of spades heahabouts. (*He pulls a bandana handkerchief from his hip pocket and mops off his perspiring face.*) Sho! Gimme air! I'se tuckered out sho' 'nuf. Dat soft Emperor job ain't no trainin' fo' a long hike ovah dat plain in de brilin' sun (*Then with a chuckle*) Cheah up, nigger, der worst is yet to come. (*He lifts his head and stares at the forest. His chuckle peters out abruptly. In a tone of awe*): My goodness, look at dem woods, will you? Dat no-count Smithers said dey'd be black an' he sho' called de turn. (*Turning away from them quickly, and looking down at his feet, he snatches at a chance to change the subject –solicitously:*) Feet, yo' is holdin' up yo' end fine an' I sutinly hopes you ain't blisterin' none. It's time you git a rest. (*He takes off his shoes, his eyes studiously avoiding the forest. He feels of the soles of his feet gingerly.*) You is still in de pink—only a little mite feverish. Cool you' self. Remember yo' done got a long journey yit befo' yo'. (*He sits in a weary attitude, listening to the rhythmic beating of the tom-tom. He grumbles in a loud tone to cover up a growing uneasiness.*) Bush niggers! Wonder dey wouldn't git sick o' beatin' dat drum. Sound louder, seem like. I wonder if dey's startin' after me? (*He scrambles to his feet, looking back across the plain.*) Couldn't see dem now, nohow, if dey was hundred feet away. (*Then shaking himself like a wet dog to get rid of these depressing thoughts.*) Sho', dey's miles an' miles behind. What yo' gittin' fidgetty about? (*But he sits down and begins to lace up his shoes in great haste, all the time muttering reassuringly.*) You know what? Yo' belly is empty, dat's what's de matter wid you. Come time to eat! Wid nothin' but wind on yo' stumach, o' course yo' feels jiggedy. Well, we eats right heah an' now soon's I gits dese pesky shoes laced up. (*He finishes lacing up his shoes.*) Dere! Now le's see! (*Gets on his hands and knees and searches the ground around him with his eyes.*) White stone, white stone, where is yo'? (*He sees the first white stone and crawls to it—with satisfaction.*) Heah yo' is! I knowed dis was de right place. Box of grub, come to me. (*He turns over the stone and feels in under it—in a tone of dismay*) Ain't heah! Gorry, is I in de right place or isn't I? Dere's 'nother stone. Guess dat's it. (*He scrambles to the next stone and turns it over.*) Ain't heah, neither! Grub, whar is yo'? Ain't heah. Gorry, has I got to go hungry into dem woods—all de night? (*While he is talking he scrambles from one stone to another, turning them over in frantic haste. Finally he jumps to his feet excitedly.*) Is I lost de place? Must have! But how dat happen when I was followin' de trail across de plain in broad daylight? (*Almost plaintively*) I'se hungry, I is! I gotta git my feed. Whar's my strength gonna come from if I doesn't? Gorry, I gotta find dat grub high an' low somehow! Why it come dark so quick like dat? Can't see nothin'. (*He scratches a match on his trousers and peers about him. The rate of the beat of the far-off tom-tom increases perceptibly as he does so. He mutters in a bewildered voice.*) How come all dese white stones come heah when I only remembers one? (*Suddenly, with a frightened gasp, he flings the match on the ground and stamps on it.*) Nigger, is yo' gone crazy mad? Is you lightin matches to show dem whar you is? Fo' Lawd's sake, use yo' haid. Gorry, I'se got to be careful! (*He stares at the plain behind him apprehensively, his hand on his revolver.*) But how come all dese white stones? And whar's dat tin box o' grub I hid all wrapped up in oilcloth?

While his back is turned, the Little Formless Fears creep out from the deeper blackness of the forest. They are black, shapeless; only their glittering little eyes can be seen. If they have any describable form at all it is that of a grubworm about the size of a creeping child. They move noiselessly, but with deliberate, painful effort, striving to raise themselves on end, failing and sinking prone again. Jones turns about to face the forest. He stares up at the tops of the trees, seeking vainly to discover his whereabouts by their conformation.

Can't tell nothin' from dem trees! Gorry, nothin' 'round heah look like I evah seed it befo'. I'se done lost de place sho' 'nuff! (*With mournful foreboding*) It's mighty queer! It's mighty queer! (*With sudden forced defiance—in an angry tone*) Woods, is yo' tryin' to put somethin' ovah on me?

From the formless creatures on the ground in front of him comes a tiny gale of low mocking laughter like a rustling of leaves. They squirm upward toward him in twisted attitudes. Jones looks down, leaps backward with a yell of terror, yanking out his revolver as he does so—in a quavering voice.

What's dat? Who's dar? What's you? Git away from me befo' I shoots yo' up! Yo' don't?—

He fires. There is a flash, a loud report, then silence, broken only by the far-off quickened throb of the tom-tom. The formless creatures have scurried back into the forest. Jones remains fixed in his position, listening intently. The sound of the shot, the reassuring feel of the revolver in his hand have somewhat restored his shaken nerve. He addresses himself with renewed confidence:

Dey're gone. Dat shot fix 'em. Dey was only little animals—little wild pigs, I reckon. Dey've maybe rooted out yo' grub an' eat it. Sho', yo' fool nigger, what you' think dey is—ha'nts? (*Excitedly*) Gorry, you give de game away when yo' fire dat shot. Dem niggers heah dat fo' su'tin! Time yo' beat it in de woods widout no long waits. (*He starts for the forest—hesitates before the plunge—then urging himself in with manful resolution.*) Git in, nigger! What yo' skeered at? Ain't nothin' dere but de trees! Git in! (*He plunges boldly into the forest.*)

SCENE THREE

*Nine o'clock. In the forest. The moon has just risen.
Its beams drifting through the canopy of leaves make
a barely perceptible, suffused eerie glow. A dense low
wall of underbrush and creepers is in the nearer foreground
fencing in a small triangular clearing. Beyond this is
the massed blackness of the forest like an encompassing
barrier. A path is dimly discerned leading down to the
clearing from left, rear, and winding away from it again
toward the right. As the scene opens nothing can be distinctly made out. Except for the beating of the tom-tom,
which is a trifle louder and quicker than in the previous
scene, there is silence, broken every few seconds by a
queer, clicking sound. Then gradually the figure of the
negro Jeff can be discerned crouching on his haunches
at the rear of the triangle. He is middle-aged, thin,
brown in color, is dressed in a Pullman porter's uniform,
cap, etc. He is throwing a pair of dice on the ground
before him, picking them up, shaking them, casting them
out with the regular, rigid, mechanical movements of
an automaton. The heavy, plodding footsteps of some
one approaching along the trail from the left are heard,
and Jones' voice, pitched in a slightly higher key and
strained in a cheering effort to overcome its own tremors.)*

De moon's rizen. Does yo' heah dat, nigger?
Yo' gits more light from dis out. No mo' buttin'
yo' fool head agin' de trunks an' scratchin' de
hide off yo' legs in de bushes. Now yo' sees
whar yo'se gwine. So cheer up! From now on
yo' has a snap. (*He steps just to the rear of the
triangular clearing and mops off his face from his sleeve.
He has lost his Panama hat. His face is scratched,
his brilliant uniform shows several large rents.*) What
10   time's it gittin' to be, I wonder? I dassent light
no match to find out. Phoo'. It's wa'm, an' dat's
a fac'! (*Warily*) How long I been makin' tracks
in dese woods? Must be hours an' hours. Seems
like fo'evah! Yit can't be, when de moon's jes'
riz. Dis am a long night fo' yo', yo' Majesty!
(*With a mournful chuckle*) Majesty! Der ain't much
majesty 'bout dis baby now. (*With attempted cheerfulness*) Never min'. It's all part o' de game. Dis
night come to an end like everythin' else. An'
20   when yo' gits dar safe an' has dat bankroll in
yo' hands, yo' laughs at all dis. (*He starts to whistle,*

but checks himself abruptly.) What yo' whistlin' for,
yo' po' dope? Want all de worl' to heah yo'?
(*He stops talking to listen.*) Heah dat ole drum!
Sho' gits nearer from de sound. Dey're packin'
it along wid 'em. Time fo' me to move. (*He takes
a step forward, then stops–worriedly.*) What's dat
odder queer clicketty sound I heah? Der it is!
Sound close! Sound like—fo' God sake, sound
like some nigger was shakin' crap! (*Frightenedly*)   30
I better beat it quick when I gits dem notions.
(*He walks quickly into the clear space–then stands
transfixed as he sees* JEFF–*in a terrified gasp.*) Who
dar? Who dat? Is dat yo', Jeff? (*Starting toward
the other, forgetful for a moment of his surroundings
and really believing it is a living man that he sees–in
a tone of happy relief.*) Jeff! I'se sho' mighty glad
to see you'! Dey tol' me yo' done died from
dat razor cut I gives you. (*Stopping suddenly, bewil-
deredly*) But how come you to be heah, nigger?   40
(*He stares fascinatedly at the other, who continues
his mechanical play with the dice.* JONES' *eyes begin
to roll wildly. He stutters*) Ain't you gwine—look
up—can't you speak to me? Is you—is you—a
ha'nt? (*He jerks out his revolver in a frenzy of terrified
rage.*) Nigger, I kills yo' dead once. Has I got
to kill yo' agin? You take it, den. (*He fires. When
the smoke clears away* JEFF *has disappeared.* JONES
stands trembling–then with a certain reassurance)
He's gone, anyway. Ha'nt or no ha'nt, dat shot   50
fix him. (*The beat of the far-off tom-tom is perceptibly
louder and more rapid.* JONES *becomes conscious of
it–with a start, look back over his shoulder.*) Dey's
gittin' near! Dey're comin' fast! An' heah I is
shootin' shots to let 'em know jes' whar I is.
Oh, Gorry, I'se got to run. (*Forgetting the path,
he plunges wildly into the underbrush in the rear and
disappears in the shadow.*)

SCENE FOUR

*Eleven o'clock. In the forest. A wide dirt road runs
diagonally from right, front, to left, rear. Rising sheer
on both sides the forest walls it in. The moon is now
up. Under its light the road glimmers ghastly and unreal.
It is as if the forest had stood aside momentarily to let
the road pass through and accomplish its veiled purpose.
This done, the forest will fold in upon itself again and*

the road will be no more. Jones stumbles in from the forest on the right. His uniform is ragged and torn. He looks about him with numbed surpirse when he sees the road, his eyes blinking in the bright moonlight. He flops down exhaustedly and pants heavily for a while. Then, with sudden anger:

I'm meltin' wid heat! Runnin' an' runnin' an' runnin'! Damn dis heah coat! Like a straitjacket! (*He tears off his coat and flings it away from him, revealing himself stripped to the waist.*) Dere! Dat's better! Now I kin breathe! (*Looking down at his feet, the spurs catch his eye.*) An' to hell wid dese high-fangled spurs. Dey're what's been a-trippin' me up an' breakin' my neck. (*He unstraps and flings then away disgustedly.*) Dere! I gits rid o'
10 dem frippety Emperor trappin's an' I travels lighter. Lawd! I'se tired! (*After a pause, listening to the insistent beat of the tom-tom in the distance.*) I must 'a put some distance between myself an' dem—runnin' like dat—an' yet—dat damn drum sound jes' de same—nearer, even. Well, I guess I a'most holds my lead, anyhow. Dey won't never kotch up. (*With a sigh*) If on'y my fool legs stands up. Oh, I'se sorry I evah went in for dis. Dat Emperor job is sho' hard to shake.
20 (*He looks around him suspiciously.*) How'd dis road evah git heah? Good, level road, too. I never remembers seein' it befo'. (*Shaking his head apprehensively.*) Dese woods is sho' full o' de queerest things at night. (*With sudden terror*) Lawd God, don't let me see no more o' dem ha'nts. Dey gits my goat! (*Then trying to talk himself into confidence.*) Ha'nts! Yo' fool nigger, dey ain't no such things! Don't de Baptist parson tell you dat many times? Is yo' civilized, or is
30 yo' like dese ign'rent black niggers heah? Sho'! Dat was all in yo' own head. Wasn't nothin' there! Wasn't no Jeff! Know what? Yo' jus' get seein' dem thing 'cause yo' belly's empty an' you's sick wid hunger inside. Hunger 'fects yo' head an' yo' eyes. Any fool know dat. (*Then pleading fervently*) But bless God, I don't come across no more o' dem, whatever dey is! (*Then cautiously*) Rest! Don't talk! Rest! You needs it. Den yo' gits on yo' way again. (*Looking at the
40 moon*) Night's half gone a'most. Yo' hits de coast in de mawning! Den you'se all safe.

From the right forward a small gang of negroes enter. They are dressed in striped convicts suits, their heads are shaven, one leg drags limpingly, shackled to a heavy ball and chain. Some carry picks, the others shovels. They are followed by a white man dressed in the uniform of a prison guard. A Winchester rifle is slung across his shoulders and he carries a heavy whip. At a signal from the guard they stop on the road opposite to where JONES *is sitting.* JONES, *who has been staring up at the sky,* 50 *unmindful of their noiseless approach, suddenly looks down and sees them. His eyes pop out, he tries to get to his feet and fly, but sinks back, too numbed by fright to move. His voice catches in a choking prayer.*

Lawd Jesus!

The prison guard cracks his whip—noiselessly—and at that signal all the convicts start to work on the road. They swing their picks, they shovel, but not a sound comes from their labor. Their movements, like those of Jeff in the preceding scene, are those of automatons—rigid, slow, and mechanical. The prison guard points sternly 60 *at Jones with his whip, motions him to take his place among the other shovelers.* JONES *gets to his feet in a hypnotized stupor. He mumbles subserviently:*)

Yes, suh! Yes, suh! I'se comin'!

As he shuffles, dragging one foot, over to his place, he curses under his breath with rage and hatred.

God damn yo' soul, I gits even wid yo' yit, some-time.

As if there was a shovel in his hands, he goes through weary, mechanical gestures of digging up dirt and throw- 70 *ing it to the roadside. Suddenly the guard approaches him angrily, threateningly. He raises his whip and lashes* JONES *viciously across the shoulders with it.* JONES *winces with pain and cowers abjectly. The guard turns his back on him and walks away contemptuously. Instantly* JONES *straightens up. With arms upraised, as if his shovel were a club in his hands, he springs murderously at the unsuspecting guard. In the act of crashing down his shovel on the white man's skull, Jones suddenly becomes aware that his hands are empty. He cries despairingly:* 80

Whar's my shovel? Gimme my shovel 'till I splits his damn head! (*Appealing to his fellow convicts*) Gimme a shovel, one o' yo' fo' God's sake!

They stand fixed in motionless attitudes, their eyes on the ground. The guard seems to wait expectantly, his back turned to the attacker. Jones bellows with baffled terrified rage, tugging frantically at his revolver.

I kills you, you white debil, if it's de last thing I evah does! Ghost or debil, I kill you agin!

90 *He frees the revolver and fires point blank at the guard's back. Instantly the walls of the forest close in from both sides, the road and the figures of the convict gang are blotted out in an enshrouding darkness. The only sounds are a crashing in the underbrush as JONES leaps away in mad flight and the throbbing of the tom-tom, still far distant, but increased in volume of sound and rapidity of beat.*

SCENE FIVE

One o'clock. A large circular clearing, enclosed by the serried ranks of lofty, gigantic trunks of tall trees whose tops are lost to view. In the center is a big dead stump, worn by the time into a curious resemblance to an auction block. The moon floods the clearing with a clear light. JONES forces his way in through the forest on the left. He looks wildly about the clearing with hunted, fearful glances. His pants are in tatters, his shoes cut and misshapen, flapping about his feet. He slinks cautiously to the stump in the center and sits down in a tense position, ready for instant flight. Then he holds his head in his hands and rocks back and forth, moaning to himself miserably.

Oh, Lawd, Lawd! Oh Lawd, Lawd! (*Suddenly he throws himself on his knees and raises his clasped hands to the sky—in a voice of agonized pleading.*) Lawd, Jesus, heah my prayer! I'se a poor sinner, a poor sinner! I knows I done wrong, I knows it! When I cotches Jeff cheatin' wid loaded dice my anger overcomes me an' I kills him dead! Lawd, I done wrong! When dat guard hits me wid de whip, my anger overcomes me, and I
10 kills him dead. Lawd, I done wrong! An' down heah war dese fool bush niggers raises me up to the seat o' de mighty, I steals all I could grab. Lawd, I done wrong! I knows it! I'se sorry! Forgive me, Lawd! Forgive dis po' sinner! (*Then beseeching terrifiedly*) An' keep dem away, Lawd! Keep dem away from me! An' stop dat drum soundin' in my ears! Dat begin to sound ha'nted,

too. (*He gets to his feet, evidently slightly reassured by his prayer—with attempted confidence*) De Lawd'll preserve me from dem ha'nts after dis. (*Sits down* 20 *on the stump again.*) I ain't skeered o' real men. Let dem come. But dem odders— (*He shudders—then looks down at his feet, working his toes inside the shoes—with a groan*) Oh, my po' feet! Dem shoes ain't no use no more 'ceptin' to hurt. I'se better off without dem. (*He unlaces them and pulls them off—holds the wrecks of the shoes in his hand and regards them mournfully.*) You was real A-one patin' leather, too. Look at yo' now. Emperor, you'se gittin' mighty low! 30

He sighs dejectedly and remains with bowed shoulders, staring down at the shoes in his hands as if reluctant to throw them away. While his attention is thus occupied, a crowd of figures silently enter the clearing from all sides. All are dressed in Southern costumes of the period of the fifties of the last century. There are middle-aged men who are evidently well-to-do planters. There is one spruce, authoritative individual—the Auctioneer. There are a crowd of curious spectators, chiefly young belles and dandies who have come to the slave market for diver- 40 *sion. All exchange courtly greetings in dumb show and chat silently together. There is something stiff, rigid, unreal, marionettish about their movements. They group themselves about the stump. Finally a batch of slaves are led in from the left by an attendant—three men of different ages, two women, one with a baby in her arms, nursing. They are placed to the left of the stump, beside JONES.*

The white planters look them over appraisingly as if they were cattle, and exchange judgments on each. The 50 *dandies point with their fingers and make witty remarks. The belles titter bewitchingly. All this in silence save for the ominous throb of the tom-tom. The Auctioneer holds up his hand, taking his place at the stump. The groups strain forward attentively. He touches JONES on the shoulder peremptorily, motioning for him to stand on the stump—the auction block.*
JONES *looks up, sees the figures on all sides, looks wildly for some opening to escape, sees none, screams and leaps madly to the top of the stump to get as far away from* 60 *them as possible. He stands there, cowering, paralyzed with horror. The Auctioneer begins his silent spiel. He points to* JONES, *appeals to the planters to see for themselves. Here is a good field hand, sound in wind and limb, as they can see. Very strong still, in spite of his*

*being middle-aged. Look at that back. Look at those shoul-
ders. Look at the muscles in his arms and his sturdy
legs. Capable of any amount of hard labor. Moreover,
of a good disposition, intelligent and tractable. Will any*
70   *gentleman start the bidding? The planters raise their
fingers, make their bids. They are apparently all eager
to possess* JONES. *The bidding is lively, the crowd
interested. While this has been going on,* JONES *has been
seized by the courage of desperation. He dares to look
down and around him. Over his face abject terror gives
way to mystification, to gradual realization—stutter-
ingly:*

What yo' all doin', white folks? What's all dis?
What yo' all lookin' at me fo'?. What yo' doin'
80   wid me, anyhow? (*Suddenly convulsed with raging
hatred and fear*) Is dis a auction? Is yo' sellin'
me like dey uster befo' de war? (*Jerking out his
revolver just as* THE AUCTIONEER *knocks him down
to one of the planters—glaring from him to the purchaser*)
An' *you* sells me? An' *you* buys me? I shows
you I'se a free nigger, damn yo' souls! (*He fires
at* THE AUCTIONEER *and at* THE PLANTER *with such
rapidity that the two shots are almost simultaneous.
As if this were a signal, the walls of the forest fold*
90   *in. Only blackness remains and silence broken by* JONES
*as he rushes off, crying with fear—and by the quickened,
ever louder beat of the tom-tom.*)

SCENE SIX

*Three o'clock. A cleared space in the forest. The limbs
of the trees meet over it, forming a low ceiling about
five feet from the ground. The interlocked ropes of creepers
reaching upward to entwine the tree trunks give an arched
appearance to the sides. The space this encloses is like
the dark, noisome hold of some ancient vessel. The moonlight is almost completely shut out and only a vague,
wan light filters through. There is the noise of some
one approaching from the left, stumbling and crawling
through the undergrowth. Jones' voice is heard between
chattering moans.*

Oh, Lawd, what I gwine do now? Ain't got
no bullet left on'y de silver one. If mo' o' dem
ha'nts come after me, how I gwine skeer dem
away? Oh, Lawd, on'y de silver one left—an'
I gotta save dat fo' luck. If I shoots dat one
I'm a goner sho'! Lawd, it's black heah! Whar's
de moon? Oh, Lawd, don't dis night evah come
to an end? (*By the sounds he is feeling his way cautiously forward.*) Dere! Dis feels like a clear space.
I gotta lie down an' rest. I don't care if dem   10
niggers does catch me. I gotta rest.

*He is well forward now where his figure can be dimly
made out. His pants have been so torn away that what
is left of them is no better than a breech cloth. He flings
himself full length, face downward on the ground, panting
with exhaustion. Gradually it seems to grow lighter in
the enclosed space, and two rows of seated figures can
be seen behind* JONES. *They are sitting in crumpled,
despairing attitudes, hunched facing one another, with
their backs touching the forest walls as if they were shackled   20
to them. All are negroes, naked save for loin cloths.
At first they are silent and motionless. Then they begin
to sway slowly forward toward each other and back again
in unison, as if they were laxly letting themselves follow
the long roll of ship at sea. At the same time, a low,
melancholy murmur rises among them, increasing gradually by rhythmic degrees, which seem to be directed and
controlled by the throb of the tom-tom in the distance,
to a long, tremendous wail of despair that reaches a
certain pitch, unbearably acute, then falls by slow grada-   30
tions of tone into silence and is taken up again.* JONES
*starts, looks up, sees the figures, and throws himself down
again to shut out the sight. A shudder of terror shakes
his whole body as the wail rises up about him again.
But the next time, his voice, as if under some uncanny
compulsion, starts with the others. As their chorus lifts
he rises to a sitting posture similar to the others, swaying
back and forth. His voice reaches the highest pitch of
sorrow, of desolation. The light fades out, the other voices
cease, and only darkness is left. Jones can be heard scram-   40
bling to his feet and running off, his voice sinking down
the scale and receding as he moves farther and farther
away in the forest. The tom-tom beats louder, quicker,
with a more insistent, triumphant pulsation.*

SCENE SEVEN

*Five o'clock. The foot of a gigantic tree by the edge
of a great river. A rough structure of boulders like an
altar is by the tree. The raised river bank is in the*

nearer background. Beyond this the surface of the river spreads out brilliant and unruffled in the moonlight, blotted out and merged into a veil of bluish mist in the distance. JONES' *voice is heard from the left, rising and falling in the long, despairing wail of the chained slaves, to the rhythmic beat of the tom-tom. As his voice sinks into silence he enters the open space. The expression of his face is fixed and stony, his eyes have an obsessed glare, he moves with a strange deliberation like a sleepwalker or one in a trance. He looks around at the tree, the rough stone altar, the moonlit surface of the river beyond, and passes his hand over his head with a vague gesture of puzzled bewilderment. Then, as if in obedience to some obscure impulse, he sinks into a kneeling, devotional posture before the altar. Then he seems to come to himself partly, to have an uncertain realization of what he is doing, for he straightens up and stares about him horrifiedly—in an incoherent mumble.*

What—what is I doin'? What is—dis place? Seems like—seems like I know dat tree—an' dem stones—an' de river. I remember—seems like I been heah befo'. (*Tremblingly*) Oh, Gorry, I'se skeered in dis place! I'se skeered! Oh, Lawd, pertect dis sinner!

Crawling away from the altar, he cowers close to the ground, his face hidden, his shoulders heaving with sobs of hysterical fright. From behind the trunk of the tree,
10 *as if he had sprung out of it, the figure of the Congo witch-doctor appears. He is wizened and old, naked except for the fur of some small animal tied about his waist, its bushy tail hanging down in front. His body is stained all over a bright red. Antelope horns are on each side of his head, branching upward. In one hand he carries a bone rattle, in the other a charm stick with a bunch of white cockatoo feathers tied to the end. A great number of glass beads and bone ornaments are about his neck, ears, wrists, and ankles. He struts noiselessly with a*
20 *queer prancing step to a position in the clear ground between* JONES *and the altar. Then with a preliminary, summoning stamp of his foot on the earth, he begins to dance and to chant. As if in response to his summons the beating of the tom-tom grows to a fierce, exultant boom whose throbs seem to fill the air with vibrating rhythm.* JONES *looks up, starts to spring to his feet, reaches a half-kneeling, half-squatting position, and*

remains rigidly fixed there, paralyzed with awed fascination by this new apparition. The witch-doctor sways, stamping with his foot, his bone rattle clicking the time. 30 *His voice rises and falls in a weird, monotonous croon, without articulate word division. Gradually his dance becomes clearly one of a narrative in pantomime, his croon is an incantation, a charm to allay the fierceness of some implacable deity demanding sacrifice. He flees, he is pursued by devils, he hides, he flees, he flees again. Ever wilder and wilder becomes his flight, nearer and nearer draws the pursuing evil, more and more the spirit of terror gains possession of him. His croon, rising to intensity, is punctuated by shrill cries.* JONES *has become* 40 *completely hypnotized. His voice joins in the incantation, in the cries; he beats time with his hands and sways his body to and fro from the waist. The whole spirit and meaning of the dance has entered into him, has become his spirit. Finally the theme of the pantomime halts, on a howl of despair, and is taken up again in a note of savage hope. There is a salvation. The forces of evil demand sacrifice. They must be appeased. The witch-doctor points with his wand to the sacred tree, the river beyond, to the altar, and finally to* JONES *with a ferocious* 50 *command.* JONES *seems to sense the meaning of this. It is he who must offer himself for sacrifice. He beats his forehead abjectly to the ground, moaning hysterically.*

Mercy, Oh Lawd! Mercy! Mercy on dis po' sinner!

The witch-doctor springs to the river bank. He stretches out his arms and calls to some god within its depths. Then he starts backward slowly, his arms remaining out. A huge head of a crocodile appears over the bank and its eyes, glittering greenly, fastens upon JONES. *He* 60 *stares into them fascinatedly. The witch-doctor prances up to him, touches him with his wand, motions with hideous command toward the waiting monster.* JONES *squirms on his belly nearer and nearer, moaning continually:*

Mercy, Lawd! Mercy!

The crocodile heaves more of his enormous bulk onto the land. JONES *squirms toward him. The witch-doctor's voice shrills out in furious exultation, the tom-tom beats madly.* JONES *cries out in fierce, exhausted spasms of* 70 *anguished pleading:*

Lawd, save me! Lawd Jesus, heah my prayer!

Immediately, in answer to his prayer, comes the thought of the one bullet left him. He snatches at his hip, shouting defiantly:

De silver bullet! Yo' don't git me yit!

He fires at the green eyes in front of him. The head of the crocodile sinks back behind the river bank, the witch-doctor springs behind the sacred tree and disappears.
80 JONES *lies with his face to the ground, his arms outstretched, whimpering with fear as the throb of the tom-tom fills the silence about him with a somber pulsation, a baffled but revengeful power.*

SCENE EIGHT

Dawn. Same as Scene Two, the dividing line of forest and plain. The nearest tree trunks are dimly revealed, but the forest behind them is still a mass of glooming shadow. The tom-tom seems on the very spot, so loud and continuously vibrating are its beats. Lem enters from the left, followed by a small squad of his soldiers, and by the Cockney trader, Smithers. Lem is a heavyset, ape-faced old savage of the extreme African type, dressed only in a loin cloth. A revolver and cartridge belt are about his waist. His soldiers are in different degrees of rag-concealed nakedness. All wear broad palm leaf hats. Each one carries a rifle. Smithers is the same as in Scene One. One of the soldiers, evidently a tracker, is peering about keenly on the ground. He grunts and points to the spot where JONES *entered the forest. Lem and Smithers come to look.*

———————

SMITHERS: (*after a glance, turns away in disgust*) That's where 'e went in right enough. Much good it'll do yer. 'E's miles orf by this an' safe to the coast, damn 'is 'ide! I tole yer ye'd lose 'im, didn't I?—wastin' the 'ole bloomin' night beatin' yer bloody drum and castin' yer silly spells! Gawd blimey, wot a pack!

LEM: (*gutterally*) We kotch him. You see. (*He makes a motion to his soldiers, who squat down on their*
10   *haunches in a semi-circle.*)

SMITHERS: (*exasperatedly*) Well, ain't yer goin' in an' 'unt 'im in the woods? What the 'ell's the good of waitin'?

LEM: (*imperturbably—squatting down himself*) We kotch him.

SMITHERS: (*turning away from him contemptuously*) Aw! Garn! 'E's a better man than the lot o' you put together. I 'ates the sight o' 'im, but I'll say that for 'im.

A sound of snapping twigs comes from the forest. The 20 *soldiers jump to their feet, cocking their rifles alertly. Lem remains sitting with an imperturbable expression, but listening intently. The sound from the woods is repeated. Lem makes a quick signal with his hand. His followers creep quickly but noiselessly into the forest, scattering so that each enters at a different spot.*

SMITHERS: (*in the silence that follows—in a contemptuous whisper*) You ain't thinkin' that would be 'im, I 'ope?

LEM: (*calmly*) We kotch him.   30

SMITHERS: Blarsted fat 'eads! (*Then after a second's thought—wonderingly*) Still an' all, it might happen. If 'e lost 'is bloody way in these stinkin' woods 'e'd likely turn in a circle without 'is knowin' it. They all does.

LEM: (*peremptorily*) S-s-s-h-h?

The report of several rifles sounds from the forest, followed a second later by savage, exultant yells. The beating of the tom-tom abruptly ceases. Lem looks up at the white man with a grin of satisfaction.   40

We kotch him. Him dead.

SMITHERS: (*with a snarl*) 'Ow d'yer know it's 'im an' 'ow d'yer know 'e's dead?

LEM: My men's dey got 'um silver bullets. Dey kill him shore.

SMITHERS: (*astonished*) They got silver bullets?

LEM: Lead bullet no kill him. He got um strong charm. I took um money, make um silver bullet, make um strong charm, too.

SMITHERS: (*light breaking upon him*) So that's wot   50 you was up to all night, wot? You was scared to put after 'im till you'd molded silver bullets, eh?

LEM: (*simply stating a fact*) Yes. Him got strong charm. Lead no good.

SMITHERS: (*slapping his thigh and guffawing*) Haw-haw! If yer don't beat al 'ell! (*Then recovering himself—scornfully*) I'll bet you it ain't 'im they shot at all, yer bleedin' looney!

LEM: (*calmly*) Dey come bring him now.   60

The soldiers come out of the forest, carrying JONES' *limp body. There is a little reddish-purple hole under his left breast. He is dead. They carry him to Lem, who examines his body with great satisfaction. Smithers leans over his shoulder—in a tone of frightened awe:*

Well, they did for yer right enough, Jonesy, me lad! Dead as a 'erring! (*Mockingly*) Where's yer 'igh an' mighty airs now, yer bloomin' Majesty? (*Then with a grin*) Silver bullets! Gawd
70   blimey, but yer died in the 'eight o' style, any'ow!

Lem makes a motion to the soldiers to carry the body out left. Smithers speaks to him sneeringly.

SMITHERS: And I s'pose you think it's yer bleedin' charms and yer silly beatin' the drum that made 'im run in a circle when 'e'd lost 'imself, don't yer?

But LEM *makes no reply, does not seem to hear the question, walks out left after his men.* SMITHERS *looks after him with contemptuous scorn.*

Stupid as 'ogs, the lot of 'em! Blarsted niggers!   80

CURTAIN FALLS

O'NEILL'S *THE EMPEROR JONES*

by *Thomas E. Cook*

The relation between Jung's psychology and O'Neill's dramatic art lies in their common quest for "fixed points of human significance" and their common discovery of these significances in image patterns which they thought of as formative and meaningful. O'Neill called the patterns "dramatic arresting visual symbol(s)" by means of which he could get "fixed form into outer structure"; Jung called them archetypes, manifest in the conscious mind as "formative principles." Without ignoring the difference between an empirical psychology and a dramatic art, it is possible to profit from analogies between them.

The analogies, once they are considered, reveal the interaction O. W. Firkins and other reviewers missed in *The Emperor Jones*. It is an interaction between instinctual forces and spiritual forces which are at the same time outside and inside the protagonist's self. O'Neill casts the interaction in shadows, in dramatic imagery, against the background of a psychoid "Force Behind." Brutus Jones fails to integrate his personality. He fails to make the Force express himself, or, in Jung's terms, he fails to fulfill the potentialities in his proto-image, his pattern of human significance. In him the process of individuation is reversed; the movement of the self is retrogressive. The dramatic images are like archetypal images which would have enabled Jones to discover and realize himself. Having rejected their guidance, having failed to integrate them into his personality, Jones must be haunted by them as by evil spirits, for they take the form of their opposites, the instinctual images Jones encounters in the forest. The "ha'nts" are images of forces once outside himself, environmental forces. But in the course of his life they have moved inside and are now projected outside again to haunt him. In other words, he is haunted not only by disorder in himself, but also and ultimately, by disorder in the substrate out of which he

From *Eugene O'Neill's Use of Dramatic Imagery, 1920-1930: A Study of Six Plays* by Thomas Edwin Cook (unpublished dissertation, Tulane University, 1962). Reprinted by permission.

arose as a potential self. He is a victim of the worst in himself and in the world. Yet, at the very moment of Jones's destruction O'Neill wants his audience to glimpse the permanent possibility of Jones's human significance.

The dramatic images by means of which O'Neill represents Jones's transformations are not "archetypal" in the strict sense of Jung's term. Nonetheless the seven forest tableaux, the silver bullet, the imperial trappings, the formless fears and the "ha'nts," the beat of the drums, the green-eyed crocodile, and so on, are symbols of transformation in the fullest sense. They are formative, arresting, and visual, and they recur in situations different yet the same, as O'Neill in his notes for *Electra* said they should. They form patterns which gradually reveal opposed motives in a struggle for control of a self. The struggle is like that in the process of individuation as Jung observed it:

> A dark impulse is the ultimate arbiter of the pattern, an unconscious a priori precipitates itself into plastic form. . . . Over the whole procedure there seems to reign a dim foreknowledge not only of the pattern, but of its meaning. Image and meaning are identical; and as the first takes shape, so the latter becomes clear.[1]

The Emperor is definitely a play that takes shape. At times, indeed, its shapeliness is almost obtrusive. The set as a whole may be aptly described as the "plastic form" of an "unconscious a priori," a mystical force partly outside yet working in and through the protagonist's personality, a plastic image gradually identified with his growing awareness of its meaning. The word "plastic" is good because it suggests the ways O'Neill could bend his set into squares, triangles, circles, and straight lines as the case required, shaping and reshaping a scene which remained essentially the same, molding it around the changing phases of his character's development. It suggests that "repetition of the same scene—in its essential spirit" which he sought later to achieve in *Mourning Becomes Electra*.

These thoughts lead to the conclusion that the eight scenes of *The Emperor* are best viewed as large-scale dramatic images intended to build an exoskeleton for the play. They are images of "outer structure" designed to give "architectural fixed form" to the action. Between these images of outer structure and those of "inner structure" ("composition[in musical sense]") there is a dramatic interaction analogous to that between the psychoid "Force Behind" and Jones's self. The articulation of the scenes is like the articulation of the words in a poem. What O'Neill achieves is Cocteau's poetry *of* the theater, a coarse and by lyric standards a heavy poetry, but a theatrical poetry nevertheless. He uses what Francis Fergusson has called "the Pirandellesque stage: i.e., the stage as an art medium like that of the painter or musician; the stage as Pirandello's characters use it, to present a brilliant and final image of their tragedies." The Pirandellesque stage, as Fergusson notes, goes back to the Baroque sets of Racine. But given the modern physical and psychological resources available to Pirandello and O'Neill, wonderful new things could be done

---

[1]Jung, Carl, "The Spirit of Psychology," *Spirit and Nature, Papers from the Eranos Yearbooks*, vol. 1, ed. by Joseph Campbell, trans. by Ralph Manheim, New York: Pantheon Books, 1954, p. 414.

with the stage as an art medium. A recent observation of Jung's suggests how the resources of psychology and the Pirandellesque stage complement one another "expressionistically" in *The Emperor*. He notes that in the unconscious "individuation process" the fantasies of a patient can be developed freely in many ways, "dramatic, dialectic, visual, acoustic, or in the form of dancing, painting, drawing, or modeling." This is a fair summary of the resources of the modern stage as a meta-realistic art medium in general. O'Neill outlines the image of Brutus Jones's tragedy visually and acoustically in eight blocks of scenery. . . .

All these images—the seven Forest tableaux, the great circle, the alternating lights and darknesses, the tom-tom beat, the silver bullets, the reversed birth, the imperial clothes, the mother moon—are masks of the "true fated reality," O'Neill's inclusive term for motive. As they recur, a pattern of motives takes shape behind them, the connections between them become clearer, and they become comprehensible as the framework of an idea and a feeling. Images of outer structure and inner composition mesh: the tom-tom beat outlines the action and at the same time composes it; images of light and darkness frame the play which at the same time they are painting. For these interactions of images and meanings O'Neill has the name "unreal-realism."

He objectified his "double-vision" in the two stages of action for *The Emperor:* The forest and the clearings (the Plain), the outer world and the inner, the "background pattern" and the "drama of the recognizable human beings" In *The Infernal Machine*, Cocteau tries at the end "to comprehend the two levels of his scene together." He envisages the passage of Oedipus and his family from the literal world of a central platform into the timeless world of the mythic machine, the world behind "nocturnal curtains." There is a similar peripety in the seventh scene of *The Emperor Jones*. It begins with the firing of the silver bullet at the green-eyed crocodile and ends in the last act with Smithers' parting remarks on Jones's death. The silver bullet is the image of Brutus Jones. When he fires it, he accomplishes two things: he casts out the worst of a rapacious self, represented by one connotation of the silver bullet, and he asserts the best of a royal self, represented by its other connotation, against a *"revengeful power."* This power is imaged in the crocodile god. It is the power of unformed, undirected instincts, the power of an environment which would alienate Jones. But his silver bullet, at once his curse and his last treasure, leaves this god *"baffled."* O'Neill discovers a fixed point of human significance in Jones's last effort to impose order upon an instinctual world, for the effort argues the reality of another power, one which has lain dormant in the seed of Jones's self. This power is the object of O'Neill's search. By retracing the steps in the evolution of that self, O'Neill exposes the best in a bad man, his power to give form and meaning to his being, his power to order and direct a disordered and undirected world. And after Lem's soldiers have destroyed Jones's misspent life and yet honored what he might have been with a death in silver, Smithers' final tribute seems only just. At the fixed point he has discovered, O'Neill, like Cocteau, tries to comprehend together the little powers of erring man and the great powers behind, the frantic world of the clearings and the timeless world of the Great Forest. He tries to make peace between the "unreal" scene of man's follies and failures on the Plain and the ultimately "real" scene of his significant acts in the Forest. This is the meaning of "unreal-realism."

O'Neill made the point himself in an interview he granted Mary B. Mullet for *The American Magazine*. The interview was published as "The Extraordinary Story of Eugene O'Neill." "Man's struggle," he said, "is his success! He is an example of the spiritual significance which life attains when it aims high enough, when the individual fights all the hostile forces within and without himself to achieve a future of nobler values. . . . If a person is to get the meaning of life he must 'learn to like' the facts about himself—ugly as they seem to his sentimental vanity—before he can lay hold on the truth *behind* the facts; and that truth is never ugly!" O'Neill would teach men to like anti-heroes, the Brutus Joneses of this world, for what is spiritually significant in them. The facts of Jones's life are ugly; the truth is not.

So viewed *The Emperor Jones* is, like the plays Aristotle knew, more philosophical than historical, for it speaks of universals. Jones's circular journey through the forest is a quest for the unique principles of his individual personality, but much more important, it is a quest for first principles which apply to all men. A worm lies at the core of his being. Yet as O'Neill and his audience approach the rotten nest they approach also the fresh and potent seed. *Les extrêmes se touchent*. In his letter to Arthur Hobson Quinn, O'Neill said he wanted to develop "symbols in the theatre which may to some degree bring home to members of a modern audience their ennobling identity with the tragic figures on the stage." Jung would have called these heroes symbols of the self. Brutus Jones is such a symbol. As his name suggests, he is one who, however misguided and however unsuccessful, tries to set things right.

THE CAUCASIAN CHALK CIRCLE

Bertolt Brecht (1898-1956)

Adapted by Eric Bentley

The attitudes and career of Brecht, a German, were shaped not only by the violent upheaval of Communism, Nazism, and two world wars but also by his earlier study of medicine and service during World War I in the medical corps of the German army. He has emerged as one of the most remarkable and stimulating of twentieth-century playrights.

His first period of writing was an expression of his disillusionment which characterized the intellectual life of post-war Germany. He anticipated the absurdists in his treatment of the disintegration of human values and the impossibility of communication with *The Wedding* and *In the Jungle of Cities*. The most successful of his early works was *The Three Penny Opera*, which was based on the 18th century English ballad opera of John Gay.

Brecht's middle period shows him politically committed to Marxism, which he frankly espouses in such plays as *Saint Joan of the Stockyards*. In his final period, Brecht's plays show a maturation of his concept of "epic theater," in which didactic purpose gives way to artistic considerations, as in *Mother Courage*, *The Good Woman of Setzuan*, and *The Caucasian Chalk Circle*. After World War II, Brecht gave a vivid demonstration of his gifts in his productions at the Berliner Ensemble.

Two terms are important in considering the production of Brecht's plays—"epic" and "alienation." Brecht called his plays epic

---

433

because of their narrative or cinematic form. He does not narrowly confine the audience's attention to a few characters engaged in a tightly structured sequence of cumulative action. Rather, as one famous European director, Piscator, said, Brecht's interest is "No longer the individual with his private, personal destiny, but the age itself." As a consequence of his social commitment, the playwright wants to challenge his audience to "complex seeing." The resulting succession of episodes made new demands on the stage in the use of music, light, sound and such pictorial devices as slides, motion pictures, maps and charts—all used in a frankly theatrical way in which actor, spectator and stage are all a part of the same theater, devoid of illusion or separation by a fourth wall. As for the actor, Brecht's intention was to present him free from emotional attachment with his role in order that "alienation" might take place—the audience will not enter into the play empathically because a distance will be maintained. Character identification, the objective of the "method" actor, was rejected because the actor became too absorbed in "psychological truth" to be aware of "social truth." All aspects of epic theater—the play, the production and the acting—were intended to neutralize the audience's emotional attachment so as to awaken them to the playwright's ideas.

The rabble meet the governor on his way to church on Easter Sunday.
Photographs in this sequence are of the 1972 production
at the University of California, Santa Barbara,
directed by T. W. Hatlen,
with sets designed by Donald J. Childs.

PHOTOGRAPH BY WILL SWALLING

Above. The governor's wife and child in the Easter procession.

Below. The Fat Prince pays his respects to the governor.

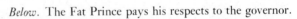

PHOTOGRAPH BY T. W. HATLEN

Opposite page. Simon proposes to Grusha as she flees
from the revolt with the governor's child.

Below. Grusha flees from the Ironshirts
across the "Rotten Bridge."

CHARACTERS

OLD MAN, *on the right*
PEASANT WOMAN, *on the right*
YOUNG PEASANT
A VERY YOUNG WORKER
OLD MAN, *on the left*
PEASANT WOMAN, *on the left*
AGRICULTURIST KATO
GIRL TRACTORIST
WOUNDED SOLDIER
THE DELEGATE *from the capital*
THE SINGER
GEORGI ABASHWILI, *the Governor*
NATELLA, *the Governor's wife*
MICHAEL, *their son*
SHALVA, *an adjutant*
ARSEN KAZBEKI, *a fat prince*
MESSENGER, *from the capital*
NIKO MIKADZE *and* MIKA LOLADZE, *doctors*
SIMON SHASHAVA, *a soldier*
GRUSHA VASHNADZE, *a kitchen maid*
OLD PEASANT, *with the milk*
CORPORAL *and* PRIVATE
PEASANT *and his wife*
LAVRENTI VASHNADZE, GRUSHA'S *brother*

ANIKO, *his wife*
PEASANT WOMAN, *for a while* GRUSHA'S *mother-in-law*
JUSSUP, *her son*
MONK
AZDAK, *village recorder*
SHAUWA, *a policeman*
GRAND DUKE
DOCTOR
INVALID
LIMPING MAN
BLACKMAILER
LUDOVICA
INNKEEPER, *her father-in-law*
STABLEBOY
POOR OLD PEASANT WOMAN
IRAKLI, *her brother-in-law, a bandit*
THREE WEALTHY FARMERS
ILLO SHUBOLADZE *and* SANDRO OBOLADZE, *lawyers*
OLD MARRIED COUPLE
SOLDIERS, SERVANTS,
PEASANTS, BEGGARS,
MUSICIANS, MERCHANTS,
NOBLES, ARCHITECTS

THE CAUCASIAN CHALK CIRCLE

PROLOGUE

Among the ruins of a war-ravaged Caucasian village the members of two Kolkhoz* villages, mostly women and older men, are sitting in a circle, smoking and drinking wine. With them is a delegate of the state reconstruction commission from Nuka, the capital.

PEASANT WOMAN: (*Left*) (*Pointing*). In those hills over there we stopped three Nazi tanks, but the apple orchard was already destroyed.

OLD MAN: (*Right*). Out beautiful dairy farm: a ruin.

GIRL TRACTORIST: I laid the fire, Comrade. (*Pause*)

THE DELEGATE: Now listen to the report. Delegates from the goat-breeding Kolkhoz "Rosa Luxemburg" have been to Nuka. When Hitler's armies approached, the Kolkhoz had moved its goat-herds further east on orders from the authorities. They are now thinking of returning. Their delegates have investigated the village and the land and found a lot of it destroyed.

DELEGATES *on right nod*

The neighboring fruit-culture Kolkhoz (*To the left*) "Galinsk" is proposing to use the former grazing land of Kolkhoz "Rosa Luxemburg," a valley with scanty growth of grass, for orchards and vineyards. As a delegate of the Reconstruction Commission, I request that the two Kolkhoz villages decide between themselves whether Kolkhoz "Rosa Luxemburg" shall return here or not.

OLD MAN: (*Right*.) First of all, I want to protest against the restriction of time for discussion. We of Kolkhoz "Rosa Luxemburg" have spent three days and three nights getting here. And now discussion is limited to half a day.

WOUNDED SOLDIER: (*Left*). Comrade, we haven't as many villages as we used to have. We haven't as many hands. We haven't as much time.

GIRL TRACTORIST: All pleasures have to be rationed. Tobacco is rationed, and wine. Discussion should be rationed.

OLD MAN: (*Right*) (*Sighing*). Death to the fascists! But I will come to the point and explain why we want our valley back. There are a great many reasons, but I'll begin with one of the simplest. Makina Abakidze, unpack the goat cheese. (*A* PEASANT WOMAN *from right takes from a basket an enormous cheese wrapped in a cloth. Applause and laughter*) Help yourselves, Comrades, start in!

OLD MAN: (*Left*) (*Suspiciously*). Is this a way of influencing us?

OLD MAN: (*Right*) (*Amid laughter*). How could it be a way of influencing you, Surab, you valley-thief? Everyone knows you will take the cheese and the valley, too. (*Laughter*) All I expect from you is an honest answer. Do you like the cheese?

---

*Kolkhoz a collective farm in the Soviet Union.

439

50   OLD MAN: (*Left*). The answer is: yes.

OLD MAN: (*Right*). Really. (*Bitterly*) I ought to have known you know nothing about cheese.

OLD MAN: (*Left*). Why not? When I tell you I like it?

OLD MAN: (*Right*). Because you can't like it. Because it's not what it was in the old days. And why not? Because our goats don't like the new grass as they did the old. Cheese is not cheese because grass is not grass, that's the thing. Please
60   put that in your report.

OLD MAN: (*Left*). But your cheese is excellent.

OLD MAN: (*Right*). It isn't excellent. It's just passable. The new grazing land is no good, whatever the young people may say. One can't live there. It doesn't even smell of morning in the morning. (SEVERAL PEOPLE *laugh*)

THE DELEGATE: Don't mind their laughing: they understand you. Comrades, why does one love one's country? Because the bread tastes better
70   there, the air smells better, voices sound stronger, the sky is higher, the ground is easier to walk on. Isn't that so?

OLD MAN: (*Right*). The valley has belonged to us from all eternity.

SOLDIER: (*Left*). What does *that* mean—from all eternity? Nothing belongs to anyone from all eternity. When you were young you didn't even belong to yourself. You belonged to the Kazbeki princes.

80   OLD MAN: (*Right*). Doesn't it make a difference, though, what kind of trees stand next to the house you are born in? Or what kind of neighbors you have? Doesn't that make a difference? We want to go back just to have you as our neighbors, valley-thieves! Now you can all laugh again.

OLD MAN: (*Left*). (*Laughing*). Then why don't you listen to what your neighbor, Kato Wachtang, our agriculturist, has to say about the valley?

PEASANT WOMAN: (*Right*). We've not said all there
90   is to be said about our valley. By no means. Not all the houses are destroyed. As for the dairy farm, at least the foundation wall is still standing.

DELEGATE: You can claim State support—here and there—you know that. I have suggestions here in my pocket.

PEASANT WOMAN: (*Right*). Comrade Specialist, we haven't come here to bargain. I can't take your

cap and hand you another, and say "This one's better." The other one might *be* better; but you   100
like yours better.

GIRL TRACTORIST: A piece of land is not a cap—not in our country, Comrade.

DELEGATE: Don't get angry. It's true we have to consider a piece of land as a tool to produce something useful, but it's also true that we must recognize love for a particular piece of land. As far as I'm concerned, I'd like to find out more exactly what you (*To those on the left*) want to do with the valley.   110

OTHERS: Yes, let Kato speak.

DELEGATE: Comrade Agriculturist!

KATO: (*Rising*, SHE'S *in military uniform*). Comrades, last winter, while we were fighting in these hills as Partisans, we discussed how, after the expulsion of the Germans, we could build up our fruit culture to ten times its original size. I've prepared a plan for an irrigation project. By means of a cofferdam on our mountain lake, 300 hectares of unfertile land can be irrigated. Our   120 Kolkhoz could not only cultivate more fruit, but also have vineyards. The project, however, would pay only if the disputed valley of Kolkhoz "Galinsk" were also included. Here are the calculations. (SHE *hands the* DELEGATE *a briefcase*)

OLD MAN: (*Right*). Write into a report that our Kolkhoz plans to start a new stud farm.

GIRL TRACTORIST: Comrades, the project was conceived during days and nights when we had to take cover in the mountains. We were often with-   130 out ammunition for our half-dozen rifles. Even getting a pencil was difficult. (*Applause from both sides*)

OLD MAN: (*Right*). Our thanks to the Comrades of Kolkhoz "Galinsk" and all who have defended our country! (THEY *shake hands and embrace*)

PEASANT WOMAN: (*Left*). In doing this our thought was that our soldiers—both your men and our men—should return to a still more productive homeland.   140

GIRL TRACTORIST: As the poet Mayakovsky said: "The home of the Soviet people shall also be the home of Reason"!

(*The* DELEGATES *including the* OLD MAN *have got up, and with the* DELEGATE *specified proceed to study the Agriculturist's drawings ... exclamations such as: "Why*

*is the altitude of all 22 meters?"–"This rock must be
blown up"–"Actually, all they need is cement and
dynamite"–"They force the water to come down here,*
150 *that's clever!")*

A VERY YOUNG WORKER: (*Right*) (*To* OLD MAN, *right*)
They're going to irrigate all the fields between
the hills, look at that, Aleko!

OLD MAN: (*Right*). I'm not going to look. I knew
the project would be good. I won't have a
revolver aimed at my chest.

DELEGATE: But they only want to aim a pencil at
your chest. (*Laughter*)

OLD MAN: (*Right*) (*Gets up gloomily, and walks over
160 to look at the drawings*) These valley-thieves know
only too well that we can't resist machines and
projects in this country.

PEASANT WOMAN: (*Right*) Aleko Bereshwili, you
have a weakness for new projects. That's well
known.

DELEGATE: What about my report? May I write
that you will all support the cession of your old
valley in the interests of this project when you
get back to your Kolkhoz?

170 PEASANT WOMAN: (*Right*). I will. What about you,
Aleko?

OLD MAN: (*Right*) (*Bent over drawings*). I suggest that
you give us copies of the drawings to take along.

PEASANT WOMAN: (*Right*). Then we can sit down
and eat. Once he has the drawings and he's ready
to discuss them, the matter is settled. I know
him. And it will be the same with the rest of
us. (DELEGATES *laughingly embrace again*)

OLD MAN: (*Left*). Long live the Kolkhoz "Rosa Lux-
180 emburg" and much luck to your horsebreeding
project!

PEASANT WOMAN: (*Left*). In honor of the visit of the
delegates from Kolkhoz "Rosa Luxemburg" and
of the Specialist, the plan is that we all hear
a presentation of the Singer Arkadi Tscheidse.
(*Applause.* GIRL TRACTORIST *has gone off to bring
the* SINGER)

PEASANT WOMAN: (*Right*). Comrades, your entertainment had better be good. We're going to pay
190 for it with a valley.

PEASANT WOMAN: (*Left*). Arkadi Tscheidse knows
about our discussion. He's promised to perform
something that has a bearing on the problem.

KATO: We wired to Tiflis three times. The whole
thing nearly fell through at the last minute
because his driver had a cold.

PEASANT WOMAN: (*Left*). Arkadi Tscheidse knows
21,000 lines of verse.

OLD MAN: (*Left*). It's very difficult to get him. You
and the Planning Commission should see to it   200
that you get him to come North more often,
Comrade.

DELEGATE: We are more interested in economics,
I'm afraid.

OLD MAN: (*Left*) (*Smiling*). You arrange the redistribution of vines and tractors, why not of songs?

(*Enter the* SINGER ARKADI TSCHEIDSE *led by* GIRL
TRACTORIST. *He is a well-built man of simple manners,
accompanied by* FOUR MUSICIANS *with their instruments.
The* ARTISTS *are greeted with applause*)   210

GIRL TRACTORIST: This is the Comrade Specialist,
Arkadi. (*The* SINGER *greets them all*)

DELEGATE: I'm honored to make your acquaintance.
I heard about your songs when I was a boy at
school. Will it be one of the old legends?

THE SINGER: A very old one. It's called The Chalk
Circle and comes from the Chinese. But we'll
do it, of course, in a changed version. Comrades,
it's an honor for me to entertain you after a difficult debate. We hope you will find that the   220
voice of the old poet also sounds well in the
shadow of Soviet tractors. It may be a mistake
to mix different wines, but old and new wisdom
mix admirably. Now I hope we'll get something
to eat before the performance begins—it would
certainly help.

VOICES: Surely. Everyone into the Club House!
(*While* EVERYONE *begins to move, the* DELEGATE
turns to the GIRL TRACTORIST)

DELEGATE: I hope it won't take long. I've got to   230
get back tonight.

GIRL TRACTORIST: How long will it last, Arkadi?
The Comrade Specialist must get back to Tiflis
tonight.

THE SINGER: (*Casually*). It's actually two stories. An
hour or two.

GIRL TRACTORIST: (*Confidentially*). Couldn't you
make it shorter?

THE SINGER: No.

VOICE: Arkadi Tscheidse's performance will take   240
place here in the square after the meal. (*And
THEY ALL go happily to eat*)

1. THE NOBLE CHILD

As the lights go up, THE SINGER *is seen sitting on the floor, a black sheepskin cloak round his shoulders, and a little well-thumbed notebook in his hand. A small group of listeners—the* CHORUS—*sits with him. The manner of his recitation makes it clear that he has told his story over and over again. He mechanically fingers the pages, seldom looking at them. With appropriate gestures, he gives the signal for each scene to begin.*

THE SINGER:

In olden times, in a bloody time,
There ruled in a Caucasian city—
Men called it City of the Damned—
A governor.
His name was Georgi Abashwili.
He was rich as Croesus
He had a beautiful wife
He had a healthy baby.
10   No other governor in Grusinia
Had so many horses in his stable
So many beggars on his doorstep
So many soldiers in his service
So many petitioners in his courtyard.
Georgi Abashwili—how shall I describe him
   to you?
He enjoyed his life.
On the morning of Easter Sunday
The governor and his family went to church.

20   *At the left a large doorway, at the right an even larger gateway.* BEGGARS *and* PETITIONERS *pour from the gateway, holding up thin* CHILDREN, *crutches, and petitions. They are followed by* IRONSHIRTS, *and then, expensively dressed, the* GOVERNOR'S FAMILY

BEGGARS AND PETITIONERS:

Mercy! Mercy, Your Grace! The taxes are
   too high.
—I lost my leg in the Persian War, where
   can I get . . .

—My brother is innocent, Your Grace, a mis-   30
   understanding . . .
—The child is starving in my arms!
—Our petition is for our son's discharge from
   the army, our last remaining son!
—Please, Your Grace, the water inspector
   takes bribes.

ONE SERVANT *collects the petitions,* ANOTHER *distributes coins from a purse.* SOLDIERS *push the* CROWD *back, lashing at them with thick leather whips*

THE SOLDIER: Get back! Clear the church door!   40
   (*Behind the* GOVERNOR, HIS WIFE, *and the* ADJU-
   TANT, *the* GOVERNOR'S CHILD *is brought through
   the gateway in an ornate carriage*)
THE CROWD:
—The baby!
—I can't see it, don't shove so hard!
—God bless the child, Your Grace!
THE SINGER: (*While the* CROWD *is driven back with
   whips*).
   For the first time on that Easter Sunday,   50
      the people saw the Governor's heir.
   Two doctors never moved from the noble
      child, apple of the Governor's eye.
   Even the mighty Prince Kazbeki bows before
      him at the church door. (*A* FAT PRINCE
steps forward and greets the family)
THE FAT PRINCE: Happy Easter, Natella Abashwili!
   What a day! When it was raining last night,
   I thought to myself, gloomy holidays! But this
   morning the sky was gay. I love a gay sky, a   60
   simple heart, Natella Abashwili. And little
   Michael is a governor from head to foot! Tititi!
   (*He tickles the* CHILD)
THE GOVERNOR'S WIFE: What do you think Arsen,
   at last Georgi has decided to start building the
   wing on the east side. All those wretched slums
   are to be torn down to make room for the garden.
THE FAT PRINCE: Good news after so much bad!
   What's the latest on the war, Brother Georgi?
   (*The* GOVERNOR *indicates a lack of interest*)   70

THE FAT PRINCE: Strategical retreat, I hear. Well, minor reverses are to be expected. Sometimes things go well, sometimes not. Such is war. Doesn't mean a thing, does it?

THE GOVERNOR'S WIFE: He's coughing. Georgi, did you hear? (*She speaks sharply to the* DOCTORS, *two dignified men standing close to the little carriage*) He's coughing!

80 THE FIRST DOCTOR: (*To the* SECOND). May I remind you, Niko Mikadze, that I was against the lukewarm bath? (*To the* GOVERNOR'S WIFE) There's been a little error over warming the bath water, Your Grace.

THE SECOND DOCTOR: (*Equally polite*). Mika Loladze, I'm afraid I can't agree with you. The temperature of the bath water was exactly what our great, beloved Mishiko Oboladze prescribed. More likely a slight draft during the night, Your Grace.

90 THE GOVERNOR'S WIFE: But do pay more attention to him. He looks feverish, Georgi. .

THE FIRST DOCTOR: (*Bending over the* CHILD). No cause for alarm, Your Grace. The bath water will be warmer. It won't occur again.

THE SECOND DOCTOR: (*With a venomous glance at the* FIRST). I won't forget that, my dear Mika Loladze. No cause for concern, Your Grace.

THE FAT PRINCE: Well, well, well! I always say: "A pain in my liver? Then the doctor gets fifty
100 strokes on the soles of his feet." We live in a decadent age. In the old days one said: "Off with his head!"

THE GOVERNOR'S WIFE: Let's go into church. Very likely it's the draft here.

The procession of FAMILY *and* SERVANTS *turns into the doorway. The* FAT PRINCE *follows, but the* GOVERNOR *is kept back by the* ADJUTANT, *a handsome young man. When the crowd of* PETITIONERS *has been driven off, a young dust-stained* RIDER, *his arm in a sling, remains*
110 *behind*

THE ADJUTANT: (*Pointing at the Rider, who steps forward*). Won't you hear the messenger from the capital, your Excellency? He arrived this morning. With confidential papers.

THE GOVERNOR: Not before Service, Shalva. But did you hear Brother Kazbeki wish me a happy Easter? Which is all very well, but I don't believe it did rain last night.

THE ADJUTANT: (*Nodding*). We must investigate.

THE GOVERNOR: Yes, at once. Tomorrow.   120

*They pass through the doorway. The Rider, who has waited in vain for an audience, turns sharply round and, muttering a curse, goes off. Only one of the palace guards–*SIMON SHASHAVA*–remains at the door*

THE SINGER:
> The city is still.
> Pigeons strut in the church square.
> A soldier of the Palace Guard
> Is joking with a kitchen maid
> As she comes up from the river with a bundle.   130

*A girl–*GRUSHA VASHADZE*–comes through the gateway with a bundle made of large green leaves under her arm*

SIMON: What, the young lady is not in church? Shirking?

GRUSHA: I was dressed to go. But they needed another goose for the banquet. And they asked me to get it. I know about geese.

SIMON: A goose? (*He feigns suspicion*) I'd like to see that goose. (GRUSHA *does not understand*) One has to be on one's guard with women. "I only went   140 for a fish," they tell you, but it turns out to be something else.

GRUSHA: (*Walking resolutely toward him and showing him the goose*). There! If it isn't a fifteen-pound goose stuffed full of corn, I'll eat the feathers.

SIMON: A queen of a goose! The Governor himself will eat it. So the young lady has been down to the river again?

GRUSHA: Yes, at the poultry farm.

SIMON: Really? At the poultry farm, down by the   150 river . . . not higher up maybe? Near those willows?

GRUSHA: I only go to the willows to wash the linen.

SIMON: (*Insinuatingly*). Exactly.

GRUSHA: Exactly what?

SIMON: (*Winking*). Exactly that.

GRUSHA: Why shouldn't I wash the linen by the willows?

SIMON: (*With exaggerated laughter*). "Why shouldn't I wash the linen by the willows!" That's good,   160 really good!

GRUSHA: I don't understand the soldier. What's so good about it?

SIMON: (*Slyly*). "If something I know someone learns, she'll grow hot and cold by turns!"

GRUSHA: I don't know what I could learn about those willows.

SIMON: Not even if there was a bush opposite? That one could see everything from? Everything that goes on there when a certain person is—"washing linen"?

GRUSHA: What goes on? Won't the soldier say what he means and have done?

SIMON: Something goes on. And something can be seen.

GRUSHA: Could the soldier mean I dip my toes in the water when it is hot? There is nothing else.

SIMON: More. Your toes. And more.

GRUSHA: More what? At most my foot?

SIMON: Your foot. And a little more. (*He laughs heartily*)

GRUSHA: (*Angrily*). Simon Shashava, you ought to be ashamed of yourself! To sit in a bush on a hot day and wait till someone comes and dips her leg in the river! And I bet you bring a friend along too! (*She runs off*)

SIMON: (*Shouting after her*). I didn't bring any friend along! (*As the* SINGER *resumes his tale, the* SOLDIER *steps into the doorway as though to listen to the service*)

THE SINGER:

The city lies still
But why are there armed men?
The Governor's palace is at peace
But why is it a fortress?
And the Governor returned to his palace
And the fortress was a trap
And the goose was plucked and roasted
But the goose was not eaten this time
And noon was no longer the hour to eat:
Noon was the hour to die.

From the doorway at the left the FAT PRINCE *quickly appears, stands still, looks around. Before the gateway at the right* TWO IRONSHIRTS *are squatting and playing dice. The* FAT PRINCE *sees them, walks slowly past, making a sign to them. They rise: One goes through the gateway, the other goes off at the right. Muffled voices are heard from various directions in the rear: "To your posts!" The palace is surrounded. The* FAT PRINCE *quickly goes off. Church bells in the distance. Enter, through the doorway, the* GOVERNOR'S FAMILY *and* PROCESSION, *returning from church*

THE GOVERNOR'S WIFE: (*Passing the* ADJUTANT). It's impossible to live in such a slum. But Georgi, of course, will only build for his little Michael. Never for me! Michael is all! All for Michael!

The PROCESSION *turns into the gateway. Again the* ADJUTANT *lingers behind. He waits. Enter the* WOUNDED RIDER *from the doorway.* TWO IRONSHIRTS *of the palace guard have taken up positions by the gateway*

THE ADJUTANT: (*To the rider*). The Governor does not wish to receive military reports before dinner—especially if they're depressing, as I assume. In the afternoon His Excellency will confer with prominent architects. They're coming to dinner too. And here they are! (*Enter* THREE GENTLEMEN *through the doorway*) Go in the kitchen and get yourself something to eat, my friend. (*As the rider goes, the* ADJUTANT *greets the* ARCHITECTS) Gentlemen, His Excellency expects you at dinner. He will devote all his time to you and your great new plans. Come!

ONE OF THE ARCHITECTS: We marvel that His Excellency intends to build. There are disquieting rumors that the war in Persia has taken a turn for the worse.

THE ADJUTANT: All the more reason to build! There's nothing to those rumors anyway. Persia is a long way off, and the garrison here would let itself be hacked to bits for its Governor. (*Noise from the palace. The shrill scream of a woman. Someone is shouting orders. Dumbfounded, the* ADJUTANT *moves toward the gateway. An* IRONSHIRT *steps out, points his lance at him*) What's this? Put down that lance, you dog.

ONE OF THE ARCHITECTS: It's the Princes! Don't you know the Princes met last night in the capital? And they're against the Grand Duke and his Governors? Gentlemen, we'd better make ourselves scarce. (*They rush off. The* ADJUTANT *remains helplessly behind*)

THE ADJUTANT: (*Furiously to the Palace Guard*). Down with those lances! Don't you see the Governor's life is threatened?

The IRONSHIRTS *of the Palace Guard refuse to obey.*

THEY *stare coldly and indifferently at the* ADJUTANT *and follow the next events without interest*

THE SINGER:

O blindness of the great!
They go their way like gods,
Great over bent backs,
Sure of hired fists,
Trusting in the power
Which has lasted so long.

But long is not forever.
O change from age to age!
Thou hope of the people!

Enter the GOVERNOR, *through the gateway, between*
TWO SOLDIERS *armed to the teeth. He is in chains. His*
270 *face is gray*

Up, great sir, deign to walk upright!
From your palace the eyes of many foes follow
you!
And now you don't need an architect, a
carpenter will do.
You won't be moving into a new palace
But into a little hole in the ground.
Look about you once more, blind man!

The arrested man looks round

280 Does all you had please you?
Between the Easter Mass and the Easter meal
You are walking to a place whence no one
returns.

The GOVERNOR *is led off. A horn sounds an alarm.*
Noise behind the gateway

When the house of a great one collapses
Many little ones are slain.
Those who had no share in the *good* fortunes
of the mighty
290 Often have a share in their *mis*fortunes.
The plunging wagon
Drags the sweating oxen down with it
Into the abyss.

The SERVANTS *come rushing through the gateway in*
panic

THE SERVANTS: *(Among themselves).*
—The baskets!
—Take them all into the third courtyard!
Food for five days!
300 —The mistress has fainted! Someone must
carry her down.
—She must get away.
—What about us? We'll be slaughtered like
chickens, as always.
—Goodness, what'll happen? There's
bloodshed already in the city, they say.
—Nonsense, the Governor has just been
asked to appear at a Princes' meeting. All
very correct. Everything'll be ironed out.
310 I heard this on the best authority . . .

The TWO DOCTORS *rush into the courtyard*

THE FIRST DOCTOR: *(Trying to restrain the other)* Niko
Mikadze, it is your duty as a doctor to attend
Natella Abashwili.
THE SECOND DOCTOR: My duty! It's yours!
THE FIRST DOCTOR: Whose turn is it to look after
the child today, Niko Mikadze, yours or mine?
THE SECOND DOCTOR: Do you really think, Mika
Loladze, I'm going to stay a minute longer in
this accursed house on that little brat's account? 320

They start fighting. All one hears is: "You neglect your
duty!" and "Duty, my foot!" Then the SECOND DOCTOR
knocks the FIRST *down*

Go to hell!   *(Exit)*

Enter the SOLDIER, SIMON SHASHAVA. *He searches in*
the crowd for GRUSHA

SIMON: Grusha! There you are at last! What are
you going to do?
GRUSHA: Nothing. If worst comes to worst, I've
a brother in the mountains. How about you? 330
SIMON: Forget about me. *(Formally again)* Grusha
Vashnadze, your wish to know my plans fills
me with satisfaction. I've been ordered to
accompany Madam Natella Abashwili as her
guard.
GRUSHA: But hasn't the Palace Guard mutinied?
SIMON: *(Seriously).* That's a fact.
GRUSHA: Isn't it dangerous to go with her?
SIMON: In Tiflis, they say: Isn't the stabbing dan-
gerous for the knife?   340
GRUSHA: You're not a knife, you're a man, Simon
Shashava, what has that woman to do with you?
SIMON: That woman has nothing to do with me.
I have my orders, and I go.
GRUSHA: The soldier is pigheaded: he is getting
himself into danger for nothing—nothing at all.
I must get into the third courtyard, I'm in a
hurry.
SIMON: Since we're both in a hurry we shouldn't
quarrel. You need time for a good quarrel. May 350
I ask if the young lady still has parents?
GRUSHA: No, just a brother.
SIMON: As time is short—my second question is
this: Is the young lady as healthy as a fish in
water?
GRUSHA: I may have a pain in the right shoulder
once in a while. Otherwise I'm strong enough
for my job. No one has complained. So far.
SIMON: That's well-known. When it's Easter Sun-

360 day, and the question arises who'll run for the goose all the same, she'll be the one. My third question is this: Is the young lady impatient? Does she want apples in winter?

GRUSHA: Impatient? No. But if a man goes to war without any reason and then no message comes —that's bad.

SIMON: A message will come. And now my final question...

370 GRUSHA: Simon Shashave, I must get to the third courtyard at once. My answer is yes.

SIMON: (Very embarrassed). Haste, they say, is the wind that blows down the scaffolding. But they also say: The rich don't know what haste is. I'm from...

GRUSHA: Kutsk...

SIMON: So the young lady has been inquiring about me? I'm healthy, I have no dependants, I make ten piasters a month, as paymaster twenty pias-

380 ters, and I'm asking—very sincerely—for your hand.

GRUSHA: Simon Shashava, it suits me well.

SIMON: (Taking from his neck a thin chain with a little cross on it). My mother gave me this cross, Grusha Vashnadze. The chain is silver. Please wear it.

GRUSHA: Many thanks, Simon.

SIMON: (Hangs it round her neck). It would be better for the young lady to go to the third courtyard now. Or there'll be difficulties. Anyway, I must harness the horses. The young lady will under-

390 stand?

GRUSHA: Yes, Simon. (They stand undecided)

SIMON: I'll just take the mistress to the troops that have stayed loyal. When the war's over, I'll be back. In two weeks. Or three. I hope my intended won't get tired, awaiting my return.

GRUSHA:
Simon Shashava, I shall wait for you.
Go calmly into battle, soldier
The bloody battle, the bitter battle

400 From which not everyone returns:
When you return I shall be there.
I shall be waiting for you under the green elm
I shall be waiting for you under the bare elm
I shall wait until the last soldier has returned
and longer.
When you come back from the battle

No boots will stand at my door
The pillow beside mine will be empty   410
And my mouth will be unkissed.
When you return, when you return
You will be able to say: It is just as it was.

SIMON: I thank you, Grusha Vashnadze. And goodbye! (He bows low before her. She does the same before him. Then she runs quickly off without looking round. Enter the ADJUTANT from the gateway)

THE ADJUTANT: (Harshly). Harness the horses to the carriage! Don't stand there doing nothing, louse! (SIMON SHASHAVA stands to attention and   420 goes off)

TWO SERVANTS crowd from the gateway, bent low under huge trunks. Behind them, supported by her WOMEN, stumbles NATELLA ABASHWILI. She is followed by a WOMAN carrying the CHILD

THE GOVERNOR'S WIFE: I hardly know if my head's still on. Where's Michael? Don't hold him so clumsily. Pile the trunks onto the carriage. Shalva, is there no news from the city?

THE ADJUTANT: None. All's quiet so far, but there's   430 not a minute to lose. No room for all these trunks in the carriage. Pick out what you need.

(Exit quickly)

THE GOVERNOR'S WIFE: Only essentials! Quick, open the trunks! I'll tell you what I need. (The trunks are lowered and opened. She points at some brocade dresses) The green one! And, of course, the one with the fur trimming. Where are Niko Mikadze and Mika Loladze? I've suddenly got the most terrible migraine again. It always starts   440 in the temples.

Enter GRUSHA

Taking your time, eh? Go at once and get the hot water bottles! (GRUSHA runs off, returns later with hot water bottles; THE GOVERNOR'S WIFE orders her about by signs) Don't tear the sleeves.

A YOUNG WOMAN: Pardon, madam, no harm has come to the dress.

THE GOVERNOR'S WIFE: Because I stopped you. I've been watching you for a long time. Nothing in   450 your head but making eyes at Shalva Tzereteli. I'll kill you, you bitch! (She beats the WOMAN)

THE ADJUTANT: (Appearing in the gateway). Please make haste, Natella Abashwili. Firing has broken out in the city.

(Exit)

THE GOVERNOR'S WIFE: (*Letting go of the* YOUNG
WOMAN*).* Oh dear, do you think they'll lay hands
on us? Why should they? Why? (*She herself begins
to rummage in the trunks*) How's Michael? Asleep?
460
THE WOMAN WITH THE CHILD: Yes, madam.
THE GOVERNOR'S WIFE: Then put him down a
moment and get my little saffron-colored boots
from the bedroom. I need them for the green
dress. (*The* WOMAN *puts down the* CHILD *and goes
off*) Just look how these things have been packed!
No love! No understanding! If you don't give
them every order yourself... At such moments
you realize what kind of servants you have! They
470
gorge themselves at your expense, and never a
word of gratitude! I'll remember this.
THE ADJUTANT: (*Entering, very excited*). Natella, you
must leave at once!
THE GOVERNOR'S WIFE: Why? I've got to take this
silver dress—it cost a thousand piasters. And
that one there, and where's the wine-colored
one?
THE ADJUTANT: (*Trying to pull her away*). Riots have
broken out! We must leave at once. Where's the
480
baby?
THE GOVERNOR'S WIFE: (*calling to the* YOUNG WOMAN
who was holding the baby). Maro, get the baby
ready! Where on earth are you?
THE ADJUTANT: (*Leaving*). We'll probably have to
leave the carriage behind and go ahead on horse-
back.

The GOVERNOR'S WIFE *rummages again among her
dresses, throws some onto the heap of chosen clothes, then
takes them off again. Noises, drums are heard. The* YOUNG
490
WOMAN *who was beaten creeps away. The sky begins
to grow red*

THE GOVERNOR'S WIFE: (*Rummaging desperately*). I
simply cannot find the wine-colored dress. Take
the whole pile to the carriage. Where's Asja?
And why hasn't Maro come back? Have you
all gone crazy?
THE ADJUTANT: (*Returning*). Quick! Quick!
THE GOVERNOR'S WIFE: (*To the* FIRST WOMAN). Run!
Just throw them into the carriage!
500
THE ADJUTANT: We're not taking the carriage. And
if you don't come now, I'll ride off on my own.
THE GOVERNOR'S WIFE: (*As the* FIRST WOMAN *can't
carry everything*). Where's the bitch Asja? (*The*
ADJUTANT *pulls her away*) Maro, bring the baby!

(*To the* FIRST WOMAN) Go and look for Masha.
No, first take the dresses to the carriage. Such
nonsense! I wouldn't dream of going on horse-
back.

*Turning round, she sees the red sky, and starts back
rigid. The fire burns. She is pulled out by the* ADJUTANT. 510
Shaking, the FIRST WOMAN *follows with the dresses*

MARO: (*From the doorway with the boots*). Madam!
(*She sees the trunks and dresses and runs toward the
baby, picks it up, and holds it a moment*) They left
it behind, the beasts. (*She hands it to* GRUSHA)
Hold it a moment. (*She runs off, following the*
GOVERNOR'S WIFE)

Enter SERVANTS *from the gateway*

THE COOK: Well, so they've actually gone. Without
the food wagons, and not a minute too early. 520
It's time for us to clear out.
A GROOM: This'll be an unhealthy neighborhood
for quite a while. (*To one of the* WOMEN) Suliko,
take a few blankets and wait for me in the foal
stables.
GRUSHA: What have they done with the governor?
THE GROOM: (*Gesturing throat cutting*). Ffffft.
A FAT WOMAN: (*Seeing the gesture and becoming hysteri-* 530
cal). Oh dear, oh dear, oh dear, oh dear! Our
master Georgi Abashwili! A picture of health
he was, at the Morning Mass—and now! Oh,
take me away, we're all lost, we must die in
sin like our master, Georgi Abashwili!
THE OTHER WOMAN: (*Soothing her*). Calm down,
Nina! You'll be taken to safety. You've never
hurt a fly.
THE FAT WOMAN: (*Being led out*). Oh dear, oh dear,
oh dear! Quick! Let's all get out before they 540
come, before they come!
A YOUNG WOMAN: Nina takes it more to heart than
the mistress, that's a fact. They even have to
have their weeping done for them.
THE COOK: We'd better get out, all of us.
ANOTHER WOMAN: (*Glancing back*). That must be
the East Gate burning.
THE YOUNG WOMAN: (*Seeing the* CHILD *in* GRUSHA's
arms). The baby! What are you doing with it?
GRUSHA: It got left behind. 550
THE YOUNG WOMAN: She simply left it there.
Michael, who was kept out of all the drafts!

The SERVANTS *gather round the* CHILD

GRUSHA: He's waking up.

THE GROOM: Better put him down, I tell you. I'd rather not think what'd happen to anybody who was found with that baby.

THE COOK: That's right. Once they get started, they'll kill each other off, whole families at a time. Let's go.

Exeunt all but GRUSHA, *with the* CHILD *on her arm, and* TWO WOMEN

THE TWO WOMEN: Didn't you hear? Better put him down.

GRUSHA: The nurse asked me to hold him a moment.

THE OLDER WOMAN: She's not coming back, you simpleton.

THE YOUNGER WOMAN: Keep your hands off it.

THE OLDER WOMAN: (*Amiably*). Grusha, you're a good soul, but you're not very bright, and you know it. I tell you, if he had the plague he couldn't be more dangerous.

GRUSHA: (*Stubbornly*). He hasn't got the plague. He looks at me! He's human!

THE OLDER WOMAN: Don't look at *him*. You're a fool—the kind that always gets put upon. A person need only say, "Run for the salad, you have the longest legs," and you run. My husband has an ox cart—you can come with us if you hurry! Lord, by now the whole neighborhood must be in flames.

BOTH WOMEN *leave, sighing. After some hesitation,* GRUSHA *puts the sleeping* CHILD *down, looks at it for a moment, then takes a brocade blanket from the heap of clothes and covers it. Then* BOTH WOMEN *return, dragging bundles.* GRUSHA *starts guiltily away from the* CHILD *and walks a few steps to one side*

THE YOUNGER WOMAN: Haven't you packed anything yet? There isn't much time, you know. The Ironshirts will be here from the barracks.

GRUSHA: Coming. (*She runs through the doorway.* BOTH WOMEN *go to the gateway and wait. The sound of horses is heard. They flee, screaming*)

Enter the FAT PRINCE *with drunken* IRONSHIRTS. *One of them carries the governor's head on a lance*

THE FAT PRINCE: Here! In the middle! (*ONE SOLDIER climbs onto the other's back, takes the head, holds it tentatively over the door*) That's not the middle.

Farther to the right. That's it. What I do, my friends, I do well. (*While, with hammer and nail, the* SOLDIER *fastens the head to the wall by its hair*) This morning at the church door I said to Georgi Abashwili: "I love a clear sky." Actually, I prefer the lightning that comes out of a clear sky. Yes, indeed. It's a pity they took the brat along, though, I need him, urgently.

Exit with IRONSHIRTS *through the gateway. Trampling of horses again. Enter* GRUSHA *through the doorway looking cautiously about her. Clearly she has waited for the* IRONSHIRTS *to go. Carrying a bundle, she walks toward the gateway. At the last moment, she turns to see if the* CHILD *is still there. Catching sight of the head over the doorway, she screams. Horrified, she picks up her bundle again, and is about to leave when the* SINGER *starts to speak. She stands rooted to the spot*

THE SINGER:

As she was standing between courtyard and gate,
She heard or she thought she heard a low voice calling.
The child called to her,
Not whining, but calling quite sensibly,
Or so it seemed to her.
"Woman," it said, "help me."
And it went on, not whining, but saying quite sensibly:
"Know, woman, he who hears not a cry for help
But passes by with troubled ears will never hear
The gentle call of a lover nor the blackbird at dawn
Nor the happy sigh of the tired grape-picker as the Angelus rings."

She walks a few steps toward the CHILD *and bends over it*

Hearing this she went back for one more look at the child:
Only to sit with him for a moment or two,
Only till someone should come,
His mother, or anyone.

Leaning on a trunk, she sits facing the CHILD

Only till she would have to leave, for the danger was too great,
The city was full of flame and crying.

*The light grows dimmer, as though evening and night
were coming on*

Fearful is the seductive power of goodness!

650   GRUSHA *now settles down to watch over the* CHILD
*through the night. Once, she lights a small lamp to look
at it. Once, she tucks it in with a coat. From time
to time she listens and looks to see whether someone is
coming*

And she sat with the child a long time,
Till evening came, till night came, till dawn
came.

She sat too long, too long she saw
The soft breathing, the small clenched fists,
Till toward morning the seduction was   660
complete
And she rose, and bent down and, sighing,
took the child
And carried it away.

She does what the SINGER *says as he describes it*

As if it was stolen goods she picked it up.
As if she was a thief she crept away.

2. THE FLIGHT INTO THE NORTHERN MOUNTAINS

THE SINGER:
When Grusha Vashnadze left the city
On the Grusinian highway
On the way to the Northern Mountains
She sang a song, she bought some milk.
THE CHORUS:
How will this human child escape
The bloodhounds, the trap-setters?
Into the deserted mountains she journeyed
10   Along the Grusinian highway she journeyed
She sang a song, she bought some milk.

GRUSHA VASHNADZE *walks on. On her back she carries
the* CHILD *in a sack, in one hand is a large stick, in
the other a bundle. She sings*

THE SONG OF THE FOUR GENERALS
Four generals
Set out for Iran.
With the first one, war did not agree.
The second never won a victory.
20   For the third the weather never was right.
For the fourth the men would never fight.
Four generals
And not a single man!

Sosso Robakidse
Went marching to Iran

With him the war did so agree
He soon had won a victory.
For him the weather was always right.
For him the men would always fight.
Sosso Robakidse,   30
He is our man!

A peasant's cottage appears

GRUSHA: *(To the* CHILD*)*. Noontime is meal time.
Now we'll sit hopefully in the grass, while the
good Grusha goes and buys a little pitcher of
milk. *(She lays the* CHILD *down and knocks at the
cottage door. An* OLD MAN *opens it)* Grandfather,
could I have a little pitcher of milk? And a corn
cake, maybe?
THE OLD MAN: Milk? We have no milk. The soldiers   40
from the city have our goats. Go to the soldiers
if you want milk.
GRUSHA: But grandfather, you must have a little
pitcher of milk for a baby?
THE OLD MAN: And for a God-bless-you, eh?
GRUSHA: Who said anything about a God-
bless-you? *(She shows her purse)* We'll pay like
princes. "Head in the clouds, backside in the
water." *(The* PEASANT *goes off, grumbling, for milk)*
How much for the milk?   50
THE OLD MAN: Three piasters. Milk has gone up.

GRUSHA: Three piasters for this little drop? *(Without a word the* OLD MAN *shuts the door in her face)* Michael, did you hear that? Three piasters! We can't afford it! *(She goes back, sits down again, and gives the* CHILD *her breast)* Suck. Think of the three piasters. There's nothing there, but you *think* you're drinking, and that's something. *(Shaking her head, she sees that the* CHILD *isn't sucking any more. She gets up, walks back to the door, and knocks again)* Open grandfather, we'll pày. *(Softly)* May lightning strike you! *(When the* OLD MAN *appears)* I thought it would be half a piaster. But the baby must be fed. How about one piaster for that little drop?

THE OLD MAN: Two.

GRUSHA: Don't shut the door again. *(She fishes a long time in her bag)* Here are two piasters. The milk better be good. I still have two days' journey ahead of me. It's a murderous business you have here—and sinful, too!

THE OLD MAN: Kill the soldiers if you want milk.

GRUSHA: *(Giving the* CHILD *some milk).* This is an expensive joke. Take a sip, Michael, it's a week's pay. Around here they think we earned our money just sitting around. Oh, Michael, Michael, you're a nice little load for a girl to take on! *(Uneasy, she gets up, puts the* CHILD *on her back, and walks on. The* OLD MAN, *grumbling, picks up the pitcher and looks after her unmoved)*

THE SINGER:

As Grusha Vashnadze went northward
The Princes' Ironshirts went after her.

THE CHORUS:

How will the barefoot girl escape the
    Ironshirts,
The bloodhounds, the trap-setters?
They hunt even by night.
Pursuers never tire.
Butchers sleep little.

TWO IRONSHIRTS *are trudging along the highway*

THE CORPORAL: You'll never amount to anything, blockhead, your heart's not in it. Your senior officer sees this in little things. Yesterday, when I made the fat gal, yes, you grabbed her husband as I commanded, and you did kick him in the stomach, at my request, but did you *enjoy* it, like a loyal Private, or were you just doing your duty? I've kept an eye on you blockhead, you're a hollow reed and a tinkling cymbal, you won't get promoted. *(They walk a while in silence)* Don't think I've forgotton how insubordinate you are, either. Stop limping! I forbid you to limp! You limp because I sold the horses, and I sold the horses because I'd never have got that price again. You limp to show me you don't like marching. I know you. It won't help. You wait. Sing!

THE TWO IRONSHIRTS: *(Singing).*

Sadly to war I went my way
Leaving my loved one at her door.
My friends will keep her honor safe
Till from the war I'm back once more.

THE CORPORAL: Louder!

THE TWO IRONSHIRTS: *(Singing).*

When 'neath a headstone I shall be
My love a little earth will bring:
"Here rest the feet that oft would run to me
And here the arms that oft to me would cling."

They begin to walk again in silence

THE CORPORAL: A good soldier has his heart and soul in it. When he receives an order, he gets a hard on, and when he drives his lance into the enemy's guts, he comes. *(He shouts for joy)* He lets himself be torn to bits for his superior officer, and as he lies dying he takes note that his corporal is nodding approval, and that is reward enough, it's his dearest wish. You won't get any nod of approval, but you'll croak all right. Christ, how'm I to get my hands on the Governor's bastard with the help of a fool like you! *(They stay on stage behind)*

THE SINGER:

When Grusha Vashnadze came to the River
    Sirra
Flight grew too much for her, the helpless
    child too heavy.
In the cornfields the rosy dawn
Is cold to the sleepless one, only cold.
The gay clatter of the milk cans in the farm-
    yard where the smoke rises
Is only a threat to the fugitive.
She who carries the child feels its weight
    and little more.

GRUSHA *stops in front of a farm. A* FAT PEASANT
WOMAN *is carrying a milk can through the door.* GRUSHA
*waits until she has gone in, then approaches the house
cautiously*

GRUSHA: (*To the* CHILD). Now you've wet yourself
again, and you know I've no linen. Michael, this
150   is where we part company. It's far enough from
the city. They wouldn't want you *so* much that
they'd follow you all *this* way, little good-
for-nothing. The peasant woman is kind, and
can't you just smell the milk? (*she bends down
to lay the* CHILD *on the threshold*) So farewell,
Michael, I'll forget how you kicked me in the
back all night to make me walk faster. And you
can forget the meager fare—it was meant well.
I'd like to have kept you—your nose is so
160   tiny—but it can't be. I'd have shown you your
first rabbit, I'd have trained you to keep dry,
but now I must turn around. My sweetheart
the soldier might be back soon, and suppose he
didn't find me? You can't ask that, can you?

She creeps up to the door and lays the CHILD *on the
threshold. Then, hiding behind a tree, she waits until
the* PEASANT WOMAN *opens the door and sees the bundle*

THE PEASANT WOMAN: Good heavens, what's this?
Husband!

170   THE PEASANT: What is it? Let me finish my soup.

THE PEASANT WOMAN: (*To the* CHILD). Where's your
mother then? Haven't you got one? It's a boy.
Fine linen. He's from a good family, you can
see that. And they just leave him on our doorstep.
Oh, these are times!

THE PEASANT: If they think we're going to feed
it, they're wrong. You can take it to the priest
in the village. That's the best we can do.

THE PEASANT WOMAN: What'll the priest do with
180   him? He needs a mother. There, he's waking
up. Don't you think we could keep him, though?

THE PEASANT: (*Shouting*). No!

THE PEASANT WOMAN: I could lay him in the corner
by the armchair. All I need is a crib. I can take
him into the fields with me. See him laughing?
Husband, we have a roof over our heads. We
can do it. Not another word out of you!

She carries the CHILD *into the house. The* PEASANT *follows
protesting.* GRUSHA *steps out from behind the tree, laughs,*
190   *and hurries off in the opposite direction*

THE SINGER:
Why so cheerful, making for home?

THE CHORUS:
Because the child has won new parents with
a laugh,
Because I'm rid of the little one, I'm cheerful.

THE SINGER:
And why so sad?

THE CHORUS:
Because I'm single and free, I'm sad   200
Like someone who's been robbed
Someone who's newly poor.

She walks for a short while, then meets the TWO
IRONSHIRTS, *who point their lances at her*

THE CORPORAL: Lady, you are running straight into
the arms of the Armed Forces. Where are you
coming from? And when? Are you having illicit
relations with the enemy? Where is he hiding?
What movements is he making in your rear?
How about the hills? How about the valleys?   210
How are your stockings fastened? (GRUSHA *stands
there frightened*) Don't be scared, we always stage
a retreat, if necessary . . . what, blockhead? I
always stage retreats. In that respect at least,
I can be relied on. Why are you staring like
that at my lance? In the field no soldier drops
his lance, that's a rule. Learn it by heart, blockhead. Now, lady, where are you headed?

GRUSHA: To meet my intended, one Simon
Shashava, of the Palace Guard in Nuka.   220

THE CORPORAL: Simon Shashava? Sure, I know
him. He gave me a key so I could look you
up once in a while. Blockhead, we are getting
to be unpopular. We must make her realize we
have honorable intentions. Lady, behind apparent frivolity I conceal a serious nature, so let
me tell you officially: I want a child from you.
(GRUSHA *utters a little scream*) Blockhead, she
understood me. Uh-huh, isn't it a sweet shock?
"Then first I must take the noodles out of the   230
oven, Officer. Then first I must change my torn
shirt, Colonel." But away with jokes, away with
my lance! We are looking for a baby. A baby
from a good family. Have you heard of such
a baby, from the city, dressed in fine linen, and
suddenly turning up here?

GRUSHA: No, I haven't heard a thing.

*Suddenly she turns round and runs back, panic-stricken.
The* IRONSHIRTS *glance at each other, then follow her,
cursing*

240

THE SINGER:
Run, kind girl! The killers are coming!
Help the helpless babe, helpless girl!
And so she runs!

THE CHORUS:
In the bloodiest times
There are kind people.

As GRUSHA *rushes into the cottage, the* PEASANT
WOMAN *is bending over the* CHILD'S *crib*

250   GRUSHA: Hide him. Quick! The Ironshirts are
coming! I laid him on your doorstep. But he
isn't mine. He's from a good family.

THE PEASANT WOMAN: Who's coming? What
Ironshirts?

GRUSHA: Don't ask questions. The Ironshirts that
are looking for it.

THE PEASANT WOMAN: They've no business in my
house. But I must have a little talk with you,
it seems.

260   GRUSHA: Take off the fine linen. It'll give us away.

THE PEASANT WOMAN: Linen, my foot! In this
house I make the decisions! "*You* can't vomit
in *my* room!" Why did you abandon it? It's a
sin.

GRUSHA: (*Looking out of the window*) Look, they're
coming out from behind those trees! I shouldn't
have run away, it made them angry. Oh, what
shall I do?

THE PEASANT WOMAN: (*Looking out of the window
and suddenly starting with fear*). Gracious!
270   Ironshirts!

GRUSHA: They're after the baby.

THE PEASANT WOMAN: Suppose they come in!

GRUSHA: You mustn't give him to them. Say he's
yours.

THE PEASANT WOMAN: Yes.

GRUSHA: They'll run him through if you hand him
over.

THE PEASANT WOMAN: But suppose they ask for
280   it? The silver for the harvest is in the house.

GRUSHA: If you let them have him, they'll run him
through, right here in this room! You've got to
say he's yours!

THE PEASANT WOMAN: Yes. But what if they don't
believe me?

GRUSHA: You must be firm.

THE PEASANT WOMAN: They'll burn the roof over
our heads.

GRUSHA: That's why you must say he's yours. His
name's Michael. But I shouldn't have told you.   290
(*The* PEASANT WOMAN *nods*) Don't nod like that.
And don't tremble—they'll notice.

THE PEASANT WOMAN: Yes.

GRUSHA: And stop saying yes, I can't stand it. (*She
shakes the* WOMAN) Don't you have any children?

THE PEASANT WOMAN: (*Muttering*). He's in the war.

GRUSHA: Then maybe *he's* an Ironshirt? Do you
want *him* to run children through with a lance?
You'd bawl him out. "No fooling with lances
in *my* house!" you'd shout, "is that what I've   300
reared you for? Wash your neck before you speak
to your mother!"

THE PEASANT WOMAN: That's true, he couldn't get
away with anything around here!

GRUSHA: So you'll say he's yours?

THE PEASANT WOMAN: Yes.

GRUSHA: Look! They're coming!

(*There is a knocking at the door. The* WOMEN *don't
answer. Enter* IRONSHIRTS. *The* PEASANT WOMAN *bows
low*)   310

THE CORPORAL: Well, here she is. What did I tell
you? What a nose I have! I *smelt* her. Lady,
I have a question for you. Why did you run
away? What did you think I would do to you?
I'll bet it was something dirty. Confess!

GRUSHA: (*While the* PEASANT WOMAN *bows again and
again*). I'd left some milk on the stove, and I
suddenly remembered it.

THE CORPORAL: Or maybe you imagined I looked
at you in a dirty way? Like there could be some-   320
thing between us? A lewd sort of look, know
what I mean?

GRUSHA: I didn't see it.

THE CORPORAL: But it's possible, huh? You admit
that much. After all, I might be a pig. I'll be
frank with you: I could think of all sorts of things
if we were alone. (*To the* PEASANT WOMAN)
Shouldn't you be busy in the yard? Feeding the
hens?

THE PEASANT WOMAN: (*falling suddenly to her knees*).   330
Soldier, I didn't know a thing about it. Please
don't burn the roof over our heads.

THE CORPORAL: What are you talking about?

THE PEASANT WOMAN: I had nothing to do with it. She left it on my doorstep, I swear it!

THE CORPORAL: (*Suddenly seeing the* CHILD *and whistling*). Ah, so there's a little something in the crib! Blockhead, I smell a thousand piasters. Take the old girl outside and hold on to her.
340 It looks like I have a little cross-examining to do.

The PEASANT WOMAN *lets herself be led out by the* PRIVATE, *without a word*

So, you've got the child I wanted from you!
    (*He walks toward the crib*)
GRUSHA: Officer, he's mine. He's not the one you're after.
THE CORPORAL: I'll just take a look. (*He bends over the crib.* GRUSHA *looks round in despair*)
350 GRUSHA: He's mine! He's mine!
THE CORPORAL: Fine linen!

GRUSHA *dashes at him to pull him away. He throws her off and again bends over the crib. Again looking round in despair, she sees a log of wood, seizes it, and hits the* CORPORAL *over the head from behind. The* CORPORAL *collapses. She quickly picks up the* CHILD *and rushes off*

THE SINGER:
    And in her flight from the Ironshirts
360   And after twenty-two days of journeying
    At the foot of the Janga-Tu Glacier
    Grusha Vashnadze decided to adopt the child.
THE CHORUS:
    The helpless girl adopted the helpless child.

GRUSHA *squats over a half-frozen stream to get the* CHILD *water in the hollow of her hand*

GRUSHA:
    Since no one else will take you, son,
    I must take you.
370   Since no one else will take you, son,
    You must take me.
    O black day in a lean, lean year,
    The trip was long, the milk was dear,
    My legs are tired, my feet are sore:
    But I wouldn't be without you anymore.
    I'll throw your silken shirt away
    And dress you in rags and tatters.
    I'll wash you, son, and christen you in glacier water.
380   We'll see it through together.

She has taken off the CHILD'S *fine linen and wrapped it in a rag*

THE SINGER:
    When Grusha Vashnadze
    Pursued by the Ironshirts
    Came to the bridge on the glacier
    Leading to the villages of the Eastern Slope
    She sang the Song of the Rotten Bridge
    And risked two lives.

A wind has risen. The bridge on the glacier is visible 390 *in the dark. One rope is broken and half the bridge is hanging down the abyss.* MERCHANTS, TWO MEN *and a* WOMAN, *stand undecided before the bridge as* GRUSHA *and the* CHILD *arrive.* ONE MAN *is trying to catch the hanging rope with a stick*

THE FIRST MAN: Take your time, young woman. You won't get across here anyway.
GRUSHA: But I *have* to get the baby to the east side. To my brother's place.
THE MERCHANT WOMAN: Have to? How d'you 400 mean, "have to"? I have to get there too—because I have to buy carpets in Atum—carpets a woman had to sell because her husband had to die. But can *I* do what I have to? Can she? Andrei's been fishing for that rope for hours. And I ask you, how are we going to fasten it, even if he gets it up?
THE FIRST MAN: (*Listening*). Hush, I think I hear something.
GRUSHA: The bridge isn't quite rotted through. I 410 think I'll try it.
THE MERCHANT WOMAN: *I* wouldn't—if the devil himself were after me. It's suicide.
THE FIRST MAN: (*Shouting*). Hi!
GRUSHA: Don't shout! (*to the* MERCHANT WOMAN) Tell him not to shout.
THE FIRST MAN: But there's someone down there calling. Maybe they've lost their way.
THE MERCHANT WOMAN: Why shouldn't he shout? Is there something funny about you? Are they 420 after you?
GRUSHA: All right, I'll tell. The Ironshirts are after me. I knocked one down.
THE SECOND MAN: Hide our merchandise!

The WOMAN *hides a sack behind a rock*

THE FIRST MAN: Why didn't you say so right away? (*To the others*) If they catch her they'll make mincemeat out of her!

430 GRUSHA: Get out of my way. I've got to cross that bridge.

THE SECOND MAN: You can't. The precipice is two thousand feet deep.

THE FIRST MAN: Even with the rope it'd be no use. We could hold it up with our hands. But then we'd have to do the same for the Ironshirts.

GRUSHA: Go away.

There are calls from the distance: "Hi, up there!"

THE MERCHANT WOMAN: They're getting near. But you can't take the child on that bridge. It's sure
440 to break. And look!

GRUSHA *looks down into the abyss. The* IRONSHIRTS *are heard calling again from below*

THE SECOND MAN: Two thousand feet!

GRUSHA: But those men are worse.

THE FIRST MAN: You can't do it. Think of the baby. Risk your life but not a child's.

THE SECOND MAN: With the child she's that much heavier!

THE MERCHANT WOMAN: Maybe she's *really* got to
450 get across. Give *me* the baby. I'll hide it. Cross the bridge alone!

GRUSHA: I won't. We belong together. (*To the* CHILD) "Live together, die together."

(*She sings*)

THE SONG OF THE ROTTEN BRIDGE

Deep is the abyss, son,
I see the weak bridge sway
But it's not for us, son,
To choose the way.
460 The way I know
Is the one you must tread,
And all you will eat
Is my bit of bread.
Of every four pieces
You shall have three.
Would that I knew
How big they will be!

Get out of my way, I'll try it without the rope.

THE MERCHANT WOMAN: You are tempting God!

There are shouts from below 470

GRUSHA: Please, throw that stick away, or they'll get the rope and follow me.

Pressing the CHILD *to her, she steps onto the swaying bridge. The* MERCHANT WOMAN *screams when it looks as though the bridge is about to collapse. But* GRUSHA *walks on and reaches the far side.*

THE FIRST MAN: She made it!

THE MERCHANT WOMAN: (*Who has fallen on her knees and begun to pray, angrily*). I still think it was a sin. 480

The IRONSHIRTS *appear; the* CORPORAL'S *head is bandaged*

THE CORPORAL: Seen a woman with a child?

THE FIRST MAN: (*While the* SECOND MAN *throws the stick into the abyss*). Yes, there! But the bridge won't carry you!

THE CORPORAL: You'll pay for this, blockhead!

GRUSHA, *from the far bank, laughs and shows the* CHILD *to the* IRONSHIRTS. *She walks on. The wind blows*

GRUSHA: (*Turning to the* CHILD). You mustn't be 490 afraid of the wind. He's a poor thing too. He has to push the clouds along and he gets quite cold doing it. (*Snow starts falling*) And the snow isn't so bad, either, Michael. It covers the little fir trees so they won't die in winter. Let me sing you a little song. (*She sings*)

THE SONG OF THE CHILD

Your father is a bandit
A harlot the mother who bore you.
Yet honorable men 500
Shall kneel down before you.

Food to the baby horses
The tiger's son will take.
The mothers will get milk
From the son of the snake.

3. IN THE NORTHERN MOUNTAINS

THE SINGER:
>   Seven days the sister, Grusha Vashnadze,
>   Journeyed across the glacier
>   And down the slopes she journeyed.
>   "When I enter my brother's house," she
>   thought
>   "He will rise and embrace me."
>   "Is that you, sister?" he will say,
>   "I have long expected you.
> 10 This is my dear wife,
>   And this is my farm, come to me by marriage,
>   With eleven horses and thirty-one cows. Sit
>   down.
>   Sit down with your child at our table and
>   eat."
>   The brother's house was in a lovely valley.
>   When the sister came to the brother,
>   She was ill from walking.
>   The brother rose from the table.

20 *A* FAT PEASANT COUPLE *rise from the table.* LAVRENTI VASHNADZE *still has a napkin round his neck, as* GRUSHA, *pale and supported by a* SERVANT, *enters with the* CHILD

LAVRENTI: Where've *you* come from, Grusha?

GRUSHA: *(Feebly).* Across the Janga-Tu Pass, Lavrenti.

THE SERVANT: I found her in front of the hay barn. She has a baby with her.

THE SISTER-IN-LAW: Go and groom the mare.

30   *(Exit the* SERVANT*)*

LAVRENTI: This is my wife Aniko.

THE SISTER-IN-LAW: I thought you were in service in Nuka.

GRUSHA: *(Barely able to stand).* Yes, I was.

THE SISTER-IN-LAW: Wasn't it a good job? We were told it was.

GRUSHA: The Governor got killed.

LAVRENTI: Yes, we heard there were riots. Your aunt told us. Remember, Aniko?

40 THE SISTER-IN-LAW: Here with us, it's very quiet.

City people always want something going on. *(She walks toward the door, calling)* Sosso, Sosso, don't take the cake out of the oven yet, d'you hear? Where on earth are you?

                                    (Exit, calling)

LAVRENTI: *(Quietly, quickly).* Is there a father? *(As she shakes her head)* I thought not. We must think up something. She's religious.

THE SISTER-IN-LAW: *(Returning).* Those servants! *(To* GRUSHA*)* You have a child.   50

GRUSHA: It's mine.

She collapses. LAVRENTI *rushes to her assistance*

THE SISTER-IN-LAW: Heavens, she's ill—what are we going to do?

LAVRENTI: *(Escorting her to a bench near the stove).* Sit down, sit. I think it's just weakness, Aniko.

THE SISTER-IN-LAW: As long as it's not scarlet fever!

LAVRENTI: She'd have spots if it was. It's only weakness. Don't worry, Aniko. *(To* GRUSHA*)* Better, sitting down?   60

THE SISTER-IN-LAW: Is the child hers?

GRUSHA: Yes, mine.

LAVRENTI: She's on her way to her husband.

THE SISTER-IN-LAW: I see. Your meat's getting cold. *(*LAVRENTI *sits down and begins to eat)* Cold food's not good for you, the fat mustn't get cold, you know your stomach's your weak spot. *(To* GRUSHA*)* If your husband's not in the city, where is he?

LAVRENTI: She got married on the other side of   70 the mountain, she says.

THE SISTER-IN-LAW: On the other side of the mountain. I see. *(She also sits down to eat)*

GRUSHA: I think I should lie down somewhere, Lavrenti.

THE SISTER-IN-LAW: If it's consumption we'll all get it. *(She goes on cross-examining her)* Has your husband got a farm?

GRUSHA: He's a soldier.

LAVRENTI: But he's coming into a farm—a small   80 one—from his father.

THE SISTER-IN-LAW: Isn't he in the war? Why not?

GRUSHA: (With effort). Yes, he's in the war.

THE SISTER-IN-LAW: Then why d'you want to go to the farm?

LAVRENTI: When he comes back from the war, he'll return to his farm.

THE SISTER-IN-LAW: But you're going there now?

LAVRENTI: Yes, to wait for him.

90 THE SISTER-IN-LAW: (Calling shrilly). Sosso, the cake!

GRUSHA: (Murmuring feverishly). A farm—a soldier—waiting—sit down, eat.

THE SISTER-IN-LAW: It's scarlet fever. ·

GRUSHA: (Starting up). Yes, he's got a farm!

LAVRENTI: I think it's just weakness, Aniko. Would you look after the cake yourself, dear?

THE SISTER-IN-LAW: But when will he come back if war's broken out again as people say? (She waddles 100 off, shouting) Sosso! Where on earth are you? Sosso!

LAVRENTI: (Getting up quickly and going to GRUSHA). You'll get a bed in a minute. She has a good heart. But wait till after supper.

GRUSHA: (Holding out the CHILD to him) Take him.

LAVRENTI: (Taking it and looking around). But you can't stay here long with the child. She's religious, you see.

GRUSHA collapses. LAVRENTI catches her

110 THE SINGER:
The sister was so ill,
The cowardly brother had to give her shelter.
Summer departed, winter came.
The winter was long, the winter was short
People mustn't know anything,
Rats mustn't bite,
Spring mustn't come.

GRUSHA sits over the weaving loom in a workroom. She and the CHILD, who is squatting on the floor, are 120 wrapped in blankets.

(She sings)

THE SONG OF THE CENTER
And the lover started to leave
And his betrothed ran pleading after him
Pleading and weeping, weeping and teaching:
"Dearest mine, dearest mine
When you go to war as now you do
When you fight the foe as soon you will

Don't lead with the front line
And don't push with the rear line   130
At the front is red fire
In the rear is red smoke
Stay in the war's center
Stay near the standard bearer
The first always die
The last are also hit
Those in the center come home."

Michael, we must be clever. If we make ourselves as small as cockroaches, the sister-in-law will forget we're in the house, and then we can stay   140 till the snow melts.

Enter LAVRENTI. He sits down beside his sister

LAVRENTI: Why are you sitting there muffled up like coachmen, you two? Is it too cold in the room?

GRUSHA: (Hastily removing one shawl). It's not too cold, Lavrenti.

LAVRENTI: If it's too cold, you shouldn't be sitting here with the child. Aniko would never forgive herself! (Pause) I hope our priest didn't question   150 you about the child?

GRUSHA: He did, but I didn't tell him anything.

LAVRENTI: That's good. I wanted to speak to you about Aniko. She has a good heart but she's very, very sensitive. People need only mention our farm and she's worried. She takes everything hard, you see. One time our milkmaid went to church with a hole in her stocking. Ever since, Aniko has worn two pairs of stockings in church. It's the old family in her. (He listens) Are you   160 sure there are no rats around? If there are rats, you couldn't live here.

There are sounds as of dripping from the roof

What's that, dripping?

GRUSHA: It must be a barrel leaking.

LAVRENTI: Yes, it must be a barrel. You've been here six months, haven't you? Was I talking about Aniko? (They listen again to the snow melting) You can't imagine how worried she gets about your soldier-husband. "Suppose he comes back   170 and can't find her!" she says and lies awake. "He can't come before the spring," I tell her. The dear woman! (The drops begin to fall faster) When d'you think he'll come? What do you think? (GRUSHA is silent) Not before the spring, you agree? *(GRUSHA is silent)* You don't believe he'll come at all? *(GRUSHA is silent)* But when the spring comes and the snow melts here and on the passes, you can't stay on. They may come and look for you. There's already talk of an illegitimate child. *(The "glockenspiel" of the falling drops has grown faster and steadier)* Grusha, the snow is melting on the roof. Spring is here.

GRUSHA: Yes.

LAVRENTI: *(Eagerly)*. I'll tell you what we'll do. You need a place to go, and, because of the child, *(He sighs)* you have to have a husband, so people won't talk. Now I've made cautious inquiries to see if we can find you a husband. Grusha, I *have* one. I talked to a peasant woman who has a son. Just the other side of the mountain. A small farm. And she's willing.

GRUSHA: But I *can't* marry! I must wait for Simon Shashava.

LAVRENTI: Of course. That's all been taken care of. You don't need a man in bed—you need a man on paper. And I've found you one. The son of this peasant woman is going to die. Isn't that wonderful? He's at his last gasp. And all in line with our story—a husband from the other side of the mountain! And when you met him he was at the last gasp. So you're a widow. What do you say?

GRUSHA: It's true I could use a document with stamps on it for Michael.

LAVRENTI: Stamps make all the difference. Without something in writing the Shah couldn't prove he's a Shah. And you'll have a place to live.

GRUSHA: How much does the peasant woman want?

LAVRENTI: Four hundred piasters.

GRUSHA: Where will you find it?

LAVRENTI: *(Guiltily)*. Aniko's milk money.

GRUSHA: No one would know us there. I'll do it.

LAVRENTI: *(Getting up)*. I'll let the peasant woman know.

(Quick exit)

GRUSHA: Michael, you cause a lot of fuss. I came to you as the pear tree comes to the sparrows. And because a Christian bends down and picks up a crust of bread so nothing will go to waste. Michael, it would have been better had I walked quickly away on that Easter Sunday in Nuka in the second courtyard. Now I *am* a fool.

THE SINGER:

The bridegroom was lying on his deathbed when the bride arrived.
The bridegroom's mother was waiting at the door, telling her to hurry.
The bride brought a child along.
The witness hid it during the wedding.

On one side of the bed. Under the mosquito net lies a very SICK MAN. GRUSHA *is pulled in at a run by her future* MOTHER-IN-LAW. *They are followed by* LAVRENTI *and the* CHILD

THE MOTHER-IN-LAW: Quick! Quick! Or he'll die on us before the wedding. *(To LAVRENTI)* I was never told she had a child already.

LAVRENTI: What difference does it make? *(Pointing toward the DYING MAN)* It can't matter to him—in his condition.

THE MOTHER-IN-LAW: To him? But *I'll* never survive the shame! We are honest people. *(She begins to weep)* My Jussup doesn't have to marry a girl with a child!

LAVRENTI: All right, make it another two hundred piasters. You'll have it in writing that the farm will go to you: but she'll have the right to live here for two years.

THE MOTHER-IN-LAW: *(Drying her tears)*. It'll hardly cover the funeral expenses. I hope she'll really lend a hand with the work. And what's happened to the monk? He must have slipped out through the kitchen window. We'll have the whole village round our necks when they hear Jussup's end is come! Oh dear! I'll run and get the monk. But he mustn't see the child!

LAVRENTI: I'll take care he doesn't. But why only a monk? Why not a priest?

THE MOTHER-IN-LAW: Oh, he's just as good. I only made one mistake: I paid half his fee in advance. Enough to send him to the tavern. I only hope. . . . *(She runs off)*

LAVRENTI: She saved on the priest, the wretch! Hired a cheap monk.

GRUSHA: You *will* send Simon Shashava over to see me if he turns up after all?

LAVRENTI: Yes. *(Pointing at the SICK MAN)* Won't you take a look at him?

GRUSHA, *taking* MICHAEL *to her, shakes her head*

He's not moving an eyelid. I hope we aren't too late.

They listen. On the opposite side enter NEIGHBORS *who look around and take up positions against the walls, thus forming another wall near the bed, yet leaving an opening so that the bed can be seen. They start murmuring prayers. Enter the* MOTHER-IN-LAW *with a* MONK. *Showing some annoyance and surprise, she bows to the* GUESTS

280 THE MOTHER-IN-LAW: I hope you won't mind waiting a few moments? My son's bride has just arrived from the city. An emergency wedding is about to be celebrated. *(To the* MONK *in the bedroom)* I might have known you couldn't keep your trap shut. *(To* GRUSHA*)* The wedding can take place at once. Here's the license. I myself and the bride's brother *(*LAVRENTI *tries to hide in the background, after having quietly taken* MICHAEL *back from* GRUSHA. *The* MOTHER-IN-LAW *waves him*
290 *away)*, who will be here in a moment, are the witnesses.

GRUSHA *has bowed to the* MONK. *They go to the bed. The* MOTHER-IN-LAW *lifts the mosquito net. The* MONK *starts reeling off the marriage ceremony in Latin. Meanwhile, the* MOTHER-IN-LAW *beckons to* LAVRENTI *to get rid of the* CHILD, *but fearing that it will cry he draws its attention to the ceremony.* GRUSHA *glances once at the* CHILD, *and* LAVRENTI *waves the* CHILD'S *hand in a greeting*

300 THE MONK: Are you prepared to be a faithful, obedient, and good wife to this man, and to cleave to him until death you do part?
GRUSHA: *(Looking at the* CHILD*)*. I am.
THE MONK: *(To the* SICK PEASANT*)*. And are you prepared to be a good and loving husband to your wife until death you do part?

As the SICK PEASANT *does not answer, the* MONK *looks inquiringly around*

THE MOTHER-IN-LAW: Of course he is! Didn't you
310 hear him say yes?
THE MONK: All right. We declare the marriage contracted! How about extreme unction?
THE MOTHER-IN-LAW: Nothing doing! The wedding cost quite enough. Now I must take care of the mourners. *(To* LAVRENTI*)* Did we say seven hundred?
LAVRENTI: Six hundred. *(He pays)* Now I don't

want to sit with the guests and get to know people. So farewell, Grusha, and if my widowed
320 sister comes to visit me, she'll get a welcome from my wife, or I'll show my teeth. *(Nods, gives the* CHILD *to* GRUSHA, *and leaves)*

The MOURNERS *glance after him without interest*

THE MONK: May one ask where this child comes from?
THE MOTHER-IN-LAW: Is there a child? I don't see a child. And you don't see a child either—you understand? Or it may turn out I saw all sorts of things in the tavern! Now come on.

After GRUSHA *has put the* CHILD *down and told him*
330 *to be quiet, they move over left,* GRUSHA *is introduced to the* NEIGHBORS

This is my daughter-in-law. She arrived just in time to find dear Jussup still alive.
ONE WOMAN: He's been ill now a whole year, hasn't he? When our Vassili was drafted he was there to say goodbye.
ANOTHER WOMAN: Such things are terrible for a farm. The corn all ripe and the farmer in bed! It'll really be a blessing if he doesn't suffer too
340 long, I say.
THE FIRST WOMAN: *(Confidentially)*. You know why we thought he'd taken to his bed? Because of the draft! And now his end is come!
THE MOTHER-IN-LAW: Sit yourselves down, please! And have some cakes!

She beckons to GRUSHA *and* BOTH WOMEN *go into the bedroom, where they pick up the cake pans off the floor. The* GUESTS, *among them the* MONK, *sit on the floor and begin conversing in subdued voices*
350

ONE PEASANT: *(To whom the* MONK *has handed the bottle which he has taken from his soutane)*. There's a child, you say! How can that have happened to Jussup?
A WOMAN: She was certainly lucky to get herself hitched, with him so sick!
THE MOTHER-IN-LAW: They're gossiping already. And gorging themselves on the funeral cakes at the same time! If he doesn't die today, I'll have to bake some more tomorrow!
360
GRUSHA: I'll bake them for you.
THE MOTHER-IN-LAW: Yesterday some horsemen rode by, and I went out to see who it was. When I came in again he was lying there like a corpse!

So I sent for you. It can't take much longer.
(She listens)

THE MONK: Dear wedding and funeral guests!
Deeply touched, we stand before a bed of death
and marriage. The bride gets a veil; the groom,
a shroud: how varied, my children, are the fates
of men! Alas! One man dies and has a roof over
his head and the other is married and the flesh
turns to dust from which it was made. Amen.

THE MOTHER-IN-LAW: He's getting his own back.
I shouldn't have hired such a cheap one. It's
what you'd expect. A more expensive monk
would behave himself. In Sura there's one with
a real air of sanctity about him, but of course
he charges a fortune. A fifty-piaster monk like
that has no dignity, and as for piety, just fifty
piasters' worth and no more! When I came to
get him in the tavern he'd just made a speech,
and he was shouting: "The war is over, beware
of the peace!" We must go in.

GRUSHA: *(Giving* MICHAEL *a cake)*. Eat this cake,
and keep nice and still, Michael.

The TWO WOMEN *offer cakes to the* GUESTS. *The* DYING
MAN *sits up in bed. He puts his head out from under
the mosquito net, stares at the* TWO WOMEN, *then sinks
back again. The* MONK *takes two bottles from his soutane
and offers them to the* PEASANT *beside him. Enter* THREE
MUSICIANS *who are greeted with a sly wink by the* MONK

THE MOTHER-IN-LAW: *(To the* MUSICIANS*)* What are
you doing here? With instruments?

ONE MUSICIAN: Brother Anastasius here *(Points at
the* MONK*)* told us there was a wedding on.

THE MOTHER-IN-LAW: What? You brought them?
Three more on my neck! Don't you know there's
a dying man in the next room?

THE MONK: A very tempting assignment for a musician: something that could be either a subdued
Wedding March or a spirited Funeral Dance.

THE MOTHER-IN-LAW: Well, you might as well play.
Nobody can stop you eating in any case.

The MUSICIANS *play a potpouri. The* WOMEN *serve cakes*

THE MONK: The trumpet sounds like a whining
baby. And you, little drum, what have you got
to tell the world?

THE DRUNKEN PEASANT: *(Beside the* MONK, *sings)*.
Miss Roundass took the old old man
And said that marriage was the thing

To everyone who met 'er.
She later withdrew from the contract because
Candles are better.

The MOTHER-IN-LAW *throws the* DRUNKEN PEASANT
out. The music stops. The GUESTS *are embarrassed*

THE GUESTS: *(Loudly)*.
—Have you heard? The Grand Duke is back!
But the Princes are against him.
—They say the Shah of Persia has lent him
a great army to restore order in Grusinia.
—But how is that possible? The Shah of Persia
is the enemy . . .
—The enemy of Grusinia, you donkey, not the
enemy of the Grand Duke!
—In any case, the war's over, so our soldiers
are coming back.

GRUSHA *drops a cake pan,* GUESTS *help her pick up
the cake*

AN OLD WOMAN: *(To* GRUSHA*)*. Are you feeling bad?
It's just excitement about dear Jussup. Sit down
and rest a while, my dear. *(*GRUSHA *staggers)*

THE GUESTS: Now everything'll be the way it was.
Only the taxes'll go up because now we'll have
to pay for the war.

GRUSHA: *(Weakly)*. Did someone say the soldiers
are back?

A MAN: I did.

GRUSHA: It can't be true.

THE FIRST MAN: *(To a* WOMAN*)*. Show her the shawl.
We bought it from a soldier. It's from Persia.

GRUSHA: *(Looking at the shawl)*. They are here. *(She
gets up, takes a step, kneels down in prayer, takes
the silver cross and chain out of her blouse, and kisses
it)*

THE MOTHER-IN-LAW: *(While the* GUESTS *silently
watch* GRUSHA*)*. What's the matter with you?
Aren't you going to look after our guests? What's
all this city nonsense got to do with us?

THE GUESTS: *(Resuming conversation while* GRUSHA
remains in prayer).
—You can buy Persian saddles from the
soldiers too. Though many want crutches
in exchange for them.
—The big shots on one side can win a war,
the soldiers on both sides lose it.
—Anyway, the war's over. It's something they
can't draft you any more.

The DYING MAN *sits bolt upright in bed. He listens*

460 —What we need is two weeks of good weather.
—Our pear trees are hardly bearing a thing
this year.

THE MOTHER-IN-LAW: *(Offering cakes).* Have some
more cakes and welcome! There are more!

The MOTHER-IN-LAW *goes to the bedroom with the empty
cake pans. Unaware of the* DYING MAN, *she is bending
down to pick up another tray when he begins to talk
in a hoarse voice*

THE PEASANT: How many more cakes are you going
470 to stuff down their throats? Think I'm a fucking
goldmine?

The MOTHER-IN-LAW *starts, stares at him aghast, while
he climbs out from behind the mosquito net*

THE FIRST WOMAN: *(Talking kindly to* GRUSHA *in the
next room).* Has the young wife got someone at
the front?

A MAN: It's good news they're on their way home,
huh?

THE PEASANT: Don't stare at me like that! Where's
480 this wife you've hung round my neck?

*Receiving no answer, he climbs out of bed and in his
nightshirt staggers into the other room. Trembling, she
follows him with the cake pan*

THE GUESTS: *(Seeing him and shrieking).* Good God!
Jussup!

EVERYONE *leaps up in alarm. The* WOMEN *rush to the
door.* GRUSHA, *still on her knees, turns round and stares
at the* MAN

THE PEASANT: A funeral supper! You'd enjoy that,
490 wouldn't you? Get out before I throw you out!
(As the GUESTS *stampede from the house, gloomily to*
GRUSHA) I've upset the apple cart, huh? *(Receiving
no answer, he turns round and takes a cake from the
pan which his* MOTHER *is holding)*

THE SINGER:
O confusion! The wife discovers she has a
husband.
By day there's the child, by night there's the
husband.
The lover is on his way both day and night.
500 Husband and wife look at each other.
The bedroom is small.

Near the bed the PEASANT *is sitting in a high wooden
bathtub, naked, the* MOTHER-IN-LAW *is pouring water*

from a pitcher. Opposite GRUSHA *cowers with* MICHAEL,
who is playing at mending straw mats

THE PEASANT: *(To his* MOTHER). That's her work,
not yours. Where's she hiding out now?

THE MOTHER-IN-LAW: *(Calling).* Grusha! The peasant wants you!   510

GRUSHA: *(To* MICHAEL). There are still two holes
to mend.

THE PEASANT: *(When* GRUSHA *approaches).* Scrub my
back!

GRUSHA: Can't the peasant do it himself?

THE PEASANT: "Can't the peasant do it himself?"
Get the brush! To hell with you! Are you the
wife here? Or are you a visitor? *(To the* MOTHER-
IN-LAW). It's too cold!

THE MOTHER-IN-LAW: I'll run for hot water.   520

GRUSHA: Let me go.

THE PEASANT: You stay here. *(The* MOTHER-IN-LAW
exits) Rub harder. And no shirking. You've seen
a naked fellow before. That child didn't come
out of thin air.

GRUSHA: The child was not conceived in joy, if
that's what the peasant means.

THE PEASANT: *(Turning and grinning).* You don't
look the type. *(GRUSHA *stops scrubbing him, starts
back)*   530

Enter the MOTHER-IN-LAW

THE PEASANT: A nice thing you've hung around
my neck! A simpleton for a wife!

THE MOTHER-IN-LAW: She just isn't co-operative.

THE PEASANT: Pour—but go easy! Ow! Go easy,
I said. *(To* GRUSHA) Maybe you did something
wrong in the city . . . I wouldn't be surprised.
Why else should you be here? But I won't talk
about that. I've not said a word about the
illegitimate object you brought into my house   540
either. But my patience has limits! It's against
nature. *(To the* MOTHER-IN-LAW) More! *(To
GRUSHA) And even if your soldier does come
back, you're married.

GRUSHA: Yes.

THE PEASANT: But your soldier won't come back.
Don't you believe it.

GRUSHA: No.

THE PEASANT: You're cheating me. You're my wife
and you're not my wife. Where you lie, nothing   550
lies, and yet no other woman can lie there. When
I go to work in the morning I'm tired—when

I lie down at night I'm awake as the devil. God has given you sex—and what d'you do? I don't have ten piasters to buy myself a woman in the city. Besides, it's a long way. Woman weeds the fields and opens up her legs, that's what our calendar says. D'you hear?

GRUSHA: *(Quietly)*. Yes. I didn't mean to cheat you out of it.

THE PEASANT: She didn't mean to cheat me out of it! Pour some more water! *(The* MOTHER-IN-LAW *pours)* Ow!

THE SINGER:

As she sat by the stream to wash the linen
She saw his image in the water
And his face grew dimmer with the passing moons.
As she raised herself to wring the linen
She heard his voice from the murmuring maple
And his voice grew fainter with the passing moons.
Evasions and sighs grew more numerous,
Tears and sweat flowed.
With the passing moons the child grew up.

GRUSHA *sits by a stream, dipping linen into the water. In the rear, a few* CHILDREN *are standing*

GRUSHA: *(To* MICHAEL*)*. You can play with them, Michael, but don't let them boss you around just because you're the littlest.

MICHAEL *nods and joins the* CHILDREN. *They start playing*

THE BIGGEST BOY: Today it's the Heads-Off Game. *(To a* FAT BOY*)* You're the Prince and you laugh. *(To* MICHAEL*)* You're the Governor. *(To a* GIRL*)* You're the Governor's wife and you cry when his head's cut off. And I do the cutting. *(He shows his wooden sword)* With this. First, they lead the Governor into the yard. The Prince walks in front. The Governor's wife comes last.

They form a procession. The FAT BOY *is first and laughs. Then comes* MICHAEL, *then the* BIGGEST BOY, *and then the* GIRL, *who weeps*

MICHAEL: *(Standing still)*. Me cut off head!

THE BIGGEST BOY: That's my job. You're the littlest. The Governor's the easy part. All you do is kneel down and get your head cut off—simple.

MICHAEL: Me want sword!

THE BIGGEST BOY: It's mine! *(He gives him a kick)*

THE GIRL: *(Shouting to* GRUSHA*)*. He won't play his part!

GRUSHA: *(Laughing)*. Even the little duck is a swimmer, they say.

THE BIGGEST BOY: You can be the Prince if you can laugh.

MICHAEL *shakes his head*

THE FAT BOY: I laugh best. Let him cut off the head just once. Then you do it, then me.

Reluctantly, the BIGGEST BOY *hands* MICHAEL *the wooden sword and kneels down. The* FAT BOY *sits down slaps his thigh, and laughs with all his might. The* GIRL *weeps loudly.* MICHAEL *swings the big sword and "cuts off" the head. In doing so, he topples over*

THE BIGGEST BOY: Hey! I'll show you how to cut heads off!

MICHAEL *runs away. The* CHILDREN *run after him.* GRUSHA *laughs, following them with her eyes. On looking back, she sees* SIMON SHASHAVA *standing on the opposite bank. He wears a shabby uniform*

GRUSHA: Simon!

SIMON: Is that Grusha Vashnadze?

GRUSHA: Simon!

SIMON: *(Formally)*. A good morning to the young lady. I hope she is well.

GRUSHA: *(Getting up gaily and bowing low)*. A good morning to the soldier. God be thanked he has returned in good health.

SIMON: They found better fish, so they didn't eat me, said the haddock.

GRUSHA: Courage, said the kitchen boy. Good luck, said the hero.

SIMON: How are things here? Was the winter bearable? The neighbor considerate?

GRUSHA: The winter was a trifle rough, the neighbor as usual, Simon.

SIMON: May one ask if a certain person still dips her foot in the water when rinsing the linen?

GRUSHA: The answer is no. Because of the eyes in the bushes.

SIMON: The young lady is speaking of soldiers. Here stands a paymaster.

GRUSHA: A job worth twenty piasters?

SIMON: And lodgings.

GRUSHA: *(With tears in her eyes)*. Behind the barracks under the date trees.

SIMON: Yes, there. A certain person has kept her eyes open.

GRUSHA: She has, Simon.

650 SIMON: And has not forgotten (*Grusha shakes her head*) So the door is still on its hinges as they say? (GRUSHA *looks at him in silence and shakes her head again*) What's this? Is something not as it should be?

GRUSHA: Simon Shashava, I can never return to Nuka. Something has happened.

SIMON: What can have happened?

GRUSHA: For one thing, I knocked an Ironshirt down.

660 SIMON: Grusha Vashnadze must have had her reasons for that.

GRUSHA: Simon Shashava, I am no longer called what I used to be called.

SIMON: (*After a pause*). I do not understand.

GRUSHA: When do women change their names, Simon? Let me explain. Nothing stands between us. Everything is just as it was. You must believe that.

SIMON: Nothing stands between us and yet there's
670 something?

GRUSHA: How can I explain it so fast and with the stream between us? Couldn't you cross the bridge there?

SIMON: Maybe it's no longer necessary.

GRUSHA: It is very necessary. Come over on this side, Simon. Quick!

SIMON: Does the young lady wish to say someone has come too late?

GRUSHA *looks up at him in despair, her face streaming*
680 *with tears.* SIMON *stares before him. He picks up a piece of wood and starts cutting it*

THE SINGER:
So many words are said, so many left unsaid.
The soldier has come.
Where he comes from, he does not say.
Hear what he thought and did not say:
"The battle began, gray at dawn, grew bloody at noon.
The first man fell in front of me, the second
690   behind me, the third at my side.
I trod on the first, left the second behind,
the third was run through by the captain.
One of my brothers died by steel, the other by smoke.

My neck caught fire, my hands froze in my gloves, my toes in my socks.
I fed on aspen buds, I drank maple juice, I slept on stone, in water."

SIMON: I see a cap in the grass. Is there a little
700 one already?

GRUSHA: There is, Simon. There's no keeping that from you. But please don't worry, it is not mine.

SIMON: When the wind once starts to blow, they say, it blows through every cranny. The wife need say no more.

GRUSHA *looks into her lap and is silent*

THE SINGER:
There was yearning but there was no waiting.
The oath is broken. Neither could say why.
Hear what she thought but did not say: 710
"While you fought in the battle, soldier,
The bloody battle, the bitter battle
I found a helpless infant
I had not the heart to destroy him
I had to care for a creature that was lost
I had to stoop for breadcrumbs on the floor
I had to break myself for that which was not mine
That which was other people's.
Someone must help!   720
For the little tree needs water
The lamb loses its way when the shepherd is asleep
And its cry is unheard!"

SIMON: Give me back the cross I gave you. Better still, throw it in the stream. (*He turns to go*)

GRUSHA: (*Getting up*). Simon Shashava, don't go away! He isn't mine! He isn't mine! (*She hears the* CHILDREN *calling*) What's the matter, children?

VOICES: Soldiers! And they're taking Michael   730 away!

GRUSHA *stands aghast as* TWO IRONSHIRTS, *with* MICHAEL *between them, come toward her*

ONE OF THE IRONSHIRTS: Are you Grusha? (*She nods*) Is this your child?

GRUSHA: Yes.   (SIMON *goes*) Simon!

THE IRONSHIRT: We have orders, in the name of the law, to take this child, found in your custody, back to the city. It is suspected that the child   740

is Michael Abashwili, son and heir of the late
Governor Georgi Abashwili, and his wife,
Natella Abashwili. Here is the document and
the seal. *(They lead the* CHILD *away)*
GRUSHA: *(Running after them, shouting).* Leave him
here. Please! He's mine!
THE SINGER:
> The Ironshirts took the child, the beloved
> child.
> The unhappy girl followed them to the city,
750 > the dreaded city.

She who had borne him demanded the child.
She who had raised him faced trial.
Who will decide the case?
To whom will the child be assigned?
Who will the judge be? A good judge? A bad?
The city was in flames
In the judge's seat sat Azdak.

---

758 The name *Azdak* should be accented on the second
syllable.

4. THE STORY OF THE JUDGE

THE SINGER:
> Hear the story of the judge
> How he turned judge, how he passed judg-
> ment, what kind of judge he was.
> On that Easter Sunday of the great revolt,
> when the Grand Duke was overthrown
> And his Governor Abashwili, father of our
> child, lost his head
> The Village Scrivener Azdak found a fugitive
10 > in the woods and hid him in his hut.

AZDAK, *in rags and slightly drunk, is helping an* OLD
BEGGAR *into his cottage*

AZDAK: Stop snorting, you're not a horse. And it
won't do you any good with the police, to run
like a snotty nose in April. Stand still, I say.
(He catches the OLD MAN *who has marched into the
cottage as if he'd like to go through the walls)* Sit
down. Feed. Here's a hunk of cheese. *(From under
some rags, in a chest, he fishes out some cheese, and
20 the* OLD MAN *greedily begins to eat)* Haven't eaten
in a long time, huh? *(The* OLD MAN *growls)* Why
were you running like that, asshole? The cop
wouldn't even have seen you.
THE OLD MAN: Had to! Had to!
AZDAK: Blue Funk? *(The* OLD MAN *stares, uncom-
prehending)* Cold feet? Panic? Don't lick your
chops like a Grand Duke. Or an old sow. I can't
stand it. We have to accept respectable stinkers
as God made them, but not you! I once heard
30 of a senior judge who farted at a public dinner

to show an independent spirit! Watching you
eat like that gives me the most awful ideas. Why
don't you say something? *(Sharply)* Show me
your hand. Can't you hear? *(The* OLD MAN *slowly
puts out his hand)* White! So you're not a beggar
at all! A fraud, a walking swindle! And I'm hiding you from the cops as though you were an
honest man! Why were you running like that
if you're a landowner? For that's what you are.
Don't deny it! I see it in your guilty face! *(He
gets up)* Get out! *(The* OLD MAN *looks at him uncertainly)* What are you waiting for, peasant-
flogger?
THE OLD MAN: Pursued. Need undivided attention.
Make proposition...
AZDAK: Make what? A proposition? Well, if that
isn't the height of insolence. He's making me
a proposition! The bitten man scratches his fingers bloody, and the leech that's biting him
makes him a proposition! Get out, I tell you!
THE OLD MAN: Understand point of view! Persuasion! Pay hundred thousand piasters one night!
Yes?
AZDAK: What, you think you can buy me? For
a hundred thousand piasters? Let's say a hundred
and fifty thousand. Where are they?
THE OLD MAN: Have not them here. Of course.
Will be sent. Hope do not doubt.
AZDAK: Doubt very much. Get out!

60 The OLD MAN *gets up, waddles to the door. A* VOICE
is heard off stage

A VOICE: Azdak!

The OLD MAN *turns, waddles to the opposite corner,
stands still*

AZDAK: *(Calling out).* I'm not in! *(He walks to door)*
So you're sniffing around here again, Shauwa?

POLICEMAN SHAUWA: *(Reproachfully).* You've caught
another rabbit, Azdak. And you promised me
it wouldn't happen again!

70 AZDAK: *(Severely).* Shauwa, don't talk about things
you don't understand. The rabbit is a dangerous
and destructive beast. It feeds on plants, especially on the species of plants known as weeds.
It must therefore be exterminated.

SHAUWA: Azdak, don't be so hard on me. I'll lose
my job if I don't arrest you. I know you have
a good heart.

AZDAK: I do not have a good heart! How often
must I tell you I'm a man of intellect?

80 SHAUWA: *(Slyly).* I know, Azdak. You're a superior
person. You say so yourself. I'm just a Christian
and an ignoramus. So I ask you: When one of
the Prince's rabbits is stolen, and I'm a policeman, what should I do with the offending party?

AZDAK: Shauwa, Shauwa, shame on you. You
stand and ask me a question, than which nothing
could be more seductive. It's like you were a
woman—let's say that bad girl Nunowna, and
you showed me your thigh—Nunowna's thigh,

90 that would be—and asked me: "What shall I
do with my thigh, it itches?" Is she as innocent
as she pretends? Of course not. I catch a rabbit,
but you catch a man. Man is made in God's
image. Not so a rabbit, you know that. I'm a
rabbit-eater, but you're a man-eater, Shauwa.
And God will pass judgment on you. Shauwa,
go home and repent. No, stop, there's something . . . *(He looks at the* OLD MAN *who stands trembling in the corner)* No, it's nothing. Go home and

100 repent. *(He slams the door behind* SHAUWA*)* Now
you're surprised, huh? Surprised I didn't hand
you over? I couldn't hand over a bedbug to that
animal. It goes against the grain. Now don't
tremble because of a cop! So old and still so
scared? Finish your cheese, but eat it like a poor
man, or else they'll still catch you. Must I even
explain how a poor man behaves? *(He pushes him*

down, and then gives him back the cheese) That box
is the table. Lay your elbows on the table. Now,
encircle the cheese on the plate like it might   110
be snatched from you at any moment—what
right have you to be safe, huh?—now, hold your
knife like an undersized sickle, and give your
cheese a troubled look because, like all beautiful
things, it's already fading away. *(*AZDAK *watches
him)* They're after you, which speaks in your
favor, but how can we be sure they're not mistaken about you? In Tiflis one time they hanged
a landowner, a Turk, who could prove he quar-
tered his peasants instead of merely cutting them   120
in half, as is the custom, and he squeezed twice
the usual amount of taxes out of them, his zeal
was above suspicion. And yet they hanged him
like a common criminal—because he was a Turk
—a thing he couldn't do much about. What injustice! He got onto the gallows by a sheer fluke.
In short, I don't trust you.

THE SINGER:

Thus Azdak gave the old beggar a bed,
And learned that old beggar was the old   130
butcher, the Grand Duke himself,
And was ashamed.

He denounced himself and ordered the policeman to take him to Nuka, to court, to be
judged.

In the court of justice THREE IRONSHIRTS *sit drinking.
From a beam hangs a man in judge's robes. Enter* AZDAK,
in chains, dragging SHAUWA *behind him*

AZDAK: *(Shouting).* I've helped the Grand Duke,
the Grand Thief, the Grand Butcher, to escape!   140
In the name of justice I ask to be severely judged
in public trial!

THE FIRST IRONSHIRT: Who's this queer bird?

SHAUWA: That's our Village Scrivener, Azdak.

AZDAK: I am contemptible! I am a traitor! A
branded criminal! Tell them, flat-foot, how I
insisted on being chained up and brought to the
capital. Because I sheltered the Grand Duke,
the Grand Swindler, by mistake. And how I
found out afterwards. See the marked man   150
denounce himself! Tell them how I forced you
to walk with me half the night to clear the whole
thing up.

SHAUWA: And all by threats. That wasn't nice of
you, Azdak.

AZDAK: Shut your mouth, Shauwa. You don't understand. A new age is upon us! It'll go thundering over you. You're finished. The police will be wiped out—poof! Everything will be gone into, everything will be brought into the open. The guilty will give themselves up. Why? They couldn't escape the people in any case. *(To* SHAUWA*)* Tell them how I shouted all along Shoemaker Street: *(With big gestures, looking at the* IRONSHIRTS*)* "In my ignorance I let the Grand Swindler escape!" So tear me to pieces, brothers! I wanted to get it in first.

THE FIRST IRONSHIRT: And what did your brothers answer?

SHAUWA: They comforted him in Butcher Street, and they laughed themselves sick in Shoemaker Street. That's all.

AZDAK: But with you it's different. I can see you're men of iron. Brothers, where's the judge? I must be tried.

THE FIRST IRONSHIRT: *(Points at the hanged man).* There's the judge. And please stop "bothering" us. It's rather a sore spot this evening.

AZDAK: "There's the judge." An answer never heard in Grusinia before. Townsman, where's His Excellency the Governor? *(Pointing to the floor)* There's His Excellency, stranger. Where's the Chief Tax Collector? Where's the official Recruiting Officer? The Patriarch? The Chief of Police? There, there, there—all there. Brothers, I expected no less of you.

THE SECOND IRONSHIRT: What? *What* was it you expected, funny man?

AZDAK: What happened in Persia, brother, what happened in Persia?

THE SECOND IRONSHIRT: What did happen in Persia?

AZDAK: Everybody was hanged. Viziers, tax collectors. Everybody. Forty years ago now. My grandfather, a remarkable man by the way, saw it all. For three whole days. Everywhere.

THE SECOND IRONSHIRT: And who ruled when the Vizier was hanged?

AZDAK: A peasant ruled when the Vizier was hanged.

THE SECOND IRONSHIRT: And who commanded the army?

AZDAK: A soldier, a soldier.

THE SECOND IRONSHIRT: And who paid the wages?

AZDAK: A dyer. A dyer paid the wages.

THE SECOND IRONSHIRT: Wasn't it a weaver, maybe?

THE FIRST IRONSHIRT: And why did all this happen, Persian?

AZDAK: Why did all this happen? Must there be a special reason? Why do you scratch yourself, brother? War! Too long a war! And no justice! My grandfather brought back a song that tells how it was. I will sing it for you. With my friend the policeman. *(To* SHAUWA*)* And hold the rope tight. It's very suitable.

He sings, with SHAUWA *holding the rope tight around him*

THE SONG OF INJUSTICE IN PERSIA

Why don't our sons bleed any more? Why don't our daughters weep?
Why do only the slaughter-house cattle have blood in their veins?
Why do only the willows shed tears on Lake Urmi?

The king must have a new province, the peasant must give up his savings.
That the roof of the world might be conquered, the roof of the cottage is torn down.
Our men are carried to the ends of the earth, so that great ones can eat at home.
The soldiers kill each other, the marshals salute each other.
They bite the widow's tax money to see if it's good, their swords break.
The battle was lost, the helmets were paid for.

Refrain

Is it so? Is it so?

Refrain by SHAUWA

Yes, yes, yes, yes, yes it's so.

AZDAK: Do you want to hear the rest of it? *(The* FIRST IRONSHIRT *nods)*

THE SECOND IRONSHIRT: *(To* SHAUWA*).* Did he teach you that song?

SHAUWA: Yes, only my voice isn't very good.

THE SECOND IRONSHIRT: No. *(To* AZDAK*)* Go on singing.

AZDAK: The second verse is about the peace.

(He sings)

The offices are packed, the streets overflow
with officials.
The rivers jump their banks and ravage the
fields.
Those who cannot let down their own trousers
rule countries.
They can't count up to four, but they devour
eight courses.
The corn farmers, looking round for buyers,
260   see only the starving.
The weavers go home from their looms in
rags.

Refrain

Is it so? Is it so?

Refrain by SHAUWA

Yes, yes, yes, yes, yes it's so.

AZDAK:

That's why our sons don't bleed any more,
that's why our daughters don't weep.
270   That's why only the slaughter-house cattle
have blood in their veins,
And only the willows shed tears by Lake
Urmi toward morning.

THE FIRST IRONSHIRT: Are you going to sing that
song here in town?

AZDAK: Sure. What's wrong with it?

THE FIRST IRONSHIRT: Have you noticed that the
sky's getting red? *(Turning round,* AZDAK *sees the
sky red with fire)* It's the people's quarters. On
280   the outskirts of town. The carpet weavers have
caught the "Persian Sickness," too. And they've
been asking if Prince Kazbeki isn't eating too
many courses. This morning they strung up the
city judge. As for us we beat them to pulp.
We were paid one hundred piasters per man,
you understand?

AZDAK: *(After a pause).* I understand.

*He glances shyly round and, creeping away, sits down
in a corner, his head in his hands*

290   THE IRONSHIRTS: *(To each other).*
—If there ever was a trouble-maker it's him.
—He must've come to the capital to fish in the
troubled waters.

SHAUWA: Oh, I don't think he's a really bad character, gentlemen. Steals a few chickens here and
there. And maybe a rabbit.

THE SECOND IRONSHIRT: *(Approaching* AZDAK*).*
Came to fish in the troubled waters, huh?

AZDAK: *(Looking up).* I don't know why I came.

THE SECOND IRONSHIRT: Are you in with the carpet   300
weavers maybe? *(*AZDAK *shakes his head)* How
about that song?

AZDAK: From my grandfather. A silly and ignorant
man.

THE SECOND IRONSHIRT: Right. And how about the
dyer who paid the wages?

AZDAK: *(Muttering).* That was in Persia.

THE FIRST IRONSHIRT: And this denouncing of
yourself? Because you didn't hang the Grand
Duke with your own hands?   310

AZDAK: Didn't I tell you I let him run? *(He creeps
farther away and sits on the floor)*

SHAUWA: I can swear to that: he let him run.

The IRONSHIRTS *burst out laughing and slap* SHAUWA
on the back. AZDAK *laughs loudest. They slap* AZDAK
too, and unchain him. They all start drinking as the
FAT PRINCE *enters with a* YOUNG MAN

THE FIRST IRONSHIRT: *(To* AZDAK, *pointing at the* FAT
PRINCE*).* There's your "new age" for you! *(More
laughter)*   320

THE FAT PRINCE: Well my friends, what is there
to laugh about? Permit me a serious word. Yesterday morning the Princes of Grusinia over-
threw the war-mongering government of the
Grand Duke and did away with his Governors.
Unfortunately the Grand Duke himself escaped.
In this fateful hour our carpet weavers, those
eternal trouble-makers, had the effrontery to stir
up a rebellion and hang the universally loved
city judge, our dear Illo Orbeliani. Ts-ts-ts. My   330
friends, we need peace, peace, peace in Grusinia!
And Justice! So I've brought along my dear
nephew Bizergan Kazbeki. He'll be the new
judge, hm? A very gifted fellow. What do you
say? I want your opinion. Let the people decide!

THE SECOND IRONSHIRT: Does this mean *we* elect
the judge?

THE FAT PRINCE: Precisely. Let the people propose
some very gifted fellow! Confer among yourselves, my friends. *(The* IRONSHIRTS *confer)* Don't   340
worry, my little fox. The job's yours. And when

we catch the Grand Duke we won't have to kiss this rabble's ass any longer.

THE IRONSHIRTS: *(Between themselves).*

—Very funny: they're wetting their pants because they haven't caught the Grand Duke.

—When the outlook isn't so bright, they say: "My friends!" and "Let the people decide!"

350 —Now he even wants justice for Grusinia! But fun is fun as long as it lasts!

Pointing at AZDAK

—*He* knows all about justice. Hey, rascal, would you like this nephew fellow to be the judge?

AZDAK: Are you asking me? You're not asking *me*?

THE FIRST IRONSHIRT: Why not? Anything for a laugh!

AZDAK: You'd like to test him to the marrow, correct? Have you a criminal on hand? An experi-

360 enced one? So the candidate can show what he knows?

THE SECOND IRONSHIRT: Let's see. We do have a couple of doctors downstairs. Let's use them.

AZDAK: Oh, no, that's no good, we can't take real criminals till we're sure the judge will be appointed. He may be dumb, but he must be appointed, or the Law is violated. And the Law is a sensitive organ. It's like the spleen, you mustn't hit it—that would be fatal. Of course

370 you can hang those two without violating the Law, because there was no judge in the vicinity. But Judgment, when pronounced, must be pronounced with absolute gravity—it's all such nonsense. Suppose, for instance, a judge jails a woman—let's say she's stolen a corncake to feed her child—and this judge isn't wearing his robes—or maybe he's scratching himself while passing sentence and half his body is uncovered—a man's thigh *will* itch once in a

380 while—the sentence this judge passes is a disgrace and the Law is violated. In short it would be easier for a judge's robe and a judge's hat to pass judgment than for a man with no robe and no hat. If you don't treat it with respect, the Law just disappears on you. Now you don't try out a bottle of wine by offering it to a dog; you'd only lose your wine.

THE FIRST IRONSHIRT: Then what do you suggest, hair-splitter?

AZDAK: I'll be the defendant.   390

THE FIRST IRONSHIRT: You? *(He bursts out laughing)*

THE FAT PRINCE: What have you decided?

THE FIRST IRONSHIRT: We've decided to stage a rehearsal. Our friend here will be the defendant. Let the candidate be the judge and sit there.

THE FAT PRINCE: It isn't customary, but why not? *(To the* NEPHEW*)* A mere formality, my little fox. What have I taught you? Who got there first —the slow runner or the fast?

THE NEPHEW: The silent runner, Uncle Arsen.   400

The NEPHEW *takes the chair. The* IRONSHIRTS *and the* FAT PRINCE *sit on the steps. Enter* AZDAK, *mimicking the gait of the Grand Duke*

AZDAK: *(In the Grand Duke's accent).* Is any here knows me? Am Grand Duke.

THE IRONSHIRTS:

—*What* is he?

—The Grand Duke. He knows him, too.

—Fine. So get on with the trial.

AZDAK: Listen! Am accused instigating war?   410 Ridiculous! Am saying ridiculous! That enough? If not, have brought lawyers. Believe five hundred. *(He points behind him, pretending to be surrounded by lawyers)* Requisition all available seats for lawyers!

The IRONSHIRTS *laugh, the* FAT PRINCE *joins in*

THE NEPHEW: *(To the* IRONSHIRTS*).* You really wish me to try this case? I find it rather unusual. From the taste angle, I mean.

THE FIRST IRONSHIRT: Let's go!   420

THE FAT PRINCE: *(Smiling).* Let him have it, my little fox!

THE NEPHEW: All right. People of Grusinia versus Grand Duke. Defendant, what have you got to say for yourself?

AZDAK: Plenty. Naturally, have read war lost. Only started on the advice of patriots. Like Uncle Arsen Kazbeki. Call Uncle Arsen as witness.

THE FAT PRINCE: *(To the* IRONSHIRTS, *delightedly).* What a screw-ball!   430

THE NEPHEW: Motion rejected. One cannot be arraigned for declaring a war, which every ruler has to do once in a while, but only for running a war badly.

AZDAK: Rubbish! Did not run it at all! Had it run! Had it run by Princes! Naturally, they messed it up.

THE NEPHEW: Do you by any chance deny having been commander-in-chief?

440 AZDAK: Not at all! Always *was* commander-in-chief. At birth shouted at wet nurse. Was trained drop turds in toilet, grew accustomed to command. Always commanded officials rob my cash box. Officers flog soldiers only on command. Landowners sleep with peasants' wives only on strictest command. Uncle Arsen here grew his belly at *my* command!

THE IRONSHIRTS: *(Clapping).* He's good! Long live the Grand Duke!

450 THE FAT PRINCE: Answer him, my little fox. I'm with you.

THE NEPHEW: I shall answer him according to the dignity of the law. Defendant, preserve the dignity of the law!

AZDAK: Agreed. Command you to proceed with the trial!

THE NEPHEW: It is not your place to command me. You claim that the Princes forced you to declare war. How can you claim, then, that they

460 —er—"messed it up"?

AZDAK: Did not send enough people. Embezzled funds. Sent sick horses. During attack, drinking in whorehouse. Call Uncle Arsen as witness.

THE NEPHEW: Are you making the outrageous suggestion that the Princes of this country did not fight?

AZDAK: No Princes fought. Fought for war contracts.

THE FAT PRINCE: *(Jumping up).* That's too much!

470 This man talks like a carpet weaver!

AZDAK: Really? I told nothing but the truth.

THE FAT PRINCE: Hang him! Hang him!

THE FIRST IRONSHIRT: *(Pulling the PRINCE down).* Keep quiet! Go on, Excellency!

THE NEPHEW: Quiet! I now render a verdict: You must be hanged! By the neck! Having lost war!

AZDAK: Young man, seriously advise not fall publicly into jerky clipped manner of speech. Cannot be employed as watchdog if howl like wolf. Got

480 it? If people realize Princes speak same language

as Grand Duke, may hang Grand Duke *and* Princes, huh? By the way, must overrule verdict. Reason? War lost, but not for Princes. Princes won their war. Got 3,863,000 piasters for horses not delivered, 8,240,000 piasters for food supplies not produced. Are therefore victors. War lost only for Grusinia, which as such is not present in this court.

THE FAT PRINCE: I think that will do, my friends.
490 *(To AZDAK)* You can withdraw, funny man. *(To the IRONSHIRTS)* you may now ratify the new judge's appointment, my friends.

THE FIRST IRONSHIRT: Yes, we can. Take down the judge's gown.

ONE IRONSHIRT *climbs on the back of the* OTHER, *pulls the gown off the hanged man*

THE FIRST IRONSHIRT: *(To the NEPHEW).* Now you run away so the right ass can get on the right chair. *(To AZDAK)* Step forward! Go to the judge's seat! Now sit in it!   500

AZDAK *steps up, bows, and sits down*

The judge was always a rascal! Now the rascal shall be a judge!

The judge's gown is placed round his shoulders, the hat on his head

And what a judge!

THE SINGER:
And there was civil war in the land.
The mighty were not safe.
And Azdak was made a judge by the Iron-   510
shirts.
And Azdak remained a judge for two years.

THE SINGER AND CHORUS:
When the towns were set afire
And rivers of blood rose higher and higher,
Cockroaches crawled out of every crack.
And the court was full of schemers
And the church of foul blasphemers.
In the judge's cassock sat Azdak.

AZDAK *sits in the judge's chair, peeling an apple.* SHAUWA   520
is sweeping out the hall. On one side an INVALID *in a wheelchair. Opposite, a* YOUNG MAN *accused of blackmail. An* IRONSHIRT *stands guard, holding the Ironshirt's banner*

AZDAK: In consideration of the large number of

cases, the Court today will hear two cases at a time. Before I open the proceedings, a short announcement—I accept.

He stretches out his hand. The BLACKMAILER *is the only one to produce any money. He hands it to* AZDAK

I reserve the right to punish one of the parties for contempt of court. (*He glances at the* INVALID) You (*To the* DOCTOR) are a doctor, and you (*To the* INVALID) are bringing a complaint against him. Is the doctor responsible for your condition?

THE INVALID: Yes. I had a stroke on his account.

AZDAK: That would be professional negligence.

THE INVALID: Worse than negligence. I gave this man money for his studies. So far, he hasn't paid me back a cent. It was when I heard he was treating a patient free that I had my stroke.

AZDAK: Rightly. (*To a* LIMPING MAN) And what are *you* doing here?

THE LIMPING MAN: I'm the patient, your honor.

AZDAK: He treated your leg for nothing?

THE LIMPING MAN: The wrong leg! My rheumatism was in the left leg, and he operated on the right. That's why I limp now.

AZDAK: And you were treated free?

THE INVALID: A five-hundred-piaster operation free! For nothing! For a God-bless-you! And I paid for this man's studies! (*To the* DOCTOR) Did they teach you to operate free?

THE DOCTOR: Your Honor, it is actually the custom to demand the fee before the operation, as the patient is more willing to pay before an operation than after. Which is only human. In the case in question I was convinced when I started the operation, that my servant had already received the fee. In this I was mistaken.

THE INVALID: He was mistaken! A good doctor doesn't make mistakes! He examines before he operates!

AZDAK: That's right. (*To* SHAUWA) Public Prosecutor, what's the other case about?

SHAUWA: (*Busily sweeping*). Blackmail.

THE BLACKMAILER: High Court of Justice, I'm innocent. I only wanted to find out from the landowner concerned if he really *had* raped his niece. He informed me very politely that this was not the case, and gave me the money only so I could pay for my uncle's studies.

AZDAK: Hm. (*To the* DOCTOR) You, on the other hand, can cite no extenuating circumstances for your offense, huh?

THE DOCTOR: Except that to err is human.

AZDAK: And you are aware that in money matters a good doctor is a highly responsible person? I once heard of a doctor who got a thousand piasters for a sprained finger by remarking that sprains have something to do with blood circulation, which after all a less good doctor might have overlooked, and who, on another occasion made a real gold mine out of a somewhat disordered gall bladder, he treated it with such loving care. You have no excuse, Doctor. The corn merchant, Uxu, had his son study medicine to get some knowledge of trade, our medical schools are so good. (*To the* BLACKMAILER) What's the landowner's name?

SHAUWA: He doesn't want it mentioned.

AZDAK: In that case I will pass judgment. The Court considers the blackmail proved. And you (*To the* INVALID) are sentenced to a fine of one thousand piasters. If you have a second stroke, the doctor will have to treat you free. Even if he has to amputate. (*To the* LIMPING MAN) As compensation, you will receive a bottle of rubbing alcohol. (*To the* BLACKMAILER) You are sentenced to hand over half the proceeds of your deal to the Public Prosecutor to keep the landowner's name secret. You are advised, moreover, to study medicine—you seem well suited to that calling. (*To the* DOCTOR) You have perpetrated an unpardonable error in the practice of your profession: you are acquitted. Next cases!

THE SINGER AND CHORUS:
Men won't do much for a shilling.
For a pound they may be willing.
For 20 pounds the verdict's in the sack.
As for the many, all too many,
Those who've only got a penny—
They've one single, sole recourse: Azdak.

Enter AZDAK *from the caravansary on the high-road, followed by an old bearded* INNKEEPER. *The judge's chair is carried by a* STABLEMAN *and* SHAUWA. *An* IRONSHIRT, *with a banner, takes up his position*

AZDAK: Put me down. Then we'll get some air, maybe even a good stiff breeze from the lemon

620 grove there. It does justice good to be done in the open: the wind blows her skirts up and you can see what she's got. Shauwa, we've been eating too much. These official journeys are exhausting. (*To the* INNKEEPER) It's a question of your daughter-in-law?

THE INNKEEPER: Your Worship, it's a question of the family honor. I wish to bring an action on behalf of my son, who's on business on the other side of the mountain. This is the offending

630 stableman, and here's my daughter-in-law.

Enter the DAUGHTER-IN-LAW, *a voluptuous wench. She is veiled*

AZDAK: (*Sitting down*). I accept.

Sighing, the INNKEEPER *hands him some money*

Good. Now the formalities are disposed of. This is a case of rape?

THE INNKEEPER: Your Honor, I caught the fellow in the act. Ludovica was in the straw on the stable floor.

640 AZDAK: Quite right, the stable. Lovely horses! I specially liked the little roan.

THE INNKEEPER: The first thing I did, of course, was to question Ludovica. On my son's behalf.

AZDAK: (*Seriously*) I said I specially liked the little roan.

THE INNKEEPER: (*Coldly*). Really? Ludovica confessed the stableman took her against her will.

AZDAK: Take your veil off, Ludovica. (*She does so*) Ludovica, you please the Court. Tell us how

650 it happened.

LUDOVICA: (*Well-schooled*). When I entered the stable to see the new foal the stableman said to me on his own accord: "It's hot today!" and laid his hand on my left breast. I said to him: "Don't do that!" But he continued to handle me indecently, which provoked my anger. Before I realized his sinful intentions, he got much closer. It was all over when my father-in-law entered and accidentally trod on me.

660 THE INNKEEPER: (*Explaining*). On my son's behalf.

AZDAK: (*To the* STABLEMAN). You admit you started it?

THE STABLEMAN: Yes.

AZDAK: Ludovica, you like to eat sweet things?

LUDOVICA: Yes, sunflower seeds!

AZDAK: You like to lie a long time in the bathtub?

LUDOVICA: Half an hour or so.

AZDAK: Public Prosecutor, drop your knife—there—on the ground. (SHAUWA *does so*) Ludovica, pick up that knife. (LUDOVICA, *swaying* 670 *her hips, does so*) See that? (*He points at her*) The way it moves? The rape is now proven. By eating too much—sweet things, especially—by lying too long in warm water, by laziness and too soft a skin, you have raped that unfortunate man. Think you can run around with a behind like that and get away with it in court? This is a case of intentional assault with a dangerous weapon! You are sentenced to hand over to the Court the little roan which your father liked to 680 ride "on his son's behalf." And now, come with me to the stables, so the Court may inspect the scene of the crime, Ludovica.

THE SINGER AND THE CHORUS:
When the sharks the sharks devour
Little fishes have their hour.
For a while the load is off their back.
On Grusinia's highways faring
Fixed-up scales of justice bearing
Strode the poor man's magistrate: Azdak.   690
And he gave to the forsaken
All that from the rich he'd taken.
And a bodyguard of roughnecks was Azdak's.
And our good and evil man, he
Smiled upon Grusinia's Granny.
His emblem was a tear in sealing wax.
All mankind should love each other
But when visiting your brother
Take an ax along and hold it fast.
Not in theory but in practice   700
Miracles are wrought with axes
And the age of miracles is not past.

AZDAK'S *judge's chair is in a tavern.* THREE RICH FARMERS *stand before* AZDAK. SHAUWA *brings him wine. In a corner stands an* OLD PEASANT WOMAN. *In the open doorway, and outside, stand* VILLAGERS *looking on. An* IRONSHIRT *stands guard with a banner*

AZDAK: The Public Prosecutor has the floor.

SHAUWA: It concerns a cow. For five weeks the defendant has had a cow in her stable, the prop-   710 erty of the farmer Suru. She was also found to be in possession of a stolen ham, and a number of cows belonging to Shutoff were killed after he asked the defendant to pay the rent on a piece of land.

THE FARMERS:

—It's a matter of my ham, Your Honor.

—It's a matter of my cow, Your Honor.

—It's a matter of my land, Your Honor.

720 AZDAK: Well, Granny, what have *you* got to say to all this?

THE OLD WOMAN: Your Honor, one night toward morning, five weeks ago, there was a knock at my door, and outside stood a bearded man with a cow. "My dear woman," he said, "I am the miracle-working Saint Banditus and because your son has been killed in the war, I bring you this cow as a souvenir. Take good care of it."

730 THE FARMERS:

—The robber, Irakli, Your Honor!

—Her brother-in-law, Your Honor!

—The cow-thief!

—The incendiary!

—He must be beheaded!

Outside, a woman screams. The CROWD *grows restless, retreats. Enter the* BANDIT IRAKLI *with a huge ax*

THE BANDIT: A very good evening, dear friends! A glass of vodka!

740 THE FARMERS: (*Crossing themselves*). Irakli!

AZDAK: Public Prosecutor, a glass of vodka for our guest. And who are you?

THE BANDIT: I'm a wandering hermit, Your Honor. Thanks for the gracious gift.

He empties the glass which SHAUWA *has brought*

Another!

AZDAK: I am Azdak. (*He gets up and bows. The* BANDIT *also bows*) The Court welcomes the foreign hermit. Go on with your story, Granny.

750 THE OLD WOMAN: Your Honor, that first night I didn't yet know Saint Banditus could work miracles, it was only the cow. But one night a few days later, the farmer's servants came to take the cow away again. Then they turned round in front of my door and went off without the cow. And bumps as big as a fist sprouted on their heads. So I knew that Saint Banditus had changed their hearts and turned them into friendly people. (*The* BANDIT *roars with laughter*)

760 THE FIRST FARMER: I know what changed them.

AZDAK: That's fine. You can tell us later. Continue.

THE OLD WOMAN: Your Honor, the next one to become a good man was the farmer Shutoff—a devil, as everyone knows. But Saint Banditus arranged it so he let me off the rent on the little piece of land.

THE SECOND FARMER: Because my cows were killed in the field. (*The* BANDIT *laughs*)

THE OLD WOMAN: (*Answering* AZDAK'S *sign to continue*). Then one morning the ham came flying 770 in at my window. It hit me in the small of the back. I'm still lame, Your Honor, look. (*She limps a few steps*) (*The* BANDIT *laughs*) Your Honor, was there ever a time when a poor old woman could get a ham *without* a miracle?

The BANDIT *starts sobbing*

AZDAK: (*Rising from his chair*). Granny, that's a question that strikes straight at the Court's heart. Be so kind as to sit here.

The OLD WOMAN, *hesitating, sits in the judge's chair* 780

AZDAK: (*Sits on the floor, glass in hand, reciting*).
Granny
We could almost call you Granny Grusinia
The Woebegone
The Bereaved Mother
Whose sons have gone to war
Receiving the present of a cow
She bursts out crying.
When she is beaten
She remains hopeful. 790
When she's not beaten
She's surprised.
On us
Who are already damned
May you render a merciful verdict
Granny Grusinia!

Bellowing at the FARMERS

Admit you don't believe in miracles, you atheists! Each of you is sentenced to pay five hundred piasters! For godlessness! Get out! 800

The FARMERS *slink out*

And you Granny, and you (*To the* BANDIT) pious man, empty a pitcher of wine with the Public Prosecutor and Azdak!

THE SINGER AND THE CHORUS:

> And he broke the rules to save them.
> Broken law like bread he gave them,
> Brought them to shore upon his crooked back.
> At long last the poor and lowly
> Had someone who was not too holy
> To be bribed by empty hands: Azdak.
> For two years it was his pleasure
> To give the beasts of prey short measure:
> He became a wolf to fight the pack.
> From All Hallows to All Hallows
> On his chair beside the gallows
> Dispensing justice in his fashion sat Azdak.

810

THE SINGER:

> But the era of disorder came to an end.
> The Grand Duke returned.
> The Governor's wife returned.
> A trial was held.
> Many died.
> The people's quarters burned anew.
> And fear seized Azdak.

820

AZDAK's *judge's chair stands again in the court of justice.* AZDAK *sits on the floor, shaving and talking to* SHAUWA. *Noises outside. In the rear the* FAT PRINCE'S *head is carried by on a lance*

830 AZDAK: Shauwa, the days of your slavery are numbered, maybe even the minutes. For a long time now I have held you in the iron curb of reason, and it has torn your mouth till it bleeds. I have lashed you with reasonable arguments, I have manhandled you with logic. You are by nature a weak man, and if one slyly throws an argument in your path, you *have* to snap it up, you can't resist. It is your nature to lick the hand of some superior being. But superior beings can be of
840 very different kinds. And now, with your liberation, you will soon be able to follow your natural inclinations, which are low. You will be able to follow your infallible instinct, which teaches you to plant your fat heel on the faces of men. Gone is the era of confusion and disorder, which I find described in the Song of Chaos. Let us now sing that song together in memory of those terrible days. Sit down and don't do violence to the music. Don't be afraid. It sounds all right.
850 And it has a fine refrain.

(*He sings*)

THE SONG OF THE CHAOS

> Sister, hide your face! Brother, take your knife!
> The times are out of joint!
> Big men are full of complaint
> And small men full of joy.
> The city says:
> "Let us drive the strong ones from our midst!"
> Offices are raided. Lists of serfs are destroyed.
> They have set Master's nose to the grindstone.
> They who lived in the dark have seen the light.
> The ebony poor box is broken.
> Magnificent sesnem wood is sawed up for beds.
> Who had no bread have barns full.
> Who begged for alms of corn now mete it out.

860

870

SHAUWA: (*Refrain*). Oh, oh, oh, oh.
AZDAK: (*Refrain*).

> Where are you, General, where are you?
> Please, please, please, restore order!
> The nobleman's son can no longer be recognized;
> The lady's child becomes the son of her slave.
> The councilors meet in a shed.
> Once, this man was barely allowed to sleep on the wall;
> Now, he stretches his limbs in a bed.
> Once, this man rowed a boat; now, he owns ships.
> Their owner looks for them, but they're his no longer.
> Five men are sent on a journey by their master.
> "Go yourself," they say, "we have arrived."

880

SHAUWA: (*Refrain*). Oh, oh, oh, oh.
AZDAK: (*Refrain*).

> Where are you, General, where are you?
> Please, please, please, restore order!

890

Yes, so it might have been, had order been neglected much longer. But now the Grand Duke has returned to the capital, and the Persians have lent him an army to restore order with. The suburbs are already aflame. Go and get me the big book I always sit on. (SHAUWA *brings the big book from the judge's chair.* AZDAK *opens it*) This is the Statute Book and I've always used it, as you can testify. Now I'd better look in this book and see what they can do to me. I've let the down-and-outs get away with murder, and I'll have to pay for it. I helped poverty onto its skinny legs, so they'll hang me for drunkedness. I peeped into the rich man's pocket, which is bad taste. And I can't hide anywhere—everybody knows me because I've helped everybody.

SHAUWA: Someone's coming!

AZDAK: (*In panic, he walks trembling to the chair*). It's the end. And now they'd enjoy seeing what a Great Man I am. I'll deprive them of that pleasure. I'll beg on my knees for mercy. Spittle will slobber down my chin. The fear of death is in me.

Enter NATELLA ABASHWILI, *the* GOVERNOR'S WIFE, *followed by the* ADJUTANT *and an* IRONSHIRT

THE GOVERNOR'S WIFE: What sort of a creature is that, Shalva?

AZDAK: A willing one, Your Highness, a man ready to oblige.

THE ADJUTANT: Natella Abashwili, wife of the late Governor, has just returned. She is looking for her two-year-old son, Michael. She has been informed that the child was carried off to the mountains by a former servant.

AZDAK: The child will be brought back, Your Highness, at your service.

THE ADJUTANT: They say that the person in question is passing it off as her own.

AZDAK: She will be beheaded, Your Highness, at your service.

THE ADJUTANT: That is all.

THE GOVERNOR'S WIFE: (*Leaving*). I don't like the man.

AZDAK: (*Following her to door, bowing*) At your service, Your Highness, it will all be arranged.

5. THE CHALK CIRCLE

THE SINGER:
　　Hear now the story of the trial
　　Concerning Governor Abashwili's child
　　And the establishing of the true mother
　　By the famous test of the Chalk Circle.

The court of justice in Juka. IRONSHIRTS *lead* MICHAEL *across stage and out at the back.* IRONSHIRTS *hold* GRUSHA *back with their lances under the gateway until the* CHILD *has been led through. Then she is admitted. She is accompanied by the former governor's* COOK. *Distant noises and a fire-red sky*

GRUSHA: (*Trying to hide*). He's brave, he can wash himself now.

THE COOK: You're lucky. It's not a real judge. It's Azdak, a drunk who doesn't know what he's doing. The biggest thieves have got by through him. Because he gets everything mixed up and the rich never offer him big enough bribes, the likes of us sometimes do pretty well.

GRUSHA: I *need* luck right now.

THE COOK: Touch wood. (*She crosses herself*) I'd better offer up another prayer that the judge may be drunk.

She prays with motionless lips, while GRUSHA *looks around, in vain, for the* CHILD

Why must you hold on to it at any price if it isn't yours? In days like these?

GRUSHA: He's mine. I brought him up.

THE COOK: Have you never thought what'd happen when she came back?

GRUSHA: At first I thought I'd give him to her. Then I thought she wouldn't come back.

THE COOK: And even a borrowed coat keeps a man warm, hm? (GRUSHA *nods*) I'll swear to anything for you. You're a decent girl. (*She sees the soldier* SIMON SHASHAVA *approaching*) You've done wrong by Simon, though. I've been talking with him. He just can't understand.

GRUSHA: (*Unaware of* SIMON's *presence*). Right now I can't be bothered whether he understands or not!

THE COOK: He knows the child isn't yours, but you married and not free "til death you do part" —he can't understand *that*.

GRUSHA *sees* SIMON *and greets him*

SIMON: (*Gloomily*). I wish the lady to know I will swear I am the father of the child.

GRUSHA: (*Low*). Thank you, Simon.

SIMON: At the same time I wish the lady to know my hands are not tied—nor are hers.

THE COOK: You needn't have said that. You know she's married.

SIMON: And it needs no rubbing in.

Enter an IRONSHIRT

THE IRONSHIRT: Where's the judge? Has anyone seen the judge?

ANOTHER IRONSHIRT: (*stepping forward*). The judge isn't here yet. Nothing but a bed and a pitcher in the whole house!

(*Exeunt* IRONSHIRTS)

THE COOK: I hope nothing has happened to him. With any other judge you'd have about as much chance as a chicken has teeth.

GRUSHA: (*Who has turned away and covered her face*). Stand in front of me. I shouldn't have come to Nuka. If I run into the Ironshirt, the one I hit over the head ...

She screams. An IRONSHIRT *had stopped and, turning his back, had been listening to her. He now wheels around. It is the* CORPORAL, *and he has a huge scar across his face.*

THE IRONSHIRT: (*In the gateway*). What's the matter, Shotta? Do you know her?

THE CORPORAL: (*After staring for some time*). No.

THE IRONSHIRT: She's the one who stole the Abashwili child, or so they say. If you know anything about it you can make some money, Shotta. (*Exit the* CORPORAL, *cursing*)

THE COOK: Was it him? (GRUSHA *nods*) I think he'll keep his mouth shut, or he'd be admitting he was after the child.

GRUSHA: I'd almost forgotten him.

Enter THE GOVERNOR'S WIFE, *followed by the* ADJUTANT *and* TWO LAWYERS)

THE GOVERNOR'S WIFE: At least there are no common people here, thank God. I can't stand their smell. It always gives me migraine.

THE FIRST LAWYER: Madam, I must ask you to be careful what you say until we have another judge.

THE GOVERNOR'S WIFE: But I didn't say anything, Illo Shuboladze. I love the people with their simple straightforward minds. It's only that their smell brings on my migraine.

THE SECOND LAWYER: There won't be many spectators. The whole population is sitting at home behind locked doors because of the riots on the outskirts of town.

THE GOVERNOR'S WIFE: (*Looking at* GRUSHA) Is that the creature?

THE FIRST LAWYER: Please, most gracious Natella Abashwili, abstain from invective until it is certain the Grand Duke has appointed a new judge and we're rid of the present one, who's about the lowest fellow ever seen in judge's gown. Things are all set to move, you see.

Enter IRONSHIRTS *from the courtyard*

THE COOK: Her Grace would pull your hair out on the spot if she didn't know Azdak is for the poor. He goes by the face.

IRONSHIRTS *begin fastening a rope to a beam.* AZDAK, *in chains, is led in, followed by* SHAUWA, *also in chains. The* THREE FARMERS *bring up the rear*

AN IRONSHIRT: Trying to run away, were you? (*He strikes* AZDAK)

ONE FARMER: Off with his judge's gown before we string him up!

IRONSHIRTS *and* FARMERS *tear off* AZDAK's *gown. His torn underwear is visible. Then someone kicks him*

AN IRONSHIRT: (*Pushing him into someone else*). If you want a heap of justice, here it is!

Accompanied by shouts of "You take it!" and "Let me have him, Brother!" THEY *throw* AZDAK *back and forth until he collapses. Then he is lifted up and dragged under the noose*

THE GOVERNOR'S WIFE: (*Who, during this "Ball-game," has clapped her hands hysterically*). I disliked that man from the moment I first saw him.

AZDAK: (*Covered with blood, panting*). I can't see.
130 Give me a rag.

AN IRONSHIRT: What is it you want to see?

AZDAK: You, you dogs! (*He wipes the blood out of his eyes with his shirt*) Good morning, dogs! How goes it, dogs! How's the dog world! Does it smell good? Got another boot for me to lick? Are you back at each other's throats, dogs?

Accompanied by a CORPORAL, *a dust-covered* RIDER *enters. He takes some documents from a leather case, looks at them, then interrupts*

140 THE RIDER: Stop! I bring a dispatch from the Grand Duke, containing the latest appointments.

THE CORPORAL: (*Bellowing*). Atten-shun!

THE RIDER: Of the new judge it says: "We appoint a man whom we have to thank for saving a life indispensable to the country's welfare—a certain Azdak of Nuka." Which is he?

SHAUWA: (*Pointing*). That's him, Your Excellency.

THE CORPORAL: (*Bellowing*). What's going on here?

AN IRONSHIRT: I beg to report that His Honor
150 Azdak was already His Honor Azdak, but on these farmers' denunciation was pronounced the Grand Duke's enemy.

THE CORPORAL: (*Pointing at the* FARMERS). March them off! (*They are marched off. They bow all the time*) See to it that His Honor Azdak is exposed to no more violence.

(*Exeunt* RIDER *and* CORPORAL)

THE COOK: (*To* SHAUWA). She clapped her hands! I hope he saw it!

160 THE FIRST LAWYER: It's a catastrophe.

AZDAK *has fainted. Coming to, he is dressed again in judge's robes. He walks, swaying, toward the* IRONSHIRTS

AN IRONSHIRT: What does Your Honor desire?

AZDAK: Nothing, fellow dogs, or just an occasional boot to lick. (*To* SHAUWA) I pardon you. (*He is unchained*) Get me some red wine, the sweet kind.

(SHAUWA *stumbles off*)

Get out of here, I've got to judge a case.

170 *Exeunt* IRONSHIRTS. SHAUWA *returns with a pitcher of wine.* AZDAK *gulps it down*

AZDAK: Something for my backside. (SHAUWA *brings the Statute Book, puts it on the judge's chair.* AZDAK *sits on it*) I accept.

The PROSECUTORS, *among whom a worried council has been held, smile with relief. They whisper*

THE COOK: Oh dear!

SIMON: A well can't be filled with dew, they say.

THE LAWYERS: (*Approaching* AZDAK, *who stands up, expectantly*). A quite ridiculous case, Your 180
Honor. The accused has abducted a child and refuses to hand it over.

AZDAK: (*Stretching out his hand, glancing at* GRUSHA). A most attractive person. (*He fingers the money, then sits down, satisfied*) I declare the proceedings open and demand the whole truth. (*To* GRUSHA) Especially from you.

THE FIRST LAWYER: High Court of Justice! Blood, as the popular saying goes, is thicker than water. This old adage . . . 190

AZDAK: (*Interrupting*). The Court wants to know the lawyers' fee.

THE FIRST LAWYER: (*Surprised*). I beg your pardon? (AZDAK, *smiling, rubs his thumb and index finger*) Oh, I see. Five hundred piasters, Your Honor, to answer the Court's somewhat unusual question.

AZDAK: Did you hear? The question is unusual. I ask it because I listen in quite a different way when I know you're good. 200

THE FIRST LAWYER: (*Bowing*). Thank you, Your Honor. High Court of Justice, of all ties the ties of blood are strongest. Mother and child—is there a more intimate relationship? Can one tear a child from its mother? High Court of Justice, she has conceived it in the holy ecstasies of love. She has carried it in her womb. She has fed it with her blood. She has borne it with pain. High Court of Justice, it has been observed that even the wild tigress, robbed of her young, roams 210
restless through the mountains, shrunk to a shadow. Nature herself . . .

AZDAK: (*Interrupting, to* GRUSHA). What's your answer to all this and anything else that lawyer might have to say?

GRUSHA: He's mine.

AZDAK: Is that all? I hope you can prove it. Why should I assign the child to you in any case?

GRUSHA: I brought him up like the priest says "according to my best knowledge and conscience." I always found him something to eat. Most of the time he had a roof over his head. And I went to such trouble for him. I had expenses too. I didn't look out for my own comfort. I brought the child up to be friendly with everyone, and from the beginning taught him to work. As well as he could, that is. He's still very little.

THE FIRST LAWYER: Your Honor, it is significant that the girl herself doesn't claim any tie of blood between her and the child.

AZDAK: The Court takes note of that

THE FIRST LAWYER: Thank you, Your Honor. And now permit a woman bowed in sorrow—who has already lost her husband and now has also to fear the loss of her child—to address a few words to you. The gracious Natella Abashwili is . . .

THE GOVERNOR'S WIFE: (*Quietly*). A most cruel fate, Sir, forces me to describe to you the tortures of a bereaved mother's soul, the anxiety, the sleepless nights, the . . .

THE SECOND LAWYER: (*Bursting out*). It's outrageous the way this woman is being treated! Her husband's palace is closed to her! The revenue of her estates is blocked, and she is cold-bloodedly told that it's tied to the heir. She can't do a thing without that child. She can't even pay her lawyers!! (*To the* FIRST LAWYER, *who, desperate about this outburst, makes frantic gestures to keep him from speaking*) Dear Illo Shuboladze, surely it can be divulged now that the Abashwili estates are at stake?

THE FIRST LAWYER: Please, Honored Sandro Oboladze! We agreed . . . (*To* AZDAK) Of course it is correct that the trial will also decide if our noble client can dispose of the Abashwili estates, which are rather extensive. I say "also" advisedly, for in the foreground stands the human tragedy of a mother, as Natella Abashwili very properly explained in the first words of her moving statement. Even if Michael Abashwili were not heir to the estates, he would still be the dearly beloved child of my client.

AZDAK: Stop! The Court is touched by the mention of estates. It's a proof of human feeling.

THE SECOND LAWYER: Thanks, Your Honor. Dear Illo Shuboladze, we can prove in any case that the woman who took the child is not the child's mother. Permit me to lay before the Court the bare facts. High Court of Justice, by an unfortunate chain of circumstances, Michael Abashwili was left behind on that Easter Sunday while his mother was making her escape. Grusha, a palace kitchen maid, was seen with the baby . . .

THE COOK: All her mistress was thinking of was what dresses she'd take along!

THE SECOND LAWYER: (*Unmoved*). Nearly a year later Grusha turned up in a mountain village with a baby and there entered into the state of matrimony with . . .

AZDAK: How did you get to that mountain village?

GRUSHA: On foot, Your Honor. And it was mine.

SIMON: I am the father, Your Honor.

THE COOK: I used to look after it for them, Your Honor. For five piasters.

THE SECOND LAWYER: This man is engaged to Grusha, High Court of Justice: his testimony is not trustworthy.

AZDAK: Are you the man she married in the mountain village?

SIMON: No, Your Honor, she married a peasant.

AZDAK: (*To* GRUSHA). Why? (*Pointing at* SIMON) Is he no good in bed? Tell the truth.

GRUSHA: We didn't get that far. I married because of the baby. So it'd have a roof over his head. (*Pointing at* SIMON) He was in the war, Your Honor.

AZDAK: And now he wants you back again, huh?

SIMON: I wish to state in evidence . . .

GRUSHA: (*Angrily*). I am no longer free, Your Honor.

AZDAK: And the child, you claim, comes from whoring? (GRUSHA *doesn't answer*) I'm going to ask you a question: What kind of child is it? Is it a ragged little bastard or from a well-to-do family?

GRUSHA: (*Angrily*). He's just an ordinary child.

AZDAK: I mean—did he have refined features from the beginning?

GRUSHA: He had a nose on his face.

AZDAK: A very significant comment! It has been said of me that I went out one time and sniffed at a rosebush before rendering a verdict—tricks like that are needed nowadays. Well, I'll make it short, and not listen to any more lies. (*To* GRUSHA) Especially not yours. (*To all the accused*) I can imagine what you've cooked up to cheat me! I know you people. You're swindlers.

GRUSHA: (*Suddenly*). I can understand your wanting to cut it short, now I've seen what you accepted!

AZDAK: Shut up! Did I accept anything from you?

GRUSHA: (*While the* COOK *tries to restrain her*). I haven't got anything.

AZDAK: True. Quite true. From starvelings I never get a thing. I might just as well starve, myself. You want justice, but do you want to pay for it, hm? When you go to a butcher you know you have to pay, but you people go to a judge as if you were going to a funeral supper.

SIMON: (*Loudly*). When the horse was shod, the horse-fly held out its leg, as the saying is.

AZDAK: (*Eagerly accepting the challenge*). Better a treasure in manure than a stone in a mountain stream.

SIMON: A fine day. Let's go fishing, said the angler to the worm.

AZDAK: I'm my own master, said the servant, and cut off his foot.

SIMON: I love you as a father, said the Czar to the peasants, and had the Czarevitch's head chopped off.

AZDAK: A fool's worst enemy is himself.

SIMON: However, a fart has no nose.

AZDAK: Fined ten piasters for indecent language in court! That'll teach you what justice is.

GRUSHA: (*Furiously*). A fine kind of justice! You play fast and loose with us because we don't talk as refined as that crowd with their lawyers!

AZDAK: That's true. You people are too dumb. It's only right you should get it in the neck.

GRUSHA: You want to hand the child over to her, and she wouldn't even know how to keep it dry, she's so "refined"! You know about as much about justice as I do!

AZDAK: There's something in that. I'm an ignorant man. Haven't even a decent pair of pants on under this gown. Look! With me, everything goes for food and drink—I was educated at a convent. Incidentally, I'll fine you ten piasters for contempt of court. And you're a very silly girl, to turn me against you, instead of making eyes at me and wiggling your backside a little to keep me in a good temper. Twenty piasters!

GRUSHA: Even if it was thirty, I'd tell you what I think of your justice, you drunken onion! (*Incoherently*) How dare you talk to me like the cracked Isaiah on the church window? As if you were somebody? For you weren't born to this. You weren't born to rap your own mother on the knuckles if she swipes a little bowl of salt someplace. Aren't you ashamed of yourself when you see how I tremble before you? You've made yourself their servant so no one will take their houses from them—houses they had stolen! Since when have houses belonged to the bed-bugs? But you're on the watch, or they couldn't drag our men into their wars! You bribe-taker! (AZDAK *half gets up, starts beaming. With his little hammer he half-heartedly knocks on the table as if to get silence. As* GRUSHA'S *scolding continues, he only beats time with his hammer*). I've no respect for you. No more than for a thief or a bandit with a knife! You can do what you want. You can take the child away from me, a hundred against one, but I tell you one thing: only extortioners should be chosen for a profession like yours, and men who rape children! As punishment! Yes, let *them* sit in judgment on their fellow creatures. It is worse than to hang from the gallows.

AZDAK: (*Sitting down*). Now it'll be thirty! And I won't go on squabbling with you—we're not in a tavern. What'd happen to my dignity as a judge? Anyway, I've lost interest in your case. Where's the couple who wanted a divorce? (*To* SHAUWA) bring 'em in. This case is adjourned for fifteen minutes.

THE FIRST LAWYER: (*To the* GOVERNOR'S WIFE). Even without using the rest of the evidence, Madam, we have the verdict in the bag.

THE COOK: (*To* GRUSHA). You've gone and spoiled your chances with him. You won't get the child now.

THE GOVERNOR'S WIFE: Shalva, my smelling salts!

Enter a VERY OLD COUPLE

AZDAK: I accept. (*The* OLD COUPLE *don't understand*) I hear you want to be divorced. How long have you been together?

410 THE OLD WOMAN: Forty years, Your Honor.

AZDAK: And why do you want a divorce?

THE OLD MAN: We don't like each other, Your Honor.

AZDAK: Since when?

THE OLD WOMAN: Oh, from the very beginning, Your Honor.

AZDAK: I'll think about your request and render my verdict when I'm through with the other case. (SHAUWA *leads them back*) I need the child.
420 (*He beckons* GRUSHA *to him and bends not unkindly toward her*) I've noticed you have a soft spot for justice. I don't believe he's your child, but if he *were* yours, woman, wouldn't you want him to be rich? You'd only have to say he wasn't yours, and he'd have a palace and many horses in his stable and many beggars on his doorstep and many soldiers in his service and many petitioners in his courtyard, wouldn't he? What do you say—don't you want him to be rich?

430   (GRUSHA *is silent*)

THE SINGER:

Hear now what the angry girl thought but did not say:

> Had he golden shoes to wear
> He'd be cruel as a bear.
> Evil would his life disgrace.
> He'd laugh in my face.
> Carrying a heart of flint
> Is too troublesome a stint.
440 Being powerful and bad
> Is hard on a lad.
> Then let hunger be his foe!
> Hungry men and women, no.
> Let him fear the darksome night
> But not daylight!

AZDAK: I think I understand you, woman.

GRUSHA: (*Suddenly and loudly*). I won't give him up. I've raised him, and he knows me.

Enter SHAUWA *with the* CHILD

450 THE GOVERNOR'S WIFE: It's in rags!

GRUSHA: That's not true. But I wasn't given time to put his good shirt on.

THE GOVERNOR'S WIFE: It must have been in a pigsty.

GRUSHA: (*Furiously*). I'm not a pig, but there are some who are! Where did you leave your baby?

THE GOVERNOR'S WIFE: I'll show you, you vulgar creature! (*She is about to throw herself on* GRUSHA, *but is restrained by her* LAWYERS) She's a criminal, she must be shipped. Immediately! 460

THE SECOND LAWYER: (*Holding his hand over her mouth*). Natella Abashwili, your promised ... Your Honor, the plaintiff's nerves ...

AZDAK: Plaintiff and defendant! The Court has listened to your case, and has come to no decision as to who the real mother is, therefore, I, the judge, am obliged to *choose* a mother for the child. I'll make a test. Shauwa, get a piece of chalk and draw a circle on the floor.

SHAUWA *does so*   470

AZDAK: Now place the child in the center. (SHAUWA *puts* MICHAEL, *who smiles at* GRUSHA, *in the center of the circle*) Stand near the circle, both of you. (THE GOVERNOR'S WIFE *and* GRUSHA *step up to the circle*) Now each of you take the child by one hand. (*They do so*) The true mother is she who can pull the child out of the circle.

THE SECOND LAWYER: (*Quickly*). High Court of Justice, I object! The fate of the great Abashwili estates, which are tied to the child, as the heir, 480 should not be made dependent on such a doubtful duel. In addition, my client does not command the strength of this person, who is accustomed to physical work.

AZDAK: She looks pretty well fed to me. Pull! (THE GOVERNOR'S WIFE *pulls the* CHILD *out of the circle on her side;* GRUSHA *has let go and stands aghast*) What's the matter with you? You didn't pull!

GRUSHA: I didn't hold on to him.

THE FIRST LAWYER: (*Congratulating* THE GOVERNOR'S 490 WIFE). What did I say! The ties of blood!

GRUSHA: (*Running to* AZDAK). Your Honor, I take back everything I said against you. I ask your forgiveness. But could I keep him till he can speak all the words? He knows a few.

AZDAK: Don't influence the Court. I bet you only know about twenty words yourself. All right, I'll make the test once more, just to be certain. (*The* TWO WOMEN *take up their positions again*) Pull! (*Again* GRUSHA *lets go of the* CHILD) 500

GRUSHA: (*In despair*). I brought him up! Shall I also tear him to pieces? I can't!

AZDAK: (*Rising*). And in this manner the Court has established the true mother. (*To* GRUSHA) Take

your child and be off. I advise you not to stay in the city with him. (*To* THE GOVERNOR'S WIFE) And you disappear before I fine you for fraud. Your estates fall to the city. They'll be converted into a playground for the children. They need one, and I've decided it shall be called after me:
510 Azdak's Garden. (THE GOVERNOR'S WIFE *has fainted and is carried out by the* LAWYERS *and the* ADJUTANT. GRUSHA *stands motionless.* SHAUWA *leads the* CHILD *toward her*) Now I'll take off this judge's gown—it's grown too hot for me. I'm not cut out for a hero. In token of farewell I invite you all to a little dance outside on the meadow. Oh, I'd almost forgotten something in my excitement . . . to sign the divorce decree.

520 *Using the judge's chair as a table, he writes something on a piece of paper, and prepares to leave. Dance music has started*

SHAUWA: (*Having read what is on the paper*). But that's not right. You've not divorced the old people. You've divorced Grusha!

AZDAK: Have I divorced the wrong couple? What a pity! And I never retract! If I did, how could we keep order in the land? (*To the* OLD COUPLE) I'll invite you to my party instead. You don't
530 mind dancing with each other, do you? (*To* GRUSHA *and* SIMON) I've got forty piasters coming from you.

SIMON: (*Pulling out his purse*). Cheap at the price, Your Honor. And many thanks.

AZDAK: (*Pocketing the cash*). I'll be needing this.

GRUSHA: (*To* MICHAEL). So we'd better leave the city tonight, Michael. (*To* SIMON) You like him?

SIMON: With my respects, I like him.

GRUSHA: Now I can tell you: I took him because on that Easter Sunday I got engaged to you. 540 So he's a child of love. Michael, let's dance.

She dances with MICHAEL, SIMON *dances with the* COOK, *the* OLD COUPLE *with each other.* AZDAK *stands lost in thought. The* DANCERS *soon hide him from view. Occasionally he is seen, but less and less as more couples join the dance*

THE SINGER:
> And after that evening Azdak vanished and
>   was never seen again.
> The people of Grusinia did not forget him 550
>   but long remembered
> The period of his judging as a brief golden
>   age,
> Almost an age of justice.

All the couples dance off. AZDAK *has disappeared*

THE SINGER:
> But you, you who have listened to the Story
>   of the Chalk Circle,
> Take note what men of old concluded:
> That what there is shall go to those who are 560
>   good for it,
> Children to the motherly, that they prosper,
> Carts to good drivers, that they be driven well,
> The valley to the waterers, that it yield fruit.

THEATRE FOR PLEASURE OR THEATRE FOR INSTRUCTION

by Bertolt Brecht

A few years back, anybody talking about the modern theatre meant the theatre in Moscow, New York and Berlin. He might have thrown in a mention of one of Jouvet's productions in Paris or Cochran's in London, or *The Dybbuk* as given by the Habima (which is to all intents and purposes part of the Russian theatre, since Vakhtangov was its director). But broadly speaking there were only three capitals so far as modern theatre was concerned.

Russian, American and German theatres differed widely from one another, but were alike in being modern, that is to say in introducing technical and artistic innovations. In a sense they even achieved a certain stylistic resemblance, probably because technology is international (not just that part which is directly applied to the stage but also that which influences it, the film for instance), and because large progressive cities in large industrial countries are involved. Among the older capitalist countries it is the Berlin theatre that seemed of late to be in the lead. For a period all that is common to the modern theatre received its strongest and (so far) maturest expression there.

The Berlin theatre's last phase was the so-called epic theatre, and it showed the modern theatre's trend of development in its purest form. Whatever was labelled 'Zeitstück' or 'Piscatorbühne' or 'Lehrstück' belongs to the epic theatre.

THE EPIC THEATRE

Many people imagine that the term 'epic theatre' is self-contradictory, as the epic and dramatic ways of narrating a story are held, following Aristotle, to be basically distinct. The difference between the two forms was never thought simply to lie in the fact that the one is performed by living beings while the other operates via the written word; epic works such as those of Homer and the medieval singers were at the same time theatrical performances, while dramas like Goethe's *Faust* and Byron's *Manfred* are agreed to have been more effective as books. Thus even by Aristotle's definition the difference between the dramatic and epic forms was attributed to their different methods of construction, whose laws were dealt with by two different branches of aesthetics. The method of construction depended on the different way of presenting the work to the public, sometimes via the stage, sometimes through a book; and independently of that there was the 'dramatic element' in epic works and the 'epic element' in dramatic. The bourgeois novel in the last century developed much that was 'dramatic', by which was meant the strong centralization of the story, a momentum that drew the separate parts into a common relationship. A particular passion of utterance, a certain emphasis on the clash of forces are hallmarks of the 'dramatic'. The epic writer Döblin provided an excellent criterion when he said that with an epic work, as opposed to a dramatic, one can as it were take a pair of scissors and cut it into individual pieces, which remain fully capable of life.

This is no place to explain how the opposition of epic and dramatic lost its rigidity after having long been held to be irreconcilable. Let us just point out that the technical advances alone were enough to permit the stage to incorporate an element of narrative in its dramatic productions. The possibility of projections, the greater adaptability of the stage due to mechanization, the film, all completed the theatre's equipment, and did so at a point where the most important transactions between people could no longer be shown simply by personifying the motive forces or subjecting the characters to invisible metaphysical powers.

To make these transactions intelligible the environment in which the people lived had to be brought to bear in a big and 'significant' way.

This environment had of course been shown in the exisitng drama, but only as seen from the central figure's point of view, and not as an independent element. It was defined by the hero's reactions to it. It was seen as a storm can be seen when one sees the ships on a sheet of water unfolding their sails, and the sails filling out. In the epic theatre it was to appear standing on its own.

The stage began to tell a story. The narrator was no longer missing, along with the fourth wall. Not only did the background adopt an attitude to the events on the stage—by big screens recalling other simultaneous events elsewhere, by projecting documents which confirmed or contradicted what the characters said, by concrete and intelligible figures to accompany abstract conversations, by figures and sentences to support mimed transactions whose sense was unclear—but the actors too refrained from going over wholly into their role, remaining detached from the character they were playing and clearly inviting criticism of him.

The spectator was no longer in any way allowed to submit to an experience uncritically (and without practical consequences) by means of simple empathy with the characters in a play. The production took the subject-matter and the incidents shown and put them through a process of alienation: the alienation that is necessary to all understanding. When something seems 'the most obvious thing in the world' it means that any attempt to understand the world has been given up.

What is 'natural' must have the force of what is startling. This is the only way to expose the laws of cause and effect. People's activity must simultaneously be so and be capable of being different.

It was all a great change.

The dramatic theatre's spectator says: Yes, I have felt like that too—Just like me—It's only natural—It'll never change—The sufferings of this man appal me, because they are inescapable—That's great art; it all seems the most obvious thing in the world—I weep when they weep, I laugh when they laugh.

The epic theatre's spectator says: I'd never have thought it—That's not the way—That's extraordinary, hardly believable—It's got to stop—The sufferings of this man appal me, because they are unnecessary—That's great art: nothing obvious in it—I laugh when they weep, I weep when they laugh.

THE INSTRUCTIVE THEATRE

The stage began to be instructive.

Oil, inflation, war, social struggles, the family, religion, wheat, the meat market, all became subjects for theatrical representation. Choruses enlightened the spectator about facts unknown to him. Films showed a montage of events from all over the world. Projections added statistical material. And as the 'background' came to the front of the stage so people's activity was subjected to criticism. Right and wrong courses of action were shown. People were shown who knew what they were doing, and others who did not. The theatre became an affair for philosophers, but only for such philosophers as wished not just to explain the world but also to change it. So we had philosophy, and we had instruction. And where was the amusement in all that? Were they sending us back to school, teaching us to read and write? Were we supposed to pass exams, work for diplomas?

Generally there is felt to be a very sharp distinction between learning and amusing oneself. The first may be useful, but only the second is pleasant. So we have to defend the epic theatre against the suspicion that it is a highly disagreeable, humourless, indeed strenuous affair.

Well: all that can be said is that the contrast between learning and amusing oneself is not laid down by divine rule; it is not one that has always been and must continue to be.

Undoubtedly there is much that is tedious about the kind of learning familiar to us from school, from our professional training, etc. But it must be remembered under what conditions and to what end that takes place.

It is really a commercial transaction. Knowledge is just a commodity. It is acquired in order to be resold. All those who have grown out of going to school have to do their learning virtually in secret, for anyone who admits that he still has something to learn devalues himself as a man whose knowledge is inadequate. Moreover the usefulness of learning is very much limited by factors outside the learner's control. There is unemployment, for instance, against which no knowledge can protect one. There is the division of labour, which makes generalized knowledge unnecessary and impossible. Learning is often among the concerns of those whom no amount of concern will get any forwarder. There is not much knowledge that leads to power, but plenty of knowledge to which only power can lead.

Learning has a very different function for different social strata. There are strata who cannot imagine any improvement in conditions: they find the conditions good enough for them. Whatever happens to oil they will benefit from it. And: they feel the years beginning to tell. There can't be all that many years more. What is the point of learning a lot now? They have said their final word: a grunt. But there are also strata 'waiting their turn' who are discontented with conditions, have a vast interest in the practical side of learning, want at all costs to find out where they stand, and know that they are lost without learning; these are the best and keenest learners. Similar differences apply to countries and peoples. Thus the pleasure of learning depends on all sorts of things; but none the less there is such a thing as pleasurable learning, cheerful and militant learning.

If there were not such amusement to be had from learning the theatre's whole structure would unfit it for teaching.

Theatre remains theatre even when it is instructive theatre, and in so far as it is good theatre it will amuse.

THEATRE AND KNOWLEDGE

But what has knowledge got to do with art? We know that knowledge can be amusing, but not everything that is amusing belongs in the theatre.

I have often been told, when pointing out the invaluable services that modern knowledge and science, if properly applied, can perform for art and specially for the theatre, that art and knowledge are two estimable but wholly distinct fields of human activity. This is a fearful truism, of course, and it is as well to agree quickly that, like most truisms, it is perfectly true. Art and science work in quite different ways: agreed. But, bad as it may sound, I have to admit that I cannot get along as an artist without the use of one or two sciences. This may well arouse serious doubts as to my artistic capacities. People are used to seeing poets as unique and slightly unnatural beings who reveal with a truly godlike assurance things that other people can only recognize after much sweat and toil. It is naturally distasteful to have to admit that one does not belong to this select band. All the same, it must be admitted. It must at the same time be made clear that the scientific occupations just confessed to are not pardonable side interests, pursued on days off after a good week's work. We all know how Goethe was interested in natural history, Schiller in history: as a kind of hobby, it is charitable to assume. I have no wish promptly to accuse these two of having needed these sciences for their poetic activity; I am not trying to shelter behind them; but I must say that I do need the sciences. I have to admit, however, that I look askance at all sorts of people who I know do not operate on the level of scientific understanding: that is to say, who sing as the birds sing, or as people imagine the birds to sing. I don't mean by that that I would reject a charming poem about the taste of fried fish or the delights of a boating party just because the writer had not studied gastronomy or navigation. But in my view the great and complicated things that go on in the world cannot be adequately recognized by people who do not use every possible aid to understanding.

Let us suppose that great passions or great events have to be shown which influence the fate of nations. The lust for power is nowadays held to be such a passion. Given that a poet 'feels' this lust and wants to have someone strive for power, how is he to show the exceedingly complicated machinery within which the struggle for power nowadays takes place? If his hero is a politician, how do politics work? If he is a business man, how does business work? And yet there are writers who find business and politics nothing like so passionately interesting as the individual's lust for power. How are they to acquire the necessary knowledge? They are scarcely likely to learn enough by going round and keeping their eyes open, though even then it is more than they would get by just rolling their eyes in an exalted frenzy. The foundation of a paper like the *Völkischer Beobachter* or a business like Standard Oil is a pretty complicated affair, and such things cannot be conveyed just like that. One important field for the playwright is psychology. It is taken for granted that a poet, if not an ordinary man, must be able without further instruction to discover the motives that lead a man to commit murder; he must be able to give a picture of a murderer's mental state 'from within himself'. It is taken for granted that one only has to look inside oneself in such a case; and then there's always one's imagination. . . . There are various reasons why I can no longer surrender to this agreeable hope of getting a result quite so simply. I can no longer find in myself all those motives which the press or scientific reports show to have been observed in people. Like the average judge when pronouncing sentence, I cannot without further ado conjure up an adequate picture of a murderer's mental state. Modern psychology, from psychoanalysis to behaviourism, acquaints me with facts that lead me to judge the case quite differently, especially if I bear in mind the findings of sociology and do not overlook economics and history. You will say: but that's getting complicated. I have to answer that it *is* complicated. Even if you let yourself be convinced, and agree with me that a large slice of literature is exceedingly primitive, you may still ask with profound concern: won't an evening in such a theatre be a most alarming affair? The answer to that is: no.

Whatever knowledge is embodied in a piece of poetic writing has to be wholly transmuted into poetry. Its utilization fulfils the very pleasure that the poetic element provokes. If it does not at the same time fulfil that which is fulfilled by the scientific element, none the less in an age of great discoveries and inventions one must have a certain inclination to penetrate deeper into things—a desire to make the world controllable—if one is to be sure of enjoying its poetry.

IS THE EPIC THEATRE SOME KIND OF 'MORAL INSTITUTION'?

According to Friedrich Schiller the theatre is supposed to be a moral institution. In making this demand it hardly occurred to Schiller that by moralizing from the stage he might drive the audience out of the theatre. Audiences had no objection to moralizing in his day. It was only later that Friedrich Nietzsche attacked him for blowing a moral trumpet. To Nietzsche any concern with morality was a depressing affair; to Schiller it seemed thoroughly enjoyable. He knew of nothing that could give greater amusement and satisfaction than the propagation of ideas. The bourgeoisie was setting about forming the ideas of the nation.

Putting one's house in order, patting oneself on the back, submitting one's account, is something highly agreeable. But describing the collapse of one's house, having pains in the back, paying one's account, is indeed a depressing affair, and that was how Friedrich Nietzsche saw things a century later. He was poorly disposed towards morality, and thus towards the previous Friedrich too.

The epic theatre was likewise often objected to as moralizing too much. Yet in the epic theatre moral arguments only took second place. Its aim was less to moralize than to observe. That is to say it observed, and then the thick end of the wedge followed: the story's moral. Of course we cannot pretend that we started our observations out of a pure passion for observing and without any more practical motive, only to be completely staggered by their results. Undoubtedly there were some painful discrepancies in our environment, circumstances that were barely tolerable, and this not merely on account of moral considerations. It is not only moral considerations that make hunger, cold and oppression hard to bear. Similarly the object of our inquiries was not just to arouse moral objections to such circumstances (even though they could easily be felt—though not by all the audience alike; such objections were seldom for instance felt by those who profited by the circumstances in question) but to discover means for their elimination. We were not in fact speaking in the name of morality but in that of the victims. These truly are two distinct matters, for the victims are often told that they ought to be contented with their lot, for moral reasons. Moralists of this sort see man as existing for morality, not morality for man. At least it should be possible to gather from the above to what degree and in what sense the epic theatre is a moral institution.

CAN EPIC THEATRE BE PLAYED ANYWHERE?

Stylistically speaking, there is nothing all that new about the epic theatre. Its expository character and its emphasis on virtuosity bring it close to the old Asiatic theatre. Didactic tendencies are to be found in the medieval mystery plays and the classical Spanish theatre, and also in the theatre of the Jesuits.

These theatrical forms corresponded to particular trends of their time, and vanished with them. Similarly the modern epic theatre is linked with certain trends. It cannot by any means be practised universally. Most of the great nations today are not disposed to use the theatre for ventilating their problems. London, Paris, Tokyo and Rome maintain their theatres for quite different purposes. Up to now favourable circumstances for an epic and didactic theatre have only been found in a few places and for a short period of time. In Berlin Fascism put a very definite stop to the development of such a theatre.

It demands not only a certain technological level but a powerful movement in society which is interested to see vital questions freely aired with a view to their solution, and can defend this interest against every contrary trend.

The epic theatre is the broadest and most far-reaching attempt at large-scale modern theatre, and it has all those immense difficulties to overcome that always confront the vital forces in the sphere of politics, philosophy, science and art.

['Vergnügungstheater oder Lehrtheater?',
from *Schriften zum Theater*, 1957]

NOTE: This essay was unpublished in Brecht's lifetime, and its exact date and purpose are unknown. Dr. Unseld, editing it for *Schriften zum Theater*, suggested that it was written 'about 1936'. Brecht's bibliographer Mr. Walter Nubel thinks that notes or drafts may have existed earlier. Unlike the items that follow, it bears no evidence of Brecht's visits to Moscow and New York during 1935, and it is tempting to think of it as having been prepared for one of these, for instance as a possible contribution to that conference of producers to which Piscator invited Brecht in Moscow: what he called (in a letter of 27 January 1935, in the Brecht-Archiv) 'collecting a few good people for a constructive discussion'.

This was to take place in April, and there are fragments of a 'Brecht-Piscator conversation' in the Brecht-Archiv (334/04-05) which evidently date from then. In these Piscator is seen referring to productions by Okhlopkhov (*Aristocrats* and Serafimovitch's *Iron Stream*) and Meyerhold (*La Dame aux Camélias* and a programme of one-act plays by Tchekov), while Brecht mentions the plans for a *'Total-Theater'* which Piscator had had drawn up by Walter Gropius before 1933. So far as the present essay goes, however, all that can really be said is that some of its arguments and actual words are also to be found in the next piece.

The term here translated as 'alienation' is *Entfremdung* as used by Hegel and Marx, and not the *Verfremdung* which Brecht himself was soon to coin and make famous. The former also occurs in a short note (*Schriften zum Theater 3*, pp. 196-7) called 'Episches Theater, Entfremdung', which refers to the need for any situation to be 'alienated' if it is to be seen socially. Alfred Döblin, the friend of Brecht's referred to early in the essay, wrote *Die drei Sprünge des Wang-lun*, *Berlin Alexanderplatz* and other novels which critics of the time likened to Joyce and Dos Passos. He too was interested in the theory of epic form. The *Völkischer Beobachter* was the chief Nazi daily paper.

BRECHT'S COMPARISON OF THE DRAMATIC & EPIC THEATERS

The modern theatre is the epic theatre. The following table shows certain changes of emphasis as between the dramatic and the epic theatre.[1]

DRAMATIC THEATRE	EPIC THEATRE
plot	narrative
implicates the spectator in a stage situation	turns the spectator into an observer, but
wears down his capacity for action	arouses his capacity for action
provides him with sensations	forces him to take decisions
experience	picture of the world
the spectator is involved in something	he is made to face something
suggestion	argument
instinctive feelings are preserved	brought to the point of recognition
the spectator is in the thick of it, shares the experience	the spectator stands outside, studies
the human being is taken for granted	the human being is the object of the inquiry
he is unalterable	he is alterable and able to alter
eyes on the finish	eyes on the course
one scene makes another	each scene for itself
growth	montage
linear development	in curves
evolutionary determinism	jumps
man as a fixed point	man as a process
thought determines being	social being determines thought
feeling	reason

---

[1]This table does not show absolute antitheses but mere shifts of accent. In a communication of fact, for instance, we may choose whether to stress the element of emotional suggestion or that of plain rational argument.

LOOK BACK IN ANGER

John Osborne (b. 1929)

"I want to make people feel . . . to give them lessons in feeling. They can think afterwards." In these words, John Osborne describes his intentions as a playwright. That his intentions were fully realized was evidenced by the reception accorded his first play produced in London in May, 1956. *Look Back in Anger* exploded like a bomb in the midst of the unsuspecting London public. Theatergoers were shell-shocked by the fury of Osborne's scathing attack on nearly all aspects of contemporary British life. This play is seen now as the opening salvo of a revolution that brought to the English stage a neo-naturalism reminiscent of those heady days when George Bernard Shaw was championing Ibsenism and delightedly scandalizing Victorian propriety by his plays, *Mrs. Warren's Profession* and *Widowers' Houses*.

Although *Look Back in Anger* was given mixed reviews, it made an enormous impact on the British theater, opening the way for other strident voices clamoring to be heard. Osborne was recognized as the spokesman for a generation who were frustrated and discontented by the shape of their world.

Osborne came from a lower-class London environment and was painfully familiar with the problems that set Jimmy Porter's teeth on edge. He gained valuable first-hand knowledge of the theater by working as an actor in the provinces, where he also turned his hand to playwriting. *Look Back in Anger* was followed by a series of other plays, most notably *The Entertainer*, *Luther*, and *Inadmissable Evidence*.

The importance of Osborne's *Look Back in Anger* is that he revived the theater as a place for discussion of serious questions—a public forum for vigorous dispute and experiment. He opened the British theater to controversy. He also introduced a new kind of stage hero—a discontented, abrasive, irreverent young man who spoke out with a sincere and vivid eloquence against the forces that held him in check. Osborne's most significant achievement was, to use Adlai Stevenson's phrase, that he brought the British theater "kicking and screaming into the twentieth century."

Below. Jimmy (left) and Cliff engage in their dance routine while Alison does the weekly ironing.
Photographs in this sequence are of the original 1956 production at the Royal Court Theatre in London,
with Kenneth Haigh as Jimmy Porter, Mary Ure as Alison Porter,
Alan Bates as Cliff Lewis, and Helena Hughes as Helena Charles.

Above. Jimmy finds an outlet for his anger in his trumpet.

Below. Alison is a victim of Jimmy's anger.

Cliff and Jimmy clown through a song-and-dance routine
for Helena, now Jimmy's mistress.

Cliff and Jimmy return to their newspapers,
this time with Helena at the ironing board.

CHARACTERS

IN ORDER OF APPEARANCE

JIMMY PORTER
CLIFF LEWIS
ALISON PORTER
HELENA CHARLES
COLONEL REDFERN

LOOK BACK IN ANGER

ACT I

The Porters' one-room flat in a large Midland town. Early evening. April. The scene is a fairly large attic room, at the top of a large Victorian house. The ceiling slopes down quite sharply from L. to R. Down R. are two small low windows. In front of these is a dark oak dressing table. Most of the furniture is simple, and rather old. Up R. is a double bed, running the length of most of the back wall, the rest of which is taken up with a shelf of books. Down R. below the bed is a heavy chest of drawers, covered with books, neckties and odds and ends, including a large, tattered toy teddy bear and soft, woolly squirrel. Up L. is a door. Below this a small wardrobe. Most of the wall L. is taken up with a high, oblong window. This looks out on to the landing, but light comes through it from a skylight beyond. Below the wardrobe is a gas stove, and, beside this, a wooden food cupboard, on which is a small, portable radio. Down C. is a sturdy dining table and three chairs, and, below this, L. and R., two deep, shabby leather armchairs.

At rise of curtain, JIMMY and CLIFF are seated in the two armchairs R. and L., respectively. All that we can see of either of them is two pairs of legs, sprawled way out beyond the newspapers which hide the rest of them from sight. They are both reading. Beside them, and between them, is a jungle of newspapers and weeklies. When we do eventually see them, we find that JIMMY is a tall, thin young man about twenty-five, wearing a very worn tweed jacket and flannels. Clouds of smoke fill the room from the pipe he is smoking. He is a disconcerting mixture of sincerity and cheerful malice, of tenderness

and freebooting cruelty; restless, importunate, full of pride, a combination which alienates the sensitive and insensitive alike. Blistering honesty, or apparent honesty, like his, makes few friends. To many he may seem sensitive to the point of vulgarity. To others, he is simply a loudmouth. To be as vehement as he is is to be almost noncommittal. CLIFF is the same age, short, dark, big boned, wearing a pullover and grey, new, but very creased trousers. He is easy and relaxed, almost to lethargy, with the rather sad, natural intelligence of the self-taught. If JIMMY alienates love, CLIFF seems to exact it–demonstrations of it, at least, even from the cautious. He is a soothing, natural counterpoint to JIMMY. Standing L., below the food cupboard, is ALISON. She is leaning over an ironing board. Beside her is a pile of clothes. Hers is the most elusive personality to catch in the uneasy polyphony of these three people. She is turned in a different key, a key of well-bred malaise that is often drowned in the robust orchestration of the other two. Hanging over the grubby, but expensive, skirt she is wearing is a cherry red shirt of JIMMY'S, but she manages somehow to look quite elegant in it. She is roughly the same age as the men. Somehow, their combined physical oddity makes her beauty more striking than it really is. She is tall, slim, dark. The bones of her face are long and delicate. There is a surprising reservation about her eyes, which are so large and deep they should make equivocation impossible. The room is still, smoke filled. The only sound is the occasional thud of ALISON'S iron on the board. It is one of those chilly Spring evenings, all cloud and shadows.

Presently, JIMMY throws his paper down.

JIMMY: Why do I do this every Sunday? Even the book reviews seem to be the same as last week's. Different books—same reviews. Have you finished that one yet?

CLIFF: Not yet.

JIMMY: I've just read three whole columns on the English Novel. Half of it's in French. Do the Sunday papers make *you* feel ignorant?

CLIFF: Not 'arf.

10 JIMMY: Well, you *are* ignorant. You're just a peasant. *(To* ALISON.*)* What about you? You're not a peasant are you?

ALISON: *(absently).* What's that?

JIMMY: I said do the papers make you feel you're not so brilliant after all?

ALISON: Oh—I haven't read them yet.

JIMMY: I didn't ask you that. I said—

CLIFF: Leave the poor girlie alone. She's busy.

JIMMY: Well, she can talk, can't she? You can talk,

20 can't you? You can express an opinion. Or does the White Woman's Burden make it impossible to think?

ALISON: I'm sorry. I wasn't listening properly.

JIMMY: You bet you weren't listening. Old Porter talks, and everyone turns over and goes to sleep. And Mrs. Porter gets 'em all going with the first yawn.

CLIFF: Leave her alone, I said.

JIMMY: *(shouting).* All right, dear. Go back to sleep.

30 It was only me talking. You know? Talking? Remember? I'm sorry.

CLIFF: Stop yelling. I'm trying to read.

JIMMY: Why do you bother? You can't understand a word of it.

CLIFF: Uh huh.

JIMMY: You're too ignorant.

CLIFF: Yes, and uneducated. Now shut up, will you?

JIMMY: Why don't you get my wife to explain it

40 to you? She's educated. *(To her.)* That's right isn't it?

CLIFF: *(kicking out at him from behind his paper).* Leave her alone, I said.

JIMMY: Do that again, you Welsh ruffian, and I'll pull your ears off.

(He bangs CLIFF's *paper out of his hands.)*

CLIFF: *(leaning forward).* Listen—I'm trying to bet-

ter myself. Let me get on with it, you big, horrible man. Give it me. *(Puts his hand out for paper.)*

ALISON: Oh, give it to him, Jimmy, for heaven's   50
sake! I can't think!

CLIFF: Yes, come on, give me the paper. She can't think.

JIMMY: Can't think! *(Throws the paper back at him.)*
She hasn't had a thought for years! Have you?

ALISON: No.

JIMMY: *(Picks up a weekly.)* I'm getting hungry.

ALISON: Oh no, not already!

CLIFF: He's a bloody pig.

JIMMY: I'm not a pig. I just like food—that's all.   60

CLIFF: Like it! You're like a sexual maniac—only with you it's food. You'll end up in the *News of the World,* boyo, you wait. James Porter, aged twenty-five, was bound over last week after pleading guilty to interfering with a small cabbage and two tins of beans on his way home from the Builder's Arms. The accused said he hadn't been feeling well for some time, and had been having black-outs. He asked for his good record as an air-raid warden, second class, to   70
be taken into account.

JIMMY: *(Grins.)* Oh, yes, yes, yes. I like to eat. I'd like to live too. Do you mind?

CLIFF: Don't see any use in your eating at all. You never get any fatter.

JIMMY: People like me don't get fat. I've tried to tell you before. We just burn everything up. Now shut up while I read. You can make me some more tea.

CLIFF: Good God, you've just had a great potful!   80
I only had one cup.

JIMMY: Like hell! Make some more.

CLIFF: *(to* ALISON*).* Isn't that right? Didn't I only have one cup?

ALISON: *(without looking up).* That's right.

CLIFF: There you are. And she only had one cup too. I saw her. You guzzled the lot.

JIMMY: *(reading his weekly).* Put the kettle on.

CLIFF: Put it on yourself. You've creased up my paper.   90

JIMMY: I'm the only one who knows how to treat a paper, or anything else, in this house. *(Picks up another paper.)* Girl here wants to know whether her boy friend will lose all respect for her if she gives him what he asks for. Stupid bitch.

CLIFF: Just let me get at her, that's all.

JIMMY: Who buys this damned thing? *(Throws it down.)* Haven't you read the other posh paper yet?

CLIFF: Which?

JIMMY: Well, there are only two posh papers on a Sunday—the one you're reading, and this one. Come on, let me have that one, and you take this.

CLIFF: Oh, all right.

(They exchange.)

I was only reading the Bishop of Bromley. *(Puts out his hand to* ALISON.) How are you, dullin'?

ALISON: All right thank you, dear.

CLIFF: *(Grasping her hand).* Why don't you leave all that, and sit down for a bit? You look tired.

ALISON: *(smiling).* I haven't much more to do.

CLIFF: *(kisses her hand, and puts her fingers in his mouth).* She's a beautiful girl, isn't she?

JIMMY: That's what they all tell me.

(His eyes met hers.)

CLIFF: It's a lovely, delicious paw you've got. Ummmmm. I'm going to bite it off.

ALISON: Don't! I'll burn his shirt.

JIMMY: Give her her finger back, and don't be so sickening. What's the Bishop of Bromley say?

CLIFF: *(letting go of* ALISON). Oh, it says here that he makes a very moving appeal to all Christians to do all they can to assist in the manufacture of the H-Bomb.

JIMMY: Yes, well, that's quite moving, I suppose. *(To* ALISON.) Are you moved, my darling?

ALISON: Well, naturally.

JIMMY: There you are: even my wife is moved. I ought to send the Bishop a subscription. Let's see. What else does he say. Dumdidumdidum-didum. Ah yes. He's upset because someone has suggested that he supports the rich against the poor. He says he denies the difference of class distinctions. "This idea has been persistently and wickedly fostered by—the working classes!" Well!

(He looks up at both of them for reaction, but CLIFF *is reading, and* ALISON *is intent on her ironing.)*

JIMMY: *(to* CLIFF). Did you read that bit?

CLIFF: Um?

(He has lost them, and he knows it, but he won't leave it.)

JIMMY: *(to* ALISON). You don't suppose your father could have written it, do you?

ALISON: Written what?

JIMMY: What I just read out, of course.

ALISON: Why should my father have written it?

JIMMY: Sounds rather like Daddy, don't you think?

ALISON: Does it?

JIMMY: Is the Bishop of Bromley his nom de plume, do you think?

CLIFF: Don't take any notice of him. He's being offensive. And it's so easy for him.

JIMMY: *(quickly).* Did you read about the woman who went to the mass meeting of a certain American evangelist at Earls Court? She went forward, to declare herself for love or whatever it is, and, in the rush of converts to get to the front, she broke four ribs and got kicked in the head. She was yelling her head off in agony, but with 50,000 people putting all they'd got into "Onward Christian Soldiers", nobody even knew she was there.

(He looks up sharply for a response, but there isn't any.)

Sometimes, I wonder if there isn't something wrong with me. What about that tea?

CLIFF: *(still behind paper).* What tea?

JIMMY: Put the kettle on.

(ALISON *looks up at him.)*

ALISON: Do you want some more tea?

JIMMY: I don't know. No, I don't think so.

ALISON: Do you want some, Cliff?

JIMMY: No, he doesn't. How much longer will you be doing that?

ALISON: Won't be long.

JIMMY: God, how I hate Sundays! It's always so depressing, always the same. We never seem to get any further, do we? Always the same ritual. Reading the papers, drinking tea, ironing. A few more hours, and another week gone. Our youth is slipping away. Do you know that?

CLIFF: *(throws down the paper).* What's that?

JIMMY: *(casually).* Oh, nothing, nothing. Damn you, damn both of you, damn them all.

CLIFF: Let's go to the pictures. *(To* ALISON.) What do you say, lovely?

190   ALISON: I don't think I'll be able to. Perhaps Jimmy would like to go.*(To* JIMMY.*)* Would you like to?

JIMMY: And have my enjoyment ruined by the Sunday night yobs in the front row? No, thank you. *(Pause.)* Did you read Priestley's piece this week? Why on earth I ask, I don't know. I know damned well you haven't. Why do I spend nine-pence on that damned paper every week? Nobody reads it except me. Nobody can be bothered. No one can raise themselves out of their delicious
200   sloth. You two will drive me round the bend soon—I know it, as sure as I'm sitting here. I know you're going to drive me mad. Oh heavens, how I long for a little ordinary human enthusiasm. Just enthusiasm—that's all. I want to hear a warm, thrilling voice cry out Hallelujah! *(He bangs his breast theatrically.)* Hallelujah! I'm alive! I've an idea. Why don't we have a little game? Let's pretend that we're human beings, and that we're actually alive. Just
210   for a while. What do you say? Let's pretend we're human. *(He looks from one to the other.)* Oh, brother, it's such a long time since I was with anyone who got enthusiastic about anything.

CLIFF: What did he say?

JIMMY: *(resentful of being dragged away from his pursuit of* ALISON*)*. What did who say?

CLIFF: Mr. Priestley.

JIMMY: What he always says, I suppose. He's like Daddy—still casting well-fed glances back to the
220   Edwardian twilight from his comfortable, disenfranchised wilderness. What the devil have you done to those trousers?

CLIFF: Done?

JIMMY: Are they the ones you bought last weekend? Look at them. Do you see what he's done to those new trousers?

ALISON: You are naughty, Cliff. They look dreadful.

JIMMY: You spend good money on a new pair of
230   trousers, and then sprawl about in them like a savage. What do you think you're going to do when I'm not around to look after you? Well, what are you going to do? Tell me?

CLIFF: *(grinning)*. I don't know. *(To* ALISON.*)* What am I going to do, lovely?

ALISON: You'd better take them off.

JIMMY: Yes, go on. Take 'em off. And I'll kick your behind for you.

ALISON: I'll give them a press while I've got the iron on.
240

CLIFF: O.K. *(Starts taking them off.)* I'll just empty the pockets. *(Takes out keys, matches, handkerchief.)*

JIMMY: Give me those matches, will you?

CLIFF: Oh, you're not going to start up that old pipe again, are you? It stinks the place out. *(To* ALISON.*)* Doesn't it smell awful?

*(*JIMMY *grabs the matches, and lights up.)*

ALISON: I don't mind it. I've got used to it.

JIMMY: She's a great one for getting used to things. If she were to die, and wake up in paradise—after
250   the first five minutes, she'd have got used to it.

CLIFF: *(hands her the trousers)*. Thank you, lovely. Give me a cigarette, will you?

JIMMY: Don't give him one.

CLIFF: I can't stand the stink of that old pipe any longer. I must have a cigarette.

JIMMY: I thought the doctor said no cigarettes?

CLIFF: Oh, why doesn't he shut up?

JIMMY: All right. They're your ulcers. Go ahead,
260   and have a bellyache, if that's what you want. I give up. I give up. I'm sick of doing things for people. And all for what?

*(*ALISON *gives* CLIFF *a cigarette. They both light up, and she goes on with her ironing.)*

Nobody thinks, nobody cares. No beliefs, no convictions and no enthusiasm. Just another Sunday evening.

*(*CLIFF *sits down again, in his pullover and shorts.)*

Perhaps there's a concert on. *(Picks up* Radio
270   Times*)* Ah. *(Nudges* CLIFF *with his foot.)* Make some more tea.

*(*CLIFF *grunts. He is reading again.)*

Oh, yes. There's a Vaughan Williams. Well, that's something, anyway. Something strong, something simple, something English. I suppose people like me aren't supposed to be very patriotic. Somebody said—what was it—we get our cooking from Paris (that's a laugh), our politics from Moscow, and our morals from Port Said.
280   Something like that, anyway. Who was it? *(Pause.)* Well, you wouldn't know anyway. I hate to admit it, but I think I can understand how

her Daddy must have felt when he came back from India, after all those years away. The old Edwardian brigade do make their brief little world look pretty tempting. All homemade cakes and croquet, bright ideas, bright uniforms. Always the same picture: high summer, the long days in the sun, slim volumes of verse, crisp linen, the smell of starch. What a romantic picture. Phoney too, of course. It must have rained sometimes. Still, even I regret it somehow, phoney or not. If you've no world of your own, it's rather pleasant to regret the passing of someone else's. I must be getting sentimental. But I must say it's pretty dreary living in the American Age—unless you're an American of course. Perhaps all our children will be Americans. That's a thought isn't it?

(He gives CLIFF *a kick, and shouts at him.)*

I said that's a thought!

CLIFF: You did?

JIMMY: You sit there like a lump of dough. I thought you were going to make me some tea.

*(*CLIFF *groans.* JIMMY *turns to* ALISON.*)*

Is your friend Webster coming tonight?

ALISON: He might drop in. You know what he is.

JIMMY: Well, I hope he doesn't. I don't think I could take Webster tonight.

ALISON: I thought you said he was the only person who spoke your language.

JIMMY: So he is. Different dialect but same language. I like him. He's got bite, edge, drive—

ALISON: Enthusiasm.

JIMMY: You've got it. When he comes here, I begin to feel exhilarated. He doesn't like me, but he gives me something, which is more than I get from most people. Not since—

ALISON: Yes, we know. Not since you were living with Madeline.

(She folds some of the clothes she has already ironed, crosses to the bed with them.)

CLIFF: *(behind paper again).* Who's Madeline?

ALISON: Oh, wake up, dear. You've heard about Madeline enough times. She was his mistress. Remember? When he was fourteen. Or was it thirteen?

JIMMY: Eighteen.

ALISON: He owes just about everything to Madeline.

CLIFF: I get mixed up with all your women. Was she the one all those years older than you?

JIMMY: Ten years.

CLIFF: Proper little Marchbanks, you are!

JIMMY: What time's that concert on? *(Checks paper.)*

CLIFF: *(yawns).* Oh, I feel so sleepy. Don't feel like standing behind that blinking sweet-stall again tomorrow. Why don't you do it on your own, and let me sleep in?

JIMMY: I've got to be at the factory first thing, to get some more stock, so you'll have to put it up on your own. Another five minutes.

*(*ALISON *has returned to her ironing board. She stands with her arms folded, smoking, staring thoughtfully.)*

She had more animation in her little finger than you two put together.

CLIFF: Who did?

ALISON: Madeline.

JIMMY: Her curiosity about things, and about people was staggering. It wasn't just a naïve nosiness. With her, it was simply the delight of being awake, and watching.

*(*ALISON *starts to press* CLIFF'S *trousers.)*

CLIFF: *(behind paper).* Perhaps I will make some tea, after all.

JIMMY: *(quietly).* Just to be with her was an adventure. Even to sit on the top of a bus with her was like setting out with Ulysses.

CLIFF: Wouldn't have said Webster was much like Ulysses. He's an ugly little devil.

JIMMY: I'm not talking about Webster, stupid. He's all right though, in his way. A sort of female Emily Brontë. He's the only one of your friends *(to* ALISON) who's worth tuppence, anyway. I'm surprised you get on with him.

ALISON: So is he, I think.

JIMMY: *(rising to window R., and looking out).* He's not only got guts, but sensitivity as well. That's about the rarest combination I can think of. None of your other friends have got either.

ALISON: *(very quietly and earnestly).* Jimmy, please—don't go on.

(He turns and looks at her. The tired appeal in her

voice has pulled him up suddenly. But he soon gathers himself for a new assult. He walks C., behind CLIFF, *and stands, looking down at his head.)*

JIMMY: Your friends—there's a shower for you.

380 CLIFF: *(mumbling).* Dry up. Let her get on with my trousers.

JIMMY: *(musingly).* Don't think I could provoke her. Nothing I could do would provoke her. Not even if I were to drop dead.

CLIFF: Then drop dead.

JIMMY: They're either militant like her Mummy and Daddy. Militant, arrogant and full of malice. Or vague. She's somewhere between the two.

CLIFF: Why don't you listen to that concert of
390 yours? And don't stand behind me. That blooming droning on behind me gives me a funny feeling down the spine.

*(*JIMMY *gives his ears a twist and* CLIFF *roars with pain.* JIMMY *grins back at him.)*

That hurt, you rotten sadist! *(To* ALISON.*)* I wish you'd kick his head in for him.

JIMMY: *(moving in between them).* Have you ever seen her brother? Brother Nigel? The straight-backed, chinless wonder from Sandhurst? I only
400 met him once myself. He asked me to step outside when I told his mother she was evil minded.

CLIFF: And did you?

JIMMY: Certainly not. He's a big chap. Well, you've never heard so many well-bred commonplaces come from beneath the same bowler hat. The Platitude from Outer Space—that's brother Nigel. He'll end up in the Cabinet one day, make no mistake. But somewhere at the back of that mind is the vague knowledge that he
410 and his pals have been plundering and fooling everybody for generations. *(Going upstage, and turning.)* Now Nigel is just about as vague as you can get without being actually invisible. And invisible politicians aren't much use to any-one—not even to *his* supporters! And nothing is more vague about Nigel than his knowledge. His knowledge of life and ordinary human beings is so hazy, he really deserves some sort of decoration for it—a medal inscribed "For Vaguery in
420 the Field". But it wouldn't do for him to be troubled by any stabs of conscience, however vague. *(Moving down again.)* Besides, he's a pat-

riot and an Englishman, and he doesn't like the idea that he may have been selling out his countryman all these years, so what does he do? The only thing he *can* do—seek sanctuary in his own stupidity. The only way to keep things as much like they always have been as possible, is to make any alternative too much for your poor, tiny brain to grasp. It takes some doing nowadays.   430
It really does. But they knew all about character building at Nigel's school, and he'll make it all right. Don't you worry, he'll make it. And, what's more, he'll do it better than anybody else!

(There is no sound, only the plod of ALISON's *iron. Her eyes are fixed on what she is doing.* CLIFF *stares at the floor. His cheerfulness has deserted him for the moment.* JIMMY *is rather shakily triumphant. He cannot allow himself to look at either of them to catch their response to his rhetoric, so he moves across to the window, to*   440
recover himself, and look out.)

It's started to rain. That's all it needs. This room and the rain.

(He's been cheated out of his response, but he's got to draw blood somehow.)

(Conversationally). Yes, that's the little woman's family. You know Mummy and Daddy, of course. And don't let the Marquess of Queens-berry manner fool you. They'll kick you in the groin while you're handing your hat to the maid.   450
As for Nigel and Alison—*(In a reverent, Stuart Hibberd voice.)* Nigel and Alison. They're what they sound like: sycophantic, phlegmatic and pusillanimous.

CLIFF: I'll bet that concert's started by now. Shall I put it on?

JIMMY: I looked up that word the other day. It's one of those words I've never been quite sure of, but always thought I knew.

CLIFF: What was that?   460

JIMMY: I told you—pusillanimous. Do you know what it means?

*(*CLIFF *shakes his head.)*

Neither did I really. All this time, I have been married to this woman, this monument to non-attachment, and suddenly I discover that there is actually a word that sums her up. Not just an adjective in the English language to describe her with—it's her name! Pusillanimous! It sounds like some fleshy Roman matron, doesn't it? The Lady Pusillanimous seen here with her husband Sextus, on their way to the Games.

(CLIFF *looks troubled, and glances uneasily at* ALISON.)

Poor old Sextus! If he were put into a Hollywood film, he's so unimpressive, they'd make some poor British actor play the part. He doesn't know it, but those beefcake Christians will make off with his wife in the wonder of stereophonic sound before the picture's over.

(ALISON *leans against the board, and closes her eyes.*)

The Lady Pusillanimous has been promised a brighter easier world than old Sextus can ever offer her. Hi, Pusey! What say we get the hell down to the Arena, and maybe feed ourselves to a couple of lions, huh?

ALISON: God help me, if he doesn't stop, I'll go out of my mind in a minute.

JIMMY: Why don't you? That would be something, anyway. (*Crosses to chest of drawers R.*) But I haven't told you what it means yet, have I? (*Picks up the dictionary.*) I don't have to tell her—she knows. In fact, if my pronunciation is at fault, she'll probably wait for a suitably public moment to correct it. Here it is. I quote: Pusillanimous. Adjective. Wanting of firmness of mind, of small courage, having a little mind, mean spirited, cowardly, timid of mind. From the Latin pusillus, very little, and animus, the mind. (*Slams the book shut.*) That's my wife! That's *her* isn't it? Behold the Lady Pusillanimous. (*Shouting hoarsely*) Hi, Pusey! When's your next picture?

(JIMMY *watches her, waiting for her to break. For no more than a flash,* ALISON's *face seems to contort, and it looks as though she might throw her head back, and scream. But it passes in a moment. She is used to these carefully rehearsed attacks, and it doesn't look as though he will get his triumph tonight. She carries on with her ironing.* JIMMY *crosses, and switches on the radio. The Vaughan Williams concert has started. He goes back to his chair, leans back in it, and closes his eyes.*)

ALISON: (*handing* CLIFF *his trousers*). There you are, dear. They're not very good, but they'll do for now.

(CLIFF *gets up and puts them on.*)

CLIFF: Oh, that's lovely.

ALISON: Now try and look after them. I'll give them a real press later on.

CLIFF: Thank you, you beautiful, darling girl.

(*He puts his arms round her waist, and kisses her. She smiles, and gives his nose a tug.* JIMMY *watches from his chair.*)

ALISON: (*to* CLIFF). Let's have a cigarette, shall we?

CLIFF: That's a good idea. Where are they?

ALISON: On the stove. Do you want one Jimmy?

JIMMY: No thank you, I'm trying to listen. Do you mind?

CLIFF: Sorry, your lordship.

(*He puts a cigarette in* ALISON's *mouth, and one in his own, and lights up.* CLIFF *sits down, and picks up his paper.* ALISON *goes back to her board.* CLIFF *throws down paper, picks up another, and thumbs through that.*)

JIMMY: Do you have to make all that racket?

CLIFF: Oh, sorry.

JIMMY: It's quite a simple thing, you know—turning over a page. Anyway, that's my paper.

(*Snatches it away.*)

CLIFF: Oh, don't be so mean!

JIMMY: Price ninepence, obtainable from any newsagent's. Now let me hear the music, for God's sake.

(*Pause.*)

(*to* ALISON). Are you going to be much longer doing that?

ALISON: Why?

JIMMY: Perhaps you haven't noticed it, but it's interfering with the radio.

ALISON: I'm sorry. I shan't be much longer.

(*A pause. The iron mingles with the music.* CLIFF *shifts restlessly in his chair,* JIMMY *watches* ALISON, *his foot beginning to twitch dangerously. Presently, he gets up quickly, crossing below* ALISON *to the radio, turns it off.*)

What did you do that for?

JIMMY: I wanted to listen to the concert, that's all.

ALISON: Well, what's stopping you?

JIMMY: Everyone's making such a din—that's what's stopping me.

ALISON: Well, I'm very sorry, but I can't just stop everything because you want to listen to music.

560   JIMMY: Why not?

ALISON: Really, Jimmy, you're like a child.

JIMMY: Don't try and patronise me. (*Turning to* CLIFF.) She's so clumsy. I watch for her to do the same things every night. The way she jumps on the bed, as if she were stamping on someone's face, and draws the curtains back with a great clatter, in that casually destructive ways of hers. It's like someone launching a battleship. Have you ever noticed how noisy women are? (*Crosses*

570   *below chairs to L.C.*) Have you? The way they kick the floor about, simply walking over it? Or have you watched them sitting at their dressing tables, dropping their weapons and banging down their bits of boxes and brushes and lipsticks?

(*He faces her dressing table.*)

I've watched her doing it night after night. When you see a woman in front of her bedroom mirror, you realise what a refined sort of a butcher she

580   is. (*Turns in.*) Did you ever see some dirty old Arab, sticking his fingers into some mess of lamb fat and gristle? Well, she's just like that. Thank God they don't have many women surgeons! Those primitive hands would have your guts out in no time. Flip! Out it comes, like the powder out of its box. Flop! Back it goes, like the powder puff on the table.

CLIFF: (*grimacing cheerfully*). Ugh! Stop it!

JIMMY: (*moving upstage*). She'd drop your guts like

590   hair clips and fluff all over the floor. You've got to be fundamentally insensitive to be as noisy and as clumsy as that.

(*He moves C., and leans against the table.*)

I had a flat underneath a couple of girls once. You heard every damned thing those bastards did, all day and night. The most simple, everyday actions were a sort of assault course on your sensibilities. I used to plead with them. I even got to screaming the most ingenious obscenities I could think of, up the stairs at them.

600   But nothing, nothing, would move them. With those two, even a simple visit to the lavatory sounded like a medieval siege. Oh, they beat me in the end—I had to go. I expect they're

still at it. Or they're probably married by now, and driving some other poor devils out of their minds. Slamming their doors, stamping their high heels, banging their irons and saucepans—the eternal flaming racket of the female.

(*Church bells start ringing outside.*)   610

JIMMY: Oh, hell! Now the bloody bells have started!

(*He rushes to the window.*)

Wrap it up, will you? Stop ringing those bells! There's somebody going crazy in here! I don't want to hear them!

ALISON: Stop shouting! (*Recovering immediately.*) You'll have Miss Drury up here.

JIMMY: I don't give a damn about Miss Drury—that mild old gentlewoman doesn't fool me, even if   620 she takes in you two. She's an old robber. She gets more than enough out of us for this place every week. Anyway, she's probably in church, (*points to the window*) swinging on those bloody bells!

(CLIFF *goes to the window, and closes it.*)

CLIFF: Come on now, be a good boy. I'll take us all out, and we'll have a drink.

JIMMY: They're not open yet. It's Sunday. Remember? Anyway, it's raining.   630

CLIFF: Well, shall we dance?

(*He pushes* JIMMY *round the floor, who is past the mood for this kind of fooling.*)

Do you come here often?

JIMMY: Only in the mating season. All right, all right, very funny.

(*He tries to escape, but* CLIFF *holds him like a vice.*)

Let me go.

CLIFF: Not until you've apologised for being so nasty to everyone. Do you think bosoms will   640 be in or out, this year?

JIMMY: Your teeth will be out in a minute, if you don't let go!

(*He makes a great effort to wrench himself free, but* CLIFF *hangs on. They collapse to the floor C., below the table, struggling.* ALISON *carries on with her ironing. This is routine, but she is getting close to breaking point,*

all the same. CLIFF *manages to break away, and finds himself in front of the ironing board.* JIMMY *springs up.*
650   *They grapple.)*

ALISON: Look out, for heaven's sake! Oh, it's more like a zoo every day!

(JIMMY *makes a frantic, deliberate effort, and manages to push* CLIFF *on the ironing board, and into* ALISON. *The board collapses.* CLIFF *falls against her, and they end up in a heap on the floor.* ALISON *cries out in pain.* JIMMY *looks down at them, dazed and breathless.)*

CLIFF: *(picking himself up).* She's hurt. Are you all right?
660   ALISON: Well, does it look like it!

CLIFF: She's burnt her arm on the iron.

JIMMY: Darling, I'm sorry.

ALISON: Get out!

JIMMY: I'm sorry, believe me. You think I did it on pur—

ALISON: *(her head shaking helplessly.)* Clear out of my sight!

(He stares at her uncertainly. CLIFF *nods to him, and he turns and goes out of the door.)*

670   CLIFF: Come and sit down.

(He leads her to the armchair. R.)

You look a bit white. Are you all right?

ALISON: Yes. I'm all right now.

CLIFF: Let's have a look at your arm. *(Examines it.)* Yes, it's quite red. That's going to be painful. What should I do with it?

ALISON: Oh, it's nothing much. A bit of soap on it will do. I never can remember what you do with burns.

680   CLIFF: I'll just pop down to the bathroom and get some. Are you sure you're all right?

ALISON: Yes.

CLIFF: *(crossing to door).* Won't be a minute.

(Exit.)

(She leans back in the chair, and looks up at the ceiling. She breathes in deeply, and brings her hands up to her face. She winces as she feels the pain in her arm, and she lets it fall. She runs her hand through hair.)

ALISON: *(in a clenched whisper).* Oh, God!

690   (CLIFF *re-enters with a bar of soap.)*

CLIFF: It's this scented muck. Do you think it'll be all right?

ALISON: That'll do.

CLIFF: Here we are then. Let's have your arm.

(He kneels down beside her, and she holds out her arm.)

I've put it under the tap. It's quite soft. I'll do it ever so gently.

(Very carefully, he rubs the soap over the burn.)

All right? *(She nods.)* You're a brave girl.

ALISON: I don't feel very brave. *(Tears harshening   700 her voice.)* I really don't, Cliff. I don't think I can take much more. *(Turns her head away.)* I think I feel rather sick.

CLIFF: All over now. *(Puts the soap down.)* Would you like me to get you something?

(She shakes her head. He sits on the arm of the chair, and puts his arm round her. She leans her head back on to him.)

Don't upset yourself, lovely.

(He massages the back of her neck, and she lets her head   710 fall forward.)

ALISON: Where is he?

CLIFF: What's he doing?

CLIFF: Lying on the bed. Reading, I think. *(Stroking her neck.)* That better?

(She leans back, and closes her eyes again.)

ALISON: Bless you.

(He kisses the top of her head.)

CLIFF: I don't think I'd have the courage to live on my own again—in spite of everything. I'm   720 pretty rough, and pretty ordinary really, and I'd seem worse on my own. And you get fond of people too, worse luck.

ALISON: I don't think I want anything more to do with love. Any more. I can't take it on.

CLIFF: You're too young to start giving up. Too young, and too lovely. Perhaps I'd better put a bandage on that—do you think so?

ALISON: There's some on my dressing table.

(CLIFF *crosses to the dressing table R.)*   730

I keep looking back, as far as I remember, and

I can't think what it was to feel young, really young. Jimmy said the same thing to me the other day. I pretended not to be listening—because I knew that would hurt him, I suppose. And—of course—he got savage, like tonight. But I knew just what he meant. I suppose it would have been so easy to say "Yes, darling, I know just what you mean. I know what you're feeling." (*Shrugs.*) It's those easy things that seem to be so impossible with us.

(CLIFF *stands down R., holding the bandage, his back to her.*)

CLIFF: I'm wondering how much longer I can go on watching you two tearing the insides out of each other. It looks pretty ugly sometimes.

ALISON: You wouldn't seriously think of leaving us, would you?

CLIFF: I suppose not. (*Crosses to her.*)

ALISON: I think I'm frightened. If only I knew what was going to happen.

CLIFF: (*kneeling on the arm of her chair*). Give it here. (*She holds out her arm.*) Yell out if I hurt you. (*He bandages it for her.*)

ALISON: (*staring at her outstretched arm*). Cliff—

CLIFF: Um? (*Slight pause.*) What is it, lovely?

ALISON: Nothing.

CLIFF: I said: what is it?

ALISON: You see—(*Hesitates.*) I'm pregnant.

CLIFF: (*after a few moments*). I'll need some scissors.

ALISON: They're over there.

CLIFF: (*crossing to the dressing table*). That is something, isn't it? When did you find this out?

ALISON: Few days ago. It was a bit of a shock.

CLIFF: Yes, I dare say.

ALISON: After three years of married life, I have to get caught out now.

CLIFF: None of us infallible, I suppose. (*Crosses to her.*) Must say I'm surprised though.

ALISON: It's always been out of the question. What with—this place, and no money, and oh—everything. He's resented it, I know. What can you do?

CLIFF: You haven't told him yet.

ALISON: Not yet.

CLIFF: What are you going to do?

ALISON: I've no idea.

CLIFF: (*having cut her bandage, he starts tying it*). That too tight?

ALISON: Fine, thank you.

(*She rises, goes to the ironing board, folds it up, and leans it against the food cupboard R.*)

CLIFF: Is it . . . Is it . . .?

ALISON: Too late to avert the situation? (*Places the iron on the rack of the stove.*) I'm not certain yet. Maybe not. If not, there won't be any problem, will there?

CLIFF: And if it is too late?

(*Her face is turned away from him. She simply shakes her head.*)

Why don't you tell him now?

(*She kneels down to pick up the clothes on the floor, and folds them up.*)

After all, he does love you. You don't need me to tell you that.

ALISON: Can't you see? He'll suspect my motives at once. He never stops telling himself that I know how vulnerable he is. Tonight it might be all right—we'd make love. But later, we'd both lie awake, watching for the light to come through that little window, and dreading it. In the morning, he'd feel hoaxed, as if I were trying to kill him in the worst way of all. He'd watch me growing bigger every day, and I wouldn't dare to look at him.

CLIFF: You may have to face it, lovely.

ALISON: Jimmy's got his own private morality, as you know. What my mother calls "loose". It is pretty free, of course, but it's very harsh too. You know, it's funny, but we never slept together before we were married.

CLIFF: It certainly is—knowing him!

ALISON: We knew each other such a short time, everything moved at such a pace, we didn't have much opportunity. And, afterwards, he actually taunted me with my virginity. He was quite angry about it, as if I had deceived him in some strange way. He seemed to think an untouched woman would defile him.

CLIFF: I've never heard you talking like this about him. He'd be quite pleased.

ALISON: Yes, he would.

(She gets up, the clothes folded over her arm.)

Do you think he's right?

CLIFF: What about?

ALISON: Oh—everything.

CLIFF: Well, I suppose he and I think the same
830 about a lot of things, because we're alike in some
ways. We both come from working people, if
you like. Oh I know some of his mother's relatives are pretty posh, but he hates them as much
as he hates yours. Don't quite know why. Anyway, he gets on with me because I'm common.
(Grins.) Common as dirt, that's me.

*(She puts her hand on his head, and strokes it thought-
fully.)*

ALISON: You think I should tell him about the
baby?

840 *(He gets up, and puts his arm round her.)*

CLIFF: It'll be all right—you see. Tell him.

*(He kisses her. Enter JIMMY. He looks at them curiously,
but without surprise. They are both aware of him, but
make no sign of it. He crosses to the armchair L., and
sits down next to them. He picks up a paper, and starts
looking at it. CLIFF glances at him, ALISON's head against
his cheek.)*

There you are, you old devil, you! Where have
you been?

850 JIMMY: You know damn well where I've been.
(Without looking at her.) How's your arm?

ALISON: Oh, it's all right. It wasn't much.

CLIFF: She's beautiful, isn't she?

JIMMY: You seem to think so.

*(CLIFF and ALISON still have their arms round one
another.)*

CLIFF: Why the hell she married you, I'll never
know.

JIMMY: You think she'd have been better off with
860 you?

CLIFF: I'm not her type. Am I, dullin'?

ALISON: I'm not sure what my type is.

JIMMY: Why don't you both get into bed, and have
done with it.

ALISON: You know, I think he really means that.

JIMMY: I do. I can't concentrate with you two standing there like that.

CLIFF: He's just an old Puritan at heart.

JIMMY: Perhaps I am, at that. Anyway, you both
look pretty silly slobbering over each other. 870

CLIFF: I think she's beautiful. And so do you, only
you're too much of a pig to say so.

JIMMY: You're just a sexy little Welshman, and you
know it! Mummy and Daddy turn pale, and
face the east every time they remember she's
married to me. But if they saw all this going
on, they'd collapse. Wonder what they would
do, incidentally. Send for the police I expect.
(Genuinely friendly.) Have you got a cigarette?

ALISON: *(disengaging).* I'll have a look. 880

(She goes to her handbag on the table C.)

JIMMY: *(pointing at CLIFF).* He gets more like a little
mouse every day, doesn't he?

(He is trying to re-establish himself.)

He really does look like one. Look at those ears,
and that face, and the little short legs.

ALISON: *(looking through her bag).* That's because he
is a mouse.

CLIFF: Eek! Eek! I'm a mouse.

JIMMY: A randy little mouse. 890

CLIFF: *(dancing round the table, and squeaking).* I'm
a mouse, I'm a mouse, I'm a randy little mouse.
That's a mourris dance.

JIMMY: A what?

CLIFF: A *Mourris Dance.* That's a Morris Dance
strictly for mice.

JIMMY: You stink. You really do. Do you know
that?

CLIFF: Not as bad as you, you horrible old bear.

(Goes over to him, and grabs his foot.) 900

You're a stinking old bear, you hear me?

JIMMY: Let go of my foot, you whimsy little half-
wit. You're making my stomach heave. I'm rest-
ing! If you don't let go, I'll cut off your nasty,
great, slimy tail!

*(CLIFF gives him a tug, and JIMMY falls to the floor.
ALISON watches them, relieved and suddenly full of affection.)*

ALISON: I've run out of cigarettes.

(CLIFF is dragging JIMMY along the floor by his feet.) 910

JIMMY: *(yelling).* Go out and get me some cigarettes,
and stop playing the fool!

CLIFF: O.K.

(He lets go of JIMMY's *legs suddenly, who yells again as his head bangs on the floor.)*

ALISON: Here's half a crown. *(Giving it him.)* The shop on the corner will be open.

CLIFF: Right you are. *(Kisses her on the forehead quickly.)* Don't forget. *(Crosses upstage to door.)*

920 JIMMY: Now get to hell out of here!

CLIFF: *(at door)*. Hey, shorty!

JIMMY: What do you want?

CLIFF: Make a nice pot of tea.

JIMMY: *(getting up)*. I'll kill you first.

CLIFF: *(grinning)*. That's my boy!

(Exit.)

*(*JIMMY *is now beside* ALISON, *who is still looking through her handbag. She becomes aware of his nearness, and, after a few moments, closes it. He takes hold of her ban-*

930 *daged arm.)*

JIMMY: How's it feeling?

ALISON: Fine. It wasn't anything.

JIMMY: All this fooling about can get a bit danger-ous.

(He sits on the edge of the table, holding her hand.) I'm sorry.

ALISON: I know.

JIMMY: I mean it.

ALISON: There's no need.

940 JIMMY: I did it on purpose.

ALISON: Yes.

JIMMY: There's hardly a moment when I'm not—watching and wanting you. I've got to hit out somehow. Nearly four years of being in the same room with you, night and day, and I still can't stop my sweat breaking out when I see you doing—something as ordinary as leaning over an ironing board.

(She strokes his head, not sure of herself yet.)

950 *(sighing)*. Trouble is—Trouble is you get used to people. Even their trivialities become indis-pensable to you. Indispensable, and a little mys-terious.

(He slides his head forward, against her, trying to catch his thoughts.)

I think . . . I must have a lot of—old stock. . . . Nobody wants it. . . .

(He puts his face against her belly. She goes on stroking his head, still on guard a little. Then he lifts his head, and they kiss passionately.)   960

What are we going to do tonight?

ALISON: What would you like to do? Drink?

JIMMY: I know what I want now.

(She takes his head in her hands and kisses him.)

ALISON: Well, you'll have to wait till the proper time.

JIMMY: There's no such thing.

ALISON: Cliff will be back in a minute.

JIMMY: What did he mean by "don't forget"?

ALISON: Something I've been meaning to tell you.   970

JIMMY: *(kissing her again)*. You're fond of him, aren't you?

ALISON: Yes, I am.

JIMMY: He's the only friend I seem to have left now. People go away. You never see them again. I can remember lots of names—men and women. When I was at school—Watson, Roberts, Davies. Jenny, Madeline, Hugh . . . *(Pause.)* And there's Hugh's mum, of course. I'd almost forgot-ten her. She's been a good friend to us, if you   980 like. She's even letting me buy the sweet-stall off her in my own time. She only bought it for us, anyway. She's so fond of you. I can never understand why you're so—distant with her.

ALISON: *(alarmed at this threat of a different mood)*. Jimmy—please no!

JIMMY: *(staring at her anxious face)*. You're very beautiful. A beautiful, great-eyed squirrel.

(She nods brightly, relieved.)

Hoarding, nut-munching squirrel. *(She mimes this   990 delightedly.)* With highly polished, gleaming fur, and an ostrich feather of a tail.

ALISON: Wheeeeeeeeeee!

JIMMY: How I envy you.

(He stands, her arms around her neck.)

ALISON: Well, you're a jolly super bear, too. A really soooooooooooooooooooooper, marvellous bear.

JIMMY: Bears and squirrels *are* marvellous.

ALISON: Marvellous *and* beautiful.   1000

(She jumps up and down excitedly, making little "paw gestures".)

Ooooooooooh! Oooooooooh!

JIMMY: What the hell's that?

ALISON: That's a dance squirrels do when they're happy.

(They embrace again.)

JIMMY: What makes you think you're happy?

ALISON: Everything just seems all right suddenly.
1010   That's all. Jimmy—

JIMMY: Yes?

ALISON: You know I told you I'd something to tell you?

JIMMY: Well?

(Cliff appears in the doorway.)

CLIFF: Didn't get any further than the front door. Miss Drury hadn't gone to church after all. I couldn't get away from her. *(To* ALISON.*)* Someone on the phone for you.

1020   ALISON: On the phone? Who on earth is it?

CLIFF: Helena something.

*(*JIMMY *and* ALISON *look at each other quickly.)*

JIMMY: *(to* CLIFF*).* Helena Charles?

CLIFF: That's it.

ALISON: Thank you, Cliff. *(Moves upstage.)* I won't be a minute.

CLIFF: You will. Old Miss Drury will keep you down there forever. She doesn't think we keep this place clean enough. *(Comes and sits in the*
1030   *armchair down R.)* Thought you were going to make me some tea, you rotter.

*(*JIMMY *makes no reply.)*

What's the matter, boyo?

JIMMY: *(slowly).* That bitch.

CLIFF: Who?

JIMMY: *(to himself).* Helena Charles.

CLIFF: Who is this Helena?

JIMMY: One of her old friends. And one of my natural enemies. You're sitting on my chair.

1040   CLIFF: Where are we going for a drink?

JIMMY: I don't know.

CLIFF: Well, you were all for it earlier on.

JIMMY: What does she want? What would make her ring up? It can't be for anything pleasant. Oh well, we shall soon know. *(He settles on the table.)* Few minutes ago things didn't seem so bad either. I've just about had enough of this

"expense of spirit" lark, as far as women are concerned. Honestly, it's enough to make you become a scoutmaster or something isn't it? 1050 Sometimes I almost envy old Gide and the Greek Chorus boys. Oh, I'm not saying that it mustn't be hell for them a lot of the time. But, at least, they do seem to have a cause—not a particularly good one, it's true. But plenty of them do seem to have a revolutionary fire about them, which is more than you can say for the rest of us. Like Webster, for instance. He doesn't like me—they hardly ever do.

(He is talking for the sake of it, only half listening to 1060 *what he is saying.)*

I dare say he suspects me because I refuse to treat him either as a clown or as a tragic hero. He's like a man with a strawberry mark—he keeps thrusting it in your face because he can't believe it doesn't interest or horrify you particularly. *(Picks up Alison's handbag thoughtfully, and starts looking through it.)* As if I give a damn which way he likes his meat served up. I've got my own strawberry mark—only it's in a different 1070 place. No, as far as the Michaelangelo Brigade's concerned, I must be a sort of right-wing deviationist. If the Revolution ever comes, I'll be the first to be put up against the wall, with all the other poor old liberals.

CLIFF: *(indicating* ALISON's *handbag).* Wouldn't you say that was her private property?

JIMMY: You're quite right. But do you know something? Living night and day with another human being has made me predatory and suspicious. 1080 I know that the only way of finding out exactly what's going on is to catch them when they don't know you're looking. When she goes out, I go through everything—trunks, cases, drawers, bookcase, everything. Why? To see if there is something of me somewhere, a reference to me. I want to know if I'm being betrayed.

CLIFF: You look for trouble, don't you?

JIMMY: Only because I'm pretty certain of finding it. 1090

(Brings out a letter from the handbag.)

Look at that! Oh, I'm such a fool. This is happening every five minutes of the day. She gets letters. *(He holds it up.)* Letters from her mother, letters in which I'm not mentioned at all because my name is a dirty word. And what does she do?

(Enter ALISON. *He turns to look at her.)*

She writes long letters back to Mummy, and never mentions me at all, because I'm just a dirty
1100   word to her too.

(He throws the letter down at her feet.)

Well, what did your friend want?

ALISON: She's at the station. She's—coming over.

JIMMY: I see. She said "Can I come over?" And you said "My husband, Jimmy—if you'll forgive me using such a dirty word, will be delighted to see you. He'll kick your face in!"

(He stands up, unable to sustain his anger, poised on the table.)

1120   ALISON: *(quietly).* She's playing with the company at the Hippodrome this week, and she's got no digs. She can't find anywhere to stay——

JIMMY: That I don't believe!

ALISON: So I said she could come here until she fixes something else. Miss Drury's got a spare room downstairs.

JIMMY: Why not have her in here? Did you tell her to bring her armour? Because she's going to need it!

1130   ALISON: *(vehemently.)* Oh why don't you shut up, please!

JIMMY: Oh, my dear wife, you've got so much to learn. I only hope you learn it one day. If only something—something would happen to you, and wake you out of your beauty sleep! *(Coming*

in close to her.) If you could have a child, and it would die. Let it grow, let a recognisable human face emerge from that little mass of indiarubber and wrinkles. *(She retreats away from him.)* Please—if only I could watch you face that.   1140
I wonder if you might even become a recognisable human being yourself. But I doubt it.

(She moves away, stunned, and leans on the gas stove down L. He stands rather helplessly on his own.)

Do you know I have never known the great pleasure of lovemaking when I didn't desire it myself. Oh, it's not that she hasn't her own kind of passion. She has the passion of a python.
She just devours me whole every time, as if I   1150
were some over-large rabbit. That's me. That bulge around her navel—if you're wondering what it is—it's me. Me, buried alive down there, and going mad, smothered in that peaceful looking coil. Not a sound, not a flicker from her—she doesn't even rumble a little. You'd think that this indigestible mess would stir up some kind of tremor in those distended, overfed tripes—but not her!

(Crosses up to the door.)   1160

She'll go on sleeping and devouring until there's nothing left of me.

(Exit.)

ALISON's *head goes back as if she were about to make some sound. But her mouth remains open and trembling, as* CLIFF *looks on.)*

Curtain

ACT II

SCENE ONE

Two weeks later. Evening. ALISON *is standing over the gas stove, pouring water from the kettle into a large teapot. She is only wearing a slip, and her feet are bare.*

In the room across the hall, JIMMY *is playing on his jazz trumpet, in intermittent bursts.* ALISON *takes the pot to the table C., which is laid for four people. The Sunday paper jungle around the two armchairs is as luxuriant as ever. It is late afternoon, the end of a hot day. She wipes her forehead. She crosses to the dressing table R., takes out a pair of stockings from one of the drawers, and sits down on the small chair beside it to put them on. While she is doing this, the door opens and* HELENA *enters. She is the same age as* ALISON, *medium height, carefully and expensively dressed. Now and again, when she allows her rather judicial expression of alertness to soften, she is very attractive. Her sense of matriarchal authority makes most men who meet her anxious, not only to please but impress, as if she were the gracious representative of visiting royalty. In this case, the royalty of that middle-class womanhood, which is so eminently secure in its divine rights, that it can afford to tolerate the parliament, and reasonably free assembly of its menfolk. Even from other young women, like* ALISON, *she receives her due of respect and admiration. In* JIMMY, *as one would expect, she arouses all the rabble-rousing instincts of his spirit. And she is not accustomed to having to defend herself against catcalls. However, her sense of modestly exalted responsibility enables her to behave with an impressive show of strength and dignity, although the strain of this is beginning to tell on her a little. She is carrying a large salad colander.*

———————

ALISON: Did you manage all right?

HELENA: Of course. I've prepared most of the meals in the last week, you know.

ALISON: Yes, you have. It's been wonderful having someone to help. Another woman, I mean.

HELENA: *(crossing down L.)* I'm enjoying it. Although I don't think I shall ever get used to having to go down to the bathroom every time I want some water for something.

10 ALISON: It is primitive, isn't it?

HELENA: Yes. It is rather.

(She starts tearing up green salad on to four plates, which she takes from the food cupboard.)

Looking after one man is really enough, but two is rather an undertaking.

ALISON: Oh, Cliff looks after himself, more or less. In fact, he helps me quite a lot.

HELENA: Can't say I'd noticed it.

ALISON: You've been doing it instead, I suppose.

20 HELENA: I see.

ALISON: You've settled in so easily somehow.

HELENA: Why shouldn't I?

ALISON: It's not exactly what you're used to, is it?

HELENA: And are you used to it?

ALISON: Everything seems very different here now —with you here.

HELENA: Does it?

ALISON: Yes. I was on my own before——

HELENA: Now you've got me. So you're not sorry 30 you asked me to stay?

ALISON: Of course not. Did you tell him his tea was ready?

HELENA: I banged on the door of Cliff's room, and yelled. He didn't answer, but he must have heard. I don't know where Cliff is.

ALISON: *(leaning back in her chair).* I thought I'd feel cooler after a bath, but I feel hot again already. God, I wish he'd lose that damned trumpet.

HELENA: I imagine that's for my benefit. 40

ALISON: Miss Drury will ask us to go soon, I know it. Thank goodness she isn't in. Listen to him.

HELENA: Does he drink?

ALISON: Drink? *(Rather startled.)* He's not an alcoholic, if that's what you mean.

(They both pause, listening to the trumpet.)

He'll have the rest of the street banging on the door next.

HELENA: *(pondering).* It's almost as if he wanted to kill someone with it. And me in particular. 50 I've never seen such hatred in someone's eyes before. It's slightly horrifying. Horrifying *(crossing to food cupboard for tomatoes, beetroot and cucumber)* and oddly exciting.

*(*ALISON *faces her dressing mirror, and brushes her hair.)*

ALISON: He had his own jazz band once. That was when he was still a student, before I knew him. I rather think he'd like to start another, and give up the stall altogether.

HELENA: Is Cliff in love with you? 60

ALISON: *(stops brushing for a moment).* No . . . I don't think so.

HELENA: And what about you? You look as though I've asked you a rather peculiar question. The way things are, you might as well be frank with me. I only want to help. After all, your behaviour together is a little strange—by most people's standards, to say the least.

ALISON: You mean you've seen us embracing each
other?

HELENA: Well, it doesn't seem to go on as much
as it did, I admit. Perhaps he finds my presence
inhibiting—even if Jimmy's isn't.

ALISON: We're simply fond of each other—there's
no more to it than that.

HELENA: Darling, really! It can't be as simple as
that.

ALISON: You mean there must be something physical too? I suppose there is, but it's not exactly
a consuming passion with either of us. It's just
a relaxed, cheerful sort of thing, like being warm
in bed. You're too comfortable to bother about
moving for the sake of some other pleasure.

HELENA: I find it difficult to believe anyone's
that lazy!

ALISON: I think *we* are.

HELENA: And what about Jimmy? After all, he is
your husband. Do you mean to say he actually
approves of it?

ALISON: It isn't easy to explain. It's what he would
call a question of allegiances, and he expects you
to be pretty literal about them. Not only about
himself and all the things he believes in, his present and his future, but his past as well. All
the people he admires and loves, and has loved.
The friends he used to know, people I've never
even known—and probably wouldn't have liked.
His father, who died years ago. Even the other
women he's loved. Do you understand?

HELENA: Do you?

ALISON: I've tried to. But I still can't bring myself
to feel the way he does about things. I can't
believe that he's right somehow.

HELENA: Well, that's something, anyway.

ALISON: If things have worked out with Cliff, it's
because he's kind and lovable, and I've grown
genuinely fond of him. But it's been a fluke.
It's worked because Cliff is such a nice person
anyway. With Hugh, it was quite different.

HELENA: Hugh?

ALISON: Hugh Tanner. He and Jimmy were
friends almost from childhood. Mrs. Tanner is
his mother—

HELENA: Oh yes—the one who started him off in
the sweet business.

ALISON: That's right. Well, after Jimmy and I were
married, we'd no money—about eight pounds
ten in actual fact—and no home. He didn't even
have a job. He'd only left the university about
a year. *(Smiles.)* No—left. I don't think one
"comes down" from Jimmy's university. According to him, it's not even red brick, but white
tile. Anyway, we went off to live in Hugh's
flat. It was over a warehouse in Poplar.

HELENA: Yes. I remember seeing the postmark on
your letters.

ALISON: Well, that was where I found myself on
my wedding night. Hugh and I disliked each
other on sight, and Jimmy knew it. He was so
proud of us both, so pathetically anxious that
we should take to each other. Like a child showing off his toys. We had a little wedding celebration, and the three of us tried to get tight on
some cheap port they'd brought in. Hugh got
more and more subtly insulting—he'd a rare talent for that. Jimmy got steadily depressed, and
I just sat there, listening to their talk, looking
and feeling very stupid. For the first time in
my life, I was cut off from the kind of people
I'd always known, my family, my friends, everybody. And I'd burnt my boats. After all those
weeks of brawling with Mummy and Daddy
about Jimmy, I knew I couldn't appeal to them
without looking foolish and cheap. It was just
before the General Election, I remember, and
Nigel was busy getting himself into Parliament.
He didn't have time for anyone but his con-
stituents. Oh, he'd have been sweet and kind,
I know.

HELENA: *(moving in C.).* Darling, why didn't you
come to me?

ALISON: You were away on tour in some play, I
think.

HELENA: So I was.

ALISON: Those next few months at the flat in Poplar
were a nightmare. I suppose I must be soft and
squeamish, and snobbish, but I felt as though
I'd been dropped in a jungle. I couldn't believe
that two people, two educated people could be
so savage, and so—so uncompromising. Mummy
has always said that Jimmy is utterly ruthless,
but she hasn't met Hugh. He takes the first prize

for ruthlessness—from all comers. Together, they were frightening. They both came to regard me as a sort of hostage from those sections of society they had declared war on.

HELENA: How were you living all this time?

ALISON: I had a tiny bit coming in from a few shares I had left, but it hardly kept us. Mummy had made me sign everything else over to her, in trust, when she knew I was really going to marry Jimmy.

HELENA: Just as well, I imagine.

ALISON: They soon thought of a way out of that. A brilliant campaign. They started inviting themselves—through me—to people's houses, friends of Nigel's and mine, friends of Daddy's, oh everyone: The Arksdens, the Tarnatts, the Wains——

HELENA: Not the Wains?

ALISON: Just about everyone I'd ever known. Your people must have been among the few we missed out. It was just enemy territory to them, and, as I say, they used me as a hostage. We'd set out from headquarters in Poplar, and carry out our raids on the enemy in W.1, S.W.1, S.W.3. and W.8. In my name, we'd gatecrash everywhere—cocktails, week-ends, even a couple of houseparties. I used to hope that one day, somebody would have the guts to slam the door in our faces, but they didn't. They were too well-bred, and probably sorry for me as well. Hugh and Jimmy despised them for it. So we went on plundering them, wolfing their food and drinks, and smoking their cigars like ruffians. Oh, they enjoyed themselves.

HELENA: Apparently.

ALISON: Hugh fairly revelled in the role of the barbarian invader. Sometimes I thought he might even dress the part—you know, furs, spiked helmet, sword. He even got a fiver out of old Man Wain once. Blackmail, of course. People would have signed almost anything to get rid of us. He told him that we were about to be turned out of our flat for not paying the rent. At least it was true.

HELENA: I don't understand you. You must have been crazy.

ALISON: Afraid more than anything.

HELENA: But letting them do it! Letting them get away with it! You managed to stop them stealing the silver, I suppose?

ALISON: Oh, they knew their guerrilla warfare better than that. Hugh tried to seduce some freshfaced young girl at the Arksdens' once, but that was the only time we were more or less turned out.

HELENA: It's almost unbelievable. I don't understand your part in it all. Why? That's what I don't see. Why did you——

ALISON: Marry him? There must be about six different answers. When the family came back from India, everything seemed, I don't know—unsettled? Anyway, Daddy seemed remote and rather irritable. And Mummy—well, you know Mummy. I didn't have much to worry about. I didn't know I was born as Jimmy says. I met him at a party. I remember it so clearly. I was almost twenty-one. The men there all looked as though they distrusted him, and as for the women, they were all intent on showing their contempt for this rather odd creature, but no one seemed quite sure how to do it. He'd come to the party on a bicycle, he told me, and there was oil all over his dinner jacket. It had been such a lovely day, and he'd been in the sun. Everything about him seemed to burn, his face, the edges of his hair glistened and seemed to spring off his head, and his eyes were so blue and full of the sun. He looked so young and frail, in spite of the tired line of his mouth. I knew I was taking on more than I was ever likely to be capable of bearing, but there never seemed to be any choice. Well, the howl of outrage and astonishment went up from the family, and that did it. Whether or no he was in love with me, that did it. He made up his mind to marry me. They did just about everything they could think of to stop us.

HELENA: Yes, it wasn't a very pleasant business. But you can see their point.

ALISON: Jimmy went into battle with his axe swinging round his head—frail, and so full of fire. I had never seen anything like it. The old story of the knight in shining armour—except that his armour didn't really shine very much.

HELENA: And what about Hugh?

ALISON: Things got steadily worse between us. He and Jimmy even went to some of Nigel's political meetings. They took bunches of their Poplar cronies with them, and broke them up for him.

HELENA: He's really a savage, isn't he?

ALISON: Well, Hugh was writing some novel or other, and he made up his mind he must go abroad—to China, or some God-forsaken place. He said that England was finished for us anyway. All the old gang was back—Dame Alison's Mob, as he used to call it. The only real hope was to get out, and try somewhere else. He wanted us to go with him, but Jimmy refused to go. There was a terrible, bitter row over it. Jimmy accused Hugh of giving up, and he thought it was wrong of him to go off forever, and leave his mother all on her own. He was upset by the whole idea. They quarrelled for days over it. I almost wished they'd both go, and leave me behind. Anyway, they broke up. A few months later we came up here, and Hugh went off to find the New Millennium on his own. Sometimes, I think Hugh's mother blames me for it all. Jimmy too, in a way, although he's never said so. He never mentions it. But whenever that woman looks at me, I can feel her thinking "If it hadn't been for you, everything would have been all right. We'd have all been happy." Not that I dislike her—I don't. She's very sweet, in fact. Jimmy seems to adore her principally because she's been poor almost all her life, and she's frankly ignorant. I'm quite aware how snobbish that sounds, but it happens to be the truth.

HELENA: Alison, listen to me. You've got to make up your mind what you're going to do. You're going to have a baby, and you have a new responsibility. Before, it was different—there was only yourself at stake. But you can't go on living in this way any longer. (To her.)

ALISON: I'm so tired. I dread him coming into the room.

HELENA: Why haven't you told him you're going to have a child?

ALISON: I don't know. (Suddenly anticipating HELENA's train of thought.) Oh, it's his all right. There couldn't be any doubt of that. You see——(she smiles). I've never really wanted anyone else.

HELENA: Listen, darling—you've got to tell him. Either he learns to behave like anyone else, and looks after you——

ALISON: Or?

HELENA: Or you must get out of this mad-house. (Trumpet crescendo.) This menagerie. He doesn't seem to know what love or anything else means.

ALISON: (pointing to chest of drawers up R.). You see that bear, and that squirrel? Well, that's him and that's me.

HELENA: Meaning?

ALISON: The game we play: bears and squirrels, squirrels and bears.

(HELENA looks rather blank.)

Yes, it's quite mad, I know. Quite mad. (Picks up the two animals.) That's him.... And that's me....

HELENA: I didn't realise he was a bit fey, as well as everything else!

ALISON: Oh, there's nothing fey about Jimmy. It's just all we seem to have left. Or had left. Even bears and squirrels seem to have gone their own ways now.

HELENA: Since I arrived?

ALISON: It started during those first months we had alone together—after Hugh went abroad. It was the one way of escaping from everything—a sort of unholy priest-hole of being animals to one another. We could become little furry creatures with little furry brains. Full of dumb, uncomplicated affection for each other. Playful, careless creatures in their own cosy zoo for two. A silly symphony for people who couldn't bear the pain of being human beings any longer. And now, even they are dead, poor little silly animals. They were all love, and no brains. (Puts them back.)

HELENA: (gripping her arm). Listen to me. You've got to fight him. Fight, or get out. Otherwise, he will kill you.

(Enter CLIFF.)

CLIFF: There you are, dullin'. Hullo, Helena. Tea ready?

350 ALISON: Yes, dear, it's all ready. Give Jimmy a call, will you?

CLIFF: Right. *(Yelling back through door.)* Hey, you horrible man! Stop that bloody noise, and come and get your tea! *(Coming in C.)* Going out?

HELENA: *(crossing to L.).* Yes.

CLIFF: Pictures?

HELENA: No. *(Pause.)* Church.

CLIFF: *(really surprised).* Oh! I see. Both of you?

HELENA: Yes. Are you coming?

360 CLIFF: Well. . . . I—I haven't read the papers properly yet. Tea, tea, tea! Let's have some tea, shall we?

(He sits at the upstage end of the table. HELENA puts the four plates of salad on it, sits down L., and they begin the meal. ALISON is making up her face at her dressing table. Presently, JIMMY enters. He places his trumpet on the bookcase, and comes above the table.)

Hullo, boyo. Come and have your tea. That blinkin' trumpet—why don't you stuff it away
370 somewhere?

JIMMY: You like it all right. Anyone who doesn't like real jazz, hasn't any feeling either for music or people.

(He sits R. end of table.)

HELENA: Rubbish.

JIMMY: *(to CLIFF).* That seems to prove my point for you. Did you know that Webster played the banjo?

CLIFF: No, does he really?

380 HELENA: He said he'd bring it along next time he came.

ALISON: *(muttering).* Oh, no!

JIMMY: Why is it that nobody knows how to treat the papers in this place? Look at them. I haven't even glanced at them yet—not the posh ones, anyway.

CLIFF: By the way, can I look at your *New*——

JIMMY: No, you can't! *(Loudly.)* You want anything, you pay for it. Like I have to. Price——

390 CLIFF: Price ninepence, obtainable from any bookstall! You're a mean old man, that's what you are.

JIMMY: What do you want to read it for, anyway? You've no intellect, no curiosity. It all just washes over you. Am I right?

CLIFF: Right.

JIMMY: What are you, you Welsh trash?

CLIFF: Nothing, that's what I am.

JIMMY: Nothing are you? Blimey you ought to be
400 Prime Minister. You must have been talking to some of my wife's friends. They're a very intellectual set, aren't they? I've seen 'em.

(CLIFF and HELENA carry on with their meal.)

They all sit around feeling very spiritual, with their mental hands on each other's knees, discussing sex as if it were the Art of Fugue. If you don't want to be an emotional old spinister, just you listen to you dad!

*(He starts eating. The silent hostility of the two women
410 has set him off on the scent, and he looks quite cheerful, although the occasional thick edge of his voice belies it.)*

You know your trouble, son? Too anxious to please.

HELENA: Thank heavens somebody is!

JIMMY: You'll end up like one of those chocolate meringues my wife is so fond of. My wife—that's the one with the tom-toms behind me. Sweet and sticky on the outside, and sink your teeth in it, *(savouring every word)* inside, all white,
420 messy and disgusting. *(Offering teapot sweetly to HELENA.)* Tea?

HELENA: Thank you.

(He smiles, and pours out a cup for her.)

JIMMY: That's how you'll end up, my boy—black hearted, evil minded and vicious.

HELENA: *(taking cup.)* Thank you.

JIMMY: And those old favourites, your friends and mine: sycophantic, phlegmatic, and, of course, top of the bill—pusillanimous.

HELENA: *(to ALISON).* Aren't you going to have your
430 tea?

ALISON: Won't be long.

JIMMY: Thought of the title for a new song today. It's called "You can quit hanging round my counter Mildred 'cos you'll find my position is closed". *(Turning to ALISON suddenly.)* Good?

ALISON: Oh, very good.

JIMMY: Thought you'd like it. If I can slip in a religious angle, it should be a big hit. *(To
440 HELENA.)* Don't you think so? I was thinking

you might help me there. *(She doesn't reply.)* It
might help you if I recite the lyrics. Let's see
now, it's something like this:

    I'm so tired of necking,
    of pecking, home wrecking,
    of empty bed blues—
    just pass me the booze.
    I'm tired of being hetero
    Rather ride on the metero
450   Just pass me the booze.
    This perpetual whoring
    Gets quite dull and boring
    So avoid that old python coil
    And pass me the celibate oil.
    You can quit etc.

No?

CLIFF: Very good, boyo.

JIMMY: Oh, yes, and I know what I meant to tell
you—I wrote a poem while I was at the market
460 yesterday. If you're interested, which you obviously are. *(To* HELENA.*)* It should appeal to you,
in particular. It's soaked in the theology of
Dante, with a good slosh of Eliot as well. It
starts off "There are no dry cleaners in Cambodia!"

CLIFF: What do you call it?

JIMMY: "The Cess Pool". Myself being a stone
dropped in it, you see——

CLIFF: You should be dropped in it, all right.

470 HELENA: *(to* JIMMY*).* Why do you try so hard to
be unpleasant?

*(He turns very deliberately, delighted that she should
rise to the bait so soon–he's scarcely in his stride yet.)*

JIMMY: What's that?

HELENA: Do you have to be so offensive?

JIMMY: You mean now? You think I'm being offensive? You under-estimate me. *(Turning to*
ALISON.*)* Doesn't she?

HELENA: I think you're a very tiresome young man.

480 *(A slight pause as his delight catches up with him. He
roars with laughter.)*

JIMMY: Oh dear, oh dear! My wife's friends! Pass
Lady Bracknell the cucumber sandwiches, will
you?

(He returns to his meal, but his curiosity about ALISON's
*preparations at the mirror won't be denied any longer.
He turns round casually, and speaks to her.)*

Going out?

ALISON: That's right.

JIMMY: On a Sunday evening in this town? Where   490
on earth are you going?

ALISON: *(rising).* I'm going out with Helena.

JIMMY: That's not a direction—that's an affliction.

*(She crosses to the table, and sits down C. He leans
forward, and addresses her again.)*

I didn't ask you what was the matter with you.
I asked you where you were going.

HELENA: *(steadily).* She's going to church.

*(He has been prepared for some plot, but he is as genuinely
surprised by this as* CLIFF *was a few minutes earlier.)*   500

JIMMY: You're doing what?

(Silence.)

Have you gone out of your mind or something?
(To HELENA.*)* You're determined to win her,
aren't you? So it's come to this now! How feeble
can you get? *(His rage mounting within.)* When
I think of what I did, what I endured, to get
you out——

ALISON: *(recognising an onslaught on the way, starts
to panic).* Oh yes, we all know what you did   510
for me! You rescued me from the wicked clutches
of my family, and all my friends! I'd still be
rotting away at home, if you hadn't ridden up
on your charger, and carried me off!

*(The wild note in her voice has re-assured him. His anger
cools and hardens. His voice is quite calm when he speaks.)*

JIMMY: The funny thing is, you know, I really did
have to ride up on a white charger—off white,
really. Mummy locked her up in their eight bedroomed castle, didn't she. There is no limit to   520
what the middle-aged mummy will do in the
holy crusade against ruffians like me. Mummy
and I took one quick look at each other, and,
from then on, the age of chivalry was dead. I
knew that, to protect her innocent young, she
wouldn't hesitate to cheat, lie, bully and blackmail. Threatened with me, a young man without
money, background or even looks, she'd bellow
like a rhinoceros in labour—enough to make
every male rhino for miles turn white, and pledge   530
himself to celibacy. But even I under-estimated
her strength. Mummy may look over-fed and

a bit flabby on the outside, but don't let that well-bred guzzler fool you. Underneath all that, she's armour plated——

(He clutches wildly for something to shock HELENA *with.)*

She's as rough as a night in the Bombay brothel, and as tough as a matelot's arms. She's probably in that bloody cistern, taking down every word we say. *(Kicks cistern.)* Can you 'ear me, mother. *(Sits on it, beats like bongo drums.)* Just about get her in there. Let me give you an example of this lady's tactics. You may have noticed that I happen to wear my hair rather long. Now, if my wife is honest, or concerned enough to explain, she could tell you that this is not due to any dark, unnatural instincts I possess, but because (a) I can usually think of better things than a haircut to spend two bob on, and (b) I prefer long hair. But that obvious, innocent explanation didn't appear to Mummy at all. So she hires detectives to watch me, to see if she can't somehow get me into the *News of the World*. All so that I shan't carry off her daughter on that poor old charger of mine, all tricked out and caparisoned in discredited passions and ideals! The old grey mare that actually once led the charge against the old order—well, she certainly ain't what she used to be. It was all she could do to carry me, but your weight *(to* ALISON*)* was too much for her. She just dropped dead on the way.

CLIFF: *(quietly).* Don't let's brawl, boyo. It won't do any good.

JIMMY: Why *don't* we brawl? It's the only thing left I'm any good at.

CLIFF: Jimmy, boy——

JIMMY: *(to* ALISON*).* You've let this genuflecting sin jobber win you over, haven't you? She's got you back, hasn't she?

HELENA: Oh for heaven's sake, don't be such a bully! You've no right to talk about her mother like that!

JIMMY: *(capable of anything now).* I've got every right. That old bitch should be dead! *(To* ALISON.*)* Well? Aren't I right?

(CLIFF and HELENA *look at* ALISON *tensely, but she just gazes at her plate.)*

I said she's an old bitch, and should be dead!

What's the matter with you? Why don't you leap to her defence!

(CLIFF gets up quickly, and takes his arm.)

CLIFF: Jimmy, don't!

(JIMMY pushes him back savagely, and he sits down helplessly, turning his head away on to his hand.)

JIMMY: If someone said something like that about me, she'd react soon enough—she'd spring into her well known lethargy, and say nothing! I say she ought to be dead. *(He brakes for a fresh spurt later. He's saving his strength for the knock-out.)* My God, those worms will need a dose of salts the day they get through her! Oh what a bellyache you've got coming to you, my little wormy ones! Alison's mother is on the way! *(In what he intends to be a comic declamatory voice.)* She will pass away, my friends, leaving a trail of worms gasping for laxatives behind her—from purgatives to purgatory.

(He smiles down at ALISON, *but still she hasn't broken.* CLIFF *won't look at them. Only* HELENA *looks at him. Denied the other two he addresses her.)*

Is anything the matter?

HELENA: I feel rather sick, that's all. Sick with contempt and loathing.

(He can feel her struggling on the end of his line, and he looks at her rather absently.)

JIMMY: One day, when I'm no longer spending my days running a sweet-stall, I may write a book about us all. It's all here. *(Slapping his forehead.)* Written in flames a mile high. And it won't be recollected in tranquillity either, picking daffodils with Auntie Wordsworth. It'll be recollected in fire, and blood. My blood.

HELENA: *(thinking patient reasonableness may be worth a try).* She simply said that she's going to church with me. I don't see why that calls for this incredible outburst.

JIMMY: Don't you? Perhaps you're not as clever as I thought.

HELENA: You think the world's treated you pretty badly, don't you?

ALISON: *(turning her face away L.)* Oh, don't try and take his suffering away from him—he'd be lost without it.

(He looks at her in surprise, but he turns back to HELENA. ALISON *can have her turn again later.)*

JIMMY: I thought this play you're touring in finished up on Saturday week?

HELENA: That's right.

630   JIMMY: Eight days ago, in fact.

HELENA: Alison wanted me to stay.

JIMMY: What are you plotting?

HELENA: Don't you think we've had enough of the heavy villian?

JIMMY: *(to* ALISON*)*. You don't believe in all that stuff. Why you don't believe in anything. You're just doing it to be vindictive, aren't you? Why—why are you letting her influence you like this?

640   ALISON: *(starting to break)*. Why, why, why, why! *(Putting her hands over her ears.)* That word's pulling my head off!

JIMMY: And as long as you're around, I'll go on using it.

(He crosses down to the armchair, and seats himself on the back of it. He addresses HELENA's *back.)*

JIMMY: The last time she was in a church was when she was married to me. I expect that surprises you, doesn't it? It was expediency, pure and
650   simple. We were in a hurry, you see. *(The comedy of this strikes him at once, and he laughs.)* Yes, we were actually in a hurry! Lusting for the slaughter! Well, the local registrar was a particular pal of Daddy's, and we knew he'd spill the beans to the Colonel like a shot. So we had to seek out some local vicar who didn't know him quite so well. But it was no use. When my best man—a chap I'd met in the pub that morning—and I turned up, Mummy and Daddy were in the
660   church already. They'd found out at the last moment, and had come to watch the execution carried out. How I remember looking down at them, full of beer for breakfast, and feeling a bit buzzed. Mummy was slumped over her pew in a heap—the noble, female rhino, pole-axed at last! And Daddy sat beside her, upright and unafraid, dreaming of his days among the Indian Princes, and unable to believe he'd left his horse-whip at home. Just the two of them in that empty
670   church—them and me. *(Coming out of his remembrance suddenly.)* I'm not sure what happened after that. We must have been married, I suppose. I think I remember being sick in the vestry. *(To* ALISON.*)* Was I?

HELENA: Haven't you finished?

(He can smell blood again, and he goes on calmly, cheerfully.)

JIMMY: *(to* ALISON*)*. Are you going to let yourself be taken in by this saint in Dior's clothing? I will tell you the simple truth about her. *(Ar-*   680
ticulating with care.) She is a cow. I wouldn't mind that so much, but she seems to have become a sacred cow as well!

CLIFF: You've gone too far, Jimmy. Now dry up!

HELENA: Oh, let him go on.

JIMMY: *(to* CLIFF*)*. I suppose you're going over to that side as well. Well, why don't you? Helena will help to make it pay off for you. She's an expert in the New Economics—the Economics of the Supernatural. It's all a simple matter of   690
payments and penalties. *(Rises.)* She's one of those apocalyptic share pushers who are spreading all those rumours about a transfer of power.

(His imagination is racing, and the words pour out.)

Reason and Progress, the old firm, is selling out! Everyone get out while the going's good. Those forgotten shares you had in the old traditions, the old beliefs are going up—up and up and up. *(Moves up L.)* There's going to be a change over. A new Board of Directors, who are going   700
to see that the dividends are always attractive, and that they go to the right people. *(Facing them.)* Sell out everything you've got: all those stocks in the old, free inquiry. *(Crosses to above table.)* The Big Crash is coming, you can't escape it, so get in on the ground floor with Helena and her friends while there's still time. And there isn't much of it left. Tell me, what could be more gilt-edged than the next world! It's a capital gain, and it's all yours.   710

(He moves round the table, back to his chair R.)

You see, I know Helena and her kind so very well. In fact, her kind are everywhere, you can't move for them. They're a romantic lot. They spend their time mostly looking forward to the past. The only place they can see the light is the Dark Ages. She's moved long ago into a lovely little cottage of the soul, cut right off from the ugly problems of the twentieth century altogether. She prefers to be cut off from all the conveniences we've fought to get for centuries. She'd rather go down to the ecstatic little shed at the bottom of the garden to relieve her sense of guilt. Our Helena is full of ecstatic wind——*(he leans across the table at her)* aren't you?

(He waits for her to reply.)

HELENA: *(quite calmly).* It's a pity you've been so far away all this time. I would probably have slapped your face.

(They look into each other's eyes across the table. He moves slowly up, above CLIFF, *until he is beside her.)*

You've behaved like this ever since I first came.
JIMMY: Helena, have you ever watched somebody die?

(She makes a move to rise.)

No, don't move away.

(She remains seated, and looks up at him.)

It doesn't look dignified enough for you.
HELENA: *(like ice).* If you come any nearer, I will slap your face.

(He looks down at her, a grin smouldering round his mouth.)

JIMMY: I hope you won't make the mistake of thinking for one moment that I am a gentleman.
HELENA: I'm not very likely to do that.
JIMMY: *(bringing his face close to hers).* I've no public school scruples about hitting girls. *(Gently.)* If you slap my face—by God, I'll lay you out!
HELENA: You probably would. You're the type.
JIMMY: You bet I'm the type. I'm the type that detests physical violence. Which is why, if I find some woman trying to cash in on what she thinks is my defenceless chivalry by lashing out with her frail little fists, I lash back at her.
HELENA: Is that meant to be subtle, or just plain Irish?

(His grin widens.)

JIMMY: I think you and I understand one another

all right. But you haven't answered my question. I said: have you watched somebody die?
HELENA: No, I haven't.
JIMMY: Anyone who's never watched somebody die is suffering from a pretty bad case of virginity.

(His good humour of a moment ago deserts him, as he begins to remember.)

For twelve months, I watched my father dying—when I was ten years old. He'd come back from the war in Spain, you see. And certain god-fearing gentlemen there had made such a mess of him, he didn't have long left to live. Everyone knew it—even I knew it.

(He moves R.)

But, you see, I was the only one who cared. *(Turns to the window.)* His family were embarrassed by the whole business. Embarrassed and irritated. *(Looking out.)* As for my mother, all she could think about was the fact that she had allied herself to a man who seemed to be on the wrong side in all things. My mother was all for being associated with minorities, provided they were the smart, fashionable ones.

(He moves up C. again.)

We all of us waited for him to die. The family sent him a cheque every month, and hoped he'd get on with it quietly, without too much vulgar fuss. My mother looked after him without complaining, and that was about all. Perhaps she pitied him. I suppose she was capable of that. *(With a kind of appeal in his voice.)* But *I* was the only one who cared!

(He moves L., behind the armchair.)

Every time I sat on the edge of his bed, to listen to him talking or reading to me, I had to fight back my tears. At the end of twelve months, I was a veteran.

(He leans forward on the back of the armchair.)

All that that feverish failure of a man had to listen to him was a small, frightened boy. I spent hour upon hour in that tiny bedroom. He would talk to me for hours, pouring out all that was left of his life to one, lonely, bewildered little boy, who could barely understand half of what he said. All he could feel was the despair and the bitterness, the sweet, sickly smell of a dying man.

(He moves around the chair.)

810   You see, I learnt at an early age what it was to be angry—angry and helpless. And I can never forget it. *(Sits.)* I knew more about—love . . . betrayal . . . and death, when I was ten years old than you will probably ever know all your life.

(They all sit silently. Presently, HELENA *rises.)*
HELENA: Time we went.

*(*ALISON *nods.)*

I'll just get my things together. *(Crosses to door.)* I'll see you downstairs.

(Exit.)

820   *(A slight pause.)*

JIMMY: *(not looking at her, almost whispering.)* Doesn't it matter to you—what people do to me? What are you trying to do to me? I've given you just everything. Doesn't it mean *anything* to you?

(Her back stiffens. His axe-swinging bravado has vanished, and his voice crumples in disabled rage.)

You Judas! You phlegm! She's taking you with her, and you're so bloody feeble, you'll let her do it!

830   *(*ALISON *suddenly takes hold of her cup, and hurls it on the floor. He's drawn blood at last. She looks down at the pieces on the floor, and then at him. Then she crosses, R., takes out a dress on a hanger, and slips it on. As she is zipping up the side, she feels giddy, and she has to lean against the wardrobe for support. She closes her eyes.)*

ALISON: *(softly).* All I want is a little peace.
JIMMY: Peace! God! She wants peace! *(Hardly able to get his words out.)* My heart is so full, I feel 840   ill—and she wants peace!

(She crosses to the bed to put on her shoes. CLIFF *gets up from the table, and sits in the armchair R. He picks up a paper, and looks at that.* JIMMY *has recovered slightly, and manages to sound almost detached.)*

I rage, and shout my head off, and everyone thinks "poor chap!" or "what an objectionable young man!" But that girl there can twist your arm off with her silence. I've sat in this chair in the dark for hours. And, although she knows 850   I'm feeling as I feel now, she's turned over, and gone to sleep. *(He gets up and faces* CLIFF, *who doesn't look up from his paper.)* One of us is crazy. One of us is mean and stupid and crazy. Which is it? Is it me? Is it me, standing here like an hysterical girl, hardly able to get my words out? Or is it her? Sitting there, putting on her shoes to go out with that——(But inspiration has deserted him by now.)* Which is it?

*(*CLIFF *is still looking down at his paper.)*

I wish to heaven you'd try loving her, that's 860   all.

(He moves up C., watching her look for her gloves.)

Perhaps, one day, you may want to come back. I shall wait for that day. I want to stand up in your tears, and splash about in them, and sing. I want to be there when you grovel. I want to be there, I want to watch it, I want the front seat.

*(*HELENA *enters, carrying two prayer books.)*

I want to see your face rubbed in the mud—that's 870   all I can hope for. There's nothing else I want any longer.
HELENA: *(after a moment).* There's a 'phone call for you.
JIMMY: *(turning).* Well, it can't be anything good, can it?

(He goes out.)

HELENA: All ready?
ALISON: Yes—I think so.
HELENA: You feel all right, don't you? *(She nods.)* 880   What's he been raving about now? Oh, what does it matter? He makes me want to claw his hair out by the roots. When I think of what you will be going through in a few months' time—and all for him! It's as if you'd done *him* wrong! These *men!* *(Turning on* CLIFF.)* And all the time you just sit there, and do nothing!

CLIFF: *(looking up slowly).* That's right—I just sit here.

890 HELENA: What's the matter with you? What sort of a man are you?

CLIFF: I'm not the District Commissioner, you know. Listen, Helena—I don't feel like Jimmy does about you, but I'm not exactly on your side either. And since you've been here, everything's certainly been worse than it's ever been. This has always been a battlefield, but I'm pretty certain that if I hadn't been here, everything would have been over between these two long 900 ago. I've been a—a no-man's land between them. Sometimes, it's been still and peaceful, no incidents, and we've all been reasonably happy. But most of the time, it's simply a very narrow strip of plain hell. But where I come from, we're used to brawling and excitement. Perhaps I even enjoy being in the thick of it. I love these two people very much. *(He looks at her steadily, and adds simply)* And I pity all of us.

HELENA: Are you including me in that? *(But she* 910 *goes on quickly to avoid his reply.)* I don't understand him, you or any of it. All I know is that none of you seems to know how to behave in a decent, civilised way. *(In command now.)* Listen, Alison—I've sent your father a wire.

ALISON: *(numbed and vague by now).* Oh!

(HELENA looks at her, and realizes quickly that everything now will have to depend on her own authority. She tries to explain patiently.)

HELENA: Look, dear—he'll get it first thing in the 920 morning. I thought it would be better than trying to explain the situation over the 'phone. I asked him to come up, and fetch you home tomorrow.

ALISON: What did you say?

HELENA: Simply that you wanted to come home, and would he come up for you.

ALISON: I see.

HELENA: I knew that would be quite enough. I told him there was nothing to worry about, so they won't worry and think there's been an acci- 930 dent or anything. I had to do something, dear. *(Very gently.)* You didn't mind, did you?

ALISON: No, I don't mind. Thank you.

HELENA: And you will go when he comes for you?

ALISON: *(Pause.)* Yes. I'll go.

HELENA: *(relieved).* I expect he'll drive up. He should be here about tea-time. It'll give you plenty of time to get your things together. And, perhaps, after you've gone—Jimmy *(saying the word almost with difficulty)* will come to his senses, and face up to things. 940

ALISON: Who was on the 'phone?

HELENA: I didn't catch it properly. It rang after I'd sent the wire off—just as soon as I put the receiver down almost. I had to go back down the stairs again. Sister somebody, I think.

ALISON: Must have been a hospital or something. Unless he knows someone in a convent—*that* doesn't seem very likely, does it? Well, we'll be late, if we don't hurry. *(She puts down one of the prayer books on the table.)* 950

(Enter JIMMY. He comes down C., between the two women.)

CLIFF: All right, boyo?

JIMMY: *(to ALISON).* It's Hugh's mum. She's—had a stroke.

(Slight pause.)

ALISON: I'm sorry.

(JIMMY sits on the bed.)

CLIFF: How bad is it?

JIMMY: They didn't say much. But I think she's 960 dying.

CLIFF: Oh dear....

JIMMY: *(rubbing his fist over his face).* It doesn't make any sense at all. Do you think it does?

ALISON: I'm sorry—I really am.

CLIFF: Anything I can do?

JIMMY: The London train goes in half an hour. You'd better order me a taxi.

CLIFF: Right. *(He crosses to the door, and stops.)* Do you want me to come with you, boy? 970

JIMMY: No thanks. After all, you hardly knew her. It's not for you to go.

(HELENA looks quickly at ALISON.)

She may not even remember me, for all I know.

CLIFF: O.K.

(Exit.)

JIMMY: I remember the first time I showed her your photograph—just after we were married. She looked at it, and the tears just welled up in her eyes, and she said: "But she's so beautiful! She's so beautiful!" She kept repeating it as if she couldn't believe it. Sounds a bit simple and senti- mental when you repeat it. But it was pure gold the way she said it.

(He looks at her. She is standing by the dressing table, her back to him.)

She got a kick out of you, like she did out of everything else. Hand me my shoes, will you?

(She kneels down, and hands them to him.)

(looking down at his feet.) You're coming with me, aren't you? She *(he shrugs)* hasn't got anyone else now. I... need you... to come with me.

(He looks into her eyes, but she turns away, and stands up. Outside, the church bells start ringing. HELENA *moves up to the door, and waits watching them closely.* ALISON *stands quite still,* JIMMY'S *eyes burning into her. Then she crosses in front of him to the table where she picks up the prayer book, her back to him. She wavers, and seems about to say something, but turns upstage instead, and walks quickly to the door.)*

ALISON: *(hardly audible).* Let's go.

(She goes out, HELENA *following.* JIMMY *gets up, looks about him unbelievingly, and leans against the chest of drawers. The teddy bear is close to his face, and he picks it up gently, looks at it quickly, and throws it downstage. It hits the floor with a thud, and it makes a rattling, groaning sound—as guaranteed in the advertisement.* JIMMY *falls forward on to the bed, his face buried in the covers.)*

Quick Curtain

SCENE TWO

The following evening. When the curtain rises, ALISON *is discovered R., going from her dressing table to the bed, and packing her things into a suitcase. Sitting down L. is her father,* COLONEL REDFERN, *a large handsome man, about sixty. Forty years of being a soldier sometimes conceals the essentially gentle, kindly man underneath.*

Brought up to command respect, he is often slightly with- drawn and uneasy now that he finds himself in a world where his authority has lately become less and less unques- tionable. His wife would relish the present situation, but he is only disturbed and bewildered by it. He looks around him, discreetly scrutinising everything.

———————

COLONEL: *(partly to himself).* I'm afraid it's all beyond me. I suppose it always will be. As for Jimmy—he just speaks a different language from any of us. Where did you say he'd gone?

ALISON: He's gone to see Mrs. Tanner.

COLONEL: Who?

ALISON: Hugh Tanner's mother.

COLONEL: Oh, I see.

ALISON: She's been taken ill—a stroke. Hugh's abroad, as you know, so Jimmy's gone to London to see her.

(He nods.)

He wanted me to go with him.

COLONEL: Didn't she start him off in this sweet-stall business?

ALISON: Yes.

COLONEL: What is she like? Nothing like her son, I trust?

ALISON: Not remotely. Oh—how can you describe her? Rather—ordinary. What Jimmy insists on calling working class. A Charwoman who mar- ried an actor, worked hard all her life, and spent most of it struggling to support her husband and her son. Jimmy and she are very fond of each other.

COLONEL: So you didn't go with him?

ALISON: No.

COLONEL: Who's looking after the sweet-stall?

ALISON: Cliff. He should be in soon.

COLONEL: Oh yes, of course—Cliff. Does he live here too?

ALISON: Yes. His room is just across the landing.

COLONEL: Sweet-stall. It does seem an extraordi- nary thing for an educated young man to be occupying himself with. Why should he want to do that, of all things. I've always thought he must be quite clever in his way.

ALISON: *(no longer interested in this problem).* Oh, he tried so many things—journalism, advertising,

40 even vacuum cleaners for a few weeks. He seems
to have been as happy doing this as anything
else.
COLONEL: I've often wondered what it was
like—where you were living, I mean. You didn't
tell us very much in your letters.
ALISON: There wasn't a great deal to tell you.
There's not much social life here.
COLONEL: Oh, I know what you mean. You were
afraid of being disloyal to your husband.
50 ALISON: Disloyal! (She laughs.) He thought it was
high treason of me to write to you at all! I used
to have to dodge downstairs for the post, so that
he wouldn't see I was getting letters from home.
Even then I had to hide them.
COLONEL: He really does hate us doesn't he?
ALISON: Oh yes—don't have any doubts about
that. He hates all of us.
COLONEL: (sighs). It seems a great pity. It was all
so unfortunate—unfortunate and unnecessary.
60 I'm afraid I can't help feeling that he must have
had a certain amount of right on his side.
ALISON: (puzzled by this admission). Right on his side?
COLONEL: It's a little late to admit it, I know, but
your mother and I weren't entirely free from
blame. I have never said anything—there was
no point afterwards—but I have always believed
that she went too far over Jimmy. Of course,
she was extremely upset at the time—we both
were—and that explains a good deal of what
70 happened. I did my best to stop her, but she
was in such a state of mind, there was simply
nothing I could do. She seemed to have made
up her mind that if he was going to marry you,
he must be a criminal, at the very least. All
those inquiries, the private detectives—the
accusations. I hated every moment of it.
ALISON: I suppose she was trying to protect me—in
a rather heavy-handed way, admittedly.
COLONEL: I must confess I find that kind of thing
80 rather horrifying. Anyway, I try to think now
that it never happened. I didn't approve of
Jimmy at all, and I don't suppose I ever should,
but, looking back on it, I think it would have
been better, for all concerned, if we had never
attempted to interfere. At least, it would have
been a little more dignified.
ALISON: It wasn't your fault.
COLONEL: I don't know. We were all to blame, in

our different ways. No doubt Jimmy acted in
good faith. He's honest enough, whatever else 90
he may be. And your mother—in her heavy-
handed way, as you put it—acted in good faith
as well. Perhaps you and I were the ones most
to blame.
ALISON: You and I!
COLONEL: I think you may take after me a little,
my dear. You like to sit on the fence because
it's comfortable and more peaceful.
ALISON: Sitting on the fence! I married him, didn't
I. 100
COLONEL: Oh yes, you did.
ALISON: In spite of all the humiliating scenes and
the threats! What did you say to me at the time?
Wasn't I letting you down, turning against you,
how could I do this to you etcetera?
COLONEL: Perhaps it might have been better if you
hadn't written letters to us—knowing how we
felt about your husband, and after everything
that had happened. (He looks at her uncomfortably.)
Forgive me, I'm a little confused, what with 110
everything—the telegram, driving up here suddenly. . . .

(He trails off rather helplessly. He looks tired. He glances
at her nervously, a hint of accusation in his eyes, as
if he expected her to defend herself further. She senses
this, and is more confused than ever.)

ALISON: Do you know what he said about
Mummy? He said she was an overfed, over-
privileged old bitch. "A good blow-out for the
worms" was his expression, I think. 120
COLONEL: I see. And what does he say about me?
ALISON: Oh, he doesn't seem to mind you so much.
In fact, I think he rather likes you. He likes
you because he can feel sorry for you. (Conscious
that what she says is going to hurt him.) "Poor old
Daddy—just one of those sturdy old plants left
over from the Edwardian Wilderness that can't
understand why the sun isn't shining any more."
(Rather lamely.) Something like that, anyway.
COLONEL: He has quite a turn of phrase, hasn't 130
he? (Simply, and without malice.) Why did you
ever have to meet this young man?
ALISON: Oh, Daddy, please don't put me on trial
now. I've been on trial every day and night of
my life for nearly four years.

COLONEL: But why should he have married you, feeling as he did about everything?

ALISON: That is the famous American question—you know, the sixty-four dollar one! Perhaps it was revenge.

(*He looks up uncomprehendingly.*)

Oh yes. Some people do actually marry for revenge. People like Jimmy, anyway. Or perhaps he should have been another Shelley, and can't understand now why I'm not another Mary, and you're not William Godwin. He thinks he's got a sort of genius for love and friendship—on his own terms. Well, for twenty years, I'd lived a happy, uncomplicated life, and suddenly, this—this spiritual barbarian—throws down the gauntlet at me. Perhaps only another woman could understand what a challenge like that means—although I think Helena was as mystified as you are.

COLONEL: I am mystified. (*He rises, and crosses to the window R.*). Your husband has obviously taught you a great deal, whether you realise it or not. What any of it means, I don't know. I always believed that people married each other because they were in love. That always seemed a good enough reason to me. But apparently, that's too simple for young people nowadays. They have to talk about challenges and revenge. I just can't believe that love between men and women is really like that.

ALISON: Only some men and women.

COLONEL: But why you? My daughter. ... No. Perhaps Jimmy is right. Perhaps I am a—what was it? an old plant left over from the Edwardian Wilderness. And I can't understand why the sun isn't shining any more. You can see what he means, can't you? It was March, 1914, when I left England, and, apart from leaves every ten years or so, I didn't see much of my own country until we all came back in '47. Oh, I knew things had changed, of course. People told you all the time the way it was going—going to the dogs, as the Blimps are supposed to say. But it seemed very unreal to me, out there. The England I remembered was the one I left in 1914, and I was happy to go on remembering it that way. Beside, I had the Maharajah's army to command

—that was my world, and I loved it, all of it. At the time, it looked like going on forever. When I think of it now, it seems like a dream. If only it could have gone on forever. Those long, cool evenings up in the hills, everything purple and golden. Your mother and I were so happy then. It seemed as though we had everything we could ever want. I think the last day the sun shone was when that dirty little train steamed out of that crowded, suffocating Indian station, and the battalion band playing for all it was worth. I knew in my heart it was all over then. Everything.

ALISON: You're hurt because everything is changed. Jimmy is hurt because everything is the same. And neither of you can face it. Something's gone wrong somewhere, hasn't it?

COLONEL: It looks like it, my dear.

(*She picks up the squirrel from the chest of drawers, is about to put it in her suitcase, hesitates, and then puts it back. The* COLONEL *turns and looks at her. She moves down towards him, her head turned away. For a few moments, she seems to be standing on the edge of choice. The choice made, her body wheels round suddenly, and she is leaning against him, weeping softly.*)

(*presently*) This is a big step you're taking. You've made up your mind to come back with me? Is that really what you want?

(*Enter* HELENA.)

HELENA: I'm sorry. I came in to see if I could help you pack, Alison. Oh, you look as though you've finished.

(ALISON *leaves her father, and moves to the bed, pushing down the lid of her suitcase.*)

ALISON: All ready.

HELENA: Have you got everything?

ALISON: Well, no. But Cliff can send the rest on sometime, I expect. He should have been back by now. Oh, of course, he's had to put the stall away on his own today.

COLONEL: (*crossing and picking up the suitcase*). Well, I'd better put this in the car then. We may as well get along. Your mother will be worried, I know. I promised her I'd ring her when I got here. She's not very well.

HELENA: I hope my telegram didn't upset her too
much. Perhaps I shouldn't have—

230 COLONEL: Not at all. We were very grateful that
you did. It was very kind of you, indeed. She
tried to insist on coming with me, but I finally
managed to talk her out of it. I thought it would
be best for everyone. What about your case,
Helena? If you care to tell me where it is, I'll
take it down with this one.

HELENA: I'm afraid I shan't be coming tonight.

ALISON: (*very surprised*). Aren't you coming with
us? (*Enter* CLIFF.)

240 HELENA: I'd like to, but the fact is I've an appointment tomorrow in Birmingham—about a job.
They've just sent me a script. It's rather important, and I don't want to miss it. So it looks
as though I shall have to stay here tonight.

ALISON: Oh, I see. Hullo, Cliff.

CLIFF: Hullo there.

ALISON: Daddy—this is Cliff.

COLONEL: How do you do, Cliff.

CLIFF: How do you do, sir.

250 (*Slight pause.*)

COLONEL:Well, I'd better put this in the car, hadn't
I? Don't be long, Alison. Good-bye, Helena.
I expect we shall be seeing you again soon, if
you're not busy.

HELENA: Oh, yes, I shall be back in a day or two.

(CLIFF *takes off his jacket.*)

COLONEL: Well, then—good-bye, Cliff.

CLIFF: Good-bye, sir.

(*The* COLONEL *goes out.* CLIFF *comes down* L. HELENA
260 *moves* C.)

You're really going then?

ALISON: Really going.

CLIFF: I should think Jimmy would be back pretty
soon. You won't wait?

ALISON: No, Cliff.

CLIFF: Who's going to tell him?

HELENA: I can tell him. That is, if I'm here when
he comes back.

CLIFF: (*quietly*). You'll be here. (*To* ALISON.) Don't
270 you think you ought to tell him yourself?

(*She hands him an envelope from her handbag. He takes
it.*)

Bit conventional, isn't it?

ALISON: I'm a conventional girl.

(*He crosses to her, and puts his arms round her.*)

CLIFF: (*back over his shoulder, to* HELENA). I hope
you're right, that's all.

HELENA: What do you mean? You hope *I'm* right?

CLIFF: (*to* ALISON). The place is going to be really
cock-eyed now. You know that, don't you? 280

ALISON: Please, Cliff—

(*He nods. She kisses him.*)

I'll write to you later.

CLIFF: Good-bye, lovely.

ALISON: Look after him.

CLIFF: We'll keep the old nut-house going somehow.

(*She crosses* C., *in between the two of them, glances
quickly at the two armchairs, the papers still left around
them from yesterday.* HELENA *kisses her on the cheek,* 290
and squeezes her hand.)

HELENA: See you soon.

(ALISON *nods, and goes out quickly.* CLIFF *and* HELENA
are left looking at each other.)

Would you like me to make you some tea?

CLIFF: No, thanks.

HELENA: Think I might have some myself, if you
don't mind.

CLIFF: So you're staying?

HELENA: Just for tonight. Do you object? 300

CLIFF: Nothing to do with me. (*Against the table
C.*) Of course he may not be back until later
on.

(*She crosses* L., *to the window, and lights a cigarette.*)

HELENA: What do you think he'll do? Perhaps he'll
look out one of his old girl friends. What about
this Madeline?

CLIFF: What about her?

HELENA: Isn't she supposed to have done a lot for
him? Couldn't he go back to her? 310

CLIFF: I shouldn't think so.

HELENA: What happened?

CLIFF: She was nearly old enough to be his mother.
I expect that's something to do with it! Why
the hell should I know!

(*For the first time in the play, his good humour has
completely deserted him. She looks surprised.*)

HELENA: You're his friend, aren't you? Anyway, he's not what you'd call reticent about himself, is he? I've never seen so many souls stripped to the waist since I've been here.

(He turns to go.)

HELENA: Aren't you staying?

CLIFF: No, I'm not. There was a train in from London about five minutes ago. And, just in case he may have been on it, I'm going out.

HELENA: Don't you think you ought to be here when he comes?

CLIFF: I've had a hard day, and I don't think I want to see anyone hurt until I've had something to eat first, and perhaps a few drinks as well. I think I might pick up some nice, pleasant little tart in a milk bar, and sneak her in past old mother Drury. Here! *(Tossing the letter at her.)* You give it to him! *(Crossing to door.)* He's all yours. *(At door.)* And I hope he rams it up your nostrils!

(Exit.)

(She crosses to the table, and stubs out her cigarette. The front door downstairs is heard to slam. She moves to the wardrobe, opens it idly. It is empty, except for one dress, swinging on a hanger. She goes over to the dressing table, now cleared but for a framed photograph of JIMMY. Idly, she slams the empty drawers open and shut. She turns upstage to the chest of drawers, picks up the toy bear, and sits on the bed, looking at it. She lays her head back on the pillow, still holding the bear. She looks up quickly as the door crashes open, and JIMMY enters. He stands looking at her, then moves down C., taking off his raincoat, and throwing it over the table. He is almost giddy with anger, and has to steady himself on the chair. He looks up.)

JIMMY: That old bastard nearly ran me down in his car! Now, if he'd killed me, that really would have been ironical. And how right and fitting that my wife should have been a passenger. A passenger! What's the matter with everybody? *(Crossing up to her.)* Cliff practically walked into me, coming out of the house. He belted up the other way, and pretended not to see me. Are you the only one who's not afraid to stay?

(She hands him ALISON's note. He takes it.)

Oh, it's one of these, is it? *(He rips it open.)*

(He reads a few lines, and almost snorts with disbelief.)

Did you write this for her! Well, listen to this then! *(Reading.)* "My dear—I must get away. I don't suppose you will understand, but please try. I need peace so desperately, and, at the moment, I am willing to sacrifice everything just for that. I don't know what's going to happen to us. I know you will be feeling wretched and bitter, but try to be a little patient with me. I shall always have a deep loving need of you—Alison." Oh, how could she be so bloody wet! Deep loving need! That makes me puke! *(Crossing to R.)* She couldn't say "You rotten bastard! I hate your guts, I'm clearing out, and I hope you rot!" No, she has to make a polite, emotional mess out of it! *(Seeing the dress in the wardrobe, he rips it out, and throws it in the corner up L.)* Deep, loving need! I never thought she was capable of being as phoney as that. What is that—a line from one of those plays you've been in? What are you doing here anyway? You'd better keep out of my way, if you don't want your head kicked in.

HELENA: *(calmly).* If you'll stop thinking about yourself for one moment, I'll tell you something I think you ought to know. Your wife is going to have a baby.

(He just looks at her.)

Well? Doesn't that mean anything? Even to you?

(He is taken aback, but not so much by the news, as by her.)

JIMMY: All right—yes. I am surprised. I give you that. But, tell me. Did you honestly expect me to go soggy at the knees, and collapse with remorse! *(Leaning nearer.)* Listen, if you'll stop breathing your female wisdom all over me, I'll tell you something: I don't care. *(Beginning quietly.)* I don't care if she's going to have a baby. I don't care if it has two heads! *(He knows her fingers are itching.)* Do I disgust you? Well, go on—slap my face. But remember what I told you before, will you? For eleven hours, I have been watching someone I love very much going through the sordid process of dying. She was

alone, and I was the only one with her. And
when I have to walk behind that coffin on Thurs-
410   day, I'll be on my own again. Because that bitch
won't even send her a bunch of flowers—I know!
She made the great mistake of all her kind. She
thought that because Hugh's mother was a deprived and ignorant old woman, who said all the
wrong things in all the wrong places, she couldn't
be taken seriously. And you think I should be
overcome with awe because that cruel, stupid
girl is going to have a baby! (*Anguish in his voice.*)

I can't believe it! I can't. (*Grabbing her shoulders.*)
Well, the performance is over. Now leave me   420
alone, and *get out*, you evil-minded little virgin.

(*She slaps his face savagely. An expression of horror and
disbelief floods his face. But it drains away, and all
that is left is pain. His hand goes up to his head, and
a muffled cry of despair escapes him.* HELENA *tears his
hand away, and kisses him passionately, drawing him
down beside her.*)

Curtain

ACT III

SCENE ONE

Several months later. A Sunday evening. ALISON'S
*personal belongings, such as her make-up things on the
dressing table, for example, have been replaced by*
HELENA'S. *At rise of curtain, we find* JIMMY *and* CLIFF
*sprawled in their respective armchairs, immersed in the
Sunday newspapers.* HELENA *is standing down L. leaning
over the ironing board, a small pile of clothes beside
her. She looks more attractive than before, for the setting
of her face is more relaxed. She still looks quite smart,
but in an unpremeditated, careless way; she wears an
old shirt of* JIMMY'S.

CLIFF: That stinking old pipe!

(*Pause.*)

JIMMY: Shut up.
CLIFF: Why don't you do something with it?
JIMMY: Why do I spend half of Sunday reading
    the papers?
CLIFF: (*kicks him without lowering his paper*). It stinks!
JIMMY: So do you, but I'm not singing an aria about
    it. (*Turns to the next page.*) The dirty ones get
10   more and more wet round the mouth, and the
    posh ones are more pompous than ever. (*Lowering

paper, and waving pipe at* HELENA.) Does this
    bother you?)
HELENA: No. I quite like it.
JIMMY: (*to* CLIFF). There you are—she likes it!

(*He returns to his paper.* CLIFF *grunts.*)

Have you read about the grotesque and evil prac-
    tices going on in the Midlands?
CLIFF: Read about the what?
JIMMY: Grotesque and evil practices going on in   20
    the Midlands.
CLIFF: No, what about 'em?
JIMMY: Seems we don't know the old place. It's
    all in here. Startling Revelations this week! Pic-
    tures too. Reconstructions of midnight invoca-
    tions to the Coptic Goddess of fertility.
HELENA: Sounds madly depraved.
JIMMY: Yes, it's rather us, isn't it? My gosh, look
    at 'em! Snarling themselves silly. Next week a
    well-known debutante relates how, during an   30
    evil orgy in Market Harborough, she killed and
    drank the blood of a white cockerel. Well—I'll
    bet Fortnums must be doing a roaring line in
    sacrificial cocks! (*Thoughtful.*) Perhaps that's
    what Miss Drury does on Sunday evenings. She
    puts in a stint as evil high priestess down at
    the Y.W.—probably having a workout at this

very moment. (*To* HELENA.) You never dabbled in this kind of thing did you?

40   HELENA: (*laughs*). Not lately!

JIMMY: Sounds rather your cup of tea—cup of blood, I should say. (*In an imitation of a midlands accent.*) Well, I mean, it gives you something to do, doesn't it? After all, it wouldn't do if we was all alike, would it? It'd be a funny world if we was all the same, that's what *I* always say! (*Resuming in his normal voice.*) All I know is what somebody's been sticking pins into *my* wax image for years. (*Suddenly.*) Of course:

50   Alison's mother! Every Friday, the wax arrives from Harrods, and all through the week-end, she's stabbing away at it with a hatpin! Ruined her bridge game, I dare say.

HELENA: Why don't *you* try it?

JIMMY: Yes, it's an idea. (*Pointing to* CLIFF.) Just for a start, we could roast him over the gas stove. Have we got enough shillings for the meter? It seems to be just the thing for these Autumn evenings. After all the whole point of a sacrifice

60   is that you give up something you never really wanted in the first place. You know what I mean? People are doing it around you all the time. They give up their careers, say—or their beliefs—or sex. And everyone thinks to themselves: how wonderful to be able to do that. If only I were capable of doing that! But the truth of it is that they've been kidding themselves, and they've been kidding you. It's not awfully difficult—giving up something you were incapable of ever

70   really wanting. We shouldn't be admiring them. We should feel rather sorry for them. (*Coming back from this sudden, brooding excursion, and turning to* CLIFF.) You'll make an admirable sacrifice.

CLIFF: (*mumbling*). Dry up! I'm trying to read.

JIMMY: Afterwards, we can make a loving cup from his blood. Can't say I fancy that so much. I've seen it—it looks like cochineal, ever so common. (*To* HELENA.) Yours would be much better—pale Cambridge blue, I imagine. No? And after-

80   wards, we could make invocations to the Coptic Goddess of fertility. Got any idea how you do that? (*To* CLIFF.) Do you know?

CLIFF: Shouldn't have thought *you* needed to make invocations to the Coptic whatever-she-is!

JIMMY: Yes, I see what you mean. (*To* HELENA.) Well, we don't want to *ask* for trouble, do we? Perhaps it might appeal to the lady here—she's written a long letter all about artificial insemination. It's headed: Haven't we tried God's pati-

90   ence enough! (*Throws the paper down.*) Let's see the other posh one.

CLIFF: Haven't finished yet.

JIMMY: Well, hurry up. I'll have to write and ask them to put hypens in between the syllables for you. There's a particularly savage correspondence going on in there about whether Milton wore braces or not. I just want to see who gets shot down this week.

CLIFF: Just read that. Don't know what it was

100   about, but a Fellow of All Souls seems to have bitten the dust, and the Athenaeum's going up in flames, so the Editor declares that this correspondence is now closed.

JIMMY: I think you're actually acquiring yourself a curiosity, my boy. Oh yes, and then there's an American professor from Yale or somewhere, who believes that when Shakespeare was writing *The Tempest*, he changed his sex, Yes, he was obliged to go back to Stratford because the other actors couldn't take him seriously any longer.

110   This professor chap is coming over here to search for certain documents which will prove that poor old W.S. ended up in someone else's second best bed—a certain Warwickshire farmer's, whom he married after having three children by him.

(HELENA *laughs.* JIMMY *looks up quizzically.*)

Is anything the matter?

HELENA: No, nothing. I'm only beginning to get used to him. I never (*this is to* CLIFF) used to be sure when he was being serious, or when

120   he wasn't.

CLIFF: Don't think he knows himself half the time. When in doubt, just mark it down as an insult.

JIMMY: Hurry up with that paper, and shut up! What are we going to do tonight? There's isn't even a decent concert on. (*To* HELENA.) Are you going to Church?

HELENA: (*rather taken aback*). No. I don't think so. Unless you want to.

JIMMY: Do I detect a growing, satanic glint in her   130

eyes lately? Do you think it's living in sin with me that does it? (*To* HELENA.) Do you feel very sinful my dear? Well? Do you?

(*She can hardly believe that this is an attack, and she can only look at him, uncertain of herself.*)

Do you feel sin crawling out of your ears, like stored up wax or something? Are you wondering whether I'm joking or not? Perhaps I ought to wear a red nose and funny hat. I'm just curious, 140   that's all.

(*She is shaken by the sudden coldness in his eyes, but before she has time to fully realise how hurt she is, he is smiling at her, and shouting cheerfully at* CLIFF.)

Let's have that paper, stupid!

CLIFF: Why don't you drop dead!

JIMMY: (*To* HELENA). Will you be much longer doing that?

HELENA: Nearly finished.

JIMMY: Talking of sin, wasn't that Miss Drury's 150   Reverend friend I saw you chatting with yesterday. Helena darling, I said wasn't that. . . .

HELENA: Yes it was.

JIMMY: My dear, you don't have to be on the defensive you know.

HELENA: I'm not on the defensive.

JIMMY: After all, there's no reason why we shouldn't have the parson to tea up here. Why don't we? Did you find that you had much in common?

HELENA: No I don't think so.

160   JIMMY: Do you think that some of this spiritual beefcake would make a man of me? Should I go in for this moral weight lifting and get myself some over-developed muscle? I was a liberal skinny weakling. I too was afraid to strip down to my soul, but now everyone looks at my superb physique in envy. I can perform any kind of press there is without betraying the least sign of passion or kindliness.

HELENA: All right Jimmy.

170   JIMMY: Two years ago I couldn't even lift up my head—now I have more uplift than a film starlet.

HELENA: Jimmy, can we have one day, just one day, without tumbling over religion or politics?

CLIFF: Yes, change the record old boy, or pipe down.

JIMMY: (*rising*). Thought of the title for a new song today. It's called "My mother's in the madhouse—that's why I'm in love with you." The lyrics are catchy too. I was thinking we might work it into the act.   180

HELENA: Good idea.

JIMMY: I was thinking we'd scrub Jock and Day, and call ourselves something else. "And jocund day stands tiptoed on the misty mountain tops." It's too intellectual! Anyway, I shouldn't think people will want to be reminded of that peculiar man's plays after Harvard and Yale have finished with him. How about something bright and snappy? I know—— What about—T. S. Eliot and Pam!   190

CLIFF: (*casually falling in with this familiar routine*). Mirth, mellerdy and madness!

JIMMY: (*sitting at the table R. and "strumming" it*). Bringing quips and strips for you?

(*They sing together.*)

"For we may be guilty, darling. . . . But we're both insane as well!"

(JIMMY *stands up, and rattles his lines off at almost unintelligible speed.*)

Ladies and gentlemen, as I was coming to the   200   theatre tonight, I was passing through the stage door, and a man comes up to me, and 'e says:

CLIFF: 'Ere! Have you seen nobody?

JIMMY: Have I seen who?

CLIFF: Have you seen nobody?

JIMMY: Of course, I haven't seen nobody! Kindly don't waste my time! Ladies and gentlemen, a little recitation entitled "She said she was called a little Gidding, but she was more like a gelding iron!" Thank you "She said she was called little   210   Gidding——"

CLIFF: Are you quite sure you haven't seen nobody?

JIMMY: Are you still here?

CLIFF: I'm looking for nobody!

JIMMY: *Will* you kindly go away! "She said she was called little Gidding——"

CLIFF: Well, I can't find nobody anywhere, and I'm supposed to give him this case!

JIMMY: Will you kindly stop interrupting per*lease*!   220

Can't you see I'm trying to entertain these ladies and gentlemen? Who is this nobody you're talking about?

CLIFF: I was told to come here and gives this case to nobody.

JIMMY: You were told to come here and give this case to nobody.

CLIFF: That's right. And when I gave it to him, nobody would give me a shilling.

230   JIMMY: And when you gave it to him, nobody would give you a shilling.

CLIFF: That's right.

JIMMY: Well, what about it?

CLIFF:. Nobody's not here!

JIMMY: Now, let me get this straight: when you say nobody's here, you don't mean nobody's here?

CLIFF: No.

JIMMY: No.

240   JIMMY: You mean—nobody's here.

CLIFF: That's right.

JIMMY: Well, why didn't you say so before?

HELENA: (not quite sure if this is really her cue). Hey! You down there!

JIMMY: Oh, it goes on for hours yet, but never mind. What is it, sir?

HELENA: (shouting). I think your sketch stinks! I say—I think your sketch stinks!

JIMMY: He thinks it stinks. And, who, pray, might you be?

250   HELENA: Me? Oh—(with mock modesty) I'm nobody.

JIMMY: Then here's your bloody case!

(He hurls a cushion at her, which hits the ironing board.)

HELENA: My ironing board!

(The two men do a Flanagan and Allen, moving slowly in step, as they sing.)

Now there's a certain little lady, and you all know who I mean,

She may have been to Roedean, but to me she's still a queen.

260   Someday I'm goin' to marry her, When times are not so bad,

Her mother doesn't care for me So I'll 'ave to ask 'er dad.

We'll build a little home for two, And have some quiet menage,

We'll send our kids to public school

And live on bread and marge.

Don't be afraid to sleep with your sweetheart, Just because she's better than you.   270

Those forgotten middle-classes may have fallen on their noses,

But a girl who's true blue, Will still have something left for you,

The angels up above, will know that you're in love

So don't be afraid to sleep with your sweetheart,

Just because she's better than you. . . .

They call me Sydney,   280

Just because she's better than you.

(But JIMMY has had enough of this gag by now, and he pushes CLIFF away.)

JIMMY: Your damned great feet! That's the second time you've kicked my ankle! It's no good—Helena will have to do it. Go on, go and make some tea, and we'll decide what we're going to do.

CLIFF: Make some yourself!

(He pushes him back violently, JIMMY loses his balance,   290
and falls over.)

JIMMY: You rough bastard!

(He leaps up, and they grapple, falling on to the floor with a crash. They roll about, grunting and gasping. CLIFF manages to kneel on JIMMY's chest.)

CLIFF: (breathing heavily). I want to read the papers!

JIMMY: You're a savage, a hooligan! You really are! Do you know that! You don't deserve to live in the same house with decent, sensitive people!

CLIFF: Are you going to dry up, or do I read the   300
papers down here?

(JIMMY makes a supreme effort, and CLIFF topples to the floor.)

JIMMY: You've made me wrench my guts!

(He pushes the struggling CLIFF down.)

CLIFF: Look what you're doing! You're ripping my shirt. Get off!

JIMMY: Well, what do you want to wear a shirt for? (Rising.) A tough character like you! Now go and make me some tea.   310

CLIFF: It's the only clean one I've got. Oh, you big oaf! (Getting up from the floor, and appealing to HELENA.) Look! It's filthy!

HELENA: Yes, it is. He's stronger than he looks. If you like to take it off now, I'll wash it through for you. It'll be dry by the time we want to go out.

(CLIFF *hesitates.*)

What's the matter, Cliff?

320 CLIFF: Oh, it'll be all right.

JIMMY: Give it to her, and quit moaning!

CLIFF: Oh, all right.

(*He takes it off, and gives it to her.*)

Thanks, Helena.

HELENA: (*taking it*). Right. I won't be a minute with it.

(*She goes out.* JIMMY *flops into his armchair. R.*)

JIMMY: (*amused*). You look like Marlon Brando or something. (*Slight pause.*) You don't care for
330 Helena, do you?

CLIFF: You didn't seem very keen yourself once. (*Hesitating, then quickly.*) It's not the same, is it?

JIMMY: (*irritably*). No, of course it's not the same, you idiot! It never is! Today's meal is always different from yesterday's and the last woman isn't the same as the one before. If you can't accept that, you're going to be pretty unhappy, my boy.

CLIFF: (*sits on the arm of his chair, and rubs his feet*).
340 Jimmy—I don't think I shall stay here much longer.

JIMMY: (*rather casually*). Oh, why not?

CLIFF: (*picking up his tone*). Oh, I don't know. I've just thought of trying somewhere different. The sweet-stall's all right, but I think I'd like to try something else. You're highly educated, and it suits you, but I need something a bit better.

JIMMY: Just as you like, my dear boy. It's your business, not mine.

350 CLIFF: And another thing—I think Helena finds it rather a lot of work to do with two chaps about the place. It won't be so much for her if there's just the two of you. Anyway, I think I ought to find some girl who'll just look after me.

JIMMY: Sounds like a good idea. Can't think who'd be stupid enough to team themselves up with you though. Perhaps Helena can think of some-body for you—one of her posh girl friends with lots of money, and no brains. That's what you
360 want.

CLIFF: Something like that.

JIMMY: Any idea what you're going to do?

CLIFF: Not much.

JIMMY: That sounds like you all right! Shouldn't think you'll last five minutes without me to explain the score to you.

CLIFF: (*grinning*). Don't suppose so.

JIMMY: You're such a scruffy little beast—I'll bet some respectable little madam from Pinner or
370 Guildford gobbles you up in six months. She'll marry you, send you out to work, and you'll end up as clean as a new pin.

CLIFF: (*chuckling*). Yes, I'm stupid enough for that too!

JIMMY: (*to himself*). I seem to spend my life saying good-bye.

(*Slight pause.*)

CLIFF: My feet hurt.

JIMMY: Try washing your socks. (*Slowly.*) It's a
380 funny thing. You've been loyal, generous and a good friend. But I'm quite prepared to see you wander off, find a new home, and make out on your own. And all because of something I want from that girl downstairs, something I know in my heart she's incapable of giving. You're worth a half a dozen Helenas to me or to anyone. And, if you were in my place, you'd do the same thing. Right?

CLIFF: Right.
390
JIMMY: Why, why, why, why do we let these women bleed us to death? Have you ever had a letter, and on it is franked "Please Give Your Blood Generously"? Well, the Postmaster-General does that, on behalf of all the women of the world. I suppose people of our generation aren't able to die for good causes any longer. We had all that done for us, in the thirties and the forties, when we were still kids. (*In his familiar, semi-serious mood.*) There aren't any good,
400 brave causes left. If the big bang does come, and we all get killed off, it won't be in aid of the old-fashioned, grand design. It'll just be for the Brave New-nothing-very-much-thank-you. About as pointless and inglorious as stepping in front of a bus. No, there's nothing left for

it, me boy, but to let yourself be butchered by the women.

(Enter HELENA.)

410 HELENA: Here you are, Cliff. (Handing him the shirt.)

CLIFF: Oh, thanks, Helena, very much. That's decent of you.

HELENA: Not at all. I should dry it over the gas—the fire in your room would be better. There won't be much room for it over that stove.

CLIFF: Right, I will. (Crosses to door.)

JIMMY: And hurry up about it, stupid. We'll all go out, and have a drink soon. (To HELENA.)

420 O.K.?

HELENA: O.K.

JIMMY: (shouting to CLIFF on his way out). But make me some tea first, you madcap little Charlie.

(She crosses down L.)

JIMMY: Darling, I'm sick of seeing you behind that damned ironing board!

HELENA: (wryly). Sorry.

JIMMY: Get yourself glammed up, and we'll hit the town. See you've put a shroud over Mummy,

430 I think you should have laid a Union Jack over it.

HELENA: Is anything wrong?

JIMMY: Oh, don't frown like that—you look like the presiding magistrate!

HELENA: How should I look?

JIMMY: As if your heart stirred a little when you looked at me.

HELENA: Oh, it does that all right.

JIMMY: Cliff tells me he's leaving us.

440 HELENA: I know. He told me last night.

JIMMY: Did he? I always seem to be at the end of the queue when they're passing information out.

HELENA: I'm sorry he's going.

JIMMY: Yes, so am I. He's a sloppy, irritating bastard, but he's got a big heart. You can forgive somebody almost anything for that. He's had to learn how to take it, and he knows how to hand it out. Come here.

450 (He is sitting on the arm of his chair. She crosses to him, and they look at each other. Then she puts out her hand, and runs it over his head, fondling his ear and neck.)

Right from that first night, you have always put out your hand to me first. As if you expected nothing, or worse than nothing, and didn't care. You made a good enemy, didn't you? What they call a worthy opponent. But then, when people put down their weapons, it doesn't mean they've necessarily stopped fighting. 460

HELENA: (steadily). I love you.

JIMMY: I think perhaps you do. Yes, I think perhaps you do. Perhaps it means something to lie with your victorious general in your arms. Especially, when he's heartily sick of the whole campaign, tired out, hungry and dry.

(His lips find her fingers, and he kisses them. She presses his head against her.)

You stood up, and came out to meet me. Oh, Helena— 470

(His face comes up to hers, and they embrace fiercely.)

Don't let anything go wrong!

HELENA: (softly). Oh, my darling——

JIMMY: Either you're with me or against me.

HELENA: I've always wanted you—always!

(They kiss again.)

JIMMY: T. S. Eliot and Pam, we'll make a good double. If you'll help me. I'll close that damned sweet-stall, and we'll start everything from scratch. What do you say? We'll get away from 480 this place.

HELENA: (nodding happily). I say that's wonderful.

JIMMY: (kissing her quickly). Put all that junk away, and we'll get out. We'll get pleasantly, joyfully tiddly, we'll gaze at each other tenderly and lecherously in "The Builder's Arms", and then we'll come back here, and I'll make such love to you, you'll not care about anything else at all.

(She moves away L., after kissing his hand.) 490

HELENA: I'll just change out of your old shirt. (Folding ironing board.)

JIMMY: (moving U.S. to door). Right. I'll hurry up the little man.

(But before he reaches the door, it opens and ALISON enters. She wears a raincoat, her hair is untidy, and she looks rather ill. There is a stunned pause.)

ALISON: (*quietly*). Hullo.

JIMMY: (*to* HELENA, *after a moment*). Friend of yours
500   to see you.

(*He goes out quickly, and the two women are left looking
at each other.*)

Quick Curtain

SCENE TWO

It is a few minutes later. From CLIFF'S *room, across
the landing, comes the sound of* JIMMY'S *jazz trumpet.
At rise of the Curtain,* HELENA *is standing L. of the
table, pouring out a cup of tea.* ALISON *is sitting on
the armchair R. She bends down and picks up* JIMMY'S
*pipe. Then she scoops up a little pile of ash from the
floor, and drops it in the ashtray on the arm of the
chair.*

ALISON: He still smokes this foul old stuff. I used
to hate it at first, but you get used to it.

HELENA: Yes.

ALISON: I went to the pictures last week, and some
old man was smoking it in front, a few rows
away. I actually got up, and sat right behind
him.

HELENA: (*coming down with cup of tea*). Here, have
this. It usually seems to help.

10 ALISON: (*taking it*). Thanks.

HELENA: Are you sure you feel all right now?

ALISON: (*nods*). It was just—oh, everything. It's my
own fault—entirely. I must be mad, coming here
like this. I'm sorry, Helena.

HELENA: Why should you be sorry—you of all
people?

ALISON: Because it was unfair and cruel of me to
come back. I'm afraid a sense of timing is one
of the things I seem to have learnt from Jimmy.

20 But it's something that can be in very bad taste.
(*Sips her tea.*) So many times, I've just managed
to stop myself coming here—right at the last
moment. Even today, when I went to the book-
ing office at St. Pancras, it was like a charade,
and I never believed that I'd let myself walk
on to that train. And when I was on it, I got
into a panic. I felt like a criminal. I told myself

I'd turn round at the other end, and come straight
back. I couldn't even believe that this place
existed any more. But once I got here, there   30
was nothing I could do. I had to convince myself
that everything I remembered about this place
had really happened to me once.

(*She lowers her cup, and her foot plays with the newspapers
on the floor.*)

How many times in these past few months I've
thought of the evenings we used to spend here
in this room. Suspended and rather remote. You
make a good cup of tea.

HELENA: (*sitting L. of table*). Something Jimmy   40
taught *me*.

ALISON: (*covering her face*). Oh, why am I here! You
must all wish me a thousand miles away!

HELENA: I don't wish anything of the kind. You've
more right to be here than I.

ALISON: Oh, Helena, don't bring out the book of
rules——

HELENA: You are his wife, aren't you? Whatever
I have done, I've never been able to forget that
fact. You have all the rights——   50

ALISON: Helena—even I gave up believing in the
divine rights of marriage long ago. Even before
I met Jimmy. They've got something different
now—constitutional monarchy. You are where
you are by consent. And if you start trying any
strong arm stuff, you're out. And I'm out.

HELENA: Is that something you learnt from him?

ALISON: Don't make me feel like a blackmailer or
something, please! I've done something foolish,
and rather vulgar in coming here tonight. I regret   60
it, and I detest myself for doing it. But I did
not come here in order to gain anything.
Whatever it was—hysteria or just macabre
curiosity, I'd certainly no intention of making
any kind of breach between you and Jimmy.
You must believe that.

HELENA: Oh, I believe it all right. That's why
everything seems more wrong and terrible than
ever. You didn't even reproach me. You should
have been outraged, but you weren't. (*She leans*   70
back, as if she wanted to draw back from herself.)
I feel so—*ashamed*.

ALISON: You talk as though he were something
you'd swindled me out of——

HELENA: (*fiercely*). And you talk as if he were a

book or something you pass around to anyone who happens to want it for five minutes. What's the matter with you? You sound as though you were quoting *him* all the time. I thought you
80   told me once you couldn't bring yourself to believe in him.

ALISON: I don't think I ever believed in your way either.

HELENA: At least, I still believe in right and wrong! Not even the months in this madhouse have stopped me doing that. Even though everything I have done is wrong, at least I have known it was wrong.

ALISON: You loved him, didn't you? That's what
90   you wrote, and told me.

HELENA: And it was true.

ALISON: It was pretty difficult to believe at the time. I couldn't understand it.

HELENA: I could hardly believe it myself.

ALISON: Afterwards, it wasn't quite so difficult. You used to say some pretty harsh things about him. Not that I was sorry to hear them—they were rather comforting then. But you even shocked me sometimes.

100   HELENA: I suppose I was a little over-emphatic. There doesn't seem much point in trying to explain everything, does there?

ALISON: Not really.

HELENA: Do you know—I have discovered what is wrong with Jimmy? It's very simple really. He was born out of his time.

ALISON: Yes. I know.

HELENA: There's no place for people like that any longer—in sex, or politics, or anything. That's
110   why he's so futile. Sometimes, when I listen to him, I feel he thinks he's still in the middle of the French Revolution. And that's where he ought to be, of course. He doesn't know where he is, or where he's going. He'll never do anything, and he'll never amount to anything.

ALISON: I suppose he's what you'd call an Eminent Victorian. Slightly comic—in a way.... We seem to have had this conversation before.

HELENA: Yes, I remember everything you said
120   about him. It horrified me. I couldn't believe that you could have married someone like that. Alison—it's all over between Jimmy and me. I can see it now. I've got to get out. No—listen

to me. When I saw you standing there tonight, I knew that it was all utterly wrong. That I didn't believe in any of this, and not Jimmy or anyone could make me believe otherwise. (*Rising*.) How could I have ever thought I could get away with it! He wants one world and I want another, and lying in that bed won't ever
130   change it! I believe in good and evil, and I don't have to apologise for that. It's quite a modern, scientific belief now, so they tell me. And, by everything I have ever believed in, or wanted, what I have been doing is wrong and evil.

ALISON: Helena—you're not going to leave him?

HELENA: Yes, I am. (*Before* ALISON *can interrupt she goes on.*) Oh, I'm not stepping aside to let you come back. You can do what you like. Frankly, I think you'd be a fool—but that's your own
140   business. I think I've given you enough advice.

ALISON: But he—he'll have no one.

HELENA; Oh, my dear, he'll find somebody. He'll probably hold court here like one of the Renaissance popes. Oh, I know I'm throwing the book of rules at you, as you call it, but, believe me, you're never going to be happy without it. I tried throwing it away all these months, but I know now it just doesn't work. When you came in at that door, ill and tired and hurt, it was
150   all over for me. You see—I didn't know about the baby. It was such a shock. It's like a judgment on us.

ALISON: You saw me, and I had to tell you what had happened. I lost the child. It's a simple fact. There is no judgment, there's no blame——

HELENA: Maybe not. But I feel it just the same.

ALISON: But don't you see? It isn't logical!

HELENA: No, it isn't. (*Calmly.*) But I know it's right.
160

(*The trumpet gets louder.*)

ALISON: Helena, (*going to her*) you mustn't leave him. He needs you, I know he needs you——

HELENA: Do you think so?

ALISON: Maybe you're not the right one for him—we're neither of us right——

HELENA: (*moving upstage*). Oh, why doesn't he stop that damned noise!

ALISON: He wants something quite different from us. What it is exactly I don't know—a kind of
170

cross between a mother and a Greek courtesan, a henchwoman, a mixture of Cleopatra and Boswell. But give him a little longer——

HELENA: (*wrenching the door open*). Please! Will you stop that! I can't think!

(*There is a slight pause, and the trumpet goes on. She puts her hands to her head.*)

Jimmy, for God's sake!

(*It stops.*)

180   Jimmy, I want to speak to you.

JIMMY: (*off*). Is your friend still with you?

HELENA: Oh, don't be an idiot, and come in here!

(*She moves down L.*)

ALISON: (*rising*). He doesn't want to see me.

HELENA: Stay where you are, and don't be silly. I'm sorry. It won't be very pleasant, but I've made up my mind to go, and I've got to tell him now.

(*Enter* JIMMY.)

190   JIMMY: Is this another of your dark plots? (*He looks at* ALISON.) Hadn't she better sit down? She looks a bit ghastly.

HELENA: I'm so sorry, dear. Would you like some more tea, or an aspirin or something?

(ALISON *shakes her head, and sits. She can't look at either of them.*)

(*to* JIMMY, *the old authority returning*). It's not very surprising, is it? She's been very ill, she's——

JIMMY: (*quietly*). You don't have to draw a diagram

200   for me—I can see what's happened to her.

HELENA: And doesn't it mean anything to you?

JIMMY: I don't exactly relish the idea of anyone being ill, or in pain. It was my child too, you know. But (*he shrugs*) it isn't my first loss.

ALISON: (*on her breath*). It was mine.

(*He glances at her, but turns back to* HELENA *quickly.*)

JIMMY: What are you looking so solemn about? What's she doing here?

ALISON: I'm sorry, I'm—— (*Presses her hand over*

210   *her mouth.*)

(HELENA *crosses to* JIMMY *C., and grasps his hand.*)

HELENA: Don't please. Can't you see the condition she's in? She's done nothing, she's said nothing, none of it's her fault.

(*He takes his hand away, and moves away a little downstage.*)

JIMMY: What isn't her fault?

HELENA: Jimmy—I don't want a brawl, so please—

JIMMY: Let's hear it, shall we?

HELENA: Very well. I'm going downstairs to pack   220 my things. If I hurry, I shall just catch the 7.15 to London.

(*They both look at him, but he simply leans forward against the table, not looking at either of them.*)

This is not Alison's doing—you must understand that. It's my own decision entirely. In fact, she's just been trying to talk me out of it. It's just that suddenly, tonight, I see what I have really known all along. That you can't be happy when what you're doing is wrong, or is hurting some-   230 one else. I suppose it could never have worked, anyway, but I do love you, Jimmy. I shall never love anyone as I have loved you. (*Turns away L.*) But I can't go on. (*Passionately and sincerely.*) I can't take part—in all this suffering. I can't!

(*She appeals to him for some reaction, but he only looks down at the table, and nods.* HELENA *recovers, and makes an effort to regain authority.*)

(*to* ALISON). You probably won't feel up to making that journey again tonight, but we can fix   240 you up at an hotel before I go. There's about half an hour. I'll just make it.

(*She turns up to the door, but* JIMMY'S *voice stops her.*)

JIMMY: (*in a low, resigned voice*). They all want to escape from the pain of being alive. And, most of all, from love. (*Crosses to the dressing table.*) I always knew something like this would turn up—some problem, like an ill wife—and it would be too much for those delicate hot-house feelings of yours.   250

(*He sweeps up* HELENA'S *things from the dressing table, and crosses over to the wardrobe. Outside, the church bells start ringing.*)

It's no good trying to fool yourself about love.

You can't fall into it like a soft job, without dirtying up your hands. (*Hands her the make-up things, which she takes. He opens the wardrobe.*) It takes muscle and guts. And if you can't bear the thought (*takes out a dress on a hanger*) of messing up your nice, clean soul, (*crossing back to her*) you'd better give up the whole idea of life, and become a saint. (*Puts the dress in her arms.*) Because you'll never make it as a human being. It's either this world or the next.

(*She looks at him for a moment, and then goes out quickly. He is shaken, and he avoids* ALISON's *eyes, crossing to the window. He rests against it, then bangs his fist against the frame.*)

Oh, those bells!

(*The shadows are growing around them.* JIMMY *stands, his head against the window pane.* ALISON *is huddled forward in the armchair R. Presently, she breaks the stillness, and rises to above the table.*)

ALISON: I'm ... sorry. I'll go now.

(*She starts to move upstage. But his voice pulls her up.*)

JIMMY: You never even sent any flowers to the funeral. Not—a little bunch of flowers. You had to deny me that too, didn't you?

(*She starts to move, but again he speaks.*)

The injustice of it is almost perfect! The wrong people going hungry, the wrong people being loved, the wrong people dying.

(*She moves to the gas stove. He turns to face her.*)

Was I really wrong to believe that there's a—a kind of—burning virility of mind and spirit that looks for something as powerful as itself? The heaviest, strongest creatures in this world seem to be the loneliest. Like the old bear, following his own breath in the dark forest. There's no warm pack, no herd to comfort him. That voice that cries out doesn't *have* to be a weakling's, does it?

(*He moves in a little.*)

Do you remember that first night I saw you at that grisly party? You didn't really notice me, but I was watching you all the evening. You seemed to have a wonderful relaxation of spirit.

I knew that was what I wanted. You've got to be really brawny to have that kind of strength—the strength to relax. It was only after we were married that I discovered that it wasn't relaxation at all. In order to relax, you've first got to sweat your guts out. And, as far as you were concerned, you'd never had a hair out of place, or a bead of sweat anywhere.

(*A cry escapes from her, and her fist flies to her mouth. She moves down to below the table, leaning on it.*)

I may be a lost cause, but I thought if you loved me, it needn't matter.

(*She is crying silently. He moves down to face her.*)

ALISON: It doesn't matter! I was wrong, I was wrong! I don't want to be neutral, I don't want to be a saint. I want to be a lost cause. I want to be corrupt and futile!

(*All he can do is watch her helplessly. Her voice takes on a little strength, and rises.*)

Don't you understand? It's gone! It's gone! That—that helpless human being inside my body. I thought it was so safe, and secure in there. Nothing could take it from me. It was mine, my responsibility. But it's lost.

(*She slides down against the leg of the table to the floor.*)

All I wanted was to die. I never knew what it was like. I didn't know it could be like that! I was in pain, and all I could think of was you, and what I'd lost. (*Scarcely able to speak.*) I thought: if only—if only he could see me now, so stupid, and ugly and ridiculous. That is what he's been longing for me to feel. This is what he wants to splash about in! I'm in the fire, and I'm burning, and all I want is to die! It's cost him his child, and any others I might have had! But what does it matter—this is what he wanted from me!

(*She raises her face to him.*)

Don't you see! I'm in the mud at last! I'm grovelling! I'm crawling! Oh, God——

(*She collapses at his feet. He stands, frozen for a moment, then he bends down and takes her shaking body in his arms. He shakes his head, and whispers:*)

JIMMY: Don't. Please don't. ... I can't——
(*She gasps for her breath against him.*)
You're all right. You're all right now. Please,
I—I. ... Not any more. ...

(*She relaxes suddenly. He looks down at her, full of
fatigue, and says with a kind of mocking, tender irony:*)

We'll be together in our bear's cave, and our
squirrel's drey, and we'll live on honey, and nuts
—lots of nuts. And we'll sing songs about our-
350 selves—about warm trees and snug caves, and
lying in the sun. And you'll keep those big eyes
on my fur, and help me keep my claws in order,
because I'm a bit of a soppy, scruffy sort of
a bear. And I'll see that you keep that sleek,
bushy tail glistening as it should, because you're
a very beautiful squirrel, but you're none too
bright either, so we've got to be careful. There
are cruel steel traps lying about everywhere, just
waiting for rather mad, slightly satanic, and very
timid little animals. Right?   360

(ALISON *nods.*)

(*pathetically*). Poor squirrels!
ALISON: (*with the same comic emphasis*). Poor bears!
(*She laughs a little. Then looks at him very tenderly, and adds very, very softly.*) Oh, poor,
poor bears!

(*Slides her arms around him.*)

Curtain

ON *LOOK BACK IN ANGER*

by Simon Trussler

. . . *Look Back in Anger* adapts the familiar mechanics of the naturalistic problem play comfortably enough. A first-act exposition culminates in the arrival of an outsider to develop the situation, as Helena duly develops it in Act Two, and the final act restores a kind of precarious *status quo*. Osborne has considerably more confidence now in curtains, which are—with one notable exception—logical rather than cliffhanging culminations. The exception is Helena's instant-seduction of Jimmy at the end of Act Two, in the immediate aftermath of Alison's departure; and her equally sudden renunciation, which brings Jimmy and Alison together again near the close of the play, is no more satisfactory. The indisputable dramatic quality of both twists lends them theatrical viability, but it is a viability in a vacuum.

Part of the trouble is that both Cliff and Helena function rather as chemical agents than as characters. Cliff even describes himself as a "no-man's land" between Alison and Jimmy:

> This has always been a battlefield, but I'm pretty certain that if I hadn't been here, everything would have been over between these two long ago. I've been a—a no-man's land between them. Sometimes, it's been still and peaceful, no incidents, and we've all been reasonably happy. But most of the time, it's simply a very narrow strip of plain hell. But where I come from, we're used to brawling and excitement. Perhaps I even enjoy being in the thick of it. I love these two people very much. And I pity all of us.

As the self-consistent idiom here suggests, Cliff is a much more credible person than Helena, and he does instil both stability and a sense of pity into the play,

---

without which Jimmy's astringency might fall victim to a law of diminishing returns. The very incongruity of Cliff's friendship with Jimmy makes it, in a sense, more acceptable. But Helena is an altogether too-perfect embodiment of everything Jimmy despises. The affair between them is necessary to the formal shape of the play; but their mutual attraction is given very little dramatic substance. To talk about an attraction of opposites is only to give a name to the cliché that is being employed; and Osborne's quasi-psychological clues—the passionate clinch following the moment of violence, the shared sado-masochism of a sexual encounter between social enemies—are too neat to be true. Helena's seduction of Jimmy would seem trite even if she were adequately conceived as the upright Anglican she proclaims herself—a reversion to which role is the lame excuse for her final departure. As it is, her whole existence seems little more than a dramatic convenience.

Perhaps it's worth remembering that in *Epitaph* there is a moment of casually motivated passion between George and Ruth similar to that which occurs between Jimmy and Helena. George's kiss leads to the long conversation at the core of the play. But Helena's leads straight to bed, and to a third act "several months later" in which the growth of the resultant relationship can be taken for granted—just as the gradual blossoming of George and Josie's relationship in *Epitaph* had to be *assumed* at the same stage of the action. In terms of their patterning of emotional events, in fact, Osborne's two earliest plays develop with a marked similarity. Both have intervals at opportune moments, saving a lot of work in routine character-fulfillment; and Ruth's departure occurs at the same moment before the close of *Epitaph* as does Helena's at the end of *Look Back in Anger*. Both leave-takings are in part symbolic, and both are followed by just enough of an anti-climax before the final curtain to suggest the nature of the dramatic resolution.

Helena, however is no such potential soul-mate to Jimmy as Ruth was to George—but it does appear that Jimmy is reconciling himself to the same kind of animal relationship with Alison as George was contemplating with Josie. Isn't Alison in her squirrel's drey precisely that "warm, generous, honest-to-goodness animal lying at your side every night," which George sought as a "kind of euthanasia"? But the conclusion to *Epitaph* is conceived as a kind of defeat, and the conclusion to *Look Back in Anger* as a kind of triumph; for Jimmy and Alison achieve a self-realisation that George and Josie are never likely to share. Hence the climatic game of bears-and-squirrels—an animal relationship indeed. So where *does* the difference between George and Jimmy begin? It begins, surely, along the line that divides the characters from their creator: the divide between generalising and particularising minds. To George and Jimmy, there are no special cases; each is a creature of sweeping condemnations and of fixed allegiances. But to Osborne every case is a special case; and Jimmy Porter's is a very special case indeed.

Jimmy, in his wife's words, has never known "what it was to feel young, really young." Emotionally, he later suggests, he was old at the age of ten. Watching his father's slow death, he "learnt at an early age what it was to be angry—angry and helpless." He tells Helena:

> I knew more about—love ... betrayal ... and death, when I was
> ten years old than you will probably ever know all your life.

Now none of this is necessarily *true*; but it is the persona Jimmy projects, and which has become inseparable—certainly inseparable on stage—from whatever kernel of unarticulated self remains beneath his protective shell of verbiage. Thus Jimmy has remained rooted in the past—a past of his own reshaping, created in the process of self-rationalisation. John Beavan, in an early review of the play, complained that Jimmy's chosen lot was that of a thirties-intellectual going slumming rather than that of a disenchanted socialist in the early fifties. But this is just the point. Only the *mythical* Jimmy Porter, the jounalist's angry young man, is of the fifties. In reality, Jimmy's slumming takes the form of running a sweet-stall and choosing to live in much more squalid surroundings than the economics of any confectioner cashing-in on the abolition of sweet-rationing could possibly dictate. He chooses his squalor existentially; he is created and identified by it. He is not a *representative* character at all, still less morally detestable or exemplary; he has been shaped by personal circumstances which have left him self-consciously proletarian and sexually uncertain.

In fact, Jimmy's ethical system is so entirely a product of sentimentalised working-class puritanism that, for all his veneer of forthright sophistication, he is almost Victorian in his insistence upon keeping a sexual relationship in its proper place—in bed. Outside bed, brawling is "the only thing left I'm any good at." Jimmy doesn't *talk* to his wife, except in anger or in allegory; and this is not really because he's "too much of a pig," as Cliff suggests, but because he's too much of a puritan to pay her any sexual compliment other than copulation. His own hypergamous marriage has apparently damned him in the eyes of his former friends; and he is no doubt well aware that his wife's social condescension resembles that of his own mother—bourgeois intellectual as she was, "all for being associated with minorities, provided they were the smart, fashionable ones."

To redeem that maternal guilt, Jimmy has sought a working-class mother-substitute in Hugh's mum, over whom he tear-jerks unashamedly. Thus, of his marriage to Alison he recalls

> the first time I showed her your photograph—just after we were married. She looked at it, and the tears just welled up in her eyes, and she said: "But she's so beautiful! She's so beautiful!" She kept repeating it as if she couldn't believe it. Sounds a bit simple and sentimental when you repeat it. But it was pure gold the way she said it.

This is no longer Osborne forestalling criticism of a possible lapse in emotional taste. The lapse is Jimmy's, who really does believe that the "simple and sentimental" is purified by its proletarian source. His own verbal introversion leads him into a curt defence of his words, for he would otherwise be the first to condemn such self-indulgence as is here transmuted into gold: he demands, in short, that others recognise his own exceptions to his own rules.

Cliff is another exception: he is permitted, to Helena's mystification, to be quite actively fond of Alison, who admits:

> It isn't easy to explain. It's what he would call a question of allegiances, and he expects you to be pretty literal about them. Not only about himself and all the things he believes in, his present and his future, but his past as well. All the people he admires and loves, and has loved. The friends he used to know, people I've never even known —and probably wouldn't have liked. His father, who died years ago. Even the other women he's loved. Do you understand?

A demand for allegiance to his own past: if one *is* to understand Jimmy—and therefore the play—this is something that has to be appreciated and accepted. Because Alison loves and consequently needs Jimmy, and is prepared for coexistence on almost any terms, she tries to offer the allegiance he requires. Verbally, she is therefore made to stumble across an endless assault-course—relieved only by occasional oases of bears-and-squirrels fantasy. Osborne chooses such an oasis as his climax, but only a few lines earlier, Alison has been "grovelling," and there can be little doubt that she will grovel again. For the bears-and-squirrels are inextricably woven into the "texture of ordinary despair" that is the fabric of the play.

Perhaps this was what a *Times Literary Supplement* leader was misunderstanding when it pontificated at the time of *Look Back in Anger*'s first production as follows:

> His maladjusted characters only really exist in the vortex of emotional vindictiveness which the writer creates with such uncomfortable vividness. All the externals of the misalliance, including the famous sweet-stall which the young man operates for his livelihood, do not seem quite integral.

Of course the sweet-stall is not integral; it is part of a complex process of self-identification with a lost, proletarian innocence, as alien to the actual, university-educated Jimmy as the Spanish Civil War. And it is surely in this conflict between actual alienation and "applied" identification that *Look Back in Anger* did strike a chord in many radical breasts of the mid-fifties. What is *typical* about the play is its hero's consciousness of the conflict; what is eccentric is his attempt to reconcile it by means of a sort of enacted nostalgia. And his foredoomed failure to find fulfillment in such an attempt is at the root of his malaise. Jimmy's scorn, and his apparently unmotivated outbreaks of anger, derive from this failure, and in turn nourish it. He is caught in a vicious circle; and in this sense the play's return to what is effectively a *status quo* is both formally and thematically appropriate.

Look Back in Anger, then, seems to me to be basically a well-made problem play of considerable psychological insight. I hope I have not over-psychologised it; if I have, it is an attempt to correct the usual tendency to over-socialise it. But what must one really make of the "little ordinary human enthusiasm" and the "good, brave causes" for which Jimmy says he longs, and from which have been woven so much of the subsequent mythology? It may help to recall the actual contexts of these over-familiar quotations. Jimmy's desire for "ordinary human enthusiasm" is an ironical plea for interest in an article in one of the posh newspapers; and his comment on the absence of good causes is an afterthought to an assertion that he is being bled to death by all the women in the world, not to mention the postmaster-general. The irony, in context, inevitably modifies the response; but this is not to suggest that the emotional *need* for brave causes, expressed out of context, wasn't entirely characterisitc of a prevailing mood in the year of the Suez War and the Hungarian Revolution.

Look Back in Anger therefore became, in spite of itself, a harbinger of the New Left, of Anti-Apartheid, and of the Campaign for Nuclear Disarmament. But I don't think Jimmy Porter would have been clamouring for his membership cards; his emotional needs may have been typical, but his response to them was exceptional—a word Osborne has himself used to describe the condition of his heroes. At once more sensitive and more skewed than George Dillon, Jimmy Porter could have found no more permanent an identity on a protest march than in the warm, animal comfort of his squirrel's drey; and given a few more years, he might well have found himself reduced to the refuges of an Archie Rice—to gin, to a succession of casual mistresses, and to looking back in increasingly hopeless nostalgia over the years that divided him from his instinctive heritage.

A NEW WORD

by Mary McCarthy

At first glance, the main actors in *Look Back in Anger* appear to be three newspapers and an ironing-board. When the curtain goes up, on a cheap one-room flat, the audience sees a pair of Sunday papers, a cloud of pipesmoke, and some men's feet and legs protruding; more papers are scattered on the floor, and, off to one side, a woman is silently ironing a shirt. "Why do I do this every Sunday?" exclaims Jimmy Porter, throwing his paper down. "Even the book reviews seem to be the same as last week's. Different books—same reviews." At the rise of the third-act curtain, months later, the two male figures are still enveloped in the Sunday papers, while a woman is silently ironing a shirt. Same scene—different girl. Nothing really changes; nothing can change. That is the horror of Sunday. Jimmy's wife, Alison, a colonel's daughter, has finally left him, but her girl-friend, Helena, has stepped into her shoes. Jimmy, a working-class intellectual, still has a hostage from the ruling class doing the washing and the cooking, and his friend, Cliff, an uneducated Welsh boy, who boards with them, is still looking on. There has been a swap of upper-class women, like the swap of posh newspapers: you put down *The Observer* and pick up *The Sunday Times*—same contents, different make-up. A blonde is replaced by a brunette, and there is a different set of make-up on the dressing-table. The two "class" newspapers, one liberal, one Tory, are interchangeable, and the mass newspaper, *The News of the World*, is a weekly Psychopathia Sexualis. Other fixtures in the cast of characters are some church bells outside, the unseen landlady downstairs, and a storage-tank in the middle of the flat that represents Jimmy Porter's mother-in-law—in the third act, the new girl at the ironing-board, a home-maker, has put a slipcover on "Mummy," which does not alter the fact that Mummy is still present, built in to the apartment, as she is built in to English life.

The stagnant boredom of Sundays in a provincial town, with the pubs closed and nothing to do but read the papers, is a travesty of the day of rest—the day which officially belongs to the private person, who is here seen as half an inert object and half a restless phantom staring through the bars of his prison. Nobody can deny that this feeling of being pent-up is characteristic of Sunday, perhaps for the majority of people in Anglo-Saxon countries. Jimmy Porter is still young enough to feel that something *ought* to happen, something a little different, to break the monotony. He believes that Sunday has a duty to be interesting. John Osborne's critics, on the contrary, believe that Jimmy has a duty not to be bored or at least not to show it, not to keep talking about it. As Helena, who marches into the play waving the standard of criticism, tells her friend Alison, Jimmy will have to learn to behave like everybody else.

"Why can't you be like other people?" This extreme demand, which always rises to the surface in quarrels between married couples, leaps from behind the footlights to confront Jimmy Porter; the play alerts a kind of intimate antagonism in its audiences, as though audience and hero were a wedded pair, headed straight for the divorce court, recriminations, lawyers, ugly charges. Criticism has picked the play to pieces, as though it were a trumped-up story; imagined discrepancies or improbabilities are pounced on ("The play is not true to life; people do their ironing on Mondays," or "They would have finished reading the papers by four o'clock in the afternoon"). One critic, writing in *The New Republic*, thinks he knows why Jimmy Porter can't be like other people: homosexual tendencies. Nor would Jimmy Porter, if he could reply, change a single feature of his conduct to avoid the drawing of this inference. The play almost asks to be misunderstood, like an infuriated, wounded person; out of bravado, it coldly refuses to justify itself.

Jimmy Porter's boredom is a badge of freedom, and he will not be passive about it; for him, boredom is a positive activity, a proclamation. To be actively, angrily, militantly bored is one of the few forms of protest open to him that do not compromise his independence and honesty. At the same time, it is one of the few forms of recreation that he can afford; his boredom becomes an instrument on which he plays variations, as he does on his trumpet, in the next room. But other people suffer, it is said. He ought not to make other people suffer because *he* is unhappy and out of sorts. No doubt, but this is unfortunately the way unhappy people are; they are driven to distribute the suffering.

For Jimmy Porter, moreover, there is a principle involved. He is determined to stay alive, which means that he must struggle against the soporific substitutes for real life that make up the Sunday program: the steady soft thud of the iron and the regular rustle of newsprint. His friend, Cliff, keeps telling him to shut up; his badgered wife, Alison, only wants peace, a little peace, but that is what Jimmy or a part of Jimmy, his needling, cruel voice, has decided that she shall not have. He is fighting to keep her awake, to keep himself and his friend awake, as though all three were in the grip of a deathly coma or narcosis that had been spread over all of England by the gases emanating from the press, the clergy, the political parties, the BBC. Jimmy Porter's jibes are a therapeutic method designed to keep a few people alive, whether they like it or not, and patterned on the violent procedures used with patients who have taken an overdose of drugs and whose muttered plea, like Alison's, is always to be left alone.

This, at any rate, is what Jimmy thinks he is doing. His voice is a calculated irritant that prevents the other characters from lapsing into torpor. For his own part, he is tired of listening to himself and would be glad to tune in on another station, where something was really happening, where there was a little enthusiasm: he would like, some time, just once, to hear "a warm, thrilling voice cry out Hallelujah!" Instead, there is only the deadly static provided by the Sunday weeklies, the Bishop of Bromley blessing the hydrogen bomb, and the church bells ringing outside. He thinks he would like to listen to a concert of Vaughan Williams' music, but the ironing interferes with the reception, and he irritably shuts the radio off.

"Interference" is what Jimmy detests, whether it comes from the iron, his mother-in-law, his wife's girl-friend or the church bells. He is morbidly suspicious in any case and morbidly sensitive to "foreign" noises. At the same time, he is unnerved by silence. The only sound he really trusts is the sound of his own voice, which he keeps turned on mechanically, almost absently, as other people keep a phonograph going. This voice is very droll and funny, which is how it placates censure; it is "as good as a show." But the other characters sometimes plead with Jimmy to be quiet; they cannot "hear themselves think" or read the papers in peace or go on with the ironing because of that voice. And if it stops talking, it moves into the next room and starts blowing on a trumpet. It never runs down and when it seems to flag for a moment, it is only to gather fresh energy, like a phonograph that pauses to let the record turn over. Jimmy demands an undivided attention, even when he is absent, and he is quick to know when no one is listening. "I'm sorry; I wasn't listening properly," says Alison at the beginning of the play. "You bet you weren't listening," he retorts, "Old Porter talks and everyone turns over and goes to sleep. And Mrs. Porter gets 'em going with the first yawn."

Behind all this is more than egotism or a childish insistence on being the center of the stage. Jimmy Porter is a completely isolated person whose profoundest, quickest, most natural instinct is mistrust. This is the automatic, animal wariness of a creature that feels itself surrounded. Solidarity, a working-class virtue, is for him the only virtue that is real; he exacts complete allegiance and fealty from anyone who enters his life. His women appear, so to speak, wearing his colors; both girls, while they *are* his, are seen wearing one of his old shirts over their regular clothes. When Alison is found in a slip, dressing to go out, in the second act, this is proof that she is about to revert, away from him, back to her own kind. Jimmy would make his women into men if he could, *not* because he is a covert homosexual, but because, if they were men, he could trust them. Women do not have that natural quality of solidarity that exists between men, and they have always been suspected by men for precisely this reason; women live in the artificial realm of the social and are adepts at transferring allegiances ("making new friends") and at all the arts of deception and camouflage of which the dressing-table, stage left, is the visible sign. Alison lets Jimmy down at the crucial moment of the play—a thing he finds unthinkable, as does Alison's father, Colonel Redfern. This is followed, appropriately, by another betrayal: Alison's girl-friend, Helena, seizes Jimmy for herself.

The story of *Look Back in Anger* has, from this point of view, a great deal in common with *Hamlet*. Cliff, the working-class Welsh boy, is Jimmy Porter's Horatio, who sticks to him without understanding all the fine points of Jimmy's philosophy; and the scenes Jimmy makes Alison have the same candid brutality that Hamlet showed to Ophelia. In both cases, the frenzied mockery springs from an expectation of betrayal. Ophelia is felt to be the ally of the corrupt court with the murderer-king at its head, of her dull brother, Laertes, and her father, that ass Polonius. In *Look Back in Anger*, brother Nigel is Laertes and Alison's mother is cast in the role of Polonius, lurking behind the arras. The fact that Alison is secretly exchanging letters with her means that she is in communication with the enemy, like that other docile daughter, Ophelia. Women cannot be trusted because they do not understand that such an act is treachery; they do it "in all innocence." Apart from anything else, they do not take in the meaning of a declaration of war.

Both Hamlet and Jimmy Porter have declared war on a rotten society; both have been unfitted by a higher education from accepting their normal place in the world. They think too much and criticize too freely. Jimmy, like Hamlet, might have become a species of courtier or social sycophant; that is, he might have "got ahead." Critics complain that he ought to have found a job at a provincial university, instead of torturing himself and his nice wife by running a sweet stall. Hamlet, too, might have settled down to a soft berth in the court of Denmark, married Ophelia, and waited for the succession. Hamlet's tirades and asides are plainly calculated to disturb and annoy the court. He too cannot stop talking and, like Jimmy Porter, who practices vaudeville routines, he turns to the players for relief from the "real" world of craft, cunning and stupidity. Both heroes are naturally histrionic, and in both cases the estrangement, marked by histrionics, is close at moments to insanity. Both have no fixed purpose beyond that of awakening the people around them from their trance of acceptance and obliging them to be conscious of the horror and baseness of the world. Both (though this is clearer in Hamlet's case) suffer from a horrible self-doubt that alternates with wild flashes of conviction, and neither wholly wills the events he himself is causing. Yet neither wants to repent whatever it is that is driving him to destroy everything in sight, and both repel pity. "He wouldn't *let* me pity him," said a young woman, sadly, coming out of *Look Back in Anger*. That is just the concession the play refuses to make; if the audience pitied Jimmy Porter, this would be interference.

THE LEADER

Eugene Ionesco (b. 1912)

Translated by Derek Prouse

Rumanian-born Ionesco first attracted critical attention with his play *The Chairs* in 1952 and soon came to be recognized as one of the most important of the "absurdist" playwrights. The "theater of the absurd" projects a nihilistic philosophy in which the traditional views of man and his universe are rejected. The "anti-theater" approach of the absurdists caused them to ignore the conventions of dramatic structure and the usual processes of communication. Ionesco usually begins his plays by establishing a familiar situation into which he introduces unfamiliar elements leading to disintegration. He has been widely produced in the *avant-garde* theater. His best-known works are *The Rhinoceros, The Killer, The Bald Soprano, The Lesson, Amedée* and *The New Tenant.*

Ionesco's point of view is indicated in his remarks about *The Chairs:*

I have tried to deal with themes that obsess me; with emptiness, with frustration, with this world, at once fleeting and crushing, with despair and death. The characters I have used are not fully conscious of their spiritual rootlessness, but they feel it instinctively and emotionally.[1]

Ionesco's approach to the theater is further evident from the following excerpt of his "Experience of the Theatre."

So if the essence of the theatre lay in magnifying its effects, they had to be magnified still further, underlined and stressed to the maximum. To push drama out of that intermediate zone where it is neither theatre nor literature is to restore it to its own domain, to its natural frontiers. It was not for me to conceal the devices of the theatre, but rather make them still more evident, deliberately obvious, go all-out for caricature and the grotesque,

---

From *Rhinoceros and Other Plays,* by Eugene Ionesco. Reprinted by permission of Grove Press, Inc. Copyright © by John Calder (Publisher) Ltd. 1960

[1]These remarks and the passage quoted in the following paragraph appear in Ionesco's "Experience of the Theatre," in *Notes and Counter Notes,* trans. Donald Watson (New York: Grove Press, 1964), p. 26.

way beyond the pale of witty drawing-room comedies. No drawing-room comedies, but farce, the extreme exaggeration of parody. Humor, yes, but using methods of burlesque. Comic effects that are firm, broad and outrageous. No dramatic comedies either. But back to the unendurable. Everything raised to paroxysm, where the source of tragedy lies. A theatre of violence; violently comic, violently dramatic.

Avoid psychology or rather give it a meta-physical dimension. Drama lies in extreme exaggeration of the feelings, exaggeration that dislocates flat everyday reality. Dislocation, disarticulation of language too.

Moreover, if the actors embarrassed me by not seeming natural enough, perhaps it was because they also were, or tried to be, *too* natural; by trying to be, perhaps they will appear natural, but in a different way. They must not be afraid of not being natural.

Below. The announcer prepares the way for the Leader's coming.
Photographs in this sequence are of the American premiere of Ionesco's play
at the 1965 Buffalo Festival of the Arts Today,
staged at the State University College of Buffalo,
with James Harwood as the announcer.

ALBRIGHT-KNOX ART GALLERY, BUFFALO, NEW YORK

Above. The Girl Admirer
anticipates the Leader's entrance.

Right. The Leader arrives.

CHARACTERS

THE ANNOUNCER
THE YOUNG LOVER
THE GIRL-FRIEND
THE ADMIRER
THE GIRL ADMIRER
THE LEADER

THE LEADER

Standing with his back to the public, centre-stage, and with his eyes fixed on the up-stage exit, the ANNOUNCER *waits for the arrival of the* LEADER. *To right and left, riveted to the walls, two of the* LEADER'S ADMIRERS, *a man and a girl, also wait for his arrival.*

ANNOUNCER: *(after a few tense moments in the same position).* There he is! There he is! At the end of the street! *(Shouts of 'Hurrah!' etc., are heard.)* There's the leader! He's coming, he's coming nearer! *(Cries of acclaim and applause are heard from the wings.)* It's better if he doesn't see us ... *(The* TWO ADMIRERS *hug the wall even closer.)* Watch out! *(The* ANNOUNCER *gives vent to a brief display of enthusiasm.)* Hurrah! Hurrah! The leader! The
10 leader! Long live the leader! *(The* TWO ADMIRERS, *with their bodies rigid and flattened against the wall, thrust their necks and heads as far forward as they can to get a glimpse of the* LEADER.) The leader! The leader! *(The* TWO ADMIRERS *in unison:)* Hurrah! Hurrah! *(Other 'Hurrahs!' mingled with 'Hurrah! Bravo!' come from the wings and gradually die down.)* Hurrah! Bravo!

The ANNOUNCER *takes a step up-stage, stops, then up-stage, followed by the* TWO ADMIRERS, *saying as he goes:*
20 'Ah! Too bad! He's going away! He's going away! Follow me quickly! After him!' *The* ANNOUNCER *and the* TWO ADMIRERS *leave, crying: 'Leader! Leeeeader! Lee-ee-eader!' (This last 'Lee-ee-eader!' echoes in the wings like a bleating cry.)*

Silence. The stage is empty for a few brief moments.

The YOUNG LOVER *enters right, and his* GIRL-FRIEND *left; they meet centre-stage.*

YOUNG LOVER: Forgive me, Madame, or should I say Mademoiselle?
GIRL-FRIEND: I beg your pardon, I'm afraid I don't 30 happen to know you!
YOUNG LOVER: And I'm afraid I don't know you either!
GIRL-FRIEND: Then neither of us knows each other.
YOUNG LOVER: Exactly. We have something in common. It means that between us there is a basis of understanding on which we can build the edifice of our future.
GIRL-FRIEND: That leaves me cold, I'm afraid.

She makes as if to go. 40

YOUNG LOVER: Oh, my darling, I adore you.
GIRL-FRIEND: Darling, so do I!

They embrace.

YOUNG LOVER: I'm taking you with me, darling. We'll get married straightaway.

They leave left. The stage is empty for a brief moment.

ANNOUNCER: *(enters up-stage followed by the* TWO ADMIRERS). But the leader swore that he'd be passing here.
ADMIRER: Are you absolutely sure of that? 50
ANNOUNCER: Yes, yes, of course.
GIRL ADMIRER: Was it really on his way?
ANNOUNCER: Yes, yes. He should have passed by here, it was marked on the Festival programme ...

ADMIRER: Did you actually see it yourself and hear it with your own eyes and ears?

ANNOUNCER: He told someone. Someone else!

ADMIRER: But who? Who was this someone else?

60 GIRL ADMIRER: Was it a reliable person? A friend of yours?

ANNOUNCER: A friend of mine who I know very well. *(Suddenly in the background one hears renewed cries of 'Hurrah!' and 'Long live the leader!')* That's him now! There he is! Hip! Hip! Hurrah! There he is! Hide yourselves! Hide yourselves!

The TWO ADMIRERS *flatten themselves as before against the wall, stretching their necks out towards the wings from where the shouts of acclamation come; the*
70 ANNOUNCER *watches fixedly upstage his back to the public.*

ANNOUNCER: The leader's coming. He approaches. He's bending. He's unbending. *(At each of the* ANNOUNCER'S *words, the* ADMIRERS *give a start and stretch their necks even farther; they shudder.)* He's jumping. He's crossed the river. They're shaking his hand. He sticks out his thumb. Can you hear? They're laughing. *(The* ANNOUNCER *and the* TWO ADMIRERS *also laugh.)* Ah...! they're giving
80 him a box of tools. What's he going to do with them? Ah...! he's signing autographs. The leading is stroking a hedgehog, a superb hedgehog! The crowd applauds. He's dancing, with the hedgehog in his hand. He's embracing his dancer. Hurrah! Hurrah! *(Cries are heard in the wings)* He's being photographed, with his dancer on one hand and the hedgehog on the other... He greets the crowd... He spits a tremendous distance.

90 GIRL ADMIRER: Is he coming past here? Is he coming in our direction?

ADMIRER: Are we really on his route?

ANNOUNCER: *(turns his head to the* TWO ADMIRERS*).* Quite, and don't move, you're spoiling everything...

GIRL ADMIRER: But even so...

ANNOUNCER: Keep quiet, I tell you! Didn't I tell you he'd promised, that he had fixed his itinerary himself.... *(He turns back up-stage and cries.)* Hur-
100 rah! Hurrah! Long live the leader! *(Silence)* Long live, long live, the leader! *(Silence)* Long live, long live, long live the lead-er! *(The* TWO

ADMIRERS, *unable to contain themselves, also give a sudden cry of:)* Hurrah! Long live the leader!

ANNOUNCER: *(to the* ADMIRERS*).* Quiet, you two! Calm down! You're spoiling everything! *(Then, once more looking up-stage, with the* ADMIRERS *silenced.)* Long live the leader! *(Wildly enthusiastic.)* Hurrah! Hurrah! He's changing his shirt. He disappears behind a red screen. He reappears! 110 *(The applause intensifies.)* Bravo! Bravo! *(The* ADMIRERS *also long to cry 'Bravo' and applaud; they put their hands to their mouths to stop themselves.)* He's putting his tie on! He's reading his newspaper and drinking his morning coffee! He's still got his hedgehog... He's leaning on the edge of the parapet. The parapet breaks. He gets up... he gets up unaided! *(Applause, shouts of 'Hurrah!')* Bravo! Well done! He brushes his soiled clothes. 120

TWO ADMIRERS: *(stamping their feet).* Oh! Ah! Oh! Oh! Ah! Ah!

ANNOUNCER: He's mounting the stool! He's climbing piggyback, they're offering him a thin-ended wedge, he knows it's meant as a joke, and he doesn't mind, he's laughing.

Applause and enormous acclaim.

ADMIRER: *(to the* GIRL ADMIRER*).* You hear that? You hear? Oh! If I were king...

GIRL ADMIRER: Ah...! the leader! 130

This is said in an exalted tone.

ANNOUNCER: *(still with his back to the public).* He's mounting the stool. No. He's getting down. A little girl offers him a bouquet of flowers... What's he going to do? He takes the flowers... He embraces the little girl... calls her 'my child'...

ADMIRER: He embraces the little girl... calls her 'my child'...

GIRL ADMIRER: He embraces the little girl... calls 140 her 'my child'...

ANNOUNCER: He gives her the hedgehog. The little girl's crying... Long live the leader! Long live the leead-er!

ADMIRER: Is he coming past here?

GIRL ADMIRER: Is he coming past here?

ANNOUNCER: *(with a sudden run, dashes out up-stage).*

He's going away! Hurry! Come on!

He disappears, followed by the TWO ADMIRERS, *all crying
'Hurrah! Hurrah!'*

150

The stage is empty for a few moments. The TWO LOVERS
*enter, entwined in an embrace; they halt centre-stage
and separate; she carries a basket on her arm.*

GIRL-FRIEND: Let's go to the market and get some
eggs!

YOUNG LOVER: Oh! I love them as much as you
do!

She takes his arm. From the right the ANNOUNCER *arrives
running, quickly regaining his place, back to the public,*
160   *followed closely by the* TWO ADMIRERS, *arriving one
from the left and the other from the right; the* TWO
ADMIRERS *knock into the* TWO LOVERS *who were about
to leave right.*

ADMIRER: Sorry!

YOUNG LOVER: Oh! Sorry!

GIRL ADMIRER: Sorry! Oh! Sorry!

GIRL-FRIEND: Oh! Sorry, sorry, sorry, so sorry!

ADMIRER: Sorry, sorry, sorry, oh! sorry, sorry, so
sorry!

170   YOUNG LOVER: Oh, oh, oh, oh, oh, oh! So sorry,
everyone!

GIRL-FRIEND: *(to her* LOVER*).* Come along, Adolphe!
(To the TWO ADMIRERS:*)* No harm done!

She leaves, leading her LOVER *by the hand.*

ANNOUNCER: *(watching up-stage).* The leader is
being pressed forward, and pressed back, and
now they're pressing his trousers! *(The* TWO
ADMIRERS *regain their places.)* The leader is smiling. Whilst they're pressing his trousers, he
180   walks about. He tastes the flowers and the fruits
growing in the stream. He's also tasting the roots
of the trees. He suffers the little children to come
unto him. He has confidence in everybody. He
inaugurates the police force. He pays tribute to
justice. He salutes the great victors and the great
vanquished. Finally he recites a poem. The
people are very moved.

TWO ADMIRERS: Bravo! Bravo! *(Then, sobbing:)* Boo!
Boo! Boo!

190   ANNOUNCER: All the people are weeping. *(Loud cries
are heard from the wings; the* ANNOUNCER *and the*
ADMIRERS *also start to bellow.)* Silence! *(The* TWO

ADMIRERS *fall silent; and there is silence from the
wings.)* They've given the leader's trousers back.
The leader puts them on. He looks happy! Hurrah! *('Bravos', and acclaim from the wings. The* TWO
ADMIRERS *also shout their acclaim, jump about, without being able to see anything of what is presumed
to be happening in the wings.)* The leader's sucking
his thumb! *(To the* TWO ADMIRERS:*)* Back, back   200
to your places, you two, don't move, behave
yourselves and shout: 'Long live the leader!'

TWO ADMIRERS: *(flattened against the wall, shouting).*
Long live, long live the leader!

ANNOUNCER: Be quiet, I tell you, you'll spoil everything! Look out, the leader's coming!

ADMIRER: *(in the same position).* The leader's coming!

GIRL ADMIRER: The leader's coming!

ANNOUNCER: Watch out! And keep quiet! Oh! The
leader's going away! Follow him! Follow me!   210

The ANNOUNCER *goes out up-stage, running; the* TWO
ADMIRERS *leave right and left, whilst in the wings the
acclaim mounts, then fades. The stage is momentarily
empty. The* YOUNG LOVER, *followed by his* GIRL-FRIEND,
appear left running across the stage right.

YOUNG LOVER: *(running).* You won't catch me! You
won't catch me!

Goes out.

GIRL-FRIEND: *(running).* Wait a moment! Wait a
moment!   220

*She goes out. The stage is empty for a moment; then
once more the* TWO LOVERS *cross the stage at a run,
and leave.*

YOUNG LOVER: You won't catch me!

GIRL-FRIEND: Wait a moment!

They leave right. The stage is empty. The ANNOUNCER
reappears up-stage, the ADMIRER *from the right, the* GIRL
ADMIRER *from the left. They meet centre.*

ADMIRER: We missed him!

GIRL ADMIRER: Rotten luck!   230

ANNOUNCER: It was your fault!

ADMIRER: That's not true!

GIRL ADMIRER: No, that's not true!

ANNOUNCER: Are you suggesting it was mine?

ADMIRER: No, we didn't mean that!

GIRL ADMIRER: No, we didn't mean that!

Noise of acclaim and 'Hurrahs' from the wings.

ANNOUNCER: Hurran!
GIRL ADMIRER: It's from over there! *(She points up-*
240   *stage.)*
ADMIRER: Yes, it's from over there! *(He points left.)*
ANNOUNCER: Very well. Follow me! Long live the
      leader!

He runs out right, followed by the TWO ADMIRERS *also,*
shouting.

TWO ADMIRERS: Long live the leader!

They leave. The stage is empty for a moment. The YOUNG
LOVER *and his* GIRL-FRIEND *appear left; the* YOUNG
LOVER *exits up-stage; the* GIRL-FRIEND, *after saying 'I'll*
250   *get you!', runs out right. The* ANNOUNCER *and the*
TWO ADMIRERS *appear from up-stage. The* ANNOUNCER
says to the ADMIRERS: Long live the leader! *This is*
repeated by the ADMIRERS. *Then, still talking to the*
ADMIRERS, *he says:* Follow me! Follow the leader!
He leaves up-stage, still running and shouting: Follow
him!

The ADMIRER *exits right, the* GIRL ADMIRER *left into*
the wings. During the whole of this, the acclaim is heard
louder or fainter according to the rhythm of the stage
260   *action; the stage is empty for a moment, then the* LOVERS
appear from right and left, crying:

YOUNG LOVER: I'll get you!
GIRL-FRIEND: You won't get me!

They leave at a run, shouting: Long live the leader!
The ANNOUNCER *and the* TWO ADMIRERS *emerge from*
up-stage, also shouting: 'Long live the leader', followed
by the TWO LOVERS. *They all leave right, in single*
file, crying as they run: 'The leader! Long live the leader!
We'll get him! It's from over here! You won't get me!
270   *They enter and leave, employing all the exits; finally,*
entering from left, from right, and from up-stage they
all meet centre, whilst the acclaim and the applause from
the wings becomes a fearful din. They embrace each other
feverishly, crying at the tops of their voices: Long live
the leader! Long live the leader! Long live the
leader!

Then, abruptly, silence falls.

ANNOUNCER: The leader is arriving. Here's the
      leader. To your places! Attention!

280   *The* ADMIRER *and the* GIRL-FRIEND *flatten themselves*
against the wall right; the GIRL ADMIRER *and the* YOUNG

LOVER *against the wall left; the two couples are in each*
      other's arms, embracing.

ADMIRER *and*
GIRL-FRIEND: My dear, my darling!
GIRL ADMIRER *and*
YOUNG LOVER: My dear, my darling!

Meanwhile the ANNOUNCER *has taken up his place, back*
to the audience, looking fixedly up-stage; a lull in the
      applause.   290

ANNOUNCER: Silence. The leader has eaten his
      soup. He is coming. He is nigh.

The acclaim redoubles its intensity; the TWO ADMIRERS
      and the TWO LOVERS *shout:*

ALL: Hurrah! Hurrah! Long live the leader!

They throw confetti before he arrives. Then the
ANNOUNCER *hurls himself suddenly to one side to allow*
the LEADER *to pass; the other four characters freeze with*
outstretched arms holding confetti; but still say: Hurrah!
The LEADER *enters from up-stage, advances down-stage*   300
to centre, to the footlights, hesitates, makes a step to
left, then takes a decision and leaves with great, energetic
strides by right, to the enthusiastic 'Hurrahs!' of the
ANNOUNCER *and the feeble, somewhat astonished 'Hur-*
rahs!' of the other four; these, in fact, have some reason
to be surprised, as the LEADER *is headless, though wearing*
a hat. This is simple to effect: the actor playing the
LEADER *needing only to wear an overcoat with the collar*
turned up round his forehead and topped with a hat.
The-man-in-an-overcoat-with-a-hat-without-a-head is   310
a somewhat surprising apparition and will doubtless pro-
duce a certain sensation. After the LEADER'S *disappear-*
ance, the GIRL ADMIRER *says:*

GIRL ADMIRER: But ... but ... the leader hasn't got
      a head!
ANNOUNCER: What's he need a head for when he's
      got genius!
YOUNG LOVER: That's true! *(To the* GIRL-FRIEND:)
      What's your name?

The YOUNG LOVER *to the* GIRL ADMIRER, *the* GIRL   320
ADMIRER *to the* ANNOUNCER, *the* ANNOUNCER *to the*
GIRL-FRIEND, *the* GIRL-FRIEND *to the* YOUNG LOVER:
What's yours? What's yours? What's yours? *(Then,*
all together, one to the other:) What's your name?

Curtain

FROM *NOTES AND COUNTER NOTES*

by Eugene Ionesco

I have never quite succeeded in getting used to existence, whether it be the existence of the world or of other people, or above all of myself. Sometimes it seems to me that the forms of life are suddenly emptied of their contents, reality is unreal, words are nothing but sounds bereft of sense, these houses and this sky are no longer anything but facades concealing nothing, people appear to be moving about automatically and without reason; everything seems to melt into thin air, everything is threatened—myself included—by a silent and imminent collapse into I know not what abyss, where there is no more night or day. What magic power still holds it all together? And what does it all mean, this appearance of movement, this appearance of light, these sorts of objects, this sort of world? And yet here I am, surrounded by the halo of creation, unable to embrace these insubstantial shades, lost to understanding, out of my element, cut off from something undefinable without which everything spells deprivation. I examine myself and see myself invaded by inconceivable distress, by nameless regrets and inexplicable remorse, by a kind of love, by a kind of hate, by a semblance of joy, by a strange pity (for what? for whom?); I see myself torn apart by blind forces rising from my innermost self and clashing in some desperate unresolved conflict; and it seems I can identify myself with one or other of these, although I know quite well I am not entirely this one or that one (what do they want from me?), for it is clear I can never know who I am, or why I am.

No event, no magical occurrence surprises me, no new train of thought excites me (no interest in culture), not a single thing ever seems to me stranger than another, for everything is evened out and blurred by the all-embracing strangeness and improba-

---

bility of the universe. The very idea that we exist and can express ourselves seems to me incongruous. Those who do not share my belief that the fact of existence is unthinkable, may find in accepting existence that only a part of it is intrinsically sensible and logical, right or wrong. Whereas for me, the whole idea of existence being inconceivable, anything that actually exists seems intrinsically possible. No private frontiers, for me, can separate the real from the unreal, the true from the false. I have no standards, no references. I feel that I am there, on the fringe of existence, a stranger to the march of history, not all "with it," bemused, paralyzed into a state of primordial stupefaction. The gates are closed to me, or perhaps they have all disappeared together with the walls and all sense of distinction.

Doubtless what I have just said describes my state of mind only when it has reached the most complete moment of truth. In spite of everything, I am still alive. And I even manage to write... plays for example. You even do me the honor of asking me what I think I believe about the theatre. So what I have said up to now may seem irrelevant to the subject. I do in fact feel convinced that I have spoken of nothing else, that I have never strayed from the heart of the matter. However, whether this be true or not, the theatre, like literature or any other manifestation of cultural life, has an only limited interest for me, only partially affects me; I do not really attribute much value to what is communicable, or rather to what has been communicated already, to anything extraneous, to the passage of events, to deeds or doing.

For me the theatre—my own drama—is usually a confession; I do nothing but make admissions (incomprehensible to the deaf, that is inevitable), for what else can I do? I try to project onto the stage an inner drama (incomprehensible to myself) and tell myself that in any case, the microcosm being a small-scale reproduction of the macrocosm, it may happen that this tattered and disjointed inner world is in some way reflection or a symbol of universal disruption. So there is no plot, no architectural construction, no puzzles to be solved. Only the inscrutable enigma of the unknown; no real characters, just people without identity (at any moment they may contradict their own nature or perhaps one will change places with another), simply a sequence of events without sequence, a series of fortuitous incidents unlinked by cause and effect, inexplicable adventures, emotional states, an indescribable tangle, but alive with intentions, impulses and discordant passions, steeped in contradiction. This may appear tragic or comic or both at the same time, for I am incapable of distinguishing one from the other. I want only to render my own strange and improbable universe.

Perhaps, however, I could make a certain distinction: when I gaze attentively, from the outside, at what seems to appear before me, from which I am completely detached, then the insubstantial texture of creation, the behavior of those human creatures and their languages—which I just seem able to make out and which is for me hermetic or empty and as though *arbitrarily invented*—all their activities, everything falls apart, becomes nonsensical, infallibly turns to derision and is transformed into a bitter burlesque. It is out of this existential vacuum that my comedies can then be born.

But when, on the other hand, one lets one's own apparitions blossom into life, still faintly colored with dark traces of passions as violent as they are incoherent, one knows that these rival forces in their vehemence will tear at one another and give birth to a work of high drama. And so I do after all feel myself carried away by the mobility of drama. But as stories are never interesting, I long to rediscover the basic and purest principles of the theatre, and to reproduce them in pure scenic movement.

ACT WITHOUT WORDS, I

Mime for one Player

Samuel Beckett (b. 1906)

Translated from the French by the Author

Like George Bernard Shaw, Beckett was born in Ireland of Protestant middle-class stock. He was an exceptional student in boarding school and at Trinity College, Dublin, where he received his B.A. in 1927. The following year he took a position as a lecturer at Ecole Normale in Paris. He met James Joyce and began his career as a writer, at first with essays and poetry. After returning to Dublin, his wanderlust caught up with him until he made a permanent home in Paris in 1937. His reputation as a playwright began with his *Waiting for Godot*, which was given its *première* in Paris in 1953. It had a wide appeal and played more than four hundred performances to establish Beckett as one of the foremost playwrights in the world. His other best-known plays are *Endgame*, *Krapp's Last Tape* and *Happy Days*.

Act Without Words was first produced at the Royal Court Theater in London on April 3, 1957, as a companion piece to *Endgame*.

Above. The man seeks shelter
in the desert.
Photographs are of the 1973
production at Lincoln Center
in New York,
starring Hume Cronyn.

Right. The man sits in the shadow
of the tree and trims his nails.

Left. Water to slake his thirst is out of reach.

ALL PHOTOGRAPHS IN THIS SECTION
BY MARTHA SWOPE

Right. He labors to reach the water.

Left. He climbs the rope
to reach the water.

Opposite page. He remains
lying on his side.

ACT WITHOUT WORDS, I

Desert. Dazzling light.

The man is flung backwards on stage from right wing. He falls, gets up immediately, dusts himself, turns aside, reflects.

Whistle from right wing.

He reflects, goes out right.

Immediately flung back on stage he falls, gets up immediately, dusts himself, turns aside, reflects.

Whistle from left wing.

10 He reflects, goes out left.

Immediately flung back on stage he falls, gets up immediately, dusts himself, turns aside, reflects.

Whistle from left wing.

He reflects, goes towards left wing, hesitates, thinks better of it, halts, turns aside, reflects.

A little tree descends from flies, lands. It has a single bough some three yards from ground and at its summit a meager tuft of palms casting at its foot a circle of shadow.

20 He continues to reflect.

Whistle from above.

He turns, sees tree, reflects, goes to it, sits down in its shadow, looks at his hands.

A pair of tailor's scissors descends from flies, comes to rest before tree, a yard from ground.

He continues to look at his hands.

Whistle from above.

He looks up, sees scissors, takes them and starts to trim his nails.

The palms close like a parasol, the shadow disap-   30
pears.

He drops scissors, reflects.

A tiny carafe, to which is attached a huge label inscribed WATER, descends from flies, comes to rest some three yards from ground.

He continues to reflect.

Whistle from above.

He looks up, sees carafe, reflects, gets up, goes and stands under it, tries in vain to reach it, renounces, turns aside, reflects.   40

A big cube descends from flies, lands.

He continues to reflect.

Whistle from above.

He turns, sees cube, looks at it, at carafe, reflects, goes to cube, takes it up, carries it over and sets it down under carafe, tests its stability, gets up on it, tries in vain to reach carafe, renounces, gets down, carries cube back to its place, turns aside, reflects.

50   A second smaller cube descends from flies, lands.

He continues to reflect.

Whistle from above.

He turns, sees second cube, looks at it, at carafe, goes to second cube, takes it up, carries it over and sets it down under carafe, tests its stability, gets up on it, tries in vain to reach carafe, renounces, gets down, takes up second cube to carry it back to its place, hesitates, thinks better of it, sets it down, goes to big cube, takes it up,
60   carries it over and puts it on small one, tests their stability, gets up on them, the cubes collapse, he falls, gets up immediately, brushes himself, reflects.

He takes up small cube, puts it on big one, tests their stability, gets up on them and is about to reach carafe when it is pulled up a little way and comes to rest beyond his reach.

He gets down, reflects, carries cubes back to their place, one by one, turns aside, reflects.

70   A third still smaller cube descends from flies, lands.

He continues to reflect.

Whistle from above.

He turns, sees third cube, looks at it, reflects, turns aside, reflects.

The third cube is pulled up and disappears in flies.

Beside carafe a rope descends from flies, with knots to facilitate ascent.

He continues to reflect.

Whistle from above.

He turns, sees rope, reflects, goes to it, climbs   80
up it and is about to reach carafe when rope is let out and deposits him back on ground.

He reflects, looks around for scissors, sees them, goes and picks them up, returns to rope and starts to cut it with scissors.

The rope is pulled up, lifts him off ground, he hangs on, succeeds in cutting rope, falls back on ground, drops scissors, falls, gets up again immediately, brushes himself, reflects.

The rope is pulled up quickly and disappears in   90
flies.

With length of rope in his possession he makes a lasso with which he tries to lasso carafe.

The carafe is pulled up quickly and disappears in flies.

He turns aside, reflects.

He goes with lasso in his hand to tree, looks at bough, turns and looks at cubes, looks again at bough, drops lasso, goes to cubes, takes up small one, carries it over and sets it down under bough,   100
goes back for big one, takes it up and carries it over under bough, makes to put it on small one, hesitates, thinks better of it, sets it down, takes up small one and puts it on big one, tests their stability, turns aside and stoops to pick up lasso.

The bough folds down against trunk.

He straightens up with lasso in his hand, turns and sees what has happened.

He drops lasso, turns aside, reflects.

He carries back cubes to their place, one by one,   110
goes back for lasso, carries it over to cubes and lays it in a neat coil on small one.

He turns aside, reflects.

Whistle from right wing.

He reflects, goes out right.

Immediately flung back on stage he falls, gets up immediately, brushes himself, turns aside, reflects.

Whistle from left wing.

He does not move.

120   He looks at his hands, looks around for scissors, sees them, goes and picks them up, starts to trim his nails, stops, reflects, runs his finger along blade of scissors, goes and lays them on small cube, turns aside, opens his collar, frees his neck and fingers it.

The small cube is pulled up and disappears in flies, carrying away rope and scissors.

He turns to take scissors, sees what has happened.

He turns aside, reflects.

130   He goes and sits down on big cube.

The big cube is pulled from under him. He falls. The big cube is pulled up and disappears in flies.

He remains lying on his side, his face towards auditorium, staring before him.

The carafe descends from flies and comes to rest a few feet from his body.

He does not move.

Whistle from above.

He does not move.

The carafe descends further, dangles and plays   140 about his face.

He does not move.

The carafe is pulled up and disappears in flies.

The bough returns to horizontal, the palms open, the shadow returns.

Whistle from above.

He does not move.

The tree is pulled up and disappears in flies.

He looks at his hands.

Curtain

SAMUEL BECKETT

by Leonard Pronko

Beckett's view of life and man's tragic place in the universe is illuminated by a passage from his study of Proust:

> Tragedy is not concerned with human justice. Tragedy is the statement of an expiation, but not the miserable expiation of a codified breach of a local arrangement, organized by the knaves for the fools. The tragic figure represents the expiation of original sin, of the original and eternal sin of him and all his "soci malorum," the sin of having been born.

The picture presented is an elemental one, in which social relationships are but one aspect of man's metaphysical anguish. He is a creature paying for a sin he did not commit or was unaware of committing. God, the villain, either does not show up for his promised appointment, or what is worse, he does not exist, and man is left alone in a meaningless universe, attempting to find the reason for it all. His moments of lucidity bring no revelation, only suffering, and he tends to sink into habits that, although boring, are at least a "great deadener." But unfortunately man is a thinking animal.... He cannot avoid moments of lucidity in which he asks certain embarrassing and unanswerable questions: Who am I? Where am I going?

Many critics have pointed out that Beckett's works constitute a search for the self, that they exploit the mystery of self-identification. The answer to the mystery seems to be, as Richard Eastman states, that the true self is so much of a myth that people, like certain actors, can exist only by devising their roles." We have already noted how Gogo and Didi improvise scenes as they go along, how Hamm,

From *Avante-Garde: The Experimental Theater in France* by Leonard C. Pronko, University of California Press, 1962. Originally published by the University of California Press; reprinted by permission of The Regents of the University of California.

like many characters in the novels, is obsessed with telling a story. Beckett's creatures must build a screen of words between themselves and nothingness—or rather, between a fancied image of themselves and their ultimate unreality. And yet they are frequently aware of what they are doing, and comment, "We're getting on," or "How boring!" . . .

Beckett's view of life is basically a religious one: it is the view of a man who seeks some meaning beyond the trivial happenings of everyday life, a purpose beyond the physical needs of a specific time and place. The painful recognition of the absurd, and the ensuing struggle for meaning, reflect a more profoundly religious attitude than any facile acceptance of inherited beliefs. Beckett appears to be struggling within the framework of the Christian religion, but has apparently not found a valid attitude aside from that lucid awareness of man's miserable condition and the ever-present threat of annihilation.

One would expect a rather sober reaction to such a pessimistic outlook, but Beckett is a comic writer of great skill and originality. "Nothing is funnier than unhappiness," says Nell in *Endgame*, and she adds, "Yes, yes, it's the most comical thing in the world." Beckett almost succeeds in convincing us that Nell is right, for his humor is invariably based upon man's wretchedness. . . .

Many of the stock methods for inducing laughter are used, such as repetition of words and even entire sentences, misunderstandings, surprising contrasts and contradictions, and of course the slapstick humor of the circus. The laughter they elicit is not usually the loud guffaw, but the wry chuckle. In most of the situations we are laughing at the characters of the drama. But there is another kind of laughter in which we join the characters as they themselves laugh grimly at their own dismal situation. It is based upon irony and disillusionment, a laugh of awareness.

THE PHYSICISTS

Friedrich Dürrenmatt (b. 1921)

Translated from the German by James Kirkup

Friedrich Dürrenmatt is regarded as one of the most important playwrights now writing in the German language. He was born in Bern, Switzerland, in 1921. The fact that his father was a Lutheran minister and his grandfather was a poet and satirist has not escaped the critical assessment of Dürrenmatt's work. He writes in a variety of forms, detective story novels as well as material for film, television, radio, and of course the stage. His first play produced was *It Is Decreed* in 1947, which caused a considerable stir because of its unorthodoxy. While further recognition came with the Munich production of *The Marriage of Mr. Mississippi*, it was not until *The Visit of the Old Lady* was premiered at the Zurich Schauspielhaus in 1956 that he achieved the reputation of being one of the outstanding European dramatists. *The Visit* was widely produced and after the New York production in 1959 Dürrenmatt won the Drama Critics Award for the best foreign play. In the same year he was given the prestigious German award for drama, the Schiller prize. He has continued to write a series of provocative plays and novels, most notably *The Meteor*, *Play Strindberg*, and *The Physicists*.

In his statement "What man has once thought cannot be taken back" Dürrenmatt capsulizes one of the seminal ideas that pervades much of his work. It is impossible, he says, to escape the consequences of man's scientific thought, and while man is well intentioned in his quest for truth, he, like Oedipus, is on a collision course that inevitably leads to catastrophe. While Dürrenmatt raises serious issues such as these, as does Shaw, the spectator finds himself entertained by a sharp, critical intelligence coupled with a biting sense of humor that, in contrast to Shaw, encompasses the bizarre and the grotesque. And like Pirandello, Dürrenmatt has a deft theatrical facility for engaging the theatergoer in an intriguing journey of discovery as he attempts to sort out truth from unreality, comedy from tragedy.

Opposite page. Möbius learns that his wife has married and is taking his sons away.

Below. The Doktor brings Möbius's sons to visit him. Photographs are of the 1964 Broadway production, with Jessica Tandy as Doktor Mathilde, Hume Cronyn as Newton, and Robert Shaw as Möbius.

Above. Newton and Möbius disclose their true identities.

Left. Möbius informs Newton that they must remain permanently in the madhouse.

Below. Newton discovers that his future
is in the hands of Doktor Mathilde.

CHARACTERS

FRAULEIN DOKTOR MATHILDE VON ZAHND   *Alienist*

MARTA BOLL   *Head Nurse*

MONIKA STETTLER   *Nurse*

UWE SIEVERS   *Chief Male Attendant*

MC ARTHUR   *Male Attendant*

MURILLO   *Male Attendant*

HERBERT GEORG BEUTLER ("NEWTON")   *Patient*

ERNST HEINRICH ERNESTI ("EINSTEIN")   *Patient*

JOHANN WILHELM MÖBIUS   *Patient*

OSKAR ROSE   *A Missionary*

FRAU LINA ROSE   *His Wife*

ADOLF-FRIEDRICH

WILFRIED-KASPAR   } *Their Sons*

JÖRG-LUKAS

RICHARD VOSS   *Inspector of Police*

POLICE DOCTORS

GUHL   *Policeman*

BLOCHER   *Policeman*

THE PHYSICISTS

ACT ONE

The drawing room of a comfortable though somewhat dilapidated "villa" belonging to the private sanatorium known as "Les Cerisiers." Surroundings: in the immediate neighborhood, an unspoiled lakeside which gradually deteriorates into a built-up area and then into a medium-sized or even smaller town. This formerly neat and charming little spot with its castle and Old Town is now adorned by the hideous edifices of insurance companies and exists chiefly on account of a modest university with a recently added theological faculty and summer courses in foreign languages; in addition there are a business college and a Dental School, a boarding school for young ladies and light industries of no great importance: the town for the most part steers clear of the hurly-burly of modern life.

So the landscape is, in a superficial way, restful to the nerves; there are blue mountain ranges, hills geometrically forested and a fairly large lake, as well as a broad plain, once a dismal moor, which turns misty in the evening and is now crisscrossed by canals and irrigation ditches and is therefore very fertile. There is a house of correction somewhere in the vicinity which has undertaken large-scale agricultural schemes, so that everywhere there are to be seen silent and shadowy bands and little groups of criminals hoeing and digging. Yet these general surroundings really play no part in what follows, and are only mentioned in order to lend precision to the setting, the "villa" of the madhouse (alas, the word slipped out). Even there, we never leave the drawing room, and we have decided to adhere strictly to the Aristotelian unities of place, time, and action. The action takes place among madmen and therefore requires a classical framework to keep it in shape.

The "villa" was where once all the patients of the establishment's founder, FRÄULEIN DOKTOR MATHILDE VON ZAHND, were housed—decayed aristocrats, arteriosclerotic politicians (unless still in office), debilitated millionaires, schizophrenic writers, manic-depressive industrial barons and so on: in short, the mentally disturbed elite of half the Western world, for the Fräulein Doktor is a very celebrated person, not just because the hunchbacked spinster in her eternal white coat is descended from a great and very ancient family, of which she is the last presentable member, but because she is also a philanthropist and a psychiatrist of enormous repute; one might almost call her world-famous – her correspondence with C. G. Jung has just been published.

But now the distinguished but not always very pleasant patients have been transferred long since to the elegant, light, and airy new building, where for terrific fees even the most disastrous past experiences are turned into blissful memories. The new building spreads over the southern section of the extensive park, branching out into various wings and pavilions (stained-glass windows by Erni in the chapel) that descend toward the plain, while the "villa's" lawns, dotted with gigantic trees, slope down to the lake. There is a stone embankment along the edge of the lake.

Now only three patients at the very most occupy the drawing room of the sparsely inhabited "villa": as it happens, they are all three physicists, though this is not entirely due to chance, for humane principles are put into practice here, and it is felt that "birds of a feather" should "flock together." They live for themselves, each one wrapped in the cocoon of his own little world of the imagination; they take their meals together in the drawing room, from time to time discuss scientific matters or just sit gazing dully before them – harmless, lovable lunatics, amenable, easily handled and unassuming. In fact, they would be model patients were it not that certain serious, nay, hideous events have recently taken place: three months ago, one of them throttled a nurse, and now the very same thing has just happened again. So once more the police are back in the house and the drawing room is more than usually animated.

The dead nurse is lying on the parquet floor in a tragic and quite unmistakable attitude, somewhat in the background, so as not to distress the public too much. But it is impossible not to see that a struggle has taken place. The furniture is in great disorder. A standard lamp and two chairs have been knocked over, and downstage left a round table has been overturned so that it presents only its legs to the spectator.

Apart from all this, the transformation into an asylum has left painful traces on the salon. (The villa was once the Zahnd summer residence.) The walls have been covered to a height of six feet with hygienic, washable, glossy paint: above this, the original plaster emerges, with some remnants of stucco moldings. The three doors in the background, which lead from a small hall into the physicists' sick rooms, are upholstered with black leather. Moreover, they are numbered from one to three. To the left of the little hall is an ugly central-heating unit; to the right there is a washbasin with towels on a rail.

The sound of a violin, with piano accompaniment, comes from Room Number 2 (the middle room). Beethoven. Kreutzer Sonata. To the left is the wall overlooking the park, with very high windows that reach right down to the linoleum-covered parquet floor. Heavy curtains hang to right and left of the high windows. The glass doors lead on to a terrace, whose stone balustrade is silhouetted against the green of the park and the relatively sunny November light. It is a little after half past four in the afternoon. To the right, over a fireplace which is never used and is covered by a wire guard, there hangs the portrait of an old man with a pointed beard, enclosed in a heavy, gilded frame. Downstage right, a massive oak door. A ponderous chandelier is suspended from the brown, coffered ceiling.

Furniture: beside the round table there stand – when the room is in order – three chairs, all painted white like the table. The remaining furniture, with well-worn upholstery, belongs to various periods. Downstage right, a sofa and a small table flanked by two easy chairs. The standard lamp should really be behind the sofa, when the room should not appear overcrowded. Little is required for the furnishing of a stage on which, contrary to the plays of the ancients, the satire precedes the tragedy. We can begin.

Police officials in plain clothes are busied round the corpse: stolid, good-natured fellows who have already downed a glass or two of white wine: their breaths smell of it. In the center of the drawing room stands the INSPECTOR OF POLICE, RICHARD VOSS, wearing coat and hat; on the left is the head nurse, MARTA BOLL, looking as resolute as she really is. In the armchair on the far right sits a policeman taking everything down in shorthand. The inspector takes a cigar out of a brown leather cigar case.

INSPECTOR: All right if I smoke?

SISTER BOLL: It's not usual.

INSPECTOR: I beg your pardon. (He puts the cigar back in the case.)

SISTER BOLL: A cup of tea?

INSPECTOR: No brandy?

SISTER BOLL: You're in a medical establishment.

INSPECTOR: Then nothing. Blocher, you can take the photographs now.

BLOCHER: Yes, sir. (He begins taking photographs.   10
Flashes.)

INSPECTOR: What was the nurse's name?

SISTER BOLL: Irene Straub.

INSPECTOR: Age?

SISTER BOLL: Twenty-two. From Kohlwang.

INSPECTOR: Relatives?

SISTER BOLL: A brother in Liechenstein.

INSPECTOR: Informed?

SISTER BOLL: By telephone.

INSPECTOR: The murderer?   20

SISTER BOLL: Please, Inspector — the poor man's ill, you know.

INSPECTOR: Well, the assailant?

SISTER BOLL: Ernst Heinrich Ernesti. We call him Einstein.

INSPECTOR: Why?

SISTER BOLL: Because he thinks he is Einstein.

INSPECTOR *(turns to the police stenographer):* Have you got the statement down, Guhl?

30   GUHL: Yes, sir.

INSPECTOR: Strangled, doctor?

POLICE DOCTOR: Quite definitely. With the flex of the standard lamp. These madmen often have gigantic reserves of strength. It's phenomenal.

INSPECTOR: Oh. Is that so? In that case I consider it most irresponsible to leave these madmen in the care of female nurses. This is the second murder —

SISTER BOLL: Please, Inspector.

40   INSPECTOR: — the second accident within three months in the medical establishment known as Les Cerisiers. *(He takes out a notebook.)* On the twelfth of August a certain Herbert Georg Beutler, who believes himself to be the great physicist Sir Isaac Newton, strangled Dorothea Moser, a nurse. *(He puts the notebook back.)* And in this very room. If they'd had male attendants such a thing would never have happened.

SISTER BOLL: Do you really think so?

50   INSPECTOR: I do.

SISTER BOLL: Nurse Moser was a member of the League of Lady Wrestlers and Nurse Straub was District Champion of the National Judo Association.

INSPECTOR: And what about you?

SISTER BOLL: Weight-lifter.

INSPECTOR: Now I'd like to see the murderer.

SISTER BOLL: Please, Inspector.

INSPECTOR: I mean — the assailant.

60   SISTER BOLL: He's playing his fiddle.

INSPECTOR: Doing what?

SISTER BOLL: Can't you hear him?

INSPECTOR: Then kindly request him to stop.

(SISTER BOLL does not react.)

I have to ask him some questions.

SISTER BOLL: Definitely not.

INSPECTOR: And why not?

SISTER BOLL: We cannot allow it, on medical grounds. Herr Ernesti has to play his fiddle, and 70   play it now.

INSPECTOR: But damn it, the man's just strangled a nurse!

SISTER BOLL: Inspector. He's not just any man, but a sick man who needs calming down. And because he thinks he is Einstein he can only calm down when he's playing the fiddle.

INSPECTOR: Can I be going mad?

SISTER BOLL: No.

INSPECTOR: I'm getting confused. *(He wipes the sweat from his forehead.)* Warm in here.   80

SISTER BOLL: I don't think so.

INSPECTOR: Sister Boll. Kindly fetch the doctor in charge.

SISTER BOLL: Quite out of the question. The Fräulein Doktor is accompanying Einstein on the piano. Einstein can only calm down when the Fräulein Doktor plays his accompaniments.

INSPECTOR: And three months ago the Fräulein Doktor had to play chess with Sir Isaac Newton, to calm *him* down. We can't have any more of   90 this, Sister. I simply must speak to the doctor in charge.

SISTER BOLL: Certainly —

INSPECTOR: Thank you.

SISTER: — but you'll have to wait.

INSPECTOR: How long's this fiddling going to last?

SISTER BOLL: Fifteen minutes, an hour. It all depends.

(The INSPECTOR controls his impatience.)

INSPECTOR: Very well, I'll wait. *(He roars:)* I'll wait!   100

BLOCHER: We're just about finished, sir.

INSPECTOR: So am I. *(Silence. The INSPECTOR wipes his forehead.)* You can take away the body.

BLOCHER: Very well, sir.

SISTER BOLL: I'll show them the way through the park to the chapel.

(She opens the French windows. The body is carried out. Equipment also. The INSPECTOR takes off his hat and sinks exhaustedly into the easy chair to the left of the sofa. The fiddling continues, with piano accompaniment.   110 *Then out of Room Number 3 comes HERBERT GEORG BEUTLER in early eighteenth-century costume. He wears a full-bottomed wig.)*

NEWTON: Sir Isaac Newton.

INSPECTOR: Inspector Richard Voss. *(He remains seated.)*

NEWTON: I'm so glad. Really very glad. Truly. I

heard a noise in here, groans and gurglings, and then people coming and going. May I inquire just what has been going on?

120 INSPECTOR: Nurse Straub was strangled.

NEWTON: The District Champion of the National Judo Association?

INSPECTOR: The District Champion.

NEWTON: Gruesome.

INSPECTOR: By Ernst Heinrich Ernesti.

NEWTON: But he's playing his fiddle.

INSPECTOR: He has to calm himself down.

NEWTON: The tussle must have taken it out of him.
130 He's rather highly strung, poor boy. How did he —?

INSPECTOR: With the cord of the standard lamp.

NEWTON: With the cord of the standard lamp. Yes. That's another possibility. Poor Ernesti. I'm sorry for him. Truly sorry. And I'm sorry for the Ladies' Judo Champion too. Now you'll have to excuse me. I must put things straight.

INSPECTOR: Do. We've got everything we want.

(NEWTON rights the table and chairs.)

140 NEWTON: I simply can't stand disorder. Really it was my love of order that made me become a physicist — *(He rights the standard lamp.)* — to interpret the apparent disorder of Nature in the light of a more sublime order. *(He lights a cigarette.)* Will it disturb you if I smoke?

INSPECTOR: On the contrary, I was just thinking, . . . *(He takes a cigar out of his case.)*

NEWTON: Excuse me, but we were talking about order just now, so I must tell you that the patients
150 are allowed to smoke here but not the visitors. If they did it would stink the place out.

INSPECTOR: I see. *(He puts the cigar away.)*

NEWTON: Will it disturb you if I have a nip of brandy?

INSPECTOR: No. Not at all.

(From behind the wire guard in front of the fire NEWTON takes a bottle of brandy and a glass.)

NEWTON: That poor Ernesti. I'm really upset. How on earth could anyone bring himself to strangle
160 a nurse? *(He sits down on the sofa and pours out a glass of brandy.)*

INSPECTOR: I believe you strangled one yourself.

NEWTON: Did I?

INSPECTOR: Nurse Dorothea Moser.

NEWTON: The lady wrestler?

INSPECTOR: On the twelfth of August. With the curtain cord.

NEWTON: But that was something quite different, Inspector. I'm not mad, you know. Your health.

INSPECTOR: And yours. 170

(NEWTON drinks.)

NEWTON: Dorothea Moser. Let me cast my mind back. Blonde hair. Enormously powerful. Yet, despite her bulk, very flexible. She loved me and I loved her. It was a dilemma that could only be resolved by the use of a curtain cord.

INSPECTOR: Dilemma?

NEWTON: My mission is to devote myself to the problems of gravitation, not the physical requirements of a woman. 180

INSPECTOR: Quite.

NEWTON: And then there was this tremendous difference in our ages.

INSPECTOR: Granted. You must be well on the wrong side of two hundred.

(NEWTON stares at him uncomprehendingly.)

NEWTON: How do you mean?

INSPECTOR: Well, being Sir Isaac Newton —

NEWTON: Are you out of your mind, Inspector, or are you just having me on? 190

INSPECTOR: Now look —

NEWTON: Do you really think I'm Sir Isaac Newton?

INSPECTOR: Well, don't you?

(NEWTON looks at him suspiciously.)

NEWTON: Inspector, may I tell you a secret? In confidence?

INSPECTOR: Of course.

NEWTON: Well, it's this. I am not Sir Isaac Newton. I only pretend to be Sir Isaac Newton. 200

INSPECTOR: What for?

NEWTON: So as not to confuse poor Ernesti.

INSPECTOR: I don't get it.

NEWTON: You see, unlike me, Ernesti is really sick. He thinks he's Albert Einstein.

INSPECTOR: But what's that got to do with you?

NEWTON: Well, if Ernesti were to find out that *I* am the real Albert Einstein, all hell would be let loose.

INSPECTOR: Do you mean to say — 210

NEWTON: I do. I am he. The celebrated physicist and discover of the theory of relativity, born March 14th, 1879, in the city of Ulm.

(The INSPECTOR *rises in some confusion of mind.)*

INSPECTOR: How do you do?

*(*NEWTON *also rises.)*

NEWTON: Just call me — Albert.
INSPECTOR: And you can call me Richard.

(They shake hands.)

220 NEWTON: I could give you a Kreutzer with a good deal more dash than Ernesti. The way he plays the Andante — simply barbarous! Simply barbarous!
INSPECTOR: I don't understand anything about music.
NEWTON: Let's sit down, shall we? *(He draws the* INSPECTOR *down beside him on the sofa.* NEWTON *puts his arm around the* INSPECTOR'S *shoulders.)* Richard.
230 INSPECTOR: Yes, Albert?
NEWTON: You're cross, aren't you, because you can't arrest me?
INSPECTOR: But Albert —
NEWTON: Is it because I strangled the nurse that you want to arrest me, or because it was I who paved the way for the atomic bomb?
INSPECTOR: But Albert —
NEWTON: When you work that switch by the door, what happens, Richard?
240 INSPECTOR: The light goes on.
NEWTON: You establish an electrical contact. Do you understand anything about electricity, Richard?
INSPECTOR: I am no physicist.
NEWTON: I don't understand much about it either. All I do is to elaborate a theory about it on the basis of natural observation. I write down this theory in the mathematical idiom and obtain several formulae. Then the engineers come
250 along. They don't care about anything except the formulae. They treat electricity as a pimp treats a whore. They simply exploit it. They build machines — and a machine can only be used when it becomes independent of the knowledge that led to its invention. So any fool nowadays can switch on a light or touch off the atomic

bomb. *(He pats the* INSPECTOR'S *shoulders.)* And that's what you want to arrest me for, Richard. It's not fair.

INSPECTOR: But I don't want to arrest you, Albert. 260
NEWTON: It's all because you think I'm mad. But, if you don't understand anything about electricity, why don't you refuse to turn on the light? It's you who are the criminal, Richard. But I must put my brandy away; if Sister Boll comes there will be wigs on the green. *(*NEWTON *hides the bottle of brandy behind the wire guard in front of the fire, but leaves the glass where it is.)* Well, goodbye.
INSPECTOR: Goodbye, Albert. 270
NEWTON: Oh, Richard. You're the one who should be arrested.

(He disappears into Room Number 3.)

INSPECTOR: Now I will have a smoke.

(He takes a cigar firmly out of his cigar case, lights it and smokes. BLOCHER *comes through the French windows.)*

BLOCHER: We're ready to leave, sir.

(The INSPECTOR *stamps his foot.)*

Yes, sir. 280

(The INSPECTOR *calms down and growls.)*

INSPECTOR: Go back to town with the men, Blocher. I'll come on later. I'm waiting for the doctor in charge!
BLOCHER: Very well, sir. *(*BLOCHER *goes.)*

(The INSPECTOR *puffs out great clouds of smoke, stands up, goes to the chimney piece and stands looking at the portrait. Meanwhile the violin and piano have stopped. The door to Room Number 2 opens and* FRAULEIN DOKTOR 290
MATHILDE VON ZAHND *comes out. She is hunchbacked, about fifty-five, wearing a white surgical overall-coat and stethoscope.)*

FRL. DOKTOR: My father, August von Zahnd, Privy Councillor. He used to live in this villa before I turned it into a sanatorium. He was a great man, a real person. I am his only child. He hated me like poison; indeed he hated everybody like poison. And with good reason, for as an expert in economics, he saw, revealed in human beings, abysses which are for ever hidden from 300 psychiatrists like myself. We alienists are still hopelessly romantic philanthropists.

INSPECTOR: Three months ago there was a different portrait hanging here.

FRL. DOKTOR: That was my uncle, the politician. Chancellor Joachim von Zahnd. *(She lays the music score on the small table in front of the sofa.)* Well, Ernesti has calmed down. In the end he just flung himself on the bed and fell sound asleep. Like a little boy, not a care in the world. I can breathe again: I was afraid he'd want to fiddle through the entire Brahms G Major Sonata. *(She sits in the armchair left of sofa.)*

INSPECTOR: Excuse me, Fräulein Doktor, for smoking in here. I gather it's prohibited, but —

FRL. DOKTOR: Smoke away as much as you like, Inspector. I badly need a cigarette myself; Sister or no Sister. Give me a light. *(He lights her cigarette and she smokes.)* Poor Nurse Straub. Simply frightful. She was such a neat, pretty little thing. *(She notices the glass.)* Newton?

INSPECTOR: I had the pleasure of speaking to him.

FRL. DOKTOR: I'd better put it away.

INSPECTOR: Allow me. *(The INSPECTOR forestalls her and puts the glass away.)*

FRL. DOKTOR: On account of Sister Boll, you know.

INSPECTOR: I know.

FRL. DOKTOR: So you had a talk with Sir Isaac?

INSPECTOR: Yes, and I discovered something. *(He sits on the sofa.)*

FRL. DOKTOR: Congratulations.

INSPECTOR: Newton thinks he is really Einstein.

FRL. DOKTOR: That's what he tells everybody. But in fact he really believes he is Newton.

INSPECTOR: *(taken aback)* Are you sure?

FRL. DOKTOR: It is I who decide who my patients think they are. I know them far better than they know themselves.

INSPECTOR: Maybe so. In that case you should co-operate with us, Fräulein Doktor. The authorities are complaining.

FRL. DOKTOR: The public prosecutor?

INSPECTOR: Fuming.

FRL. DOKTOR: As if it were my business, Inspector.

INSPECTOR: But two murders—

FRL. DOKTOR: Please, Inspector.

INSPECTOR: Two accidents in three months. You must admit that the safety precautions in your establishment would seem inadequate.

FRL. DOKTOR: What sort of safety precautions have you in mind, Inspector? I am the director of a medical establishment, not a reformatory. One can't very well lock murderers up *before* they have committed their murders, can one?

INSPECTOR: It's not a question of murderers but of madmen, and they can commit murders at any time.

FRL. DOKTOR: So can the sane; and, significantly, a lot more often. I have only to think of my grandfather, Leonidas von Zahnd, the Field Marshall who lost every battle he ever fought. What age do you think we're living in? Has medical science made great advances or not? Do we have new resources at our disposal, drugs that can transform raving madmen into the gentlest of lambs? Must we start putting the mentally sick into solitary confinement again, hung up in nets, I shouldn't wonder, with boxing gloves on, as they used to? As if we were still unable to distinguish between dangerous patients and harmless ones.

INSPECTOR: You weren't much good at distinguishing between them in the cases of Beutler and Ernesti.

FRL. DOKTOR: Unfortunately, no. *That's* what disturbs me, not the fuming of your public prosecutor.

(EINSTEIN comes out of Room Number 2, carrying his violin. He is lean with long, snow-white hair and mustache.)

EINSTEIN: I just woke up.

FRL. DOKTOR: Oh, Professor!

EINSTEIN: Did I play well?

FRL. DOKTOR: Beautifully, Professor.

EINSTEIN: What about Nurse Irene? Is she—

FRL. DOKTOR: Don't give it another thought, Professor.

EINSTEIN: I'm going back to bed.

FRL. DOKTOR: Yes, do, Professor.

(EINSTEIN goes back into his room. The INSPECTOR has jumped to his feet.)

INSPECTOR: So that was him!

FRL. DOKTOR: Yes. Ernst Heinrich Ernesti.

INSPECTOR: The murderer—

FRL. DOKTOR: Please, Inspector.

INSPECTOR: I mean, the assailant, the one who

thinks he's Einstein. When was he brought in?

FRL. DOKTOR: Two years ago.

INSPECTOR: And Sir Isaac Newton?

400 FRL. DOKTOR: One year ago. Both incurable. Look here, Voss, I'm no beginner, God knows, at this sort of job. You know that, and so does the public presecutor; he has always respected my professional opinion. My sanatorium is world-famous and the fees are correspondingly high. Errors of judgment and incidents that bring the police into my house are luxuries I cannot afford. If anything was to blame here, it was medical science, not me. These incidents could
410 not have been foreseen; you or I would be just as likely to strangle a nurse. No—medically speaking there is no explanation for what has happened. Unless—(*She has taken a fresh cigarette. The* INSPECTOR *lights it for her.*) Inspector. Haven't you noticed something?

INSPECTOR: What do you mean?

FRL. DOKTOR: Consider these two patients.

INSPECTOR: Yes?

FRL. DOKTOR: They're both physicists. Nuclear
420 physicists.

INSPECTOR: Well?

FRL. DOKTOR: Inspector, you really have a very unsuspecting mind.

(*The* INSPECTOR *ponders.*)

INSPECTOR: Doktor von Zahnd.

FRL. DOKTOR: Well, Voss?

INSPECTOR: You don't think—

FRL. DOKTOR: They were both doing research on radioactive materials.

430 INSPECTOR: You suppose there was some connection?

FRL. DOKTOR: I suppose nothing. I merely state the facts. Both of them go mad, the conditions of both deteriorate, both become a danger to the public and both of them strangle their nurses.

INSPECTOR: And you think the radioactivity affected their brains?

FRL. DOKTOR: I regret to say that is a possibility I must face up to.

440 (*The* INSPECTOR *looks about him.*)

INSPECTOR: What's on the other side of the hall?

FRL. DOKTOR: The green drawing room and upstairs.

INSPECTOR: How many patients have you got here now?

FRL. DOKTOR: Three.

INSPECTOR: Only three?

FRL. DOKTOR: The rest were transferred to the new wing immediately after the first incident. For-
450 tunately I was able to complete the building just in time. Rich patients contributed to the costs. So did my own relations. They died off one by one, most of them in here. And I was left sole inheritor. Destiny, Voss. I am always sole inheritor. My family is so ancient, it's something of a miracle, in medicine, that I should be relatively normal, I mean, mentally.

(*The* INSPECTOR *thinks a moment.*)

INSPECTOR: What about the third patient?

FRL. DOKTOR: He's also a physicist.
460
INSPECTOR: Well, that's extraordinary. Don't you think so?

FRL. DOKTOR: Not at all. I put them all together. The writers with the writers, the big industrialists with the big industrialists, the millionairesses with the millionairesses, and the physicists with the physicists.

INSPECTOR: What's his name?

FRL. DOKTOR: Johann Wilhelm Möbius.

INSPECTOR: Was he working with radioactive
470 materials as well?

FRL. DOKTOR: No.

INSPECTOR: Mightn't he also perhaps—

FRL. DOKTOR: He's been fifteen years here. He's harmless. His condition has never changed.

INSPECTOR: Doktor von Zahnd, you can't get away with it like that. The public prosecutor insists that your physicists have male attendants.

FRL. DOKTOR: They shall have them.

(*The* INSPECTOR *picks up his hat.*)   480

INSPECTOR: Good. I'm glad you see it that way. This is the second visit I have paid to Les Cerisiers, Fräulein Doktor. I hope I shan't have to pay a third. Good-bye.

(*He puts on his hat, goes out left through the French windows on to the terrace and makes his way across the park.* DOKTOR MATHILDE VON ZAHND *gazes thoughtfully after him. Enter right the* SISTER, MARTA BOLL,

490 *who stops short, sniffing the air. She is carrying a patient's dossier.)*

SISTER BOLL: Please, Fräulein Doktor.

FRL. DOKTOR: Oh, I'm sorry. *(She stubs out her cigarette.)* Have they laid out Nurse Straub?

SISTER BOLL: Yes, under the organ loft.

FRL. DOKTOR: Have candles and wreaths put round her.

SISTER BOLL: I've already telephoned the florists about it.

FRL. DOKTOR: How is my Great-aunt Senta?

500 SISTER BOLL: Restless.

FRL. DOKTOR: Double her dose. And my Cousin Ulrich?

SISTER BOLL: No change.

FRL. DOKTOR: Fräulein Sister Boll, I regret to say that one of our traditions here at Les Cerisiers must come to an end. Until now I have employed female nurses only. From tomorrow the villa will be in the hands of male attendants.

SISTER BOLL: Fräulein Doktor von Zahnd. I won't

510 let my three physicists be snatched away from me. They are my most interesting cases.

FRL. DOKTOR: My decision is final.

SISTER BOLL: I'd like to know where you are going to find three male nurses, what with the demand for them these days.

FRL. DOKTOR: That's my problem. Leave it to me. Has Frau Möbius arrived?

SISTER BOLL: She's waiting in the green drawing room.

520 FRL. DOKTOR: Send her in.

SISTER BOLL: Here is Möbius's dossier. (SISTER BOLL *gives her the dossier and then goes to the door on the right, where she turns.)* But—

FRL. DOKTOR: Thank you, Sister, thank you.

(SISTER BOLL *goes. The* DOKTOR *opens the dossier and studies it at the round table,* SISTER BOLL *comes in again right leading* FRAU ROSE *and three boys of fourteen, fifteen, and sixteen. The eldest is carrying a briefcase.* HERR ROSE, *a missionary, brings up the rear. The*

530 DOKTOR *stands up.)*

My dear Frau Möbius—

FRAU ROSE: Rose. Frau Rose. It must be an awful surprise to you, Fräulein Doktor, but three weeks ago I married Herr Rose, who is a missionary. It was perhaps rather sudden. We met in September at a missionary convention. *(She*

blushes and rather awkwardly indicates her new husband.)* Oskar was a widower.

(The FRÄULEIN DOKTOR *shakes her by the hand.)*

FRL. DOKTOR: Congratulations, Frau Rose, hear- 540 tiest congratulations. And my best wishes to you, too, Herr Rose. *(She gives him a friendly nod.)*

FRAU ROSE: You do understand why we took this step?

FRL. DOKTOR: But of course, Frau Rose. Life must continue to bloom and flourish.

HERR ROSE: How peaceful it is here! What a friendly atmosphere! Truly a divine peace reigns over this house, just as the psalmist says: For the Lord heareth the needy and despiseth not 550 his prisoners.

FRAU ROSE: Oskar is such a good preacher, Fräulein Doktor. *(She blushes.)* My boys.

FRL. DOKTOR: Good afternoon, boys.

THREE BOYS: Good afternoon, Fräulein Doktor. *(The youngest picks something up from the floor.)*

JÖRG-LUKAS: A piece of electric wire, Fräulein Doktor. It was lying on the floor.

FRL. DOKTOR: Thank you, young man. Grand boys you have, Frau Rose. You can face the future 560 with confidence.

(FRAU ROSE *sits on the sofa to the right, the* DOKTOR *at the table left. Behind the sofa the three boys, and on the chair at extreme right,* HERR ROSE.)

FRAU ROSE: Fräulein Doktor, I have brought my boys with me for a very good reason. Oskar is taking over a mission in the Marianas.

HERR ROSE: In the Pacific Ocean.

FRAU ROSE: I thought it only proper that my boys should make their father's acquaintance before 570 their departure. This will be their one and only opportunity. They were still quite small when he fell ill and now, perhaps they will be saying goodbye for ever.

FRL. DOKTOR: Frau Rose, speaking as a doctor, I would say that there might be objections, but speaking as a human being I can understand your wish and gladly give my consent to a family reunion.

FRAU ROSE: And how is my dear little Johann 580 Wilhelm?

(The DOKTOR *leafs through the dossier.)*

FRL. DOKTOR: Our dear old Möbius shows signs

neither of improvement nor of relapse, Frau Rose. He's spinning his own little cocoon.

FRAU ROSE: Does he still claim to see King Solomon?

FRL. DOKTOR: Yes.

HERR ROSE: A sad and deplorable delusion.

590 FRL. DOKTOR: Your harsh judgment surprises me a bit, Herr Missionary. Nevertheless, as a theologian you must surely reckon with the possibility of a miracle.

HERR ROSE: Oh, of course—but not in the case of somone mentally sick.

FRL. DOKTOR: Whether the manifestations perceived by the mentally sick are real or not is something which psychiatry is not competent to judge. Psychiatry has to concern itself exclu-

600 sively with states of mind and with the nerves, and in this respect things are in a bad enough way with our dear old Möbius, even though his illness takes rather a mild form. As for helping him, goodness me, another course of insulin shock treatment might be indicated, but as the others have been without success I'm leaving it alone. I can't work miracles, Frau Rose, and I can't pamper our dear old Möbius back to health; but I certainly don't want to make his

610 life a misery either.

FRAU ROSE: Does he know that I've—I mean, does he know about the divorce?

FRL. DOKTOR: He has been told the facts.

FRAU ROSE: Did he understand?

FRL. DOKTOR: He takes hardly any interest in the outside world any more.

FRAU ROSE: Fräulein Doktor. Try to understand my position. I am five years older than Johann Wilhelm I first met him when he was a fifteen-

620 year-old schoolboy, in my father's house, where he had rented an attic room. He was an orphan and wretchedly poor. I helped him through high school and later made it possible for him to read physics at the university. We got married on his twentieth birthday, against my parents' wishes. We worked day and night. He was writing his dissertation and I took a job with a transport company. Four years later we had our eldest boy, Adolf-Friedrich, and then came the two

630 others. Finally there were prospects of his obtaining a professorship; we thought we could begin to relax at last. But then Johann Wilhelm

fell ill and his illness swallowed up immense sums of money. To provide for my family I went to work in a chocolate factory. Tobler's chocolate factory. (*She silently wipes away a tear.*) For years I worked my fingers to the bone. (*They are all moved.*)

FRL. DOKTOR: Frau Rose, you are a brave woman.

640 HERR ROSE: And a good mother.

FRAU ROSE: Fräulein Doktor, until now I have made it possible for Johann Wilhelm to stay in your establishment. The fees are far beyond my means, but God came to my help time and time again. All the same, I am now, financially speaking, at the end of my tether. I simply cannot raise the extra money.

FRL. DOKTOR: That's understandable, Frau Rose.

FRAU ROSE: I'm afraid now you'll think I married

650 Oskar so as to get out of providing for Johann Wilhelm. But that is not so. Things will be even more difficult for me now. Oskar brings me six sons from his previous marriage!

FRL. DOKTOR: Six?

HERR ROSE: Six.

FRAU ROSE: Oskar is a most zealous father. But now there are nine boys to feed and Oskar is by no means robust. And his salary is not high. (*She weeps.*)

660 FRL. DOKTOR: Come, now, Frau Rose, you mustn't. Don't cry.

FRAU ROSE: I reproach myself bitterly for having left my poor little Johann Wilhelm in the lurch.

FRL. DOKTOR: Frau Rose! You have no need to reproach yourself.

FRAU ROSE: My poor little Johann Wilhelm will have to go into a state institution now.

FRL. DOKTOR: No he won't, Frau Rose. Our dear old Möbius will stay on here in the villa. You

670 have my word. He's got used to being here and has found some nice, kind colleagues. I'm not a monster, you know!

FRAU ROSE: You're so good to me, Fräulein Doktor.

FRL. DOKTOR: Not at all, Frau Rose, not at all. There are such things as grants and bequests. There's the Oppel Foundation for invalid scientists, there's the Doktor Steinemann Bequest. Money's as thick as muck around here and it's my duty as his doctor to pitchfork some of it

680 in the direction of your dear little Johann Wilhelm. You can steam off to the Marianas

with a clear conscience. But now let us have a word with Möbius himself—our dear, good old Möbius. (*She goes and opens the door Number 1.* FRAU ROSE *rises expectantly.*) Dear Möbius. You have visitors. Now leave your physicist's lair for a moment and come in here.

(JOHANN WILHELM MÖBIUS *comes out of Room Number 1. He is about forty, a rather clumsy man. He looks around him uncertainly, stares at* FRAU ROSE, *then at the boys, and finally at the missionary,* HERR ROSE. *He appears not to recognize them and remains silent.*)

FRAU ROSE: Johann Wilhelm!

THREE BOYS: Papi!

(MÖBIUS *remains silent.*)

FRL. DOKTOR: My dear Möbius, you're not going to tell me you don't recognize your own wife?

(MÖBIUS *stares at* FRAU ROSE.)

MÖBIUS: Lina?

FRL. DOKTOR: That's better, Möbius. Of course it's Lina.

MÖBIUS: Hullo, Lina.

FRAU ROSE: My little Johann Wilhelm, my dear, dear little Johann Wilhelm.

FRL. DOKTOR: There we are, now. Frau Rose, Herr Rose, if you have anything else to tell me I shall be at your disposal in the new wing over there. (*She goes off through door left.*)

FRAU ROSE: These are your sons, Johann Wilhelm.

(MÖBIUS *starts.*)

MÖBIUS: Three?

FRAU ROSE: Of course, Johann Wilhelm. Three. (*She introduces the boys to him.*) Adolf-Friedrich, your eldest.

(MÖBIUS *shakes his hand.*)

MÖBIUS: How do you do, Adolf-Friedrich, my eldest.

ADOLF-FRIEDRICH: How do you do, Papi.

MÖBIUS: How old are you, Adolf-Friedrich?

ADOLF-FRIEDRICH: Sixteen, Papi.

MÖBIUS: What do you want to be?

ADOLF-FRIEDRICH: A minister, Papi.

MÖBIUS: I remember now. We were walking across St. Joseph's Square. I was holding your hand.

The sun was shining brightly and the shadows were just as if they'd been drawn with a compass. (MÖBIUS *turns to the next boy.*) And you—you are—?

WILFRIED-KASPAR: My name is Wilfried-Kaspar, Papi.

MÖBIUS: Fourteen?

WILFRIED-KASPAR: Fifteen. I should like to study philosophy.

MÖBIUS: Philosophy?

FRAU ROSE: He's an exceptionally mature boy for his age.

WILFRIED-KASPAR: I have read Schopenhauer and Nietzsche.

FRAU ROSE: This is your youngest boy, Jörg-Lukas. Fourteen.

JÖRG-LUKAS: How do you do, Papi.

MÖBIUS: How do you do, Jörg-Lukas, my youngest.

FRAU ROSE: He's the one who takes after you most.

JÖRG-LUKAS: I want to be a physicist, Papi.

(MÖBIUS *stares at his youngest in horror.*)

MÖBIUS: A physicist?

JÖRG-LUKAS: Yes, Papi.

MÖBIUS: You mustn't, Jörg-Lukas. Not under any circumstances. You get that idea right out of your head. I—I forbid it!

(JÖRG-LUKAS *looks puzzled.*)

JÖRG-LUKAS: But you became a physicist yourself, Papi—

MÖBIUS: I should never have been one, Jörg-Lukas. Never. I wouldn't be in the madhouse now.

FRAU ROSE: But Johann Wilhelm. That's not right. You are in a sanatorium, not a madhouse. You're having a little trouble with your nerves, that's all.

(MÖBIUS *shakes his head.*)

MÖBIUS: No, Lina. People say I am mad. Everybody. Even you. And my boys too. Because King Solomon appears to me.

(*They are all struck dumb with embarrassment. Then* FRAU ROSE *introduces* HERR ROSE.)

FRAU ROSE: Let me introduce Oskar Rose to you, Johann Wilhelm. He is my husband. A missionary.

770 MÖBIUS: Your husband? But *I'm* your husband.

FRAU ROSE: Not any more, my little Johann Wilhelm. (*She blushes.*) We're divorced, you know.

MÖBIUS: Divorced?

FRAU ROSE: Now you know that, surely?

MÖBIUS: No.

FRAU ROSE: Doktor von Zahnd told you. Of course she did.

MÖBIUS: Possibly.

780 FRAU ROSE: And then I married Oskar. He has six boys of his own. He was a minister at Guttannen and now he has been given a post in the Marianas.

MÖBIUS: In the Marianas?

HERR ROSE: In the Pacific Ocean.

FRAU ROSE: We're joining the ship at Bremen tomorrow.

MÖBIUS: I see. (*He stares at* HERR ROSE. *They are all embarrassed.*)

790 FRAU ROSE: Yes, that's right.

(MÖBIUS *nods to* HERR ROSE.)

MÖBIUS: I am glad to make the acquaintance of my boys' new father.

HERR ROSE: I have taken them to my bosom, Herr Möbius, all three of them. God will provide. As the psalmist says: The Lord is my shepherd, I shall not want.

FRAU ROSE: Oskar knows all the psalms off by heart. The Psalms of David, the Psalms of Solo-

800 mon.

MÖBIUS: I am glad the boys have found such an excellent father. I have not been a satisfactory father to them.

(*The three boys protest at this.*)

THREE BOYS: Ah, no, Papi.

MÖBIUS: And Lina has found a husband more worthy of her.

FRAU ROSE: But my dear little Johann Wilhelm—

MÖBIUS: I congratulate you. Heartiest congratula-

810 tions.

FRAU ROSE: We must be going soon.

MÖBIUS: To the Marianas.

FRAU ROSE: I mean, we must say goodbye to one another.

MÖBIUS: For ever.

FRAU ROSE: Your sons are remarkably musical, Johann Wilhelm. They are very gifted players on their recorders. Play your papi something, boys, as a parting present.

THREE BOYS: Yes, mama. 820

(ADOLF-FRIEDRICH *opens the briefcase and distributes recorders.*)

FRAU ROSE: Sit down, my little Johann Wilhelm.

(MÖBIUS *sits down at the round table.* FRAU ROSE *and* HERR ROSE *sit down on the sofa. The three boys take their places in the middle of the room.*)

Now. What are you going to play?

JÖRG-LUKAS: A bit of Buxtehude.

FRAU ROSE: Ready—one, two, three.

(*The boys play.*) 830

More feeling, boys, more expression!

(*The boys play with more expression.* MÖBIUS *jumps up.*)

MÖBIUS: I'd rather they didn't. Please, don't!

(*The boys stop playing, bewildered.*)

Don't play any more. Please. For King Solomon's sake. Don't play any more.

FRAU ROSE: But Johann Wilhelm!

MÖBIUS: Please, don't play any more. Please, don't play any more, please, please.

HERR ROSE: Herr Möbius, King Solomon himself 840 will rejoice to hear the piping of these innocent lads. Just think: Solomon, the Psalmist, Solomon, the singer of the Song of Songs.

MÖBIUS: Herr Missionary. I have met Solomon face to face. He is no longer the great golden king who sang of the Shulamite, and of the two young roes that are twins, which feed among the roses. He has cast away his purple robe! (MÖBIUS *suddenly dashes past his horrified family to his room and throws open the door.*) Now here in my room 850 he crouches naked and stinking, the pauper king of truth, and his psalms are horrible. Listen carefully, Herr Missionary. You love the words of the psalms and know them all by heart. Well, you can learn these by heart as well. (*He has run to the round table left, turned it over, climbed into it, and sat down.*) A Song of Solomon to be sung to the Cosmonauts.

860 We shagged off into outerspace
To the deserts of the moon. Foundered in
    her dust
Right from the start there were plenty
That soundlessly shot their bolts out there.
But most of them cooked
In the lead fumes of Mercury, were wiped
    out
In the oil-swamps of Venus and
Even on Mars we were wolfed by the sun—
Thundering, radioactive, yellow.

870 Jupiter stank
An arrow-swift rotatory methane mash
He, the almighty, slung over us
Till we spewed up our guts over Ganymede.

FRAU ROSE: But, Johann Wilhelm—
MÖBIUS:
Saturn we greeted with curses
What came next, a waste of breath

Uranus Neptune
Grayish-green, frozen to death
880 Over Pluto and Transpluto fell the final
Dirty jokes.
We had long since mistaken the sun for Sirius
Sirius for Canopus
Outcasts we cast out, up into the deep
Toward a few white stars
That we never reached anyhow

Long since mummied in our spacecraft
Caked with filth

In our deathsheads no more memories
890 Of breathing earth.

SISTER BOLL: But Herr Möbius!

(SISTER BOLL *has entered, right, with* NURSE MONICA. MÖBIUS *sits staring blankly, his face like a mask, inside the overturned table.*)

MÖBIUS: And now get yourselves off to the
    Marianas!
FRAU ROSE: My little Johann Wilhelm—
THREE BOYS: Papi!
MÖBIUS: Get yourselves away! And quick about
900   it! Off to the Marianas the whole pack of you!
    (*He stands up with a threatening look. The* ROSE
    family is nonplussed.)
SISTER BOLL: Come, Frau Rose. Come, boys. Herr
    Rose. He needs time to calm down.
MÖBIUS: Away with you! Get out!

SISTER BOLL: Just a mild attack. Nurse Monika will
    stay with him and calm him down. Just a mild
    attack.
MÖBIUS: Get out, will you! For good and all! Off
    to the Pacific with the lot of you!   910
JÖRG-LUKAS: Goodbye, Papi! Goodbye!

(SISTER BOLL *leads the overwrought and weeping family
off right.* MÖBIUS *goes on yelling unrestrainedly after
them.*)

MÖBIUS: I never want to set eyes on you again!
    You have insulted King Solomon! May you be
    damned for ever! May you and the entire
    Marianas sink and drown in the Mariana Deep!
    Four thousand fathoms down! May you sink and
    rot in the blackest hole of the sea, forgotten by   920
    God and man!
MONIKA: We're alone now. Your family can't hear
    you any more.

(MÖBIUS *stares wonderingly at* NURSE MONICA *and
finally seems to come to himself.*)

MÖBIUS: Ah, yes, of course. (NURSE MONICA *is silent.
    He is somewhat embarrassed.*) Was I a bit violent?
MONIAK: Somewhat.
MÖBIUS: I had to speak the truth.
MONIKA: Obviously.   930
MÖBIUS: I got worked up.
MONIKA: You were putting it on.
MÖBIUS: So you saw through me?
MONIKA: I've been looking after you for two years
    now.

(*He paces up and down, then stops.*)

MÖBIUS: All right. I admit I was just pretending
    to be mad.
MONIKA: Why?
MÖBIUS: So that I could say goodbye to my wife   940
    and sons for ever.
MONIKA: But why in such a dreadful way?
MÖBIUS: Oh no, it was a humane way. If you're
    in a madhouse already, the only way to get rid
    of the past is to behave like a madman. Now
    they can forget me with a clear conscience. My
    performance finally cured them of ever wanting
    to see me again. The consequences for myself
    are unimportant; life outside this establishment
    is the only thing that counts. Madness costs   950
    money. For fifteen years my Lina has been pay-
    ing out monstrous sums and an end had to be
    put to all that. This was a favorable moment.

King Solomon has revealed to me what was to be revealed; the Principle of Universal Discovery is complete, the final pages have been dictated, and my wife has found a new husband, a missionary, a good man through and through. You should feel reassured now, nurse. Everything is in order. (*He is about to go.*)

960

MONIKA: You had it all planned.

MÖBIUS: I am a physicist. (*He turns to go to his room.*)

MONIKA: Herr Möbius.

(*He stops.*)

MÖBIUS: Yes, nurse?

MONIKA: I have something to tell you.

MÖBIUS: Well?

MONIKA: It concerns us both.

MÖBIUS: Let's sit down.

970

(*They sit down: she on the sofa, he in the armchair on its left.*)

MONIKA: We must say goodbye to one another too. And for ever.

(*He is frightened.*)

MÖBIUS: Are you leaving me?

MONIKA Orders.

MÖBIUS: What has happened?

MONIKA: I'm being transferred to the main building. From tomorrow the patients here will be supervised by male attendants. Nurses won't be allowed to enter the villa any more.

980

MÖBIUS: Because of Newton and Einstein?

MONIKA: At the request of the public prosecutor. Doktor von Zahnd feared there would be difficulties and gave way.

(*Silence. He is dejected.*)

MÖBIUS: Nurse Monika, I don't know what to say. I've forgotten how to express my feelings; talking shop with the two sick men I live with can hardly be called conversation. I am afraid that I may have dried up inside as well. Yet you ought to know that for me everything has been different since I got to know you. It's been more bearable. These were two years during which I was happier than before. Because through you, Nurse Monika, I have found the courage to accept being shut away, to accept the fate of being a madman. Goodbye. (*He stands, holding out his hand.*)

990

MONIKA: Herr Möbius, I don't think you *are* mad.

1000

(MÖBIUS *laughs and sits down again.*)

MÖBIUS: Neither do I. But that does not alter my position in any way. It's my misfortune that King Solomon keeps appearing to me and in the realm of science there is nothing more repugnant than a miracle.

MONIKA: Herr Möbius, I believe in this miracle.

(MÖBIUS *stares at her, disconcerted.*)

MÖBIUS: You believe in it?

MONIKA: I believe in King Solomon.

MÖBIUS: And that he appears to me?

1010

MONIKA: That he appears to you.

MÖBIUS: Day in, day out?

MONIKA: Day in, day out.

MÖBIUS: And you believe that he dictates the secrets of nature to me? How all things connect? The Principle of Universal Discovery?

MONIKA: I believe all that. And if you were to tell me that King David and all his court appeared before you I should believe it all. I simply know that you are not sick. I can feel it.

1020

(*Silence. Then* MÖBIUS *leaps to his feet.*)

MÖBIUS: Nurse Monika! Get out of here!

(*She remains seated.*)

MONIKA: I'm staying.

MÖBIUS: I never want to see you again.

MONIKA: You need me. Apart from me, you have no one left in all the world. Not one single person.

MÖBIUS: It is fatal to believe in King Solomon.

MONIKA: I love you.

1030

(MÖBIUS *stares perplexed at* MONIKA, *and sits down again. Silence.*)

MÖBIUS: I love you too. (*She stares at him.*) That is why you are in danger. Because we love one another.

(EINSTEIN, *smoking his pipe, comes out of Room Number 2.*)

EINSTEIN: I woke up again. I suddenly remembered.

MONIKA: Now, Herr Professor.

1040

EINSTEIN: I strangled Nurse Irene.

MONIKA: Try not to think about it, Herr Professor.

(*He looks at his hands.*)

EINSTEIN: Shall I ever again be able to touch my violin with these hands?

(MÖBIUS *stands up as if to protect* MONIKA.)

MONIKA: You were playing just now.

EINSTEIN: Well, I hope?

MONIKA: The Kreutzer Sonata. While the police
1050   were here.

EINSTEIN: The Kreutzer! Well, thank God for that!
(*His face, having brightened, clouds over again.*) All
the same, I don't like playing the fiddle and I
don't like this pipe either. It's foul.

MONIKA: Then give them up.

EINSTEIN: I can't do that, not if I'm Albert Einstein.
(*He gives them both a sharp look.*) Are you two
in love?

MÖBIUS: We are in love.

1060   (EINSTEIN *proceeds thoughtfully backstage to where the
murdered nurse lay.*)

EINSTEIN: Nurse Irene and I were in love too. She
would have done anything for me. I warned her.
I shouted at her. I treated her like a dog. I
implored her to run away before it was too late.
In vain. She stayed. She wanted to take me away
into the country. To Kohlwang. She wanted
to marry me. She even obtained permission for
the wedding from Fräulein Doktor von Zahnd
1070   herself. Then I strangled her. Poor Nurse Irene.
In all the world there's nothing more absurd
than a woman's frantic desire for self-sacrifice.

(MONIKA *goes to him.*)

MONIKA: Go and lie down again, Herr Professor.

EINSTEIN: You may call me Albert.

MONIKA: Be sensible, now, Albert.

EINSTEIN: And you be sensible, too, Nurse. Obey
the man you love and run away from him; or
you're lost. (*He turns back toward Room Number
1080   2.*) I'm going back to bed. (*He disappears into Room
Number 2.*)

MONIKA: That poor, confused creature.

MÖBIUS: Well, he must have convinced you finally
of the impossibility of remaining in love with
me.

MONIKA: But you're not mad.

MÖBIUS: It would be wiser if you were to treat
me as if I were. Make your escape now! Go
on, run! Clear off! Or I'll treat you like a dog
1090   myself.

MONIKA: Why can't you treat me like a woman?

MÖBIUS: Come here Monika. (*He leads her to an
armchair, sits down opposite her, and takes her hands.*)
Listen. I have committed a grave mistake. I have
not kept King Solomon's appearances to myself.
So he is making me atone for it. For life. But
you ought not to be punished for what I did.
In the eyes of the world, you are in love with
a man who is mentally sick. You're simply asking
for trouble. Leave this place; forget me: that   1100
would be the best thing for us both.

MONIKA: Don't you want me?

MÖBIUS: Why do you talk like that?

MONIKA: I want to sleep with you. I want to have
children by you. I know I'm talking quite
shamelessly. But why won't you look at me?
Don't you find me attractive? I know these
nurses' uniforms are hideous. (*She tears off her
nurse's cap.*) I hate my profession! For five years
I've been looking after sick people out of love   1110
for my fellow-beings. I never flinched; everyone
could count on me: I sacrificed myself. But now
I want to sacrifice myself for one person alone,
to exist for one person alone, and not for everybody all the time. I want to exist for the man
I love. For you. I will do anything you ask,
work for you day and night: only you can't send
me away! I have no one else in the world! I
am as much alone as you.

MÖBIUS: Monika. I must send you away.   1120

MONIKA (*despairing*): But don't you feel any love
for me at all?

MÖBIUS: I love you, Monika. Good God, I love
you. That's what's mad.

MONIKA: Then why do you betray me? and not
only me. You say that King Solomon appears
to you. Why do you betray him too?

(MÖBIUS, *terribly worked up, takes hold of her.*)

MÖBIUS: Monika! You can believe what you like
of me. I'm a weakling; all right. I *am* unworthy   1130
of your love. But I have always remained faithful
to King Solomon. He thrust himself into my
life, suddenly, unbidden, he abused me, he
destroyed my life, but I have never betrayed
him.

MONIKA: Are you sure?

MÖBIUS: Do you doubt it?

MONIKA: You think you have to atone because you
have not kept his appearances secret. But perhaps
it is because you do not stand up for his revela-   1140
tions.

(He lets her go.)

MÖBIUS: I — I don't follow you.

MONIKA: He dictates to you the Principle of Universal Discovery. Why won't you fight for that principle?

MÖBIUS: But after all, people do regard me as a madman.

MONIKA: Why can't you show more spirit?

1150 MÖBIUS: In my case, to show spirit would be a crime.

MONIKA: Johann Wilhelm. I've spoken to Fräulein Doktor von Zahnd.

(MÖBIUS stares at her.)

MÖBIUS: You spoke to her?

MONIKA: You are free.

MÖBIUS: Free?

MONIKA: We can get married.

MÖBIUS: God.

1160 MONIKA: Fräulein Doktor von Zahnd has arranged everything. Of course, she still considers you're a sick man, but not dangerous. And it's not a hereditary sickness. She said she was madder than you, and she laughed.

MÖBIUS: That was good of her.

MONIKA: She's a great woman.

MÖBIUS: Indeed.

MONIKA: Johann Wilhelm! I've accepted a post as district nurse in Blumenstein. I've been saving

1170 up. We have no need to worry. All we need is to keep our love for each other.

(MÖBIUS has stood up. It gradually gets darker in the room.)

Isn't it wonderful?

MÖBIUS: Indeed, yes.

MONIKA: You don't sound very happy.

MÖBIUS: It's all happened so unexpectedly —

MONIKA: I've done something else.

MÖBIUS: What would that be?

1180 MONIKA: I spoke to Professor Schubert.

MÖBIUS: He was my teacher.

MONIKA: He remembered you perfectly. He said you'd been his best pupil.

MÖBIUS: And what did you talk to him about?

MONIKA: He promised he would examine your manuscripts with an open mind.

MÖBIUS: Did you explain that they have been dictated by King Solomon?

MONIKA: Naturally.

MÖBIUS: Well?   1190

MONIKA: He just laughed. He said you'd always been a bit of a joker. Johann Wilhelm! We mustn't think just of ourselves. You are a chosen being. King Solomon appeared to you, revealed himself in all his glory and confided in you the wisdom of the heavens. Now you have to take the way ordained by that miracle, turning to neither left nor right, even if that way leads through mockery and laughter, through disbelief and doubt. But the way leads out of this asylum,   1200 Johann Wilhelm, it leads into the outside world, not into loneliness, it leads into battle. I am here to help you, to fight at your side. Heaven, that sent you King Solomon, sent me too.

(MÖBIUS stares out of the window.)

Dearest.

MÖBIUS: Yes dear?

MONIKA: Aren't you happy?

MÖBIUS: Very.

MONIKA: Now we must get your bags packed. The   1210 train for Blumenstein leaves at eight twenty.

MÖBIUS: There's not much to pack.

MONIKA: It's got quite dark.

MÖBIUS: The nights are drawing in quickly now.

MONIKA: I'll switch on the light.

MÖBIUS: Wait a moment. Come here.

(She goes to him. Only their silhouettes are visible.)

MONIKA: You have tears in your eyes.

MÖBIUS: So have you.

MONIKA: Tears of happiness.   1220

(He rips down the curtain and flings it over her. A brief struggle. Their silhouettes are no longer visible. Then silence. The door to Room Number 3 opens. A shaft of light shines into the darkened room. In the doorway stands NEWTON in eighteenth-century costume. MÖBIUS rises.)

NEWTON: What's happened?

MÖBIUS: I've strangled Nurse Monika Stettler.

(The sound of a fiddle playing comes from Room Number 2.)   1230

NEWTON: Einstein's off again. Kreisler. Humoresque.

(He goes to the fireplace and gets the brandy.)

ACT TWO

One hour later. The same room. It is dark outside. The police are again present, measuring, sketching, photographing. But this time the corpse of MONIKA STETTLER *cannot be seen by the audience and it is assumed to be lying backstage right, below the window. The drawing room is brightly lit. The chandelier and the standard lamp have been switched on. On the sofa sits* FRÄULEIN DOKTOR MATHILDE VON ZAHND, *looking gloomy and pre-occupied. There is a box of cigars on the small table in front of her.* GUHL, *with his stenographer's notebook, is occupying the armchair on the extreme right.* INSPECTOR VOSS, *wearing his coat and hat, turns away from where the corpse is presumed to be lying and comes downstage.*

FRL. DOKTOR: Cigar?
INSPECTOR: No, thanks.
FRL. DOKTOR: Brandy?
INSPECTOR: Later.

(A silence.)

Blocher, you can take your photographs now.
BLOCHER: Very well, Inspector. *(Photographs and flashes.)*
INSPECTOR: What was the nurse's name?
10 FRL. DOKTOR: Monika Stettler.
INSPECTOR: Age?
FRL. DOKTOR: Twenty-five. From Blumenstein.
INSPECTOR: Any relatives?
FRL. DOKTOR: None.
INSPECTOR: Have you got the statement down, Guhl?
GUHL: Yes, sir.
INSPECTOR: Strangled again, doctor?
POLICE DOCTOR: Quite definitely. And again, tre-
20 mendous strength was used. But with the curtain cord this time.
INSPECTOR: Just like three months ago. *(He sits down wearily in the armchair downstage right.)*
FRL. DOKTOR: Would you like to have the murderer brought in?

588

INSPECTOR: Please, Fräulein Doktor.
FRL. DOKTOR: I mean, the assailant.
INSPECTOR: I don't think so.
FRL. DOKTOR: But —
INSPECTOR: Fräulein Doktor von Zahnd. I am   30
doing my duty, taking down evidence, examin-
ing the corpse, having it photographed and get-
ting the police doctor's opinion. But I do not
wish to examine Möbius. I leave him to you.
Along with the other radioactive physicists.
FRL. DOKTOR: And the public prosecutor?
INSPECTOR: He's past being angry now. He's just
brooding.

(The DOKTOR *wipes her forehead.)*

FRL. DOKTOR: Warm in here.   40
INSPECTOR: *I* don't think so.
FRL. DOKTOR: This third murder —
INSPECTOR: Please, Fräulein Doktor.
FRL. DOKTOR: This third accident is the end as far
as my work at Les Cerisiers goes. Now I can
resign. Monika Stettler was my best nurse. She
understood the patients. She could enter into
their states of mind. I loved her like a daughter.
But her death is not the worst thing that's hap-
pened. My reputation as a doctor is ruined.   50
INSPECTOR: You'll build it up again. Blocher, get
another shot from above.
BLOCHER: Very well, Herr Inspektor.

(Two enormous male attendants enter right pushing a trolley with food, plates, and cutlery on it. One of them is a Negro. They are accompanied by a chief male attendant who is equally enormous.)

CHIEF ATTNDT.: Dinner for the dear good patients,
Fräulein Doktor.

(The INSPECTOR *jumps up.)*   60

INSPECTOR: Uwe Sievers.
CHIEF ATTNDT.: Correct, Herr Inspektor. Uwe
Sievers. Former European heavyweight boxing

champion. Now chief male attendant at Les Cerisiers.

INSPECTOR: And these two other bruisers?

CHIEF ATTNDT.: Murillo, South American champion, also a heavyweight. And McArthur *(Pointing to the Negro:)*, North American middleweight champion. McArthur, the table.

(MC ARTHUR rights the overturned table.)

Murillo, the tablecloth.

(MURILLO spreads a white cloth over the table.)

McArthur, the Meissen.

(MC ARTHUR lays the plates.)

Murillo, the silver.

(MURILLO lays out the silver.)

McArthur, the soup tureen in the middle.

(MC ARTHUR sets the soup tureen in the center of the table.)

INSPECTOR: And what are the dear good patients having for dinner? *(He lifts the lid of the tureen.)* Liver-dumpling soup.

CHIEF ATTNDT.: Poulet à la broche. Cordon Bleu.

INSPECTOR: Fantastic.

CHIEF ATTNDT.: First class.

INSPECTOR: I am a mere fourteenth-class official. Plain cooking is all we can run to in my home.

CHIEF ATTNDT.: Fräulein Doktor. Dinner is served.

FRL. DOKTOR: Thank you Sievers. You may go. The patients will help themselves.

CHIEF ATTNDT.: Herr Inspektor. Glad to have made your acquaintance.

(The three attendants bow and go out right. The INSPECTOR gazes after them.)

INSPECTOR: Well I'm damned.

FRL. DOKTOR: Satisfied?

INSPECTOR: Envious. If we had them with the police —

FRL. DOKTOR: Their wages are astronomical.

INSPECTOR: With all your industrial barons and multi-millionairesses you can certainly such luxuries. Those fellows will finally set the public prosecutor's mind at rest. They wouldn't let anyone slip through their fingers.

(From Room Number 2 comes the sound of EINSTEIN playing his fiddle.)

There's Einstein at it again.

FRL. DOKTOR: Kreisler. As usual. Liebesleid. The pangs of love.

BLOCHER: We're finished now, Herr Inspektor.

INSPECTOR: Take the body out. Again.

(Two policemen lift the corpse. Then MÖBIUS rushes out of Room Number 1.)

MÖBIUS: Monika! My beloved!

(The two policemen stand still, carrying the corpse. FRÄULEIN DOKTOR rises majestically.)

FRL. DOKTOR: Möbius! How could you do it! You have killed my best nurse, my sweetest nurse!

MÖBIUS: I'm sorry, Fräulein Doktor.

FRL. DOKTOR: Sorry.

MÖBIUS: King Solomon ordained it.

FRL. DOKTOR: King Solomon. *(She sits down again, heavily. Her face is white.)* So it was His Majesty who arranged the murder.

MÖBIUS: I was standing at the window staring out into the falling dusk. Then the King came floating up out of the park over the terrace, right up close to me, and whispered his commands to me through the windowpane.

FRL. DOKTOR: Excuse me, Inspector, my nerves.

INSPECTOR: Don't mention it.

FRL. DOKTOR: A place like this wears one out.

INSPECTOR: I can well believe it.

FRL. DOKTOR: If you'll excuse me — *(She stands up.)* Herr Inspektor Voss, please express my profound regret to the public prosecutor for the incidents that have taken place in my sanatorium. Kindly assure him that everything is now well in hand again. Doctor, gentlemen, it was a pleasure. *(She first of all goes upstage right, bows her head ceremoniously before the corpse, looks at MÖBIUS and goes off right.)*

INSPECTOR: There. Now you can take the body into the chapel. Put her beside Nurse Irene.

MÖBIUS: Monika!

(The two policemen carrying the corpse and the others carrying their apparatus go out through the doors to the garden. The police doctor follows them.)

Monika, my love.

(The INSPECTOR walks to the small table beside the sofa.)

INSPECTOR: Möbius, come and sit down. Now I absolutely must have a cigar. I've earned it. *(He* takes a gigantic cigar out of the box and considers its size.) Good grief! (He bites off the end and lights the cigar.) My dear Möbius, behind the fireguard you will find a bottle of brandy hidden away by Sir Isaac Newton.

MÖBIUS: Certainly, Herr Inspektor.

160 (The INSPECTOR blows out clouds of smoke while MÖBIUS goes and gets the brandy and the glass.)

May I pour you one?

INSPECTOR: Indeed you may. (He takes the glass and drinks.)

MÖBIUS: Another?

INSPECTOR: Another.

MÖBIUS: Herr Inspektor, I must ask you to arrest me.

INSPECTOR: But what for, my dear Möbius?

170 MÖBIUS: Well, after all, Nurse Monika—

INSPECTOR: You yourself admitted that you acted under the orders of King Solomon. As long as I'm unable to arrest him you are a free man.

MÖBIUS: All the same—

INSPECTOR: There's no question of all the same. Pour me another glass.

MÖBIUS: Certainly, Herr Inspektor.

INSPECTOR: And now hide the brandy bottle away again or the attendants will be getting drunk
180 on it.

MÖBIUS: Very well, Herr Inspektor. (He puts the brandy away.)

INSPECTOR: You see, it's like this. Every year in this small town and the surrounding district, I arrest a few murderers. Not many. a bare half-dozen. Some of the these it gives me great pleasure to apprehend; others I feel sorry for. All the same I have to arrest them. Justice is Justice. And then you come along and your two
190 colleagues. At first I felt angry at not being able to proceed with the arrests. But now? All at once I'm enjoying myself. I could shout with joy. I have discovered three murderers whom I can, with an easy conscience, leave unmolested. For the first time Justice is on holiday — and it's a terrific feeling. Justice, my friend, is a terrible strain; you wear yourself out in its service, both physically and morally; I need a breathing space, that's all. Thanks to you, my dear Möbius,
200 I've got it. Well, goodbye. Give my kindest regards to Einstein and Newton.

MÖBIUS: Very well, Herr Inspektor.

INSPECTOR: And my respects to King Solomon.

(The INSPECTOR goes. MÖBIUS is left alone. He sits down on the sofa and takes his head in his hands. NEWTON comes out of Room Number 3.)

NEWTON: What's cooking?

(MÖBIUS does not reply. NEWTON takes the lid off the tureen.)

Liver-dumpling soup. (Lifts the lid off the other 210
dishes on the trolley.) Poulet à la broche, Cordon Bleu. Extraordinary. We usually only have a light supper in the evenings. And a very modest one. Ever since the other patients were moved into the new building. (He helps himself to soup.) Lost your appetite?

(MÖBIUS remains silent.)

I quite understand. I lost mine too after my nurse. (He sits and begins to drink the soup.)

(MÖBIUS rises and is about to go to his room.) 220

Stay here.

MÖBIUS: Sir Isaac?

NEWTON: I have something to say to you, Möbius.

(MÖBIUS remains standing.)

MÖBIUS: Well?

(NEWTON gestures at the food.)

NEWTON: Wouldn't you like to try just a spoonful of the liver-dumpling soup? It's excellent.

MÖBIUS: No.

NEWTON: Möbius, we are no longer lovingly 230
tended by nurses, we are being guarded by male attendants. Great hefty fellows.

MÖBIUS: That's of no consequence.

NEWTON: Perhaps not to you, Möbius. It's obvious you really want to spend the rest of your days in a madhouse. But it is of some consequence to me. The fact is, I want to get out of here. (He finishes his plate of soup.) Mmm — Now for the poulet à la broche. (He helps himself.) These new attendants have compelled me to act straight 240
away.

MÖBIUS: That's your affair.

NEWTON: Not altogether. A confession, Möbius. I am not mad.

MÖBIUS: But of course not, Sir Isaac.

NEWTON: I am not Sir Isaac Newton.

MÖBIUS: I know. Albert Einstein.

NEWTON: Fiddlesticks. Nor am I Herbert Georg Beutler, as they think here. My real name, dear boy, is Kilton.

(MÖBIUS *stares at him in horror.*)

MÖBIUS: Alec Jaspar Kilton?

NEWTON: Correct.

MÖBIUS: The author of the Theory of Equivalents?

NEWTON: The very same.

(MÖBIUS *moves over to the table.*)

MÖBIUS: So you wangled your way in here?

NEWTON: By pretending to be mad.

MÖBIUS: In order to — spy on me?

NEWTON: In order to get to the root of your madness. My impeccable German was acquired in our Intelligence Service. A frightful grind.

MÖBIUS: And because poor Nurse Dorothea stumbled on the truth, you —

NEWTON: — Yes. I am most extraordinarily sorry about the whole thing.

MÖBIUS: I understand.

NEWTON: Orders are orders.

MÖBIUS: Of course.

NEWTON: I couldn't do anything else.

MÖBIUS: Naturally.

NEWTON: My whole mission hung in the balance, the most secret undertaking of our Secret Service. I had to kill, if I wanted to avert suspicion. Nurse Dorothea no longer considered me to be demented; Fräulein Doktor von Zahnd thought I was only slightly touched; to prove my total insanity I had to commit a murder. I say, this poulet à la broche is simply superb.

(EINSTEIN *is fiddling in Room Number 2.*)

MÖBIUS: Einstein's at it again.

NEWTON: That Bach Gavotte.

MÖBIUS: His dinner's getting cold.

NEWTON: Let the old idiot get on with his fiddling.

MÖBIUS: Is that a threat?

NEWTON: I have the most immeasurable respect for you. It would grieve me to have to take violent steps.

MÖBIUS: So your mission is to abduct me?

NEWTON: Yes, if the suspicions of our Intelligence Service prove correct.

MÖBIUS: What would they be?

NEWTON: Our Intelligence Service happens to consider you to be the greatest genius among present-day physicists.

MÖBIUS: I'm a man whose nerves are sick, Kilton, that's all.

NEWTON: Our Intelligence Service has other ideas on the subject.

MÖBIUS: And what is your opinion?

NEWTON: I simply consider you to be the greatest physicist of all time.

MÖBIUS: And how did your Intelligence Service get on my trail?

NEWTON: Through me. Quite by chance I read your dissertation on the foundations of a new concept of physics. At first I thought it was a practical joke. Then the scales seemed to fall from my eyes. I realized I was reading the greatest work of genius in the history of physics. I began to make inquiries about its author but made no progress. Thereupon I informed our Intelligence Service: they got on to you.

EINSTEIN: You were not the only one who read that dissertation, Kilton. (*He has entered unnoticed from Room Number 2 with his fiddle and bow under his arm.*) As a matter of fact, I'm not mad either. May I introduce myself? I too am a physicist. Member of a certain Intelligence Service. A somewhat different one from yours, Kilton. My name is Joseph Eisler.

MÖBIUS: The discoverer of the Eisler-effect?

EINSTEIN: The very same.

NEWTON: "Disappeared" in 1950.

EINSTEIN: Of my own free will.

(NEWTON *is suddenly seen to have a revolver in his hand.*)

NEWTON: Eisler, might I trouble you to stand with your face to the wall, please?

EINSTEIN: Why of course. (*He saunters easily across to the window seat, lays his fiddle and bow on the mantelpiece, then swiftly turns with a revolver in his hand.*) My dear Kilton, we both, I suspect, know how to handle these things, so don't you think it would be better if we were to avoid a duel? If possible? I shall gladly lay down my Browning if you will do the same with your Colt.

NEWTON: Agreed.

EINSTEIN: Behind the fireguard with the brandy.

340   Just in case the attendants come in suddenly.
NEWTON: Good.

(They both put their revolvers behind the fireguard.)

EINSTEIN: You've messed up all my plans, Kilton.
I thought you really were mad.
NEWTON: Never mind: I thought you were.
EINSTEIN: Things kept going wrong. That business
with Nurse Irene, for example, this afternoon.
She was getting suspicious, and so she signed
her own death warrant. I am most extraordinar-
350   ily sorry about the whole thing.
MÖBIUS: I understand.
EINSTEIN: Orders are orders.
MÖBIUS: Of course.
EINSTEIN: I couldn't do anything else.
MÖBIUS: Naturally.
EINSTEIN: My whole mission hung in the balance;
it was the most secret undertaking of our Secret
Service. But let's sit down.
NEWTON: Yes, let's sit down.

360   *(He sits down on the left side of the table, EINSTEIN
on the right.)*

MÖBIUS: Eisler, I presume that you, too, want to
compel me now to —
EINSTEIN: Now Möbius —
MÖBIUS: — want to persuade me to visit your country.
EINSTEIN: We also consider you to be the greatest
physicist of all time. But just at the moment
all I'm interested in is my dinner. It's a real
370   gallows-feast. *(He ladles soup into his plate.)* Still
no appetite, Möbius?
MÖBIUS: Yes; it's suddenly come back. Now that
you've both got to the bottom of things. *(He
sits down between them at the table and helps himself
to the soup.)*
NEWTON: Burgundy, Möbius?
MÖBIUS: Go ahead.

(NEWTON pours out the wine.)

NEWTON: I'll attack the Cordon Bleu, what?
380   MÖBIUS: Make yourselves perfectly at home.
NEWTON: Bon appétit.
EINSTEIN: Bon appétit.
MÖBIUS: Bon appétit.

*(They eat. The three male attendants come in right,
the CHIEF ATTENDANT carrying a notebook.)*

CHIEF ATTNDT.: Patient Beutler!
NEWTON: Here.
CHIEF ATTNDT.: Patient Ernesti!
EINSTEIN: Here.
CHIEF ATTNDT.: Patient Möbius!   390
MÖBIUS: Here.
CHIEF ATTNDT.: Head Nurse Sievers, Nurse
Murillo, Nurse McArthur. *(He puts the notebook
away.)* On the recommendation of the
authorities, certain security measures are to be
observed. Murillo. The grille.

*(MURILLO lets down a metal grille over the window.
The room now suddenly has the aspect of a prison.)*

McArthur. Lock up.

(MC ARTHUR locks the grille.)   400

Have the gentlemen any further requests before
retiring for the night? Patient Beutler?
NEWTON: No.
CHIEF ATTNDT.: Patient Ernesti?
EINSTEIN: No.
CHIEF ATTNDT.: Patient Möbius?
MÖBIUS: No.
CHIEF ATTNDT.: Gentlemen, we take our leave.
Good night.

(The three attendants go. Silence.)   410

EINSTEIN: Monsters.
NEWTON: They've got more of the brutes lurking
in the park. I've been watching them from my
window for some time.

(EINSTEIN goes up and inspects the grille.)

EINSTEIN: Solid steel. With a special lock.

*(NEWTON goes to the door of his room, opens it, and
looks in.)*

NEWTON: They've put a grille over my window.
Quick work. *(He opens the other two doors.)* Same   420
for Eisler. And for Möbius. *(He goes to the door
right.)* Locked. *(He sits down again. So does
EINSTEIN.)*
EINSTEIN: Prisoners.
NEWTON: Only logical. What with our nurses and
everything.
EINSTEIN: We'll never get out of this madhouse
now unless we act together.
MÖBIUS: I do not wish to escape.

430 EINSTEIN: Möbius —

MÖBIUS: I see no reason for it at all. On the contrary. I am quite satisfied with my fate.

(Silence.)

NEWTON: But I'm not satisfied with it. That's a fairly decisive element in the case, don't you think? With all respect to your personal feelings, you are a genius and therefore common property. You mapped out new directions in physics. But you haven't a monopoly of knowledge. It is your

440 duty to open the doors for us, the non-geniuses. Come on out: within a year, we'll have you in a top hat, white tie and tails, fly you to Stockholm and give you the Nobel prize.

MÖBIUS: Your Intelligence Service is very altruistic.

NEWTON: I don't mind telling you, Möbius, they have a suspicion that you've solved the problem of gravitation.

MÖBIUS: I have.

450 *(Silence.)*

EINSTEIN: You say that as if it were nothing.

MÖBIUS: How else should I say it?

EINSTEIN: *Our* Intelligence Service believed you would discover the Unitary Theory of Elementary Particles.

MÖBIUS: Then I can set their minds at rest as well. I have discovered it.

(NEWTON mops his forehead.)

NEWTON: The basic formula.

460 EINSTEIN: It's ludicrous. Here we have hordes of highly paid physicists in gigantic state-supported laboratories working for years and years and years vainly trying to make some progress in the realm of physics while you do it quite casually at your desk in this madhouse. *(He too mops his forehead.)*

NEWTON: Möbius. What about the — the Principle of Universal Discovery?

MÖBIUS: Yes, something on those lines, too. I did

470 it out of curiosity, as a practical corollary to my theoretical investigations. Why play the innocent? We have to face the consequences of our scientific thinking. It was my duty to work out the effects that would be produced by my Unitary Theory of Elementary Particles and by

my discoveries in the field of gravitation. The result is — devastating. New and inconceivable forces would be unleashed, making possible a technical advance that would transcend the wildest flights of fantasy if my findings were to fall 480 into the hands of mankind.

EINSTEIN: And that can scarcely be avoided.

NEWTON: The only question is: who's going to get at them first?

(MÖBIUS laughs.)

MÖBIUS: You'd like that for your own Intelligence Service, wouldn't you, Kilton, and the miltary machine behind it?

NEWTON: And why not? It seems to me, if it can restore the greatest physicist of all time to the 490 confraternity of the physical sciences, any military machine is a sacred instrument. It's nothing more nor less than a question of the freedom of scientific knowledge. It doesn't matter who guarantees that freedom. I give my services to any system, providing that system leaves me alone. I know there's a lot of talk nowadays about physicists' moral responsibilities. We suddenly find ourselves confronted with our own fears and we have a fit of morality. This is nonsense. 500 We have far-reaching, pioneering work to do and that's all that should concern us. Whether or not humanity has the wit to follow the new trails we are blazing is its own look-out, not ours.

EINSTEIN: Admittedly we have pioneer work to do. I believe that too. But all the same we cannot escape our responsibilities. We are providing humanity with colossal sources of power. That gives us the right to impose conditions. If we 510 are physicists, then we must become power politicians. We must decide in whose favor we shall apply our knowledge, and I for one have made my decision. Whereas you, Kilton, are nothing but a lamentable aesthete. If you feel so strongly about the freedom of knowledge why don't you come over to our side? We too for some time now have found it impossible to dictate to our physicists. We too need results. Our political system too must eat out of the scientist's 520 hand.

NEWTON: Both our political systems, Eisler, must now eat out of Möbius's hand.

EINSTEIN: On the contrary. He must do what we tell him. We have finally got him in check.

NEWTON: You think so? It looks more like stalemate to me. Our Intelligence Services, unfortunately, both hit upon the same idea. So don't let's delude ourselves. Let's face the impossible situation we've got ourselves into. If Möbius goes with you, I can't do anything about it because you would stop me. And similarly you would be helpless if Möbius decided in my favor. It isn't we who have the choice, it's him.

(EINSTEIN *rises ceremoniously.*)

EINSTEIN: Let us retrieve our revolvers.

(NEWTON *rises likewise.*)

NEWTON: Let us do battle. (NEWTON *brings the two revolvers and hands* EINSTEIN *his weapon.*)

EINSTEIN: I'm sorry this affair is moving to a bloody conclusion. But we must fight it out, between us and then with the attendants. If need be with Möbius himself. He may well be the most important man in the world, but his manuscripts are more important still.

MÖBIUS: My manuscripts? I've burned them.

(*Dead silence.*)

EINSTEIN: Burned them?

MÖBIUS (*embarrassed*): I had to. Before the police came back. So as not to be found out.

(EINSTEIN *bursts into despairing laughter.*)

EINSTEIN: Burned.

(NEWTON *screams with rage.*)

NEWTON: Fifteen years' work.

EINSTEIN: I shall go mad.

NEWTON: Officially, you already are.

(*They put their revolvers in their pockets and sit down, utterly crushed, on the sofa.*)

EINSTEIN: We've played right into your hands, Möbius.

NEWTON: And to think that for this I had to strangle a nurse and learn German!

EINSTEIN: And I had to learn to play the fiddle. It was torture for someone like me with no ear for music.

MÖBIUS: Shall we go on with dinner?

NEWTON: I've lost my appetite.

EINSTEIN: Pity about the Cordon Bleu.

(MÖBIUS *stands.*)

MÖBIUS: Here we are, three physicists. The decision we have to make is one that we must make as physicists; we must go about it therefore in a scientific manner. We must not let ourselves be influenced by personal feelings but by logical processes. We must endeavor to find a rational solution. We cannot afford to make mistakes in our thinking, because a false conclusion would lead to catastrophe. The basic facts are clear. All three of us have the same end in view, but our tactics differ. Our aim is the advancement of physics. You, Kilton, want to preserve the freedom of that science, and argue that it has no responsibility but to itself. On the other hand you, Eisler, see physics as responsible to the power politics of one particular country. What is the real position now? That's what I must know if I have to make a decision.

NEWTON: Some of the world's most famous physicists are waiting to welcome you. Remuneration and accommodation could not be better. The climate is murderous, but the air-conditioning is excellent.

MÖBIUS: But are these physicists free men?

NEWTON: My dear Möbius, these physicists declare they are ready to solve scientific problems which are decisive for the defense of the country. Therefore, you must understand—

MÖBIUS: So they are not free. (*He turns to* EINSTEIN:) Joseph Eisler, your line is power politics. But that requires power. Have you got it?

EINSTEIN: You misunderstand me, Möbius. My political power, to be precise, lies in the fact that I have renounced my own power in favor of a political party.

MÖBIUS: Would you be able to persuade that party to take on your responsibility, or is there a risk of the party persuading you?

EINSTEIN: Möbius, that's ridiculous. I can only hope that the party will follow my recommendations, nothing more. In any case, without hope, all political systems are untenable.

MÖBIUS: Are your physicists free at least?

EINSTEIN: Well, naturally, they too are needed for the defense of the country—

MÖBIUS: Extraordinary. Each of you is trying to palm off a different theory, yet the reality you offer me is the same in both cases: a prison. I'd prefer the madhouse. Here at least I feel safe from the exactions of power politicians.

620 EINSTEIN: But after all, one must take certain risks.

MÖBIUS: There are certain risks that one may not take: the destruction of humanity is one. We know what the world has done with the weapons it already possesses; we can imagine what it would do with those that my researches make possible, and it is these considerations that have governed my conduct. I was poor. I had a wife and three children. Fame beckoned from the university; industry tempted me with money. Both 630 courses were too dangerous. I should have had to publish the result of my researches, and the consequences would have been the overthrow of all scientific knowledge and the breakdown of the economic structure of our society. A sense of responsibility compelled me to choose another course. I threw up my academic career, said no to industry, and abandoned my family to its fate. I took on the fool's cap and bells. I let it be known that King Solomon kept appear- 640 ing to me, and before long, I was clapped into a madhouse.

NEWTON: But that couldn't solve anything.

MÖBIUS: Reason demanded the taking of this step. In the realm of knowledge we have reached the farthest frontiers of perception. We know a few precisely calculable laws, a few basic connections between incomprehensible phenomena and that is all. The rest is mystery closed to the rational mind. We have reached the end of our journey. 650 But humanity has not yet got as far as that. We have battled onwards, but now no one is following in our footsteps; we have encountered a void. Our knowledge has become a frightening burden. Our researches are perilous, our discoveries are lethal. For us physicists there is nothing left but to surrender to reality. It has not kept up with us. It disintegrates on touching us. We have to take back our knowledge and I have taken it back. There is no other way out, 660 and that goes for you as well.

EINSTEIN: What do you mean by that?

MÖBIUS: You must stay with me here in the madhouse.

NEWTON: What! Us?

MÖBIUS: Both of you.

(Silence.)

NEWTON: But Möbius, surely you can't expect us to — for the rest of our days to—

MÖBIUS: I expect you have secret radio trans- 670 mitters.

EINSTEIN: Well?

MÖBIUS: You inform your superior that you have made a mistake, that I really am mad.

EINSTEIN: Then we'd be stuck here for the rest of our lives. Nobody's going to lose any sleep over a broken-down spy.

MÖBIUS: But it's the one chance I have to remain undetected. Only in the madhouse can we be free. Only in the madhouse can we think our own thoughts. Outside they would be dynamite. 680

NEWTON: But damn it all, we're not mad.

MÖBIUS: But we *are* murderers.

(They stare at him in perplexity.)

NEWTON: I resent that!

EINSTEIN: You shouldn't have said that, Möbius!

MÖBIUS: Anyone who takes life is a murderer, and we have taken life. Each of us came to this estab- lishment for a definite purpose. Each of us killed his nurse, again for a definite purpose. You two did it so as not to endanger the outcome of your 690 secret mission; and I, because Nurse Monika believed in me. She thought I was an unrecog- nized genius. She did not realize that today it's the duty of a genius to remain unrecognized. Killing is a terrible thing. I killed in order to avoid an even more dreadful murder. Then you come along. I can't do away with you, but perhaps I can bring you round to my way of thinking. Are those murders we committed to stand for nothing? Either they were sacrificial 700 killings, or just plain murders. Either we stay in this madhouse or the world becomes one. Either we wipe ourselves out of the memory of mankind or mankind wipes out itself.

(Silence.)

NEWTON: Möbius!

MÖBIUS: Kilton.

NEWTON: This place. These ghastly male atten- dants. That hunchback of a doctor!

710 MÖBIUS: Well?

EINSTEIN: We're caged in, like wild beasts!

MÖBIUS: We are wild beasts. We ought not to be let loose on humanity.

(*Silence.*)

NEWTON: Is there really no other way out?

MÖBIUS: None.

(*Silence.*)

EINSTEIN: Johann Wilhelm Möbius, I am a man of integrity. I'm staying.

720 (*Silence.*)

NEWTON: I'm staying too, for ever.

(*Silence.*)

MÖBIUS: Thank you. Thank you for leaving the world this faint chance of survival. (*He raises his glass.*) To our nurses!

(*They have gravely risen to their feet.*)

NEWTON: I drink to Dorothea Moser.

THE OTHERS: Nurse Dorothea!

NEWTON: Dorothea! You had to be sacrificed. In 730 return for your love, I gave you death! Now I want to prove myself worthy of you.

EINSTEIN: I drink to Irene Straub!

THE OTHERS: Nurse Irene!

EINSTEIN: Irene! You had to be sacrificed. As a tribute to your memory and your devotion, I am now going to behave like a rational human being.

MÖBIUS: I drink to Monika Stettler.

THE OTHERS: Nurse Monika!

740 MÖBIUS: Monika! You had to be sacrificed. May your love bless the friendship which we three have formed in your name. Give us the strength to be fools, that we may guard faithfully the secrets of our knowledge.

(*They drink and put the glasses on the table.*)

NEWTON: Let us be changed to madmen once again. Let us put on the shade of Newton.

EINSTEIN: Let us once again scrape away at Kreisler and Beethoven.

750 MÖBIUS: Let us have King Solomon appear before us once again.

NEWTON: Let us be mad, but wise.

EINSTEIN: Prisoners but free.

MÖBIUS: Physicists but innocent.

(*The three of them wave to each other and go back to their rooms. The drawing room stands empty. Then enter right* MC ARTHUR *and* MURILLO. *They are now wearing black uniforms, peaked caps, and pistols. They clear the table.* MC ARTHUR *wheels the trolley with the china and cutlery off right.* MURILLO *places the round table* 760 *in front of the window right, and puts on it the upturned chairs, as if the place were a restaurant closing for the night. Then* MURILLO *goes off right. The room stands empty agian. Then enters right* FRÄULEIN DOKTOR MATHILDE VON ZAHND. *As usual she is wearing a white surgical coat. Stethoscope. She looks about her. Finally* SIEVERS *comes in, also wearing a black uniform.*)

SIEVERS: Yes, boss?

FRL. DOKTOR: Sievers, the portrait.

(MC ARTHUR *and* MURILLO *carry in a large oil painting,* 770 *a portrait in a heavy gilded frame. It represents a general.* SIEVERS *takes down the old portrait and hangs up the new one.*)

It's better for General Leonidas von Zahnd to be hung in here than among the women patients. He still looks a great man, the old war-horse, despite his goiter. He loved heroic deaths and that is what there have been in this house. (*She gazes at her father's portrait.*) And so the Privy Councillor must go into the women's section 780 among the millionairesses. Put him in the corridor for the time being.

(MC ARTHUR *and* MURILLO *carry out the picture right.*)

Has my general administrator arrived with his minions?

CHIEF ATTNDT.: They are waiting in the green drawing room. Shall I serve champagne and caviar?

FRL. DOKTOR: That gang's here to work, not stuff its guts. (*She sits down on the sofa.*) Have Möbius 790 brought in, Sievers.

CHIEF ATTNDT.: Sure, boss. (*He goes to Room Number 1. Opens door.*) Möbius, out!

(MÖBIUS *appears. He is exalted.*)

MÖBIUS: A night of prayer. Deep blue and holy. The night of the mighty king. His white shadow is loosed from the wall; his eyes are shining.

(*Silence.*)

FRL. DOKTOR: Möbius, on the orders of the public
800   prosecutor I may speak to you only in the presence of an attendant.

MÖBIUS: I understand, Fräulein Doktor.

FRL. DOKTOR: What I have to say to you applies
also to your colleagues.

(MC ARTHUR *and* MURILLO *have returned.*)

McArthur and Murillo. Fetch the other two.

(MC ARTHUR *and* MURILLO *open doors Numbers 2 and
3.*)

MURILLO *and* MC ARTHUR: Out!

810   (NEWTON *and* EINSTEIN *come out, also in a state of
exaltation.*)

NEWTON: A night of secrets. Unending and sublime. Through the bars of my window glitter
Jupiter and Saturn unveiling the laws of the
infinite.

EINSTEIN: A blessed night. Comforting and good.
Riddles fall silent, questions are dumb. I should
like to play on for ever.

FRL. DOKTOR: Alec Jaspar Kilton and Joseph Eis-
820   ler—

(*They both stare at her in amazement.*)

I have something to say to you.

(*They both draw their revolvers but are disarmed by*
MURILLO *and* MC ARTHUR.)

Gentlemen, your conversation was overheard;
I had had my suspicions for a long time.
McArthur and Murillo, bring in their secret
radio transmitters.

CHIEF ATTNDT.: Hands behind your heads!

830   (MÖBIUS, EINSTEIN, *and* NEWTON *put their hands behind
their heads while* MC ARTHUR *and* MURILLO *go into rooms
Numbers 2 and 3.*)

NEWTON: It's funny! (*He laughs. The others do not.
Spooky.*)

EINSTEIN: I don't know.

NEWTON: Too funny! (*He laughs again, then falls silent.*)

(MC ARTHUR *and* MURILLO *come in with the transmitters.*)

CHIEF ATTNDT.: Hands down.   840

(*The physicists obey. Silence.*)

FRL. DOKTOR: Sievers. The searchlights.

CHIEF ATTNDT.: Okay, boss. (*He raises his hands.
Searchlights blaze in from outside, bathing the physicists in a blinding light. At the same time,* SIEVERS
switches off the lights in the room.)

FRL. DOKTOR: The villa is surrounded by guards.
Any attempt to escape would be useless. (*To
the attendants:*) You three, get out!

(*The three attendants leave the room, carrying the revol-   850
vers and radio apparatus. Silence.*)

You alone shall hear my secret. You alone among
men. Because it doesn't matter any longer
whether you know or not.

(*Silence.*)

(*Grandly:*) He has appeared before me also. Solomon, the golden king.

(*All three stare at her in perplexity.*)

MÖBIUS: Solomon?

FRL. DOKTOR: This many a long year.   860

(NEWTON *softly giggles.*)

(*Unconcerned:*) The first time was in my study.
One summer evening. Outside, the sun was still
shining, and a woodpecker was hammering away
somewhere in the park. Then suddenly the golden king came floating toward me like a tremendous angel.

EINSTEIN: She's gone mad.

FRL. DOKTOR: His gaze came to rest upon me. His
lips parted. He began to converse with his hand-   870
maiden. He had arisen from the dead, he desired
to take upon himself again the power that once
belonged to him here below, he had unveiled
his wisdom, that Möbius might reign on earth,
in his name.

EINSTEIN: She must be locked up. She should be
in a madhouse.

FRL. DOKTOR: But Möbius betrayed him. He tried
to keep secret what could not be kept secret.
For what was revealed to him was no secret.   880
Because it could be thought. Everything that
can be thought is thought at some time or
another. Now or in the future. What Solomon

had found could be found by anyone, but he wanted it to belong to himself alone, his means toward the establishment of his holy dominion over all the world. And so he did seek me out, his unworthy handmaiden.

EINSTEIN (*insistently*): You—are—mad. D'you hear, you—are—mad.

FRL. DOKTOR: He did command me to cast down Möbius, and reign in his place. I hearkened unto his command. I was a doctor and Möbius was my patient. I could do with him whatever I wished. Year in, year out, I fogged his brain and made photocopies of the golden king's proclamations, down to the last page.

NEWTON: You're raving mad! Absolutely! Get this clear once for all! (*Softly:*) We're all mad.

FRL. DOKTOR: I went cautiously about my work. At first I exploited only two or three discoveries, in order to rake in the necessary capital. Then I founded enormous plants and factories, one after the other. I've created a giant cartel. I shall exploit to the full, gentlemen, the Principle of Universal Discovery.

MÖBIUS (*insistent*): Fräulein Doktor Mathilde von Zahnd, you are sick. Solomon does not exist. He never appeared to me.

FRL. DOKTOR: Liar.

MÖBIUS: I only pretended to see him in order to keep my discoveries secret.

FRL. DOKTOR: You deny him.

MÖBIUS: Do be reasonable. Don't you see you're mad?

FRL. DOKTOR: I'm no more mad than you.

MÖBIUS: Then I must shout the truth to the whole world. You sucked me dry all these years, without shame. You even let my poor wife go on paying for me.

FRL. DOKTOR: You are powerless, Möbius. Even if your voice were to reach the outside world, nobody would believe you. Because to the public at large you are nothing but a dangerous lunatic. By the murder you committed.

(*The truth dawns on the three men.*)

MÖBIUS: Monika—

EINSTEIN: Irene—

NEWTON: Dorothea—

FRL. DOKTOR: I simply seized my opportunity. The wisdom of Solomon had to be safeguarded and your treachery punished. I had to render all three of you harmless. By the murders you committed. I drove those three nurses into your arms. I could count upon your reactions. You were as predictable as automata. You murdered like professionals.

(MÖBIUS *is about to throw himself upon her but is restrained by* EINSTEIN.)

There's no point in attacking me, Möbius. Just as there was no point in burning manuscripts which I already possess in duplicate.

(MÖBIUS *turns away.*)

What you see around you are no longer the walls of an asylum. This is the strong room of my trust. It contains three physicists, the only human beings apart from myself to know the truth. Those who keep watch over you are not medical attendants. Sievers is the head of my works police. You have taken refuge in a prison you built for yourselves. Solomon thought through you. He acted through you. And now he destroys you, through me.

(*Silence.*)

But I'm taking his power upon myself. I have no fears. My sanatorium is full of my own lunatic relatives, all of them loaded with jewels and medals. I am the last normal member of my family. No more. The last one. I am barren. I can love no one. Only humanity. And so King Solomon took pity on me. He, with his thousand brides, chose me. Now I shall be mightier than my forefathers. My cartel will dictate in each country, each continent; it will ransack the solar system and thrust out beyond the great nebula in Andromeda. It all adds up, and the answer comes out in favor, not of the world, but of an old hunchbacked spinster. (*She rings a little bell and the* CHIEF ATTENDANT *comes in right.*)

CHIEF ATTNDT.: Yes, boss?

FRL. DOKTOR: I must go, Sievers. The board of trustees is waiting. Today we go into world-wide operation. The assembly lines are rolling. (*She goes out right with* CHIEF ATTENDANT.)

(*The three physicists are alone. Silence. It is all over. Stillness.*)

NEWTON: It is all over. (*He sits down on the sofa.*)

EINSTEIN: The world has fallen into the hands of an insane, female psychiatrist. (*He sits down beside* NEWTON.)

MÖBIUS: What was once thought can never be unthought.

(MÖBIUS *sits down in the armchair on the left of the sofa. Silence. The three stare before them. Then each speaks in turn, quite calmly and naturally, simply introducing themselves to the audience.*)

NEWTON: I am Newton. Sir Isaac Newton. Born the 4th of January, 1643, at Woolsthorpe, near Grantham. I am president of the Royal Society. But there's no need to get up on my behalf. I wrote the Mathematical Principles of Natural Philosophy. I said: Hypotheses non fingo—I do not invent hypotheses. In the fields of experimental optics, theoretical mechanics, and higher mathematics my achievements are not without importance; but I had to leave unresolved certain problems concerning the nature of gravitational force. I also wrote theological works. Commentaries on the Prophet Daniel and on the Revelation of St. John the Divine. I am Newton, Sir Isaac Newton. I am the president of the Royal Society. (*He rises and goes into his room.*)

EINSTEIN: I am Einstein. Professor Albert Einstein. Born the 14th of March, 1879, at Ulm. In 1902 I started work testing inventions at the Federal patent office in Berne. It was there that I propounded my special theory of relativity which changed our whole concept of physics. Then I became a member of the Prussian Academy of Science. Later I became a refugee. Because I am a Jew. It was I who evolved the Formula $E = mc^2$, the key to the transformation of matter into energy. I love my fellow men and I love my violin, but it was on my recommendation that they built the atomic bomb. I am Einstein. Professor Albert Einstein, born the 14th of March, 1879, at Ulm. (*He rises and goes into his room. He is heard fiddling. Kreisler. Liebesleid.*)

MÖBIUS: I am Solomon. I am poor King Solomon. Once I was immeasurable rich, wise, and God-fearing. The mighty trembled at my word. I was a Prince of Peace, a Prince of Justice. But my wisdom destroyed the fear of God, and when I no longer feared God my wisdom destroyed my wealth. Now the cities over which I ruled are dead, the Kingdom that was given unto my keeping is deserted: only a blue shimmering wilderness. And somewhere round a small, yellow, nameless star there circles, pointlessly, everlastingly, the radioactive earth. I am Solomon. I am Solomon. I am Solomon. I am poor King Solomon. (*He goes into his room.*)

(*Now the drawing room is empty. Only* EINSTEIN's *fiddle is heard.*)

21 POINTS ON THE PHYSICISTS

by Friedrich Dürrenmatt

1. My point of departure is not a thesis, but a story.
2. Taking a story as a point of departure, it must be thought out to its end.
3. A story is thought out to its end if it has taken the worst possible turn.
4. The worse possible turn is not foreseeable. It happens by accident.
5. The art of a playwright consists in making the accident within the action as effective as possible.
6. The agents of a dramatic action are people.
7. The accident in a dramatic action consists of when and where and who meets whom accidentally.
8. The more people proceed according to plan the more effectively they will be struck by accident.
9. People who proceed according to plan wish to attain a definite goal. Accident strikes them hardest when they attain the opposite of their goals—that which they feared and tried hard to avoid (for example, Oedipus).
10. Such a story may be grotesque, but not absurd.
11. It is a paradox.
12. Logicians can no more avoid paradoxes than dramatists.
13. Logicians can no more avoid paradoxes than scientists.
14. A drama for scientists must be paradoxical.
15. The aim of the drama is not to express the contents of physics, but the effects.
16. The content of physics concerns the scientists, the effects concern men.
17. What concerns all men can only be resolved by all.
18. Every attempt by an individual to resolve for himself that which concerns everybody must fail.
19. Reality appears in paradoxes.
20. Whoever confronts paradoxes exposes himself to reality.
21. The playwright can deceive the spectator into exposing himself to reality, but he cannot force him to stay with it or to master it.

From *Theater: Schriften und Reden I* by Friedrich Dürrenmatt, translated by Isa Bergsohn. Verlag der Arche, Peter Schifferli, Zurich 1966.

PROBLEMS OF THE THEATRE

by Friedrich Dürrenmatt

Tragedy and comedy are but formal concepts, dramatic attitudes, figments of the esthetic imagination which can embrace one and the same thing. Only the conditions under which each is created are different, and these conditions have their basis only in small part in art.

Tragedy presupposes guilt, despair, moderation, lucidity, vision, a sense of responsibility. In the Punch-and-Judy show of our century, in this back-sliding of the white race, there are no more guilty and also, no responsible men. It is always, "We couldn't help it" and "We didn't really want that to happen." And indeed things happen without anyone in particular being responsible for them. Everything is dragged along and everyone gets caught somewhere in the sweep of events. We are all collectively guilty, collectively bogged down in the sins of our fathers and of our forefathers. We are the offspring of children. That is our misfortune, but not our guilt: guilt can exist only as a personal achievement, as a religious deed. Comedy alone is suitable for us. Our world has led to the grotesque as well as to the atom bomb, and so it is a world like that of Hieronymus Bosch whose apocalyptic paintings are also grotesque. But the grotesque is only a way of expressing in a tangible manner, of making us perceive physically the paradoxical, the form of the unformed, the face of a world without face; and just as in our thinking today we seem to be unable to do without the concept of the paradox, so also in art, and in our world which at times seems still to exist only because the atom bomb exists: out of fear of the bomb.

But the tragic is still possible even if pure tragedy is not. We can achieve the tragic out of comedy. We can bring it forth as a frightening moment, as an abyss that opens suddenly; indeed many of Shakespeare's tragedies are already really comedies out of which the tragic arises.

After all this the conclusion might easily be drawn that comedy is the expression of despair, but this conclusion is not inevitable. To be sure, whoever realizes that senselessness, the hopelessness of this world might well despair, but this despair is not a result of this world. Rather it is an answer given by an individual to this world; another answer would be not to despair, would be an individual's decision to endure this world in which we live like Gulliver among the giants. He also achieves distance, he also steps back a pace or two who takes measure of his opponent, who prepares himself to fight his opponent or to escape him. It is still possible to show man as a courageous being.

In truth this is a principal concern of mine. The blind man, Romulus, Uebelohe, Akki, are all men of courage. The lost world order is restored within them; the universal escapes my grasp. I refuse to find the universal in a doctrine. The universal for me is chaos. The world (hence the stage which represents this world) is for me something monstrous, a riddle of misfortunes which must be accepted but before which one must not capitulate. The world is far bigger than any man, and perforce threatens him constantly. If one could but stand outside the world, it would no longer be threatening. But I have neither the right nor the ability to be an outsider to this world. To find solace in poetry can also be all too cheap; it is more honest to retain one's human point of view. Brecht's thesis, that the world is an accident, which he developed in his street scene where he shows how this accident happened, may yield—as it in fact did—some magnificent theatre; but he did it by concealing most of the evidence! Brecht's thinking is inexorable, because inexorably there are many things he will not think about.

And lastly it is through the conceit, through comedy that the anonymous audience becomes possible as an audience, becomes a reality to be counted on, and also, one to be taken into account. The conceit easily transforms the crowd of theatre-goers into a mass which can be attacked, deceived, outsmarted into listening to things it would otherwise not so readily listen to. Comedy is a mousetrap in which the public is easily caught and in which it will get caught over and over again. Tragedy, on the other hand, predicated a true community, a kind of community whose existence in our day is but an embarrassing fiction. Nothing is more ludicrous, for instance, than to sit and watch the mystery plays of the Anthroposophists when one is not a participant.

CEREMONIES
IN DARK OLD MEN

Lonne Elder III

Ceremonies in Dark Old Men, Lonne Elder III's first professionally produced stage play, made an impressive debut in February, 1969, at the off-Broadway St. Mark's Theater. The playwright was fortunate in his cast—an excellent group of actors from the Negro Ensemble Company. A second production was given during the same season at The Pocket Theater. The original production was so well received by critics that it won fourteen votes in the balloting for the best play of the season from the New York Drama Critics Circle. It also received a citation for distinguished achievement from the Outer Circle Critics.

Elder's play centers about an ex-vaudeville hoofer's family as they try to eke out a precarious existence in Harlem. His story is told with sincerity and simplicity, warmed by flashes of humor and shadowed by the unhappy sequence of events that occurs as his sons reach maturity, determined to find a way out of their negative surroundings even if it means resorting to dishonest methods. Elder's gift for characterization and his ability to accurately define the circumstances of the action, free from rancor, sentiment, or self-pity, marks the talent of a playwright fully in control of his material. Moreover, *Ceremonies* provided an eminently actable vehicle that made his first play a compelling experience in the theater. Elder further enhanced his reputation with his excellent film script, *Sounder*.

Below Mr. Parker and Mr. Jenkins face the problems
of the world over a checkerboard.
Unless otherwise indicated, photographs in this sequence
are of the 1970 Minnesota Theatre Company production,
with Maxwell Glanville as Mr. Parker, Gerry Black as Mr. Jenkins,
and Bette Howard as Adele.

Above. Adele is fed up with the task of supporting grown men.

Opposite top. Mr. Parker's dance routine receives mixed reactions
in this scene from the 1971 production
at the University of California,
Santa Barbara's Studio Theater,
directed by Floyd Gaffney.

Opposite bottom. Adele objects to the bootleg scheme.

Below. Mr. Parker luxuriating on his throne, plans his future.

GUTHRIE THEATER COMPANY

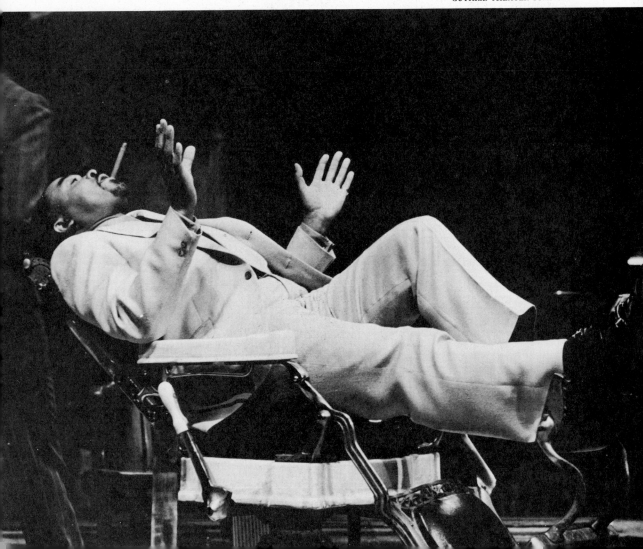

CHARACTERS

MR. RUSSELL B. PARKER
MR. WILLIAM JENKINS
THEOPOLIS PARKER
BOBBY PARKER
ADELE ELOISE PARKER
BLUE HAVEN
YOUNG GIRL

CEREMONIES
IN DARK OLD MEN

Early spring, about 4:30 in the afternoon, now.

A small, poverty-stricken barbershop on 126th Street between Seventh and Lenox avenues, Harlem U.S.A.

There is only one barber's throne in this barbershop. There is a not too lengthy mirror along the wall, and a high, broad shelf in the immediate area of the throne. There are two decks of shelves of equal width projecting just below the main shelf. These shelves are covered by small, sliding panels. On the far left corner of the shop is the street door, and on the far right corner is a door leading to a back room. Just to the right of the door,

flush against the wall, is a card table and two chairs. Farther right is a clothes rack. Against the wall to the far left of the shop, near the door, are four chairs lined up uniformly.

The back room is like any back room in a poverty-striken barbershop. It has an old refrigerator, an even older antique-type desk, and a medium-size bed. On the far right is a short flight of stairs leading up. A unique thing about this room: a door to stairs coming up from a small basement.

The action of the play takes place in the barbershop and the back room.

ACT ONE

SCENE ONE

As the curtain rises, MR. RUSSELL B. PARKER *is seated in the single barber's throne, reading the* Daily News. *He is in his early or middle fifties. He rises nervously, moves to the window, and peers out, his right hand over his eyebrows. He returns to the chair and continues to read. After checking his watch, he rises again and moves to the window for another look. Finally he sees the right person coming and moves to the door to open it.* MR. WILLIAM JENKINS *enters: early fifties, well dressed in a complete suit of clothes, and carrying a newspaper under his arm.* 10

MR. PARKER: Where have you been?

MR. JENKINS: Whatcha mean? You know where I was.

MR. PARKER: You want to play the game or not?

MR. JENKINS: That's what I came here for.

MR. PARKER: (*Slides open a panel in the counter.*) I wanted to get in at least three games before Adele got home, but this way we'll be lucky if we get in one. 20

MR. JENKINS: Stop complaining and get the board out—I'll beat you, and that will be that.

MR. PARKER: I can do without your bragging. (*Pulls out a checkerboard and a small can, quickly places them on the table, then shakes up the can.*) Close your eyes and take a man.

MR. JENKINS: (*Closing his eyes.*) You never learn. (*Reaches into the can and pulls out a checker.*) It's red.

30 MR. PARKER: All right, I get the black. (*Sits at the table and rushes to set up his men.*) Get your men down, Jenkins!

MR. JENKINS: (*Sits.*) Aw, man, take it easy, the checkers ain't gon' run away! (*Setting his men up.*) If you could play the game I wouldn't mind it—but you can't play!—Your move.

MR. PARKER: I'll start here—I just don't want Adele to catch us here playing checkers. She gave me and the boys a notice last week that we had

40 to get jobs or get out of the house.

MR. JENKINS: Don't you think it's about time you got a job? In the five years I've been knowing you, I can count the heads of hair you done cut in this shop on one hand.

MR. PARKER: This shop is gon' work yet; I know it can. Just give me one more year and you'll see . . . Going out to get a job ain't gon' solve nothing—all it's gon' do is create a lot of bad feelings with everybody. I can't work! I don't

50 know how to! (*Moves checker.*)

MR. JENKINS: I bet if all your children were living far from you like mine, you'd know how to. That's one thing I don't understand about you, Parker. How long do you expect your daughter to go on supporting you and those two boys?

MR. PARKER: I don't expect that! I just want some time until I can straighten things out. My dear Doris understood that. She understood me like a book. (*Makes another move.*)

60 MR. JENKINS: You mean to tell me your wife enjoyed working for you?

MR. PARKER: Of course she didn't, but she never worried me. You been married, Jenkins: you know what happens to a man when a woman worries him all the time, and that's what Adele been doing, worrying my head off! (*Makes another move.*)

MR. JENKINS: Whatcha gon' do about it?

MR. PARKER: I'm gon' get tough, evil and bad. 70 That's the only sign a woman gets from a man. (*Makes move.*)

(THEOPOLIS PARKER *enters briskly from street. He is in his twenties, of medium height, and has a lean, solid physique. His younger brother* BOBBY *follows, carrying a huge paper bag whose contents are heavy and fragile.*)

THEO: That's the way I like to hear you talk, Pop, but she's gon' be walking through that door soon, and I wants to see how tough you gon' be.

MR. PARKER: Leave me alone, boy.

THEO: Pop, we got six more days. You got to do 80 something!

MR. PARKER: I'll do it when the times comes.

THEO: Pop, the time is *now*.

MR. PARKER: And right now I am playing a game of checkers with Mr. Jenkins, so leave me alone!

THEO: All right—don't say I didn't warn you when she locks us out of the house!

(THEO *and* BOBBY *rush through the back room.* BOBBY *places the brown bag in the old refrigerator as they dart up the stairs leading to the apartment.* PARKER *makes* 90 *another move.*)

MR. PARKER: *You're trapped, Jenkins!*

(*Pause.*)

MR. JENKINS: (*Pondering.*) Hmmmmmm . . . It looks that way, don't it?

MR. PARKER: (*Moves to the door.*) While you're moaning over the board, I'll just make a little check to see if Adele is coming . . . Don't cheat now! (*He backs toward the window, watching that his adversary does not cheat. He quickly looks out the* 100 *window.*) Uh-uh! It's Adele! She's in the middle of the block, talking to Miss Thomas! (*Rushes to take out a towel and spreads it over the checkerboard.*) Come on, man! (*Drags* MR. JENKINS *by the arm toward the back room.*)

MR. JENKINS: *What are you doing, Parker!*

MR. PARKER: You gon' have to hide out in the back room, 'cause if Adele comes in here and sees you, she'll think that we been playing checkers all day! 110

MR. JENKINS: I don't care about that!

MR. PARKER: You want to finish the game, don't you?

MR. JENKINS: Yeah, but—

MR. PARKER: All you have to do, Jenks, is lay low for a minute, that's all. She'll stop in and ask me something about getting a job, I'll tell her I got a good line on one, and then she'll go on upstairs. There won't be nobody left here but you and me. Whatcha say, Jenks?

MR. JENKINS: (*Pause.*) All right, I'll do it. I don't like it, but I'll do it, and you better not mention this to nobody, you hear!

MR. PARKER: Not a single soul in this world will know but you and me.

MR. JENKINS: (*Moves just inside the room and stands.*) This is the most ridiculous thing I ever heard of, hiding in somebody's back room just to finish up a checker game.

MR. PARKER: Stop fighting it, man!

MR. JENKINS: All right!

MR. PARKER: Not there!

MR. JENKINS: What in the hell is it now!

MR. PARKER: *You've got to get under the bed!*

MR. JENKINS: No, I'm not gettin' under nobody's bed!

MR. PARKER: Now look ... Adele never goes through the front way. She comes through the shop and the back room, and the basement stairs to the apartment. Now you want her to catch you hiding in there, looking like a fool?

MR. JENKINS: No, I can take myself out of here and go home!

MR. PARKER: (*Pushes* JENKINS *over to the table and uncovers the checkerboard.*) Look at this! Now you just take a good look at this board! (*Releases him.*)

MR. JENKINS: I'm looking, so what?

MR. PARKER: *So what?* I got you and you know it! There ain't no way in the world you'll ever get out of that little trap I got you in. *And it's your move.* How many years we been playing against each other?

MR. JENKINS: Three.

MR. PARKER: Never won a game from you in all that time, have I?

MR. JENKINS: That ain't the half of it. You ain't gon' win one either.

MR. PARKER: Now that I finally got you, that's easy talk, comin' from a running man. All right, go on. Run. (*Moves away.*)

MR. JENKINS: Go on, hell! All I gotta do is put my king here, give you this jump here, move this man over there, and you're dead!

MR. PARKER: (*Turns to him.*) Try me then. Try me, or are you scared at last I'm gon' beat you?

MR. JENKINS: I can't do it now, there ain't enough time!

MR. PARKER: (*Strutting like a sport.*) Run, rabbit, run ...

MR. JENKINS: All right! I'll get under the bed. But I swear, Parker, I'm gon' beat you silly! (*They move into the back room.*)

MR. PARKER: Hurry it up then. We ain't got much time.

(*As* MR. PARKER *struggles to help* MR. JENKINS *get under the bed in the back room,* ADELE *comes in from the street. She is in her late twenties, well dressed in conventional New York office attire. She is carrying a smart-looking handbag and a manila envelope. She stops near the table on which checkerboard is hidden under towel.* MR. PARKER *enters from the back room.*)

MR. PARKER: Hi, honey.

(*She doesn't answer, instead busies herself putting minor things in order.*)

ADELE: You looked for work today?

MR. PARKER: All morning ...

(*Pause.*)

ADELE: No luck in the morning, and so you played checkers all afternoon.

MR. PARKER: No, I've been working on a few ideas of mine. My birthday comes up the tenth of the month, and I plan to celebrate it with an idea to shake up this whole neighborhood, and then I'm gon' really go to the country!

ADELE: Don't go to the country—go to work, huh? (*Moves toward back room.*) Oh, God, I'm tired!

MR. PARKER: (*Rushing to get her away from bed.*) Come on and let me take you upstairs. I know you must've had yourself a real tough day at the office ... and you can forget about cooking supper and all of that stuff.

ADELE: (*Breaks away, moves back into shop toward counter.*) Thank you, but I've already given myself the privilege of not cooking your supper tonight.

MR. PARKER: You did?

ADELE: The way I figure it, you should have my dinner waiting for me.

MR. PARKER: But I don't know how to cook.

210 ADELE: (*Turns sharply.*) You can learn.

MR. PARKER: Now look, Adele, if you got something on your mind, say it, 'cause you know damn well I ain't doin' no cooking.

ADELE: (*Pause.*) All right, I will. A thought came to me today as it does every day, and I'm damn tired of thinking about it—

MR. PARKER: What?

ADELE: —and that is, I've been down at that motor-license bureau so long, sometimes I forget the
220 reasons I ever took the job in the first place.

MR. PARKER: Now look, everybody knows you quit college and came home to help your mama out. Everybody knows it! What you want me to do? Write some prayers to you?

(*The two boys enter the back room from upstairs.*)

ADELE: I just want you to get a job!

(*The boys step into shop and stand apart from each other.*)

BOBBY: Hey, Adele.

ADELE: Well! From what cave did you fellows
230 crawl out of? I didn't know you hung around barbershops ... Want a haircut, boys?

THEO: For your information, this is the first time we been in this barbershop today. We been upstairs thinking.

ADELE: With what?

THEO: With our *minds*, baby!

ADELE: If the two of you found that house upstairs so attractive to keep you in it all day, then I can think of only three things: the telephone,
240 the bed, and the kitchen.

BOBBY: The kitchen, that's it: we been washing dishes all day!

ADELE: I don't like that, Bobby!

THEO: And I don't like your attitude!

ADELE: Do you like it when I go out of here every morning to work?

THEO: There you go again with that same old tired talk: work! Mama understood about us, I don't know why you gotta give everybody a hard
250 time ...

ADELE: That was one of Mama's troubles: understanding everybody.

THEO: Now don't start that junk with me!

ADELE: I have got to start that, *Mr. Theopolis Parker!*

MR. PARKER: Hold on now, there's no need for all this ... Can't we settle this later on, Adele ...

ADELE: We settle it now. You got six days left, so you gotta do something, and quick. I got a man coming here tomorrow to change the locks on the door. So for the little time you have left, 260 you'll have to cooe by me to enter this house.

THEO: Who gives you the right to do that?

ADELE: Me, Adele Eloise Parker, black, over twenty-one, and the only working person in this house!

(*Pause.*)

I am not going to let the three of you drive me into the grave the way you did Mama. And if you really want to know how I feel about that, I'll tell you: Mama killed herself because 270 there was no kind of order in this house. There was nothing but her old-fashion love for a bum like you, Theo—and this one (*points to* BOBBY) who's got nothing better to do with his time but to shoplift every time he walks into a department store. And you, Daddy, you and those fanciful stories you're always ready to tell, and all the talk of the good old days when you were the big vaudeville star, of hitting the numbers big. How? How, Daddy? The money you spent 280 on the numbers you got from Mama ... In a way, you let Mama make a bum out of you—you let her kill herself!

MR. PARKER: That's a terrible thing to say, Adele, and I'm not going to let you put that off on me!

ADELE: But the fact remains that in the seven years you've been in this barbershop you haven't earned enough money to buy two hot dogs! Most of your time is spent playing checkers with that 290 damn Mr. Jenkins.

THEO: (*Breaks in.*) Why don't you get married or something! We don't need you—Pop is here, it's HIS HOUSE!

ADELE: You're lucky I don't get married and—

THEO: Nobody wants you, baby!

ADELE: (THEO's *remark stops her for a moment. She resettles herself.*) All right, you just let someone ask me, and I'll leave you with *Pop*, to starve with Pop. Or, there's another way: why don't 300 the three of you just leave right now and try making it on your own? Why don't we try that!

MR. PARKER: What about my shop?

ADELE: Since I'm the one that has to pay the extra forty dollars a month for you to keep this place, there's going to be no more shop. It was a bad investment and the whole of Harlem knows it!

MR. PARKER: (*Grabbing her by the arm, in desperation.*) I'm fifty-four years old!

310 ADELE: (*Pulling away.*) Don't touch me!

MR. PARKER: You go ahead and do what you want, but I'm not leaving this shop! (*Crosses away from her.*)

ADELE: Can't you understand, Father? I can't go on forever supporting three grown men! *That ain't right!*

(*Long pause.*)

MR. PARKER: (*Shaken by her remarks.*) No, it's not right—it's not right at all.

320 ADELE: —It's going to be *you* or me.

BOBBY: (*After a pause.*) I'll do what I can, Adele.

ADELE: You'll do *more* than you can.

BOBBY: I'll do more than I can.

ADELE: Is that all right by you, Mr. Theopolis?

THEO: Yes.

(*Pause.*)

ADELE: That's fine. Out of this house tomorrow morning—before I leave here, or with me—suit your choice. And don't look so mournful (*gathers up her belongings at the shelf*), smile. You're going to be happier than you think, earning a living for a change. (*Moves briskly through the back room and up the stairs.*)

330

BOBBY: You do look pretty bad, Theo. A job might be just the thing for you.

(MR. JENKINS *comes rushing from the bed into the shop.*)

MR. PARKER: Jenkins! I plumb forgot—

MR. JENKINS: I let you make a fool out of me, Parker!

340 MR. PARKER: We can still play!

MR. JENKINS: (*Gathering his jacket coat.*) We can't play nothing, I'm going home where I belong!

MR. PARKER: Okay, okay, I'll come over to your place tonight.

MR. JENKINS: That's the only way. I ain't gon' have my feelings hurt by that daughter of yours.

MR. PARKER: I'll see you tonight—about eight.

MR. JENKINS: (*At the door.*) And, Parker, tell me something?

MR. PARKER: Yeah, what, Jenks?   350

MR. JENKINS: Are you positively sure Adele is your daughter?

MR. PARKER: Get out of here! (MR. JENKINS *rushes out.*) Now what made him ask a silly question like that?

THEO: I think he was trying to tell you that you ain't supposed to be taking all that stuff from Adele.

BOBBY: Yeah, Pop, he's right.

(MR. PARKER *starts putting his checker set together.*)   360

THEO: (*To* BOBBY.) I don't know what you talking about—you had your chance a few minutes ago, but all you did was poke your eyes at me and nod your head like a fool.

BOBBY: I don't see why you gotta make such a big thing out of her taking charge. Somebody's gotta do it. I think she's right!

THEO: I know what she's up to. She wants us to get jobs so she can fix up the house like she always wanted it, and then it's gon' happen.   370

BOBBY: What's that?

THEO: She gon' get married to some konkhead out on the Avenue, and then she gon' throw us out the door.

BOBBY: She wouldn't do that.

THEO: She wouldn't, huh? Put yourself in her place. She's busting thirty wide open. *Thirty years old*—that's a lot of years for a broad that's not married.

BOBBY: I never thought of it that way . . .   380

THEO: (*In half confidence.*) And you know something else, Pop? I sneaked and peeped at her bankbook, and you know what she got saved?

MR. PARKER and BOBBY: (*Simultaneously, turning their heads.*) How much!?

THEO: Two thousand two hundred and sixty-five dollars!

BOBBY: WHAT!!!

MR. PARKER: I don't believe it!

THEO: You better—and don't let her hand you that   390 stuff about how she been sacrificing all these years for the house. The only way she could've saved up that kind of money was by staying right here!

MR. PARKER: Well, I'll be damned—two thousand dollars!

THEO: She better watch out is all I gotta say, 'cause I know some guys out there on that Avenue who don't do nothing but sit around all day figuring out ways to beat working girls out of their savings.

MR. PARKER: You oughta know, 'cause you're one of them yourself. The way I figure it, Theo, anybody that can handle you the way she did a few minutes ago can very well take care of themselves. (*He occupies himself putting checkers and board away and cleaning up.*)

THEO: That's mighty big talk coming from you, after the way she treated you.

MR. PARKER: Lay off me, boy.

THEO: You going out to look for a job?

MR. PARKER: I'm giving it some serious thought.

THEO: Well, I'm not. I ain't wasting myself on no low, dirty, dead-end job. I got my paintings to think about.

BOBBY: Do you really think you're some kind of painter or something?

THEO: You've seen them.

BOBBY: Yeah, but how would I know?

THEO: (*Rushes into the back room, takes paintings from behind the refrigerator.*) All right, look at 'em.

BOBBY: Don't bring that stuff in here to me—show it to Pop!

(THEO *holds up two ghastly, inept paintings to his brother.* MR. PARKER, *sweeping the floor pays no attention.*)

THEO: Look at it! Now tell me what you see.

BOBBY: Nothing.

THEO: You've got to see something—even an idiot has impressions.

BOBBY: I ain't no idiot.

THEO: All right, fool then.

BOBBY: Now look, you better stop throwing them words "fool" and "idiot" at me any time you feel like it. I'm gon' be one more fool, and then my fists is gonna land right upside your head!

THEO: Take it easy now—I tell you what: try to see something.

BOBBY: Try?

THEO: Yeah, close your eyes and really try.

BOBBY: (*Closes his eyes.*) Okay, I'm trying, but I don't know how I'm gon' see anything with my eyes closed!

THEO: Well, open them!

BOBBY: They open.

THEO: Now tell me what you see.

BOBBY: I see paint.

THEO: I know you see paint, stupid.

BOBBY: (*Slaps him ferociously across the face.*) Now I told you about that! Every time you call me out of my name, you get hit!

THEO: You'll never understand!

BOBBY: All I know is that a picture is supposed to be pretty, but I'm sorry, that mess you got there is downright ugly!

THEO: You're hopeless.—You understand this, don't you, Pop? (*Holding the painting for him to see.*)

MR. PARKER: (*Not looking at the painting.*) Don't ask me—I don't know nothing about no painting.

THEO: You were an artist once.

MR. PARKER: That was a different kind.

THEO: Didn't you ever go out on the stage with a new thing inside of you? One of them nights when you just didn't want to do that ol' soft-shoe routine? You knew you had to do it—after all, it was your job—but when you did it, you gave it a little bite here, a little acid there, and still, with all that, they laughed at you anyway. Didn't that ever happen to you?

MR. PARKER: More than once ... But you're BSn', boy, and you know it. You been something new every year since you quit school. First you was going to be a racing-car driver, then a airplane pilot, then a office big shot, and now it's a painter. As smart a boy as you is, you should've stayed in school, but who do you think you're fooling with them pictures?—It all boils down to one thing: you don't want to work. But I'll tell you something, Theo: time done run out on you. Adele's not playing, so you might as well put all that junk and paint away.

THEO: Who the hell is Adele? You're my father, you're the man of the house.

MR. PARKER: True, and that's what I intend to be, but until I get a job, I'm gon' play it cool.

THEO: You're going to let her push you out into the streets to hustle up a job. You're an old man. You ain't used to working, it might kill you.

MR. PARKER: Yeah, but what kind of leg do I have to stand on if she puts me out in the street?

THEO: She's bluffing!

MR. PARKER: A buddy of mine who was in this

same kind of fix told me exactly what you just said. Well, the last time I saw him, he was standing on the corner of Eighth Avenue and 125th Street at four o'clock in the morning, twenty-degree weather, in nothing but his drawers, mumbling to himself, "I could've sworn she was bluffing!"

THEO: Hey, Pop! Let me put it to you this way: if none of us come up with anything in that two-week deadline she gave us—none of us, you hear me?

MR. PARKER: I hear you and that's just about all.

THEO: Don't you get the point? That's three of us—you, me, and Bobby. What she gon' do? Throw the three of us out in the street? I tell you, she ain't gon' do that!

MR. PARKER: If you want to take that chance, that's your business, but don't try to make me take it with you. Anyway, it ain't right that she has to work for three grown men. It just ain't right.

THEO: Mama did it for you.

MR. PARKER: (Sharply.) That was different. She was my wife. She knew things about me you will never know. We oughtn' talk about her at all.

THEO: I'm sorry, Pop, but ever since Mama's funeral I've been thinking. Mama was the hardest-working person I ever knew, and it killed her! Is that what I'm supposed to do? No, that's not it, I know it's not. You know what I've been doing? I've been talking to some people, to a very important person right here in Harlem, and I told him about this big idea of mine—

MR. PARKER: You're loaded with ideas, boy—bad ideas! (Puts broom away.)

THEO: WHY DON'T YOU LISTEN TO WHAT I HAVE TO SAY!

MR. PARKER: Listen to you for what? Another con game you got up your sleeve because your sister's got fed up with you lying around this house all day while she's knocking herself out. You're pulling the same damn thing on me you did with those ugly paintings of yours a few minutes ago.

THEO: Okay, I can't paint. So I was jiving, but now I got something I really want to do—something I got to do!

MR. PARKER: If you're making a point, Theo, you've gotta be smarter than you're doing to get it through to me.

THEO: (Goes to back room, opens refrigerator, and takes out brown-paper bag, then comes back into the shop.) Pop, I got something here to show how smart I really am. (Lifts an old jug out of the bag.) Check this out, Pop! Check it out!

MR. PARKER: What is it?

THEO: Whiskey—corn whiskey—you want some?

MR. PARKER: (Hovers.) Well, I'll try a little bit of it out, but we better not let Adele see us.

THEO: (Starts unscrewing cork from jug.) That girl sure puts a scare in you, Pop, and I remember when you wouldn't take no stuff off Mama, Adele, or nobody.

MR. PARKER: God is the only person I fear.

THEO: (Stops unscrewing the jug.) God! Damn, you're all alike!

MR. PARKER: What are you talking about, boy?

THEO: You, the way Mama was—ask you any question you can't answer, and you throw that Bible stuff at us.

MR. PARKER: I don't get you.

THEO: For instance, let me ask you about the black man's oppressions, and you'll tell me about some small nation in the East rising one day to rule the world. Ask you about pain and dying, and you say, "God wills it." ... Fear? — and you'll tell me about Daniel, and how Daniel wasn't scared of them lions. Am I right or wrong?

MR. PARKER: It's all in the book and you can't dispute it.

THEO: You wanta bet? If that nation in the East ever do rise, how can I be sure they won't be worse than the jokers we got running things now? —Nobody but nobody wills me to pain and dying, not if I can do something about it. That goes for John, Peter, Mary, J.C., the whole bunch of 'em! And as for ol' Daniel: sure, Daniel didn't care nothing about them lions—but them lions didn't give a damn about him either! They tore him into a million pieces!

MR. PARKER: That's a lie! That's an ungodly, unholy lie! (Takes his Bible from the shelf.) And I'll prove it!

THEO: What lie?

MR. PARKER: (Moving from the counter, thumbing through Bible.) You and those bastard ideas of yours. Here, here it is! (Reading from Bible.) "And when he came near unto the den to Daniel, he cried with a pained voice; The King spoke and

590 said to Daniel: 'O Daniel, servant of the living God, is thy God, whom thou servest continually, able to deliver thee from the lions?' Then said Daniel unto the King: 'O King, live forever! My God hath sent his angel, and hath shut the lions' mouths, and they have not hurt me; for as much as before him innocence was found in me, and also before thee, O King, have I done no hurt.' Then was the King exceeding glad, and commanded that they should take Daniel up out of 600 the den. So Daniel was taken up out of the den, and no manner of hurt was found upon him, because he trusted his God!!!" (*Slams the book closed, triumphant.*)

THEO: Hollywood, Pop, Hollywood!

MR. PARKER: Damn you! How I ever brought something like you into this world, I'll never know! You're no damn good! Sin! That's who your belief is! Sin and corruption! With you, it's nothing but women! Whiskey! Women! Whis-610 key! (*While he is carrying on,* THEO *pours out a glass of corn and puts it in* MR. PARKER'S *hand.*) Women! Whiskey! (*Takes a taste.*) Whisk—Where did you get this from? (*Sits on throne.*)

THEO: (*Slapping* BOBBY'S *hand.*) I knew you'd get the message, Pop—I just knew it!

MR. PARKER: Why, boy, this is the greatest corn I ever tasted!

BOBBY: And Theo puts that stuff together like he was born to be a whiskey maker!

620 MR. PARKER: Where did you learn to make corn like this?

THEO: Don't you remember? You taught me.

MR. PARKER: By George, I did! Why, you weren't no more'n nine years old—

THEO: Eight. Let's have another one. (*Pours another for* PARKER.) Drink up. Here's to ol' Daniel. You got to admit one thing—he had a whole lot of heart!

MR. PARKER: (*Drinks up and puts his hand out again.*) 630 Another one, please . . .

THEO: (*Pouring.*) Anything you say, Pop! *You're the boss of this house!*

MR. PARKER: Now that's the truth if you ever spoke it. (*Drinks up.*) Whew! This is good! (*Putting his glass out again, slightly tipsy.*)

THEO: About this idea of mine, Pop: well, it's got something to do with this corn.

MR. PARKER: (*Drinks up.*) Wow! Boy, people oughta pay you to make this stuff.

THEO: Well, that's what I kinda had in mind. I 640 tested some of it out the other day, and I was told this corn liquor could start a revolution —that is, if I wanted to start one. I let a preacher taste some, and he asked me to make him a whole keg for him.

MR. PARKER: (*Pauses. Then, in a sudden change of mood.*) God! Damnit!

BOBBY: What's wrong, Pop?

MR. PARKER: I miss her, boy, I tell you, I miss her! Was it really God's will? 650

THEO: Don't you believe that—*don't you ever believe that!*

MR. PARKER: But I think, boy—I think hard!

THEO: That's all right. We think hard too. We got it from you. Ain't that right, Bobby?

BOBBY: Yeah.

MR. PARKER: (*Pause.*) You know something? That woman was the first woman I ever got close to—your mama . . .

BOBBY: *How old were you?* 660

MR. PARKER: Twenty.

BOBBY: Aw, come on, Pop!

MR. PARKER: May God wipe me away from this earth . . .

THEO: Twenty years old and you had never touched a woman? You must've been in bad shape.

MR. PARKER: I'll tell you about it.

THEO: Here he goes with another one of his famous stories! 670

MR. PARKER: I can always go on upstairs, you know.

THEO: No, Pop, we want to hear it.

MR. PARKER: Well, I was working in this circus in Tampa, Florida—your mother's hometown. You remember Bob Shepard—well, we had this little dance routine of ours we used to do a sample of outside the tent. One day we was out there doing one of our numbers, when right in the middle of the number I spied this fine, foxy-looking thing, blinking her eyes at me. 'Course 680 ol' Bob kept saying it was him she was looking at, but I knew it was *me*—'cause if there was one thing that was my specialty, it was a fine-looking woman.

THEO: You live twenty years of you life not getting

anywhere near a woman, and all of a sudden they become *your specialty?*

MR. PARKER: Yeah, being that—

690   THEO: Being that you had never had a woman for all them terrible years, naturally it was on your mind all the time.

MR. PARKER: That's right.

THEO: And it being on your mind so much, you sorta became a specialist on women?

MR. PARKER: Right again.

THEO: (*Laughs.*) I don't know. But I guess you got a point there!

MR. PARKER: You want to hear this or not!?

BOBBY: Yeah, go on, Pop. *I'm* listening.

700   MR. PARKER: Well, while I was standing on the back of the platform, I motions to her with my hand to kinda move around to the side of the stand, so I could talk to 'er. She strolled 'round to the side, stood there for a while, and you know what? Ol' Bob wouldn't let me get a word in edgewise. But you know what she told him; she said Mister, you talk like a fool! (*All laugh.*)

BOBBY: That was Mama, all right.

MR. PARKER: So I asked her if she would like to
710   meet me after the circus closed down. When I got off that night, sure enough, she was waiting for me. We walked up to the main section of town, off to the side of the road, 'cause we had a hard rain that day and the road was full of muddy little ponds. I got to talking to her and telling her funny stories and she would laugh—boy, I'm telling you that woman could laugh!

THEO: That was your technique, huh? Keep 'em
720   laughing!

MR. PARKER: Believe it or not, it worked—'cause she let me kiss her. I kissed her under this big ol' pecan tree. She could kiss too. When that woman kissed me, somethin' grabbed me so hard and shook me so, I fell flat on my back into a big puddle of water! *And that woman killed herself laughing!*

(*Pause.*)

I married her two weeks later.

730   THEO: And then you started making up for lost time. I'm glad you did, Pop—'cause if you hadn't, I wouldn't be here today.

MR. PARKER: If I know you, you'd have made some kind of arrangement.

BOBBY: What happened after that?

MR. PARKER: We just lived and had fun—and children too, that part you know about. We lived bad and we lived good—and then my legs got wobbly, and my feet got heavy, I lost my feeling, and everything just stayed as it was.   740

(*Pause.*)

I only wish I had been as good a haircutter as I was a dancer. Maybe she wouldn't have had to work so hard. She might be living today.

THEO: Forget it, Pop—it's all in the gone by. Come on, you need another drink. (*Pouring.*)

MR. PARKER: Get me to talking about them old days. It hurts, I tell you, it—

THEO: Pop, you have got to stop thinking about those things. We've got work to do!   750

MR. PARKER: You said you had an idea . . .

THEO: Yes—you see, Pop, this idea has to do with Harlem. It has to do with the preservation of Harlem. That's what it's all about. So I went to see this leader, and I spoke to him about it. He thought it was great and said he would pay me to use it!

MR. PARKER: Who wants to preserve this dump! Tear it down, is what I say!

THEO: But this is a different kind of preserving.   760
Preserve it for black men—preserve it for men like you, me, and Bobby. That's what it's all about.

MR. PARKER: That sounds good.

THEO: Of course I told this leader, I couldn't promise to do anything until I had spoken to my father. I said, after straightening everything out with you I would make arrangements for the two of you to meet.

MR. PARKER: Meet him for what?   770

THEO: For making money! For business! *This man knows how to put people in business!*

MR. PARKER: All right, I'll meet him. What's his name?

THEO: —But first you gotta have a showdown with Adele and put her in her place once and for all.

MR. PARKER: Now wait just a minute. You didn't say Adele would have anything to do with this.

780   THEO: Pop, this man can't be dealing with men who let women rule them. Pop, you've got to tell that girl off or we can't call ourselves men!

MR. PARKER: (*Pause.*) All right. If she don't like it, that's too bad. Whatever you have in mind for us to do with this leader of yours, we'll do it.

THEO: Now that's the way I like to hear my old man talk! Take a drink, Pop! (*Starts popping his fingers and moves dancing about the room.*)

790
We're gonna show 'em now
We're gonna show 'em how
All over
This ol' Harlem Town!

(THEO *and* BOBBY *start making rhythmic scat sounds with their lips as they dance around the floor.*) —Come on, Pop, show us how you used to cut one of them things!

BOBBY: (*Dancing.*) This is how he did it!

THEO: Nawwww, that's not it. He did it like this!

MR. PARKER: (*Rising.*) No, no! Neither one of you
800   got it! Speed up that riff a little bit . . . (*The two boys speed up the riff, singing, stomping their feet, clapping their hands. Humped over,* MR. PARKER *looks down on the floor concentrating.*) Faster! (*They speed it up more.*)

THEO: Come on now, Pop—let 'er loose!

MR. PARKER: Give me time . . .

BOBBY: *Let that man have some time!*

(MR. PARKER *breaks into his dance.*)

THEO: Come on, Pop, take it with you!
810   BOBBY: Work, Pop!

THEO: DOWNTOWN!

(MR. PARKER *does a coasting "camel walk."*)

BOBBY: NOW BRING IT ON BACK UP-TOWN!

(MR. PARKER *really breaks loose: a rapid series of complicated dance steps.*)

THEO: YEAHHHHHHHH!

BOBBY: That's what I'm talkin' about!

(ADELE *enters, stops at the entrance to the shop, observes*
820   *the scene, bemused.* PARKER, *glimpsing her first, in one motion abruptly stops dancing and reaches for the broom.* BOBBY *looks for something to busy himself with.* THEO *just stares.*)

ADELE: Supper's ready, fellows!

Curtain

SCENE TWO

Six days later. Late afternoon.

———

BOBBY *is seated in the barber's throne, munching on a sandwich.* THEO *enters from the front of the shop.*

THEO: Did Pop get back yet?

(BOBBY *shrugs shoulders.*)

THEO: You eating again? Damn. (*Calling upstairs.*) Pop! (*No answer.* THEO *checks his watch, steps back into shop, looks through window, then crosses to* BOBBY *and snatches the sandwich from his mouth.*) You eat too damn much!

BOBBY: What the fuck you do that for?   10

THEO: (*Handing the sandwich back.*) 'Cause you always got a mouth full of peanut butter and jelly!

BOBBY: I'm hungry! And let me tell you something: don't you *ever* snatch any food from my mouth again.

THEO: You'll hit me—you don't care nothing about your brother. One of these days, I'm gon' hit back.

BOBBY: *Nigger!* The day you swing your hand at   20
me, you'll draw back a nub.

THEO: You see! That's exactly what I mean. Now when Blue gets here tonight, I don't want you talking like that, or else you gon' blow the whole deal.

BOBBY: I know how to act. I don't need no lessons from you.

THEO: Good. I got a job for you.

BOBBY: A job? Shit!

THEO: Don't get knocked out now—it ain't no real   30
job. I just want you to jump over to Smith's on 125th Street and pick me up a portable typewriter.

BOBBY: Typewriter—for what?

THEO: Don't ask questions, just go and get it.

BOBBY: Them typewriters cost a lotta money.

THEO: You ain't gon' use money.

BOBBY: You mean—

THEO: —I mean you walk in there and take one.

40 BOBBY: Naw, you don't mean I walk into nowhere and take nothing!

THEO: Now, Bobby.

BOBBY: No!

THEO: Aw, come on, Bobby. You the one been bragging about how good you are, how you can walk into any store and get anything you wanted, provided it was not too heavy to carry out.

BOBBY: I ain't gon' do it!

THEO: You know what day it is?

50 BOBBY: Thursday.

THEO: That's right. Thursday, May 10th.

BOBBY: What's that suppose to mean, Thieves' Convention on 125th Street?

THEO: It's Pop's birthday!

BOBBY: I didn't know he was still having them.

THEO: Well, let me tell you something: Adele remembered it and she's planning on busting into this shop tonight with a birthday cake to surprise him.

60 BOBBY: She suppose to be throwing us out today. That don't make no sense with her buying him a birthday cake.

THEO: He's been looking for work, I guess she changed her mind about him. Maybe it's gon' be just me and you that goes.

BOBBY: (Pause.) What's he gon' type?

THEO: Them lies he's always telling—like the one about how he met Mama. Pop can tell some of the greatest lies you ever heard of and you

70 know how he's always talking about writing them down.

BOBBY: Pop don't know nothing 'bout writing—specially no typewriting!

THEO: (Takes out his father's notebook.) Oh no? take a look at this. (Hands book to BOBBY.) All he has to do is put it down on paper the way he tells it. Who knows, somebody might get interested in it for television or movies, and we can make ourselves some money, and besides, I kinda think

80 he would get a real charge out of you thinking about him that way—don't you?

BOBBY: (Pause.) Well, ain't no use in lettin' you go over there, gettin' youself in jail with them old clumsy fingers of yours.

THEO: Good boy, Bobby! (MR. PARKER enters the shop.) Hey, Pop! Did you get that thing straightened out with Adele yet?

MR. PARKER: What?

THEO: Adele?

MR. PARKER: Oh, yeah, I'm gon' take care of that   90 right away. (Shoves BOBBY out of throne and sits.)

THEO: Where you been all day?

(BOBBY moves into back room.)

MR. PARKER: Downtown, seeing about some jobs.

THEO: You sure don't care much about yourself.

MR. PARKER: I can agree with you on that, because lookin' for a job can really hurt a man. I was interviewed five times today, and I could've shot every last one of them interviewers—the white ones and the colored ones too. I don't know if   100 I can take any more of this.

THEO: Yeah, looking for a job can be very low-grading to a man, and it gets worse after you get the job. Anyway, I'm glad you got back here on time, or you would've missed your appointment. (No response from PARKER.) Now don't tell me you don't remember! The man, the man that's suppose to come here and tell you how life in Harlem can be profitable.

MR. PARKER: (Steps out of throne, edging toward back   110 room.) Oh, that.

THEO: (Following him.) Oh, that—my foot! Today is the day we're suppose to come up with those jobs, and you ain't said one word to Adele about it—not one single word! All you do is waste your time looking for work! Now that don't make no sense at all, Pop, and you know it.

MR. PARKER: Look, son. Let me go upstairs now and tell her about all the disappointments I suffered today, soften her up a bit, and then I'll   120 come on back down here to meet your man. I promise, you won't have to worry about me going downtown any more—not after what I went through today. And I certainly ain't giving up my shop for nobody! (Exits upstairs.)

THEO: (Turns to BOBBY, who's at the mirror.) Now that's the way I like to hear my old man talk! Hey, baby, don't forget that thing. It's late, we ain't got much time.

BOBBY: All right!   130

(A jet-black-complexioned young man comes in. He is dressed all in blue and wears sunglasses. He carries a *gold-top cane and a large salesman's valise. He stops just inside the door.)*

THEO: Blue, baby!

BLUE: Am I late?

THEO: No, my father just walked in the door. He's upstairs now, but he'll be right back down in a few minutes. Let me take your things. *(Takes* BLUE'*s cane and valise.)* Sit down, man, while I fix you a drink. *(Places* BLUE'*s things on the table and moves into back room.* BOBBY *enters shop.)*

BLUE: Hey, Bobby. How's the stores been treating you?

BOBBY: I'm planning on retiring next year. *(Laughs.)*

THEO: *Returning with jug and two glasses. Moves to the table and pours.)* I was thinking, Blue—we can't let my old man know about our "piano brigade." I know he ain't going for that, but we can fix it where he will never know a thing.

BLUE: You know your father better than I do. *(Takes a drink.)*

BOBBY: What's the "piano brigade"?

THEO: Blue here has the best thieves and store burglars in this part of town, and we plan to work on those businesses over on 125th Street until they run the insurance companies out of business.

BOBBY: You mean breaking into people's stores at night and taking their stuff?

THEO: That's right, but not the way you do it. We'll be organized, we'll be revolutionary.

BOBBY: If the police catch you, they ain't gon' care what you is, and if Pop ever finds out, the police gon' seem like church girls! *(Slips out the front door.)*

THEO: *(After him.)* You just remember that the only crime you'll ever commit is the one you get caught at!

(Pause.)

Which reminds me, Blue—I don't want Bobby to be a part of that "piano brigade."

BLUE: If that's the way you want it, that's the way it shall be, Theo. How's your sister?

THEO: You mean Adele?

BLUE: You got a sister named Mary or something?

THEO: What's this with Adele?

BLUE: I want to know, how are you going to get along with her, selling bootleg whiskey in this place?

THEO: This is not her place, it's my father's. And once he puts his okay on the deal, that's it. What kind of house do you think we're living in, where we gon' let some woman tell us what to do? Come here, let me show you something. *(Moves into back room.* BLUE *follows.)* How do you like it—ain't it something?

BLUE: *(Standing in the doorway.)* It's a back room.

THEO: Yeah, I know. But I have some great plans for reshaping it by knocking down this wall, and putting—

BLUE: Like I said, it's a back room. All I wanta know is, will it do the job? It's a good room. You'll do great with that good-tasting corn of yours. You're going to be so busy here, you're going to grow to hate this place—you might not have any time for your love life, Theopolis!

THEO: *(Laughing.)* Don't you worry about that—I can manage my sex life!

BLUE: Sex! Who's talking about sex? You surprise me, Theo. Everyone's been telling me about how you got so much heart, how you so deep. I sit and talk to you about life, and you don't know the difference between sex and love.

THEO: Is it that important?

BLUE: Yes, it is, ol' buddy, if you want to hang out with me, and you do want to hang out with me, don't you?

THEO: That depends—

BLUE: It depends upon you knowing that sex's got nothing to do with anything but you and some woman laying up in some funky bed, pumping and sweating your life away all for one glad moment—you hear that, *one moment!*

THEO: I'll take that moment!

BLUE: With every woman you've had?

THEO: One out of a hundred!

BLUE: *(Laughing, and moving back into shop.)* One out of a hundred! All that sweat! All that pumping and grinding for the sake of one little dead minute out of a hundred hours!

*(*MR. PARKER *comes in from upstairs.)*

THEO: *(Pause. Stopping* PARKER.*)* Pop, you know who this is?

MR. PARKER: I can't see him.

THEO: This is Blue!

MR. PARKER: Blue who?

THEO: The man I was telling you about . . . *Mr.*
230   *Blue Haven.*

MR. PARKER: (*Extends his hand to shake* BLUE'*s.*) Please
to make your acquaintance, Mr. Haven.

BLUE: (*Shaking* MR. PARKER'*s hand.*) Same to you,
Mr. Parker.

THEO: You sure you don't know who Blue Haven
is, Pop?

MR. PARKER: I'm sorry, but I truly don't know you,
Mr. Haven. If you're a celebrity, you must
accept my apology. You see, since I got out of
240   the business, I don't read the *Variety* anymore.

THEO: I'm not talking about a celebrity.

MR. PARKER: Oh, no?

THEO: He's the leader!

MR. PARKER: Ohhhhh!

THEO: Right here in Harlem.

MR. PARKER: Where else he gon' be but in Harlem?
We got more leaders within ten square blocks
of this barbershop than they got liars down in
City Hall. That's why you dressed up that way,
250   huh, boy? So people can pick you out of a
crowded room?

THEO: Pop, this is serious!

MR. PARKER: All right, go on, don't get carried
away—there are some things I don't catch on
to right away, Mr. Blue.

THEO: Well, get to this: I got to thinking the other
day when Adele busted in here shoving everybody around—I was thinking about this barbershop, and I said to myself: Pop's gon' lose
260   this shop if he don't start making himself some
money.

MR. PARKER: Now tell me something I don't know.
(*Sits on throne.*)

THEO: Here I go. What would you say if I were
to tell you that Blue here can make it possible
for you to have a thriving business going on,
right here in this shop, for twenty-four hours
a day?

MR. PARKER: What is he—some kind of hair grower!

270   THEO: Even if you don't cut but one head of hair
a week!

MR. PARKER: Do I look like a fool to you?

THEO: (*Holds up his jug.*) Selling this!

MR. PARKER: (*Pause.*) Well, well, well. I knew it
was something like that. I didn't exactly know
what it was, but I knew it was something. And
I don't want to hear it!

THEO: Pop, you've always been a man to listen—when you didn't agree, even when
I was wrong, you listened! That's the kind of   280
man you are! You—

MR. PARKER: Okay, okay, I'm listening!

THEO: (*Pause.*) Tell him who you are, Blue.

BLUE: I am the Prime Minister of the Harlem De-
Colonization Association.

MR. PARKER: (*Pause.*) Some kind of organization?

BLUE: Yes.

MR. PARKER: (*As an aside, almost under his breath.*)
They got all kinds of committees in Harlem.
What was that name again, "De"?   290

THEO: De-Colo-ni-zation! Which means that Harlem is owned and operated by Mr. You-
Know-Who. Let me get this stuff—we gon' show
you something . . . (*Moves to the table and opens*
BLUE'*s valise.*)

BLUE: We're dead serious about this project, Mr.
Parker. I'd like you to look at this chart.

THEO: And you'll see, we're not fooling. (*Hurriedly*
pins charts taken from BLUE'*s valise on wall out in*
the shop.)   300

MR. PARKER: (*Reading from center chart.*) The Harlem
De-Colonization Association, with Future Perspective for Bedford Stuyvesant. (*Turns to* BLUE.)
All right, so you got an organization. What do
you do? I've never heard of you.

BLUE: The only reason you've never heard of us
is because we don't believe in picketing, demonstrating, rioting, and all that stuff. We always
look like we're doing something that we ain't
doing, but we are doing something—and in that   310
way nobody gets hurt. Now you may think we're
passive. To the contrary, we believe in direct
action. We are doers, enterprisers, thinkers
—and most of all, we're businessmen! Our aim
is to drive Mr. You-Know-Who out of Harlem.

MR. PARKER: Who's this Mr. You-Know-Who?

THEO: Damn, Pop! The white man!

MR. PARKER: Oh, himmm!

BLUE: We like to use that name for our members
in order to get away from the bad feelings we   320

have whenever we use the word "white." We want our members to always be objective and in this way we shall move forward. Before we get through, there won't be a single Mr. You-Know-Who left in this part of town. We're going to capture the imagination of the people of Harlem. And that's never been done before, you know.

MR. PARKER: Now, tell me how?

330 BLUE: *(Standing before the charts, pointing with his cane.)* You see this here. This is what we call a "brigade." And you see this yellow circle?

MR. PARKER: What's that for?

BLUE: My new and entertaining system for playing the numbers. You do play the numbers, Mr. Parker?

MR. PARKER: I do.

BLUE: You see, I have a lot of colors in this system and these colors are mixed up with a whole lot 340 of numbers, and the idea is to catch the right number with the right color. The right number can be anything from one to a hundred, but in order to win, the color must always be black. The name of this game is called "Black Heaven." It's the color part that gives everybody all the fun in playing this game of mine.

MR. PARKER: Anybody ever catch it?

BLUE: Sure, but not until every number and every color has paid itself off. The one thing you'll 350 find out about my whole operation: you can't lose. *(Pause for effect.)*

MR. PARKER: Keep talking.

BLUE: Now over here is the Red Square Circle Brigade, and this thing here is at the heart of my dream to create here in Harlem a symbolic life-force in the heart of the people.

MR. PARKER: You don't say . . .

BLUE: Put up that target, Theo. *(THEO hurriedly pins on wall a dart target with the face of a beefy,* 360 *Southern-looking white man as bull's-eye.)*

MR. PARKER: Why, that's that ol' dirty sheriff from that little town in Mississippi!

BLUE: *(Taking a dart from THEO.)* That's right—we got a face on a target for every need. We got governors, mayors, backwood crackers, city crackers, Southern crackers, and Northern crackers. We got all kinds of faces on these targets that any good Harlemite would be willing to buy for the sake of slinging one of these darts in that bastard's throat! *(Throws dart, puncturing* 370 *face on board.)*

MR. PARKER: Let me try it one time. *(Rising, takes dart from* BLUE *and slings it into the face on the target.)* Got him! *(A big laugh.)*

BLUE: It's like I said, Mr. Parker: the idea is to capture the imagination of the people!

MR. PARKER: You got more? Let me see more!

BLUE: Now this is our green circle—that's Theo and his corn liquor—for retail purposes will be called "Black Lightning." This whiskey of 380 Theo's can make an everlasting contribution to this life-force I've been telling you about. I've tested this whiskey out in every neighborhood in Harlem, and everybody claimed it was the best they ever tasted this side of Washington, D.C. You see, we plan to supply every after-hours joint in this area, and this will run Mr. You-Know-Who and his bonded product out of Harlem.

THEO: You see, Pop, this all depends on the bar- 390 bershop being open night and day so the people can come and go as they please, to pick up their play for the day, to get a bottle of corn, and to take one of them targets home to the kiddies. They can walk in just as if they were getting a haircut. In fact, I told Blue that we can give a haircut as a bonus for anyone who buys two quarts.

MR. PARKER: What am I suppose to say now?

THEO: You're suppose to be daring. You're suppose 400 to wake up to the times, Pop! These are urgent days—a man has to stand up and be counted!

MR. PARKER: The police might have some counting of their own to do.

THEO: Do you think I would bring you into something that was going to get us in trouble? Blue has an organization! Just like Mr. You-Know-Who. He's got members on the police force! In the city government, the state govern- ment. 410

BLUE: Mr. Parker, if you have any reservations concerning the operation of my association, I'd be only too happy to have you come to my summer home, and I'll let you in on everything—especially our protective system against being caught doing this thing.

THEO: Did you hear him, Pop, *he's got a summer home!*

MR. PARKER: Aw, shut up, boy! Let me think! *(Turns to* BLUE.*)* So you want to use my place as a headquarters for Theo's corn, the colored numbers, and them targets?

BLUE: Servicing the area of 125th to 145th, between the East and West rivers.

MR. PARKER: *(Pause.)* I'm sorry, fellows, but I can't do it. *(Moves into back room.)*

THEO: *(Following* MR. PARKER.*)* Why?

MR. PARKER: It's not right.

THEO: Not right! What are you talking about? Is it right that all that's out there for us is to go downtown and push one of them carts? I have done that, and I ain't gon' do it no more!

MR. PARKER: That still don't make it right.

THEO: I don't buy it! I'm going into this thing with Blue, with or without you!

MR. PARKER: Go on, I don't care! You quit school, I couldn't stop you! I asked you to get a job, you wouldn't work! You have never paid any attention to any of my advice, and I don't expect you to start heeding me now!

THEO: Remember what you said to me about them paintings, and being what I am—well, this is me! At last I've found what I can do, and it'll work—I know it will. Please, Pop, just—

MR. PARKER: Stop begging, Theo. *(Crosses back into shop, looks at* BLUE.*)* Why?

BLUE: I don't get you.

MR. PARKER: What kind of boy are you that you went through so much pain to dream up this cockeyed, ridiculous plan of yours?

BLUE: Mr. Parker, I was born about six blocks from here, and before I was ten I had the feeling I had been living for a hundred years. I got so old and tired I didn't know how to cry. Now you just think about that. But now I own a piece of this neighborhood. I don't have to worry about some bastard landlord or those credit crooks on 125th Street. Beautiful, black Blue—they have to worry about me! *(Reaches into his pocket and pulls out a stack of bills. Places them in* PARKER's *hands.)* Can't you see, man—I'm here to put you in business! *(*MR. PARKER *runs his fingers through the money.)* Money, Mr. Parker—brand-new money . . .

(After concentrated attention, MR. PARKER *drops money on table and moves into back room.* THEO *hurriedly follows.* MR. PARKER *sits on bed, in deep thought.)*

THEO: That's just to get us started. And if we can make a dent into Mr. You-Know-Who's goings-on in Harlem, nobody's going to think of us as crooks. We'll be heroes from 110th Street to Sugar Hill. And just think, Pop, you won't have to worry about jobs and all that. You'll have so much time for you and Mr. Jenkins to play checkers, your arms will drop off. You'll be able to sit as long as you want, and tell enough stories and lies to fit between the cover of a 500-page book. That's right! Remember you said you wanted to write all them stories down! Now you'll have time for it! You can dress up the way you used to. And the girls—remember how you used to be so tough with the girls before you got married? All that can come back to you, and some of that you never had. It's so easy! All you have to do is call Adele down those stairs and let her know that you're going into business and if she don't like it she can pack up and move out, because you're not going to let her drive you down because you're a man, and—

MR. PARKER: All right! *(Moves back into shop, where* BLUE *is putting away his paraphernalia.)* I'll do it!

(Pause.)

I'll do it under one condition—

BLUE: And that is?

MR. PARKER: If my buddy Jenkins wants to buy into this deal, you'll let him.

BLUE: Theo?

THEO: It's all right.

MR. PARKER: *(Extending his hand to* BLUE.*)* Then you got yourself some partners, Mr. Haven!

BLUE: Welcome into the association, Mr. Parker.

MR. PARKER: Welcome into my barbershop!

THEO: *(Jubilantly.)* Yehhhhhhhhhh!

*(*BLUE *checks his watch.* ADELE *comes into the back room.)*

BLUE: Well, I have to check out now, but I'll stop over tomorrow and we will set the whole thing up just as you want it, Mr. Parker. See you later, Theo.

510 MR. PARKER: *(To* BLUE *as he is walking out the front door.)* You should stick around awhile and watch my polish!

THEO: Pop, don't you think it would be better if you would let me give the word to Adele?

MR. PARKER: No. If I'm going to run a crooked house, *I'm* going to run it, and that goes for you as well as her.

THEO: But, Pop, sometimes she kinda gets by you.

520 MR. PARKER: Boy, I have never done anything like this in my life, but since I've made up my mind to it, you have nothing to say—not a word. You have been moaning about me never making it so you can have a chance. Well, this time you can say I'm with you. But let me tell you something: I don't want no more lies from you, and no more conning me about painting, airplane piloting, or nothing. If being a crook is what you want to be, you're going to be the best crook in the world—even if you have to drink mud

530 to prove it.

THEO: *(Pause.)* Okay, Pop.

MR. PARKER: *(Moves toward back room.)* Well, here goes nothing. Adele! *(Just as he calls,* ADELE *steps out of the back room, stopping him in his tracks.)*

ADELE: Yes, Father.

MR. PARKER: Oh, you're here already. Well, I want to talk to—well, I, er—

ADELE: What is it?

MR. PARKER: *(Pause.)* Nothing. I'll talk to you later.

540 *(He spots* BOBBY *entering from the outside with a package wrapped in newspaper.)* What you got there?

BOBBY: Uh... uh... —fish!

MR. PARKER: Well, you better get them in the refrigerator before they stink on you.

THEO: *(Going over to* BOBBY *and taking package from him.)* No, no. Now, Bobby, I promised Pop we would never lie to him again. It ain't fish, Pop. We've got something for you. *(Puts the pack-*

550 *age on the table and starts unwrapping it. The two boys stand over the table, and as the typewriter is revealed, both turn to him.)*

THEO and BOBBY: Happy Birthday!

MR. PARKER: Birthday? Birthday?

THEO and BOBBY: Yes, Happy Birthday!

MR. PARKER: Now hold on just a minute!

BOBBY: What are we holding on for, Pop?

MR. PARKER: *(Pause.)* That's a good question, son. We're—we're holding on for a celebration! *(Laughs loudly.)* Thanks, fellows! But what am 560 I going to do with a typewriter! I don't know nothing about no typing!

ADELE: I would like to know where they got the money to buy one!

THEO: *(Ignoring her.)* You know what you told me about writing down your stories—now you can write them down three times as fast!

MR. PARKER: But I don't know how to type!

THEO: With the money we're gonna be having, I 570 can hire somebody to teach you!

ADELE: What money you going to have?

THEO: We're going into business, baby—right here in this barbershop!

MR. PARKER: Theo—

THEO: *(Paying no attention.)* We're going to sell bootleg whiskey, numbers, and—

ADELE: You're what!?

MR. PARKER: Theo—

THEO: You heard me, and if you don't like it you 580 can pack your bags and leave!

ADELE: Leave? I pay the rent here!

THEO: No more! I pay it now!

MR. PARKER: Shut up, Theo!

THEO: We're going to show you something, girl. You think—

MR. PARKER: *I said shut up!*

ADELE: Is he telling the truth?

MR. PARKER: Yes, he is telling the truth.

ADELE: You mean to tell me you're going to turn this shop into a bootleg joint? 590

MR. PARKER: I'll turn it into anything I want to!

ADELE: Not while I'm still here!

MR. PARKER: The lease on this house has my signature, not yours!

ADELE: I'm not going to let you do this!

MR. PARKER: You got no choice, Adele. *You don't have a damn thing to say!*

ADELE: *(Turns sharply to* THEO.) You put him up to this!

MR. PARKER: Nobody puts me up to anything I 600 don't want to do! These two boys have made it up in their minds they're not going to work for nobody but themselves, and the thought in my mind is *why should they!* I did like you said, I went downtown, and it's been a long time since I did that, but *you're* down there every day, and you oughta know by now that I am too old a man to ever dream I . . . could overcome the dirt and filth they got waiting for me down there. I'm surprised at you, that you would have so little care in you to shove me into the middle of that mob.

ADELE: You can talk about caring? What about Mama? She *died* working for you! Did you ever stop to think about that! In fact, *did you ever love her?* No!!!

MR. PARKER: That's a lie!

ADELE: I hope that one day you'll be able to do one good thing to drive that doubt out of my mind. *But this is not it!* You've let this hoodlum sell you his twisted ideas of making a short cut through life. But let me tell you something—this bastard is going to ruin you!

THEO: *(Into her face.)* Start packing, baby!

ADELE: *(Strikes him across the face.)* Don't you talk to me like that!

(He raises his hand to strike her back.)

MR. PARKER: Drop your hand, boy! *(THEO does not respond.)* I said, drop your goddamn hand!

THEO: She hit me!

MR. PARKER: I don't care if she had broken your jaw. If you ever draw your hand back to hit this girl again—*as long as you* live! You better not be in my hand reach when you do, 'cause *I'll split your back in two!* (To ADELE.) We're going into business, Adele. I have come to that and I have come to it on my own. I am going to stop worrying once and for all whether I live naked in the cold or whether I die like an animal, unless I can live the best way I know how to. I am getting old and I oughta have some fun. I'm going to get me some money, and I'm going to spend it! I'm going to get drunk! I'm going to dance some more! *I'm getting old! I'm going to fall in love one more time before I die!* So get to that, girl, and if it's too much for you to bear, I wouldn't hold it against you if you walked away from here this very minute—

ADELE: *(Opens the door to the back room to show him the birthday surprise she has for him.)* Happy birthday!

MR. PARKER: *(Goes into the room and stands over table where birthday cake is.)* I guess I fooled all of you. Today is not my birthday. It never was. *(Moves up the stairs.)*

ADELE: It's not going to work! You're going to cut your throat—you hear me! You're going to rip yourself into little pieces! *(Turns to THEO.)* It's not going to be the way you want it—because I know Mr. Blue Haven, and he is not a person to put your trust in. *(THEO turns his back on her, heads for the shop door.)* . . . I am talking to you!

THEO: *(Stops and turns.)* Why don't you leave us alone. You're the one who said we had to go out and do something. Well, we did, but we're doing it our way. Me and Bobby, we're men—if we lived the way you wanted us to, we wouldn't have nothing but big fat veins popping out of our heads.

ADELE: I'll see what kind of men you are every time a cop walks through that door, every time a stranger steps into this back room and you can't be too sure about him, and the day they drag your own father off and throw him into a jail cell.

THEO: But, tell me, what else is there left for us to do. You tell me and I'll do it. You show me where I can go to spin the world around before it gets too late for somebody like Mama living fifty years just to die on 126th Street! *You tell me of a place where there are no old crippled vaudeville men!*

ADELE: There is no such place.

(Pause.)

But you don't get so hung up about it you have to plunge a knife into your own body. You don't bury yourself here in this place; you climb up out of it! Now that's something for you to wonder about, boy.

THEO: I wonder all the time—how you have lived here all your whole life on this street, and you haven't seen, heard, learned, or felt a thing in all those years. I wonder how you ever got to be such a damn fool!

Curtain

ACT TWO

SCENE ONE

Two months later. It is about 9 P.M.

As the curtain rises, the lights come up in the back room. BOBBY *is there, listening to a record of James Brown's "Money Won't Change You, But Time Will Take You On." As he is dancing out to the shop,* THEO *appears from the cellar, which has been enlarged by taking out a panel in the lower section of the wall and houses the whiskey-making operation.* THEO *brings in two boxes filled with bottles of corn whiskey and shoves them under the bed.*

BOBBY *moves past* THEO *into the shop, carrying a target rolled up in his hand, and two darts. He is wearing a fancy sports shirt, new trousers, new keen-toed shoes, and a stingy, diddy-bop hat. He pins the target up on the wall of the shop. In the center of the target is the face of a well-known American racist.*

———————

BOBBY: *(Moves away from the target, aims and hurls the dart.)* That's for Pop! Huh! *(Throws another.)* And this is for me! Huh! *(Moves to the target to pull darts out.* THEO *cuts record off abruptly. A knock at the door.)*

THEO: *(Calling out to* BOBBY *from the back room.)* Lock that door!

BOBBY: Lock it yourself!

THEO: *(With quick but measured steps moves toward* 10 *front door.)* I'm not selling another bottle, target, or anything, till I get some help! *(Locks door in spite of persistent knocking.)* We're closed!

BOBBY: I don't think Blue is gon' like you turning customers away. *(Sits in barber chair, lighting up cigar.)*

THEO: You can tell Blue I don't like standing over that stove all day, that I don't like him promising me helpers that don't show up. There are a lot of things I don't go for, like Pop taking off and

20 not showing up for two days. I make this whiskey, I sell it, I keep books, I peddle numbers and those damn targets. *And I don't like you stand-*

ing around here all day not lifting a finger to help me!

BOBBY: *(Taking a big puff on his cigar.)* I don't hear you.

THEO: Look at you—all decked out in your new togs. Look at me: I haven't been out of these dungarees since we opened this place up.

BOBBY: *(Jumps out of chair.)* I don't wanta hear 30 nothing! You do what you wanta do, and leave me alone!

THEO: What am I supposed to be, a work mule or something?

BOBBY: You're the one that's so smart—you can't answer your own stupid questions?

THEO: You done let Blue turn you against me, huh?

BOBBY: You ask the questions, and you gon' answer them—but for now, stop blowing your breath in my face! 40

THEO: You make me sick. *(Moves into back room. Sits on bed.)*

ADELE: *Enters from upstairs, dressed in a smart Saks Fifth Avenue outfit.)* Getting tired already, Theo?

THEO: No, just once in a while I'd like to have some time to see one of my women!

ADELE: You being the big industrialist and all that, I thought you had put girls off for a year or two!

THEO: Get away from me. *(Crosses to desk and sits.)* 50

ADELE: I must say, however—it is sure a good sight to see you so wrapped up in work. I never thought I'd live to see the day, but—

THEO: Don't you ever have anything good to say?

ADELE: I say what I think and feel. I'm honest.

THEO: Honest? You're just hot because Pop decided to do something my way for a change.

ADELE: That's a joke, when you haven't seen him for two whole days. Or, *do* you know where he has gone to practically every night since you 60 opened up this little store.

THEO: He's out having a little sport for himself. What's wrong with that? He hasn't had any fun in a long time.

626

ADELE: Is fun all you can think of? When *my* father doesn't show up for two days, I worry.

THEO: You're not worried about nobody but yourself—I'm on to your game. You'd give anything in the world to go back just the way we were, because you liked the idea of us being dependent on you. Well, that's all done with, baby. We're on our own. So don't worry yourself about Pop. When Blue gets here tonight with our money, he'll be here!

ADELE: If my eyes and ears are clear, then I would say that Father isn't having the kind of money troubles these days that he must rush home for your pay day.

THEO: What do you mean by that?

ADELE: I mean that he has been dipping his hands into that little drawer of yours at least two or three times a week.

THEO: You ain't telling nothing I don't know.

ADELE: What about your friend Blue?

THEO: I can handle him.

ADELE: I hope so, since it is a known fact that he can be pretty evil when he thinks someone has done him wrong—and it happened once, in a bar uptown, he actually killed a man.

THEO: You're lying. *(He moves quickly to shop entrance.)* Bobby, have you heard anything about Blue killing a man? (BOBBY, *seated in the barber's chair, looks at him, then turns away, not answering.* THEO *returns to the back room.)*

ADELE: Asking him about it is not going to help you. Ask yourself a few questions and you will know that you are no better than Blue—because it is you two who are the leaders of those mysterious store raids on 125th Street, and your ace boy on those robberies is no one other than your brother, Bobby Parker!

THEO: Bobby!

ADELE: I don't know why that should surprise you, since he is known as the swiftest and coolest young thief in Harlem.

THEO: I didn't know about Bobby—*who told you!*

ADELE: As you well know by now, I've been getting around lately, and I meet people, and people like to have something to talk about, and you know something: this place is becoming the talk along every corner and bar on the Avenue!

THEO: You're just trying to scare me.

ADELE: I wish to God I was. *(Starts out.)*

THEO: Where are you going?

ADELE: *(Stops, turns abruptly.)* Out. Do you mind?

THEO: *That's all you ever do!*

ADELE: Yes, you're right.

THEO: They tell me you're going with Wilmer Robinson?

ADELE: Yes, that's true. *(Moving through shop toward door.* BOBBY *doesn't move from the barber's throne and buries his nose in a comic book.)*

THEO: *(Following behind her.)* He's a snake.

ADELE: No better or worse than someone like you or Blue.

THEO: He'll bleed you for every dime you've got!

ADELE: So what. He treats me like a woman, and that's more than I can say for any man in this house!

THEO: He'll treat you like a woman until he's gotten everything he wants, and then he's gon' split your ass wide open!

ADELE: *(Turns sharply at door.)* Theoooooooooooo!

(Pause.)

You talk like that to me because you don't know how to care for the fact that I am your sister.

THEO: But why are you trying to break us up? Why?

ADELE: I don't have to waste that kind of good time. I can wait for you to bust it up yourself. Good night! *(Slams the door behind herself.)*

(THEO *stands with a long, deep look in his eyes, then goes down cellar.* MR. PARKER *steps into the shop, all dapper, dressed up to a fare-thee-well, holding a gold-top cane in one hand and a book in the other.* BOBBY *stares at him, bewildered.)*

BOBBY: What's that you got on?

MR. PARKER: What does it look like?

BOBBY: Nothing.

MR. PARKER: You call this nothing!

BOBBY: Nothing—I mean, I didn't mean nothing when I asked you that question.

MR. PARKER: Where's Theo?

BOBBY: In the back, working.

MR. PARKER: Good! Shows he's got his mind stretched out for good and great things. *(Hangs up hat and puts away cane.)*

BOBBY: He's been stretching his mind out to find out where you been.

MR. PARKER: Where I been is none of his business,

Blue is the man to think about. It's pay day, and I wanta know, where the hell is he! *(Checks his watch, taps* BOBBY, *indicating he should step down from chair.)*

BOBBY: *(Hops down from chair.* PARKER *sits.)* Whatcha reading?

MR. PARKER: A book I picked up yesterday. I figured since I'm in business I might as well read a businessman's book.

170 BOBBY: Let me see it. *(Takes the book in his hand.) The Thief's Journal,* by Jean Gin-nett. *(Fingering through pages.)* Is it a good story?

MR. PARKER: So far—

BOBBY: *(Hands it back.)* What's it all about?

MR. PARKER: A Frenchman who was a thief.

BOBBY: Steal things?

MR. PARKER: Uh-huh.

BOBBY: Where did he get all that time to write a book?

180 MR. PARKER: Oh, he had the time all right, 'cause he spent most of it in jail.

BOBBY: Some thief!

MR. PARKER: The trouble with this bird is that he became a thief and then he became a thinker.

BOBBY: No shucking!

MR. PARKER: No shucking. But it is my logicalism that you've got to become a thinker and then you become a crook! Or else, why is it when you read up on some of these politicians' back-

190 grounds you find they all went to one of them big law colleges? That's where you get your start!

BOBBY: Well, I be damned!

MR. PARKER: *(Jumps down out of the chair, moves briskly toward door.)* Now where is Blue! He said he would be here nine-thirty on the nose! *(Opens the door and* JENKINS *comes in.)* Hey, Jenkins! What's up!

MR. JENKINS: That Blue fellow show up yet?

MR. PARKER: No, he didn't, and I'm gon' call him

200 down about that too.

MR. JENKINS: It don't matter. I just want whatever money I got coming, and then I'm getting out of this racket.

MR. PARKER: Don't call it that, it's a committee!

MR. JENKINS: This committee ain't no committee. It ain't nothing but a racket, and I'm getting out of it!

MR. PARKER: You put your money into this thing, man. It ain't good business to walk out on an

210 investment like that.

MR. JENKINS: I can, and that's what I'm doing before I find myself in jail! Man, this thing you got going here is the talk in every bar in this neighborhood.

MR. PARKER: There ain't nothing for you to be scared of, Jenkins. Blue guaranteed me against ever being caught by the police. Now that's all right by me, but I've got some plans of my own. When he gets here tonight, I'm gon' force him to make me one of the leaders in this group, 220 and if he don't watch out, I just might take the whole operation over from him. I'll make you my right-hand man, and not only will you be getting more money, and I won't just guarantee you against getting caught, but I'll guarantee you against being scared!

MR. JENKINS: There's nothing you can say to make me change my mind. I shouldn't've let you talk me into this mess in the first place. I'm getting out, and that's it! *(Starts for the door.)* And if 230 he gets back before I do, you hold my money for me! *(Exiting.)*

MR. PARKER: *(Pursuing him to door.)* Suit yourself, but you're cutting your own throat. This little set-up is the biggest thing to hit this neighborhood since the day I started dancing! *(Slams door.)* Fool! *(Takes off coat, hangs it up. Goes to mirror to primp.)*

BOBBY: Going somewhere again?

MR. PARKER: Got myself a little date to get to if 240 Blue ever gets here with our money—*and he better get here with our money!*

BOBBY: You been dating a lot lately—nighttime dates, and day ones too—and Theo's not happy about it. He says you don't stay here long enough to cut Yul Brynner's hair.

MR. PARKER: He can complain all he wants to. I'm the boss here, and he better not forget it. He's the one that's got some explaining to do: don't talk to nobody no more, don't go nowhere, look- 250 ing like he's mad all the time . . . I've also noticed that he don't get along with you any more.

BOBBY: Well, Pop, that's another story.

MR. PARKER: Come on, boy, there's something on his mind, and you know what it is.

BOBBY: *(Moving away.)* Nothing, except he wants to tell me what to do all the time. But I've got some ideas of my own. I ain't no dumbbell; I just don't talk as much as he do. If I did, the people I talk to would know just as much as 260

I do. I just want him to go his way, and I'll go mine.

MR. PARKER: There's more to it than that, and I wanta know what it is.

BOBBY: There's nothing.

MR. PARKER: Come on now, boy.

BOBBY: That's all, Pop!

MR. PARKER: (Grabs him.) It's not, and you better say something!

270 BOBBY: He—I don't know what to tell you, Pop. He just don't like the way things are going—with you, me—Adele. He got in a fight with her today and she told him about Blue killing a man.

MR. PARKER: Is it true?

BOBBY: Yeah. Blue killed this man one time for saying something about his woman, and this woman got a child by Blue but Blue never married her and so this man started signifying about it. Blue hit him, the man reached for a gun in 280 his pocket, Blue took the gun from him, and the—man started running, but by that time Blue had fire in his eyes, and he shot the man three times.

MR. PARKER: Well...

BOBBY: Blue got only two years for it!

MR. PARKER: Two years, hunh? That's another thing I'm gon' throw in his face tonight if he tries to get smart with me. Ain't that something. Going around bumping people off, and getting 290 away with it too! What do he think he is, white or something! (THEO comes in and sits at desk. MR. PARKER checks his watch.) I'm getting tired of this! (Moves into back room.) Where's that friend of yours!? I don't have to wait around this barbershop all night for him. It's been two months now, and I want my money! When I say be here at nine-thirty, I mean be here!

THEO: (Rising from desk.) Where have you been, Pop?

300 MR. PARKER: That's none of your business! Now where is that man with my money!

THEO: Money is not your problem—you've been spending it all over town! And you've been taking it out of this desk!

MR. PARKER: So? I borrowed a little.

THEO: You call four hundred dollars a little! Now I've tried to fix these books so it don't show too big, and you better hope Blue don't notice it when he starts fingering through these pages 310 tonight.

MR. PARKER: To hell with Blue! It's been two months now, and he ain't shown us a dime!

THEO: What are you doing with all that money, Pop?

MR. PARKER: I don't have to answer to you! I'm the boss here. And another thing, there's a lot about Blue and this association I want to know about. I want a position! I don't have to sit around here every month or so, waiting for somebody to bring me *my* money.   320

THEO: Money! Money! That's all you can think about!

MR. PARKER: Well, look who's talking. You forget this was all your idea. Remember what I told you about starting something and sticking with it. What is it now, boy? The next thing you'll tell me is that you've decided to become a priest or something. What's the new plan, Theo?

THEO: No new plans, Pop. I just don't want us to mess up. Don't you understand—things must   330 be done right, or else we're going to get ourselves in jail. We have to be careful, we have to think about each other all the time. I didn't go into this business just for myself, I wasn't out to prove how wrong Adele was. I just thought the time had come for us to do something about all them years we laid around here letting Mama kill herself!

MR. PARKER: I have told you a thousand times I don't wanta hear any talk about your mama.   340 She's dead, damnit! So let it stay that way! (Moves toward shop.)

THEO: All right, let's talk about Adele then.

MR. PARKER: (Stopping at steps.) What about her?

THEO: She's out of this house every night.

MR. PARKER: Boy, you surprise me. What do you think she should do, work like a dog all day and then come to this house and bite her fingernails all night?

THEO: She's got herself a boy friend too, and—   350

MR. PARKER: (Crossing to counter.) Good! I got myself a girl friend, now that makes two of us!

THEO: (Following him.) But he's—aw, what's the use. But I wish you'd stay in the shop more!

MR. PARKER: That's too bad. I have things to do. I don't worry about where you're going when you leave here.

THEO: I don't go anywhere and you know it. If I did, we wouldn't do an hour's business. *But we have been doing great business!* And you wanta   360 know why? They love it! *Everybody* loves the way ol' Theo brews corn! Every after-hours joint is burning with it! And for us to do that kind of business, I've had to sweat myself down in this hole for something like sixteen hours a day for two whole months!

MR. PARKER: What do you want from me?

THEO: I just want you here in the shop with me, so at least we can pretend that this is a barbershop. A cop walked through that door today while I had three customers in here, and I had to put one of them in that chair and cut his hair!

MR. PARKER: How did you make out?

THEO: Pop, I don't need your jokes!

MR. PARKER: All right, don't get carried away. *(Goes to* THEO *and puts his arm around the boy's shoulders.)* I'll make it my business to stay here in the shop with you more.

THEO: And make Blue guarantee me some help.

MR. PARKER: You'll get that too. But you've got to admit one thing, though—you've always been a lazy boy. I didn't expect you to jump and all of a sudden act like John Henry!

THEO: I have never been lazy. I just didn't wanta break my back for the man!

MR. PARKER: Well, I can't blame you for that. I know, because I did it. I did it when they didn't pay me a single dime!

BOBBY: When was that?

MR. PARKER: When I was on the chain gang!

BOBBY: Now you know you ain't never been on no chain gang!

MR. PARKER: *(Holds up two fingers.)* Two months, that's all it was. Just two months.

BOBBY: Two months, my foot!

MR. PARKER: I swear to heaven I was. It was in 19-something, I was living in Jersey City, New Jersey . . . *(Crosses to throne and sits.)*

BOBBY: Here we go with another story!

MR. PARKER: That was just before I started working as a vaudeville man, and there was this ol' cousin of mine we used to call "Dub," and he had this job driving a trailer truck from Jersey City to Jacksonville, Florida. One day he asked me to come along with him for company. I weren't doing nothing at the time, and—

BOBBY: As usual.

MR. PARKER: I didn't say that! Anyway, we drove along. Everything was fine till we hit Macon,

Georgia. We weren't doing a thing, but before we knew it this cracker police stopped us, claiming we'd ran through a red light. He was yelling and hollering and, boyyy, did I get mad—I was ready to get a hold of that cracker and work on his head until . . .

BOBBY: Until what?

MR. PARKER: Until they put us on the chain gang, and the chain gang they put us on was a chain gang and a half! I busted some rocks John Wayne couldn't've busted! I was a rock-busting fool! *(Rises and demonstrates how he swung the hammer.)* I would do it like this! I would hit the rock, and the hammer would bounce—bounce so hard it would take my hand up in the air with it—but I'd grab it with my left hand and bring it down like this: Hunh! *(Carried away by the rhythm of his story, he starts twisting his body to the swing of it.)* It would get so good to me, I'd say: Hunh! Yeah! Hunh! I'd say, Ooooooooooooweeeee! I'm wide open now! *(Swinging and twisting.)* Yeah, baby, I say, Hunh! Sooner or later that rock would crack! Old Dub ran into a rock one day that was hard as Theo's head. He couldn't bust that rock for nothing. He pumped and swung, but that rock would not move. So finally he said to the captain: "I'm sorry, Cap, but a elephant couldn't break this rock." Cap didn't wanna hear nothing. He said, "Well, Dub, I wanna tell you something—your lunch and your supper is in the middle of that rock." On the next swing of the hammer, Dub busted that rock into a thousand pieces! *(Laughs.)* I'm telling you, them crackers is mean. Don't let nobody tell you about no Communists, Chinese, or anything: there ain't nothing on this earth meaner and dirtier than an American-born cracker! We used to sleep in them long squad tents on the ground, and we was all hooked up to this one big long chain: the guards had orders to shoot at random in the dark if ever one of them chains would rattle. You couldn't even turn over in your sleep! *(Sits on throne.)*

BOBBY: A man can't help but turn over in his sleep!

MR. PARKER: Not on this chain gang you didn't. You turn over on this chain gang in your sleep and your behind was shot! But if you had to, you would have to wake up, announce that you was turning over, and then you go back to sleep!

BOBBY: What!

MR. PARKER: Just like this. (*Illustrating physically.*) "Number 4 turning over!" But that made all the chains on the other convicts rattle, so they had to turn over too and shout: "Number 5 turning over! Number 6 turning over! Number 7!"

THEO: Why don't you stop it!

MR. PARKER: I ain't lying!

BOBBY: Is that all?

470 MR. PARKER: Yeah, and I'm gon' get Adele to type that up on my typewriter! (*Goes to the window.*) Now where the hell is that Blue Haven!

MR. JENKINS: (*Rushing in.*) Did he show up yet?

MR. PARKER: Naw, and when he does, I'm—

MR. JENKINS: I told you I didn't trust that boy—who knows where he is! Well, I'm going out there and get him! (*Starts back out.*)

MR. PARKER: (*Grabs him by the arm.*) Now don't go out there messing with Blue, Jenkins! If there's anybody got a reason for being mad with him,
480 it's me. Now take it easy. When he gets here, we'll all straighten him out. Come on, sit down and let me beat you a game one time. (*Takes board out quickly.*)

BOBBY: Tear him up, Pop!

MR. JENKINS: (*Pause.*) Okay, you're on. (*Moves toward* MR. PARKER *and the table.*) It's hopeless. I been playing your father for three solid years, and he has yet to beat me one game!

MR. PARKER: Yeah! But his luck done come to past!

490 MR. JENKINS: My luck ain't come to past, 'cause my luck is skill. (*Spelling the word out.*) S-K-I-L-L.

MR. PARKER: (*Shakes up the can.*) Come on now, Jenkins, let's play the game. Take one. (MR. JENKINS *pulls out a checker.*) You see there, you get the first move.

MR. JENKINS: You take me for a fool, Parker, and just for that I ain't gon' let you get a king.

MR. PARKER: Put your money where your lips is. I say I'm gon' win this game!

500 MR. JENKINS: I don't want your money, I'm just gon' beat you!

MR. PARKER: I got twenty dollars here to make a liar out of you! (*Slams down a twenty-dollar bill on the table.*) Now you doing all the bragging about how I never beat you, but I'm valiant enough to say that, from here on in, you can't win air, and I got twenty dollars up on the table to back it up.

MR. JENKINS: Oh, well, he ain't satisfied with me
510 beating him all the time for sport. He wants

me to take his money too.

MR. PARKER: But that's the difference.

MR. JENKINS: What kind of difference?

MR. PARKER: We're playing for money, and I don't think you can play under that kind of pressure. You do have twenty dollars, don't you?

MR. JENKINS: I don't know what you're laughing about, I always keep some money on me. (*Pulls out change purse and puts twenty dollars on the table.*) You get a little money in your pocket and you 520 get carried away.

MR. PARKER: It's your move.

MR. JENKINS: Start you off over here in this corner.

MR. PARKER: Give you that little ol' fellow there.

MR. JENKINS: I'll take him.

MR. PARKER: I'll take this one.

MR. JENKINS: I'll give you this man here.

MR. PARKER: I'll jump—so that you can have this one.

MR. JENKINS: I'll take him. 530

MR. PARKER: Give you this man here.

MR. JENKINS: All right. (*He moves.*)

MR. PARKER: I'll take this one. (*Series of grunts and groans as they exchange men.*) And I'll take these three. (*Jumping* MR. JENKINS's *men and laughing loud.*) Boom! Boom! Boom! (*The game is now definitely in favor of* MR. PARKER. MR. JENKINS *is pondering over his situation. Relishing* MR. JENKINS's *predicament:*) Study long, you study wrong. I'm afraid that's you, ol' buddy . . . I knew it, I knew 540 it all the time—I used to ask myself: I wonder how ol' Jenks would play if he really had some pressure on him? You remember how the Dodgers used to raise hell every year until they met the Yankees in the World Series, and how under all that pressure they would crack up? (*Laughs.*) That pressure got him!

MR. JENKINS: Hush up, man. I'm trying to think!

MR. PARKER: I don't know what you could be thinking about, 'cause the rooster done came and 550 wrote, skiddy biddy!

MR. JENKINS: (*Finally makes a move.*) There!

MR. PARKER: (*In sing-song.*) That's all—that's all . . . (*Makes another jump.*) Boom! Just like you say, Bobby—"tear him up!" (*Rears his head back in ecstatic laughter.*)

MR. JENKINS: (*Makes a move.*) It's your move.

MR. PARKER: (*His laughter trails off sickly as he realizes that the game is now going his opponent's way.*) Well,

560   I see. I guess that kinda changes the color of the game ... Let me see now ...

MR. JENKINS: *(Getting his revenge.)* Why don't you laugh some more? I like the way you laugh, Parker.

MR. PARKER: Shut up, Jenkins. I'm thinking!

MR. JENKINS: Thinking? Thinking for what? The game is over! *(Now he is laughing hard.* MR. PARKER *ruefully makes his move.)* Uh-uh! Lights out! *(Still laughing, answers* PARKER's *move.)* Game time, and

570   you know it! Take your jump! *(*MR. PARKER *is forced to take his jump.* JENKINS *takes his opponent's last three men.)* I told you about laughing and bragging in my game! Boom! Boom! Boom!

MR. PARKER: *(Rises abruptly from the table and dashes to coat rack.)* DAMNIT!!!

MR. JENKINS: Where you going—ain't we gon' play some more?

MR. PARKER: *(Putting on coat.)* I don't wanta play you no more. You too damn lucky!

580   MR. JENKINS: Aw, come on, Parker. I don't want your money, I just want to play!

MR. PARKER: You won it, you keep it—I can *afford* it! But one of these days you're going to leave that voodoo root of yours home, and that's gonna be the day—you hear me, you sonofabitch!

BOBBY: Pop!

MR. PARKER: I don't want to hear nothing from you!

MR. JENKINS: *(Realizing that* PARKER *is really upset.)*

590   It's only a game—and it don't have nothing to do with luck ... But you keep trying, Parker, and one of these days you're going to beat me. And when you do, it won't have nothing to do with luck—it just might be the unluckiest and worst day of your life. You'll be champion chekcer player of the world. Meanwhile, I'm the champ, *and you're gonna have to live with it.*

MR. PARKER: *(Smiling, grudgingly moves toward him with his hand extended.)* All right, Jenkins! You

600   win this time, but I'm gon' beat you yet. I'm gon' whip your behind until it turns white!

BOBBY: That's gon' be some strong whipping! *(There's a tap at the door.)* That must be Blue. *(Rushes to the door and opens it.)*

MR. PARKER: About time. *(*BLUE *enters.)* Hey, boy, where have you been?

BLUE: *(Moves in, carrying an attaché case.)* I got stuck with an emergency council meeting.

MR. PARKER: What kind of council?

BLUE: The council of the Association. I see you're   610 sporting some new clothes there, Mr. P. You must be rolling in extra dough these days.

MR. PARKER: Just a little something I picked up the other day. All right, where is the money, Blue?

BLUE: You'll get your money, but first I want to see those books. *(Moves to the desk in the back room and starts going over the books. In the shop an uneasy silence prevails.* JENKINS, *out of nervousness,* 620 *sets up the checkers for another game.)*

BLUE: I see. *(Takes out pencil and pad and starts scribbling on a sheet of paper.)* Uh-huh. Uh-huh ... *(Re-enters shop.)*

MR. PARKER: Well?

BLUE: Everything seems to be okay.

MR. PARKER: Of course everything is all right. What did you expect? *(Angry, impatient.)* Now come on and give me my money.

BLUE: Take it easy, Mr. Parker! *(Takes a white envelope from his case and passes it on to* PARKER.)   630 Here's your money.

MR. PARKER: Now this is what I like to see!

BLUE: *(Passes some bills to* MR. JENKINS.) And you, Mr. Jenkins.

MR. JENKINS: Thank you, young man. But from here on in, you can count me out of your operation.

BLUE: What's the trouble?

MR. JENKINS: No trouble at all. I just want to be out of it.   640

BLUE: People and headaches—that's all I ever get from all the Mr. Jenkinses in this world!

MR. JENKINS: Why don't you be quiet sometime, boy.

MR. PARKER: I'm afraid he's telling you right, Blue.

BLUE: *He's telling me that he is a damn idiot, who can get himself hurt!*

THEO: Who's going to hurt him?

(They all stare at BLUE.)

BLUE: *(Calming down.)* I'm sorry. I guess I'm work-   650 ing too hard these days. I got a call today from one of them "black committees" here in Harlem ...

THEO: What did they want?

BLUE: They wanted to know what we did. They said they had heard of us, but they never see us—meaning they never see us picketing, demonstrating, and demanding something all the time.

660   MR. PARKER: So?

BLUE: They want us to demonstrate with them next Saturday, and I have decided to set up a demonstrating committee, with you in charge, Mr. Parker.   ·

MR. PARKER: You what!

BLUE: You'd be looking good!

MR. PARKER: You hear that! (*Cynical laughter.*) *I'd be looking good!* Count me out! When I demonstrate, it's for real!

670   BLUE: You demonstrate in front of any store out there on that street, and you'll have a good sound reason for being there!

MR. PARKER: I thought you said we was suppose to be different, and we was to drive out that Mr. You-Know-Somebody—well, ain't that what we doing? Two stores already done put up "going out of business" signs.

BLUE: That's what we started this whole thing for, and that's what we're doing.

680   MR. PARKER: I got some questions about that, too. I don't see nothing that we're doing that would cause a liquor store, a clothing store, and a radio store to just all of a sudden close down like that, unless we've been raiding and looting them at night or something like that.

(BOBBY *quickly moves out of the shop into the back room and exits upstairs.*)

BLUE: It's the psychological thing that's doing it, man!

690   MR. PARKER: Psychological? Boy, you ain't telling me everything, and anyway I wanta know who made this decision about picketing.

BLUE: The council!

MR. PARKER: Who is on this council!

BLUE: You know we don't throw names around like that!

MR. PARKER: I don't get all the mystery, Blue. This is my house, and you know everything about it from top to bottom. I got my whole family

700   in this racket!

BLUE: You're getting a good share of the money—ain't that enough?

MR. PARKER: Not when I'm dealing with you in the dark.

BLUE: You're asking for something, so stop beating around corners and tell me what it is you want!

MR. PARKER: All right! You been promising my boy some help for two months now, and he's still waiting. Now I want you to give him that help starting tomorrow, and I want you to put   710 somebody in this shop who can cut hair to relieve me when I'm not here. And from here on in, I want to know everything that's to be known about this "de-colonization committee"—how it works, who's in it, who's running it—*and I want to be on that council you was talking about!*

BLUE: NO!

MR. PARKER: Then I can't cooperate with you any more!

BLUE: What does that mean?   720

MR. PARKER: It means we can call our little deal off, and you can take your junk out of here!

BLUE: Just like that?

MR. PARKER: Just any ol' way you want it. I take too many risks in this place, not to know where I stand.

BLUE: Mr. Parker—

MR. PARKER: All right, let me hear it and let me hear it quick!

BLUE: There is an opening on our council. It's a—   730

MR. PARKER: Just tell me what position is it!

BLUE: President.

MR. PARKER: President?

BLUE: The highest office on our council.

MR. PARKER: Boy, you're gonna have to get up real early to get by an old fox like me. A few minutes ago you offered me nothing, and now you say I can be president—that should even sound strange to *you!*

BLUE: There's nothing strange. A few minutes ago   740 you weren't ready to throw me out of your place, but now *I've got no other choice!*

MR. PARKER: (*Pointing his finger at him and laughing.*) That's true! You don't! All right, I'll give you a break—I accept! Just let me know when the next meeting is. (*Checks watch and grabs his hat.*) Come on, Jenkins, let's get out of here! (*Starts out with* MR. JENKINS.)

THEO: Hey, Pop—you're going out there with all that money in your pocket.   750

MR. PARKER: Don't worry about it. I'm a grown man, I can take care of myself.

THEO: But what about our part of it?

MR. PARKER: Look, son, he held me up—I'm late already. You'll get yours when I get back.

THEO: But, Pop—

MR. PARKER: Good night, Theo! *(Bolts out the door, with* MR. JENKINS *following.)*

THEO: *(Rushes to the door.)* Pop, you better be careful! I'll be waiting for you! I don't care if it's till dawn!

BLUE: You're becoming a worrier, Theo!

(Pause.)

But that's the nature of all things . . . I'm forever soothing and pacifying someone. Sometimes I have to pacify myself. You don't think that president stuff is going to mean anything, do you? He had me up-tight, so what I did was to bring him closer to me so I would be definitely sure of letting him know less and having more control over him—and over you, too.

THEO: What do you mean by that?

BLUE: It didn't take me more than one glance into those books to know that he's been spending money out of the box. And to think—you didn't bother to tell me about it.

THEO: Why should I? I trust your intelligence.

BLUE: Please don't let him do it any more.

THEO: Why don't you hire your own cashier and bookkeeper? *(He goes into back room.)*

BLUE: *(Following him.)* That's an idea! What about Adele! Now that was a thought in the back of my mind, but I'm putting that away real quick. Seems this sweet, nice-girl sister of yours has took to partying with the good-time set and keeping company with a simple ass clown like Wilmer Robinson. No, that wouldn't work, would it? I'd have more trouble with her than I'm having with you. When a girl as intelligent as your sister, who all of a sudden gets into things, and hooked up to people who just don't go with her personality, that could mean trouble. To be honest with you, I didn't think this thing was going to work, but *it is working*, Theo! I've got three places just like this one, and another on the way. A man has to care about what he does. Don't you want to get out of this place?

THEO: Yes, but lately I've been getting the feeling that I'm gonna have to hurt someone.

BLUE: I see.

THEO: You think the old man was asking you those questions about stores closing down as a joke or something?

BLUE: He asks because he thinks, but he is still in the dark!

THEO: He was playing with you! And when my father holds something inside of him and plays with a man, he's getting meaner and more dangerous by the minute.

BLUE: I don't care what he was doing—he is messing with my work! He has gotten himself into a "thing" with one of the rottenest bitches on the Avenue, who happens to be tight with a nigger who is trying to fuck up my business. Now that's something you had better get straight: it's your turn to soothe and pacify!

THEO: Why should I do anything for you when you lied to me and sent my brother out with that band of thieves of yours?

BLUE: He said he needed the money, and I couldn't stop him.

THEO: But I told you I didn't want that!

BLUE: Let's face it, baby! Bobby's the greatest thief in the world! He's been prancing around stores and stealing all of his life! And I think that's something to bow down to—because he's black and in trouble, just like you and me. So don't ride me so hard, Theo! *(They cross back into shop. He picks up attaché case, preparing to leave.)*

THEO: Blue! Now I don't care what kind of protection you got, but I say those store raids are dangerous and I don't want my brother on them, and I mean it!

BLUE: When we first made our plans, you went along with it—you knew somebody had to do it. What makes you and your brother so special?

THEO: Well, you better—

BLUE: *To hell with you, Theo!* I could take this hand and make you dead! You are nothing but what I make you be!

THEO: *(Pause.)* That just might be. But what if tomorrow this whole operation were to bust wide open in your face because of some goof-up by my father or sister—something that would be just too much for you to clean up. What would you do? Kill them?

BLUE: *(Pause. Then calmly and deliberately.)* The other day I went up on the hill to see my little boy. I took him out for a ride and as we were moving along the streets he asked me where all the people were coming from. I said from work, going home, going to the store, and coming back from the store. Then we went out to watch the river and then he asked me about the water, the ships, the weeds—everything. That kid threw so many questions at me, I got dizzy—I wanted to hit him once to shut him up. He was just a little dark boy discovering for the first time that there are things in the world like stones and trees . . . It got late and dark, so I took him home and watched him fall asleep. Then I took his mother into my arms and put her into bed. I just laid there for a while, listening to her call me all kinds of dirty mother-fuckers. After she got that out of her system, I put my hands on her and before long our arms were locked at each other's shoulders and then my thighs moved slowly down between her thighs and then we started that sweet rolling until the both of us were screaming as if the last piece of love was dying forever. After that, we just laid there, talking soft up into the air. I would tell her she was the loveliest bitch that ever lived, and all of a sudden she was no longer calling me a dirty mother-fucker, she was calling me a sweet mother-fucker. It got quiet. I sat up on the edge of the bed with my head hanging long and deep, trying to push myself out of the room and back into it at one and the same time. She looked up at me and I got that same question all over again. Will you marry me and be the father of your son! I tried to move away from her, but she dug her fingernails into my shoulders. I struck her once, twice, and again and again—with this hand! And her face was a bloody mess! And I felt real bad about that. I said, I'll marry you, Yes! Yes! Yes!

(Pause.)

I put my clothes on and I walked out into the streets, trembling with the knowledge that now I have a little boy who I must walk through the park with every Sunday, who one day just may blow my head off—and an abiding wife who on a given evening may get herself caught in the bed of some other man, and I could be sealed in a dungeon until dead! I was found lying in a well of blood on the day I was born! But I have been kind! I have kissed babies for the simple reason they were babies! I'm going to get married to some bitch and that gets me to shaking all over! *(He moves close to* THEO.*)* The last time I trembled this way *I killed a man! (Quickly and rhythmically takes out a long, shiny*

switchblade knife. *It pops open just at* THEO's *neck.* BLUE *holds it there for a moment, then withdraws and closes it. Puts it away. Then he collects his belongings, then calmly addresses* THEO.*)* Things are tight and cool on my end, Theo, and that's how you should keep it here. If not, everything gets messy and I find myself acting like a policeman, keeping order. I don't have the time for that kind of trick. *(*BLUE *exits.)*

THEO: *(After a moment of silent thought, moves decisively to the back-room stairs and calls.)* Bobby! *(*BOBBY *comes downstairs.)*

THEO: I want you to stay away from those store raids, Bobby.

BOBBY: Not as long as I can get myself some extra money. *(Moving close to him.)* You didn't say nothing to me before, when I was stealing every other day and giving you half of everything I stole. You didn't think nothing that day you sent me for that typewriter!

THEO: I don't know what you're going to do from here on in, because I'm calling the whole affair off with Blue.

BOBBY: That won't stop me, and you know it!

THEO: What is it, Bobby—we used to be so close! Bobby, don't get too far away from me!

BOBBY: *(Heatedly.)* What do you want me to do? Stick around you all the time? Hell, I'm tired of you! I stick by you and I don't know what to do! I steal and that puts clothes on my back and money in my pockets! *That's* something to do! But I sit here with you all day just thinking about the next word I'm going to say—I'm not stupid! I sit here all day thinking about what I'm going to say to you. I stuck by you and I hoped for you because whatever you became, I was gonna become. I thought about that, and that ain't shit! *(He leaves the shop.* THEO *is alone with his troubled thoughts. Suddenly he rushes into back room, gets hat and shirt, puts them on, and goes out into the street.)*

MR. PARKER: *(Stepping down into the back room from the apartment upstairs.)* Come on, girl! *(A very attractive, well-dressed* YOUNG GIRL *in her early twenties follows him into the shop.)*

MR. PARKER: You wanted to see it. Well, here it is.

GIRL: *(Looking about the place.)* So this is where you do your business. Like I keep asking you, Russell, what kind of business is it for you to make all that money you got?

MR. PARKER: (*Heading toward the refrigerator in the back room.*) Come on in here, sweetheart. I'll fix us a drink!

GIRL: (*Moves briskly after him.*) I asked you a question, Russell.

960   MR. PARKER: (*Still ignoring her question, he takes a jug out of refrigerator and grabs two glasses.*) I'm going to make you a special drink, made from my own hands. It's called "Black Lightning."

GIRL: (*Surveys the room as* PARKER *pours drink*). That should be exciting.

MR. PARKER: Here you go. (*Hands her the drink.*) *Toujours l'amour!*

GIRL: (*Gasping from the drink.*) What the fuck is this! What *is* this, Russell?

970   MR. PARKER: (*Patting her on the back.*) Knocks the tail off of you, don't it! But it gets smoother after the second swallow . . . Go on, drink up!

GIRL: Okay. (*Tries it again and scowls. Moves away as he sits on bed.*)

MR. PARKER: Now, did you think about what I asked you last night?

GIRL: About getting married?

MR. PARKER: Yes.

GIRL: Why do you want to marry me, Russell?

980   MR. PARKER: Because I love you, and I think you could make me happy.

GIRL: Well, I don't believe you. When I asked you a question about your business, you deliberately ignored me. It was like you didn't trust me, and I thought that love and trust went together.

MR. PARKER: I'm not so sure about that. My son Theo, I'm wild about him, but I wouldn't trust him no farther 'n I could throw a building.

GIRL: I'm not your son!

990   MR. PARKER: What is it you wanta know?

GIRL: Where you gettin' all that money from?

MR. PARKER: Oh, that. That's not for a girl to know, baby doll.

GIRL: Then it's time for me to go. I'm not gettin' myself hooked up with no mystery man! (*Moves as if to leave.* PARKER *stops her, then pauses for a moment.*)

MR. PARKER: All right, I'll tell you. I'm partners in a big business, which I'm the president of.

1000   GIRL: Partners with who, Russell?

MR. PARKER: That's not important, baby.

GIRL: Partners with who, Russell.

MR. PARKER: Mr. Blue Haven.

GIRL: *Blue Haven!* Then it's crooked business.

MR. PARKER: Oh no, baby, it's nothing like that. It's real straight.

GIRL: What does that mean?

MR. PARKER: That what we're doing is right!

GIRL: Tell me about it, then.

MR. PARKER: I've said enough. Now let's leave it 1010 at that! (*Tries to embrace her.*)

GIRL: (*Wards him off, sits on bed.*) All you take me for is something to play with.

MR. PARKER: That's not true, I wanna marry you. (*Sits beside her.*)

GIRL: You say you want to marry me, but how do you expect me to think about marrying somebody who won't confide in me about what they're doing. How do I know I'm not letting myself in for trouble. 1020

MR. PARKER: (*Ponders for a moment, then rises.*) All right, I'll tell you! We peddle a variety of products to the community and we sell things to people at a price they can't get nowhere else in this city. Yes, according to the law it's illegal, but we help our people, our own people. We take care of business and at the same time we make everybody happy. We take care of our people. Just like I been taking care of you.

GIRL: You take care of me? How? You've never 1030 given me more than ten dollars in cash since I've known you.

MR. PARKER: Well, I've got a big present for you coming right out of this pocket and I'm gon' take you downtown tomorrow and let you spend till the store runs out.

GIRL: Taking me to a store and giving me spending change makes me feel like a child and I don't like it and I'm not gonna stand for it any more.

MR. PARKER: Then take this and you do whatever 1040 you want with it.

GIRL: (*Taking the money and putting it away.*) Now don't get the idea I'm just in love with your money.

MR. PARKER: Now I want you to stop talking to me about money. I've got *plenty* of it! You've got to understand—I'm the most different man you ever met. I've been around this world, I danced before the King and Queen of England. I've seen and heard many a thing in my 1050 lifetime—and you know what: I'm putting it all down on paper—my story!

GIRL: Your story!

(MR. PARKER *moves into shop, gets notebook from behind one of the sliding panels. During his absence* GIRL *checks under the bed.*)

MR. PARKER: (*Re-enters.*) Here it is, right here. (*Sits next to her on the bed, giving her the notebook.*)

1060 GIRL: (*Thumbing through the pages.*) You write things too?

MR. PARKER: I certainly do—and I've been thinking about writing a poem about you.

GIRL: A poem about me!

MR. PARKER: (*Taking book from her and dropping it on floor.*) I'm gon' do it tonight before I go to sleep. (*He kisses her neck and reaches for the hem of her dress.*)

GIRL: (*Breaking out of his embrace.*) No, Russell, not here!

1070 MR. PARKER: Why not?

GIRL: Just because there's a bed wherever we go don't mean that we have to jump into it. You don't understand, Russell! You've got to start treating me the same as if I was your wife.

MR. PARKER: *That's exactly what I'm trying to do!*

GIRL: (*Rising.*) Don't yell at me!

MR. PARKER: All right. I tell you what: I'm kinda tired, let's just lie down for a while and talk. I ain't gon' try nothing.

1080 GIRL: Russell—

MR. PARKER: May the Lord smack me down this minute into hell—I swear I won't do nothing.

GIRL: What are the three biggest lies men tell to women, Russell?

MR. PARKER: I ain't just any man—I'm the man you gon' spend your life with.

GIRL: Okay, Russell, we'll lie down, but you've got to keep your word. If I'm the girl you want to marry, you've got to learn to keep your word.

1090 (*They lie on bed. To her surprise,* PARKER *is motionless, seemingly drifting off to sleep. After a moment she takes the initiative and begins love-making. He responds, and once his passion has reached an aggressive peak she breaks off abruptly.*) Where do you get these things you sell to people?

MR. PARKER: What are you talking about?

GIRL: You know what I'm saying. I overheard you tell Mr. Jenkins you suspected your son was robbing stores.

1100 MR. PARKER: You heard no such thing!

GIRL: (*Desperately.*) Where do they keep the stuff?

MR. PARKER: Now, baby, you've got to relax and stop worrying about things like that! (*Pulls her by the shoulders. She does not resist.*) Come here. (*He pulls her down to the bed, takes her into his arms and kisses her, reaching again for the hem of her dress.*)

GIRL: (*Struggling, but weakening to his ardor.*) Russell, you said you wouldn't do nothing!

MR. PARKER: I ain't! I just want to get a little closer to you! 1110

GIRL: Russell, not here!

MR. PARKER: Just let me feel it a little bit!

GIRL: You swore to God, Russell! (THEO *comes in the front door and heads toward back room.*)

MR. PARKER: I ain't gon' do nothing!

GIRL: (*Hears* THEO.) Russell! Russell! Somebody is out there!

MR. PARKER: (*Jumps up quickly.* THEO *stands before him.*) What are you doing here?

THEO: The question is, *what are you doing!* 1120

MR. PARKER: I have been having a private talk with a good friend of mine. Now get out of here!

(GIRL *jumps up, moving past* MR. PARKER.)

MR. PARKER: (*Stopping her.*) Where are you going?

GIRL: Home!

MR. PARKER: Hold it now, honey!

GIRL: I never should have come here in the first place!

MR. PARKER: No, you're not going anywhere. This is my place and you don't have to run off because 1130 of this Peeping Tom!

THEO: Pop, it's time to give us our money.

MR. PARKER: You'll get your share tomorrow and not before!

THEO: I want it now before you give it all to that girl. Pop, cut that broad loose!

MR. PARKER: What was that?

THEO: I said, cut her loose! She don't need an old man like you, she's just pumping you for information. That bitch is a hustler! 1140

MR. PARKER: (*Slaps* THEO *with the back of his hand.*) Bite your tongue!

GIRL: I think I better go, Russell. (*Heads for the front door.*)

MR. PARKER: (*Following her.*) Okay, but I'll be right with you as soon as I get things straight here. You will be waiting for me, won't you?

GIRL: Sure!

MR. PARKER: You run along now and I'll be right
over there. (GIRL *exits.* PARKER *whirls back into
shop.*) What do you think you're doing, boy?

THEO: Just be careful, Pop. Please be careful.

MR. PARKER: If there's anybody I got to be careful
of, it's you! You lying selfish sonofabitch! You
think I don't know about you and Blue running
that gang of thieves—about you sending your
own brother out there with them?

THEO: I didn't do that!

MR. PARKER: If Bobby gets hurt out on them streets,
I'm gonna kill you, boy! I'm gonna kill you.
(*Hurriedly collects hat and coat.*)

THEO: You're not worried about Bobby! All you
can think of is the money you're rolling in. The
clothes. And that stupid outfit you've got on.

(ADELE *comes in from the street, obviously distraught.*)

MR. PARKER: What's wrong with you? Are you
drunk? (*Moves in.* ADELE *doesn't answer, so he moves
off.*)

THEO: Of course she's drunk. What did you expect
—did you think everything would stop and stand
still while you were being reborn again!

MR. PARKER: What do you want from me? Call
this whole thing off? It was your idea, not mine!
But now that I've got myself something—I'm
not going to throw it away for nobody!

THEO: But can't you see what's happening here?

MR. PARKER: If she wants to be a drunken wench,
let her! I'm not going to take the blame. And
as for you—(*Fumbles in his coat pocket.*) If you
want this money, you can take it from me—I
can throw every dollar of it into the ocean if
I want to! You can call me a fool too, but I'm
a *burning fool!* I'm going to marry that little girl.
She is not a whore! She is a woman! And I'm
going to marry her! And if the two of you don't
like it, you can kiss my ass! (*Bolts out into the
street.*)

THEO: You're not drunk. What happened?

ADELE: (*Heading for the back room.*) What does it
look like. Wilmer hit me.

THEO: (*Following.*) Why?

ADELE: (*Sits on bed.*) He caught me in Morgan's
with a friend of his after I had lied about going
bowling with the girls. He just walked in and
started hitting me, over and over again. His
friend just stood there pleading with him not

to hit me, but he never did anything to stop
him. I guess he figured, "Why should I risk
getting myself killed over just another piece of
ass?" I thought he was going to kill me but then
Blue came in with some of his friends and they
just grabbed him by the arms and took him away.

THEO: Was Bobby with them?

ADELE: I couldn't tell.

THEO: Damnit! Everything gets fucked up!

ADELE: It had to, because you don't think. If you're
going to be a crook, you don't read a comic book
for research, you don't recruit an old black man
that's about to die!

THEO: No matter what you do, he's gon' die anyway. This whole place was built for him to die
in—so you bite, you scratch, you kick: you do
anything to stay alive!

ADELE: Yes, you bite! You scratch, you steal, you
kick, and you get killed anyway! Just as I was
doing, coming back here to help Momma.

THEO: Adele, I'm sick and tired of your talk about
sacrifices. You were here because you had no
other place to go. You just got scared too young
and too soon.

ADELE: You're right. All I was doing was waiting
for her to die so I could get on with what I
thought I wanted to do with myself. But, God,
she took so long to die! But then I found myself
doing the same things she had done, taking care
of three men, trying to shield them from the
danger beyond that door, *but who the hell ever
told every black woman she was some kind of goddamn
savior!* Sure, this place was built for us to die
in, but if we aren't very careful, Theo—that
can actually happen. Good night. (*Heads for the
stairs.*)

THEO: Adele—(*She stops in her tracks and turns.*) I've
decided that there's going to be no more of Blue's
business here. It's over. We're getting out.

ADELE: (*After a long pause.*) Theo, do you really
mean it? (THEO *nods yes.*)

ADELE: What about Daddy?

THEO: He will have to live with it. This set-up
can't move without me.

ADELE: And Bobby?

THEO: I'll take care of him.

ADELE: That's fine, Theo. We'll throw the old
things into the river—and we'll try something
new: I won't push and you won't call me a bitch!

(*Goes upstairs.* THEO *picks up his father's notebook from the floor beside the bed. A knock at the door.*)

THEO: We're closed!

(*The knocking continues.*)

1250   THEO: WE'RE CLOSED!

(*The knocking turns to banging and a voice calls out to* THEO. *He rushes to the door and opens.*)

THEO: I SAID WE'RE CLOSED! Oh, I'm sorry, Mr. Jenkins, I didn't know that was you ... What are you doing here this time of night?

MR. JENKINS: I want to speak to Parker.

THEO: You know him—he's been keeping late hours lately . . . .

MR. JENKINS: I'll wait for him.

1260   THEO: Suit yourself, but don't you have to work tomorrow?

MR. JENKINS: I have something to tell him, and I'll wait if it takes all night.

THEO: In that case, you can tell me about it.

(ADELE *comes downstairs and stops on steps leading to shop, looking about confusedly. She has a deadly, almost blank look on her face.*)

THEO: What's wrong with you?

ADELE: (*Pause.*) Some—somebody just called me.

1270   THEO: What did they call you about? (*She does not answer.* JENKINS *rises and seats her gently on bed.*) Didn't you hear me—what about? (*She still does not respond.*) WHAT IS IT, ADELE!!!

MR. JENKINS: THEO!!! (THEO *turns to* MR. JENKINS.) I think she probably just heard that your brother Bobby has been killed in a robbery by a night watchman.

THEO: Uh-uh, nawww, nawww, that's not true.

MR. JENKINS: Yes, it is, son.

1280   ADELE: Yes.

THEO: No.

MR. JENKINS: Yes! (*Moves toward the shop door.*)

THEO: *I don't believe you!*

MR. JENKINS: I saw him, boy, I saw him. (*Dead silence as* MR. JENKINS *slowly moves toward the street exit.*)

THEO: You should've seen this dude I caught the other day on Thirty-second Street. He had on a bright purple suit, gray shirt, yellow tie, and

1290   his hair was processed with bright purple color. What a sight he was! But I have to say one thing for him—he was clean. (*The lights are slowly dimming.*) Used to be a time when a dude like that came in numbers, but you don't see too many of them nowadays. I have to say one thing for him—he was clean. You don't see too many like—he was clean. He was—he was clean—

Blackout

SCENE TWO

About two hours later, in the shop.

————

MR. PARKER *and* MR. JENKINS *enter the shop.* MR. PARKER *is drunk, and* MR. JENKINS *helps him walk and finally seats him on the barber's throne.*)

MR. PARKER: Thank you, Jenkins. You are the greatest friend a man can have. They don't make 'em like you any more. You are one of the last of the great friends, Jenkins. Pardon me, Mister Jenkins. No more will I ever call you Jenks or Jenkins. From now on, it's Mister Jenkins!

MR. JENKINS: Thank you, but when I ran into Theo   10 and Adele tonight they said they had something important to say to you, and I think you oughta see them.

MR. PARKER: I know what they want. They want to tell me what an old fool I am.

MR. JENKINS: I don't think that's it, and you should go on upstairs and—

MR. PARKER: Never! Upstairs is for the people upstairs!

MR. JENKINS: Russell, I—   20

MR. PARKER: I am downstairs people! You ever hear of downstairs people?

MR. JENKINS: (*Pause.*) No.

MR. PARKER: Well, they're the people to watch in this world.

MR. JENKINS: If you say so.

MR. PARKER: *Put your money on 'em!*

MR. JENKINS: Come on, Mister Parker: why don't you lie down in the back room and—

MR. PARKER: Oh! No—you don't think I'd have   30 you come all the way over here just for me to go to bed, do you? I wouldn't do a thing like that to you, Jenkins. I'm busy—Mister Jenkins. Just stay with me for a little while ... (*His tone changes.*) Why did that girl lock me out? She said she would be waiting for me, but she locked me out. Why did she do a thing like that? I give her everything—money, clothes, pay her rent. I even love her!

40 MR. JENKINS: Russell—

MR. PARKER: (*Rising precariously.*) Tell me something, Mister Jenkins—since you are my friend —why do you think she locked me out?

MR. JENKINS: (*Steadying him.*) I don't know.

MR. PARKER: I'll tell you why. I'm an old man, and all I've got is a few dollars in my pocket. Ain't that it?

MR. JENKINS: I don't know . . . Good night, Parker. (*Starts out.*)

50 MR. PARKER: (*Grabs his arm.*) You think a man was in that room with my girl?

MR. JENKINS: *Yes!*

MR. PARKER: *Goddamnit! Goddamnit!*

MR. JENKINS: Russell—

MR. PARKER: I don't believe it! When I love 'em, they stay loved!

MR. JENKINS: Nobody's got that much love, man!

MR. PARKER: (*Pause.*) No, no—you're wrong. My wife—my dear Doris had more love in her than
60 life should've allowed. A hundred men couldn't have taken all that love.

MR. JENKINS: We ain't talking about Doris, Russell.

MR. PARKER: Aw, forget it! (*Crossing toward table.*) *Goddamnit!* You stumble around like an old black cow and you never get up again . . .

I have had my fun!
If I don't get well no more!
I have had my fun!
If I—

70 (PARKER *falls down.*) Get up, old bastard! Get up! (*Rises to his feet, aided by* JENKINS.) Get up and fall back down again. Come on, Mister Jenkins, let's play ourselves a game of checkers.

MR. JENKINS: I don't want to play no damn checkers.

MR. PARKER: Why do you curse my home, Mister Jenkins?

MR. JENKINS: (*Pause.*) I apologize for that.

MR. PARKER: Come on, have a game of checkers
80 with your good friend. (*Sits at table.*)

MR. JENKINS: (*Moves to the table.*) All right, one game and then I'm going home.

MR. PARKER: One game.

MR. PARKER: (*Pausing while* JENKINS *sits down.*) I said a lot of dirty things to my children tonight—the kind of things you have to live a long time to overcome.

MR. JENKINS: I know exactly what you mean. (JENKINS *sets up jumps for* PARKER. PARKER *seems unaware of it. They play briefly.* PARKER *stops.*) 90

MR. PARKER: Theo is a good boy, and a smart one too, but he lets people push him around. That's because he's always trying to con somebody out of something—you know the kind: can't see for looking. And Bobby? He wouldn't hurt a flea. A lot of people think that boy is dumb, but just let somebody try to trick or fool him if they dare! (*Begins a series of checker jumps.*)

(*Pause.*)

Got a story for you. 100

MR. JENKINS: No stories tonight, Parker . . .

MR. PARKER: Mister Parker. (*The last move is made, the game is over. His conquest slowly sinks in. And* MR. PARKER *is at long last the victor. Rising from the table.*) Call me champ! (THEO *and* ADELE *enter shop from outside, and stand just inside the door.* PARKER *is laughing.*) You're beat! I beat you! I beat you! (MR. PARKER *throws his arm around* MR. JENKINS's *waist and holds him from behind.*) . . . You fall down and you never get up! (*Still laughing.*) 110 Fall down, old man! Fall down! (*Releases* JENKINS *upon seeing* ADELE *and* THEO.) You hear that, children, I beat him! I beat him! (*His laughter subsides as he realizes they are not responding to him. Guilt-ridden, he approaches* THEO, *looks at him intently, then reaches into his inside coat pocket and pulls out the money.*) Here, Theo, here's the money, here's all of it. Take it, it's yours. Go out and try to get happy, boy. (THEO *does not move or take the money from his father's outstretched hand. He turns* 120 *to* ADELE. *Her face is almost a blank.*) WHY DON'T SOMEBODY SAY SOMETHING! (ADELE *attempts to speak but* PARKER *cuts her off.*) I know you have some trouble with me . . . (PARKER *spies the notebook in the throne, takes it in his hand, and approaches* ADELE.) You have a woman, you love her, you stop loving her, and sooner or later she ups and dies and you sit around behaving like you was a killer. I didn't have no more in me. I just didn't have no more in me! 130

(Pause.)

I know you don't believe I ever loved your mother, but it's here in this book—read it . . . *(She does not respond.)* You wanta read something, boy! *(THEO turns away. PARKER slowly crosses, hands the book to MR. JENKINS, and addresses his remarks to him.)* I got sour the day my legs got so trembly and sore on the stage of the Strand Theatre—I couldn't even walk out to take a proper bow.

140   It was then I knew nobody would ever hire me to dance again. I just couldn't run downtown to meet the Man the way she did—not after all those years of shuffling around like I was a dumb clown, with my feet hurting and aching the way they did, having my head patted as if I was some little pet animal: back of the bus, front of the train, grinning when I was bleeding to death! . . . After all of that I was going to ask for more by throwing myself into the low drag of some dusty old factory in Brooklyn. All

150   I could do was to stay here in this shop with you, my good friend. And we acted out the ceremony of a game. And you, boy—*(Turns to THEO.)* . . . You and Blue with your ideas of overcoming the evil of white men. To an old man like me, it was nothing more than an ounce of time to end my dragging about this shop. All it did was to send me out into those streets to live a time—and I did live myself a time for a while.

160   I did it amongst a bunch of murderers—all kinds of 'em—where at times it gets so bad till it seems that the only thing that's left is for you to go out there and kill somebody before they kill you. That's all—that's out there! *(Goes to ADELE.)* Adele, as for that girl that was here tonight, she's probably no good, but if at my age I was stupid enough to think that I could have stepped out of here and won that little girl, loved her, and moved through the rest of my days without

170   killing anybody, that was a victory! *(Moves to center stage, stands silently, then does a little dance.)* Be a dancer—any kind of dancer you wanta be—but dance it! *(Tries out a difficult step, but can't quite make it.)* Uh-uhhh! Can't make that one no more. *(Continues to dance.)* Be a singer— sing any song you wanta sing, but sing! *(Stops in his tracks.)* And you've got enough trouble to take you to the graveyard!

(Pause.)

180   But think of all that life you had before they buried you. *(Breaks into a frantic dance, attempting steps that just cross him up. He stumbles about until he falls. Everyone in the room rushes to help him up.)* . . . I'm okay, I'm okay . . . *(He rises from the floor, slowly.)* I'm tired, I'm going to bed and by the time tomorrow comes around, let's see if we can't all throw it into the river. *(Moves into the back room, singing.)*

I have had my fun!
If I don't get well no more   190
I have had my fun
If I don't get well no more—

(A thought strikes him. He turns and moves back to where JENKINS is standing at the entrance to the back room.) Jenkins, you said that the day I beat you playing checkers, you said it could be the unluckiest day of my life. But after all that's happened today—I'm straight—I feel just great! *(Moves to the stairs leading up, suddenly stops, turns and briskly moves back to the doorway leading to the   200 shop.)* Say, where's Bobby?

Curtain

CEREMONIES IN DARK OLD MEN: A REMARKABLE ACHIEVEMENT IN BLACK DRAMA

by William R. Reardon

To gain even a greater appreciation of the talent of Mr. Lonne Elder III and the excellence of *Ceremonies in Dark Old Men*, it may help to know a little of the history of the black man on the American stage and the enormous obstacles that he had to overcome.

In the late eighteenth and early nineteenth centuries, a black man was not allowed on the stage. If there were a black character in a play, he would be portrayed by a white man in black-face makeup. Even when a group of blacks tried to organize their own theatre—The African Company in New York in 1821—they were hounded out of existence. This policy prevented Americans from seeing Ira Aldridge, perhaps the greatest of black American actors, for he had to go to Europe around 1825 in order to perform on stage.

Even the minstrel shows, derived strictly from the songs, dances, and instruments used by slaves on the plantations, were done by white men in blackface. Thus the black suffered a double indignity. Not only was his material stolen from him, but he was also now presented on stage in such a distorted stereotype for the rest of the century that an incredible image of the black man was pounded into the American consciousness. This distortion of the black slipped automatically into the movies from the minstrel shows.

Not until after the Civil War was a black man permitted on stage, and even then the roles open to him were far from inviting. He was now permitted to perform minstrel shows himself—in essence to play the stereotype, even to distorting his features with makeup. Probably the major difference would then have been that the songs and dances would have been done correctly and perhaps some of the hidden satire brought out. Incredibly, out of such activities ultimately came such fine composers as James Bland and W. C. Handy. He could also appear in the "Tom" shows, extravagant off-shoots from *Uncle Tom's Cabin*, usually with little or no reference to Stowe's original story. In fact, the black man would rarely get to play Uncle Tom, but was usually restricted to appearing as one of a "passel of darkies."

Not until around the turn of the century did the black performer actually achieve a breakthrough. The most influential persons in this effort were Sissieretta Jones and Bob Cole. Mrs. Jones had such a brilliant voice that she was inevitably compared to Adelina Patti and in later years a musical show was formed around her talents entitled *Black Patti's Troubadours*. Bob Cole conceived and executed the first all black musical show. Since the color barrier still existed, however, black entertainers now performed on a circuit of vaudeville theatres restricted to blacks from New York to Florida and from Chicago to New Orleans.

In April, 1917, white audiences were finally made aware of black actors, when Ridgely Torrence presented three one-act plays. Although a white man, Torrence had a feeling for the black experience. His three plays—*The Rider of Dreams, Granny Maumee*, and *Simon the Cyrenian*—are distinctive in presenting the black as a genuine human being whose miseries tend to stem preeminently from the white man. In the 1920s, other works by white authors such as O'Neill, Green, Dubose, and Heyward had roles in them which helped propel such noted black artists as Charles Gilpin, Paul Robeson, Frank Wilson, and Rose McClendon to national attention. In spite of economic conditions, black theatres in Harlem were springing up to aid the black actor: The Lafayette, the Lincoln, the Alhambra, McClendon Players, and others. Even in the face of the depression in the thirties, and the approaching war, with the aid of the Federal Theatre Project several outstanding black shows appeared between 1935 and 1939 including *Haiti, Big White Fog*, and *The Swing Mikado*. Even more importantly, blacks were participating in the technical functions of theatre such as design and lighting from which they had hitherto been excluded. Still very little was being done for the black dramatist.

Although there was not much of dramatic worth in the forties, before the decade of the fifties was over, the black dramatist had gained recognition with surprising speed. Truly to understand Elder's achievement, and the achievement of black drama in general, it is essential to realize that these heights have been attained in the incredibly short span of twenty years. Forging the way for this rapid growth in the fifties were Alice Childress (*Just a Little Simple*), Loften Mitchell (*A Land Beyond the River*), William Branch (*A Medal for Willie*), Louis Petersen (*Take a Giant Step*), Charles Sebree (*Mrs. Patterson*), and Lorraine Hansberry (*A Rasin in the Sun*). Their thematic notes were varied and penetrating whether they were, respectively, discussing the genial and perceptive philosophies of a Harlem native, examining Supreme Court decisions on segregation, or the irony of awards for valor, or the difficult problems of black adolescence, or the painful fantasies of a black child, or the most intimate portrait of a troubled family.

The sixties witnessed the genuine flowering of black drama. Among the memorable comedies of the decade are Ossie Davis' *Purlie Victorious*, Langston Hughes' *Simply Heavenly* and Douglas Turner Ward's *Day of Absence* and *Happy Ending*. These men proved themselves to be excellent satirists, making their points with hilarity and incisiveness in plays which are delightfully uninhibited. Of the serious dramas, Baldwin's *Blues for Mr. Charlie* and *The Amen Corner* impressed many, as have the occasionally bitter, sardonic, and poignant dramas of Ed Bullins, particularly *Clara's Ole Man*, *A Son Come Home*, and *In the Wine Time*.

Probably the greatest theatrical impact was made by LeRoi Jones. His writing is of such merit that at one time, in 1964, he had five plays appearing simultaneously off-Broadway: *The Dutchman*, *The Toilet*, *The Slave*, *The Eighth Ditch*, and *The Baptism*. Jones is very much a moralist and preoccupied with displaying moral decay. Since he finds white people to be the source of most of this decay, and he excoriates them constantly, he has naturally aroused some irritations. But he is a most theatrically effective writer and his works flow with a passion and fire which are unremittingly dramatic. His language is often of the ghetto; his satire almost maniacal. A person may dislike Jones' writing, but he will probably not be bored by it. In the past few years, Jones has focused on works which are more revolutionary in nature and are intended for black audiences only. They are less complex than his earlier works, though effective for his thematic points. Many other young black writers have followed his recent direction, and their works are somewhat exclusively for the Black Arts Theatre.

The presence of these talented writers, as well as others such as Elder, Kennedy, Shine, Milner, and Gunn, to name but a few, bodes well for the continued growth of black drama in the seventies. Furthermore, the significant growth and success of the Negro Ensemble Company is no less encouraging for the future, both from the scope of its offerings and from the quality of its work.

It is particularly fitting that the Negro Ensemble Company should have produced Lonne Elder III's *Ceremonies in Dark Old Men*, for it indicates the level of excellence which has been reached both in production and in writing by our black artists. Elder's play is a mature work, richly textured, multi-faceted in character. He skillfully blends humor and poignancy, hilarity and anguish, romantic dreams and chilling reality to a culmination in a moment of intense pity that we feel for Mr. Parker in the blow which will now strike him.

The black experience permeates *Ceremonies in Dark Old Men* both explicitly and implicitly. Some of the thematic strands are not particularly original in themselves and have often been used by black dramatists: the dominant female and her relative emasculation of the males; the hustlers abounding in all quarters—Blue Haven, The Young Girl, Wilmer, even the boys; the get rich quick schemes; the white shopowner's economic domination of Harlem; the decent, well-meaning, but basically incompetent father. In Elder's hands these strands undergo a transformation.

Perhaps his most significant accomplishment as a playwright, is his ability in *Ceremonies* to make the Harlem environment a living force at work on this play both within the shop itself and as that outside environment which plays an inexorable role on the motivations of the characters. He makes us feel the presence of that environment; he makes us realize that it will crush these people, that there will be no escaping the inevitability of poverty, improper education, and the lack of opportunity. Yet he is compassionate and understanding of their dreams and of their needs for some bits and pieces of happiness and so we laugh and joy with them in their momentary triumphs. But because he is a singularly honest dramatist, we know that there is no escaping the destruction of hopes and dreams which will ensue. Thus he leaves us not only with pity for his characters, but also with a deep sense of indignation. These people deserved more from life.

Mr. Elder has a genius to draw his theme from character, to show and to imply it forcefully without the necessity to over-verbalize. He sets a very high standard for his fellow dramatists to equal.

BIBLIOGRAPHY

GENERAL WORKS ON THE THEATER

Artaud, Antonin, *The Theater and Its Double*, translated by Mary Caroline Richards, New York, 1958.

Bentley, Eric, *The Life of the Drama*, New York, 1964.

Bogard, Travis, and William I. Oliver (editors), *Modern Drama: Essays in Criticism*, New York, 1965.

Brockett, Oscar G., *The Theatre: An Introduction*, New York, 1964.

———, *History of the Theatre*, Boston, 1968.

Brook, Peter, *The Empty Space*, New York, 1968.

Brooks, Cleanth, and Robert B. Heilman, *Understanding Drama*, New York, 1945.

Brustein, Robert, *The Theatre of Revolt*, Boston, 1962.

Clark, Barrett H., *European Theories of Drama*, New York, 1947.

Clurman, Harold, *Lies Like Truth*, New York, 1958.

Cole, Toby (editor), *Playwrights on Playwriting*, New York, 1960.

Corrigan, Robert W. (editor), *Tragedy: Vision and Form*, San Francisco, 1965.

———, *Comedy: Meaning and Form*, San Francisco, 1965.

Downer, Alan S., *Fifty Years of American Drama, 1900-1950*, Chicago, 1951.

Enck, John, J., Elizabeth T. Forter, and Alvin Whitley (editors), *The Comic in Theory and Practice*, New York, 1960.

Esslin, Martin, *The Theatre of the Absurd*, New York, 1961.

Fergusson, Francis, *The Idea of Theater*, New York, 1953.

Fowlie, Wallace, *Dionysus in Paris, A Guide to Contemporary French Theatre*, New York, 1960.

Freedley, George, and John A. Reeves, *A History of the Theatre*, New York, 1941; revised, 1955.

Gassner, John, *Form and Idea in Modern Theatre*, New York, 1956.

———, *Masters of the Drama*, New York, 1954.

Grotowski, Jerzy, *Towards a Poor Theatre*, 1969.

Hainaux, Rene, and Yves-Bonnat, *Stage Design Throughout the World Since 1935*, New York, 1956.

———, *Stage Design Throughout the World Since 1950*, New York, 1964.

——— (editors), *Stage Design Throughout the World: 1960-1970*, New York, 1972.

Hartnoll, Phyllis, *The Oxford Companion to the Theatre*, Oxford, 1951.

Hewitt, Barnard, *Theatre U.S.A.*, *1668-1957*, New York, 1959.

Jones, Robert Edmond, *Dramatic Imagination*, New York.

Kerr, Walter, *Tragedy & Comedy*, New York, 1967.

Kitto, Humphrey D., *Form and Meaning in Drama*, London, 1956.

Lauter, Paul (editor), *Theories of Comedy*, Garden City, New York, 1964.

MacGowan, Kenneth, and William Melnitz, *The Living Stage*, New York, 1955.

Michel, Lawrence, and Richard B. Sewall (editors), *Tragedy: Modern Essays in Criticism*, New York, 1963.

Muller, Herbert, *The Spirit of Tragedy*, New York, 1956.

Mullin, Donald C., *The Development of the Playhouse*, Berkeley, California, 1970.

Nicoll, Allardyce, *The Development of the Theatre*, New York, revised, 1958.

Olson, Elder, *Tragedy and the Theory of Drama*, Detroit, 1961.

Peacock, Ronald, *The Art of Drama*, London, 1957.

Reose-Evans, James, *The Experimental Theatre*, 1970.

Styan, J. L., *The Dramatic Experience*, Cambridge, 1965.

Wellwarth, George E., *The Theatre of Protest and Paradox*, New York, 1964.

Williams, Raymond, *Drama from Ibsen to Eliot*, London, 1952.

SOPHOCLES

Goheen, Robert F., *The Imagery of Sophocles' Antigone*, Princeton, New Jersey, 1951.

Kitto, Humphrey D., *Sophocles, Dramatist and Philosopher*, London, 1958.

Waldock, A. J. A., *Sophocles, the Dramatist*, Cambridge, Massachusetts, 1951.

Webster, T. B. L., *An Introduction to Sophocles*, London, 1969.

Whitman, Cedric H., *Sophocles: A Study in Heroic Humanism*, Cambridge, Massachusetts, 1951.

Woodard, Thomas Marion, *Sophocles: A Collection of Critical Essays*, Englewood Cliffs, New Jersey, 1966.

SHAKESPEARE

Beckerman, Bernard, *Shakespeare at the Globe, 1559-1609*, New York, 1962.

Bradley, A. C., *Shakespearean Tragedy*, London, 1931.

Campbell, Lily B., *Shakespeare's Tragic Heroes: Slaves of Passion*, Cambridge, Massachusetts, 1952.

Harrison, George B., *Shakespeare's Tragedies*, London, 1951.

Knight, G. Wilson, *The Wheel of Fire*, London, 1930.

MOLIÈRE

Fernandez, Ramon, *Molière: The Man Seen Through the Plays*, New York, 1958.

Gossman, Lionel, *Men and Masks: A Study of Molière*, Baltimore, 1963.

Guicharaud, Jacques, *Molière, a Collection of Critical Essays*, Englewood Cliffs, New Jersey, 1964.

Lewis, D. B. W., *Molière, the Comic Mask*, New York, 1959.

Moore, Will G., *Molière, a New Criticism*, London, 1949.

Walker, Hallam, *Molière*, New York, 1971.

CONGREVE

Dobrée, Bonamy, *Restoration Comedy 1660-1720*, London, 1924.

Fujimura, Thomas H., *The Restoration Comedy of Wit*, Princeton, New Jersey, 1952.

Hodges, John C., *William Congreve, the Man*, New York, 1941.

Loftis, John, *Comedy and Society from Congreve to Fielding*, Stanford, California, 1959.

Lynch, Kathleen M., *The Social Mode of Restoration Comedy*, New York, 1926.

HENRIK IBSEN

Downs, Brian W., *Ibsen: The Intellectual Background*, Cambridge, Massachusetts, 1946.

Fjelde, Rolf (translator), *Henrik Ibsen: Four Major Plays*, New York, 1970.

———— (editor), *Ibsen: A Collection of Critical Essays*, Englewood Cliffs, New Jersey, 1965.

McFarlane, James Walter (editor), *Discussions of Henrik Ibsen*, Boston, 1962.

Northam, John, *Ibsen's Dramatic Method*, London, 1953.

Tennant, P. F. D., *Ibsen's Dramatic Technique*, Cambridge, Massachusetts, 1948.

Williams, Raymond, *Drama from Ibsen to Eliot*, London, 1952.

ARTHUR MILLER

Brandon, Henry, "The State of the Theatre: A Conversation with Arthur Miller," *Harper's*, 221 (November, 1960).

Miller, Arthur, "The Family in Modern Drama," *Atlantic Monthly*, 197 (April, 1956).

———, "Introduction," in *Collected Plays*, New York, 1957.

Welland, Dennis, *Arthur Miller*, London, 1961.

AUGUST STRINDBERG

Klaf, Franklin S., *Strindberg: The Origin of Psychology in Modern Drama*, New York, 1963.

Lamm, Martin, *August Strindberg*, translated by Harry G. Carlson, New York, 1971.

Lucas, Frank Laurence, *The Drama of Ibsen and Strindberg*, London, 1962.

Madsen, Borge Gedso, *Strindberg's Naturalistic Theatre*, Seattle, 1962.

Reinert, Otto (compiler), *Strindberg: A Collection of Critical Essays*, Englewood Cliffs, New Jersey, 1971.

Smedmark, Carl Reinhold, *Essays on Strindberg*, Stockholm, 1966.

Sprigge, Elizabeth, *The Strange Life of August Strindberg*, New York, 1949.

GEORGE BERNARD SHAW

Bentley, Eric, *Bernard Shaw*, New York, revised, 1957.

Henderson, Archibald, *George Bernard Shaw: Man of the Century*, New York, 1956.

Kaufmann, R. J. (editor), *G. B. Shaw: A Collection of Critical Essays*, Englewood Cliffs, New Jersey, 1965.

Kronenberger, Louis (editor), *George Bernard Shaw: A Critical Survey*, Cleveland, 1953.

West, E. J. (editor), *Shaw on Theatre*, New York, 1958.

EUGENE O'NEILL

Cargill, Oscar, et al. (editors), *O'Neill and His Plays: Four Decades of Criticism*, New York, 1961.

Falk, Doris, *Eugene O'Neill and the Tragic Vision*, New Brunswick, New Jersey, 1958.

Gassner, John (editor), *O'Neill: A Collection of Critical Essays*, Englewood Cliffs, New Jersey, 1964.

Gelb, Barbara, and Arthur Gelb, *O'Neill: A Biography*, New York, 1962.

See also O'Neill issue of *Modern Drama* (December, 1960).

BERTOLT BRECHT

Bentley, Eric, *In Search of Theater*, New York, 1953.

Demetz, Peter (editor), *Brecht: A Collection of Critical Essays*, Englewood Cliffs, New Jersey, 1962.

Esslin, Martin, *Brecht: The Man and His Work*, Garden City, New York, 1960.

Willett, John, *The Theatre of Bertolt Brecht*, London, 1959.

See also Brecht issue of *Tulane Drama Review*, (Autumn, 1961).

JOHN OSBORNE

Carter, Alan, *John Osborne*, Edinburgh, 1969.

Taylor, John Russell (editor), *Look Back in Anger: A Selection of Critical Essays*, London, 1968.

————, *Anger and After*, London, 1963.

Trussler, Simon, *The Plays of John Osborne: An Assessment*, London, 1969.

Weiss, Samuel A., "Osborne's Angry Young Play," *Educational Theater Journal*, December, 1960.

SAMUEL BECKETT

Esslin, Martin, *The Theatre of the Absurd*, Garden City, New York, 1961.

Grossvogel, David I., *Modern French Drama*, New York, 1961.

Kenner, Hugh, *Samuel Beckett*, New York, 1962.

Pronko, Leonard C., *Avante-Garde: The Experimental Theater in France*, Berkeley, California, 1962.

See Samuel Beckett Issue of *Perspective*, 11 (Autumn, 1959).

EUGENE IONESCO

Coe, Richard, *Ionesco*, Edinburgh, 1961.

Fowlie, Wallace, *Dionysus in Paris*, New York, 1960.

Esslin, Martin, *The Theatre of the Absurd*, Garden City, New York, 1961.

Ionesco, Eugène, *Notes and Counter Notes*, translated by Donald Watson, New York, 1964.

Pronko, Leonard C., *Avant-Garde: The Experimental Theater in France*, Berkeley, California, 1962.

See also Ionesco issue of *Tulane Drama Review*, October, 1958.

FRIEDRICH DÜRRENMATT

Armin, Arnold, *Friedrich Dürrenmatt*, New York, 1972.

Dürrenmatt, Friedrich, "Problems of the Theatre," *Tulane Drama Review*, 3 (October, 1958).

————, "21 Points on The Physicists," *Theater-Schriften und Reden*, Zurich, 1966, pp. 193-194.

Garten, H. F., *Modern German Drama*, Fair Lawn, New Jersey, 1959.

Goodman, Randolph, *Drama on Stage*, New York, 1961.

Klarmann, Adolf, "Friedrich Dürrenmatt and the Tragic Sense of Comedy," *Tulane Drama Review*, 4 (May, 1960), pp. 77-104.

Peppard, Murray B., *Dürrenmatt*, New York, 1969.

LONNE ELDER III

Abramson, Doris, *Negro Playwrights in American Theater, 1925-1959*, New York, 1964.

Hatch, James V., *Black Image on the American Stage*, New York, 1970.

Hughes, Langston, and Milton Meltzer, *Black Magic: A Pictorial History of the Negro in American Entertainment*, Englewood Cliffs, New Jersey, 1967.

Mitchell, Loften, *Black Drama: The Story of the American Negro in the Theater*, New York, 1967.

Patterson, Lindsay (compiler and editor), *Anthology of the American Negro in the Theater* [International Library of Negro Life and History. Under the auspices of The Association for the Study of Negro Life and History.], New York, 1967-1968.

Reardon, William, and Thomas Pawley, *The Black Teacher and the Dramatic Arts*, Westport, Connecticutt, 1970. Cf. particularly bibliography, pp. 70-121.

See also *Tulane Drama Review*, special issue on the Black Theater, T40.

LEARNING AIDS

FILMS

Antigone. Directed by George Tzavellas. Branden Films, 34 Mac Questen Parkway South, Mount Vernon, N. Y. 10550.

King Lear. Dr. Frank Baxter discusses the play and reads selected scenes. In five parts, 29 minutes each. Association Films, 347 Madison Ave., New York, N. Y. 10017.

Miss Julie, rehearsal and scenes from. 59 minutes. Indiana University Audio-Visual Center, Bloomington, Indiana 47401.

Miss Julie. Alf. Sjoberg's classic. 90 min. Janus Films, 745 Fifth Ave., New York, N. Y. 10022.

Major Barbara. Produced by Gabriel Pascal. 90 minutes. Janus Films.

The Goad, adapted from Beckett's *Act Without Words II*. 17 minutes. Grove Press Evergreen Films, 53 E. 11th St., New York, N. Y. 10003.

Waiting for Godot, by Samuel Beckett. With Zero Mostel and Burgess Meredith. 102 minutes. Grove Press Evergreen Films.

The Lesson, by Eugene Ionesco. The Emmy Award winning production with Fred Gwynne. 67 minutes. Grove Press Evergreen Films.

PLAY RECORDINGS

Antigone. Translated by Dudley Fitts and Robert Fitzgerald. With Dorothy Tutin, Max Adrian, and Jeremy Brett. Caedmon Records, 505 Eighth Ave., New York, N. Y. 10018. TRS 320 LPs. CDL 5320 cassettes.

King Lear. With Paul Scofield, Cyril Cusack, and Pamela Brown. Caedmon Records. SRS 233 LPs.

King Lear. Dublin Gate Theater production. 4 Spoken Word A9.

Shakespeare/Soul of an Age. Narrated by Ralph Richardson. With Michael Redgrave. Readings from seven histories, four comedies, and two tragedies. Caedmon Records. TCP 1170 LP.

King Lear. Cambridge University. Marlowe Society. 4—Argo—280/3.

The Miser. Repertory Theater of Lincoln Center production, directed by Jules Irving. Caedmon Records. TRS 338 LPs. CDL 5338 cassettes.

The Way of the World. National Theater production, directed by Michael Langham. Caedmon Records. TRS 339 LPs.

An Enemy of the People, Ibsen-Miller version. Repertory Theater of Lincoln Center production, directed by Jules Irving. Caedmon Records. TRS 349 LPs.

Major Barbara. With Maggie Smith, Robert Morley, Alec McCowen. Caedmon Records. TRS 319 LPs.

The Emperor Jones. Directed by Theodore Mann. With James Earl Jones. Includes rehearsal discussion. Caedmon Records. TRS 341 LPs. CDL 5341 cassettes.

Brecht on Brecht. Original Broadway cast. 2—COL. 025-203.

To Be Young, Gifted and Black, by Lorraine Hansberry and Robert Nemiroff. Caedmon Records. TRS 342 LPs. CDL 5342 cassettes.

GLOSSARY

Acting area, or "playing area." The part of the stage used for performance.

Alienation. A technique used by Bertolt Brecht in his "epic dramas" to negate the emotional involvement of his audience in order to make an intellectual appeal to his political views.

Antagonist. The character of force in opposition to the protagonist or hero.

Apron. The stage area in front of the main curtain.

Arena stage. An arrangement for "central staging" of plays with the acting area in the middle of the room surrounded by the audience.

Aside. A dramatic convention by which the actor speaks his private thoughts aloud, unnoticed by other actors.

Backing. Stage scenery used to mask the openings so as to prevent the audience from seeing the off-stage areas.

Blocking. The director's organization of the stage movement of his cast.

Business. The individual actions of the characters in a play, as for example, taking a drink, smoking a pipe, writing a letter.

Catharsis. The act of purging or cleansing, usually in connection with tragedy. Aristo-

tle says that tragedy arouses fear and pity, and that these emotions are purged away and leave the audience in a state of purification. (See pp. 29, 30-31.)

Chorus. In Greek drama, a group, varying in size from twelve to fifty, that recited lines in unison. As the first element to develop in Greek drama, it provided information and, in its most elaborate state, commentary on past actions and forebodings about future ones. With the invention of the second and third actors, the chorus became gradually less important. In later drama, the chorus was a single actor who communicated directly with the audience in giving them essential information.

Classical drama. Usually refers to the dramas of ancient Greece and Rome. See also "neoclassicism."

Climax. The strongest point of emotional tension. Most plays have a series of climaxes which cumulate in a major climax. (See p. 14.)

Comedy. Drama designed to entertain the audience, usually resulting in a happy ending.

Comedy of humours. Comedy of character based upon a dominant trait such as greed or jealousy. Popularized by the Elizabethan playwright Ben Jonson.

657

Comedy of manners.   Social comedy that satirized characters wittily in terms of their shortcomings as measured against a specific code of conduct. For example, *The Way of the World.*

Commedia dell'arte.   Improvised Italian comedy of the sixteenth, seventeenth and eighteenth centuries put together out of stock roles in formula situations. Performed during this period by small companies of professional actors who were very popular all over Europe.

Complication.   Any new force introduced into a play which affects the duration of the course of action. (See p. 13.)

Confidant.   A minor character paired with a major one and who shares the latter's confidences, usually for expository purposes.

Contamination.   The practice of combining plot materials from two or more plays to make a new one. Originally used to describe the practices of Plautus and Terence in reference to their borrowings from Greek comedy, the term was extended to the general practice of the Elizabethans in making new plays from old material.

Conventions.   Common agreements between theater-worker and spectator concerning the manner of production, that is, certain "ground rules" that determine how the game is played; for example, the physical separation of actor and spectator.

Crisis.   A time of decision; a turning point. (See p. 14.)

Cyclorama.   Drapery or canvas usually hung in a half circle to mask the wings and backstage areas. Often represents the sky, or it may be a simple drape setting.

Denouement.   The resolution or unravelling of a plot so that an equilibrium is usually restored. (See p. 15.)

Deus ex Machina.   In the Greek theater the "God of the machine." A mechanical device used for the intervention of some outside agent to resolve the plot. As a general term, it refers to the intervention of any outside force to bring about a desired ending.

Discovery.   The revelation of important information about the characters, their motivations, feelings and relationships. Discovery is often accompanied by recognition *(anagnorisis)* when a character learns the truth about himself. (See p. 12.)

Downstage.   The area of the stage closest to the audience.

Drame.   Any play that deals seriously with themes, characters and ideas of the present day and is of a keen and sober interest to a middle-class audience. (See pp. 38–40.)

Exposition.   Dramatic techniques for acquainting the audience with antecedent information and background material. (See p. 11.)

Expressionism.   A style of drama in which an attempt is made to present "inner reality," the man beneath the skin. Often distorts the normal to present symbolic action in dreamlike sequences.

Farce.   Low comedy, written for amusement, usually emphasizing physical action.

Flat.   The most useful element of stage scenery, consisting of a wooden frame generally covered with muslin or canvas to represent walls.

Flies.   The space above the stage out of sight of the audience—where scenery can be "flown."

Foreshadowing.   Techniques for preparing the audience for the action that follows (See p. 13.)

Forestage.   In the modern theater, the area in front of the proscenium arch. In the Elizabethan theater, the forestage was a large projecting platform that was the main acting area.

Gridiron, ("grid"). The open framework above the stage from which suspended scenery is hung.

High Comedy.   A general term referring to that kind of comedy which evokes "thoughtful laughter" through its concern with character, thought and dialogue.

Imagery.   Communication by means of concrete and particular meanings through the use of language devices such as metaphors, similes and clusters of related words.

Irony.   A discrepancy between what a character plans and anticipates, and what actually occurs.

Melodrama.   Pseudo-serious drama that is played at the game level and exploits exciting action.

Motivation.   A logical justification, or a showing of plausible reasons, for the behavior of the characters in a play.

Naturalism.   An exaggerated form of realism which emphasizes a sordid and deterministic view of life. First appeared in France in the late nineteenth century as a response to the scientific revolution.

Neoclassicism.   An attempt in the sixteenth, seventeenth and eighteenth centuries to "regularize" dramatic techniques by following scrupulously what were thought to be the practices of the ancients, e.g., adherence to the "unities," use of a chorus, preservation of "decorum" in language and action, avoiding acts of violence on stage, and use of only royal or noble characters.

Plot.   The structure of the incidents; that which gives drama its form; dramatic composition. (See pp. 9 ff., 29-30, 48 ff.)

Probability.   An atteempt by the playwright to establish credibility, or as Aristotle says, to make the action of a play seem "necessary and probable."

Properties, ("props"). Includes objects used by the actors in the production of a play such as letters, weapons, food.

Proscenium arch.   The architectural frame through which the spectator views the stage.

Protagonist.   The chief character in a play.

Realism.   Drama that attempts to establish authenticity through the use of the observed facts of daily existence.

Recognition.   See "discovery."

Romanticism.   In contrast with the classical drama, romantic drama adventurous, emotionally loaded characters in remote and exotic circumstances.

Reversal. An Aristotelian critical term (*peripety*) referring to a sudden change in the fortunes of the protagonist. (See p. 12.)

Skene.   Originally a small hut at the back of the orchestra in the Greek theater; later became the stage-house.

"Slice-of life" play.   An attempt to give the impression that the action of a play is unorganized actuality, without an apparent beginning, middle or end. Used principally in naturalistic drama.

Soliloquy.   A "solo" speech of a single character.

Spectacle.   The visual aspects of a produced play.

Stage left or right.   Left or right side of the stage from the actor's point of view as he faces the audience.

Thought.   The reasoning aspect of drama—the argument, the theme, the meaning.

Tragic flaw. An Aristotelian concept of an "error in judgment," a frailty in an otherwise good and prominent man that leads to his downfall.

Unity of action.   All parts of the play are essential and organic, free from sub-plots or extraneous diversions. (See p. 17.)

..y of place. All of the action occurs in one locale. (See p. 16.)

Unity of time. The action of a play takes place as Aristotle suggested "within the single revolution of the sun." The play covers a short span of time. (See p. 16.)

Upstage. The acting area farthest from the audience.

"Well-made play." Dramatic technique perfected by the French playwright, Scribe, in which all aspects of plot were carefully worked out in a logical cause and effect relationship.

Wings. The area offstage of the acting area.